# Notes on the New Testament

Albert Barnes

*Edited by*
Robert Frew

REVELATION

BAKER BOOK HOUSE
Grand Rapids, Michigan 49506

# Heritage Edition           Fourteen Volumes 0834-

| | | | |
|---|---|---|---|
| 1. Genesis (Murphy) | 0835-2 | 8. Minor Prophets (Pusey) | 0842- |
| 2. Exodus to Esther (Cook) | 0836-0 | 9. The Gospels | 0843- |
| 3. Job | 0837-9 | 10. Acts and Romans | 0844- |
| 4. Psalms | 0838-7 | 11. I Corinthians to Galatians | 0846- |
| 5. Proverbs to Ezekiel (Cook) | 0839-5 | 12. Ephesians to Philemon | 0847- |
| 6. Isaiah | 0840-9 | 13. Hebrews to Jude | 0848- |
| 7. Daniel | 0841-7 | 14. Revelation | 0849- |

When ordering by ISBN (International Standard Book Number), numbers listed above should be preceded by 0-8010-.

Reprinted from the 1884-85 edition published by Blackie & Son,
London, edited by Robert Frew

ISBN: 0-8010-0849-2

Printed and bound in the United States of America

# CONTENTS

| | PAGE |
|---|---|
| AUTHOR'S PREFACE, . . . . . . . . . . . . . . . . | v–x |

EDITOR'S PREFACE:—

INTRODUCTION.

Author's qualifications for Apocalyptic exposition—Author's plan in preparing his Commentary, affords assurance of his sobriety as an interpreter, and rebukes the scorn of hostile critics—Peculiarities of this edition, . . . . . . . . . . . . . . . xi–xiii

YEAR-DAY PRINCIPLE.

Importance of the question regarding—Protestant theory of Apocalyptic interpretation stands or falls with it—Rival schemes, nature and origin of—Advocates on both sides—Views of Dr. Davidson and Professor Stuart, . . . . . . . . . . . . . . . . xiii–xiv

ARGUMENTS IN FAVOUR OF YEAR-DAY THEORY.

1. *Concurrent Testimony of Protestant Interpreters*—Objection of Dr. Davidson—Reply—Use which the Reformers made of the Apocalypse—Views of Walter Brute—Views of Luther, . . . xiv–xvi
2. *Symbolical Character of the Predictions in Daniel and the Apocalypse*—Laws of symbolic propriety—Dr. Maitland's famous objection, that a day is no symbol for a year—General principles on which Year-day view rests—Ground occupied by Mede—Principle of Bush and Faber—True basis—View of Birks and Elliott, xvi–xx
3. *Indications of the Year-day Principle in Scripture*—The case of the spies in the book of Numbers—Ezekiel's typical siege—Objection of Professor Stuart—Professor Bush's reply—Objection of Bishop Horsley—Objections from Isaiah, ch. xx. 2, 3—Daniel's seventy weeks—Diverse views of opponents—Outlines of Discussion, . . . . . . . . . . . . . . . . . . . xx–xxiv
4. *Exigency of Passages in which Prophetic Times occur*—Saracenic woe in Rev. ix. 5–10—Turkish woe in Rev. ix. 15—The forty-two months of the Gentiles in ch. xi. 2—The times of the two witnesses in ch. xi. 3–11—The times of the woman in the wilderness, in ch. xii. 6–14—Forty-two months of the Beast, in ch. xiii. 5—Danielic periods—Objections alleged, novelty of the Year-day principle, . . . . . . . . . . . . . . . xxiv–xxviii

AUTHOR'S INTRODUCTION:—SECT. I. The Writer of the Book of Revelation.—SECT. II. The Time of Writing the Apocalypse.—SECT. III. The Place where the Book was written.—SECT. IV. The Nature and Design of the Book.—SECT. V. The Plan of the Apocalypse, xxix–lv

ANALYSIS, . . . . . . . . . . . . . . . . . . . lvi–lxii

THE BOOK OF REVELATION, . . . . . . . . . . . . . 31–464

# LIST OF ENGRAVINGS

PAGE

*Engravings Printed in the Text.*

| | | |
|---|---|---|
| Egyptian Calf-idol, . . . . . . . . . . . . . . . . | Rev. | 115 |
| Human-headed Winged Lion; from the Nineveh Sculptures, . | Rev. | 116 |
| Eagle-headed Winged Lion; from the Nineveh Sculptures, . . | Rev. | 117 |
| Medal of the Emperor Nerva wearing Crown, . . . . . . | Rev. | 145 |
| Medal of the Emperor Valentinian wearing Diadem, . . . . | Rev. | 145 |
| Symbolic Bas-reliefs from a Roman Triumphal Arch, . . . . | Rev. | 146 |
| Emblem of a Roman Procurator, . . . . . . . . . . . | Rev. | 154 |
| Symbolical Locust, according to Elliott, . . . . . . . . | Rev. | 218 |
| Standard-bearer of a Turkish Pasha, . . . . . . . . . | Rev. | 237 |
| Roman Standard, from Montfauçon, . . . . . . . . . . . | Rev. | 305 |
| Medal of Pope Leo XII., . . . . . . . . . . . . . | Rev. | 384 |

# PREFACE

WHEN I began the preparation of these "Notes" on the New Testament, now more than twenty years ago, I did not design to extend the work beyond the Gospels, and contemplated only simple and brief explanations of that portion of the New Testament, for the use of Sunday-school teachers and Bible classes. The work originated in the belief that Notes of that character were greatly needed, and that the older commentaries, having been written for a different purpose, and being, on account of their size and expense, beyond the reach of most teachers of Sunday-schools, did not meet the demand which had grown up from the establishment of such schools. These Notes, contrary to my original plan and expectation, have been extended to eleven volumes, and embrace the whole of the New Testament.

Having, at the time when these Notes were commenced, as I have ever had since, the charge of a large congregation, I had no leisure that I could properly devote to these studies, except the early hours of the morning; and I adopted the resolution—a resolution which has since been invariably adhered to—to cease writing precisely at nine o'clock in the morning. The habit of writing in this manner, once formed, was easily continued; and having been thus continued, I find myself at the end of the New Testament. Perhaps this personal allusion would not be proper, except to show that I have not intended, in these literary labours, to infringe on the proper duties of the pastoral office, or to take time for these pursuits on which there was a claim for other purposes. This allusion may perhaps also be of use to my younger brethren in the ministry, by showing them that much may be accomplished by the habit of early rising, and by a diligent use of the early morning hours. In my own case, these Notes on the New Testament, and also the Notes on the books of Isaiah, Job, and Daniel, extending in all to sixteen volumes, have all been written before nine o'clock in the morning, and are the fruit of the habit of rising between four and five o'clock. I do not know that by this practice I have neglected any duty which I should otherwise have performed; and on the score of health, and, I may add, of profit in the contemplation of a portion of divine truth at the beginning of each day, the habit has been of inestimable advantage to me.

It was not my original intention to prepare Notes on the book of Revelation, nor did I entertain the design of doing it until I *came up* to it in the regular course of my studies. Having written on all the other portions of the New Testament, there remained only this book to complete an entire commentary on this part of the Bible. That I have endeavoured to explain the book at all is to be traced to the habit which I had formed of spending the early hours of the day in the study of the sacred Scriptures. That habit, continued, has carried me forward until I have reached the end of the New Testament.

It may be of some use to those who peruse this volume, and it is proper in itself, that I should make a brief statement of the manner in which I have prepared these Notes, and of the method of interpretation on which I have proceeded; for the result which has been reached has not been the effect of any preconceived theory or plan, and if in the result I coincide in any degree with the common method of interpreting the volume, the fact may be regarded as the testimony of another witness—however unimportant the testimony may be in itself—to the correctness of that method of interpretation.

Up to the time of commencing the exposition of this book, I had no theory in my own mind as to its meaning. I may add, that I had a prevailing belief that it could *not* be explained, and that all attempts to explain it must be visionary and futile. With the exception of the work of the Rev. George Croly,[1] which I read more than twenty years ago, and which I had never desired to read again, I had perused no commentary on this book until that of Professor Stuart was published, in 1845. In my regular reading of the Bible in the family and in private, I had perused the book often. I read it, as I suppose most others do, from a sense of duty, yet admiring the beauty of its imagery, the sublimity of its descriptions, and its high poetic character; and though to me wholly unintelligible in the main, finding so many striking detached passages that were intelligible and practical in their nature, as to make it on the whole attractive and profitable, but with no definitely formed idea as to its meaning as a whole, and with a vague general feeling that all the interpretations which had been proposed were wild, fanciful, and visionary.

In this state of things, the utmost that I contemplated when I began to write on it, was to explain, as well as I could, the meaning of the language and the symbols, without attempting to apply the explanation to the events of past history, or to inquire what is to occur hereafter. I supposed that I might venture to do this without encountering the danger of adding another vain attempt to explain a book so full of mysteries, or of propounding a theory of interpretation to be set aside, perhaps, by the next person that should prepare a commentary on the book.

[1] "*The Apocalypse of St. John,* or Prophecy of the Rise, Progress, and Fall of the Church of Rome; the Inquisition; the Revolution in France; a Universal War, and the final triumph of Christianity: being a new interpretation, by the Rev. George Croly, A.M., H.R.S.L."

Beginning with this aim, I found myself soon insensibly inquiring whether, in the events which succeeded the time when the book was written, there were not historical facts of which the emblems employed would be natural and proper symbols, on the supposition that it was the divine intention, in disclosing these visions, to refer to them; and whether, therefore, there might not be a natural and proper application of the symbols to these events. In this way I examined the language used in reference to the first, second, third, fourth, fifth, and sixth seals, with no anticipation or plan in examining one as to what would be disclosed under the next seal, and in this way also I examined ultimately the whole book: proceeding step by step in ascertaining the meaning of each word and symbol as it occurred, but with no theoretic anticipation as to what was to follow. To my own surprise I found, chiefly in Gibbon's *Decline and Fall of the Roman Empire*, a series of events recorded, such as seemed to me to correspond, to a great extent, with the series of symbols found in the Apocalypse. The symbols were such as it might be supposed *would be used*, on the supposition that they were intended to refer to these events; and the language of Mr. Gibbon was often such as *he would have used*, on the supposition that he had designed to prepare a commentary on the symbols employed by John. It was such, in fact, that if it had been found in a Christian writer, professedly writing a commentary on the book of Revelation, it would have been regarded by infidels as a designed attempt to force history to utter a language that should conform to a predetermined theory in expounding a book full of symbols. So remarkable have these coincidences appeared to me in the course of this exposition, that it has almost seemed as if he had designed to write a commentary on some portions of this book; and I have found it difficult to doubt that that distinguished historian was raised up by an overruling Providence to make a record of those events which would ever afterwards be regarded as an impartial and unprejudiced statement of the evidences of the fulfilment of prophecy. The historian of the *Decline and Fall of the Roman Empire* had no belief in the divine origin of Christianity, but he brought to the performance of his work learning and talent such as few Christian scholars have possessed. He is always patient in his investigations; learned and scholar-like in his references; comprehensive in his groupings, and sufficiently minute in his details; unbiassed in his statements of facts, and usually cool and candid in his estimates of the causes of the events which he records; and, excepting his philosophical speculations, and his sneers at everything, he has probably written the most candid and impartial history of the times that succeeded the introduction of Christianity that the world possesses; and even after all that has been written since his time, his work contains the best ecclesiastical history that is to be found. Whatever use of it can be made in explaining and confirming the prophecies, will be regarded by the world as impartial and fair; for it was a result which he least of all contemplated, that he would ever be regarded as an expounder of the prophecies in the Bible, or be referred to as vindicating their truth.

It was in this manner that these Notes on the Book of Revelation assumed the form in which they are now given to the world; and it surprises me—and, under this view of the matter, may occasion some surprise to my readers—to find how nearly the views coincide with those taken by the great body of Protestant interpreters. And perhaps this fact may be regarded as furnishing some evidence that, after all the obscurity attending it, there is a natural and obvious interpretation of which the book is susceptible. Whatever may be the value or the correctness of the views expressed in this volume, the work is the result of no previously-formed theory. That it will be satisfactory to all, I have no reason to expect; that it may be useful to some, I would hope; that it may be regarded by many as only adding another vain and futile effort to explain a book which defies all attempts to elucidate its meaning, I have too much reason, judging from the labours of those who have gone before me, to fear. But as it is, I commit it to the judgment of a candid Christian public, and to the blessing of Him who alone can make any attempt to explain his Word a means of diffusing the knowledge of truth.

I cannot conceal the fact that I dismiss it, and send it forth to the world, as the last volume on the New Testament, with deep emotion. After more than twenty years of study on the New Testament, I am reminded that I am no longer a young man; and that, as I close this work, so all my work on earth must at no distant period be ended. I am sensible that he incurs no slight responsibility who publishes a commentary on the Bible; and I especially feel this now in view of the fact—so unexpected to me when I began these labours—that I have been permitted in our own country to send forth more than two hundred and fifty thousand volumes of commentary on the New Testament, and that probably a greater number has been published abroad. That there are many imperfections in these Notes no one can feel more sensibly than I do; but the views which I have expressed are those which seem to me to be in accordance with the Bible, and I send the last volume forth with the deep conviction that these volumes contain the truth as God has revealed it, and as he will bless it to the extension of his church in the world. I have no apprehension that the sentiments which I have expressed will corrupt the morals, or destroy the peace, or ruin the souls of those who may read these volumes; and I trust that they may do something to diffuse abroad a correct knowledge of that blessed gospel on which the interests of the church, the welfare of our country, and the happiness of the world depend. In language which I substantially used in publishing the revised edition of the volumes of the Gospels (Preface to the Seventeenth Edition, 1840), I can now say, "I cannot be insensible to the fact that, in the form in which these volumes now go forth to the public, I may continue, though dead, to speak to the living; and that the work may be exerting an influence on immortal minds when I am in the eternal world. I need not say that, while I am sensitive to this consideration, I earnestly desire it. There are no sentiments in these volumes which I wish to alter; none that I do not believe to be truths that will abide the investigations of the great day; none of which I am ashamed. That I may be in error, I know; that a better work than this might be prepared by a more gifted mind, and a purer heart, I know. But the truths here set forth are, I am persuaded, those which are destined to abide, and to be the means of saving millions of souls, and ultimately of converting this whole world to God. That these volumes may have a part in this great work is my earnest prayer; and with many thanks to the public for their favours, and to God, the great source of all blessing, I send them forth, committing them to His care, and leaving them to live or die, to be remembered or forgotten, to be used by the present generation and the next, or to be superseded by other works, as shall be in accordance with his will, and as he shall see to be for his glory."

ALBERT BARNES.

WASHINGTON SQUARE, PHILADELPHIA,
*March 26, 1851.*

---

The works which I have had most constantly before me, and from which I have derived most aid in the preparation of these Notes, are the following. They are enumerated here, as some of them are frequently quoted, to save the necessity of a frequent reference to the *Editions* in the Notes:—

A Commentary on the Apocalypse. By Moses Stuart, Professor of Sacred Literature in the Theological Seminary at Andover, Mass. Andover, 1845.

Horæ Apocalypticæ; or, a Commentary on the Apocalypse, Critical and Historical. By the Rev. E. B. Elliott, A.M., late Vicar of Tuxford, and Fellow of Trinity College. Third Edition. London, 1847.

The Works of Nathaniel Lardner, D.D. In ten volumes. London, 1829.

The History of the Decline and Fall of the Roman Empire. By Edward Gibbon, Esq. Fifth American, from the last London edition. Complete in four volumes. New York, J. and J. Harper, 1829.

History of Europe. By Archibald Alison, F.R.S.E. New York, Harper Brothers, 1843.

An Exposition of the Apocalypse. By David N. Lord. Harpers, 1847.

Hyponoia; or, Thoughts on a Spiritual Understanding of the Apocalypse, a Book of Revelation. New York, Leavitt, Trow, and Co., 1844.

The Family Expositor. By Philip Doddridge, D.D. London, 1831.

Ἀνάκρισις Apocalypsios Joannis Apostoli, etc. Auctore Campegio Vitringa, Theol. et Hist. Professore. Amsterdam, 1629.

Kurtzgefasstes exegetisches Handbuch zum Neuen Testament. Von Dr. W. M. L. De Wette. Leipzig, 1847.

Rosenmüller, Scholia in Novum Testamentum.

Dissertations on the Opening of the Sealed Book. Montreal, 1848.

Two New Arguments in Vindication of the Genuineness and Authenticity of the Revelation of St. John. By John Collyer Knight. London, 1842.

The Seventh Vial: being an Exposition of the Apocalypse, and in particular of the pouring out of the Seventh Vial, with special reference to the present Revolution in Europe. London, 1848.

Die Offenbarung des Heiligen Joannes. Von G. W. Hengstenberg. Berlin, 1850.

The Works of the Rev. Andrew Fuller. Newhaven, 1825.

Novum Testamentum. Editio Koppiana, 1821.

Dissertation on the Prophecies. By Thomas Newton, D.D. London, 1832.

The Apocalypse of St. John. By the Rev. George Croly, A.M. Philadelphia, 1827.

The Signs of the Times, as denoted by the fulfilment of Historical Predictions, from the Babylonian Captivity to the present time. By Alexander Keith, D.D. Eighth Edition. Edinburgh, 1847.

Christ's Second Coming: will it be Pre-millennial? By the Rev. David Brown, A.M., St. James's Free Church, Glasgow. New York, 1851.

Apocalyptical Key. An extraordinary Discourse on the Rise and Fall of the Papacy. By Robert Fleming, V.D.M. New York, American Protestant Society.

A Treatise on the Millennium. By George Bush, A.M. New York, 1832.

A Key to the Book of Revelation. By James M'Donald, minister of the Presbyterian Church, Jamaica, L. I. Second Edition. New London, 1848.

Das Alte und Neue Morgenland. Rosenmüller. Leipzig, 1820.

The Season and Time; or, an Exposition of the Prophecies which relate to the two periods subsequent to the 1200 years now recently expired, being the time of the Seventh Trumpet, &c. By W. Ettrick, A.M. London, 1816.

Einleitung in das Neue Testament. Von Johann Gottfried Eichhorn. Leipzig, 1811.

For a very full view of the history of the interpretation of the Apocalypse, and of the works that have been written on it, the reader is referred to Elliott's Horæ Apocalypticæ, vol. iv. pp. 307-487, and Prof. Stuart, vol. i. pp. 450-475. See, for a condensed view, Editor's Preface.

# EDITOR'S PREFACE

## YEAR-DAY PRINCIPLE

PROFESSOR BUSH, in the *Hierophant* for January, 1845, at the close of a review of Barnes on the Hebrews, thus wrote:—"We sincerely hope Mr. Barnes may be enabled to accomplish his plan to its very ultimatum, and furnish a commentary of equal merit on the remaining books of the New Testament; with the exception, however, of the Apocalypse, to which, we think, his rigid Calvinian austerity of reason is not so well adapted; and which, we presume to think, would fare better under our own reputed fanciful and allegorical pen."[1] The indefatigable author *has* lived to accomplish his plan, and has ventured to include within it the mysterious prophecy, for the elucidation of which the reviewer imagined the severe character of his mind disqualified him. Many will think the supposed disqualification a foremost requisite in an Apocalyptic commentator, inasmuch as the Apocalypse has been too long interpreted on fanciful and allegorical principles; and it is now "high time for principle to take the place of fancy, for exegetical proof to thrust out assumption."[2] The advocates of what has been called the Protestant Historic Scheme of Interpretation, have been supposed peculiarly liable to delusions of this nature. It is, therefore, gratifying to find that this new defender of that scheme has been distinguished by a "Calvinian austerity of reason," which may help to preserve both him and his readers from being in like manner led astray, and at the same time secure a more respectful tone from critics who have espoused opposite views. Bush, who has himself so ably defended the Protestant scheme on the other side of the Atlantic, now that he finds Barnes on the same ground, will think that the spirit of severe logic and searching inquiry which he has brought with him to the contest, render him all the more valuable an associate. In examining the former volumes of Mr. Barnes, we found it was no part of his system of interpretation to admit typical and mystical senses where the literal one could at all be adopted. We had to complain that his tendency was too strong in the opposite direction.[3]

The plan which the author tells us he adopted in preparing his commentary, is a singular illustration of his judgment and caution; and therefore affords another assurance of his sobriety as an interpreter of the symbols of John. Up to the time of commencing the exposition of this book, he tells us he had no theory in his mind as to its meaning. The utmost he contemplated, when he began, was to explain the meaning of its language and symbols, without attempting to apply that explanation to historical events. But, to his own surprise, he found a series of events, recorded chiefly in Gibbon, such as seemed to correspond, to a great extent, with the series of symbols found in the Apocalypse. Farther examination exhibited this correspondence still

[1] P. 192.   [2] Moses Stuart.   [3] See Supplementary Notes on Heb. vii

more strikingly; and the result was, that his views ultimately took the shape of those given by the great body of Protestant interpreters. He therefore justly claims to be another and independent witness in favour of the common interpretation.[1] These statements, while they cannot but increase the reader's confidence in the guide who now offers to lead him through the mazes of the Apocalypse, ought also to mitigate the scorn with which some have affected to regard *all* expositions of this school—speaking of them as "hariolations" and "surmises," which set the reader "afloat upon a boundless ocean of conjecture and fancy, without rudder or compass."[2] It is easy to say such things, and they are therefore too often said by the followers of Eichhorn and Stuart; but accurate inquiry into the non-Protestant scheme will speedily convince anyone that the hariolations do by no means all belong to one side. We venture to say, that nothing so much deserving the name occurs in the whole series of Protestant expositions, as the absurd and unfounded guesses of the last-named writer regarding the witnesses in chap. xi., and the explanation of chap. xvii. 8, by an unfounded heathen rumour regarding the reappearance of Nero after he had been slain.[3]

With this edition of the Notes on the Book of Revelation we have not found it expedient to present any accompanying or supplementary notes. The author's text has been carefully revised, and many errors which had crept both into the American and English editions have been corrected. On certain points we could have wished a little more fulness. The important question of the date of the book; the history of apocalyptic interpretation; and the principles of prophetic interpretation, particularly as regards designations of time, are matters lying at the very foundation of just views of the Apocalypse. The first of these points has, indeed, a page or two allotted to it in the "Introduction," and is also incidentally noticed in the commentary; the second is less or more touched on in the exposition of difficult passages; but the last is almost entirely overlooked, on the ground that the author intends a full discussion of the subject in his forthcoming volume on Daniel. We somewhat regret this, because of the importance of the Year-day principle itself, and because every reader of the Notes on the Book of Revelation may not possess, or have immediately at hand, those on Daniel. We have no doubt that the author's defence of this part of the Protestant citadel will prove one of the most able that has yet been given. It will, beyond a doubt, avoid the errors of those who have weakened the argument by insisting on points which, at best, are uncertain; and place the theory on a basis sufficiently broad to admit of rational and hopeful maintaining of it, in spite of numerous learned and able assaults. In the meantime, that our edition may not be without something, however brief and imperfect, on a point which on

---

[1] Author's Preface, p. vi.   [2] Stuart on Apocalypse, p. 170, Edinburgh, 1847.
[3] This view of the great philologist has deservedly met with indignant censure, both in this country and in America. "We confess," says Dr. Beecher of Boston, "that this whole effort to force Nero into chap. xvii. as the wounded beast, savours too much of that German infidelity that regards John as little better than a soothsayer himself, and does not hesitate to affirm that he believes the rumours concerning Nero. Professor Stuart of course abandons this ground, and yet he avers that John spoke as if he believed it. This theory is perfectly consistent in the hands of one who denies the inspiration of John, but it cannot be so grafted on the tree of true Christian interpretation as to appear like one of its true and genuine branches" (*Bib. Repos.*, 1847, p. 296). So also Elliott with still greater severity, vol. iv. p. 548.

all hands is allowed to be fundamental, we purpose to devote the following pages to an examination of the Year-day principle.

The importance of the question on which we now enter can scarcely be overestimated. If the prophetic periods of Daniel and John; if the famous 1260 days, the time, times, and the dividing of time, are to be understood literally, and explained of the limited term of three and a half years, during the days of Nero and Antiochus Epiphanes, or days yet to come, towards the consummation and era of the second advent,[1] then clearly the ideas that have been long current among Protestants are untenable. There is no figuration of Papal Rome, in the Apocalypse or in Daniel, existing through long and dreary ages, wearing out the saints of the Most High. There are no witnesses during that period of gloom ever and anon lifting up their testimony against the grand apostasy. There is no cheering assurance, derived from an infallible oracle, that the Papal system is doomed, that its days are numbered, and must now be drawing to a close. All the arguments against this "mystery of iniquity," derived from Daniel and John, must be abandoned; and Protestants must, with shame, retire from a field so long and so successfully occupied by them, whilst the Romanists triumph in their overthrow. "If," says Bush in his animadversions on Stuart, "your hypothesis be correct, not only has nearly the whole Christian world been led astray for ages by a mere *ignis fatuus* of false hermeneutics, but the church is at once cut loose from every chronological mooring, and set adrift in the open sea, without the vestige of a beacon, lighthouse, or star, by which to determine her bearings or distances from the desired millennial haven to which she was tending. She is deprived of the means of taking a single celestial observation, and has no possible data for ascertaining, in the remotest degree, how far she is yet floating from the Ararat of promise. Upon your theory the Christian world has no distinct intimation given it as to the date of the downfall of the Roman despotism, civil or ecclesiastical, of Mahometanism, or of Paganism; no clue to the time of the conversion of the Jews or of the introduction of the millennium. On all these points the church is shut up to a blank and dreary uncertainty, which, though it may not extinguish, will tend greatly to diminish the ardour of her present zeal in the conversion of the world."[2] Strange, indeed, it must be regarded, that while the Old Testament church was cheered by her chronological promises or predictions, marking her progress as she floated down the stream of time, and indicating, at any stage of it, how far she was yet distant from the happy times of deliverance that awaited her, everything of this kind should be systematically excluded from the sublime predictions of the New Dispensation. Strange, too, that the grand symbols of Daniel and John—that their glorious predictions, confessedly allowed to reach onwards to the consummation of all things, should embrace a brief chapter in the lives of such men as Nero or Antiochus, and give no notice of that gigantic apostasy which for ages has cast its dark

---

[1] "The first of these two counter schemes is the *Preterists'*, which would have the prophecy stop altogether short of the Popedom, explaining it of the catastrophes, one or both, of the *Jewish nation* and *Pagan Rome;* the second, the *Futurists'*, which would have it all shoot over the head of the Popedom into times yet future" (Elliott, iv. 529). The first of these schemes originated with the Jesuit *Alcassar* in A.D. 1614; the other with the Jesuit *Ribera* in A.D. 1585; and it is not a little remarkable, that both originated in the necessities of the Papal cause, oppressed by Protestant interpreters. [2] *Hierophant,* p. 242.

shadow over Christendom, and no comfort to a sorrowing church walking amid the gloom. Yet if the Protestant exposition of Daniel and the Apocalypse has proceeded on false principles, the sooner a return is made to the right path the better, however humbling may be the confession of error, and grieving the loss of imagined advantage in our controversy with Rome. Truth is great, and must prevail. None of her friends would assail even the worst cause with weapons she did not approve.

On both sides of this question, the importance of which has been set forth in the preceding paragraph, we find men of the very highest character for learning and skill in biblical science. "On one side Maitland and Burgh are the most able; on the other Faber, Elliott, and Birks. In America the indefatigable Stuart has taken up the same ground as the former, and has met with a formidable antagonist in Bush." To the first class—the literal day class, namely—must now be added the name of the author who has thus specified the chief combatants—Dr. Davidson of the Lancashire Independent College. He has taken up the subject in the third volume of his *Introduction to the New Testament*, and discussed it with all the learning and ability which his high position among English critics might have led us to anticipate. "*Si Pergama dextra defendi possent, etiam hoc defensa fuissent.*" We think we can discern in his able defence some symptoms of progress in the controversy. The line which Dr. Davidson pursues is essentially different in many respects from that of Professor Stuart. The American professor insists on many points which the English divine seems to have abandoned.[1]

Everything like dogmatism in the discussion of a question so circumstanced is of course to be carefully avoided. There are difficulties on both sides, of which no satisfactory solution has as yet been given. Our aim shall be to ascertain, if possible, on which side the greater amount of truth lies. While avowing a decided leaning to the Year-day theory, we shall endeavour to do justice to the arguments of its opponents, and shall frankly allow it whenever the arguments of its supporters seem to us weak or dubious.

First, then, it must be allowed that the concurrent testimony of the great mass of Protestant interpreters, the nearly unanimous voice of the Protestant church, furnishes a *prestige* in favour of the Year-day principle. If it do not supply an argument it creates a favourable feeling, which is worthy of a better name than "prejudice." It is a prepossession, but a prepossession founded on perfectly just ground, namely, that wherever men of learning and research, as well as Christian people at large, have long and tenaciously held any particular view, there must be something in that view that has a better foundation than its assailants are willing to allow. This is certainly very different from "calling up the names of illustrious dead, as the infallible expounders of the Bible;" and from "giving our language the semblance of

---

[1] Compare Stuart on Apocalypse, Excursus v., with Davidson's *Introduction*, vol. iii. pp. 513, 514. Dr. D. justly complains in his preface of being charged by Mr. Elliott with the sin of copying Stuart. Besides the difference mentioned above, there is between the two a difference in regard to the entire scheme of interpretation, Dr. D. condemning the Preterist scheme, of which Professor Stuart is perhaps the ablest supporter. The theory which the latter has put forth on the witnesses meets with unequivocal condemnation in the pages of the former. Dr. D. himself, in the meantime, seems to have no scheme of interpretation. After remarking on the Preterist, Continuous, and Futurist scheme, he says very candidly, "we feel disinclined to support any of the rival hypotheses till they be better supported" (vol. iii. p. 627).

assuming that, to differ from current opinions, is to disown Protestantism and favour Romanism." That there is something in this presumptive argument, which we seek to build on Protestant opinion, is obvious from the anxiety that is manifested to make out that the principle or theory in question has, in reality, no connection with the reformers and the Protestant cause. "The statement," it is said, "that certain applications of the Apocalypse caused or promoted the Reformation is wholly incorrect. It is absolutely false. *A spiritual apprehension of the simple gospel*, accompanied with the power of the Spirit, led these illustrious men to separate from the Romish church. And then it should be remembered, by those who write like Bush of the reformers and the 'Protestant' interpretation, that not one of the reformers understood a *day* in prophecy to mean a *year*. To talk of the reformers, therefore, in connection with this so-called 'Protestant' notion, is worse than trifling. It conveys a false impression."[1] Two questions are involved here:—How far the reformers made use of the Apocalypse in their controversy with Papists? and whether the Year-day principle may be regarded as a "Protestant" notion? The fact is, in regard to the first question, that the Waldenses and Wickliffites, previous to the Reformation, drew their weapons from the Apocalypse; and if we do not present references or quotations to prove it, it is just because the matter seems too plain to admit of any doubt. One testimony shall suffice, namely, that of Walter Brute, A.D. 1391. According to Foxe, the martyrologist, he was "a layman, and learned and brought up in the University of Oxford, being there a graduate." He was accused of saying, among sundry other things, that the *Pope* is Antichrist, and a seducer of the people. Being called to answer, he put in, first, certain more brief "exhibits;" then another declaration, more ample, explaining and setting forth the grounds of his opinion. *His defence was grounded very mainly on the Apocalyptic prophecy.* For he at once bases his justification on the fact, as demonstrable, of the *pope* answering alike to *the chief of the false Christs*, prophesied of by Christ as to come in his name; to the *man of sin*, prophesied of by St. Paul; and to both the *first beast* and *beast with the two lamb-like horns*, in the Apocalypse; *the city of Papal Rome*, also answering similarly to the Apocalyptic *Babylon*.[2] Indeed, we may learn much as to how far the Apocalypse had, even in these times, come to be used against the Church of Rome, from the fears of the Papists themselves, which prompted the fifth council of Lateran authoritatively to prohibit all writing or preaching on the subject of Antichrist, and all speculation regarding the time of the expected evils—"*Tempus quoque præfixum futurorum malorum vel Antichristi adventum, aut certum diem judicii predicare vel asserere nequaquan presumant.*"[3] As to the reformers, properly so called, they appear in the field next, using the same weapons with increasing skill and energy, as the two great prophecies whence they were drawn came to be better understood. The pages of Milner, D'Aubigné, or other historians of the period, abound with evidence; and Mr. Barnes has collected part of it under chap. x. 6, to which the reader is referred. Luther and his German associates seem to have drawn more upon Daniel, while in Switzerland and England the Apocalypse, for the most part, was appealed to. We might multiply proofs, were it necessary, from the writings of *Leo Juda*,

[1] *Introduction to the New Testament*, by Samuel Davidson, D.D., vol. iii. p. 513.
[2] Elliott, iv. 419.  [3] Harduin, ix. 1808; in Elliott, ii. p. 83.

*Bullinger, Latimer, Bale, Foxe,* &c. It is enough to refer to the very copious extracts given in the last volume of the *Horæ Apocalypticæ*.[1] As to the other question, namely, whether the Year-day principle can be regarded as a "Protestant" notion, opportunity will be found for the consideration of it when we come to consider the objection against that principle, drawn from its alleged novelty. Meantime we shall only remark, that while Luther certainly had arrived at no definite conclusions regarding the Apocalyptic designations of time, his mind nevertheless was in search of some principle by which he should be enabled to extend the times beyond the literal sense. Nor need it in any way surprise us, that definite ideas on this subject should only have been obtained when the notion became settled and prevalent that the Popedom was the Apocalyptic Antichrist, and the interpretation of the times on a scale suited to the duration of that system became, in consequence, imperative.

2. The next consideration we advance is, the *symbolical character* of most of the predictions in which the disputed designations of time occur. In Daniel and the Apocalypse, things pictured to the eye are the signs or representations of a hidden sense intended to be conveyed by them. Now, it seems reasonable to conclude, that in this symbolic or picture writing the times should be hidden under some veil, as well as the associated events. Nay, one would imagine that these were just the very things that specially required concealment, in accordance with the design of the predictions, especially such as relate to the future deliverance and glory of the church; which is, that the saints should understand as much as may sustain their hope, yet in a way of diligence, watchfulness, and prayer. It is said, indeed, that symbolical times are not essential to this partial concealment. It may be so, yet they are doubtless fitted to serve this purpose; and there cannot but appear a manifest impropriety in associating symbolical events with literal or natural times. Why the veil in the one case and not in the other? Is not this system of mixing the symbolic and the literal fitted to mislead? and, according to the theory of Maitland and others, has it not, in point of fact, led astray the greater part of the Protestant world? Is it wonderful, that when times are found "imbedded in symbols," a symbolical character should have been attached to them too. Let it be observed also, that in cases of what has been called *miniature symbolization,* as where an empire is represented by a man or a beast, long periods, such as might very well be attributed to an empire, or to any great political or ecclesiastical system, could not, in consistency with symbolical propriety, have been expressed otherwise than we find them. On the supposition that long periods were designed to be expressed, they must necessarily have been symbolized by shorter ones. "Nothing is more obvious than that the prophets have frequently, under divine prompting, adopted the system of hieroglyphic representation, in which a single man represents a community, or a wild beast an extended empire. Consequently, since the mystic exhibition of the community or empire is in miniature, symbolical propriety requires that the associated chronological periods should be exhibited in miniature also. The intrinsic fitness of such a mode of presentation is self-evident. In predicating of a nation a long term of 400 or even 4000 years, there is nothing revolting to verisimilitude or decorum; but to assign such a period to the actings of a

[1] P. 424, *et seq.*

symbolical man or animal would be a grievous outrage on all the proprieties of the prophetic style. The character of the adjuncts should evidently correspond with those of the principal, or the whole picture is at once marred by the most palpable incongruity."[1] It appears, then, in regard to dates occurring in passages where this principle of *miniature symbolization* is adopted, there is a strong presumption in favour of the Year-day theory, or some theory suitably extending the times.

Dr. Maitland has attempted to dislodge his antagonists from this intrenchment. His argument is subtle, and must have been deemed triumphant, for it is repeated and praised as a master-stroke by almost every subsequent writer on the same side. Allowing even that symbols of time might be expected in symbolic predictions, along with symbols of events, he denies that a day can in any way be regarded as the symbol of a year. It is not, he argues, a symbol at all. We give the argument in his own words, premising only that the advocates of the Year-day principle, as we shall by and by see, appeal to Ezek. iv. 4-9 in proof of it:—"When you speak of the beasts I know what you mean, for you admit that Daniel saw certain beasts; but when you speak of 'the days,' I know not what days you refer to, for your system admits of *no days:* you take, if I may so speak, the *word* 'goat' to mean the *thing* 'goat,' and the *thing* goat to represent the *thing* 'king;' but you take the *word* 'day' not to represent the *thing* 'day,' but at once to represent the *thing* year. And this is precisely the point which distinguishes this case from that of Ezekiel's, which has been so often brought forward as parallel to it. The whole matter lies in this, that the one is a case of *representing,* the other of *interpreting.* A *goat,* not the *word* goat, *represented* a king; a day, that is the *word* day, is *interpreted* to mean a year."[2] The pith of the argument seems to lie in this, that while, in Daniel, kingdoms are represented by certain *visible* symbols—beasts, namely—there is no *visible* symbol of a year. We may *interpret* a day of a year, but we cannot say a day *symbolizes* a year. The objector appears to have been met, in the first instance, by the alleged difficulty of symbolizing times in a visible way; but the case of Pharaoh and his officers was at once appealed to, in whose dreams three years are represented by three branches and three baskets; and seven years by seven kine, and seven ears of corn.[3] A writer in the *Investigator* rejoined, that *large* numbers, such as the 1260 or 2300, could not easily be represented in the same way; a statement which seems so very simple and obvious, that we cannot but wonder it should have elicited such a burst of indignation as this: "What! shall it be affirmed that he who called up a vision in which seven kine symbolized seven years, could not employ visible and equally intelligible representations of 1260 years? This were to limit the power of the Almighty, by arrogantly assuming, that though he presented a *few years* by outward pictures to the eye, He could not, with equal facility, and like intelligibleness to men, have painted *a much larger number* by external emblems. We refer the writer in the *Investigator* to Rev. xiv. 1, and ask him how the apostle John knew there were exactly 144,000. On his principle that large number could not have been presented to the eye. How then did he know that there were 144,000?"[4] Does the critic mean that John must have come to the knowledge of it by picture represen-

[1] *Hierophant,* p. 245.    [2] Reply to Cunninghame.
[3] Gen. xl., xli.    [4] Davidson's *Introduction,* vol. iii. p. 520.

tation? Is he sure of this? The number is the same, and the company is the same as in chap. vii. 4, and there we read, "And I *heard* the number of them which were sealed, and there were sealed an hundred and forty and four thousand of all the tribes of the children of Israel." The question is by no means one regarding what God *could* do, but one regarding merely the powers and capabilities of symbolic language; and we do not feel ourselves at all guilty of any unwarrantable "daring," when we aver that large numbers could not be visibly represented like small ones. The real solution of the difficulty which the objection presents, seems to us to have been given by Birks, in his *First Elements of Prophecy*. "The beasts were conceptions visually suggested to the eye of the prophet, and nothing more; and the days, in like manner, were conceptions suggested by the words of the vision to his ear. *The only difference is in the sense by which the mental image is conveyed;* for it is plain that a day, when used as a symbol, must be mentioned, and could not appear visibly to the eye."[1] But whatever may be thought of this, and of the preceding observations, we have still our appeal to the matter of fact. If it be the fact, that in Scripture a day *does* represent a year, we have no concern about speculations regarding *modes* of representing. The only question is, What is the Bible mode? and to that question we shall very shortly apply ourselves.

Meanwhile, we would remark, ere leaving this part of the subject, that although we affirm that wherever we find the principle of miniature symbolization of events, there we have a strong presumption in favour of the times, if such there be, being also expressed on a miniature scale, yet we do not exalt this into a principle embracing the entire case. We shall endeavour to ascertain here, what such general principle is. It need not be disguised that the ground of it has been shifted more than once during the progress of discussion. Mede himself seems to have occupied ground by far too wide; and few or none now choose to defend the Year-day principle on the platform chosen by him who has been erroneously regarded as its originator. He maintained that, "alike in Daniel, and, for aught he knew, in all the other prophets, times of things prophesied, expressed by days, are to be understood of years." But prophecies can be quoted almost without number in which the predicted times must be understood literally; and against this position, somewhat doubtingly and casually assumed by an illustrious interpreter, the artillery of Stuart and Maitland would be most successful, if any were found so foolish as to intrench themselves within it. Professor Stuart, however, chooses to write as if it were an essential part of the Year-day theory. He fights with a man of straw, and expends his logic and his ridicule alike in vain. He asks in triumph, If the 120 years, predicted as the period that should elapse before the flood, must be extended into a respite for the antediluvians of 43,200 years? and if the predicted bondage of Abraham's posterity in Egypt, for 400 years, must be extended into 144,000 years? if the seven years of plenty, and seven of famine to Egypt, must mean 2520 years of each? if Israel's forty years' wilderness-wanderings are to last 14,400 years?[2] No, truly! and yet the times in Daniel and John may be symbolical

[1] P. 343.
[2] *Commentary on Apocalypse*, p. 790, Edinburgh, 1848; where also are cited the following passages expressly from the prophetic books: Ezek. xxix. 11, 12; Jonah iii. 4; Isa. vii. 8 · xvi. 4; Jer. xxvii., xxix.

times notwithstanding. By Bush and Faber, the principle is much narrowed. The ground assumed is that of miniature symbolization. This covers a large part of the field within which the Year-day theory is applied; still, it must be allowed, that both in Daniel and the Apocalypse, there are passages where the times are construed symbolically, or according to the longer reckoning, without being associated with symbols of events. Of this kind is Daniel's famous prophecy of the seventy weeks. What, then, is the true principle or basis of the Year-day theory? We are disposed to reply, as we find Mr. Barnes in one place has done, that it is the manner of the symbolical books of Daniel and John, to express times on the scale of a day for a year; and that in regard to those places, if such there be, where the times are literal, the circumstances of the case, or some expressions in the text, prevent the possibility of mistake, and leave the principle untouched. The *circumstances of the case*, for example, forbid us to explain Dan. iv. 32 in accordance with the principle of a day for a year. "According to this, Nebuchadnezzar must have been mad and eat grass 2520 years."[1] The limited life of man renders any such extension of times here positively absurd. So also with the other case, so much insisted on by the Day-day theorists, of Daniel fasting three weeks.[2] "Surely no one will contend that Daniel fasted twenty-one years." No, but not to mention that this is not a prophecy at all, the circumstances of the case forbid it; and besides, in this place, we have the addition of יָמִים (weeks of *days*), "inserted expressly to bar any such interpretation as would assign to it, as its first sense, the meaning of years."[3] It would, therefore, be most unwise[4] to argue from these exceptive passages, where there can be no danger of mistakes, against the application of the Year-day principle to the great leading prophecies in Daniel and John, regarding the glorious epochs of the church, and the times especially of the consummation. Nor can anyone rationally contend, that because these prophets have adopted this style of a day for a year, in predictions of the character above specified —predictions which form the chief part of their writings—that they are in no single instance to depart from that style—that they are never to lay aside

[1] Stuart's *Apocalypse*, p. 791.   [2] Dan. x. 2, 3.   [3] *Hierophant*, p. 252.
[4] Elliott, however, refuses to except the "seven times" specified in Nebuchadnezzar's vision from the category of chronological prophecies to which the Year-day principle is to be applied. He regards the monarch as the mystical representative of the Assyrian empire, and Babylon, governed by him. "For my own part," says he, "considering the extraordinary nature of the judgment—the fact of its being so fully recorded by Daniel —the circumstance of Nebuchadnezzar being addressed on occasion of another prophecy as the representative of his nation ('thou art that head of gold'), and that of the symbolic tree, when cut down, being bound with a band of *brass* and *iron*, the metals significant of the *Greek* and *Roman empires*, which for ages held sway over the prostrate region of Babylon; all these considerations, united with that of the prediction that *Assyria* specifically is to recover in the latter day from its apostasy (Isa. xix. 24, 25), induce me to believe that Nebuchadnezzar's insanity and degradation typified that of his empire in its apostasy from God; and the *seven times* 360 *days* that passed over him in that state, the *seven times* 360, or 2520 *years* that would have to be completed, ere Assyria's recovery to a sound mind, at the termination of the *times of the Gentiles.*" At the same time Mr. Elliott does not deny the application of the prediction to Nebuchadnezzar as an individual, and remarks, that it is not an uncommon circumstance "for an individual person to be made the subject of a prefigurative vision, and yet himself to prefigure in that very action or character something future." If, then, we admit the truth of this representation, and set aside Dan. x. 2, 3 as not a prediction at all, both the passages insisted on by Professor Stuart are in this way removed from the list of exceptions.

the symbolic and assume the natural. Birks and Elliott, it may be noticed finally, find, in those passages where the Year-day theory is applicable, a purpose of *temporary concealment;* it being "the express design of God, that the church should be kept in the constant expectation of Christ's advent," and that, "yet as the time of the consummation drew near, there should be evidence of it sufficiently clear to each faithful inquirer." "This," adds the latter writer, "sets aside, from its very nature, the objections that have been drawn from sundry prophetic periods, known to be literally expressed, in prophecies where no such temporary concealment was intended."[1]

3. Having seen that the symbolical character of the predictions in which the disputed times for the most part occur, affords a strong presumption, amounting as nearly as possible to proof, in favour of some such principle as that involved in the Year-day theory, we inquire next *whether there be any indications of such principle in Scripture?*

The case of the spies in the book of Numbers[2] has been appealed to by nearly all writers on the Year-day side, and by some of them with no little confidence. "They returned from searching the land after forty days. . . . After the number of the days in which ye searched the land, even forty days, each day for a year, shall ye bear your iniquities, even forty years, and ye shall know my breach of promise." We confess, however, that if this passage were the only one of its kind, we should not be disposed to build much on it. It has been too much pressed; and many will find it difficult to see anything typical or mystical in it. It cannot be proved that the spies were types of the whole nation, or that the days were meant to represent years. Dr. Davidson seems to give the true account of the passage when he says, "It is a simple historical prophecy, in which God ordained that *as* the spies had wandered forty days, *so* the Israelites should wander forty years in the wilderness because of their sins."[3] Taken in connection with other passages, however, it may serve to show that the "Year-day scale" readily occurs in Scripture, when another might as easily have been adopted. The very fact of the punishment of Israel in this case being on the precise scale of a year for a day, seems to indicate something of this kind.

Ezekiel's typical siege presents a much stronger case. We give the passage at length. Ezekiel having been commanded to portray the city of Jerusalem on a tile, and conduct a symbolic siege against it, is further enjoined— "Lie thou also upon thy left side, and lay the iniquity of the house of Israel upon it: according to the number of the days that thou shalt lie upon it thou shalt bear their iniquity. For I have laid upon thee the years of their iniquity, according to the number of the days, three hundred and ninety days: so shalt thou bear the iniquity of the house of Israel. And when thou hast accomplished them, lie again on thy right side, and thou shalt bear the iniquity of the house of Judah forty days: *I have appointed thee each day for a year.*"[4] Ezekiel was ordered to assume this painful position that he might be a sign or symbol of the sufferings of the Jewish nation; and the number of days during which he lay prostrate was declared to symbolize the years of their punishment. Here, then, we have a plain precedent showing that in symbolical representations days stand for years. The argument is equally valid whether we suppose the symbolical

---

[1] *Elements of Prophecy,* p. 375, and *Horæ Apocalyp.,* vol. iii. p. 250.
[2] Chap. xiii. 25; xiv. 34.   [3] *Introduction,* p. 518.   [4] Ezek. iv. 4–6

actions represented things past or things future. The principle is the same. The probability is, that at the time of the representation a few years of the 390 had yet to run; and the design was to show that Jerusalem should be destroyed, and the inhabitants led away captive into Babylon. It is not our province, however, to enter into any exposition of the prophecy. The grand objection made to the argument from this passage is, that in it the symbolic significancy of the days "is expressly stated at the outset." [1] "It is expressly stated that God had appointed a day for a year, whereas in Daniel and John no such information is given." [2] But what if there had *not* been an "express statement" of the principle? That omission, we imagine, would have been eagerly laid hold on as an evidence that no such principle was contained in it. The "express statement," then, so far from being an argument against using this passage as a precedent, is in reality a strong argument in favour of so doing. Can anything be more unreasonable than to object to the passages furnishing a clue or key for certain difficulties elsewhere, that they are plain and express? Nothing, we apprehend, unless to object next that the passages *for* which a key is sought are *not* plain and express. We had thought that it belonged to the very nature of key-passages that they should be plain, and to the very nature of the passages for which the key was needed, that they should not be plain. The demand that there shall be the express statement in these latter which belongs to the former, is just to demand that there shall be no mystery about the times at all,—that they shall be revealed with perfect clearness, and that no wisdom and diligence be called for in evolving a principle and applying it to special cases. Bush's reply to Stuart on this point is, we think, triumphant. "The obvious reply to all this (the want of express statement in Daniel and the Apocalypse) is, that the instances now adduced are to be considered as merely giving us a clue to a general principle of interpretation. Here are two or three striking examples of predictions constructed on the plan of *miniature symbolic representation* in which the involved periods of time are reduced to a scale proportioned to that of the events themselves. What, then, more natural or legitimate, than that, when we meet with other prophecies constructed on precisely the same principle, we should interpret their chronological periods by the same rule? Instead of yielding to a demand to adduce authority for this mode of interpretation, I feel at liberty to demand the authority for departing from it. *Manente ratione manet lex* is an apothegm which is surely applicable here if anywhere. You repeatedly, in the course of your pages, appeal to the oracles of *common sense*, as the grand arbiter in deciding upon the principles of hermeneutics. I make my appeal to the same authority in the present case. I demand, in the name of common sense, a reason why the symbolical prophecies of Daniel and John should not be interpreted on the same principle with other prophecies of the same class. But however loud and urgent my demand on this head, I expect nothing else than that hill and dale will re-echo it, even to the 'crack of doom,' before a satisfactory response from your pages falls on my ear. All the answer I obtain is the following:—'Instead of being aided by an appeal to Ezekiel iv. 5, 6, we find that a principle is recognized there which makes directly against the interpretation we are calling in question. The *express exception* as to the usual modes of reckoning goes directly to show, that the

---

[1] Stuart's *Hints on the Interpretation of Prophecy*, pp. 76, 78; *Apocalypse*, Excursus v.
[2] Davidson's *Introduction*, vol. iii. p. 519.

*general rule* would necessitate a different interpretation.' I may possibly be over sanguine, but I cannot well resist the belief, that the reader will perceive that that which you regard as *the exception*, is in fact *the rule.*"[1]

Dr. Maitland's famous objection, that in Ezekiel the case is one of *representing*, whereas in Daniel and the Apocalypse it is one of *interpreting*, has already been met in a previous part of this Preface. The objection of Bishop Horsley is not very grave—namely, that because the *day* of temptation in the wilderness was *forty years*, and one *day* is with the Lord as a *thousand years*, and a thousand years as one day, we might as well conclude that a day is forty years or a thousand years, as that it represents but one year. So might we, indeed, *if* a number of passages could be produced in which a day has such significancy, and another set of passages could be produced to which the first set furnish a key that seems exactly to answer. In the meantime, we must recognize the difference between what is merely figurative language, and therefore loose and shifting, and the language of symbol.

But the case of Isaiah[2] has been supposed to neutralize any argument built upon that of Ezekiel: "The Lord spake by Isaiah, go and loose the sackcloth from off thy loins, and put off thy shoe from thy foot. And he did so, walking naked and barefoot. And the Lord said, Like as my servant Isaiah hath walked naked and barefoot *three years*, for a sign and wonder upon Egypt and upon Ethiopia, so shall the king of Assyria lead away the Egyptians prisoners." Now, it is argued that here "three *years* correspond to three *years*, not three *days* to three years. It is arbitrary to suppose with Lowth that the original reading was *three days*, or to supply *three days*, with Vitringa. The text must stand as it is."[3] But the interpretation of Lowth and Vitringa is not the only mode in which we may escape from the difficulty, as this learned writer seems to hint. We are not shut up to conjectural emendations. The "three years" in the third verse may be connected with what follows, as well as with what goes before; then the verse will run, "Like as my servant Isaiah hath walked naked and barefoot; *a three years' sign and wonder*," which relieves us entirely from the supposition that Isaiah walked three years barefoot, and, by consequence, from the objection that is founded on it. All that is intimated is, that in some way or other (the passage does not say how) the prophet was a three years' sign—a sign, that is, of a calamity that would last during that time, or commence from that time. In proof of the justice of this arrangement, it may be noticed that the Masoretic interpunction throws the *three years* into the second clause; that the Septuagint gives both solutions, by repeating $\tau\rho\iota\alpha$ $\xi\tau\eta$;[4] and that in a period of such alarm, when Ashdod was taken and the Assyrian pressing on them, it is not likely the symbolical representation would be continued so long. Indeed, this opinion seems to meet with little or no countenance.[5] The opinion that seems generally to prevail is, that Isaiah indicated the three years' captivity either by exhibiting himself in the manner described in the text for three days, which would intimate three years, or by appearing in this manner once only, and at the same time verbally *declaring* his design in so doing.

We come next to what is confessedly a main pillar of the Year-day theory, *the prophecy of the seventy weeks in Daniel.*[6] "Seventy weeks are determined

---

[1] *Hierophant*, pp. 247, 248.  
[2] Chap. xx. 2, 3.  
[3] Davidson's *Introduction*, vol. iii. p. 522.  
[4] J. A. Alexander, *in loco*.  
[5] See the *Critici Sacri*, Scott, Barnes, Alexander, &c.  
[6] Dan. ix. 24–27.

## YEAR-DAY PRINCIPLE.

upon thy people, and upon thy holy city, to finish the transgression, and to make an end of sins, and to make reconciliation for iniquity, and to bring in everlasting righteousness, and to seal up the vision and prophecy, and to anoint the most holy. Know therefore and understand, that from the going forth of the commandment to restore and to build Jerusalem, unto Messiah the prince, &c." Now, the all but universal agreement that this prophecy was fulfilled in a period of 490 years, usually reckoned from the 7th of Artaxerxes, and extending to A.D. 33, the year in which Christ died, seems at once to settle the question regarding the mode of computation. There are, indeed, those[1] who maintain that this prediction has yet to be fulfilled, and they profess to look for its fulfilment in seventy weeks of days; but the number holding this opinion is exceedingly small. The great mass of writers, even of those who contend for literal times, reject it as quite untenable. This mode of cutting the knot, however, indicates the difficulty that is felt by some "Day-dayists" in reconciling the passage with their theory, and their dissatisfaction with the more usual method of reconciliation. That method adopts a new rendering. The words, it is said, ought to be translated seventy *sevens;* and these are assumed to be sevens of *years,* because in the early part of the chapter Daniel had been meditating on Jeremiah's prophecy regarding the seventy years' captivity. By thus understanding the sevens at once of years, without the intervention of symbolic days or weeks, the argument for the Year-day principle, it will be seen, is entirely destroyed.

It would be difficult and tedious to trace the course of discussion fully to which the passage has given rise. A very general outline must suffice. It had been maintained by some who contended for "sevens of years," that the word translated weeks (שָׁבֻעִים *shabuim*) was the regular masculine plural of שֶׁבַע (*sheba*), seven, and ought, therefore, to be translated sevens.[2] But שָׁבֻעִים (*shabuim*), as was alleged in reply, "is not the normal plural of the Hebrew term for seven." The normal plural is שִׁבְעִים (*shibim*); but that is the term for *seventy,* and cannot mean sevens.[3] It seems now admitted on all hands, that both שָׁבֻעִים (*shabuim*) and the feminine form שָׁבֻעוֹת (*shabpuoth*) are plural forms of שָׁבוּעַ (*shabua*), which, according to the etymology of the word, signifies a hebdomad or septemized period.[4] The only question that remains, therefore, regards the use of the word. *What is its use?* So that after much controversy, the matter stands very much as Mede left it. "The question," says he, "lies not in the etymology, but in the use, wherein שָׁבוּעַ (*shabua*) always signifies *sevens of days,* and never *sevens of years.* Wheresoever it is *absolutely* put, it means of days; it is nowhere thus used of years."[5] Besides the places in Daniel, the word occurs absolutely elsewhere, in some one or other of its forms, *eleven* times, and *in every one of these cases with the sense of weeks of days.*[6] It is true that if we except the places in Daniel, there is no instance in Scripture where the masculine plural שָׁבֻעִים (*shabuim*) is used to denote weeks. The word elsewhere used for that purpose is uniformly שָׁבֻעוֹת (*shabpuoth*) in the feminine. But we confess ourselves at a loss to understand

---

[1] Tyso, Govett, and Todd.    [2] *Hints on the Interpretation of Prophecy,* p. 79.
[3] *Hierophant,* p. 250.    [4] Davidson's *Introduction,* vol. iii. p. 515.
[5] Mede's *Works,* book iii. chap. ix. p. 599.
[6] Gen. xxix. 27, 28; Lev. xii. 5; Exod. xxxiv. 22; Deut. xvi. 9, twice, and 10; Jer. v. 24; Deut. xvi. 16; 2 Chron. viii. 13; Num. xxviii. 26.

why so much should be made of this. The word which Daniel uses is confessedly the masculine plural[1] of the same word, which in the singular is translated "week," and in the feminine plural "weeks;" and although there are instances in various languages of the masculine and feminine plurals having different significations, yet, in the absence of anything like proof that such is the case here, we must be guided by the use of the word in its other forms throughout the Scripture, when we come to interpret the peculiar form that occurs in Daniel. What good reason can be given for departing from the analogy of the other forms? This, it must be confessed, is entirely on the side of the Year-day principle; and the objection resolves itself into nothing more than this, that it is a peculiar form of the word which Daniel uses.

As to what is said of the qualifying word יָמִים, *yamim* (days), twice occurring in chap. x. 2, 3,[2] in connection with שָׁבֻעִים (*shabuim*), giving the literal sense *three weeks, days*, or *three weeks as to days*, we cannot see that it furnishes any grave objection to our argument. It seems rather to strengthen it. For here we have two places in which the word in question, and the form of it in question, are declared to mean weeks of days. Does not this intimate that such is the ordinary and primary sense? Are we not as much entitled to draw this conclusion, as other parties to conclude that the qualifying word is added because the usual sense is sevens of years? Let us only suppose that the qualifying word had been years instead of days (sevens as to years), would it not very readily have been said in that case, Here is a plain declaration that sevens of *years* are to be understood; and certainly the places where no qualifying word occurs must be ruled by this? Gesenius supposes the addition of יָמִים (days) is merely *pleonastic;* but if any other reason must be found for it, that of Bush seems as satisfactory as any, which regards it as an intimation that the primary sense is the only admissible one in the circumstances.

4. We entitle our next head of evidence, *Exigency of the passages in which the prophetic times occur.* The very best plan of arriving at the truth in the question, whether the shorter or longer reckoning be the right one, is to test both by application to the disputed passages. Try the two keys, and see which best suits the lock. One section of the literal dayists have here, however, a great advantage over their opponents, inasmuch as their plan of placing the Apocalyptic fulfilments entirely in the future (with the exception, on the part of some of them, of the epistles to the seven churches), relieves them from every embarrassment that might arise from any specific historical application. Of course it is impossible to argue with men of this school, that their literal times do not answer to their historical events, for historical events they have none, and we cannot prove that their ideal fulfilments may not be realized.

To discuss fully this part of our subject, however, would require a volume embracing an exposition of nearly all the more important passages in Daniel and the Apocalypse. We intend only to offer a few passing remarks on one or two of these, referring such as wish to prosecute the subject, to the "Notes" in this volume.

Let us take first the *Saracenic woe*.[3] We say not, in the meantime, that the interpretation which has given rise to this name is necessarily the right one. We merely wish to institute a comparison between it and another in-

---

[1] Gesenius' *Lexicon*.  [2] See margin.  [3] Chap. ix. 5-10.

terpretation, which proceeds on the principle of the shorter dates. If the reader will turn to our author's exposition, and attentively study it, he will, we think, be disposed to acquiesce in the justice of his closing remark, that, on the supposition that it was the design of John to symbolize these events (the Arabian conquests), the symbol has been chosen which of all others is best adapted to the end. Moreover, it will be seen that the Arabian history, according to the requirements of the passage, on the Year-day principle, furnishes a period of five months, or 150 years of intense stinging oppression, and immediately thereafter exhibits a gradual decline in power, along with a disinclination to persecute. Now what have we to oppose to this view on the part of those who advocate literal times? We turn to Professor Stuart. He tells us he can find no event in history that, with any good degree of probability, will correspond to a period of 150 years. "And," adds he, "if we count five literal months, we are still involved in the same difficulty. Hence the tropical use of the expression five months, seems to be most probable and facile." His conclusion is that "the meaning must be a short period." We cannot think that this "tropical use" is very "probable;" it is however abundantly "facile;" and we know not how to argue with those who, when events will not correspond with their literal times, immediately take refuge in tropes. When Professor Stuart can find events that suit, his times are literal, as we shall immediately see; when he cannot find such events, his times are tropical. But a principle so "facile," however it may suit his convenience, is not fitted to guide us in an inquiry into the prophetic periods. "The proper laws of interpretation," our author has justly observed in his exposition of the place, "demand that one or the other of these periods should be found, either that of five months literally, or that of a hundred and fifty years."

Take next the *Turkish woe*.[1] We refer the reader again to the author's exposition, that he may see how "the hour, day, month, and year" of this prediction—that is, the 391 years, and a 12th or 24th of a year—find their fulfilment in the history of the Turkish empire. But on the supposition that the times are literal, what events can be fixed on as occupying this period of little more than a year? or how, in transactions so great, should a single hour be mentioned? These questions are evaded by assigning a new sense to the clause εἰς τὴν ὥραν καὶ ἡμέραν, &c. It is said to mean only, "that at the destined hour, and destined day, and destined month, and destined year," the calamity should happen; that is to say, it should occur simply *at the appointed time*. We venture to say that such a periphrasis for an idea so simple has no parallel elsewhere. For the criticism of the passage, we refer to Barnes and Elliott, who have successfully contended that the words completely reject this sense. The latter appeals also to the parallel passage in Dan. xii. 7, where "for a time, times, and half a time" is universally understood of the *aggregate* period of three years and a half.[2]

*The forty-two months of the Gentiles* is another and remarkable Apocalyptic period.[3] If we do not, with our author, apply the passage in which this notation of time occurs, to the trampling down of the church by the Papacy during her long and oppressive reign of 1260 years, but seek an explanation from those who deny the Year-day principle, shall we find events that will better answer on the principle of literal times? Let us try. Professor Stuart, in this place, abandons the idea he sometimes resorts to, of supposing the periods

[1] Chap. ix. 15.   [2] *Horæ Apocalyp.*, vol. i. p. 489.   [3] Chap. xi. 2.

"figurative modes of expressing a short time." He thinks a "literal and definite period" is here meant; and he even condescends, in spite of all his hatred of historical comments, on historical events answering to this definite period. "It is certain," says he, "that the invasion of the Romans lasted just about the length of the period named until Jerusalem was taken." And again, in his *Excursus on Designations of Time*, he says that in the spring of A.D. 67, Vespasian was sent by Nero to subdue Palestine; and that on the 10th of August, A.D. 70, Jerusalem was taken and destroyed by Titus. Thus he makes out the literal period of forty-two months, or three and a half years. He is, however, compelled to admit that the war actually began some time before Vespasian's mission. But allowing all this to be correct, there was, as Mr. Barnes remarks, "no precise period of three years and a half, in respect to which the language here used would be applicable to the literal Jerusalem. Judea was held in subjection, and trodden down by the Romans for centuries, and never, in fact, gained its independence." It is trodden down still. And yet we are told, in a laboured article written on purpose to set aside the Year-day principle, that *there can scarcely be a doubt* that the period in question (the forty-two months) is designed to mark the time during which the conquest of Palestine and of the Holy City was going on.

In close connection with this prediction, we have *the times of the two witnesses*.[1] They were to "prophesy a thousand two hundred and threescore days, clothed in sackcloth." Again, we think the longer reckoning meets the requirements of the passage, and is consistent with the historical events offered in explanation. During all the dark period of Papal rule, there has been a competent number of witnesses testifying in favour of the truth. The reader will find ample details in the exposition within. Let us turn now to the exposition offered by the great chief of the Literal-day theorists. His theory requires him to find the witnesses in Jerusalem immediately previous to its fall. But where the witnesses in Jerusalem prophesying during three and a half literal years? History is quite silent in regard to any such parties; nay more, the accounts which we have of the period render it exceedingly improbable that any such parties could have existed in Jerusalem at that time. The Christians, warned by their Master, had fled to Pella, and thereby escaped the calamity in which their unbelieving countrymen were overwhelmed. Yet, in the absence of history, and in spite of history, suppositions are made to stand in its place. We are told that some of the faithful and zealous teachers of Christianity would certainly remain in spite of their Lord's warning. These, it is supposed next, would be slain by the Zealots, who would, notwithstanding, be unable to destroy Christianity. The truth should ever have a resurrection. We offer no further remark on this, than that if pure imaginations are to be alleged, where history fails, there can be no difficulty in meeting the requirements of any theory, inasmuch as inventions are much more "facile" than facts. But the exposure of the dead bodies of the witnesses is supposed to be perfectly fatal to the Year-day principle in this passage. "What now," it is asked, "if we should insist on interpreting this (the three days and a half of exposure) as meaning three and a half *years?* It would bring out an absurdity; for a single month in the climate of Palestine would in one way or another destroy any dead body, not to speak of its being devoured." Doubtless this is an absurdity; but it is an absurdity ob-

---
[1] Chap. xi. 3, 11.

tained by subjecting a symbolical passage to a very singular process, in which one part of the symbol is explained, and then read along with the *unexplained* part. But explain both parts of the passage, the *lying exposed*, as well as the *days*, and then we have no incongruous sense, but an intimation, that for three and a half years the witnesses should be silenced, and be treated with great indignity, as if unworthy of Christian burial. Or if the question be regarding symbolical propriety, let the symbolical representation stand as it is—both parts unexplained; and what inconsistency is there in supposing dead bodies exposed for three and a half *days* in the climate of Palestine? If we choose to proceed on a principle like this, we may make as many absurdities as there are passages in the Apocalypse.

Next in order, we have the *times of the woman in the wilderness*,[1] the thousand two hundred and threescore days, or time, times, and half a time, during which she was protected and nourished by God. Once more we refer to the author's exposition of this passage for a defence of the Protestant interpretation, which explains it of the preservation of the church in a state of comparative obscurity during the long period of Papal oppression. But on the principle of literal days, that is, "if the period of the woman's sojourn be only three years and six months, the preparation must be either quite disproportionate to the event, or the steps of the preparation will be crowded into the narrowest compass. The spiritual deliverance, the dejection of Satan, the renewed persecution, the protection, the flood, its absorption by the friendly earth, and the persevering rage of the dragon, will all be crushed into the space of two or three years. Surely nothing but the most distinct revelation could make us receive such an exposition of the true reference of so glorious a prophecy."[2] It is difficult, indeed, to conceive that a prophecy of this nature should find its fulfilment in any three and a half years of the church's history; and our difficulties certainly are not diminished, when we come to consider the special interpretations that are constructed on this principle. We are told that the woman is the Jewish Theocratic church. But that church never dwelt 1260 days in the wilderness, nor can any historical event be alleged in illustration of such a view that does not bear its refutation on the face of it. The Christians who fled to Pella, will the reader believe it, are, for the sake of a theory, made to stand for the church, symbolized by the woman; and their protection, during the continuance of the Jewish war, is the woman's wilderness sojourn. The flight is the flight of the woman, or Jewish Theocratic church, in the first instance. But the Jewish church, to answer the necessities of the case, is at once transformed into the Christian; and finally, a comparatively small body of Christians in the neighbourhood of Jerusalem is elevated into the dignity of *the church*, to the exclusion of the numerous societies of Christians existing elsewhere. These are the assumptions set forth in antagonism to the Protestant view; set forth, too, not as modest guesses, but as certain verities, to reject which, brings down on us the charge of ignorance of history, and of exegetical science.

Our limits forbid us to speak of the forty-two months of the beast,[3] or of the periods in Daniel. Of the beast, it is manifest, that it is a power of no brief duration; but one which, existing through a long previous period, appears again at the great final battle immediately previous to the millennium, and is then destroyed. Great care is taken, in the chapter which describes

---

[1] Chap. xii. 6, 14.    [2] *Elements of Prophecy*, p. 382.    [3] Chap. xiii. 5.

the closing struggle, to identify the beast which was then slain with that which had previously appeared on the stage.[1] As to the view which explains the beast of Nero, and the times of the three and a half years of his persecution, it is certainly enough to observe, that it requires the aid of a heathen hariolation to make it out, and may, therefore, be dismissed without argument. Of the periods in Daniel, particularly those in the seventh and twelfth chapters,[2] we can only say that the mode of authoritatively asserting that the reference is to Antiochus Epiphanes, and then ridiculing the idea of any one man living through 1260 years,[3] is a mode which must be abandoned by such as would secure a favourable reception for their views. We believe the sublime predictions of Daniel and John are occupied with far higher subjects—subjects of infinitely more concern to the church and the world than the history of the two tyrants, Antiochus and Nero.

[We had intended to consider some of the current objections against the Year-day theory, particularly that founded on its alleged novelty—"The spiritual common sense of the church," according to Dr. Maitland, "being set in array against it, from the days of Daniel to those of Wickliffe." Mr. Elliott has thoroughly examined this position; and the conclusion to which he comes, after a most painstaking inquiry, is—"That from the time of Cyprian, near the middle of the 3d century, even to the time of Joachim and the Waldenses, in the 12th century, there was kept up, by a succession of expositors, a recognition of the precise *Year-day* principle." We have carefully examined the grounds of this opinion, and compared them with certain recent and able adverse criticisms, without having had our conviction shaken that, *in the main*, it is correct.]

[1] Compare chap. xiii. with xix. 19, 20.   [2] vii. 25; xii. 7.   [3] Stuart's *Commentary*.

# INTRODUCTION

TO THE

# BOOK OF REVELATION OF ST. JOHN

§ I.—*The Writer of the Book of Revelation.*

Much has been written on the question who was the author of this book. To enter into an extended investigation of this would greatly exceed the limits which I have, and would not comport with my design in these Notes. For a full examination of the question I must refer to others, and would mention particularly, Prof. Stuart, *Com.* i. 283-427; Lardner, *Works*, vi. 318-327; Hug, *Intro. to the New Testament*, pp. 650-673, Andover, 1836; Michaelis, *Intro. to the New Testament*, iv. 457-544; and the article "Revelation," in Kitto's *Cyclopædia of Biblical Literature*. I propose to exhibit, briefly, the evidence that the apostle John was the author, according to the opinion which has been commonly entertained in the church; the proof of which seems to me to be satisfactory. This may be considered under these divisions: the direct historical evidence, and the insufficiency of the reason for doubting it.

I. The direct historical evidence. The sum of all that is to be said on this point is, that to the latter half of the third century it was not doubted that the apostle John was the author. Why it was ever afterwards doubted, and what is the force and value of the doubt, will be considered in another part of this Introduction.

There may be some convenience in dividing the early historical testimony into three periods of half a century each, extending from the death of John, about A.D. 98, to the middle of the third century.

1. From the death of John, about A.D. 98 to A.D. 150. This period embraces the last of those men who conversed, or who might have conversed, with the apostles; that is, who were, for a part of their lives, the contemporaries of John. The testimony of the writers who lived then would, of course, be very important. Those embraced in this period are Hermas, Ignatius, Polycarp, and Papias. The evidence of this period is not indeed very *direct*, but it is such as it would be on the supposition that John was the author, and there is nothing contradictory to that supposition.

HERMAS, about A.D. 100.—In the *Shepherd* or *Pastor*, ascribed to this writer, there are several allusions which are supposed to refer to this book, and which resemble it so much as to make it probable that the author was acquainted with it. Dr. Lardner thus expresses the result of his examination of this point: "*It is probable* that Hermas had read the book of Revelation, and imitated it. He has many things resembling it" (vol. ii. pp. 69-72). There is no *direct* testimony, however, in this writer that is of importance.

IGNATIUS.—He was bishop of Antioch, and flourished A.D. 70-107. In the latter year he suffered martyrdom, in the time of Trajan. Little, however, can be derived from him in regard to the Apocalypse. He was a contemporary of John, and it is not a little remarkable that he has not more directly alluded to him. In the course of a forced and hurried journey to Rome, the scene of his martyrdom, he wrote several epistles to the Ephesians, Magnesians, Trallians, Romans, Philadelphians, Smyrneans, and to Polycarp. There has been much controversy respecting the authenticity of these epistles, and it is generally admitted that those which we now possess have been greatly corrupted. There is no direct mention of the Apocalypse in these epistles, and Michaelis makes this one of the strong grounds of his disbelief of its genuineness. His argument is, that the silence of Ignatius shows, either that he did not know of the existence of this book, or did not recognize it as a part of the sacred Scriptures. Little, however, can be ever inferred from the mere *silence* of an author; for there may have been many reasons why, though the book may have been in existence, and recognized as the writing of John, Ignatius did not refer to it. The whole matter of the residence of John at Ephesus, of his banishment to Patmos, and of his death, is unnoticed by him. There are, however, two or three *allusions* in the epistles of Ignatius which have been supposed to refer to the Apocalypse, or to prove that he was familiar with that work—though it must be admitted that the language is so general, that it furnishes no certain proof that he designed to quote it. They are these: Epis. to the Romans—"In the patience of Jesus Christ," comp. Rev. i. 9; and Epis. to the Ephesians—"Stones of the temple of the Father prepared for the building of God," comp. Rev. xxi. 2-19. To these Mr. John Collyer Knight, of the British Museum, in a recent publication (*Two new Arguments in Vindication of the Genuineness and Authenticity of the Revelation of St. John*, London, 1842), has added a third: Epis. to the Philadelphians—"If they do not speak concerning Jesus Christ, they are but *sepulchral pillars*, and *upon them are written only the names of men*." Comp. Rev. iii. 12, "Him that overcometh will I make a pillar in the temple of my God; and he shall go no more out: and I will write upon him the name of my God." It must be admitted, however, that this coincidence of language does not furnish any certain proof that Ignatius had seen the Apocalypse, though this is such language as he *might* have used if he had seen it. There was no known necessity, however, for his referring to this book if he was acquainted with it, and nothing can be inferred from his silence.

POLYCARP.—He was bishop of Smyrna, and suffered martyrdom, though at what time is not certain. The *Chronicon Paschale* names A.D. 163; Eusebius, 167; Usher, 169; and Pearson, 148. He died at the age of eighty-six, and consequently was contemporary with John, who died about A.D. 98. There is but one relic of his writings extant—his epistle to the Philippians. There is in Eusebius (iv. 15), an epistle from the church in Smyrna to the churches in Pontus, giving an account of the martyrdom of Polycarp. It is admitted that in neither of these is there any express mention, or any certain allusion, to the book of Revelation. But from this circumstance nothing can be inferred respecting the Apocalypse, either for or against it, since there may have been no occasion for Polycarp or his friends, in the writings now extant, to speak of this book; and from their silence nothing more should be inferred against this book than against the epistles of Paul, or the Gospel by John. There is, however, what may, without impropriety, be regarded as an important testimony of Polycarp in regard to this book. Polycarp was, as there is every reason to suppose, the personal friend of John, and Irenæus was the personal friend of Polycarp (Lardner, ii. 94-96). Now Irenæus, as we shall see, on all occasions, and in the most positive manner, gives his clear testimony that the Apocalypse was written by the apostle John. It is impossible to suppose that he would do this if Polycarp had not believed it to be true; and certainly he would not have been likely to hold this opinion if one who was his own friend, and the friend of John, had doubted or denied it. This is not indeed absolute proof, but it furnishes strong presumptive evidence in favour of the opinion that the book of Revelation was written by the apostle John. The whole history of Polycarp, and his testimony to the books of the New Testament, may be seen in Lardner, ii. 94-114.

PAPIAS.—Papias was bishop of Hierapolis, near Colosse, and flourished, according to Cave, about A.D. 110; according to others, about the year 115 or 116. How long he lived is uncertain. Irenæus asserts that he was the intimate friend—$\dot{\epsilon}\tau a\hat{\iota}\rho os$—of Polycarp, and this is also admitted by Eusebius (*Ecc. Hist.* iii. 39). He was the contemporary of John, and was probably acquainted with him. Eusebius expressly says that he was "a hearer of John" (Lardner, ii. 117). Of his writings there remain only a few fragments preserved by Eusebius, by Jerome, and in the *Commentary* of Andrew, bishop of Cæsarea, in Cappadocia. He was a warm defender of the Millennarian doctrines. In his writings preserved to us (see Lardner, ii. 120-125), there is no express mention of the Apocalypse, or direct reference to it; but the commentator Andrew of Cæsarea reckons him among the explicit witnesses in its favour. In the Preface to his *Commentary on the Apocalypse*, Andrew says, "In regard now to the inspiration of the book, we think it superfluous to extend our discourse, inasmuch as the blessed Gregory, and Cyril, and moreover the ancient [writers] *Papias, Irenœus, Methodius,* and *Hippolytus* bear testimony to its credibility." See the passage in Hug, *Intro.* p. 652; and Prof. Stuart, i. 305. And in nearly the same words does Arethas, the successor of Andrew, bear the like testimony. The evidence, therefore, in this case is the same as in the case of Polycarp, and it cannot be supposed that Papias would have been thus referred to unless it was uniformly understood that he regarded the book as the production of the apostle John.

These are all the testimonies that properly belong to the first half century after the death of John, and though not absolutely *positive* and *conclusive* in themselves, yet the following points may be regarded as established:—(*a*) The book was known; (*b*) so far as the testimony goes, it is in favour of its having been composed by John; (*c*) the fact that he was the author is not called in question or doubted; (*d*) it was generally ascribed to him; (*e*) it was *probably* the foundation of the Millennarian views entertained by Papias—that is, it is easier to account for his holding these views by supposing that the book was known, and that he founded them on this book, than in any other way. See Prof. Stuart, i. 304.

2. The second half century after the death of John, from A.D. 150 to A.D. 200. This will include the names of Justin Martyr, the Narrator of the Martyrs of Lyons, Irenæus, Melito, Theophilus, Apollonius, Clement of Alexandria and Tertullian.

JUSTIN MARTYR.—He was a Christian philosopher, born at Flavia Neapolis, anciently called Sichem, a city of Samaria, it is supposed about A.D. 103; was converted to Christianity about A.D. 133, and suffered martyrdom about A.D.

165 (Lardner, ii. 125-140). He was partly contemporary with Polycarp and Papias. He travelled in Egypt, Italy, and Asia Minor, and resided some time at Ephesus. He was endowed with a bold and inquiring mind, and was a man eminent for integrity and virtue. Tatian calls him an "admirable man." Methodius says, that he was a man "not far removed from the apostles in time or in virtue." Photius says, that he was "well acquainted with the Christian philosophy, and especially with the heathen; rich in the knowledge of history, and all other parts of learning" (Lardner). He was, therefore, well qualified to ascertain the truth about the origin of the book of Revelation, and his testimony must be of great value. He was an advocate of the doctrine of *Chiliasm*—or, the doctrine that Christ would reign a thousand years on the earth—and in defence of this he uses the following language: "And a man from among us, by name John, one of the Apostles of Christ, in a Revelation made to him—$\dot{\epsilon}\nu$ 'Αποκαλυψει γενομένη αὐτῷ—has prophesied that the believers in one Christ shall live a thousand years in Jerusalem; and after that shall be the general, and, in a word, the eternal resurrection and judgment of all men together." There can be no doubt whatever that there is an allusion here to the book of Revelation—for the very name *Revelation*—'Αποκάλυψις—is used; that Justin believed that it was written by the apostle John; and that there is express reference to what is now chap. xx. of that book. The book was, therefore, in existence in the time of Justin—that is, in about fifty years after the death of John; was believed to be the work of the apostle John; was quoted as such, and by one who had lived in the very region where John lived, and by a man whose character is unimpeached, and who, in a point like this, could not have been mistaken. The testimony of Justin Martyr, therefore, is very important. It is positive; it is given where there was every opportunity for knowing the truth, and where there was no motive for a false testimony; and it is the testimony of one whose character for truthfulness is unimpeached.

THE NARRATIVE OF THE MARTYRS OF VIENNE AND LYONS.—Lardner, ii. 160-165. In the reign of Marcus Antoninus, Christians suffered much from persecution. This persecution was particularly violent at Lyons, and the country round about. The churches of Lyons and Vienne sent an account of their sufferings, in an epistle, to the churches of Asia and Phrygia. This, according to Lardner, was about A.D. 177. The epistle has been preserved by Eusebius. In this epistle, among other undoubted allusions to the New Testament, the following occurs. Speaking of Vettius Epigathus, they say—"For he was indeed a genuine disciple of Christ, *following the Lamb whithersoever he goes.*" Comp. Rev. xiv. 2: "These are they which *follow the Lamb whithersoever he goeth.*" There can be no doubt that this passage in Revelation was referred to; and it proves that the book was then known, and that the writers were accustomed to regard it as on a level with the other sacred writings.

IRENÆUS.—The testimony of this father has already been referred to when speaking of Polycarp. He was bishop of Lyons, in Gaul. His country is not certainly known, but Lardner supposes that he was a Greek, and, from his early acquaintance with Polycarp, that he was from Asia. When a youth, he was a hearer of Polycarp, and also a disciple of Papias. He was born about the beginning of the second century, and it is commonly supposed that he suffered martyrdom in extreme old age. He became bishop of Lyons after he was seventy years of age, and wrote his principal work, *Contra Hæreses*, after this. His testimony is particularly valuable, as he was in early life acquainted with Polycarp, who was a contemporary and friend of the apostle John (Lardner, ii. 165-192). Of his reference to the book of Revelation, Lardner says: "The Apocalypse, or Revelation, is often quoted by him as the Revelation of John, the disciple of the Lord." In one place he says: "It was seen no long time ago, but almost in our age, at the end of the reign of Domitian." And again, he spoke of the exact and ancient copies of the book, as if it was important to ascertain the true reading, and as if it were then possible to do this. Thus Eusebius (Lardner, ii. 167) says of him: "In his fifth book he thus discourses of the Revelation of John, and the computation of the name of Antichrist: 'These things being thus, *and this number being in all the exact and ancient copies, and they who saw John attesting to the same things*, and reason teaching us that the number of the name of the beast, according to the acceptation of the Greeks, is expressed by the letters contained in it.'" Here is an undoubted reference to Revelation xiii. 18. This evidence is clear and positive. Its value consists in these things: (*a*) That he was familiar with one who was the friend of John; (*b*) that he must have known his views on the subject; (*c*) that he must have been intimately acquainted with the common opinion on the subject of the authorship of the book; (*d*) that a spurious work could not have been palmed upon the world as the production of John; (*e*) that he bears unequivocal testimony to the fact that it was written by John; (*f*) and that he speaks of the "most exact" copies being then in existence, and testified to by those who had seen John himself.

MELITO.—Lardner, ii. 157-160. He was bishop of Sardis, one of the churches to which the book of Revelation was directed. He is supposed to have flourished about A.D. 170. He was a man greatly distinguished for learning and piety, and Jerome says that Christians were accustomed to name him a *prophet*. He was, moreover, remarkably inquisitive respecting the sacred books; and, at the request of Onesimus, he made extracts from the Scriptures respecting the Messianic prophecies, and also a complete list of the books of the Old Testament, which is still extant in Eusebius, *Ecc. Hist.* iv. 26. He wrote a *Treatise* or *Commentary on the Book of Revelation*. Dr. Lardner says of this, "What it contained we are not informed. I will say it was a commentary on that book. It is plain he ascribed that book to John, and very likely to John the apostle. I think it very probable he esteemed it a book of canonical authority." Hug says (p. 653), "Melito himself calls it the Apocalypse of John." Even Michaelis (*Intro. to the New Testament*, iv. 466) reckons Melito among the witnesses in favour of the book. The *value* of this testimony is this: (*a*) Melito was bishop of one of the churches to which the Apocalypse was directed; (*b*) he lived near the time of John; (*c*) he was a diligent student on this very subject; (*d*) he had every opportunity of ascertaining the truth on the subject; (*e*) he regarded it as the work of the apostle John; (*f*) and he wrote a treatise or commentary on it as an inspired book. It is not easy to conceive of stronger testimony in favour of the book.

THEOPHILUS.—Lardner, ii. 203-215. He was bishop of Antioch, and flourished about A.D. 169-180. He wrote a work against the "heresy" of Hermogenes, referred to by Eusebius, *Ecc. Hist.* iv. 24. In that work he expressly speaks of the Apocalypse as the production of John; and Lardner says of his testimony, "That the book of Revelation was owned by him is undoubted from Eusebius. Eusebius has assured us that Theophilus, in his book against Hermogenes, brought testimonies from the Apocalypse of John," pp. 214, 215. The value of this testimony is, that Theophilus doubtless expressed the current opinion of his time, and that he had ample opportunity for ascertaining the truth. There is also a passage in the writings of Theophilus which *seems* to be a direct allusion to the book of Revelation: "This Eve, because she was deceived by the serpent—the evil demon, who is also called Satan, who thus spoke to her by the serpent—does not cease to accuse; this demon is also called the dragon." Comp. Rev. xii. 9.

APOLLONIUS.—Lardner, ii. 391–393. He flourished about A.D. 192. Eusebius says of him, "He makes use of testimonies out of the Revelation of John." The value of this testimony is, (a) that he quotes the book as of authority; and (b) that he ascribes it to John, evidently meaning the apostle John.

CLEMENT OF ALEXANDRIA.—Lardner, ii. 222–259. He flourished about A.D. 192–220. Many of his writings are extant. Lardner (p. 245) says of him, "The book of Revelation is several times quoted by him, and once in this manner: 'Such an one, though here on earth he be not honoured with the first seat, shall sit upon the four and twenty thrones judging the people, as John says in the Revelation.'" Comp. Rev. iv. 4; xi. 16. Lardner adds, "And that he supposed this writer to be John the apostle appears from another place, where he refers to Rev. xxi. 21, as the words of the apostle." Professor Stuart says (i. 317), "There is no good ground for doubt, from anything which is found in the work, that he received and admitted the Apocalypse as a work of John the apostle." The known character of Clement makes this testimony of great value.

TERTULLIAN.—He was the contemporary of Clement, and was the most ancient, and one of the most learned, of the Latin fathers (Lardner, ii. 267–306). He was born at Carthage about the middle of the second century, and died about A.D. 220. He was reared in the study of the Greek and Latin languages, of philosophy and the Roman law, and possessed extensive information. "His testimony to the Apocalypse is most full and ample. He quotes, or refers to it in more than seventy passages in his writings, appealing to it expressly as the work of the apostle John" (Elliott, i. 27). "The declarations of Tertullian are so frequent and plain, that no doubt can possibly remain as to his belief" (Prof. Stuart, i. 318). "The Revelation of John is often quoted. I put together two or three passages, which show his full persuasion that it was written by the apostle and evangelist of that name" (Lardner, ii. 295). One of the passages referred to by Lardner is the following: "The apostle John, in the Apocalypse, describes a sharp two-edged sword coming out of the mouth of God." Another is, "Though Marcion rejects his revelation, the succession of bishops traced to the original will assure us that John is the author." There can be no doubt, therefore, that Tertullian regarded the apostle John as the author of the book of Revelation; and his confident assertion may be considered as expressive of the prevailing opinion of his time.

Thus far, to the end of the second century, the testimony of the fathers of the church, as far as we now have it, was uniform and unbroken; and so far as historical testimony is concerned, this should be permitted to decide the question. Marcion, indeed, who lived in the time of Polycarp, and whom Polycarp called "the first-born of Satan" (Lardner, ii. 95), rejected the book of Revelation (see the declaration of Tertullian in Lardner, ii. 275); but it is also to be remembered that he rejected the whole of the Old Testament, the account of the genealogy and baptism of the Saviour, the Acts of the Apostles, the Epistles to Timothy, Titus, the Hebrews, and the Catholic Epistles (Lardner, vi. 142–151, 347–350; viii. 489–513). Besides the opinion of Marcion, the testimony was uniform, with the exception of the heretical sect of the *Alogi*, if there was any such sect, which is generally supposed to have arisen in the latter half of this century, who derived their name from their antipathy to the name of *Logos*, and who on this account denied both the Gospel of John and the book of Revelation. See Lardner, iv. 190, 191; viii. 627, 628. Lardner, however, maintains that there never was any such sect (viii. 628).

3. The third half century after the death of John, A.D. 200–250. Among the names embraced in this period are those of Hippolytus, who flourished about A.D. 220; Nepos, an Egyptian bishop; the well-known Origen, the most acute critic of all the early fathers, and who devoted his life to the study of the Scriptures; Cyprian, bishop of Carthage, who flourished about A.D. 246; and Methodius, bishop of Olympia in Lycia. All these, without exception, have left a clear and decided expression of their belief that the apostle John was the author of the Apocalypse. See that testimony at length in Prof. Stuart, i. 321–326.

It is unnecessary to pursue the historical evidence further. If the testimony in favour of the work is unbroken and clear for an hundred and fifty years, the testimony of those who lived subsequent to that period would add little to its strength. To the names already mentioned, however, there might be added those of Epiphanius, Basil, Cyril of Alexandria, Ephrem the Syrian, Ambrose, Jerome, Augustine, Hilary of Poictiers, Gregory Nazianzen, Chrysostom, and many others.

Such is the external positive testimony in favour of the opinion that the book of Revelation was written by the apostle John.

To this might be added certain internal marks, or certain facts in the life of John which accord with this supposition, and seem to confirm it. They are such that if they did *not* exist there might be some room for plausible doubt, though it must be admitted that, in themselves, they do not amount to positive proof of any considerable strength that he *was* the author. There is not room to dwell upon them, and they can only be briefly referred to. They are such as these:—(1) That the author calls himself *John*, evidently with the design of representing himself as the *apostle* of that name; for (a) his supposed relation to the churches of Asia Minor is such as the relation of the apostle John was, and (b) the name *John*, unless there was something to qualify it, would be naturally understood as referring to the apostle of that name. (2) The fact that John lived at Ephesus, and was well known to the seven churches of Asia Minor. (3) The fact that he lived to extreme old age—to the time when the book was supposed to have been written. See § II. (4) The fact that there was a persecution in the time of Domitian, when this book is supposed to have been written; and (5) what might be derived from a comparison of this book with the acknowledged writings of John.

II. To confirm the argument, it is necessary to show the insufficiency of the reasons for doubting that John was the author. This point may be considered under two heads—the alleged grounds for doubting that it was written by John by the ancients; and the reasons alleged by the moderns.

(1) The ancients.

(a) It has been maintained that it was rejected by Caius, a presbyter at Rome. He flourished, according to Cave, about A.D. 210. See Lardner, ii. 394–410. There is a single passage in his writings, from which it has been inferred that he designed to reject the Apocalypse. This is in the following words—"And Cerinthus also, who by his revelations, as if written by some great apostle, imposes upon us monstrous relations of things of his own invention, as shown him by an angel, says, 'that after the resurrection there shall be a terrestrial kingdom of Christ, and that men shall live again in Jerusalem, subject to sensual desires and pleasures. And being an enemy to the divine Scriptures, and desirous to seduce mankind, he says there will be a term of a thousand years spent in nuptial entertainments'" (Lardner, ii. 400, 401).

The whole force of this depends on the supposition that Caius meant to refer to Rev. xx. 4–6.

But in regard to this the following remarks may be made:—(a) Caius was strongly opposed to Cerinthus, and to his views; (b) he was opposed to the prevailing doctrine of Chiliasm, or the doctrine of the millennium, as then extensively held—that Christ would reign personally on the earth with his saints for a thousand years; (c) it may be *possible* that Cerinthus may have forged a work pretending to be of apostolic origin, in which these doctrines were affirmed; (d) it is possible that the book of Revelation, as left by John, may have been interpolated and corrupted by Caius thus. Some one of these suppositions is more probable than the supposition that Caius meant to reject the book of Revelation; for,

1. The views referred to by Caius, as held by Cerinthus, are *not* the views which are found in Rev. xx. He spoke of a "terrestrial kingdom of Christ;" says that "men would again live in Jerusalem;" that they "would be subject to sensual pleasures;" and that the "term of a thousand years would be spent in nuptial entertainments." None of these opinions are found in the book of Revelation as we now have it.

2. The *title* given by Caius to the book—*Revelations* instead of *Revelation*—Ἀποκάλυψις—as we find it in the book itself, chap. i. 1, would seem to indicate a different work from that of John. Eusebius always refers to the Apocalypse by the noun singular (Prof. Stuart, i. 341), and this is the general manner in which the work has been designated. If Caius had designed to refer to this, it is probable that he would have used the common term to designate it.

3. These views receive some confirmation from a passage in Theodoret, "who spoke of Cerinthus in such a way as seems to imply that he had forged an Apocalypse for the promotion of his designs." That passage is, "Cerinthus forged certain revelations *as if he himself had seen them*, and added descriptions of certain terrible things, and declares that the kingdom of the Lord will be established on the earth," &c. See Prof. Stuart, i. 342. On the whole, nothing of material importance can be derived from the testimony of Caius in proof that the Apocalypse was not believed to have been written by John.

(b) Dionysius of Alexandria doubted the genuineness of the Apocalypse as being the production of John, though he did not deny its inspiration. He was made bishop of the see of Alexandria A.D. 247 or 248, and died about A.D. 264 or 265. See Lardner, ii. 643–722. He was a pupil of Origen, and enjoyed a high reputation. The full testimony of Dionysius in regard to this book may be seen in Lardner, ii. 693–697. I will copy all that is material to show his opinion. He says, "Some who were before us have utterly rejected and confuted this book, criticising every chapter; showing it throughout unintelligible and inconsistent; adding, moreover, that the inspiration is false, forasmuch as it is not John's; nor is a revelation which is hidden under so obscure and thick a veil of ignorance." [Prof. Stuart (i. 346) translates this, "It contains, moreover, no revelation; for it is covered with a strong and thick veil of ignorance."] "And this not only no apostle, but not so much as any holy or ecclesiastical man was the author of this writing, but that Cerinthus, founder of the heresy called after him the Cerinthian, the better to recommend his own forgery, prefixed to it an honourable name. For this, they say, was one of his particular notions, that the kingdom of Christ should be earthly; consisting of those things which he himself, a carnal and sensual man, most admired, the pleasures of the belly and its concupiscence; that is, eating, and drinking, and marriage; and for the more decent procurement of these, feastings, and sacrifices, and slaughters of victims. But, for my part, I dare not reject the book, since many of the brethren have it in high esteem; but allowing it to be above my understanding, I suppose it to contain throughout some latent and wonderful meaning; for though I do not understand it, I suspect there must be some profound sense in the words; not measuring and judging these things by my own reason, but ascribing more to faith, I esteem them too sublime to be comprehended by me." Then, having quoted some passages from the book, he adds, speaking of the author, "I do not deny, then, that his name is John, and that this is John's book; for I believe it to be the work of some holy and inspired person. Nevertheless, I cannot easily grant him to be the apostle, the son of Zebedee, brother of James, whose is the Gospel ascribed to John, and the Catholic Epistle; for I conclude from the manner of each, and the term of expression, and the conduct of the book, as we call it, that he is not the same person; for the Evangelist nowhere puts down his name, nor does he speak of himself either in the Gospel or the Epistle. I think, therefore, that he [the author] is another, one of them that dwelleth in Asia; forasmuch as it is said, that there are two tombs at Ephesus, each of them called John's tomb. And from the sentiment, and words, and disposition of them, it is likely that he differed from him [who wrote the Gospel and Epistle]."

This is the sum of all that Dionysius says in regard to the genuineness of the book.

Respecting this the following remarks may be made:—

1. Dionysius, though he did not regard the work as the work of John the apostle, yet received it as an inspired book, though far above his comprehension.

2. He does not agree with those who altogether rejected it, as if it were no revelation, and contained no inspired truth.

3. He did not ascribe it, as it has been supposed by some that Caius did, to Cerinthus.

4. *All* the objections that he urges to its being the work of the apostle

John are derived from the book itself, and from the difficulty of supposing that the Gospel of John, and the First Epistle of John, should have been written by the same author. He refers to no *historical* proof on that point; and does not even intimate that its genuineness had been called in question by the early writers. It is clear, therefore, that the objections of Dionysius should not be allowed to set aside the strong and clear proofs of a historical nature already adduced from the early Christian writers. See the opinion of Dionysius examined more at length in Prof. Stuart, i. 344-354. Comp. Hug, *Intro.* pp. 654-656.

(c) It may be added, in regard to the historical testimony from the ancients, that the book is not found in many of the early catalogues of the books of the New Testament, and that this has been made an objection to its authenticity. Thus Gregory of Nazianzen, in a piece composed in verse, containing a catalogue of the canonical Scriptures, omits the book of Revelation; in the catalogue of sacred writings annexed to the canons of the council of Laodicea, A.D. 363, it is also omitted; in the so-called Canons of the Apostles, a supposititious work of the latter part of the fourth century, it is also omitted; it is also omitted in a catalogue of sacred books published by Cyril of Jerusalem, A.D. 360; and it is mentioned by Amphilocus, bishop of Iconium, A.D. 380, as among the books that were doubtful. "Some," says he, "admit the Apocalypse of John, but most persons say it is spurious." See Michaelis, *Intro. New Test.* iv. 489; Prof. Stuart, i. 357, seq.

In regard to these omissions, and the doubts entertained by later writers on the subject, it may be remarked in general, (1) That it is well known that in the latter part of the fourth century and onward many doubts were entertained as to the canonical authority of the Apocalypse, and that, together with the Epistle to the Hebrews, the Second Epistle of Peter, and the Second and Third Epistles of John, it was reckoned among the books called *Antilegomena;* that is, *books spoken against,* or books whose canonical authority was not admitted by all. (2) This fact shows, as has been often remarked, the great vigilance of the church in the early ages, in settling the canon of Scripture, and in determining what books were to be admitted, and what were to be rejected. (3) These doubts, entertained in a later age, cannot affect the clear historical testimony of the early writers, as we now have it; for the question of the origin of the Apocalypse, so far as the historical testimony is concerned, must be determined by the testimony of the writers who lived near the time when it is alleged to have been written. (4) The objections alleged against the Apocalypse in later times were wholly on *internal* grounds, and were mainly derived from the fact that it was supposed to countenance the doctrine of Chiliasm, or the doctrine of the personal reign of Christ and the saints, for a thousand years, in Jerusalem; and from the fact that the followers of Cerinthus appealed to this book in support of their pernicious errors. The book *seemed* (see chap. xx.) to countenance the views early entertained by many on the subject of the millennium, and, in accordance with a common method of controversy, its canonical authority was therefore called in question. Thus Hug (*Intro.* p. 654) says, "It was amidst the disputes concerning the millennium that the first explicit and well-authenticated denial of the Apocalypse occurred." Nepos, bishop of the Arsinoitic præfecture in Egypt, had maintained that the doctrine of the millennium could be defended from the book of Revelation by a literal exposition.

Dionysius opposed this view, and, in the violence of the dispute on the subject, the authority of the Apocalypse itself was called in question by Dionysius, on the grounds referred to above. "He did this, however," says Hug, "with such moderation, that he might not offend those who had so readily agreed to a compromise;" that is, a compromise by which, as bishop, he had endeavoured to reconcile the contending parties. Hug has shown conclusively (pp. 654-656) that this constitutes no objection to the genuineness of the book. It was on such internal grounds entirely that the authenticity of the book was called in question, and that it was ever placed among the disputed books. That objection is, of course, of no importance now. (5) It is well known that, mainly by the influence of Jerome and Augustine (see Prof. Stuart, i. 334), all these doubts were removed, and that the Apocalypse after their time was all but universally received, until Luther, for reasons derived from the book itself, in the early part of his life, again called it in question.

Such is a summary of the historical argument in favour of the genuineness of the book of Revelation; and such is the nature of the evidence which has satisfied the Christian world at large that it is the work of the apostle John, and is, therefore, entitled to a place as an inspired book in the canon of Scripture. In ancient times there were no objections to it on historical grounds, and it is unnecessary to say that there can be none on these grounds now.

(2) The objections to its genuineness and authenticity in modern times are wholly derived from the contents of the book itself. These objections, as stated by De Wette, and as expressing the substance of all that is urged by Ewald, Lücke, Credner, and others, are the following:—

1. That the Apocalyptical writer calls himself John, which the evangelist never does. It is added, also, by Ewald, Credner, and Hitzig, that in chap. xviii. 20 and xxi. 14 the writer expressly excludes himself from the number of the apostles.

2. That the language of the book is entirely different from that of the fourth Gospel, and the three Epistles of John the apostle. It is said to be characterized by strong Hebraisms, and by ruggedness; by negligence of expression, and by grammatical inaccuracies; and that it exhibits the absence of pure Greek words, and of the apostle's favourite expressions.

3. That the style is unlike that which appears in the Gospel and the Epistles. In the latter it is said there is calm, deep feeling; in the Apocalypse a lively creative power of fancy.

4. That the doctrinal aspect of the book is different from that of the apostle's acknowledged writings. It is said that we find in the latter nothing of the "sensuous expectations of the Messiah and of his kingdom," which are prominent in the Apocalypse; that the views inculcated respecting spirits, demons, and angels are foreign to John; and that there is a certain spirit of revenge flowing throughout the Apocalypse quite inconsistent with the mild and amiable disposition of the beloved disciple.

For a full consideration of these points, and a complete answer to these objections, the reader is referred to the *Commentary* of Prof. Stuart, vol. i. pp. 371-422. A more condensed reply is found in Kitto's *Cyclopædia of Biblical Literature*, in an article by the Rev. S. Davidson, LL.D., Professor of Biblical Literature and Oriental Languages in the Lancashire Independent College, vol. ii. pp. 614-618.

The objections do not seem to me to have the importance which has been attached to them by many persons, but it may be satisfactory to see the manner in which they are disposed of by Dr. Davidson; I therefore copy his answer to them.

"Let us now consider the internal evidence in favour of John the Apostle, beginning with an examination of the arguments adduced on the other side by De Wette. These do not possess all the weight that many assign to them. We shall follow the order in which they have been already stated.

"1. We attach no importance to this circumstance. Why should not a writer be at liberty to name himself or not as he pleases? above all, why should not a writer, under the immediate inspiration of the Almighty, omit the particulars which he was not prompted to record? How could he refrain from doing so? The Holy Spirit must have had some good reason for leading the writer to set forth his name, although curiosity is not gratified by assigning the reason. The Old Testament prophets usually prefixed their names to the visions and predictions which they were prompted to record; and John does the same. But instead of styling himself an apostle, which carries with it an idea of dignity and official authority, he modestly takes to himself the appellation of *a servant of Christ, the brother and companion of the faithful in tribulation*. This corresponds with the relation which he sustained to Christ in the receiving of such visions, as also with the condition of the Redeemer himself. In the Gospel John is mentioned as *the disciple whom Jesus loved*, for then he stood in an intimate relation to Christ, as the *Son of man* appearing in the form of a servant; but in the book before us Christ is announced as the glorified Redeemer who should quickly come to judgment, and John is *his servant*, intrusted with the secrets of his house. Well did it become the apostle to forget all the honour of his apostolic office, and to be abased before the Lord of glory. The resplendent vision of the Saviour had such an effect upon the seer that he fell at his feet as dead; and therefore it was quite natural for him to be clothed with profound humility, to designate himself the servant of Jesus Christ, the brother and companion of the faithful in tribulation. Again, in chap. xviii. 20 the prophets are said to be represented as already in heaven in their glorified condition, and therefore the writer could not have belonged to their number. But this passage neither affirms, nor necessarily implies, that the saints and apostles and prophets were at that time in heaven. Neither is it stated that *all* the apostles had then been glorified. Chap. xxi. 14 is alleged to be inconsistent with the modesty and humility of John. This is a questionable assumption. The official honour inseparable from the person of an apostle was surely compatible with profound humility. It was so with Paul; and we may safely draw the same conclusion in regard to John. In describing the heavenly Jerusalem it was necessary to introduce the twelve apostles. The writer could not exclude himself (see Lücke, p. 389; and Guerike's *Beiträge*, p. 37, seq.).

"2. To enter fully into this argument would require a lengthened treatise. Let us briefly notice the particular words, phrases, and expressions to which Ewald, Lücke, De Wette, and Credner specially allude. Much has been written by Ewald concerning the Hebraistic character of the language. The writer, it is alleged, strongly imbued with Hebrew modes of thought, frequently inserts Hebrew words, as in chap. iii. 14; ix. 11; xii. 9, 10; xix. 1, 3, 4, 6; xx. 2; xxii. 20; while the influence of *cabbalistic artificiality* is obvious throughout the entire book, and particularly in chap. i. 4, 5; iv. 2; xiii. 18; xvi. 14. The mode of employing the tenses is foreign to the Greek language, and moulded after the Hebrew (chap. i. 7; ii. 5, 16, 22, 23, 27; iii. 9; iv. 9–11; xii. 2–4; xvi. 15, 21; xvii. 13, 14; xviii. 11, 15; xxii. 7, 12). So also the use of the participle (chap. i. 16; iv. 1, 5, 8; v. 6, 13; vi. 2, 5; vii. 9, 10; ix. 11; x. 2; xiv. 1, 14; xix. 12, 13; xxi. 14); and of the infinitive (chap. xii. 7). The awkward disposition of words is also said to be Hebraistic; such as a genitive appended like the construct state; the stringing together of several genitives (chap. xiv. 8, 10, 19; xvi. 19; xviii. 3, 14; xix. 15; xxi. 6; xxii. 18, 19); and the use of the Greek cases, which are frequently changed for prepositions (chap. ii. 10; iii. 9; vi. 1, 8; viii. 7; ix. 19; xi. 6, 9; xii. 5; xiv. 2, 7); incorrectness in appositions (chap. i. 5; ii. 20; iii. 12; iv. 2–4; vi. 1; vii. 9; viii. 9; ix. 14; xiii. 1–3; xiv. 2, 12, 14, 20, &c.); a construction formed of an αὐτός put after the relative pronoun (chap. iii. 8; vii. 2, 9; xiii. 12; xx. 8); frequent anomalies in regard to number and gender (chap. ii. 27; iii. 4, 5; iv. 8; vi. 9, 10; ix. 13, 14; xi. 15; xiv. 1, 3; xvii. 16; xix. 14; and viii. 11; xi. 18; xv. 4; xvii. 12, 15; xviii. 14; xix. 21; xx. 12; xxi. 4, 24; also chap. xvi. 10; xix. 1, 8, 9). In addition to this, it is alleged by Credner, that the use made of the Old Testament betrays an acquaintance on the part of the writer with the Hebrew text (comp. chap. vi. 13, 14, with Isa. xxxiv. 4; chap. xviii. 2, with Isa. xiii. 21, xxi. 9, xxxiv. 14, Jer. l. 39; chap. xviii. 4, 5, with Jer. li. 6, 9, 45; chap. xviii. 7, with Isa. xlvii. 7, 8; chap. xviii. 21–23, with Jer. xxv. 10, li. 63, 64). In contrast with all this, we are reminded of the fact that, according to Acts iv. 13, John was an unlearned and ignorant man.

"The book is deficient in words and turns of expression purely Greek, such as πάντοτε πώποτε, οὐδέποτε; compound verbs, as ἀναγγέλλειν, παραλαμβάνειν, ἐπιβάλλειν; the double negation; the genitive absolute; the attraction of the relative pronoun; the regular construction of the neuter plural with the verb singular (except chap. viii. 3; ix. 20; xiv. 13; xviii. 24; xix. 14; xxi. 12); ἀκούειν with the genitive. Favourite expressions, such as occur in the Gospel and Epistles, are seldom found, as θεάομαι, θεωρέω, ἐργάζομαι, ῥήματα, πάλιν, φωνεῖν, μένειν, καθώς, ὡς (an adverb of time), οὖν, μέν μέντοι, κόσμος, φῶς, σκοτία, δοξάζεσθαι, ὑψοῦσθαι, ζωή, αἰώνιος, ἀπόλλυσθαι, οὗτος (τοῦτο) ἵνα; the historic present. There are also favourite expressions of the writer of the book, such as do not occur in John's authentic writings: οἰκουμένη, ὑπομονή, κρατεῖν τὸ ὄνομα, τὴν διδαχήν, παντοκράτωρ, θεὸς καὶ πατήρ, δύναμις, κράτος, ἰσχύς, τιμή, πρωτότοκος τῶν νεκρῶν, ἡ ἀρχὴ τῆς κτίσεως τοῦ θεοῦ, ὁ ἄρχων τῶν βασιλέων τῆς γῆς ὧδε in the beginning of a sentence. The conjunction εἰ, so common in the Gospel, does not occur in the Apocalypse; but only εἰ μή, εἰ δὲ μή, and εἴ τις. The frequent joining of a substantive with μέγας, as φωνὴ μεγάλη, θλίψις μεγάλη, φόβος μέγας, σεισμὸς μέγας, rather reminds one of Luke than John; μείζων, so frequent in the Gospel, is not found in the Revelation; and, on the contrary, ἰσχυρός, which occurs seven times in the Apocalypse, is foreign to the Gospel.

"The following discrepancies between the language of the Gospel and that of the Epistles have been noticed: ἀληθινός is used of God both in the Gospel and the Apocalypse, but in different senses; so also κύριος, and ἐργάζομαι; instead of ἴδε the Apocalypse has only ἰδού; instead of Ἱεροσόλυμα only Ἱερουσαλήμ; instead of ἐάν τις, as in the Gospel, εἴ τις; περί, so often used by John, occurs only once in the Apocalypse, and that too in relation to place; ὄχλος is used in the plural. Words denoting *seeing* are differently used in the Gospel and Apocalypse; thus, for the present we find in the latter βλέπειν, θεωρεῖν, ὁρᾶν; for the aorist of the active εἶδον, βλέπειν, and θεωρεῖν; for the future ὄπτεσθαι, and for the aorist of the passive also ὄπτεσθαι; μένειν has a different meaning from that which it bears in the Gospel; instead of ὁ ἄρχων τοῦ κόσμου, and ὁ πονηρός, we find ὁ σατανᾶς, ὁ διάβολος, ὁ δράκων ὁ μέγας.

"Such is a summary statement of an argument drawn out at great length by Lücke, De Wette, Ewald, and Credner.

"Some have attempted to turn aside its force by resorting to the hypothesis that the book was originally written in Hebrew and then translated into Greek. This, however, is contradicted by the most decisive internal evidence, and is in itself highly improbable. The Apocalypse was written in the Greek language, as all antiquity attests. How, then, are we to account for its Hebraistic idioms and solecisms of language, its negligences of diction, and ungrammatical constructions? One circumstance to be taken into account is, that the nature of the Gospel is widely different from that of the Apocalypse. The latter is a prophetic book—a poetical composition; while the former is a simple record in prose, of the discourses of Jesus in the days of his flesh. It is apparent, too, that John in the Apocalypse imitates the manner of Ezekiel and Daniel. The New Testament prophet conforms to the diction and symbolic features of the former seers. 'If the question should be urged why John chose these models, the obvious answer is, that he conformed to the taste of the times in which he lived. The numerous apocryphal works of an Apocalyptical nature, which were composed nearly at the same time with the Apocalypse—such as the book of Enoch, the Ascension of Isaiah, the Testament of the Twelve Patriarchs, many of the Sibylline Oracles, the fourth book of Ezra, the Pastor of Hermas, and many others which are lost—all testify to the taste and feelings of the times when, or near which, the Apocalypse was written. If this method of writing was more grateful to the time in which John lived, it is a good reason for his preferring it.'[1] In consequence of such imitation, the diction has an Oriental character; and the figures are in the highest style of imagery peculiar to the East. But it is said that John was an illiterate man. Illiterate, doubtless, he was as compared with Paul, who was brought up at the feet of Gamaliel; yet he may have been capable of reading the Old Testament books; and he was certainly inspired. Wrapt in ecstasy, he saw wondrous visions. He was *in the Spirit*. And when writing the things he beheld, his language was to be conformed to the nature of such marvellous revelations. It was to be adapted to the mysterious disclosures, the vivid pictures, the moving scenes, the celestial beings and scenery of which he was privileged to tell. Hence it was to be lifted up far above the level of simple prose or biographic history, so as to correspond with the sublime visions of the seer. Nor should it be forgotten that he was not in the circumstances of an ordinary writer. He was *inspired*. How often is this fact lost sight of by the German critics! It is, therefore, needless to inquire into his education in the Hebrew language, or his mental culture while residing in Asia Minor, or the smoothness of the Greek language as current in the place where he lived, before and after he wrote the Apocalypse. The Holy Spirit qualified him beyond and irrespective of ordinary means for the work of writing. However elevated the theme he undertook, he was assisted in

[1] Stuart, in the *Bibliotheca Sacra*, pp. 353, 354.

employing diction as elevated as the nature of the subject demanded. We place, therefore, little reliance upon the argument derived from *the time of life* at which the Apocalypse was composed, though Olshausen and Guerike insist upon it. Written, as they think, twenty years before the Gospel or Epistles, the Apocalypse exhibits marks of inexperience in writing, of youthful fire, and of an ardent temperament. It exhibits the first essays of one expressing his ideas in a language to which he was unaccustomed. This may be true; but we lay far less stress upon it than these authors seem inclined to do. The strong Hebraized diction of the book we account for on the ground that the writer was a Jew; and, as such, expressed his Jewish conceptions in Greek; that he imitated the later Old Testament prophets, especially the manner of Daniel; and that the only prophetic writing in the New Testament naturally approaches nearer the Old Testament, if not in subject, at least in colouring and linguistic features.

"These considerations may serve to throw light upon the language of the book, after all the extravagancies of assertion in regard to anomalies, solecisms, and ruggednesses, have been fairly estimated. For it cannot be denied that many rash and unwarrantable assumptions have been made by De Wette and others relative to the impure Greek said to be contained in the Apocalypse. Winer has done much to check such bold assertions, but with little success in the case of those who are resolved to abide by a strong and prevalent current of opinion. We venture to affirm, without fear of contradiction, that there are books in the New Testament almost as Hebraizing as the Apocalypse; and that the anomalies charged to the account of the Hebrew language may be paralleled in other parts of the New Testament, or in classical Greek. What shall be said, for instance, to the attempt of Hitzig to demonstrate from the language of Mark's Gospel, as compared with that of the Apocalypse, that both proceeded from one author, viz. John Mark? This author has conducted a lengthened investigation with the view of showing that all the peculiarities of language found in the Apocalypse are equally presented in the second Gospel, particularly that the Hebraisms of the one correspond with those of the other. Surely this must lead to new investigations of the Apocalyptic diction, and possibly to a renunciation of those extravagant assertions so often made in regard to the harsh, rugged, Hebraized Greek of the Apocalypse. Who ever dreamed before of the numerous solecisms of Mark's language? and yet Hitzig has demonstrated its similarity to the Apocalyptic as plausibly as Ewald, Lücke, and others have proved the total dissimilarity between the diction of the Apocalypse and that of John's Gospel.

"The length allotted to this article will not allow the writer to notice every term and phrase supposed to be peculiar. This can only be done with success by him who takes a concordance to the Greek Testament in his hand, with the determination to test each example; along with a good syntax of classical Greek, such as Bernhardy's. In this way he may see whether the alleged Hebraisms and anomalies have not their parallels in classical Greek. Some of the allegations already quoted are manifestly incorrect, *e.g.*, that ἀκούω with the genitive is not found in the Apocalypse. On the contrary, it occurs eight times with the genitive. Other words are adduced on the principle of their not occurring so frequently in the book before us as in the Gospel and Epistles. But by this mode of reasoning it might be shown, that the other acknowledged writings of the apostle John, for instance his First Epistle, are not authentic. Thus ῥήματα, one of the words quoted, though frequently found in the Gospel, is not in any of the three Epistles; therefore, these Epistles were not written by John. It is found *once* in the Apocalypse. Again, ἐργάζομαι, which is found seven times in the Gospel, and once in the Apocalypse, as also once in each of the Second and Third Epistles, is not in the First Epistle; therefore the First Epistle proceeded from another writer than the author of the Second and Third. The same reasoning may be applied to θεωρέω. Again, it is alleged that the regular construction of neuters plural with singular verbs is not found, with the exception of six instances. To say nothing of the large list of exceptions, let it be considered, that the plural verb is joined with plural nouns where animate beings, especially persons, are designated. Apply now this principle, which regularly holds good in classical Greek, to the Apocalypse, and nothing peculiar will appear in the latter. Should there still remain examples of neuters plural designating things without life, we shall find similar ones in the Greek writers. Another mode in which the reasoning founded upon the use of peculiar terms and expressions may be tested is the following. It is admitted that there are words which occur in the Gospel and Epistles, but not in the Apocalypse. The adverb πάντοτε is an example. On the same principle, and by virtue of the same reasoning, it may be denied, *as far as language is concerned*, that I. Timothy was written by Paul, because πάντοτε, which is found in his other epistles, does not occur in it. In this manner we might individually take up each word and every syntactical peculiarity on which the charge of harshness, or solecism, or Hebraizing has been fastened. It is sufficient to state, that there are very few *real* solecisms in the Apocalypse. *Almost all* that have been adduced may be paralleled in Greek writers, or in those of the New Testament. The words of Winer, a master in this department, are worthy of attention: 'The solecisms that appear in the Apocalypse give the diction the impress of great harshness, but they are *capable of explanation*, partly from anacoluthon and the mingling of two constructions, partly in another manner. Such explanation should have been always adopted, instead of ascribing these irregularities to the ignorance of the author, who, in other constructions of a much more difficult nature in this very book, shows that he was exceedingly well acquainted with the rules of grammar. For most of these anomalies, too, analogous examples in the Greek writers may be found, with this difference alone, that they do not follow one another so frequently as in the Apocalypse,' (*Grammatik, fünfte Auflage,* pp. 273, 274). Should the reader not be satisfied with this brief statement of Winer, he is referred to his *Exeget. Studien,* i. 154, seq., where the professor enters into details with great ability.

"The following linguistic similarities between John's Gospel and the Apocalypse deserve to be cited: μετὰ ταῦτα, Apoc. i. 19; iv. 1; vii. 1, 9; ix. 12; xv. 5; xviii. 1; xix. 1; xx. 3;—Gosp. iii. 22; v. 1, 14; vi. 1; vii. 1; xix. 38; xxi. 1. μαρτυρία, Apoc. i. 2, 9; vi. 9; xi. 7; xii. 11, 17; xix. 10; xx. 4;—Gosp. (μαρτυρέω or μαρτυρία) i. 7, 8, 15, 19, 32, 34; ii. 25; iii. 11, 26, 28, 32, 33; iv. 3, 9, 44; v. 31-34, 36, 37, 39;—1 Epist. i. 2; iv. 14; v. 6-11. ἵνα, Apoc. ii. 10, 21; iii. 9, 11, 18; vi. 2, 4, 11; vii. 1, &c.;—Gosp. vi. 5, 7, 12, 15, 28-30, 38-40, 50; xi. 4, 11, 15, 16, 19, 31, 37, 42, 50, 52, 53, 55, 57; xii. 9, 10, 20, 23, 35, &c.;—1 Epist. of John i. 3, 4, 9; ii. 1, 19, 27, 28. ὄψις, Gosp. vii. 24; xi. 44;—Apoc. i. 16. πιάζειν, Apoc. xix. 20;—Gosp. vii. 30, 32, 44; viii. 20; x. 39; xi. 57; xxi. 3, 10. τηρεῖν τὸν λόγον, τὰς ἐντολάς, or some similar expression, Apoc. iii. 8, 10; xii. 17; xiv. 12; xxii. 7, 9;—Gosp. viii. 51, 55;

xiv. 15; xxiii. 24, &c. ὁ νικῶν, Apoc. ii. 7, 11, 17, 26; iii. 5, 12, 21; xv. 2; xxi. 7. This verb is quite common in the First Epistle, chap. ii. 13, 14; iv. 4; v. 4, 5;—Gosp. xvi. 33. ὕδωρ ζωῆς, Apoc. xxi. 6; xxii. 17; comp. Gosp. vii. 38. Compare also the joining together of the present and the future in Apoc. ii. 5, and Gosp. xiv. 3. The assertion of the same thing positively and negatively, Apoc. ii. 2, 6, 8, 13; iii. 8, 17, 21; Gosp. i. 3, 6, 7, 20, 48; iii. 15, 17, 20; iv. 42; v. 19, 24; viii. 35, 45; x. 28; xv. 5-7; 1 Epist. ii. 27, &c. In several places in the Apocalypse Christ is called the Lamb; so also in the Gospel, chap. i. 29, 36. Christ is called ὁ λόγος τοῦ Θεοῦ, Apoc. xix. 13, and in the Gospel of John only has he the same epithet. τηρεῖν ἐκ τινός, Apoc. iii. 10; Gosp. xvii. 15. σφάττειν, Apoc. v. 6, 9, 12; vi. 4, 9; xiii. 3, 8; xviii. 24; only in the 1st Epistle of John, chap. iii. 12. ἔχειν μέρος, Apoc. xx. 6; Gosp. xiii. 8. περιπατεῖν μετά τινος, Apoc. iii. 4; Gosp. vi. 66. σκηνόω, Apoc. vii. 15; xii. 12; xiii. 6; xxi. 3; Gosp. i. 14. The expulsion of Satan from heaven is expressed thus in the Apoc. xii. 9: ἐβλήθη εἰς τὴν γῆν; in the Gosp. it is said, νῦν ὁ ἄρχων τοῦ κόσμου τούτου ἐκβληθήσεται ἔξω, chap. xii. 31. (See Scholz, *Die Apokalypse des heilig. Johannes übersetzt, erklärt*, u. s. w. Frankfurt am Main, 1828, 8vo; Schulz, *Ueber den Schriftsteller, Character und Werth des Johannes*, Leipzig, 1803, 8vo; Donker Curtius, *Specimen hermeneuticotheologicum de Apocalypsi ab indole, doctrina, et scribendi genere Johannis Apostoli non abhorrente*, Trajecti Batav. 1799, 8vo; Kolthoff, *Apocalypsis Joanni Apostolo vindicata*, Hafniæ, 1834, 8vo; Stein, in Winer and Engelhardt's *Kritisch. Journal*, v. i.; and the *Jena Literatur-Zeitung* for April, 1833, No. 61.) It is true that some of these expressions are said, by Lücke, De Wette, and Credner, to be used in a different sense in the Apocalypse; others not to be *characteristic*, but rather accidental and casual; others not *original*, but borrowed. Such assertions, however, proceed more from *à priori* assumption than from any inherent truth they possess. In regard to the charge of *cabbalism*, especially in the use of numbers, it is easily disposed of. The cabbala of the Jews was widely different from the instances in the Apocalypse that have been quoted. Perhaps John's use of the number 666 comes the nearest to one kind of the cabbala; but still it is so unlike as to warrant the conclusion that the apostle did not employ the cabbalistic art. His mysterious indications of certain facts, and the reasons of their being in some measure involved in darkness, are explicable on other than Jewish grounds. There is no real cause for believing that the apostle had recourse to the artificial and trifling conceits of the Rabbins. In short, this argument is by no means conclusive. As far as the language is concerned, nothing militates against the opinion that the Apocalypse proceeded from John, who wrote the Gospel. The contrary evidence is not of such a nature as to demand assent. When rigidly scrutinized, it does not sustain the conclusion so confidently built upon it.

"But it is also affirmed, that the doctrinal views and sentiments inculcated in the Apocalypse are quite different from those found in the Gospel. This may be freely allowed without any detriment to their identity of authorship. How slow the Germans are in learning that a difference in the exhibition of truths substantially the same is far from being a contradiction! A difference of subject in connection with a different plan, demands correspondent dissimilarity of treatment. Besides, there must be a gradual development of the things pertaining to the kingdom of God on earth. Sensuous expectations of the Messiah, such as are alleged to abound in the Apocalypse, may be perfectly consistent with the spirituality of his reign, though it appears to us that the representations so designated are figurative, shadowing forth spiritual realities by means of outward objects.

"But what is to be said of the pneumatological, demonological, and angelogical doctrines of the book? The object for which John's Gospel was primarily written did not lead the apostle to introduce so many particulars regarding angels and evil spirits. The intervention of good and the malignant influence of evil spirits are clearly implied in the Old Testament prophets, particularly in Zechariah and Daniel. It is therefore quite accordant with the prophetic Hebraistic character of the Apocalypse, to make angelic agency a prominent feature in the book. And that such agency is recognized in the Gospels, is apparent to the most cursory reader. The special object with which the fourth Gospel was written was different from that which prompted the composition of the Apocalypse, and therefore the subject-matter of both is exceedingly diverse. But still there is no opposition in doctrine. The same doctrinal views lie at the foundation of all the representations contained in them. In the one, the Redeemer is depicted in his humble career on earth; in the other, in his triumphs as a king—or rather, in the victorious progress of his truth in the world, notwithstanding all the efforts of Satan and wicked men to suppress it. As to a spirit of revenge in the Apocalyptic writer, it is not found. The inspired prophet was commissioned to pronounce woes and judgments as soon to befall the enemies of Christ, in consequence of their persevering, malignant efforts. As well might an evil disposition be attributed to the blessed Saviour himself, in consequence of his denunciation of the Scribes and Pharisees. The same John who wrote the Apocalypse says, in the Second Epistle, ver. 10, 'If there come any unto you and bring not this doctrine, receive him not into your house, neither bid him God speed.' It must ever strike the simple reader of the Apocalypse as a positive ground for attributing the authorship to John the apostle, that he styles himself THE *servant* of God by way of eminence, which none other at that time would have ventured to do; and that he employs the expression, *I John*, after the manner of Daniel, as if he were the only prophet and person of the name. Nor can it be well believed that a disciple of the apostle, or any other individual, should have presumed to introduce John as the speaker, thus deceiving the readers. The apostle was well known to the Christians of his time, and especially to the Asiatic churches. He did not therefore think it necessary to say John the Apostle for the sake of distinguishing himself from any other. See Züllig's *Die Offenbarung Johannis*, Stuttgart, 1834, 8vo, p. 136."

### § II.—*The Time of Writing the Apocalypse.*

The evidence as to the date of the Apocalypse may be considered as external or historical, and internal.

1. External or historical. On this point the testimony of the early Christian fathers is almost or quite uniform, that it was in the latter part of the life of the apostle John, and towards the end of the reign of Domitian; that is, about A.D. 95 or 96.

The principal testimony to this fact is that of Irenæus. It will be recollected that he was a disciple of Polycarp, bishop of Smyrna, who was himself the disciple of the apostle John. See § I. (*b*). He had, therefore, every opportunity of obtaining correct information, and doubtless expresses the common sentiment of his age on the subject. His character is unexceptionable, and he had no inducement to bear any false or perverted testimony in the case. His testimony is plain and positive that the book was written near the close of the reign of Domitian, and the testimony should be regarded as decisive unless it can be set aside. His language in regard to the book of Revelation is: "It was seen *no long time ago, but almost in our age, at the end of the reign of Domitian*" (Lardner, ii. 181). Or, as the passage is translated by Prof. Stuart: "The Apocalypse was seen not long ago, but almost in our generation, near the end of Domitian's reign." There can be no doubt, therefore, as to the meaning of the passage, or as to the time when Irenæus believed the book to have been written. Domitian was put to death A.D. 96, and consequently, according to Irenæus, the Apocalypse must have been written not far from this time.

This testimony of Irenæus is confirmed by that of Clement of Alexandria. Relating the well-known story of John and the robber, he speaks of the event as having occurred on his return from exile in Patmos "*after the death of the tyrant,*" and represents him *as then an infirm old man*. The testimony in the book itself (chap. i. 9) is clear, that John was on the island of Patmos when these visions were seen. The "*tyrant*" whose death is here referred to must necessarily be either *Nero* or *Domitian*, as these were, up to the end of the first century, the only imperial persecutors of the Christians. It cannot be supposed to be Nero, since at the time of his persecution (A.D. 64) John could not be supposed to be an "infirm old man;" being probably not much above, if indeed so much as sixty years of age. See Eusebius, *Ecc. Hist.*, b. iii. chap. 23. Of this testimony Prof. Stuart, who himself supposes that the Apocalypse was written before the death of Nero, says (i. 264), "The tyrant here meant is probably Domitian; at least, although he is not named by Clement, it is clear that Eusebius so understands the matter."

Victorinus, bishop of Pettaw and martyr in Diocletian's persecution, in his *Commentary on the Apocalypse*, written towards the close of the third century, says twice expressly that the Apocalypse was seen by the apostle John in the isle of Patmos, when banished thither by the Roman emperor Domitian. See the passages quoted in Elliott, i. 39, and in Prof. Stuart, i. 264. The testimony is unequivocal.

To these testimonies from the early fathers may be added that of Jerome, who says that "John saw the Apocalypse on the island of Patmos, to which he was sent by Domitian," and in another place he says that this occurred in the fourteenth year of the reign of Domitian (Adv. Jovin. lib. i., Lardner, iv. 446, 447).

And to these plain testimonies may be added those of Sulpicius Severus and Orosius, contemporaries of Augustine; Gregory Turonensis (cent. vi.), Isidorus Hispalensis (cent. vii.), Marianus Scotus, Primasius, and others. See Prof. Stuart, i. 264, 265, and Elliott, i. 38, 39.

Such is the *positive* testimony that the book was written near the end of the reign of Domitian and about A.D. 96. It is true, that notwithstanding this positive testimony, there were some writers who assigned it to an earlier date. Thus Epiphanius, bishop of Salamis in Cyprus, in the latter half of the fourth century, speaks of John as having prophesied in the isle of Patmos in the days of the emperor *Claudius* (A.D. 41–54); a time when, as Michaelis observes, it does not appear from history that there was any imperial persecution of Christians whatever, and when, moreover, the probability is that, of the seven Apocalyptic churches, scarcely one was in existence, and the apostle John was in no way associated with them. Lardner (iv. 190) seems to suspect that, in the passage referred to, the name *Claudius* was a fault of the transcriber. Epiphanius, however, received the Apocalypse as the work of John and as an inspired book (Lardner, iv. 190). Others have ascribed the date of the book of Revelation to the time of Nero. Thus, in the later Syriac version, the title-page declares that it was written in Patmos, *whither John was sent by Nero Cæsar*. This version, however, was made in the beginning of the sixth century, and can have little authority in determining the question. It is not known by whom the version was made, or on what authority the author relied, when he said that John was banished to Patmos in the time of Nero. So also Andreas and Arethas, commentators on the book of Revelation, one of them in the beginning of the sixth century and the other in the middle of the sixth century, make quotations from the book in such a manner as to show that they supposed that it was written before the destruction of Jerusalem. They, however, made no express declaration on that point, and their testimony at anyrate, at that late period, is of little value. A few other later writers also supposed that the book was written at an earlier period than the reign of Domitian. See Prof. Stuart, i. 268, 269.

Such is the sum of the historical testimony as to the time when the Apocalypse was written; and that testimony, it seems to me, is so clear as to settle the point so far as the historical evidence is concerned, that the book was written near the end of the reign of Domitian, that is, about A.D. 95 or 96. My exposition of the book proceeds on the supposition that it was written at that time.

2. There is another inquiry, however, as to the *internal* evidence, for on this ground it has been maintained that it must have been written before the destruction of Jerusalem and in the time of Nero. See the argument in Prof. Stuart, i. 270-282.

Now, in regard to this it may be remarked in general, that on the supposition that it was written near the close of the life of John, and in the time of Domitian, it can be shown that there is no internal improbability or inconsistency; that is, in other words, all the known circumstances in regard to John, and to the condition of the church at that time, would accord with that supposition. For,

(*a*) It is known that John spent many of the later years of his like at Ephesus, in the midst of the seven churches to which the book was addressed, and the epistles in the book are such as they would be on that supposition.

(*b*) It is admitted that there was a persecution of Christians in the time of Domitian; and of the persecution which he excited against Christians, Mosheim remarks that "he was an emperor little inferior to Nero in baseness of character and conduct. This persecution undoubtedly was severe; but it was of short continuance, as the emperor was soon murdered" (Mosheim, i. 69). It commenced about A.D. 93 or 94. It is not certainly known how far it extended, but as the *ground* of the persecution was a fear of Domitian that he would lose his empire from some person among the relatives of *Christ* who would attempt a revolution (Mosheim, i. 69; Milman, *Hist. of Christianity*, 193), there is every probability that it would be directed particularly to the East and the countries near where the Saviour lived and died.

(c) It is not improbable that John would be *banished* in this persecution. He was a man of great influence among Christians, and it is to be presumed that he would not escape the notice of those who were actively engaged in carrying on the persecution. Moreover, it is *as* probable that he would be *banished* as that he would be put to death; for, though we have few facts respecting this persecution, and few names are mentioned, yet we have one recorded instance in which banishment on account of professing the Christian religion took place. Thus Milman (*Hist. of Christianity*, p. 193), speaking of two of the cousin-germans of Domitian, says, "The one fell an early victim to his jealous apprehensions. The other, Flavius Clemens, is described as a man of the most contemptible indolence of character. His powerful kinsman, instead of exciting the fears, enjoyed for some time the favour of Domitian. He received in marriage Domitilla, the niece of the emperor; his children were adopted as heirs to his throne; Clemens himself obtained the consulship. On a sudden these harmless kinsmen became dangerous conspirators; they were arraigned on the unprecedented charge of Atheism and Jewish manners; the husband Clemens was put to death; *the wife Domitilla banished to the desert island of either Pontia or Pandataria.*" Nothing is more probable, therefore, than that John the apostle should be also *banished to a desert island*—and Patmos was admirably adapted to such a purpose. See Notes on chap. i. 9. There is, therefore, everything in the circumstances to make it *probable* that the book was written at the time in which it is so uniformly said by the early historians to have been. Those things seem to me to make it proper to acquiesce in the general opinion so long entertained in regard to the date of the Apocalypse, for there is, perhaps, no book of the New Testament whose date is better determined on historical grounds than this. These considerations also make it unnecessary to examine the alleged internal evidence from the book that it was written before the destruction of Jerusalem, especially as it will be shown in the Notes that the passages usually relied on (chap. vi. 9, 10; vii.; xi. 3, 8; xvii. 8, 11; and chap. i. 1, 3; xxii. 7, 20) are susceptible of an easy and satisfactory explanation on the supposition that the book was written in the time of Domitian, or *after* the destruction of Jerusalem. See also Editor's Preface.

§ III.—*The Place where the Book was Written.*

The book itself purports (chap. i. 9) to have been written in the island of Patmos, where the writer says he was "for the word of God, and for the testimony of Jesus Christ;" that is, clearly, where he had been banished for his attachment to the Saviour. For an account of this island, see Notes on chap. i. 9. The only question that has ever been raised on this point is, whether this was a *reality*, or a *poetical fiction*—that is, whether the writer in his visions merely *seemed* to have been transferred to the place, and this was made the imaginary scene of the vision. The latter supposition has been entertained by Eichhorn in his *Introduction to the New Testament* (1810), and by some other writers.

In favour, however, of understanding this as a literal fact, the following considerations may be suggested:—

1. The clear statement of the writer himself (chap. i. 9)—a statement that should be received as literally true, unless there is something in the character of the composition, or some intrinsic improbability in the case, to set it aside.

If the composition were avowedly fictitious or poetical, then it would be understood that such a statement was not to be received literally. And thus, in a prophetic record, it *might* be clear that it was a mere visionary representation, in which the prophet *seemed* to be transported to some place where there would be no danger of misunderstanding it. Undoubtedly, on this principle, some of the visions of Ezekiel and Jeremiah are to be regarded as located at some place remote from that where the prophet was; and thus many of the visions in this book are located in heaven or elsewhere. But these cases are wholly different from the statement in chap. i. 9. Patmos is not represented as the mere scene of a vision. The statement occurs in a plain prose narrative, and there is no intrinsic improbability that it is true.

2. This accords with the representation of history, and with the probabilities of the case, that John was actually banished to Patmos in a time of persecution. See § II. On this point the representations of history are uniform, and they are such, that if a writer had *designed* to forge a book in the name of John, he would, in all probability, have fixed on Patmos as the scene of the vision, from the fact that he was actually banished there.

3. If Patmos was merely a fictitious place, why should John select it? What was there in *that* island that would have occurred to him as a proper place to be the scene of such visions? It was little known; it had no sacred associations; it had never been represented as a place visited by the Most High, and it had no particular relation to the scenes which are referred to. One born in Judea, and trained under the influence of the Hebrew religion; one who was a disciple of Christ, and who had witnessed the scene of the transfiguration or the ascension, would have been much more likely to select Sinai, Carmel, Hermon, Tabor, or Olivet, as the scene where the visions were to be laid. These were consecrated spots. On these God had manifested himself in a peculiar manner; had conversed with men, and had given glorious exhibitions of his character and plans. Why should not one of these spots—any one of them in itself is as well adapted to be the scene of such visions as the lonely isle of Patmos — have been selected? Why was a *Grecian* island chosen—a place not once named in all the sacred writings, and so small and so desolate as to have been almost entirely, before this, unknown even in the heathen world?

4. All the circumstances have the aspect of *reality*. It was a *real* persecution to which the writer refers, and it was a *real* affliction which he was experiencing, and the concinnity of the passage requires us to understand this as a *real* transfer to a lonely island. If that were a mere vision, then we should be required also to understand the statement that he was "a companion of others in *tribulation*" as a vision also, and his affliction as an account of an *ideal* transfer to that island. But this is contrary to the spirit of the passage in chap. i. 9; and the whole, therefore, should be understood as the statement of a literal fact.

These considerations are sufficient to show, that the common opinion, that the visions were seen in the island of Patmos, has every probability in its favour, and should be received as correct. Whether the *record* was actually made on that island, or was made afterwards, is a point on which no light can be observed, and which is of no importance. From such passages, however, as those in chap. x. 4; xiv. 13; xix. 9; and xxi. 5, it would seem probable that the record was made as soon as the visions were seen, and that the book was actually *written* in Patmos.

### § IV.—*The Nature and Design of the Book.*

This must be learned from an examination of the book itself, and the views entertained on this point will be determined, in a great measure, by the principles which are adopted in interpreting it. From the examination which I have given of the book, and the methods of interpretation which I have adopted, it seems to me that the matter and design of the book may be expressed in the following specifications:—

1. It was composed in a time of persecution, and in view of the persecutions and hostilities, external and internal, to which the church was then, and would be exposed. Christianity was then in its infancy. It was comparatively feeble. It encountered the opposition of the world. The arm of the civil power was raised to crush it. It was also exposed to the attacks of internal foes, and persecutions would arise from its own bosom, and formidable enemies in future times would seem to endanger its very existence. Heresies, and divisions, and corruptions of doctrine and of practice, might be expected to exist in its own bosom; times of conflict and darkness would come; changes would occur in governments that would deeply affect the welfare of the church; and there might be periods when it would seem to be doubtful whether the true church would not become wholly extinct. The faith of Christians was, doubtless, sorely tried in the persecution which existed when the book was written, and would be in like manner often sorely tried in the corruptions and persecutions of future ages.

2. The Apocalypse is designed to meet this state of feeling by furnishing the assurance that the gospel would ultimately prevail; that all its enemies would be subdued, and the kingdom of the Messiah set up over all the world. It was intended to impart consolation to the people of God in all ages, and in all forms of persecution and trial, by the assurance that the true religion would be at last triumphant, thus furnishing an illustration of the truth of the declarations of the Saviour respecting the church, that the "gates of hell should not prevail against it," Mat. xvi. 18. Hence everything in the book tends to the final triumph of the gospel; and hence at the close (chap. xx.), we have the assurance of its far-spread diffusion over the earth, for a period of a thousand years, and (chap. xxi., xxii.) a graphic view of the state of the redeemed when they shall be delivered from sin and woe, and when all tears shall be wiped away from their eyes.

3. The method of doing this is by giving a rapid glance at the great events of history, bearing on the church in all coming times, till it should be triumphant; or by sketching a bold *outline* of the principal things that would serve to endanger the church, and the principal divine interpositions in behalf of the church, until its triumph should be secured upon the earth. This *might* have been done by direct statement, or by plain and positive assertion, as it was by many of the prophets; but the end, in this case, would be better secured by a glance at future history, in such a way, that while the great fact of the final triumph of the gospel would be kept before the church, there might be furnished a clear demonstration, in the end, of the divine origin and inspiration of the book itself. This latter object, indeed, would have been *in fact* accomplished by a plain declaration, but it would be *best*

accomplished by such *details* as would show that the whole course of events was comprehended by the Holy Spirit—the real author of the whole. A general view of these details may be seen, according to the principles which I have adopted in the interpretation of the work, in the Analysis at the close of the Introduction, § V.

4. The method in which this is mainly done in this book is by *pictures* or *symbols;* for, above all the other books in the Bible, the Apocalypse is characterized by this method of representation, and it may eminently be called a book of symbols. It is this which has made it appear to be so obscure; and this particularly which has given occasion for so great a variety in the methods of interpreting it—for there is no kind of representation that furnishes occasion for so much fanciful interpretation as that of symbolical writing. The true principle of interpreting symbolical language has been hitherto little understood, and consequently every writer has indulged his own fancy in affixing such a meaning to the symbol as he chose. The result has been, that there has been no generally admitted principle of interpretation respecting this book, and that the variety of conjectures indulged, and the wild and vain theories advanced, have produced the impression that the book is not susceptible of a plain and sensible exposition. A very common belief is, that symbolical language must, from the nature of the case, be obscure and unintelligible, and that a book, written in the manner of the Apocalypse, must always be liable to the wild vagaries of imagination which have been so commonly exhibited in the attempts to explain this book. These considerations make it proper to offer a few remarks here about the nature of symbolical language, and on the question whether a book written in that language is necessarily unintelligible, or incapable of a plausible interpretation.

A symbol is properly a representation of any moral thing by the images or properties of natural things. Thus a circle is a symbol of eternity, as having neither beginning nor end; an eye is a symbol of wisdom; a lion, of courage; a lamb, of meekness and gentleness. This general idea of symbols is found in types, enigmas, parables, fables, allegories, emblems, hieroglyphics, &c. The symbols mostly used in the book of Revelation are *pictures,* and could be painted—and, indeed, a great part of the book could be represented in a *panorama,* and would constitute a series of the most splendid drawings that the world can conceive. The following remarks may throw some light on the reason why this mode of representation was adopted, and on the question whether a book written in this manner is necessarily unintelligible.

(*a*) This method of representation is not uncommon in the ancient prophecies. A considerable portion of Daniel and Ezekiel is written in this way; and it is often resorted to by Isaiah and the other prophets. It was a method of representation which accorded well with the warm and glowing imagination of the Orientals, and with the character of mind in the early periods of the world. It was *supposed* to be capable of conveying ideas of important events, although it was doubtless understood that there might be some degree of obscurity in the representation, and that study and ingenuity might be requisite in understanding it—as is always the case with parables and enigmas. We have frequent instances in the Bible of a certain kind of trial of skill in expounding dark sayings and riddles, when the sense was intentionally so conveyed as to demand acuteness of thought in the explanation. The

## INTRODUCTION.

utterance of truths in symbolic language accorded much with this prevailing bent of mind in the ancient and the oriental world—as we see in the symbolical representations in Egypt. If the use of symbols, therefore, in the Apocalypse be urged as an objection to the book, the objection would lie with equal force against no small part of the writings of the ancient Hebrew prophets, and against a method of writing which was actually in extensive use in the early ages of the world. To object to it, must be to object that our own methods and views were not the views and methods of all past ages; that the improved modes of communication in existence now were not in existence always.

(*b*) Such a method of representation may be, however, clear and intelligible. The purpose of prophecy does not require that there should be in all cases an explicit statement of what will occur, or a particular detail of names, dates, and circumstances—for if such a statement were made, it is plain that it would be possible, on the one hand, for an impostor so to shape his conduct as to seem to fulfil the prophecy, and, on the other, for wicked men, knowing exactly what was predicted, to prevent its fulfilment. All that is demanded in such predictions is, (1) such a statement as undoubtedly *refers* to the future event; (2) such a statement as, when fairly interpreted, *describes* such an event; and (3) such a statement as that, when the event occurs, it shall be clear that this was the event referred to, or that the prediction cannot properly be referred to any other event; that is, so that they shall compare with each other as the two parts of a tally do. Now, that symbolical language may have these characteristics, and may be in these respects sufficiently clear and plain, is evident from the following considerations:—

1. A picture may be a correct representation of an event. It was thus among the Mexicans, who, by means of pictures, were enabled to give a correct representation of the landing of the Spaniards, and to convey to their monarch a correct idea of the number and character of the Spanish forces.

The following extract from Dr. Robertson's *History of America*, book v., § xii., referring to the landing of the Spaniards in Mexico, will illustrate this:—"During this interview [an interview between Cortes and the ambassadors of Montezuma], some painters in the train of the Mexican chiefs had been diligently employed in delineating, upon white cotton cloths, figures of the ships, the horses, the artillery, the soldiers, and whatever else attracted their eyes as singular. When Cortes observed this, and was informed that these *pictures* were to be sent to Montezuma, in order to convey to him a more lively idea of the strange and wonderful objects now presented to their view *than any words could communicate,* he resolved to render the representation still more animated and interesting, by exhibiting such a spectacle as might give both them and their monarch an awful impression of the extraordinary prowess of his followers, and the irresistible force of their arms."

2. A symbol may be as definite in its signification as the arbitrary character which constitutes a letter with us, or the arbitrary character which denotes a syllable or a word with the Chinese. There is some reason to believe that the letters in most languages were at first pictures or symbols; but whether this is true or not, it is easy to conceive that such *might* have been the case, and that as definite ideas might have been attached to the symbols employed as to the arbitrary marks or signs. Thus, it is easy to suppose that a circle, a lion, an eagle, a horse, a banner, an axe, a lamb, might have been so em-

ployed as always to denote the same thing, in the same way as the letters of the alphabet do, and thus, consequently, the number of symbols employed might have been very numerous, though still retaining their definite character.

3. The truth of these remarks has been illustrated by the recent investigations of the symbolical language or hieroglyphical signs in Egypt. On the celebrated Rosetta stone, an inscription was found in three compartments of the stone, in three different languages—the first in hieroglyphical or symbolical language, the language used by the priests; the second in *enchorical* or *demotic* language—the language in common use among the Egyptian people; and the third in Greek. It was conjectured that the inscription in each language was the same, and that consequently there might be a key for explaining the symbols or the hieroglyphics so common in Egypt. Acting on this suggestion, Champollion was enabled to read the inscription in the Egyptian language, and to determine the meaning of the symbols in so common use in the ancient inscriptions, and the symbolical language of Egypt became as intelligible as other ancient forms of record—as it was undoubtedly when it was at first employed. Each of the symbols had a well-known signification, and was adapted to convey a definite idea. An account of this stone, and of the symbols of Egypt generally, may be seen in Gliddon's *Ancient Egypt*, chap. i. The symbols employed by the Hebrew prophets may have had, as used by them, as definite a meaning, and may be as susceptible of as clear an interpretation now, as the symbols employed in Egypt, or as any other language. The only real difficulty in interpreting them may have arisen from the fact that they referred to future events (see Notes on Rev. xvi. 12); the employment of such methods of writing was in accordance with the genius of the Orientals, and gave great poetic beauty to their compositions.

4. It should be added, however, that peculiar care is necessary in the interpretation of writings of this character. There is much room for the indulgence of the imagination, and facts have shown that in almost nothing has so much indulgence been given to the fancy as in the interpretation of such books as Daniel and the Apocalypse. Indeed, the explanations of these books have been so loose and wild, as, with many, to bring the whole science of interpretation of the prophecies into contempt, and to produce the very common impression that a rational and consistent exposition of such books as Daniel and the Apocalypse is impossible. A better mode of interpretation, it is hoped, however, is to prevail—a mode in which there will be more careful attention to the true meaning of symbols and to the proper laws of symbolic language. The true method may not have been reached, and many errors may occur before it shall be reached. For many ages the meaning of the Egyptian hieroglyphics was entirely unknown. Thousands of conjectures had been made as to the method of reading those symbols; vast ingenuity had been exhausted; the hope was sometimes entertained that the clue had been discovered, but it was at last felt that all those proposed methods were fanciful, and the world had settled down in despair as to the possibility of deciphering their meaning. The accidental discovery of the Rosetta stone, and the patient labours of De Sacy, Akerblad, Tychsen, and especially of Champollion, have changed the views of the world on that subject, and the hieroglyphics of Egypt have become as intelligible as any other language. It is possible that the same may be true in regard to the meaning of the symbols of the sacred prophets; and that although those of Daniel and John may

have seemed to be as obscure as those of Egypt, and although the most wild and extravagant opinions may have been entertained in regard to their meaning, yet the time may come when those books shall take their place among the well-understood portions of the Bible, and when the correspondence of the predictions couched under these symbols with the events shall be so clear, that there shall be no lingering doubt on any mind that they are a part of the divine communications to mankind. Whether this attempt to explain one of those books will contribute anything to a better understanding of the true meaning of the symbolical language employed by the prophets, must be submitted to the judgment of the reader.

### § V.—*The Plan of the Apocalypse.*

The book of Revelation may be regarded as divided into seven portions, embracing the following general points: — The introduction, chap. i.; the epistles to the seven churches, chap. ii., iii.; the preparatory vision, chap. iv.; the relation of the church to the external world, embracing the outward or secular aspect of things as bearing on the church, chap. v.—xi. 1-18; the internal state of the church, embracing the rise and destiny of Antichrist— or, the internal history of the church until the overthrow of that formidable power and the permanent and triumphant establishment of the kingdom of Christ, the last temporary apostasy, and the general judgment, chap. xi. 19; xii.-xx.; the final condition of the righteous in their state of triumph and glory, chap. xxi., xxii. 1-5; and the epilogue or conclusion, chap. xxii. 6-21. This plan, as pursued in this attempt to explain the book, may be seen more in detail in the ANALYSIS on the following pages.

# ANALYSIS

OF THE

# BOOK OF REVELATION OF ST. JOHN.

SHOWING THE DESIGN AND ARGUMENT OF THE BOOK

I. GENERAL INTRODUCTION, CHAP. I.
- I. The title and design of the book, chap. i. 1-3.
- II. Dedication to the seven churches of Asia, chap. i. 4-8.
- III. Vision of the Redeemer, chap. i. 9-18.
- IV. Commission to write to the seven churches, chap. i. 19, 20.

II. EPISTLES TO THE SEVEN CHURCHES OF ASIA, CHAP. II. III.
- I. Epistle to the church at Ephesus, chap. ii. 1-7.
- II. Epistle to the church at Smyrna, chap. ii. 8-11.
- III. Epistle to the church at Pergamos, chap. ii. 12-17.
- IV. Epistle to the church at Thyatira, chap. ii. 18-29.
- V. Epistle to the church at Sardis, chap. iii. 1-6.
- VI. Epistle to the church at Philadelphia, chap. iii. 7-13.
- VII. Epistle to the church at Laodicea, chap. iii. 14-22.

III. PREPARATORY VISION, CHAP. IV.
- I. The scene laid in heaven, chap. iv. 1, 2.
- II. The vision of God, of the elders, and of the living creatures, ch. iv. 3-8.
- III. The worship rendered to God, chap. iv. 9-11.

IV. THE EXTERNAL RELATIONS OF THE CHURCH—THE RELATION TO SECULAR AFFAIRS — POLITICAL CHANGES AND REVOLUTIONS, AS BEARING ON THE CHURCH, CHAP. V.—XI. 1-18.

II. The opening of the seals.

I. The Sealed book, containing the record of these events, in the hand of him that sat on the throne. The Lamb of God only could open it. The joy in heaven that one was found who could open the seals, chap. v.

1. The opening of the first seal, chap. vi. 1, 2.
*The white horse.*—Peace, prosperity, and triumph, fulfilled in the state of the Roman empire from the death of Domitian, A.D. 96, to the accession of Commodus, A.D. 180.

2. The opening of the second seal, chap. vi. 3, 4.
*The red horse.*—Bloodshed, discord, civil strife; fulfilled in the state of the Roman empire from the death of Commodus, A.D. 193, and onward.

3. The opening of the third seal, chap. vi. 5, 6.
*The black horse.*—Calamity, distress, want, trouble; fulfilled in the Roman empire, in the scarcity of food that prevailed; the excessive taxation; the special order not to destroy the olive-yards and vine-yards; the sources of revenue, in the time of Caracalla, A.D. 211, and onward.

4. The opening of the fourth seal, chap. vi. 7, 8.
*The pale horse.*—The reign of death, in the form of famine, pestilence, disease; fulfilled in the Roman empire in the bloodshed, famine, and pestilence that prevailed in the time of Decius, Gallus, Æmilianus, Valerian, and Gallianus, A.D. 243-268.

5. The opening of the fifth seal, chap. vi. 9-11.
*The martyrs.*—Fulfilled in the Roman empire in the persecutions, particularly in the time of Diocletian, A.D. 284-304; the last of the efforts in the Pagan world to extinguish the Christian name.

6. The opening of the sixth seal, chap. vi. 12-17.
*Consternation and alarm as if the world was coming to an end;* fulfilled in the Roman empire in the threatening invasions of the Goths in the neighbourhood of the Danube, pressed on by the Huns, and producing universal alarm and consternation, A.D. 365, and onwards.

ANALYSIS OF THE BOOK OF REVELATION.   lvii

IV. THE EXTERNAL RELATIONS OF THE CHURCH—THE RELATION TO SECULAR AFFAIRS — POLITICAL CHANGES AND REVOLUTIONS, AS BEARING ON THE CHURCH, CHAP. V.—XI. 1-18.—*Continued.*

II. The opening of the seals.—*Continued.*

Intermediate vision between the opening of the sixth and seventh seals. A view of the persecution of the church, and the glory of the saints in heaven, designed to sustain the mind in the midst of so much gloom, and to furnish the assurance that innumerable multitudes of men would be brought to glory, chap. vii.

(*a*) The impending storm of wrath that seemed to threaten universal destruction is suspended in order that the servants of God might be sealed, chap. vii. 1-3.

(*b*) The sealing process, indicating the preservation of the church in these times of danger, and the influences that would designate and save the true people of God in all time to come, chap. vii. 4-8.

(*c*) A vision of an immense host before the throne, gathered out of all people and all lands, chap. vii. 9-12.

(*d*) A view of the martyrs who would be saved; a view designed to give comfort in the trials that would come upon the people of God in this world, chap. vii. 13, 14.

(*e*) A view of the happiness of heaven, where all suffering will cease, and all tears be wiped away, chap. vii. 15-17.

7. The opening of the seventh seal, chap. viii.—xi. 1-18.

Seven trumpets given to seven angels to sound, and the preparatory arrangements for sounding, chap. viii. 1-6.

Two series of events referring to the West and the East in the downfall of the Roman empire:—

A. THE WEST—to the fall of the Western empire—four trumpets.

(1) The first trumpet sounded, chap. viii. 7. The invasion of the Roman empire by Alaric, king of the Goths, A.D. 395-410.

(2) The second trumpet sounded, chap. viii. 8, 9. The invasion of the Roman empire by Genseric, king of the Vandals, A.D. 428-468.

(3) The third trumpet sounded, chap. viii. 10, 11. The invasion of the Roman empire by Attila, king of the Huns, the "Scourge of God," A.D. 433-453.

(4) The fourth trumpet sounded, chap. viii. 12, 13. The final conquest of Rome and the Western empire by Odoacer, king of the Heruli, A.D. 476-490.

B. THE EAST—to the fall of the Eastern empire—two trumpets, chap. ix.

(5) The fifth trumpet sounded, chap. ix. 1-12. The Mahometans, or Saracens.

(6) The sixth trumpet sounded, chap. ix. 13-19. The Turkish power.

The interval between the fall of the Eastern empire and the sounding of the seventh trumpet, chap. ix. 20; xi. 13:—

(*a*) The result of these judgments, chap. ix. 20, 21. They produce no change in the moral condition of the world; fulfilled in the state of the Papal world after the conquest of Constantinople, and before the Reformation.

(*b*) An angel is seen descending from heaven with emblems of majesty, joy, and peace, chap. x; fulfilled in the Reformation:—

(α) The angel with the rainbow on his head, and his face like the sun, a proper symbol of the Reformation as a work of peace, and accompanied with light and knowledge, chap. x. 1.

IV. THE EXTERNAL RELATIONS OF THE CHURCH—THE RELATION TO SECULAR AFFAIRS — POLITICAL CHANGES AND REVOLUTIONS, AS BEARING ON THE CHURCH, CHAP. V.—XI. 1-18.—*Continued.*

II. The opening of the seals.—*Continued.*

(β) The little book in his hand, a symbol of the principal agent in the Reformation —*a book*—the Bible, chap. x. 2.
(γ) His crying with a loud voice, symbolical of the Reformation as arresting the attention of the nations, chap. x. 3.
(δ) The seven thunders — the anathemas of Papal Rome—the thunder of the seven-hilled city, chap. x. 3.
(ε) The purpose of John to record what the seven thunders had uttered, and the command not to write; the mistake which the Reformers were in danger of making, by regarding the doctrine of the Papacy as the truth of God, chap. x. 4.
(ζ) The solemn oath of the angel that the time predicted would not then occur, but would occur in the time when the seventh angel should sound, chap. x. 5–7; fulfilled in the anticipations of the Reformers that the world was about to come to an end, and the reign of Christ about to commence, and the assurance of the angel that this would not *then* occur, but that a long and important interval must take place.
(η) The command given to John to go and take the little book from the hand of the angel, chap. x. 8; fulfilled in the delivery of the Bible again to the church.
(θ) The command to eat it, and the consequences—sweet in the mouth, and bitter to the belly, chap. x. 9, 10; the effect of the pure word of God on the soul indicated by the one; the bitter consequences, in persecution and opposition, that would result from the attempt to make the truth known to the world, indicated by the other.
(ι) The assurance that he would yet prophesy before many people, and nations, and tongues, and kings, chap. x. 10; fulfilled in the restoration of *preaching* in the church, founded on the Bible, and in the immediate and ultimate influence of the Bible in making the gospel known to the world.
(c) The measuring of the holy city, chap. xi. 1, 2; the determining of what constituted the true church at the time of the Reformation.
(d) The two witnesses, chap. xi. 3-13. Those who bore faithful testimony to the truth in all the corruptions of the church; their trials and their triumph; fulfilled in the succession of true and sincere Christians whom God raised up from time to time to testify to the truth. They would be persecuted, and many of them would be put to death; they would seem to be finally silenced, and would be treated with great indignity, as if their dead bodies should remain unburied; they would, however, come to life again, that is, at the time of the Reformation they would rise and testify against the corruptions of the Papacy, and would triumph *as if* they ascended visibly and gloriously to heaven.
(7) The sounding of the seventh trumpet. The final triumph of the church, and the establishment of the kingdom of God in the overthrow of all its enemies, chap. xi. 14-18. This ends the first series of visions; and this expresses in general terms what is drawn out more in detail in the next series of visions, Part V., embracing more particularly the rise and progress of Antichrist.

BOOK OF REVELATION. lix

V. THE CHURCH INTERNALLY — THE RISE OF ANTICHRIST, AND THE EFFECT OF THAT FORMIDABLE POWER ON THE INTERNAL HISTORY OF THE CHURCH, TO THE TIME OF THE OVERTHROW OF THAT GREAT POWER, AND THE TRIUMPHANT ESTABLISHMENT OF THE KINGDOM OF GOD, CHAP. XI.19; XII.-XX.

I. General Introduction to this series of visions, Chap. xi. 19; xii.

1. A new vision of the temple of God opened in heaven, chap. xi. 19
2. A representation of the church, under the image of a beautiful woman, chap. xii. 1.
3. The particular thing designed to be represented —the church about to increase and to fill the world, chap. xii. 2.
4. The deadly hostility of Satan to the church, and his purpose to destroy it, represented by a great red dragon waiting to destroy the man-child, chap. xii. 3, 4.
5. The ultimate safety of the church, represented by the child caught up to heaven, chap. xii 5.
6. The fact that the church would be a long time obscure and hidden — represented by the woman fleeing into the wilderness, chap. xii. 6.
7. A scenic representation of the great contest going on in the universe about the church— represented by a conflict in heaven between Michael, the protector of the church, with his angels, and Satan, the great enemy of the church, with his angels, chap. xii. 7.
8. The ultimate discomfiture of Satan, represented by his being overcome and cast out of heaven, chap. xii. 8, 9.
9. A song of victory in view of this triumph, chap. xii. 10, 11.
10. The fact that Satan would be allowed, for a limited time, to persecute the church, chap. xii. 12, 13.
11. The church in the wilderness, chap. xii. 14-17.
  (*a*) The church would be driven into obscurity, like a woman fleeing into a desert—representing the condition of the church while the Papacy should have the ascendency, ver. 14.
  (*b*) The church would still be preserved, though in obscurity—represented by the woman nourished by some unseen power, ver. 14.
  (*c*) Satan would still rage against the church —represented by the dragon pouring forth a flood of waters to overwhelm the woman, ver. 15.
  (*d*) The church would be protected, as if the earth should open its mouth to swallow up the water—representing the interpositions from an unexpected quarter in delivering the church from its perils, ver. 16
  (*e*) The wrath of Satan against the remnant — representing the attempts of the Papacy to cut off individuals when open and general persecution no longer raged, ver. 17.

II. The two beasts, representing the great persecuting power in the church, Chap. xiii.

1. The first beast, representing the Roman *civil* or *secular* power that sustained the Papacy in its career of persecution, chap. xiii. 1-10.
2. The second beast, representing the Papal *ecclesiastical* power, giving life to the former, and perpetuating its influence on the earth, chap. xiii. 11-18.

III. A representation designed, under a succession of symbols, to cheer and sustain the church in its present and prospective trials, with the assurance of its final triumph,

1. A vision of the redeemed in heaven, triumphant and rejoicing, ver. 1-5.
2. The ultimate spread of the gospel through all the world, ver. 6, 7.
3. The fall of Babylon, the great Antichristian power, ver. 8.
4. The final overthrow of all the *upholders* of that Antichristian power, ver. 9-12.
5. The blessed state of those who should die in the Lord in any time, whether of persecution or peace, ver. 13.
6. The consummation of all things—the final tri-

ANALYSIS OF THE

and the ultimate destruction of all its foes, Chap. xiv.

umph of the church, and the overthrow of the wicked, ver. 14-20:—
(a) The great harvest of the world by the Son of God—the gathering in of the righteous, ver. 14-16.
(b) The final overthrow and destruction of the wicked, ver. 17-20.

IV. Preparation for the final judgment on the beast and his image, Chap. xv.

1. A new wonder is seen in heaven; seven angels appear, having the seven last plagues, to fill up or complete the wrath of God, ver. 1.
2. Those who in former times had suffered from persecution by the power represented by the beast, but who, in the midst of trial and temptation, had maintained their faith steadfast, now appear to celebrate with a song of victory the prospective downfall of the great foe, ver. 2-4.
3. Arrangements made for executing the wrath of God. The temple is open in heaven; seven angels come out having the seven last plagues; one of the four living creatures gives command to them to go and execute the divine purpose, presenting seven golden bowls full of the wrath of God; the temple is forthwith filled with smoke, preventing all access to the mercy-seat, and indicating that the divine purpose was inexorable, ver. 5-8.

V. THE CHURCH INTERNALLY — THE RISE OF ANTICHRIST, AND THE EFFECT OF THAT FORMIDABLE POWER ON THE INTERNAL HISTORY OF THE CHURCH, TO THE TIME OF THE OVERTHROW OF THAT GREAT POWER, AND THE TRIUMPHANT ESTABLISHMENT OF THE KINGDOM OF GOD, CHAP. XI.19; XII.—XX. — Continued.

V. The execution of the purpose, Chap. xvi.

1. The first vial, ver. 1, 2. The first blow struck on the Papacy in the French Revolution.
2. The second vial, ver. 3. The scenes of blood and carnage in that Revolution.
3. The third vial, ver. 4-7. The calamities brought by the French invasions upon the countries where the most bloody persecutions had been waged—the north of Italy.
4. The fourth vial, ver. 8, 9. The overturning of the governments that sustained the Papal power, in the wars consequent on the French Revolution.
5. The fifth vial, ver. 10, 11. The direct assault on the Papal power; the capture of the pope himself, and the temporary entire subjugation of Rome by the French arms.
6. The sixth vial, ver. 12-16. The decline of the Turkish power; the rapid extension of the gospel in the East; the rallying of the strength of Paganism, Mahometanism, and Romanism —represented by the three frogs that came out of the mouth of the dragon, the beast, and the false prophet: the preparation of those powers as if for some great conflict, and the decisive struggle between the church and its foes, *as if* the issue were staked on a single battle—in Armageddon.
7. The seventh vial, ver. 17-21. The complete and final overthrow of the Papal power, *as if* in a tremendous storm of hail, lightning, and thunder, accompanied with an earthquake.

VI. A particular description of the judgment on this formidable Antichristian power, under a new image of a harlot (Chap. xvii.) in the form of an *explanatory Episode.*

1. Introduction to the Episode; the vision of the woman sitting on many waters, ver. 1-3.
2. A particular description of the Antichristian power referred to, under the image of an abandoned and gaily-attired woman, ver. 3-6.
3. A particular explanation of what is designed to be represented by the image of the scarlet-coloured woman, ver. 7-18:—
(a) The angel promises to explain it, ver. 7.
(b) A symbolical representation of the design of the vision, ver. 8-14.
(c) A more literal statement of what is meant, ver. 15-18. The whole designed to characterize Papal Rome, and to describe the manner of its rise and the means of its ultimate destruction.

BOOK OF REVELATION.　　　lxi

V. THE CHURCH INTERNALLY — THE RISE OF ANTICHRIST, AND THE EFFECT OF THAT FORMIDABLE POWER ON THE INTERNAL HISTORY OF THE CHURCH, TO THE TIME OF THE OVERTHROW OF THAT GREAT POWER, AND THE TRIUMPHANT ESTABLISHMENT OF THE KINGDOM OF GOD, CHAP. XI.19; XII.–XX. — *Continued.*

VII. A description of the *effect* of that judgment in pouring out the seventh vial on that formidable Antichristian power, under the image of a rich and luxurious city; a further *explanatory Episode*, Ch. xviii.

1. A vision of an angel coming from heaven, ver. 1-3.
2. A warning voice calling on the people of God to come out of the mystical Babylon, and not to partake of her sin and her doom, ver. 4-8.
3. Lamentation over her fate:—
   (*a*) By kings, that had lived delicately with her, ver. 9, 10.
   (*b*) By merchants that had been enriched by her, ver. 11-17.
   (*c*) By mariners that had trafficked with her, ver. 17-19.
4. Rejoicing over her fate, ver. 20.
5. The final destruction of the mystical Babylon— the Papal power—represented by a millstone cast by an angel into the sea, ver. 21-24.

VIII. A further *episodical representation* of the effects that would result from the fall of the powers that opposed the reign of the Son of God and the introduction of the Millennium, with an account of the final destruction of these powers, Chap. xix.

1. A hymn of the heavenly hosts in view of the destruction of the mystical Babylon, ver. 1-7:—
   (*a*) A voice of many people in heaven, shouting Hallelujah, ver. 1, 2.
   (*b*) The sound echoed and repeated as the smoke of her torment ascends, ver. 3.
   (*c*) The four and twenty elders, and the four living creatures unite in the song, ver. 4.
   (*d*) A voice heard commanding them to praise God, ver. 5.
   (*e*) The mighty shout of Hallelujah echoed and repeated from unnumbered hosts, ver. 6, 7.
2. The marriage of the Lamb as the reason of this increased joy, ver. 8, 9.
3. John, overcome with this scene, and filled with rapturous joy in view of the final triumphs of the church, prostrates himself before the angel to worship him, ver. 10.
4. The final conquest over the beast and the false prophet, ver. 11-21:—
   (*a*) A description of the conqueror—the Son of God—as he goes forth to victory, attended by the armies of heaven, ver. 11-16.
   (*b*) An angel is seen standing in the sun, calling on all the fowls of heaven to come to the great feast prepared for them in the destruction of the enemies of God, ver. 17, 18.
   (*c*) The final war, ver. 19-21. The beast and the kings of the earth and their armies gather together for the battle; the beast and the false prophet taken, and cast into the lake that burns with fire and brimstone; the remainder of the enemies of the church slain. The last enemy of the church on earth is destroyed, and the way is prepared for its universal triumph.

IX. The Millennial period and the final judgment, Ch. xx.

1. The binding of Satan, ver. 1-3.
2. The Millennium, ver. 4-6. Thrones are placed *as if* there were to be a judgment; the spirit of the martyrs and saints is revived again *as if* they were raised from the dead, and *lived* again on the earth; Satan is confined, and the church enjoys a state of repose and prosperity, for the period of a thousand years.
3. The release of Satan for a little time, ver. 7, 8. After the thousand years are expired, he is permitted to go forth again among the nations, and to awaken a new form of hostility to Christ and the church.
4. The final overthrow, subjugation, and punishment of Satan and those opposing hosts, and the final triumph, therefore, of the church, ver. 9, 10.
5. The final judgment on all mankind, ver. 11-15. All the dead are raised; the sea gives up its dead; Death and Hades give up their dead, and a solemn and just judgment is pronounced on all mankind, and the wicked are consigned to the lake of fire.

VI. THE FINAL CONDITION OF THE RIGHTEOUS—THE STATE OF FUTURE BLESSEDNESS, CHAP. XXI.; XXII. 1-5.
  I. A vision of the new heavens and new earth, as the final abode of the righteous, chap. xxi. 1.
  II. That blessed future abode represented under the image of a beautiful city descending from heaven, chap. xxi. 2-4.
  III. A particular description of the city, as the final abode of the righteous; its general appearance, its walls, its gates, its foundations, its size, its light, its inmates, &c., chap. xxi. 9-27; xxii. 1-5.

VII. THE EPILOGUE, OR CONCLUSION, CHAP. XXII. 6-20.
  I. A solemn declaration that the things revealed in this book are true, ver. 6, 7.
  II. The effect of those revelations on John, ver. 8, 9.
  III. A command not to seal up what had been revealed, ver. 10.
  IV. The unchangeable condition of the righteous and the wicked in the future state, ver. 14, 15.
  V. The blessedness of those who have a right to enter into the Holy City, ver. 15.
  VI. Jesus declares himself to be the author of all these revelations, ver. 16.
  VII. The free invitations of the gospel to all men, ver. 17.
  VIII. A solemn injunction not to change anything that had been written in this book, ver. 18, 19.
  IX. The assurance of the Saviour that he would come quickly, and the joyous assent of John to this, and prayer that it might occur, ver. 20.
  X. The benediction, ver. 21.

# THE
# REVELATION OF ST. JOHN THE DIVINE.

## CHAPTER I.
### ANALYSIS OF THE CHAPTER.

This chapter contains a general introduction to the whole book, and comprises the following parts:—

I. The announcement that the object of the book is to record a revelation which the Lord Jesus Christ had made of important events which were shortly to occur, and which were signified by an angel to the author, John, ver. 1-3. A blessing is pronounced on him who should read and understand the book, and special attention is directed to it because the time was at hand when the predicted events would occur.

II. Salutation to the seven churches of Asia, ver. 4-8. To those churches, it would seem from this, the book was originally dedicated or addressed, and two of the chapters (ii. and iii.) refer exclusively to them. Among them evidently the author had resided (ver. 9), and the whole book was doubtless sent to them, and committed to their keeping. In this salutation, the author wishes for them grace, mercy, and peace from "him which is, and which was, and which is to come"—the original fountain of all light and truth—referring to the Father; "from the seven Spirits which are before the throne"—referring to the Holy Spirit (see Note on ver. 4), by whom all grace is communicated to men; and from the Lord Jesus Christ, by whom the revelation is imparted. As it is *his* revelation, as it is designed peculiarly to glorify him, and as it predicts the final triumph of his religion, the author appends to this reference to him a special ascription of praise, ver. 5-8. He refers to the great work which he had done for his people in redeeming them, and making them kings and priests to God; he assures those to whom he wrote that he would come in glory to the world again, and that all eyes would see him; and he represents the Redeemer himself as applying to his own person a title—"Alpha and Omega," "the beginning and the ending"—which indicates his exalted nature, and his supreme authority.

III. The commission of the writer, or his authority for thus addressing the churches of Asia, ver. 9-20. His authority to do this is derived from the fact that the Lord Jesus had appeared to him personally in his exile, and had directed him to reveal what he saw in vision, and to send it to those churches. The statement of this commission is made as impressive as it well could be. (*a*) The writer was an exile—banished to a lonely island on account of the common faith, ver. 9. (*b*) On the day of Christian rest—the day set apart to the memory of the Saviour, and which he sacredly observed in his solitude as holy time—when in the spirit of calm contemplation on the truths appropriate to this day, he suddenly heard the voice of his Redeemer, like a trumpet, commanding him to record what he saw, and to send it to the seven churches of Asia, ver. 10, 11. (*c*) Then follows (ver. 12-18) a magnificent description of the appearance of the Saviour, as he appeared in his glory. He is seen standing in the midst of seven golden candlesticks, clothed in a long white robe, girded with a girdle of gold, his hair white, his eyes like a flame of fire, his feet like brass, and his voice like the roaring of mighty waters. In his hand are seven stars, and from his mouth goes a sharp sword, and his countenance is like the sun in the full splendour of its shining. John falls at his feet as if he were dead; and the Saviour lays his right hand upon him, and animates him with the assurance that though he had himself been dead he is now alive, and would for ever live, and that he has the keys of hell and death. (*d*) Then follows the commission itself, ver. 19, 20. He was to make a record of the things which he saw. He was especially to unfold the meaning of the seven stars which he saw in the right hand of the Saviour, and of the seven golden candlesticks, as referring to the seven churches of Asia Minor; and was then to describe

## CHAPTER I.

THE Revelation of Jesus Christ, which God gave unto him, to show unto his servants things which must shortly come to pass; and he sent and signified it by his angel unto his servant John:

---

the series of visions which pertained to the future history and destiny of the church at large.

In the scene represented in this chapter, there is some imagery which would be suggested by the arrangements in the temple at Jerusalem, and it has been supposed (Elliott, i. 72, 73) that the vision was laid there, and that Christ is represented as walking among the seven lamps "habited as the ancient high-priest." But the vision is not such an one as would have been presented in the holy place in the temple. In that place there was but one lamp-stand, with seven sconces; here, there were seven separate lamp-stands; there were there no "stars," and the vestments of the Jewish high-priest were not those in which the Saviour is represented as appearing. He had no mitre, no ephod, no breastplate, and no censer. The object was not to represent Christ as a priest, or as superseding the Jewish high-priest, but to represent him with costume appropriate to the Son of God —as having been raised from the dead, and received to the glory of heaven. His vestments are neither those of a prophet, a king, nor a priest; not with such garments as the ancient prophets wore, nor with crown and sceptre such as monarchs bear, nor yet with the usual habiliments of a priest. He appears as the Son of God, irrespective of the offices that he bears, and comes as the glorified Head of the Church to declare his will in regard to the seven churches of Asia, and to disclose the future for the guidance and comfort of his church at large. The scene appears to be laid at Patmos, and the apostle in the vision of the Saviour does not appear to have regarded himself as transferred to any other place. The view which is to be kept before the mind in the description of "the things that are" (ch. ii., iii.), is that of seven burning lamps, and the Son of God standing among them. Thus, amidst these lamps, representing the churches, he dictates to the apostle what he shall write to the churches; thus, with seven stars in his hand, representing the angels of the churches, he dictates what shall be said to them. Is it unnatural to suppose that the position of those lamps might have been arranged in the vision in a manner resembling the geographical position of the churches themselves? If so, the scene would be more significant, and more sublime.

1. *The Revelation of Jesus Christ.* This is evidently a title or caption of the whole book, and is designed to comprise the substance of the whole; for all that the book contains would be embraced in the general declaration that it is a revelation of Jesus Christ. The word rendered *Revelation*—'Ἀποκάλυψις, whence we have derived our word *Apocalypse*—means properly *an uncovering;* that is, *nakedness;* from ἀποκαλύπτω, to uncover. It would apply to anything which had been covered up so as to be hidden from the view, as by a veil, a darkness, in an ark or chest, and then made manifest by removing the covering. It comes then to be used in the sense of disclosing or revealing, by removing the veil of darkness or ignorance. "There is nothing covered that shall not be revealed." It may be applied to the disclosing or manifesting of anything which was before obscure or unknown. This may be done—(*a*) By instruction in regard to that which was before obscure; that is, by statements of what was unknown before the statements were made; as in Lu. ii. 32, where it is said that Christ would be "a light to lighten the Gentiles"—φῶς εἰς ἀποκάλυψιν ἐθνῶν; or when it is applied to the divine mysteries, purposes, or doctrines, before obscure or unknown, but made clear by light revealed in the gospel, Ro. xvi. 25; 1 Co. ii. 10; xiv. 6; Ep. iii. 5. (*b*) By the event itself; as the manifestation of the wrath of God at the day of judgment will disclose the true nature of his wrath. "After thy hardness and impenitent heart treasurest up unto thyself wrath against the day of wrath and *revelation* of the righteous judgment of God," Ro. ii. 5. "For the earnest expectation of the creature waiteth for the *manifestation* (Gr. *revelation*) of the sons of God," Ro. viii. 19; that is, till it shall be manifest by the event what they who are the children of God are to be. In this sense the word is frequently applied to the second advent or appearing of the Lord Jesus Christ, as disclosing him in his

glory, or showing what he truly is; "When the Lord Jesus shall be revealed," 2 Th. i. 7—ἐν τῇ ἀποκαλύψει —*in the revelation* of Jesus Christ; "Waiting for the coming (the revelation—την ἀποκάλυψιν) of our Lord Jesus Christ," 1 Co. i. 7; "At the *appearing* (Gr. *revelation*) of Jesus Christ," 1 Pe. i. 7; "When his glory shall be *revealed*," 1 Pe. iv. 13. (*c*) It is used in the sense of making known *what is to come*, whether by words, signs, or symbols, as if a veil were lifted from that which is hidden from human vision, or which is covered by the darkness of the unknown future. This is called a revelation, because the knowledge of the event is in fact made known to the world by Him who alone can see it, and in such a manner as he pleases to employ; though many of the terms or the symbols may be, from the necessity of the case, obscure, and though their full meaning may be disclosed only by the event. It is in this sense, evidently, that the word is used here: and in this sense that it is more commonly employed when we speak of a revelation. Thus the word גָּלָה (*gâlâ*) is used in Am. iii. 7, "Surely the Lord God will do nothing, but he revealeth his secret unto his servants." So Job xxxiii. 16, "Then he openeth (marg. *revealeth* or *uncovereth;* Heb. יִגְלֶה) the ears of men;" that is, in a dream, he discloses to their ears his truth before concealed or unknown. Comp. Da. ii. 22, 28, 29; x. 1; De. xxix. 29. These ideas enter into the word as used in the passage before us. The idea is that of a disclosure of an extraordinary character, beyond the mere ability of man, by a special communication from heaven. This is manifest, not only from the usual meaning of this word, but by the word *prophecy,* in ver. 3, and by all the arrangements by which these things were made known. The ideas which would be naturally conveyed by the use of this word in this connection are two: (1), that there was something which was before hidden, obscure, or unknown; and, (2), that this was so disclosed by these communications as to be seen or known. The things hidden or unknown were those which pertained to the future; the method of disclosing them was mainly by symbols. In the Greek, in this passage, the article is wanting—ἀποκάλυψις —*a* Revelation, not ἡ, *the* Revelation. This is omitted because it is the title of a book, and because the use of the article might imply that this was the only revelation, excluding other books claiming to be a revelation; or it might imply some previous mention of the book, or knowledge of it in the reader. The simple meaning is, that this was "*a* Revelation;" it was only a part of *the* revelation which God has given to mankind.

The phrase, "the Revelation of Jesus Christ," might, so far as the construction of the language is concerned, refer either to Christ as the *subject* or *object.* It might either mean that Christ is the *object* revealed in this book, and that its great purpose is to make him known, and so the phrase is understood in the commentary called *Hyponoia* (New York, 1844); or it may mean that this is a revelation which Christ *makes* to mankind, that is, it is his in the sense that he communicates it to the world. That this latter is the meaning here is clear, (1), because it is expressly said in this verse that it was a revelation which God gave to him; (2), because it is said that it pertains to things which must shortly come to pass; and, (3), because, in fact, the revelation is a disclosure of *events* which were to happen, and not of the person or work of the Lord Jesus Christ. ¶ *Which God gave unto him.* Which God imparted or communicated to Jesus Christ. This is in accordance with the representations everywhere made in the Scriptures, that God is the original fountain of truth and knowledge, and that, whatever was the original dignity of the Son of God, there was a mediatorial dependence on the Father. See Jn. v. 19, 20, "Verily, verily, I say unto you, The Son can do nothing of himself, but what he seeth the Father do: for whatsoever he doeth, these also doeth the Son likewise. For the Father loveth the Son, and *showeth him* (δείκνυσιν αὐτῷ) all things that himself doeth." "My doctrine is not mine, but his that sent me," Jn. vii. 16. "As my Father hath *taught me* (ἐδίδαξέ με), I speak these things," Jn. viii. 28. "For I have not spoken of myself; but the Father which sent me, he gave me a commandment, what I should say, and what I should speak," Jn. xii. 49. See also Jn. xiv. 10; xvii. 7, 8; Mat. xi. 27; Mar. xiii. 32. The same mediatorial dependence the apostle teaches us still subsists in heaven in his glorified state, and will continue until he has subdued all things (1 Co. xv. 24-28); and hence, even in that state, he is represented as receiving the Revelation from the Father to communicate it to men. ¶ *To show unto his servants.* That is, to his people, to Christians, often represented as the servants of God or of Christ, 1 Pe. ii. 16; Re. ii. 20; vii. 3; xix. 2; xxii. 3. It is true that the word is sometimes applied, by way of eminence, to the prophets (1 Ch. vi. 49; Da. vi. 20), and to the apostles (Ro. i. 1; Ga. i. 10; Phi. i. 1; Tit. i. 1; Ja. i. 1); but it is also applied to the mass of Christians, and there is no reason why it should not be so understood here. The book was sent to the churches of Asia, and was clearly designed for general use; and the contents of the book were evidently intended for the churches of the Redeemer in all ages and lands. Comp. ver. 3. The word rendered *to show* (δεῖξαι) commonly denotes to point out, to cause to see, to present to the sight, and is a word eminently appropriate here, as what was to be revealed was, in general, to be presented to the *sight* by sensible tokens or symbols. ¶ *Things which must shortly come to pass.* Not *all* the things that will occur, but such as it was deemed of importance for his people to be made acquainted with. Nor is it certainly implied that all the things that *are* communicated would shortly come to pass, or would soon occur. Some of them might perhaps lie in the distant future, and still it might be true that there were those which were revealed in connection with them, which soon would occur. The word rendered "*things*" (ἅ) is a pronoun, and might be rendered *what;* "he showed to his servants *what things* were about to occur," not implying that he showed *all* the things that would happen, but such as he judged to be needful that his people should know. The word would naturally embrace those things which, in the circumstances, were most desirable to be known. The phrase rendered "must come to pass" (δεῖ γενέσθαι), would imply more than mere futurity; The word used (δεῖ) means *it needs, there is need of*, and implies that there is some kind of *necessity* that the event should occur. That necessity may either arise from the felt *want* of anything, as where it is absent or wanting, Xen. *Cyr.* iv. 10; ib. vii. 5, 9; or from the nature of the case, or from a sense of duty, as Mat. xvi. 21, "Jesus began to show to his disciples that he *must go* (δεῖ ἀπελθεῖν) to Jerusalem" (comp. Mat. xxvi. 35; Mar. xiv. 31; Lu. ii. 49); or the necessity may exist, because a thing is right and just, meaning that it *ought* to be done, as Lu. xiii. 14, "There are six days in which men *ought* to work" (δεῖ ἐργάζεσθαι). "And ought not this woman (οὐκ ἔδει), whom Satan hath bound, &c., be loosed from this bond," Lu. xiii. 16 (comp. Mar. xiii. 14; Jn. iv. 20; Ac. v. 11, 29; 2 Ti. ii. 6; Mat. xviii. 33; xxv. 27); or the necessity may be that it is conformable to the divine arrangement, or is made necessary by divine appointment, as in Jn. iii. 14, "As Moses lifted up the serpent in the wilderness, even so *must* (δεῖ) the Son of man be lifted up." "For as yet they knew not the Scriptures, that he *must* (δεῖ) rise again from the dead," Jn. xx. 9; comp. Ac. iv. 12; xiv. 22, *et al.* In the passage before us, it is implied that there was some *necessity* that the things referred to should occur. They were not the result of chance, they were not fortuitous. It is not, however, stated what was the ground of the necessity; whether because there was a want of something to complete a great arrangement, or because it was right and proper in existing circumstances, or because such was the divine appointment. They were events which, on some account, *must* certainly occur, and which, therefore, it was important should be made known. The real ground of the necessity, probably, was founded in the design of God in redemption. He intended to carry out his great plans in reference to his church, and the things revealed here must necessarily occur in the completion of that design. The phrase rendered *shortly* (ἐν τάχει) is one whose meaning has been much controverted, and on which much has been made to depend in the interpretation of the whole book. The question has been whether the phrase necessarily implies that the events referred to were *soon* to occur, or whether it may have such an extent of meaning as to admit the supposition that the events referred to, though beginning soon, would embrace in their development far distant years, and would reach the end of all things. Those who maintain, as Professor Stuart, that the book was written before the destruction of Jerusalem, and that the portion in ch. iv.-xi. has special reference to Jerusalem and Judea, and the portion in ch. xii.-xix. to persecuting and heathen Rome, maintain the former opinion;

those who suppose that ch. iv.-xi. refers to the irruption of Northern barbarians in the Roman empire, and ch. xii., seq., to the rise and the persecutions of the Papal power, embrace the latter opinion. All that is proper in this place is, without reference to any theory of interpretation, to inquire into the proper meaning of the language, or to ascertain what idea it would naturally convey. (*a*) The phrase properly and literally means, *with quickness, swiftness, speed;* that is, *speedily, quickly, shortly* (Rob. *Lex.;* Stuart, *in loco*). It is the same in meaning as ταχέως. Comp. 1 Co. iv. 19, "But I will come to you *shortly*, if the Lord will." "Go out *quickly* into the streets," Lu. xiv. 21. "Sit down *quickly*, and write fifty," Lu. xvi. 6. "She rose up hastily (ταχέως) and went out," Jn. xi. 31. "That ye are so *soon* removed (ταχέως) from him that called you," Ga. i. 6. "Lay hands *suddenly* on no man," 1 Ti. v. 22. See also Phi. ii. 19, 24; 2 Th. ii. 2; 2 Ti. iv. 9. The phrase used here (ἐν τάχει) occurs in Lu. xviii. 8, "He will avenge them *speedily*" (lit. *with speed*). "Arise up *quickly*," Ac. xii. 7. "Get thee *quickly* out of Jerusalem," Ac. xxii. 18. "Would depart *shortly*," Ac. xxv. 4. "Bruise Satan under your feet *shortly*," Ro. xvi. 20; and Re. i. 1; xxii. 6. The essential idea is, that the thing which is spoken of was *soon* to occur, or it was not a remote and distant event. There is the notion of rapidity, of haste, of suddenness. It is such a phrase as is used when the thing is on the point of happening, and could not be applied to an event which was in the remote future, considered as an independent event standing by itself. The same idea is expressed, in regard to the same thing, in ver. 3, "The time is *at hand*"—ὁ γὰρ καιρὸς ἐγγύς; that is, it is near, it is soon to occur. Yet (*b*) it is not necessary to suppose that the meaning is that *all* that there is in the book was soon to happen. It may mean that the *series* of events which were to follow on in their proper order was soon to commence, though it might be that the sequel would be remote. The first in the series of events was soon to begin, and the others would follow on in their train, though a portion of them, in the regular order, might be in a remote futurity. If we *suppose* that there was such an order, that a series of transactions was about to commence, involving a long train of momentous developments, and that the beginning of this was to occur soon, the language used by John would be that which would be naturally employed to express it. Thus, in case of a revolution in a government, when a reigning prince should be driven from his kingdom, to be succeeded by a new dynasty, which would long occupy the throne, and involving, as the consequence of the revolution, important events extending far into the future, we would naturally say that these things were shortly to occur, or that the time was near. It is customary to speak of a succession of events or periods as near, however vast or interminable the series may be, when the commencement is at hand. Thus, we say that the great events of the eternal world are near; that is, the beginning of them is soon to occur. So Christians now speak often of the millennium as near, or as about to occur, though it is the belief of many that it will be protracted for many ages. (*c*) That this is the true idea here is clear, whatever general view of interpretation in regard to the book is adopted. Even Professor Stuart, who contends that the greater portion of the book refers to the destruction of Jerusalem, and the persecutions of heathen Rome, admits that "the closing part of the Revelation relates beyond all doubt to a distant period, and some of it to a future eternity" (ii. p. 5); and, if this be so, then there is no impropriety in supposing that a part of the series of predictions preceding this may lie also in a somewhat remote futurity. The true idea seems to be that the writer contemplated a *series* of events that were to occur, and that this series was about to commence. How far into the future it was to extend, is to be learned by the proper interpretation of all the parts of the series. ¶ *And he sent.* Gr., "Sending by his angel, signified it to his servant John." The idea is not precisely that he sent his angel to communicate the message, but that he sent *by* him, or employed him as an agent in doing it. The thing sent was rather the message than the angel. ¶ *And signified* it. Ἐσήμανεν. He indicated it by signs and symbols. The word occurs in the New Testament only in Jn. xii. 33; xviii. 32; xxi. 19; Ac. xi. 28; xxv. 27, and in the passage before us, in all which places it is rendered *signify, signifying,* or *signified.* It properly refers to some sign, signal, or token by which anything is made known

2 Who bare record of the word of God, and of the testimony of Jesus Christ, and of all things that he saw.

(comp. Mat. xxvi. 28; Ro. iv. 11; Ge. ix. 12, 13; xvii. 11; Lu. ii. 12; 2 Co. xii. 12; 1 Co. xiv. 22), and is a word most happily chosen to denote the manner in which the events referred to were to be communicated to John, for nearly the whole book is made up of signs and symbols. If it be asked *what* was signified to John, it may be replied that either the word "*it*" may be understood, as in our translation, to refer to the Apocalypse or Revelation, or what he saw (ὅσα εἶδε), as Professor Stuart supposes; or it may be absolute, without any object following, as Professor Robinson (*Lex.*) supposes. The general sense is, that, sending by his angel, he made to John a communication by expressive signs or symbols. ¶ *By his angel.* That is, an angel was employed to cause these scenic representations to pass before the mind of the apostle. The communication was not made directly to him, but was through the medium of a heavenly messenger employed for this purpose. Thus, in Re. xxii. 6, it is said, "And the Lord God of the holy prophets sent his angel to show unto his servants the things which must shortly be done." Comp. ver. 8, 9 of that chapter. There is frequent allusion in the Scriptures to the fact that *angels* have been employed as agents in making known the divine will, or in the revelations which have been made to men. Thus, in Ac. vii. 53, it is said, "Who have received the law by the disposition of angels." "For if the word spoken by angels was stedfast," &c., He. ii. 2; "And it was ordained by angels in the hand of a mediator," Ga. iii. 19. Comp. Notes on Ac. vii. 38, 53. There is almost no further reference to the agency of the angel employed for this service in the book, and there is no distinct specification of what he did, or of his great agency in the case. John is everywhere represented as seeing the symbols himself, and it would seem that the agency of the angel was, either to cause those symbols to pass before the apostle, or to convey their meaning to his mind. How far John himself understood the meaning of these symbols, we have not the means of knowing with certainty. The most probable supposition is, that the angel was employed to cause these visions or symbols to pass before his mind, rather than to interpret them.

If an interpretation had been given, it is inconceivable that it should not have been recorded, and there is no more probability that their meaning should have been disclosed to John himself, for his private use, than that it should have been disclosed and recorded for the use of others. It would seem probable, therefore, that John had only that view of the meaning of what he saw which anyone else might obtain from the record of the visions. Comp. Notes on 1 Pe. i. 10–12. ¶ *Unto his servant John.* Nothing could be learned from this expression as to *what* John was the author of the book, whether the apostle of that name or some other. Comp. Intro. § 1. It cannot be inferred from the use of the word *servant*, rather than *apostle*, that the apostle John was *not* the author, for it was not uncommon for the apostles to designate themselves merely by the words *servants*, or *servants of God*. Comp. Notes on Ro. i. 1.

2. *Who bare record of the word of God.* Who bore witness to, or testified of (ἐμαρτύρησε) the word of God. He regarded himself merely as a *witness* of what he had seen, and claimed only to make a fair and faithful *record* of it. "This is the disciple which *testifieth* (ὁ μαρτυρῶν) of these things, and wrote these things," Jn. xxi. 24. "And he that saw it bare record"—μεμαρτύρηκε, Jn. xix. 35. Compare also the following places, where the apostle uses the same word of himself: 1 Jn. i. 2; iv. 14. The expression here, "*the word of God*," is one the meaning of which has been much controverted, and is important in its bearing on the question who was the author of the book of Revelation. The main inquiry is, whether the writer refers to the "testimony" which he bears in this book respecting the "word of God;" or whether he refers to some testimony on that subject in some other book with which those to whom he wrote were so familiar that they would at once recognize him as the author; or whether he refers to the fact that he had borne his testimony to the great truths of religion, and especially respecting Jesus Christ, as a preacher who was well known, and who would be characterized by this expression. The phrase "the word of God" —τὸν λόγον τοῦ Θεοῦ—occurs frequently in the New Testament (comp. Jn. x. 35;

Ac. iv. 31; vi. 2, 7; xi. 1; xii. 24); and may either mean the word or doctrine *respecting* God — that which teaches what God is—or that which he speaks or teaches. It is more commonly used in the latter sense (comp. the passages referred to above), and especially refers to what God speaks or commands in the gospel. The fair meaning of this expression would be, that John had borne faithful witness to, or testimony of, the truth which God had spoken to man in the gospel of Christ. So far as the *language* here used is concerned, this might apply either to a written or an oral testimony; either to a treatise like that of his gospel, to his preaching, or to the record which he was then making. Vitringa and others suppose that the reference here is to the gospel which he had published, and which now bears his name; Lücke and others, to the revelation made to him in Patmos, the record of which he now makes in this book; Professor Stuart and others, to the fact that he was a teacher or preacher of the gospel, and that (comp. ver. 9) the allusion is to the testimony which he had borne to the gospel, and for which he was an exile in Patmos. Is it not possible that these conflicting opinions may be to some extent harmonized, by supposing that in the use of the aorist tense — ἐμαρτύρησε — the writer meant to refer to a characteristic of himself, to wit, that he was a faithful *witness* of the word of God and of Jesus Christ, whenever and however made known to him? With an eye, perhaps, to the record which he was about to make in this book, and intending to include that, may he not also refer to what had been and was his well-known character as a *witness* of what God communicated to him? He had always borne this testimony. He always regarded himself as such a witness. He had been an eye-witness of what had occurred in the life and at the death of the Saviour (see Notes on 2 Pe. i. 17, 18), and had, in all his writings and public administrations, borne witness to what he had seen and heard; for that (ver. 9) he had been banished to Patmos: and he was now about to carry out the same characteristic of himself by bearing witness to what he saw in these new revelations. This would be much in the manner of John, who often refers to this characteristic of himself (comp. Jn. xix. 35; xxi. 24; 1 Jn. i. 2), as well as harmonize the different opinions. The meaning, then, of the expression, "who bare record of the word of God," as I understand it, is, that it was a characteristic of the writer to bear simple but faithful testimony to the truth which God communicated to men in the gospel. If this be the correct interpretation, it may be remarked, (*a*) that this is such language as John the apostle would be *likely* to use, and yet (*b*) that it is not such language as an author would be likely to adopt if there was an attempt to forge a book in his name. The artifice would be too refined to occur probably to anyone, for although perfectly natural for John, it would not be so natural for a forger of a book to select this circumstance and weave it thus unostentatiously into his narrative. ¶ *And of the testimony of Jesus Christ.* That is, in accordance with the interpretation above, of the testimony *which Jesus Christ bore for the truth;* not of a testimony *respecting* Jesus Christ. The idea is, that Jesus Christ was himself *a witness* to the truth, and that the writer of this book was a witness merely of the testimony which Christ had borne. Whether the testimony of Jesus Christ was borne in his preaching when in the flesh, or whether made known to the writer by him at any subsequent period, it was *his* office to make a faithful record of that testimony. As he had always before done that, so he was about to do it now in the new revelation made to him in Patmos, which he regarded as a new testimony of Jesus Christ to the truth, ver. 1. It is remarkable that, in confirmation of this view, John so often describes the Lord Jesus as *a witness,* or represents him as having come to bear his faithful *testimony* to the truth. Thus in ver. 5: "And from Jesus Christ, who is the faithful and true witness." "I am one that bear witness— ὁ μαρτυρῶν—of myself," Jn. viii. 18. "To this end was I born, and for this cause came I into the world, that I should bear witness — ἵνα μαρτυρήσω — to the truth," Jn. xviii. 37. "These things saith the Amen, the faithful and true witness"— ὁ μάρτυς ὁ πιστός, κ.τ.λ., Re. iii. 14. Of this testimony which the Lord Jesus came to bring to man respecting eternal realities, the writer of this book says that he regarded *himself* as a witness. To the office of bearing such testimony he had been dedicated; that testimony he was now to bear, as he had always done. ¶ *And of all things that he saw.* "Ὅσα τε εἶδε. This

3 Blessed[a] *is* he that readeth, and they that hear the words of this prophecy, and keep those things which are written therein: [b]for the time *is* at hand.

a Lu.11.28.
b Ja.5.8,9; 1 Pe.4.7.

is the common reading in the Greek, and according to this reading it would properly mean, "*and* whatsoever he saw;" that is, it would imply that he bore witness to "the word of God," *and* to "the testimony of Jesus Christ," *and* to "whatever he saw"—meaning that the things which he saw, and to which he refers, were things *additional* to those to which he had referred by "the word of God," and the "testimony of Christ." From this it has been supposed that in the former part of the verse he refers to some testimony which he had formerly borne, as in his gospel or in his preaching, and that here he refers to what he "saw" in the visions of the Revelation as something *additional* to the former. But it should be remembered that the word rendered *and* —τε—is wanting in a large number of manuscripts (see Wetstein), and that it is now omitted in the best editions of the Greek Testament—as by Griesbach, Tittmann and Hahn. The evidence is clear that it should be omitted; and if so omitted, the reference is to whatever he had at any time borne his testimony to, and not particularly to what passed before him in the visions of this book. It is a general affirmation that he had always borne a faithful testimony to whatever he had seen respecting the word of God and the testimony of Christ. The correct rendering of the whole passage then would be, "And sending by his angel, he signifies it to his servant John, who bare record of" [*i.e.* whose character and office it was to bear his testimony to] "the word of God" [the message which God has sent to me], "and the testimony of Jesus Christ" [the testimony which Christ bore to the truth], "whatsoever he saw." He concealed nothing; he held nothing back; he made it known precisely as it was seen by him. Thus interpreted, the passage refers to what was a general characteristic of the writer, and is designed to embrace *all* that was made known to him, and to affirm that he was a faithful witness to it. There were doubtless special *reasons* why John was employed as the medium through which this communication was to be made to the church and the world. Among these reasons may have been the following: (*a*) That he was the "beloved disciple." (*b*) That he was the only surviving apostle. (*c*) That his character was such that his statements would be readily received. Comp. Jn. xix. 35; xxi. 24; 3 Jn. 12. (*d*) It *may be* that his mind was better fitted to be the medium of these communications than that of any other of the apostles—even if they had been then alive. There is almost no one whose mental characteristics are less correctly understood than those of the apostle John. Among the most gentle and amiable of men; with a heart so fitted for *love* as to be known as "the beloved disciple"—he yet had mental characteristics which made it proper that he should be called "a son of thunder" (Mar. iii. 17); a mind fitted to preserve and record the profound thoughts in his gospel; a mind of high poetic order, fitted for the magnificent conceptions in this book.

3. *Blessed* is *he that readeth.* That is, it is to be regarded as a privilege attended with many blessings, to be permitted to mark the disclosures to be made in this book; the important revelations respecting future times. Professor Stuart supposes that this refers to a public reading, and that the phrase "those who hear the words of this prophecy," refers to those who listened to the public reader, and that both the reader and hearer should regard themselves as highly favoured. It is, however, more in accordance with the usual meaning of the word rendered "read," to suppose that it refers to the act of one's reading for himself; to learn by reading. So Robinson (*Lex.*) understands it. The Greek word, indeed, would bear the other interpretation (see Lu. iv. 16; Ac. xiii. 27; xv. 21; 2 Co. iii. 15); but as this book was sent abroad to be read by Christians, and not merely to be in the hands of the ministers of religion to be read by them to others, it is more natural to interpret the word in the usual sense. ¶ *And hear the words of this prophecy.* As they shall be declared or repeated by others; or perhaps the word *hear* is used in a sense that is not uncommon, that of giving attention to; taking heed to. The general sense is, that they were to be regarded as highly favoured who be-

## CHAPTER I.

4 JOHN to the *seven churches which are in Asia: Grace *be* unto you, and peace, ᵈfrom him which is, and which was, and which is to come; and from the *seven Spirits which are before his throne;

*c* ver.11.  *d* ver.8.  *e* ch.3.1; 4.5; Zec.4.10.

came acquainted in any way with what is here communicated. The writer does not *say* that they were blessed who *understood* it, or that they who read or heard it *would* fully understand it; but it is clearly implied, that there would be so far an understanding of its meaning as to make it a felicitous condition to have been made acquainted with it. An author could not be supposed to say that one should regard his condition as a favoured one who merely heard words that he could not understand, or who had placed before him magnificent symbols that had to him no meaning. The word *prophecy* is used here in its more strict sense as denoting the disclosure of future events—a large portion of the book being of this nature. It is here synonymous with *Revelation* in ver. 1. ¶ *And keep those things which are written therein.* Keep in mind those things which relate to the future; and obey those things which are required as truth and duty. The blessing which results from having in possession the revealed truth of God is not merely in reading it, or in hearing it: it results from the fact that the truth is properly regarded, and exerts a suitable influence over our lives. Comp. Ps. xix. 11: "And in keeping of them there is great reward." ¶ *For the time is at hand.* See ver. 1. The word here used—ἐγγύς—has the same signification substantially as the word "*shortly*" in ver. 1. It would apply to any event whose beginning was soon to occur, though the end might be remote, for the series of events might stretch far into the future. It cannot be doubted, however, that the writer meant to press upon them the importance of attending to these things, from the fact that either entirely or in part these things were soon to happen. It may be inferred from this verse, that it is possible so to *understand* this book, as that it may convey useful instruction. This is the only book in the Bible of which a special blessing is pronounced on him who reads it; but assuredly a blessing would not be pronounced on the perusal of a book which is entirely unintelligible. While, therefore, there may be many obscurities in this book, it is also to be assumed that it may be so far understood as to be useful to Christians, in supporting their faith, and giving them elevated views of the final triumph of religion, and of the glory of the world to come. Anything is a blessing which enables us with well-founded hope and joy to look forward to the heavenly world.

4. *John to the seven churches which are in Asia.* The word *Asia* is used in quite different senses by different writers. It is used (1) as referring to the whole eastern continent now known by that name; (2) either Asia or Asia Minor; (3) that part of Asia which Attalus III., king of Pergamos, gave to the Romans, viz. Mysia, Phrygia, Lycaonia, Lydia, Caria, Pisidia, and the southern coast—that is, all in the western, south-western, and southern parts of Asia Minor; and (4), in the New Testament, usually the south-western part of Asia Minor, of which Ephesus was the capital. See Notes, Ac. ii. 9. The word *Asia* is not found in the Hebrew Scriptures, but it occurs often in the books of Maccabees, and in the New Testament. In the New Testament it is not used in the large sense in which it is now, as applied to the whole continent, but in its largest signification it would include only Asia Minor. It is also used, especially by Luke, as denoting the country that was called *Ionia*, or that which embraced the provinces of Caria and Lydia. Of this region Ephesus was the principal city, and it was in this region that the "seven churches" were situated. Whether there were more than seven churches in this region is not intimated by the writer of this book, and on that point we have no certain knowledge. It is evident that these seven were the principal churches, even if there were more, and that there was some reason why they should be particularly addressed. There is mention of some other churches in the neighbourhood of these. Colosse was near to Laodicea; and from Col. iv. 13, it would seem not improbable that there was a church also at Hierapolis. But there may have been nothing in their circumstances that demanded particular instruction or admonition, and they may have been on that account omitted. There is also some reason to sup-

pose that, though there had been other churches in that vicinity besides the seven mentioned by John, they had become extinct at the time when he wrote the book of Revelation. It appears from Tacitus (*Annal.* xiv. 27; comp. also Pliny, *N. H.* v. 29), that in the time of Nero, A.D. 61, the city of Laodicea was destroyed by an earthquake, in which earthquake, according to Eusebius, the adjacent cities of Colosse and Hierapolis were involved. Laodicea was, indeed, immediately rebuilt, but there is no evidence of the re-establishment of the church there before the time when John wrote this book. The earliest mention we have of a church there, after the one referred to in the New Testament by Paul (Col. ii. 1; iv. 13, 15, 16), is in the time of Trajan, when Papias was bishop there, sometime between A.D. 98 and 117. It would appear, then, to be not improbable that at the time when the Apocalypse was written, there were in fact but seven churches in the vicinity. Professor Stuart (i. 219) supposes that "seven, and only so many, may have been named, because the sevenfold divisions and groups of various objects constitute a conspicuous feature in the Apocalypse throughout." But this reason seems too artificial; and it can hardly be supposed that it would influence the mind of John, in the specification *by name* of the churches to which the book was sent. If no *names* had been mentioned, and if the statement had occurred in glowing poetic description, it is not inconceivable that the number *seven* might have been selected for some such purpose. ¶ *Grace be unto you and peace.* The usual form of salutation in addressing a church. See Notes on Rom. i. 7. ¶ *From him which is, and which was, and which is to come.* From him who is everlasting —embracing all duration, past, present, and to come. No expression could more strikingly denote eternity than this. He now exists; he has existed in the past; he will exist in the future. There is an evident allusion here to the name JEHOVAH, the name by which the true God is appropriately designated in the Scriptures. That name יְהֹוָה, from הָיָה, *to be, to exist,* seems to have been adopted because it denotes *existence,* or *being,* and as denoting simply one who *exists;* and has reference merely to the *fact* of existence. The word has no variation of form, and has no reference to time, and would embrace all time: that is, it is as true at one time as another that he exists. Such a word would not be inappropriately paraphrased by the phrase "who is, and who was, and who is to come," or who is to be; and there can be no doubt that John referred to him here as being himself the eternal and uncreated *existence,* and as the great and original fountain of all being. They who desire to find a full discussion in regard to the origin of the name JEHOVAH, may consult an article by Prof. Tholuck, in the *Biblical Repository,* vol. iv. pp. 89–108. It is remarkable that there are some passages in heathen incriptions and writings which bear a very strong resemblance to the language here used by John respecting God. Thus Plutarch (*De Is. et Osir.*, p. 354), speaking of a temple of Isis, at Sais, in Egypt, says, "It bore this inscription—'I am all that was, and is, and shall be, and my vail no mortal can remove.'"—'Ἐγώ εἰμι πᾶν τὸ γεγονός, καὶ ὄν, καὶ ἐσόμενον· καὶ τὸν ἐμὸν πέπλον οὐδείς πω θνητὸς ἀνεκάλυψεν. So Orpheus (in *Auctor. Lib. de Mundo*), "Jupiter is the head, Jupiter is the middle, and all things are made by Jupiter." So in Pausanias (*Phocic.* 12), "Jupiter was; Jupiter is; Jupiter shall be." The reference in the phrase before us is to God as such, or to God considered as the Father. ¶ *And from the seven Spirits which are before his throne.* After all that has been written on this very difficult expression, it is still impossible to determine with certainty its meaning. The principal opinions which have been held in regard to it are the following:—I. That it refers to God, as such. This opinion is held by Eichhorn, and is favoured by Ewald. No arguments derived from any parallel passages are urged for this opinion, nor can any such be found, where God is himself spoken of under the representation of a sevenfold Spirit. But the objections to this view are so obvious as to be insuperable. (1) If it refers to God as such, then it would be mere tautology, for the writer had just referred to him in the phrase "from him who was," &c. (2) It is difficult to perceive in what sense "seven spirits" could be ascribed to God, or how he could be described *as* a being of "Seven Spirits." At least, if he could be spoken of as such, there would be no objection to applying the phrase to the Holy

## CHAPTER I.

Spirit. (3) How could it be said of God himself that he was "before the throne?" He is everywhere represented as sitting *on* the throne, not as *before* it. It is easy to conceive of angels as standing before the throne; and of the Holy Spirit it is *more* easy to conceive as being represented thus as ready to go forth and convey a heavenly influence from that throne, but it is impossible to conceive in what sense this could be applied to God as such. II. The opinion held by Grotius, and by John Henry Heinrichs, that it refers to "the multiform providence of God," or to God considered as operating in seven or many different ways. In support of this Grotius appeals to ch. v. 12; vii. 12. But this opinion is so far-fetched, and it is so destitute of support, as to have found, it is believed, no other advocates, and to need no further notice. It cannot be supposed that John meant to personify the attributes of the Deity, and then to unite them with God himself, and with the Lord Jesus Christ, and to represent them as real subsistences from which important blessings descend to men. It is clear that as by the phrase, "who is, and who was, and who is to come," and by "Jesus Christ, the faithful and true witness," he refers to real subsistences, so he must here. Besides, if the attributes of God, or the modes of divine operation, are denoted, why is the number *seven* chosen? And why are they represented as standing before the throne? III. A third opinion is, that the reference is to seven attending and ministering presence-angels—angels represented as standing before the throne of God, or in his presence. This opinion was adopted among the ancients by Clemens of Alexandria; Andreas of Cesarea, and others; among the moderns by Beza, Drusius, Hammond, Wetstein, Rosenmüller, Clarke, Professor Stuart, and others. This opinion, however, has been held in somewhat different forms; some maintaining that the seven angels are referred to because it was a received opinion among the Hebrews that there were seven angels standing in the presence of God, as seven princes stood in the Persian court before the king; others, that the angels of the seven churches are particularly referred to, represented now as standing in the presence of God; others, that seven angels, represented as the principal angels employed in the government of the world, are referred to; and others, that seven archangels are particularly designated. Compare Poole, *Synop. in loco*. The *arguments* which are relied on by those who suppose that seven angels are here referred to are briefly these: (1) The nature of the expression here used. The expression, it is said, is such as would naturally denote beings who were before his throne—beings who were different from him who was *on* the throne—and beings more than one in number. That it could not refer to one *on* the throne, but must mean those distinct and separate from one on the throne, is argued from the use of the phrases "before the throne," and "before God," in Re. iv. 5; vii. 9, 15; viii. 2; xi. 4, 16; xii. 10; xiv. 3; xx. 12; in all which places the representation denotes those who were in the presence of God, and standing before him. (2) It is argued from other passages in the book of Revelation which, it is said (Professor Stuart), go directly to confirm this opinion. Thus in Re. viii. 2: "And I saw the seven angels which stood before God." So Re. iv. 5: the seven lamps of fire burning before the throne, are said to be "the seven Spirits of God." In these passages, it is alleged that the article "*the*" designates the *well-known* angels; or those which had been before specified, and that this is the first mention of any such angels after the designation in the passage before us. (3) It is said that this is in accordance with what was usual among the Hebrews, who were accustomed to speak of seven presence-angels, or angels standing in the presence of Jehovah. Thus in the book of Tobit (xii. 15), Raphael is introduced as using this language: "I am Raphael, one of the seven holy angels, which present the prayers of the saints, and which go in and out before the glory of the Holy One." The apocryphal book of Enoch (chap. xx.) gives the names of the seven angels who *watch;* that is, of the watchers (comp. Notes on Da. iv. 13, 17) who stand in the presence of God waiting for the divine commands, or who watch over the affairs of men. So in the Zendavesta of Zoroaster, seven amshaspends, or archangels, are mentioned. See Professor Stuart, *in loco*.

To these views, however, there are objections of great weight, if they are not in fact quite insuperable. They are such as the following: (1) That the same rank should be given to them as to God, as the source of blessings. According to the view which represents this expression as referring to angels, they are placed on the same level, so far as the matter before us is concerned, with "him who was, and is, and is to come," and with the Lord Jesus Christ—a doctrine which does not elsewhere occur in the Scriptures, and which we cannot suppose the writer designed to teach. (2) That blessings should be *invoked* from angels—as if they could impart "grace and peace." It is evident that, whoever is referred to here by the phrase "the seven Spirits," he is placed on the same level with the others mentioned as the source of "grace and peace." But it cannot be supposed that an inspired writer would invoke that grace and peace from any but a divine being. (3) That as two persons of the Trinity are here mentioned, it is to be presumed that the third would not be omitted; or to put this argument in a stronger form, it cannot be supposed that an inspired writer would mention two of the persons of the Trinity in this connection, and then not only *not* mention the third, but refer to *angels*—to creatures—as bestowing that which would be appropriately sought from the Holy Spirit. The incongruity would be not merely in omitting all reference to the Spirit—which might indeed occur, as it often does in the Scriptures—but in putting in the place which that Spirit would naturally occupy an allusion to *angels* as conferring blessings. (4) If this refer to angels, it is impossible to avoid the inference that angel-worship, or invocation of angels, is proper. To all intents and purposes, this is an act of worship; for it is an act of solemn invocation. It is an acknowledgment of the "seven Spirits," as the source of "grace and peace." It would be impossible to resist this impression on the popular mind; it would not be possible to meet it if urged as an argument in favour of the propriety of angel-invocation, or angel-worship. And yet, if there is anything clear in the Scriptures, it is that God alone is to be worshipped. For these reasons, it seems to me that this interpretation cannot be well founded.

IV. There remains a fourth opinion, that it refers to the Holy Spirit, and in favour of that opinion it may be urged, (1) That it is most natural to suppose that the Holy Spirit *would* be invoked on such an occasion, in connection with him "who was, and is, and is to come," and with "Jesus Christ." If two of the persons of the Trinity were addressed on such an occasion, it would be properly supposed that the Holy Spirit would not be omitted, as one of the persons from whom the blessing was to descend. Comp. 2 Co. xiii. 14: "The grace of the Lord Jesus Christ, and the love of God, and the communion of the Holy Ghost, be with you all." (2) It would be unnatural and improper, in such an invocation, to unite angels with God as imparting blessings, or as participating with God and with Christ in communicating blessings to man. An invocation to God to *send* his angels, or to impart grace and favour *through* angelic help, would be in entire accordance with the usage in Scripture, but it is not in accordance with such usage to invoke such blessings *from* angels. (3) It cannot be denied that an invocation of grace from "him who is, and was, and is to come," is of the nature of worship. The address to him is *as God*, and the attitude of the mind in such an address is that of one who is engaged in an act of devotion. The effect of uniting any other being with him in such a case, would be to lead to the worship of one thus associated with him. In regard to the Lord Jesus, "the faithful and true witness," it is from such expressions as these that we are led to the belief that he is divine, and that it is proper to worship him as such. The same effect must be produced in reference to what is here called "the seven Spirits before the throne." We cannot well resist the impression that some one with divine attributes is intended; or, if it refer to angels, we cannot easily show that it is not proper to render divine worship to them. If they were thus invoked by an apostle, can it be improper to worship them now? (4) The word used here is not *angels*, but *spirits;* and though it is true that angels are spirits, and that the word spirit is applied to them (He. i. 7), yet it is also true that that is not a word which would be understood to refer to them without designating that angels were meant. If angels had been intended here, that word would naturally have been used, as is the case elsewhere in this book. (5) In Re. iv. 5, where there is a reference to "the seven lamps before the throne," it is said of them that they "are," that is, they represent "the seven Spirits of God." This passage may be understood as referring to

# CHAPTER I.

**5 And from Jesus Christ,** *who is the* ᶠ*faithful witness, and the* ᵍ*first-begotten of the dead, and the prince of the kings of the*

*f* Jn. 8. 14.   *g* Col. 1. 18.

the same thing as that before us, but it cannot be well understood of angels; for, (*a*) if it did, it would have been natural to use that language for the reason above mentioned; (*b*) the angels are nowhere called "the spirits *of God*," nor would such language be proper. The phrase, "Spirit of God" naturally implies divinity, and could not be applied to a creature. For these reasons it seems to me that the interpretation which applies the phrase to the Holy Spirit is to be preferred; and though that interpretation is not free from difficulties, yet there are *fewer* difficulties in that than in either of the others proposed. Though it may not be possible wholly to remove the difficulties involved in that interpretation, yet perhaps something may be done to diminish their force. (1) First, as to the reason why the number *seven* should be applied to the Holy Spirit. (*a*) There would be as much propriety certainly in applying it to the Holy Spirit as to God as such. And yet Grotius, Eichhorn, Ewald, and others saw no difficulty in such an application considered as representing a sevenfold mode of operation of God, or a manifold divine agency. (*b*) The word *seven* often denotes a full or complete number, and may be used to denote that which is full, complete, or manifold; and might thus be used in reference to an all-perfect Spirit, or to a spirit which was manifold in its operations. (*c*) The number seven is evidently a favourite number in the book of Revelation, and it might be used by the author in places, and in a sense, such as it would not be likely to be used by another writer. Thus there are seven epistles to the seven churches; there are seven seals, seven trumpets, seven vials of the wrath of God, seven last plagues; there are seven lamps, and seven Spirits of God; the Lamb has seven horns and seven eyes. In ch. i. 16, seven stars are mentioned; in ch. v. 12, seven attributes of God; ch. xii. 3, the dragon has seven heads; ch. xiii. 1, the beast has seven heads. (*d*) The number seven, therefore, *may* have been given to the Holy Spirit with reference to the *diversity* or the *fulness* of his operations on the souls of men, and to his *manifold* agency on the affairs of the world, as further developed in this book. (2) As to his being represented as "*before* the throne," this may be intended to designate the fact that the Divine Spirit was, as it were, prepared to go forth, or to be *sent* forth, in accordance with a common representation in the Scriptures, to accomplish important purposes on human affairs. The posture does not necessarily imply inferiority of nature, any more than the language does respecting the Son of God, when he is represented as being *sent* into the world to execute an important commission from the Father.

5. *And from Jesus Christ,* who is *the faithful witness.* See Notes on ver. 2. He is faithful in the sense that he is one on whose testimony there may be entire reliance, or who is entirely worthy to be believed. From him "grace and peace" are appropriately sought, as one who bears such a testimony, and as the first-begotten from the dead, and as reigning over the kings of the earth. Thus grace and peace are invoked from the infinite God in all his relations and operations :—as the Father, the Source of all existence; as the Sacred Spirit, going forth in manifold operations upon the hearts of men; and as the Son of God, the one appointed to bear faithful testimony to the truth respecting God and future events. ¶ And *the first-begotten of the dead.* The same Greek expression—πρωτότοκος—occurs in Col. i. 18. See it explained in the Notes on that passage. Comp. Notes, 1 Co. xv. 20. ¶ *And the prince of the kings of the earth.* Who has over all the kings of the earth the pre-eminence which kings have over their subjects. He is the Ruler *of* rulers; King *of* kings. In ch. xvii. 14, xix. 16, the same thought is expressed by saying that he is the "King of kings." No language could more sublimely denote his exalted character, or his supremacy. Kings and princes sway a sceptre over the millions of the earth, and the exaltation of the Saviour is here expressed by supposing that all those kings and princes constitute a community over which he is the head. The exaltation of the Redeemer is elsewhere expressed in different language, but the idea is one that everywhere prevails in regard to him in the Scriptures. Comp. Mat.

earth. Unto *h*him that loved us, and *i*washed us from our sins in his own blood,

6 And hath made us *k*kings and priests unto God and his Father; *l*to him *be* glory and dominion for ever and ever. Amen.

*h* Jn.13.1.   *i* He.9.14.   *k* Ex.19.6; 1 Pe.2.5-9.   *l* He.13.21.

xxviii. 18; xi. 27; Jn. xvii. 2; Ep. i. 20-22; Phi. ii. 9-11; Col. i. 15-18. The word *prince*—ὁ ἄρχων—means properly, *ruler, leader, the first in rank.* We often apply the word *prince* to an heir to a throne who is not invested with absolute sovereignty. The word here, however, denotes that he actually exercises dominion over the rulers of the earth. As this is an authority which is claimed by God (comp. Is. x. 5, seq.; xlv. 1, seq.; Ps. xlvii. 2; xcix. 1; ciii. 19; Da. iv. 34), and which can only appertain to God, it is clear that in ascribing this to the Lord Jesus it is implied that he is possessed of divine attributes. As much of the revelations of this book pertained to the assertion of power over the princes and rulers of this world, there was a propriety that, in the commencement, it should be asserted that he who was to exert that power was invested with the prerogative of a ruler of the nations, and that he had this right of control. ¶ *Unto him that loved us.* This refers undoubtedly to the Lord Jesus, whose *love* for men was so strong that nothing more was necessary to characterize him than to speak of him as the one "who loved us." It is manifest that the division in the verses should have been made here, for this commences a new subject, not having any special connection with that which precedes. In ver. 4, and the first part of this verse, the writer had invoked grace from the Father, the Spirit, and the Saviour. In the latter clause of the verse there commences an ascription of praise to the Redeemer; an ascription to him particularly, because the whole book is regarded as a revelation from him (ver. 1); because he was the one who especially appeared to John in the visions of Patmos; and because he was to be the great agent in carrying into execution the purposes revealed in this book. ¶ *And washed us from our sins in his own blood.* He has removed the pollution of sin from our souls by his blood; that is, his blood has been applied to cleanse us from sin. Blood can be represented as having a cleansing power *only* as it makes an expiation for sin, for considered literally its effect would be the reverse. The language is such as would be used only on the supposition that he had made an atonement, and that it was *by* the atonement that we are cleansed; for in what sense could it be said of a martyr that he "had washed us from our sins in his blood?" How could this language be used of Paul or Polycarp; of Ridley or Cranmer? The doctrine that the blood of Christ *cleanses* us from sin, or *purifies* us, is one that is common in the Scriptures. Comp. 1 Jn. i. 7; He. ix. 14. The specific idea of *washing,* however—representing that blood as *washing* sin away—is one which does not elsewhere occur. It is evidently used in the sense of *cleansing* or *purifying,* as we do this by *washing,* and as the blood of Christ accomplishes in respect to our souls, what washing with water does in respect to the body.

6. *And hath made us kings and priests unto God.* In 1 Pe. ii. 9 the same idea is expressed by saying of Christians that they are "*a royal priesthood.*" See Notes on that verse. The quotation in both places is from Ex. xix. 6: "And ye shall be unto me a kingdom of priests." This idea is expressed here by saying that Christ had made us in fact kings *and* priests; that is, Christians are exalted to the dignity and are invested with the office, implied in these words. The word *kings*, as applied to them, refers to the exalted rank and dignity which they will have; to the fact that they, in common with their Saviour, will reign triumphant over all enemies; and that, having gained a victory over sin and death and hell, they may be represented as reigning together. The word *priests* refers to the fact that they are engaged in the holy service of God, or that they offer to him acceptable worship. See Notes on 1 Pe. ii. 5. ¶ *And his Father.* Even his Father; that is, the Saviour has redeemed them, and elevated them to this exalted rank, in order that they may thus be engaged in the service of his Father. ¶ *To him* be *glory.* To the Redeemer; for so the construction (ver. 5) demands. The word

A.D. 96.　　　　　　　　　CHAPTER I.　　　　　　　　　　45

7 Behold, he <sup>m</sup>cometh with clouds; and every eye shall see him, and <sup>n</sup>they *also* which pierced

*m* Da.7.13; Mat.26.64.　　*n* Zec.12.10.

him: and all kindreds of the earth <sup>o</sup>shall wail because of him. <sup>p</sup>Even so, Amen.

Mat 24.30.　　　　*p* ch.22 20.

"glory" here means praise, or honour, implying a wish that all honour should be shown him. ¶ *And dominion.* This word means literally *strength—κράτος*; but it here means the strength, power, or authority which is exercised over others, and the expression is equivalent to a wish that he may *reign.*
7. *Behold he cometh with clouds.* That is, the Lord Jesus, when he returns, will come accompanied with clouds. This is in accordance with the uniform representation respecting the return of the Saviour. See Notes on Mat. xxiv. 30. Comp. Mat. xxvi. 64; Mar. xiii. 26; xiv. 62; Ac. i. 9, 11. Clouds are appropriate symbols of majesty, and God is often represented as appearing in that manner. See Ex. xix. 18; Ps. xviii. 11, seq.; Is. xix. 1. So, among the heathen, it was common to represent their divinities as appearing clothed with a cloud:

"tandem venias, precamur,
Nube candentes humeros amictus
　　　　　　　　　Augur Apollo."

The *design* of introducing this representation of the Saviour, and of the manner in which he would appear, seems to be to impress the mind with a sense of the majesty and glory of that being from whom John received his revelations. His rank, his character, his glory were such as to demand respect; all should reverence him, and all should feel that his communications about the future were important to them, for they must soon appear before him. ¶ *And every eye shall see him.* He will be made visible in his glory to all that dwell upon the earth; to all the children of men. Everyone, therefore, has an interest in what he says; everyone has this in certain prospect, that he shall see the Son of God coming as a Judge. ¶ *And they* also *which pierced him.* When he died; that is, they who pierced his hands, his feet, and his side. There is probably an allusion here to Zec. xii. 10: "They shall look upon me whom they have pierced, and they shall mourn." The language here is so general that it may refer to *any* act of looking upon the pierced Saviour, and might be applied to those who would see him on the cross and to their compunctious visitings then; or to their subsequent reflections, as they might look by faith on him whom they had crucified; or to the feeling of any sinners who should reflect that their sins had been the cause of the death of the Lord Jesus; or it might be applied, as it is here, more specifically to the feelings which his murderers will have when they shall see him coming in his glory. All sinners who have pierced his heart by their crimes will then behold him and will mourn over their treatment of him; they, in a special manner, who imbrued their hands in his blood will then remember their crime and be overwhelmed with alarm. The *design* of what is here said seems to be, to show that the coming of the Saviour will be an event of great interest to all mankind. None can be indifferent to it, for all will see him. His friends will hail his advent (comp. ch. xxii. 20), but all who were engaged in putting him to death, and all who in any manner have pierced his heart by sin and ingratitude, unless they shall have repented, will have occasion of bitter lamentation when he shall come. There are none who have a more fearful doom to anticipate than the murderers of the Son of God, including those who actually put him to death, and those who would have engaged in such an act had they been present, and those who, by their conduct, have done all they could to pierce and wound him by their ingratitude. ¶ *And all kindreds of the earth.* Gr., "All the tribes — φυλαὶ — of the earth." This language is the same which the Saviour uses in Mat. xxiv. 30. See Notes on that passage. The word *tribes* is that which is commonly applied to the twelve tribes of Israel, and thus used, it would describe the inhabitants of the Holy Land; but it may be used to denote nations and people in general, as descended from a common ancestor, and the connection requires that it should be understood in this sense here, since it is said that "every eye shall see him;" that is, all that dwell on the face of the earth. ¶ *Shall wail because of him.* On account of him; on account of their treatment of him. The word rendered *wail—κόπτω* —means properly to beat, to cut; then

8 I *am Alpha and Omega, the beginning and the ending,
*q* Is. 41. 4.

saith the Lord, which is, and which was, and which is to come, *r* the Almighty.
*r* Is. 9. 6.

to beat or cut one's self in the breast as an expression of sorrow; and then to lament, to cry aloud in intense grief. The coming of the Saviour will be an occasion of this, (*a*) because it will be an event which will call the sins of men to remembrance, and (*b*) because they will be overwhelmed with the apprehension of the wrath to come. Nothing would fill the earth with greater consternation than the coming of the Son of God in the clouds of heaven; nothing could produce so deep and universal alarm. This fact, which no one can doubt, is proof that men *feel* that they are guilty, since, if they were innocent, they would have nothing to dread by his appearing. It is also a proof that they believe in the doctrine of future punishment, since, if they do not, there is no reason why they should be alarmed at his coming. Surely men would not dread his appearing if they really believed that all will be saved. Who dreads the coming of a benefactor to bestow favours on him? Who dreads the appearing of a jailer to deliver him from prison; of a physician to raise him up from a bed of pain; of a deliverer to knock off the fetters of slavery? And how *can* it be that men should be alarmed at the coming of the Saviour, unless their consciences tell them that they have much to fear in the future? The presence of the Redeemer in the clouds of heaven would destroy all the hopes of those who believe in the doctrine of universal salvation — as the approach of death now often does. Men *believe* that there is much to be dreaded in the future world, or they would not fear the coming of Him who shall wind up the affairs of the human race. ¶ *Even so, Amen*—ναὶ, ἀμήν. "A double expression of *so be it, assuredly, certainly*, one in Greek and the other in Hebrew" (Professor Stuart). Comp. Ro. viii. 16, "Abba, Father"—ἀββᾶ, ὁ πατήρ. The idea which John seems to intend to convey is, that the coming of the Lord Jesus, and the consequences which he says will follow, are events which are altogether *certain*. This is not the expression of a wish that it *may* be so, as our common translation would seem to imply, but a strong affirmation that it *will* be so. In some passages, however, the word (ναὶ) expresses *assent* to what is said, implying approbation of it as true, or as desirable. "*Even so*, Father: for so it seemed good in thy sight," Mat. xi. 26; Lu. x. 21. So in Re. xvi. 7, "*Even so* (ναὶ), Lord God Almighty." So in Re. xxii. 20, "*Even so* (ναὶ), come, Lord Jesus." The word *Amen* here seems to determine the meaning of the phrase, and to make it the affirmation of a *certainty*, rather than the expression of a *wish*.

8. *I am Alpha and Omega.* These are the first and the last letters of the Greek alphabet, and denote properly the first and the last. So in Re. xxii. 13, where the two expressions are united, "I am Alpha and Omega, the beginning and the end, the first and the last." So in ch. i. 17, the speaker says of himself, "I am the first and the last." Among the Jewish Rabbins it was common to use the first and the last letters of the Hebrew alphabet to denote the whole of anything, from beginning to end. Thus it is said, "Adam transgressed the whole law, from א to ת"— from Aleph to Tâv. "Abraham kept the whole law, from א to ת." The language here is that which would properly denote *eternity* in the being to whom it is applied, and could be used in reference to no one but the true God. It means that he is the beginning and the end of all things; that he was at the commencement, and will be at the close; and it is thus equivalent to saying that he has always existed, and that he will always exist. Comp. Is. xli. 4, "I the Lord, the first, and with the last;"—xliv. 6, "I am the first and I am the last; and beside me there is no God;"—xlviii. 12, "I am he; I am the first, I also am the last." There can be no doubt that the language here would be naturally understood as implying divinity, and it could be properly applied to no one but the true God. The obvious interpretation here would be to apply this to the Lord Jesus; for (*a*) it is he who is spoken of in the verses preceding, and (*b*) there can be no doubt that the same language is applied to him in ver. 11. As there is, however, a difference of reading in this place in the Greek text, and as it cannot be absolutely certain that the writer meant to refer to the Lord Jesus speci-

**9 I John, who also am your brother, and companion in tribulation, and in the kingdom and patience of Jesus Christ, was in**

fically here, this cannot be adduced with propriety as a proof-text to demonstrate his divinity. Many MSS., instead of "*Lord*," κυριος, read "*God*," θεὸς; and this reading is adopted by Griesbach, Tittman, and Hahn, and is now regarded as the correct reading. There is no real incongruity in supposing, also, that the writer here meant to refer to God as such, since the introduction of a reference to him would not be inappropriate to his manifest design. Besides, a portion of the language here used, "which is, and was, and is to come," is that which would more naturally suggest a reference to God as such, than to the Lord Jesus Christ. See ver. 4. The *object* for which this passage referring to the "first and the last —to him who was, and is, and is to come," is introduced here evidently is, to show that as he was clothed with omnipotence, and would continue to exist through all ages to come as he had existed in all ages past, there could be no doubt about his ability to execute all which it is said he would execute. ¶ *Saith the Lord.* Or, saith God, according to what is now regarded as the correct reading. ¶ *Which is, and which was*, &c. See Notes on ver. 4. ¶ *The Almighty.* An appellation often applied to God, meaning that he has all power, and used here to denote that he is able to accomplish what is disclosed in this book.

9. *I John, who also am your brother.* Your Christian brother; who am a fellow-Christian with you. The reference here is doubtless to the members of the seven churches in Asia, to whom the epistles in the following chapters were addressed, and to whom the whole book seems to have been sent. In the previous verse, the writer had closed the salutation, and he here commences a description of the circumstances under which the vision appeared to him. He was in a lonely island, to which he had been banished on account of his attachment to religion; he was in a state of high spiritual enjoyment on the day devoted to the sacred remembrance of the Redeemer; he suddenly heard a voice behind him, and turning saw the Son of man himself, in glorious form, in the midst of seven golden lamps, and fell at his feet as dead. ¶ *And companion in tribulation.* Your partner in affliction. That is, he and they were suffering substantially the same kind of trials on account of their religion. It is evident from this that some form of persecution was then raging, in which they were also sufferers, though in their case it did not lead to banishment. The leader, the apostle, the aged and influential preacher, was banished; but there were many other forms of trial which they might be called to endure who remained at home. What they were we have not the means of knowing with certainty. ¶ *And in the kingdom and patience of Jesus Christ.* The meaning of this passage is, that he, and those whom he addressed, were not only companions in affliction, but were fellow-partners in the kingdom of the Redeemer; that is, they shared the honour and the privileges pertaining to that kingdom; and that they were fellow-partners in the *patience* of Jesus Christ, that is, in enduring with patience whatever might follow from their being his friends and followers. The general idea is, that alike in privileges and sufferings they were united. They shared alike in the results of their attachment to the Saviour. ¶ *Was in the isle that is called Patmos.* Patmos is one of the cluster of islands in the Ægean Sea anciently called the *Sporades.* It lies between the island of Icaria and the promontory of Miletus. It is merely mentioned by the ancient geographers (Plin. *Hist. Nat.* iv. 23; Strabo, x. 488). It is now called Patino or Patmoso. It is some six or eight miles in length, and not more than a mile in breadth, being about fifteen miles in circumference. It has neither trees nor rivers, nor has it any land for cultivation, except some little nooks among the ledges of rocks. On approaching the island, the coast is high, and consists of a succession of capes, which form so many ports, some of which are excellent. The only one in use, however, is a deep bay, sheltered by high mountains on every side but one, where it is protected by a projecting cape. The town attached to this port is situated upon a high rocky mountain, rising immediately from the sea, and this, with the Scala below upon the shore, consisting of some ships and houses, forms the only inhabited site of the island. Though Patmos is deficient in trees, it abounds in flowery plants

the isle that is called Patmos, for the word of God, and for the testimony of Jesus Christ.

and shrubs. Walnuts and other fruit trees are raised in the orchards, and the wine of Patmos is the strongest and the best flavoured in the Greek islands. Maize and barley are cultivated, but not in a quantity sufficient for the use of the inhabitants and for a supply of their own vessels, and others which often put into their good harbour for provisions. The inhabitants now do not exceed four or five thousand; many of whom are emigrants from the neighbouring continent. About half-way up the mountain there is shown a natural grotto in a rock, where John is *said* to have seen his visions and to have written this book. Near this is a small church, connected with which is a school or college, where the Greek language is taught; and on the top of the hill, and in the centre of the island, is a monastery, which, from its situation, has a very majestic appearance (Kitto's *Cyclopædia of Bib. Lit.*). The annexed engraving is supposed to give a good representation of the appearance of the island. It is commonly supposed that John was banished to this island by Domitian, about A.D. 94. No place could have been selected for banishment which would accord better with such a design than this. Lonely, desolate, barren, uninhabited, seldom visited, it had all the requisites which could be desired for a place of punishment; and banishment to that place would accomplish all that a persecutor could wish in silencing an apostle, without putting him to death. It was no uncommon thing, in ancient times, to banish men from their country; either sending them forth at large, or specifying some particular place to which they were to go. The whole narrative leads us to suppose that this place was *designated* as that to which John was to be sent. Banishment to an island was a common mode of punishment; and there was a distinction made by this act in favour of those who were thus banished. The more base, low, and vile of criminals were commonly condemned to work in the mines; the more decent and respectable were *banished* to some lonely island. See the authorities quoted in Wetstein, *in loco*. ¶ *For the word of God.* On account of the word of God; that is, for holding and preaching the gospel. See Notes

10 I was *s*in the Spirit on the *t*Lord's day, and heard behind

*s* 2 Co.12.2.　　*t* Jn.20.26; Ac.20.7; 1 Co.16.2.

on ver. 2. It cannot mean that he was sent there with a view to his *preaching* the word of God; for it is inconceivable that he should have been sent from Ephesus to preach in such a little, lonely, desolate place, where indeed there is no evidence that there were any inhabitants; nor can it mean that he was sent there by the Spirit of God to receive and record this revelation, for it is clear that the revelation could have been made elsewhere, and such a place afforded no peculiar advantages for this. The fair interpretation is, in accordance with all the testimony of antiquity, that he was sent there in a time of persecution, as a punishment for preaching the gospel. ¶ *And for the testimony of Jesus Christ.* See Notes on ver. 2. He did not go there to bear testimony to Jesus Christ on that island, either by preaching or recording the visions in this book, but he went because he *had* preached the doctrines which testified of Christ.

10. *I was in the Spirit.* This cannot refer to his own spirit, for such an expression would be unintelligible. The language then must refer to some unusual state, or to some influence that had been brought to bear upon him from without, that was appropriate to such a day. The word *Spirit* may refer either to the Holy Spirit, or to some state of mind such as the Holy Spirit produces —a spirit of elevated devotion, a state of high and uncommon religious enjoyment. It is clear that John does not mean here to say that he was under the influence of the Holy Spirit in such a sense as that he was *inspired*, for the command to make a record, as well as the visions, came subsequently to the time referred to. The fair meaning of the passage is, that he was at that time favoured, in a large measure, with the influences of the Holy Spirit—the spirit of true devotion; that he had a high state of religious enjoyment, and was in a condition not inappropriate to the remarkable communications which were made to him on that day. The state of mind in which he was at the time here referred to, is not such as the prophets are often represented to have been in when under the prophetic inspiration (comp. Eze. i. 1; viii. 3; xl. 2; Je. xxiv. 1), and which was often accom-

panied with an entire prostration of bodily strength (comp. Nu. xxiv. 4); 1 Sa. xix. 24; Eze. i. 28; Da. x. 8-10; Re. i. 17), but such as any Christian may experience when in a high state of religious enjoyment. He was not *yet* under the prophetic ecstasy (comp. Ac. x. 10; xi. 5; xxii. 17), but was, though in a lonely and barren island, and far away from the privileges of the sanctuary, permitted to enjoy, in a high degree, the consolations of religion—an illustration of the great truth that God can meet his people anywhere; that, when in solitude and in circumstances of outward affliction, when persecuted and cast out, when deprived of the public means of grace and the society of religious friends, He can meet them with the abundant consolations of His grace, and pour joy and peace into their souls. This state was not inappropriate to the revelations which were about to be made to John, but this itself was not that state. It was a state which seems to have resulted from the fact, that on that desert island he devoted the day to the worship of God, and, by honouring the day dedicated to the memory of the risen Saviour, found, what all will find, that it was attended with rich spiritual influences on his soul. ¶ *On the Lord's day.* The word here rendered *Lord's* ($\kappa\nu\varrho\iota\alpha\kappa\tilde{\eta}$), occurs only in this place and in 1 Co. xi. 20, where it is applied to the Lord's supper. It properly means *pertaining to the Lord;* and, so far as this *word* is concerned, it might mean a day pertaining to the Lord, in any sense, or for any reason; either because he claimed it as his own, and had set it apart for his own service, or because it was designed to commemorate some important event pertaining to him, or because it was observed in honour of him. It is clear, (1) That this refers to some one day which was distinguished from all other days of the week, and which would be sufficiently designated by the use of this term. (2) That it was a day which was for some reason regarded as peculiarly a day of the Lord, or peculiarly devoted to him. (3) It would further appear that this was a day particularly devoted to the Lord Jesus; for, (*a*) that is the natural meaning of the word *Lord* as used in the New Testament (comp. Notes on Ac. i. 24); and (*b*) if the Jewish Sabbath were intended to be designated, the word *Sabbath* would have been used. The term was used generally by the early Christians to denote the first day of the week. It occurs twice in the Epistle of Ignatius to the Magnesians (about A.D. 101), whc calls the Lord's day "the queen and prince of all days." Chrysostom (on Ps. cxix.) says, "It was called the Lord's day because the Lord rose from the dead on that day." Later fathers make a marked distinction between the *Sabbath* and the *Lord's day;* meaning by the former the Jewish Sabbath, or the seventh day of the week, and by the latter the first day of the week, kept holy by Christians. So Theodoret (*Fab. Haeret.* ii. 1), speaking of the Ebionites, says, "They keep the *Sabbath* according to the Jewish law, and sanctify the *Lord's day* in like manner as we do" (Professor Stuart). The strong probability is, that the name was given to this day in honour of the Lord Jesus, and because he rose on that day from the dead. No one can doubt that it was an appellation given to the first day of the week; and the passage, therefore, proves (1) that that day was thus early distinguished in some peculiar manner, so that the mere mention of it would be sufficient to identify it in the minds of those to whom the apostle wrote; (2) that it was in some sense regarded as devoted to the Lord Jesus, or was designed in some way to commemorate what he had done; and (3) that if this book were written by the apostle John, the observance of that day has the apostolic sanction. He had manifestly, in accordance with a prevailing custom, set apart this day in honour of the Lord Jesus. Though alone, he was engaged on that day in acts of devotion. Though far away from the sanctuary, he enjoyed what all Christians *hope* to enjoy on such a day of rest, and what not a few *do* in fact enjoy in its observance. We may remark, in view of this statement, (*a*) that when away from the sanctuary, and deprived of its privileges, we should nevertheless not fail to observe the Christian Sabbath. If on a bed of sickness, if in a land of strangers, if on the deep, if in a foreign clime, if on a lonely island, as John was, where we have none of the advantages of public worship, we should yet honour the Sabbath. We should worship God alone, if we have none to unite with us; we should show to those around us, if we are with strangers, by our dress and our conversation, by a serious and devout manner, by abstinence from labour, me a great voice, as of a trumpet,

11 Saying, I am Alpha and Omega, the first and the last: and, What thou seest, write in a book, and send *it* unto the seven churches which are in Asia; unto *u* Ephesus, and unto *v* Smyrna, and unto *w* Pergamos, and unto *x* Thyatira, and unto *y* Sardis, and unto *z* Philadelphia, and unto *a* Laodicea.

*u* ch.2.1.   *v* ch.2.8.   *w* ch.2.12.   *x* ch.2.18.
*y* ch.3.1.   *z* ch.3.7.   *a* ch.3.14.

and by a resting from travel, that we devoutly regard this day as set apart for God. (*b*) We may expect, in such circumstances, and with such a devout observance of the day, that God will meet with us and bless us. It was on a lonely island, far away from the sanctuary and from the society of Christian friends, that the Saviour met "the beloved disciple," and we may trust it will be so with us. For on such a desert island, in a lonely forest, on the deep, or amid strangers in a foreign land, he can as easily meet us as in the sanctuary where we have been accustomed to worship, and when surrounded by all the privileges of a Christian land. No man, at home or abroad, among friends or strangers, enjoying the privileges of the sanctuary, or deprived of those privileges, ever kept the Christian Sabbath in a devout manner without profit to his own soul; and, when deprived of the privileges of public worship, the visitations of the Saviour to the soul may be more than a compensation for all our privations. Who would not be willing to be banished to a lonely island like Patmos, if he might enjoy such a glorious vision of the Redeemer as John was favoured with there? ¶ *And heard behind me a great voice.* A loud voice. This was of course sudden, and took him by surprise. ¶ *As of a trumpet.* Loud as a trumpet. This is evidently the only point in the comparison. It does not mean that the tones of the voice resembled a trumpet, but only that it was clear, loud, and distinct like a trumpet. A trumpet is a well-known wind-instrument, distinguished for the clearness of its sounds, and was used for calling assemblies together, for marshalling hosts for battle, &c. The Hebrew word employed commonly to denote a trumpet (שׁוֹפָר—*shophar*) means *bright* and *clear*, and is supposed to have been given to the instrument on account of its clear and shrill sound, as we now give the name "clarion" to a certain wind-instrument. The Hebrew trumpet is often referred to as employed, on account of its clearness, to summon people together, Ex. xix. 13; Nu. x. 10; Ju. vii. 18, &c.; 1 Sa. xiii. 3; 2 Sa. xv. 10.

11. *Saying.* That is, literally, "the trumpet saying." It was, however, manifestly the *voice* that addressed these words to John, though they *seemed* to come through a trumpet, and hence the trumpet is represented as uttering them. ¶ *I am Alpha and Omega.* Ver. 8. ¶ *The first and the last.* An explanation of the terms Alpha and Omega. See Notes on ver. 8. ¶ *And, What thou seest.* The voice, in addition to the declaration, "I am Alpha and Omega," gave this direction that he should record what he saw. The phrase, "what thou seest," refers to what would pass before him in vision, what he there saw, and what he would see in the extraordinary manifestations which were to be made to him. ¶ *Write in a book.* Make a fair record of it all; evidently meaning that he should describe things as they occurred, and implying that the vision would be held so long before the eye of his mind that he would be able to transfer it to the "book." The fair and obvious interpretation of this is, that he was to make the record in the island of Patmos, and then send it to the churches. Though Patmos was a lonely and barren place, and though probably there were few or no inhabitants there, yet there is no improbability in supposing that John could have found writing materials there, nor even that he may have been permitted to take such materials with him. He seems to have been banished for *preaching*, not for *writing;* and there is no evidence that the materials for writing would be withheld from him. John Bunyan, in Bedford jail, found materials for writing the *Pilgrim's Progress*, and there is no evidence that the apostle John was denied the means of recording his thoughts when in the island of Patmos. The word *book* here (βιβλίον), would more properly mean *a roll* or *scroll*, that being the form in which books were anciently made. See Notes on Lu. iv. 17. ¶ *And send* it *unto the seven churches which are in Asia.*

A.D. 96.] CHAPTER I. 51

12 And I turned to see the voice that spake with me. And being turned, I saw *b* seven golden candlesticks;
13 And in the midst of the seven candlesticks *c* one like unto the Son of man, clothed with a garment down to the foot, and girt about the paps with a golden girdle.

*b* Ex.25.37; Zec.4.2.     *c* Eze.1.26-28; Da.7.9,13; 10.5,6.

The churches which are immediately designated, not implying that there were no other churches in Asia, but that there were particular reasons for sending it to these. He was to send *all* that he should "see;" to wit, all that is recorded in this volume or book of "Revelation." Part of this (ch. ii., iii.) would appertain particularly to them; the remainder (ch. iv.–xxii.) would appertain to them no more than to others, but still they would have the common interest in it which all the church would have, and, in their circumstances of trial, there might be important reasons why *they* should see the assurance that the church would ultimately triumph over all its enemies. They were to derive from it themselves the consolation which it was fitted to impart in time of trial, and to transmit it to future times, for the welfare of the church at large. ¶ *Unto Ephesus.* Perhaps mentioned first as being the capital of that portion of Asia Minor; the most important city of the seven; the place where John had preached, and whence he had been banished. For a particular description of these seven churches, see the Notes on the epistles addressed to them in ch. ii., iii.

12. *And I turned to see the voice that spake with me.* He naturally turned round to see who it was that spake to him in this solitary and desolate place, where he thought himself to be alone. To see *the voice* here means to see *the person* who spake. ¶ *And being turned, I saw seven golden candlesticks.* These were the *first* things that met his eye. This must have been in *vision*, of course, and the meaning is, that there seemed to be there seven such lamps or candelabras. The word rendered *candlesticks* (λυχνία) means properly a light-stand, lamp-stand — something to bear up a light. It would be applied to anything that was used for this purpose; and nothing is intimated, in the use of the word, in regard to the form or dimensions of the light-bearers. Lamps were more commonly used at that time than candles, and it is rather to be supposed that these were designed to be lamp-bearers, or lamp-sustainers, than *candlesticks*. They were seven in number; not one branching into seven, but seven standing apart, and so far from each other that he who appeared to John could stand among them. The lamp-bearers evidently sustained each a light, and these gave a peculiar brilliancy to the scene. It is not improbable that, as they were designed to represent the seven churches of Asia, they were arranged in an order resembling these churches. The scene is not laid in the temple, as many suppose, for there is nothing that resembles the arrangements in the temple except the mere fact of the *lights*. The scene as yet is in Patmos, and there is no evidence that John did not regard himself as there, or that he fancied for a moment that he was translated to the temple in Jerusalem. There can be no doubt as to the *design* of this representation, for it is expressly declared (ver. 20) that the seven lamp-bearers were intended to represent the seven churches. Light is often used in the Scriptures as an emblem of true religion; Christians are represented as "the light of the world" (Mat. v. 14; comp. Phi. ii. 15; Jn. viii. 12), and a Christian church may be represented as a light standing in the midst of surrounding darkness.

13. *And in the midst of the seven candlesticks.* Standing among them, so as to be encircled with them. This shows that the representation could not have been like that of the vision of Zechariah (Zec. iv. 2), where the prophet sees "a candlestick all of gold, with a bowl upon the top of it, and his seven lamps thereon." In the vision as it appeared to John, there was not *one* lamp-bearer, with seven lamps or branches, but there were *seven* lamp-bearers, so arranged that one in the likeness of the Son of man could stand in the midst of them. ¶ One *like unto the Son of man.* This was evidently the Lord Jesus Christ himself, elsewhere so often called "the Son of man." That it was the Saviour himself is apparent from ver. 18. The expression rendered "like unto *the* Son of man," should have been "like unto

14 His head and *his* hairs *were* white like wool, as white as snow; and *a*his eyes *were* as a flame of fire;

*d* ch.2.18; 19.12.

*a* son of man;" that is, like a man, a human being, or in a human form. The reasons for so interpreting it are, (*a*) that the Greek is without the article, and (*b*) that, as it is rendered in our version, it seems to make the writer say that he was *like himself*, since the expression "*the* Son of man" is in the New Testament but another name for the Lord Jesus. The phrase is often applied to him in the New Testament, and always, except in three instances (Ac. vii. 56; Re. i. 13; xiv. 14), by the Saviour himself, evidently to denote his warm interest *in* man, or his relationship to man; to signify that he was a man, and wished to designate himself eminently as such. See Notes on Mat. viii. 20. In the use of this phrase in the New Testament, there is probably an allusion to Da. vii. 13. The idea would seem to be, that he whom he saw resembled "the Son of man"—the Lord Jesus, as he had seen him in the days of his flesh —though it would appear that he did not *know* that it was he until he was informed of it, ver. 18. Indeed, the costume in which he appeared was so unlike that in which John had been accustomed to see the Lord Jesus in the days of his flesh, that it cannot be well supposed that he would at once recognize him as the same. ¶ *Clothed with a garment down to the foot*. A robe reaching down to the feet, or to the ankles, yet so as to leave the feet themselves visible. The allusion here, doubtless, is to a long, loose, flowing robe, such as was worn by kings. Comp. Notes on Is. vi. 1. ¶ *And girt about the paps*. About the breast. It was common, and is still, in the East, to wear a girdle to confine the robe, as well as to form a beautiful ornament. This was commonly worn about the middle of the person, or "the loins," but it would seem also that it was sometimes worn around the breast. See Notes on Mat. v. 38–41. ¶ *With a golden girdle*. Either wholly made of gold, or, more probably, richly ornamented with gold. This would naturally suggest the idea of one of rank, probably one of princely rank. The raiment here assumed was not that of a *priest*, but that of a *king*. It was very far from being that in which the Redeemer appeared when he dwelt upon the earth, and was rather designed to denote his royal state as he is exalted in heaven. He is not indeed represented with a crown and sceptre here, and perhaps the leading idea is that of one of exalted rank, of unusual dignity, of one fitted to inspire awe and respect. In other circumstances, in this book, this same Redeemer is represented as wearing a crown, and going forth to conquest. See ch. xix. 12–16. Here the representation seems to have been designed to impress the mind with a sense of the greatness and glory of the personage who thus suddenly made his appearance.

14. *His head and* his *hairs were white like wool, as white as snow*. Exceedingly or perfectly white—the first suggestion to the mind of the apostle being that of wool, and then the thought occurring of its *extreme* whiteness resembling snow —the purest white of which the mind conceives. The comparison with wool and snow to denote anything peculiarly *white* is not uncommon. See Is. i. 18. Professor Stuart supposes that this means, not that his hairs were literally white, as if with age, which he says would be incongruous to one just risen from the dead, clothed with immortal youth and vigour, but that it means radiant, bright, resplendent—similar to what occurred on the transfiguration of the Saviour, Mat. xvii. 2. But to this it may be replied, (*a*) That this would not accord well with that with which his hair is compared—*snow* and *wool*, particularly the latter. (*b*) The usual meaning of the word is more obvious here, and not at all inappropriate. The representation was fitted to signify majesty and authority; and this would be best accomplished by the image of one who was venerable in years. Thus, in the vision that appeared to Daniel (ch. vii. 9), it is said of him who is there called the "Ancient of Days," that "his garment was white as snow, and the hair of his head like the pure wool." It is not improbable that John had that representation in his eye, and that therefore he would be impressed with the conviction that this was a manifestation of a divine person. We are not necessarily to suppose that this is the form in which the Saviour always appears now in heaven, any more than we are to suppose that God appears always in the form in which he was manifested

A.D. 96.]  CHAPTER I.  53

15 And *e*his feet like unto fine brass, as if they burned in a furnace; and *f*his voice as the sound of many waters.

16 And he had in his right hand seven stars; and out of his mouth went *g*a sharp two-edged sword: and his countenance was as *h*the sun shineth in his strength.

*e* Eze.1.7.   *f* Eze.43.2.   *g* Is.49.2; He.4.12.   *h* ch.10.1; Ac.26.13.

to Isaiah (ch. vi. 1), to Daniel (ch. vii. 9), or to Moses and Aaron, Nadab and Abihu in the mount, Ex. xxiv. 10, 11. The representation is, that this form was assumed for the purpose of impressing the mind of the apostle with a sense of his majesty and glory. ¶ *And his eyes were as a flame of fire.* Bright, sharp, penetrating; as if everything was light before them, or they would penetrate into the thoughts of men. Such a representation is not uncommon. We speak of a lightning glance, a fiery look, &c. In Da. x. 6, it is said of the man who appeared to the prophet on the banks of the river Hiddekel, that his eyes were "as lamps of fire." Numerous instances of this comparison from the Greek and Latin classics may be seen in Wetstein, *in loco.*

15. *And his feet like unto fine brass.* Comp. Da. x. 6, "And his arms and his feet like in colour to polished brass." See also Eze. i. 7, "and they" [the feet of the living creatures] "sparkled like the colour of burnished brass." The word here used — χαλκολιβάνω — occurs in the New Testament only here and in ch. ii. 18. It is not found in the Septuagint. The word properly means *white brass* (probably compounded of χαλκός, *brass*, and λιβανός, *whiteness*, from the Hebrew לבן, *white*). Others regard it as from χαλκός, *brass*, and λιπαρόν, *clear*. The *metal* referred to was undoubtedly a species of brass distinguished for its clearness or whiteness. Brass is a compound metal, composed of copper and zinc. The colour varies much according to the different proportions of the various ingredients. The Vulgate here renders the word *aurichalcum*, a mixture of gold and of brass — perhaps the same as the ἤλεκτρον — the *electrum* of the ancients, composed of gold and of silver, usually in the proportion of four parts gold and one part silver, and distinguished for its brilliancy. See Robinson, *Lex.*, and Wetstein, *in loco.* The kind of metal here referred to, however, would seem to be some compound of brass — of a whitish and brilliant colour. The exact proportion of the ingredients in the metal here referred to cannot now be determined. ¶ *As if they burned in a furnace.* That is, his feet were so bright that they seemed to be like a beautiful metal glowing intensely in the midst of a furnace. Anyone who has looked upon the dazzling and almost insupportable brilliancy of metal in a furnace, can form an idea of the image here presented. ¶ *And his voice as the sound of many waters.* As the roar of the ocean, or of a cataract. Nothing could be a more sublime description of majesty and authority than to compare the voice of a speaker with the roar of the ocean. This comparison often occurs in the Scriptures. See Eze. xliii. 2, "And behold the glory of the God of Israel came from the east: and his voice was like the sound of many waters: and the earth shined with his glory." So Re. xiv. 2; xix. 6. Comp. Eze. i. 24; Da. x. 6.

16. *And he had in his right hand seven stars.* Emblematic of the angels of the seven churches. *How* he held them is not said. It may be that they seemed to rest on his open palm; or it may be that he seemed to hold them as if they were arranged in a certain order, and with some sort of attachment, so that they could be grasped. It is not improbable that, as in the case of the seven lamp-bearers (Notes, ver. 13), they were so arranged as to represent the relative position of the seven churches. ¶ *And out of his mouth went a sharp two-edged sword.* On the form of the ancient two-edged sword, see Notes on Ep. vi. 17. The two edges were designed to cut both ways; and such a sword is a striking emblem of the penetrating power of *truth*, or of words that proceed from the mouth; and this is designed undoubtedly to be the representation here — that there was some symbol which showed that his words, or his truth, had the power of cutting deep, or penetrating the soul. So in Is. xlix. 2, it is said of the same personage, "And he hath made my mouth like a sharp sword."

**17** And when I saw him, I fell at his feet as dead. And he laid his right hand upon me, saying unto me, Fear not; I am the first and the last:

See Notes on that verse. So in He. iv. 12, "The word of God is quick and powerful, sharper than any two-edged sword," &c. So it is said of Pericles by Aristophanes:

"His powerful speech
Pierced the hearer's soul, and left behind
Deep in his bosom its keen point infixt."

A similar figure often occurs in Arabic poetry. "As arrows his words enter into the heart." See Gesenius, *Comm. zu*, Is. xlix. 2. The only difficulty here is in regard to the apparently incongruous representation of a *sword* seeming to proceed from the mouth; but it is not perhaps necessary to suppose that John means to say that he *saw* such an image. He heard him speak; he felt the penetrating power of his words; and they were *as if* a sharp sword proceeded from his mouth. They penetrated deep into the soul, and as he looked on him it seemed as if a sword came from his mouth. Perhaps it is not necessary to suppose that there was even *any* visible representation of this —either of a sword or of the breath proceeding from his mouth appearing to take this form, as Professor Stuart supposes. It may be wholly a figurative representation, as Heinrichs and Ewald suppose. Though there were visible and impressive symbols of his majesty and glory presented to the eyes, it is not necessary to suppose that there were visible symbols of his *words*. ¶ *And his countenance.* His face. There had been before particular descriptions of some parts of his face—as of his eyes—but this is a representation of his whole aspect; of the general splendour and brightness of his countenance. ¶ Was *as the sun shineth in his strength.* In his full splendour when unobscured by clouds; where his rays are in no way intercepted. Comp. Ju. v. 31: "But let them that love him [the Lord] be as the sun when he goeth forth in his might;" 2 Sa. xxiii. 4, "And he shall be as the light of the morning, when the sun ariseth, even a morning without clouds;" Ps. xix. 5, "Which [the sun] is as a bridegroom coming out of his chamber, and rejoiceth as a strong man to run a race." There could be no more striking description of the majesty and glory of the countenance than to compare it with the overpowering splendour of the sun.—This closes the description of the personage that appeared to John. The design was evidently to impress him with a sense of his majesty and glory, and to prepare the way for the authoritative nature of the communications which he was to make. It is obvious that this appearance must have been *assumed*. The representation is not that of the Redeemer as he rose from the dead—a middle-aged man; nor is it clear that it was the same as on the mount of transfiguration—where, for anything that appears, he retained his usual aspect and form though temporarily invested with extraordinary brilliancy; nor is it the form in which we may suppose he ascended to heaven —for there is no evidence that he was thus transformed when he ascended; nor is it that of a priest—for all the peculiar habiliments of a Jewish priest are wanting in this description. The appearance assumed is, evidently, in accordance with various representations of God as he appeared to Ezekiel, to Isaiah, and to Daniel—that which was a *suitable* manifestation of a divine being—of one clothed in the majesty and power of God. We are not to infer from this, that this is in fact the appearance of the Redeemer now in heaven, or that this is the form in which he will appear when he comes to judge the world. Of his appearance in heaven we have no knowledge; of the aspect which he will assume when he comes to judge men we have no certain information. We are necessarily quite as ignorant of this as we are of what will be *our own* form and appearance after the resurrection from the dead.

**17.** *And when I saw him, I fell at his feet as dead.* As if I were dead; deprived of sense and consciousness. He was overwhelmed with the suddenness of the vision; he saw that this was a divine being; but he did not as yet know that it was the Saviour. It is not probable that in this vision he would immediately recognize any of the familiar features of the Lord Jesus as he had been accustomed to see him some sixty years before; and if he *did*, the effect would have been quite as overpowering as is here described. But the subsequent revelations of this divine

# CHAPTER I.

18 *I am* ⁱhe *that liveth, and was dead; and, behold, I am alive* for evermore, Amen; *and have* ᵏ*the keys of hell and of death.*

*i* Ro.6.9.   *k* ch.20.1,2; Ps.68.20.

personage would rather seem to imply that John did not at once recognize him as the Lord Jesus. The effect here described is one that often occurred to those who had a vision of God. See Da. viii. 18, "Now as he was speaking with me, I was in a deep sleep on my face toward the ground; but he touched me, and set me upright;" ver. 27, "And I Daniel fainted, and was sick certain days; afterwards I rose up, and did the king's business." Comp. Ex. xxxiii. 20; Is. vi. 5; Eze. i. 28; xliii. 3; Da. x. 7–9, 17. ¶ *And he laid his right hand upon me.* For the purpose of raising him up. Comp. Da. viii. 18, "He touched me and set me upright." We usually stretch out the *right* hand to raise up one who has fallen. ¶ *Saying unto me, Fear not.* Comp. Mat. xiv. 27, "It is I; be not afraid." The fact that it was the Saviour, though he appeared in this form of overpowering majesty, was a reason why John should not be afraid. *Why* that was a reason, he immediately adds—that he was the first and the last; that though he had been dead he was now alive, and would continue ever to live, and that he had the keys of hell and of death. It is evident that John was overpowered with that awful emotion which the human mind must feel at the evidence of the presence of God. Thus men feel when God seems to come near them by the impressive symbols of his majesty—as in the thunder, the earthquake, and the tempest. Comp. Hab. iii. 16; Lu. ix. 34. Yet, amidst the most awful manifestations of divine power, the simple assurance that our Redeemer is near us is enough to allay our fears, and diffuse calmness through the soul. ¶ *I am the first and the last.* Notes, ver. 8. This is stated to be one of the reasons why he should not fear —that he was *eternal:* "I always live—have lived through all the past, and will live through all which is to come—and therefore I can accomplish all my promises, and execute all my purposes."

18. I am *he that liveth, and was dead.* I was indeed once dead, but now I live, and shall continue to live for ever. This would at once identify him who thus appeared as the Lord Jesus Christ, for to no one else could this apply. He had been put to death; but he had risen from the grave. This also is given as a reason why John should not fear; and nothing would allay his fears more than this. He now saw that he was in the presence of that Saviour whom more than half a century before he had so tenderly loved when in the flesh, and whom, though now long absent, he had faithfully served, and for whose cause he was now in this lonely island. His faith in his resurrection had not been a delusion; he saw the very Redeemer before him who had once been laid in the tomb. ¶ *Behold, I am alive for evermore.* I am to live for ever. Death is no more to cut me down, and I am never again to slumber in the grave. As he was always to live, he could accomplish all his promises, and fulfil all his purposes. The Saviour is never to die again. He can, therefore, always sustain us in our troubles; he can be with us in our death. Whoever of our friends die, he will not die; when we die, he will still be on the throne. ¶ *Amen.* A word here of strong affirmation—as if he had said, it is *truly,* or *certainly so.* See Notes on ver. 7. This expression is one that the Saviour often used when he wished to give emphasis, or to express anything strongly. Comp. Jn. iii. 3; v. 25. ¶ *And have the keys of hell and of death.* The word rendered *hell*—ᾅδης, *hades*—refers properly to the underworld; the abode of departed spirits; the region of the dead. This was represented as dull and gloomy; as inclosed with walls; as entered through gates which were fastened with bolts and bars. For a description of the views which prevailed among the ancients on the subject, see Notes on Lu. xvi. 23, and Job x. 21, 22. To hold the *key* of this, was to hold the power over the invisible world. It was the more appropriate that the Saviour should represent himself as having this authority, as he had himself been raised from the dead by his own power (comp. Jn. x. 18), thus showing that the dominion over this dark world was intrusted to him. ¶ *And of death.* A personification. Death reigns in that world. But to his wide-extended realms the Saviour holds the key, and can have access to his empire when he pleases, releasing all whom he chooses, and confining there still

56 REVELATION. [A.D. 96.

19 Write the things which thou hast seen, and the things which are, and the things which shall be hereafter;

20 The mystery of $^l$the seven stars which thou sawest in my right hand, and the seven golden candlesticks. The seven stars are the angels of the seven churches: and $^m$the seven candlesticks which thou sawest, are the seven churches.

$l$ ver. 16.

$m$ Mat. 5. 15, 16.

---

such as he shall please. It is probably in part from such hints as these that Milton drew his sublime description of the gates of hell in the *Paradise Lost*. As Christ always lives; as he always retains this power over the regions of the dead, and the whole world of spirits, it may be further remarked that *we* have nothing to dread if we put our trust in him. We need not fear to enter a world which he has entered, and from which he has emerged, achieving a glorious triumph; we need not fear what the dread king that reigns there can do to us, for his power extends not beyond the permission of the Saviour, and in his own time that Saviour will call us forth to life, to die no more.

19. *Write the things which thou hast seen.* An account of the vision which thou hast had, ver. 10–18. ¶ *And the things which are.* Give an account of those things which thou hast seen as designed to represent the condition of the seven churches. He had seen not only the Saviour, but he had seen seven lamp-stands, and seven stars in the hand of the Saviour, and he is now commanded to record the meaning of these symbols as referring to things then actually existing in the seven churches. This interpretation is demanded by ver. 20. ¶ *And the things which shall be hereafter.* The Greek phrase rendered *hereafter* — μετὰ ταῦτα — means "*after these things;*" that is, he was to make a correct representation of the things which then were, and then to record what would occur "*after* these things:" to wit, of the images, symbols, and truths, which would be disclosed to him after what he had already seen. The expression refers to future times. He does not say for *how long* a time; but the revelations which were to be made referred to events which were to occur beyond those which were then taking place. Nothing can be argued from the use of this language in regard to the length of time embraced in the revelation—whether it extended only for a few years or whether it embraced all coming time. The more natural interpretation, however, would seem to be, that it would stretch far into future years, and that it was designed to give at least *an outline* of what would be the character of the future in general.

20. *The mystery of the seven stars.* On the word *mystery*, see Notes on Ep. i. 9. The word means, properly, that which is hidden, obscure, unknown—until it is disclosed by one having the ability to do it, or by the course of events. *When* disclosed, it may be as clear, and as capable of comprehension, as any other truth. The meaning here, as applied to the seven stars, is, that they were symbols, and that their meaning as symbols, without a suitable explanation, would remain hidden or unknown. They were designed to represent important truths, and John was directed to write down what they were intended in the circumstances to signify, and to send the explanation to the churches. It is evidently implied that the meaning of these symbols would be beyond the ordinary powers of the human mind to arrive at with certainty, and hence John was directed to explain the symbol. The general and obvious truths which they would serve to convey would be that the ministers of the churches, and the churches themselves, were designed to be lights in the world, and should burn clearly and steadily. Much important truth would be couched under these symbols, indeed, if nothing had been added in regard to their signification as employed here by the Saviour; but there were particular truths of great importance in reference to each of these "stars" and "lamp-bearers," which John was more fully to explain. ¶ *Which thou sawest in my right hand.* Gr., "*upon* my right hand" —ἐπὶ τῆς δεξιᾶς μου: giving some support to the opinion that the stars, as they were seen, appeared to be placed *on* his hand—that is, on the *palm* of his hand as he stretched it out. The expression in ver. 16 is, that they were "*in* (ἐν) his right hand;" but the language here used is not decisive as to the position of the stars. They *may* have been held in some way *by* the hand, or

A.D. 96.]  CHAPTER I.  57

represented as scattered on the open hand. ¶ *The seven golden candlesticks.* The truth which these emblematic representations are designed to convey. ¶ *The seven stars are.* That is, they represent, or they denote—in accordance with a common usage in the Scriptures. See Notes on Mat. xxvi. 26. ¶ *The angels of the seven churches.* Gr., "Angels of the seven churches:" the article being wanting. This does not refer to them as a collective or associated body, for the addresses are made to them as individuals—an epistle being directed to "the angel" of each particular church, ch. ii. 1, 12, &c. The evident meaning, however, is, that what was recorded should be directed to them, not as pertaining to them exclusively as individuals, but as presiding over or representing the churches, for what is recorded pertains *to* the churches, and was evidently designed to be laid before them. It was *for* the churches, but was committed to the "angel" as representing the church, and to be communicated to the church under his care. There has been much diversity of opinion in regard to the meaning of the word *angels* here. By the advocates of Episcopacy, it has been argued that the use of this term proves that there was a presiding bishop over a circle or group of churches in Ephesus, in Smyrna, &c., since it is said that it cannot be supposed that there was but a single church in a city so large as Ephesus, or in the other cities mentioned. A full examination of this argument may be seen in my work on the *Apostolic Church* [pp. 191–199, London ed.]. The word *angel* properly means a messenger, and is thus applied to celestial beings *as* messengers sent forth from God to convey or to do his will. This being the common meaning of the word, it may be employed to denote anyone who is a messenger, and hence, with propriety, anyone who is employed to communicate the will of another; to transact his business, or, more remotely, to act in his place—to be a representative. In order to ascertain the meaning of the word as used in this place, and in reference to these churches, it may be remarked, (1) That it cannot mean literally an *angel*, as referring to a heavenly being, for no one can suppose that such a being presided over these churches. (2) It cannot be shown to mean, as Lord (*in loco*) supposes, messengers that the churches had sent *to* John, and that these letters were given to them to be returned by them to the churches; for, (*a*) there is no evidence that any such messenger had been sent to John; (*b*) there is no probability that while he was a banished exile in Patmos such a thing would be permitted; (*c*) the message was not sent *by* them, it was sent *to* them— "*Unto* the angel of the church in Ephesus *write,*" &c. (3) It cannot be proved that the reference is to a prelatical bishop presiding over a group or circle of churches, called a *diocese;* for, (*a*) There is nothing in the word *angel*, as used in this connection, which would be peculiarly applicable to such a personage—it being *as* applicable to a pastor of a single church, as to a bishop of many churches. (*b*) There is no evidence that there *were* any such groups of churches then as constitute an episcopal diocese. (*c*) The use of the word "*church*" in the singular, as applied to Ephesus, Smyrna, &c., rather implies that there was but a single church in each of those cities. Comp. ch. ii. 1, 8, 12, 18; see also similar language in regard to the *church* in Corinth, 1 Co. i. 2; in Antioch, Ac. xiii. 1; at Laodicea, Col. iv. 16; and at Ephesus, Ac. xx. 28. (*d*) There is no evidence, as Episcopalians must suppose, that a successor to John had been appointed at Ephesus, if, as they suppose, he was "bishop" of Ephesus; and there is no probability that they would *so soon* after his banishment show him such a want of respect as to regard the see as vacant, and appoint a successor. (*e*) There is no improbability in supposing that there was a *single* church in each of these cities—as at Antioch, Corinth, Rome. (*f*) If John was a prelatical "bishop," it is probable that he was "bishop" of the whole group of churches embracing the seven: yet here, if the word "angel" means "bishop," we have no less than seven such bishops immediately appointed to succeed him. And (*g*) the supposition that this refers to prelatical bishops is so forced and unnatural that many Episcopalians are compelled to abandon it. Thus Stillingfleet—than whom an abler man, or one whose praise is higher in Episcopal churches, as an advocate of prelacy, is not to be found—says of these angels: "If many things in the epistles be directed to the angels, but yet so as to concern the whole body, then, of necessity, the angel must be taken as a *representative* of the whole body; and then why may not the angel be taken by way of representation of the body itself, either of the whole church, or, *which is far more probable*, of the *concessors*, or order of *presbyters* in this church?" (4) If the word does not mean literally an angel; if it does not refer to messengers sent to John in Patmos by the churches; and if it does not refer to a prelatical bishop, then it follows that it must refer to some one who presided over the church as its pastor, and through whom a message might be properly sent to the church. Thus understood, the pastor or "angel" would be regarded as the representative of the church; that is, as delegated by the church to manage its affairs, and as the authorized person to whom communications should be made in matters pertaining to it—as pastors are now. A few considerations will further confirm this interpretation, and throw additional light on the meaning of the word. (*a*) The word *angel* is employed in the Old Testament to denote a *prophet;* that is, a minister of religion as sent by God to communicate his will. Thus in Haggai (i. 13) it is said, "Then spake Haggai, the Lord's *messenger* [Heb. *angel*, מַלְאַךְ יְהוָה—Sept. ἄγγελος κυρίου], in the Lord's message unto the people," &c. (*b*) It is applied to a *priest*, as one sent by God to execute the functions of that office, or to act in the name of the Lord. Mal. ii. 7, "For the priest's lips should keep knowledge, for he is the *messenger of the Lord of hosts*"—מַלְאַךְ יְהוָה צְבָאוֹת—that is, "*angel* of the Lord of hosts." (*c*) The name *prophet* is often given in the New Testament to the ministers of religion, as being appointed by God to proclaim or communicate his will to his people, and as occupying a place resembling, in some respects, that of the prophets in the Old Testament. (*d*) There was no reason why the word might not be thus employed to designate a pastor of a Christian church, as well as to designate a prophet or a priest under the Old Testament dispensation. (*e*) The supposition that a pastor of a church is intended will meet all the circumstances of the case: for, (1) it is an appropriate appellation; (2) there is no reason to suppose that there was more than one church in each of the cities referred to; (3) it is a term which would designate the respect in which the office was held; (4) it would impress upon those to whom it was applied a solemn sense of their responsibility. Further, it would be more *appropriately* applied to a pastor of a single church than to a prelatical bishop; to the tender, intimate, and endearing relation sustained by a pastor to his people, to the blending of sympathy, interest, and affection, where he is with them continually, meets them frequently in the sanctuary, administers to them the bread of life, goes into their abodes when they are afflicted, and attends their kindred to the grave, than to the union subsisting between the people of an extended *diocese* and a *prelate*—the formal, unfrequent, and, in many instances, stately and pompous visitations of a diocesan bishop—to the unsympathizing relation between him and a people scattered in many churches, who are visited at distant intervals by one claiming a "superiority in ministerial rights and powers," and who must be a stranger to the ten thousand ties of endearment which bind the hearts of a pastor and people together. The conclusion, then, to which we have come is, that the "angel of the church" was the pastor, or the presiding presbyter in the church; the minister who had the pastoral charge of it, and who was therefore a proper representative of it. He was a man who, in some respects, performed the functions which the angels of God do; that is, who was appointed to execute his will, to communicate his message, and to convey important intimations of his purposes to his people. To no one could the communications in this book, intended for the churches, be more properly intrusted than to such an one; for to no one now would a communication be more properly intrusted than to a pastor.

Such is the sublime vision under which this book opens; such the solemn commission which the penman of the book received. No more appropriate introduction to what is contained in the book could be imagined; no more appropriate circumstances for making such a sublime revelation could have existed. To the most beloved of the apostles, now the only surviving one of the number; to him who had been a faithful labourer for a period not far from sixty years after the death of the Lord Jesus, who had been the bosom friend of the Saviour when in the flesh, who had seen him in the mount of transfiguration, who had seen him die, and who had seen him ascend into heaven; to him who had lived while the church was founded, and while it had spread into all lands; and to him who was now suffering persecution on account of the Saviour and his cause, it was appropriate that such communications should be made. In a lonely island; far away from the abodes of men; surrounded by the ocean, and amid barren rocks; on the day consecrated to the purposes of sacred repose and the holy duties of religion — the day observed in commemoration of the resurrection of his Lord, it was most fit that the Redeemer should appear to the "beloved disciple" in the last Revelation which he was ever to make to mankind. No more appropriate time or circumstance could be conceived for disclosing, by a series of sublime visions, what would occur in future times; for sketching out the history of the church or the consummation of all things.

## CHAPTER II.

### ANALYSIS OF THE CHAPTER.

THIS chapter comprises four of the seven epistles addressed to the seven churches; those addressed to Ephesus, Smyrna, Pergamos, and Thyatira. A particular view of the contents of the epistles will be more appropriate as they come separately to be considered, than in this place. There are some general remarks in regard to their structure, however, which may be properly made here.

(1) They all begin with a reference to some of the attributes of the Saviour, in general some attribute that had been noted in the first chapter; and while they are all adapted to make a deep impression on the mind, perhaps each one was selected in such a way as to have a special propriety in reference to each particular church. Thus in the address to the church at Ephesus (ch. ii. 1), the allusion is to the fact that he who speaks to them "holds the seven stars in his right hand, and walks in the midst of the seven golden candlesticks;" in the epistle to the church at Smyrna (ch. ii. 8), it is he who "is the first and the last, who was dead and is alive;" in the epistle to the church at Pergamos (ch. ii. 12), it is he "which hath the sharp sword with the two edges;" in the epistle to the church at Thyatira (ch. ii. 18), it is "the Son of God, who hath his eyes like unto a flame of fire, and his feet like fine brass;" in the epistle to the church at Sardis (ch. iii. 1), it is he who "hath the seven Spirits of God, and the seven stars;" in the epistle to the church at Philadelphia (ch. iii. 7), it is "he that is holy, he that is true, he that hath the key of David, he that openeth and no man shutteth, and shutteth and no man openeth;" in the epistle to the church at Laodicea (ch. iii. 14), it is he who is the "Amen, the faithful and true witness, the beginning of the creation of God."

(2) These introductions are followed with the formula, "I know thy works." The peculiar characteristics, then, of each church are referred to, with a sentiment of approbation or disapprobation expressed in regard to their conduct. Of two of the churches, that at Smyrna (ii. 9), and that at Philadelphia (iii. 10), he expresses his entire approbation; to the churches of Sardis (iii. 3), and Laodicea (iii. 15-18), he administers a decided rebuke; to the churches of Ephesus (ii. 3-6), Pergamos (ii. 13-16), and Thyatira (iii. 19, 20, 24, 25), he intermingles praise and rebuke, for he saw much to commend, but, at the same time, not a little that was reprehensible. In all cases, however, the approbation precedes the blame; showing that he was more disposed to find that which was good than that which was evil.

(3) After the statement of their characteristics, there follows in each case counsel, advice, admonition, or promises, such as their circumstances demanded—encouragement in trial, and injunctions to put away their sins. The admonitions are addressed to the churches as if Christ were at hand, and would ere long come and sit in judgment on them and their deeds.

(4) There is a solemn admonition to hear what the Spirit has to say to the churches. This is in each case expressed in the same manner, as "He that hath an ear, let him hear what the Spirit saith unto the churches" (ch. ii. 7, 11, 17, 29; iii. 6, 13, 22). These admonitions were designed to call the attention of the churches to these things, and, at the same time, they seemed designed to show that they were not intended for them alone. They are addressed to any-one who "has an ear," and therefore had some principles of general application to others, and to which all should attend who were disposed to learn the will of the Redeemer. What was addressed to one church, at any time, would be equally applicable to all

## CHAPTER II.

UNTO the angel of the church of Ephesus write; These things saith *a*he that holdeth the

*a* ch.1.16,20.

churches in the same circumstances; what was adapted to rebuke, elevate, or comfort Christians in any one age or land, would be adapted to be useful to Christians of all ages and lands.

(5) There then is, either following or preceding that call on all the churches to hear, some promise or assurance designed to encourage the church, and urge it forward in the discharge of duty, or in enduring trial. This is found in each one of the epistles, though not always in the same relative position.

THE EPISTLE TO THE CHURCH AT EPHESUS.

The contents of the epistle to the church at Ephesus—the first addressed —are these: (1) The attribute of the Saviour referred to is, that he "holds the stars in his right hand, and walks in the midst of the golden candlesticks," ch. ii. 1. (2) He commends them for their patience, and for their opposition to those who are evil, and for their zeal and fidelity in carefully examining into the character of some who claimed to be apostles, but who were, in fact, impostors; for their perseverance in bearing up under trial, and not fainting in his cause, and for their opposition to the Nicolaitanes, whom, he says, he hates, ver. 2, 3, 6. (3) He reproves them for having left their first love to him, ver. 4. (4) He admonishes them to remember whence they had fallen, to repent, and to do their first works, ver. 5. (5) He threatens them that, if they do not repent, he will come and remove the candlestick out of its place, ver. 5; and (6) he assures them, and all others, that whosoever overcomes, he will "give him to eat of the tree of life, which is in the midst of the paradise of God," ver. 7.

1. *Unto the angel.* The minister; the presiding presbyter; the bishop— in the primitive sense of the word bishop —denoting one who had the spiritual charge of a congregation. See Notes on ch. i. 20. ¶ *Of the church.* Not of the *churches* of Ephesus, but of the *one church* of that city. There is no evidence that the word is used in a collective sense to denote a group of churches, like a diocese; nor is there any evidence that there *was* such a group of churches in Ephesus, or that there was more than one church in that city. It is probable that all who were Christians there were regarded as members of one church—though for convenience they may have met for worship in different places. Thus there was one church in Corinth (1 Co. i. 1); one church in Thessalonica (1 Th. i. 1), &c. ¶ *Of Ephesus.* On the situation of Ephesus, see Notes on Ac. xviii. 19, and the Intro. to the Notes on the Epistle to the Ephesians, § 1, and the engraving there. It was the capital of Ionia; was one of the twelve Ionian cities of Asia Minor in the Mythic times, and was *said* to have been founded by the Amazons. It was situated on the river Cayster, not far from the Icarian Sea, between Smyrna and Miletus. It was one of the most considerable cities of Asia Minor, and while, about the epoch when Christianity was introduced, other cities declined, Ephesus rose more and more. It owed its prosperity, in part, to the favour of its governors; for Lysimachus named the city Arsinöe, in honour of his second wife, and Attalus Philadelphus furnished it with splendid wharves and docks. Under the Romans it was the capital not only of Ionia, but of the entire province of Asia, and bore the honourable title of *the first and greatest metropolis of Asia.* John is supposed to have resided in this city, and to have preached the gospel there for many years; and on this account, perhaps, it was, as well as on account of the relative importance of the city, that the first epistle of the seven was addressed to that church. On the present condition of the ruins of Ephesus, see Notes on ver. 5. We have no means whatever of ascertaining the size of the church when John wrote the book of Revelation. From the fact, however, that Paul, as is supposed (see Intro. to the Epistle to the Ephesians, § 2), laboured there for about three years; that there was a body of "elders" who presided over the church there (Ac. xx. 17); and that the apostle John seems to have spent a considerable part of his life there in preaching the gospel, it may be presumed that there was a large and flourishing church in that city. The epistle before us shows also that it was charac-

A.D. 96.]  CHAPTER II.  61

2 I[b] know thy works, and thy labour, and thy patience, and how thou canst not bear them which are

*b* ver.9,13,19; ch.3.1,8,15; Ps.1.6.

evil: and [c]thou hast tried them which say they are apostles,[d] and are not, and hast found them liars:

*c* 1 Jn.4.1.  *d* 2 Co.11.13.

terized by distinguished piety. ¶ *These things saith he that holdeth the seven stars in his right hand.* See Notes on ch. i. 16. The object here seems to be to turn the attention of the church in Ephesus to some attribute of the Saviour which deserved their special regard, or which constituted a special reason for attending to what he said. To do this, the attention is directed, in this case, to the fact that he held the seven stars—emblematic of the ministers of the churches—in his hand, and that he walked in the midst of the lamp-bearers — representing the churches themselves; intimating that they were dependent on him, that he had power to continue or remove the ministry, and that it was by his presence only that those lamp-bearers would continue to give light. The absolute control over the ministry, and the fact that he walked amidst the churches, and that his presence was necessary to their perpetuity and their welfare, seem to be the principal ideas implied in this representation. These truths he would impress on their minds, in order that they might feel how easy it would be for him to punish any disobedience, and in order that they might do what was necessary to secure his continual presence among them. These views seem to be sanctioned by the character of the punishment threatened (ver. 5), "that he would remove the candlestick representing *their* church out of its place." See Notes on ver. 5. ¶ *Who walketh in the midst,* &c. In ch. i. 13 he is represented simply as *being seen* amidst the golden candlesticks. See Notes on that place. Here there is the additional idea of his "*walking*" in the midst of them, implying perhaps constant and vigilant supervision. He went from one to another, as one who inspects and surveys what is under his care; perhaps also with the idea that he went among them as a friend to bless them.

2. *I know thy works.* The common formula with which all the epistles to the seven churches are introduced. It is designed to impress upon them deeply the conviction that he was intimately acquainted with all that they did, good and bad, and that therefore he was abundantly qualified to dispense rewards or administer punishments according to truth and justice. It may be observed that, as many of the things referred to in these epistles were things pertaining to the heart—the feelings, the state of the mind—it is implied that he who speaks here has an intimate acquaintance with the heart of man, a prerogative which is always attributed to the Saviour. See Jn. ii. 25. But no one can do this who is not divine; and this declaration, therefore, furnishes a strong proof of the divinity of Christ. See Ps. vii. 9; Je. xi. 20; xvii. 10; 1 Sa. xvi. 7; 1 Ki. viii. 39. ¶ *And thy labour.* The word here used (κόπος) means properly a *beating*, hence wailing, grief, with beating the breast; and then it means excessive labour or toil adapted to produce grief or sadness, and is commonly employed in the New Testament in the latter sense. It is used in the sense of *trouble* in Mat. xxvi. 10, "Why *trouble* ye [literally, why give ye *trouble* to] the woman?" (comp. also Mar. xiv. 6; Lu. xi. 7; xviii. 5; Ga. vi. 17); and in the sense of *labour*, or wearisome toil, in Jn. iv. 38; 1 Co. iii. 8; xv. 58; 2 Co. vi. 5; x. 15; xi. 23, 27, *et al.* The connection here would admit of either sense. It is commonly understood, as in our translation, in the sense of *labour*, though it would seem that the other signification, that of *trouble*, would not be inappropriate. If it means *labour*, it refers to their faithful service in his cause, and especially in opposing error. It seems to me, however, that the word *trouble* would better suit the connection. ¶ *And thy patience.* Under these trials; to wit, in relation to the efforts which had been made by the advocates of error to corrupt them, and to turn them away from the truth. They had patiently borne the opposition made to the truth, they had manifested a spirit of firm endurance amidst many arts of those opposed to them to draw them off from simple faith in Christ. ¶ *And how thou canst not bear them which are evil.* Canst not *endure* or *tolerate* them. Comp. Notes on 2 Jn. 10, 11. That is, they had no sympathy with their doctrines or their practices, they were utterly opposed to them. They had lent them no countenance, but had in every way shown that they

**3 And hast borne, and hast patience, and for my name's sake** had no fellowship with them. The evil persons here referred to were, doubtless, those mentioned in this verse as claiming that "they were apostles," and those mentioned in ver. 6 as the Nicolaitanes. ¶ *And thou hast tried them which say they are apostles.* Thou hast thoroughly examined their claims. It is not said in what way they had done this, but it was probably by considering attentively and candidly the evidence on which they relied, whatever that may have been. Nor is it certainly known who these persons were, or on what grounds they advanced their pretensions to the apostolic office. It cannot be supposed that they claimed to have been of the number of apostles selected by the Saviour, for that would have been too absurd; and the only solution would seem to be that they claimed either (1) that they had been called to that office after the Saviour ascended, as Paul was; or (2) that they claimed the honour due to this name or office, in virtue of some election to it; or (3) that they claimed to be the *successors* of the apostles, and to possess and transmit their authority. If the first of these, it would seem that the only ground of claim would be that they had been called in some miraculous way to the rank of apostles, and, of course, an examination of their claims would be an examination of the alleged miraculous call, and of the evidence on which they would rely that they had such a call. If the second, then the claim must have been founded on some such plea as that the apostolic office was designed to be elective, as in the case of Matthias (Ac. i. 23–26), and that they maintained that this arrangement was to be continued in the church; and then an examination of their claims would involve an investigation of the question, whether it was contemplated that the apostolic office was designed to be perpetuated in that manner, or whether the election of Matthias was only a temporary arrangement, designed to answer a particular purpose. If the third, then the claim must have been founded on the plea that the apostolic office was designed to be perpetuated by a regular succession, and that they, by ordination, were in a line of that succession; and then the examination and refutation of the claim must have consisted in showing, from the nature of the office, and

**hast laboured, and** *e* **hast not fainted.**

*e* Ga.6.9.

the necessary qualifications for the office of apostle, that it was designed to be temporary, and that there could be properly no successors of the apostles, as such. On either of these suppositions, such a line of argument would be fatal to all claims to any succession in the apostolic office now. If each of these points should fail, of course their claims to the rank of apostles would cease; just as all claims to the dignity and rank of the apostles must fail now. The passage becomes thus a strong argument against the claims of *any* persons to be "apostles," or to be the "successors" of the apostles, in the peculiarity of their office. ¶ *And are not.* There were never any *apostles* of Jesus Christ but the original twelve whom he chose, Matthias, who was chosen in the place of Judas (Ac. i. 26), and Paul, who was specially called to the office by the Saviour after his resurrection. On this point, see my work on the *Apostolic Church* [pp. 49–57, London ed.]. ¶ *And hast found them liars.* Hast discovered their pretensions to be unfounded and false. In 2 Co. xi. 13, "false apostles" are mentioned; and, in an office of so much honour as this, it is probable that there would be not a few claimants to it in the world. To set up a claim to what they *knew* they were not entitled to would be a falsehood, and as this seems to have been the character of these men, the Saviour, in the passage before us, does not hesitate to designate them by an appropriate term, and to call them *liars.* The point here commended in the Ephesian church is, that they had sought to have a *pure ministry*, a ministry whose claims were well founded. They had felt the importance of this, had carefully examined the claims of pretenders, and had refused to recognize those who could not show, in a proper manner, that they had been designated to their work by the Lord Jesus. The same zeal, in the same cause, would be commended by the Saviour now.

3. *And hast borne.* Hast borne up under trials; or hast borne with the evils with which you have been assailed. That is, you have not given way to murmuring or complaints in trial, you have not abandoned the principles of truth and yielded to the prevalence of error. ¶ *And hast patience.* That is,

4 Nevertheless I have *somewhat* against thee, because thou hast left thy first love.

in this connection, hast shown that thou canst bear up under these things with patience. This is a repetition of what is said in ver. 2, but in a somewhat different connection. There it rather refers to the trouble which they had experienced on account of the pretensions of false apostles, and the patient, persevering, and enduring spirit which they had shown in that form of trial; here the expression is more general, denoting a patient spirit in regard to *all* forms of trial. ¶ *And for my name's sake hast laboured.* On account of me, and in my cause. That is, the *labour* here referred to, whatever it was, was to advance the cause of the Redeemer. In the word rendered "*hast laboured*" (κεκοπιακας) there is a reference to the word used in the previous verse—"thy labour" (κόπον σου); and the design is to show that the "labour," or trouble there referred to, was on account of him. ¶ *And hast not fainted.* Hast not become exhausted, or wearied out, so as to give over. The word here used (κάμνω) occurs in only three places in the New Testament: "Lest ye be *wearied,* and faint," He. xii. 3; "The prayer of faith shall save the *sick,*" Ja. v. 15; and in the passage before us. It means properly to become weary and faint from toil, &c.; and the idea here is, that they had not become so wearied out as to give over from exhaustion. The sense of the whole passage is thus rendered by Professor Stuart:—"Thou canst not bear with false teachers, but thou canst bear with troubles and perplexities on account of me; thou hast undergone wearisome toil, but thou art not wearied out thereby." The state of mind, considered as the state of mind appropriate to a Christian, here represented, is, that we should not tolerate error and sin, but that we should bear up under the trials which they may incidentally occasion us; that we should have such a repugnance to evil that we cannot endure it, as evil, but that we should have such love to the Saviour and his cause as to be willing to bear anything, even in relation to that, or springing from that, that we may be called to suffer *in* that cause; that while we may be weary *in* his work, for our bodily strength may become exhausted (comp. Mat. xxvi. 41), we should not be weary *of* it; and that

5 Remember therefore from whence thou art fallen; and repent,

though we may have many perplexities, and may meet with much opposition, yet we should not relax our zeal, but should persevere with an ardour that never faints, until our Saviour calls us to our reward.

4. *Nevertheless I have* somewhat *against thee.* Notwithstanding this general commendation, there are things which I cannot approve. ¶ *Because thou hast left thy first love.* Thou hast *remitted* (ἀφῆκας) or let down thy early love; that is, it is less glowing and ardent than it was at first. The love here referred to is evidently love to the Saviour; and the idea is, that, as a church, they had less of this than formerly characterized them. In this respect they were in a state of declension; and, though they still maintained the doctrines of his religion, and opposed the advocates of error, they showed less ardour of affection towards him directly than they had formerly done. In regard to this we may remark, (1) That what is here stated of the church at Ephesus is not uncommon. (*a*) Individual Christians often lose much of their first love. It is true, indeed, that there is often an *appearance* of this which does not exist in reality. Not a little of the ardour of young converts is often nothing more than the excitement of animal feeling, which will soon die away of course, though 'their *real* love may not be diminished, or may be constantly growing stronger. When a son returns home after a long absence, and meets his parents and brothers and sisters, there is a glow, a warmth of feeling, a joyousness of emotion, which cannot be expected to continue always, and which he may never be able to recall again, though he may be ever growing in *real* attachment to his friends and to his home. (*b*) Churches remit the ardour of their first love. They are often formed under the reviving influences of the Holy Spirit when many are converted, and are warm-hearted and zealous young converts. Or they are formed from other churches that have become cold and dead, from which the new organization, embodying the life of the church, was constrained to separate. Or they are formed under the influence of some strong and mighty truth that has taken possession of the mind, and that gives a peculiar character to the church

and *f* do the first works; or else I will come unto thee quickly, and will *g* remove thy candlestick out of his place, except thou repent.

*f* Je.2.2,3.   *g* Mat. 21.41,43.

at first. Or they are formed with a distinct reference to promoting some one great object in the cause of the Redeemer. So the early Christian churches were formed. So the church in Germany, France, Switzerland, and England came out from the Roman communion under the influence of the doctrine of justification by faith. So the Nestorians in former ages, and the Moravians in modern times, were characterized by warm zeal in the cause of missions. So the Puritans came out from the established church of England at one time, and the Methodists at another, warmed with a holier love to the cause of evangelical religion than existed in the body from which they separated. So many a church is formed now amidst the exciting scenes of a revival of religion, and in the early days of its history puts to shame the older and the slumbering churches around them. But it need scarcely be said that this early zeal may die away, and that the church, once so full of life and love, may become as cold as those that went before it, or as those from which it separated, and that there may be a necessity for the formation of new organizations that shall be fired with ardour and zeal. One has only to look at Germany, at Switzerland, at various portions of the reformed churches elsewhere; at the Nestorians, whose zeal for missions long since departed; or even at the Moravians, among whom it has so much declined; at various portions of the Puritan churches, and at many an individual church formed under the warm and exciting feelings of a revival of religion, to see that what occurred at Ephesus may occur elsewhere. (2) The same thing that occurred there may be expected to follow in all similar cases. The Saviour governs the church always on essentially the same principles; and it is no uncommon thing that, when a church has lost the ardour of its first love, it is suffered more and more to decline, until "the candlestick is removed"—until either the church becomes wholly extinct, or until vital piety is wholly gone, and all that remains is the religion of forms.

5. *Remember therefore from whence thou art fallen.* The eminence which you once occupied. Call to remembrance the state in which you once were.

The duty here enjoined is, when religion has declined in our hearts, or in the church, to call to distinct recollection the former state—the ardour, the zeal, the warmth of love which once characterized us. The *reason* for this is, that such a recalling of the former state will be likely to produce a happy influence on the heart. Nothing is better adapted to affect a backsliding Christian, or a backsliding church, than to call to distinct recollection the former condition—the happier days of piety. The joy then experienced, the good done, the honour reflected on the cause of religion, the peace of mind of that period, will contrast strongly with the present, and nothing will be better fitted to recall an erring church, or an erring individual, from their wanderings than such a reminiscence of the past. The *advantages* of thus "remembering" their former condition would be many; for some of the most valuable impressions which are made on the mind, and some of the most important lessons learned, are from the recollections of a former state. Among those advantages, in this case, would be such as the following:—(*a*) It would show how much they might have *enjoyed* if they had continued as they began, how much more real happiness they would have had than they actually have enjoyed. (*b*) How much *good* they might have done, if they had only persevered in the zeal with which they commenced the Christian life. How much more good might most Christians do than they actually accomplish, if they would barely, even without increasing it, *continue* with the degree of zeal with which they begin their course. (*c*) How much greater *attainments* they might have made in the divine life, and in the knowledge of religion, than they have made; that is, how much more elevated and enlarged might have been their views of religion, and their knowledge of the Word of God. And (*d*) such a recollection of their past state as, contrasted with what they now are, would exert a powerful influence in producing true repentance; for there is nothing better adapted to do this than a just view of what we might have been, as compared with what we now are. If a man has become cold towards his wife, nothing is better fitted to reclaim him than to recall to his recollection the time when he led her to the altar, the solemn vow then made, and the rapture of his heart when he pressed her to his bosom and called her his own. ¶ *And repent.* The word here used means to change one's mind and purposes, and, along with that, the conduct or demeanour. The *duty* of repentance here urged would extend to all the points in which they had erred. ¶ *And do the first works.* The works which were done when the church was first established. That is, manifest the zeal and love which were formerly evinced in opposing error, and in doing good. This is the true counsel to be given to those who have backslidden, and have "left their first love," now. Often such persons, sensible that they have erred, and that they have not the enjoyment in religion which they once had, profess to be willing and desirous to return, but they know not how to do it—how to revive their ardour, how to rekindle in their bosom the flame of extinguished love. They suppose it must be by silent meditation, or by some supernatural influence, and they wait for some visitation from above to call them back, and to restore to them their former joy. The counsel of the Saviour to all such, however, is to *do their first works.* It is to engage at once in *doing* what they did in the first and best days of their piety, the days of their "espousals" (Je. ii. 2) to God. Let them read the Bible as they did then; let them pray as they did then; let them go forth in the duties of active benevolence as they did then; let them engage in teaching a Sabbath-school as they did then; let them relieve the distressed, instruct the ignorant, raise up the fallen, as they did then; let them open their heart, their purse, and their hand, to bless a dying world. As it was in this way that they manifested their love then, so this would be better fitted than all other things to rekindle the flame of love when it is almost extinguished. The weapon that is used keeps bright; that which has become rusty will become bright again if it is used. ¶ *Or else I will come unto thee quickly.* On the word rendered *quickly* ($\tau \acute{\alpha} \chi \epsilon \iota$), see Notes on ch. i. 1. The meaning is, that he would come as a Judge, at no distant period, to inflict punishment in the manner specified—by removing the candlestick out of its place. He does not say in what way it would be done; whether by some sudden judgment, by a direct act of power, or by a gradual process that would certainly lead to that result. ¶ *And will remove thy candlestick out of his place, except thou repent.* On the meaning of the word *candlestick* see Notes on ch. i. 12. The meaning is, that the church gave light in Ephesus; and that what he would do in regard to that place would be like removing a lamp, and leaving a place in darkness. The expression is equivalent to saying that the church there would cease to exist. The proper idea of the passage is, that the church would be wholly extinct; and it is observable that this is a judgment more distinctly disclosed in reference to this church than to any other of the seven churches. There is not the least evidence that the church at Ephesus did repent, and the threatening has been most signally fulfilled. Long since the church has become utterly extinct, and for ages there was not a single professing Christian there. Every memorial of there having been a church there has departed, and there are nowhere, not even in Nineveh, Babylon, or Tyre, more affecting demonstrations of the fulfilment of ancient prophecy than in the present state of the ruins of Ephesus. A remark of Mr. Gibbon (*Decline and Fall,* iv. 260) will show with what exactness the prediction in regard to this church has been accomplished. He is speaking of the conquests of the Turks. "In the loss of Ephesus the Christians deplored the fall of the first angel, the extinction of the first candlestick of the Revelations; the desolation is complete; and the temple of Diana, or the Church of Mary will equally elude the search of the curious traveller." Thus the city, with the splendid temple of Diana, and the church that existed there in the time of John, has disappeared, and nothing remains but unsightly ruins. These ruins lie about ten days' journey from Smyrna, and consist of shattered walls, and remains of columns and temples. The soil on which a large part of the city is supposed to have stood, naturally rich, is covered with a rank, burnt-up vegetation, and is everywhere deserted and solitary, though bordered by picturesque mountains. A few cornfields are scattered along the site of the ancient city. Towards the sea extends the ancient port, a pestilential marsh. Along the slope of the mountain, and over the plain, are scattered fragments of masonry and detached ruins, but no-

6 But this thou hast, that thou hatest the deeds of the *h* Nicolaitanes, which I also hate.

*h* ver. 15.

thing can now be fixed on as the great temple of Diana. There are ruins of a theatre; there is a circus, or stadium, nearly entire; there are fragments of temples and palaces scattered around; but there is nothing that marks the site of a church in the time of John; there is nothing to indicate even that such a church then existed there. About a mile and a half from the principal ruins of Ephesus there is indeed now a small village called *Asalook*, a Turkish word, which is associated with the same idea as Ephesus, meaning, The City of the Moon. A church, dedicated to John, is supposed to have stood near, if not on the site of the present mosque. Dr. Chandler (p. 150, 4to) gives us a striking description of Ephesus as he found it in 1764:—"Its population consisted of a few Greek peasants, living in extreme wretchedness, dependence, and insensibility, the representatives of an illustrious people, and inhabiting the wreck of their greatness. Some reside in the substructure of the glorious edifices which they raised; some beneath the vaults of the stadium, and the crowded scenes of these diversions; and some in the abrupt precipice, in the sepulchres which received their ashes. Its streets are obscured and overgrown. A herd of goats was driven to it for shelter from the sun at noon, and a noisy flight of crows from the quarries seemed to insult its silence. We heard the partridge call in the area of the theatre and of the stadium. . . . Its fate is that of the entire country; a garden has become a desert. Busy centres of civilization, spots where the refinements and delights of the age were collected, are now a prey to silence, destruction, and death. Consecrated first of all to the purposes of idolatry, Ephesus next had Christian temples almost rivalling the Pagan in splendour, wherein the image of the great Diana lay prostrate before the cross; after the lapse of some centuries Jesus gives way to Mahomet, and the crescent glittered on the dome of the recently Christian church. A few more scores of years, and Ephesus has neither temple, cross, crescent, nor city, but is desolation, a dry land, and a wilderness." See the article "Ephesus" in Kitto's *Cyclopedia*, and the authorities there referred to. What is affirmed here of Ephesus has often been illustrated in the history of the world, that when a church has declined in piety and love, and has been called by faithful ministers to repent, and has not done it, it has been abandoned more and more, until the last appearance of truth and piety has departed, and it has been given up to error and to ruin. And the same principle is as applicable to individuals, for they have as much reason to dread the frowns of the Saviour as churches have. If they who have "left their first love" will not repent at the call of the Saviour, they have every reason to apprehend some fearful judgment, some awful visitation of his Providence that shall overwhelm them in sorrow, as a proof of his displeasure. Even though they should finally be saved, their days may be without comfort, and perhaps their last moments without a ray of conscious hope. The accompanying engraving, representing the present situation of Ephesus, will bring before the eye a striking illustration of the fulfilment of this prophecy, that the candlestick of Ephesus would be removed from its place. See also the engravings prefixed to the Notes on the Epistle to the Ephesians.

6. *But this thou hast.* This thou hast that I approve of, or that I can commend. ¶ *That thou hatest the deeds of the Nicolaitanes.* Gr., *works* (τὰ ἔργα). The word *Nicolaitanes* occurs only in this place, and in the 15th verse of this chapter. From the reference in the latter place it is clear that the doctrines which they held prevailed at Pergamos as well as at Ephesus; but from neither place can anything now be inferred in regard to the nature of their doctrines or their practices, unless it be supposed that they held the same doctrine that was taught by Balaam. See Notes on ver. 15. From the two passages, compared with each other, it would seem that they were alike corrupt in doctrine and in practice, for in the passage before us their *deeds* are mentioned, and in ver. 15 their *doctrine*. Various conjectures, however, have been formed respecting this class of people, and the reasons why the name was given to them. I. In regard to the origin of the *name*, there have been three opinions. (1) That mentioned by Irenæus, and by some of the other fathers, that the name was derived from Nicolas, one

of the deacons ordained at Antioch, Ac. vi. 5. Of those who have held this opinion, some have supposed that it was given to them because he became apostate and was the founder of the sect, and others because they *assumed* his name, in order to give the greater credit to their doctrine. But neither of these suppositions rests on any certain evidence, and both are destitute of probability. There is no proof whatever that Nicolas the deacon ever apostatized from the faith, and became the founder of a sect; and if a name had been *assumed*, in order to give credit to a sect and extend its influence, it is much more probable that the name of an apostle would have been chosen, or of some other prominent man, than the name of an obscure deacon of Antioch. (2) Vitringa, and most commentators since his time, have supposed that the name Nicolaitanes was intended to be symbolical, and was not designed to designate any sect of people, but to denote those who resembled Balaam, and that this word is used in the same manner as the word *Jezebel* in ch. ii. 20, which is supposed to be symbolical there. Vitringa supposes that the word is derived from νίκος, *victory*, and λαός, *people*, and that thus it corresponds with the name Balaam, as meaning either בַּעַל עָם, *lord of the people*, or בָּלַע עָם, *he destroyed the people;* and that, as the same effect was produced by their doctrines as by those of Balaam, that the people were led to commit fornication and to join in idolatrous worship, they might be called *Balaamites* or *Nicolaitanes*, that is, corrupters of the people. But to this it may be replied, (*a*) that it is far-fetched, and is adopted only to remove a difficulty; (*b*) that there is every reason to suppose that the word here used refers to a class of people who bore that name, and who were well known in the two churches specified; (*c*) that in ch. ii. 15 they are expressly distinguished from those who held the doctrine of Balaam, ver. 14, "So hast thou *also* (καὶ) those that hold the doctrine of the Nicolaitanes." (3) It has been supposed that some person now unknown, probably of the name *Nicolas*, or *Nicolaus*, was their leader, and laid the foundation of the sect. This is by far the most probable opinion, and to this there can be no objection. It is in accordance with what usually occurs in regard to sects, orthodox or heretical, that they derive their origin from some person whose name they continue to bear; and as there is no evidence that this sect prevailed extensively, or was indeed known beyond the limits of these churches, and as it soon disappeared, it is easily accounted for that the character and history of the founder were so soon forgotten. II. In regard to the *opinions* which they held, there is as little certainty. Irenæus (*Adv. Hæres.* i. 26) says that their characteristic tenets were the lawfulness of promiscuous intercourse with women, and of eating things offered to idols. Eusebius (*Hist. Eccl.* iii. 29) states substantially the same thing, and refers to a tradition respecting Nicolaus, that he had a beautiful wife, and was jealous of her, and being reproached with this, renounced all intercourse with her, and made use of an expression which was misunderstood, as implying that illicit pleasure was proper. Tertullian speaks of the Nicolaitanes as a branch of the Gnostic family, and as, in his time, extinct. Mosheim (*De Rebus Christian Ante. Con.* § 69) says that "the questions about the Nicolaitanes have difficulties which cannot be solved." Neander (*History of the Christian Religion*, as translated by Torrey, i. pp. 452, 453) numbers them with Antinomians; though he expresses some doubt whether the actual existence of such a sect can be proved, and rather inclines to an opinion noticed above, that the name is symbolical, and that it is used in a mystical sense, according to the usual style of the book of Revelation, to denote corrupters or seducers of the people, like Balaam. He supposes that the passage relates simply to a class of persons who were in the practice of seducing Christians to participate in the sacrificial feasts of the heathens, and in the excesses which attended them—just as the Jews were led astray of old by the Moabites, Nu. xxv. What was the origin of the name, however, Neander does not profess to be able to determine, but suggests that it was the custom of such sects to attach themselves to some celebrated name of antiquity, in the choice of which they were often determined by circumstances quite accidental. He supposes also that the sect may have possessed a life of Nicolas of Antioch, drawn up by themselves or others from fabulous accounts and traditions, in which what had been imputed to Nicolas was embodied. Everything,

**7** He*i* that hath an ear, let him hear what the Spirit saith unto the churches; To him that overcometh will I give to eat of the *k*tree of life, which is in the midst of the paradise of God.

*i* ver.11,17,29; Mat.11.15.  *k* ch.22.2,14; Ge.2.9.

however, in regard to the origin of this sect, and the reason of the name given to it, and the opinions which they held, is involved in great obscurity, and there is no hope of throwing light on the subject. It is generally agreed, among the writers of antiquity who have mentioned them, that they were distinguished for holding opinions which countenanced gross social indulgences. This is all that is really necessary to be known in regard to the passage before us, for this will explain the strong language of aversion and condemnation used by the Saviour respecting the sect in the epistles to the churches of Ephesus and Pergamos. ¶ *Which I also hate.* If the view above taken of the opinions and practices of this people is correct, the reasons why he hated them are obvious. Nothing can be more opposed to the personal character of the Saviour, or to his religion, than such doctrines and deeds.

**7.** *He that hath an ear, let him hear,* &c. This expression occurs at the close of each of the epistles addressed to the seven churches, and is substantially a mode of address often employed by the Saviour in his personal ministry, and quite characteristic of him. See Mat. xi. 15; Mar. iv. 23; vii. 16. It is a form of expression designed to arrest the attention, and to denote that what was said was of special importance. ¶ *What the Spirit saith unto the churches.* Evidently what the Holy Spirit says—for he is regarded in the Scriptures as the Source of inspiration, and as appointed to disclose truth to man. The "Spirit" may be regarded either as speaking through the Saviour (comp. Jn. iii. 34), or as imparted to John, through whom he addressed the churches. In either case it is the same Spirit of inspiration, and in either case there would be a claim that his voice should be heard. The language here used is of a general character—"He that hath an ear;" that is, what was spoken was worthy of the attention not only of the members of these churches, but of all others. The truths were of so general a character as to deserve the attention of mankind at large. ¶ *To him that overcometh.* Gr., "To him that gains the victory, or is a conqueror"—τῷ νικῶντι. This may refer to any victory of a moral character, and the expression used would be applicable to one who should triumph in any of these respects:—(*a*) over his own easily-besetting sins; (*b*) over the world and its temptations; (*c*) over prevalent error; (*d*) over the ills and trials of life, so as, in all these respects, to show that his Christian principles are firm and unshaken. Life, and the Christian life especially, may be regarded as a warfare. Thousands fall in the conflict with evil; but they who maintain a steady warfare, and who achieve a victory, shall be received as conquerors in the end. ¶ *Will I give to eat of the tree of life.* As the reward of his victory. The meaning is, that he would admit him to heaven, represented as paradise, and permit him to enjoy its pleasures—represented by being permitted to partake of its fruits. The phrase "the tree of life" refers undoubtedly to the language used respecting the Garden of Eden, Ge. ii. 9; iii. 22—where the "tree of life" is spoken of as that which was adapted to make the life of man perpetual. Of the nature of that tree nothing is known, though it would seem probable that, like the tree of the knowledge of good and evil, it was a mere emblem of life—or a tree that was set before man in connection with the tree of the knowledge of good and evil, and that his destiny turned on the question whether he partook of the one or the other. That God should make the question of life or death depend on that, is no more absurd or improbable than that he should make it depend on what man does now—it being a matter of fact that life and death, happiness and misery, joy and sorrow, *are* often made to depend on things quite as arbitrary apparently, and quite as unimportant as an act of obedience or disobedience in partaking of the fruit of a designated tree. Does it not appear probable that in Eden there were two trees designated to be of an emblematic character, of life and death, and that as man partook of the one or the other he would live or die? Of all the others he might freely partake without their affecting his condition; of one of these—the tree of life—he might have partaken before the fall, and lived for ever. One was forbidden on pain of death. When the law forbidding that was violated, it was still *possible* that he might partake of the other; but, since the sentence of death had been passed upon him, that would not now be proper, and he was driven from the garden, and the way was guarded by the flaming sword of the cherubim. The reference in the passage before us is to the *celestial* paradise—to heaven—spoken of under the beautiful image of a garden; meaning that the condition of man, in regard to life, will still be the same *as if* he had partaken of the tree of life in Eden. Comp. Notes on ch. xxii. 2. ¶ *Which is in the midst of the paradise of God.* Heaven, represented as paradise. To be permitted to eat of that tree, that is, of the fruit of that tree, is but another expression implying the promise of eternal life, and of being happy for ever. The word *paradise* is of Oriental derivation, and is found in several of the Eastern languages. In the Sanskrit the word *paradêsha* and *paradisha* is used to denote a land elevated and cultivated; in the Armenian the word *pardes* denotes a garden around the house planted with grass, herbs, trees for use and ornament; and in the Hebrew form פַּרְדֵּס, and Greek παράδεισος, it is applied to the pleasure gardens and parks, with wild animals, around the country residences of the Persian monarchs and princes, Ne. ii. 8. Comp. Ec. ii. 5; Ca. iv. 13; Xen. *Cyro.* i. 3, 14 (Rob. *Lex.*). Here it is used to denote heaven—a world compared in beauty with a richly cultivated park or garden. Comp. 2 Co. xii. 4. The meaning of the Saviour is, that he would receive him that overcame to a world of happiness; that he would permit him to taste of the fruit that grows there, imparting immortal life, and to rest in an abode fitted up in a manner that would contribute in every way to enjoyment. Man, when he fell, was not permitted to reach forth his hand and pluck of the fruit of the tree of life in the first Eden, as he might have done if he had not fallen; but he is now permitted to reach forth his hand and partake of the tree of life in the paradise above. He is thus restored to what he might have been if he had not transgressed by eating of the fruit of the tree of the knowledge of good and evil; and in the Paradise Regained, the blessings of the Paradise Lost will be more than recovered—for man may now live for ever in a far higher and more blessed state than his would have been in Eden.

THE EPISTLE TO THE CHURCH AT SMYRNA.

The contents of the epistle to the church at Smyrna are these: (1) A statement, as in the address to the church at Ephesus, of some of the attributes of the Saviour, ver. 8. The attributes here referred to are, that he was "the first and the last," that "he had been dead, but was alive"—attributes fitted to impress the mind deeply with reverence for him who addressed them, and to comfort them in the trials which they endured. (2) A statement (ver. 9), as in the former epistle, that he well knew their works and all that pertained to them—their tribulation, their poverty, and the opposition which they met with from wicked men. (3) An exhortation not to be afraid of any of those things that were to come upon them, for, although they were to be persecuted, and some of them were to be imprisoned, yet, if they were faithful, they should have a crown of life, ver. 10. (4) A command to hear what the Spirit said to the churches, as containing matter of interest to all persons, with an assurance that any who would "overcome" in these trials would not be hurt by the second death, ver. 11. The language addressed to the church of Smyrna is throughout that of commiseration and comfort. There is no intimation that the Saviour disapproved of what they had done; there is no threat that he would remove the candlestick out of its place. *Smyrna* was a celebrated commercial town of Ionia (Ptolem. v. 2), situated near the bottom of that gulf of the Ægean Sea which received its name from it (Mela, i. 17, 3), at the mouth of the small river Meles, 320 stadia, or about forty miles north of Ephesus (Strabo, xv. p. 632). It was a very ancient city; but having been destroyed by the Lydians, it lay waste four hundred years to the time of Alexander the Great, or, according to Strabo, to that of Antigonus. It was rebuilt at the distance of twenty stadia from the ancient city, and in the time of the first Roman emperor it was one of the most flourishing cities of Asia. It was destroyed by an earthquake, A.D. 177, but the emperor Marcus Aurelius caused it to be rebuilt with more than its former splendour. It afterwards, however, suffered greatly from earthquakes and conflagrations, and has

8 And unto the angel of the church in Smyrna write; These things saith *l* the first and the last, which was dead, and is alive;
9 I know thy works, and tribulation, and poverty, (but *m* thou art rich,) and *I know* the blasphemy of *n* them which say they are Jews, and are not, but *are* the *o* synagogue of Satan.

*l* ch.1.8,17.   *m* 1 Ti.6.18.   *n* Ro.2.28,29.   *o* ch.3.9.

declined from these causes, though, from its commercial advantages, it has always been a city of importance as the central emporium of the Levantine trade, and its relative rank among the cities of Asia Minor is probably greater than it formerly bore. The engraving in this vol. will give a representation of Smyrna. The Turks now call it Izmir. It is better built than Constantinople, and its population is computed at about 130,000, of which the Franks compose a greater proportion than in any other town in Turkey, and they are generally in good circumstances. Next to the Turks, the Greeks form the most numerous portion of the inhabitants, and they have a bishop and two churches. The unusually large portion of Christians in the city renders it peculiarly unclean in the eyes of strict Moslems, and they call it Giaour Izmir, or the Infidel Smyrna. There are in it about 20,000 Greeks, 8000 Armenians, 1000 Europeans, and 9000 Jews. It is now the seat of important missionary operations in the East, and much has been done there to spread the gospel in modern times. Its history during the long tract of time since John wrote is not indeed minutely known, but there is no reason to suppose that the light of Christianity there has ever been wholly extinct. Polycarp suffered martyrdom there, and the place where he is supposed to have died is still shown. The Christians of Smyrna hold his memory in great veneration, and go annually on a visit to his supposed tomb, which is at a short distance from the place of his martyrdom. See the article "Smyrna" in Kitto's *Cyclopedia*, and the authorities referred to there.

8. *And unto the angel of the church in Smyrna write.* On the meaning of the word *angel*, see Notes on ch. i. 20. ¶ *These things saith the first and the last.* See Notes on ch. i. 8, 17. ¶ *Which was dead, and is alive.* See Notes on ch. i. 18. The idea is, that he is a *living* Saviour; and there was a propriety in referring to that fact here from the nature of the promise which he was about to make to the church at Smyrna: "He that overcometh shall not be hurt of the second death," ver. 11. As he had himself triumphed over death in all its forms, and was now alive for ever, it was appropriate that he should promise to his true friends the same protection from the second death. He who was wholly beyond the reach of death could give the assurance that they who put their trust in him should come off victorious.

9. *I know thy works.* The uniform method of introducing these epistles, implying a most intimate acquaintance with all that pertained to the church. See Notes on ver. 2. ¶ *And tribulation.* This word is of a general signification, and probably includes all that they suffered in any form, whether from persecution, poverty, or the blasphemy of opposers. ¶ *And poverty.* It would seem that this church, at that time, was eminently poor, for this is not specified in regard to any one of the others. No reason is suggested why *they* were particularly poor. It was not, indeed, an uncommon characteristic of early Christians (comp. 1 Cor. i. 26-28), but there might have been some special reasons why that church was eminently so. It is, however, the only church of the seven which has survived, and perhaps in the end its poverty was no disadvantage. ¶ *But thou art rich.* Not in this world's goods, but in a more important respect —in the grace and favour of God. These things are not unfrequently united. Poverty is no hindrance to the favour of God, and there are some things in it favourable to the promotion of a right spirit towards God which are not found where there is abundant wealth. The Saviour was eminently poor, and not a few of his most devoted and useful followers have had as little of this world's goods as he had. The poor should always be cheerful and happy, if they can hear their Saviour saying unto them, "I know thy poverty—but thou art rich." However keen the feeling arising from the reflection "I am a poor man," the edge of the sorrow is taken off if the mind can be turned to a brighter image—"*but* thou art rich."

10 Fear none of those things which thou shalt suffer: behold, the devil shall cast *some* of you into prison, that ye may be tried; and ye shall have tribulation ten days: be thou *p*faithful unto death, and I will give thee a *q*crown of life.

*p* Mat.10.22.   *q* Ja.1.12.

¶ *And* I know *the blasphemy.* The reproaches; the harsh and bitter revilings. On the word *blasphemy,* see Notes on Mat. ix. 3; xxvi. 65. The word here does not seem to refer to blasphemy *against God,* but to bitter reproaches against themselves. The reason of these reproaches is not stated, but it was doubtless on account of their religion. ¶ *Of them which say they are Jews.* Who profess to be Jews. The idea seems to be that though they were of Jewish extraction, and professed to be Jews, they were not *true Jews;* they indulged in a bitterness of reproach, and a severity of language, which showed that they had not the spirit of the Jewish religion; they had nothing which became those who were under the guidance of the spirit of their own Scriptures. That would have inculcated and fostered a milder temper; and the meaning here is, that although they were of Jewish origin, they were not worthy of the name. That spirit of bitter opposition was indeed often manifested in their treatment of Christians, as it had been of the Saviour, but still it was foreign to the true nature of their religion. There were Jews in all parts of Asia Minor, and the apostles often encountered them in their journeyings, but it would seem that there was something which had particularly embittered those of Smyrna against Christianity. What this was is now unknown. It may throw some light on the passage, however, to remark that at a somewhat later period—in the time of the martyrdom of Polycarp — the Jews of Smyrna were among the most bitter of the enemies of Christians, and among the most violent in demanding the death of Polycarp. Eusebius (*Eccl. Hist.* iv. 15) says, that when Polycarp was apprehended, and brought before the proconsul at Smyrna, the Jews were the most furious of all in demanding his condemnation. When the mob, after his condemnation to death, set about gathering fuel to burn him, "the Jews," says he, "being especially zealous, as was their custom — μάλιστα προθύμως, ὡς ἔθος αὐτοῖς—ran to procure fuel." And when, as the burning failed, the martyr was transfixed with weapons, the Jews urged and besought the magistrate that his body might not be given up to Christians. Possibly at the time when this epistle was directed to be sent to Smyrna, there were Jews there who manifested the same spirit which those of their countrymen did afterwards, who urged on the death of Polycarp. ¶ *But are the synagogue of Satan.* Deserve rather to be called the synagogue of Satan. The *synagogue* was a Jewish place of worship (comp. Notes on Mat. iv. 23), but the word originally denoted the *assembly* or *congregation.* The meaning here is plain, that though they worshipped in a synagogue, and professed to be the worshippers of God, yet they were not worthy of the name, and deserved rather to be regarded as in the service of Satan. *Satan* is the word that is properly applied to the great evil spirit, elsewhere called the devil. See Notes on Lu. xxii. 3, and Job i. 6.

10. *Fear none of those things which thou shalt suffer.* He did not promise them exemption from suffering. He saw that they were about to suffer, and he specifies the manner in which their affliction would occur. But he entreats and commands them not to be afraid. They were to look to the "crown of life," and to be comforted with the assurance that if they were faithful unto death, that would be theirs. We need not dread suffering if we can hear the voice of the Redeemer encouraging us, and if he assures us that in a little while we shall have the crown of life. ¶ *Behold, the devil shall cast* some *of you into prison.* Or, shall cause some of you to be cast into prison. He had just said that their persecutors were of the "synagogue of Satan." He here represents Satan, or the devil—another name of the same being—as about to throw them into prison. This would be done undoubtedly by the hands of men, but still Satan was the prime mover, or the instigator in doing it. It was common to cast those who were persecuted into prison. See Ac. xii. 3, 4; xvi. 23. It is not said on what pretence, or by what authority, this would be done; but, as John had been banished to Patmos from Ephesus, it is probable

11 He that hath an ear, let him hear what the Spirit saith unto the churches; He that overcometh shall not be hurt of the ʳsecond death.

*r* ch. 20. 14.

that this persecution was raging in the adjacent places, and there is no improbability in supposing that many might be thrown into prison. ¶ *That ye may be tried.* That the reality of your faith may be subjected to a test to show whether it is genuine. The *design* in the case is that of the Saviour, though Satan is allowed to do it. It was common in the early periods of the church to suffer religion to be subjected to trial amidst persecutions, in order to show that it was of heavenly origin, and to demonstrate its value in view of the world. This is, indeed, one of the designs of trial at all times, but this seemed eminently desirable when a new system of religion was about to be given to mankind. Comp. Notes on 1 Pe. i. 6, 7. ¶ *And ye shall have tribulation ten days.* A short time; a brief period; a few days. It is *possible*, indeed, that this might have been literally ten days, but it is much more in accordance with the general character of this book, in regard to numbers, to suppose that the word *ten* here is used to denote *a few.* Comp. Ge. xxiv. 55; 1 Sa. xxv. 38; Da. i. 12, 14. We are wholly ignorant how long the trial actually lasted; but the assurance was that it would not be long, and they were to allow this thought to cheer and sustain them in their sorrows. Why should not the same thought encourage us now? Affliction in this life, however severe, can be but brief; and in the hope that it will soon end, why should we not bear it without murmuring or repining? ¶ *Be thou faithful unto death.* Implying, perhaps, that though, in regard to the church, the affliction would be brief, yet that it might be fatal to some of them, and they who were thus about to die should remain faithful to their Saviour until the hour of death. In relation to all, whether they were to suffer a violent death or not, the same injunction and the same promise was applicable. It is true of everyone who is a Christian, in whatever manner he is to die, that if he is faithful unto death, a crown of life awaits him. Comp. Notes on 2 Ti. iv. 8. ¶ *And I will give thee a crown of life.* See Notes on Ja. i. 12. Comp. 1 Pe. v. 4; 1 Co. ix. 24–27. The promise here is somewhat different from that which was made to the faithful in Ephesus (ver. 7), but the same thing substantially is promised them—happiness hereafter, or an admission into heaven. In the former case it is the peaceful image of those admitted into the scenes of paradise; here it is the triumph of the crowned martyr.

11. *He that hath an ear,* &c. See Notes on ver. 7. ¶ *He that overcometh.* See Notes on ver. 7. The particular promise here is made to him that should "overcome;" that is, that would gain the victory in the persecutions which were to come upon them. The reference is to him who would show the sustaining power of religion in times of persecution; who would not yield his principles when opposed and persecuted; who would be triumphant when so many efforts were made to induce him to apostatize and abandon the cause. ¶ *Shall not be hurt of the second death.* By a second death. That is, he will have nothing to fear in the future world. The punishment of hell is often called *death*, not in the sense that the soul will cease to exist, but (*a*) because death is the most fearful thing of which we have any knowledge, and (*b*) because there is a striking similarity, in many respects, between death and future punishment. Death cuts off from life—and so the second death cuts off from eternal life; death puts an end to all our hopes here, and the second death to all our hopes for ever; death is attended with terrors and alarms—the faint and feeble emblem of the terrors and alarms in the world of woe. The phrase, "the second death," is three times used elsewhere by John in this book (ch. xx. 6, 14; xxi. 8), but does not occur elsewhere in the New Testament. The words *death* and *to die*, however, are not unfrequently used to denote the future punishment of the wicked.

The promise here made would be all that was necessary to sustain them in their trials. Nothing more is requisite to make the burdens of life tolerable than an assurance that, when we reach the end of our earthly journey, we have arrived at the close of suffering, and that beyond the grave there is no power that can harm us. Religion, indeed, does not promise to its friends exemption from death in one form. To none of the race has such a promise ever been made, and to but two has the favour been granted to pass to heaven without tasting death. It could have been granted to all the redeemed, but there were good reasons why it should not be; that is, why it would be better that even they who are to dwell in heaven should return to the dust, and sleep in the tomb, than that they should be removed by perpetual miracle, translating them to heaven. Religion, therefore, does not come to us with any promise that we shall not die. But it comes with the assurance that we shall be sustained in the dying hour; that the Redeemer will accompany us through the dark valley; that death to us will be a calm and quiet slumber, in the hope of awakening in the morning of the resurrection; that we shall be raised up again with bodies incorruptible and undecaying; and that beyond the grave we shall never fear death in any form. What more is needful to enable us to bear with patience the trials of this life, and to look upon death when it does come, disarmed as it is of its sting (1 Co. xv. 55-57), with calmness and peace?

### THE EPISTLE TO THE CHURCH AT PERGAMOS.

The contents of this epistle (ver. 12-17) are as follows: (1) A reference, as is usual in these epistles, to some attribute of Him who addressed them, fitted to inspire respect, and adapted to a state of things existing in the church, ver. 12. That to which the Saviour here directs their attention is, that he has "the sharp sword with two edges"—implying (ver. 16) that he had the power of punishing. (2) A statement, in the usual form, that he was thoroughly acquainted with the state of the church; that he saw all their difficulties; all that there was to commend, and all that there was to reprove, ver. 13. (3) A commendation to the church for its fidelity, especially in a time of severe persecution, when one of her faithful friends was slain, ver. 13. (4) A reproof of the church for tolerating some who held false and pernicious doctrines—doctrines such as were taught by Balaam, and the doctrines of the Nicolaitanes, ver. 14, 15. (5) A solemn threat that, unless they repented, he would come against them, and inflict summary punishment on them, ver. 16. (6) The usual call upon all to hear what the Spirit says to the churches, and a promise to those who should overcome, ver. 17.

Pergamos was a city in the southern part of Mysia, the capital of a kingdom of that name, and afterwards of the Roman province of Asia Propria. It was on the bank of the river Caicus, which is formed by the union of two branches meeting thirty or forty miles above its mouth, and watering a valley not exceeded in beauty and fertility by any in the world. The city of Pergamos stood about twenty miles from the sea. It was on the northern bank of the river, at the base and on the declivity of two high and steep mountains. About two centuries before the Christian era, Pergamos became the residence of the celebrated kings of the family of Attalus, and a seat of literature and the arts. King Eumenes, the second of the name, greatly beautified the town, and so increased the number of volumes in the library that they amounted to 200,000. This library remained at Pergamos after the kingdom of the Attali had lost its independence, until Antony removed it to Egypt, and presented it to Queen Cleopatra (Pliny, *Hist. Nat.* iii. 2). It is an old tradition, that, as the papyrus plant had not begun to be exported from Egypt (Kitto), or as Ptolemy refused to sell it to Eumenes (Professor Stuart), sheep and goat skins, prepared for the purpose, were used for manuscripts; and as the art of preparing them was brought to perfection at Pergamos, they, from that circumstance, obtained the name of *pergamena* (περγαμηνή) or *parchment*. The last king of Pergamos bequeathed his treasures to the Romans, who took possession of the kingdom also, and created it into a province by the name of Asia Propria. Under the Romans, it retained that authority over the cities of Asia which it had acquired under the successors of Attalus. The present name of the place is Bergamos, and it is of considerable importance, containing a population of about 14,000, of whom about 3000 are Greeks, 300 Armenians, and the rest Turks. Macfarlane describes the approach to the town as very beautiful: "The approach to this ancient and decayed city was as impressive as well might be. After crossing the Caicus, I saw, looking over three vast tumuli, or sepulchral barrows, similar to those on the plains of Troy, the Turkish city of Pergamos, with its tall minarets, and its taller cypresses, situated on the lower declivities and at the foot of the Acropolis, whose bold gray brow was crowned by the rugged

12 And to the angel of the church in Pergamos write; These things saith *he which hath the sharp sword with two edges;

13 I*t* know thy works, and where thou dwellest, *even* where

*s* ch.1.16.     *t* ver.9.

Satan's seat *is:* and thou holdest fast my name, and *u*hast not denied my faith, even in those days wherein Antipas *was* my faithful martyr, who was slain among you, where Satan dwelleth.

*u* 2 Ti.2.12.

walls of a barbarous castle, the usurper of the site of a magnificent Greek temple. The town consists, for the most part, of small and mean wooden houses, among which appear the remains of early Christian churches. None of these churches have any scriptural or apocalyptic interest connected with them, having been erected several centuries after the ministry of the apostles, and when Christianity was not an humble and despised creed, but the adopted religion of a vast empire. The Pagan temples have fared worse than these Christian churches. The fanes of Jupiter and Diana, of Æsculapius and Venus, are prostrate in the dust; and where they have not been carried away by the Turks, to be cut up into tombstones or to pound into mortar, the Corinthian and Ionic columns, the splendid capitals, the cornices and the pediments, all in the highest ornament, are thrown into unsightly heaps" (*Visit to the Seven Apocalyptic Churches*, 1832. Comp. *Missionary Herald* for 1839, pp. 228-230). The engraving represents the ruins of one of the ancient churches in Pergamos.

12. *And to the angel of the church in Pergamos.* See Notes on ch. i. 20. ¶ *These things saith he which hath the sharp sword*, &c. See Notes on ch. i. 16. Comp. He. iv. 12; Ec. xii. 11; Is. xlix. 2. Professor Stuart suggests that when the Saviour, as represented in the vision, "uttered words, as they proceeded from his mouth, the halitus which accompanied them assumed, in the view of John, the form of an igneous two-edged sword." It is more probable, however, that the words which proceeded from his mouth did not assume anything like a form or substance, but that John means to represent them *as if* they were a sharp sword. His words cut and penetrate deep, and it was easy to picture him as having a sword proceeding from his mouth; that is, his words were as piercing as a sharp sword. As he was about to reprove the church at Pergamos, there was a propriety in referring to this power of the Saviour. Reproof cuts deep; and this is the idea represented here.

13. *I know thy works.* The uniform mode of addressing the seven churches in these epistles. See Notes on ch. ii. 2. ¶ *And where thou dwellest.* That is, I know all the temptations to which you are exposed; all the allurements to sin by which you are surrounded; all the apologies which might be made for what has occurred arising from those circumstances; and all that could be said in commendation of you for having been as faithful as you have been. The sense of the passage is, that it does much to enable us to judge of character to know where men live. It is much more easy to be virtuous and pious in some circumstances than in others; and in order to determine how much credit is due to a man for his virtues, it is necessary to understand how much he has been called to resist, how many temptations he has encountered, what easily-besetting sins he may have, or what allurements may have been presented to his mind to draw him from the path of virtue and religion. In like manner, in order to judge correctly of those who have embraced error, or have been led into sin, it is necessary to understand what there may have been in their circumstances that gave to error what was plausible, and to sin what was attractive; what there was in their situation in life that exposed them to these influences, and what arguments may have been employed by the learned, the talented, and the plausible advocates of error, to lead them astray. We often judge harshly where the Saviour would be far less severe in his judgments; we often commend much where in fact there has been little to commend. It is possible to conceive that in the strugglings against evil of those who have ultimately fallen, there may be more to commend than in cases where the path of virtue has been pursued as the mere result of circumstances, and where there never has been a conflict with temptation. The adjudications of the great day will do much to reverse

14 But I have a few things against thee, because thou hast there them that hold the doctrine of Balaam, *ᵛ*who taught Balac to cast a stumbling-block before the children of Israel, to *ʷ*eat things sacrificed unto idols, and to *ˣ*commit fornication.

*v* Nu.31.16.     *w* Ac.15.29.     *x* 1 Co.6.13,18.

the judgments of mankind. ¶ Even *where Satan's seat* is. A place of peculiar wickedness, as if Satan dwelt there. Satan is, as it were, enthroned there. The influence of Satan in producing persecution is that which is *particularly* alluded to, as is apparent from the reference which is immediately made to the case of Antipas, the "faithful martyr." ¶ *And thou holdest fast my name.* They had professed the name of Christ; that is, they had professed to be his followers, and they had steadfastly adhered to him and his cause in all the opposition made to him. The name *Christian*, given in honour of Christ, and indicating that they were his disciples, they had not been ashamed of or denied. It was this *name* that subjected the early Christians to reproach. See 1 Pe. iv. 14. ¶ *And hast not denied my faith.* That is, hast not denied my religion. The great essential element in the Christian religion is *faith*, and this, since it is so important, is often put for the whole of religion. ¶ *Even in those days wherein Antipas* was *my faithful martyr.* Of Antipas we know nothing more than is here stated. "In the *Acta Sanctorum* (ii. pp. 3, 4) is a martyrology of Antipas from a Greek MS.; but it is full of fable and fiction, which a later age had added to the original story" (Professor Stuart, *in loco*). ¶ *Who was slain among you.* It would seem from this, that, though the persecution had raged there, but one person had been put to death. It would appear also that the persecution was of a local character, since Pergamos is described as "Satan's seat;" and the death of Antipas is mentioned in immediate connection with that fact. All the circumstances referred to would lead us to suppose that this was a popular outbreak, and not a persecution carried on under the authority of government, and that Antipas was put to death in a popular excitement. So Stephen (Ac. vii.) was put to death, and so Paul at Lystra was stoned until it was supposed he was dead, Ac. xiv. 19. ¶ *Where Satan dwelleth.* The repetition of this idea —very much in the manner of John— showed how intensely the mind was fixed on the thought, and how much alive the feelings were to the malice of Satan as exhibited at Pergamos.

14. *But I have a few things against thee.* As against the church at Ephesus, ch. ii. 4. The charge against this church, however, is somewhat different from that against the church at Ephesus. The charge there was, that they had "left their first love;" but it is spoken in commendation of them that they "hated the deeds of the Nicolaitanes," ch. ii. 6. Here the charge is, that they tolerated that sect among them, and that they had among them also those who held the doctrine of Balaam. Their general course had been such that the Saviour could approve it; he did not approve, however, of their tolerating those who held to pernicious practical error—error that tended to sap the very foundation of morals. ¶ *Because thou hast there them that hold the doctrine of Balaam.* It is not necessary to suppose that they professedly held to the same opinion as Balaam, or openly taught the same doctrines. The meaning is, that they taught substantially the same doctrine which Balaam did, and deserved to be classed with him. What that doctrine was is stated in the subsequent part of the verse. ¶ *Who taught Balac to cast a stumbling-block before the children of Israel.* The word *stumbling-block* properly means anything over which one falls or stumbles, and then anything over which anyone may fall into sin, or which becomes the occasion of one's falling into sin. The meaning here is, that it was through the instructions of Balaam that Balak learned the way by which the Israelites might be led into sin, and might thus bring upon themselves the Divine malediction. The main circumstances in the case were these: (1) Balak, king of Moab, when the children of Israel approached his borders, felt that he could not contend successfully against so great a host, for his people were dispirited and disheartened at their numbers, Nu. xxii. 3, 4. (2) In these circumstances he resolved to send for one who had a

distinguished reputation as a prophet, that he might "curse" that people, or might utter a malediction over them, in order, at the same time, to ensure their destruction, and to inspirit his own people in making war on them: in accordance with a prevalent opinion of ancient times, that prophets had the power of blighting anything by their curse. Comp. Notes on Job iii. 8. For this purpose he sent messengers to Balaam to invite him to come and perform this service, Nu. xxii. 5, 6. (3) Balaam professed to be a prophet of the Lord, and it was obviously proper that he should inquire of the Lord whether he should comply with this request. He did so, and was positively forbidden to go, Nu. xxii. 12. (4) When the answer of Balaam was reported to Balak, he supposed that he might be prevailed to come by the offer of rewards, and he sent more distinguished messengers with an offer of ample honour if he would come, Nu. xxii. 15-17. (5) Balaam was evidently strongly inclined to go, but, in accordance with his character as a prophet, he said that if Balak would give him his house full of silver and gold he could do no more, and say no more, than the Lord permitted, and he proposed again to consult the Lord, to see if he could obtain permission to go with the messengers of Balak. He obtained permission, but with the express injunction that he was only to utter what God should say; and when he came to Balak, notwithstanding his own manifest desire to comply with the wish of Balak, and notwithstanding all the offers which Balak made to him to induce him to do the contrary, he only continued to bless the Hebrew people, until, in disgust and indignation, Balak sent him away again to his own land, Nu. xxii., xxiii., xxiv. 10, seq. (6) Balaam returned to his own house, but evidently with a desire still to gratify Balak. Being forbidden to curse the people of Israel; having been overruled in all his purposes to do it; having been, contrary to his own desires, constrained to bless them when he was himself more than willing to curse them; and having still a desire to comply with the wishes of the King of Moab, he cast about for some way in which the object might yet be accomplished—that is, in which the curse of God might *in fact* rest upon the Hebrew people, and they might become exposed to the divine displeasure.

To do this, no way occurred so plausible, and that had such probability of success, as to lead them into idolatry, and into the sinful and corrupt practices connected with idolatry. It was, therefore, resolved to make use of the charms of the females of Moab, that through their influence the Hebrews might be drawn into licentiousness. This was done. The abominations of idolatry spread through the camp of Israel; licentiousness everywhere prevailed, and God sent a plague upon them to punish them, Nu. xxv. 1, seq. That also this was planned and instigated by Balaam is apparent from Nu. xxxi. 16: "Behold these [women] caused the children of Israel, through the counsel of Balaam, to commit trespass against the Lord, in the matter of Peor, and there was a plague among the congregation of the Lord." The *attitude* of Balaam's mind in the matter was this: I. He had a strong desire to do that which he knew was wrong, and which was forbidden expressly by God. II. He was restrained by internal checks and remonstrances, and prevented from doing what he wished to do. III. He cast about for some way in which he might do it, notwithstanding these internal checks and remonstrances, and finally accomplished the same thing in fact, though in form different from that which he had first prepared. This is not an unfair description of what often occurs in the plans and purposes of a wicked man. The meaning in the passage before us is, that in the church at Pergamos there were those who taught, substantially, the same thing that Balaam did; that is, the tendency of whose teaching was to lead men into idolatry, and the ordinary accompaniment of idolatry—licentiousness. ¶ *To eat things sacrificed unto idols.* Balaam taught the Hebrews to do this—perhaps in some way securing their attendance on the riotous and gluttonous feasts of idolatry celebrated among the people among whom they sojourned. Such feasts were commonly held in idol temples, and they usually led to scenes of dissipation and corruption. By plausibly teaching that there could be no harm in eating what had been offered in sacrifice—since an idol was nothing, and the flesh of animals offered in sacrifice was the same as if slaughtered for some other purpose, it would seem that these teachers at Pergamos had induced professing Chris-

A.D. 96.] CHAPTER II. 77

15 So hast thou also them that hold the doctrine of the Nicolaitanes, which thing I hate.
16 Repent; or else I will come unto thee quickly, and ʸ will fight against them with the sword of my mouth.

y Is.11.4.

tians to attend on those feasts—thus lending their countenance to idolatry, and exposing themselves to all the corruption and licentiousness that commonly attended such celebrations. See the banefulness of thus eating the meat offered in sacrifice to idols considered in the Notes on 1 Co. viii. ¶ *And to commit fornication.* Balaam taught this; and that was the tendency of the doctrines inculcated at Pergamos. On what pretence this was done is not said; but it is clear that the church had regarded this in a lenient manner. So accustomed had the heathen world been to this vice, that many who had been converted from idolatry might be disposed to look on it with less severity than we do now, and there was a necessity of incessant watchfulness lest the members of the church should fall into it. Comp. Notes on Ac. xv. 20.

15. *So hast thou also them,* &c. That is, there are those among you who hold those doctrines. The meaning here may be, either that, in addition to those who held the doctrine of Balaam, they had also another class who held the doctrine of the Nicolaitanes; or that the Nicolaitanes held the same doctrine, and taught the same thing as Balaam. If but one class is referred to, and it is meant that the Nicolaitanes held the doctrines of Balaam, then we know what constituted their teaching; if two classes of false teachers are referred to, then we have no means of knowing what was the peculiarity of the teaching of the Nicolaitanes. The more natural and obvious construction, it seems to me, is to suppose that the speaker means to say that the Nicolaitanes taught the same things which Balaam did—to wit, that they led the people into corrupt and licentious practices. This interpretation seems to be demanded by the proper use of the word "so"— οὕτως —meaning, *in this manner, on this wise, thus;* and usually referring to what precedes. If this be the correct interpretation, then we have, in fact, a description of what the Nicolaitanes held, agreeing with all the accounts given of them by the ancient fathers. See Notes on ver. 6. If this is so, also, then it is clear that the same kind of doctrines was held at Smyrna, at Pergamos, and at Thyatira (ver. 20), though mentioned in somewhat different forms. It is not quite certain, however, that this is the correct interpretation, or that the writer does not mean to say that, *in addition* to those who held the doctrine of Balaam, they had also another class of errorists who held the doctrine of the Nicolaitanes. ¶ *Which thing I hate.* So the common Greek text—ὁ μισῶ. But the best-supported reading, and the one adopted by Griesbach, Tittmann, and Hahn, is ὁμοίως—*in like manner;* that is, "as Balak retained a false prophet who misled the Hebrews, so thou retainest those who teach things like to those which Balaam taught."

16. *Repent.* See ver. 5. ¶ *Or else I will come unto thee quickly.* On the word *quickly,* see Notes on ch. i. 1. The meaning here is, that he would come against them in judgment, or to punish them. ¶ *And will fight against them.* Against the Nicolaitanes. He would come against the church for tolerating them, but his opposition would be principally directed against the Nicolaitanes themselves. The church would excite his displeasure by retaining them in its bosom, but it was in its power to save them from destruction. If the church would repent, or if it would separate itself from the evil, then the Saviour would not come against them. If this were *not* done, they would feel the vengeance of his sword, and be subjected to punishment. The church always suffers when it has offenders in its bosom; it has the power of saving them if it will repent of its own unfaithfulness, and will strive for their conversion. ¶ *With the sword of my mouth.* Notes on ch. i. 16; ii. 12. That is, he would give the order, and they would be cut as if by a sword. Precisely in what way it would be done he does not say; but it might be by persecution, or by heavy judgments. To see the force of this, we are to remember the power which Christ has to punish the wicked by a word of his mouth. By a word in the last day he will turn all the wicked into hell.

17. *He that hath an ear,* &c. Notes on ver. 7. ¶ *To him that overcometh.*

17 He[z] that hath an ear, let him hear what the Spirit saith unto the churches; To him that overcometh will I give to eat of the [a]hidden manna, and will give him a white stone, and in the stone a [b]new name written,[c] which no man knoweth saving he that receiveth it.

[z] ver.7; ch.3.6,13,22.
[a] Ps.25.14.  [b] ch.3.12; 19.12,13; Is.56.4,5; 65.15.
[c] 1 Co.2.14.

Notes on ver. 7. ¶ *Will I give to eat of the hidden manna.* The true spiritual food; the food that nourishes the soul. The idea is, that the souls of those who "overcame," or who gained the victory in their conflict with sin, and in the persecutions and trials of the world, would be permitted to partake of that spiritual food which is laid up for the people of God, and by which they will be nourished for ever. The Hebrews were supported by manna in the desert (Ex. xvi. 16-35); a pot of that manna was laid up in the most holy place, to be preserved as a memorial (Ex. xvi. 32-34); it is called "angels' food" (Ps. lxxviii. 25), and "corn of heaven" (Ps. lxxviii. 24); and it would seem to have been emblematical of that spiritual food by which the people of God are to be fed from heaven, in their journey through this world. By the word "*hidden,*" there would seem to be an allusion to that which was laid up in the pot before the ark of the testimony, and the blessing which is promised here is that they would be nourished *as if* they were sustained by that manna thus laid up before the ark: by food from the immediate presence of God. The language thus explained would mean that they who overcome will be nourished through this life *as if* by that "hidden manna;" that is, that they will be supplied all along through the "wilderness of this world" by that food from the immediate presence of God which their souls require. As the parallel places in the epistles to the churches, however, refer rather to the heavenly world, and to the rewards which they who are victors shall have there, it seems probable that this has immediate reference to that world also, and that the meaning is, that, as the most holy place was a type of heaven, they will be admitted into the immediate presence of God, and nourished for ever by the food of heaven—that which the angels have; that which the soul will need to sustain it there. Even in this world their souls may be nourished with this "hidden manna;" in heaven it will be their constant food for ever.

¶ *And will give him a white stone.* There has been a great variety of opinion in regard to the meaning of this expression, and almost no two expositors agree. Illustrations of its meaning have been sought from Grecian, Hebrew, and Roman customs, but none of these have removed all difficulty from the expression. The general sense of the language seems plain, even though the allusion on which it is founded is obscure, or even unknown. It is, that the Saviour would give him who overcame a token of his favour which would have some word or name inscribed on it, and which would be of use to him alone, or intelligible to him only: that is, some secret token which would make him sure of the favour of his Redeemer, and which would be unknown to other men. The idea here would find a correspondence in the evidences of his favour granted to the soul of the Christian himself; in the pledge of heaven thus made to him, and which he would understand, but which no one else would understand. The *things*, then, which we are to look for in the explanation of the emblem are two—that which would thus be a token of his favour, and that which would explain the fact that it would be intelligible to no one else. The question is, whether there is any known thing pertaining to ancient customs which would convey these ideas. The word rendered *stone* — ψῆφον — means, properly, a small stone, as worn smooth by water — a gravel-stone, a pebble; then any polished stone, the stone of a gem, or ring (Rob. *Lex.*). Such a stone was used among the Greeks for various purposes, and the word came to have a signification corresponding to these uses. The following uses are enumerated by Dr. Robinson, *Lex.* : — the *stones* or *counters* for reckoning; *dice, lots,* used in a kind of magic; a *vote,* spoken of the black and white stones or pebbles anciently used in voting—that is, the white for approval, and the black for condemning. In regard to the use of the word here, some have supposed that the reference is to a custom of the Roman emperors, who, in the games

A.D. 96.] CHAPTER II. 81

**18 And unto the angel of the church in Thyatira write; These things saith the Son of God, who** hath $^a$his eyes like unto a flame of fire, and his feet *are* like fine brass;

*d* ch.1.14,15.

cotton and a kind of reddish root [madder], used for dyeing red, are raised abundantly. I observed that this root is extensively cultivated in all that region, and forms an important article of export to England, where it is used for dyeing purposes. In Ac. xvi. 14 we read of Lydia, a seller of purple, of the city of Thyatira. May not this root be the very article with which her purple was coloured, which she was selling at Philippi, when the Lord opened her heart to attend to the things spoken by Paul? It seems to me probable. But, if it was so, this art of colouring appears to have been lost, for I could not find that it is now at all practised in that place or that region.

"The Christian traveller and missionary naturally looks for something interesting in a place where once existed a true church of Christ. But, alas! how sadly is he disappointed! The place presents an appearance in nothing different from other Turkish towns. Everything wears a Mussulman aspect. The houses, streets, dress, occupation, and language of the inhabitants all indicate a predominating Turkish influence. Christianity exists there in name, but it is the bare name. Its spirit has long since fled. The Greeks, especially, seem to be peculiarly superstitious. I visited their church, and found it full of pictures and other marks of degenerate Christianity. A long string of these images, extending from one side of the church to the other, was suspended so low as to permit the worshipper to approach and kiss them; and so frequently had this adoration been bestowed on them, that all appeared soiled from the frequent contact of the lips. Over the entrance of the church I observed a representation of a grave old man, with a silvery beard, surrounded by angels. Suspecting the object designed to be shadowed forth, I inquired of a lad standing by what that figure meant. He instantly replied, 'It is God.' I observed two similar representations of the Deity in the interior of the church. The churchyard is used as a burying-place; but only those whose friends are able to pay for the privilege of entombing their dead can enjoy it. Candles are lighted at the heads of the graves in the night, and incense is often burned. When the process of decay has proceeded so far as to leave nothing but the bones, these are taken up and thrown into a sealed vault, over which a chapel is fitted up, in which mass is said over these relics of the dead for the benefit of their souls! A feeling of abhorrence came over me as I stood in the place where such abominations are committed.

"The Armenians are far less superstitious. Comparatively only a few pictures are to be seen in their church, and three or four individuals are more or less enlightened, and in an inquiring state of mind. We had a long interview with one of them, the teacher, and left some books with him. I am not without hopes that a little gospel leaven has been deposited here, the effects of which will appear at some future day" (*Miss. Herald*, Feb. 1848). The engraving in this volume will give a representation of this city as it now exists.

18. *And unto the angel of the church.* See Notes on ch. i. 20. ¶ *These things saith the Son of God.* This is the first time, in these epistles, that the *name* of the speaker is referred to. In each other instance there is merely some *attribute* of the Saviour mentioned. Perhaps the severity of the rebuke contemplated here made it proper that there should be a more impressive reference to the authority of the speaker; and hence he is introduced as the "Son of God." It is not a reference to him as the "Son of man"—the common appellation which he gave to himself when on earth—for that might have suggested his humanity only, and would not have conveyed the same impression in regard to his authority; but it is to himself as sustaining the rank, and having the authority, of the Son of God —one who, therefore, has a right to speak, and a right to demand that what he says shall be heard. ¶ *Who hath his eyes like unto a flame of fire.* Comp. Notes on ch. i. 14. Before the glance of his eye all is light, and nothing can be concealed from his view. Nothing would be better fitted to inspire awe then, as nothing should be now, than such a reference to the Son of God as being able to penetrate the secret re-

19 I*e* know thy works, and charity, and service, and faith, and thy patience, and thy works; and the last *to be* more than the first.

20 Notwithstanding, I have a few things against thee, because

*e* ver. 2.

thou sufferest that woman *f* Jezebel, which calleth herself a prophetess, to teach and to seduce my servants to commit fornication, and to *g* eat things sacrificed unto idols.

*f* 1 Ki.16.31.   *g* Ex.34.15; 1 Co.10.20,28.

---

cesses of the heart. ¶ *And his feet* are *like fine brass*. See Notes on ch. i. 15. Perhaps indicative of majesty and glory as he walked in the midst of the churches.

19. *I know thy works.* See Notes on ch. ii. 2. He knew all they had done, good and bad. ¶ *And charity.* Love; love to God, and love to man. There is no reason for restricting this word here to the comparatively narrow sense which it now bears. Comp. Notes on 1 Co. xiii. 1. ¶ *And service.* Gr., *ministry*—διακονίαν. The word would seem to include all the service which the church had rendered in the cause of religion; all which was the proper fruit of love, or which would be a carrying out of the principles of love to God and man. ¶ *And faith.* Or, fidelity in the cause of the Redeemer. The word here would include not only trust in Christ for salvation, but that which is the proper result of such trust — fidelity in his service. ¶ *And thy patience.* Patient endurance of the sorrows of life—of all that God brought upon them in any way, to test the reality of their religion. ¶ *And thy works.* Thy works as the fruit of the virtues just mentioned. The word is repeated here, from the first part of the verse, perhaps to specify more particularly that their works had been recently more numerous and praiseworthy even than they had formerly been. In the beginning of the verse, as in the commencement of each of the epistles, the word is used, in the most general sense, to denote *all* that they had done; meaning that he had so thorough an acquaintance with them in all respects that he could judge of their character. In the latter part of the verse the word seems to be used in a more specific sense, as referring to *good* works, and with a view to say that they had latterly abounded in these more than they had formerly. ¶ *And the last* to be *more than the first.* Those which had been recently performed were more numerous, and more commendable, than those which had been rendered formerly.

That is, they were making progress; they had been acting more and more in accordance with the nature and claims of the Christian profession. This is a most honourable commendation, and one which every Christian, and every church, should seek. Religion in the soul, and in a community, is designed to be progressive; and while we should seek to live in such a manner always that we may have the commendation of the Saviour, we should regard it as a thing to be greatly desired that we may be approved as making *advances* in knowledge and holiness; that as we grow in years we may grow alike in the disposition to do good, and in the ability to do it; that as we gain in experience, we may also gain in a readiness to apply the results of our experience in promoting the cause of religion. He would deserve little commendation in religion who should be merely stationary; he alone properly develops the nature of true piety, and shows that it has set up its reign in the soul, who is constantly making advances.

20. *Notwithstanding, I have a few things against thee.* Comp. Notes on ver. 4. ¶ *Because thou sufferest that woman Jezebel.* Thou dost tolerate, or countenance her. Comp. Notes on ver. 14. Who the individual here referred to by the name *Jezebel* was, is not known. It is by no means probable that this was her real name, but seems to have been given to her as expressive of her character and influence. Jezebel was the wife of Ahab; a woman of vast influence over her husband—an influence which was uniformly exerted for evil. She was a daughter of Ethbaal, king of Tyre and Sidon, and lived about 918 years before Christ. She was an idolater, and induced her weak husband not only to connive at her introducing the worship of her native idols, but to become an idolater himself, and to use all the means in his power to establish the worship of idols instead of the worship of the true God. She was highly gifted, persuasive, and artful; was resolute in the accomplishment of

and spectacles which they gave to the people in imitation of the Greeks, are said to have thrown among the populace *dice* or *tokens* inscribed with the words, "Frumentum, vestes," &c.; that is, "Corn, clothing," &c.; and whosoever obtained one of these received from the emperor whatever was marked upon it. Others suppose that allusion is made to the mode of casting lots, in which sometimes dice or tokens were used with names inscribed on them, and the lot fell to him whose name first came out. The "*white* stone" was a symbol of good fortune and prosperity; and it is a remarkable circumstance that, among the Greeks, persons of distinguished virtue were said to receive a ψῆφον, *stone*, from the gods, *i.e.*, as an approving testimonial of their virtue. See Robinson's *Lex.*, and the authorities there referred to; Wetstein, N. T., *in loco*, and Stuart, *in loco*. Professor Stuart supposes that the allusion is to the fact that Christians are said to be kings and priests to God, and that as the Jewish high-priest had a mitre or turban, on the front of which was a plate of gold inscribed "Holiness to the Lord," so they who were kings and priests under the Christian dispensation would have that by which they would be known, but that, instead of a plate of gold, they would have a pellucid stone, on which the *name* of the Saviour would be engraved as a token of his favour. It is *possible*, in regard to the explanation of this phrase, that there has been too much effort to find *all* the circumstances alluded to in some ancient custom. Some well-understood fact or custom may have suggested the general thought, and then the filling up may have been applicable to this case alone. It is quite clear, I think, that none of the customs to which it has been supposed there is reference correspond fully with what is stated here, and that though there may have been a general allusion of that kind, yet something of the particularity in the circumstances may be regarded as peculiar to this alone. In accordance with this view, perhaps the following points will embody all that need be said: (1) A white stone was regarded as a token of favour, prosperity, or success everywhere—whether considered as a vote, or as given to a victor, &c. As such, it would denote that the Christian to whom it is said to be given would meet with the favour of the Redeemer, and would have a token of his approval. (2) The name written on this stone would be designed also as a token or pledge of his favour—as a name engraved on a signet or seal would be a pledge to him who received it of friendship. It would be not merely a *white* stone—emblematic of favour and approval—but it would be so *marked* as to indicate its origin, with the name of the giver on it. This would appropriately denote, when explained, that the victor Christian would receive a token of the Redeemer's favour, as if his name were engraven on a stone, and given to him as a pledge of his friendship; that is, that he would be as *certain* of his favour *as if* he had such a stone. In other words, the victor would be assured from the Redeemer, who distributes rewards, that his welfare would be secure. (3) This would be to him *as if* he should receive a stone so marked that its letters were invisible to all others, but apparent to him who received it. It is not needful to suppose that in the Olympic games, or in the prizes distributed by Roman emperors, or in any other custom, such a case had actually occurred, but it is conceivable that a name *might* be so engraved—with characters so small, or in letters so unknown to all others, or with marks so unintelligible to others—that no other one into whose hands it might fall would understand it. The meaning then probably is, that to the true Christian—the victor over sin—there is given some pledge of the divine favour which has to him all the effect of assurance, and which others do not perceive or understand. This consists of favours shown directly to the soul—the evidence of pardoned sin; joy in the Holy Ghost; peace with God; clear views of the Saviour; the possession of a spirit which is properly that of Christ, and which is the gift of God to the soul. The true Christian understands this; the world perceives it not. The Christian receives it as a pledge of the divine favour, and as an evidence that he will be saved; to the world, that on which he relies seems to be enthusiasm, fanaticism, or delusion. The Christian bears it about with him as he would a precious stone given to him by his Redeemer, and on which the name of his Redeemer is engraved, as a pledge that he is accepted of God, and that the rewards of heaven shall be his; the world does not understand it, or attaches no value to it. ¶ *And in the stone a new name written.* A name indicating a *new* relation, new hopes and triumphs. Probably the *name* here referred to is the name of the Redeemer, or the name Christian, or some such appellation. It would be some name which he would understand and appreciate, and which would be a pledge of acceptance. ¶ *Which no man knoweth,* &c. That is, no one would understand its import, as no one but the Christian estimates the value of that on which he relies as the pledge of his Redeemer's love.

### THE EPISTLE TO THE CHURCH AT THYATIRA.

The contents of this epistle (ver. 18–29) are as follows: (1) A reference, as is usual in these epistles, to some attribute of the Saviour which demanded their particular attention, or which was especially appropriate to the nature of the message which he was about to send to them, ver. 18. The attributes which he fixes on here are, that his eyes are like a flame of fire—as if they would pierce and penetrate to the recesses of the heart; and that his feet are like fine brass—perhaps indicative of majesty as he moved among the churches. (2) A statement, in the usual form, that he was entirely acquainted with the church, and that therefore the judgment which he was about to pronounce was founded on a thorough knowledge of what the church was; and a general commendation of them for their charity, service, faith, and patience, ver. 19. (3) A severe reproof of the church, notwithstanding, for their tolerating a teacher of dangerous doctrine, whom he calls Jezebel, with the assurance that she and her children should not go unpunished, ver. 20–23. (4) An assurance to all the rest in Thyatira that no other calamity or burden would come upon the church than what was inevitable in delivering it from the dangerous influence of these doctrines, and a solemn charge to them to hold fast all the truth which they had until he should come, ver. 24, 25. (5) A promise, as usual, to those who should overcome, or who should be victorious, ver. 26–29. They would have power over the nations; they would be associated with the Redeemer in ruling them; they would have the morning star. (6) A call, as usual, on all who had ears to hear, to attend to what the Spirit said to the churches.

Thyatira was a city of Asia Minor, on the northern border of Lydia, and commonly reckoned as belonging to Lydia. It was about twenty-seven miles from Sardis; about a day's journey from Pergamos, and about the same distance from the sea-coast. Its modern name is Ak-hissar, or *the white castle*. According to Pliny, it was known in earlier times by the name of Pelopia (*Hist. Nat.* v. 29). Strabo (xiii. p. 928) says that it was a Macedonian colony. The Roman road from Pergamos to Sardis passed through it. It was noted for the art of dyeing (Ac. xvi. 14), and Luke's account in the Acts has been confirmed by the discovery of an inscription in honour of Antonius Claudius Alphenus, which concludes with the words οἱ βαφεῖς—*the dyers.*

The Rev. Pliny Fisk, the American missionary, who visited the city, thus describes it: "Thyatira is situated near a small river, a branch of the Caicus, in the centre of an extensive plain. At the distance of three or four miles it is almost completely surrounded by mountains. The houses are low; many of them of mud or earth. Excepting the motsellim's palace, there is scarcely a decent house in the place. The streets are narrow and dirty, and everything indicates poverty and degradation. We had a letter of introduction to Economo, the bishop's procurator, and a principal man among the Greeks of this town. . . . He says the Turks have destroyed all remnants of the ancient church; and even the place where it stood is now unknown. At present there are in the town one thousand houses, for which taxes are paid to the government" (*Memoir of the Rev. P. Fisk;* Boston, Mass., 1828).

The following description, by the Rev. Mr. Schneider, missionary of the American Board, will give a correct view of Thyatira, as it existed in 1848: "From Magnesia we proceeded to Thyatira, the site of one of the Apocalyptic churches, now called Ak-hissar. The population consists of about seven hundred Mussulman houses, two hundred and fifty Greek, and fifty Armenian. The town is located in a plain of considerable size, and is hardly visible on being approached, by reason of the profusion of foliage. The plain itself is bounded on all sides by mountains, and

84                     REVELATION.                [A.D. 96.

23 And I will *l*kill her children with death; and *m*all the churches shall know that *n*I am he which searcheth the reins and hearts; and *o*I will give unto every one of you according to your works.

*l* ch.6.8.    *m* Zep.1.11.
*n* 1 Ch.28.9; 2 Ch.6.30; Ps.7.9; Je.17.10.
*o* Ps.62.12.

how almost uniformly is this the case with those who thus live! Sooner or later, sorrow always comes upon the licentious; and God has evinced by some of his severest judgments, in forms of frightful disease, his displeasure at the violation of the laws of purity. There is no sin that produces a more withering and desolating effect upon the soul than that which is here referred to; none which is more certain to be followed with sorrow. ¶ *Except they repent of their deeds.* It is only by repentance that we can avoid the consequences of sin. The word *repent* here evidently includes both sorrow for the past, and abandonment of the evil course of life.

23. *And I will kill her children with death.* A strong Hebraistic mode of expression, meaning that he would certainly destroy them. It has been made a question whether the word *children* here is to be taken literally or figuratively. The word itself would admit of either interpretation; and there is nothing in the connection by which its meaning here can be determined. If it is to be taken literally, it is in accordance with what is often threatened in the Scriptures, that children shall be visited with calamity for the sins of parents, and with what often occurs in fact, that they *do* thus suffer. For it is no uncommon thing that whole families are made desolate on account of the sin and folly of the parent. See Notes on Ro. v. 19. If it is to be taken figuratively, then it refers to those who had imbibed her doctrines, and who, of course, would suffer in the punishment which would follow from the propagation of such doctrines. The reference in the word *death* here would seem to be to some heavy judgment, by plague, famine, or sword, by which they would be cut off. ¶ *And all the churches shall know,* &c. That is, the design of this judgment will be so apparent that it will convince all that I know what is in the hearts of men, even the secret acts of wickedness that are

24 But unto you I say, and unto the rest in Thyatira, as many as have not this doctrine, and which have not known the *p*depths of Satan, as they speak; I will put upon you none other burden.

*p* 2 Th.2.9-12.

concealed from human view. ¶ *I am he which searcheth the reins and hearts.* This is clearly a claim to omniscience; and as it is the Lord Jesus who speaks in all these epistles, it is a full proof that he claims this for himself. There is nothing which more clearly appertains to God than the power of searching the heart, and nothing that is more constantly claimed by him as his peculiar prerogative, 1 Ch. xxviii. 9; Ps. vii. 9; xi. 4; xliv. 21; cxxxix. 2; Pr. xv. 3; Je. xi. 20; xvii. 10; xx. 12; xxxii. 19; He. iv. 13. The word *reins*—νεφροὺς—means, literally, *the kidney,* and is commonly used in the plural to denote the kidneys, or the loins. In the Scriptures it is used to denote the inmost mind, the secrets of the soul; probably because the parts referred to by the word are as *hidden* as any other part of the frame, and would seem to be the repository of the more secret affections of the mind. It is not to be supposed that it is taught in the Scriptures that the reins are the real seat of any of the affections or passions; but there is no more impropriety in using the term in a popular signification than there is in using the word *heart,* which all continue to use, to denote the seat of love. ¶ *And I will give unto every one of you according to your works.* To every one of you; not only to those who have embraced these opinions, but to all the church. This is the uniform rule laid down in the Bible by which God will judge men.

24. *But unto you I say, and unto the rest in Thyatira.* The word—"*and*"—καὶ—is omitted in many MSS. and versions, and in the critical editions of Griesbach, Tittmann, and Hahn, and the connection demands that it should be omitted. As it stands in the received text, it would seem that what he here says was addressed to those who *had* received that doctrine, and to all others as well as to them; whereas the declaration here made pertains manifestly to those who had *not* received the doctrine. With that particle omitted the passage will read, as

21 And I gave her *h*space to repent of her fornication; and *i*she repented not.

*h* Ro.2.4; 2 Pe.3.9.  *i* ch.9.20.

her purposes; ambitious of extending and perpetuating her power, and unscrupulous in the means which she employed to execute her designs. See 1 Ki. xvi. 31, seq. The kind of *character*, therefore, which would be designated by the term as used here, would be that of a woman who was artful and persuasive in her manner; who was capable of exerting a wide influence over others; who had talents of a high order; who was a thorough advocate of error; who was unscrupulous in the means which she employed for accomplishing her ends; and the tendency of whose influence was to lead the people into the abominable practices of idolatry. The opinions which she held, and the practices into which she led others, appear to have been the same which are referred to in ver. 6 and ver. 14, 15 of this chapter. The difference was, that the teacher in this case was a *woman*—a circumstance which by no means lessened the enormity of the offence; for, besides the fact that it was contrary to the whole genius of Christianity that a woman should be a public teacher, there was a special incongruity that she should be an advocate of such abominable opinions and practices. Every sentiment of our nature makes us feel that it is right to expect that if a woman teaches at all in a public manner, she should inculcate only that which is true and holy—she should be an advocate of a pure life. We are shocked; we feel that there is a violation of every principle of our nature, and an insult done to our common humanity, if it is otherwise. We have in a manner become accustomed to the fact that *man* should be a teacher of pollution and error, so that we do not shrink from it with horror; we never can be reconciled to the fact that a *woman* should. ¶ *Which calleth herself a prophetess.* Many persons set up the claim to be prophets in the times when the gospel was first preached, and it is not improbable that many females would lay claim to such a character, after the example of Miriam, Deborah, Huldah, &c. ¶ *To teach and to seduce my servants to commit fornication.* Comp. ver. 14. Whether she herself practised what she taught is not expressly affirmed, but seems to be

22 Behold, *k* I will cast her into a bed, and them that commit adultery with her into great tribulation, except they repent of their deeds.

*k* Eze.16.37; 23.29.

implied in ver. 22. It is not often that persons *teach* these doctrines without practising what they teach; and the fact that they *desire* and *design* to live in this manner will commonly account for the fact that they inculcate such views. ¶ *And to eat things sacrificed unto idols.* See Notes on ver. 14. The custom of attending on the festivals of idols led commonly to licentiousness, and they who were gross and sensual in their lives were fit subjects to be persuaded to attend on idol feasts—for nowhere else would they find more unlimited toleration for the indulgence of their passions.

21. *And I gave her space to repent of her fornication.* Probably after some direct and solemn warning of the evil of her course. The error and sin had been of long standing, but he now resolved to bear with it no longer. It is true of almost every great sinner, that sufficient time is given for repentance, and that vengeance is delayed after crime is committed. But it cannot always be deferred, for the period must arrive when no reason shall exist for longer delay, and when punishment must come upon the offender. ¶ *And she repented not.* As she did not do it; as she showed no disposition to abandon her course; as all plea of having had no time to repent would now be taken away, it was proper that he should rise in his anger and cut her down.

22. *Behold, I will cast her into a bed.* Not into a bed of ease, but a bed of pain. There is evidently a purpose to contrast this with her former condition. The harlot's bed and a sick-bed are thus brought together, as they are often, in fact, in the dispensations of Providence and the righteous judgments of God. One cannot be indulged without leading on, sooner or later, to the horrid sufferings of the other: and how soon no one knows. ¶ *And them that commit adultery with her.* Those who are seduced by her doctrines into this sin; either they who commit it with her literally, or who are led into the same kind of life. ¶ *Into great tribulation.* Great suffering; disease of body or tortures of the soul. How often—

rendered by Professor Stuart, "But I say unto you, the remainder in Thyatira, so many as hold not this doctrine," &c. That is, he addresses now all the members of the church who were not involved in the charges already made. He does not say how large a portion of the church had escaped the contaminating influence of those opinions, but to that portion, whether great or small, he addresses only words of exhortation and comfort. ¶ *As many as have not this doctrine.* To all who have not embraced it, or been contaminated with it. It may be presumed that there was a considerable portion of the church which had not. ¶ *And which have not known the depths of Satan.* The deep art and designs of Satan. Deep things are those which are hidden from view— as of things which are far underground; and hence the word is used to denote mysteries, or profound designs and purposes. The allusion here is not to any *trials* or *sufferings* that Satan might bring upon anyone, or to any temptations of which he might be the author, but to his profound art in inculcating error and leading men astray. There are doctrines of error, and arguments for sin, to originate which seems to lie beyond the power of men, and which would appear almost to have exhausted the talent of Satan himself. They evince such a profound knowledge of man; of the divine government; of the course of events on earth; and of what our race needs; and they are defended with so much eloquence, skill, learning, and subtlety of argumentation, that they appear to lie beyond the compass of the human powers. ¶ *As they speak.* This cannot mean that the defenders of these errors themselves called their doctrines "the depths of Satan," for no teachers would choose so to designate their opinions; but it must mean, either that they who were opposed to those errors characterized them as "the depths of Satan," or that they who opposed them said that *they* had not known "the depths of Satan." Professor Stuart understands it in the latter sense. A somewhat more natural interpretation, it seems to me, however, is to refer it to what the opposers of these heretics said of these errors. They called them "the depths of Satan," and they professed not to have known anything of them. The meaning, perhaps, would be expressed by the familiar words, "as they say," or "as they call them," in the following manner: "As many as have not known the depths of Satan, as they say," or, "to use their own language." Doddridge paraphrases it, "as they proverbially speak." Tyndale incloses it in a parenthesis. ¶ *I will put upon you none other burden.* That is, no other than that which you now experience from having these persons with you, and that which must attend the effort to purify the church. He had not approved their conduct for suffering these persons to remain in the church, and he threatens to punish all those who had become contaminated with these pernicious doctrines. He evidently designed to say that there was *some* token of his displeasure proper in the case, but he was not disposed to bring upon them any *other* expression of his displeasure than that which grew naturally and necessarily out of the fact that they had been tolerated among them, and those troubles and toils which must attend the effort to deliver the church from these errors. Under any circumstances the church must suffer. It would suffer in reputation. It would suffer in respect to its internal tranquillity. Perhaps, also, there were those who were implicated in these errors, and who would be implicated in the punishment, who had friends and kindred in the church; and the judgments which were to come upon the advocates of these errors must, therefore, come in a measure upon the church. A kind Saviour says, that he would bring upon them no other and no weightier burden, than *must* arise from his purpose to inflict appropriate vengeance on the guilty themselves. The trouble which would grow out of that would be a sufficient expression of his displeasure. This is, in fact, often now all that is necessary as a punishment on a church for harbouring the advocates of error and of sin. The church has trouble enough ultimately in getting rid of them; and the injury which such persons do to its piety, peace, and reputation, and the disorders of which they are the cause, constitute a sufficient punishment for having tolerated them in its bosom. Often the most severe punishment that God can bring upon men is to "lay upon them no other burden" than to leave them to the inevitable consequences of their own folly, or to the trouble and vexation incident to the effort to free themselves

86          REVELATION.          [A.D. 96.

25 But *that which ye have *already* hold fast till I come.

26 And *r* he that overcometh, and keepeth *s* my works unto the end, to him will I give power over the nations:

27 And *t* he shall rule them with a rod of iron; as the vessels of a potter shall they be *u* broken to shivers: even as I received of my Father.

28 And I will give him *v* the morning star.

29 He that hath an ear, let him hear what the Spirit saith unto the churches.

*q* ch.3.11.    *r* ver.7,11,17; ch.3.5,12,21; 21.7.
*s* Jn.6.29; Ja.2.20.    *t* Ps.49.14; 149.5-9.
*u* Ps.2.9.    *v* ch.22.16.

from what they had for a long time tolerated or practised.

25. *But that which ye have,* &c. All that there is of truth and purity remaining among you, retain faithfully. Comp. ch. iii. 11. ¶ *Till I come.* To receive you to myself, Jn. xiv. 3.

26. *And he that overcometh.* Notes on ch. ii. 7. ¶ *And keepeth my works unto the end.* The works that I command and that I require, to the end of his life. Comp. Jn. xiii. 1. ¶ *To him will I give power over the nations.* The evident meaning of what is said here, and in the next verse, is, that in accordance with the uniform promise made to the redeemed in the New Testament, they would partake of the final triumph and glory of the Saviour, and be associated with him. It is not said that they would have exclusive power over the nations, or that they would hold offices of trust under him during a personal reign on the earth; but the meaning is, that they would be associated with him in his future glory. Comp. Notes on Ro. viii. 17; 1 Co. vi. 2, 3.

27. *And he shall rule them with a rod of iron.* There is an allusion here to Ps. ii. 9: "Thou shalt break them with a rod of iron; thou shalt dash them in pieces like a potter's vessel." There is a slight change in the passage, "he shall *rule,*" instead of "thou shalt *break,*" in order to adapt the language to the purpose of the speaker here. The allusion in the Psalm is to the Messiah as reigning triumphant over the nations, or subduing them under him; and the idea here, as in the previous verse, is, that his redeemed people will be associated with him in this dominion. To rule with a sceptre of iron, is not to rule with a harsh and tyrannical sway, but with power that is firm and invincible. It denotes a government of strength, or one that cannot be successfully opposed; one in which the subjects are effectually subdued. ¶ *As the vessels of a potter shall they be broken to shivers.* The image here is that of the vessel of a potter—a fragile vessel of clay—struck with a rod of iron and broken into fragments. That is, as applied to the nations, there would be no power to oppose his rule; the enemies of his government would be destroyed. Instead of remaining firm and compacted together, they would be broken like the clay vessel of a potter when struck with a rod of iron. The speaker does not intimate *when* this would be; but all that is said here would be applicable to that time when the Son of God will come to judge the world, and when his saints will be associated with him in his triumphs. As, in respect to all the others of the seven epistles to the churches, the rewards promised refer to heaven, and to the happy state of that blessed world, it would seem also that this should have a similar reference, for there is no reason why "to him that overcame" in Thyatira a temporal reward and triumph should be promised more than in the cases of the others. If so, then this passage should not be adduced as having any reference to an imaginary personal reign of the Saviour and of the saints on the earth. ¶ *Even as I received of my Father.* As he has appointed me, Ps. ii. 6-9.

28. *And I will give him the morning star.* The "morning star" is that bright planet—Venus—which at some seasons of the year appears so beautifully in the east, leading on the morning —the harbinger of the day. It is one of the most beautiful objects in nature, and is susceptible of a great variety of uses for illustration. It appears as the darkness passes away; it is an indication that the morning comes; it is intermingled with the first rays of the light of the sun; it seems to be a herald to announce the coming of that glorious luminary; it is a pledge of the faithfulness of God. In which of these senses, if any, it is referred to here, is not stated; nor is it said what is implied by its being *given* to him that

overcomes. It would seem to be used here to denote a bright and brilliant ornament; something with which he who "overcame" would be adorned, resembling the bright star of the morning. It is observable that it is not said that he would *make* him *like* the morning star, as in Da. xii. 3; nor that he would be compared with the morning star, like the king of Babylon, Is. xiv. 12; nor that he would resemble a star which Balaam says he saw in the distant future, Nu. xxiv. 17. The idea seems to be, that the Saviour would give him something that would resemble that morning planet in beauty and splendour—perhaps meaning that it would be placed as a gem in his diadem, and would sparkle on his brow —bearing some such relation to him who is called " the Sun of Righteousness," as the morning star does to the glorious sun on his rising. If so, the meaning would be that he would receive a beautiful ornament, bearing a near relation to the Redeemer himself as a bright sun—a pledge that the darkness was past—but one whose beams would melt away into the superior light of the Redeemer himself, as the beams of the morning star are lost in the superior glory of the sun.

29. *He that hath an ear,* &c. See Notes on ver. 7.

## CHAPTER III.

### THE EPISTLE TO THE CHURCH AT SARDIS.

The contents of the epistle to the church at Sardis (ver. 1-6) are: (1) The usual salutation to the angel of the church, ver. 1. (2) The usual reference to the attributes of the Saviour—those referred to here being that he had the seven Spirits of God, and the seven stars, ver. 1. (3) The assurance that he knew their works, ver. 1. (4) The statement of the peculiarity of the church, or what he saw in it—that it had a name to live and was dead, ver. 1. (5) A solemn direction to the members of the church, arising from their character and circumstances, to be watchful, and to strengthen the things which remained, but which were ready to die; to remember what they had received, and to hold fast that which had been communicated to them, and to repent of all their sins, ver. 2, 3. (6) A threat that if they did not do this, he would come suddenly upon them, at an hour which they could not anticipate, ver. 3. (7) A commendation of the church as far as it could be done, for there were still a few among them who had not defiled their garments, and a promise that they should walk before him in white, ver. 4. (8) A promise, as usual, to him that should be victorious. The promise here is, that he should walk before him in white; that his name should not be blotted out of the book of life; that he should be acknowledged before the Father, and before the angels, ver. 5. (9) The usual call on all persons to hear what the Spirit said to the churches.

Sardis was the capital of the ancient kingdom of Lydia, one of the provinces of Asia Minor, and was situated at the foot of Mount Tmolus, in a fine plain watered by the river Pactolus, famous for its golden sands. It was the capital where the celebrated Crœsus, proverbial for his wealth, reigned. It was taken by Cyrus (B.C. 548), when Crœsus was king, and was at that time one of the most splendid and opulent cities of the East. It subsequently passed into the hands of the Romans, and under them sank rapidly in wealth and importance. In the time of Tiberius it was destroyed by an earthquake, but was rebuilt by order of the emperor. The inhabitants of Sardis bore an ill repute among the ancients for their voluptuous modes of life. *Perhaps* there may be an allusion to this fact in the words which are used in the address to the church there: "Thou hast a few names *even in Sardis* which have not defiled their garments." Successive earthquakes, and the ravages of the Saracens and the Turks, have reduced this once-celebrated city to a heap of ruins, though exhibiting still many remains of former splendour. The name of the village which now occupies the place of this ancient capital is Sart. It is a miserable village, comprising only a few wretched cottages, occupied by Turks and Greeks. There are ruins of the theatre, the stadium, and of some ancient churches. The most remarkable of the ruins are two pillars supposed to have belonged to the temple of Cybele; and if so, they are among the most ancient in the world, the temple of Cybele having been built only three hundred years after that of Solomon. The Acropolis serves well to define the site of the city. Several travellers have recently visited the remains of Sardis, and its appearance will be indicated by a few extracts from their writings. Arundell, in his *Discoveries*

## CHAPTER III.

AND unto the angel of the church in Sardis write; These things saith he that hath the [a]seven

*a* ch.5.6.

Spirits of God, and the seven stars; [b]I know thy works, that thou hast [c]a name that thou livest, and art dead.

*b* ch.2.2,&c.     *c* 1 Ti.5.6.

*in Asia Minor*, says: "If I were asked what impresses the mind most strongly in beholding Sardis, I should say its indescribable *solitude*, like the darkness of Egypt—darkness that could be *felt*. So the deep solitude of the spot, once the 'lady of kingdoms,' produces a corresponding feeling of *desolate abandonment* in the mind, which can never be forgotten."

The Rev. J. Hartley, in regard to these ruins, remarks: "The ruins are, with one exception, more entirely gone to decay than those of most of the ancient cities which we have visited. No Christians reside on the spot: two Greeks only work in a mill here, and a few wretched Turkish huts are scattered among the ruins. We saw the churches of St. John and the Virgin, the theatre, and the building styled the Palace of Crœsus; but the most striking object at Sardis is the temple of Cybele. I was filled with wonder and awe at beholding the two stupendous columns of this edifice, which are still remaining: they are silent but impressive witnesses of the power and splendour of antiquity."

The impression produced on the mind is vividly described in the following language of a recent traveller, who lodged there for a night: "Every object was as distinct as in a northern twilight; the snowy summit of the mountain [Tmolus], the long sweep of the valley, and the flashing current of the river [Pactolus]. I strolled along towards the banks of the Pactolus, and seated myself by the side of the half-exhausted stream.

"There are few individuals who cannot trace on the map of their memory some moments of overpowering emotion, and some scene, which, once dwelt upon, has become its own painter, and left behind it a memorial that time could not efface. I can readily sympathize with the feelings of him who wept at the base of the pyramids; nor were my own less powerful, on that night when I sat beneath the sky of Asia to gaze upon *the ruins of Sardis*, from the banks of the golden-sanded Pactolus. Beside me were the cliffs of the Acropolis, which, centuries before, the hardy Median scaled, while leading on the conquering Persians, whose tents had covered the very spot on which I was reclining. Before me were the vestiges of what had been the palace of the gorgeous Crœsus; within its walls were once congregated the wisest of mankind, Thales, Cleobulus, and Solon. It was here that the wretched father mourned alone the mangled corse of his beloved Atys; it was here that the same humiliated monarch wept at the feet of the Persian boy who wrung from him his kingdom. Far in the distance were the gigantic *tumuli* of the Lydian monarchs, Candaules, Halyattys, and Gyges; and around them were spread those very plains once trodden by the countless hosts of Xerxes, when hurrying on to find a sepulchre at Marathon.

"There were more varied and more vivid remembrances associated with the sight of Sardis than could possibly be attached to any other spot of earth; but all were mingled with a feeling of disgust at the littleness of human glory. All—all had passed away! There were before me the fanes of a dead religion, the tombs of forgotten monarchs, and the palm-tree that waved in the banquet-hall of kings; while the feeling of desolation was doubly heightened by the calm sweet sky above me, which, in its unfading brightness, shone as purely now as when it beamed upon the golden dreams of Crœsus" (Emerson's *Letters from the Ægean*, p. 113, seq.). The present appearance of the ruins is shown by the engraving in this volume.

1. *And unto the angel of the church in Sardis.* Notes on ch. i. 20. ¶ *These things saith he that hath the seven Spirits of God.* See Notes on ch. i. 4. If the phrase, "the seven Spirits of God," as there supposed, refers to the Holy Spirit, there is great propriety in saying of the Saviour, that he has that Spirit, inasmuch as the Holy Spirit is represented as sent forth by him into the world, Jn. xv. 26, 27; xvi. 7, 13, 14. It was one of the highest characteristics that could be given of the Saviour to say, that the Holy Ghost was his to send forth into the world, and that that great Agent, on whose gracious influences all were dependent for the possession of true religion, could

A.D. 96.]  CHAPTER III.  89

2 Be watchful and <sup>d</sup>strengthen the things which remain, that are ready to die: for I have not found thy works <sup>e</sup>perfect before God.

3 Remember<sup>f</sup> therefore how

d ch.2.5.  e Da.5.27.  f He.2.1.

be given or withheld by him at his pleasure. ¶ *And the seven stars.* See Notes on ch. i. 16. These represented the angels of the seven churches (Notes on ch. i. 20); and the idea which the Saviour would seem to intend to convey here is, that he had entire control over the ministers of the churches, and could keep or remove them at pleasure. ¶ *I know thy works.* See Notes on ch. ii. 2. ¶ *That thou hast a name that thou livest.* Thou dost profess attachment to me and my cause. The word *life* is a word that is commonly employed, in the New Testament, to denote religion, in contradistinction from the natural state of man, which is described as *death* in sin. By the profession of religion they expressed the purpose to live unto God, and for another world; they professed to have true, spiritual life. ¶ *And art dead.* That is, spiritually. This is equivalent to saying that their profession was merely *in name;* and yet this must be understood comparatively, for there were some even in Sardis who truly lived unto God, ver. 4. The meaning is, that in general, the profession of religion among them was a mere name. The Saviour does not, as in the case of the churches of Ephesus and Thyatira, specify any prevailing form of error or false doctrine; but it would seem that here it was a simple *want* of religion.

2. *Be watchful.* Be wakeful; be attentive and earnest—in contradistinction from the drowsy condition of the church. ¶ *Strengthen the things which remain.* The true piety that still lives and lingers among you. Whatever there was of religion among them, it was of importance to strengthen it, that the love of the Saviour might not become wholly extinct. An important duty in a low and languishing state of religion is, to "strengthen the things that still survive." It is to cultivate all the graces which do exist; to nourish all the love of truth which may linger in the church; and to confirm, by warm exhortation, and by a reference to the gracious promises of God's word, the few who may be endeavouring to do their duty, and who, amidst many discouragements, are aiming to be faithful to the Saviour. In the lowest state of religion in a church there may be a few, perhaps quite obscure and of humble rank, who are mourning over the desolations of Zion, and who are sighing for better times. All such it is the duty of the ministers of religion to comfort and encourage; for it is in their hearts that piety may be kept alive in the church—it is through them that it may be hoped religion may yet be revived. In the apparent hopelessness of doing much good to others, good may always be done to the cause itself by preserving and strengthening what there may be of life among those few, amidst the general desolation and death. It is much to preserve life in grain sown in a field through the long and dreary winter, when all seems to be dead—for it will burst forth, with new life and beauty, in the spring. When the body is prostrate with disease, and life just lingers, and death seems to be coming on, it is much to preserve the little strength that remains; much to keep the healthful parts from being invaded, that there may be strength yet to recover. ¶ *That are ready to die.* That seem just ready to become extinct. So, sometimes, in a plant, there seems to be but the least conceivable life remaining, and it appears that it must die. So, when we are sick, there seems to be but the feeblest glimmering of life, and it is apparently just ready to go out. So, when a fire dies away, there seems but a spark remaining, and it is just ready to become extinct. And thus, in religion in the soul—religion in a church—religion in a community—it often seems as if it were just about to go out for ever. ¶ *For I have not found thy works perfect before God.* I have not found them *complete* or *full.* They come short of that which is required. Of what church, of what individual Christian, is not this true? Whom might not the Saviour approach with the same language? It was true, however, in a marked and eminent sense, of the church at Sardis.

3. *Remember therefore how thou hast received.* This may refer either to some peculiarity in the manner in which the gospel was conveyed to them—as, by the labours of the apostles, and by

thou hast received and heard; and hold fast, and *repent.* If therefore thou shalt not watch, I will come on thee *as a thief, and thou

*g* ver.19.  *h* ch.16.15.

the remarkable effusions of the Holy Spirit; or to the ardour and love with which they embraced it; or to the greatness of the favours and privileges conferred on them; or to their own understanding of what the gospel required, when they were converted. It is not possible to determine in which sense the language is used; but the general idea is plain, that there was something marked and unusual in the way in which they had been led to embrace the gospel, and that it was highly proper in these circumstances to look back to the days when they gave themselves to Christ. It is always well for Christians to call to remembrance the "day of their espousals," and their views and feelings when they gave their hearts to the Saviour, and to compare those views with their present condition, especially if their conversion was marked by anything unusual. ¶ *And heard.* How thou didst hear the gospel in former times; that is, with what earnestness and attention thou didst embrace it. This would rather seem to imply that the reference in the whole passage is to the fact that they embraced the gospel with great ardour and zeal. ¶ *And hold fast.* (1) Hold fast the truths which thou didst then receive; (2) hold fast what remains of true religion among you. ¶ *And repent.* Repent in regard to all that in which you have departed from your views and feelings when you embraced the gospel. ¶ *If therefore thou shalt not watch.* The speaker evidently supposed that it was possible that they would not regard the warning; that they would presume that they would be safe if they refused to give heed to it, or that by mere inattention and indifference they might suffer the warning to pass by unheeded. Similar results have been so common in the world as to make such a supposition not improbable, and to make proper, in other cases as well as that, the solemn threatening that he would come suddenly upon them. ¶ *I will come on thee as a thief.* In a sudden and unexpected manner. See Notes on 1 Th. v. 2. ¶ *And ye shall not know*

shalt not know what hour I will come upon thee.

4 Thou hast a few names even in Sardis which have not defiled their

*what hour I will come upon thee.* You shall not know beforehand; you shall have no warning of my immediate approach. This is often the way in which God comes to men in his heavy judgments. Long beforehand, he admonishes us, indeed, of what must be the consequences of a course of sin, and warns us to turn from it; but when sinners refuse to attend to his warning, and still walk in the way of evil, he comes suddenly, and cuts them down. Every man who is warned of the evil of his course, and who refuses or neglects to repent, has reason to believe that God will come suddenly in his wrath, and call him to his bar, Pr. xxix. 1. No such man can presume on impunity; no one who is warned of his guilt and danger can feel that he is for one moment safe. No one can have any basis of calculation that he will be spared; no one can flatter himself with any probable anticipation that he will have time to repent when God comes to take him away. Benevolence has done its appropriate work in warning him—how can the Great Judge of all be to blame, if he comes then, and suddenly cuts the sinner off?

4. *Thou hast a few names even in Sardis.* See the analysis of the chapter. The word *names* here is equivalent to *persons;* and the idea is, that even in a place so depraved, and where religion had so much declined, there were a few persons who had kept themselves free from the general contamination. In most cases, when error and sin prevail, there may be found a few who are worthy of the divine commendation; a few who show that true religion may exist even when the mass are evil. Comp. Notes on Ro. xi. 4. ¶ *Which have not defiled their garments.* Comp. Notes on Jude 23. The meaning is, that they had not defiled themselves by coming in contact with the profane and the polluted; or, in other words, they had kept themselves free from the prevailing corruption. They were like persons clothed in white walking in the midst of the defiled, yet keeping their raiment from being soiled. ¶ *And they shall walk with me in white.* White is the emblem of innocence, and is hence

garments; and they shall walk with me *i* in white: for they are worthy.

5 He that overcometh, the same shall be clothed in white raiment; and I will not blot out his name out of the *k* book of life, but I will *l* confess his name before my Father, and before his angels.

6 He that hath an ear, let him hear what the Spirit saith unto the churches.

*i* ch.7.9; 19.8.　　　　*k* ch.17.8.　　*l* Lu.12.8.

appropriately represented as the colour of the raiment of the heavenly inhabitants. The persons here referred to had kept their garments uncontaminated on the earth, and as an appropriate reward it is said that they would appear in white raiment in heaven. Comp. ch. vii. 9; xix. 8. ¶ *For they are worthy.* They have shown themselves worthy to be regarded as followers of the Lamb; or, they have a character that is fitted for heaven. The declaration is not that they have any *claim* to heaven on the ground of their own merit, or that it will be in virtue of their own works that they will be received there; but that there is a *fitness* or *propriety* that they should thus appear in heaven. We are all personally unworthy to be admitted to heaven, but we may evince such a character as to show that, according to the arrangements of grace, it is *fit* and *proper* that we should be received there. We have the character to which God has promised eternal life.

5. *He that overcometh.* See Notes on ch. ii. 7. ¶ *The same shall be clothed in white raiment.* Whosoever he may be that shall overcome sin and the temptations of this world, shall be admitted to this glorious reward. The promise is made not only to those in Sardis who should be victorious, but to all in every age and every land. The hope that is thus held out before us, is that of appearing with the Redeemer in his kingdom, clad in robes expressive of holiness and joy. ¶ *And I will not blot out his name out of the book of life.* The book which contains the names of those who are to live with him for ever. The names of his people are thus represented as enrolled in a book which he keeps—a register of those who are to live for ever. The phrase "book of life" frequently occurs in the Bible, representing this idea. See Notes on Phi. iv. 3. Comp. Re. xv. 3; xx. 12, 15; xxi. 27; xxii. 19. The expression "I will not blot out" means, that the names would be found there on the great day of final account, and would be found there for ever. It may be remarked, that as no one can have access to that book but he who keeps it, there is the most positive assurance that it will never be done, and the salvation of the redeemed will be, therefore, secure. And let it be remembered that the period is coming when it will be felt to be a higher honour to have the name enrolled in that book than in the books of heraldry —in the most splendid catalogue of princes, poets, warriors, nobles, or statesmen that the world has produced. ¶ *But I will confess his name,* &c. I will acknowledge him to be my follower. See Notes on Mat. x. 32.

6. *He that hath an ear,* &c. See Notes on ch. ii. 7.

THE EPISTLE TO THE CHURCH IN PHILADELPHIA.

This epistle (ver. 7-13) comprises the following subjects: (1) The usual address to the angel of the church, ver. 7. (2) The reference to some attribute or characteristic of the speaker, ver. 7. He here addresses the church as one who is holy and true; as he who has the key of David, and who can shut and no one can open, and open and no one can shut. The representation is that of one who occupies a royal palace, and who can admit or exclude anyone whom he pleases. The reference to such a palace is continued through the epistle. (3) The usual declaration that he knows their works, and that he has found that they had strength, though but a little, and had kept his word, ver. 8. (4) A declaration that he would constrain some who professed that they were Jews, but who were of the synagogue of Satan, to come and humble themselves before them, ver. 9. (5) The particular promise to that church. He would keep them in the hour of temptation that was coming to try all that dwelt upon the earth, ver. 10. (6) The command addressed to them as to the other churches. He solemnly enjoins it on them to see that no one should take their crown, or deprive them of the reward which he would give to his faithful followers,

7 And to the angel of the church in Philadelphia write; These things saith ᵐhe that is holy, ⁿhe that is true, ᵒhe that hath the key of David, he that openeth, and no man shutteth; and ᵖshutteth, and no man openeth;

m Ac.3.14.　　n 1 Jn.5.20.　　o Is.22.22.

p Job 12.14.

ver. 11. (7) A general promise, in view of the circumstances in Philadelphia, to *all* who should overcome, ver. 12. They would be made a pillar in the temple of God, and go no more out. They would have written on themselves the name of his God, and the name of the holy city—showing that they were inhabitants of the heavenly world. (8) The usual call on all to attend to what was said to the churches, ver. 13.

Philadelphia stood about twenty-five miles south-east from Sardis, in the plain of Hermus, and about midway between the river of that name and the termination of Mount Tmolus. It was the second city in Lydia, and was built by King Attalus Philadelphus, from whom it received its name. In the year 133 B.C. the place passed, with the country in the vicinity, under the dominion of the Romans. The site is reported by Strabo to be liable to earthquakes, but it continued to be a place of importance down to the Byzantine age; and, of all the towns in Asia Minor, it withstood the Turks the longest. It was taken by Bajazat, A.D. 1392. "It still exists as a Turkish town, under the name of Allah Shehr, 'City of God,' *i.e.* the 'High Town.' It covers a considerable extent of ground, running up the slopes of four hills, or rather of one hill with four flat summits. The country, as viewed from these hills, is extremely magnificent—gardens and vineyards lying at the back and sides of the town, and before it one of the most beautiful and extensive plains of Asia. The missionaries Fisk and Parsons were informed by the Greek bishop that the town contained 3000 houses, of which he assigned 250 to the Greeks, and the rest to the Turks. On the same authority it is stated that there are five churches in the town, besides twenty others which were too old or too small for use. Six minarets, indicating as many mosques, are seen in the town, and one of these mosques is believed by the native Christians to have been the church in which assembled the primitive Christians addressed in the Apocalypse. There are few ruins; but in one part are four pillars, which are supposed to have been columns of a church. One solitary pillar has been often noticed, as reminding beholders of the remarkable words in the Apocalypse—'Him that overcometh I will make *a pillar* in the temple of my God'" (*Kitto's Encyclo.* See also the *Missionary Herald* for 1821, p. 253; 1839, pp. 210-212). The town is the seat of a Greek archbishop, with about twenty inferior clergy. The streets are narrow, and are described as remarkably filthy. The engraving in this volume will give a representation of the town as it now appears.

7. *And to the angel of the church in Philadelphia.* See Notes on ch. i. 20. ¶ *These things saith he that is holy.* This refers undoubtedly to the Lord Jesus. The appellation *holy*, or *the holy one*, is one that befits him, and is not unfrequently given to him in the New Testament, Lu. i. 35; Ac. ii. 27; iii. 14. It is not only an appellation appropriate to the Saviour, but well adapted to be employed when he is addressing the churches. Our impression of what is said to us will often depend much on our idea of the character of him who addresses us, and solemnity and thoughtfulness always become us when we are addressed by a holy Redeemer. ¶ *He that is true.* Another characteristic of the Saviour well fitted to be referred to when he addresses men. It is a characteristic often ascribed to him in the New Testament (Jn. i. 9, 14, 17; viii. 40, 45; xiv. 6; xviii. 37; 1 Jn. v. 20), and one which is eminently adapted to impress the mind with solemn thought in view of the fact that he is to pronounce on our character, and to determine our destiny. ¶ *He that hath the key of David.* This expression is manifestly taken from Is. xxii. 22, "And the key of the house of David will I lay upon his shoulder." See the passage explained in the Notes on that place. As used by Isaiah, the phrase is applied to Eliakim; and it is not to be inferred, because the language here is applied to the Lord Jesus, that originally it had any such reference. "The application of the same terms," says Professor Alexander on Is. xxii. 22, "to Peter (Mat. xvi. 19), and to Christ himself (Re. iii. 7), does not

A.D. 96.]   CHAPTER III.   93

8 I know thy works: behold, I have set before thee an *q* open door, and no man can shut it: for thou hast a little strength, and hast kept my word, and hast not denied my name.

*q* 1 Co. 16. 9.

prove that they here refer to either, or that Eliakim was a type of Christ, but merely that the same words admit of different applications." The language is that which properly denotes authority or control—as when one has the key of a house, and has unlimited access to it; and the meaning here is, that as David is represented as the king of Israel residing in a palace, so he who had the key to that palace had *regal authority.* ¶ *He that openeth, and no man shutteth,* &c. He has free and unrestrained access to the house; the power of admitting anyone, or of excluding anyone. Applied here to the Saviour, as king in Zion, this means that in his kingdom he has the absolute control in regard to the admission or exclusion of anyone. He can prescribe the terms; he can invite whom he chooses; he can exclude those whom he judges should not be admitted. A reference to this absolute control was every way proper when he was addressing a church, and is every way proper for us to reflect on when we think of the subject of our personal salvation.

8. *I know thy works.* See Notes on ch. ii. 2. ¶ *Behold, I have set before thee an open door.* Referring to his authority as stated in ver. 7. The "open door" here evidently refers to the enjoyment of some privilege or honour; and, so far as the *language* is concerned, it may refer to any one of the following things: either, (1) the ability to do good—represented as the "opening of the door." Comp. Ac. xiv. 27; 1 Co. xvi. 9; 2 Co. ii. 12; Col. iv. 3. (2) The privilege of access to the heavenly palace; that is, that they had an abundant opportunity of securing their salvation, the door being never closed against them by day or by night. Comp. Re. xxi. 25. Or (3) it may mean that they had before them an open way of egress from danger and persecution. This latter Professor Stuart supposes to be the true meaning; and argues this because it is immediately specified that those Jewish persecutors would be made to humble themselves, and that the church would but lightly experience the troubles which were coming upon the world around them. But the more natural interpretation of the phrase "an open door" is that it refers to access *to* a thing rather than egress *from* a thing; that we may come to that which we desire to approach, rather than escape from that which we dread. There is no objection, it seems to me, to the supposition that the language may be used here in the largest sense—as denoting that, in regard to the church at Philadelphia, there was no restraint. He had given them the most unlimited privileges. The temple of salvation was thrown open to them; the celestial city was accessible; the whole world was before them as a field of usefulness, and anywhere, and everywhere, they might do good, and at all times they might have access to the kingdom of God. ¶ *And no man can shut it.* No one has the power of preventing this, for he who has control over all things concedes these privileges to you. ¶ *For thou hast a little strength.* This would imply that they had not *great* vigour, but still that, notwithstanding there were so many obstacles to their doing good, and so many temptations to evil, there still remained with them some degree of energy. They were not wholly dead; and as long as that was the case, the door was still open for them to do good. The words "little strength" may refer either to the smallness of the *number*—meaning that they were few; or it may refer to the spiritual life and energy of the church—meaning that, though feeble, their vital energy was not wholly gone. The more natural interpretation seems to be to refer it to the latter; and the sense is, that although they had not the highest degree of energy, or had not all that the Saviour desired they should have, they were not *wholly* dead. The Saviour saw among them the evidences of spiritual life; and in view of that he says he had set before them an open door, and there was abundant opportunity to employ all the energy and zeal which they had. It may be remarked that the same thing is true now; that wherever there is *any* vitality in a church, the Saviour will furnish ample opportunity that it may be employed in his service. ¶ *And hast not denied my name.* When Christians were brought before heathen magistrates in times of persecution, they were required to re-

9 Behold, I will make them of the synagogue of Satan, which *r*say they are Jews, and are not, but do lie; behold, I will make them to *s*come and worship before thy

*r* ch.2.9.   *s* Is.60.14.

10 Because thou hast kept the word of my patience, *t* I also will keep thee from the hour of tempta-

*t* 2 Pe.2.9.

nounce the name of Christ, and to disown him in a public manner. It is possible that, amidst the persecutions that raged in the early times, the members of the church at Philadelphia had been summoned to such a trial, and they had stood the trial firmly. It would seem from the following verse, that the efforts which had been made to induce them to renounce the name of Christ had been made by those who professed to be Jews, though they evinced the spirit of Satan. If so, then the attempt was probably to convince them that Jesus was not the Christ. This attempt would be made in all places where there were Jews.

9. *Behold, I will make.* Greek, "I give"— διδωμι; that is, I will arrange matters so that this shall occur. The word implies that he had power to do this, and consequently proves that he has power over the heart of man, and can secure such a result as he chooses. ¶ *Them of the synagogue of Satan, which say they are Jews.* Who profess to be Jews, but are really of the synagogue of Satan. See Notes on ch. ii. 9. The meaning is, that, though they were of Jewish extraction, and boasted much of being Jews, yet they were really under the influence of Satan, and their assemblages deserved to be called his "synagogue." ¶ *And are not, but do lie.* It is a false profession altogether. Comp. Notes on 1 Jn. i. 6. ¶ *Behold, I will make them to come and worship before thy feet.* The word rendered *worship* here, means, properly, *to fall prostrate;* and then to do homage, or to worship in the proper sense, as this was commonly done by falling prostrate. See Notes on Mat. ii. 2. So far as the *word* is concerned, it may refer either to spiritual homage, that is, the worship of God; or it may mean respect as shown to superiors. If it is used here in the sense of divine worship properly so called, it means that they would be constrained to come and worship "*before* them," or in their very presence; if it is used in the more general signification, it means that they would be constrained to show them honour and respect. The latter is the probable meaning; that is, that they would be constrained to acknowledge that they were the children of God, or that God regarded them with his favour. It does not mean necessarily that they would themselves be converted to Christ, but that, as they had been accustomed to revile and oppose those who were true Christians, they would be constrained to come and render them the respect due to those who were sincerely endeavouring to serve their Maker. The *truth* taught here is, that it is in the power of the Lord Jesus so to turn the hearts of all the enemies of religion that they shall be brought to show respect to it; so to incline the minds of all people that they shall honour the church, or be at least outwardly its friends. Such homage the world shall yet be constrained to pay to it. ¶ *And to know that I have loved thee.* This explains what he had just said, and shows that he means that the enemies of his church will yet be constrained to acknowledge that it enjoys the smiles of God, and that instead of being persecuted and reviled, it should be respected and loved.

10. *Because thou hast kept the word of my patience.* My word commanding or enjoining patience; that is, thou hast manifested the patience which I require. They had shown this in the trials which they had experienced; he promises now, that in return he will keep them in the future trials that shall come upon the world. One of the highest rewards of patience in one trial is the grace that God gives us to bear another. The fact that we *have been* patient and submissive may be regarded as proof that he will give us grace that we *may be* patient and submissive in the trials that are to come. God does not leave those who have shown that they will not leave him. ¶ *I also will keep thee.* That is, I will so keep you that you shall not sink under the trials which will prove a severe temptation to many. This does not mean that they would be actually kept from calamity of all kinds, but that they would be kept from the *temptation of apostasy* in calamity. He

## CHAPTER III.

tion, which shall come upon all the world, to try them that dwell upon the earth.

11 Behold, *u* I come *v* quickly: hold that fast which thou hast, that no man take thy crown.

*u* Zep.1.14.   *v* ver.3.

12 Him that overcometh will I make a pillar in the temple of my God; and he shall go no more out: and I will write upon him the name of my God, and the name of the city of my God, *which is w* New

*w* ch.21.2,10.

would give them grace to bear up under trials with a Christian spirit, and in such a manner that their salvation should not be endangered. ¶ *From the hour of temptation.* The season; the time; the period of temptation. You shall be so kept that that which will prove to be a time of temptation to so many, shall not endanger your salvation. Though others fall, you shall not; though you may be afflicted with others, yet you shall have grace to sustain you. ¶ *Which shall come upon all the world.* The phrase here used — "*all the world*"—may either denote the whole world; or the whole Roman empire; or a large district of country; or the land of Judæa. See Notes on Lu. ii. 1. Here, perhaps, all that is implied is, that the trial would be very *extensive* or *general*—so much so as to embrace the *world*, as the word was understood by those to whom the epistle was addressed. It need not be supposed that the whole world literally was included in it, or even all the Roman empire, but what was the world to them — the region which they would embrace in that term. If there were some far-spreading calamity in the country where they resided, it would probably be all that would be fairly embraced in the meaning of the word. It is not known to what trial the speaker refers. It may have been some form of persecution, or it may have been some calamity by disease, earthquake, or famine that was to occur. Tacitus (see Wetstein, *in loco*) mentions an earthquake that sank twelve cities in Asia Minor, in one night, by which, among others, Philadelphia was deeply affected; and it is *possible* that there may have been reference here to that overwhelming calamity. But nothing can be determined with certainty in regard to this. ¶ *To try them that dwell upon the earth.* To test their character. It would rather seem from this that the affliction was some form of persecution as adapted to test the fidelity of those who were affected by it. The persecutions in the Roman empire would furnish abundant occasions for such a trial.

11. *Behold, I come quickly.* That is, in the trials referred to. Comp. Notes on ch. i. 1, 11, 16. ¶ *Hold that fast which thou hast.* That is, whatever of truth and piety you now possess. See Notes on ver. 3. ¶ *That no man take thy crown.* The crown of life appointed for all who are true believers. See Notes on 2 Ti. iv. 8. The truth which is taught here is, that by negligence or unfaithfulness in duty we may be deprived of the glory which we might have obtained if we had been faithful to our God and Saviour. We need to be on our constant guard, that, in a world of temptation, where the enemies of truth abound, we may not be robbed of the crown that we might have worn for ever. Comp. Notes on 2 Jn. 8.

12. *Him that overcometh.* See Notes on ch. ii. 7. ¶ *Will I make a pillar in the temple of my God.* See the introductory remarks to this epistle. The promised reward of faithfulness here is, that he who was victorious would be honoured as if he were a pillar or column in the temple of God. Such a pillar or column was partly for ornament, and partly for support; and the idea here is, that in that temple he would contribute to its beauty and the justness of its proportions, and would at the same time be honoured as if he were a pillar which was necessary for the support of the temple. It is not uncommon in the New Testament to represent the church as a temple, and Christians as parts of it. See 1 Co. iii. 16, 17; vi. 19; 2 Co. vi. 16; 1 Pe. ii. 5. ¶ *And he shall go no more out.* He shall be permanent as a part of that spiritual temple. The idea of "going out" does not properly belong to a *pillar;* but the speaker here has in his mind the *man*, though represented as a column. The description of some parts would be applicable more directly to a pillar; in others more properly to a man. Comp. Jn. vi. 37; x. 28, 29; 1 Jn. ii. 19, for an illustration of the sentiment here. The main truth here is, that if we reach

heaven, our happiness will be secure for ever. We shall have the most absolute certainty that the welfare of the soul will no more be perilled; that we shall never be in danger of falling into temptation; that no artful foe shall ever have power to alienate our affections from God; that we shall never die. Though we may change our place, and may roam from world to world till we shall have surveyed all the wonders of creation, yet we shall never "go out of the temple of God." Comp. Notes on Jn. xiv. 2. When we reach the heavenly world our conflicts will be over, our doubts at an end. As soon as we cross the threshold we shall be greeted with the assurance, "he shall go no more out for ever." That is to be our eternal abode, and whatever of joy, or felicity, or glory, that bright world can furnish, is to be ours. Happy moment when, emerging from a world of danger and of doubt, the soul shall settle down into the calmness and peace of that state where there is the assurance of God himself that that world of bliss is to be its eternal abode! ¶ *And I will write upon him the name of my God.* Considered as a pillar or column in the temple. The name of God would be conspicuously recorded on it to show that he belonged to God. The allusion is to a public edifice, on the columns of which the names of distinguished and honoured persons were recorded; that is, where there is a public testimonial of the respect in which one whose name was thus recorded was held. The honour thus conferred on him "who should overcome" would be as great *as if* the name of that God whom he served, and whose favour and friendship he enjoyed, were inscribed on him in some conspicuous manner. The *meaning* is, that he would be known and recognized as belonging to God; the God of the Redeemer himself—indicated by the phrase, "the name of *my* God." ¶ *And the name of the city of my God.* That is, indicating that he belongs to that city, or that the New Jerusalem is the city of his habitation. The idea would seem to be, that in this world, and in all worlds wherever he goes and wherever he abides, he will be recognized as belonging to that holy city; as enjoying the rights and immunities of such a citizen. ¶ Which is *New Jerusalem.* Jerusalem was the place where the temple was reared, and where the worship of God was celebrated. It thus came to be synonymous with the church—the dwelling-place of God on earth. ¶ *Which cometh down out of heaven from my God.* See this explained in the Notes on ch. xxi. 2, seq. Of course this must be a figurative representation, but the idea is plain. It is, (1) that the church is, in accordance with settled Scripture language, represented as a city—the abode of God on earth. (2) That is, instead of being built here, or having an earthly origin, it has its origin in heaven. It is *as if* it had been constructed there, and then sent down to earth ready formed. The type, the form, the whole structure is heavenly. It is a departure from all proper laws of interpretation to explain this *literally*, as if a city should be actually let down from heaven; and equally so to infer from this passage, and the others of similar import in this book, that a city will be literally *reared* for the residence of the saints. If the passage proves anything on either of these points, it is, that a great and splendid city, such as that described in ch. xxi., will *literally come down from heaven.* But who can believe that? Such an interpretation, however, is by no means necessary. The comparison of the church with a beautiful city, and the fact that it has its origin in heaven, is all that is fairly implied in the passage. ¶ *And* I will write upon him *my new name.* See Notes on ch. ii. 17. The *reward*, therefore, promised here is, that he who, by persevering fidelity, showed that he was a real friend of the Saviour, would be honoured with a permanent abode in the holy city of his habitation. In the church redeemed and triumphant he would have a perpetual dwelling; and wherever he should be, there would be given him sure pledges that he belonged to him, and was recognized as a citizen of the heavenly world. To no higher honour could any man aspire; and yet that is an honour to which the most humble and lowly may attain by faith in the Son of God.

THE EPISTLE TO THE CHURCH AT LAODICEA.

The contents of the epistle to the church at Laodicea (ver. 14-22) are as follows: (1) The usual salutation to the angel of the church, ver. 14. (2) The reference to the attributes of the speaker—the one here referred to being that he was the "Amen," "the faithful

Jerusalem, which cometh down out of heaven from my God: and *I will write upon him* my new name.

13 He that hath an ear, let him hear what the Spirit saith unto the churches.

14 And unto the angel of the church ¹of the Laodiceans write;

¹ or, *in Laodicea.*

and true witness," and "the beginning of the creation of God," ver. 14. (3) The claim that he knew all their works, ver. 15. (4) The characteristic of the church: it was "lukewarm"—neither "cold nor hot," ver. 15. (5) The punishment threatened, that he would "spue them out of his mouth," ver. 16. (6) A solemn reproof of their self-confidence, of their ignorance of themselves, and of their pride, when they were in fact poor, and blind, and naked; and a solemn counsel to them to apply to him for those things which would make them truly rich—which would cover up the shame of their nakedness, and which would give them clear spiritual vision, ver. 17, 18. (7) A command to repent, in view of the fact that he rebukes and chastens those whom he loves. (8) An assurance that an opportunity is still offered for repentance, represented by his standing at the door and praying for admittance, ver. 20. (9) A promise to him that should be victorious—in this case, that he should sit down with him on his throne, ver. 21; and (10) the usual call on those who had ears to hear, to attend to what the Spirit said to the churches.

Laodicea was situated in the southern part of Phrygia, near the junction of the small rivers Asopus and Carpus, on a plain washed at its edges by each. It was about forty miles from Ephesus, and not far from Colosse and Hierapolis. In the time of Strabo it was a large city; but the frequency of earthquakes, to which this district has been always liable, demolished, long since, a large part of the city, and destroyed many of the inhabitants, and the place was abandoned, and now lies in ruins. It is now a deserted place, called by the Turks Eski-hissar, or Old Castle. From its ruins, which are numerous, consisting of the remains of temples, theatres, &c., it seems to have been situated on six or seven hills, taking up a large space of ground. The whole rising ground on which the city stood is one vast tumulus of ruins, abandoned entirely to the owl and the fox. Col. Leake says, "There are few ancient sites more likely than Laodicea to preserve many curious remains of antiquity beneath the surface of the soil; its opulence, and the earthquakes to which it was subject, rendering it probable that valuable works of art were there buried beneath the ruins of the public and private edifices." The neighbouring village contains some fifty or sixty people, among whom, on a visit of a recent traveller there, there were but two nominal Christians. "The name of Christianity," says Emerson (p. 101), "is forgotten, and the only sounds that disturb the silence of its desertion are the tones of the Muezzin, whose voice from the distant village (Eski-hissar) proclaims the ascendency of Mahomet. Laodicea is even more solitary than Ephesus; for the latter has the prospect of the rolling sea or of a whitening sail to enliven its decay; while the former sits in widowed loneliness, its walls are grass-grown, its temples desolate, its very name has perished." A thunderstorm gathered on the mountains at a distance while this traveller was examining the ruins of Laodicea. He returned to Eski-hissar, and waited until the fury of the storm had abated, but set off on his journey again before it had entirely ceased to blow and to rain. "We preferred," says he, "hastening on, to a farther delay in that melancholy spot, where everything whispered desolation, and where the very wind that swept impetuously through the valley sounded like the fiendish laugh of time exulting over the destruction of man and his proudest monuments." See Professor Stuart, vol. ii. pp. 44, 45; Kitto's *Encyclo.;* Smith's *Journey to the Seven Churches,* 1671; Leake, Arundell, Hartley, MacFarlane, Pococke, &c. The engraving in this vol. will furnish a representation of the ruins of Laodicea.

14. *And unto the angel of the church of the Laodiceans write.* See Notes on ch. i. 20. ¶ *These things saith the Amen.* Referring, as is the case in every epistle, to some attribute of the speaker adapted to impress their minds, or to give peculiar force to what he was about to say to that particular church. Laodicea was characterized by lukewarmness, and the reference to the fact that he who was about to address them was the

"Amen"—that is, was characterized by the simple earnestness and sincerity denoted by that word—was eminently fitted to make an impression on the minds of such a people. The word *Amen* means *true, certain, faithful;* and, as used here, it means that he to whom it is applied is eminently true and faithful. What he affirms is true; what he promises or threatens is certain. Himself characterized by sincerity and truth (Notes on 2 Co. i. 20), he can look with approbation only on the same thing in others: and hence he looks with displeasure on the lukewarmness which, from its very nature, always approximates insincerity. This was an attribute, therefore, every way appropriate to be referred to in addressing a lukewarm church. ¶ *The faithful and true witness.* This is presenting the idea implied in the word *Amen* in a more complete form, but substantially the same thing is referred to. He is a witness for God and his truth, and he can approve of nothing which the God of truth would not approve. See Notes on ch. i. 5. ¶ *The beginning of the creation of God.* This expression is a very important one in regard to the rank and dignity of the Saviour, and, like all similar expressions respecting him, its meaning has been much controverted. Comp. Notes on Col. i. 15. The phrase here used is susceptible, properly, of only one of the following significations, viz.: either (*a*) that he was the beginning of the creation in the sense that he caused the universe to begin to exist —that is, that he was the author of all things; or (*b*) that he was the first created being; or (*c*) that he holds the primacy over all, and is at the head of the universe. It is not necessary to examine any other proposed interpretations, for the only other senses supposed to be conveyed by the words, that he is the beginning of the creation in the sense that he rose from the dead as the firstfruits of them that sleep, or that he is the head of the *spiritual* creation of God, are so foreign to the natural meaning of the words as to need no special refutation. As to the three significations suggested above, it may be observed, that the *first* one—that he is the *author* of the creation, and in that sense the *beginning*—though expressing a scriptural doctrine (Jn. i. 3; Ep. iii. 9; Col. i. 16), is not in accordance with the proper meaning of the word here used —ἀρχή. The word properly refers to the *commencement* of a thing, not its *authorship*, and denotes properly primacy in time, and primacy in rank, but not primacy in the sense of causing anything to exist. The two ideas which run through the word as it is used in the New Testament are those just suggested. For the former—primacy in regard to time—that is properly the commencement of a thing, see the following passages where the word occurs: Mat. xix. 4, 8; xxiv. 8, 21; Mar. i. 1; x. 6; xiii. 8, 19; Lu. i. 2; Jn. i. 1, 2; ii. 11; vi. 64; viii. 25, 44; xv. 27; xvi. 4; Ac. xi. 15; 1 Jn. i. 1; ii. 7, 13, 14, 24; iii. 8, 11; 2 Jn. 5, 6. For the latter signification, primacy of rank or authority, see the following places: Lu. xii. 11; xx. 20; Ro. viii. 38; 1 Co. xv. 24; Ep. i. 21; iii. 10; vi. 12; Col. i. 16, 18; ii. 10, 15; Tit. iii. 1. The word is not, therefore, found in the sense of *authorship*, as denoting that one is the *beginning* of anything in the sense that he caused it to have an existence. As to the *second* of the significations suggested, that it means that he was the *first created being*, it may be observed (*a*) that this is not a *necessary* signification of the phrase, since no one can show that this is the *only* proper meaning which could be given to the words, and therefore the phrase cannot be adduced to prove that he is himself a created being. If it *were* demonstrated from other sources that Christ was, in fact, a created being, and the first that God had made, it cannot be denied that this language would appropriately *express* that fact. But it cannot be made out from the mere use of the language here; and as the language is susceptible of other interpretations, it cannot be employed to prove that Christ is a created being. (*b*) Such an interpretation would be at variance with all those passages which speak of him as uncreated and eternal; which ascribe Divine attributes to him; which speak of him as himself the Creator of all things. Comp. Jn. i. 1-3; Col. i. 16; He. i. 2, 6, 8, 10-12. The *third* signification, therefore, remains, that he is "the beginning of the creation of God," in the sense that he is the head or prince of the creation; that is, that he presides over it so far as the purposes of redemption are to be accomplished, and so far as is necessary for those purposes. This is (1) in accordance with the meaning of the word, Lu. xii. 11; xx. 20, *et al. ut supra;* and (2) in accordance with the uniform

A.D. 96.] CHAPTER III. 99

These things saith the *ˣAmen, the faithful and true witness, the beginning of the creation of God;*

*x* Is. 65. 16.

15 I know thy works, that thou art neither cold nor hot: ʸI would thou wert cold or hot.

*y* 1 Ki. 18. 21.

statements respecting the Redeemer, that "all power is given unto him in heaven and in earth" (Mat. xxviii. 18); that God has "given him power over all flesh" (Jn. xvii. 2); that all things are "put under his feet" (He. ii. 8; 1 Co. xv. 27); that he is exalted over all things, Ep. i. 20-22. Having this rank, it was proper that he should speak with authority to the church at Laodicea.

15. *I know thy works.* Notes on ch. ii. 2. ¶ *That thou art neither cold nor hot.* The word *cold* here would seem to denote the state where there was no pretension to religion; where everything was utterly lifeless and dead. The language is obviously figurative, but it is such as is often employed, when we speak of one as being *cold* towards another, as having a cold or icy heart, &c. The word *hot* would denote, of course, the opposite — warm and zealous in their love and service. The very words that we are constrained to use when speaking on this subject — such words as *ardent* (i.e. *hot* or *burning*); *fervid* (i.e. *very hot*, *burning*, *boiling*) — show how necessary it is to use such words, and how common it is. The state indicated here, therefore, would be that in which there was a profession of religion, but no warm-hearted piety; in which there was not, on the one hand, open and honest opposition to him, and, on the other, such warm-hearted and honest love as he had a right to look for among his professed friends; in which there was a profession of that religion which *ought* to warm the heart with love, and fill the soul with zeal in the cause of the Redeemer; but where the only result, in fact, was deadness and indifference to him and his cause. Among those who made no profession he had reason to expect nothing but coldness; among those who made a profession he had a right to expect the glow of a warm affection; but he found nothing but indifference. ¶ *I would thou wert cold or hot.* That is, I would prefer *either* of those states to that which now exists. Anything better than this condition, where love is professed, but where it does not exist; where vows have been assumed which are not fulfilled. Why he would prefer that they should be "hot" is clear enough; but why would he prefer a state of utter coldness — a state where there was no profession of real love? To this question the following answers may be given: (1) Such a state of open and professed coldness or indifference is more *honest*. There is no disguise; no concealment; no pretence. We know where one in this state "may be found;" we know with whom we are dealing; we know what to expect. Sad as the state is, it is at least honest; and we are so made that we all prefer such a character to one where professions are made which are never to be realized — to a state of insincerity and hypocrisy. (2) Such a state is more *honourable*. It is a more elevated condition of mind, and marks a higher character. Of a man who is false to his engagements, who makes professions and promises never to be realized, we can make nothing. There is essential meanness in such a character, and there is nothing in it which we can respect. But in the character of the man who is openly and avowedly opposed to anything; who takes his stand, and is earnest and zealous in his course, though it be wrong, there are traits which may be, under a better direction, elements of true greatness and magnanimity. In the character of Saul of Tarsus there were always the elements of true greatness; in that of Judas Iscariot there were never. The one was capable of becoming one of the noblest men that has ever lived on the earth; the other, even under the personal teaching of the Redeemer for years, was nothing but a traitor — a man of essential meanness. (3) There is more hope of conversion and salvation in such a case. There could always have been a ground of hope that Saul would be converted and saved, even when "breathing out threatening and slaughter;" of Judas, when numbered among the professed disciples of the Saviour, there was no hope. The most hopeless of all persons, in regard to salvation, are those who are members of the church without any true religion; who have made a profession without any evidence of personal piety; who are content with a name to live. This is so, because (*a*) the essential character of

16 So then because thou art lukewarm, and neither cold nor hot, I will spue thee out of my mouth.

17 Because thou sayest, *I am rich, and increased with goods, and have need of nothing; and knowest not that thou art wretched, and miserable, and poor, and blind, and naked:

z Ho.12.8.

---

anyone who will allow himself to *do this* is eminently unfavourable to true religion. There is a lack of that thorough honesty and sincerity which is so necessary for true conversion to God. He who is content to profess to be what he really is not, is not a man on whom the truths of Christianity are likely to make an impression. (*b*) Such a man never applies the truth to himself. Truth that is addressed to impenitent sinners he does not apply to himself, of course; for he does not rank himself in that class of persons. Truth addressed to hypocrites he *will* not apply to himself; for no one, however insincere and hollow he may be, chooses to act on the presumption that he is himself a hypocrite, or so as to leave others to suppose that he regards himself as such. The means of grace adapted to save a *sinner*, as such, he will not use; for he is in the church, and chooses to regard himself as safe. Efforts made to reclaim him he will resist; for he will regard it as proof of a meddlesome spirit, and an uncharitable judging in others, if they consider him to be anything different from what he professes to be. What right have they to go *back* of his profession, and assume that he is insincere? As a consequence, there are probably fewer persons by far converted of those who come into the church without any religion, than of any other class of persons of similar number; and the most hopeless of all conditions, in respect to conversion and salvation, is when one enters the church deceived. (*c*) It may be presumed that, for these reasons, God himself will make less direct effort to convert and save such persons. As there are fewer appeals that can be brought to bear on them; as there is less in their character that is noble, and that can be depended on in promoting the salvation of a soul; and as there is special guilt in hypocrisy, it may be presumed that God will more frequently leave such persons to their chosen course, than he will those who make no professions of religion. Comp. Ps. cix. 17, 18; Je. vii. 16; xi. 14; xiv. 11; Is. i. 15; Ho. iv. 17.

16. *So then because thou art lukewarm—I will spue thee out of my mouth.* Referring, perhaps, to the well-known fact that tepid water tends to produce sickness at the stomach, and an inclination to vomit. The image is intensely strong, and denotes deep disgust and loathing at the indifference which prevailed in the church at Laodicea. The idea is, that they would be utterly rejected and cast off as a church—a threatening of which there has been an abundant fulfilment in subsequent times. It may be remarked, also, that what was threatened to that church may be expected to occur to all churches, if they are in the same condition; and that all professing Christians, and Christian churches, that are lukewarm, have special reason to dread the indignation of the Saviour.

17. *Because thou sayest, I am rich.* So far as the *language* here is concerned, this may refer either to riches literally, or to spiritual riches; that is, to a boast of having religion enough. Professor Stuart supposes that it refers to the former, and so do Wetstein, Vitringa, and others. Doddridge, Rosenmüller, and others, understand it in the latter sense. There is no doubt that there was much wealth in Laodicea, and that, as a people, they prided themselves on their riches. See the authorities in Wetstein on Col. ii. 1, and Vitringa, p. 160. It is not easy to determine *which* is the true sense; but may it not have been that there was an allusion to *both*, and that, *in every respect*, they boasted that they had enough? May it not have been so much the characteristic of that people to boast of their wealth, that they carried the spirit into everything, and manifested it even in regard to religion? Is it not true that they who have much of this world's goods, when they make a profession of religion, are very apt to suppose that they are well off in everything, and to feel self-complacent and happy? And is not the possession of much wealth by an individual Christian, or a Christian church, likely to produce just the lukewarmness which it is said existed in the church at Laodicea? If we thus understand it,

there will be an accordance with the well-known fact that Laodicea was distinguished for its riches, and, at the same time, with another fact, so common as to be almost universal, that the possession of great wealth tends to make a professed Christian self-complacent and satisfied in every respect; to make him feel that, although he may not have much *religion*, yet he is on the whole well off; and to produce, in religion, a state of just such lukewarmness as the Saviour here says was loathsome and odious. ¶ *And increased with goods.* πεπλούτηκα—"I am enriched." This is only a more emphatic and intensive way of saying the same thing. It has no reference to the *kind* of riches referred to, but merely denotes the confident manner in which they affirmed that they were rich. ¶ *And have need of nothing.* Still an emphatic and intensive way of saying that they were rich. In all respects their wants were satisfied; they had enough of everything. They felt, therefore, no stimulus to effort; they sat down in contentment, self-complacency, and indifference. It is almost unavoidable that those who are rich in this world's goods should feel that they have need of *nothing.* There is no more common illusion among men than the feeling that if one has wealth he has everything; that there is no want of his nature which cannot be satisfied with that; and that he may now sit down in contentment and ease. Hence the almost universal desire *to be* rich; hence the common feeling among those who *are* rich that there is no occasion for solicitude or care for anything else. Comp. Lu. xii. 19. ¶ *And knowest not.* There is no just impression in regard to the real poverty and wretchedness of your condition. ¶ *That thou art wretched.* The word *wretched* we now use to denote the actual consciousness of being miserable, as applicable to one who is sunk into deep distress or affliction. The word here, however, refers rather to the condition itself than to the consciousness of that condition, for it is said that they did not *know* it. Their state was, in fact, a miserable state, and was fitted to produce actual distress if they had had any just sense of it, though they thought that it was otherwise. ¶ *And miserable.* This word has, with us now, a similar signification; but the term here used— ἐλεεινὸς—rather means a *pitiable* state than one actually *felt* to be so. The meaning is, that their condition was one that was fitted to excite *pity* or *compassion;* not that they were actually miserable. Comp. Notes on 1 Co. xv. 19. ¶ *And poor.* Notwithstanding all their boast of having enough. They really had not that which was necessary to meet the actual wants of their nature, and, therefore, they were poor. Their worldly property could not meet the wants of their souls; and, with all their pretensions to piety, they had not religion enough to meet the necessities of their nature when calamities should come, or when death should approach; and they were, therefore, in the strictest sense of the term, *poor.* ¶ *And blind.* That is, in a spiritual respect. They did not see the reality of their condition; they had no just views of themselves, of the character of God, of the way of salvation. This seems to be said in connection with the boast which they made in their own minds—that they had *everything;* that they wanted nothing. One of the great blessings of life is clearness of vision, and their boast that they had everything must have included that; but the speaker here says that they lacked that indispensable thing to completeness of character and to full enjoyment. With all their boasting, they were actually *blind*,— and how could one who was in that state say that he "had need of nothing?" ¶ *And naked.* Of course, *spiritually.* Salvation is often represented as a garment (Mat. xxii. 11, 12; Re. vi. 11; vii. 9, 13, 14); and the declaration here is equivalent to saying that they had no religion. They had nothing to cover the nakedness of the soul, and in respect to the real wants of their nature they were like one who had no clothing in reference to cold, and heat, and storms, and to the shame of nakedness. How could such an one be regarded as rich? We may learn from this instructive verse, (1) That men may think themselves to be rich, and yet, in fact, be miserably poor. They may have the wealth of this world in abundance, and yet have nothing that really will meet their wants in disappointment, bereavement, sickness, death; the wants of their never-dying soul; their wants in eternity. What had the "rich fool," as he is commonly termed, in the parable, when he came to die? Lu. xii. 16,

18 I counsel thee to *a* buy of me gold tried in the fire, that thou mayest be rich; and white raiment, that thou mayest be clothed, and

*a* Is.55.1.

that *b* the shame of thy nakedness do not appear; and anoint thine eyes with eye-salve, that thou mayest see.

*b* ch.16.15.

seq. What had "Dives," as he is commonly termed, to meet the wants of his nature when he went down to hell? Lu. xvi. 19, seq. (2) Men may have much property, and think that they have all they want, and yet be *wretched*. In the sense that their *condition* is a wretched condition, this is always true; and in the sense that they are consciously wretched, this may be, and often is, true also. (3) Men may have great property, and yet be *miserable*. This is true in the sense that their condition is a *pitiable* one, and in the sense that they are actually *unhappy*. There is no more pitiable *condition* than that where one has great property, and is self-complacent and proud, and who has nevertheless no God, no Saviour, no hope of heaven, and who perhaps that very day may "lift up his eyes in hell, being in torments;" and it need not be added that there is no greater actual *misery* in this world than that which sometimes finds its way into the palaces of the rich. He greatly errs who thinks that misery is confined to the cottages of the poor. (4) Men may be rich, and think they have all that they want, and yet be *blind* to their condition. They really have no distinct vision of anything. They have no just views of God, of themselves, of their duty, of this world, or of the next. In most important respects they are in a worse condition than the inmates of an asylum for the blind, for they may have clear views of God and of heaven. Mental darkness is a greater calamity than the loss of natural vision; and there is many an one who is surrounded by all that affluence can give, who never yet had one correct view of his own character, of his God, or of the reality of his condition, and whose condition might have been far better if he had actually been born blind. (5) There may be gorgeous robes of adorning, and yet real nakedness. With all the decorations that wealth can impart, there may be a nakedness of the soul as real as that of the body would be if, without a rag to cover it, it were exposed to cold, and storm, and shame. The soul destitute of the robes of salvation, is in a worse condition than the body without raiment; for how can it bear the storms of wrath that shall beat upon it for ever, and the shame of its exposure in the last dread day?

18. *I counsel thee to buy of me gold tried in the fire.* Pure gold; such as has been subjected to the action of heat to purify it from dross. See Notes on 1 Pe. i. 7. Gold here is emblematic of religion—as being the most precious of the metals, and the most valued by men. They professed to be rich, but were not; and he counsels them to obtain from him that which would make them truly rich. ¶ *That thou mayest be rich.* In the true and proper sense of the word. With true religion; with the favour and friendship of the Redeemer, they would have all that they really needed, and would never be in want. ¶ *And white raiment.* The emblem of purity and salvation. See Notes on ver. 4. This is said in reference to the fact (ver. 17) that they were then *naked*. ¶ *That thou mayest be clothed.* With the garments of salvation. This refers, also, to true religion, meaning that that which the Redeemer furnishes will answer the same purpose in respect to the soul which clothing does in reference to the body. Of course it cannot be understood literally, nor should the language be pressed too closely, as if there was too strict a resemblance. ¶ *And that the shame of thy nakedness do not appear.* We clothe the body as well for decency as for protection against cold, and storm, and heat. The soul is to be clothed that the "shame" of its sinfulness may not be exhibited, and that it may not be offensive and repellant in the sight. ¶ *And anoint thine eyes with eye-salve.* In allusion to the fact that they were *blind*, ver. 17. The word *eye-salve*—κολλούριον—occurs nowhere else in the New Testament. It is a diminutive from κολλύρα—*collyra*—a coarse bread or cake, and means properly a small cake or cracknel. It is applied to eye-salve as resembling such a cake, and refers to a medicament prepared for sore or weak eyes. It was compounded of various substances supposed to have a healing

A.D. 96.]  CHAPTER III.  103

19 As<sup>c</sup> many as I love, I rebuke and chasten: be zealous therefore, and repent.
20 Behold, I stand at the door,

*c* He.12.5,6.

and <sup>d</sup>knock: <sup>e</sup>if any man hear my voice, and open the door, I will come in to him, and will sup with him, and he with me.

*d* Ca.5.2; Lu.12.36.  *e* Jn.14.23.

quality. See Wetstein, *in loco*. The reference here is to a spiritual healing — meaning that, in respect to their spiritual vision, what he would furnish would produce the same effect as the collyrium or eye-salve would in diseased eyes. The idea is, that the grace of the gospel enables men who were before blind to see clearly the character of God, the beauty of the way of salvation, the loveliness of the person and work of Christ, &c. See Notes on Ep. i. 18.

19. *As many as I love, I rebuke and chasten*. Of course, only on the supposition that they deserve it. The meaning is, that it is a proof of love on his part, if his professed friends go astray, to recall them by admonitions and by trials. So a father calls back his children who are disobedient; and there is no higher proof of his love than when, with great pain to himself, he administers such chastisement as shall save his child. See the sentiment here expressed fully explained in the Notes on He. xii. 6, seq. The language is taken from Pr. iii. 12. ¶ *Be zealous, therefore, and repent.* Be earnest, strenuous, ardent in your purpose to exercise true repentance, and to turn from the error of your ways. Lose no time; spare no labour, that you may obtain such a state of mind that it shall not be necessary to bring upon you the severe discipline which always comes on those who continue lukewarm in religion. The *truth* taught here is, that when the professed followers of Christ have become lukewarm in his service, they should lose no time in returning to him, and seeking his favour again. As sure as he has any true love for them, if this is not done he will bring upon them some heavy calamity, alike to rebuke them for their errors, and to recover them to himself.

20. *Behold, I stand at the door, and knock*. Intimating that, though they had erred, the way of repentance and hope was not closed against them. He was still willing to be gracious, though their conduct had been such as to be loathsome, ver. 16. To see the real force of this language, we must remember how disgusting and offensive their conduct had been to him. And yet he was willing, notwithstanding this, to receive them to his favour; nay more, he stood and pled with them that he might be received with the hospitality that would be shown to a friend or stranger. The *language* here is so plain that it scarcely needs explanation. It is taken from an act when we approach a dwelling, and, by a well-understood sign—*knocking*—announce our presence, and ask for admission. The act of *knocking* implies two things: (*a*) that we desire admittance; and (*b*) that we recognize the right of him who dwells in the house to open the door to us or not, as he shall please. We would not obtrude upon him; we would not force his door; and if, after we are sure that we are heard, we are not admitted, we turn quietly away. Both of these things are implied here by the language used by the Saviour when he approaches man as represented under the image of knocking at the door: that he *desires* to be admitted to our friendship; and that he recognizes our *freedom* in the matter. He does not obtrude himself upon us, nor does he employ force to find admission to the heart. If admitted, he comes and dwells with us; if rejected, he turns quietly away—perhaps to return and knock again, perhaps never to come back. The language here used, also, may be understood as applicable to all persons, and to all the methods by which the Saviour seeks to come into the heart of a sinner. It would properly refer to anything which would announce his presence: — his word; his Spirit; the solemn events of his providence; the invitations of his gospel. In these and in other methods he comes to man; and the manner in which these invitations ought to be estimated would be seen by supposing that he came to us personally and solicited our friendship, and proposed to be our Redeemer. It may be added here, that this expression proves that the attempt at reconciliation begins with the Saviour. It is not that the sinner goes out to meet him, or to seek for him; it is that the Saviour *presents himself* at the door of the heart, as if he were de-

21 To him that *overcometh will I grant to ᵍsit with me in my throne, even as ʰI also overcame, and am set down with my Father in his throne.

*f* ch.12.11; 1 Jn.5.4,5.　　*g* Lu.22.30.　　*h* Jn.16.33.

sirous to enjoy the friendship of man. This is in accordance with the uniform language of the New Testament, that "God so loved the world as to *give* his only-begotten Son;" that "Christ came to *seek* and to save the lost;" that the Saviour says, "Come unto me, all ye that labour and are heavy laden," &c. Salvation, in the Scriptures, is never represented as originated by man. ¶ *If any man hear my voice.* Perhaps referring to a custom then prevailing, that he who knocked spake, in order to let it be known who it was. This might be demanded in the night (Lu. xi. 5), or when there was apprehension of danger, and it may have been the custom when John wrote. The language here, in accordance with the uniform usage in the Scriptures (comp. Is. lv. 1; Jn. vii. 37; Re. xxii. 17), is universal, and proves that the invitations of the gospel are made, and are *to be* made, not to a part only, but fully and freely to all men; for, although this originally had reference to the members of the church in Laodicea, yet the language chosen seems to have been of design so universal (ἰάν τις) as to be applicable to every human being; and anyone, of any age and in any land, would be authorized to apply this to himself, and, under the protection of this invitation, to come to the Saviour, and to plead this promise as one that fairly included himself. It may be observed farther, that this also recognizes the freedom of man. It is submitted to him whether he will hear the voice of the Redeemer or not; and whether he will open the door and admit him or not. He speaks loud enough, and distinctly enough, to be heard, but he does not force the door if it is not voluntarily opened. ¶ *And open the door.* As one would when a stranger or friend stood and knocked. The meaning here is simply, if anyone will *admit* me; that is, receive me as a friend. The act of receiving him is as voluntary on our part as it is when we rise and open the door to one who knocks. It may be added, (1) that this is an *easy* thing. Nothing is more easy than to open the door when one knocks; and so everywhere in the Scriptures it is represented as an easy thing, if the heart is will-

ing, to secure the salvation of the soul. (2) This is a *reasonable* thing. We invite him who knocks at the door to come in. We always assume, unless there is reason to suspect the contrary, that he applies for peaceful and friendly purposes. We deem it the height of rudeness to let one stand and knock long; or to let him go away with no friendly invitation to enter our dwelling. Yet how different does the sinner treat the Saviour! How long does he suffer him to knock at the door of his heart, with no invitation to enter—no act of common civility such as that with which he would greet even a stranger! And with how much coolness and indifference does he see him turn away—perhaps to come back no more, and with no desire that he ever should return! ¶ *I will come in to him, and will sup with him, and he with me.* This is an image denoting intimacy and friendship. Supper, with the ancients, was the principal social meal; and the idea here is, that between the Saviour and those who would receive him there would be the intimacy which subsists between those who sit down to a friendly meal together. In all countries and times, to eat together, to break bread together, has been the symbol of friendship, and this the Saviour promises here. The *truths*, then, which are taught in this verse, are, (1) that the invitation of the gospel is made to all—"if *any* man hear my voice;" (2) that the movement towards reconciliation and friendship is originated by the Saviour—"behold, I stand at the door and knock;" (3) that there is a recognition of our own free agency in religion—"if any man will hear my voice, and open the door;" (4) the *ease* of the terms of salvation, represented by "hearing his voice," and "opening the door;" and (5) the blessedness of thus admitting him, arising from his friendship—"I will sup with him, and he with me." What friend can man have who would confer so many benefits on him as the Lord Jesus Christ? Who is there that he should so gladly welcome to his bosom?

21. *To him that overcometh.* See Notes on ch. ii. 7. ¶ *Will I grant to sit with me in my throne.* That is,

**22** He[i] that hath an ear, let him hear what the Spirit saith unto the churches.

[i] ch.2.7.

---

they will share his honours and his triumphs. See Notes on ch. ii. 26, 27; comp. Notes on Ro. viii. 17. ¶ *Even as I also overcame.* As I gained a victory over the world, and over the power of the tempter. As the reward of this, he is exalted to the throne of the universe (Phi. ii. 6-11), and in these honours, achieved by their great and glorious Head, all the redeemed will share. ¶ *And am set down with my Father in his throne.* Comp. Notes on Phi. ii. 6-11. That is, he has dominion over the universe. All things are put under his feet, and in the strictest unison and with perfect harmony he is united with the Father in administering the affairs of all worlds. The dominion of the Father is that of the Son—that of the Son is that of the Father; for they are one. See Notes on Jn. v. 19; comp. Notes on Ep. i. 20-22; 1 Co. xv. 24-28.

22. *He that hath an ear,* &c. See Notes on ch. ii. 7.

This closes the epistolary part of this book, and the "visions" properly commence with the next chapter. Two remarks may be made in the conclusion of this exposition. (1) The first relates to the truthfulness of the predictions in these epistles. As an illustration of that truthfulness, and of the present correspondence of the condition of those churches with what the Saviour said to John they would be, the following striking passage may be introduced from Mr. Gibbon. It occurs in his description of the conquests of the Turks (*Decline and Fall,* iv. 260, 261). "Two Turkish chieftains, Sarukhan and Aidin left their names to their conquests, and their conquests to their posterity. The captivity or ruin of the *seven* churches of Asia was consummated; and the barbarous lords of Ionia and Lydia still trample on the monuments of classic and Christian antiquity. In the loss of Ephesus, the Christians deplored the fall of the first angel, the extinction of the first candlestick of the Revelations: the desolation is complete; and the temple of Diana, or the church of Mary, will equally elude the search of the curious traveller. The circus and three stately theatres of Laodicea are now peopled with wolves and foxes; Sardis is reduced to a miserable village; the God of Mahomet, without a rival or a son, is invoked in the mosques of Thyatira and Pergamos; and the populousness of Smyrna is supported by the foreign trade of Franks and Armenians. Philadelphia alone has been saved by prophecy or courage. At a distance from the sea, forgotten by the emperors, encompassed on all sides by the Turks, her valiant citizens defended their religion and freedom above fourscore years, and at length capitulated with the proudest of the Ottomans. Among the Greek colonies and churches of Asia, Philadelphia is still erect, a column in a scene of ruins; a pleasing example that the paths of honour and safety may sometimes be the same."

(2) The second remark relates to the applicability of these important truths to us. There is perhaps no part of the New Testament more searching than these brief epistles to the seven churches; and though those to whom they were addressed have long since passed away, and the churches have long since become extinct; though darkness, error, and desolation have come over the places where these churches once stood, yet the principles laid down in these epistles still live, and they are full of admonition to Christians in all ages and all lands. It is a consideration of as much importance to us as it was to these churches, that the Saviour now knows our works; that he sees in the church, and in any individual, all that there is to commend and all that there is to reprove; that he has power to reward or punish now as he had then; that the same rules in apportioning rewards and punishments will still be acted on; that he who overcomes the temptations of the world will find an appropriate reward; that those who live in sin must meet with the proper recompense, and that those who are lukewarm in his service will be spurned with unutterable loathing. His rebukes are awful; but his promises are full of tenderness and kindness. While they who have embraced error, and they who are living in sin, have occasion to tremble before him, they who are endeavouring to perform their duty may find in these epistles enough to cheer their hearts, and to animate them with the hope of final victory, and of the most ample and glorious reward.

## CHAPTER IV.

### ANALYSIS OF THE CHAPTER.

This chapter properly commences the series of visions respecting future events, and introduces those remarkable symbolical descriptions which were designed to cheer the hearts of those to whom the book was first sent, in their trials, and the hearts of all believers in all ages, with the assurance of the final triumph of the gospel. See the Introduction.

In regard to the *nature* of these visions, or the state of mind of the writer, there have been different opinions. Some have supposed that all that is described was made only to pass before the mind, with no visible representation; others, that there were visible representations so made to him that he could copy them; others, that all that is said or seen was only the production of the author's imagination. The latter is the view principally entertained by German writers on the book. All that would seem to be apparent on the face of the book—and that is all that we can judge by—is, that the following things occurred: (1) The writer was in a devout frame of mind—a state of holy contemplation—when the scenes were represented to him, ch. i. 10. (2) The representations were supernatural; that is, they were something which was disclosed to him, in that state of mind, beyond any natural reach of his faculties. (3) These things were so made to pass before him that they had the aspect of reality, and he could copy and describe them as real. It is not necessary to suppose that there was any representation to the bodily eye; but they had, to his mind, such a reality that he could describe them as pictures or symbols—and his office was limited to that. He does not attempt to *explain* them, nor does he intimate that he understood them; but his office pertains to an accurate *record*—a fair transcript—of what passed before his mind. For anything that appears, he may have been as ignorant of their signification as any of his readers, and may have subsequently studied them with the same kind of attention which we now give to them (comp. Notes on 1 Pe. i. 11, 12), and may have, perhaps, remained ignorant of their signification to the day of his death. It is no more necessary to suppose that he understood all that was implied in these symbols, than it is that one who can describe a beautiful landscape understands all the laws of the plants and flowers in the landscape; or, that one who copies all the designs and devices of armorial bearings in heraldry, should understand all that is meant by the symbols that are used; or, that one who should copy the cuneiform inscriptions of Persepolis, or the hieroglyphics of Thebes, should understand the meaning of the symbols. All that is demanded or expected, in such a case, is, that the *copy* should be accurately made; and, *when* made, this copy may be as much an object of study to him who made it as to anyone else. (4) Yet there was a sense in which these symbols were *real;* that is, they were a real and proper delineation of future events. They were not the mere workings of the imagination. He who saw them in vision though there may have been no representation to the eye, had before him what was a real and appropriate representation of coming events. If not, the visions are as worthless as dreams are.

The visions open (ch. iv.) with a *Theophany*, or a representation of God. John is permitted to look into heaven, and to have a view of the throne of God, and of the worship celebrated there. A *door* (θύρα) or opening is made into heaven, so that he, as it were, looks *through* the concave above, and sees what is beyond. He sees the throne of God, and him who sits on the throne, and the worshippers there; he sees the lightnings play around the throne, and hears the thunder's roar; he sees the rainbow that encompasses the throne, and hears the songs of the worshippers. In reference to this vision, at the commencement of the series of symbols which he was about to describe, and the *reason* why this was vouchsafed to him, the following remarks may be suggested: (1) There is, in some respects, a striking resemblance between this and the visions of Isaiah (ch. vi.) and Ezekiel (ch. i.). As those prophets, when about to enter on their office, were solemnly inaugurated by being permitted to have a vision of the Almighty, so John was inaugurated to the office of making known future things—the last prophet of the world—by a similar vision. We shall see, indeed, that the representation made to John was not precisely the same as that which was made to Isaiah or that which was made to Ezekiel; but the most striking symbols are retained, and that of John is as much adapted to impress the mind as either of the others. Each of them describes the throne, and the attending circumstances of sublimity and majesty; each of them speaks of one on the throne, but neither of them has attempted any description of the Almighty. There is no delineation of an image, or a figure representing God, but everything respecting him is veiled in such obscurity as to fill the mind with awe. (2) The representation is such as to produce deep solemnity on the mind of the writer and the reader. Nothing could have been better adapted to prepare the mind of John for the important communications which he was about to make than to be permitted to look, as it were, directly into heaven, and to see the throne of God. And nothing is better fitted to impress the mind of the reader than the view which is furnished, in the opening vision, of the majesty and glory of God. Brought, as it were, into his very presence; permitted to look upon his burning throne; seeing the reverent and profound worship of the inhabitants of heaven, we feel our minds awed, and our souls subdued, as we hear the God of heaven speak, and as we see seal after seal opened, and hear trumpet after trumpet utter its voice. (3) The form of the manifestation—the opening vision—is eminently fitted to show us that the communications in this book proceed from heaven. Looking into heaven, and seeing the vision of the Almighty, we are prepared to feel that what follows has a higher than any human origin; that it has come direct from the throne of God. And (4) there was a propriety that the visions should open with a manifestation of the throne of God in heaven, or with a vision of heaven, because that, also, is the *termination* of the whole; it is that to which all the visions in the book tend. It begins in heaven, as seen by the exile in Patmos; it terminates in heaven, when all enemies of the church are subdued, and the redeemed reign triumphant in glory.

The substance of the introductory vision in this chapter can be stated in few words: (*a*) A door is opened, and John is permitted to look into heaven, and to see what is passing there, ver. 1, 2. (*b*) The first thing that strikes him is a throne, with one sitting on the throne, ver. 2. (*c*) The appearance of him who sits upon the throne is described, ver. 3. He is "like a jasper and a sardine stone." There is no attempt to portray his form; there is no description from which an image could be formed that could become an object of idolatrous worship—for who would undertake to chisel anything so indefinite as that which is merely "*like* a jasper or a sardine stone?" And yet the description is distinct enough to fill the mind with emotions of awe and sublimity, and to leave the impression that he who sat on the throne was a pure and holy God. (*d*) Round about the throne there was a bright rainbow: a symbol of peace, ver. 3. (*e*) Around the throne are gathered the elders of the church, having on their heads crowns of gold: symbols of the ultimate triumph of the church, ver. 4. (*f*) Thunder and lightning, as at Sinai, announce the presence of God, and seven burning lamps before the throne represent the Spirit of God, in his diversified operations, as going forth through the world to enlighten, sanctify, and save, ver. 5. (*g*) Before the throne there is a pellucid pavement, as of crystal, spread out like a sea: emblem of calmness, majesty, peace, and wide dominion, ver. 6. (*h*) The throne is supported by four living creatures, full of eyes: emblems of the all-seeing power of him that sits upon the throne, and of his ever-watchful providence, ver. 6. (*i*) To each one of these living creatures there is a peculiar symbolic face: respectively emblematic of the authority, the power, the wisdom of God, and of the rapidity with which the purposes of Providence are executed, ver. 7. All are furnished with wings: emblematic of their readiness to do the will of God (ver. 8), but each one individually with a peculiar form. (*j*) All these creatures pay ceaseless homage to God, whose throne they are represented as supporting: emblematic of the fact that all the operations of the divine government do, in fact, promote his glory, and, as it were, render him praise, ver. 8, 9. (*k*) To this the elders, the representatives of the church, respond: representing the fact that the church acquiesces in all the arrangements of Providence, and in the execution of all the divine purposes, and finds in them all ground for adoration and thanksgiving, ver. 10, 11.

1. *After this.* Gr., "After these things;" that is, after what he had seen,

## CHAPTER IV.

AFTER this I looked, and, behold, a door *was* opened in heaven; and the first [a] voice which I heard *was* as it were of a trumpet talking with me; which said, [b] Come

a ch.1.10.   b ch.11.12.

up hither, and I will show thee things which must be hereafter.

2 And immediately I was [c] in the Spirit: and, behold, a [d] throne was set in heaven, and [e] *one* sat on the throne.

c ch.17.3; 21.10; Eze.3.12-14.
d Is.6.1; Je.17.12; Eze.1.26,28.   e Da.7.9; He.8.1.

---

and after what he had been directed to record in the preceding chapters. How long after these things this occurred, he does not say—whether on the same day, or at some subsequent time; and conjecture would be useless. The *scene*, however, is changed. Instead of seeing the Saviour standing before him (ch. i.), the scene is transferred to heaven, and he is permitted to look in upon the throne of God, and upon the worshippers there. ¶ *I looked*. Gr., *I saw*—εἶδον. Our word *look* would rather indicate *purpose* or *intention*, as if he had *designedly* directed his attention to heaven, to see what could be discovered there. The meaning, however, is simply that he saw a new vision, without intimating whether there was any *design* on his part, and without saying how his thoughts came to be directed to heaven. ¶ *A door was opened*. That is, there was apparently an opening in the sky like a door, so that he could look into heaven. ¶ *In heaven*. Or, rather, in the expanse above—in the visible heavens as they appear to spread out over the earth. So Eze. i. 1, "The heavens were opened, and I saw visions of God." The Hebrews spoke of the sky above as a solid expanse; or as a curtain stretched out; or as an extended arch above the earth—describing it as it *appears* to the eye. In that expanse, or arch, the stars are set as gems (comp. Notes on Is. xxxiv. 4); through apertures or windows in that expanse the rain comes down, Ge. vii. 11; and that is opened when a heavenly messenger comes down to the earth, Mat. iii. 16. Comp. Lu. iii. 21; Ac. vii. 56; x. 11. Of course, all this is figurative, but it is such language as all men naturally use. The simple meaning here is, that John had a vision of what is in heaven *as if* there had been such an opening made through the sky, and he had been permitted to look into the world above. ¶ *And the first voice which I heard*. That is, the first sound which he heard was a command to come up and see the glories of that world. He afterwards heard other sounds—the sounds of praise; but the first notes that fell on his ear were a direction to come up there and receive a revelation respecting future things. This does not seem to me to mean, as Professor Stuart, Lord, and others suppose, that he now recognized the voice which had *first*, or formerly spoken to him (ch. i. 10), but that this was the *first* in contradistinction from other voices which he afterwards heard. It resembled the former "voice" in this, that it was "like the sound of a trumpet," but besides that there does not seem to have been anything that would suggest to him that it came from the same source. It is certainly possible that the Greek would admit of that interpretation, but it is not the most obvious or probable. ¶ *Was as it were of a trumpet*. It resembled the sound of a trumpet, ch. i. 10. ¶ *Talking with me*. As of a trumpet that seemed to speak directly to me. ¶ *Which said*. That is, the voice said. ¶ *Come up hither*. To the place whence the voice seemed to proceed—heaven. ¶ *And I will show thee things which must be hereafter*. Gr., "after these things." The reference is to future events; and the meaning is, that there would be disclosed to him events that were to occur at some future period. There is no intimation here *when* they would occur, or what would be embraced in the period referred to. All that the words would properly convey would be, that there would be a disclosure of things that were to occur in some future time.

2. *And immediately I was in the Spirit.* See Notes on ch. i. 10. He does not affirm that he was caught up into heaven, nor does he say what impression was on his own mind, if any, as to the place where he was; but he was at once absorbed in the contemplation of the visions before him. He was doubtless still in Patmos, and these things were made to pass before his mind as a reality; that is, they appeared as real to him as if he saw them, and they were in fact a real symbolical representation

3 And he that sat was to look upon like a jasper and a sardine stone: and *there was* a rainbow round about the throne, in sight like unto an emerald.

---

of things occurring in heaven. ¶ *And, behold, a throne was set in heaven.* That is, a throne was *placed* there. The first thing that arrested his attention was a throne. This was "in heaven"—an expression which proves that the scene of the vision was not the temple in Jerusalem, as some have supposed. There is no allusion to the temple, and no imagery drawn from the temple. Isaiah had his vision (Is. vi.) in the holy of holies of the temple; Ezekiel (ch. i. 1), by the river Chebar; but John looked directly into heaven, and saw the throne of God, and the encircling worshippers there. ¶ *And* one *sat on the throne.* It is remarkable that John gives no description of him who sat on the throne, nor does he indicate who he was by name. Neither do Isaiah or Ezekiel attempt to describe the appearance of the Deity, nor are there any intimations of that appearance given from which a picture or an image could be formed. So much do their representations accord with what is demanded by correct taste; and so sedulously have they guarded against any encouragement of idolatry. 3. *And he that sat was to look upon.* Was in appearance; or, as I looked upon him, this seemed to be his appearance. He does not describe his form, but his splendour. ¶ *Like a jasper*—ἰάσπιδι. The jasper, properly, is "an opaque, impure variety of quartz, of red, yellow, and also of some dull colours, breaking with a smooth surface. It admits of a high polish, and is used for vases, seals, snuff-boxes, &c. When the colours are in stripes or bands, it is called *striped jasper*" (Dana, in Webster's *Dictionary*). The *colour* here is not designated, whether red or yellow. As the red was, however, the common colour worn by princes, it is probable that that was the colour that appeared, and that John means to say that he appeared like a prince in his royal robes. Comp. Is. vi. 1. ¶ *And a sardine stone*—σαρδίῳ. This denotes a precious stone of a blood-red, or sometimes of a flesh-colour, more commonly known by the name of *carnelian* (Rob. *Lex.*). Thus it corresponds with the jasper, and this is only an additional circumstance to convey the exact idea in the mind of John, that the appearance of him who sat on the throne was that of a prince in his scarlet robes. This is all the description which he gives of his appearance; and this is (*a*) entirely appropriate, as it suggests the idea of a prince or a monarch; and (*b*) it is well adapted to impress the mind with a sense of the majesty of Him who cannot be described, and of whom no image should be attempted. Comp. De. iv. 12: "Ye heard the voice of the words, but saw no similitude." ¶ *And* there was *a rainbow round about the throne.* This is a beautiful image, and was probably designed to be emblematical as well as beautiful. The previous representation is that of majesty and splendour; this is adapted to temper the majesty of the representation. The rainbow has always, from its own nature, and from its associations, been an emblem of peace. It appears on the cloud as the storm passes away. It contrasts beautifully with the tempest that has just been raging. It is seen as the rays of the sun again appear clothing all things with beauty—the more beautiful from the fact that the storm has come, and that the rain has fallen. If the rain has been gentle, nature smiles serenely, and the leaves and flowers refreshed appear clothed with new beauty: if the storm has raged violently, the appearance of the rainbow is a pledge that the war of the elements has ceased, and that God smiles again upon the earth. It reminds us, too, of the "covenant" when God did "set his bow in the cloud," and solemnly promised that the earth should no more be destroyed by a flood, Ge. ix. 9–16. The appearance of the rainbow, therefore, around the throne, was a beautiful emblem of the mercy of God, and of the peace that was to pervade the world as the result of the events that were to be disclosed to the vision of John. True, there were lightnings and thunderings and voices, but there the bow abode calmly above them all, assuring him that there was to be mercy and peace. ¶ *In sight like unto an emerald.* The emerald is green, and this colour so predominated in the bow that it seemed to be made of this species of precious stone. The modified and mild colour of green appears to every one to predominate in the rainbow. Ezekiel (i. 28) has introduced the image of the rainbow, also, in his description of the vision that appeared to

**4** And round about the throne were *f* four and twenty seats: and upon the seats I saw four and twenty elders sitting, *g* clothed in white raiment; and they had on their heads *h* crowns of gold.

*f* ch.11.16.  *g* ch.3.4,5.  *h* ver.10.

him, though not as calmly encircling the throne, but as descriptive of the general appearance of the scene. "As is the appearance of the bow that is on the cloud in the day of rain, so was the appearance of the brightness round about." Milton, also, has introduced it, but it is also as a part of the colouring of the throne:—

"Over their heads a crystal firmament,
Whereon a sapphire throne, inlaid with pure
Amber, and colours of the showery arch."
*Par. Lost*, b. vii.

**4.** *And round about the throne were four and twenty seats.* Or rather thrones—θρόνοι—the same word being used as that which is rendered *throne*—θρόνος. The word, indeed, properly denotes *a seat*, but it came to be employed to denote particularly the seat on which a monarch sat, and is properly translated thus in ver. 2, 3. So it is rendered in Mat. v. 34; xix. 28; xxiii. 22; xxv. 31; Lu. i. 32; and uniformly elsewhere in the New Testament (fifty-three places in all), except in Lu. i. 52; Re. ii. 13; iv. 4; xi. 16; xvi. 10, where it is rendered *seat* and *seats*. It should have been rendered *thrones* here, and is so translated by Professor Stuart. Coverdale and Tyndale render the word *seat* in each place in ver. 2-5. It was undoubtedly the design of the writer to represent those who sat on those seats as, in some sense, *kings*—for they have on their heads crowns of gold—and that idea should have been retained in the translation of this word. ¶ *And upon the seats I saw four and twenty elders sitting.* Very various opinions have been entertained in respect to those who thus appeared sitting around the throne, and to the question why the number twenty-four is mentioned. Instead of examining those opinions at length, it will be better to present, in a summary manner, what seems to be probable in regard to the intended reference. The following points, then, would appear to embrace all that can be known on this subject. (1) These elders have a regal character, or are of a kingly order. This is apparent, (*a*) because they are represented as sitting on "thrones," and (*b*) because they have on their heads "crowns of gold." (2) They are emblematic. They are designed to symbolize or represent some class of persons. This is clear, (*a*) because it cannot be supposed that so small a number would compose the whole of those who are in fact around the throne of God, and (*b*) because there are *other* symbols there designed to represent something pertaining to the homage rendered to God, as the four living creatures and the angels, and this supposition is necessary in order to complete the symmetry and harmony of the representation. (3) They are human beings, and are designed to have some relation to the race of man, and somehow to connect the human race with the worship of heaven. The four living creatures have another design; the angels (ch. v.) have another; but these are manifestly of our race—persons from this world before the throne. (4) They are designed in some way to be symbolic of the church as redeemed. Thus they say (ch. v. 9), "Thou hast redeemed us to God by thy blood." (5) They are designed to represent the *whole* church in every land and every age of the world. Thus they say (ch. v. 9), "Thou hast redeemed us to God by thy blood, *out of every kindred, and tongue, and people, and nation.*" This shows, further, that the whole representation is emblematic; for otherwise in so small a number—twenty-four—there could not be a representation out of every nation. (6) They represent the church triumphant—the church victorious. Thus they have crowns on their heads; they have harps in their hands (ch. v. 8); they say that they are "kings and priests," and that they will "reign on the earth," ch. v. 10. (7) The design, therefore, is to represent the church triumphant—redeemed—saved—as rendering praise and honour to God; as uniting with the hosts of heaven in adoring him for his perfections and for the wonders of his grace. As representatives of the church, they are admitted near to him; they encircle his throne; they appear victorious over every foe; and they come, in unison with the living creatures, and the angels, and the whole universe (ch. v. 13), to ascribe power and dominion to God. (8) As to the reason why the

A.D. 96.]  CHAPTER IV.  111

5 And out of the throne proceeded *ⁱ*lightnings and thunderings and voices: and *there were*

*i* ch.8.5; 16.18.

seven *ᵏ*lamps of fire burning before the throne, which are the *ˡ*seven Spirits of God.

*k* Ge.15.17; Ex.37.23; Zec.4.2.   *l* ch.1.4.

number "twenty-four" is mentioned, perhaps nothing certain can be determined. Ezekiel, in his vision (Eze. viii. 16; xi. 1), saw twenty-five men between the porch and the altar, with their backs toward the temple, and their faces toward the earth—supposed to be representations of the twenty-four "courses" into which the body of priests was divided (1 Ch. xxiv. 3–19), with the high-priest among them, making up the number twenty-five. It is *possible* that John in this vision may have designed to refer to the church considered *as* a priesthood (comp. Notes on 1 Pe. ii. 9), and to have alluded to the fact that the priesthood under the Jewish economy was divided into twenty-four courses, each with a presiding officer, and who was a representative of that portion of the priesthood over which he presided. If so, then the ideas which enter into the representation are these: (*a*) That the whole church may be represented as a priesthood, or a community of priests—an idea which frequently occurs in the New Testament. (*b*) That the church, as such a community of priests, is employed in the praise and worship of God—an idea, also, which finds abundant countenance in the New Testament. (*c*) That, in a series of visions having a designed reference to the church, it was natural to introduce some symbol or emblem representing the church, and representing the fact that this is its office and employment. And (*d*) that this would be well expressed by an allusion derived from the ancient dispensation—the division of the priesthood into classes, over each one of which there presided an individual who might be considered as the representative of his class. It is to be observed, indeed, that in *one* respect they are represented as "kings," but still this does not forbid the supposition that there might have been intermingled also *another* idea, that they were also "priests." Thus the two ideas are blended by these same elders in ch. v. 10: "And hath made us unto our God *kings* and *priests.*" Thus understood, the vision is designed to denote the fact that the representatives of the church, ultimately to be triumphant, are properly engaged in ascribing praise to God. The word *elders* here seems to be used in the sense of aged and venerable men, rather than as denoting office. They were such as by their *age* were qualified to preside over the different divisions of the priesthood. ¶ *Clothed in white raiment.* Emblem of purity, and appropriate, therefore, to the representatives of the sanctified church. Comp. ch. iii. 4; vi. 11; vii. 9. ¶ *And they had on their heads crowns of gold.* Emblematic of the fact that they sustained a kingly office. There was blended in the representation the idea that they were both "kings and priests." Thus the idea is expressed by Peter (1 Pe. ii. 9), "*a royal priesthood*"— βασίλειον ἱεράτευμα.

5. *And out of the throne proceeded lightnings and thunderings and voices.* Expressive of the majesty and glory of Him that sat upon it. We are at once reminded by this representation of the sublime scene that occurred at Sinai (Ex. xix. 16), where "there were thunders and lightnings, and a thick cloud upon the mount, and the voice of the trumpet exceeding loud." Comp. Eze. i. 13, 24. So Milton:

"Forth rushed with whirlwind sound
The chariot of Paternal Deity,
Flashing thick flames."

"And from about him fierce effusion rolled
Of smoke, and lightning flame, and sparkles dire." *Par. Lost*, b. vi.

The word "*voices*" here connected with "*thunders*" perhaps means "voices even thunders"—referring to the sound made by the thunder. The meaning is, that these were echoing and re-echoing sounds, as it were a multitude of voices that seemed to speak on every side. ¶ *And* there were *seven lamps of fire burning before the throne.* Seven burning lamps that constantly shone there, illuminating the whole scene. These steadily burning lamps would add much to the beauty of the vision. ¶ *Which are the seven Spirits of God.* Which represent, or are emblematic of, the seven Spirits of God. On the meaning of the phrase, "the seven Spirits of God," see Notes on chap. i. 4. If these lamps are designed to be symbols of the Holy Spirit, according to the interpretation proposed in chap. i. 4, it may

6 And before the throne *there was* a <sup>m</sup>sea of glass like unto crystal: and in the midst of the throne, and round about the throne, were <sup>n</sup>four beasts, full of eyes before and behind.

*m* ch.15.2.   *n* Eze.1.5,&c.; 10.14.

be perhaps in the following respects: (1) They may represent the manifold influences of that Spirit in the world— as imparting light; giving consolation; creating the heart anew; sanctifying the soul, &c. (2) They may denote that all the operations of that Spirit are of the nature of *light*, dissipating darkness, and vivifying and animating all things. (3) *Perhaps* their being placed here before the throne, in the midst of thunder and lightning, may be designed to represent the idea that—amidst all the scenes of magnificence and grandeur; all the storms, agitations, and tempests on the earth; all the political changes; all the convulsions of empire under the providence of God; and all the commotions in the soul of man, produced by the thunders of the law—the Spirit of God beams calmly and serenely, shedding a steady influence over all, like lamps burning in the very midst of lightnings, and thunderings, and voices. In all the scenes of majesty and commotion that occur on the earth, the Spirit of God is present, shedding a constant light, and undisturbed in his influence by all the agitations that are abroad.

6. *And before the throne* there was *a sea of glass.* An expanse spread out like a sea composed of glass: that is, that was pellucid and transparent like glass. It is not uncommon to compare the sea with glass. See numerous examples in Wetstein, *in loco.* The point of the comparison here seems to be its transparent appearance. It was perfectly clear—apparently stretching out in a wide expanse, as if it were a *sea.* ¶ *Like unto crystal.* The word *crystal* means properly anything congealed and pellucid, as ice; then anything resembling that, particularly a certain species of stone distinguished for its clearness— as the transparent crystals of quartz; limpid and colourless quartz; rock or mountain quartz. The word *crystal* now, in mineralogy, means an inorganic body which, by the operation of affinity, has assumed the form of a regular solid, by a certain number of plane and smooth faces. It is here used manifestly in its popular sense to denote anything that is perfectly clear like ice. The comparison, in the representation of the expanse spread around the throne, turns on these points: (1) It appeared like a sea—stretching afar. (2) It resembled, in its general appearance, glass; and this idea is strengthened by the addition of another image of the same character—that it was like an expanse of crystal, perfectly clear and pellucid. This would seem to be designed to represent the floor or pavement on which the throne stood. If *this* is intended to be emblematical, it *may* denote (*a*) that the empire of God is vast—as if it were spread out like the sea; or (*b*) it may be emblematic of the *calmness*, the *placidity* of the divine administration — like an undisturbed and unruffled ocean of glass. Perhaps, however, we should not press such circumstances too far to find a symbolical meaning. ¶ *And in the midst of the throne.* ἐν μέσῳ τοῦ θρόνου. Not occupying the throne, but so as to appear to be intermingled with the throne, or "in the midst" of it, in the sense that it was beneath the centre of it. The meaning would seem to be, that the four living creatures referred to occupied such a position collectively that they at the same time appeared to be *under* the throne, so that it rested on them, and *around* it, so that they could be seen from any quarter. This would occur if their bodies were under the throne, and if they stood so that they faced outward. To one approaching the throne they would seem to be *around* it, though their bodies were *under*, or "in the midst" of it as a support. The form of their bodies is not specified, but it is not improbable that though their *heads* were different, their *bodies*, that were under the throne, and that sustained it, were of the same form. ¶ *And round about the throne.* In the sense above explained—that, as they stood, they would be seen on every side of the throne. ¶ Were *four beasts.* This is a very unhappy translation, as the word *beasts* by no means conveys a correct idea of the original word. The Greek word—ζῶον—means properly *a living thing;* and it is thus indeed applied to animals, or to the living creation, but the notion of their being *living things*, or *living creatures*, should be retained in the translation. Professor Stuart renders it, "living creatures." Isaiah (vi.), in his vision of Jehovah,

saw two seraphim; Ezekiel, whom John more nearly resembles in his description, saw four "living creatures"—הָיוֹת (ch. i. 5)—that is, living, animated, moving beings. The words "living beings" would better convey the idea than any other which could be employed. They are evidently, like those which Ezekiel saw, symbolical beings; but the nature and purpose of the symbol is not perfectly apparent. The "four and twenty elders" are evidently human beings, and are representatives, as above explained, of the church. In ch. v. 11, *angels* are themselves introduced as taking an important part in the worship of heaven: and these living beings, therefore, cannot be designed to represent either angels or men. In Ezekiel they are either designed as poetic representations of the majesty of God, or of his providential government, showing what *sustains* his throne; symbols denoting intelligence, vigilance, the rapidity and directness with which the divine commands are executed, and the energy and firmness with which the government of God is administered. The nature of the case, and the similarity to the representation in Ezekiel, would lead us to suppose that the same idea is to be found substantially in John; and there would be no difficulty in such an interpretation were it not that these "living creatures" are apparently represented in ch. v. 8, 9, as uniting with the redeemed from the earth in such a manner as to imply that they were themselves redeemed. But perhaps the language in ch. v. 9, "And *they* sung a new song," &c., though apparently connected with the "four beasts" in ver. 8, is not designed to be so connected. John may intend there merely to advert to the fact that a new song was sung, without meaning to say that the "four living beings" *united* in that song. For, if he designed merely to say that the "four living beings" and the "four and twenty elders" fell down to worship, and then that a song was heard, though in fact sung only by the four and twenty elders, he might have employed the language which he actually has done. If this interpretation be admitted, then the most natural explanation to be given of the "four living beings" is to suppose that they are symbolical beings designed to furnish some representation of the government of God—to illustrate, as it were, that on which the divine government *rests*, or which constitutes its support—to wit, power, intelligence, vigilance, energy. This is apparent, (*a*) because it was not unusual for the thrones of monarchs to be supported by carved animals of various forms, which were designed undoubtedly to be somehow emblematic of government—either of its stability, vigilance, boldness, or firmness. Thus Solomon had twelve lions carved on each side of his throne—no improper emblems of government—1 Ki. x. 10, 20. (*b*) These living beings are described as the *supports* of the throne of God, or as that on which it rests, and would be, therefore, no improper symbols of the great principles or truths which give support or stability to the divine administration. (*c*) They are, in themselves, well adapted to be representatives of the great principles of the divine government, or of the divine providential dealings, as we shall see in the more particular explanation of the symbol. (*d*) Perhaps it might be added, that, so understood, there would be *completeness* in the vision. The "elders" appear there as representatives of the church redeemed; the angels in their own proper persons render praise to God. To this it was not improper to add, and the completeness of the representation seems to make it necessary to add, that all the doings of the Almighty unite in his praise; his various acts in the government of the universe harmonize with redeemed and unfallen intelligences in proclaiming his glory. The vision of the "living beings," therefore, is not, as I suppose, a representation of the *attributes* of God as such, but an emblematic representation of the divine government—of the throne of Deity resting upon, or sustained by, those things of which these living beings are emblems—intelligence, firmness, energy, &c. This supposition seems to combine more probabilities than any other which has been proposed; for, according to this supposition, all the acts, and ways, and creatures of God unite in his praise. It is proper to add, however, that expositors are by no means agreed as to the design of this representation. Professor Stuart supposes that the attributes of God are referred to; Mr. Elliott (i. 93), that the "twenty-four elders and the four living creatures symbolize the church, or the collective body of the saints of God; and that as there are two grand

7 And the first beast *was* like a lion, and the second beast like a calf, and the third beast had a face as a man, and the fourth beast *was* like a flying eagle.

divisions of the church, the larger one that *of the departed in Paradise*, and the other that *militant on earth*, the former is depicted by the twenty-four elders, and the latter by the living creatures;" Mr. Lord (pp. 53, 54), that the living creatures and the elders are both of one race; the former perhaps denoting those like Enoch and Elijah, who were translated, and those who were raised by the Saviour after his resurrection, or those who have been raised to special eminence—the latter the mass of the redeemed; Mr. Mede, that the living creatures are symbols of the church worshipping on earth; Mr. Daubuz, that they are symbols of the ministers of the church on earth; Vitringa, that they are symbols of eminent ministers and teachers in every age; Dr. Hammond regards him who sits on the throne as the metropolitan bishop of Judea, the representative of God, the elders as diocesan bishops of Judea, and the living creatures as four apostles, symbols of the saints who are to attend the Almighty as assessors in judgment! See Lord on the Apocalypse, pp. 58, 59. ¶ *Full of eyes.* Denoting omniscience. The ancients fabled Argus as having one hundred eyes, or as having the power of seeing in any direction. The emblem here would denote an ever-watchful and observing Providence; and, in accordance with the explanation proposed above, it means that, in the administration of the divine government, everything is distinctly contemplated; nothing escapes observation; nothing can be concealed. It is obvious that the divine government could not be administered unless this were so; and it is the perfection of the government of God that all things are seen just as they are. In the vision seen by Ezekiel (ch. i. 18), the "rings" of the wheels on which the living creatures moved are represented as "full of eyes round about them," emblematic of the same thing. So Milton—

"As with stars their bodies all,
And wings were set with eyes; with eyes the wheels
Of beryl, and careening fires between."

¶ *Before.* In front. As one looked on their faces, from whatever quarter the throne was approached, he could see a multitude of eyes looking upon him.

¶ *And behind.* On the parts of their bodies which were under the throne. The meaning is, that there is universal vigilance in the government of God. Whatever is the form of the divine administration; whatever part is contemplated; however it is manifested—whether as activity, energy, power, or intelligence—it is based on the fact that *all things are seen from every direction.* There is nothing that is the result of blind fate or of chance.

7. *And the first beast was like a lion.* A *general* description has been given, applicable to all, denoting that in whatever form the divine government is administered, *these things* will be found; a particular description now follows, contemplating that government under particular aspects, as symbolized by the living beings on which the throne rests. The first is that of a lion. The lion is the monarch of the woods, the king of beasts, and he becomes thus the emblem of dominion, of authority, of government in general. Comp. Ge. xlix. 9; Am. iii. 8; Joel iii. 16; Da. vii. 4. As emblematic of the divine administration, this would signify that He who sits on the throne is the ruler over all, and that his dominion is absolute and entire. It has been made a question whether the *whole* body had the form of a lion, or whether it had the appearance of a lion only as to its face or front part. It would seem probable that the latter only is intended, for it is expressly said of the "third beast" that it had "the *face* of a man," implying that it did not resemble a man in other respects, and it is probable that, as these living creatures were the supports of the throne, they had the same form in all other particulars except the front part. The writer has not informed us what was the appearance of these living creatures in other respects, but it is most natural to suppose that it was in the form of an ox, as being adapted to sustain a burden. It is hardly necessary to say that the *thing* supposed to be symbolical here in the government of God—his absolute rule—actually exists, or that it is important that this should be fairly exhibited to men. ¶ *And the second beast like a calf.* Or, more properly, a young bullock,

for so the word—μόσχος—means. The term is given by Herodotus (ii. 41; iii. 28) to the Egyptian god Apis, that is, a young bullock. Such an emblem, standing under a throne as one of its supports, would symbolize firmness, endurance, strength (comp. Pr. xiv. 4); and, as used to represent qualities pertaining to him who sat on the throne, would denote stability, firmness, perseverance: qualities that are found abundantly in the divine administration. There was clearly, in the apprehension of the ancients, some natural fitness or propriety in such an emblem A young bullock was worshipped in Egypt as a god. Jeroboam set up two idols in the form of a calf, the one in Dan and the other in Bethel, 1 Ki. xii. 28, 29. A similar object of worship was found in the Indian, Greek, and Scandinavian mythologies, and the image appears to have been adopted early and extensively

Egyptian Calf-idol.

to represent the divinity. The above figure is a representation of a calf-idol, copied from the collection made by the artists of the French Institute at Cairo. It is recumbent, with human eyes, the skin flesh-coloured, and the whole after-parts covered with a white and sky-blue drapery: the horns not on the head, but above it, and containing within them the symbolical globe surmounted by two feathers. The meaning of the emblems on the back is not known. It is copied here merely to show that, for some cause, the calf was regarded as an emblem of the Divinity. It may illustrate this, also, to remark that among the sculptures found by Mr. Layard, in the ruins of Nineveh, were not a few winged bulls, some of them of large structure, and probably all of them emblematic. One of these was removed with great difficulty, to be deposited in the British Museum. See Mr. Layard's *Nineveh and its Remains*, vol. ii. pp. 64-75. Such emblems were common in the East; and, being thus common, they would be readily understood in the time of John. ¶ *And the third beast had a face as a man.* There is no intimation as to what was the form of the remaining portion of this living creature; but as the beasts were "in the midst of the throne," that is, under it as a support, it may be presumed that they had such a form as was adapted to that purpose —as supposed above, perhaps the form of an ox. To this living creature there was attached the head of a man, and *that* would be what would be particularly visible to one looking on the throne. The aspect of a *man* here would denote intelligence—for it is this which distinguishes man from the creation beneath him; and if the explanation of the symbol above given be correct, then the meaning of this emblem is, that the operations of the government of God are conducted with intelligence and wisdom. That is, the divine administration is not the result of blind fate or chance; it is founded on a clear knowledge of things, on what is best to be done, on what will most conduce to the common good. Of the *truth* of this there can be no doubt; and there was a propriety that, in a vision designed to give to man a view of the government of the Almighty, this should be appropriately symbolized. It may illustrate this to observe, that in ancient sculptures it was common to unite the head of a man with the figure of an animal, as *combining* symbols. Among the most remarkable figures discovered by Mr. Layard, in the ruins of Nineveh, were winged, human-headed lions. These lions are thus described by Mr. Layard: —"They were about twelve feet in height, and the same number in length. The body and limbs were admirably portrayed; the muscles and bones, although strongly developed, to display the strength of the animal, showed, at the same time, a correct knowledge of its anatomy and form. Expanded wings sprung from the shoulder and spread over the back; a knotted girdle, ending in tassels, encircled the loins. These sculptures, forming an entrance, were partly in full, and partly in relief. The head and forepart, facing the chambers, were in full; but only one side of the rest of the slab was sculptured, the back being placed against the wall of sun-dried bricks" (*Nineveh and its Remains*, vol. i. p. 75). The following engraving will give an idea

Human-headed Winged Lion.

of one of these human-headed animals, and will serve to illustrate the passage before us — alike in reference to the *head*, indicating intelligence, and the *wings*, denoting rapidity. On the use of these figures, found in the ruins of Nineveh, Mr. Layard makes the following sensible remarks—remarks admirably illustrating the view which I take of the symbols before us:—" I used to contemplate for hours these mysterious emblems, and muse over their intent and history. What more noble forms could have ushered the people into the temple of their gods? What more sublime images could have been borrowed from nature by men who sought, unaided by the light of revealed religion, to embody their conceptions of the wisdom, power, and ubiquity of a Supreme Being? They could find no better type of intellect and knowledge than the head of a man; of strength, than the body of the lion; of rapidity of motion, than the wings of a bird. These winged, human-headed lions were not idle creations, the offspring of mere fancy; their meaning was written upon them. They had awed and instructed races which flourished 3000 years ago. Through the portals which they guarded, kings, priests, and warriors had borne sacrifices to their altars, long before the wisdom of the East had penetrated into Greece, and had furnished its mythology with symbols long recognized by the Assyrian votaries" (*Nineveh and its Remains*, vol. i. p. 75, 76). ¶ *And the fourth beast was like a flying eagle.* All birds, indeed, fly; but the epithet *flying* is here employed to add intensity to the description. The eagle is distinguished, among the feathered race, for the rapidity, the power, and the elevation of its flight. No other bird is supposed to fly so high; none ascends with so much power; none is so majestic and grand in his ascent towards the sun. That which would be properly symbolized by this would be the rapidity with which the commands of God are executed; or this characteristic of the divine government, that the purposes of God are carried into prompt execution. There is, as it were, a vigorous, powerful, and rapid flight towards the accomplishment of the designs of God —as the eagle ascends unmolested towards the sun. Or, it *may* be that this symbolizes protecting care, or is an emblem of that protection which God, by his providence, extends over those who put their trust in him. Thus in Ex. xix. 4, " Ye have seen how I bare you on eagles' wings." " Hide me under the shadow of thy wings," Ps. xvii. 8. " In the shadow of thy wings will I rejoice," Ps. lxiii. 7. " As an eagle stirreth up her nest, fluttereth over her young, spreadeth abroad her wings, taketh them, beareth them on her wings: so the Lord alone did lead him," De. xxxii. 11, 12, &c. As in the case of the other living beings, so it is to be remarked of the fourth living creature also, that the form of the *body* is unknown. There is no impropriety in supposing that it is only its front aspect that John here speaks of, for that was sufficient for the symbol. The remaining portion "in the midst of the throne" may have corresponded with that of the other living beings, as being adapted to a support. In further illustration of this it may be remarked, that symbols of this description were common in the Oriental world. Figures in the human form, or in the form of animals, with the head of an eagle or a vulture, are found in the ruins of Nineveh, and were undoubtedly designed to be symbolic. "On the earliest Assyrian monuments," says Mr. Layard (*Nineveh and its Remains*, vol. ii. p. 348, 349), "one of the most prominent sacred types is the eagle-headed, or the vulture-headed, human figure. Not only is it found in colossal proportions on the walls, or guarding the portals of the chambers, but it is also constantly represented in the groups on the em-

A.D. 96.]   CHAPTER IV.   117

8 And the four beasts had each of them °six wings about *him;* and *they were* full of eyes within: and

*o* Is.6.2,&c.

broidered robes. When thus introduced, it is generally seen contending with other mythic animals — such as the human-headed lion or bull; and in these contests it is always the conqueror. It may hence be inferred that it was a type of the Supreme Deity, or of one of his principal attributes. A fragment of the Zoroastrian oracles, preserved by Eusebius, declares that 'God is he that has *the head of a hawk.* He is the first, indestructible, eternal, unbegotten, indivisible, dissimilar; the dispenser of all good; incorruptible; the best of the good, the wisest of the wise; he is the father of equity and justice, self-taught, physical and perfect, and wise, and the only inventor of the sacred philosophy.' Sometimes the head of this bird is added to the body of a lion. Under this form of the Egyptian hieracosphinx it is the conqueror in combats with other symbolical figures, and is frequently represented as striking down a gazelle or wild goat. It also clearly resembles the gryphon of the Greek mythology, avowedly an Eastern symbol, and connected with Apollo, or with the sun, of which the Assyrian form was probably an emblem." The following figure found in Nimroud, or ancient

Eagle-headed Winged Lion.

Nineveh, may furnish an illustration of one of the usual forms. If these views of the meaning of these symbols are correct, then the idea which would be conveyed to the mind of John, and the idea, therefore, which should be conveyed to our minds, is, that the government of God is energetic, firm, intelligent, and that in the execution of its purposes it is *rapid* like the unobstructed flight of an eagle, or *protective* like

they ¹rest not day and night, saying, Holy, holy, holy, Lord God Almighty, which was, and is, and is to come.

¹ *have no rest.*

the care of the eagle for its young. When, in the subsequent parts of the vision, these living creatures are represented as offering praise and adoration to Him that sits on the throne (ver. 8; ch. v. 8, 14), the meaning would be, in accordance with this representation, that all the acts of divine government do, as if they were personified, unite in the praise which the redeemed and the angels ascribe to God. All living things, and all acts of the Almighty, conspire to proclaim his glory. The church, by her representatives, the "four and twenty elders," honours God; the angels, without number, unite in the praise; all creatures in heaven, in earth, under the earth, and in the sea (ch. v. 13), join in the song; and all the acts and ways of God declare also his majesty and glory: for around his throne, and beneath his throne, are expressive symbols of the firmness, energy, intelligence, and power with which his government is administered.

8. *And the four beasts had each of them six wings about* him. An emblem common to them all, denoting that, in reference to each and all the things here symbolized, there was one common characteristic—that in heaven there is the utmost promptness in executing the divine commands. Comp. Is. vi. 2; Ps. xviii. 10; civ. 3; Je. xlviii. 40. No mention is made of the manner in which these wings were arranged, and conjecture in regard to that is vain. The seraphim, as seen by Isaiah, had each one six wings, with two of which the face was covered, to denote profound reverence; with two the feet, or lower parts—emblematic of modesty; and with two they flew—emblematic of their celerity in executing the commands of God, Is. vi. 2. Perhaps without impropriety we may suppose that, in regard to these living beings seen by John, two of the wings of each were employed, as in Isaiah, to cover the face—token of profound reverence; and that the remainder were employed in flight—denoting the rapidity with which the divine commands are executed. Mercury, the messenger of Jupiter among the heathen, was represented with wings, and nothing is

118 REVELATION. [A.D. 96.

9 And when those beasts give glory and honour and thanks to him that sat on the throne, *p* who liveth for ever and ever,

10 The four and twenty elders fall down before him that sat on the throne, and worship him that liveth for ever and ever, and cast

*p* ch.5.14.

their *q* crowns before the throne, saying,

11 Thou art *r* worthy, O Lord, to receive glory and honour and power; *s* for thou hast created all things, and for thy pleasure they are and were created.

*q* ver.4.    *r* ch.5.12.    *s* Col.1.16.

more common in the paintings and bas-reliefs of antiquity than such representations. ¶ *And they were full of eyes within.* Professor Stuart more correctly renders this, "around and within are full of eyes;" connecting the word "around" ["about"], not with the *wings*, as in our version, but with the *eyes*. The meaning is, that the portions of the beasts that were visible from the outside of the throne, and the portions under or within the throne, were covered with eyes. The obvious design of this is to mark the universal vigilance of divine providence. ¶ *And they rest not.* Marg., *have no rest.* That is, they are constantly employed; there is no intermission. The meaning, as above explained, is, that the works and ways of God are constantly bringing praise to him. ¶ *Day and night.* Continually. They who are employed day and night fill up the whole time—for this is all. ¶ *Saying, Holy, holy, holy.* For the meaning of this, see Notes on Is. vi. 3. ¶ *Lord God Almighty.* Isaiah (vi. 3) expresses it, "Jehovah of hosts." The reference is to the true God, and the epithet *Almighty* is one that is often given him. It is peculiarly appropriate here, as there were to be, as the sequel shows, remarkable exhibitions of *power* in executing the purposes described in this book. ¶ *Which was, and is, and is to come.* Who is eternal—existing in all past time; existing now; and to continue to exist for ever. See Notes on ch. i. 4.

9. *And when those beasts give glory,* &c. As often as those living beings ascribe glory to God. They did this continually (ver. 8); and, if the above explanation be correct, then the idea is that the ways and acts of God in his providential government are continually of such a nature as to honour him.

10. *The four and twenty elders fall down before him,* &c. The representatives of the redeemed church in heaven (Notes, ver. 4) also unite in the praise. The meaning, if the explanation of the symbol be correct, is, that the church universal unites in praise to God for all that characterizes his administration. In the connection in which this stands here, the sense would be, that as often as there is any *new* manifestation of the principles of the divine government, the church ascribes *new* praise to God. Whatever may be thought of this explanation of the meaning of the symbols, of the *fact* here stated there can be no doubt. The church of God always rejoices when there is any new manifestation of the principles of the divine administration. As all these acts, in reality, bring glory and honour to God, the church, *as often* as there is any new manifestation of the divine character and purposes, renders praise anew. Nor can it be doubted that the view here taken is one that is every way appropriate to the general character of this book. The great design was to disclose what God was to do in future times, in the various revolutions that were to take place on the earth, until his government should be firmly established, and the principles of his administration should everywhere prevail; and there was a propriety, therefore, in describing the representatives of the church as taking part in this universal praise, and as casting every crown at the feet of Him who sits upon the throne. ¶ *And cast their crowns before the throne.* They are described as "crowned" (ver. 4), that is, as triumphant, and as kings (comp. ch. v. 10), and they are here represented as casting their crowns at his feet, in token that they owe their triumph to Him. To his providential dealings, to his wise and merciful government, they owe it that they are crowned at all; and there is, therefore, a propriety that they should acknowledge this in a proper manner by placing their crowns at his feet.

11. *Thou art worthy, O Lord.* In thy character, perfections, and government, there is that which makes it

# CHAPTER V. 119

proper that universal praise should be rendered. The feeling of all true worshippers is, that God is *worthy* of the praise that is ascribed to him. No man worships him aright who does not feel that there is that in his nature and his doings which makes it *proper* that he should receive universal adoration. ¶ *To receive glory.* To have praise or glory ascribed to thee. ¶ *And honour.* To be honoured; that is, to be approached and adored as worthy of honour. ¶ *And power.* To have power ascribed to thee, or to be regarded as having infinite power. Man can *confer* no power on God, but he may acknowledge that which he has, and adore him for its exertion in his behalf and in the government of the world. ¶ *For thou hast created all things.* Thus laying the foundation for praise. No one can contemplate this vast and wonderful universe without seeing that He who has made it is *worthy* to "receive glory, and honour, and power." Comp. Notes on Job xxxviii. 7. ¶ *And for thy pleasure they are.* They exist by thy will — διὰ τὸ θέλημά. The meaning is, that they owe their existence to the *will* of God, and therefore their creation lays the foundation for praise. He "spake, and it was done; he commanded, and it stood fast." He said, "Let there be light; and there was light." There is no other reason why the universe exists at all than that such was the will of God; there is nothing else that is to be adduced as explaining the fact that anything has now a being. The putting forth of that will explains all; and, consequently, whatever wisdom, power, goodness, is manifested in the universe, is to be traced to God, and is the expression of what was in him from eternity. It is proper, then, to "look up through nature to nature's God," and wherever we see greatness or goodness in the works of creation, to regard them as the faint expression of what exists essentially in the Creator. ¶ *And were created.* Bringing more distinctly into notice the fact that they owe their existence to his will. They are not eternal; they are not self-existent; they were formed from nothing.

This concludes the magnificent introduction to the principal visions in this book. It is beautifully appropriate to the solemn disclosures which are to be made in the following portions of the book, and, as in the case of Isaiah and Ezekiel, was eminently adapted to impress the mind of the holy seer with awe. Heaven is opened to his view; the throne of God is seen; there is a vision of Him who sits upon that throne; thunders and voices are heard around the throne; the lightnings play; and a rainbow, symbol of peace, encircles all; the representatives of the redeemed church, occupying subordinate thrones, and in robes of victory, and with crowns on their heads, are there; a vast smooth expanse like the sea is spread out before the throne; and the emblems of the wisdom, the power, the vigilance, the energy, the strength of the divine administration are there, represented as in the act of bringing honour to God, and proclaiming his praise. The mind of John was doubtless prepared by these august visions for the disclosures which follow; and the mind of the reader should in like manner be deeply and solemnly impressed when he contemplates them, as if *he* looked into heaven, and saw the impressive grandeur of the worship there. Let us fancy ourselves, therefore, with the holy seer looking into heaven, and listen with reverence to what the great God discloses respecting the various changes that are to occur until every foe of the church shall be subdued, and the earth shall acknowledge his sway, and the whole scene shall close in the triumphs and joys of heaven.

## CHAPTER V.
### ANALYSIS OF THE CHAPTER.

This chapter introduces the disclosure of future events. It is done in a manner eminently fitted to impress the mind with a sense of the importance of the revelations about to be made. The proper state of mind for appreciating this chapter is that when we look on the future, and are sensible that important events are about to occur; when we feel that that future is wholly impenetrable to us; and when the efforts of the highest created minds fail to lift the mysterious veil which hides those events from our view; it is in accordance with our nature that the mind should be impressed with solemn awe under such circumstances; it is not a violation of the laws of our nature that one who had an earnest desire to penetrate that future, and who saw the volume before him which contained the mysterious revelation, and who yet felt that there was no one in heaven or earth who could break the seals, and disclose what was to come, should weep. Comp.

ver. 4. The *design* of the whole chapter is evidently to honour the Lamb of God, by showing that the power was intrusted to him which was confided to no one else in heaven or earth, of disclosing what is to come. Nothing else would better illustrate this than the fact that he alone could break the mysterious seals which barred out the knowledge of the future from all created eyes; and nothing would be better adapted to impress this on the mind than the representation in this chapter —the exhibition of a mysterious book in the hand of God; the proclamation of the angel, calling on any who could do it to open the book; the fact that no one in heaven or earth could do it; the tears shed by John when it was found that no one could do it; the assurance of one of the elders that the Lion of the tribe of Judah had power to do it; and the profound adoration of all in heaven, and in earth, and under the earth in view of the power intrusted to him of breaking these mysterious seals.

The main points in the chapter are these: (1) Having in ch. iv. described God as sitting on a throne, John here (ver. 1) represents himself as seeing in his right hand a mysterious volume; written all over on the inside and the outside, yet sealed with seven seals; a volume manifestly referring to the future, and containing important disclosures respecting coming events. (2) A mighty angel is introduced making a proclamation, and asking who is worthy to open that book, and to break those seals; evidently implying that none unless of exalted rank could do it, ver. 2. (3) There is a pause: no one in heaven, or in earth, or under the earth, approaches to do it, or claims the right to do it, ver. 3. (4) John, giving way to the expressions of natural emotion—indicative of the longing and intense desire in the human soul to be made acquainted with the secrets of the future—pours forth a flood of tears because no one is found who is worthy to open the seals of this mysterious book, or to read what was recorded there, ver. 4. (5) In his state of suspense and of grief, one of the elders— the representatives of that church for whose benefit these revelations of the future were to be made (Note on ch. iv. 4)—approaches him and says that there *is* one who is able to open the book; one who has the power to loose its seals, ver. 5. This is the Messiah— the Lion of the tribe of Judah, the Root of David—coming now to make the disclosure for which the whole book was given, ch. i. 1. (6) Immediately the attention of John is attracted by the Messiah, appearing as a Lamb in the midst of the throne; with horns, the symbols of strength; and eyes, the symbols of all-pervading intelligence. He approaches and takes the book from the hand of Him that sits on the throne; symbolical of the fact that it is the province of the Messiah to make known to the church and the world the events which are to occur, ver. 6, 7. He appears here in a different form from that in which he manifested himself in ch. i., for the purpose is different. There he appears clothed in majesty, to impress the mind with a sense of his essential glory. Here he appears in a form that recalls the memory of his sacrifice; to denote, perhaps, that it is in virtue of his atonement that the future is to be disclosed; and that therefore there is a special propriety that *he* should appear and do what no other one in heaven or earth could do. (7) The approach of the Messiah to unfold the mysteries in the book, the fact that he had "prevailed" to accomplish what there was so strong a desire should be accomplished, furnishes an occasion for exalted thanksgiving and praise, ver. 8-10. (8) This ascription of praise in heaven is instantly responded to, and echoed back, from all parts of the universe—all joining in acknowledging the Lamb as worthy of the exalted office to which he was raised, ver. 11-13. The angels around the throne—amounting to thousands of myriads—unite with the living creatures and the elders; and to these are joined the voices of every creature in heaven, on the earth, under the earth, and in the sea, ascribing to Him that sits upon the throne and the Lamb universal praise. (9) To this loud ascription of praise from far-distant worlds the living creatures respond a hearty *Amen*, and the elders fall down and worship him that lives for ever and ever, ver. 14. The universe is held in wondering expectation of the disclosures which are to be made, and from all parts of the universe there is an acknowledgment that the Lamb of God alone has the right to break the mysterious seals. The *importance* of the developments justifies the magnificence of

# CHAPTER V.

AND I saw in the right hand of him that sat on the throne this representation; and it would not be possible to imagine a more sublime introduction to these great events.

1. *And I saw in the right hand of him that sat on the throne.* Of God, ch. iv. 3, 4. His *form* is not described there, nor is there any intimation of it here except the mention of his "right hand." The book or roll seems to have been so held in his hand that John could see its shape, and see distinctly how it was written and sealed. ¶ *A book*—βιβλίον. This word is properly a diminutive of the word commonly rendered book (βίβλος), and would strictly mean a small book, or a book of diminutive size—a tablet, or a letter (Liddell and Scott, *Lex.*). It is used, however, to denote a book of any size—a roll, scroll, or volume; and is thus used (*a*) to denote the Pentateuch, or the Mosaic law, He. ix. 19; x. 7; (*b*) the book of life, Re. xvii. 8; xx. 12; xxi. 27; (*c*) epistles which were also rolled up, Re. i. 11; (*d*) documents, as a bill of divorce, Mat. xix. 7; Mar. x. 4. When it is the express design to speak of a small book, another word is used (βιβλαρίδιον), Re. x. 2, 8, 9, 10. The book or roll referred to here was that which contained the revelation in the subsequent chapters, to the end of the description of the opening of the seventh seal—for the communication that was to be made was all included in the seven seals; and to conceive of the *size* of the book, therefore, we are only to reflect on the amount of parchment that would naturally be written over by the communications here made. The *form* of the book was undoubtedly that of a scroll or roll; for that was the usual form of books among the ancients, and such a volume could be more easily sealed with a number of seals, in the manner here described, than a volume in the form in which books are made now. On the ancient form of books, see Notes on Lu. iv. 17. The engraving in Job, ch. xix., will furnish an additional illustration of their form. ¶ *Written within and on the back side.* Gr., "within and behind." It was customary to write only on one side of the paper or vellum, for the sake of convenience in reading the volume as it was unrolled. If, as sometimes was the case, the book was in the same form as books are now a *a*book written within and on the back side, *b*sealed with seven seals.

*a* Eze.2.9,10.   *b* Is.29.11.

—of leaves bound together—then it was usual to write on both sides of the leaf, as both sides of a page are printed now. But in the other form it was a very uncommon thing to write on both sides of the parchment, and was never done unless there was a scarcity of writing material; or unless there was an amount of matter beyond what was anticipated; or unless something had been omitted. It is not necessary to suppose that John saw both sides of the parchment as it was held in the hand of him that sat on the throne. That it was written on the *back* side he would naturally see, and, as the book was sealed, he would infer that it was written in the usual manner on the inside. ¶ *Sealed with seven seals.* On the ancient manner of sealing, see Notes on Mat. xxvii. 66; comp. Notes on Job xxxviii. 14. The fact that there were *seven* seals—an unusual number in fastening a volume—would naturally attract the attention of John, though it might not occur to him at once that there was anything significant in the number. It is not stated in what manner the seals were attached to the volume, but it is clear that they were so attached that each seal closed one part of the volume, and that when one was broken and the portion which that was designed to fasten was unrolled, a second would be come to, which it would be necessary to break in order to read the next portion. The outer seal would indeed bind the whole; but when that was broken it would not give access to the whole volume unless each successive seal were broken. May it not have been intended by this arrangement to suggest the idea that the whole future is unknown to us, and that the disclosure of any one portion, though necessary if the whole would be known, does not disclose all, but leaves seal after seal still unbroken, and that they are all to be broken one after another if we would know all? *How* these were arranged, John does not say. All that is necessary to be supposed is, that the seven seals were put successively upon the *margin* of the volume as it was rolled up, so that each opening would extend only as far as the next seal, when the unrolling would be arrested. Anyone, by rolling up a sheet of paper, could

2 And I saw a strong angel proclaiming with a loud voice, Who is worthy to open the book, and to loose the seals thereof?

3 And no man in heaven, nor in earth, neither under the earth, was able to open the book, neither to look thereon.

so fasten it with pins, or with a succession of seals, as to represent this with sufficient accuracy.

2. *And I saw a strong angel.* An angel endowed with great strength, as if such strength was necessary to enable him to give utterance to the loud voice of the inquiry. "Homer represents his heralds as powerful, robust men, in order consistently to attribute to them deep-toned and powerful voices" (Prof. Stuart). The inquiry to be made was one of vast importance; it was to be made of all in heaven, all on the earth, and all under the earth, and hence an angel is introduced so mighty that his voice could be heard in all those distant worlds. ¶ *Proclaiming with a loud voice.* That is, as a herald or crier. He is rather introduced here as *appointed* to this office than as *self-moved*. The *design* undoubtedly is to impress the mind with a sense of the importance of the disclosures about to be made, and at the same time with a sense of the impossibility of penetrating the future by any created power. That one of the highest angels should make such a proclamation would sufficiently show its importance; that such an one, by the mere act of making such a proclamation, should practically confess his own inability, and consequently the inability of all of similar rank, to make the disclosures, would show that the revelations of the future were beyond mere created power. ¶ *Who is worthy to open the book*, &c. That is, who is "worthy" in the sense of having a rank so exalted, and attributes so comprehensive, as to authorize and enable him to do it. In other words, who has the requisite endowments of all kinds to enable him to do it? It would require moral qualities of an exalted character to justify him in approaching the seat of the holy God, to take the book from his hands; it would require an ability beyond that of any created being to penetrate the future, and disclose the meaning of the symbols which were employed. The fact that the book was held in the hand of him that was on the throne, and sealed in this manner, was in itself a sufficient proof that it was not his purpose to make the disclosure directly,

and the natural inquiry arose whether there was anyone in the wide universe who, by rank, or character, or office, would be empowered to open the mysterious volume.

3. *And no man in heaven.* No one —οὐδεὶς. There is no limitation in the original to *man.* The idea is, that there was no one in heaven—evidently alluding to the created beings there—who could open the volume. Is it not taught here that *angels* cannot penetrate the future, and disclose what is to come? Are not their faculties limited in this respect like those of man? ¶ *Nor in earth.* Among all classes of men—sages, divines, prophets, philosophers—who among those have ever been able to penetrate the future, and disclose what is to come? ¶ *Neither under the earth.* These divisions compose, in common language, the universe: what is in heaven above; what is on the earth; and whatever there is under the earth—the abodes of the dead. May there not be an allusion here to the supposed science of *necromancy*, and an assertion that even the dead cannot penetrate the future, and disclose what is to come? Comp. Notes on Is. viii. 19. In all these great realms no one advanced who was qualified to undertake the office of making a disclosure of what the mysterious scroll might contain. ¶ *Was able to open the book.* Had ability—ἠδύνατο—to do it. It was a task beyond their power. Even if anyone had been found who had a rank and a moral character which might have seemed to justify the effort, there was no one who had the power of reading what was recorded respecting coming events. ¶ *Neither to look thereon.* That is, so to open the seals as to have a view of what was written therein. That it was not beyond their power merely to *see* the book is apparent from the fact that John himself saw it in the hand of him that sat on the throne; and it is evident also (ver. 5) that in that sense the elders saw it. But no one could prevail to inspect the contents, or so have access to the interior of the volume as to be able to see what was written there. It could be seen, indeed (ver. 1), that it was written on

A.D. 96.] CHAPTER V. 123

4 And I wept much, because no man was found worthy to open and to read the book, neither to look thereon.

5 And one of the elders saith unto me, Weep not: behold, the ᶜLion of the tribe of Judah, the ᵈRoot of David, hath prevailed to open the book, and to loose the seven seals thereof.

c Ge.49.9,10; Nu.24.9; He.7.14.
d ch.22.16; Is.11.1,10.

both sides of the parchment, but *what* the writing was no one could know.
4. *And I wept much, because no man was found worthy*, &c. Gr., as in ver. 3, *no one*. It would seem as if there was a pause to see if there were any response to the proclamation of the angel. There being none, John gave way to his deep emotions in a flood of tears. The tears of the apostle here may be regarded as an illustration of two things which are occurring constantly in the minds of men: (1) The strong desire to penetrate the future; to lift the mysterious veil which shrouds that which is to come; to find some way to pierce the dark wall which seems to stand up before us, and which shuts from our view that which is to be hereafter. There have been no more earnest efforts made by men than those which have been made to read the sealed volume which contains the record of what is yet to come. By dreams, and omens, and auguries, and astrology, and the flight of birds, and necromancy, men have sought anxiously to ascertain what is to be hereafter. Compare, for an expression of that intense desire, Foster's Life and Correspondence, vol. i. p. 111, and vol. ii. pp. 237, 238. (2) The weeping of the apostle may be regarded as an instance of the deep grief which men often experience when all efforts to penetrate the future fail, and they feel that after all they are left completely in the dark. Often is the soul overpowered with grief, and often are the eyes filled with sadness at the reflection that there is an absolute limit to the human powers; that all that man can arrive at by his own efforts is uncertain conjecture, and that there is no way possible by which he can make nature speak out and disclose what is to come. Nowhere does man find himself more fettered and limited in his powers than here; nowhere does he feel that there is such an intense disproportion between his desires and his attainments. In nothing do *we* feel that we are more absolutely in need of divine help than in our attempts to unveil the future; and were it not for revelation man might weep in despair.

5. *And one of the elders saith unto me.* See Notes on ch. iv. 4. No particular reason is assigned why this message was delivered by one of the *elders* rather than by an angel. If the elders were, however (see Notes on ch. iv. 4), the representatives of the church, there was a propriety that they should address John in his trouble. Though they were in heaven, they were deeply interested in all that pertained to the welfare of the church, and they had been permitted to understand what as yet was unknown to him, that the power of opening the mysterious volume which contained the revelation of the future was intrusted particularly to the Messiah. Having this knowledge, they were prepared to comfort him with the hope that what was so mysterious would be made known. ¶ *Weep not.* That is, there is no occasion for tears. The object which you so much desire can be obtained. There is one who can break those seals, and who can unroll that volume and read what is recorded there. ¶ *Behold the Lion of the tribe of Judah.* This undoubtedly refers to the Lord Jesus; and the points needful to be explained are, why he is called a *Lion*, and why he is spoken of as the Lion *of the tribe of Judah.* (*a*) As to the first: This appellation is not elsewhere given to the Messiah, but it is not difficult to see its propriety as used in this place. The lion is the king of beasts, the monarch of the forest, and thus becomes an emblem of one of kingly authority and of power (see Notes on ch. iv. 7), and as such the appellation is used in this place. It is because Christ has *power* to open the seals—as if he ruled over the universe, and all events were under his control, as the lion rules in the forest—that the name is here given to him. (*b*) As to the other point: He is called the "*Lion of the tribe of Judah*," doubtless, with reference to the prophecy in Ge. xlix. 9—"Judah is a lion's whelp: from the prey, my son, thou art gone up: he stooped down, he couched as a lion, and as an old lion;" and from the fact that the Messiah was of the tribe of Judah. Comp. Ge. xlix. 10. This use of the term would connect

6 And I beheld, and, lo, in the midst of the throne and of the four beasts, and in the midst of the elders, stood a *Lamb, as it had been slain, having seven horns and

e Is.53.7; Jn.1.29,36.

him in the apprehension of John with the prophecy, and would suggest to him the idea of his being a ruler, or having dominion. As such, therefore, it would be appropriate that the power of breaking these seals should be committed to him. ¶ *The Root of David.* Not the Root of David in the sense that David sprung from him as a tree does from a root, but in the sense that *he himself* was a "root-shoot" or sprout *from* David, and had sprung from him as a shoot or sprout springs up from a decayed and fallen tree. See Notes on Is. xi. 1. This expression would connect him directly with David, the great and glorious monarch of Israel, and as having a right to occupy his throne. As one thus ruling over the people of God, there was a propriety that to him should be intrusted the task of opening these seals. ¶ *Hath prevailed.* That is, he has acquired this power as the result of a conflict or struggle. The word used here—ἐνίκησεν—refers to such a conflict or struggle, properly meaning to come off victor, to overcome, to conquer, to subdue; and the idea here is, that his power to do this, or the reason why he does this, is the result of a conflict in which he was a victor. As the series of events to be disclosed, resulting in the final triumph of religion, was the effect of his conflicts with the powers of evil, there was a special propriety that the disclosure should be made by him. The *truths* taught in this verse are, (1) that the power of making disclosures, in regard to the future, is intrusted to the Messiah; and (2) that this, so far as he is concerned, is the result of a conflict or struggle on his part.

6. *And I beheld, and, lo, in the midst of the throne.* We are not to suppose that he was in the centre of the throne itself, but he was a conspicuous object when the throne and the elders and the living beings were seen. He was so placed as to seem to be in the midst of the *group* made up of the throne, the living beings, and the elders. ¶ *And of the four beasts.* See Notes, ch. iv. 6. ¶ *Stood a Lamb.* An appellation often given to the Messiah, for two reasons: (1) because the lamb was an emblem of innocence; and (2) because a lamb was offered commonly in sacrifice. Comp. Notes on Jn. i. 29. ¶ *As it had been slain.* That is, in some way having the appearance of having been slain; having some marks or indications about it that it had been slain. What those were the writer does not specify. If it were covered with blood, or there were marks of mortal wounds, it would be all that the representation demands. The great work which the Redeemer performed —that of making an atonement for sin —was thus represented to John in such a way that he at once recognized him, and saw the reason why the office of breaking the seals was intrusted to him. It should be remarked that this representation is merely *symbolic*, and we are not to suppose that the Redeemer really *assumed* this form, or that he appears in this form in heaven. We should no more suppose that the Redeemer appears literally as a lamb in heaven with numerous eyes and horns, than that there is a literal throne and a sea of glass there; that there are "seats" there, and "elders," and "crowns of gold." ¶ *Having seven horns.* Emblems of authority and power—for the *horn* is a symbol of power and dominion. Comp. De. xxxiii. 17; 1 Ki. xxii. 11; Je. xlviii. 25; Zec. i. 18; Da. vii. 24. The propriety of this symbol is laid in the fact that the strength of an animal is in the horn, and that it is by this that he obtains a victory over other animals. The number *seven* here seems to be designed, as in other places, to denote *completeness*. See Notes on ch. i. 4. The meaning is, that he had so large a number as to denote complete dominion. ¶ *And seven eyes.* Symbols of intelligence. The number *seven* here also denotes *completeness;* and the idea is, that he is able to survey all things. John does not say anything as to the relative arrangement of the horns and eyes on the "Lamb," and it is vain to attempt to conjecture how it was. The whole representation is symbolical, and we may understand the meaning of the symbol without being able to form an exact conception of the figure as it appeared to him. ¶ *Which are the seven Spirits of God sent forth into all the earth.* See Notes on ch. i. 4. That is, which *represent* the seven Spirits of God; or the manifold operations of the one Divine Spirit. As the eye is

seven*ˊ* eyes, which are the seven Spirits of God sent forth into all the earth.

*f* Zec.4.10.

the symbol of intelligence—outward objects being made visible to us by that--so it may well represent an all-pervading spirit that surveys and sees all things. The eye, in this view, among the Egyptians was an emblem of the Deity. By the "seven Spirits" here the same thing is doubtless intended as in ch. i. 4; and if, as there supposed, the reference is to the Holy Spirit considered with respect to his manifold operations, the meaning here is, that the operations of that Spirit are to be regarded as connected with the work of the Redeemer. Thus, all the operations of the Spirit are connected with, and are a part of, the work of redemption. The expression "sent forth into all the earth," refers to the fact that that Spirit prevades all things. The Spirit of God is often represented as sent or poured out; and the meaning here is, that his operations are *as if* he was sent out to survey all things and to operate everywhere. Comp. 1 Co. xii. 6–11.

7. *And he came and took the book out of the right hand,* &c. As if it pertained to him by virtue of rank or office. There is a difficulty here, arising from the incongruity of what is said of a *lamb,* which it is not easy to solve. The difficulty is in conceiving how a *lamb* could take the book from the hand of Him who held it. To meet this several solutions have been proposed. (1) Vitringa supposes that the Messiah appeared as a lamb only in some such sense as the four living beings (ch. iv. 7) resembled a lion, a calf, and an eagle; that is, that they bore this resemblance only in respect to the head, while the body was that of a man. He thus supposes, that though in respect to the upper part the Saviour resembled a lamb, yet that to the front part of the body hands were attached by which he could take the book. But there are great difficulties in this supposition. Besides that nothing of this kind is intimated by John, it is contrary to every appearance of probability that the Redeemer would be represented as a monster. In his being represented as a lamb there is nothing that strikes the mind as inappropriate or unpleasant,

7 And he came and took the book out of the right hand of him that sat upon the throne.

for he is often spoken of in this manner, and the image is one that is agreeable to the mind. But all this beauty and fitness of representation is destroyed, if we think of him as having human hands proceeding from his breast or sides, or as blending the form of a man and an animal together. The representation of having an unusual number of horns and eyes does not strike us as being incongruous in the same sense; for though the *number* is increased, they are such as pertain properly to the animal to which they are attached. (2) Another supposition is that suggested by Professor Stuart, that the form was changed, and a human form resumed when the Saviour advanced to take the book and open it. This would relieve the whole difficulty, and the only objection to it is, that John has not given any express notice of such a change in the form; and the only question can be whether it is right to *suppose* it in order to meet the difficulty in the case. In support of this it is said that all is symbol; that the Saviour is represented in the book in various forms; that as his appearing as a lamb was designed to represent in a striking manner the fact that he was slain, and that all that he did was based on the atonement, so there would be no impropriety in supposing that when an action was attributed to him he assumed the form in which that act would be naturally or is usually done. And as in taking a book from the hand of another it is wholly incongruous to think of its being done by a *lamb*, is it not most natural to suppose that the usual form in which the Saviour is represented as appearing would be resumed, and that he would appear again as a man?—But is it absolutely certain that he appeared in the form of a lamb at all? May not all that is meant be, that John saw him near the throne, and among the elders, and was struck at once with his appearance of meekness and innocence, and with the marks of his having been slain as a sacrifice, and spoke of him in strong figurative language as a lamb? And where his "seven horns" and "seven eyes" are spoken of, is it necessary to suppose that there was any real assumption of such horns and eyes?

8 And when he had taken the book, the *g* four beasts and four *and* twenty elders fell down before the Lamb, having every one of

*g* ch.4.4,8,10.

them *h* harps, and golden vials full of ¹odours, which are the *i* prayers of saints.

*h* ch.15.2.   ¹ or, *incense*.   *i* Ps.141.2.

May not all that is meant be that John was struck with that in the appearance of the Redeemer of which these *would be* the appropriate symbols, and described him *as if* these had been visible? When John the Baptist saw the Lord Jesus on the banks of the Jordan, and said, "Behold the Lamb of God which taketh away the sin of the world" (Jn. i. 29), is it necessary to suppose that he actually appeared in the form of a lamb? Do not all at once understand him as referring to traits in his character, and to the work which he was to accomplish, which made it proper to speak of him as a lamb? And why, therefore, may we not suppose that John in the Apocalypse designed to use language in the same way, and that he did not intend to present so incongruous a description as that of a *lamb* approaching a throne and taking a book from the hand of Him that sat on it, and a lamb, too, with many horns and eyes? If this supposition is correct, then all that is meant in this passage would be expressed in some such language as the following: "And I looked, and lo there was one in the midst of the space occupied by the throne, by the living creatures, and by the elders, who, in aspect, and in the emblems that represented his work on the earth, was spotless, meek, and innocent as a lamb; one with marks on his person which brought to remembrance the fact that he had been slain for the sins of the world, and yet one who had most striking symbols of power and intelligence, and who was therefore worthy to approach and take the book from the hand of Him that sat on the throne." It may do something to confirm this view to recollect that when we use the term "Lamb of God" now, as is often done in preaching and in prayer, it never suggests to the mind the idea of a *lamb*. We think of the Redeemer as resembling a lamb in his moral attributes and in his sacrifice, but never as to form. This supposition relieves the passage of all that is incongruous and unpleasant, and may be all that John meant.

8. *And when he had taken the book, the four beasts,* &c. The acts of adoration here described as rendered by the four living creatures and the elders are, according to the explanation given in ch. iv. 4-7, emblematic of the honour done to the Redeemer by the church, and by the course of providential events in the government of the world. ¶ *Fell down before the Lamb.* The usual posture of profound worship. Usually in such worship there was entire prostration on the earth. See Notes on Mat. ii. 2; 1 Co. xiv. 25. ¶ *Having every one of them harps.* That is, as the construction, and the propriety of the case would seem to demand, the *elders* had each of them harps. The whole prostrated themselves with profound reverence; the elders had harps and censers, and broke out into a song of praise for redemption. This construction is demanded, because (*a*) the Greek word—ἔχοντες—more properly agrees with the word *elders*—πρεσβύτεροι —and not with the word *beasts*—ζῶα; (*b*) there is an incongruity in the representation that the living creatures, in the form of a lion, a calf, an eagle, should have harps and censers; and (*c*) the song of praise that is sung (ver. 9) is one that properly applies to the elders as the representatives of the church, and not to the living creatures—"Thou hast redeemed us to God by thy blood." The *harp* was a well-known instrument used in the service of God. Josephus describes it as having ten strings, and as struck with a key (*Ant.* vii. 12, 3). See Notes on Is. v. 12. ¶ *And golden vials.* The word *vial* with us, denoting a small slender bottle with a narrow neck, evidently does not express the idea here. The article here referred to was used for offering incense, and must have been a vessel with a large open mouth. The word *bowl* or *goblet* would better express the idea, and it is so explained by Professor Robinson, *Lex.*, and by Professor Stuart, *in loco*. The Greek word—φιάλη—occurs in the New Testament only in Revelation (v. 8; xv. 7; xvi. 1-4, 8, 10, 12, 17; xvii. 1; xxi. 9), and is uniformly rendered *vial* and *vials*, though the idea is always that of a bowl or goblet. ¶ *Full of odours.* Or rather, as in the margin, full of *incense*— θυμιαμάτων. See Notes on Lu. i. 9. ¶ *Which are the prayers of saints.*

9 And they sung a ᵏnew song, saying, Thou art worthy to take the book, and to open the seals thereof: for thou wast slain, and hast redeemed us to God ˡby thy blood, out of ᵐevery kindred, and tongue, and people, and nation;

*k* ch.14.3.   *l* Ac.20.28; Ep.1.7; He.9.12; 1 Pe.1.18,19.   *m* ch.7.9.

Which represent or denote the prayers of saints. Comp. Ps. cxli. 2, "Let my prayer be set forth before thee as incense." The meaning is, that incense was a proper emblem of prayer. This seems to have been in two respects: (*a*) as being acceptable to God—as being produced an agreeable fragrance; and (*b*) in its being wafted towards heaven—ascending towards the eternal throne. In ch. viii. 3, an angel is represented as having a golden censer: "And there was given unto him much incense, that he should offer it with the prayers of all saints upon the golden altar which was before the throne. The representation there undoubtedly is, that the angel is employed in *presenting* the prayers of the saints which were offered on earth before the throne. See Notes on that passage. It is most natural to interpret the passage before us in the same way. The allusion is clearly to the temple service, and to the fact that incense was offered by the priest in the temple itself at the time that prayer was offered by the people in the courts of the temple. See Lu. i. 9, 10. The idea here is, therefore, that the representatives of the church in heaven—the elders—spoken of as "priests" (ver. 10), are described as officiating in the temple above in behalf of the church still below, and as offering incense while the church is engaged in prayer. It is not said that *they* offer the prayers themselves, but that they offer *incense* as representing the prayers of the saints. If this be the correct interpretation, as it seems to be the obvious one, then the passage lays no foundation for the opinion expressed by Professor Stuart, as derived from this passage (*in loco*), that prayer is offered by the redeemed in heaven. Whatever may be the truth on that point—on which the Bible seems to be silent—it will find no support from the passage before us. Adoration, praise, thanksgiving, are represented as the employment of the saints in heaven: the only representation respecting *prayer* as pertaining to that world is, that there are emblems there which symbolize its ascent before the throne, and which show that it is acceptable to God. It is an interesting and beautiful representation that there *are* in heaven appropriate symbols of ascending prayer, and that while in the outer courts here below *we* offer prayer, incense, emblematic of it, ascends in the holy of holies above. The *impression* which this should leave on our minds ought to be, that our prayers are wafted before the throne, and are acceptable to God.

9. *And they sung a new song.* Comp. ch. xiv. 3. *New* in the sense that it is a song consequent on redemption, and distinguished therefore from the songs sung in heaven before the work of redemption was consummated. We may suppose that songs of adoration have always been sung in heaven; we know that the praises of God were celebrated by the angelic choirs when the foundations of the earth were laid (Job xxxviii. 7); but the song of redemption was a different song, and is one that would never have been sung there if man had not fallen, and if the Redeemer had not died. This song strikes notes which the other songs do not strike, and refers to glories of the divine character which, but for the work of redemption, would not have been brought into view. In this sense the song was new; it will continue to be new in the sense that it will be sung afresh as redeemed millions continue to ascend to heaven. Comp. Ps. xl. 3; xcvi. 1; cxliv. 9; Is. xlii. 10. ¶ *Thou art worthy to take the book,* &c. This was the occasion or ground of the "new song," that by his coming and death he had acquired a right to approach where no other one could approach, and to do what no other one could do. ¶ *For thou wast slain.* The *language* here is such as would be appropriate to a lamb slain as a sacrifice. The idea is, that the fact that he was thus slain constituted the ground of his worthiness to open the book. It could not be meant that there was in him no *other* ground of worthiness, but that this was that which was most conspicuous. It is just the outburst of the grateful feeling resulting from redemption, that he who has died to save the soul is worthy

of *all* honour, and is fitted to accomplish what no other being in the universe *can* do. However this may appear to the inhabitants of other worlds, or however it may appear to the dwellers on the earth who have no interest in the work of redemption, yet all who are redeemed will agree in the sentiment that He who has ransomed them with his blood has performed a work to do which every other being was incompetent, and that now all honour in heaven and on earth may appropriately be conferred on him. ¶ *And hast redeemed us.* The word here used—ἀγοράζω—means properly to purchase, to buy; and is thus employed to denote redemption, because redemption was accomplished by the payment of a price. On the meaning of the word, see Notes on 2 Pe. ii. 1. ¶ *To God.* That is, so that we become *his*, and are to be henceforward regarded as such; or so that he might possess us as his own. See Notes on 2 Co. v. 15. This is the true nature of redemption, that by the price paid we are rescued from the servitude of Satan, and are henceforth to regard ourselves as belonging unto God. ¶ *By thy blood.* See Notes on Ac. xx. 28. This is such language as they use who believe in the doctrine of the atonement, and is such as would be used by them alone. It would not be employed by those who believe that Christ was a mere martyr, or that he lived and died merely as a teacher of morality. If he was truly an atoning sacrifice, the language is full of meaning; if not, it has no significance, and could not be understood. ¶ *Out of every kindred.* Literally, " of every tribe "—φυλῆς. The word *tribe* means properly a comparatively small division or class of people associated together (Professor Stuart). It refers to a family, or race, having a common ancestor, and usually associated or banded together —as one of the tribes of Israel; a tribe of Indians; a tribe of plants; a tribe of animals, &c. This is such language as a Jew would use, denoting one of the smaller divisions that made up a nation of people; and the meaning would seem to be, that it will be found ultimately to be true that the redeemed will have been taken from all such minor divisions of the human family—not only from the different *nations*, but from the smaller *divisions* of those nations. This can only be true from the fact that the knowledge of the true religion will yet be diffused among all those smaller portions of the human race; that is, that its diffusion will be universal. ¶ *And tongue.* People speaking all languages. The word here used would seem to denote a division of the human family larger than a tribe, but smaller than a nation. It was formerly a fact that a nation might be made up of those who spoke many different languages—as, for example, the Assyrian, the Babylonian, or the Roman nations. Comp. Da. iii. 29; iv. 1. The meaning here is, that no matter what language the component parts of the nations speak, the gospel will be conveyed to them, and in their own tongue they will learn the wonderful works of God. Comp. Ac. ii. 8-11. ¶ *And people.* The word here used — λαός — properly denotes a people considered as *a mass*, made up of smaller divisions—as an association of smaller bodies—or as a multitude of such bodies united together. It is distinguished from another word commonly applied to a people—δῆμος—for that is applied to a community of free citizens, considered as on a level, or without reference to any minor divisions or distinctions. The words here used would apply to an army, considered as made up of regiments, battalions, or tribes; to a mass-meeting, made up of societies of different trades or professions; to a nation, made up of different associated communities, &c. It denotes a *larger* body of people than the previous words; and the idea is, that no matter of what *people* or *nation*, considered as made up of such separate portions, one may be, he will not be excluded from the blessings of redemption. The sense would be well expressed, by saying, for instance, that there will be found there those of the Gaelic race, the Celtic, the Anglo-Saxon, the Mongolian, the African, &c. ¶ *And nation.* Ἔθνους. A word of still larger signification; the people in a still wider sense; a people or nation considered as distinct from all others. The word would embrace all who come under one sovereignty or rule; as, for example, the British nation, however many minor *tribes* there may be; however many different *languages* may be spoken; and however many separate *people* there may be—as the Anglo-Saxon, the Scottish, the Irish, the people of Hindoostan, of Labrador, of New South Wales, &c. The words here used by John would together denote nations of every kind, great and

A.D. 96.]  CHAPTER V.  129

10 And hast made us unto our God ⁿkings and priests: and we shall ᵒreign on the earth.
11 And I beheld, and I heard the voice of many angels round about the throne and the beasts

*n* ch.1.6.   *o* ch.22.5.

and the elders: and the ᵖnumber of them was ten thousand times ten thousand, and thousands of thousands;
12 Saying with a loud voice, ᑫWorthy is the Lamb that was

*p* Da.7.10; He.12.22.   *q* ch.4.11.

small; and the sense is, that the blessings of redemption will be extended to all parts of the earth.
10. *And hast made us unto our God kings and priests.* See Notes on ch. i. 6. ¶ *And we shall reign on the earth.* The redeemed, of whom we are the representatives. The idea clearly is, in accordance with what is so frequently said in the Scriptures, that the dominion on the earth will be given to the saints; that is, that there will be such a prevalence of true religion, and the redeemed will be so much in the ascendency, that the affairs of the nations will be in their hands. Righteous men will hold the offices; will fill places of trust and responsibility; will have a controlling voice in all that pertains to human affairs. See Notes on Da. vii. 27, and Re. xx. 1-6. To such a prevalence of religion all things are tending; and to this, in all the disorder and sin which now exist, are we permitted to look forward. It is not said that this will be a reign under the Saviour in a literal kingdom on the earth; nor is it said that the saints will descend from heaven, and occupy thrones of power under Christ as a visible king. The simple affirmation is, that they will *reign* on the earth; and as this seems to be spoken in the name of the redeemed, all that is necessary to be understood is, that there will be such a prevalence of true religion on the earth that it will become a vast kingdom of holiness, and that, instead of being in the minority, the saints will everywhere have the ascendency.
11. *And I beheld.* And I looked again. ¶ *And I heard the voice of many angels.* The inhabitants of heaven uniting with the representatives of the redeemed church in ascribing honour to the Lamb of God. The design is to show that there is universal sympathy and harmony in heaven, and that all worlds will unite in ascribing honour to the Lamb of God. ¶ *Round about the throne and the beasts and the elders.* In a circle or area *beyond* that which was occupied by the throne, the living creatures, and the elders. They occu-

pied the centre, as it appeared to John, and this innumerable company of angels surrounded them. The angels are represented here, as they are everywhere in the Scriptures, as taking a deep interest in all that pertains to the redemption of men, and it is not surprising that they are here described as uniting with the representatives of the church in rendering honour to the Lamb of God. Comp. Notes on 1 Pe. i. 12. ¶ *And the number of them was ten thousand times ten thousand.* One hundred millions — a general term to denote either a countless number, or an exceedingly great number. We are not to suppose that it is to be taken literally. ¶ *And thousands of thousands.* Implying that the number before specified was not large enough to comprehend all. Besides the "ten thousand times ten thousand," there was a vast uncounted host which one could not attempt to enumerate. The language here would seem to be taken from Da. vii. 10: "Thousand thousands ministered unto him, and ten thousand times ten thousand stood before him." Comp. Ps. lxviii. 17: "The chariots of God are twenty thousand, even thousands of angels." See also De. xxxiii. 2; 1 Ki. xxii. 19.
12. *Saying with a loud voice, Worthy is the Lamb that was slain.* See Notes on ver. 2, 9. The idea here is, that the fact that he was slain, or was made a sacrifice for sin, was the ground or reason for what is here ascribed to him. Comp. Notes on ver. 5. ¶ *To receive power.* Power or authority to rule over all things. Comp. Notes on Mat. xxviii. 18. The meaning here is, that he was worthy that these things should be ascribed to him, or to be addressed and acknowledged as possessing them. A part of these things were his in virtue of his very nature—as wisdom, glory, riches; a part were conferred on him as the result of his work—as the mediatorial dominion over the universe, the honour resulting from his work, &c. In view of all that he was, and of all that he has done, he is here spoken

slain to receive power, and riches, and wisdom, and strength, and honour, and glory, and blessing.

13 And ʳevery creature which is in heaven, and on the earth, and under the earth, and such as are in the sea, and all that are in them, heard I saying, Blessing, and honour, and glory, and power, *be* unto him that sitteth upon the throne, and unto the Lamb for ever and ever.

ʳ Phi.2.10.   ˢ 1 Ch.29.11; 1 Ti.6.16; 1 Pe.4.11.

of as "*worthy*" of all these things. ¶ *And riches.* Abundance. That is, he is worthy that whatever contributes to honour, and glory, and happiness, should be conferred on him *in abundance.* Himself the original proprietor of all things, it is fit that he should be recognized as such; and having performed the work which he has, it is proper that whatever may be made to contribute to his honour should be regarded as his. ¶ *And wisdom.* That he should be esteemed as eminently wise; that is, that as the result of the work which he has accomplished, he should be regarded as having ability to choose the best ends and the best means to accomplish them. The feeling here referred to is that which arises from the contemplation of the work of salvation by the Redeemer, as a work eminently characterized by *wisdom*—wisdom manifested in meeting the evils of the fall; in honouring the law; in showing that mercy is consistent with justice; and in adapting the whole plan to the character and wants of man. If wisdom was anywhere demanded, it was in reconciling a lost world to God; if it has been anywhere displayed, it has been in the arrangements for that work, and in its execution by the Redeemer. See Notes on 1 Co. i. 24; comp. Mat. xiii. 54; Lu. ii. 40, 52; 1 Co. i. 20, 21, 30; Ep. i. 8; iii. 10. ¶ *And strength.* Ability to accomplish his purposes. That is, it is meet that he should be regarded as having such ability. This *strength* or *power* was manifested in overcoming the great enemy of man; in his control of winds, and storms, and diseases, and devils; in triumphing over death; in saving his people. ¶ *And honour.* He should be esteemed and treated with honour for what he has done. ¶ *And glory.* This word refers to a *higher* ascription of praise than the word *honour.* Perhaps that might refer to the honour which we feel in our hearts; this to the expression of that by the language of praise. ¶ *And blessing.* Everything which would express the desire that he might be happy, honoured, and adored. To bless one is to desire that he may have happiness and prosperity; that he may be successful, respected, and honoured. To bless God, or to ascribe blessing to him, is that state where the heart is full of love and gratitude, and where it desires that he may be everywhere honoured, loved, and obeyed as he should be. The words here express the wish that the universe would ascribe to the Redeemer all honour, and that he might be everywhere loved and adored.

13. *And every creature which is in heaven.* The meaning of this verse is, that all created things seemed to unite in rendering honour to Him who sat on the throne, and to the Lamb. In the previous verse a certain number — a vast host—of angels are designated as rendering praise as they stood round the area occupied by the throne, the elders, and the living creatures; here it is added that *all* who were in heaven united in this ascription of praise. ¶ *And on the earth.* All the universe was heard by John ascribing praise to God. A voice was heard from the heavens, from all parts of the earth, from under the earth, and from the depths of the sea, *as if* the entire universe joined in the adoration. It is not necessary to press the language literally, and still less is it necessary to understand by it, as Professor Stuart does, that *the angels* who presided over the earth, over the under-world, and over the sea, are intended. It is evidently *popular* language; and the sense is, that John heard a universal ascription of praise. All worlds seemed to join in it; all the dwellers on the earth, and under the earth, and in the sea, partook of the spirit of heaven in rendering honour to the Redeemer. ¶ *Under the earth.* Supposed to be inhabited by the shades of the dead. See Notes on Job x. 21, 22; Is. xiv. 9. ¶ *And such as are in the sea.* All that dwell in the ocean. In Ps. cxlviii. 7-10, "dragons, and all deeps; beasts, and all cattle; creeping things, and flying fowl," are called on to praise the

14 And the *four beasts said, Amen. And the four *and* twenty

*t* ch.19.4.

elders fell down and worshipped him that liveth for ever and ever.

Lord; and there is no more incongruity or impropriety in one description than in the other. In the Psalm, the universe is called on to render praise; in the passage before us it is described as actually doing it. The hills, the streams, the floods; the fowls of the air, the dwellers in the deep, and the beasts that roam over the earth; the songsters in the grove, and the insects that play in the sunbeam, in fact, declare the glory of their Creator; and it requires no very strong effort of the fancy to imagine the universe as sending up a constant voice of thanksgiving. ¶ *Blessing, and honour*, &c. There is a slight change here from ver. 12, but it is the same thing substantially. It is an ascription of all glory to God and to the Lamb.

14. *And the four beasts said, Amen.* The voice of universal praise came to them from abroad, and they accorded with it, and ascribed honour to God. ¶ *And the four* and *twenty elders fell down*, &c. The living creatures and the elders *began* the work of praise (ver. 8), and it was proper that it should conclude with them; that is, they give the last and final response (Professor Stuart). The whole universe, therefore, is sublimely represented as in a state of profound adoration, waiting for the developments to follow on the opening of the mysterious volume. All feel an interest in it; all feel that the secret is with God; all feel that there is but One who *can* open this volume; and all gather around, in the most reverential posture, awaiting the disclosure of the great mystery.

The truths taught in this chapter are the following: (1) The knowledge of the future is with God, ver. 1. It is as in a book held in his hand, fully written over, yet sealed with seven seals. (2) It is impossible for man or angel to penetrate the future, ver. 2, 3. It seems to be a law of created being, that the ability to penetrate the future is placed beyond the reach of any of the faculties by which a creature is endowed. Of the past we have a record, and we can remember it; but no created being seems to have been formed with a power in reference to the future corresponding with that in reference to the past—with no faculty of *foresight* corresponding to *memory*. (3) It is natural that the mind should be deeply affected by the fact that we *cannot* penetrate the future, ver. 4. John *wept* in view of this; and how often is the mind borne down with heaviness in view of that fact! What things there are, there must be, in that future of interest to us! What changes there may be for us to experience; what trials to pass through; what happiness to enjoy; what scenes of glory to witness! What progress may we make in knowledge; what new friendships may we form; what new displays of the divine perfections may we witness! All our great interests are in the future — in that which is to us now unknown. There is to be all the happiness which we are to enjoy, all the pain that we are to suffer; all that we hope, all that we fear. All the friends that we are to have are to be there; all the sorrows that we are to experience are to be there. Yet an impenetrable veil is set up to hide all that from our view. We cannot remove it; we cannot penetrate it. There it stands to mock all our efforts, and in all our attempts to look into the future we soon come to the barrier, and are repelled and driven back. Who has not felt his heart sad that he cannot look into that which is to come? (4) The power of laying open the future to mortals has been intrusted to the Redeemer, ver. 5-7. It is a part of the work which was committed to him to make known to men *as much* as it was proper to be known. Hence he is at once a prophet, and is the inspirer of the prophets. Hence he came to teach men what is to be in the future pertaining to them, and hence he has caused to be recorded by the sacred writers all that *is* to be known of what is to come until it is slowly unfolded as events develop themselves. The Saviour alone takes the mysterious book and opens the seals; he only unrolls the volume and discloses to man what is to come. (5) The fact that he does this is the foundation of joy and gratitude for the church, ver. 8-10. It is impossible that the church should contemplate what the Saviour has revealed of the future without gratitude and joy; and how often, in times of persecution and trouble, has the church joyfully turned to the developments made by the

Saviour of what is to be when the gospel shall spread over the world, and when truth and righteousness shall be triumphant. (6) This fact is of interest to the angelic beings, and for them also it lays the foundation of praise, ver. 11, 12. This may arise from these causes: (*a*) from the interest which they take in the church, and the happiness which they have from anything that increases its numbers or augments its joy; (*b*) from the fact that in the disclosures of the future made by the Redeemer, there may be much that is new and of interest to them (comp. Notes on 1 Pe. i. 12); and (*c*) from the fact that they cannot but rejoice in the revelations which are made of the final triumphs of truth in the universe. (7) The universe at large has an interest in these disclosures, and the fact that they are to be made by the Redeemer lays the foundation for universal joy, ver. 13, 14. These events pertain to all worlds, and it is proper that all the inhabitants of the universe should join in the expressions of adoration and thanksgiving. The universe is one; and what affects one portion of it really pertains to every part of it. Angels and men have one and the same God and Father, and may unite in the same expressions of praise.

## CHAPTER VI.

### ANALYSIS OF THE CHAPTER.

This chapter contains an account of the opening of six of the seven seals. It need hardly be said to anyone who is at all familiar with the numerous—not to say numberless—expositions of the Apocalypse, that it is at this point that interpreters begin to differ, and that here commences the divergence towards those various, discordant, and many of them wild and fantastic theories, which have been proposed in the exposition of this wonderful book. Up to this point, though there may be unimportant diversities in the exposition of words and phrases, there is no material difference of opinion as to the general meaning of the writer. In the epistles to the seven churches, and in the introductory scenes to the main visions, there can be no doubt, in the main, as to what the writer had in view, and what he meant to describe. He addressed churches then existing (ch. i.–iii.), and set before them their sins and their duties; and he described scenes passing before his eyes as then present (ch. iv. v.), which were merely designed to impress his own mind with the importance of what was to be disclosed, and to bring the great actors on the stage, and in reference to which there could be little ground for diversity in the interpretation. Here, however, the scene opens into the future, comprehending all the unknown period until there shall be a final triumph of Christianity, and all its foes shall be prostrate. The actors are the Son of God, angels, men, Satan, storms, tempests, earthquakes, the pestilence and fire; the scene is heaven, earth, hell. There is no certain designation of places; there is no mention of names—as there is in Isaiah (xlv. 1) of Cyrus, or as there is in Daniel (viii. 21; x. 20; xi. 2) of the "king of Grecia;" there is no designation of time that is necessarily unambiguous; and there are no characteristics of the symbols used that make it antecedently certain that they could be applied only to one class of events. In the boundless future that was to succeed the times of John, there would be, of necessity, many events to which these symbols might be applied, and the result has shown that it has required but a moderate share of pious ingenuity to apply them, by different expositors, to events differing widely from each other in their character, and in the times when they would occur. It would be too long to glance even at the various theories which have been proposed and maintained in regard to the interpretation of the subsequent portions of the Apocalypse, and wholly impossible to attempt to examine those theories. Time, in its developments, has already exploded many of them; and time, in its future developments, will doubtless explode many more, and each one must stand or fall as, in the disclosures of the future, it shall be found to be true or false. It would be folly to add another to those numerous theories, even if I had any such theory (see the Preface), and perhaps equal folly to pronounce with certainty on any one of those which have been advanced. Yet this seems to be an appropriate place to state, in few words, what principles it is designed to pursue in the interpretation of the remainder of the book.

(1) It may be assumed that large portions of the book relate to *the future;* that is, to that which was future when John wrote. In this all expositors are agreed, and this is manifest indeed on the very face of the representation. It would be impossible to attempt an in-

terpretation on any other supposition, and somewhere in that vast future the events are to be found to which the symbols here used had reference. This is assumed, indeed, on the supposition that the book is *inspired*—a fact which is assumed all along in this exposition, and which should be allowed to control our interpretation. But assuming that the book relates to the future, though that supposition will do something to determine the true method of interpretation, yet it leaves many questions still unsolved. Whether it refers to the destruction of Jerusalem, on the supposition that the work was written before that event, or to the history of the church subsequent to that; whether it is designed to describe events minutely, or only in the most general manner; whether it is intended to furnish a *syllabus* of civil and ecclesiastical history, or only a very general outline of future events; whether the *times* are so designated that we can fix them with entire certainty; or whether it was intended to furnish any certain indication of the periods of the world when these things should occur;—all these are still open questions, and it need not be said that on these the opinions of expositors have been greatly divided.

(2) It may be assumed that there *is* meaning in these symbols, and that they were not used without an intention to convey some important ideas to the mind of John and to the minds of his readers—to the church then, and to the church in future times. Comp. Notes on ch. i. 3. The book is indeed surpassingly sublime. It abounds with the highest flights of poetic language. It is Oriental in its character, and exhibits everywhere the proofs of a most glowing imagination in the writer. But it is also to be borne in mind that it is an *inspired* book, and this fact is to determine the character of the exposition. *If* inspired, it is to be assumed that there is a *meaning* in these symbols; an idea in each one of them, and in all combined, of importance to the church and the world. Whether we can ascertain the meaning is another question; but it is never to be doubted by an expositor of the Bible that there *is* a meaning in the words and images employed, and that to find out that meaning is worthy of earnest study and prayer.

(3) Predictions respecting the future are often necessarily obscure to man. It cannot be doubted, indeed, that God *could* have foretold future events in the most clear and unambiguous language. He who knows all that is to come as intimately as he does all the past, could have caused a record to have been made, disclosing names, and dates, and places, so that the most minute statements of what is to occur might have been in the possession of man as clearly as the records of the past now are. But there were obvious reasons why this should not occur, and in the prophecies it is rare that there is any such specification. To have done this might have been to defeat the very end in view; for it would have given to man, a free agent, the power of embarrassing or frustrating the divine plans. But if this course is *not* adopted, then prophecy must, from the nature of the case, be obscure. The knowledge of any one particular fact in the future is so connected with many other facts, and often implies so much knowledge of other things, that without that other knowledge it could not be understood. Suppose that it had been predicted, in the time of John, that at some future period some contrivance should be found out by which what was doing in one part of the world could be instantaneously known in another remote part of the world, and spread abroad by thousands of copies in an hour, to be read by a nation. Suppose, for instance, that there had been some symbol or emblem representing what actually occurs now, when in a morning newspaper we read what occurred last evening at St. Louis, Dubuque, Galena, Chicago, Cincinnati, Charleston, New Orleans; it is clear that at a time when the magnetic telegraph and the printing-press were unknown, any symbol or language describing it that could be employed must be obscure, and the impression must have been that this could be accomplished only by miracle—and it would not be difficult for one who was disposed to scepticism to make out an argument to prove that this could *not* occur. It would be impossible to explain any symbol that could be employed to represent this until these wonderful descriptions should become reality, and in the meantime the book in which the symbols were found might be regarded as made up of mere riddles and enigmas; but when these inventions should be actually found out, however much ridicule or contempt had been poured on the book before, it

might be perfectly evident that the symbol was the most appropriate that could be used, and no one could doubt that it was a divine communication of what was to be in the future. Something of the same kind *may* have occurred in the symbols used by the writer of the book before us.

(4) It is not necessary to suppose that a prophecy will be understood in all its details until the prediction is accomplished. In the case just referred to, though the *fact* of the rapid spread of intelligence might be clear, yet nothing would convey any idea of the *mode*, or of the actual meaning of the *symbols* used, unless the inventions were themselves anticipated by a direct revelation. The trial of *faith* in the case would be the belief that *the fact would occur*, but would not relate to the *mode* in which it was to be accomplished, or the *language* employed to describe it. There might be great obscurity in regard to the symbols and language, and yet the knowledge of the fact be perfectly plain. When, however, the fact should occur as predicted, all would be clear. So it is in respect to prophecy. Many recorded predictions that are now clear as noon-day, were once as ambiguous and uncertain in respect to their meaning as in the supposed case of the press and the telegraph. Time has made them plain; for the event to which they referred has so entirely corresponded with the symbol as to leave no doubt in regard to the meaning. Thus many of the prophecies relating to the Messiah were obscure at the time when they were uttered; were apparently so contradictory that they could not be reconciled; were so unlike anything that then existed, that the fulfilment seemed to be impossible; and were so enigmatical in the symbols employed, that it seemed in vain to attempt to disclose their meaning. The advent of the long-promised Messiah, however, removed the obscurity; and now they are read with no uncertainty as to their meaning, and with no doubt that those predictions, once so obscure, had a divine origin.

The view just suggested may lead us to some just conceptions of what is necessary to be done in attempting to explain the prophecies. Suppose, then, *first*, that there had been, say in the dark ages, some predictions that claimed to be of divine origin, of the invention of the art of printing and of the magnetic telegraph. The proper business of an interpreter, if he regarded this as a divine communication, would have consisted in four things: (*a*) to explain, as well as he could, the fair meaning of the symbols employed, and the language used; (*b*) to admit the *fact* referred to, and implied in the fair interpretation of the language employed, of the rapid spread of intelligence in that future period, though he could not explain *how* it was to be done; (*c*) in the meantime it would be a perfectly legitimate object for him to inquire whether there were any events occurring in the world, or whether there had been any, to which these symbols were applicable, or which would meet all the circumstances involved in them; (*d*) if there were, then his duty would be ended; if there were not, then the symbols, with such explanation as could be furnished of their meaning, should be handed on to future times, *to be* applied when the predicted events should actually occur. Suppose, then, *secondly*, the case of the predictions respecting the Messiah, scattered along through many books, and given in various forms, and by various symbols. The proper business of an interpreter would have been, as in the other case, (*a*) to explain the fair meaning of the language used, and to bring together all the circumstances in one connected whole, that a distinct conception of the predicted Messiah might be before the mind; (*b*) to admit the *facts* referred to, and thus predicted, however incomprehensible and apparently contradictory they might appear to be; (*c*) to inquire whether anyone had appeared who combined within himself all the characteristics of the description; and (*d*) if no one had thus appeared, to send on the prophecies, with such explanations of words and symbols as could be ascertained to be correct, to future times, to have their full meaning developed when the object of all the predictions should be accomplished, and the Messiah should appear. Then the meaning of all would be plain; and then the argument from prophecy would be complete. This is obviously now the proper state of the mind in regard to the predictions in the Bible, and these are the principles which should be applied in examining the book of Revelation.

(5) It may be assumed that new light *will* be thrown upon the prophecies by time, and by the progress of events. It cannot be supposed that

the investigations of the meaning of the prophetic symbols will all be in vain. Difficulties, it is reasonable to hope, may be cleared up; errors may be detected in regard to the application of the prophecies to particular events; and juster views on the prophecies, as on all other subjects, will prevail as the world grows older. We become wiser by seeing the errors of those who have gone before us, and an examination of the causes which led them astray may enable us to avoid such errors in the future. Especially may it be supposed that light will be thrown on the prophecies as they shall be in part or wholly fulfilled. The prophecies respecting the destruction of Babylon, of Petra, of Tyre, of Jerusalem, are now fully understood; the prophecies respecting the advent of the Messiah, and his character and work, once so obscure, are now perfectly clear. So, we have reason to suppose, it will be with *all* prophecy in the progress of events, and sooner or later the world will settle down into some uniform belief in regard to the design and meaning of these portions of the sacred writings. Whether the time has yet come for this, or whether numerous other failures are to be added to the melancholy catalogue of past failures on this subject, is another question; but ultimately all the now unfulfilled prophecies will be as clear as to their meaning as are those which have been already fulfilled.

(6) The plan, therefore, which I propose in the examination of the remaining portion of the Apocalypse is the following: (*a*) To explain the meaning of the symbols; that is, to show, as clearly as possible, what those symbols properly express, independently of any attempt to apply them. This opens, of itself, an interesting field of investigation, and one where essential service may be done, even if nothing further is intended. Without any reference to the *application* of those symbols, this, of itself, is an important work of criticism, and, if successfully done, would be rendering a valuable service to the readers of the sacred volume. (*b*) To state, as briefly as possible, what others who have written on this book, and who have brought eminent learning and talent to bear on its interpretation, have supposed to be the true interpretation of the symbols employed by John, and in regard to the times in which the events referred to would occur. It is in this way only that we can be made acquainted with the real progress made in interpreting this book, and it will be useful at least to know how the subject has struck other minds, and how and why they have failed to perceive the truth. I propose, therefore, to state, as I go along, some of the theories which have been held as to the meaning of the Apocalypse, and as to the events which have been supposed by others to be referred to. My limits require, however, that this should be briefly done, and forbid my attempting to examine those opinions at length. (*c*) To state, in as brief and clear a manner as possible, the view which I have been led to entertain as to the proper application of the symbols employed in the book, with such historical references as shall seem to me to confirm the interpretation proposed. (*d*) Where I cannot form an opinion as to the meaning, to confess my ignorance. He does no service in a professed interpretation of the Bible who passes over a difficulty without *attempting* to remove it, or who, to save his own reputation, conceals the fact that there *is* a real difficulty; and he does as little service who is unwilling to confess his ignorance on many points, or who attempts an explanation where he has no clear and settled views. As his opinion can be of no value to anyone else unless it is based on reasons in his own mind that will bear examination, so it can usually be of little value unless those reasons are stated. It is as important for his readers to have those reasons before their own minds as it is for him; and unless he has it in his power to *state* reasons for what he advances, his opinions can be worth nothing to the world. He who lays down this rule of interpretation may expect to have ample opportunity, in interpreting such a book as the Apocalypse, to confess his ignorance; but he who interprets a book which he believes to be inspired, may console himself with the thought that what is now obscure will be clear hereafter, and that he performs the best service which he can if he endeavours to explain the book *up to* the time in which he lives. There will be developments hereafter which will make that clear which is now obscure; developments which will make this book, in all past ages apparently so enigmatical, as clear as any other portion of the inspired volume, as it is now, even with

## CHAPTER VI.

AND I saw when *a*the Lamb opened one of the seals; and

*a* ch.5.5.

the imperfect view which we may have of its meaning, beyond all question one of the most sublime books that has ever been written.

This chapter describes the opening of the first six seals. (1) The first discloses a white horse, with a rider armed with a bow. A crown is given to him, symbolical of triumph and prosperity, and he goes forth to conquer, ver. 1, 2. (2) The second discloses a red-coloured horse, with a rider. The emblem is that of blood — of sanguinary war. Power is given him to take peace from the earth, and a sword is given him—emblem of war, but not of certain victory. Triumph and prosperity are denoted by the former symbol; war, discord, bloodshed, by this, ver. 3, 4. (3) The third discloses a black horse, with a rider. He has a pair of balances in his hand, as if there were *scarcity* in the earth, and he announces the price of grain in the times of this calamity, and a command is given not to hurt the oil and the wine, ver. 5, 6. The emblem is that of scarcity—as if there were oppression, or as a consequence of war or discord, while at the same time there is care bestowed to preserve certain portions of the produce of the earth from injury. (4) The fourth discloses a pale horse, with a rider. The name of this rider is Death, and Hell (or Hades) follows him—as if the hosts of the dead came again on the earth. Power is given to the rider over the fourth part of the earth, to kill with sword, with hunger, with death, and with wild beasts. This emblem would seem to denote war, wide-wasting pestilence, famine, and desolation—as if wild beasts were suffered to roam over lands that had been inhabited; something of which *paleness* would be an emblem. Here ends the array of *horses;* and it is evidently intended by these four symbols to refer to a series of events that have a general resemblance —something that could be made to stand by themselves, and that could be grouped together. (5) The fifth seal opens a new scene. The horse and the rider no longer appear. It is not a scene of war, and of the consequences of war, but a scene of persecution. The souls of those who were slain for the word of God and the testimony which they held are seen under the altar, praying to God that he would avenge their blood. White robes are given them—tokens of the divine favour, and emblems of their ultimate triumph; and they are commanded to "rest for a little season, till their fellow-servants and their brethren that should be killed as they were should be fulfilled;" that is, that they should be *patient* until the number of the martyrs was filled up. In other words, there was (*a*) the assurance of the divine favour towards them; (*b*) vengeance, or the punishment of those who had persecuted them, would not be *immediate;* but (*c*) there was the implied assurance that just punishment would be inflicted on their persecutors, and that the cause for which they had suffered would ultimately triumph, ver. 9–11. (6) The opening of the sixth seal, ver. 12–17. There was an earthquake, and the sun became dark, and the moon was turned to blood, and the stars fell, and all kings and people were filled with consternation. This symbol properly denotes the time of public commotion, of revolution, of calamity; and it was evidently to be fulfilled by some great changes on the earth, or by the overturning of the seats of power, and by such sudden revolutions as would fill the nations with alarm.

1. *And I saw.* Or, I looked. He fixed his eye attentively on what was passing, as promising important disclosures. No one had been found in the universe who could open the seals but the Lamb of God (ch. v. 2–4); and it was natural for John, therefore, to look upon the transaction with profound interest. ¶ *When the Lamb opened one of the seals.* See Notes on ch. v. 1, 5. This was the first or outermost of the seals, and its being broken would permit a certain portion of the volume to be unrolled and read. See Notes on ch. v. 1. The representation in this place is, therefore, that of a volume with a small portion unrolled, and written on both sides of the parchment. ¶ *And I heard, as it were the noise of thunder.* One of the four living creatures speaking as with a voice of thunder, or with a loud voice. ¶ *One of the four beasts.* Notes on ch. iv. 6, 7.

I heard, as it were the noise of thunder, one of the four beasts saying, Come and see.

# CHAPTER VI.

2 And I saw, and behold [b]a white horse: and he that sat on him had a bow; and a crown was given unto him: and he went forth [c]conquering, and to conquer.

[b] Zec.6.3,&c.
[c] Ps.45.3-5.

The particular one is not mentioned, though what is said in the subsequent verses leaves no doubt that it was the first in order as seen by John—the one like a lion, ch. iv. 7. In the opening of the three following seals, it is expressly said that it was the second, the third, and the fourth of the living creatures that drew near, and hence the conclusion is certain that the one here referred to was the first. If the four living creatures be understood to be emblematic of the divine providential administration, then there was a propriety that they should be represented as summoning John to witness what was to be disclosed. These events pertained to the developments of the divine purposes, and these emblematic beings would therefore be interested in what was occurring. ¶ *Come and see.* Addressed evidently to John. He was requested to approach and *see* with his own eyes what was disclosed in the portion of the volume now unrolled. He had wept much (ch. v. 4) that no one was found who was worthy to open that book, but he was now called on to approach and see for himself. Some have supposed (Lord, *in loco*) that the address here was not to John, but to the horse and his rider, and that the command to them was not to "come and see," but to *come forth*, and appear on the stage, and that the act of the Redeemer in breaking the seal, and unrolling the scroll, was nothing more than an emblem signifying that it was by his act that the divine purposes were to be unfolded. But, in order to this interpretation, it would be necessary to omit from the received text the words καὶ βλέπε—"*and see.*" This is done, indeed, by Hahn and Tittmann, and this reading is followed by Professor Stuart, though he says that the received text has "probability" in its favour, and is followed by some of the critical editions. The most natural interpretation, however, is that the words were addressed to John. John saw the Lamb open the seal; he heard the loud voice; he looked and beheld a white horse—that is, evidently, he looked on the unfolding volume, and saw the representation of a horse and his rider. That the voice was addressed to John is the common interpretation, is the most natural, and is liable to no real objection.

2. *And I saw, and behold.* A question has arisen as to the mode of representation here: whether what John saw in these visions was a series of *pictures*, drawn on successive portions of the volume as one seal was broken after another; or whether the description of the horses and of the events was *written* on the volume, so that John read it himself, or heard it read by another; or whether the opening of the seal was merely the *occasion* of a scenic representation, in which a succession of horses was introduced, with a written statement of the events which are referred to. Nothing is indeed said by which this can be determined with certainty; but the most probable supposition would seem to be that there was some pictorial representation in form and appearance, such as he describes in the opening of the six seals. In favour of this it may be observed, (1) that, according to the interpretation of ver. 1, it was something *in* or *on* the volume—since he was invited to draw nearer, in order that he might contemplate it. (2) Each one of the things under the first five seals, where John uses the word "saw," is capable of being represented by a picture or painting. (3) The language used is not such as would have been employed if he had merely *read* the description, or had *heard* it read. (4) The supposition that the pictorial representation was not *in* the volume, but that the opening of the seal was the occasion merely of causing a scenic representation to pass before his mind, is unnatural and forced. What would be the use of a sealed *volume* in that case? What the use of the *writing* within and without? On this supposition the representation would be that, as the successive seals were broken, nothing was disclosed in the volume but a succession of blank portions, and that the mystery or the difficulty was not in anything in the volume, but in the want of ability to summon forth these successive scenic representations. The most obvious interpretation is, undoubtedly, that what John proceeds to describe was in some way represented in the volume; and

the idea of a succession of pictures or drawings better accords with the whole representation, than the idea that it was a mere written description. In fact, these successive scenes could be well represented now in a pictorial form on a scroll. ¶ *And behold a white horse.* In order to any definite understanding of what was denoted by these symbols, it is proper to form in our minds, in the first place, a clear conception of what the symbol properly represents, or an idea of what it would naturally convey. It may be assumed that the symbol was significant, and that there was some reason why that was used rather than another; why, for instance, a *horse* was employed rather than an eagle or a lion; why a *white* horse was employed in one case, and a red one, a black one, a pale one in the others; why in this case a bow was in the hand of the rider, and a crown was placed on his head. Each one of these particulars enters into the constitution of the symbol; and we must find something in the event which *fairly* corresponds with each—for the symbol is made up of all these things grouped together. It may be farther observed, that where the general symbol is the same—as in the opening of the first four seals—it may be assumed that the same object or class of objects is referred to; and the *particular* things denoted, or the diversity in the general application, is to be found in the *variety* in the representation—the colour, &c., of the horse, and the arms, apparel, &c., of the rider. The specifications under the first seal are four: (1) the general symbol of the horse—common to the first four seals; (2) the colour of the horse; (3) the fact that he that sat on him had a bow; and (4) that a crown was given him by some one, as indicative of victory. The question now is, what these symbols would naturally denote.

(1) The horse. The meaning of this symbol must be drawn from the natural use to which the symbol is applied, or the characteristics which it is known to have; and it may be added, that there might have been something for which that was best known in the time of the writer who uses it, which would not be so prominent at another period of the world, or in another country, and that it is necessary to have that before the mind in order to obtain a correct understanding of the symbol. The use of the horse, for instance, may have varied at different times to some degree; at one time the prevailing use of the horse may have been for battle; at another for rapid marches—as of cavalry; at another for draught; at another for races; at another for conveying messages by the establishment of posts or the appointment of couriers. To an ancient Roman the horse might suggest prominently one idea; to a modern Arab another; to a teamster in Holland another. The things which would be most naturally suggested by the horse as a symbol, as distinguished, for instance, from an eagle, a lion, a serpent, &c., would be the following: (*a*) War, as this was probably one of the first uses to which the horse was applied. So, in the magnificent description of the horse in Job xxxix. 19-25, no notice is taken of any of his qualities but those which pertain to war. See, for a full illustration of this passage, and of the frequent reference in the classic writers to the horse as connected with war, Bochart, *Hieroz.* lib. ii. c. viii., particularly p. 149. Comp. Virg. *Geor.* iii. 83, 84:

"Si qua sonum procul arma dedêre,
Stare loco nescit, micat auribus, et tremit artus."

Ovid, *Metam.* iii. :

"Ut fremit acer equus, cum bellicus, aere canoro
Signa dedit tubicen, pugnæque assumit amorem."

*Silius*, lib. xiii. :

"Is trepido alituum tinnitu, et stare neganti,
Imperitans violenter equo."

So Solomon says (Pr. xxi. 31), "The horse is prepared against the day of battle." So in Zec. x. 3, the prophet says, God had made the house of Judah "as his goodly horse in the battle;" that is, he had made them like the victorious war-horse. (*b*) As a consequence of this, and of the conquests achieved by the horse in war, he became the symbol of conquest—of a people that could not be overcome. Comp. the above reference in Zec. Thus in Carthage the horse was an image of victorious war, in contradistinction to the *ox*, which was an emblem of the arts of peaceful agriculture. This was based on a tradition respecting the foundation of the city, referred to by Virgil, *Æn.* i. 442-445:

"Quo primum jactati undis et turbine Poeni
Effodêre loco signum, quod regia Juno
Monstrârat, *caput acris equi:* sic nam fore bello
Egregiam, et facilem victu per Sæcula gentem."

## CHAPTER VI.

In reference to this circumstance Justin (lib. xviii. 5) remarks, that "in laying the foundations of the city the head of an ox was found, which was regarded as an emblem of a fruitful land, but of the necessity of labour and of dependence; on which account the city was transferred to another place. Then the head of a horse was found, and this was regarded as a happy omen that the city would be warlike and prosperous." Comp. Creuzer, *Symbolik*, vol. ii. p. 456. (c) The horse was an emblem of *fleetness*, and, consequently, of the rapidity of conquest. Comp. Joel ii. 4: "The appearance of them is as the appearance of horses; and as horsemen, so shall they run." Je. iv. 13: "Behold, he shall come up as clouds, and his chariots shall be as the whirlwind; his horses are swifter than eagles." Compare Job xxxix. 18. (d) The horse is an emblem of strength, and consequently of safety. Ps. cxlvii. 10: "He delighteth not in the strength of the horse." In general, then, the horse would properly symbolize war, conquest, or the rapidity with which a message is conveyed. The particular character or complexion of the event— as peaceful or warlike, prosperous or adverse—is denoted by the colour of the horse, and by the character of the rider.

(2) The colour of the horse: *a white horse*. It is evident that this is designed to be significant, because it is distinguished 'from the red, the black, and the pale horse, referred to in the following verses. In general, it may be observed that *white* is the emblem of innocence, purity, prosperity—as the opposite is of sickness, sin, calamity. If the significance of the emblem turned alone on the *colour*, we should look to something cheerful, prosperous, happy as the thing that was symbolized. But the significance in the case is to be found not only in the colour—*white*—but in the horse that was white; and the inquiry is, what would *a horse of that colour* properly denote; that is, on what occasions, and with reference to what ends, was such a horse used? Now, the general notion attached to the mention of a white horse, according to ancient usage, would be that of state and triumph, derived from the fact that white horses were rode by conquerors on the days of their triumph; that they were used in the marriage cavalcade; that they were employed on coronation occasions, &c. In the triumphs granted by the Romans to their victorious generals, after a procession composed of musicians, captured princes, spoils of battle, &c., came the conqueror himself, seated on a high chariot drawn by four white horses, robed in purple, and wearing a wreath of laurel (Eschenburg, *Man. of Class. Literature*, p. 283. Comp. Ovid *de Arte Amandi*, lib. v. 214). The name of λεύκιππος—*leucippos*—was given to Proserpine, because she was borne from Hades to Olympus in a chariot drawn by white horses (*Scol. Pind. Ol.* vi. 161. See Creuzer's *Symbol.* iv. 253). White horses are supposed, also, to excel others in fleetness. So Horace, *Sat.* lib. i. vii. 8:

"Sisennas, Barrosque ut equis præcurreret albis."

So Plaut. *Asin.* ii. 2, 12. So Homer, *Il.* K. 437:

Λευκότεροι χιονος, θείειν δ' ἀνέμοισιν ὁμοῖοι.

—"Whiter than the snow, and swifter than the winds." And in the *Æneid*, where Turnus was about to contend with Æneas, he demanded horses:

"Qui candore nives anteirent cursibus auras."

—"Which would surpass the snow in whiteness, and the wind in fleetness" (*Æn.* xii. 84). So the poets everywhere describe the chariot of the sun as drawn by white horses (Bochart, *ut supra*). So conquerors and princes are everywhere represented as borne on white horses. Thus Propertius, lib. iv. eleg. i.:

"Quatuor huic albos Romulus egit equos."

So Claudian, lib. ii. ,.*de Laudibus Stilichonis:*

"Deposito mitis clypeo, candentibus urbem
Ingreditur trabeatus equis."

And thus Ovid (lib. i. *de Arte*) addresses Augustus, auguring that he would return a victor:

"Ergo erit illa dies, quâ tu, Pulcherrime rerum,
Quatuor in niveis aureus ibis equis."

The preference of *white* to denote triumph or victory was early referred to among the Hebrews. Thus, Ju. v. 10, in the Song of Deborah:

"Speak, ye that ride on white asses,
Ye that sit in judgment,
And walk by the way."

The expression, then, in the passage before us, would properly refer to some kind of *triumph;* to some joyous occasion; to something where there was success or victory; and, so far as *this* expression is concerned, would refer to *any kind* of triumph, whether of the gospel or of victory in war.

(3) The bow: *and he that sat on him had a bow.* The bow would be a natural emblem of war—as it was used in war; or of hunting—as it was used for that purpose. It was a common instrument of attack or defence, and seems to have been early invented, for it is found in all rude nations. Comp. Ge. xxvii. 3; xlviii. 22; xlix. 24; Jos. xxiv. 12; 1 Sa. xviii. 4; Ps. xxxvii. 15; Is. vii. 24. The *bow* would be naturally emblematic of the following things: (*a*) *War*. See the passages above. (*b*) *Hunting*. Thus it was one of the emblems of Apollo as the god of hunting. (*c*) *The effect of truth*—as that which secured conquest, or overcame opposition in the heart. So far as *this* emblem is concerned, it might denote a warrior, a hunter, a preacher, a ruler—anyone who exerted power over others, or who achieved any kind of conquest over them.

(4) The crown: *and a crown was given unto him.* The word here used—στέφανος—means a circlet, chaplet, or crown—usually such as was given to a victor, 1 Co. ix. 25. It would properly be emblematic of victory or conquest—as it was given to victors in war, or to the victors at the Grecian games, and as it is given to the saints in heaven regarded as victors, Re. iv. 4, 10; 2 Ti. iv. 8. The crown or chaplet here was "given" to the rider as significant that he *could be* victorious, not that he *had been;* and the proper reference of the emblem was to some conquest yet to be made, not to any which had been made. It is not said *by whom* this was given to the rider; the material fact being only that such a diadem *was* conferred on him.

(5) The going forth to conquest: *and he went forth, conquering and to conquer.* He went forth *as a conqueror, and that he might conquer.* That is, he went forth with the spirit, life, energy, determined purpose of one who was confident that he would conquer, and who had the port and bearing of a conqueror. John saw in him two things: one, that he had the aspect or port of a conqueror—that is, of one who had been accustomed to conquest, and who was confident that he could conquer; the other was, that this was clearly the design for which he went forth, and this would be the result of his going forth.

Having thus inquired into the natural meaning of the emblems used, perhaps the proper work of an expositor is done, and the subject might be left here. But the mind naturally asks what was this designed to signify, and to what events are these things to be applied? On this point it is scarcely necessary to say, that the opinions of expositors have been almost as numerous as the expositors themselves, and that it would be a hopeless task, and as useless as hopeless, to attempt to enumerate all the opinions entertained. They who are desirous of examining those opinions must be referred to the various books on the Apocalypse where they may be found. Perhaps all the opinions entertained, though presented by their authors under a great variety of forms, might be referred to three: (1) That the whole passage in ch. vi.–xi. refers to the destruction of Jerusalem and the wasting of Judæa, principally by the Romans—and particularly the humiliation and prostration of the Jewish persecuting enemies of the church: on the supposition that the book was written before the destruction of Jerusalem. This is the opinion of Professor Stuart, and of those generally who hold that the book was written at that time. (2) The opinion of those who suppose that the book was written in the time of Domitian, about A.D. 95 or 96, and that the symbols refer to the Roman affairs subsequent to that time. This is the opinion of Mede, Elliott, and others. (3) The opinions of those who suppose that the different horses and horsemen refer to the Saviour, to ministers of the gospel, and to the various results of the ministry. This is the opinion of Mr. David C. Lord and others. My purpose does not require me to examine these opinions in detail. Justice could not be done to them in the limited compass which I have; and it is better to institute a direct inquiry whether any events are known which can be regarded as corresponding with the symbols here employed. In regard to this, then, the following things may be referred to:—

(*a*) It will be assumed here, as elsewhere in these Notes, that the Apocalypse was written in the time of Domitian, about A.D. 95 or 96. For the reasons for this opinion, see Intro. § 2. Comp. an article by Dr. Geo. Duffield in the *Biblical Repository*, July, 1847, pp. 385–411. It will also be assumed that the book is inspired, and

## CHAPTER VI.

that it is not to be regarded and treated as a work of mere human origin. These suppositions will preclude the necessity of any reference in the opening of the seals to the time of Nero, or to the events pertaining to the destruction of Jerusalem and the overthrow of the Jewish persecuting enemies of the church — for the opinion that those events are referred to can be held only on one of two suppositions: either that the work was written in the time of Nero, and before the Jewish wars, as held by Professor Stuart and others; or that it was penned *after* the events referred to had occurred, and is such a description of the past as could have been made by one who was uninspired.

(*b*) It is to be presumed that the events referred to, in the opening of the first seal, would occur *soon* after the time when the vision appeared to John in Patmos. This is clear, not only because that would be the most natural supposition, but because it is fairly implied in ch. i. 1: "The Revelation of Jesus Christ, which God gave unto him to show unto his servants things which must *shortly* come to pass." See Notes on that verse. Whatever may be said of *some* of those events—those lying most remotely in the series—it would not accord with the fair interpretation of the language to suppose that the *beginning* of the series would be far distant, and we therefore naturally look for that beginning in the age succeeding the time of the apostle, or the reign of Domitian.

(*c*) The inquiry then occurs whether there *were* any such events in that age as would properly be symbolized by the circumstances before us—the horse; the colour of the horse; the bow in the hand of the rider; the crown given him; the state and bearing of the conqueror.

(*d*) Before proceeding to notice what seems to me to be the interpretation which best accords with all the circumstances of the symbol, it may be proper to refer to the only other one which has any plausibility, and which is adopted by Grotius, by the author of *Hyponoia*, by Dr. Keith (*Signs of the Times*, i. 181, seq.), by Mr. Lord, and others, that this refers to Christ and his church — to Christ and his ministers in spreading the gospel. The objections to this class of interpretations seem to me to be insuperable: (1) The whole description, so far as it is a representation of triumph, is a representation of the triumph of war, not of the gospel of peace. All the symbols in the opening of the first four seals are warlike; all the consequences in the opening of each of the seals where the horseman appears, are such as are usually connected with war. It is the march of empire, the movement of military power. (2) A horseman thus armed is not the usual representation of Christ, much less of his ministers or of his church. Once indeed (ch. xix. 14-16) Christ himself is thus represented; but the ordinary representation of the Saviour in this book is either that of a man—majestic and glorious, holding the stars in his right hand—or of a lamb. Besides, if it *were* the design of the emblem to refer to Christ, it must be a representation of him *personally* and *literally* going forth in this manner; for it would be incongruous to suppose that this relates to him, and then to give it a metaphorical application, referring it not to himself, but to his truth, his gospel, his ministers. (3) If there is little probability that this refers to Christ, there is still less that it refers to ministers of the gospel—as held by Lord and others—for such a symbol is employed nowhere else to represent an order of ministers, nor do the circumstances find a fulfilment in them. The minister of the gospel is a herald of peace, and is employed in the service of the Prince of Peace. He cannot well be represented by a warrior, nor is he in the Scriptures. In itself considered, there is nothing more unlike or incongruous than a warrior going forth to conquest with hostile arms, and a minister of Christ. (4) Besides, this representation of a horse and his rider, when applied in the following verses, on this principle becomes most forced and unnatural. If the warrior on the white horse denotes the ministry, then the warrior on the red horse, the black horse, the pale horse, must denote the ministry also, and nothing is more fanciful and arbitrary than to attempt to apply these to teachers of various kinds of error—error denoted by the red, black, and pale colour—as must be done on that supposition. It seems plain, therefore, to me, that the representation was not designed to symbolize the ministry, or the state of the church considered with reference to its extension, or the various forms of belief which prevailed. But if so, it only remains to inquire whether a state of things existed in the Roman world of which these would be appropriate symbols. We have, then, the following facts, which are of such a nature as would properly be symbolized by the horse of the first seal; that is, they are such facts that if one were to undertake to devise an appropriate symbol of them *since* they occurred, they would be well represented by the image here employed.

(1) It was in general a period of prosperity, of triumph, of conquest—well represented by the horseman on the white horse going forth to conquest. I refer now to the period immediately succeeding the time of John's banishment, embracing some ninety years, and extending through the successive reigns of Nerva, Trajan, Adrian, and the two Antonines, from the death of Domitian, A.D. 96, to the accession of Commodus, and the peace made by him with the Germans, A.D. 180. As an *illustration* of this period, and of the pertinency of the symbol, I will first copy from an historical chart drawn up with no reference to the symbol here, and in the mind of whose author the application to this symbol never occurred. The chart, distinguished for accuracy, is that of A. S. Lyman, published A.D. 1845. The following is the account of this period, beginning at the death of Domitian:—" Domitian, a cruel tyrant, the last of the twelve Cæsars." (His death, therefore, was an important epoch.) " A.D. 96 : Nerva, noted for his virtues, but enfeebled by age." "A.D. 98 : Trajan, *a great general, and popular emperor; under him the empire attains its greatest extent.*" " A.D. 117: Adrian, an able sovereign; spends thirteen years travelling through the empire, reforming abuses and rebuilding cities." " A.D. 138: Antoninus Pius, celebrated for his wisdom, virtue, and humanity." " A.D. 161: Marcus Aurelius Antoninus, the Stoic Philosopher, noted for his virtues." Then begins a new era—a series of wicked princes and of great calamities. The *next* entry in the series is, " A.D. 180: Commodus, profligate and cruel." Then follows a succession of princes of the same general description. Their character will be appropriately considered under the succeeding seals. But in regard to the period now supposed to be represented by the opening of the first seal, and the general applicability of the description here to that period, we have the fullest testimony in Mr. Gibbon, in his *Decline and Fall of the Roman Empire:* a writer who, sceptic as he was, seems to have been raised up by Divine Providence to search deeply into historic records, and to furnish an inexhaustible supply of materials in confirmation of the fulfilment of the prophecies, and of the truth of revelation. For (1) he was eminently endowed by talent, and learning, and patience, and general candour, and accuracy, to prepare a history of that period of the world, and to place his name in the very first rank of historians. (2) His history commences at about the period supposed in this interpretation to be referred to by these symbols, and extends over a very considerable portion of the time embraced in the book of Revelation. (3) It cannot be alleged that he was biassed in his statements of facts by a desire to favour revelation; nor can it be charged on him that he perverted *facts* with a view to overthrow the authority of the volume of inspired truth. He was, indeed, thoroughly sceptical as to the truth of Christianity, and he lost no opportunity to express his feelings towards it by a sneer—for it seems to have been an unfortunate characteristic of his mind to sneer at everything—but there is no evidence that he ever designedly perverted a *fact* in history to press it into the service of infidelity, or that he designedly falsified a statement for the purpose of making it bear against Christianity. It cannot be suspected that he had any *design*, by the statements which he makes, to confirm the truth of Scripture prophecies. Infidels, at least, are bound to admit his testimony as impartial. (4) Not a few of the most clear and decisive proofs of the fulfilment of prophecies are to be found in his history. They are frequently such statements as would be expected to occur in the writings of a partial friend of Christianity who was endeavouring to make the records of history speak out in favour of his religion; and if they had been found in such a writer, they would be suspected of having been shaped with a view to the confirmation of the prophecies, and it may be added also with an intention to defend some favourite interpretation of the Apocalypse. In regard to the passage before us—the opening of the first seal and the general explanation of the meaning of that seal, above given, there is a striking resemblance between that representation and the state of the Roman empire as given by Mr. Gibbon at the period

under consideration—from the end of the reign of Domitian to the accession of Commodus. By a singular coincidence Mr. Gibbon *begins* his history at about the period supposed to be referred to by the opening of the seal — the period following the death of Domitian, A.D. 96. Thus in the opening sentences of his work he says: "In the second century of the Christian era the empire of Rome comprehended the fairest part of the earth, and the most civilized portion of mankind. During a happy period of more than fourscore years the public administration was conducted by the virtue and abilities of Nerva, Trajan, Adrian, and the two Antonines. It is the design of this and the two succeeding chapters to describe the prosperous condition of their empire; and afterwards, from the death of Marcus Antoninus, to deduce the most important circumstances of its decline and fall; a revolution which will ever be remembered, and is still felt by the nations of the earth," vol. i. 1. Before Mr. Gibbon proceeds to give the history of the fall of the empire, he pauses to describe the happy condition of the Roman world during the period now referred to—for this is substantially his object in the first three chapters of his history. The *titles* of these chapters will show their object. They are respectively the following:—Ch. i., "The Extent and Military Force of the Empire, *in the Age of the Antonines;*" ch. ii., "Of the Union and Internal Prosperity of the Roman Empire, *in the Age of the Antonines;*" ch. iii., "Of the Constitution of the Roman Empire, *in the Age of the Antonines.*" In the language of another, this is "the bright ground of his historic picture, from which afterwards more effectively to throw out in deep colouring the successive traits of the empire's corruption and decline" (Elliott). The introductory remarks of Mr. Gibbon, indeed, professedly refer to "the age of the Antonines" (A.D. 138-180); but that he designed to describe, under this general title, the actual condition of the Roman world during the period which I suppose to be embraced under the first seal, as a time of prosperity, triumph, and happiness—from Domitian to Commodus—is apparent (*a*) from a remarkable statement which there will be occasion again to quote, in which he expressly designates this period in these words: "If a man were called to fix the period in the history of the world during which the condition of the human race was most happy and prosperous, he would, without hesitation, name that which elapsed *from the death of Domitian to the accession of Commodus,*" i. 47. The same thing is apparent also from a remark of Mr. Gibbon in the general summary which he makes of the Roman affairs, showing that this period constituted, in his view, properly an *era* in the condition of the world. Thus he says (i. 4): "Such was the state of the Roman frontiers, and such the maxims of imperial policy, from the death of Augustus *to the accession of Trajan.*" This was A.D. 98. The question now is, whether, during this period, the events in the Roman empire were such as accord with the representation in the first seal. There was nothing in the first century that could accord with this; and if John wrote the Apocalypse at the time supposed (A.D. 95 or 96), of course it does not refer to that. Respecting that century Mr. Gibbon remarks: "The only accession which the Roman empire received, during the first century of the Christian era, was the province of Britain. In this single instance the successors of Cæsar and Augustus were persuaded to follow the example of the former rather than the precept of the latter. After a war of about forty years, undertaken by the most stupid, maintained by the most dissolute, and terminated by the most timid of all the emperors, the far greater part of the island submitted to the Roman yoke," i. 2, 3. Of course the representation in the first seal *could not* be applied to such a period as this. In the second century, however, and especially in the early part of it—the beginning of the period supposed to be embraced in the opening of the first seal — a different policy began to prevail, and though the main characteristic of the period, as a whole, was comparatively peaceful, yet it began with a career of conquests, and its general state might be characterized as triumph and prosperity. Thus Mr. Gibbon speaks of Trajan on his accession after the death of Nerva: "That virtuous and active prince had received the education of a soldier, and possessed the talents of a general. The peaceful system of his predecessors *was interrupted by scenes of war and conquest;* and the legions, after a long interval, beheld a military emperor at their head. The first exploits of Trajan were against the

Dacians, the most warlike of men, who dwelt beyond the Danube, and who, during the reign of Domitian, had insulted the majesty of Rome. This memorable war, with a very short suspension of hostilities, lasted five years; and as the emperor could exert, without control, the whole force of the state, it was terminated by an absolute submission of the barbarians. The new province of Dacia, which formed a second exception to the precept of Augustus, was about thirteen hundred miles in circumference," i. 4. Speaking of Trajan (p. 4), he says farther: "The praises of Alexander, transmitted by a succession of poets and historians, had kindled a dangerous emulation in the mind of Trajan. Like him, the Roman emperor undertook an expedition against the nations of the East; but he lamented with a sigh that his advanced age scarcely left him any hopes of equalling the renown of the son of Philip. Yet the success of Trajan, however transient, was rapid and specious. The degenerate Parthians, broken by intestine discord, fled before his arms. He descended the river Tigris, *in triumph*, from the mountains of Armenia to the Persian Gulf. He enjoyed the honour of being the first, as he was the last, of the Roman generals who ever navigated that remote sea. His fleets ravaged the coasts of Arabia; and Trajan vainly flattered himself that he was approaching towards the confines of India. Every day the astonished senate received the intelligence *of new names and new nations* that acknowledged his sway. They were informed that the kings of Bosphorus, Colchis, Iberia, Albania, Osrhoene, and even the Parthian monarch himself, had accepted their diadems from the hand of the emperor; that the independent tribes of the Median and Carduchian hills had implored his protection; and that the rich countries of Armenia, Mesopotamia, and Assyria were reduced into the state of provinces." Of such a reign what more appropriate symbol could there be than the horse and the rider of the first seal? If Mr. Gibbon had been writing a designed commentary on this, what more appropriate language could he have used in illustration of it? The reign of Hadrian, the successor of Trajan (A.D. 117–138), was comparatively a reign of peace— though one of his first acts was to lead an expedition into Britain: but though comparatively a time of peace, it was a reign of prosperity and triumph. Mr. Gibbon, in the following language, gives a general characteristic of that reign: — "The life of [Hadrian] was almost a perpetual journey; and as he possessed the various talents of the soldier, the statesman, and the scholar, he gratified his curiosity in the discharge of his duty. Careless of the difference of seasons and of climates, he marched on foot, and bareheaded, over the snows of Caledonia and the sultry plains of Upper Egypt; nor was there a province of the empire which, in the course of his reign, was not honoured with the presence of the monarch," p. 5. On p. 6 Mr. Gibbon remarks of this period: "The Roman name was revered amongst the remote nations of the earth. The fiercest barbarians frequently submitted their differences to the arbitration of the emperor; and we are informed by a contemporary historian that he had seen ambassadors who were refused the honour which they came to solicit, of being admitted into the rank of subjects." And again, speaking of the reign of Hadrian, Mr. Gibbon remarks (i. 45): "Under his reign, as has been already mentioned, the empire flourished in peace and prosperity. He encouraged the arts, reformed the laws, asserted military discipline, and visited all the provinces in person." Hadrian was succeeded by the Antonines, Antoninus Pius and Marcus Aurelius (the former from A.D. 138 to 161; the latter from A.D. 161 to the accession of Commodus, A.D. 180). The general character of their reigns is well known. It is thus stated by Mr. Gibbon: "The two Antonines governed the world forty-two years with the same invariable spirit of wisdom and virtue. Their united reigns are possibly the only period of history in which the happiness of a great people was the sole object of government," i. 46. And after describing the state of the empire in respect to its military and naval character, its roads, and architecture, and constitution, and laws, Mr. Gibbon sums up the whole description of this period in the following remarkable words (vol. i. p. 47):—"*If a man were called to fix the period in the history of the world during which the condition of the human race was most happy and prosperous, he would, without hesitation, name that which elapsed from the death of Domitian to the accession of Commodus. The vast extent of the Roman empire was governed by absolute* power, under the guidance of virtue and wisdom. The armies were restrained by the firm but gentle hands of four successive emperors, whose characters and authority commanded involuntary respect. The forms of the civil administration were carefully preserved by Nerva, Trajan, Hadrian, and the Antonines, who delighted in the image of liberty, and were pleased with considering themselves as the accountable ministers of the laws. Such princes deserved the honour of restoring the republic, had the Romans of their days been capable of enjoying a rational freedom." If it be supposed now that John *designed* to represent this period of the world, could he have chosen a more expressive and significant emblem of it than occurs in the horseman of the first seal? If Mr. Gibbon had intended to prepare a commentary on it, could he have shaped the facts of history so as better to furnish an illustration?

(2) The particular things represented in the symbol. (*a*) The bow—a symbol of war. Mr. Elliott has endeavoured to show that the *bow* at that period was *peculiarly* the badge of the Cretians, and that Nerva, who succeeded Domitian, was a Cretian by birth. The argument is too long to be abridged here, but, if well founded, the fulfilment is remarkable; for although the sword or the javelin was usually the badge of the Roman emperor, if this were so there would be a peculiar propriety in making the *bow* the badge during this period. See Elliott, vol. i. pp. 133–140. But whatever may be said of this, the *bow* was so generally the badge of a warrior, that there would be no impropriety in

Medal of the Emperor Nerva wearing Crown.

using it as a symbol of Roman victory. (*b*) The crown—στέφανος—was, up to the time of Aurelian, A.D. 270 (see Spanheim, p. 60), the distinguishing badge of the Roman emperor; after that, the *diadem*, set with pearls and other jewels, was adopted and worn. The crown, composed usually of laurel, was properly the badge of the emperor considered as

Medal of the Emperor Valentinian wearing Diadem.

a military leader or commander. See Elliott, i. 130. At the period now under consideration the proper badge of the Roman emperor would be the *crown;* after the time of Aurelian, it would have been the *diadem*. In illustration of this, two engravings have been introduced, the first representing the emperor Nerva with the *crown*, or στέφανος, the second the emperor Valentinian, with the *diadem*. (*c*) The fact that the crown was *given* to the rider. It was common among the Romans to represent an emperor in this manner; either on medals, bas-reliefs, or triumphal arches. The emperor appears going forth on horseback, and with Victory represented as either crowning him, or as preceding him with a crown in her hand to present to him. The engraving on p. 146, copied from one of the bas-reliefs on a triumphal arch erected to Claudius Drusus on occasion of his victories over the Germans, will furnish a good illustration of this, and, indeed, is so similar to the symbol described by John, that the one seems almost a copy of the other. Except that the bow is wanting, nothing could have a closer resemblance; and the fact that such symbols were employed, and were well understood by the Romans, may be admitted to be a confirmation of the view above taken of the meaning of the first seal. Indeed, so many things combine to confirm this, that it seems im-

**3** And when he had opened the second seal, I heard the second beast say, Come and see.

**4** And there went out another horse *that was* red: and *power* was given to him that sat thereon to take peace from the earth, and that they should kill one another: and there was given unto him a great sword.

---

possible to be mistaken in regard to it: for if it should be supposed that John lived *after* this time, and that he *meant*

Symbolic Bas-reliefs from a Roman Triumphal Arch.

to furnish a striking emblem of this period of Roman history, he could not have employed a more significant and appropriate symbol than he has done.

**3.** *And when he had opened the second seal.* So as to disclose another portion of the volume. Notes, ch. v. 1. ¶ *I heard the second beast say.* The second beast was like a calf or an ox. Notes, ch. iv. 7. It cannot be supposed that there is any special significancy in the fact that the *second* beast addressed the seer on the opening of the *second* seal, or that, so far as the symbol was concerned, there was any reason why this living creature should approach on the opening of this seal rather than on either of the others. All that seems to be designed is, that as the living creatures are intended to be emblems of the providential government of God, it was proper to represent that government as concerned in the opening of each of these four seals, indicating important events among the nations. ¶ *Come and see.* See Notes on ver. 1.

**4.** *And there went out another horse.* In this symbol there were, as in the others, several particulars which it is proper to explain in order that we may be able to understand its application. The particular things in the symbol are the following: (*a*) The horse. See this explained in the Notes on ver. 2. (*b*) The colour of the horse: *another horse that was red.* This symbol cannot be mistaken. As the white horse denoted prosperity, triumph, and happiness, so this would denote carnage, discord, bloodshed. This is clear, not only from the nature of the emblem, but from the explanation immediately added: "And power was given to him that sat thereon to take peace from the earth, and that they should kill one another." On the *colour*, compare Bochart, *Hieroz.* P. i. lib. ii. c. vii. p. 104. See also Zec. i. 8. There is no possibility of mistaking this, that a time of *slaughter* is denoted by this emblem. (*c*) The power given to him that sat on the horse: *and power was given to him that sat thereon to take peace from the earth, and that they should kill one another.* This would seem to indicate that the condition immediately preceding this was a condition of tranquillity, and that this was now disturbed by some cause producing discord and bloodshed. This idea is confirmed by the original words — τὴν εἰρήνην —" *the* peace;" that is, the previously existing peace. When peace in general is referred to, the word is used without the article: Mat. x. 34, "Think not that I am come to send peace—βαλεῖν εἰρήνην—upon the earth." Comp.—Lu. i. 79; ii. 14; xix. 38; Mar. v. 34; Jn. xiv. 27; xvi. 33; Ac. vii. 26; ix. 31, *et al.* in the Greek. In these cases the word peace is without the article. The characteristics of the period referred to by this are: (*a*) that peace and tranquillity existed before; (*b*) that such peace and tranquillity were now taken away, and were succeeded by confusion and bloodshed; and (*c*) that the particular form of that confusion was civil discord, producing mutual slaughter: "that they should kill one another." (*d*) The presentation of a sword: *and there was given unto him a great sword.* As an emblem of what he was to do, or of the period that was referred to by the opening of the seal. The sword is an emblem of war, of slaughter, of authority (Ro. xiii. 4), and is here used as signifying that that period would be characterized by carnage. Comp. Is. xxxiv. 5; Re. xix. 17, 18; Lc. xxvi. 25; Ge. xxvii. 40; Mat. x. 34; xxvi. 52. It is not said *by whom* the sword was presented, but *the fact* is merely referred to, that the rider *was* presented with a sword as a symbol of what would occur.

In inquiring now into the period referred to by this symbol, we naturally look to that which immediately succeeded the one which was represented by the opening of the first seal; that is, the period which followed the accession of Commodus, A.D. 180. We shall find, in the events which succeeded his accession to the empire, a state of things which remarkably accords with the account given by John in this emblem —so much so, that if it were supposed that the book was written *after* these events had occurred, and that John had *designed* to represent them by this symbol, he could not have selected a more appropriate emblem. The only authority which it is necessary to refer to here is Mr. Gibbon; who, as before remarked, seems to have been raised up by a special Providence to make a record of those events which were referred to by some of the most remarkable prophecies in the Bible. As he had the highest qualifications for an historian, his statements may be relied on as accurate; and as he had no belief in the inspiration of the prophetic records, his testimony will not be charged with partiality in their favour. The following particulars, therefore, will furnish a full illustration of the opening of the second seal: (*a*) The previous state of peace. This is implied in the expression, "and power was given to him to *take peace* from the earth." Of this we have had a full confirmation in the peaceful reign of Hadrian and the Antonines. See the Notes on the exposition of the first seal. Mr. Gibbon, speaking of the accession of Commodus to the imperial throne, says that he "had nothing to wish, and everything to enjoy. The beloved son of Marcus [Commodus] succeeded his father amidst the acclamations of the senate and armies; and when he ascended the throne, the happy youth saw around him neither competitor to remove, nor enemies to punish. In this calm elevated station, it was surely natural that he should prefer the love of mankind to their detestation; the mild glories of his five predecessors to the ignominious fate of Nero and Domitian," i. 51. So again, on the same page, he says of Commodus, "His graceful person, popular address, and imagined virtues attracted the public favour; the honourable peace which he had recently granted to the barbarians diffused an universal joy." No one can doubt that the accession of Commodus was preceded by a remarkable prevalence of peace and prosperity. (*b*) Civil war and bloodshed: *to take peace from the earth, and that they should kill one another.* Of the applicability of this to the time supposed to be represented by this seal, we have the fullest confirmation in the series of civil wars commencing with the assassination of the emperor Commodus, A.D. 193, and continued, with scarcely any intervals of intermission, for eighty or ninety years. So Sismondi, on the fall of the Roman empire (i. 36), says, "With Commodus' death commenced the third and most calamitous period. It lasted ninety-two years, from 193 to 284. During that time, thirty-two emperors, and twenty-seven pretenders to the empire, alternately hurried each other from the throne, by incessant civil warfare. Ninety-two years of almost incessant civil warfare taught the world *on what a frail foundation the virtue of the Antonines had reared the felicity of the empire.*" The full history of this period may be seen in Gibbon, i. pp. 50-197. Of course it is impossible in these Notes to present anything like a complete account of the characteristics of those times. Yet the briefest summary may well show the general condition of the Roman empire then, and the propriety of representing it by the symbol of a red horse, as a period when peace would be taken from the earth, and when men would kill one another. Commodus himself is represented by Mr. Gibbon in the following words:—" Commodus was not, as he has been represented, a tiger, born with an insatiate thirst of human blood, and capable, from his infancy, of the most inhuman actions. Nature had formed him of a weak, rather than a wicked disposition. His simplicity and timidity rendered him the slave of his attendants, who gradually corrupted his mind. His cruelty, which at first obeyed the dictates of others, degenerated into habit, and at length became the ruling passion of his soul," i. 51. During the first three years of his reign "his hands were yet unstained with blood" (*Ibid.*), but he soon degenerated into a most severe and bloody tyrant, and "when Commodus had once tasted human blood, he was incapable of pity or remorse," i. 52. "The tyrant's rage," says Mr. Gibbon (i. 52), "after having shed the noblest blood of the senate, at length recoiled on the principal instrument of his cruelty. While Commodus *was immersed in blood and luxury* he devolved the detail of public business on Perennis, a servile and ambitious minister, who had obtained his post by the murder of his predecessor," &c. "Every sentiment of virtue and humanity was extinct in the mind of Commodus," i. 55. After detailing the history of his crimes, his follies, and his cruelties, Mr. Gibbon remarks of him: "His cruelty proved at last fatal to himself. He had shed with impunity the best blood of Rome: he perished as soon as he was dreaded by his own domestics. Marcia, his favourite concubine, Eclectus, his chamberlain, and Lætus, his pretorian prefect, alarmed by the fate of their companions and predecessors, resolved to prevent the destruction which every hour hung over their heads, either from the mad caprice of the tyrant, or the sudden indignation of the people. Marcia seized the occasion of presenting a draught of wine to her lover, after he had fatigued himself with hunting some wild beasts. Commodus retired to sleep; but while he was labouring with the effects of poison and drunkenness, a robust youth, by profession a wrestler, entered his chamber, and strangled him without resistance," i. 57. The immediate consequence of the assassination of Commodus was the elevation of Pertinax to the throne, and his murder eighty-six days after (*Decline and Fall*, i. 60). Then followed the public setting-up of the empire to sale by the pretorian guards, and its purchase by a wealthy Roman senator, Didius Julianus, or Julian, who, "on the throne of the world, found himself without a friend and without an adherent," i. 63. "The streets and public places in Rome resounded with clamours and imprecations." "The public discontent was soon diffused from the centre to the frontiers of the empire," i. 63. In the midst of this universal indignation Septimius Severus, who then commanded the army in the neighbourhood of the Danube, resolved to avenge the death of Pertinax, and to seize upon the imperial crown. He marched to Rome, overcame the feeble Julian, and placed himself on the throne. Julian, after having reigned sixty-six days, was beheaded in a private apartment of the baths of the palace, i. 67. "In less than four years Severus subdued the riches of the East, and the valour of the West. He vanquished two competitors of reputation and ability, and defeated numerous armies provided with weapons and discipline equal to his own," i. 68. Mr. Gibbon then enters into a detail of "the two *civil wars* against Niger and Albinus"—rival competitors for the empire (i. 68–70), both of whom were vanquished, and both of whom were put to death "in their flight from the field of battle." Yet he says, "Although the wounds of civil war were apparently healed, its mortal poison still lurked in the vitals of the constitution," i. 71. After the death of Severus, then follows an account of the contentions between his sons, Geta and Caracalla, and of the death of the former by the instigation of the latter (i. 77); then of the remorse of Caracalla, in which it is said that "his disordered fancy often beheld the angry forms of his father and his brother rising into life to threaten and upbraid him" (i. 77); then of the cruelties which Caracalla inflicted on the friends of Geta, in which "it was computed that, under the vague appellation of the friends of Geta, above twenty thousand persons of both sexes suffered death" (i. 78); then of the departure of Caracalla from the capital, and his cruelties in other parts of the empire, concerning which Mr. Gibbon remarks (i. 78, 79), that "Caracalla was the common enemy of mankind. Every province was by turns the scene of his rapine and cruelty. In the midst of peace and repose, upon the slightest provocation, he issued his commands at Alexandria in Egypt for a general massacre. From a secure post in the temple of Serapis he viewed and directed the slaughter of many thousand citizens, as well as strangers, without distinguishing either the number or the crime of the sufferers," &c. Then follows the account of the assassination of Caracalla (i. 80); then, and in consequence of that, of the civil war which crushed Macrinus, and raised Elagabalus to the throne (i. 83); then of the life and follies of that wretched voluptuary, and of his massacre by the pretorian guards

5 And when he had opened the third seal, I heard the third beast say, Come and see. And I beheld, (i. 86); then, after an interval of thirteen years, of the murder of his successor, the second Severus, on the Rhine; then of the civil wars excited against his murderer and successor, Maximin, in which the two emperors of a day—the Gordians, father and son—perished in Africa, and Maximin himself, and his son, in the siege of Aquileia; then of the murder at Rome of the two joint emperors, Maximus and Balbinus; and quickly after that an account of the murder of their successor in the empire, the third and youngest Gordian, on the banks of the river Aboras; then of the slaughter of the next emperor Philip, together with his son and associate in the empire, in the battle near Verona:—and this state of things may be said to have continued until the accession of Diocletian to the empire, A.D. 284. See *Decline and Fall*, i. 110–197. Does any portion of the history of the world present a similar period of connected history that would be so striking a fulfilment of the symbols used here of "peace being taken from the earth," and "men killing one another?" In regard to this whole period it is sufficient, after reading Mr. Gibbon's account, to ask two questions: (1) If it were supposed that John lived *after* this period, and designed to represent this by an expressive symbol, could he have found one that would have characterized it better than this does? (2) And if it should be supposed that Mr. Gibbon *designed* to write a commentary on this "seal," and to show the exact fulfilment of the symbol, could he have selected a better portion of history to do it, or could he have better described facts that would be a complete fulfilment? It is only necessary to observe further, (c) that this is a *marked* and *definite* period. It has such a beginning, and such a continuance and ending, as to show that this symbol was applicable to this *as* a period of the world. For it was not only preceded by a state of peace, as is supposed in the symbol, but no one can deny that the condition of things in the empire, from Commodus onward through many years, was such as to be appropriately designated by the symbol here used.

5, 6. *And when he had opened the third seal.* Unfolding another portion of the volume. See Notes on ch. v. 1. ¶ *I heard the third beast say, Come and see.* See Notes on ch. iv. 7. It is not apparent why the *third* beast is represented as taking a particular interest in the opening of *this* seal (comp. Notes on ver. 3), nor is it necessary to show why it was so. The general design seems to have been, to represent each one of the four living creatures as interested in the opening of the seals, but the *order* in which they did this does not seem to be a matter of importance. ¶ *And I beheld, and lo, a black horse.* The specifications of the symbol here are the following: (*a*) As before, the horse. See Notes on ver. 2. (*b*) The *colour* of the horse: *lo, a black horse.* This would properly denote distress and calamity—for *black* has been regarded always as such a symbol. So Virgil speaks of *fear* as black: "atrumque timorem" (*Æn.* ix. 619). So again, *Georg.* iv. 468:

"Caligantem nigra formidine lucum."

So, as applied to the dying Acca, *Æn.* xi. 825:

"Tenebris nigrescunt omnia circum."

Black, in the Scriptures, is the image of fear, of famine, of death. La. v. 10: "Our skin was black like an oven, because of the terrible famine." Je. xiv. 2: "Because of the drought Judah mourneth, and the gates thereof languish; they are in deep mourning [literally, *black*] for the land." Joel ii. 6: "All faces shall gather blackness." Na. ii. 10: "The knees smite together, and there is great pain in all loins, and the faces of them all gather blackness." Comp. Re. vi. 12; Eze. xxxii. 7. See also Bochart, *Hieroz.* P. i. lib. ii. c. vii. pp. 106, 107. From the *colour* of the horse here introduced we should naturally look for some dire calamity, though the *nature* of the calamity would not be designated by the mere use of the word *black*. What the calamity was to be must be determined by what follows in the symbol. Famine, pestilence, oppression, heavy taxation, tyranny, invasion—any of these might be denoted by the colour of the horse. (*c*) The balances: *and he that sat on him had a pair of balances in his hand.* The original word here rendered *a pair*

150  REVELATION.  [A.D. 96.

6 And I heard a voice in the midst of the four beasts say, ¹A measure of wheat for a penny, and three measures of barley for a penny; and *see* thou ᵈhurt not the oil and the wine.

¹ The word *chœnix* signifieth a measure containing one wine quart, and the twelfth part of a quart.

d ch.9.4.

*of balances*, is ζυγὸν. This word properly means *a yoke*, serving to couple anything together, as a yoke for cattle. Hence it is used to denote the *beam* of a balance, or of a pair of scales—and is evidently so used here. The idea is, that something was to be *weighed*, in order to ascertain either its *quantity* or its *value*. Scales or balances are the emblems of justice or equity (comp. Job xxxi. 6; Ps. lxii. 9; Pr. xi. 1; xvi. 11); and when joined with symbols that denote the sale of corn and fruit by weight, become the symbol of scarcity. Thus "bread by weight" (Le. xxvi. 26) denotes scarcity. So in Eze. iv. 16, "And they shall eat bread by weight." The use of balances here as a symbol would signify that something was to be accurately and carefully weighed out. The connection leads us to suppose that this would appertain to the necessaries of life, and that it would occur either in consequence of scarcity, or because there would be an accurate or severe exaction, as in collecting a revenue on these articles. The balance was commonly the symbol of equity and justice; but it was also, sometimes, the symbol of exaction and oppression, as in Ho. xii. 7: "The balance of deceit is in his hands; he loveth to oppress." If the balances stood alone, and there were no proclamation as to what was to occur, we should look, under this seal, to a time of the exact administration of justice, as scales or balances are now used as emblems of the rigid application of the laws and of the principles of justice in courts, or in public affairs. If *this* representation stood alone, or if the black horse and the scales constituted the whole of the symbol, we should look for some severe administration, or perhaps some heavy calamity under a rigorous administration of laws. The reference, however, to the "wheat and barley," and to the price for which they were to be weighed out, serves still further to limit and define the meaning of the symbol as having reference to the necessaries of life —to the productions of the land—to the actual capital of the country. Whether this refers to scarcity, or to taxation, or both, must be determined by the other parts of the symbol. (*d*) The proclamation: *And I heard a voice in the midst of the four beasts say.* That is, from the throne, ch. iv. 6. The voice was not that of one of the four beasts, but it seemed to come from among them. As the rider went forth, this was the proclamation that was made in regard to him; or this is that which is symbolized in his going forth, to wit, that there would be such a state of things that a measure of wheat would be sold for a penny, &c. The proclamation consists essentially of two things —that which refers to the price or value of wheat and barley, and that which requires that care shall be taken not to injure the oil and the wine. Each of these demands explanation. ¶ *A measure of wheat for a penny.* See the margin. The word rendered *measure*— χοῖνιξ, *chœnix*—denotes an Attic measure for grain and things dry, equal to the forty-eighth part of the Attic medimnus, or the eighth part of the Roman modius, and consequently was nearly equivalent to one quart English (Rob. *Lex.*). The word rendered *penny*, δηναρίον—Lat. *denarius*—was of the same value as the Greek δραχμή, *drachmē*, and was equivalent to about fourteen cents or sevenpence. This was the usual price of a day's labour, Mat. xx. 2, 9. The chœnix, or measure of grain here referred to, was the ordinary daily allowance for one man (*Odyss.*, xix. 27, 28). See Stuart, *in loco*. The common price of the Attic medimnus of wheat was five or six denarii; but here, as that contained forty-eight chœnixes or quarts, the price would be augmented to forty-eight denarii—or it would be about eight times as dear as ordinary; that is, there would be a scarcity or famine. The price of a *bushel* of wheat at this rate would be about four dollars and a half or 18 shillings—a price which would indicate great scarcity, and which would give rise to much distress. ¶ *And three measures of barley for a penny.* It would seem from this that barley usually bore about one-third the price of wheat. It was a less valuable grain, and perhaps was produced in greater abundance. This is not far from the proportion which the price of this grain usually bears to that of wheat, and here, as in the case of the wheat, the thing which would be indicated would be scarcity. This proclamation of "a measure of wheat for a penny" was heard either as addressed *to* the horseman, as a rule of action for him, or as addressed *by* the horseman as he went forth. If the former is the meaning, it would be an appropriate address to one who was going forth to collect tribute—with reference to the *exact* manner in which this tribute was to be collected, implying some sort of severity of exaction; or to one who should distribute wheat and barley out of the public granaries at an advanced price, indicating scarcity. Thus it would mean that a severe and heavy tax—represented by the scales and the scarcity—or a tax so severe as to *make* grain dear, was referred to. If the latter is the meaning, then the idea is that there would be a scarcity, and that grain would be dealt out by the government at a high and oppressive price. The latter idea would be as consonant with the symbol of the scales and the price mentioned as the other, if it were not for the *additional* injunction not to "hurt the oil and the wine"—which cannot be well applied to the idea of dealing out grain at a high price. It can, however, be connected, by a fair interpretation of that passage, with such a severity of taxation that there would be a propriety in such a command—for, as we shall see, under the explanation of that phrase, such a law was actually promulgated as resulting from severity of taxation. The idea, then, in the passage before us, would seem to be, (*a*) that there would be a rigid administration of the law in regard to the matter under consideration—that pertaining to the productions of the earth—represented by the balances; and (*b*) that that would be connected with general scarcity, or such an exercise of this power as to determine the price of grain, so that the price would be some three times greater than ordinary. ¶ *And* see *thou hurt not the oil and the wine.* There has been a great variety of interpretations proposed of this passage, and it is by no means easy to determine the true sense. The first inquiry in regard to it is, to whom is it addressed? Perhaps the most common impression on reading it would be, that it is addressed to the horseman with the balances, commanding *him* not to injure the oliveyards and the vineyards. But this is not probably the correct view. It does not appear that the horseman goes forth to destroy anything, or that the effect of his going forth is directly to injure anything. This, therefore, should not be understood as addressed to the horseman, but should be regarded as a general command to any and all *not* to injure the oliveyards and vineyards; that is, an order that nothing should be done essentially to injure them. If thus regarded as addressed to others, a fair and congruous meaning would be furnished by either of the following interpretations: either (*a*) considered as addressed to those who were disposed to be prodigal in their manner of living, or careless as to the destruction of the crop of the oil and wine, as they would now be needed; or (*b*) as addressed to those who raised such productions, on the supposition that they would be *taxed* heavily, or that large quantities of these productions would be extorted for revenue, that they should not mutilate their fruit-trees in order to evade the taxes imposed by the government. In regard to the things specified here—oil and wine—it may be remarked, that they were hardly considered as articles of luxury in ancient times. They were almost as *necessary* articles as wheat and barley. They constituted a considerable part of the food and drink of the people, as well as furnished a large portion of the revenue, and it would seem to be with reference to that fact that the command here is given that they should not be injured; that is, that nothing should be done to diminish the quantity of oil and wine, or to impair the productive power of oliveyards and vineyards. The state of things thus described by this seal, as thus interpreted, would be, (*a*) a rigid administration of the laws of the empire, particularly in reference to taxation, producing a scarcity among the necessary articles of living; (*b*) a strong tendency, *from* the severity of the taxation, to mutilate such kinds of property, with a view either of concealing the real amount of property, or of diminishing the amount of taxes; and (*c*) a solemn command from some authoritative quarter *not* to do this. A command from the ruling power *not* to do this would meet all that would be fairly demanded in the *interpretation* of the passage; and what is necessary in its *application*, is to find such a state of things as would correspond with these predictions; that is, such as a writer *would have* described by such symbols on the supposition that they were referred to.

Now it so happens that there *were* important events which occurred in the Roman empire, and connected with its decline and fall, of sufficient importance to be noticed in a series of calamitous events, which corresponded with the symbol here, as above explained. They were such as these: (*a*) The *general* severity of taxation, or the oppressive burdens laid on the people by the emperors. In the account which Mr. Gibbon gives of the operation of the *Indictions*, and *Superindictions*, though the specific laws on this subject pertained to a subsequent period, the general nature of the taxation of the empire and its oppressive character may be seen (*Decline and Fall*, i. 357–359). A general estimate of the amount of revenue to be exacted was made out, and the collecting of this was committed to the pretorian prefects, and to a great number of subordinate officers. "The lands were measured by surveyors who were sent into the provinces; their nature, whether arable, or pasture, or woods, was distinctly reported; and an estimate made of their common value, from the average produce of five years. The number of slaves and of cattle constituted an essential part of the report; an oath was administered to the proprietors, which bound them to disclose the true state of their affairs; and their attempts to prevaricate or elude the intention of the legislature were severely watched, and punished as a capital crime, which included the double guilt of treason and of sacrilege. According to the different nature of lands, their real produce in the various articles of *wine or oil, corn or barley*, wood or iron, was transported by the labour or at the expense of the provincials to the imperial magazines, from whence they were occasionally distributed for the use of the court or of the army, and of the two capitals, Rome and Constantinople," i. p. 358. Comp. Lactant. *de Mort. Persecut.*, c. 23. (*b*) The particular order, under this oppressive system of taxation, respecting the preservation of vineyards and oliveyards, may be referred to, also, as corresponding to the command sent forth under this rider, not to "hurt the oil and the wine." That order was in the following words: —" If any one shall sacrilegiously cut a vine, or stint the fruit of prolific boughs, and craftily feign poverty in order to avoid a fair assessment, he shall, immediately on detection, suffer death, and his property be confiscated" (*Cod. Theod.* l. xiii. lib. xi. seq.; Gibbon, i. 358, note). Mr. Gibbon remarks: "Although this law is not without its studied obscurity, it is, however, clear enough to prove the minuteness of the inquisition, and the disproportion of the penalty." (*c*) Under this general subject of the severity of taxation—as a fact far-spreading and oppressive, and as so important as to hasten the downfall of the empire, may be noticed a distinct edict of Caracalla as occurring more directly in the period in which the rider with the balances may be supposed to have gone forth. This is stated by Mr. Gibbon (i. 91) as one of the important causes which contributed to the downfall of the empire. "The personal characters of the emperors, their victories, laws, and fortunes," says he, "can interest us no farther than they are connected with the general history of the decline and fall of the monarchy. Our constant attention to that object will not suffer us to overlook a most important edict of Antoninus Caracalla, which communicated to all the free inhabitants of the empire the name and privileges of Roman citizens. His unbounded liberality, however, flowed not from the sentiments of a generous mind; it was the sordid result of avarice," &c. He then proceeds at length to state the nature and operations of that law, by which a heavy tax, under the pretence of liberality, was in fact imposed on all the citizens of the empire—a fact which, in its ultimate results, the historian of the *Decline and Fall* regards as so closely connected with the termination of the empire. See Gibbon, i. pp. 91–95. After noticing the laws of Augustus, Nero, and the Antonines, and the real privileges conferred by them on those who became entitled to the rank of Roman citizens—privileges which were a compensation in the honour, dignity, and offices of that rank for the measure of taxation which it involved—he proceeds to notice the fact that the *title* of "Roman citizen" was conferred by Caracalla on all the free citizens of the empire, involving the subjection to all the heavy taxes usually imposed on those who sustained the rank expressed by the title, but with nothing of the compensation connected with the title when it was confined to the inhabitants of Italy. "But the favour," says he, "which implied a distinction, was lost in the prodigality of Caracalla, and the reluctant provincials were compelled to assume *the vain title*, and the real *obligations*, of Roman citizens. Nor was the rapacious son of Severus [Caracalla] contented with such a measure of taxation as had appeared sufficient to his moderate predecessors. Instead of a twentieth, he exacted a tenth of all legacies and inheritances; and during his reign he crushed alike every part of the empire under the weight of his iron sceptre," i. 95. So again (*Ibid.*), speaking of the taxes which had been lightened somewhat by Alexander, Mr. Gibbon remarks: "It is impossible to conjecture the motive that engaged him to spare so trifling a remnant of the evil; but the noxious weed, which had not been totally eradicated, again sprung up with the most luxuriant growth, and in the succeeding age darkened the Roman world with its deadly shade. In the course of this history we shall be too often summoned to explain the land-tax, the capitation, and the heavy contributions of *corn, wine, oil*, and meat, which were exacted from the provinces for the use of the court, the army, and the capital." In reference to this whole matter of *taxation* as being one of the things which contributed to the downfall of the empire, and which spread woe through the falling empire—a woe worthy to be illustrated by one of the seals—a confirmation may be derived from the reign of Galerius, who, as Cæsar, acted under the authority of Diocletian; who excited Diocletian to the work of persecution (*Decline and Fall*, i. 317, 318); and who, on the abdication of Diocletian, assumed the title of Augustus (*Decline and Fall*, i. 222). Of his administration in general Mr. Gibbon (i. 226) remarks: "About that time the avarice of Galerius, or perhaps the exigencies of the state, had induced him to make a very strict and rigorous inquisition into the property of his subjects for the purpose of a general taxation, both on their lands and on their persons. A very minute survey appears to have been taken of their real estates; and wherever there was the slightest suspicion of concealment, torture was very freely employed to obtain a sincere declaration of their personal wealth." Of the nature of this exaction under Galerius; of the cruelty with which the measure was prosecuted —particularly in its bearing on Christians, towards whom Galerius cherished a mortal enmity (*Decline and Fall*, i. 317); and of the extent and severity of the suffering among Christians and others, caused by it—the following account of Lactantius (*De Mort. Persecut.*, c. 23) will furnish a painful but most appropriate illustration:— "Swarms of exactors sent into the provinces and cities filled them with agitation and terror, as though a conquering enemy were leading them into captivity. The fields were separately measured, the trees and vines, the flocks and herds numbered, and an examination made of the men. In the cities the cultivated and rude were united as of the same rank. The streets were crowded with groups of families, and every one required to appear with his children and slaves. Tortures and lashes resounded on every side. Sons were gibbeted in the presence of their parents, and the most confidential servants harassed that they might make disclosures against their masters, and wives that they might testify unfavourably of their husbands. If there were a total destitution of property, they were still tortured to make acknowledgments against themselves, and, when overcome by pain, inscribed for what they did not possess. Neither age nor ill-health was admitted as an excuse for not appearing. The sick and weak were borne to the place of inscription, a reckoning made of the age of each, and years added to the young and deducted from the old, in order to subject them to a higher taxation than the law imposed. The whole scene was filled with wailing and sadness. In the meantime individuals died, and the herds and the flocks diminished, yet tribute was none the less required to be paid for the dead, so that it was no longer allowed either to live or die without a tax. Mendicants alone escaped, where nothing could be wrenched, and whom misfortune and misery had made incapable of farther oppression. These the impious wretch affecting to pity, that they might not suffer want, ordered to be assembled, borne off in vessels, and plunged into the sea." See Lord on the Apoc., pp. 128, 129. These facts in regard to the severity of taxation, and the rigid nature of the law enforcing it; to the sources of the revenue exacted in the provinces, and to the care that none

7 And when he had opened the fourth seal, I heard the voice of the fourth beast say, Come and see.

8 And I looked, and behold a pale horse; and his name that sat on him was Death, and Hell followed with him. And power was given ²unto them over the fourth part of the earth, to kill ᵉ with sword, and with hunger, and with death, and with the beasts of the earth.

² or, *to him.*   *e* Eze.14.21.

of those sources should be diminished; and to the actual and undoubted bearing of all this on the decline and fall of the empire, are so strikingly applicable to the symbol here employed, that if it be supposed that it was *intended* to refer to them, no more natural or expressive symbol could have been used; if it were supposed that the historian *meant* to make a record of the fulfilment, he could not well have made a search which would more strikingly accord with the symbol. Were we *now* to represent these things by a symbol, we could scarcely find one that would be more expressive than that of a rider on a black horse with a pair of scales, sent forth under a proclamation which indicated that there would be a most rigid and exact administration of severe and oppressive laws, and with a special command, addressed to the people, not for the purposes of concealment, or from opposition to the government, to injure the sources of revenue. It may serve further to illustrate this, to copy one of

Emblem of a Roman Procurator.

the usual emblems of a Roman procurator or questor. It is taken from Spanheim, *De Usu Num. Diss.*, vi. 545. See Elliott, i. 169. It has a balance as a symbol of exactness or justice, and an ear of grain as a symbol employed with reference to procuring or exacting grain from the provinces.

7. *And when he had opened the fourth* seal. See Notes, ch. v. 1. ¶ *I heard the voice of the fourth beast say.* The flying eagle. Notes, ch. iv. 7. As in the other cases, there does not appear to have been any particular reason why the *fourth* of the living creatures should have made this proclamation rather than either of the others. It was poetic and appropriate to represent each one in his turn as making proclamation. ¶ *Come and see.* See Notes, ver. 1.

8. *And I looked, and behold a pale horse*—ἵππος χλωρός. On the *horse*, as an emblem, see Notes on ver. 2. The *peculiarity* of this emblem consists in the *colour* of the horse, the rider, and the power that was given unto him. In these there is entire harmony, and there can be comparatively little difficulty in the explanation and application. The *colour* of the horse was *pale*—χλωρός This word properly means *pale-green, yellowish-green*, like the colour of the first shoots of grass and herbage; then *green, verdant*, like young herbage, Mar. vi. 39; Re. viii. 7; ix. 4; and then *pale yellowish* (Rob. *Lex.*). The colour here would be an appropriate one to denote the reign of death—as one of the most striking effects of death is *paleness*—and, of course, of death produced by any cause, famine, pestilence, or the sword. From this portion of the symbol, if it stood with nothing to limit and define it, we should naturally look for some condition of things in which death would prevail in a remarkable manner, or in which multitudes of human beings would be swept away. And yet, perhaps, from the very nature of *this* part of the symbol, we should look for the prevalence of death in some such peaceful manner as by famine or disease. The *red* colour would more naturally denote the ravages of death in war; the black, the ravages of death by sudden calamity; the pale would more obviously suggest famine or wasting disease. ¶ *And his name that sat on him was Death.* No description is given of his aspect; nor does he appear with any emblem—as sword, or spear,

or bow. There is evident scope for the fancy to picture to itself the form of the destroyer; and there is just that kind of obscurity about it which contributes to sublimity. Accordingly, there has been ample room for the exercise of the imagination in the attempts to paint "Death on the pale horse," and the opening of this seal has furnished occasion for some of the greatest triumphs of the pencil. The simple *idea* in this portion of the symbol is, that death would reign or rule under the opening of this seal—whether by sword, by famine, or by pestilence, is to be determined by other descriptions in the symbol. ¶ *And Hell followed with him.* Attended him as he went forth. On the meaning of the word here rendered *hell*—ἅδης, *hades*—see Notes on Lu. xvi. 23, comp. Notes on Job x. 21, 22; Is. xiv. 9. It is here used to denote the abode of the dead, considered as a place where they dwell, and not in the more restricted sense in which the word is now commonly used as a place of punishment. The idea is, that the dead would be so numerous at the going forth of this horseman, that it would seem as if the pale nations of the dead had come again upon the earth. A vast retinue of the dead would accompany him; that is, it would be a time when death would prevail on the earth, or when multitudes would die. ¶ *And power was given unto them.* Marg., *to him.* The common Greek text is αὐτοῖς — *to them.* There are many MSS., however, which read αὐτῷ—*to him*. So Professor Stuart reads it. The authority, however, is in favour of *them* as the reading; and according to this, death and his train are regarded as grouped together, and the power is considered as given to them collectively. The sense is not materially varied. ¶ *Over the fourth part of the earth.* That is, of the Roman world. It is not absolutely necessary to understand this as extending over *precisely* a fourth part of the world. Comp. Re. viii. 7-10, 12; ix. 15, *et al*. Undoubtedly we are to look in the fulfilment of this to some far-spread calamity; to some severe visitations which would sweep off great multitudes of men. The *nature* of that visitation is designated in the following specifications. ¶ *To kill with sword*. In war and discord—and we are, therefore, to look to a period of war. ¶ *And with hunger.* With famine—one of the accompaniments of war—where armies ravage a nation, trampling down the crops of grain; consuming the provisions laid up; employing in war, or cutting off, the men who would be occupied in cultivating the ground; making it necessary that they should take the field at a time when the grain should be sown or the harvest collected; and shutting up the people in besieged cities to perish by hunger. Famine has been not an unfrequent accompaniment of war; and we are to look for the fulfilment of this in its extensive prevalence. ¶ *And with death.* Each of the other forms—"with the sword and with hunger"—imply that *death* would reign; for it is said that "power was given to *kill* with sword and with hunger." This word, then, must refer to death in some other form —to death that seemed to reign without any such *visible* cause as the "sword" and "hunger." This would well denote the pestilence—not an unfrequent accompaniment of war. For nothing is better fitted to produce this than the unburied bodies of the slain; the filth of a camp; the want of food; and the crowding together of multitudes in a besieged city; and, accordingly, the pestilence, especially in Oriental countries, has been often closely connected with war. That the *pestilence* is referred to here is rendered more certain by the fact that the Hebrew word דֶּבֶר, *pestilence*, which occurs about fifty times in the Old Testament, is rendered θάνατος, *death*, more than thirty times in the Septuagint. ¶ *And with the beasts of the earth.* With wild beasts. This, too, would be one of the consequences of war, famine, and pestilence. Lands would be depopulated, and wild beasts would be multiplied. Nothing more is necessary to make them formidable than a prevalence of these things; and nothing, in the early stages of society, or in countries ravaged by war, famine, and the pestilence, is more formidable. Homer, at the very beginning of his *Iliad*, presents us with a representation similar to this. Comp. Eze. xiv. 21: "I send my four sore judgments upon Jerusalem, the sword, and the famine, and the noisome beast, and the pestilence," דֶּבֶר—Sept., as here, θάνατον. See also 2 Ki. xvii. 26.

In regard to the fulfilment of this there can be little difficulty, if the principles adopted in the interpretation of the first three seals are correct. We may turn to Gibbon, and, as in the other cases, we shall find that he has been an unconscious witness of the fidelity of the representation in this seal. Two *general* remarks may be made before there is an attempt to illustrate the particular things in the symbol. (*a*) The first relates to *the place* in the order of time, or in history, which this seal occupies. If the three former seals have been located with any degree of accuracy, we should expect that this would follow, not very remotely, the severe laws pertaining to taxation, which, according to Mr. Gibbon, contributed so essentially to the downfall of the empire. And if it be admitted to be probable that the fifth seal refers to a time of persecution, it would be most natural to fix this period between those times and the times of Diocletian, when the persecution ceased. I may be permitted to say, that I was led to fix on this period without having any definite view beforehand of what occurred *in* it, and was surprised to find in Mr. Gibbon what *seems* to be so accurate a correspondence with the symbol. (*b*) The second remark is, that the *general* characteristics of this period, as stated by Mr. Gibbon, agree remarkably with what we should expect of the period from the symbol. Thus speaking of this whole period (A.D. 248-268), embracing the reigns of Decius, Gallus, Æmilianus, Valerian, and Gallienus, he says, "From the great secular games celebrated by Philip to the death of the emperor Gallienus, there elapsed twenty years of shame and misfortune. During this calamitous period every instant of time was marked, every province of the Roman world was afflicted by barbarous invaders and military tyrants, and the ruined empire seemed to approach the last and fatal moment of its dissolution," i. 135.

In regard to the *particular* things referred to in the symbol, the following specifications may furnish a sufficient confirmation and illustration: (*a*) The killing with the sword. A fulfilment of this, so far as the *words* are concerned, might be found indeed in many portions of Roman history, but no one can doubt that it was eminently true of this period. It was the period of the *first* Gothic invasion of the Roman empire; the period when those vast hordes, having gradually come down from the regions of Scandinavia, and having moved along the Danube towards the Ukraine and the countries bordering on the Borysthenes, invaded the Roman territories from the East, passed over Greece, and made their appearance almost, as Mr. Gibbon says, within sight of Rome. Of this invasion Mr. Gibbon says, "This is the first considerable occasion [the fact that the emperor Decius was summoned to the banks of the Danube, A.D. 250, by the invasion of the Goths] in which history mentions that great people, who afterwards broke the Roman power, sacked the Capitol, and reigned in Gaul, Spain, and Italy. So memorable was the part which they acted in the subversion of the Western empire, that the name of GOTHS is frequently, but improperly, used as a general appellation of rude and warlike barbarism," i. p. 136. As one of the illustrations that the "sword" would be used by "Death" in this period, we may refer to the siege and capture of Philippolis. "A hundred thousand persons are reported to have been massacred in the sack of that great city" (*Dec. and Fall*, i. 140). "The whole period," says Mr. Gibbon, speaking of the reigns of Valerian and Gallienus, "was one uninterrupted series of confusion and calamity. The Roman empire was, at the same time, and on every side, attacked by the blind fury of foreign invaders, and the wild ambition of domestic usurpers," i. 144. "Such were the barbarians," says Mr. Gibbon in the close of his description of the Goths at this period, and of the tyrants that reigned, "and such the tyrants, who, under the reigns of Valerian and Gallienus, dismembered the provinces, and reduced the empire to the lowest pitch of disgrace and ruin, from whence it seemed impossible that it should ever emerge," i. 158. (*b*) Famine: "Shall kill with hunger." This would naturally be the consequence of long-continued wars, and of such invasions as those of the Goths. Mr. Gibbon says of this period: "Our habits of thinking so fondly connect the order of the universe with the fate of man, that this gloomy period of history has been decorated with inundations, earthquakes, uncommon meteors, preternatural darkness, and a crowd of prodigies, fictitious or exaggerated. But *a long and general famine* was a calamity of a more serious kind. It was the inevitable consequence of rapine and oppression, which extirpated the produce of the present, and the hope of future harvests," i. p. 159. Prodigies, and preternatural darkness, and earthquakes, were *not* seen in the vision of the opening of the *seal*—but *war* and *famine* were; and the facts stated by Mr. Gibbon are such as would be now appropriately symbolized by Death on the pale horse. (*c*) Pestilence: "And shall kill with death." Of the pestilence which raged in this period Mr. Gibbon makes the following remarkable statement, in immediate connection with what he says of the famine:—"Famine is almost always followed by epidemical diseases, the effect of scanty and unwholesome food. Other causes must, however, have contributed to the furious plague, which, from the year 250 to the year 265, *raged without interruption in every province, every city, and almost every family of the Roman empire*. During some time five thousand persons died daily at Rome; and many towns that had escaped the hands of the barbarians were entirely depopulated," i. 159. (*d*) Wild beasts: "And shall kill with the beasts of the earth." As already remarked, these are formidable enemies in the early stages of society, and when a country becomes, from any cause, depopulated. They are not mentioned by Mr. Gibbon as contributing to the decline and fall of the empire, or as connected with the calamities that came upon the world at that period. But no one can doubt that in such circumstances they would be likely to abound, especially if the estimate of Mr. Gibbon be correct (i. 159), when speaking of these times, and making an estimate of the proportion of the inhabitants of Alexandria that had perished—which he says was more than one-half—he adds, "Could we venture to extend the analogy to the other provinces, we might suspect that *war, pestilence*, and *famine* had consumed in a few years the moiety of the human species." Yet, though not adverted to by Mr. Gibbon, there *is* a record pertaining to this very period, which shows that this was one of the calamities with which the world was then afflicted. It occurs in Arnobius, *Adv. Gentes*, lib. i. p. 5. Within a few years after the death of Gallienus (about A.D. 300) he speaks of wild beasts in such a manner as to show that they were regarded as a sore calamity. The public peril and suffering on this account were so great, that in common with other evils this was charged on Christians as one of the judgments of heaven which they brought upon the world. In defending Christians against the general charge that these judgments were sent from heaven on their account, he adverts to the prevalence of wild beasts, and shows that they could not have been sent as a judgment on account of the existence of Christianity, by the fact that they had prevailed also in the times of heathenism, long before Christianity was introduced into the empire. "Quando cum feris bella, et proelia cum leonibus gesta sunt? Non ante nos? Quando pernicies populis venenatis ab anguibus data est? Non ante nos?" "When were wars waged with wild beasts, and contests with lions? Was it not before our times? When did a plague come upon men poisoned by serpents? Was it not before our times?" In regard to the *extent* of the destruction which these causes would bring upon the world, there is a remarkable confirmation in Gibbon. To say, as is said in the account of the seal, that "a *fourth* part of the earth" would be subjected to the reign of death by the sword, by famine, by pestilence, and by wild beasts, may seem to many to be an improbable statement—a statement for the fulfilment of which we should look in vain to any historical records. Yet Mr. Gibbon, without expressly mentioning the plague of wild beasts, but referring to the three others—"war, pestilence, and famine"—goes into a calculation, in a passage already referred to, by which he shows that it is probable that from these causes *half* the human race was destroyed. The following is his estimate:—"We have the knowledge of a very curious circumstance, of some use perhaps in the melancholy calculation of human calamities. An exact register was kept at Alexandria of all the citizens entitled to receive the distribution of corn. It was found that the ancient number of those comprised between the ages of forty and seventy had been equal to the whole sum of claimants, from fourteen to fourscore years of age, who remained alive after the reign of Gallienus. Applying this authentic fact to the most correct tables of mortality, it evidently proves that above half the people of Alexandria had perished; and could we venture to extend the analogy to the other provinces, *we might suspect that war, pestilence, and famine had consumed in a few years the moiety of the human species*," i. 159. The historian says that it might be "*suspected*" from these data that one-half of the

158   REVELATION.   [A.D. 96.

9 And when he had opened the fifth seal, I saw under the *f* altar the *g* souls of them that were slain for *h* the word of God, and for the testimony which they held:

10 And they cried with a loud

*f* ch.8.3.   *g* ch.20.4.   *h* ch.1.9; 12.17.

voice, saying, *i* How long, O Lord, holy and true, dost thou not judge and *k* avenge our blood on them that dwell on the earth?

11 And *l* white robes were given unto every one of them; and it

*i* Zec.1.12.   *k* ch.11.18; De.32.41-43.   *l* ch.7.9,14.

human race had been cut off in a few years, from these causes; in the Apocalyptic vision it is said that power was given over one "*fourth*" of the earth. We may remark, (*a*) that the description in the symbol is as *likely* to be correct as the "suspicion" of the historian; and (*b*) that his statement that in this period "a moiety of the race," or one-half of the race, perished, takes away all improbability from the prediction, and gives a most graphic confirmation of the symbol of *Death on the pale horse*. If such a desolation in fact occurred, there is no improbability in the supposition that it might have been prefigured by the opening of a prophetic seal. Such a wide-spread desolation would be *likely* to be referred to in a series of symbols that were designed to represent the downfall of the Roman power, and the great changes in human affairs that would affect the welfare of the church.

9-11. *And when he had opened the fifth seal.* Notes, ch. v. 1; vi. 1. ¶ *I saw under the altar.* The four living creatures are no longer heard as in the opening of the first four seals. No reason is given for the change in the manner of the representation; and none can be assigned, unless it be, that having represented each one of the four living creatures in their turn as calling attention to the remarkable events about to occur, there seemed to be no necessity or propriety in introducing them again. In itself considered, it cannot be supposed that they would be any less interested in the events about to be disclosed than they were in those which preceded. This seal pertains to *martyrs* —as the former successively did to a time of prosperity and triumph; to discord and bloodshed; to oppressive taxation; to war, famine, and pestilence. In the series of woes, it was natural and proper that there should be a vision of martyrs, if it was intended that the successive seals should refer to coming and important periods of the world; and accordingly we have here a striking representation of the martyrs crying to God to interpose in their behalf and to avenge their blood. The points which require elucidation are: (*a*) their position —under the altar; (*b*) their invocation —or their prayer that they might be avenged; (*c*) the clothing of them with robes; and (*d*) the command to wait patiently a little time. (1) The position of the martyrs—*under the altar*. There were in the temple at Jerusalem two altars—the altar of burnt sacrifices, and the altar of incense. The altar here referred to was probably the former. This stood in front of the temple, and it was on this that the daily sacrifice was made. Comp. Notes on Mat. v. 23, 24. We are to remember, however, that the temple and the altar were both destroyed before the time when this book was written, and this should, therefore, be regarded merely as a vision. John saw these souls *as if* they were collected under the altar—the place where the sacrifice for sin was made—offering their supplications. *Why* they are represented as being there is not so apparent; but probably two suggestions will explain this: (*a*) The altar was the place where sin was expiated, and it was natural to represent these redeemed martyrs as seeking refuge there; and (*b*) it was usual to offer prayers and supplications *at* the altar, in connection with the sacrifice made for sin, and on the ground of that sacrifice. The idea is, that they who were suffering persecution would naturally seek a refuge in the place where expiation was made for sin, and where prayer was appropriately offered. The *language* here is such as a Hebrew would naturally use; the *idea* is appropriate to anyone who believes in the atonement, and who supposes that that is the appropriate refuge for those who are in trouble. But while the language here is such as a Hebrew would use, and while the reference in the language is to the altar of burnt sacrifice, the scene should be regarded as undoubtedly laid in heaven —the temple where God resides. The whole representation is that of fleeing to the atonement, and pleading with

A.D. 96.]  CHAPTER VI.  159

was said unto them, that they should ᵐrest yet for a little season, until ⁿ their fellow-servants also

*m* ch.14.13.   *n* He.11.40.

God in connection with the sacrifice for sin. ¶ *The souls of them that were slain.* That had been put to death by persecution. This is one of the incidental proofs in the Bible that the soul does not cease to exist at death, and also that it does not cease to be conscious, or does not sleep till the resurrection. These souls of the martyrs are represented as still in existence; as remembering what had occurred on the earth; as interested in what was now taking place; as engaged in prayer; and as manifesting earnest desires for the divine interposition to avenge the wrongs which they had suffered. ¶ *For the word of God.* On account of the word or truth of God. See Notes on ch. i. 9. ¶ *And for the testimony which they held.* On account of their testimony to the truth, or being faithful witnesses of the truth of Jesus Christ. See Notes on ch. i. 9.  (2) The invocation of the martyrs, ver. 10: *And they cried with a loud voice.* That is, they pleaded that their blood might be avenged. ¶ *Saying, How long, O Lord, holy and true.* They did not doubt that God *would* avenge them, but they inquired *how long* the vengeance would be delayed. It seemed to them that God was slow to interpose, and to check the persecuting power. They appeal therefore to him as a God of holiness and truth; that is, as one who could not look with approval on sin, and in whose sight the wrongs inflicted by the persecuting power must be infinitely offensive; as one who was true to his promises, and faithful to his people. On the ground of his own hatred of wrong, and of his plighted faithfulness to his church, they pleaded that he would interpose. ¶ *Dost thou not judge and avenge our blood.* That is, dost thou *forbear* to judge and avenge us; or dost thou delay to punish those who have persecuted and slain us. They do not speak as if they had any doubt that it would be done, nor as if they were actuated by a spirit of *revenge*; but as if it would be *proper* that there should be an expression of the divine sense of the wrongs that had been done them. It is not right to desire vengeance or revenge; it is to

and their brethren, that should be killed as they *were*, should be fulfilled.

desire that justice should be done, and that the government of God should be vindicated. The word *"judge"* here may either mean "judge *us*," in the sense of "vindicate *us*," or it may refer to their persecutors, meaning "judge *them*." The more probable sense is the latter: "How long dost thou forbear to execute judgment on our account on those that dwell on the earth?" The word *avenge*—ἐκδικέω— means to do justice; to execute punishment. ¶ *On them that dwell on the earth.* Those who are still on the earth. This shows that the scene here is laid in heaven, and that the souls of the martyrs are represented as there. We are not to suppose that this *literally* occurred, and that John actually saw the souls of the martyrs beneath the altars—for the whole representation is symbolical; nor are we to suppose that the injured and the wronged in heaven actually pray for vengeance on those who wronged them, or that the redeemed in heaven will continue to pray with reference to things on the earth; but it may be fairly inferred from this that there will be *as real* a remembrance of the wrongs of the persecuted, the injured, and the oppressed, *as if* such prayer were offered there; and that the oppressor has as much to dread from the divine vengeance *as if* those whom he has injured should cry in heaven to the God who hears prayer, and who takes vengeance. The wrongs done to the children of God; to the orphan, the widow, the down-trodden; to the slave and the outcast, will be as certainly remembered in heaven as if they who are wronged should plead for vengeance there, for every act of injustice and oppression goes to heaven and pleads for vengeance. Every persecutor should dread the death of the persecuted *as if* he went to heaven to plead against him; every cruel master should dread the death of his slave that is crushed by wrongs; every seducer should dread the death and the cries of his victim; every one who does wrong in any way should remember that the sufferings of the injured cry to heaven with a martyr's pleadings, saying, "How long, O Lord, holy and true, dost thou not judge and avenge our blood?" (3) The robes that were given to the martyrs: *And white robes were given unto every one of them.* Emblems of purity or innocence. See Notes on ch. iii. 5. Here the robes would be an emblem of their innocence as martyrs; of the divine approval of their testimony and lives, and a pledge of their future blessedness. (4) The command to wait: *And it was said unto them, that they should rest yet for a little season.* That is, that they must wait for a little season before they could be avenged as they desired, ver. 10. They had pleaded that their cause might be at once vindicated, and had asked how long it would be before it should be done. The reply is, that the desired vindication would not at once occur, but that they must wait until other events were accomplished. Nothing definite is determined by the phrase "a little season," or a short time. It is simply an intimation that this would not *immediately* occur, or was not soon to take place. Whether it refers to an existing persecution, and to the fact that they were to wait for the divine interposition until that was over, and those who were then suffering persecution should be put to death and join them; or whether to a series of persecutions stretching along in the history of the world, in such a sense that the promised vengeance would take place only when all those persecutions were passed, and the number of the martyrs completed, cannot be determined from the meaning of their words. Either of these suppositions would accord well with what the language naturally expresses. ¶ *Until their fellow-servants also.* Those who were then suffering persecution, or those who should afterwards suffer persecution, grouping all together. ¶ *And their brethren.* Their brethren as Christians, and their brethren in trial: those then living, or those who would live afterwards and pass through similar scenes. ¶ *Should be fulfilled.* That is, till these persecutions were passed through, and the number of the martyrs was complete. The state of things represented here would seem to be, that there was then a persecution raging on the earth. Many had been put to death, and their souls had fled to heaven, where they pleaded that their cause might be vindicated, and that their oppressors and persecutors might be punished. To this the answer was, that *they* were now safe and happy —that God approved their course, and that in token of his approbation they should be clothed in white raiment; but that the invoked vindication could not at once occur. There were others who would yet be called to suffer as they had done, and they must wait until all that number was completed. *Then*, it is implied, God would interpose, and vindicate his name. The scene, therefore, is laid in a time of persecution, when many had already died, and when there were many more that were exposed to death; and a sufficient fulfilment of the passage, so far as the *words* are concerned, would be found in *any* persecution, where many might be represented as having already gone to heaven, and where there was a certainty that many more would follow. We naturally, however, look for the fulfilment of it in some period succeeding those designated by the preceding symbols. There would be no difficulty, in the early history of the church, in finding events that would correspond with all that is represented by the symbol; but it is natural to look for it in a period succeeding that represented, under the fourth seal, by Death on the pale horse. If the previous seals have been correctly interpreted we shall not be much in danger of erring in supposing that this refers to the persecution under Diocletian; and perhaps we may find in one who never intended to write a word that could be construed as furnishing a proof of the fulfilment of the prophecies of the New Testament, what should be regarded as a complete verification of all that is represented here. The following particulars may justify this application: (*a*) The *place* of that persecution in history, or the time when it occurred. As already remarked, if the previous seals have been rightly explained, and the fourth seal denotes the wars, the famine, and the pestilence, under the invasion of the Goths, and in the time of Valerian and Gallienus, then the last great persecution of the church under Diocletian would well accord with the period in history referred to. Valerian died in A.D. 260, being flayed alive by Sapor, king of Persia; Gallienus died in A.D. 268, being killed at Milan. Diocletian ascended the throne A.D. 284, and resigned the purple A.D. 304. It was during this period, and chiefly at the instigation of Galerius, that the tenth persecution of the Christians occurred — the last under the Roman power; for in A.D. 306 Constantine ascended the throne, and ultimately be-

## CHAPTER VI.

came the protector of the church. (*b*) The *magnitude* of this persecution under Diocletian is as consonant to the representation here as its place in history. So important was it, that, in a general chapter on the persecutions of the Christians, Mr. Gibbon has seen fit, in his remarks on the nature, causes, extent, and character of the persecutions, to give a prominence to this which he has not assigned to any others, and to attach an importance to it which he has not to any other. See vol. i. pp. 317–322. The *design* of this persecution, as Mr. Gibbon expresses it (i. 318), was "to set bounds to the progress of Christianity;" or, as he elsewhere expresses it (on the same page), "the destruction of Christianity." Diocletian, himself naturally averse from persecution, was excited to this by Galerius, who urged upon the emperor every argument by which he could persuade him to engage in it. Mr. Gibbon says in regard to this, "Galerius at length extorted from him [Diocletian] the permission of summoning a council, composed of a few persons, the most distinguished in the civil and military departments of the state. It may be presumed that they insisted on every topic which might interest the pride, the piety, the fears of their sovereign *in the destruction of Christianity,*" i. 318. The *purpose* evidently in the persecution, was, to make a last and desperate effort, through the whole Roman empire, for the destruction of the Christian religion; for Mr. Gibbon (i. 320) says that "the edict against the Christians was designed for a general law *of the whole empire.*" Other efforts had failed. The religion still spread, notwithstanding the rage and fury of nine previous persecutions. It was resolved to make one more effort. This was designed by the persecutors to be the last, in the hope that then the Christian name would cease to be: in the providence of God it *was* the last —for then even these opposing powers became convinced that the religion could not be destroyed in this manner —and as this persecution was to establish this fact, it was an event of sufficient magnitude to be symbolized by the opening of one of the seals. (*c*) The *severity* of this persecution accorded with the description here, and was such as to deserve a place in the series of important events which were to occur in the world. We have seen above, from the statement of Mr. Gibbon, that it was designed for the "whole empire," and it in fact raged with fury throughout the empire. After detailing some of the events of local persecutions under Diocletian, Mr. Gibbon says, "The resentment or the fears ot Diocletian at length transported him beyond the bounds of moderation, which he had hitherto preserved, and he declared, in a series of edicts, his intention of abolishing the Christian name. By the first of these edicts the governors of the provinces were directed to apprehend all persons of the ecclesiastical order; and the prisons destined for the vilest criminals were soon filled with a multitude of bishops, presbyters, deacons, and exorcists. By a second edict the magistrates were commanded to employ every method of severity which might reclaim them from their odious superstition, and oblige them to return to the established worship of the gods. This rigorous order was extended, by a subsequent edict, to the whole body of Christians, who were exposed to a violent and general persecution. Instead of those salutary restraints which had required the direct and solemn testimony of an accuser, it became the duty as well as the interest of the imperial officers to discover, to pursue, and to torment the most obnoxious among the faithful. Heavy penalties were denounced against all who should presume to save a proscribed sectary from the just indignation of the gods, and of the emperors," i. 322. The first decree against the Christians, at the instigation of Galerius, will show the general nature of this fiery trial of the church. That decree was to the following effect: "All assembling of the Christians for the purposes of religious worship was forbidden; the Christian churches were to be demolished to their foundations; all manuscripts of the Bible should be burned; those who held places of honour or rank must either renounce their faith or be degraded; in judicial proceedings the torture might be used against all Christians, of whatever rank; those belonging to the lower walks of private life were to be divested of their rights as citizens and as freemen; Christian slaves were to be incapable of receiving their freedom, so long as they remained Christians" (Neander, *Hist. of the Church*, Torrey's Trans. i. 148). This persecution was the last against the Christians by the Roman emperors; the

12 And I beheld when he had opened the sixth seal, and, lo, there was a great *earthquake; and the

*ch.16.18.

---

last that was waged by that mighty Pagan power. Diocletian soon resigned the purple, and after the persecution had continued to rage, with more or less severity, under his successors, for ten years, the peace of the church was established. "Diocletian," says Mr. Gibbon (i. 322), "had no sooner published his edicts against the Christians, than, as if he had been committing to other hands his work of persecution, he divested himself of the imperial purple. The character and situation of his colleagues and successors sometimes urged them to enforce, and sometimes to suspend, the execution of these rigorous laws; nor can we acquire a just and distinct idea of this important period of ecclesiastical history, unless we separately consider the state of Christianity in the different parts of the empire, during the space of ten years which elapsed between the first edicts of Diocletian *and the final peace of the church.*" For this detail consult Gibbon, i. 322–329, and the authorities there referred to; and Neander, *Hist. of the Church,* i. 147–156. Respecting the details of the persecution, Mr. Gibbon remarks (i. 326), " It would have been an easy task, from the history of Eusebius, from the declamations of Lactantius, and from the most ancient acts, to collect a long series of horrid and disgustful pictures, and to fill many pages with racks and scourges, with iron-hooks, and red-hot beds, and with the variety of tortures which fire and steel, savage beasts, and more savage executioners, could inflict on the human body." It is true that Mr. Gibbon professes to doubt the truth of these records, and attempts to show that the account of the number of the martyrs has been greatly exaggerated; yet no one, in reading his own account of this persecution, can doubt that it was the result of a determined effort to blot out the Christian religion, and that the whole of the imperial power was exerted to accomplish this end. At length the last of the imperial persecutions ceased, and the great truth was demonstrated that Christianity could not be extinguished by power, and that "the gates of hell could not prevail against it." "In the year 311," says Neander (i. 156), "the remarkable edict appeared which put an end to the last sanguinary conflict of the Christian church and the Roman empire." This decree was issued by the author and instigator of the persecution, Galerius, who, "softened by a severe and painful disease, the consequence of his excesses, had been led to think that the God of the Christians might, after all, be a powerful being, whose anger punished him, and whose favour he must endeavour to conciliate." This man suspended the persecution, and gave the Christians permission "once more to hold their assemblies, provided they did nothing contrary to the good order of the Roman state." "Ita ut ne quid contra disciplinam agant" (Neander, *ibid.*).

12–17. *And I beheld when he had opened the sixth seal.* See Notes, ch. v. 1; vi. 1. ¶ *And, lo, there was a great earthquake.* Before endeavouring to ascertain to what the sixth seal was designed to refer, it is proper, as in the previous cases, to furnish a particular explanation of the meaning of the symbols. All the symbols represented in the opening of this seal denote consternation, commotion, changes; but still they are all significant, and we are to suppose that something would occur corresponding with each one of them. It cannot be supposed that the things here described were represented on the part of the roll or volume that was now unfolded in any other way than that they were pictures, or that the whole was a species of panoramic representation made to pass before the eyes. Thus understood, it would not be difficult to represent each one of these things in a painting: as the heaving ground—the agitated forests—the trembling hills—the falling cities and houses—the sun blackened, and the moon turned to blood.

(*a*) The earthquake, ver. 12: *There was a great earthquake.* The word here used denotes a shaking or agitation of the earth. The effect, when violent, is to produce important changes—opening chasms in the earth; throwing down houses and temples; sinking hills, and elevating plains; causing ponds and lakes to dry up, or forming them where none existed; elevating the ocean from its bed, rending rocks, &c. As all that occurs in the opening of the other seals is symbolical, it is to be presumed that this is also, and that for the fulfilment sun*p* became black as sackcloth of hair, and the moon became as blood;

*p* Joel 2.10,31; 3.15.

of this we are not to look for a literal earthquake, but for such agitations and changes in the world as would be properly symbolized by this. The earthquake, as a symbol, would merely denote great agitations or overturnings on the earth. The particular character of those changes must be determined by other circumstances in the symbol that would limit and explain it. There are, it is said, but three literal earthquakes referred to in the Scripture: that mentioned in 1 Ki. xix. 11; that in Uzziah's time, Am. i. 1; Zec. xiv. 5; and that which took place at the Saviour's death. All the rest are emblematical or symbolical—referring mostly to civil commotions and changes. Then in Hag. ii. 6, 7: "Yet once, it is a little while, and I will shake the heavens and the earth, and the sea, and the dry land, and I will shake all nations, and the desire of all nations shall come; and I will fill this house with glory, saith the Lord of hosts." That is, there would be great agitations in the world before he came. See Notes on He. xii. 26–28. So also great changes and commotions are referred to in Is. xxiv. 19, 20: "The earth is utterly broken down, the earth is clean dissolved, the earth is moved exceedingly. The earth shall reel to and fro like a drunkard, and shall be removed like a cottage." An *earthquake*, if there were no other circumstances limiting and explaining the symbol, would merely denote great agitation and commotion—*as if* states and empires were tumbling to ruin. As this is here a mere *symbol*, it is not necessary to look for a literal fulfilment, or to expect to find in history actual earthquakes to which this had reference, any more than when it is said that "the heavens departed as a scroll" we are to expect that they will be literally rolled up; but if, in the course of history, earthquakes preceded remarkable political convulsions and revolutions, it would be proper to represent such events in this way.

(*b*) The darkening of the sun: *And the sun became black as sackcloth of hair.* Sackcloth was a coarse black cloth, commonly, though not always, made of hair. It was used for sacks, for strainers, and for mourning garments; and as thus worn it was not an improper em-

13 And the *q* stars of heaven fell unto the earth, even as a fig-tree

*q* ch.8.10.

blem of sadness and distress. The idea here is, that the sun put on a dark, dingy, doleful appearance, *as if* it were in mourning. The general image, then, in this emblem, is that of calamity—*as if* the very sun should put on the robes of mourning. We are by no means to suppose that this was *literally* to occur, but that *some* great calamity would happen, of which this would be an appropriate emblem. See Notes on Is. xiii. 10; Mat. xxiv. 29. Comp. Is. xxiv. 23; xxxiv. 4; l. 3; lx. 19, 20; Eze. xxxii. 7, 8; Joel ii. 10; iii. 15, 16; Am. viii. 9. What is the particular nature of the calamity is to be learned from other parts of the symbol.

(*c*) The discoloration of the moon: *And the moon became as blood.* Red like blood—either from the smoke and vapour that usually precedes an earthquake, or as a mere emblem. This also would betoken calamity, and *perhaps* the symbol may be so far limited and modified by this as to denote *war*, for that would be most naturally suggested by the colour—*red*. Comp. Notes on ver. 4 of this chapter. But *any* great calamity would be appropriately represented by this—as the change of the moon to such a colour would be a natural emblem of distress.

(*d*) The falling of the stars, ver. 13: *And the stars of heaven fell unto the earth.* This *language* is derived from the poetic idea that the sky seems to be a solid concave, in which the stars are *set*, and that when any convulsion takes place, that concave will be shaken, and the stars will be loosened and fall from their places. See this language explained in the Notes on Is. xxxiv. 4. Sometimes the expanse above us is spoken of as a curtain that is spread out, and that may be rolled up; sometimes as a solid crystalline expanse in which the stars are fixed. According to either representation the stars are described as falling to the earth. If the expanse is *rolled up*, the stars, having nothing to support them, fall; if violent tempests or concussions shake the heavens, the stars, loosened from their fixtures, fall to the earth. Stars, in the Scriptures, are symbols of princes and rulers (see Da. viii. 10; Re. viii. 10, 11; ix. 1); and the natural meaning of this symbol is, that there would be commotions which would casteth her ³untimely figs, when she is shaken of a mighty wind.

14 And the ʳheaven departed as a scroll when it is rolled together; and ˢevery mountain and

³ or, *green.*  ʳ Ps.102.26; Is.34.4.
ˢ ch.16.20; Je.4.23,24; Hab.3.6,10.

island were moved out of their places.

15 And the kings of the earth and the great men, and the rich men, and the chief captains, and the mighty men, and every bond-

---

unsettle princes, and bring them down from their thrones — like stars falling from the sky. ¶ *Even as a fig-tree casteth her untimely figs.* Marg., *green;* Gr., ὀλύνθους. This word properly denotes *winter-figs,* or such as grow under the leaves, and do not ripen at the proper season, but hang upon the trees during the winter (Rob. *Lex.*). This fruit seldom matures, and easily falls off in the spring of the year (Stuart, *in loco*). A violent wind shaking a plantation of fig-trees would of course cast many such figs to the ground. The point of the comparison is, the ease with which the stars would seem to be shaken from their places, and hence the ease with which, in these commotions, princes would be dethroned.

(*e*) The departing of the heavens, ver. 14: *And the heaven departed as a scroll.* That is, as a book or volume—βιβλίον—rolled up. The heavens are here described as spread out, and their passing away is represented by the idea that they might be rolled up, and thus disappear. See Notes on Is. xxxiv. 4. This, too, is a symbol, and we are not to suppose that it will literally occur. Indeed it never *can* literally occur; and we are not, therefore, to look for the fulfilment of this in any physical fact that would correspond with what is here said. The plain meaning is, that there would be changes *as if* such an event would happen; that is, that revolutions would occur in the high places of the earth, and among those in power, *as if* the stars should fall, and the very heavens were swept away. This is the natural meaning of the symbol, and this accords with the usage of the language elsewhere.

(*f*) The removal of mountains and islands, ver. 14: *And every mountain and island were moved out of their places.* This would denote convulsions in the political or moral world, as great as would occur in the physical world if the very mountains were removed and the islands should change their places. We are not to suppose that this would literally occur; but we should be authorized from this to expect that, in regard to those things which seemed to be permanent and fixed on an immovable basis, like mountains and islands, there would be violent and important changes. If thrones and dynasties long established were overthrown; if institutions that seemed to be fixed and permanent were abolished; if a new order of things should rise in the political world, the meaning of the symbol, so far as the language is concerned, would be fulfilled.

(*g*) The universal consternation, ver. 15-17: *And the kings of the earth,* &c. The design of these verses (15-17), in the varied language used, is evidently to denote universal consternation and alarm—*as if* the earth should be convulsed, and the stars should fall, and the heavens should pass away. This consternation would extend to all classes of men, and fill the world with alarm, *as if* the end of all things were coming. ¶ *The kings of the earth.* Rulers—all who occupied thrones. ¶ *The great men.* High officers of state. ¶ *And the rich men.* Their wealth would not secure them from destruction, and they would be alarmed like others. ¶ *And the chief captains.* The commanders of armies, who tremble like other men when God appears in judgment. ¶ *And the mighty men.* Men of great prowess in battle, but who feel now that they have no power to withstand God. ¶ *And every bondman.* Servant—δοῦλος. This word does not necessarily denote a *slave* (comp. Notes on Ep. vi. 5; 1 Ti. vi. 1; Phile. 16), but here the connection seems to demand it, for it stands in contrast with *freeman.* There were, in fact, slaves in the Roman empire, and there is no objection in supposing that they are here referred to. There is no reason why they should not be filled with consternation as well as others; and as this does not refer to the end of the world, or the day of judgment, the word here determines nothing as to the question whether slavery is to continue on the earth. ¶ *And every freeman.* Whether the master of slaves or not. The idea is, man, and every freeman, *hid themselves in the dens and in the rocks of the mountains;

16 And "said to the mountains and rocks, Fall on us, and hide us from the face of him that sitteth on

*t* Is. 2. 19   *u* ch. 9. 6; Ho. 10. 8; Lu. 23. 30.

the throne, and from the wrath of the Lamb:

17 For the *v*great day of his wrath is come; and *w* who shall be able to stand?

*v* ch. 16. 14; Is. 13. 6, &c.; Zep. 1. 14, &c.
*w* Ps. 76. 7.

that all classes of men, high and low, would be filled with alarm. ¶ *Hid themselves in the dens.* Among the caves or caverns in the mountains. See Notes on Is. ii. 19. These places were resorted to for safety in times of danger. Comp. 1 Sa. xiii. 6; xxiv.; Ju. vi. 2; Je. xli. 9; Jos. *Ant.* book xiv. ch. xv.; *Jewish Wars*, book i. ch. xvi. ¶ *And in the rocks of the mountains.* Among the crags or the fastnesses of the mountains—also natural places of refuge in times of hostile invasion or danger. See Notes on Is. ii. 21. ¶ *And said to the mountains and rocks, Fall on us*, &c., ver. 16. This language is found substantially in Ho. x. 8: "And they shall say to the mountains, Cover us; and to the hills, Fall on us." It is also used by the Saviour as denoting the consternation which would occur at his coming: "Then shall they begin to say to the mountains, Fall on us; and to the hills, Cover us," Lu. xxiii. 30. It is language denoting consternation, and an awful fear of impending wrath. The state of mind is that where there is an apprehension that God himself is coming forth with the direct instruments of his vengeance, and where there is a desire rather to be crushed by falling rocks and hills than by the vengeance of his uplifted arm. ¶ *From the face of him that sitteth on the throne.* The face of God—for he seems to be coming forth with the displays of his vengeance. It is not said that God would actually come forth in a visible form, but their consternation would be as great as if he were to do this; the state of mind indicated by this was an apprehension that it would be so. ¶ *And from the wrath of the Lamb.* The Lamb of God; the Lord Jesus. See Notes on ch. v. 6. There seems to be an incongruity between the words *wrath* and *Lamb;* but the word *Lamb* here is so far a proper name as to be used only to designate the Redeemer. He comes forth to execute wrath, not as a Lamb, but as the Son of God, who bore that name. It would seem from this that they who thus dreaded the impending terrors were aware of their source, or had knowledge enough to understand by whom they were to be inflicted. They would see that these were *divine* judgments, and would apprehend that the end of the world drew near. ¶ *For the great day of his wrath is come,* ver. 17. The threatening judgments would be so severe and awful that they would suppose that the end of the world was coming. ¶ *And who shall be able to stand?* To stand before him, or to withstand his judgments.

It is unnecessary to say that there has been, in this case, as in reference to every other part of the book of Revelation, a great diversity of opinion respecting the events symbolized by this seal. Grotius applied it to the wars between the Jews and Romans under Nero and Vespasian; Dr. Hammond supposed that the defeat of the Jewish leaders in those wars was particularly symbolized; Mr. Brightman referred these symbols to the persecution under Diocletian; Mr. Mede, Dr. Cressner, Dr. More, Mr. Whiston, Mr. Jurien, Mr. Daubuz, Mr. Lowman, Bishop Newton, Mr. Elliott, and others, refer it to the defeat of the Pagan powers, and the final suppression of those powers as opposed to Christianity; Vitringa regarded it as foreshadowing the overthrow of the antichristian powers of the western Roman empire; Cocceius explains it of the wars of the Emperor Frederick against the German princes in the sixteenth century; Dean Woodhouse, of the day of vengeance at the end of the world; Mr. Cunninghame, of the same period as the seventh trumpet, commencing with the French revolution, and to be consummated by the visible advent of the Son of God; Professor Stuart, of the destruction of Jerusalem; and Mr. Lord, of a series of events, part of which are fulfilled, three of them corresponding with the first three vials—the first expressive of the revolution of France, the second of a despotism extending through several years, and the third of the overthrow of that violent dynasty, at the fall of

Bonaparte, in 1815. It is not my purpose to examine these views; but, amidst this great variety of opinion, it seems to me that the obvious and natural application of the opening of the seal has not been adverted to. I shall suggest it because it *is* the most natural and obvious, and seems to be demanded by the explanations given of the previous seals. It is, in one word, the impending judgments from the invasions of the northern hordes of Goths and Vandals, threatening the breaking up of the Roman empire—the gathering of the storm, and the hovering of those barbarians on the borders of the empire; the approaches which they made from time to time towards the capital, though restrained as yet from taking it; the tempest of wrath that was, as it were, *suspended* yet on the frontiers, until the events recorded in the next chapter should occur, then bursting forth in wrath in successive blasts, as denoted by the first four trumpets of the seventh seal (ch. viii.), when the empire was entirely overthrown by the Goths and Vandals. The precise point of time which I suppose this seal occupies is that *succeeding* the last persecution. It embraces the preparatory arrangements of these hordes of invaders—their gathering on the frontiers of the empire—their threatened approaches toward the capital—and the formation of such vast armies as would produce universal consternation. A brief notice of these preparatory scenes, as adapted to produce the alarm referred to in the opening of the sixth seal, is all that will be necessary here; the more complete detail must be reserved for the explanation of the four trumpets of the seventh seal, when the work of destruction was consummated. These preparations and threatened invasions were events sufficiently important in their relation to the church, to what preceded, and to the future history of the world, to be symbolized here; and they are events in which all the particulars of the symbol may find a fulfilment. Anyone has only to look on a chart of history to see how appropriately this application of the symbol follows, if the previous explanations have been correct. In the illustration of this, in order to show the probability that these events are referred to by the symbols of the sixth seal, I would submit the following remarks:—

(1) The *time* is that which would be naturally suggested by this seal in its relation to the others. If the fifth referred to the persecutions under Diocletian—the last great persecution of the Pagan powers in attempting to extinguish the Christian name—then we should naturally look for the fulfilment of the opening of the next in some event, or series of events, which would succeed that at no very distant interval, and that pertained to the empire or power that had been the prominent subject of the predictions in the previous seals. It would also be natural to look for some events that might be regarded as conveying an expression of the divine feeling in regard to that power, or that would present it in such an aspect that it would be seen that its power to persecute was at an end. This natural *expectation* would be answered either by some symbol that would refer to the complete triumph of the Christian system, or by such a series of judgments as would break the persecuting power itself in pieces. Now the threatened irruption of the northern barbarians followed the series of events already described with sufficient *nearness* to make it proper to regard that series of events as referred to.

(2) The events were of sufficient *importance* in the history of the empire to deserve this notice in the foreshadowing of what would occur. They were connected with the breaking up of that mighty power, and the complete change of the aspect of the world, in a political and religious point of view. A new order of things arose in the world's history. A new religion became established. New kingdoms from the fragments of the once-mighty Roman empire were founded, and the affairs of the world were put on a new footing. These mighty northern hordes not only spread consternation and alarm, as if the world were coming to an end, but they laid the foundations of kingdoms which continue to this day. In fact, few more important events have occurred in history.

(3) This series of events was *introduced* in the manner described in the opening of the sixth seal. I have already said that it is not *necessary* to suppose, in the fulfilment of the symbol, that there would be a literal earthquake; but nothing in the symbol forbids us to suppose that there might be, and if there were we could not but consider it as remarkable. Now it so happens that the series of events per-

taining to the Gothic invasions is introduced by Mr. Gibbon in the following language: "A.D. 365. In the second year of the reign of Valentinian and Valens, on the morning of the twenty-first day of July, the greatest part of the Roman world was shaken by a violent and destructive earthquake. The impression was communicated to the waters; the shores of the Mediterranean were left dry by the sudden retreat of the sea; great quantities of fish were caught with the hand; large vessels were stranded on the mud; and a curious spectator amused his eye, or rather his fancy, by contemplating the various appearances of valleys and mountains which had never before, since the formation of the globe, been exposed to the sun. But the tide soon returned, with the weight of an immense and irresistible deluge, which was severely felt on the coasts of Sicily, of Dalmatia, of Greece, and of Egypt; large boats were transported, and lodged on the roofs of houses, or at the distance of two miles from the shore; the people, with their habitations, were swept away by the waters; and the city of Alexandria annually commemorated the day on which fifty thousand persons had lost their lives in the inundation. This calamity, the report of which was magnified from one province to another, *astonished and terrified the subjects of Rome;* and their affrighted imagination enlarged the real extent of the momentary evil. They recollected the preceding earthquakes which had subverted the cities of Palestine and Bithynia; they considered these alarming strokes as the prelude only of still more dreadful calamities, and their fearful vanity was disposed to confound *the symptoms of a declining empire and a sinking world*," vol. ii. pp. 115, 116. Mr. Gibbon then proceeds to detail the evils of war, as greatly surpassing the calamities produced by any natural causes, and adds (p. 116), "In the disastrous period of the fall of the Roman empire, which may be justly dated from the reign of Valens, the happiness and security of each individual was personally attacked; and the arts and labours of ages were rudely defaced by the barbarians of Scythia and Germany." He then proceeds with an exceedingly interesting description of the origin, the habits, and the movements of the Tartar nations, particularly the Huns, as they moved to the West, and precipitated the Gothic nations on the provinces of the Roman empire, until Rome itself was thrice besieged, was taken, and was sacked (ii. 116–266). The earthquake referred to occurred in A.D. 365. The movements of the Huns from their territories in the neighbourhood of China had commenced about A.D. 100, and in A.D. 375 they overcame the Goths lying along the Danube. The Goths, pressed and overcome by these savage invaders, asked permission of the Romans to cross the Danube, to find protection in the Roman empire, and to cultivate the waste lands of Thrace (Gibbon, ii. 129, 130). In the year 376 they were transported over the Danube, by the permission of the Roman emperor Valens; an event which, according to Mr. Gibbon, in its ultimate result, was the cause of the downfall of the empire; for they learned their own strength; they were attracted by the riches of the capital and the hope of reward, until they finally drew the Western emperor to Ravenna, sacked Rome, and took possession of Italy.

(4) A slight reference to the *series* of events in these periods of consternation and conquest may show more closely the nature of the alarms which would be caused by the prospect of these dreadful invasions, and may prepare us for a better understanding of the successive calamities which occurred under these invaders, when the empire fell, as described by the four first trumpets of the seventh seal. I shall copy from the tables of contents of Mr. Gibbon's history, under the twenty-sixth, thirtieth, and thirty-first chapters:—

"A.D.
365. Earthquakes.
376. The Huns and Goths.
100. The emigration of the Huns.
375. Their victories over the Goths.
376. The Goths implore the protection of Valens.
,, They are transported over the Danube into the Roman empire.
,, They penetrate into Thrace.
377. Union of the Goths with Huns, Alani, &c.
378. Battle of Hadrianople.
,, The defeat of the Romans.
383–395. The settlement of the Goths in Thrace and Asia.
395. Revolt of the Goths.
396. Alaric marches into Greece.
398. Is proclaimed king of the Visigoths.
400–403. He invades Italy.
406. Radagaisus invades Italy.
,, Besieges Florence.
,, Threatens Rome.
,, The remainder of the Germans invade Gaul.
407. Desolation of Gaul.
408. Alaric marches to Rome.
,, First siege of Rome by the Goths.

168    REVELATION.    [A.D. 96.

"A.D.
408. Famine, plague, superstition.
409. Alaric accepts a ransom and raises the siege.
„  Fruitless negotiations for peace.
„  Second siege of Rome by the Goths.
410. Third siege and sack of Rome by the Goths.
„  Respect of the Goths for the Christian religion.
„  Pillage and fire of Rome.
„  Captives and fugitives.
411-416. Fall of the usurpers Jovinus, Sebastian, and Attalus.
409. Invasion of Spain by the Suevi, Vandals, Alani, &c.
415-418. The Goths conquer and restore Spain."

(5) This would coincide, in the *effects* produced on the empire, with the consternation and alarm described in the passage before us. The symbols are such as *would be* employed on the supposition that these are the events referred to; they are such as the events are fitted to suggest. The mighty preparations in the East and North—the report of which could not but spread through the empire—would be appropriately symbolized by the earthquake, the darkened sun, the moon becoming like blood, the stars falling, the departing heavens, and the kings and great men of the earth fleeing in alarm to find a place of safety, as if the end of the world were drawing near. Nothing could have been so well adapted to produce the consternation described in the opening of the sixth seal, as the dreaded approach of vast hosts of barbarians from the regions of the North. This alarm would be increased by the fact that their numbers were unknown; that their origin was hidden; and that the advancing multitudes would sweep everything before them. As in other cases, also, rumour would increase their numbers and augment their ferocity. The sudden shock of an earthquake, the falling stars, the departing heavens, the removal of mountains and islands, and the consternation of kings and all classes of people, would be the appropriate emblems to represent these impending calamities. In confirmation of this, and as showing the *effect* produced by the approach of the Goths, and the dread of the Gothic arms, in causing universal consternation, the following extracts may be adduced from Mr. Gibbon, when describing the threatened invasion of Alaric, king of the Visigoths. He quotes from Claudian. "'Fame,' says the poet, 'encircling with terror her gloomy wings, proclaimed the march of the barbarian army, and filled Italy with consternation.'" Mr. Gibbon adds, "the apprehensions of each individual were increased in just proportion to the measure of his fortune; and the most timid, who had already embarked their valuable effects, meditated their escape to the island of Sicily, or to the African coast. The public distress was aggravated by the fears and reproaches of superstition. Every hour produced some horrid tale of strange and portentous accidents; the Pagans deplored the neglect of omens and the interruption of sacrifices; but the Christians still derived some comfort from the powerful intercession of the saints and martyrs," ii. 218, 219. See further illustrations in the Notes on ch. viii. 7-13.

## CHAPTER VII.

### ANALYSIS OF THE CHAPTER.

The state of things represented in this chapter is, that where there had been awful consternation and alarm, as if the end of the world were coming, and where the signs of the approaching consummation of all things are, as it were, held back until there should be an opportunity of sealing the number that was to be saved. This is symbolized by four angels standing in the four quarters of the earth, and holding the winds and the storms that they should not blow on the earth until the servants of God should be sealed in their foreheads. The idea is that of sudden destruction about to burst on the world, which, if unrestrained, would apparently bring on the consummation of all things, but which is held back until the purposes of God in regard to his people shall be accomplished—that is, until those who are the true servants of God shall be designated by some appropriate mark. This furnishes an opportunity of disclosing a glorious vision of those who will be saved, alike among the Jews and the Gentiles. The *fact*, as seen in the symbol, is, that the end of the world does *not* come at the opening of the sixth seal, as it seemed as if it would, and as it was anticipated in the time of the consternation. The number of the chosen was not complete, and the impending wrath was therefore suspended. God interposes in favour of his people, and discloses in vision a vast number from all lands who will yet be saved, and the winds and storms are held back as if by angels.

The *points*, then, that are apparent in this chapter, without any reference now to the question of the application, are the following: (1) The impending ruin that seemed about to spread over the earth, apparently bringing on the consummation of all things, restrained or suspended, ver. 1. This impending ruin is symbolized by the four winds of heaven that seemed about to sweep over the world; the interposition of God is represented by the four angels who have power over those winds to hold them back, as if it depended on their will to let them loose and to spread ruin over the earth or not. (2) A suspension of these desolating influences and agents until another important purpose could be accomplished—that is, until the servants of God could be sealed in their foreheads, ver. 2, 3. Another angel, acting independently of the four first seen, and having power to command, appears in the east, having the seal of the living God; and he directs the four angels having the four winds not to let them loose upon the earth until the servants of God should be sealed in their foreheads. This obviously denotes some suspension of the impending wrath, and for a specific purpose, that something might be done by which the true servants of God would be so marked as to be publicly known—*as if* they had a mark or brand to that effect imprinted on their foreheads. Whatever would serve to designate them, to determine who they were, to ascertain their number, would be a fulfilment of this act of the sealing angel. The length of *time* during which it would be done is not designated; the essential thing is, that there would be a suspension of impending judgments, *in order* that it might be done. Whether this was to occupy a longer or a shorter period is not determined by the symbol; nor is it determined *when* the winds thus held back would be suffered to blow. (3) The number of the sealed, ver. 4-8. The seer does not represent himself as actually beholding the process of sealing, but he says that he heard the number of those who were sealed. That number was an hundred and forty-four thousand, and they were selected from the twelve tribes of the children of Israel—Levi being reckoned, who was not usually numbered with the tribes, and the tribe of Dan being omitted. The number from each tribe, large or small, was the same; the entire portion selected being but a very small part of the whole. The general idea here, whatever may be the particular application, is, that there would be a *selection*, and that the whole number of the tribe would not be embraced; that the selection would be made from *each* tribe, and that all would have the same mark, and be saved by the same means. It would not be in accordance with the nature of symbolic representation to suppose that the saved would be the precise number here referred to; but *some* great truth is designed to be represented by this fact. We should look, in the fulfilment, to some process by which the true servants of God would be designated; we should expect that a portion of them would be found in each one of the classes here denoted by a tribe; we should suppose that the true servants of God thus referred to would be *as safe* in the times of peril as if they were designated by a visible mark. (4) After this, another vision presents itself to the seer. It is that of a countless multitude before the throne, redeemed out of all nations, with palms in their hands, ver. 9-17. The scene is transferred to heaven, and there is a vision of *all* the redeemed—not only of the hundred and forty-four thousand, but of all who would be rescued and saved from a lost world. The *design* is doubtless to cheer the hearts of the true friends of God in times of gloom and despondency, by a view of the great numbers that will be saved, and the glorious triumph that awaits the redeemed in heaven. This portion of the vision embraces the following particulars:—(*a*) A vast multitude, which no man can number, is seen before the throne in heaven. They are clad in white robes—emblems of purity; they have palms in their hands—emblems of victory, ver. 9. (*b*) They are engaged in ascribing praise to God, ver. 10. (*c*) The angels, the elders, and the four living creatures, fall down before the throne, and unite with the redeemed in ascriptions of praise, ver. 11, 12. (*d*) A particular inquiry is made of the seer—evidently to call his attention to it—respecting those who appear there in white robes, ver. 13. (*e*) To this inquiry it is answered, that they were those who had come up out of great tribulation, and who had washed their robes, and had made them pure in the blood of the Lamb, ver. 14. (*f*) Then follows a description of their condition and employment in heaven, ver. 15-17. They are

## CHAPTER VII.

AND after these things I saw four angels standing on the four corners of the earth, holding the *a*four winds of the earth, that the wind should not blow on the earth, nor on the sea, nor on any tree.

*a* Da.7.2.

constantly before the throne; they serve God continually; they neither hunger nor thirst; they are not subjected to the burning heat of the sun; they are provided for by the Lamb in the midst of the throne; and all tears are for ever wiped away from their eyes. This must be regarded, I think, as an episode, having no *immediate* connection with what precedes or with what follows. It seems to be thrown in here—while the impending judgments of the sixth seal are suspended, and before the seventh is opened—to furnish a *relief* in the contemplation of so many scenes of woe, and to cheer the soul with inspiring hopes from the view of the great number that would ultimately be saved. While these judgments, therefore, are suspended, the mind is directed on to the world of triumph, as a view fitted to sustain and comfort those who would be partakers in the scenes of woe. At the same time it is one of the most touching and beautiful of all the representations of heaven ever penned, and is eminently adapted to comfort those, in all ages, who are in a vale of tears.

In the exposition it will be proper (ver. 1-8) to inquire into the fair meaning of the *language* employed in the symbols; and then to inquire whether there are any known facts to which the description is applicable. The first inquiry may and should be pursued independently of the other; and it may be added, that the explanation offered on this may be correct, even if the other should be erroneous. The same remark, also, is applicable to the remainder of the chapter (ver. 9-17), and indeed is of general applicability in the exposition of this book.

1. *And after these things.* After the vision of the things referred to in the opening of the sixth seal. The natural interpretation would be, that what is here said of the angels and the winds occurred *after* those things which are described in the previous chapter. The exact chronology may not be always observed in these symbolical representations, but doubtless there is a general order which is observed. ¶ *I saw four angels.* He does not describe their forms, but merely mentions their agency. This is, of course, a symbolical representation. We are not to suppose that it would be *literally* fulfilled, or that, at the time referred to by the vision, four celestial beings would be stationed in the four quarters of the world for the purpose of checking and restraining the winds that blow from the four points of the compass. The meaning is, that events would occur which would be properly *represented* by four angels standing in the four quarters of the world, and having power over the winds. ¶ *Standing on the four corners of the earth.* This language is, of course, accommodated to the prevailing mode of speaking of the earth among the Hebrews. It was a common method among them to describe it as a vast plain, having four corners, those corners being the prominent points—north, south, east, and west. So we speak now of the four winds, the four quarters of the world, &c. The Hebrews spoke of the earth, as we do of the rising and setting of the sun and of the motions of the heavenly bodies, according to appearances, and without aiming at philosophical exactness. Comp. Notes on Job xxvi. 7. With this view they spoke of the earth as an extended plain, and as having boundaries or corners, as a plain or field naturally has. Perhaps, also, they used this language with some allusion to an edifice, as having four corners; for they speak also of the earth as having *foundations*. The language which the Hebrews used was in accordance with the prevailing ideas and language of the ancients on the subject. ¶ *Holding the four winds of the earth.* The winds blow in fact from every quarter, but it is convenient to speak of them as coming from the four principal points of the compass, and this method is adopted probably in every language. So among the Greeks and Latins, the winds were arranged under four classes —Zephyrus, Boreas, Notus, and Eurus —considered as under the control of a king, Æolus. See Eschenburg, *Man. Class. Lit.* § 78, comp. § 108. The angels here are represented as "*holding*" the winds—κρατοῦντας. That is, they held them back when about to sweep over

## CHAPTER VII.

2 And I saw another angel ascending from the east, having the *b*seal of the living God; and he cried with a loud voice to the four angels, to whom it was given to hurt the earth and the sea,

*b* 2 Ti. 2. 19.

the earth, and to produce far-spread desolation. This is an allusion to a popular belief among the Hebrews, that the agency of the angels was employed everywhere. It is not suggested that the angels had *raised* the tempest here, but only that they now restrained and controlled it. The essential idea is, that they had *power* over those winds, and that they were now exercising that power by keeping them back when they were about to spread desolation over the earth. ¶ *That the wind should not blow on the earth.* That there should be a calm, *as if* the winds were held back. ¶ *Nor on the sea.* Nowhere—neither on sea nor land. The sea and the land constitute the surface of the globe, and the language here, therefore, denotes that there would be a universal calm. ¶ *Nor on any tree.* To injure it. The *language* here used is such as would denote a state of profound quiet; as when we say that it is so still that not a leaf of the trees moves.

In regard to the literal meaning of the symbol here employed there can be no great difficulty; as to its application there may be more. The winds are the proper symbols of wars and commotions. Comp. Da. vii. 2. In Je. xlix. 36, 37 the symbol is both used and explained: "And upon Elam will I bring the four winds from the four quarters of heaven, and will scatter them toward all those winds; and there shall be no nation whither the outcasts of Elam shall not come. For I will cause Elam to be dismayed before their enemies, and before them that seek their life." So in Je. li. 1, 2, a destroying wind is an emblem of destructive war: "I will raise up against Babylon a destroying wind, and will send unto Babylon fanners, that shall fan her, and shall empty her land." Comp. Horace, *Odes*, b. i. 14. The essential ideas, therefore, in this portion of the symbol, cannot be mistaken. They are two: (1) that at the period of time here referred to—after the opening of the sixth seal and before the opening of the seventh—there would be a state of things which would be well represented by rising tempests and storms, which if unrestrained would spread desolation afar; and (2) that this impending ruin was held back as if by angels having control of those winds; that is, those tempests were not suffered to go forth to spread desolation over the world. A suspended tempest; calamity held in check; armies hovering on the borders of a kingdom, but not allowed to proceed for a time; hordes of invaders detained, or stayed in their march, as if by some restraining power not their own, and from causes not within themselves—any of these things would be an obvious fulfilling of the meaning of the symbol.

2. *And I saw another angel.* Evidently having no connection with the four, and employed for another purpose. This angel, also, must have been symbolic; and all that is implied is, that something would be done *as if* an angel had done it. ¶ *Ascending from the east.* He appeared in the east, and seemed to rise like the sun. It is not easy to determine what is the special significancy, if any, of the *east* here, or why this quarter of the heavens is designated rather than the north, the south, or the west. It may be that as light begins in the east, this would be properly symbolic of something that could be compared with the light of the morning; or that some influence in "sealing" the servants of God would in fact go out from the east; or perhaps no special significance is to be attached to the quarter from which the angel is seen to come. It is not necessary to suppose that every minute thing in a symbol is to receive a complete fulfilment, or that there will be some particular thing to correspond with it. Perhaps all that is meant here is, that as the sun comes forth with splendour from the east, so the angel came with magnificence to perform a task—that of sealing the servants of God—cheerful and joyous like that which the sun performs. It is certain that from no other quarter of the heavens would it be so appropriate to represent an angel as coming forth to perform a purpose of light, and mercy, and salvation. It does not seem to me, therefore, that we are to look, in the fulfilment of this, for any special influence setting in *from the east* as that which is symbolized here. ¶ *Having the seal of the living God.* Bearing it in his hands. In regard to this seal the following remarks may be made:—(*a*)

3 Saying, *c*Hurt not the earth, neither the sea, nor the trees, till we have *d*sealed the servants of our God *e*in their foreheads.

*c* ch. 6. 6.     *d* Eze. 9. 4.     *e* ch. 22. 4.

The phrase "*seal of the living God*" doubtless means that which God had appointed, or which he would use; that is, if God himself came forth in this manner, he would use this seal for these purposes. Men often have a seal of their own, with some name, symbol, or device, which designates it as theirs, and which no other one has a right to use. A seal is sometimes used by the person himself; sometimes intrusted to a high officer of state; sometimes to the secretary of a corporation; and sometimes, as a mark of special favour, to a friend. In this case it was intrusted to an angel, who was authorized to use it, and whose use of it would be sanctioned, of course, wherever he applied it, by the living God, as if he had employed it himself. (*b*) As to the *form* of the seal, we have no information. It would be most natural to suppose that the *name* " of the living God" would be engraven on it, so that that name would appear on anyone to whom it might be affixed. Comp. Notes on 2 Ti. ii. 19. It was customary in the East to brand the name of the master on the forehead of a slave (Grotius, *in loco*); and such an idea would meet all that is implied in the *language* here, though there is no certain evidence that there is an allusion to that custom. In subsequent times, in the church, it was common for Christians to impress the sign of the cross on their foreheads (Tertullian *de Corona;* Cyrill. lib. vi. See Grotius). As nothing is said here, however, about any mark or device on the seal, conjecture is useless as to what it was. (*c*) As to what was to be designated by the seal, the main idea is clear, that it was to place some such mark upon his friends that they would be known to be his, and that they would be safe in the impending calamities. There is perhaps allusion here to Eze. ix. 4–6, where the following direction to the prophet occurs:—" Go through the midst of the city, through the midst of Jerusalem, and set a mark upon the foreheads of the men that sigh, and that cry, for all the abominations that be done in the midst thereof. And to the others he said in mine hearing, Go ye after him through the city, and smite; let not your eye spare, neither have ye pity: slay utterly old and young, both maids and little children, and women; but come not near any man upon whom is the mark." The essential ideas in the *sealing*, in the passage before us, would therefore seem to be, (1) that there would be some mark, sign, or token, by which they who were the people of God would be known; that is, there would be *something* which would answer, in this respect, the same purpose *as if* a seal had been impressed upon their foreheads. Whether this was an outward badge, or a religious rite, or the doctrines which they would hold and by which they would be known, or something in their spirit and manner which would characterize his true disciples, may be a fair subject of inquiry. It is not specifically designated by the use of the word. (2) It would be something that would be conspicuous or prominent, *as if* it were impressed on the forehead. It would not be merely some *internal* sealing, or some designation by which they would be known to themselves and to God, but it would be something *apparent*, as if engraved on the forehead. What this would be, whether a profession, or a form of religion, or the holding of some doctrine, or the manifestation of a particular spirit, is not here designated. (3) This would be something appointed by God himself. It would not be of human origin, but would be *as if* an angel sent from heaven should impress it on the forehead. If it refers to the doctrines which they would hold, they could not be doctrines of human origin; if to the spirit which they would manifest, it would be a spirit of heavenly origin; if to some outward protection, it would be manifest that it was from God. (4) This would be a pledge of safety. The design of sealing the persons referred to seems to have been to secure their safety in the impending calamities. Thus the winds were held back until those who were to be sealed could be designated, and then they were to be allowed to sweep over the earth. These things, therefore, we are to look for in the fulfilment of the symbol. ¶ *And he cried with a loud voice.* As if he had authority to command, and as if the four winds were about to be let forth upon the world. ¶ *To whom it was given to hurt the earth and the sea.* Who had power committed

# CHAPTER VII.

4 And I heard the number of them which were sealed: *and there*

---

to them to do this by means of the four winds.

3. *Saying, Hurt not the earth, neither the sea,* &c. Let the winds be restrained until what is here designated shall be done. These destroying angels were commanded to suspend the work of destruction until the servants of God could be rendered secure. The division here, as in ver. 1, of the "earth, the sea, and the trees," seems to include everything —water, land, and the productions of the earth. Nothing was to be injured until the angel should designate the true servants of God. ¶ *Till we have sealed the servants of our God.* The use of the plural "*we*" seems to denote that he did not expect to do it alone. Who were to be associated with him, whether angels or men, he does not intimate; but the work was evidently such that it demanded the agency of more than one. ¶ *In their foreheads.* See Notes on ver. 2; comp. Eze. ix. 4, 5. A mark thus placed on the forehead would be conspicuous, and would be something which could at once be recognized if destruction should spread over the world. The fulfilment of this is to be found in two things: (*a*) in something which would be conspicuous or prominent — so that it could be seen; and (*b*) in the mark being of such a nature or character that it would be a proper designation of the fact that they were the true servants of God.

4. *And I heard the number of them which were sealed.* He does not say *where* he heard that, or *by whom* it was communicated to him, or *when* it was done. The material point is, that he *heard* it; he did not *see* it done. Either by the angel, or by some direct communication from God, he was *told* of the number that would be sealed, and of the distribution of the whole number into twelve equal parts, represented by the tribes of the children of Israel. ¶ *And there were sealed an hundred and forty and four thousand of all the tribes of the children of Israel.* In regard to this number, the first and the main question is, whether it is meant that this was to be the *literal* number, or whether it was *symbolical;* and, if the latter, of what it is a symbol. I. As to the first of these inquiries, there does not appear to be any good reason for doubt. The fair

*were sealed* *f* an hundred *and* forty *and* four thousand of all the tribes of the children of Israel.
*f* ch.14.1.

---

interpretation seems to require that it should be understood as symbolical, or as designed not to be literally taken; for (*a*) the whole scene is symbolical— the winds, the angels, the sealing. (*b*) It cannot be supposed that this number will include *all* who will be sealed and saved. In whatever way this is interpreted, and whatever we may suppose it to refer to, we cannot but suppose that more than this number will be saved. (*c*) The number is too exact and artificial to suppose that it is literal. It is inconceivable that exactly the same number — precisely twelve thousand — should be selected from each tribe of the children of Israel. (*d*) If literal, it is necessary to suppose that this refers to the twelve tribes of the children of Israel. But on every supposition this is absurd. Ten of their tribes had been long before carried away, and the distinction of the tribes was lost, no more to be recovered, and the Hebrew people never have been, since the time of John, in circumstances to which the description here could be applicable. These considerations make it clear that the description here is symbolical. But, II. Of *what* is it symbolical? Is it of a large number, or of a small number? Is it of those who would be saved from among the Jews, or of all who would be saved in the Christian church —represented as the "tribes of the children of Israel?" To these inquiries we may answer, (1) that the representation seems to be rather that of a comparatively *small* number than a *large* one, for these reasons: (*a*) The number *of itself* is not large. (*b*) The number is not large as *compared* with those who must have constituted the tribes here referred to—the number twelve thousand, for example, as compared with the whole number of the tribe of Judah, of the tribe of Reuben, &c. (*c*) It would seem from the language that there would be some *selection* from a much greater number. Thus, not *all* in the tribes were sealed, but those who were sealed were "of all the tribes" —ἐκ πάσης φυλῆς; that is, *out of* these tribes. So in the specification in each tribe—ἐκ φυλῆς Ἰούδα, Ῥουβὴν, &c. Some *out of* the tribe, to wit, twelve thousand, were sealed. It is not said of the twelve thousand of the tribes of Judah, Reuben, &c., that they *constituted* the tribe, but that they were sealed *out of* the tribe, as a part of it preserved and saved. "When the preposition ἐκ, or *out of*, stands after any such verb as *sealed*, between a definite numeral and a noun of multitude in the genitive, sound criticism requires, doubtless, that the numeral should be thus construed as signifying, not the whole, but a part taken out" (Elliott, i. 237). Comp. Ex. xxxii. 28; Nu. i. 21; 1 Sa. iv. 10. The phrase, then, would properly denote those taken *out of* some other and greater number—as a portion of a tribe, and not the whole tribe. If the reference here is to the church, it would seem to denote that a portion only of that church would be sealed. (*d*) For the same reason the idea would seem to be, that comparatively a *small* portion is referred to—as twelve thousand would be comparatively a small part of one of the tribes of Israel; and if this refers to the church, we should expect to find its fulfilment in a state of things in which the largest proportion would *not* be sealed; that is, in a corrupt state of the church in which there would be many professors of religion, but comparatively few who had real piety. (2) To the other inquiry — whether this refers to those who would be sealed and saved among the Jews, or to those in the Christian church—we may answer, (*a*) that there are strong reasons for supposing the latter to be the correct opinion. Long before the time of John all these distinctions of tribe were abolished. The ten tribes had been carried away and scattered in distant lands, never more to be restored; and it cannot be supposed that there was any such *literal* selection from the twelve tribes as is here spoken of, or any such designation of twelve thousand from each. There was no occasion—either when Jerusalem was destroyed, or at any other time—on which there were such transactions as are here referred to occurring in reference to the children of Israel. (*b*) The language is such as a Christian, who had been by birth and education a Hebrew, would naturally use if he wished to designate the church. Comp. Notes on Ja. i. 1. Accustomed to speak of the people of God as "the twelve tribes of Israel," nothing was more natural than to transfer this language to the church of the Redeemer, and to speak of it in that figurative manner. Accordingly, from the necessity of the case, the language is universally understood to have reference to the Christian church. Even Professor Stuart, who supposes that the reference is to the siege and destruction of Jerusalem by the Romans, interprets it of the preservation of Christians, and their flight to Pella, beyond Jordan. Thus interpreted, moreover, it accords with the entire symbolical character of the representation. (*c*) The reference to the particular *tribes* may be a designed allusion to the Christian church as it would be divided into denominations, or known by different names; and the fact that a certain portion would be sealed from every tribe would not be an unfit representation of the fact that a portion of all the various churches or denominations would be sealed and saved. That is, salvation would be confined to no one church or denomination, but among them all there would be found true servants of God. It would be improper to suppose that the division into tribes among the children of Israel was designed to be a *type* of the sects and denominations in the Christian church, and yet the fact of such a division may not improperly be employed as an *illustration* of that; for the whole church is made up not of any one denomination alone, but of all who hold the truth combined, as the people of God in ancient times consisted not solely of any one tribe, however large and powerful, but of all combined. Thus understood, the symbol would point to a time when there would be various denominations in the church, and yet with the idea that true friends of God would be found among them all. (*d*) Perhaps nothing can be argued from the fact that exactly twelve thousand were selected from each of the tribes. In language so figurative and symbolical as this, it could not be maintained that this proves that the same definite number would be taken from each denomination of Christians. Perhaps all that *can be* fairly inferred is, that there would be no partiality or preference for one more than another; that there would be no favouritism on account of the tribe or denomination to which any one belonged; but that the seal would be impressed on all, of any denomination, who had the true spirit of religion. No one would receive the token of the divine favour *because* he was of the tribe

5 Of the tribe of Juda *were* sealed twelve thousand. Of the tribe of Reuben *were* sealed twelve thousand. Of the tribe of Gad *were* sealed twelve thousand.

6 Of the tribe of Aser *were* sealed twelve thousand. Of the tribe of Nepthalim *were* sealed twelve thousand. Of the tribe of Manasses *were* sealed twelve thousand.

7 Of the tribe of Simeon *were* sealed twelve thousand. Of the tribe of Levi *were* sealed twelve thousand. Of the tribe of Issachar *were* sealed twelve thousand.

8 Of the tribe of Zabulon *were* sealed twelve thousand. Of the tribe of Joseph *were* sealed twelve thousand. Of the tribe of Benjamin *were* sealed twelve thousand.

---

of Judah or Reuben; no one *because* he belonged to any particular denomination of Christians. Large numbers from every branch of the church would be sealed; none would be sealed because he belonged to one form of external organization rather than to another; none would be excluded because he belonged to any one tribe, if he had the spirit and held the sentiments which made it proper to recognize him as a servant of God. These views seem to me to express the true sense of this passage. No one can seriously maintain that the writer meant to refer literally to the Jewish people; and if he referred to the Christian church, it seems to be to some selection that would be made out of the whole church, in which there would be no favouritism or partiality, and to the fact that, in regard to them, there would be some something which, in the midst of abounding corruption or impending danger, would designate them as the chosen people of God, and would furnish evidence that they would be safe.

5–8. *Of the tribe of Juda* were *sealed twelve thousand*. That is, a selection was made, or a number sealed, *as if* it had been made from one of the tribes of the children of Israel—the tribe of Judah. If the remarks above made are correct, this refers to the Christian church, and means, in connection with what follows, that each portion of the church would furnish a definite part of the whole number sealed and saved. We are not required to understand this of the exact number of twelve thousand, but that the designation would be made from all parts and branches of the church *as if* a selection of the true servants of God were made from the whole number of the tribes of Israel.—There seems to be no particular reason why the tribe of Judah was mentioned first. Judah was not the oldest of the sons of Jacob, and there was no settled order in which the tribes were usually mentioned. The order of their birth, as mentioned in Ge. xxix. xxx., is as follows: Reuben, Simeon, Levi, Judah, Dan, Naphtali, Gad, Asher, Issachar, Zebulun, Joseph, Benjamin. In the blessing of Jacob, Ge. xlix., this order is changed, and is as follows:—Reuben, Simeon, Levi, Judah, Zebulun, Issachar, Dan, Gad, Asher, Naphtali, Joseph, Benjamin. In the blessing of Moses, De. xxxiii., a different order still is observed: Reuben, Judah, Levi, Benjamin, Joseph, Zebulun, Issachar, Gad, Dan, Naphtali, Asher; and in this last, moreover, Simeon is omitted. So, again, in Eze. xlviii., there are two enumerations of the twelve tribes, differing from each other, and both differing from the arrangements above referred to: viz., in ver. 31–34, where Levi is reckoned as one, and Joseph as only one; and in ver. 1–27, referring to the division of the country, where Levi, who had no heritage in land, is omitted, and Ephraim and Manasseh are counted as two tribes (Professor Stuart, ii. 172, 173). From facts like these it is clear that there was no certain and settled order in which the tribes were mentioned by the sacred writers. The same thing seems to have occurred in the enumeration of the tribes, which would occur, for example, in the enumeration of the several States of the American Union. There is indeed an order which is usually observed, beginning with Maine, &c., but almost no two writers would observe throughout the same order; nor should we deem it strange if the order should be materially varied by even the same writer in enumerating them at different times. Thus, at one time it might be convenient to enumerate them according to their geographical position; at another, in the order of their settlement; at another, in the order of their admission into the Union; at another, in the order of their size and importance; at another, in the order in which they are arranged in reference to political parties, &c. Something of the same kind may have occurred in the order in which the tribes were mentioned among the Jews. *Perhaps* this may have occurred also of design, in order that no one tribe might claim the precedence or the pre-eminence by being always placed at the head of the list. If, as is supposed above, the allusion in this enumeration of the tribes was to the various portions of the Christian church, then perhaps the idea intended to be conveyed is, that no one division of that church is to have any preference on account of its locality, or its occupying any particular country, or because it has more wealth, learning, or numbers than others; but that all are to be regarded, where there is the true spirit of religion, as on a level.

There are, however, three peculiarities in this enumeration of the tribes which demand a more particular explanation. The number indeed is twelve, but that number is made up in a peculiar manner. (1) *Joseph* is mentioned, and also *Manasseh*. The matter of fact was, that Joseph had two sons, Ephraim and Manasseh (Ge. xlviii. 1), and that these two sons gave name to two of the tribes, the tribes of Ephraim and Manasseh. There was, properly speaking, no tribe of the name of *Joseph*. In Nu. xiii. the name Levi is omitted, as it usually is, because that tribe had no inheritance in the division of the land; and in order that the number twelve might be complete, Ephraim *and* Joseph are mentioned as two tribes, ver. 8, 11. In ver. 11 the writer states expressly that by the tribe Joseph he meant Manasseh— "Of the tribe of Joseph, *namely*, of the tribe of Manasseh," &c. From this it would seem that, as Manasseh was the oldest (Ge. xlviii. 14), the name *Joseph* was sometimes given to that tribe. As Ephraim, however, became the largest tribe, and as Jacob in blessing the two sons of Joseph (Ge. xlviii. 14) laid his right hand on Ephraim, and pronounced a special blessing on him (ver. 19, 20), it would seem not improbable that, when not particularly designated, the name *Joseph* was given to that tribe, as it is evidently in this place. Possibly the name *Joseph* may have been a general name which was occasionally applied to *either* of these tribes. In the long account of the original division of Canaan in Jos. xiii.–xix., Levi is omitted, because he had no heritage, and Ephraim and Manasseh are mentioned as two tribes. The name Joseph in the passage before us (ver. 8) is doubtless designed, as remarked above, to refer to Ephraim. (2) In this list (ver. 7) the name of *Levi* is inserted among the tribes. As already remarked, this name is not commonly inserted among the tribes of the children of Israel, because that tribe, being devoted to the sacerdotal office, had no inheritance in the division of the country, but was scattered among the other tribes. See Jos. xiv. 3, 4; xviii. 7. It may have been inserted here, if this refers to the Christian church, to denote that the ministers of the gospel, as well as other members of the church, would share in the protection implied by the sealing; that is, to denote that no class in the church would be excluded from the blessings of salvation. (3) The name of one of the tribes—*Dan*—is omitted; so that by this omission, and the insertion of the tribe of Levi, the original number of twelve is preserved. There have been numerous conjectures as to the reason why the tribe of *Dan* is omitted here, but none of the solutions proposed are without difficulty. All that can be known, or regarded as probable, on the subject, seems to be this:—(*a*) As the tribe of Levi was usually omitted in an enumeration of the tribes, because that tribe had no part in the inheritance of the Hebrew people in the division of the land of Canaan, so there appear to have been instances in which the names of some of the other tribes were omitted, the reason for which is not given. Thus, in De. xxxiii., in the blessing pronounced by Moses on the tribes just before his death, the name Simeon is omitted. In 1 Ch. iv.–viii. the names of Zebulun and Dan. are both omitted. It would seem, therefore, that the name of a tribe might be sometimes omitted without any particular reason being specified. (*b*) It has been supposed by some that the name *Dan* was omitted because that tribe was early devoted to idolatry, and continued idolatrous to the time of the captivity. Of that *fact* there can be no doubt, for it is expressly affirmed in Ju. xviii. 30; and that fact seems to be a sufficient reason for the omission of the name. As being thus idolatrous, it was in a measure separated from the people of God, and deserved not to be reckoned among them; and in enumerating those who were the servants of God, there seemed to be a propriety that a tribe devoted to idolatry should not be reckoned among the number. This will account for the omission, without resorting to the supposition of Grotius, that the tribe of Dan was extinct at the time when the Apocalypse was written—a fact which also existed in regard to all the ten tribes; or to the supposition of Andreas and others, that Dan is omitted because Antichrist was to spring from that tribe — a supposition which is alike without proof and without probability. The fact that Dan was omitted cannot be supposed to have any special significancy in the case before us. Such an omission is what, as we have seen, might have occurred at any time in the enumeration of the tribes.

In reference to the application of this portion of the book (ver. 1-8), or of what is designed to be here represented, there has been, as might be expected, a great variety of opinions. From the exposition of the words and phrases which has been given, it is manifest that we are to look for a series of events like the following:—(1) Some impending danger, or something that threatened to sweep everything away —like winds that were ready to blow on the earth. (2) That tempest restrained or held back, as if the winds were held in check by an angel, and were not suffered to sweep over the world. (3) Some new influence or power, represented by an angel coming from the east — the great source of light—that should designate the true church of God—the servants of the Most High. (4) Some mark or note by which the true people of God could be designated, or by which they could be known—*as if* some name were impressed on their foreheads. (5) A selection or election of the number from a much greater number who were the professed, but were not the true servants of God. (6) A definite, though comparatively a small number thus designated out of the whole mass. (7) This number taken from all the divisions of the professed people of God, in such numbers and in such a manner, that it would be apparent that there would be no partiality or favouritism; that is, that wherever the true servants of God were found, they would be sealed and saved. These are things which lie on the face of the passage, if the interpretation above given is correct, and in its application it is necessary to find some facts that will properly correspond with these things.

If the interpretation of the sixth seal proposed above is correct, then we are to look for the fulfilment of this in events that soon succeeded those which are there referred to, or at least which had their commencement at about that time; and the inquiry now is, whether there *were* any events that would accord properly with the interpretation here proposed: that is, any impending and spreading danger; any restraining of that danger; any process of designating the servants of God so as to preserve them; anything like a designation or selection of them from among the masses of the professed people of God? Now, in respect to this, the following facts accord so well with what is demanded in the interpretation that it may be regarded as morally certain that they were the things which were thus made to pass in vision before the mind of John. They have at least this degree of probability, that if it were admitted that he intended to describe them, the symbols which are actually employed are those which it would have been proper to select to represent them.

1. The impending danger, like winds restrained, that threatened to sweep everything away, and to hasten on the end of the world. In reference to this, there may have been two classes of impending danger—that from the invasion of the northern hordes, referred to in the sixth seal (ch. vi.), and that from the influx of error, that threatened the ruin of the church. (*a*) As to the former, the language used by John will accurately express the state of things as it existed at the period supposed at the time of the sixth seal—the series of events introduced, now suspended, like the opening of the seventh seal. The idea is that of nations pressing on to conquest; heaving like tempests on the borders of the empire; overturning everything in their way; spreading desolation by fire and sword, *as if* the world were about to come to an end. The language used by Mr. Gibbon in describing the times here referred to is so applicable, that it would seem almost as if he had the symbols used by John in his eye. Speaking of the time of Constantine, he says, "The *threatening*

*tempest* of barbarians, which so soon subverted the foundations of Roman greatness, was still repelled, *or suspended on the frontiers*" (i. 362). This language accurately expresses the condition of the Roman world at the period succeeding the opening of the sixth seal; the period of suspended judgments, in order that the servants of God might be sealed. See the Notes on ch. vi. 12-17. The nations which ultimately spread desolation through the empire hovered around its borders, making occasional incursions into its territory; even carrying their arms, as we have seen in some instances, as far as Rome itself, but still restrained from accomplishing the final purpose of overthrowing the city and the empire. The church and the state alike were threatened with destruction, and the impending wrath seemed only to be held back *as if* to give time to accomplish some other purpose. (*b*) At the same time there was another class of evils which threatened to sweep like a tempest over the church—the evils of error in doctrine that sprang up on the establishment of Christianity by Constantine. That fact was followed with a great increase of professors of religion, who, for various purposes, crowded into a church patronized by the state—a condition of things which tended to do more to destroy the church than all that had been done by persecution had accomplished. This effect was natural; and the church became filled with those who had yielded themselves to the Christian faith from motives of policy, and who, having no true spiritual piety, were ready to embrace the most lax views of religion, and to yield themselves to any form of error. Of this period, and of the effect of the conversion of Constantine in this respect, Mr. Gibbon makes the following remarks, strikingly illustrative of the view now taken of the meaning of this passage:— " The hopes of wealth and honours, the example of an emperor, his exhortations, his irresistible smiles, diffused conviction among the venal and obsequious crowds which usually fill the apartments of a palace. The cities which signalized a forward zeal, by the voluntary destruction of their temples, were distinguished by municipal privileges, and rewarded with popular donatives; and the new capital of the East gloried in the singular advantage, that Constantinople was never profaned by the worship of idols. As the lower ranks of society are governed by imitation, the conversion of those who possessed any eminence of birth, of power, or of riches, was soon followed by dependent multitudes. The salvation of the common people was purchased at an easy rate, if it be true that, in one year, twelve thousand men were baptized at Rome, besides a proportionable number of women and children, and that a white garment, with twenty pieces of gold, had been promised by the emperor to every convert" (i. 425). At a time, therefore, when it might have been supposed that, under the patronage of a Christian emperor, the truth would have spread around the world, the church was exposed to one of its greatest dangers—that arising from the fact that it had become united with the state. About the same time, also, there sprang up many of those forms of error which have spread farthest over the Christian world, and which then threatened to become the universal form of belief in the church. Of this class of doctrine were the views of Arius, and the views of Pelagius—forms of opinion which, there were strong reasons to fear, might become the prevailing belief of the church, and essentially change its character. About this time, also, the church was passing into the state in which the Papacy would arise—that dark and gloomy period in which error would spread over the Christian world, and the true servants of God would retire for a long period into obscurity. " We are now but a little way off from the commencement of that noted period —obscurely hinted at by Daniel, plainly announced by John—the twelve hundred and sixty prophetic days or years, for which preparations of a very unusual kind, but requisite, doubtless, are made. This period was to form the gloomiest, without exception, in the annals of the world—the period of Satan's highest success, and of the church's greatest depression; and lest she should become during it utterly extinct, her members, never so few as then, were all specially sealed. The long night passes on, darkening as it advances; but the sealed company are not visible; they disappear from the Apocalyptic stage, just as they then disappeared from the observation of the world; for they fled away to escape the fire and the dungeons of their persecutors, to hide in the hoary caves of the earth, or to inhabit the untrodden regions of the wilderness, or to dwell beneath the shadow of the Alps, or to enjoy fellowship with God, emancipated and unknown, in the deep seclusion and gloom of some convent" (*The Seventh Vial*, London, 1848, pp. 27, 28). These facts seem to me to show, with a considerable degree of probability, what was designated by the *suspense* which occurred after the opening of the sixth seal—when the affairs of the world *seemed* to be hastening on to the great catastrophe. At that period the prophetic eye sees the tendency of things suddenly arrested; the winds held back, the church preserved, and a series of events introduced, intended to designate and to save from the great mass of those who professedly constituted the "tribes of Israel," a definite number who should be in fact the true church of God.

II. The facts, then, to which there is reference in checking the tendency of things, and sealing the servants of God, may have been the following:—(*a*) The preservation of the church from extinction during those calamitous periods when ruin seemed about to sweep over the Roman world. Not only as a matter of fact was there a suspension of those impending judgments that seemed to threaten the very extinction of the empire by the invasion of the northern hordes (see Notes on ch. vi.), but there were *special* acts in favour of the church, by which these fierce barbarians appeared not only to be restrained from destroying the church, but to be influenced by tenderness and sympathy for it, as if they were raised up to preserve it when Rome had done all it could to destroy it. It would seem *as if* God restrained the rage of these hordes for the sake of preserving his church; *as if* he had touched their hearts that they might give to Christians an opportunity to escape in the impending storm. We may refer here particularly to the conduct of Alaric, king of the Goths, in the attack on Rome already referred to; and, as usual, we may quote from Mr. Gibbon, who will not be suspected of a design to contribute anything to the illustration of the Apocalypse. "At the hour of midnight," says he (vol. ii. pp. 260, 261), "the Salarian Gate was silently opened, and the inhabitants were awakened by the tremendous sound of the Gothic trumpet. Eleven hundred and sixty-three years after the foundation of Rome, the imperial city, which had subdued and civilized so considerable a part of mankind, was delivered to the licentious fury of the tribes of Germany and Scythia. The proclamation of Alaric, when he forced his entrance into the vanquished city, discovered, however, some regard for the laws of humanity and religion. He encouraged his troops boldly to seize the rewards of valour, and to enrich themselves with the spoils of a wealthy and effeminate people; but he exhorted them at the same time to spare the lives of the unresisting citizens, *and to respect the churches of the apostles St. Peter and St. Paul as holy and inviolable sanctuaries*. While the barbarians roamed through the city in quest of prey, the humble dwelling of an aged virgin, who had devoted her life to the service of the altar, was forced open by one of the powerful Goths. He immediately demanded, though in civil language, all the gold and silver in her possession; and was astonished at the readiness with which she conducted him to a splendid hoard of massy plate, of the richest materials and the most curious workmanship. The barbarian viewed with wonder and delight this valuable acquisition, till he was interrupted by a serious admonition, addressed to him in the following words: 'These,' said she, 'are the consecrated vessels belonging to St. Peter; if you presume to touch them, the sacrilegious deed will remain on your conscience: for my part, I dare not keep what I am unable to defend.' The Gothic captain, struck with reverential awe, despatched a messenger to inform the king of the treasure which he had discovered; and received a peremptory order from Alaric, that all the consecrated plate and ornaments should be transported, without damage or delay, to the church of the apostle. From the extremity, perhaps, of the Quirinal hill, to the distant quarter of the Vatican, a numerous detachment of the Goths, marching in order of battle through the principal streets, protected, with glittering arms, the long train of their devout companions, who bore aloft on their heads the sacred vessels of gold and silver; and the martial shouts of the barbarians were mingled with the sound of religious psalmody. From all the adjacent houses a crowd of Christians hastened to join this edifying procession; and a multitude of fugitives, without distinction of age or rank, or even of sect, had the good fortune to escape to the secure and hospitable sanctuary of the Vatican." In a note Mr. Gibbon adds: "According to Isidore, Alaric himself was heard to say, that he waged war with the Romans, and not with the apostles." He adds also (p. 261), "The learned work concerning the *City of God* was professedly composed by St. Augustine to justify the ways of Providence in the destruction of the Roman greatness. He celebrates with peculiar satisfaction this memorable triumph of Christ; and insults his adversaries by challenging them to produce some similar example of a town taken by storm, in which the fabulous gods of antiquity had been able to protect either themselves or their deluded votaries." We may refer here, also, to that work of Augustine as illustrating the passage before us. In book i. ch. 2, he defends this position, that "there never was war in which the conquerors would spare them whom they conquered for the gods they worshipped"—referring particularly to the sacking of Troy; in ch. 3 he appeals to the example of Troy; in ch. 4 he appeals to the sanctuary of Juno, in Troy; in ch. 5 he shows that the Romans never spared the temples of those cities which they destroyed; and in ch. 6 he maintains that the fact that mercy was shown by the barbarians in the sacking of Rome, was "through the power of the name of Jesus Christ." In illustration of this he says, "Therefore, all the spoil, murder, violence, and affliction, that in this fresh calamity came upon Rome, were nothing but the ordinary effects following the custom of war. But that which was so unaccustomed, that the savage nature of the barbarians should put on a new shape, and appear so merciful that it would make choice of great and spacious churches to fill with such as it meant to show pity on, from which none should be haled to slaughter or slavery, in which none should be hurt, to which many by their courteous foes should be conducted, and out of which none should be led into bondage; this is due to the name of Christ, this is due to the Christian profession; he that seeth not is blind; he that seeth and praiseth it not is unthankful; he that hinders him that praiseth it is mad" (*City of God*, p. 11; London, 1620). Such a preservation of Christians; such a suspension of judgments, when all things seemed to be on the verge of ruin, would not be *inappropriately* represented by winds that threatened to sweep over the world; by the staying of those winds by some remarkable power, as by an angel; and by the special interposition which spared the church in the tumults and terrors of a siege, and of the sacking of a city. (*b*) There *may* have been a reference to another class of Divine interpositions at about the same time, to designate the true servants of God. It has been already remarked, that from the time when Constantine took the church under his patronage, and it became connected with the state, there was a large accession of nominal professors in the church, producing a great corruption in regard to spiritual religion, and an extended prevalence of error. Now the delay here referred to, between the opening of the sixth and seventh seals, *may* have referred to the fact, that during this period the true doctrines of Christianity would be vindicated and established in such a way that the servants of God would be "sealed" and designated in contradistinction from the great mass of the professed followers of Christ, and from the numerous advocates of error. *From* that mass a certain and definite number was to be sealed—implying, as we have seen, that there would be a *selection*, or that there would be something which would *discriminate* them from the multitudes as the true servants of God. This is represented by an angel coming from the east: the angel representing the new heavenly influence coming upon the church; and the coming from the east—as the east is the quarter where the sun rises—denoting that it came from the source and fountain of light—that is, God. The "sealing" would denote anything in this new influence or manifestation which would mark the true children of God, and would be appropriately employed to designate any doctrines which would keep up true religion in the world; which would preserve correct views about God, the way of salvation, and the nature of true religion, and which would thus determine where the church of God really was. If there should be a tendency in the church to degenerate into formality; if the rules of discipline should be relaxed; if error should prevail as to what constitutes spiritual religion; and if there should be a new influence at that time which would distinguish those who were the children of God from those who were not, *this* would be appropriately represented by the angel from the east, and by the sealing of the servants of God. Now it requires but a slight knowledge of the history of the Roman empire, and of the church at the period supposed here to be referred to, to perceive that all this occurred. There was a large influx of professed converts. There was a vast increase of worldliness. There was a wide diffusion of error. Religion was fast becoming mere formalism. The true church was apparently fast verging to ruin. At this period God raised up distinguished men—as if they had been angels ascending from the east—who came as with the "seal of the living God"—the doctrines of grace, and just views of spiritual religion—to designate who were, and who were not, the "true servants of God" among the multitudes who professed to be his followers. Such were the doctrines of Athanasius and Augustine—those great doctrines on which the very existence of the true church has in all ages depended. The doctrines thus illustrated and defended were fitted to make a broad line of distinction between the true church and the world, and this would be well represented by the symbol employed here—for it is by these doctrines that the true people of God are sealed and confirmed. On this subject comp. Elliott, i. 279-292. The general sense here intended to be expressed is, that there was at the period referred to, after the conversion of Constantine, a decided tendency to a worldly, formal, lax kind of religion in the church; a very prevalent denial of the doctrine of the Trinity and of the doctrines of grace; a lax mode of admitting members to the church, with little or no evidence of true conversion; a disposition to attribute saving grace to the ordinances of religion, and especially to baptism; a disposition to rely on the outward ceremonies of religion, with little acquaintance with its spiritual power; and a general breaking down of the barriers between the church and the world, as there is usually in a time of outward prosperity, and especially when the church is connected with the state. At this time there arose another set of influences well represented by the angel coming from the east, and sealing the true servants of God, in illustration and confirmation of the true doctrines of Christianity—doctrines on which the spirituality of the church has always depended: the doctrines of the Trinity, the atonement, the depravity of man, regeneration by the agency of the Holy Spirit, justification by faith, the sovereignty of God, and kindred doctrines. Such doctrines have in all ages served to determine where the true church is, and to designate and "seal" the servants of the Most High. (*c*) This process of "sealing" may be regarded as continued during the long night of Papal darkness that was coming upon the church, when error would abound, and the religion of forms would be triumphant. Even then, in places obscure and unknown, the work of sealing the true servants of God might be going forward—for even in those times of gloomy night there *were* those, though comparatively few in number, who loved the truth, and who were the real servants of God. The number of the elect was filling up, for even in the darkest times there were those who loved the cause of spiritual religion, and who bore upon them the impress of the "seal of the living God." Such appears to have been the intent of this sealing vision: a staying of the desolation that, in various forms, was sweeping over the world, in order that the true church might be safe, and that a large number, from all parts of the church, might be sealed and designated as the true servants of God. The winds that blowed from all quarters were stayed as if by mighty angels. A new influence, from the great source of light, came in to designate those who were the true servants of the Most High, as if an angel had come from the rising sun with the seal of the living God, to impress it on their foreheads. A selection was made out of a church filling up with formalists, and in which the true doctrines of spiritual religion were fast fading away, of those who could be designated as the true servants of God. By their creed, and their lives, and their spirit, and their profession, they could be designated as the true servants of God, as if a visible mark were impressed on their foreheads. This selection was confined to no place, no class, no tribe, no denomination. It was taken from the whole of Israel, in such numbers that it could be seen that none of the tribes were excluded from the honour, but that, wherever the true spirit of religion was, God was acknowledging these tribes—or churches—as his, and there he was gathering a people

**9** After this I beheld, and, lo, a great multitude, which no man could number, *g* of all nations, and

*g* ch.5.9; Ro.11.25.

to himself. This would be long continued, until new scenes would open, and the eye would rest on other developments in the series of symbols, revealing the glorious host of the redeemed emerging from darkness, and in countless numbers triumphing before the throne.

**9.** *After this.* Gr., "After these things" —Μετὰ ταῦτα: that is, after I saw these things thus represented I had another vision. This would undoubtedly imply, not only that he *saw* these things after he had seen the sealing of the hundred and forty-four thousand, but that they would *occur* subsequently to that. But he does not state whether they would immediately occur, or whether other things might not intervene. As a matter of fact, the vision seems to be transferred from earth to heaven—for the multitudes which he saw appeared "before the throne" (ver. 9); that is, before the throne of God in heaven. The design seems to be to carry the mind forward quite beyond the storms and tempests of earth—the scenes of woe and sorrow—the days of error, darkness, declension, and persecution—to that period when the church should be triumphant in heaven. Instead, therefore, of leaving the impression that the hundred and forty-four thousand would be *all* that would be saved, the eye is directed to an innumerable host, gathered from all ages, all climes, and all people, triumphant in glory. The multitude that John thus saw was not, therefore, I apprehend, the same as the hundred and forty-four thousand, but a far greater number—the whole assembled host of the redeemed in heaven, gathered there as *victors*, with palm-branches, the symbols of triumph, in their hands. The *object* of the vision is to cheer those who are desponding in times of religious declension and in seasons of persecution, and when the number of true Christians seems to be small, with the assurance that an immense host shall be redeemed from our world, and be gathered triumphant before the throne. ¶ *I beheld.* That is, he saw them before the throne. The vision is transferred from earth to heaven; from the contemplation of the scene when desolation seemed to impend over the world, and when comparatively few in number were "sealed" as the servants of God, to the time when the redeemed would be triumphant, and when a host which no man can number would stand before God. ¶ *And, lo.* Indicating surprise. A vast host burst upon the view. Instead of the comparatively few who were sealed, an innumerable company were presented to his vision, and surprise was the natural effect. ¶ *A great multitude.* Instead of the comparatively small number on which the attention had been fixed. ¶ *Which no man could number.* The number was so great that no one could count them, and John, therefore, did not attempt to do it. This is such a statement as one would make who should have a view of all the redeemed in heaven. It would appear to be a number beyond all power of computation. This representation is in strong contrast with a very common opinion that only a few will be saved. The representation in the Bible is, that immense hosts of the human race will be saved; and though vast numbers will be lost, and though at any particular period of the world hitherto it may seem that few have been in the path to life, yet we have every reason to believe that, taking the race at large, and estimating it as a whole, a vast majority of the whole will be brought to heaven. For the true religion is yet to spread all over the world, and perhaps for many, many thousands of years, piety is to be as prevalent as sin has been; and in that long and happy time of the world's history we may hope that the numbers of the saved may surpass all who have been lost in past periods, beyond any power of computation. See Notes on ch. xx. 3-6. ¶ *Of all nations.* Not only of Jews; not only of the nations which, in the time of the sealing vision, had embraced the gospel, but of all the nations of the earth. This implies two things: (*a*) that the gospel would be preached among all nations; and (*b*) that even when it was thus preached to them they would keep up their national characteristics. There can be no hope of blending all the nations of the earth under one visible sovereignty. They may all be subjected to the spiritual reign of the Redeemer, but still there is no reason to suppose that they will not have their distinct organizations and laws. ¶ *And kindreds*—φυλῶν. This word properly refers to those who are

A.D. 96.]  CHAPTER VII.  183

kindreds, and people, and tongues, stood before the throne, and before descended from a common ancestry, and hence denotes a race, lineage, kindred. It was applied to the tribes of Israel, as derived from the same ancestor, and for the same reason might be applied to a *clan*, and thence to any division in a nation, or to a nation itself—properly retaining the notion that it was descended from a common ancestor. Here it would seem to refer to a smaller class than a nation—the different clans of which a nation might be composed. ¶ *And people*—λαῶν. This word refers properly to a people or community as a *mass*, without reference to its origin or any of its divisions. The former word would be used by one who should look upon a nation as made up of portions of distinct languages, clans, or families; this word would be used by one who should look on such an assembled people as a mere mass of human beings, with no reference to their difference of clanship, origin, or language. ¶ *And tongues*. Languages. This word would refer also to the inhabitants of the earth, considered with respect to the fact that they speak different languages. The use of particular languages does not designate the precise boundaries of nations—for often many people speaking different languages are united as one nation, and often those who speak the same language constitute distinct nations. The view, therefore, with which one would look upon the dwellers on the earth, in the use of the word *tongues* or *languages*, would be, not as divided into nations; not with reference to their lineage or clanship; and not as a mere mass without reference to any distinction, but as divided by *speech*. The meaning of the whole is, that persons from all parts of the earth, as contemplated in these points of view, would be among the redeemed. Comp. Notes on Da. iii. 4; iv. 1. ¶ *Stood before the throne*. The throne of God. See Notes on ch. iv. 2. The throne is there represented as set up in heaven, and the vision here is a vision of what will occur in heaven. It is designed to carry the thoughts beyond *all* the scenes of conflict, strife, and persecution on earth, to the time when the church shall be triumphant in glory—when all storms shall have passed by; when all persecutions shall have ceased; when all revolutions shall have occurred; when all the elect—not the Lamb, *h*clothed with white robes, and *i*palms in their hands;

*h* ch.6.11.  *i* Le.23.40.

only the hundred and forty-four thousand of the sealed, but of all nations and times—shall have been gathered in. There was a beautiful propriety in this vision. John saw the tempests stayed, as by the might of angels. He saw a new influence and power that would seal the true servants of God. But those tempests were stayed only for a time, and there were more awful visions in reserve than any which had been exhibited—visions of woe and sorrow, of persecution and of death. It was appropriate, therefore, just at this moment of calm suspense—of delayed judgments —to suffer the mind to rest on the triumphant close of the whole in heaven, when a countless host would be gathered there with palms in their hands, uniting with angels in the worship of God. The mind, by the contemplation of this beautiful vision, would be refreshed and strengthened for the disclosure of the awful scenes which were to occur on the sounding of the trumpets under the seventh seal. The simple idea is, that, amidst the storms and tempests of life —scenes of existing or impending trouble and wrath—it is well to let the eye rest on the scene of the final triumph, when innumerable hosts of the redeemed shall stand before God, and when sorrow shall be known no more. ¶ *And before the Lamb*. In the midst of the throne—in heaven. See Notes on ch. v. 6. ¶ *Clothed with white robes*. The emblems of innocence or righteousness, uniformly represented as the raiment of the inhabitants of heaven. See Notes on ch. iii. 4; vi. 11. ¶ *And palms in their hands*. Emblems of victory. Branches of the palm-tree were carried by the victors in the athletic contests of Greece and Rome, and in triumphal processions. See Notes on Mat. xxi. 8. The palm-tree—straight, elevated, majestic—was an appropriate emblem of triumph. The portion of it which was borne in victory was the long *leaf* which shoots out from the top of the tree. Comp. Notes on Is. iii. 26. See Eschenberg, *Manual of Class. Lit.* p. 243, and Le. xxiii. 40: "And ye shall take you on the first day the boughs of goodly trees, *branches of palm-trees*," &c. So in the Saviour's triumphal entry into Jerusalem (Jn. xii. 12, 13)—"On the next day much people took branches of

10 And ᵏcried with a loud voice, saying, ˡSalvation to our God which sitteth upon the throne, and unto the Lamb.

11 And all the angels stood round about the throne, and *about* the elders and the four beasts, and fell before the throne on their faces, and worshipped God,

12 Saying, ᵐAmen: Blessing, and glory, and wisdom, and thanksgiving, and honour, and power, and might, *be* unto our God for ever and ever. Amen.

k Zec.4.7.  l ch.19.1; Is.43.11.  m ch.5.13,14; Jude 25.

---

palm-trees, and went forth to meet him, and cried, Hosanna."

10. *And cried with a loud voice.* Comp. Zec. iv. 7. This is expressive of the greatness of their joy; the ardour and earnestness of their praise. ¶ *Salvation to our God.* The word rendered salvation — σωτηρία — means properly safety, deliverance, preservation; then welfare or prosperity; then victory; then, in a Christian sense, deliverance from punishment and admission to eternal life. Here the idea seems to be that their deliverance from sin, danger, persecution, and death, was to be ascribed solely to God. It cannot be meant, as the words would seem to imply, that they desired that God might have salvation; but the sense is, that *their* salvation was to be attributed entirely to him. This will undoubtedly be the song of the released for ever, and all who reach the heavenly world will feel that they owe their deliverance from eternal death, and their admission to glory, wholly to him. Professor Robinson (*Lex.*) renders the word here *victory.* The fair meaning is, that *whatever* is included in the word *salvation* will be due to God alone—the deliverance from sin, danger, and death; the triumph over every foe; the resurrection from the grave; the rescue from eternal burnings; the admission to a holy heaven—*victory* in all that that word implies will be due to God. ¶ *Which sitteth upon the throne.* Notes on ch. iv. 2. ¶ *And unto the Lamb.* Notes on ch. v. 6. God the Father, and He who is the Lamb of God, alike claim the honour of salvation. It is observable here that the redeemed ascribe their salvation to the Lamb as well as to Him who is on the throne. Could they do this if he who is referred to as the "Lamb" were a mere man? Could they if he were an angel? Could they if he were not equal with the Father? Do those who are in heaven worship a creature? Will they unite a created being with the Anointed One in acts of solemn adoration and praise?

11. *And all the angels stood round about the throne.* Notes on ch. v. 11. ¶ *And* about *the elders.* Notes on ch. iv. 4. ¶ *And the four beasts.* Notes on ch. iv. 6. The meaning is, that the angels stood in the *outer* circle, or *outside* of the elders and the four living creatures. The redeemed, it is manifest, occupied the inner circle, and were near the throne, though their precise location is not mentioned. The angels sympathize with the church redeemed and triumphant, as they did with the church in its conflicts and trials, and they now appropriately unite with that church in adoring and praising God. They see in that redemption new displays of the character of God, and they rejoice that that church is rescued from its troubles, and is now brought triumphant to heaven. ¶ *And fell before the throne on their faces.* The usual position of profound adoration, ch. iv. 10; v. 8. ¶ *And worshipped God.* Notes on ch. v. 11, 12.

12. *Saying, Amen.* See Notes on ch. i. 7. The word *Amen* here is a word strongly affirming the truth of what is said, or expressing hearty assent to it. It may be uttered, as expressing this, either in the beginning or end of a sentence. Thus *wills* are commonly commenced, "In the name of God, *Amen.*" ¶ *Blessing, and glory,* &c. Substantially the same ascription of praise occurs in ch. v. 12. See Notes on that verse. The general idea is, that the highest kind of praise is to be ascribed to God; everything excellent in character is to be attributed to him; every blessing which is received is to be traced to him. The *order* of the words indeed is changed, but the sense is substantially the same. In the former case (ch. v. 12) the ascription of praise is to the Lamb—the Son of God; here it is to God. In both instances the worship is described as rendered in heaven; and the use of the language shows that God and the Lamb are regarded in heaven as entitled to equal praise. The only words found here which do not occur in

A.D. 96.]  CHAPTER VII.  185

13 And one of the elders answered, saying unto me, What are these which are arrayed in white robes? and whence came they?

14 And I said unto him, Sir, thou knowest. And he said to me, These are they which ⁿcame out of great tribulation, and have ᵒwashed their robes, and made them white ᵖin the blood of the Lamb.

n ch.6.9; Jn.16.33.
o 1 Co.6.11; He.9.14.   p ch.1.5; 1 Jn.1.7.

---

ch. v. 12 are *thanksgiving* and *might*—words which require no particular explanation.

13. *And one of the elders.* See Notes on ch. iv. 4. That is, as there understood, one of the representatives of the church before the throne. ¶ *Answered.* The word *answer*, with us, means to reply to something which has been said. In the Bible, however, the word is not unfrequently used in the *beginning* of a speech, where nothing has been said—as if it were a reply to something that *might* be said on the subject; or to something that is passing through the mind of another; or to something in the case under consideration which suggests an inquiry. Comp. Is. lxv. 24; Da. ii. 26; Ac. v. 8. Thus it is used here. John was looking on the host, and reflecting on the state of things; and to the train of thought passing through his mind the angel *answered* by an inquiry as to a part of that host. Professor Stuart renders it *accosted me*. ¶ *What are these which are arrayed in white robes? Who are these?* The object evidently is to bring the case of these persons more particularly into view. The vast host with branches of palm had attracted the attention of John, but it was the object of the speaker to turn his thoughts to a particular part of the host—the martyrs who stood among them. He would seem, therefore, to have turned to a particular portion of the immense multitude of the redeemed, and by an emphasis on the word *these*—"Who are *these*"—to have fixed the eye upon them. All those who are before the throne are represented as clothed in white robes (ver. 9), but the eye might be directed to a particular part of them as grouped together, and as having something peculiar in their position or appearance. There was a *propriety* in thus directing the mind of John to the martyrs as triumphing in heaven in a time when the churches were suffering persecution, and in view of the vision which he had had of times of darkness and calamity coming upon the world at the opening of the sixth seal. Beyond all the scenes of sorrow and grief, he was permitted to see the martyrs triumphing in heaven. ¶ *Arrayed in white robes.* Notes on ver. 9. ¶ *And whence came they?* The object is to fix the attention more distinctly on what is said of them, that they came up out of great tribulation.

14. *And I said unto him, Sir, thou knowest.* The word *sir* in this place—κύριε, *lord*—is a form of respectful address, such as would be used when speaking to a superior, Ge. xliii. 20; Mat. xiii. 27; xxi. 30; xxvii. 63; Jn. iv. 11, 15, 19, 49; v. 7; xii. 21; xx. 15. The simple meaning of the phrase "thou knowest" is, that he who had asked the question must be better informed than he to whom he had proposed it. It is, on the part of John, a modest confession that he did not know, or could not be presumed to know, and at the same time the respectful utterance of an opinion that he who addressed this question to him must be in possession of this knowledge. ¶ *And he said unto me.* Not offended with the reply, and ready, as he had evidently intended to do, to give him the information which he needed. ¶ *These are they which came out of great tribulation.* The word rendered *tribulation*—θλίψις—is a word of general character, meaning *affliction*, though perhaps there is here an allusion to persecution. The sense, however, would be better expressed by the phrase *great trials*. The object seems to have been to set before the mind of the apostle a view of those who had suffered much, and who by their sufferings had been sanctified and prepared for heaven, in order to encourage those who might be yet called to suffer. ¶ *And have washed their robes.* To wit, in the blood of the Lamb. ¶ *And made them white in the blood of the Lamb.* There is some incongruity in saying that they had made them *white* in the *blood* of the Lamb; and the meaning therefore must be, that they had *cleansed* or *purified* them in that blood. Under the ancient ritual, various things about the sanctuary were *cleansed* from ceremonial defilement by the sprinkling of blood on them—the

15 Therefore are they before the throne of God, and serve him day and night in his temple: and he that sitteth on the throne *q*shall dwell among them.
16 They shall *r*hunger no more,

*q* ch.21.3,4.   *r* Is.49.10.

blood of sacrifice. In accordance with that usage, the blood of the Lamb—of the Lord Jesus—is said to cleanse and purify. John sees a great company with white robes. The means by which it is said they became white or pure is the blood of the Lamb. It is not said that they were made white as the result of their sufferings or their afflictions, but by the blood of the Lamb. The course of thought here is such that it would be natural to suppose that, if at any time the great deeds or the sufferings of the saints could contribute to the fact that they will wear white robes in heaven, this is an occasion on which there might be such a reference. But there is no allusion to that. It is not by their own sufferings and trials, their persecutions and sorrows, that they are made holy, but by the blood of the Lamb that had been shed for sinners. This reference to the blood of the Lamb is one of the incidental proofs that occur so frequently in the Scriptures of the reality of the atonement. It could be only in allusion to that, and with an implied belief in that, that the blood of the Lamb could be referred to as cleansing the robes of the saints in heaven. If he shed his blood merely as other men have done; if he died only as a martyr, what propriety would there have been in referring to his blood more than to the blood of any other martyr? And what influence could the blood of *any* martyr have in cleansing the robes of the saints in heaven? The fact is, that if that were all, such language would be unmeaning. It is never used except in connection with the blood of Christ; and the language of the Bible everywhere is such as would be employed on the supposition that he shed his blood to make expiation for sin, and on no other supposition. On the general meaning of the language used here, and the sentiment expressed, see Notes on He. ix. 14 and 1 Jn. i. 7.

15. *Therefore are they before the throne of God.* The reason why they are there is to be traced to the fact that the Lamb shed his blood to make expiation for sin. No other reason can be given why any one of the human race is in heaven; and that is reason enough why any of that race are there.

¶ *And serve him day and night in his temple.* That is, continually or constantly. Day and night constitute the whole of time, and this expression, therefore, denotes constant and uninterrupted service. On earth, toil is suspended by the return of night, and the service of God is intermitted by the necessity of rest; in heaven, as there will be no weariness, there will be no need of intermission, and the service of God, varied doubtless to meet the state of the mind, will be continued for ever. The phrase, "to serve him in his temple," refers undoubtedly to heaven, regarded as the temple or holy dwelling-place of God. See Notes on ch. i. 6.   ¶ *And he that sitteth on the throne.* God. Notes, ch. iv. 2.   ¶ *Shall dwell among them*—σκηνώσει. This word properly means, *to tent, to pitch a tent;* and, in the New Testament, to dwell as in tents. The meaning here is, that God would dwell among them as in a tent, or would have his abode with them. Perhaps the allusion is to the tabernacle in the wilderness. That was regarded as the peculiar dwelling-place of God, and that always occupied a central place among the tribes of Israel. So in heaven there will be the consciousness always that God dwells there among his people, and that the redeemed are gathered around him in his own house. Professor Stuart renders this, it seems to me, with less beauty and propriety, " will spread his tent over them," as meaning that he would receive them into intimate connection and union with him, and offer them his protection. Comp. ch. xxi. 3.

16. *They shall hunger no more.* A considerable portion of the redeemed who will be there, were, when on earth, subjected to the evils of famine; many who perished with hunger. In heaven they will be subjected to that evil no more, for there will be no want that will not be supplied. The bodies which the redeemed will have—spiritual bodies (1 Co. xv. 44)—will doubtless be such as will be nourished in some other way than by food, if they require any nourishment; and whatever that nourishment may be, it will be fully supplied. The passage here is taken from Is. xlix. 10:

# CHAPTER VII.

neither thirst any more; neither shall the sun light on them, *nor any heat.

17 For the Lamb, which is in the midst of the throne, shall *t*feed them, and shall lead them unto living fountains of waters: and God shall *u*wipe away all tears from their eyes.

*s* Ps.121.6; Is.4.6.    *t* Ps.23.1,2,5; 36.8; Is.40.11.    *u* Is.25.8.

"They shall not hunger nor thirst; neither shall the heat nor sun smite them." See Notes on that passage. ¶ *Neither thirst any more.* As multitudes of the redeemed have been subjected to the evils of hunger, so have multitudes also been subjected to the pains of thirst. In prison; in pathless deserts; in times of drought, when wells and fountains were dried up, they have suffered from this cause—a cause producing as intense suffering perhaps as any that man endures. Comp. Ex. xvii. 3; Ps. lxiii. 1; La. iv. 4; 2 Co. xi. 27. It is easy to conceive of persons suffering so intensely from thirst that the highest vision of felicity would be such a promise as that in the words before us—"neither thirst any more." ¶ *Neither shall the sun light on them.* It is hardly necessary, perhaps, to say that the word *light* here does not mean to enlighten, to give light to, to shine on. The Greek is πέση—*fall on*—and the reference, probably, is to the intense and burning heat of the sun, commonly called a *sunstroke*. Excessive heat of the sun, causing great pain or sudden death, is not a very uncommon thing among us, and must have been more common in the warm climates and burning sands of the countries in the vicinity of Palestine. The meaning here is, that in heaven they would be free from this calamity. ¶ *Nor any heat.* In Is. xlix. 10, from which place this is quoted, the expression is שָׁרָב, *sharab*, properly denoting heat or burning, and particularly the *mirage*, the excessive heat of a sandy desert producing a vapour which has a striking resemblance to water, and which often misleads the unwary traveller by its deceptive appearance. See Notes on Is. xxxv. 7. The expression here is equivalent to intense heat; and the meaning is, that in heaven the redeemed will not be subjected to any such suffering as the traveller often experiences in the burning sands of the desert. The language would convey a most grateful idea to those who had been subjected to these sufferings, and is one form of saying that, in heaven, the redeemed will be delivered from the ills which they suffer in this life. Perhaps the whole image here is that of travellers who have been on a long journey, exposed to hunger and thirst, wandering in the burning sands of the desert, and exposed to the fiery rays of the sun, at length reaching their quiet and peaceful home, where they would find safety and abundance. The believer's journey from earth to heaven is such a *pilgrimage*.

17. *For the Lamb, which is in the midst of the throne.* Notes on ch. v. 6. He is still the great agent in promoting the happiness of the redeemed in heaven. ¶ *Shall feed them.* Rather, shall exercise over them the office of a shepherd —ποιμανεῖ. This includes much more than mere *feeding*. It embraces all the care which a shepherd takes of his flock—watching them, providing for them, guarding them from danger. Comp. Ps. xxiii. 1, 2, 5; xxxvi. 8. See this fully illustrated in the Notes on Is. xl. 11. ¶ *And shall lead them unto living fountains of waters.* Living fountains refer to running streams, as contrasted with standing water and stagnant pools. See Notes on Jn. iv. 10. The allusion is undoubtedly to the happiness of heaven, represented as fresh and everflowing, like streams in the desert. No image of happiness, perhaps, is more vivid, or would be more striking to an Oriental, than that of such fountains flowing in sandy and burning wastes. The word *living* here must refer to the fact that that happiness will be perennial. These fountains will always bubble; these streams will never dry up. The thirst for salvation will always be gratified; the soul will always be made happy. ¶ *And God shall wipe away all tears from their eyes.* This is a new image of happiness taken from another place in Isaiah (ch. xxv. 8), "The Lord God will wipe away tears from off all faces." The expression is one of exquisite tenderness and beauty. The poet Burns said that he could never read this without being affected to weeping. Of all the *negative* descriptions of heaven, there is no one perhaps that would be better adapted to produce consolation than this. This is a world of weeping—a

vale of tears. Philosophers have sought a brief definition of man, and have sought in vain. Would there be any better description of him, as representing the reality of his condition here, than to say that he is *one who weeps?* Who is there of the human family that has not shed a tear? Who that has not wept over the grave of a friend; over his own losses and cares; over his disappointments; over the treatment he has received from others; over his sins; over the follies, vices, and woes of his fellow-men? And what a change would it make in our world if it could be said that henceforward not another tear would be shed; not a head would ever be bowed again in grief! Yet this is to be the condition of heaven. In that world there is to be no pain, no disappointment, no bereavement. No friend is to lie in dreadful agony on a sick-bed; no grave is to be opened to receive a parent, a wife, a child; no gloomy prospect of death is to draw tears of sorrow from the eyes. To that blessed world, when our eyes run down with tears, are we permitted to look forward; and the prospect of such a world should contribute to wipe away our tears here—for all our sorrows will soon be over. As already remarked, there was a beautiful propriety, at a time when such calamities impended over the church and the world—when there was such a certainty of persecution and sorrow—in permitting the mind to rest on the contemplation of these happy scenes in heaven, where all the redeemed, in white robes, and with palms of victory in their hands, would be gathered before the throne. To us also now, amidst the trials of the present life — when friends leave us; when sickness comes; when our hopes are blasted; when calumnies and reproaches come upon us; when, standing on the verge of the grave, and looking down into the cold tomb, the eyes pour forth floods of tears—it is a blessed privilege to be permitted to look forward to that brighter scene in heaven, where not a pang shall ever be felt, and not a tear shall ever be shed.

## CHAPTER VIII.

### ANALYSIS OF THE CHAPTER.

One seal of the mysterious roll (ch. v. 1) remains to be broken—six having already disclosed the contents of the volume relating to the future. It was natural that the opening of the seventh, and the last, should be attended with circumstances of peculiar solemnity, as being all that remained in this volume to be unfolded, and as the events thus far had been evidently preparatory to some great catastrophe. It would have been natural to expect that, like the six former, this seal would have been opened at once, and would have disclosed all that was to happen at one view. But, instead of that, the opening of this seal is followed by a series of events, seven also in number, which succeed each other, represented by new symbols—the blowing of as many successive trumpets. These circumstances retard the course of the action, and fix the mind on a new order of events--events which could be appropriately grouped together, and which, for some reason, might be thus more appropriately represented than they could be in so many successive seals. What was the reason of this arrangement will be more readily seen on an examination of the particular events referred to in the successive trumpet-blasts.

The points in the chapter are the following: — (1) The opening of the seventh seal, ver. 1. This is attended, not with an immediate exhibition of the events which are to occur, as in the case of the former seals, but with a solemn silence in heaven for the space of half an hour. The *reason* of this silence, apparently, is found in the solemn nature of the events which are anticipated. At the opening of the sixth seal (ch. vi. 12, seq.) the grand catastrophe of the world's history seemed about to occur. This had been suspended for a time, as if by the power of angels holding the winds and the storm (ch. vii.), and now it was natural to expect that there would be a series of overwhelming calamities. In view of these apprehended terrors, the inhabitants of heaven are represented as standing in awful silence, as if anticipating and apprehending what was to occur. This circumstance adds much to the interest of the scene, and is a forcible illustration of the position which the mind naturally assumes in the anticipation of dreaded events. Silence—solemn and awful silence—is the natural state of the mind under such circumstances. In accordance with this expectation of what was to come, a series of new representations is introduced, adapted to prepare the mind for the fearful disclosures which are yet to be made. (2) Seven angels appear, on the opening of the seal, to whom are given seven trumpets, as if they were appointed to perform an important part in introducing the series of events which was to follow, ver. 2. (3) As a still farther preparation, another angel is introduced, standing at the altar with a golden censer, ver. 3-5. He is represented as engaged in a solemn act of worship, offering incense and the prayers of the saints before the throne. This unusual representation seems to be designed to denote that some extraordinary events were to occur, making it proper that incense should ascend, and prayer be offered to deprecate the wrath of God. After the offering of the incense, and the prayers, the angel takes the censer and casts it to the earth; and the effect is, that there are voices, and thunderings, and lightnings, and an earthquake. All these would seem to be symbolical of the fearful events which are to follow. The silence; the incense-offering; the prayers; the fearful agitations produced by the casting of the censer upon the earth, as if the prayer was not heard, and as if the offering of the incense did not avail to turn away the impending wrath,—all are appropriate symbols to introduce the series of fearful calamities which were coming upon the world on the sounding of the trumpets. (4) The first angel sounds, ver. 7. Hail and fire follow, mingled with blood. The third part of the trees and of the green grass—that is, of the vegetable world—is consumed. (5) The second angel sounds, ver. 8, 9. A great burning mountain is cast into the sea, and the third part of the sea becomes blood, and a third part of all that is in the sea — fishes and ships — is destroyed. (6) The third angel sounds, ver. 10, 11. A great star, burning like a lamp, falls from heaven upon a third part of the rivers, and upon the fountains of waters, and the waters become bitter, and multitudes of people die from drinking the waters. (7) The fourth angel sounds, ver. 12. The calamity falls on the sources of light —the sun, the moon, and the stars— and the third part of the light is extinguished, and for the third part of the day there is no light, and for the third part of the night also there is no light. (8) At this stage of things, after the sounding of the four trumpets, there is a pause, and an angel flies through the midst of heaven, thrice crying *woe*, by reason of the remaining trumpets which are to sound, ver. 13. Here would seem to be some natural interval, or something which would separate the events which had occurred from those which were to follow. These four, from some cause, are grouped together, and are distinguished from those which are to follow—as if the latter appertained to a new class of events, though under the same general *group* introduced by the opening of the seventh seal.

A few *general* remarks are naturally suggested by the analysis of the chapter, which may aid us in its exposition and application. (*a*) These events, in their order, undoubtedly *succeed* those which are referred to under the opening of the first six seals. They are a continuation of the *series* which is to occur in the history of the world. It has been supposed by some that the events here symbolized are substantially the same as those already referred to under the first six seals, or that, at the opening of the sixth seal, there is a catastrophe; and, one series being there concluded, the writer, by a new set of symbols, goes back to the same point of time, and passes over the same period by a new and parallel set of symbols. But this is manifestly contrary to the whole design. At the first (ch. v. 1) a volume was exhibited, sealed with seven seals, the unrolling of which would manifestly develop *successive* events, and the whole of which would embrace *all* the events which were to be disclosed. When *all* these seven seals were broken, and the contents of *that* volume were disclosed, there might indeed be *another* set of symbols going over the same ground with another design, or giving a representation of future events in some other point of view; but clearly the series should not be broken until the whole seven seals are opened, nor should it be supposed that there is, in the opening of the same volume, an arresting of the course of events, in order to go back again to the same beginning. The representation in this series of symbols is like drawing out a telescope. A telescope might be divided into seven parts, as well as into the usual number, and the drawing out of the seventh part, for example, might be regarded as a representation of the opening of the seventh seal. But the seventh part, instead of being one unbroken piece like the other six, might be so constructed as to be subdivided

## CHAPTER VIII.

AND when he had opened the ᵃseventh seal, there was silence in heaven about the space of half and hour.

ᵃ ch.5.1.

into seven minor parts, each representing a smaller portion of the seventh part. In such a case, the drawing out of the seventh division would *succeed* that of the others, and would be designed to represent a subsequent order of events. (*b*) There was some reason, manifestly, why these seven last events, or the series represented by the seven trumpets, should be grouped together, as coming under the same general classification. They were sufficiently distinct to make it proper to represent them by different symbols, and yet they had so much of the same general character as to make it proper to group them together. If this had not been so, it would have been proper to represent them by a succession of *seals* extending to thirteen in number, instead of representing six seals in succession, and then, under the seventh, a new series extending also to the number seven. In the fulfilment, it will be proper to look for some events which have some such natural connection and bearing that, for some reason, they can be classed together, and yet so distinct that, under the same general symbol of the *seal*, they can be represented under the particular symbol of the *trumpets*. (*c*) For some reason there was a further distinction between the events represented by the first four trumpets and those which were to follow. There was some reason why *they* should be more particularly grouped together, and placed in close connection, and why there should be an interval (ch. viii. 13) before the other trumpet should sound. In the fulfilment of this we should naturally look for such an order of events as would be designated by four successive symbols, and then for such a change, in some respects, as to make an interval proper, and a proclamation of *woe*, before the sounding of the other three, ch. viii. 13. Then it would be natural to look for such events as could properly be grouped under the three remaining symbols—the three succeeding trumpets. (*d*) It is natural, as already intimated, to suppose that the *entire* group would extend, in some general manner at least, to the consummation of all things; or that there would be, *under* the last one, a reference to the consummation of all things—the end of the world. The *reason* for this has already been given, that the apostle saw a volume (ch. v. 1), which contained a sealed account of the future, and it is natural to suppose that there would be a reference to the great leading events which were to occur in the history of the church and of the world. This *natural* anticipation is confirmed by the events disclosed under the sounding of the seventh trumpet (ch. xi. 15, seq.): "And the seventh angel sounded; and there were great voices in heaven, saying, The kingdoms of this world are become the kingdoms of our Lord, and of his Christ, and he shall reign for ever and ever. And the four and twenty elders, which sat before God on their seats, fell upon their faces, and worshipped God, saying, We give thee thanks, O Lord God Almighty, which art, and wast, and art to come; because thou hast taken thy great power, and hast reigned," &c. At all events, this would lead us on to the final triumph of Christianity—to the introduction of the millennium of glory—to the period when the Son of God should reign on the earth. After that (ch. xi. 19, seq.) a new series of visions commences, disclosing, through the same periods of history, a new view of the church to the time also of its final triumph:—the church internally; the rise of Antichrist, and the effect of the rise of this formidable power. See the Analysis of the Book, part fifth.

1. *And when he had opened the seventh seal.* See Notes on ch. v. 1. ¶ *There was silence in heaven.* The whole scene of the vision is laid in heaven (ch. iv.), and John represents things as they seem to be passing there. The meaning here is, that on the opening of this seal, instead of voices, thunderings, tempests, as perhaps was expected from the character of the sixth seal (ch. vi. 12, seq.), and which seemed only to have been suspended for a time (ch. vii.), there was an awful stillness, as if all heaven was reverently waiting for the development. Of course this is a symbolical representation, and is designed not to represent a pause in the events themselves, but only the impressive and fearful nature of the events which are now to be disclosed. ¶ *About the space of half an hour.* He did not profess to

A.D. 96.] CHAPTER VIII. 191

2 And I saw the seven angels which *b*stood before God; and to them were given seven *c*trumpets.

*b* Lu.1.19.     *c* 2 Ch.29.25-28.

designate the time exactly. It was a brief period—yet a period which in such circumstances would appear to be long —*about* half an hour. The word here used—ἡμιωριον—does not occur elsewhere in the New Testament. It is correctly rendered *half an hour;* and as the day was divided into twelve parts from the rising to the setting of the sun, the time designated would not vary much from half an hour with us. Of course, therefore, this denotes a brief period. In a state, however, of anxious suspense, the moments would seem to move slowly; and to see the exact force of this, we are to reflect on the scenes represented —the successive opening of seals disclosing most important events—increasing in interest as each new one was opened; the course of events which seemed to be leading to the consummation of all things, arrested after the opening of the sixth seal; and now the last in the series to be opened, disclosing what the affairs of the world would be at the consummation of all things. John looks on this; and in this state of suspense the half hour may have seemed an age. We are not, of course, to suppose that the silence in heaven is produced by the *character* of the events which are now to follow—for they are as yet unknown. It is caused by what, from the nature of the previous disclosures, was naturally apprehended, and by the fact that this is the last of the series—the finishing of the mysterious volume. This seems to me to be the obvious interpretation of this passage, though there has been here, as in other parts of the book of Revelation, a great variety of opinion as to the meaning. Those who suppose that the whole book consists of a *triple series* of visions designed to prefigure future events, parallel with each other, and each leading to the consummation of all things—the series embracing the seals, the trumpets, and the vials, each seven in number—regard this as the proper ending of the first of this series, and suppose that we have on the opening of the seventh seal the beginning of a new symbolical representation, going over the same ground, under the representations of the trumpets, in a new aspect or point of view. Eichhorn and Rosenmüller suppose that the silence introduced by the apostle is merely for effect, and that, therefore, it is without any special signification. Grotius applies the whole representation to the destruction of Jerusalem, and supposes that the silence in heaven refers to the restraining of the winds referred to in ch. vii. 1—the wrath in respect to the city, which was now suspended for a short time. Professor Stuart also refers it to the destruction of Jerusalem, and supposes that the seven trumpets refer to seven gradations in the series of judgments that were coming upon the persecutors of the church. Mr. Daubuz regards the silence here referred to as a symbol of the liberty granted to the church in the time of Constantine; Vitringa interprets it of the peace of the millennium which is to succeed the overthrow of the beast and the false prophet; Dean Woodhouse and Mr. Cunninghame regard it as the termination of the series of events which the former seals denote, and the commencement of a new train of revelations; Mr. Elliott, as the suspension of the winds during the sealing of the servants of God; Mr. Lord, as the period of repose which intervened between the close of the persecution by Diocletian and Galerius, in 311, and the commencement, near the close of that year, of the civil wars by which Constantine the Great was elevated to the imperial throne. It will be seen at once how arbitrary and unsatisfactory most of those interpretations are, and how far from harmony expositors have been as to the meaning of this symbol. The most simple and obvious interpretation is likely to be the true one; and that is, as above suggested, that it refers to silence in heaven as expressive of the fearful anticipation felt on opening the last seal that was to close the series, and to wind up the affairs of the church and the world. Nothing would be more natural than such a state of solemn awe on such an occasion; nothing would introduce the opening of the seal in a more impressive manner; nothing would more naturally express the anxiety of the church, the probable feelings of the pious on the opening of these successive seals, than the representation that incense, accompanied with their prayers, was continually offered in heaven.

192  REVELATION.  [A.D. 96.

3 And another angel came and stood at the altar, having a golden censer; and there was given unto him much incense, that he should ¹offer *it* with the ᵈprayers of all saints upon the ᵉgolden altar which was before the throne.

¹ or, *add it to*.   d ch.5.8.   e ch.6.9.

2. *And I saw the seven angels which stood before God.* Professor Stuart supposes that by these angels are meant the "presence-angels" which he understands to be referred to, in ch. i. 4, by the "seven spirits which are before the throne." If, however, the interpretation of that passage above proposed, that it refers to the Holy Spirit, with reference to his multiplied agency and operations, be correct, then we must seek for another application of the phrase here. The only difficulty in applying it arises from the use of the article—"*the* seven angels"—τοὺς—as if they were angels already referred to; and as there has been no previous mention of "*seven* angels," unless it be in the phrase "the seven spirits which are before the throne," in ch. i. 4, it is argued that this must have been such a reference. But this interpretation is not absolutely necessary. John might use this language either because the angels had been spoken of before; or because it would be sufficiently understood, from the common use of language, who would be referred to—as we now might speak of "*the seven* members of the cabinet of the United States," or "*the* thirty-one governors of the states of the Union," though they had not been particularly mentioned; or he might speak of them as just then disclosed to his view, and because his meaning would be sufficiently definite by the circumstances which were to follow — their agency in blowing the trumpets. It would be entirely in accordance with the usage of the article for one to say that he saw an army, and *the* commander-in-chief, and *the* four staff-officers, and *the* five bands of music, and *the* six companies of sappers and miners, &c. It is not absolutely necessary, therefore, to suppose that these angels had been before referred to. There is, indeed, in the use of the phrase "which stood before God," the idea that they are to be regarded as permanently standing there, or that that is their proper place—as if they were angels who were particularly designated to this high service. Comp. Lu. i. 19: "I am Gabriel, that stand in the presence of God." If this idea is involved in the phrase, then there is a sufficient reason why the article is used, though they had not before been mentioned. ¶ *And to them were given seven trumpets.* One to each. By whom the trumpets were given is not said. It may be supposed to have been done by Him who sat on the throne. Trumpets were used then, as now, for various purposes; to summon an assembly; to muster the hosts of battle; to inspirit and animate troops in conflict. Here they are given to announce a series of important events producing great changes in the world—as if God summoned and led on his hosts to accomplish his designs.

3. *And another angel came.* Who this angel was is not mentioned, nor have we any means of determining. Of course a great variety of opinion has been entertained on the subject (see Poole's *Synopsis*)—some referring it to angels in general; others to the ministry of the church; others to Constantine; others to Michael; and many others to the Lord Jesus. All that we know is, that it was an *angel* who thus appeared, and there is nothing inconsistent in the supposition that anyone of the angels in heaven may have been appointed to perform what is here represented. The design seems to be, to represent the prayers of the saints as ascending in the anticipation of the approaching series of wonders in the world—and there would be a beautiful propriety in representing them as offered by an angel, feeling a deep interest in the church, and ministering in behalf of the saints. ¶ *And stood at the altar.* In heaven—represented as a temple, with an altar, and with the usual array of things employed in the worship of God. The altar was the appropriate place for him to stand when about to offer the prayers of the saints—for that is the place where the worshipper stood under the ancient dispensation. Comp. Notes on Mat. v. 23, 24; Lu. i. 11. In the latter place an angel is represented as appearing to Zacharias "on the right side of the altar of incense." ¶ *Having a golden censer.* The *fire-pan*, made for the purpose of carrying fire, on which to burn incense in time of worship. See it described and illustrated in the Notes on He. ix. 4. There

4 And the smoke of the *f* incense, which came with the prayers of the saints, ascended up before God out of the angel's hand.

5 And the angel took the censer,

*f* Ex.30.1.

and filled it with fire of the altar, and cast it ²into the earth: and there were *g* voices, and thunderings, and lightnings, and an *h* earthquake.

² or, *upon*. *g* ch.16.18. *h* 2 Sa.22.8.

seems reason to suppose that the incense that was offered in the ancient worship was designed to be emblematic of the prayers of saints, for it was the custom for worshippers to be engaged in prayer at the time the incense was offered by the priest. See Lu. i. 10. ¶ *And there was given unto him much incense.* See Notes on Lu. i. 9. A large quantity was here given to him, because the occasion was one on which many prayers might be expected to be offered. ¶ *That he should offer it with the prayers.* Marg., "*add it to.*" Gr., "that he should *give* it with"—δώση. The idea is plain, that, when the prayers of the saints ascended, he would also burn the incense, that it might go up at the same moment, and be emblematic of them. Comp. Notes on ch. v. 8. ¶ *Of all saints.* Of all who are holy; of all who are the children of God. The idea seems to be, that, at this time, all the saints would unite in calling on God, and in deprecating his wrath. As the events which were about to occur were a matter of common interest to the people of God, it was to be supposed that they would unite in common supplication. ¶ *Upon the golden altar.* The altar of incense. This in the tabernacle and in the temple was overlaid with gold. ¶ *Which was before the throne.* This is represented as a temple-service, and the altar of incense is, with propriety, placed before his seat or throne, as it was in the tabernacle and temple. In the temple, God is represented as occupying the mercy-seat in the holy of holies, and the altar of incense is in the holy place before that. See the description of the temple in the Notes on Mat. xxi. 12.

4. *And the smoke of the incense*, &c. The smoke caused by the burning incense. John, as he saw this, naturally interpreted it of the prayers of the saints. The meaning of the whole symbol, thus explained, is that, at the time referred to, the anxiety of the church in regard to the events which were about to occur would naturally lead to much prayer. It is not necessary to attempt to verify this by any distinct historical facts, for no one can doubt that, in a time of such impending calamities, the church would be earnestly engaged in devotion. Such has always been the case in times of danger; and it may always be assumed to be true, that when danger threatens, whether it be to the church at large or to an individual Christian, there will be a resort to the throne of grace.

5. *And the angel took the censer.* Ver. 3. This is a new symbol, designed to furnish a new representation of future events. By the former it had been shown that there would be much prayer offered; by this it is designed to show that, notwithstanding the prayer that would be offered, great and fearful calamities would come upon the earth. This is symbolized by casting the censer upon the earth, *as if* the prayers were not heard any longer, or as if prayer were now in vain. ¶ *And filled it with fire of the altar.* An image similar to this occurs in Eze. x. 2, where the man clothed in linen is commanded to go between the wheels under the cherub, and fill his hands with coals of fire from between the cherubims, and to scatter them over the city as a symbol of its destruction. Here the coals are taken, evidently, from the altar of sacrifice. Comp. Notes on Is. vi. 1. On these coals no incense was placed, but they were thrown at once to the earth. The new emblem, therefore, is the taking of coals, and scattering them abroad as a symbol of the destruction that was about to ensue. ¶ *And cast it into the earth.* Marg., *upon.* The margin expresses undoubtedly the meaning. The symbol, therefore, properly denoted that fearful calamities were about to come upon the earth. Even the prayers of saints did not prevail to turn them away, and now the symbol of the scattered coals indicated that terrible judgments were about to come upon the world. ¶ *And there were voices.* Sounds, noises. See Notes on ch. iv. 5. The *order* is not the same here as there, but lightnings, thunderings, and voices are mentioned in both.

194　　　　　　　　REVELATION.　　　　　　　[A.D. 96.

6 And the seven angels which had the seven trumpets prepared themselves to sound.

7 The first angel sounded, and *there followed hail and fire

*i* Eze. 38. 22.

¶ *And an earthquake.* Ch. vi. 12. This is a symbol of commotion. It is not necessary to look for a literal fulfilment of it, any more than it is for literal "voices," "lightnings," or "thunderings."

6. *And the seven angels which had the seven trumpets prepared themselves to sound.* Ver. 7. Evidently in succession, perhaps by arranging themselves in the order in which they were to sound. The way is now prepared for the sounding of the trumpets, and for the fearful commotions and changes which would be indicated by that. The last seal is opened; heaven stands in suspense to know what is to be disclosed; the saints, filled with solicitude, have offered their prayers; the censer of coals has been cast to the earth, as if these judgments could be no longer stayed by prayer; and the angels prepare to sound the trumpets indicative of what is to occur.

7. *The first angel sounded.* The first in order, and indicating the first in the series of events that were to follow. ¶ *And there followed hail.* Hail is usually a symbol of the divine vengeance, as it has often been employed to accomplish the divine purposes of punishment. Thus in Ex. ix. 23, "And the Lord sent thunder and hail, and the fire ran along the ground; and the Lord rained hail upon the land of Egypt." So in Ps. cv. 32, referring to the plagues upon Egypt, it is said, " He gave them hail for rain, and flaming fire in their land." So again, Ps. lxxviii. 48, " He gave up their cattle also to the hail, and their flocks to hot thunderbolts." As early as the time of Job hail was understood to be an emblem of the divine displeasure, and an instrument in inflicting punishment:

*"Hast thou entered into the treasures of the snow,
Or hast thou seen the treasure of the hail?
Which I have reserved against *the time of trouble*,
Against *the day of battle and war?*"
Job xxxviii. 22, 23.

So also the same image is used in Ps. xviii. 13:

"The Lord also thundered in the heaven,
And the Most High gave forth his voice,
Hailstones and coals of fire."

Comp. Hag., ch. ii. 17. The destruction of the Assyrian army, it is said, would be accomplished in the same way, Is. xxx. 30. Comp. Eze. xiii. 11; xxxviii. 22. ¶ *And fire.* Lightning. This also is an instrument and an emblem of destruction. ¶ *Mingled with blood.* By blood "we must naturally understand," says Professor Stuart, "in this case, a shower of coloured rain; that is, rain of a rubidinous aspect, an occurrence which is known sometimes to take place, and which, like falling stars, eclipses, &c., was viewed with terror by the ancients, because it was supposed to be indicative of blood that was to be shed." The appearance, doubtless, was that of a red shower, apparently of *hail*, or snow—for *rain* is not mentioned. It is not a *rain*-storm, it is a *hail*-storm that is the image here; and the image is that of a driving hail-storm, where the lightnings flashed, and where there was the intermingling of a reddish substance that resembled blood, and that was an undoubted symbol of blood that was to be shed. I do not know that there is red *rain*, or red *hail*, but red *snow* is not very uncommon; and the image here would be complete if we suppose that there was an intermingling of red snow in the driving tempest. This species of snow was found by Captain Ross at Baffin's Bay on the 17th of August, 1819. The mountains that were dyed with the snow were about eight miles long, and six hundred feet high. The red colour reached to the ground in many places ten or twelve feet deep, and continued for a great length of time. Although red snow had not until this attracted much notice, yet it had been long before observed in Alpine countries. Saussure discovered it on Mount St. Bernard in 1778. Ramond found it on the Pyrenees; and Summerfield discovered it in Norway. "In 1818 red snow fell on the Italian Alps and Apennines. In March, 1808, the whole country about Cadore, Belluno, and Feltri was covered with a red-coloured snow to the depth of six and a half feet; but a white snow had fallen both before and after it, the red formed a stratum in the middle of the white. At the same time a similar fall took place in the mountains of the Valteline, Brescia, Carinthia, and Tyrol" (*Edin. Encyclo.* art. "Snow"). These facts show that mingled with blood, and they were cast upon the earth: and the third part of *ᵏtrees was burnt up, and all green grass was burnt up.

k Is. 2.13.

what is referred to here in the symbol might possibly occur. Such a symbol would be properly expressive of blood and carnage. ¶ *And they were cast upon the earth.* The hail, the fire, and the blood—denoting that the fulfilment of this was to be *on the earth.* ¶ *And the third part of trees was burnt up.* By the fire that came down with the hail and the blood. ¶ *And all green grass was burnt up.* Wherever this lighted on the earth. The meaning would seem to be, that wherèver this tempest beat the effect was to destroy a third part — that is, a large portion of the *trees,* and to consume *all* the grass. A portion of the trees—strong and mighty—would stand against it; but that which was so tender as grass is, would be consumed. The sense does not seem to be that the tempest would be confined to a third part of the world, and destroy *all* the trees and the grass *there;* but that it would be a sweeping and general tempest, and that wherever it spread it would prostrate a third part of the trees and consume all the grass. Thus understood, it would seem to mean, that in reference to those things in the world which were firm and established like *trees,* it would not sweep them *wholly* away, though it would make great desolation; but in reference to those which were delicate and feeble — like grass — it would sweep them wholly away. — This would not be an inapt description of the ordinary effects of invasion in time of war. A few of those things which seem most firm and established in society—like trees in a forest—weather out the storm; while the gentle virtues, the domestic enjoyments, the arts of peace, like tender grass, are wholly destroyed. The fulfilment of this we are undoubtedly to expect to find in the terrors of invasion; the evils of war; the effusion of blood; the march of armies. So far as the language is concerned, the symbol would apply to *any* hostile invasion; but in pursuing the exposition on the principles on which we have thus far conducted it, we are to look for the fulfilment in one or more of those invasions of the northern hordes that preceded the downfall of the Roman empire and that contributed to it.—In the "Analysis" of the chapter, some reasons were given why these four trumpet signals were placed together, as pertaining to a series of events of the same general character, and as distinguished from those which were to follow. The natural place which they occupy, or the events which we should suppose, from the views taken above of the first six seals, would be represented, would be the successive invasions of the northern hordes which ultimately accomplished the overthrow of the Roman empire. There are *four* of these "trumpets," and it would be a matter of inquiry whether there were *four* events of sufficient distinctness that would mark these invasions, or that would constitute *periods* or *epochs* in the destruction of the Roman power. At this point in writing, I looked on a chart of history, composed without any reference to this prophecy, and found a singular and unexpected prominence given to *four* such events extending from the first invasion of the Goths and Vandals at the beginning of the fifth century, to the fall of the Western empire, A.D. 476. The first was the invasion of Alaric, king of the Goths, A.D. 410; the second was the invasion of Attila, king of the Huns, "scourge of God," A.D. 447; a third was the sack of Rome by Genseric, king of the Vandals, A.D. 455; and the fourth, resulting in the final conquest of Rome, was that of Odoacer, king of the Heruli, who assumed the title of King of Italy, A.D. 476. We shall see, however, on a closer examination, that although two of these—Attila and Genseric — were, during a part of their career, contemporary, yet the most prominent place is due to Genseric in the events that attended the downfall of the empire, and that the second trumpet probably related to him; the third to Attila. These were, beyond doubt, four great periods or events attending the fall of the Roman empire, which synchronize with the period before us. If, therefore, we regard the opening of the sixth seal as denoting the threatening aspect of these invading powers—the gathering of the dark cloud that hovered over the borders of the empire, and the consternation produced by that approaching storm; and if we regard the transactions in the seventh chapter —the holding of the winds in check, and the sealing of the chosen of God— as denoting the *suspension* of the impending judgments in order that a work might be done to save the church, and as referring to the divine interposition in behalf of the church; then the appropriate place of these four trumpets, under the seventh seal, will be when that delayed and restrained storm burst in successive blasts upon different parts of the empire—the successive invasions which were so prominent in the overthrow of that vast power. History marks four of these events—four heavy blows—four sweepings of the tempest and the storm—under Alaric, Genseric, Attila, and Odoacer, whose movements could not be better symbolized than by these successive blasts of the trumpet.

The first of these is the invasion of Alaric; and the inquiry now is, whether his invasion is such as would be properly symbolized by the first trumpet. In illustrating this, it will be proper to notice some of the movements of Alaric, and the alarm consequent on his invasion of the empire; and then to inquire how far this corresponds with the images employed in the description of the first trumpet. For these illustrations I shall be indebted mainly to Mr. Gibbon. Alaric, the Goth, was at first employed in the service of the emperor Theodosius, in his attempt to oppose the usurper Arbogastes, after the murder of Valentinian, emperor of the West. Theodosius, in order to oppose the usurper, employed, among others, numerous barbarians—Iberians, Arabs, and Goths. One of them was Alaric, who, to use the language of Mr. Gibbon (ii. 179), "acquired in the school of Theodosius the knowledge of the art of war, which he afterwards so fatally exerted for the destruction of Rome," A.D. 392-394. After the death of Theodosius (A.D. 395) the Goths revolted from the Roman power, and Alaric, who had been disappointed in his expectations of being raised to the command of the Roman armies, became their leader (*Decline and Fall*, ii. 213). "That renowned leader was descended from the noble race of the Balti; which yielded only to the royal dignity of the Amali; he had solicited the command of the Roman armies; and the imperial court provoked him to demonstrate the folly of their refusal, and the importance of their loss. In the midst of a divided court and a discontented people the emperor Arcadius was terrified by the aspect of the Gothic arms," &c. Alaric then invaded and conquered Greece, laying it waste in his progress, until he reached Athens, ii. 214, 215. "The fertile fields of Phocis and Bœotia were instantly covered by a deluge of barbarians, who massacred the males of age to bear arms, and drove away the beautiful females, with the spoil and cattle of the flaming villages." Alaric then concluded a treaty with Theodosius, the emperor of the East (ii. 216); was made master-general of Eastern Illyricum, and created a magistrate (ii. 217); soon united under his command the barbarous nations that had made the invasion, and was solemnly declared to be the king of the Visigoths, ii. 217. "Armed with this double power, seated on the verge of two empires, he alternately sold his deceitful promises to the courts of Arcadius and Honorius, till he declared and executed his purpose of invading the dominions of the West. The provinces of Europe which belonged to the Eastern empire were already exhausted; those of Asia were inaccessible; and the strength of Constantinople had resisted his attack. But he was tempted by the beauty, the wealth, and the fame of Italy, which he had twice visited; and he secretly aspired to plant the Gothic standard on the walls of Rome; and to enrich his army with the accumulated spoils of three hundred triumphs," ii. 217, 218. In describing his march to the Danube, and his progress towards Italy, having increased his army with a large number of barbarians, Mr. Gibbon uses the remarkable language expressive of the general consternation, already quoted in the description of the sixth seal. Alaric approached rapidly towards the imperial city, resolved to "conquer or die before the gates of Rome." But he was checked by Stilicho, and compelled to make peace, and retired (*Decline and Fall*, ii. 222), and the threatening storm was for a time suspended. See Notes on ch. vii. 1, seq. So great was the consternation, however, that the Roman court, which then had its seat at Milan, thought it necessary to remove to a safer place, and became fixed at Ravenna, ii. 224. This calm, secured by the retreat of Alaric, was, however, of short continuance. In A.D. 408 he again invaded Italy in a more successful manner, attacked the capital, and more than once pillaged Rome. The following facts, for which I am indebted to Mr. Gibbon, will illustrate the progress of the events, and the effects of this blast of the "first trumpet" in the series that announced the destruction of the Western empire:—

(a) The effect, on the destiny of the empire, of removing the Roman court to Ravenna from the dread of the Goths. As early as A.D. 303 the court of the emperor of the West was, for the most part, established at Milan. For some time before, the "sovereignty of the capital was gradually annihilated by the extent of conquest," and the emperors were required to be long absent from Rome on the frontiers, until in the time of Diocletian and Maximian the seat of government was fixed at Milan, "whose situation at the foot of the Alps appeared far more convenient than that of Rome for the important purpose of watching the motions of the barbarians of Germany" (Gibbon, i. 213). "The life of Diocletian and Maximian was a life of action, and a considerable portion of it was spent in camps, or in their long and frequent marches; but whenever the public business allowed them any relaxation, they seem to have retired with pleasure to their favourite residences of Nicomedia and Milan. Till Diocletian, in the twentieth year of his reign, celebrated his Roman triumph, it is extremely doubtful whether he ever visited the ancient capital of the empire" (Gibbon, i. 214). From this place the court was driven away, by the dread of the northern barbarians, to Ravenna, a safer place, which thenceforward became the seat of government, while Italy was ravaged by the northern hordes, and while Rome was besieged and pillaged. Mr. Gibbon, under date of A.D. 404, says, "The recent danger to which the person of the emperor had been exposed in the defenceless palace of Milan [from Alaric and the Goths] urged him to seek a retreat in some inaccessible fortress in Italy, where he might securely remain, while the open country was covered by a deluge of barbarians" (vol. ii. p. 224). He then proceeds to describe the situation of Ravenna, and the removal of the court thither, and then adds (p. 225), "The fears of Honorius were not without foundation, nor were his precautions without effect. While Italy rejoiced in her deliverance from the Goths, a furious tempest was excited among the nations of Germany, who yielded to the irresistible impulse that appears to have been gradually communicated from the eastern extremity of the continent of Asia." That mighty movement of the Huns is then described, as the storm was preparing to burst upon the Roman empire, ii. 225. The agitation and the removal of the Roman government were events not inappropriate to be described by symbols relating to the fall of that mighty power.

(b) The particulars of that invasion, the consternation, the siege of Rome, and the capture and pillage of the imperial city, would confirm the propriety of this application to the symbol of the first trumpet. It would be too long to copy the account — for it extends through many pages of the *History of the Decline and Fall of the Empire;* but a few selected sentences may show the general character of the events, and the propriety of the symbols, on the supposition that they referred to these things. Thus Mr. Gibbon (ii. 226, 227) says, "The correspondence of nations was, in that age, so imperfect and precarious, that the revolutions of the North might escape the knowledge of the court of Ravenna, till the dark cloud which was collected along the coast of the Baltic burst in thunder upon the banks of the Upper Danube. The king of the confederate Germans passed, without resistance, the Alps, the Po, and the Apennines; leaving on the one hand the inaccessible palace of Honorius securely buried among the marshes of Ravenna, and on the other the camp of Stilicho, who had fixed his head-quarters at Ticinum, or Pavia, but who seems to have avoided a decisive battle till he had assembled his distant forces. Many cities of Italy were pillaged or destroyed. The senate and people trembled at their approach within a hundred and eighty miles of Rome; and anxiously compared the danger which they had escaped with the new perils to which they were exposed,"&c. Rome was besieged for the first time by the Goths A.D. 408. Of this siege Mr. Gibbon (ii. 252-254) has given a graphic description. Among other things, he says, "That unfortunate city gradually experienced the distress of scarcity, and at length the horrid calamities of famine." "A dark suspicion was entertained, that some desperate wretches fed on the bodies of their fellow-creatures whom they had secretly murdered; and even mothers —such were the horrid conflicts of the two most powerful instincts implanted by nature in the human breast—even mothers are said to have tasted the flesh of their slaughtered infants. Many thousands of the inhabitants of Rome expired in their houses, or in the streets, for want of sustenance; and as the public sepulchres without the walls were in the power of the enemy, the stench which arose from so many putrid and unburied carcasses infected the air; and the miseries of famine were succeeded and aggravated by a pestilential disease." The first siege was raised by the payment of an enormous ransom (Gibbon, ii. 254). The second siege of Rome by the Goths occurred A.D. 409. *This* siege was carried on by preventing the supply of provisions, Alaric having seized upon *Ostia*, the Roman port, where the provisions for the capital were deposited. The Romans finally consented to receive a new emperor at the hand of Alaric, and Attalus was appointed in the place of the feeble Honorius, who was then at Ravenna, and who had abandoned the capital. Attalus, an inefficient prince, was soon publicly stripped of the robes of office, and Alaric, enraged at the conduct of the court at Ravenna towards him, turned his wrath a third time on Rome, and laid siege to the city. This occurred A.D. 410. "The king of the Goths, who no longer dissembled his appetite for plunder and revenge, appeared in arms under the walls of the capital; and the trembling senate, without any hope of relief, prepared, by a desperate effort, to delay the ruin of their country. But they were unable to guard against the conspiracy of their slaves and domestics, who, either from birth or interest, were attached to the cause of the enemy. At the hour of midnight the Salarian Gate was silently opened, and the inhabitants were awakened by the tremendous sound of the Gothic trumpet. Eleven hundred and sixty-three years after the foundation of Rome, the imperial city, which had subdued and civilized so considerable a part of mankind, was delivered to the licentious fury of the tribes of Germany and Scythia" (Gibbon, ii. 260).

(c) It is, perhaps, only necessary to add that the invasion of Alaric was in fact but *one* of the great events that led to the fall of the empire, and that, in announcing that fall, where a succession of events was to occur, it would properly be represented by the blast of one of the trumpets. The expressions employed in the symbol are, indeed, such as might be applied to *any* invasion of hostile armies, but they are such as *would* be used if the design were admitted to be to describe the invasion of the Gothic conqueror. For (1) that invasion, as we have seen, would be well represented by the storm of hail and lightning that was seen in vision; (2) by the *red* colour mingled in that storm —indicative of blood; (3) by the fact that it consumed the trees and the grass. This, as we saw in the exposition, would properly denote the desolation produced by war—applicable, indeed, to *all* war, but *as* applicable to the invasion of Alaric as *any* war that has occurred, and it is such an emblem as would be used if it were admitted that it was the design to represent his invasion. The sweeping storm, prostrating the trees of the forest, is an apt emblem of the evils of war, and, as was remarked in the exposition, no more striking illustration of the consequences of a hostile invasion could be employed than the destruction of the "green grass." What is here represented in the symbol cannot, perhaps, be better expressed than in the language of Mr. Gibbon, when describing the invasion of the Roman empire under Alaric. Speaking of that invasion, he says—"While the peace of Germany was secured by the attachment of the Franks and the neutrality of the Alemanni, the subjects of Rome, unconscious of their approaching calamities, enjoyed the state of quiet and prosperity which had seldom blessed the frontiers of Gaul. Their flocks and herds were permitted to graze in the pastures of the barbarians; their huntsmen penetrated, without fear or danger, into the darkest recesses of the Hercynian wood. The banks of the Rhine were crowned, like those of the Tiber, with elegant houses and well-cultivated farms; and if a poet descended the river, he might express his doubt on which side was situated the territory of the Romans. This scene of peace and plenty was suddenly changed into a desert; and the prospect of the smoking ruins could alone distinguish the solitude of nature from the desolation of man. The flourishing city of Mentz was surprised and destroyed; and many thousand Christians were inhumanly massacred in the church. Worms perished after a long and obstinate siege; Strasburg, Spires, Rheims,

**8 And the second angel sounded, and as it were a great *l* mountain burning with fire was *m* cast into the sea: and the third part of the sea *n* became blood;**

*l* Je.51.25.   *m* Am.7.4.   *n* ch.16.3,&c.; Ex.7.19-21.

Tournay, Arras, Amiens, experienced the cruel oppression of the German yoke; and the consuming flames of war spread from the banks of the Rhine over the greatest part of the seventeen provinces of Gaul. That rich and extensive country, as far as the ocean, the Alps, and the Pyrenees, was delivered to the barbarians, who drove before them, in a promiscuous crowd, the bishop, the senator, and the virgin, laden with the spoils of their houses and altars,'' ii. 230. In reference, also, to the invasion of Alaric, and the particular nature of the desolation depicted under the first trumpet, a remarkable passage which Mr. Gibbon has quoted from Claudian, as describing the effects of the invasion of Alaric, may be here introduced. "The *old* man," says he, speaking of Claudian, "who had passed his simple and innocent life in the neighbourhood of Verona, was a stranger to the quarrels both of kings and of bishops; *his* pleasures, his desires, his knowledge, were confined within the little circle of his paternal farm; and a staff supported his aged steps on the same ground where he had sported in infancy. Yet even this humble and rustic felicity (which Claudian describes with so much truth and feeling) was still exposed to the undistinguishing rage of war. His trees, his old *contemporary*\* trees, must blaze in the conflagration of the whole country; a detachment of Gothic cavalry must sweep away his cottage and his family; and the power of Alaric could destroy that happiness which he was not able either to taste or to bestow. 'Fame,' says the poet, 'encircling with terror or gloomy wings, proclaimed the march of the barbarian army, and filled Italy with consternation,'" ii. 218. And (4) as to the *extent* of the calamity, there is also a striking propriety in the language of the symbol as applicable to the invasion of Alaric. I do not suppose, indeed, that it is necessary, in order to find a proper fulfilment of the symbol, to be able to show that exactly one-third part of the empire was made desolate in this way; but it is a sufficient fulfilment if desolation spread over a considerable portion of the Roman world—*as if* a third part had been destroyed. No one who reads the account of the invasion of Alaric can doubt that it would be an apt description of the ravages of his arms to say that a third part was laid waste. That the desolations produced by Alaric were such as would be *properly* represented by this symbol may be fully seen by consulting the whole account of that invasion in Gibbon, ii. 213-266.

8. *And the second angel sounded.* Comp. Notes on ver. 2-7. This, according to the interpretation proposed above, refers to the second of the four great events which contributed to the downfall of the Roman empire. It will be proper in this case, as in the former, to inquire into the literal meaning of the symbol, and then whether there was any event that corresponded with it. ¶ *And as it were a great mountain.* A *mountain* is a natural symbol of strength, and hence becomes a symbol of a strong and powerful kingdom; for mountains are not only places of strength in themselves, but they anciently answered the purposes of fortified places, and were the seats of power. Hence they are properly symbols of strong nations. "The stone that smote the image became *a great mountain*, and filled the whole earth," Da. ii. 35. Comp. Zec. iv. 7; Je. li. 25. We naturally, then, apply this part of the symbol to some strong and mighty nation—not a nation, necessarily, that issued *from* a mountainous region, but a nation that in strength *resembled* a mountain. ¶ *Burning with fire.* A mountain in a blaze; that is, with all its woods on fire, or, more probably, a *volcanic* mountain. There would perhaps be no more sublime image than such a mountain lifted suddenly from its base and thrown into the sea. One of the sublimest parts of the *Paradise Lost* is that where the poet represents the angels in the great battle in heaven as lifting the mountains—tearing them from their base—and hurling them on the foe:—

"From their foundations heaving to and fro,
They plucked the seated hills, with all their load,
Rocks, waters, woods, and by the shaggy tops
Uplifting, bore them in their hands," &c.
Book vi.

\* Ingentem meminit parvo qui germine quercum
Æquævumque videt consenuisse nemus.
A neighbouring wood born with himself he sees
And loves his old contemporary trees.—COWLEY.

9 And the third part of the creatures which were in the sea, and had life, died; and the third part of the ships were destroyed.

The poet, however, has not, as John has, represented a volcano borne along and cast into the sea. The symbol employed here would denote some fiery, impetuous, destructive power. If used to denote a nation, it would be a nation that was, as it were, burning with the desire of conquest—impetuous, and fierce, and fiery in its assaults—and consuming all in its way. ¶ *Cast into the sea.* The image is very sublime; the scene, should such an event occur, would be awfully grand. As to the fulfilment of this, or the thing that was intended to be represented by it, there cannot be any material doubt. It is not to be understood literally, of course; and the natural application is to some *nation*, or *army*, that has a resemblance in some respects to such a blazing mountain, and the effect of whose march would be like casting such a mountain into the ocean. We naturally look for agitation and commotion, and particularly in reference to the sea, or to some maritime coasts. It is undoubtedly required in the application of this, that we should find its fulfilment in some country lying beyond the sea, or in some sea-coast or maritime country, or in reference to commerce. ¶ *And the third part of the sea became blood.* Resembled blood; became *as red as blood.* The figure here is, that as such a blazing mountain cast into the sea would, by its reflection on the waters, seem to tinge them with red, so there would be something corresponding with this in what was referred to by the symbol. It would be fulfilled if there was a fierce maritime warfare, and if in some desperate naval engagement the sea should be tinged with blood.

9. *And the third part of the creatures which were in the sea, and had life, died.* The effect was *as if* one-third of all the fish in the sea were cut off. Of course this is not to be taken literally. It is designed to describe an effect, pertaining to the maritime portion of the world, *as if* a third portion of all that was in the sea should perish. The *natural* interpretation would be to apply it to some invasion or calamity pertaining to the sea—to the islands, to the maritime regions, or to commerce. If the whole description pertains to the Roman empire, then this might be supposed to have particular reference to something that would have a bearing on the maritime parts of that empire. ¶ *And the third part of the ships were destroyed.* This also pertains to the same general calamity, affecting the *commerce* of the empire. The destruction of the "ships" was produced, in some way, by casting the mountain into the sea—either by their being consumed by the contact with the burning mass, or by being sunk by the agitation of the waters. The essential idea is, that the calamity would be of such a nature as would produce the destruction of vessels at sea—either naval armaments, or ships of commerce. In looking now for the application or fulfilment of this, it is necessary (*a*) to find some event or events which would have a particular bearing on the maritime or commercial part of the world; and (*b*) some such event or events that, on the supposition that they were the things referred to, would be properly symbolized by the image here employed. (1) If the first trumpet had reference to the invasion of Alaric and the Goths, then in this we naturally look for the next succeeding act of invasion which shook the Roman empire, and contributed to its fall. (2) The next invasion was that under Genseric, at the head of the Vandals (Gibbon, ii. 306, seq.). This occurred A.D. 428-468. (3) The symbol of a blazing or burning mountain, torn from its foundation, and precipitated into the ocean, would well represent this mighty nation moved from its ancient seat, and borne along towards the maritime parts of the empire, and its desolations there—as will be shown in the following remarks. (4) The acts of the Vandals, under Genseric, corresponded with the ideas expressed by the symbol. In illustrating this I shall be indebted, as heretofore, principally to Mr. Gibbon. (*a*) His general account of the Vandals is this: they are supposed (i. 138) to have been originally the same people with the Goths, the Goths and Vandals constituting one great nation living on the shores of the Baltic. They passed in connection with them over the Baltic; emigrated to Prussia and the Ukraine; invaded the Roman provinces; received tribute from the Romans; subdued the countries about the Bosphorus; plundered the cities of Bithynia; ravaged Greece and

Illyrium, and were at last settled in Thrace under the emperor Theodosius (Gibbon, i. 136-166; ii. 110-150). They were then driven forward by the Huns, and having passed through France and Spain into Africa, conquered the Carthaginian territory, established an independent government, and thence through a long period harassed the neighbouring islands, and the coasts of the Mediterranean by their predatory incursions, destroying the ships and the commerce of the Romans, and were distinguished in the downfall of the empire by their ravages on the islands and the sea. Thus they were moved along from place to place until the scene of their desolations became more distinctly in the maritime parts of the empire; and the effect of their devastations might be well compared with a burning mountain moved from its ancient base, and then thrown into the sea. (*b*) This will be apparent from the statements of Mr. Gibbon in regard to their ravages under their leader Genseric. "Seville and Carthagena became the reward, or rather the prey of the ferocious conquerors" [after they had defeated the Roman Castinus], "and the vessels which they found in the harbour of Carthagena might easily transport them to the isles of Majorca and Minorca, where the Spanish fugitives, as in a secure recess, had vainly concealed their families and fortunes. The experience of navigation, and perhaps the prospect of Africa, encouraged the Vandals to accept the invitation which they received from Count Boniface" [to aid him in his apprehended difficulties with Rome, and to enter into an alliance with him by settling permanently in Africa (Gibbon, ii. 305, 306)]: "and the death of Gonderic" [the Vandal king] "served only to forward and animate the bold enterprise. In the room of a prince, not conspicuous for any superior powers of the mind or body, they acquired his bastard brother, the terrible Genseric—*a name which, in the destruction of the Roman empire, has deserved an equal rank with the names of Alaric and Attila.*" "The ambition of Genseric was almost without bounds, and without scruples; and the warrior could dexterously employ the dark engines of policy to solicit the allies who might be useful to his success, or to scatter among his enemies the seeds of enmity and contention. Almost in the moment of his departure he was informed that Hermanric, king of the Suevi, had presumed to ravage the Spanish territories, which he was resolved to abandon. Impatient of the insult, Genseric pursued the hasty retreat of the Suevi as far as Merida; precipitated the king and his army into the river Anas, and calmly returned to the sea-shore to embark his troops. The vessels which transported the Vandals over the modern Straits of Gibraltar, a channel only twelve miles in breadth, were furnished by the Spaniards, who anxiously wished for their departure; and by the African general who had implored their formidable assistance" (Gibbon, ii. 306. Genseric, in the accomplishment of *his* purposes, soon took possession of the northern coast of Africa, defeating the armies of Boniface, and "Carthage, Cirta, and Hippo Regius were the only cities that appeared to rise above the general inundation" (Gibbon, ii. 308). "On a sudden," says Mr. Gibbon (ii. 309), "the seven fruitful provinces, from Tangier to Tripoli, were overwhelmed by the invasion of the Vandals; whose destructive rage has perhaps been exaggerated by popular animosity, religious zeal, and extravagant declamation. War in its fairest form implies a perpetual violation of humanity and justice; and the hostilities of barbarians are inflamed by the fierce and lawless spirit which perpetually disturbs their peaceful and domestic society. The Vandals, where they found resistance, seldom gave quarter; and the deaths of their valiant countrymen were expiated by the ruin of the cities under whose walls they had fallen," &c. The result of the invasion was the conquest of all northern Africa; the reduction of Hippo and Carthage, and the establishment of a government under Genseric in Africa that waged a long war with Rome (Gibbon, ii. 310, 311). The symbol before us has particular reference to *maritime* or *naval* operations and desolations, and the following extracts from Mr. Gibbon will show with what propriety, if this symbol was designed to refer to him, these images were employed. "The discovery and conquest of the black nations [in Africa] that might dwell beneath the torrid zone could not tempt the rational ambition of Genseric; but he cast his eyes *towards the sea;* he resolved to create a naval power, and his bold resolution was executed with steady and active perseverance. The woods of Mount Atlas afforded an inexhaustible supply of timber; his new subjects were skilled in the arts of navigation and ship-building; he animated his daring Vandals to embrace a mode of warfare which would render every maritime country accessible to their arms; the Moors and Africans were allured by the hope of plunder; and after an interval of six centuries the fleets that issued from the port of Carthage again claimed the empire of the Mediterranean. The success of the Vandals, the conquest of Sicily, the sack of Palermo, and the frequent descents on the coasts of Lucania, awakened and alarmed the mother of Valentinian and the sister of Theodosius. Alliances were formed; and armaments, expensive and ineffectual, were prepared for the destruction of the common enemy, who reserved his courage to encounter those dangers which his policy could not prevent or elude. The revolutions of the palace, which left the Western empire without a defender and without a lawful prince, dispelled the apprehension and stimulated the avarice of Genseric. He immediately equipped a numerous fleet of Vandals and Moors, and cast anchor at the mouth of the Tiber," &c. (Gibbon, ii. 352). "On the third day after the tumult [A.D. 455, on the death of Maximus] Genseric boldly advanced from the port of Ostia to the gates of the defenceless city. Instead of a sally of the Roman youth, there issued from the gates an unarmed and venerable procession of the bishop at the head of the clergy. But Rome and its inhabitants were delivered to the licentiousness of the Vandals and the Moors, whose blind passions revenged the injuries of Carthage. The pillage lasted fourteen days and nights; and all that yet remained of public or private wealth, of sacred or profane treasure, was diligently transported to the vessels of Genseric," &c. See the account of this pillage in Gibbon, ii. 355-366. The emperor Majorian (A.D. 457) endeavoured to "restore the happiness of the Romans," but he encountered the arms of Genseric, from his character and situation their most formidable enemy. A fleet of Vandals and Moors landed at the mouth of the Liris, or Garigliano; but the imperial troops surprised and attacked the disorderly barbarians, who were encumbered with the spoils of Campania; they were chased with slaughter to their ships; and their leader, the king's brother-in-law, was found in the number of the slain. Such vigilance might announce the character of the new reign; but the strictest vigilance, and the most numerous forces, were insufficient to protect the long-extended coast of Italy from the depredations of a naval war" (Gibbon, ii. 363). "The emperor had foreseen that it was impossible, without a maritime power, to achieve the conquest of Africa. In the first Punic war the republic had exerted such incredible diligence, that within sixty days after the first stroke of the axe had been given in the forest a fleet of one hundred and sixty galleys proudly rode at anchor in the sea. Under circumstances much less favourable Majorian equalled the spirit and perseverance of the ancient Romans. The woods of the Apennines were felled, the arsenals and manufactures of Ravenna and Misenium were restored, Italy and Gaul vied with each other in liberal contributions to the public service; and the imperial navy of three hundred large galleys, with an adequate proportion of transports and smaller vessels, was collected in the secure and capacious harbour of Carthagena in Spain" (Gibbon, ii. 363, 364). The fate of this large navy is thus described by Mr. Gibbon:—"Genseric was saved from impending and inevitable ruin by the treachery of some powerful subjects; envious or apprehensive of their master's success. Guided by their secret intelligence, he surprised the unguarded fleet in the bay of Carthagena; many of the ships were sunk, or taken, or burnt; and the preparations of three years were destroyed in a single day," ii. 364. The farther naval operations and maritime depredations of the Vandals under Genseric are thus stated by Mr. Gibbon:— "The kingdom of Italy, a name to which the Western empire was gradually reduced, was afflicted, under the reign of Ricimer, by the incessant depredations of Vandal pirates. In the spring of each year they equipped a formidable navy in the port of Carthage; and Genseric himself, though in very advanced age, still commanded in person the most important expeditions. His designs were concealed with impenetrable secrecy till the moment that he hoisted sail. When he was asked by the pilot what course he should steer—'Leave the determination to the winds,' replied the barbarian, with pious

**A.D. 96.]** **CHAPTER VIII.** **203**

10 And the third angel sounded, and there °fell a great star from heaven, burning as it were a lamp, and it fell upon the third part of the rivers, and upon the fountains of waters:

*o* ch.9.1; Is.14.12.

arrogance; '*they* will transport us to the guilty coast whose inhabitants have provoked the divine justice;' but if Genseric himself deigned to issue more precise orders, he judged the most wealthy to be the most criminal. The Vandals repeatedly visited the coasts of Spain, Liguria, Tuscany, Campania, Lucania, Bruttium, Apulia, Calabria, Venetia, Dalmatia, Epirus, Greece, and Sicily; they were tempted to subdue the island of Sardinia, so advantageously placed in the centre of the Mediterranean; and their arms spread desolation, or terror, from the Columns of Hercules to the mouth of the Nile. As they were more ambitious of spoil than of glory, they seldom attacked any fortified cities, or engaged any regular troops in the open field. But the celerity of their motions enabled them, almost at the same time, to threaten and to attack the most distant objects which attracted their desires; and as they always embarked a sufficient number of horses, they had no sooner landed than they swept the dismayed country with a body of light cavalry," ii. 366. How far this description agrees with the symbol in the passage before us—"a great mountain burning with fire cast into the sea;" "the third part of the ships were destroyed"—must be left to the reader to judge. It may be asked, however, with at least some show of reason, whether, if it be admitted that it was the *design* of the author of the book of Revelation to refer to the movements of the Vandals under Genseric as one of the important and immediate causes of the ruin of the Roman empire, he could have found a more expressive symbol than this? Indeed, is there now any symbol that would be more striking and appropriate? If one should now undertake to represent this as one of the causes of the downfall of the empire *by a symbol*, could he easily find one that would be more expressive? It is a matter that is in itself perhaps of no importance, but it may serve to show that the interpretation respecting the second trumpet was not *forced*, to remark that I had gone through with the interpretation of the *language* of the symbol before I looked into Mr. Gibbon with any reference to the application.

10. *And the third angel sounded.* Indicating, according to the interpretation above proposed, some important event in the downfall of the Roman empire. ¶ *And there fell a great star from heaven.* A *star* is a natural emblem of a prince, of a ruler, of one distinguished by rank or by talent. Comp. Notes on ch. ii. 28. See Nu. xxiv. 17, and the Notes on Is. xiv. 12. A star falling from heaven would be a natural symbol of one who had left a higher station, or of one whose character and course would be like a meteor shooting through the sky. ¶ *Burning as it were a lamp.* Or, as a torch. The language here is such as would describe a meteor blazing through the air; and the reference in the symbol is to something that would have a *resemblance* to such a meteor. It is not a *lurid* meteor (livid, pale, ghastly) that is here referred to, but a bright, intense, blazing star—emblem of fiery energy; of rapidity of movement and execution; of splendour of appearance—such as a chieftain of high endowments, of impetuousness of character, and of richness of apparel, would be. In all languages, probably, a *star* has been an emblem of a prince whose virtues have shone brightly, and who has exerted a beneficial influence on mankind. In all languages also, probably, a meteor flaming through the sky has been an emblem of some splendid genius causing or threatening desolation and ruin; of a warrior who has moved along in a brilliant but destructive path over the world; and who has been regarded as sent to execute the vengeance of heaven. This usage occurs because a meteor is so bright; because it appears so suddenly; because its course cannot be determined by any known laws; and because, in the apprehensions of men, it is either sent as a proof of the divine displeasure, or is adapted to excite consternation and alarm. In the application of this part of the symbol, therefore, we naturally look for some prince or warrior of brilliant talents, who appears suddenly and sweeps rapidly over the world; who excites consternation and alarm; whose path is marked by desolation, and who is regarded as sent from heaven to execute the divine purposes—who comes not to bless the world by brilliant tal-

11 And the name of the star is called *p* Wormwood: and the third part of the *q* waters became wormwood; and many men died of the waters, because they were made bitter.

*p* De.29.18; Am.5.7; He.12.15.
*q* Ex.15.23; Jer.9.15; 23.15.

ents well directed, but to execute vengeance on mankind. ¶ *And it fell upon the third part of the rivers, and upon the fountains of waters.* On the phrase, "the third part," see Notes on ver. 7. This reference to the "rivers" and to the "fountains of waters" seems, in part, to be for the purpose of saying that *everything* would be affected by this series of judgments. In the previous visions the trees and the green grass, the sea and the ships, had been referred to. The rivers and the fountains of waters are not less important than the trees, the grass, and the commerce of the world, and hence this judgment is mentioned as particularly bearing on them. At the same time, as in the case of the other trumpets, there is a propriety in supposing that there would be something in the event referred to by the symbol which would make it more appropriate to use this symbol in this case than in the others. It is natural, therefore, to look for some desolations that would particularly affect the portions of the world where rivers abound, or where they take their rise; or, if it be understood as having a more metaphorical sense, to regard it as affecting those things which *resemble* rivers and fountains—the sources of influence; the morals, the religion of a people, the institutions of a country, which are often so appropriately compared with running fountains or flowing streams.

11. *And the name of the star is called Wormwood.* Is *appropriately* so called. The writer does not say that it would be *actually* so called, but that this name would be properly descriptive of its qualities. Such expressions are common in allegorical writings. The Greek word —ἄψινθος—denotes *wormwood*, a well-known bitter herb. That word becomes the proper emblem of bitterness. Comp. Je. ix. 15; xxiii. 15; La. iii. 15, 19. ¶ *And the third part of the waters became wormwood.* Became bitter as wormwood. This is doubtless an emblem of the calamity which *would* occur if the waters should be thus made bitter. Of course they would become useless for the purposes to which they are mostly applied, and the destruction of life would be inevitable. To conceive of the extent of such a calamity we have only to imagine a large portion of the wells, and rivers, and fountains of a country made bitter as wormwood. Comp. Ex. xv. 23, 24. ¶ *And many men died of the waters, because they were made bitter.* This effect would naturally follow if any considerable portion of the fountains and streams of a land were changed by an infusion of wormwood. It is not necessary to suppose that this is intended to be *literally* true; for as, by the use of a symbol, it is not to be supposed that literally a part of the waters would be turned into wormwood by the baleful influence of a falling meteor, so it is not necessary to suppose that there is intended to be represented a literal destruction of human life by the use of waters. Great destruction and devastation are undoubtedly intended to be denoted by this—destruction that would be well represented in a land by the natural effects if a considerable part of the waters were, by their bitterness, made unfit to drink.

In the interpretation and application, therefore, of this passage, we may adopt the following principles and rules:—(*a*) It may be assumed, in *this* exposition, that the previous symbols, under the first and second trumpet-blasts, referred respectively to Alaric and his Goths, and to Genseric and his Vandals. (*b*) That the next great and decisive event in the downfall of the empire is the one that is here referred to. (*c*) That there would be some chieftain or warrior who might be compared with a blazing meteor; whose course would be singularly brilliant; who would appear suddenly *like* a blazing star, and then disappear like a star whose light was quenched in the waters. (*d*) That the desolating course of that meteor would be mainly on those portions of the world that abounded with springs of water and running streams. (*e*) That an effect would be produced *as if* those streams and fountains were made bitter; that is, that many persons would perish, and that wide desolations would be caused in the vicinity of those rivers and streams, *as if* a bitter and baleful star should fall into the waters, and death should spread over the lands adjacent to them, and watered by them.

Whether any events occurred of which this would be the proper emblem is now the question. Among expositors there has been a considerable degree of unanimity in supposing that Attila, the king of the Huns, is referred to; and if the preceding expositions are correct, there can be no doubt on the subject. After Alaric and Genseric, Attila occupies the next place as an important agent in the overthrow of the Roman empire, and the only question is, whether *he* would be properly symbolized by this baleful star. The following remarks may be made to show the propriety of the symbol:—(1) As already remarked, the *place* which he occupies in history, as immediately succeeding Alaric and Genseric in the downfall of the empire. This will appear in any chronological table, or in the table of contents of any of the histories of those times. A full detail of the career of Attila may be found in Gibbon, vol. ii. pp. 314-351. His career extended from A.D. 433 to A.D. 453. It is true that he was contemporary with Genseric, king of the Vandals, and that a portion of the operations of Genseric in Africa were subsequent to the death of Attila (A.D. 455—A.D. 467); but it is *also* true that Genseric *preceded* Attila in the career of conquest, and was properly the first in order, being pressed forward in the Roman warfare by the Huns, A.D. 428. See Gibbon, ii. 306, seq. (2) In the manner of his appearance he strongly resembled a brilliant meteor flashing in the sky. He came from the east, gathering his Huns, and poured them down, as we shall see, with the rapidity of a flashing meteor, suddenly on the empire. He regarded himself also as devoted to Mars, the god of war, and was accustomed to array himself in a peculiarly brilliant manner, so that his appearance, in the language of his flatterers, was such as to dazzle the eyes of beholders. One of his followers perceived that a heifer that was grazing had wounded her foot, and curiously followed the track of blood, till he found in the long grass the point of an ancient sword, which he dug out of the ground and presented to Attila. "That magnanimous, or rather that artful prince," says Mr. Gibbon, "accepted with pious gratitude this celestial favour; and, as the rightful possessor of *the sword of Mars*, asserted his divine and indefeasible claim to the dominion of the earth. The favourite of Mars soon acquired a sacred character, which rendered his conquests more easy and more permanent; and the barbarian princes confessed, in the language of devotion or flattery, that they could not presume to gaze, with a steady eye, on the divine majesty of the king of the Huns," ii. 317. How appropriate would it be to represent such a prince by the symbol of a bright and blazing star—or a meteor flashing through the sky! (3) There may be propriety, as applicable to him, in the expression—"a great star *from heaven* falling upon the earth." Attila was regarded as an instrument in the divine hand in inflicting punishment. The common appellation by which he has been known is "the scourge of God." This title is supposed by the modern Hungarians to have been first given to Attila by a hermit of Gaul, but it was "inserted by Attila among the titles of his royal dignity" (Gibbon, ii. 321, foot-note). To no one could the title be more applicable than to him. (4) His career as a conqueror, and the effect of his conquests on the downfall of the empire, were such as to be properly symbolized in this manner. (*a*) The *general* effect of the invasion was worthy of an important place in describing the series of events which resulted in the overthrow of the empire. This is thus stated by Mr. Gibbon: "The western world was oppressed by the Goths and Vandals, who fled before the Huns; but the achievements of the Huns themselves were not adequate to their power and prosperity. Their victorious hordes had spread from the Volga to the Danube, but the public force was exhausted by the discord of independent chieftains; their valour was idly consumed in obscure and predatory excursions; and they often degraded their national dignity by condescending, for the hopes of spoil, to enlist under the banners of their fugitive enemies. In the reign of Attila the Huns again became the terror of the world; and I shall now describe the character and actions of that formidable barbarian who alternately invaded and insulted the East and the West, *and urged the rapid downfall of the Roman empire*," vol. ii. pp. 314, 315. (*b*) The parts of the earth affected by the invasion of the Huns were those which would be properly symbolized by the things specified at the blowing of this trumpet. It is said particularly that the effect would be on "the rivers," and on "the fountains of waters." If this has a literal application, or if, as was supposed in the case of the second trumpet, the language used was such as had reference to the portion of the empire that would be particularly affected by the hostile invasion, then we may suppose that this refers to those portions of the empire that abounded in rivers and streams, and more particularly those in which the rivers and streams had their origin—for the effect was permanently in the "*fountains* of waters." As a matter of fact, the principal operations of Attila were in the regions of the Alps, and on the portions of the empire whence the rivers flow down into Italy. The invasion of Attila is described by Mr. Gibbon in this general language: "The whole breadth of Europe, as it extends above five hundred miles from the Euxine to the Adriatic, was at once invaded, and occupied, and desolated, by the myriads of barbarians whom Attila led into the field," ii. 319, 320. After describing the progress and the effects of this invasion (pp. 320-331) he proceeds more particularly to detail the events in the invasion of Gaul and Italy, pp. 331-347. After the terrible battle of Châlons, in which, according to one account, one hundred and sixty-two thousand, and, according to other accounts, three hundred thousand persons were slain, and in which Attila was defeated, he recovered his vigour, collected his forces, and made a descent on Italy. Under pretence of claiming Honoria, the daughter of the Empress of Rome, as his bride, "the indignant lover took the field, passed the Alps, invaded Italy, and besieged Aquileia with an innumerable host of barbarians." After endeavouring in vain for three months to subdue the city, and when about to abandon the siege, Attila took advantage of the appearance of a stork as a favourable omen to arouse his men to a renewed effort, "a large breach was made in the part of the wall where the stork had taken her flight; the Huns mounted to the assault with irresistible fury; and the succeeding generation could scarcely discover the ruins of Aquileia. After this dreadful chastisement Attila pursued his march; and as he passed, the cities of Altinum, Concordia, and Padua were reduced into heaps of stones and ashes. The inland towns, Vicenza, Verona, and Bergamo, were exposed to the rapacious cruelty of the Huns; Milan and Pavia submitted without resistance to the loss of their wealth, and applauded the unusual clemency which preserved from the flames the public as well as the private buildings, and spared the lives of the captive multitude. The popular traditions of Comum, Turin, or Modena, may be justly suspected, yet they concur with more authentic evidence to prove that Attila spread his ravages over the rich plains of modern Lombardy, which are divided by the Po, and bounded by the Alps and the Apennines," ii. pp. 343, 344. "It is a saying worthy of the ferocious pride of Attila, that the grass never grew on the spot where his horse had trod" (*ibid.* p. 345). Anyone has only to look on a map, and to trace the progress of those desolations and the chief seats of his military operations to see with what propriety this symbol would be employed. In these regions the great rivers that water Europe have their origin, and are swelled by numberless streams that flow down from the Alps; and about the fountains whence these streams flow were the principal military operations of the invader. (*c*) With equal propriety is he represented in the symbol as affecting "*a third*" part of these rivers and fountains. At least a third part of the empire was invaded and desolated by him in his savage march, and the *effects* of his invasion were as disastrous *on* the empire as if a bitter star had fallen into a third part of those rivers and fountains, and had converted them into wormwood. (*d*) There is one other point which shows the propriety of this symbol. It is, that the meteor, or star, seemed to be *absorbed* in the waters. It fell into the waters; embittered them; and was seen no more. Such would be the case with a meteor that should thus fall upon the earth—flashing along the sky, and then disappearing for ever. Now, it was remarkable in regard to the Huns, that their power was concentrated under Attila; that he alone appeared as the leader of this formidable host; and that when he died all the concentrated power of the Huns was dissipated, or became absorbed and lost. "The revolution," says Mr. Gibbon (ii. 348), "which subverted the empire of the Huns, established the fame of Attila, *whose genius alone had sustained the huge and disjointed fabric*. After his death the boldest chieftains aspired to the rank of kings; the most powerful kings refused to acknowledge a superior; and

12 And the fourth angel sounded, and the third part of ʳthe sun was smitten, and the third part of the moon, and the third part of the stars; so as the third part of them was darkened, and the day shone not for a third part of it, and the night likewise.

*r* Is.13.10; Je.4.23; Eze.32.7,8; Joel 2.10; Am.8.9.

---

the numerous sons, whom so many various mothers bore to the deceased monarch, divided and disputed, like a private inheritance, the sovereign command of the nations of Germany and Scythia." Soon, however, in the conflicts which succeeded, the empire passed away, and the empire of the *Huns* ceased. The people that composed it were absorbed in the surrounding nations, and Mr. Gibbon makes this remark, after giving a summary account of these conflicts, which continued but for a few years: "The Igours of the north, issuing from the cold Siberian regions, which produced the most valuable furs, spread themselves over the desert, as far as the Borysthenes and the Caspian gates, *and finally extinguished the empire of the Huns.*" These facts may, perhaps, show with what propriety Attila would be compared with a bright but beautiful meteor; and that, if the design was to symbolize him as acting an important part in the downfall of the Roman empire, there is a fitness in the symbol here employed.

12. *And the fourth angel sounded.* Notes, ver. 6, 7. ¶ *And the third part of the sea was smitten.* On the phrase *the third part*, see Notes on ver. 7. The darkening of the heavenly luminaries is everywhere an emblem of any great calamity—*as if* the light of the sun, moon, and stars should be put out. See Notes on ch. vi. 12, 13. There is no certain evidence that this refers to *rulers*, as many have supposed, or to anything that would particularly affect the *government* as such. The meaning is, that calamity would come *as if* darkness should spread over the sun, the moon, and the stars, leaving the world in gloom. What is the precise *nature* of the calamity is not indicated by the language, but anything that would diffuse gloom and disaster would accord with the fair meaning of the symbol. There are a few circumstances, however, in regard to this symbol which may aid us in determining its application. (1) It would follow in the *series* of calamities that were to occur. (2) It would be *separated* in some important sense—of time, place, or degree—from those which were to follow, for there is a *pause* here (ver. 13), and the angel proclaims that more terrible woes are to succeed this series. (3) Like the preceding, it is to affect "one third part" of the world; that is, it is to be a calamity *as if* a third part of the sun, the moon, and the stars were suddenly smitten and darkened. (4) It is not to be *total*. It is not as if the sun, the moon, and the stars were entirely blotted out, for there was still some remaining light; that is, there was a continuance of the existing state of things—as if these heavenly bodies should still give an obscure and partial light. (5) Perhaps it is also intended by the symbol that there would be light again. The world was not to go into a state of total and permanent night. For a third part of the day, and a third part of the night, this darkness reigned; but does not this imply that there would be light again—that the obscurity would pass away, and that the sun, and moon, and stars would shine again? That is, is it not implied that there would still be prosperity in some future period?

Now, in regard to the application of this, if the explanation of the preceding symbols is correct, there can be little difficulty. If the previous symbols referred to Alaric, to Genseric, and to Attila, there can be no difficulty in applying this to Odoacer, and to his reign—a reign in which, in fact, the Roman dominion in the West came to an end, and passed into the hands of this barbarian. Anyone has only to open the *Decline and Fall of the Roman Empire*, to see that this is the next event that *should* be symbolized if the design were to represent the downfall of the empire. These four great barbarian leaders succeed each other in order, and under the last, Odoacer, the barbarian dominion was established; for it is here that the existence of the Roman power, as such, ended. The Western empire terminated, according to Mr. Gibbon (ii. p. 380), about A.D. 476 or 479. Odoacer was "King of Italy" from A.D. 476 to A.D. 490 (Gibbon, ii. 379). The Eastern empire still lingered, but calamity, like blotting out the sun, and moon, and stars, had come over that part of the world which for so many centuries had constituted the seat of power and dominion.—Odoacer was the son of Edecon, a barbarian, who was in the service of Attila, and who left two sons—Onulf and Odoacer. The former directed his steps to Constantinople; Odoacer "led a wandering life among the barbarians of Noricum, with a mind and fortune suited to the most desperate adventures; and when he had fixed his choice, he piously visited the cell of Severinus, the popular saint of the country, to solicit his approbation and blessing. The lowness of the door would not admit the lofty stature of Odoacer; he was obliged to stoop; but in that humble attitude the saint could discern the symptoms of his future greatness; and addressing him in a prophetic tone, 'Pursue,' said he, 'your design; proceed to Italy; you will soon cast away this coarse garment of skins; and your wealth will be adequate to the liberality of your mind.' The barbarian, whose daring spirit accepted and ratified this prediction, was admitted into the service of the Western empire, and soon obtained an honourable rank in the guards. His manners were gradually polished, his military skill improved; and the confederates of Italy would not have elected him for their general unless the exploits of Odoacer had established a high opinion of his courage and capacity. Their military acclamations saluted him with the title of king; but he abstained during his whole reign from the use of the purple and the diadem, lest he should offend those princes whose subjects, by their accidental mixture, had formed the victorious army which time and policy might insensibly unite into a great nation" (Gibbon, ii. 379, 380). In another place Mr. Gibbon says: "Odoacer was the first barbarian who reigned in Italy, over a people who had once asserted their superiority above the rest of mankind. The disgrace of the Romans still excites our respectful compassion, and we fondly sympathize with the imaginary grief and indignation of their degenerate posterity. But the calamities of Italy had gradually subdued the proud consciousness of freedom and glory. In the age of Roman virtue the provinces were subject to the arms, and the citizens to the laws, of the republic; till those laws were subverted by civil discord, and both the city and the provinces became the servile property of a tyrant. The forms of the constitution which alleviated or disguised their abject slavery were abolished by time and violence; the Italians alternately lamented the presence or the absence of the sovereigns whom they detested or despised; and the succession of five centuries inflicted the various evils of military license, capricious despotism, and elaborate oppression. During the same period the barbarians had emerged from obscurity and contempt, and the warriors of Germany and Scythia were introduced into the provinces, as the servants, the allies, and at length the masters of the Romans, whom they insulted or protected," ii. 381, 382. Of the effect of the reign of Odoacer Mr. Gibbon remarks: "In the division and decline of the empire the tributary harvests of Egypt and Africa were withdrawn; the numbers of the inhabitants continually decreased with the means of subsistence; and the country was exhausted by the irretrievable losses of war, famine, and pestilence. St. Ambrose has deplored the ruin of a populous district, which had been once adorned with the flourishing cities of Bologna, Modena, Rhegium, and Placentia. Pope Gelasius was a subject of Odoacer; and he affirms, with strong exaggeration, that in Æmilia, Tuscany, and the adjacent provinces the human species was almost extirpated. *One-third* of those ample estates, to which the ruin of Italy is originally imputed, was extorted for the use of the conquerors," ii. 383. Yet the light was not *wholly* extinct. It was "a third part" of it which was put out; and it was still true that some of the forms of the ancient constitution were observed —that the light still lingered before it wholly passed away. In the language of another, "The authority of the Roman name had not yet entirely ceased. The senate of Rome continued to assemble as usual. The consuls were appointed yearly, one by the Eastern emperor, one by Italy and Rome. Odoacer himself governed Italy under a title—that of *Patrician*—conferred on him by the Eastern emperor. There was still a certain, though often faint, recognition of the supreme imperial authority. The moon and the stars might seem still to shine in the West, with a dim reflected light. In the course of the events, however, which rapidly followed in the next half-century, these too were extinguished. After above a century and a half of calamities unex-

13 And I beheld, and heard an *angel flying through the midst of heaven, saying with a loud voice, Woe, woe, woe, to the inhabiters of the earth, by reason of the other voices of the trumpet of the three angels, which are yet to sound!

*s* ch.14.6.

ampled almost, as Dr. Robertson most truly represents it,[1] in the history of nations, the statement of Jerome — a statement couched under the very Apocalyptic figure of the text, but prematurely pronounced on the first taking of Rome by Alaric — might be considered at length accomplished: 'Clarissimum terrarum *lumen* extinctum est' — 'The world's glorious *sun* has been extinguished;' or, as the modern poet Byron (*Childe Harold*, canto iv.) has expressed it, still under the Apocalyptic imagery:—

'She saw her glories star by star expire,'

till not even one star remained to glimmer in the vacant and dark night" (Elliott, i. 360, 361).

I have thus endeavoured to explain the meaning of the four first trumpets under the opening of the seventh seal, embracing the successive severe blows struck on the empire by Alaric, Genseric, Attila, and Odoacer, until the empire fell, to rise no more. I cannot better conclude this part of the exposition than in the words of Mr. Gibbon, in his reflections on the fall of the empire. "I have now accomplished," says he, "the laborious narrative of the decline and fall of the Roman empire, from the fortunate age of Trajan and the Antonines to its total extinction in the West, about five centuries after the Christian era. At that unhappy period the Saxons fiercely struggled with the natives for the possession of Britain; Gaul and Spain were divided between the powerful monarchies of the Franks and the Visigoths, and the dependent kingdoms of the Suevi and the Burgundians; Africa was exposed to the cruel persecution of the Vandals, and the savage insults of the Moors; Rome and Italy, as far as the banks of the Danube, were afflicted by an army of barbarian mercenaries, whose lawless tyranny was succeeded by the reign of Theodoric the Ostrogoth. All the subjects of the empire, who, by the use of the Latin language, more particularly deserved the name and privileges of Romans, were oppressed by the disgrace and calamities of foreign conquest; and the victorious nations of Germany established a new system of manners and government in the western countries of Europe. The majesty of Rome was faintly represented by the princes of Constantinople, the feeble and imaginary successors of Augustus" (vol. ii. pp. 440, 441). "The splendid days of Augustus and Trajan *were eclipsed by a cloud of ignorance* [a fine illustration of the language 'the third part of the sun was smitten, and the day shone not, and the night likewise']; and the barbarians subverted the laws and palaces of Rome" (*ibid.* p. 446).

Thus ended the history of the Gothic period, and, as I suppose, the immediate symbolic representation of the affairs of the Western empire. An interval now occurs (ver. 13) in the sounding of the trumpets, and the scene is transferred, in the three remaining trumpets, to the Eastern parts of the empire. After that the attention is directed again to the West, to contemplate Rome under a new form, and exerting a new influence in the nations, under the Papacy, but destined ultimately to pass away in its spiritual power, as its temporal power had yielded to the elements of internal decay in its bosom, and to the invasions of the northern hordes.

13. *And I beheld.* My attention was attracted by a new vision. ¶ *And I heard an angel flying,* &c. I heard the voice of an angel making this proclamation. ¶ *Woe, woe, woe.* That is, there will be *great* woe. The repetition of the word is intensive, and the idea is, that the sounding of the three remaining trumpets would indicate great and fearful calamities. These three are grouped together as if they pertained to a similar series of events, as the first four had been. The two classes are separated from each other by this interval and by this proclamation — implying that the first series had been completed, and that there would be some interval, either of space or time, before the other series would come upon the world. All that is fairly implied here would be fulfilled by the supposition that the former referred to the

[1] "If we were called on to fix a period most calamitous, it would be that from the death of Theodosius to the establishment of the Lombards" (*Charles V* pp. 11, 12).

## CHAPTER IX.

AND the fifth angel sounded, and I saw a *a*star fall from

<small>a ch.8.10; Lu.10.18.</small>

heaven unto the earth: and to him was given the key of the *b*bottomless pit.

<small>b ch.17.8; 20.1.</small>

West, and that the latter pertained to the *East*, and were to follow when those should have been completed.

## CHAPTER IX.
### ANALYSIS OF THE CHAPTER.

The three remaining trumpets (ch. ix.-xi.) are usually called the *woe-trumpets*, in reference to the proclamation of woes, ch. viii. 13 (Professor Stuart). The three extend, as I suppose, to the end of time, or, as it is supposed by the writer himself (ch. xi. 15), to the period when "the kingdoms of this world shall have become the kingdoms of Christ," embracing a succinct view of the most material events that were to occur, particularly in a *secular* point of view. See the Analysis prefixed to the book. In ch. xi. 19, as I understand it, a new view is commenced, referring to the church internally; the rise of Antichrist, and the effect of the rise of that formidable power on the internal history of the church, to the time of its overthrow, and the triumphant establishment of the kingdom of God. This, of course, synchronizes in its beginning and its close with the portion already passed over, but with a different view. See the Analysis prefixed to ch. xi. 19, seq.

This chapter contains properly three parts. *First*, a description of the first of those trumpets, or the fifth in the order of the whole, ver. 1-12. This woe is represented under the figure of calamities brought upon the earth by an immense army of locusts. A star is seen to fall from heaven—representing some mighty chieftain, and to him is given the key of the bottomless pit. He opens the pit, and then comes forth an innumerable swarm of locusts that darken the heavens, and they go forth upon the earth. They have a command given them to do a certain work. They are not to hurt the earth, or any green thing, but they are sent against those men which have not the seal of God on their foreheads. Their main business, however, was not to kill them, but to torment them for a limited time—for five months. A description of the appearance of the locusts then follows. Though they are *called* locusts, because in their general appearance, and in the ravages they commit, they resemble them, yet, in the main, they are imaginary beings, and combine in themselves qualities which are never found united in reality. They had a strong resemblance to horses prepared for battle; they wore on their heads crowns of gold; they had the faces of men but the hair of women and the teeth of lions. They had breastplates of iron, and tails like scorpions, with stings in their tails. They had a mighty king at their head, with a name significant of the destruction which he would bring upon the world. These mysterious beings had their origin in the bottomless pit, and they are summoned forth to spread desolation upon the earth. *Second*, a description of the second of these trumpets, the sixth in order, ver. 13-19. When this is sounded, a voice is heard from the four horns of the altar which is before God. The angel is commanded to loose the four angels which are bound in the great river Euphrates. These angels are loosed—angels which had been prepared for a definite period—a day, and a month, and a year, to slay the third part of men. The number of the army that would appear—composed of cavalry—is stated to amount to two hundred thousand, and the *peculiarities* of these horsemen are then stated. They are remarkable for having breastplates of fire, and jacinth, and brimstone; the heads of the horses resemble lions; and they breathe forth fire and brimstone. A third part of men fall before them, by the fire, and the smoke, and the brimstone. Their power is in their mouth and in their tails, for their tails are like serpents. *Third*, a statement of the effect of the judgments brought upon the world under these trumpets, ver. 20, 21. The effect, so far as the reasonable result could have been anticipated, is lost. The nations are not turned from idolatry. Wickedness still abounds, and there is no disposition to repent of the abominations which had been so long practised on the earth.

1. *And the fifth angel sounded.* See Notes on ch. viii. 6, 7. ¶ *And I saw a star fall from heaven unto the earth.* This denotes, as was shown in the Notes on ch. viii. 10, a leader, a military

## CHAPTER IX.

**2 And he opened the bottomless pit; and there arose a smoke out of the pit, as the smoke of a great furnace; and the sun and the air were ᶜdarkened by reason of the smoke of the pit.**

*c* Joel 2.2.

chieftain, a warrior. In the fulfilment of this, as in the former case, we look for the appearance of some mighty prince and warrior, to whom is given power, as it were, to open the bottomless pit, and to summon forth its legions. That some such agent is denoted by the *star* is farther apparent from the fact that it is immediately added, that "to *him* [the star] was given the key of the bottomless pit." It could not be meant that a key would be given to a literal *star*, and we naturally suppose, therefore, that some intelligent being of exalted rank, and of baleful influence, is here referred to. Angels, good and bad, are often called stars; but the reference here, as in ch. viii. 10, seems to me not to be to angels, but to some mighty leader of armies, who was to collect his hosts, and to go through the world in the work of destruction. ¶ *And to him was given the key of the bottomless pit.* Of the under-world, considered particularly of the abode of the wicked. This is represented often as a dark prison-house, inclosed with walls, and accessible by gates or doors. These gates or doors are fastened, so that none of the inmates can come out, and the key is in the hand of the keeper or guardian. In ch. i. 18 it is said that the keys of that world are in the hand of the Saviour (comp. Notes on that passage); here it is said that for a time, and for a temporary purpose, they are committed to another. The word *pit* —φρέαρ—denotes properly a well, or a pit for water dug in the earth; and then any pit, cave, abyss. The reference here is doubtless to the nether world, considered as the abode of the wicked dead, the prison-house of the guilty. The word *bottomless*, ἄβυσσος —whence our word *abyss*—means properly *without any bottom* (from α, pr., and βύθος, *depth, bottom*). It would be applied properly to the ocean, or to any deep and dark dell, or to any obscure place whose depth was unknown. Here it refers to Hades—the region of the dead—the abode of wicked spirits—as a deep, dark place, whose bottom was unknown. Having the *key* to this, is to have the power to confine those who are there, or to permit them to go at large. The meaning here is, that this master-spirit would have power to evoke the dead from these dark regions; and it would be fulfilled if some mighty genius, that could be compared with a fallen star, or a lurid meteor, should summon forth followers which would *appear* like the dwellers in the nether world called forth to spread desolation over the earth.

2. *And he opened the bottomless pit.* It is represented before as wholly confined, so that not even the smoke or vapour could escape. ¶ *And there arose a smoke out of the pit.* Comp. ch. xiv. 11. The meaning here is, that the pit, as a place of punishment, or as the abode of the wicked, was filled with burning sulphur, and consequently that it emitted smoke and vapour as soon as opened. The common image of the place of punishment, in the Scriptures, is that of a "lake that burns with fire and brimstone." Comp. ch. xiv. 10; xix. 20; xx. 10; xxi. 8. See also Ps. xi. 6; Is. xxx. 33; Eze. xxxviii. 22. It is not improbable that this image was taken from the destruction of Sodom and Gomorrah, Ge. xix. 24. Such burning sulphur would produce, of course, a dense smoke or vapour; and the idea here is, that the pit had been closed, and that as soon as the door was opened a dense column escaped that darkened the heavens. The purpose of this is, probably, to indicate the *origin* of the plague that was about to come upon the world. It would be of such a character that it would appear as if it had been emitted from hell; as if the inmates of that dark world had broke loose upon the earth. Comp. Notes on ch. vi. 8. ¶ *As the smoke of a great furnace.* So in Ge. xix. 28, whence probably this image is taken: "And he looked towards Sodom and Gomorrah, and all the land of the plain, and beheld, and lo, the smoke of the country went up as the smoke of a furnace." ¶ *And the sun and the air were darkened*, &c. As will be the case when a smoke ascends from a furnace. The meaning here is, that an effect would be produced *as if* a dense and dark vapour should ascend from the under-world. We are not, of course, to understand this literally.

3. *And there came out of the smoke locusts upon the earth.* That is, they escaped from the pit with the smoke.

3 And there came out of the smoke $^d$ locusts upon the earth: and unto them was given power, as the $^e$ scorpions of the earth have power.

$d$ Ex.10.4,&c.    $e$ ver.10.

At first they were mingled with the smoke, so that they were not distinctly seen, but when the smoke cleared away they appeared in great numbers. The idea seems to be, that the bottomless pit was filled with vapour and with those creatures, and that as soon as the gate was opened the whole contents expanded and burst forth upon the earth. The sun was immediately darkened, and the air was full, but the smoke soon cleared away, so that the locusts became distinctly visible. The *appearance* of these locusts is described in another part of the chapter, ver. 7, seq. The locust is a voracious insect belonging to the grasshopper or grylli genus, and is a great scourge in Oriental countries. A full description of the locust may be seen in Robinson's *Calmet*, and in Kitto's *Encyclo.* vol. ii. pp. 258, seq. There are ten Hebrew words to denote the locust, and there are numerous references to the destructive habits of the insect in the Scriptures. In fact, from their numbers and their destructive habits, there was scarcely any other plague that was so much dreaded in the East. Considered as a *symbol*, or *emblem*, the following remarks may be made in explanation:—(1) The symbol is *Oriental*, and would most naturally refer to something that was to occur in the East. As locusts have appeared chiefly in the East, and as they are in a great measure an *Oriental* plague, the mention of this symbol would most naturally turn the thoughts to that portion of the earth. The symbols of the first four trumpets had no especial locality, and would suggest no particular part of the world; but on the mention of this, the mind would be naturally turned to the East, and we should expect to find that the scene of this woe would be located in the regions where the ravages of locusts most abounded. Compare, on this point, Elliott, *Horæ Apoc.* i. 394–406. He has made it probable that the prophets, when they used symbolical language to denote any events, commonly, at least, employed those which had a local or geographical reference; thus, in the symbols derived from the vegetable kingdom, when Judah is to be symbolized, the olive, the vine, and the fig-tree are selected; when Egypt is referred to, the reed is chosen; when Babylon, the willow. And so, in the animal kingdom, the lion is the symbol of Judah; the wild ass, of the Arabs; the crocodile, of Egypt, &c. Whether this theory could be wholly carried out or not, no one can doubt that the symbol of locusts would most naturally suggest the Oriental world, and that the natural interpretation of the passage would lead us to expect its fulfilment there. (2) Locusts were remarkable for their *numbers*—so great often as to appear like clouds, and to darken the sky. In this respect they would naturally be symbolical of numerous armies or hosts of men. This natural symbol of numerous armies is often employed by the prophets. Thus, in Je. xlvi. 23:—

"Cut down her forests [*i.e.* her people, or cities],
   saith Jehovah,
That it may not be found on searching;
Although they surpass the locusts in multitude,
And they are without number."

So in Na. iii. 15:—

"There shall the fire devour thee;
The sword shall cut thee off; it shall devour thee
   as the locust,
Increase thyself as the numerous locusts."

So also in Na. iii. 17:—

"Thy crowned princes are as the numerous locusts,
And thy captains as the grasshoppers;
Which encamp in the fences in the cold day,
But when the sun ariseth they depart,
And their place is not known where they were."

See also De. xxviii. 38, 42; Ps. lxxviii. 46; Am. vii. 1. Comp. Ju. vi. 3–6; vii. 12; and Joel, ch. i. ii. (3) Locusts are an emblem of desolation or destruction. No symbol of desolation could be more appropriate or striking than this, for one of the most remarkable properties of locusts is, that they devour every green thing and leave a land perfectly waste. They do this even when what they destroy is not necessary for their own sustenance. "Locusts seem to devour not so much from a ravenous appetite as from a rage for destroying. Destruction, therefore, and not food, is the chief impulse of their devastations, and in this consists their utility; they are, in fact, omnivorous. The most poisonous plants are indifferent to them; they will prey even upon the crowfoot, whose causticity burns even the hides of beasts. They simply consume *every-*

A.D. 96.] CHAPTER IX. 213

4 And it was *commanded them that they should not hurt the grass of the earth, neither any green

*f* ch.6.6.

thing, neither any tree; but only those men which have not the *g* seal of God in their foreheads.

*g* ch.7.3; Ex.12.23; Job 2.6; Eze.9.4.

thing, without predilection—vegetable matter, linens, woollens, silk, leather, &c.; and Pliny does not exaggerate when he says, *fores quoque tectorum*—'even the doors of houses'—for they have been known to consume the very varnish of furniture. They reduce everything indiscriminately to shreds, which become manure" (Kitto's *Encyclo.* ii. 263). Locusts become, therefore, a most striking symbol of an all-devouring army, and as such are often referred to in Scripture. So also in Josephus, *de Bello Jud.* book v. ch. vii.:—"As after locusts we see the woods stripped of their leaves, so, in the rear of Simon's army, nothing but devastation remained." The *natural* application of this symbol, then, is to a numerous and destructive army, or to a great multitude of people committing ravages, and sweeping off everything in their march. ¶ *And unto them was given power.* This was something that was *imparted* to them beyond their ordinary nature. The locust in itself is not strong, and is not a symbol of strength. Though destructive in the extreme, yet neither as individuals, nor as combined, are they distinguished for strength. Hence it is mentioned as a remarkable circumstance that they had such power conferred on them. ¶ *As the scorpions of the earth have power.* The phrase "the earth" seems to have been introduced here because these creatures are said to have come up from "the bottomless pit," and it was natural to compare them with some well-known objects found on the earth. The scorpion is an animal with eight feet, eight eyes, and a long, jointed tail, ending in a pointed weapon or sting. It is the largest and the most malignant of all the insect tribes. It somewhat resembles the lobster in its general appearance, but is much more hideous. See Notes on Lu. x. 19. Those found in Europe seldom exceed four inches in length, but in tropical climates, where they abound, they are often found twelve inches long. There are few animals more formidable, and none more irascible, than the scorpion. Goldsmith states that Maupertuis put about a hundred of them together in the same glass, and that as soon as they came into contact they began to exert all their rage in mutual destruction, so that in a few days there remained but fourteen, which had killed and devoured all the rest. The sting of the scorpion, Dr. Shaw states, is not always fatal; the malignity of their venom being in proportion to their size and complexion. The torment of a scorpion, when he strikes a man, is thus described by Dioscorides, lib. vii. cap. 7, as cited by Mr. Taylor:—"When the scorpion has stung, the place becomes inflamed and hardened; it reddens by tension, and is painful by intervals, being now chilly, now burning. The pain soon rises high, and rages, sometimes more, sometimes less. A sweating succeeds, attended by a shivering and trembling; the extremities of the body become cold, the groin swells, the hair stands on end, the members become pale, and the skin feels throughout the sensation of a perpetual pricking, as if by needles" (Fragments to Calmet's *Dic.* vol. iv. p. 376, 377). "The tail of the scorpion is long, and formed after the manner of a string of beads, the last larger than the others, and longer; at the end of which are, sometimes, two stings which are hollow, and filled with a cold poison, which it ejects into the part which it stings" (Calmet's *Dic.*). The sting of the scorpion, therefore, becomes the emblem of that which causes acute and dangerous suffering. On this comparison with *scorpions* see the remark of Niebuhr, quoted in the Notes on ver. 7.

4. *And it was commanded them.* The writer does not say *by whom* this command was given, but it is clearly by some one who had the direction of them. As they were evoked from the "bottomless pit" by one who had the key to that dark abode, and as they are represented in ver. 11 as under the command of one who is there called Abaddon, or Apollyon—the Destroyer—it would seem most probable that the command referred to is one that is given by him; that is, that this expresses one of the principles on which he would act in his devastations. At all events, this denotes what would be one of the characteristics of these destroyers. Their pur-

5 And to them it was given that they should not kill them, but that they should be tormented five months: and their torment *was* as the torment of a scorpion, when he striketh a man.

pose would be to vex and trouble men; not to spread desolation over vineyards, olive-yards, and fields of grain. ¶ *That they should not hurt the grass of the earth*, &c. See Notes on ch. viii. 7. The meaning here is plain. There would be some sense in which these invaders would be characterized in a manner that was not common among invaders, to wit, that they would show particular care not to carry their devastations into the vegetable world. Their warfare would be with men, and not with orchards and green fields. ¶ *But only those men which have not the seal of God in their foreheads*. See Notes on ch. vii. 2, 3. They commenced war against that part of the human race only. The *language* here properly denotes those who were not the friends of God. It may here refer, however, either to those who *in reality* were not such, or to those who were regarded by him who gave this command as not being such. In the former case, the commission would have respect to real infidels in the sight of God—that is, to those who rejected the true religion; in the latter it would express the sentiment of the leader of this host, as referring to those who in *his* apprehension were infidels or enemies of God. The true interpretation must depend on the sense in which we understand the phrase "it was commanded;" whether as referring to God, or to the leader of the host himself. The language, therefore, is ambiguous, and the meaning must be determined by the other parts of the passage. Either method of understanding the passage would be in accordance with its fair interpretation.

5. *And to them it was given.* There is here the same indefiniteness as in the former verse, the impersonal verb being here also used. The writer does not say *by whom* this power was given, whether by God, or by the leader of the host. It may be admitted, however, that the most natural interpretation is to suppose that it was given them by God, and that this was the execution of *his* purpose in this case. Still it is remarkable that this is not directly affirmed, and that the language is so general as to admit of the other application. The *fact* that they did not kill them, but tormented them—if such a fact should be found to exist—would be in every sense a fulfilment of what is here said. ¶ *That they should not kill them.* This is in accordance with the nature of the symbol. The locusts do not themselves destroy any living creature; and the sting of the scorpion, though exceedingly painful, is not usually fatal. The proper fulfilment of this would be found in that which would not be generally fatal, but which would diffuse misery and wretchedness. (Comp. ver. 6.) *Perhaps* all that would be necessarily meant by this would be, not that individual *men* would not be killed, but that they would be sent to inflict plagues and torments rather than to take life, and that the characteristic effects of their appearing would be distress and suffering rather than death. There may be included in the fair interpretation of the words, general distress and sorrow; acts of oppression, cruelty, and violence; such a condition of public suffering that men would regard death as a relief if they could find it. ¶ *But that they should be tormented.* That is, that they should be subjected to ills and troubles which might be properly compared with the sting of a scorpion. ¶ *Five months.* So far as the *words* here are concerned this might be taken literally, denoting five months or one hundred and fifty days; or as a prophetic reckoning, where a day stands for a year. Comp. Notes on Da. ix. 24, seq. The latter is undoubtedly the correct interpretation here, for it is the character of the book thus to reckon time. See Notes on ver. 15. [See also Editor's Preface, pp. xi-xv.] If this be the true method of reckoning here, then it will be necessary to find some events which will embrace the period of one hundred and fifty years, during which this distress and sorrow would continue. The proper laws of interpretation demand that one or the other of these periods should be found—either that of five months literally, or that of a hundred and fifty years. It may be true, as Professor Stuart suggests (*in loco*), that "the usual time of locusts is from May to September inclusive—five months." It may be true, also, that this symbol was chosen partly *because* that was the fact, and they would, from that fact, be well adapted to symbolize

6 And in those days shall *h* men seek death, and shall not find it; and shall desire to die, and death shall flee from them.

7 And the *i* shapes of the locusts *were* like unto horses prepared unto battle; and on their heads *were* as it were *k* crowns like gold, and their *l* faces *were* as the faces of men.

*h* Job 3.21; Je.8.3.    *i* Joel 2.4.    *k* Na.3.17.    *l* Da.7.4,8.

a period that could be spoken of as "five months;" but still the meaning must be more than simply it was "*a short period*," as he supposes. The phrase *a few months* might designate such a period; but if that had been the writer's intention, he would not have selected the definite number *five*. ¶ *And their torment was as the torment of a scorpion*, &c. See Notes on ver. 3. That is, it would be painful, severe, dangerous.

6. *And in those days shall men seek death*, &c. See Notes on ver. 5. It is very easy to conceive of such a state of things as is here described, and, indeed, this has not been very uncommon in the world. It is a state where the distress is so great that men would consider death a relief, and where they anxiously look to the time when they may be released from their sufferings by death. In the case before us it is not intimated that they would lay violent hands on themselves, or that they would take any positive measures to end their sufferings; and this, perhaps, *may be* a circumstance of some importance to show that the persons referred to were servants of God. When it is said that "they would *seek* death," it can only be meant that they would look out for it—or desire it—as the end of their sorrows. This is descriptive, as we shall see, of a particular period of the world; but the *language* is beautifully applicable to what occurs in all ages and in all lands. There is always a great number of sufferers who are looking forward to death as a relief. In cells and dungeons; on beds of pain and languishing; in scenes of poverty and want; in blighted hopes and disappointed affections, how many are there who would be glad to die, and who have no hope of an end of suffering but in the grave! A few, by the pistol, by the halter, by poison, or by drowning, seek thus to end their woes. A large part look forward to death as a release, when, if the reality were known, death would furnish no such relief, for there are deeper and longer woes beyond the grave than there are this side of it.

Comp. Notes on Job iii. 20-22. But to a portion death *will* be a relief. It will be an end of sufferings. They will find peace in the grave, and are assured they shall suffer no more. Such bear their trials with patience, for the end of *all* sorrow to them is near, and death will come to release their spirits from the suffering clay, and to bear them in triumph to a world where a pang shall never be felt, and a tear never shed.

7. *And the shapes of the locusts were like unto horses prepared for battle.* The resemblance between the locust and the horse, dissimilar as they are in most respects, has been often remarked. Dr. Robinson (*Bib. Research.* i. 59) says: "We found to-day upon the shrubs an insect, either a species of black locust, or much resembling them, which our Bedouin called *Farras el Jundy*, 'soldiers' horses.' They said these insects were common on Mount Sinai, of a green colour, and were found on dead trees, but did them no injury." The editor of the *Pictorial Bible* makes the following remarks:—"The first time we saw locusts browsing with their wings closed, the idea of comparing them to horses arose spontaneously to our minds —as we had not previously met with such a comparison, and did not at that time advert to the present text [Joel ii. 4]. The resemblance in the head first struck our attention; and this notion having once arisen, other analogies were found or imagined in its general appearance and action in feeding. We have since found the observation very common. The Italians, indeed, from this resemblance, called the locust *cavaletta*, or *little horse*. Sir W. Ouseley reports: 'Zakaria Cazvine divides the locusts into two classes, like horsemen and footmen—mounted and pedestrian.' Niebuhr says that he heard from a Bedouin, near Bussorah, a particular comparison of the locust to other animals; but as this passage of Scripture did not occur to him at the time he thought it a mere fancy of the Arab's, till he heard it repeated at Bagdad. He compared the head of the locust to that of the horse; the feet to those of the camel;

8 And they had hair as the hair of women, and their ᵐteeth were as *the teeth* of lions.

9 And they had breastplates, as

m Ps.57.4; Joel 1.6.

the belly with that of a serpent; the tail with that of a scorpion; and the feelers (if Niebuhr remembered rightly) to the hair of a virgin" (*Pict. Bib.* on Joel ii. 4). The resemblance to horses would naturally suggest the idea of *cavalry*, as being referred to by the symbol. ¶ *And on their heads were as it were crowns like gold*. The writer does not say either that these were literally *crowns*, or that they were actually made of *gold*. They were "*as it were*" (ὡς) crowns, and they were *like* (ὅμοιοι) *gold*. That is, as seen by him, they had a resemblance to crowns or diadems, and they also resembled gold in their colour and brilliancy. The word *crown* — στέφανος — means properly a circlet, chaplet, encircling the head (*a*) as an emblem of royal dignity, and as worn by kings; (*b*) as conferred on victors in the public games—a chaplet, a wreath; (*c*) as an ornament, honour, or glory, Phi. iv. 1. No particular *shape* is designated by the word στέφανος—*stephanos*—and perhaps the word *crown* does not quite express the meaning. The word *diadem* would come nearer to it. The true notion in the word is that of something that is passed around the head, and that encircles it, and as such it would well describe the appearance of a *turban* as seen at a distance. On the supposition that the symbolic beings here referred to had turbans on their heads, and on the supposition that something was referred to which was not much worn in the time of John, and, therefore, that had no name, the word *stephanos*, or *diadem*, would be likely to be used in describing it. This, too, would accord with the use of the phrase "*as it were*" —ὡς. The writer saw such head-ornaments as he was accustomed to see. They were not *exactly* crowns or diadems, but they had a resemblance to them, and he therefore uses this language: "and on their heads were *as it were* crowns." Suppose that these were *turbans*, and that they were not in common use in the time of John, and that they had, therefore, no name, would not this be the exact language which he would use in describing them? The same remarks may be made respecting

it were breastplates of iron; and the sound of their wings *was* as the ⁿsound of chariots of many horses running to battle.

n Na.2.4.

the other expression. ¶ *Like gold.* They were not pure gold, but they had a resemblance to it. Would not a yellow turban correspond with all that is said in this description? ¶ *And their faces were as the faces of men.* They had a human countenance. This would indicate that, after all, they were human beings that the symbol described, though they had come up from the bottomless pit. Horsemen, in strange apparel, with a strange head-dress, would be all that would be properly denoted by this.

8. *And they had hair as the hair of women.* Long hair; not such as men commonly wear, but such as women wear. See Notes on 1 Co. xi. 14. This struck John as a peculiarity, that, though warriors, they should have the appearance of effeminacy indicated by allowing their hair to grow long. It is clear from this, that John regarded their appearance as unusual and remarkable. Though manifestly designed to represent an army, yet it was not the usual appearance of men who went forth to battle. Among the Greeks of ancient times, indeed, long hair was not uncommon (see the Notes above referred to on 1 Co. xi. 14), but this was by no means the usual custom among the ancients; and the fact that these warriors had long hair like women was a circumstance that would distinguish them particularly from others. On this comparison of the appearance of the locusts with the hair of women see the remarks of Niebuhr, in the Notes on ver. 7. ¶ *And their teeth were as the teeth of lions.* Strong; fitted to devour. The teeth of the locust are by no means prominent, though they are strong, for they readily cut down and eat up all vegetable substances that come in their way. But it is evident that John means to say that there was much that was unusual and remarkable in the teeth of these locusts. They would be ravenous and fierce, and would spread terror and desolation like the lions of the desert.

9. *And they had breastplates, as it were breastplates of iron.* Hard, horny, impenetrable, *as if* they were made of

10 And they had tails like unto scorpions, and there were stings in their tails: and °their power was to hurt men five months.

11 And they had a ᵖking over them, *which is* the angel of the bottomless pit, whose name in the Hebrew tongue *is* Abaddon, but in the Greek tongue hath *his* name ¹Apollyon.

o ver.5.   p Ep.2.2.   1 That is, *a destroyer*.

iron. The locust *has* a firm and hard cuticle on the forepart of the breast, which serves for a shield or defence while it moves in the thorny and furzy vegetation. On those which John saw this was peculiarly hard and horny, and would thus be well adapted to be an emblem of the breastplates of iron commonly worn by ancient warriors. The meaning is, that the warriors referred to would be well clad with defensive armour. ¶ *And the sound of their wings was as the sound of chariots of many horses running to battle.* The noise made by locusts is often spoken of by travellers, and the comparison of that noise with that of chariots rushing to battle, is not only appropriate, but also indicates clearly what was symbolized. It was *an army* that was symbolized, and everything about them served to represent hosts of men well armed, rushing to conflict. The same thing here referred to is noticed by Joel, ch. ii. 4, 5, 7:—

"The appearance of them is as the appearance of horses;
And as horsemen so shall they run.
Like the noise of chariots on the tops of mountains, shall they leap;
Like the noise of a flame of fire that devoureth the stubble;
As a strong people set in battle array.
They shall run like mighty men;
They shall climb the wall like men of war;
And they shall march every one his ways, and shall not break their ranks," &c.

It is remarkable that Volney, who had no intention of illustrating the truth of Scripture, has given a description of locusts, *as if* he meant to confirm the truth of what is here said. "Syria," says he, "as well as Egypt, Persia, and almost all the south of Asia, is subject to another calamity no less dreadful [than earthquakes]; I mean those *clouds* of locusts so often mentioned by travellers. The quantity of these insects is incredible to all who have not themselves witnessed their astounding numbers; the whole earth is covered with them for the space of several leagues. The *noise* they make in browsing on the trees and herbage may be heard to a great distance, and resembles that of an army foraging in secret" (*Travels in Egypt and Syria*, vol. i. pp. 283, 284).

10. *And they had tails like unto scorpions.* The fancy of an Arab now often discerns a resemblance between the tail of the locust and the scorpion. See the remark of Niebuhr, quoted in the Notes on ver. 7. ¶ *And there were stings in their tails.* Like the stings of scorpions. See Notes on ver. 3. This made the locusts which appeared to John the more remarkable, for though the fancy may imagine a resemblance between the tail of a locust and a scorpion, yet the locusts have properly no sting. The only thing which they have resembling a sting is a hard bony sub-substance like a needle, with which the female punctures the bark and wood of trees in order to deposit her eggs. It has, however, no adaptation, like a sting, for conveying poison into a wound. These, however, appeared to be armed with stings properly so called. ¶ *And their power* was *to hurt men*. Not primarily to *kill* men, but to inflict on them various kinds of tortures. See Notes on ver. 5. The word here used —ἀδικῆσαι, rendered *to hurt*—is different from the word in ver. 5—βασανισθῶσι, rendered *should be tormented*. This word properly means *to do wrong, to do unjustly, to injure, to hurt;* and the two words would seem to convey the idea that they would produce distress by *doing wrong* to others, or by dealing unjustly with them. It does not appear that the wrong would be by inflicting bodily torments, but would be characterized by that injustice towards others which produces distress and anguish. ¶ *Five months.* See Notes on ver. 5; [also Editor's Preface, page xxiv].

11. *And they had a king over them.* A ruler who marshalled their hosts. Locusts often, and indeed generally, move in bands, though they do not appear to be under the direction of any one as a particular ruler or guide. In this case it struck John as a remarkable peculiarity that they *had* a king —a king who, it would seem, had the absolute control, and to whom was to

be traced all the destruction which would ensue from their emerging from the bottomless pit. ¶ *Which is the angel of the bottomless pit.* See Notes on ver. 1. The word *angel* here would seem to refer to the chief of the evil angels, who presided over the dark and gloomy regions from whence the locusts seemed to emerge. This may either mean that this evil angel seemed to command them personally, or that his spirit was infused into the leader of these hosts. ¶ *Whose name in the Hebrew tongue is Abaddon.* The name Abaddon means literally *destruction,* and is the same as Apollyon. ¶ *But in the Greek tongue hath his name Apollyon.* From ἀπόλλυμι—*to destroy.* The word properly denotes a destroyer, and the name is given to this king of the hosts, represented by the locusts, because this would be his principal characteristic.

After this minute explanation of the literal meaning of the symbol, it may be useful, before attempting to apply it, and to ascertain the *events* designed to be represented, to have a distinct impression of the principal image—the locust. It is evident that this is, in many respects, a creature of the imagination, and that we are not to expect the exact representation to be found in any forms of actual existence in the animal creation. The following engraving, prepared by Mr. Elliott (vol. i. p. 410), will give a sufficiently accurate representation of this symbolical figure as it appeared to John.

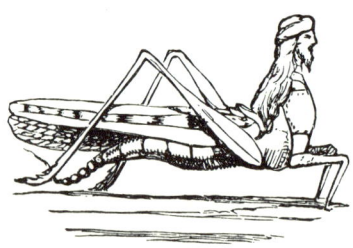

Symbolical Locust, according to Elliott.

The question now is, whether any events occurred in history, subsequent to and succeeding those supposed to be referred to in the fourth trumpet, to which this symbol would be applicable. Reasons have already been suggested for supposing that there was a transfer of the seat of the operations to another part of the world. The first four trumpets referred to a continual series of events of the same general character, and having a proper close. These have been explained as referring to the successive shocks which terminated in the downfall of the Western empire. At the close of that series there is a pause in the representation (ch. viii. 13), and a solemn proclamation that other scenes were to open distinguished for woe. These were to be symbolized in the sounding of the remaining three trumpets, embracing the whole period till the consummation of all things — or sketching great and momentous events in the future, until the volume sealed with the seven seals (ch. v. 1) should have been wholly unrolled and its contents disclosed. The whole scene now is changed. Rome has fallen. It has passed into the hands of strangers. The power that had spread itself over the world has, in that form, come to an end, and is to exist no more—though, as we shall see (ch. xi. seq.), *another* power, quite as formidable, existing there, is to be described by a new set of symbols. But here (ch. ix.) a new power appears. The scenery is all Oriental, and clearly has reference to events that were to spring up in the East. With surprising unanimity, commentators have agreed in regarding this as referring to the empire of the Saracens, or to the rise and progress of the religion and the empire set up by Mahomet. The inquiry now is, whether the circumstances introduced into the symbol find a proper fulfilment in the rise of the Saracenic power, and in the conquests of the Prophet of Mecca.

(1) *The country where the scene is laid.* As already remarked, the scene is Oriental—for the mention of locusts naturally suggests the East—that being the part of the world where they abound, and they being in fact peculiarly an Oriental plague. It may now be added, that in a more strict and proper sense Arabia may be intended; that is, if it be admitted that the design was to symbolize events pertaining to Arabia, or the gathering of the hosts of Arabia for conquest, the symbol of *locusts* would have been employed for the locust, the groundwork of the symbol is peculiarly Arabic. It was the east wind which brought the locusts on Egypt (Ex. x. 13), and they must therefore have come from some portion of Arabia—for Arabia is the land that lies over against Egypt in the east. Such, too, is the testimony

of Volney; "the most judicious," as Mr. Gibbon calls him, "of modern travellers." "The inhabitants of Syria," says he, "have remarked that locusts come constantly from the desert of Arabia," ch. xx. sect. 5. All that is necessary to say further on this point is, that on the supposition that it was the design of the Spirit of inspiration in the passage before us to refer to the followers of Mahomet, the image of the locusts was that which would be naturally selected. There was no other one so appropriate and so striking; no one that would so naturally designate the country of Arabia. As some confirmation of this, or as showing how *natural* the symbol would be, a remark may be introduced from Mr. Forster. In his *Mohammedanism Unveiled*, vol. i. p. 217, he says, "In the Bedoween romance of *Antar*, the *locust* is introduced as the national emblem of the Ishmaelites. And it is a remarkable coincidence that Mohammedan tradition speaks of locusts having dropped into the hands of Mohammed, bearing on their wings this inscription—'We are the army of the Great God.'" These circumstances will show the propriety of the symbol on the supposition that it refers to Arabia and the Saracens.

(2) *The people.* The question is, whether there was anything in the symbol, as described by John, which would properly designate the followers of Mahomet, on the supposition that it was designed to have such a reference. (*a*) As to *numbers.* "They (the Midianite Arabs) came as locusts for multitude," Ju. vi. 5. See Notes on ver. 3. Nothing would better represent the *numbers* of the Saracenic hordes that came out of Arabia, and that spread over the East—over Egypt, Libya, Mauritania, Spain, and that threatened to spread over Europe—than such an army of locusts. "One hundred years after his flight [Mahomet] from Mecca," says Mr. Gibbon, "the arms and the reign of his successors extended from India to the Atlantic Ocean, over the various and distant provinces which may be comprised under the names of Persia, Syria, Egypt, Africa, and Spain," vol. iii. p. 410. "At the end of the first century of the Hegira the caliphs were the most potent and absolute monarchs on the globe. Under the last of the Ommiades the Arabian empire extended two hundred days' journey from east to west, from the confines of Tartary and India to the shores of the Atlantic Ocean" (*ibid.* p. 460). In regard to the immense *hosts* employed in these conquests, an idea may be formed by a perusal of the whole fifty-first chapter in Gibbon (vol. iii. pp. 408-461). Those hosts issued primarily from Arabia, and in their numbers would be well compared with the swarms of locusts that issued from the same country, so numerous as to darken the sky. (*b*) The *description* of the people. ¶ *Their faces were as the faces of men.* This would seem to be in contrast with other people, or to denote something that was peculiar in the appearance of the persons represented. In other words, the meaning would seem to be, that there was something manly and warlike in their appearance, so far as their *faces* were concerned. It is remarkable that the appearance of the Goths (represented, as I suppose, under the previous trumpets) is described by Jerome (comp. on Is. viii.) as quite the reverse. They are described as having faces shaven and smooth; faces, in contrast with the bearded Romans, *like women's faces.*\* Is it fancy to suppose that the reference here is to the beard and moustache of the Arabic hosts? We know with what care they regarded the beard; and *if* a representation was made of them, especially in contrast with nations that shaved their faces, and who thus resembled women, it would be natural to speak of those represented in the symbol as "having faces as the faces of *men.*" ¶ *They had hair as the hair of women.* A strange mingling of the appearance of effeminacy with the indication of manliness and courage. See Notes on ver. 8. And yet this strictly accords with the appearance of the Arabs or Saracens. Pliny, the contemporary of John, speaks of the Arabs then as having the hair long and uncut, with the moustache on the upper lip, or the beard: Arabes mitrati sunt, aut *intonso crine.* Barba abraditur, *præterquam in superiore labro.* Aliis et *hac intonsa* (*Nat. Hist.* vol. vi. p. 28). So Solinus describes them in the third century (Plurimis crinis intonsus, mitrata capita, pars rasâ in cutem barbâ, c. 53); so Ammianus Marcellinus, in the fourth century (*Crinitus* quidam a Saracenorum cuneo, vol. xxxi. p. 16); and so Claudian, Theodore of Mopsuesta, and Jerome, in the fifth. Jerome lived

---

\* Fœmineas incisas facies præferentes, virorum et bene barbatorum fugientia terga confodiunt.

about two centuries before the great Saracen invasion; and as he lived at Bethlehem, on the borders of Arabia, he must have been familiar with the appearance of the Arabs. Still later, in that most characteristic of Arab poems, *Antar*, a poem written in the time of Mahomet's childhood, we find the moustache, and the beard, and the long flowing hair on the shoulder, and the turban, all specified as characteristic of the Arabians: "He adjusted himself properly, twisted his whiskers, *and folded up his hair under his turban*, drawing it from off his shoulders," vol. i. p. 340. "His hair flowed down on his shoulders," vol. i. p. 169. "Antar cut off Maudi's hair in revenge and insult," vol. iii. p. 117. "We will hang him up by his hair," vol. iv. p. 325. See Elliott, vol. i. pp. 411, 412. Comp. *Newton on the Prophecies*, p. 485. ¶ *And on their heads were as it were crowns of gold.* See Notes on ver. 7. That is, diadems, or something that appeared like crowns, or chaplets. This will agree well with the *turban* worn by the Arabs or Saracens, and which was quite characteristic of them in the early periods when they became known. So in the passage already quoted, Pliny speaks of them as Arabes *mitrati;* so Solinus, *mitrata capita;* so in the poem of *Antar*, "he folded up his hair *under his turban*." It is remarkable also that Ezekiel (ch. xxiii. 42) describes the turbans of the Sabean or Keturite Arabs under the very appellation here used by John: "Sabeans from the wilderness, which put beautiful *crowns* upon their heads." So in the preface to *Antar*, it is said, "It was a usual saying among them, that God had bestowed four peculiar things on the Arabs; that their *turbans* should be unto them instead of *diadems*, their tents instead of walls and houses, their swords instead of intrenchments, and their poems instead of written laws." Mr. Forster, in his *Mohammedanism Unveiled*, quotes as a precept of Mahomet: "Make a point of wearing *turbans*, because it is the way of angels." Turbans might then with propriety be represented as crowns, and no doubt these were often so gilded and ornamented that they might be spoken of as "*crowns of gold.*" ¶ *They had breastplates, as it were breastplates of iron.* See Notes on ver. 9. As a *symbol*, this would be properly descriptive of the Arabians or Saracens. In the poem *Antar* the steel and iron cuirasses of the Arab warriors are frequently noticed: "A warrior immersed in *steel armour,*" vol. ii. p. 203. "Fifteen thousand men armed with cuirasses, and well accoutred for war," vol. ii. p. 42. "They were clothed in iron armour, and brilliant cuirasses," vol. i. p. 23. "Out of the dust appeared horsemen clad in iron," vol. iii. p. 274. The same thing occurs in the Koran: "God hath given you coats of mail to defend you in your wars," vol. ii. p. 104. In the history of Mahomet we read expressly of the cuirasses of himself and of his Arab troops. Seven cuirasses are noted in the list of Mahomet's private armoury (Gagnier, vol. iii. p. 328-334). In his second battle with the Koreish, seven hundred of his little army are spoken of by Mr. Gibbon as armed with cuirasses. See Elliott, vol. i. p. 413. These illustrations will show with what propriety the locusts in the symbol were represented as having breastplates like breastplates of iron. On the supposition that this referred to the Arabs and the Saracens this would have been the very symbol which would have been used. Indeed, all the features in the symbol are precisely such as *would* properly be employed on the supposition that the reference was to them. It is true that beforehand it might not have been practicable to describe exactly what people were referred to; but (*a*) it would be easy to see that some fearful calamity was to be anticipated from the ravages of hosts of fearful invaders; and (*b*) when the events occurred, there would be no difficulty in determining to whom this application should be made.

(3) *The time when this would occur.* As to this there can be no difficulty in the application to the Saracens. On the supposition that the four first trumpets refer to the downfall of the Western empire, then the proper time supposed to be represented by this symbol is subsequent to that; and yet the manner in which the last three trumpets are introduced (ch. viii. 13) shows that there would be an *interval* between the sounding of the last of the four trumpets and the sounding of the fifth. The events referred to, as I have supposed, as represented by the fourth trumpet, occurred in the close of the fifth century (A.D. 476-490). The principal events in the seventh century were connected with the invasions and conquests of the Saracens. The interval of a century is not more than the fair

interpretation of the proclamation in ch. viii. 13 would justify.

(4) *The commission given to the symbolical locusts.* This embraces the following things:—(*a*) They were not to hurt the grass of the earth, nor any green thing; (*b*) they were especially to go against those who had not the seal of God in their foreheads; (*c*) they were not to *kill* them, but were to *torment* them. ¶ *They were not to hurt the grass of the earth,* &c. Notes, ver. 4. This agrees remarkably with an express command in the Koran. The often-quoted order of the Caliph Aboubekir, the father-in-law and successor of Mahomet, issued to the Saracen hordes on their invasion of Syria, shows what was understood to be the spirit of their religion: "Remember that you are always in the presence of God, on the verge of death, in the assurance of judgment, and the hope of paradise. Avoid injustice and oppression; consult with your brethren, and study to preserve the love and confidence of your troops. When you fight the battles of the Lord, acquit yourselves like men, without turning your backs; *but let not the victory be stained with the blood of women or children. Destroy no palm-trees, nor burn any fields of corn. Cut down no fruit-trees, nor do any mischief to cattle, only such as you kill to eat.* When you make any covenant or article, stand to it, and be as good as your word. As you go on, you will find some religious persons who live retired in monasteries, and propose to themselves to serve God in that way; let them alone, and *neither kill them* ['and to them it was given that they should not kill them,' ver 5], nor destroy their monasteries," &c. (Gibbon, iii. 417, 418). So Mr. Gibbon notices this precept of the Koran: "In the siege of Tayaf," says he, "sixty miles from Mecca, Mohammed violated *his own laws* by the extirpation of the fruit-trees," ii. 392. The same order existed among the Hebrews, and it is not improbable that Mahomet derived his precept from the command of Moses (De. xx. 19), though what was *mercy* among the Hebrews was probably mere *policy* with him. This precept is the more remarkable because it has been the usual custom in war, and particularly among barbarians and semi-barbarians, to destroy grain and fruit, and especially to cut down fruit-trees, in order to do greater injury to an enemy. Thus we have seen (Notes on ch. viii. 7), that in the invasion of the Goths their course was marked by desolations of this kind. Thus, in more modern times, it has been common to carry the desolations of war into gardens, orchards, and vineyards. In the single province of Upper Messenia the troops of Mahomet Ali, in the war with Greece, cut down half a million of olive-trees, and thus stripped the country of its means of wealth. So Scio was a beautiful spot, the seat of delightful villas, and gardens, and orchards; and in one day all this beauty was destroyed. On the supposition, therefore, that this prediction had reference to the Saracens, nothing could be more appropriate. Indeed, in all the history of barbarous and savage warfare it would be difficult to find another distinct command that no injury should be done to gardens and orchards. (*d*) Their commission was expressly against "those men who had not the seal of God in their foreheads." See Notes on ver. 4. That is, they were to go either against those who were not *really* the friends of God, or those who *in their estimation* were not. Perhaps, if there were nothing in the connection to demand a different interpretation, the former would be the most natural explanation of the passage; but the language *may be* understood as referring to the purpose which they considered themselves as called upon to execute: that is, that they were to go against those whom they regarded as being strangers to the true God, to wit, idolaters. Now it is well known that Mahomet considered himself called upon, principally, to make war with idolaters, and that he went forth, professedly, to bring them into subjection to the service of the true God. "The means of persuasion," says Mr. Gibbon, "had been tried, the season of forbearance was elapsed, and he was now commanded to propagate his religion by the sword, to destroy the monuments of idolatry, and, without regarding the sanctity of days or months, to pursue the unbelieving nations of the earth," iii. 387. "The fair option of friendship, or submission, or battle, was proposed to the enemies of Mahomet" (*ibid.*). "The sword," says Mahomet, "is the key of heaven and hell; a drop of blood shed in the cause of God, a night spent in arms, is of more avail than two months of fasting and prayer: whosoever falls in battle, his sins are forgiven; at the day of judgment his wounds shall be resplendent

as vermilion, and odoriferous as musk; and the loss of his limbs shall be supplied by the wings of angels and cherubim" (Gibbon, iii. 387). The first conflicts waged by Mahomet were against the *idolaters* of his own country—those who can, on no supposition, be regarded as "having the seal of God in their foreheads;" his subsequent wars were against *infidels* of all classes; that is, against those whom he regarded as not having the "seal of God in their foreheads," or as being the enemies of God. (*e*) The other part of the commission was "not to kill, but to torment them." Notes, ver. 5. Compare the quotation from the command of Aboubekir, as quoted above: "Let not the victory be stained with the blood of women and children." "Let them alone, and neither kill them nor destroy their monasteries." The meaning of this, if understood as applied to their commission against Christendom, would seem to be, that they were not to go forth to "kill," but to "torment" them; to wit, by the calamities which they would bring upon Christian nations for a definite period. Indeed, as we have seen above, it was an express command of Aboubekir that they should not put those to death who were found leading quiet and peaceable lives in monasteries, though against another class he *did* give an express command to "cleave their skulls." See Gibbon, iii. 418. As applicable to the conflicts of the Saracens with Christians, the meaning here would seem to be, that the power conceded to those who are represented by the locusts was not to cut off and to destroy the church, but it was to bring upon it various calamities to continue for a definite period. Accordingly, some of the severest afflictions which have come upon the church have undoubtedly proceeded from the followers of the Prophet of Mecca. There were times in the early history of that religion when, to all human appearance, it would universally prevail, and wholly supplant the Christian church. But the church still survived, and no power was at any time given to the Saracenic hosts to destroy it altogether. In respect to this, some remarkable facts have occurred in history. The followers of the false prophet contemplated the subjugation of Europe, and the destruction of Christianity, from two quarters—the East and the West—expecting to make a junction of the two armies in the north of Italy, and to march down to Rome. Twice did they attack the *vital* part of Christendom by besieging Constantinople: first, in the seven years' siege, which lasted from A.D. 668 to A.D. 675; and, secondly, in the years 716-718, when Leo the Isaurian was on the imperial throne. But on both occasions they were obliged to retire defeated and disgraced.—Gibbon, iii. 461, seq. Again, they renewed their attack on the West. Having conquered Northern Africa, they passed over into Spain, subdued that country and Portugal, and extended their conquests as far as the Loire. At that time they designed to subdue France, and having united with the forces which they expected from the East, they intended to make a descent on Italy, and complete the conquest of Europe. This purpose was defeated by the valour of Charles Martel, and Europe and the Christian world were saved from subjugation (Gibbon, iii. 467, seq.). "A victorious line of march," says Mr. Gibbon, "had been prolonged above a thousand miles, from the rock of Gibraltar to the banks of the Loire; the repetition of an equal space would have carried the Saracens to the confines of Poland and the Highlands of Scotland. The Rhine is not more impassable than the Nile or the Euphrates, and the Arabian fleet might have sailed without a naval combat into the mouth of the Thames. Perhaps the interpretation of the Koran would now be taught in the schools of Oxford, and her pulpits might demonstrate to a circumcised people the sanctity and truth of the revelations of Mohammed." The arrest of the Saracen hosts before Europe was subdued, was what there was no reason to anticipate, and it even yet perplexes historians to be able to account for it. "The calm historian," says Mr. Gibbon, "who strives to follow the rapid course of the Saracens, must study to explain by what means the church and state were saved from this impending, and, as it should seem, inevitable danger." "These conquests," says Mr. Hallam, "which astonish the careless and superficial, are less perplexing to a calm inquirer than their cessation—the loss of half the Roman empire than the preservation of the rest" (*Middle Ages*, ii. 3, 169). These illustrations may serve to explain the meaning of the symbol—that their grand commission was not to annihilate or root out, but to annoy and afflict. Indeed, they did not go forth with a primary design to *destroy.* The announcement of the Mussulman always was "the Koran, the tribute, or the sword," and when there was submission, either by embracing his religion or by tribute, life was always spared. "The fair option of friendship, or submission, or battle," says Mr. Gibbon (iii. 387), "was proposed to the enemies of Mohammed." Comp. also vol. iii. 453, 456. The *torment* mentioned here, I suppose, refers to the calamities brought upon the Christian world—on Egypt, and Northern Africa, and Spain, and Gaul, and the East—by the hordes which came out of Arabia, and which swept over all those countries like a troublesome and destructive host of locusts. Indeed, would *any* image better represent the effects of the Saracenic invasions than such a countless host of locusts? Even now, can we find an image that would better represent this?

(5) *The leader of this host.* (*a*) He was like a star that fell from heaven, (ver. 1), a bright and illustrious prince, *as if* heaven-endowed, but fallen. Would anything better characterize the genius, the power, and the splendid but perverted talent of Mahomet? Mahomet was, moreover, by birth, of the princely house of the Koreish, governors of Mecca, and to no one could the term be more appropriate than to one of that family. (*b*) He was a king. That is, there was to be one monarch—one ruling spirit to which all these hosts were subject. And never was anything more appropriate than this title as applied to the leader of the Arabic hosts. All those hosts were subject to one mind—to the command of the single leader that originated the scheme. (*c*) The name *Abaddon,* or *Apollyon—Destroyer,* ver. 11. This name would be appropriate to one who spread his conquests so far over the world; who wasted so many cities and towns; who overthrew so many kingdoms; and who laid the foundation of ultimate conquests by which so many human beings were sent to the grave. (*d*) The description of the leader "as the angel of the bottomless pit," ver. 11. If this be regarded as meaning that "the angel of the bottomless pit"—the spirit of darkness himself—originated the scheme, and animated these hosts, what term would better characterize the leader? And if it be a poetic description of Mahomet as sent out by that presiding spirit of evil, how could a better representative of the spirit of the nether world have been sent out upon the earth than he was—one more talented, more sagacious, more powerful, more warlike, more wicked, more fitted to subdue the nations of the earth to the dominion of the Prince of Darkness, and to hold them for ages under his yoke?

(6) *The duration of the torment.* It is said (ver. 5) that this would be five months; that is, prophetically, a hundred and fifty years. See Notes on ver. 5. The Hegira, or flight of Mahomet, occurred A.D. 622; the Saracens first issued from the desert into Syria, and began their series of wars on Christendom, A.D. 629. Reckoning from these periods respectively, the five months, or the hundred and fifty years, would extend to A.D. 772 or 779. It is not necessary to understand this period of a hundred and fifty years of the actual continued existence of the bodies symbolized by the locusts, but only of the period in which they would inflict their "torment"—"that they should be tormented five months." That is, this would be the period of the *intensity* of the woe inflicted by them; there would be at that time some marked intermission of the torrent. The question then is, whether, in the history of the Saracens, there was any period after their career of conquest had been continued for about a hundred and fifty years, which would mark the intermission or cessation of these "torments." If so, then this is all that is necessary to determine the applicability of the symbol to the Arabian hordes. Now, in reply to this question, we have only to refer to Mr. Gibbon. The table of contents prefixed to chapters forty-one and forty-two of his work would supply all the information desired. I looked at that table, after making the estimate as to what period the "five months," or hundred and fifty years, would conduct us to, to see whether anything occurred at about that time in the Mahometan power and influence, which could be regarded as marking the time of the intermission or cessation of the calamities inflicted by the Arabic hordes on the Christian world. After Mr. Gibbon had recorded in detail (vol. iii. 360-460) the character and conquests of the Arabian

hordes under Mahomet and his successors, I find the statement of the decline of their power at just about the period to which the hundred and fifty years would lead us, for at that very time an important change came over the followers of the prophet of Mecca, turning them from the love of conquest to the pursuits of literature and science. From that period they ceased to be formidable to the church; their limits were gradually contracted; their power diminished; and the Christian world, in regard to them, was substantially at peace. This change in the character and purposes of the Saracens is thus described by Mr. Gibbon, at the close of the reign of the caliph Abdalrahman, whose reign commenced A.D. 755, and under whom the *peaceful* sway of the Ommiades of Spain began, which continued for a period of two hundred and fifty years. "The luxury of the caliphs, so useless to their private happiness, relaxed the nerves, and terminated the progress, of the Arabian empire. Temporal and spiritual conquest had been the sole occupation of the first successors of Mahomet; and after supplying themselves with the necessaries of life, the whole revenue was scrupulously devoted to that salutary work. The Abassides were impoverished by the multitude of their wants, and their contempt of economy. Instead of pursuing the great object of ambition, their leisure, their affections, and the powers of their minds were diverted by pomp and pleasure: the rewards of valour were embezzled by women and eunuchs, and the royal camp was encumbered by the luxury of the palace. A similar temper was diffused among the subjects of the caliph. Their stern enthusiasm was softened by time and prosperity: they sought riches in the occupations of industry, fame in the pursuits of literature, and happiness in the tranquillity of domestic life. War was no longer the passion of the Saracens; and the increase of pay, the repetition of donatives, were insufficient to allure the posterity of those voluntary champions who had crowded to the standard of Aboubekir and Omar for the hopes of spoil and of paradise," iii. 477, 478. Of the Ommiades, or princes who succeeded Abdalrahman, Mr. Gibbon remarks in general—"Their mutual designs or declarations of war evaporated without effect; but instead of opening a door to the conquest of Europe, Spain was dissevered from the trunk of the monarchy, engaged in perpetual hostility with the East, *and inclined to peace and friendship with the Christian sovereigns of Constantinople and France,*" iii. p. 472. How much does this look like some change occurring by which they would cease to be a source of "torment" to the nations with whom they now dwelt! From this period they gave themselves to the arts of peace; cultivated literature and science; lost entirely their spirit of conquest, and their ambition for universal dominion, until they gradually withdrew, or were driven, from those parts of the Christian world where they had inspired most terror, and which in the days of their power and ambition they had invaded. By turning merely to the "table of contents" of Mr. Gibbon's history, the following periods, occurring at about the time that would be embraced in the "five months," or hundred and fifty years, are distinctly marked:—

"A.D.
668–675. First siege of Constantinople by the Arabs.
677. Peace and tribute.
716–718. Second siege of Constantinople.
„ Failure and retreat of the Saracens.
„ Invention and use of the Greek fire.
721. Invasion of France by the Arabs.
732. Defeat of the Saracens by Charles Martel.
„ They retreat before the Franks.
746–750. The elevation of the Abassides.
750. Fall of the Ommiades.
755. Revolt of Spain.
„ Triple division of the caliphate.
750–960. Magnificence of the caliphs.
„ Its consequences on private and public happiness.
754, &c. Introduction of learning among the Arabians.
„ Their real progress in the sciences."

It will be seen from this that the decline of their military and civil power; their defeats in their attempts to subjugate Europe; their turning their attention to the peaceful pursuits of literature and science, synchronize remarkably with the period that would be indicated by the five months, or the hundred and fifty years. It should be added, also, that in the year 762, Almanzor, the caliph, built Bagdad, and made it the capital of the Saracen empire. Henceforward that became the seat of Arabic learning, luxury, and power, and the wealth and talent of the Saracen empire were gradually drawn to that capital, and they ceased to vex and annoy the Christian world. The

12 One*q* woe is past; *and*, behold, there come two woes more hereafter.

13 And the sixth angel sounded,

*q* ch.8.13.

and I heard a voice from the four horns of the golden altar which is before God,

14 Saying to the sixth angel, which had the trumpet, Loose the

building of Bagdad occurred within just ten years of the time indicated by the "five months"—reckoning that from the Hegira, or flight of Mahomet; or reckoning from the time when Mahomet began to preach (A.D. 609—Gibbon, iii. 383), it wanted but three years of coinciding exactly with the period.

These considerations show with what propriety the fifth trumpet—the symbol of the locusts—is referred to the Arabian hordes under the guidance of Mahomet and his successors. On the supposition that it was the design of John to symbolize these events, the symbol has been chosen which of all others was best adapted to the end. If, now that these events are past, we should endeavour to find some symbol which would appropriately represent them, we could not find one that would be more striking or appropriate than that which is here employed by John.

12. *One woe is past.* The *woe* referred to in ver. 1-11. In ch. viii. 13 three woes are mentioned which were to occur successively, and which were to embrace the whole of the period comprised in the seven seals and the seven trumpets. Under the last of the seals we have considered four successive periods, referring to events connected with the downfall of the Western empire; and then we have found one important event worthy of a place in noticing the things which would permanently affect the destiny of the world—the rise, the character, and the conquests of the Saracens. This was referred to by the first *woe-trumpet*. We enter now on the consideration of the second. This occupies the remainder of the chapter, and in illustrating it the same method will be pursued as heretofore: first, to explain the literal meaning of the words, phrases, and symbols; and then to inquire what events in history, if any, succeeding the former, occurred, which would correspond with the language used. ¶ *And, behold, there come two woes more hereafter.* Two momentous and important events that will be attended with sorrow to mankind. It cannot be intended that there would be no *other* evils that would visit mankind; but the eye, in glancing along the future, rested on these as having a special pre-eminence in affecting the destiny of the church and the world.

13. *And the sixth angel sounded.* See Notes on ch. viii. 2, 7. ¶ *And I heard a voice from the four horns of the golden altar which is before God.* In the language here used there is an allusion to the temple, but the scene is evidently laid in heaven. The temple in its arrangements was designed, undoubtedly, to be in important respects a symbol of heaven, and this idea constantly occurs in the Scriptures. Comp. the Epistle to the Hebrews *passim*. The golden altar stood in the holy place, between the table of show-bread and the golden candlestick. See Notes on He. ix. 1, 2. This altar, made of shittim or acacia wood, was ornamented at the four corners, and overlaid throughout with laminæ of gold. Hence it was called "the golden altar," in contradistinction from the altar for sacrifice, which was made of stone. Comp. Notes on Mat. xxi. 12, seq. On its four corners it had projections which are called *horns* (Ex. xxx. 2, 3), which seem to have been intended mainly for ornaments. See Jahn, *Arch*. § 332; Joseph. *Ant*. iii. 6, 8. When it is said that this was "before God," the meaning is, that it was directly before or in front of the symbol of the divine presence in the most holy place. This image, in the vision of John, is transformed to heaven. The voice seemed to come from the very presence of the Deity; from the place where offerings are made to God.

14. *Saying to the sixth angel, which had the trumpet.* Notes, ch. viii. 2. ¶ *Loose*, &c. This power, it would seem, was given to the sixth angel in addition to his office of blowing the trumpet. All this, of course, was in vision, and cannot be literally interpreted. The meaning is, that the effect of his blowing the trumpet would be the same *as if* angels that had been bound should be suddenly loosed and suffered to go forth over the earth; that is, some event would occur which would be properly symbolized by

four angels which are bound in the great river *r* Euphrates.

*r* ch.16.12; Ge.2.14; Je.51.63.

such an act. ¶ *The four angels.* Comp. Notes, ch. viii. 2. It was customary to represent important events as occurring under the ministry of angels. The general meaning here is, that in the vicinity of the river Euphrates there were mighty powers which had been bound or held in check, which were now to be let loose upon the world. What we are to look for in the fulfilment is evidently this—some power that seemed to be kept back by an invisible influence as if by angels, now suddenly let loose and suffered to accomplish the purpose of desolation mentioned in the subsequent verses. It is not necessary to suppose that angels were actually employed in these restraints, though no one can demonstrate that their agency was *not* concerned in the transactions here referred to. Comp. Notes on Da. x. 12, 13. It has been made a question why the number *four* is specified, and whether the forces were in any sense made up of four divisions, nations, or people. While nothing certain can be determined in regard to that, and while the number four *may* be used merely to denote a great and strong force, yet it must be admitted that the most obvious interpretation would be to refer it to some combination of forces, or to some union of powers, that was to accomplish what is here said. If it had been a single nation, it would have been more in accordance with the usual method in prophecy to have represented them as restrained by an angel, or by angels in general, without specifying any number. ¶ *Which are bound.* That is, they *seemed* to be bound. There was something which held them, and the forces under them, in check, until they were thus commanded to go forth. In the fulfilment of this it will be necessary to look for something of the nature of a check or restraint on these forces, until they were commissioned to go forth to accomplish the work of destruction. ¶ *In the great river Euphrates.* The well-known river of that name, commonly called, in the Scriptures, "the great river," and, by way of eminence, "*the* river," Ex. xxiii. 31; Is. viii. 7. This river was on the east of Palestine; and the language here used naturally denotes that the power referred to under the sixth trumpet would spring

15 And the four angels were loosed, which were prepared ²for

² or, *at.*

up in the East, and that it would have its origin in the vicinity of that river. Those interpreters, therefore, who apply this to the invasion of Judæa by the Romans have great difficulty in explaining this—as the forces employed in the destruction of Jerusalem came from the West, and not from the East. The fair interpretation is, that there were forces in the vicinity of the Euphrates which were, up to this period, bound or restrained, but which were now suffered to spread woe and sorrow over a considerable portion of the world.

15. *And the four angels were loosed.* Who had this mighty host under restraint. The loosening of the angels was, in fact, also a letting loose of all these hosts, that they might accomplish the work which they were commissioned to do. ¶ *Which were prepared.* See ver. 7. The word here used properly refers to that which is made ready, fitted up, arranged for anything: as persons prepared for a journey, horses for battle, a road for travellers, food for the hungry, a house to live in, &c. See Rob. *Lex.*, sub. voce 'Ετοιμάζω. As used here, the word means that whatever was necessary to *prepare* these angels —the leaders of this host—for the work which they were commissioned to perform, was now done, and that they stood in a state of readiness to execute the design. In the fulfilment of this it will be necessary to look for some arrangements existing in the vicinity of the Euphrates, by which these restrained hosts were *in a state of readiness* to be summoned forth to the execution of this work, or in such a condition that they *would* go forth spontaneously if the restraints existing were removed. ¶ *For an hour*, &c. Marg., *at.* The Greek—εἰς—means properly *unto*, *with reference to;* and the sense is, that, with reference to that hour, they had all the requisite preparation. Professor Stuart explains it as meaning that they were "prepared for the particular year, month, day, and hour, destined by God for the great catastrophe which is to follow." The meaning, however, rather seems to be that they were prepared, not for the *commencement* of such a period, but they were prepared for *the whole period* indicated by the hour, the day, the month, and the year; that is,

an hour, and a day, and a month, and a year, for to *s*slay the third part of men.

16 And the number of the *t*army

*s* ch.8.7–9.   *t* Eze.38.4; Da.11.40.

that the continuance of this "woe" would extend along through the whole period. For (*a*) this is the natural interpretation of the word "for"—εἰς; (*b*) it makes the whole sentence intelligible—for though it might be proper to say of anything that it was "prepared for an hour," indicating the commencement of what was to be done, it is not usual to say of anything that it is "prepared for an hour, a month, a day, a year," when the design is merely to indicate the *beginning* of it; and (*c*) it is in accordance with the prediction respecting the first "woe" (ver. 5), where the time is specified in language similar to this, to wit, "five months." It seems to me, therefore, that we are to regard the time here mentioned as a prophetic indication of the period during which this woe would continue. ¶ *An hour, and a day, and a month, and a year.* If this were to be taken literally, it would, of course, be but little more than a year. If it be taken, however, in the common prophetic style, where a day is put for a year (see Notes on Da. ix. 24, seq.; also Editor's Preface, p. xxv. &c.), then the amount of time (360 + 30 + 1 + an hour) would be three hundred and ninety-one years, and the portion of a year indicated by an hour —a twelfth or twenty-fourth part, according as the day was supposed to be divided into twelve or twenty-four hours. That this is the true view seems to be clear, because this accords with the usual style in this book; because it can hardly be supposed that the "preparation" here referred to would have been for so brief a period as the time would be if literally interpreted; and because the mention of so small a portion of time as an " hour," if literally taken, would be improbable in so great transactions. The fair interpretation, therefore, will require us to find some events that will fill up the period of about three hundred and ninety-one years. ¶ *For to slay the third part of men.* Comp. ch. viii. 7, 9, 12. The meaning here is, that the immense host which was restrained on the Euphrates would, when loosed, spread desolation over about a third part of the world. We are not to suppose that this is to be of the horsemen *were* *u*two hundred thousand thousand: and *v*I heard the number of them.

17 And thus I saw the horses

*u* Ps.68.17.   *v* ch.7.4.

understood in exactly a literal sense; but the meaning is, that the desolation would be so widespread that it would seem to embrace a third of the world. No such event as the cutting off of a few thousands of Jews in the siege of Jerusalem would correspond with the language here employed, and we must look for events more general and more disastrous to mankind at large.

16. *And the number of the army of the horsemen.* It is to be observed here that the strength of the army seemed to be cavalry. In the former plagues there is no distinct mention of horsemen; but here that which struck the beholder was the immense and unparalleled number of horsemen. ¶ Were *two hundred thousand thousand.* A thousand thousand are a million, and consequently the number here referred to would be two hundred millions. This would be a larger army than was ever assembled, and it cannot be supposed that it is to be taken literally. That it would be a very large host—so large that it would not be readily numbered—is clear. The expression in the original, while it naturally conveys the idea of an immense number, would seem also to refer to some peculiarity in the manner of reckoning them. The language is, *two myriads of myriads* — δύο μυριάδες μυριάδων. The myriad was ten thousand. The idea would seem to be this. John saw an immense host of cavalry. They appeared to be divided into large bodies that were in some degree separate, and that might be reckoned by ten thousands. Of these different squadrons there were many, and to express their great and unusual numbers he said that there seemed to be *myriads* of them— two myriads of myriads, or twice ten thousand myriads. The army thus would seem to be immense—an army, as we should say, to be reckoned *by tens of thousands.* ¶ *And I heard the number of them.* They were so numerous that he did not pretend to be able to estimate the number himself, for it was beyond his power of computation; but he heard it stated in these round numbers, that there were "two myriads of myriads" of them.

17. *And thus I saw the horses in the*

in the vision, and them that sat on them, having breastplates of fire, and of jacinth, and brimstone: and the heads of the horses *were* as *w* the

*w* 1 Ch. 12.8; Is 5.28,29.

*vision.* That is, he saw them as he proceeds to describe them, for the word *thus* — οὕτως — refers to what follows. Comp. Rob. *Lex.* on the word, (*b*), and see Mat. i. 18; ii. 5; Jn. xxi. 1; He. iv. 4. Professor Stuart, however, refers to what precedes. The meaning, as it seems to me, is, that he fixed his attention on the appearance of the immense army—the horses and their riders, and proceeded to describe them as they struck him. ¶ *And them that sat on them.* He fixed the attention on horse and rider. Their appearance was unusual, and deserved a particular description. ¶ *Having breastplates of fire.* That is, those who sat on them had such breastplates. The word here rendered breastplate denoted properly a coat of mail that covered the body from the neck to the thighs. See Notes on Ep. vi. 14. This would be a prominent object in looking at a horseman. This was said to be composed of "fire, and jacinth, and brimstone;" that is, the part of the body usually incased in the coat of mail had these three colours. The word "fire" here simply denotes *red*. It was burnished and bright, and seemed to be a blaze of fire. The word "jacinth"—ὑακίνθινους—means hyacinthine. The colour denoted is that of the hyacinth—a flower of a deep purple or reddish blue. Then it refers to a gem of the same colour, nearly related to the *zircon* of the mineralogists, and the colour here mentioned is deep purple or reddish blue. The word rendered "brimstone"—θειώδης—means properly sulphurous, that is, made of sulphur, and means here simply *yellow*. The meaning of the whole then is, that these horsemen appeared to be clad in a peculiar kind of armour—armour that shone like fire, mingled with blue and yellow. It will be necessary to look for the fulfilment of this in cavalry that was so caparisoned. ¶ *And the heads of the horses* were *as the heads of lions.* Resembled, in some respects, the heads of lions. He does not say that they *were* the heads of lions, or that the riders were on monsters, but only that they, in some respects, *resembled* the heads of lions. It would be easy to give this general appearance by the heads of lions: and out of their mouths issued fire and smoke and brimstone.

18 By these three was the third part of men killed, by the fire, and

way in which the head-dress of the horses was arrayed. ¶ *And out of their mouths issued.* That is, *appeared* to issue. It is not necessary to understand this as affirming that it actually came from their *mouths*, but only that, to one looking on such an approaching army, it would have this *appearance.* The heathen poets often speak of horses breathing out fire and smoke (Virg. *Geor.* vol. ii. p. 140; iii. 85; Ovid, *Met.* vol. vii. p. 104), meaning that their *breath* seemed to be mingled smoke and fire. There is an image superadded here not found in any of the classic descriptions, that this was mingled with *brimstone.* All this *seemed* to issue from their mouths—that is, it was breathed forth in front of the host, as if the horses emitted it from their mouths. ¶ *Fire and smoke and brimstone.* The *exact* idea, whether that was intended or not, would be conveyed by the discharge of musketry or artillery. The fire, the smoke, and the sulphurous smell of such a discharge would correspond precisely with this language; and if it be supposed that the writer *meant* to describe such a discharge, this would be the very language that would be used. Moreover, in describing a battle nothing would be more proper than to say that this *appeared* to issue from the horses' mouths. If, therefore, it should be found that there were any events where firearms were used, in contradistinction from the ancient mode of warfare, this *language* would be appropriate to describe that; and if it were ascertained that the writer meant to refer to some such fact, then the language here used would be that which he would adopt. One thing is certain, that this is *not* language which would be employed to describe the onset of ancient cavalry in the mode of warfare which prevailed then. No one describing a charge of cavalry among the Persians, the Greeks, or the Romans, when the only armour was the sword and the spear, would think of saying that there seemed to be emitted from the horses' mouths fire, and smoke, and brimstone.

18. *By these three.* Three things—

A.D. 96.] CHAPTER IX. 229

by the smoke, and by the brimstone, which issued out of their mouths.

19 For their power is in their mouth, and in their tails: for *their tails were like unto serpents, and had heads, and with them they do hurt.

20 And the rest of the men which were not killed by these plagues, *y*yet repented not of the works of their hands, that they should not *z*worship devils, and *a*idols of gold, and silver, and brass, and stone, and of wood: which neither can see, nor hear, nor walk.

21 Neither repented they of their murders, nor of their *b*sorceries, nor of their fornication, nor of their thefts.

*x* Is.9.15; Ep.4.14.   *y* Je.5.3; 8.6.
*z* Le.17.7; 1 Co.10.20.
*a* Ps.135.15; Is.40.19,20.   *b* ch.22.15.

explained immediately as referring to the fire, the smoke, and the brimstone. ¶ *Was the third part of men killed.* See Notes on ch. viii. 7–12, on each of which verses we have notices of calamities that came upon the third part of the race, of the sea, of rivers, &c. We are not to suppose that this is to be taken literally, but the description is given as it *appeared* to John. Those immense numbers of horsemen would sweep over the world, and a full third part of the race of men would seem to fall before them.

19. *For their power is in their mouth.* That is, as described in the fire, smoke, and brimstone that proceeded out of their mouths. What struck the seer as remarkable on looking on the symbol was, that this immense destruction seemed to proceed out of their mouths. It was not that they trampled down their enemies; nor that they destroyed them with the sword, the bow, or the spear: it was some new and remarkable power in warfare—in which the destruction seemed to proceed from fire, and smoke, and sulphur issuing from the mouths of the horses themselves. ¶ *And in their tails.* The tails of the horses. This, of course, was something unusual and remarkable in horses, for naturally they have no power there. The power of a fish, or a scorpion, or a wasp, may be said to be in their tails, for their strength or their means of defence or of injury are there; but we never think of speaking in this way of horses. It is not necessary, in the interpretation of this, to suppose that the reference is literally to the tails of the horses, any more than it is to suppose that the smoke, and fire, and brimstone literally proceeded from their mouths. John describes things as they *appeared* to him in looking at them from a considerable distance. From their mouths the horses belched forth fire, and smoke, and sulphur, and even their tails seemed to be armed for the work of death. ¶ *For their tails* were *like unto serpents.* Not like the tails of serpents, but like serpents themselves. ¶ *And had heads.* That is, there was something remarkable in the position and appearance of their *heads.* All serpents, of course, have heads; but John saw something unusual in this— or something so peculiar in their heads as to attract special attention. It would seem most probable that the heads of these serpents appeared to extend in every direction—as if the hairs of the horses' tails had been converted into snakes, presenting a most fearful and destructive image. Perhaps it may illustrate this to suppose that there is reference to the Amphisbæna, or two-headed snake. It is said of this reptile that its tail resembles a head, and that with this it throws out its poison (Lucan, vol. ix. p. 179; Pliny's *Hist. Nat.* vol. viii. p. 35). It really has but one head, but its tail has the appearance of a head, and it has the power of moving in either direction to a limited degree. If we suppose these snakes fastened to the tail of a horse, the appearance of *heads* would be very prominent and remarkable. The image is that of the power of destruction. They seemed like ugly and poisonous serpents instead of tails. ¶ *And with them they do hurt.* Not the main injury, but they have the power of inflicting *some* injury by them.

20, 21. *And the rest of the men which were not killed by these plagues,* &c. One third part is represented as swept off, and it might have been expected that a salutary effect would have been produced on the remainder, in reforming them, and restraining them from error and sin. The writer proceeds to state, however, that these judgments did *not* have the effect which might reasonably have been anticipated. No reformation followed; there was no abandonment of the prevailing forms of iniquity; there was no change in their idolatry and superstition. In regard to the *exact* meaning of what is here stated (ver. 20, 21), it will be a more convenient arrangement to consider it *after* we have ascertained the proper application of the passage relating to the sixth trumpet. What is here stated (ver. 20, 21) pertains to the state of the world *after* the desolations which would occur under this woe-trumpet; and the explanation of the words may be reserved, therefore, with propriety, until the inquiry shall have been instituted as to the general design of the whole.

With respect to the fulfilment of this symbol—the sixth trumpet—it will be necessary to inquire whether there has been any event, or class of events, occurring at such a time, and in such a manner, as would be properly denoted by such a symbol. The examination of this question will make it necessary to go over the leading points *in* the symbol, and to endeavour to apply them. In doing this I shall simply state, with such illustrations as may occur, what seems to me to have been the design of the symbol. It would be an endless task to examine all the explanations which have been proposed, and it would be useless to do so.

The reference, then, seems to me to be to the Turkish power, extending from the time of the first appearance of the Turks in the neighbourhood of the Euphrates, to the final conquest of Constantinople in 1453. The general reasons for this opinion are such as the following:—(*a*) If the previous trumpet referred to the Saracens, or to the rise of the Mahometan power among the Arabs, then the Turkish dominion, being the next in succession, would be that which would most naturally be symbolized. (*b*) The Turkish power rose on the decline of the Arabic, and was the next important power in affecting the destinies of the world. (*c*) This power, like the former, had its seat in the East, and would be properly classified under the events occurring there as affecting the destiny of the world. (*d*) The introduction of this power was *necessary*, in order to complete the survey of the downfall of the Roman empire—the great object kept in view all along in these symbols. In the first four of these trumpets, under the seventh seal, we found the decline and fall of the *Western* empire; in the first of the remaining three—the fifth in order—we found the rise of the Saracens, materially affecting the condition of the *Eastern* portion of the Roman world; and the notice of the Turks, under whom the empire at last fell to rise no more, seemed to be demanded in order to the completion of the picture. As a leading design of the whole vision was to describe the ultimate destiny of that formidable power—the Roman— which, in the time when the Revelation was given to John, ruled over the whole world; under which the church was then oppressed; and which, either as a civil or ecclesiastical power, was to exert so important an influence on the destiny of the church, it was proper that its history should be sketched until it ceased—that is, until the conquest of the capital of the Eastern empire by the Turks. Here the termination of the empire, as traced by Mr. Gibbon, closes; and these events it was important to incorporate in this series of visions.

The rise and character of the Turkish people may be seen stated in full in Gibbon, *Decline and Fall*, iii. 101–103, 105, 486; iv. 41, 42, 87, 90, 91, 93, 100, 127, 143, 151, 258, 260, 289, 350. The leading facts in regard to the history of the Turks, so far as they are necessary to be known before we proceed to apply the symbols, are the following:—(1) The Turks, or Turkmans, had their origin in the vicinity of the Caspian Sea, and were divided into two branches, one on the east, and the other on the west. The latter colony, in the tenth century, could muster forty thousand soldiers; the other numbered a hundred thousand families (Gibbon, iv. 90). By the latter of these, Persia was invaded and subdued, and soon Bagdad also came into their possession, and the seat of the caliph was occupied by a Turkish prince. The various details respecting this, and respecting their conversion to the faith of the Koran, may be seen in Gibbon, iv. 90–93. A mighty Turkish and Moslem power was thus concentrated under Togrul, who had subdued the caliph, in the vicinity of the Tigris and the Euphrates, extending east over Persia and the countries adjacent to the Caspian Sea, but it had not yet crossed the Euphrates to carry its conquests to the west. The conquest of Bagdad by Togrul, the first prince of the Seljuk race, was an important event, not only in itself, but as it was by this event that the Turk was constituted temporal lieutenant of the prophet's vicar, and so the head of the temporal power of the religion of Islam. "The conqueror of the East kissed the ground, stood some time in a modest posture, and was led toward the throne by the vizier and an interpreter. After Togrul had seated himself on another throne his commission was publicly read, which declared him the temporal lieutenant of the prophet. He was successively invested with seven robes of honour, and presented with seven slaves, the natives of the seven climates of the Arabian empire, &c. Their alliance [of the sultan and the caliph] was cemented by the marriage of Togrul's sister with the successor of the prophet," &c. (Gibbon, iv. 93). The conquest of Persia, the subjugation of Bagdad, the union of the Turkish power with that of the caliph, the successor of Mahomet, and the foundation of this powerful kingdom in the neighbourhood of the Euphrates, is all that is necessary to explain the sense of the phrase "which were *prepared* for an hour," &c., ver. 15. The arrangements were then made for the important series of events which were to occur when that formidable power should be summoned from the East, to spread the predicted desolation over so large a part of the world. A mighty dominion had been forming in the East that had subdued Persia, and that, by union with the caliphs, by the subjugation of Bagdad, and by embracing the Mahometan faith, had become "*prepared*" to play its subsequent important part in the affairs of the world. (2) The next important event in their history was the crossing of the Euphrates, and the invasion of Asia Minor. The account of this invasion can be best given in the words of Mr. Gibbon: "Twenty-five years after the death of Basil [the Greek emperor], his successors were suddenly assaulted by an unknown race of barbarians, who united the Scythian valour with the fanaticism of new proselytes, and the art and riches of a powerful monarchy. The myriads of Turkish horse overspread a frontier of six hundred miles from Taurus to Arzeroum, and the blood of one hundred and thirty thousand Christians was a grateful sacrifice to the Arabian prophet. Yet the arms of Togrul did not make any deep or lasting impression on the Greek empire. The torrent rolled away from the open country; the sultan retired without glory or success from the siege of an Armenian city; the obscure hostilities were continued or suspended with a vicissitude of events; and the bravery of the Macedonian legions renewed the fame of the conqueror of Asia. The name of Alp Arslan, the valiant lion, is expressive of the popular idea of the perfection of man; and the successor of Togrul displayed the fierceness and generosity of the royal animal. ['The heads of the horses were as the heads of lions.'] He passed the Euphrates at the head of the Turkish cavalry, and entered Cæsarea, the metropolis of Cappadocia, to which he had been attracted by the fame and the wealth of the temple of St. Basil" (vol. iv. 93, 94; comp. also p. 95). (3) The next important event was the establishing of the kingdom of *Roum* in Asia Minor. After a succession of victories and defeats; after being driven once and again from Asia Minor, and compelled to retire beyond its limits; and after subjecting the East to their arms (Gibbon, iv. 95–100) in the various contests for the crown of the Eastern empire, the aid of the Turks was invoked by one party or the other until they secured for themselves a firm foothold in Asia Minor, and established themselves there in a permanent kingdom — evidently with the purpose of seizing upon Constantinople itself when an opportunity should be presented (Gibbon, iv. 100, 101). Of this kingdom of *Roum* Mr. Gibbon (iv. 101) gives the following description, and speaks thus of the effect of its establishment on the destiny of the Eastern empire : "Since the first conquests of the caliphs, the establishment of the Turks in Anatolia, or Asia Minor, was the most deplorable loss which the church and empire had sustained. By the propagation of the Moslem faith Soliman deserved the name of Gazi, a holy champion; and his new kingdom of the Romans, or of *Roum*, was added to the table of Oriental geography. It is described as extending *from the Euphrates to Constantinople*, from the Black Sea to the confines of Syria; pregnant with mines of silver and iron, of alum and copper, fruitful in corn and wine, and productive of cattle and excellent horses. The wealth of Lydia, the arts of the Greeks, the splendour of the Augustan age, existed only in books and ruins, which were equally obscure in the eyes of the Scythian conquerors. By the choice of the Sultan, Nice, the metropolis of Bithynia, was preferred for his palace and fortress—the seat of the Seljukian dynasty of Roum was planted one hundred miles from Constantinople; and the divinity of Christ was denied and derided in the same temple in which it had been pronounced by the first general synod of the Catholics. The unity of God and the mission of Mahomet were preached in the mosques; the Arabian learning was taught in the schools; the cadis judged according to the law of the Koran; the Turkish manners and language prevailed in the cities; and Turkman camps were scattered over the plains and mountains of Anatolia," &c. (4) The next material event in the history of the Turkish power was the conquest of Jerusalem. See this described in Gibbon, iv. 102-106. By this the attention of the Turks was turned for a time from the conquest of Constantinople—an event at which the Turkish power all along aimed, and in which they doubtless expected to be ultimately successful. Had they not been diverted from it by the wars connected with the Crusades, Constantinople would have fallen long before it did fall, for it was too feeble to defend itself if it had been attacked. (5) The conquest of Jerusalem by the Turks, and the oppressions which Christians experienced there, gave rise to the Crusades, by which the destiny of Constantinople was still longer delayed. The war of the Crusades was made on the Turks, and as the crusaders mostly passed through Constantinople and Anatolia, all the power of the Turks in Asia Minor was requisite to defend themselves, and they were incapable of making an attack on Constantinople until after the final defeat of the crusaders and restoration of peace. See Gibbon, iv. 106-210. (6) The next material event in the history of the Turks was the conquest of Constantinople in A.D. 1453—an event which established the Turkish power in Europe and completed the downfall of the Roman empire (Gibbon, iv. 333-359).

After this brief reference to the general history of the Turkish power, we are prepared to inquire more particularly whether the symbol in the passage before us is applicable to this series of events. This may be considered in several particulars.

(1) *The time.* If the first woe-trumpet referred to the Saracens, then it would be natural that the rise and progress of the Turkish power should be symbolized as the next great fact in history, and as that under which the empire fell. As we have seen, the Turkish power rose immediately after the power of the Saracens had reached its height, and identified itself with the Mahometan religion; and was, in fact, the next great power that affected the Roman empire, the welfare of the church, and the history of the world. There can be no doubt, therefore, that the *time* is such as is demanded in the proper interpretation of the symbol.

(2) *The place.* We have seen (in the remarks on ver. 14) that this was on or near the river Euphrates, and that this power was long forming and consolidating itself on the east of that river before it crossed it in the invasion of Asia Minor. It had spread over Persia, and had even invaded the region of the East as far as the Indies; it had secured, under Togrul, the conquest of Bagdad, and had united itself with the caliphate, and was, in fact, a mighty power "*prepared*" for conquest before it moved to the west. Thus Mr. Gibbon (iv. 92) says, "The more rustic, perhaps the wisest, portion of the Turkmans continued to dwell in the tents of their ancestors; and from the Oxus to the *Euphrates* these military colonies were protected and propagated by their native princes." So again, speaking of Alp Arslan, the son and successor of Togrul, he says (iv. 94), "He passed the *Euphrates* at the head of the Turkish cavalry, and entered Cæsarea, the metropolis of Cappadocia, to which he was attracted by the fame and the wealth of the temple of St. Basil." If it be admitted that it was *intended* by John to refer to the Turkish power, it could not have been better represented than as a power that had been forming in the vicinity of that great river, and that was prepared to precipitate itself on the Eastern empire. To one contemplating it in the time of Togrul or Alp Arslan, it would have *appeared* as a mighty power growing up in the neighbourhood of the Euphrates.

(3) *The four angels:* "Loose the four angels which are bound." That is, loose the powers which are in the vicinity of the Euphrates, *as if* they were under the control of four angels. The most natural construction of this would

be, that under the mighty power that was to sweep over the world, there were four subordinate powers, or that there were such subdivisions that it might be supposed they were ranged under *four* angelic powers or leaders. The question is, whether there was any such division or arrangement of the Turkish power, that, to one looking on it at a distance, there would *seem* to be such a division. In the *History of the Decline and Fall of the Roman Empire* (iv. 100) we find the following statement:—"The greatness and unity of the Turkish empire expired in the person of Malek Shah. The vacant throne was disputed by his brother and his four sons; and, after a series of civil wars, the treaty which reconciled the surviving candidates confirmed a lasting separation in the Persian dynasty, the oldest and principal branch of the house of Seljuk. The three younger dynasties were those of *Kerman*, of *Syria*, and of *Roum;* the first of these commanded an extensive, though obscure dominion, on the shores of the Indian Ocean; the second expelled the Arabian princes of Aleppo and Damascus; and the third (our peculiar care) invaded the Roman provinces of Asia Minor. The generous policy of Malek contributed to their elevation; he allowed the princes of his blood, even those whom he had vanquished in the field, to seek new kingdoms worthy of their ambition; nor was he displeased that they should draw away the more ardent spirits who might have disturbed the tranquillity of his reign. As the supreme head of his family and nation, the great Sultan of Persia commanded the obedience and tribute of his royal brethren: the thrones of Kerman and Nice, of Aleppo and Damascus; the atabeks and emirs of Syria and Mesopotamia erected their standards under the shadow of his sceptre, and the hordes of Turkmans overspread the plains of Western Asia. After the death of Malek the bands of union and subordination were gradually relaxed and dissolved; the indulgence of the house of Seljuk invested their slaves with the inheritance of kingdoms; and, in the Oriental style, a crowd of princes arose from the dust of their feet." Here it is observable, that, at the period when the Turkman hordes were about to precipitate themselves on Europe, and to advance to the destruction of the Eastern empire, we have distinct mention of *four* great departments of the Turkish power: the original power that had established itself in Persia, under Malek Shah, and the three subordinate powers that sprung out of that of Kerman, Syria, and Roum. It is observable (*a*) that this occurs at the period when that power would appear in the East as advancing in its conquests to the West; (*b*) that it was in the vicinity of the great river Euphrates; (*c*) that it had never before occurred—the Turkish power having been before united as one; and (*d*) that it never afterwards occurred—for, in the words of Mr. Gibbon, "after the death of Malek the bands of union and subordination were relaxed and finally dissolved." It would not be improper, then, to look upon this one mighty power as under the control of four spirits that were held in check in the East, and that were "prepared" to pour their energies on the Roman empire.

(4) *The preparation:* "Prepared for an hour," &c. That is, arranged; made ready—as if by previous discipline—for some mighty enterprise. Applied to the Turkmans, this would mean that the preparation for the ultimate work which they executed had been making as that power increased and became consolidated under Togrul, Alp Arslan, and Malek Shah. In its successful strides Persia and the East had been subdued; the caliph at Bagdad had been brought under the control of the sultan; a union had been formed between the Turks and the Saracens; and the sultanies of Kerman, Syria, and Roum had been established—embracing together all the countries of the East, and constituting this by far the most mighty nation on the globe. All this would seem to be a work of *preparation* to do what was afterwards done as seen in the visions of John.

(5) *The fact that they were bound:* "Which are bound in the great river Euphrates." That is, they were, as it were, *restrained* and *kept back* for a long time in that vicinity. It would have been natural to suppose that that vast power would at once move on toward the West to the conquest of the capital of the Eastern empire. Such had been the case with the Huns, the Goths, and the Vandals. But these Turkish hordes had been long restrained in the East. They had subdued Persia. They had then achieved the conquest of India. They had conquered Bagdad, and the entire East was under their control.

Yet for a long time they had now been inactive, and it would seem as if they had been *bound* or *restrained* by some mighty power from moving in their conquests to the West.

(6) *The material that composed the army:* "And the number of the army *of the horsemen.*" "And thus I saw *the horses* in the vision.—And the heads of *the horses* were as the heads of lions." From this it appears that this vast host was composed mainly of cavalry; and it is hardly necessary to say that this description would apply better to the Turkish hordes than to any other body of invaders known in history. Thus Mr. Gibbon (vol. iv. p. 94) says, "The myriads of the Turkish *horse* overspread a frontier of six hundred miles, from Taurus to Arzeroum," A.D. 1050. So again, speaking of Togrul (vol. iv. p. 94), "He passed the Euphrates at the head of the Turkish *cavalry*" (*ibid.*). So again (vol. iii. p. 95), "Alp Arslan flew to the scene of action at the head of forty thousand horse." A.D. 1071. So in the attack of the crusaders on Nice, the capital of the Turkish kingdom of Roum, Mr. Gibbon (vol. iv. p. 127) says of the sultan Soliman: "Yielding to the first impulse of the torrent, he deposited his treasure and family in Nice; retired to the mountains with fifty thousand horse," &c. And so again (*ibid.*), speaking of the Turks who rallied to oppose the "strange" invasion of "the Western barbarians," he says, "The Turkish emirs obeyed the call of loyalty or religion; the Turkman hordes encamped round his standard; and his whole force is loosely stated by the Christians at two hundred, or even three hundred and sixty thousand horse," A.D. 1097. Every student of history knows that the Turks, or Turkmans, in the early periods of their history, were remarkable for their cavalry.

(7) *Their numbers:* "And the number of the army of the horsemen were two hundred thousand thousand." That is, it was *vast*, or it was such as to be reckoned by *myriads*, or by tens of thousands — δύο μυριάδες μυριάδων — *two myriads of myriads*. Thus Mr. Gibbon (vol. iv. p. 94) says, "The *myriads* of Turkish horse overspread," &c. It has been suggested by Daubuz that in this there may be probably an allusion to the Turkman custom of numbering by *tomans*, or *myriads*. This custom, it is true, has existed elsewhere, but there is probably none with whom it has been so familiar as with the Tartars and Turks. In the Seljukian age the population of Samarcand was rated at seven *tomans* (*myriads*), because it could send out 70,000 warriors. The dignity and rank of Tamerlane's father and grandfather was thus described, that "they were the hereditary chiefs of a *toman*, or 10,000 horse"—*a myriad* (Gibbon, vol. iv. p. 270); so that it is not without his usual propriety of language that Mr. Gibbon speaks of the *myriads* of the Turkish horse, or of the cavalry of the earlier Turks of Mount Altai, "being, both men and horses, proudly computed by *myriads.*" One thing is clear, that to no other invading hosts could the language here used be so well applied, and if it were supposed that John was writing *after* the event, this would be the language which he would be likely to employ—for this is nearly the identical language employed by the historian Gibbon.

(8) *Their personal appearance:* "Them that sat on them having breastplates of fire, and of jacinth, and brimstone"—as explained above, in a "uniform" of red, and blue, and yellow. This might, undoubtedly, be applicable to other armies besides the Turkish hordes; but the proper question here is, whether it *would be* applicable to them. The fact of the application of the symbol to the Turks in general must be determined from other points in the symbol which designate them clearly; the only natural inquiry here is, whether this description would apply to the Turkish hosts; for if it would not, that would be fatal to the whole interpretation. On the application of this passage to the Turks Mr. Daubuz justly remarks, that "from their first appearance the Ottomans have affected to wear warlike apparel of scarlet, blue, and yellow—a descriptive trait the more marked from its contrast to the military appearance of the Greeks, Franks, or Saracens contemporarily." Mr. Elliott adds: "It only needs to have seen the Turkish cavalry (as they *were* before the late innovations), whether in war itself, or in the djerrid war's mimicry, to leave an impression of the absolute necessity of some such notice of their rich and varied colourings, in order to give in description at all a just impression of their appearance," vol. i. p. 481.

(9) *The remarkable appearance of the cavalry:* "Having breastplates of fire, and of jacinth, and brimstone; and the

heads of the horses were as the heads of lions; and out of their mouths issued fire, and smoke, and brimstone." It was remarked in the exposition of this passage that this is just such a description as would be given of an army to which the use of gunpowder was known, and which made use of it in these wars. Looking now upon a body of cavalry in the heat of an engagement, it would seem, if the cause were not known, that the horses belched forth smoke and sulphurous flame. The only question now is, whether in the warfare of the Turks there was anything which would peculiarly or remarkably justify this description. And here it is impossible not to advert to the historical fact that they were among the first to make use of gunpowder in their wars, and that to the use of this destructive element they owed much of their success and their ultimate triumphs. The historical truth of this it is necessary now to advert to, and this will be done by a reference to Mr. Gibbon, and to the account which he has given of the final conquest of Constantinople by the Turks. It will be seen how he puts this new instrumentality of war into the foreground in his account; how prominent this seemed to *him* to be in describing the victories of the Turks; and how probable, therefore, it is that John, in describing an invasion by them, would refer to the "fire and smoke and brimstone," that seemed to be emitted from the mouths of their horses. As preparatory to the account of the siege and conquest of Constantinople by the Turks, Mr. Gibbon gives a description of the invention and use of gunpowder. "The chemists of China or Europe had found, by casual or elaborate experiments, that a mixture of saltpetre, sulphur, and charcoal produces, with a spark of fire, a tremendous explosion. It was soon observed that if the expansive force were compressed in a strong tube, a ball of stone or iron might be expelled with irresistible and destructive velocity. The precise era of the invention and application of gunpowder is involved in doubtful traditions and equivocal language; yet we may clearly discern that it was known before the middle of the fourteenth century; and that before the end of the same the use of artillery in battles and sieges, by sea and land, was familiar to the states of Germany, Italy, Spain, France, and England. The priority of nations is of small account; none could derive any exclusive benefit from their previous or superior knowledge; and in the common improvement they stood on the same level of relative power and military science. Nor was it possible to circumscribe the secret within the pale of the church; it was disclosed *to the Turks* by the treachery of apostates and the selfish policy of rivals; and the sultans had sense to adopt, and wealth to reward, the talents of a Christian engineer. By the Venetians the use of gunpowder was communicated without reproach to the sultans of Egypt and Persia, their allies against the Ottoman power; the secret was soon propagated to the extremities of Asia; and the advantage of the European was confined to his easy victories over the savages of the New World," vol. iv. p. 291. In the description of the conquest of Constantinople Mr. Gibbon makes frequent mention of their artillery, and of the use of gunpowder, and of its important agency in securing their final conquests, and in the overthrow of the Eastern empire. "Among the implements of destruction he [the Turkish sultan] studied with peculiar care the recent and tremendous discovery of the Latins; and his artillery surpassed whatever had yet appeared in the world. A founder of cannon, a Dane or Hungarian, who had almost starved in the Greek service, deserted to the Moslems, and was liberally entertained by the Turkish sultan. Mahomet was satisfied with the answer to his first question, which he eagerly pressed on the artist: 'Am I able to cast a cannon capable of throwing a ball or stone of sufficient size to batter the walls of Constantinople? I am not ignorant of their strength, but, were they more solid than those of Babylon, I could oppose an engine of superior power; the position and management of that engine must be left to your engineers.' On this assurance a foundry was established at Adrianople; the metal was prepared; and at the end of three months Urban produced a piece of brass ordnance of stupendous and almost incredible magnitude: a measure of twelve palms is assigned to the bore; and the stone bullet weighed above six hundred pounds. A vacant place before the new palace was chosen for the first experiment; but to prevent the sudden and mischievous effects of astonishment and fear, a proclamation was issued that the cannon would be discharged the ensuing day. The explosion was felt or heard in a circuit of a hundred furlongs; the ball, by force of gunpowder, was driven above a mile; and on the spot where it fell it buried itself a fathom deep in the ground," vol. iv. p. 339. So, in speaking of the siege of Constantinople by the Turks, Mr. Gibbon says of the defence by the Christians (vol. iv. p. 343): "The incessant volleys of lances and arrows were accompanied with the smoke, the sound, and the fire of their musketry and cannon." "The same destructive secret," he adds, "had been revealed to the Moslems, by whom it was employed with the superior energy of zeal, riches, and despotism. The great cannon of Mahomet has been separately noticed —an important and visible object in the history of the times; but that enormous engine was flanked by two fellows almost of equal magnitude; the long order of the Turkish artillery was pointed against the walls; fourteen batteries thundered at once on the most accessible places; and of one of these it is ambiguously expressed that it was mounted with one hundred and thirty guns, or that it discharged one hundred and thirty bullets," vol. iv. pp. 343, 344. Again: "The first random shots were productive of more sound than effect; and it was by the advice of a Christian that the engineers were taught to level their aim against the two opposite sides of the salient angles of a bastion. However imperfect, the weight and repetition of the fire made some impression on the walls," vol. iv. p. 344. And again: "A circumstance that distinguishes the siege of Constantinople is the reunion of the ancient and modern artillery. The cannon were intermingled with the mechanical engines for casting stones and darts; the bullet and the battering-ram were directed against the same walls; nor had the discovery of gunpowder superseded the use of the liquid and inextinguishable fire," vol. iv. p. 344. So again, in the description of the final conflict when Constantinople was taken, Mr. Gibbon says, "From the lines, the galleys, and the bridge, the Ottoman artillery thundered on all sides; and the camp and city, the Greeks and the Turks, were involved in a cloud of smoke which could only be dispelled by the final deliverance or destruction of the Roman empire," vol. iv. p. 350. Assuredly, if such was *the fact* in the conquests of the Turks, it was not unnatural in one who was looking on these warriors in vision to describe them as if they seemed to belch out "fire and smoke and brimstone." If Mr. Gibbon had *designed* to describe the conquest of the Turks as a fulfilment of the prediction, could he have done it in a style more clear and graphic than that which he has employed? If this had occurred in a *Christian* writer, would it not have been charged on him that he had shaped his facts to meet his notions of the meaning of the prophecy?

(10) The statement that "their power was in their mouth, and in their tails," ver. 19. The former part of this has been illustrated. The inquiry now is, what is the meaning of the declaration that "their power was in their tails?" In ver. 19 their tails are described as resembling "serpents, having heads," and it is said that "with them they do hurt." See Notes on that verse. The allusion to the "serpents" would seem to imply that there was something in the horses' tails, as compared with them, or in some *use* that was made of them, which would make this language proper; that is, that their appearance would so suggest the idea of death and destruction, that the mind would easily imagine they were a bundle of serpents. The following remarks may show how applicable this was to the Turks: (*a*) In the Turkish hordes there was *something*, whatever it was, that naturally suggested *some* resemblance to serpents. Of the Turkmans when they began to spread their conquests over Asia, in the eleventh century, and an effort was made to rouse the people against them, Mr. Gibbon makes the following remark: "Massoud, the son and successor of Mahmoud, had too long neglected the advice of his wisest Omrahs. 'Your enemies' [the Turkmans], they repeatedly urged, 'were in their origin a swarm of ants; they are now little snakes; and unless they be instantly crushed, they will acquire the venom and magnitude of serpents," vol. iv. p. 91. (*b*) It is a remarkable fact that the horse's tail is a well-known Turkish standard—a symbol of office and authority. "The pashas are distinguished, after a Tartar custom, by three horse-tails on the side of their tents, and receive by courtesy the title of *beyler beg*, or prince of princes. The next in rank are the pashas of two tails, the beys who are honoured with one tail."—

*Edin. Ency.* (art. "Turkey"). In the times of their early warlike career the principal standard was once lost in battle, and the Turkman commander, in default, cut off his horse's tail, lifted it on a pole, made it the rallying ensign, and so gained the victory. So Tournefort in his *Travels* states. The following is Ferrario's account of the origin of this ensign:—"An author acquainted with their customs says, that a general of theirs, not knowing how to rally his troops that had lost their standards, cut off a horse's tail, and fixed it to the end of a spear; and the soldiers rallying at that signal, gained the victory." He adds farther, that whereas "on his appointment a pasha of the three tails *used* to receive a drum and a standard, now for the *drum* there have been substituted three horses' tails, tied at the end of a spear, round a gilded haft. One of the first officers of the palace presents him these three tails as a standard" (Elliott, vol. i. pp. 485, 486). This remarkable standard or ensign is found only among the Turks, and, if there was an intended reference to them, the symbol here would be the proper one to be adopted. The *meaning* of the passage where it is said that "their *power* is in their tails" would seem to

Standard-bearer of a Turkish Pasha.

be, that their tails were the symbol or emblem of their authority—as in fact the horse's tail is in the appointment of a pasha. The *image* before the mind of John would seem to have been, that he saw the horses belching out fire and smoke, and, what was equally strange, he saw that their power of spreading desolation was connected with the tails of horses. Anyone looking on a body of cavalry with such banners or ensigns would be struck with this unusual and remarkable appearance, and would speak of their banners as concentrating and directing their power. The above engraving, representing the standard of a Turkish pasha, will illustrate the passage before us.

(11) The number slain, ver. 18. That is said to have been "the third part of men." No one in reading the accounts of the wars of the Turks, and of the ravages which they have committed, would be likely to feel that this is an exaggeration. It is not necessary to suppose that it is *literally* accurate, but it is such a representation as would strike one in looking over the world, and contemplating the effect of their invasions. If the other specifications in the symbol are correct, there would be no hesitation in admitting the propriety of this.

(12) The time of the continuance of this power. This is a material, and a more difficult point. It is said (ver. 15) to be "an hour, and a day, and a month, and a year;" that is, as explained, three hundred and ninety-one years, and the portion of a year indicated by the expression "an hour;" to wit, an additional twelfth or twenty-fourth part of a year. The question now is, whether, supposing the time to which this reaches to be the capture of Constantinople, and the consequent downfall of the Roman empire—the object in view in this series of visions—in reckoning *back* from that period for 391 years, we should reach an epoch that would properly denote the moving forward of this power towards its final conquest; that is, whether there was any such marked epoch that, if the 391 years were added to it, it would reach the year of the conquest of Constantinople, A.D. 1453. The period that would be indicated by taking the number 391 from 1453 would be 1062—and that is the time in which we are to look for the event referred to. This is on the supposition that the year consisted of 360 days, or twelve months of thirty days each. If, however, instead of this, we reckon 365 days and six hours, then the length of time would be found to amount to 396 years and

106 days.* This would make the time of the "loosening of the angels," or the moving forward of this power, to be A.D. 1057. In the uncertainty on this point, and in the unsettled state of ancient chronology, it would, perhaps, be vain to hope for minute accuracy, and it is not reasonable to demand it of an interpreter. On any fair principle of interpretation it would be sufficient if at *about* one of these periods—A.D. 1062 or A.D. 1057—there was found such a definite or strongly marked event as would indicate a movement of the hitherto restrained power toward the West. This is the real point, then, to be determined. Now, in a common work on chronology I find this record: "A.D. 1055, Turks reduce Bagdad, and overturn the empire of the caliphs." In a work still more important to our purpose (Gibbon, iv. 92, 93), under the date of A.D. 1055, I find a series of statements which will show the propriety of referring to that event as the one by which this power, so long restrained, was "let loose;" that is, was placed in such a state that its final conquest of the Eastern empire certainly followed. The event was the union of the Turkish power with the caliphate in such a way that the sultan was regarded as "the temporal lieutenant of the vicar of the prophet." Of this event Mr. Gibbon gives the following account. After mentioning the conversion of the Turks to the Moslem faith, and especially the zeal with which the son of Seljuk had embraced that faith, he proceeds to state the manner in which the Turkish sultan Togrul came in possession of Bagdad, and was invested with the high office of the "temporal lieutenant of the vicar of the prophet." There were two caliphs, those of Bagdad and Egypt, and "the sublime character of the successor of the prophet" was "disputed" by them, iv. 93. Each of them became "solicitous to prove his title in the judgment of the strong though illiterate barbarians." Mr. Gibbon then says, "Mahmoud the Gaznevide had declared himself in favour of the line of Abbas; and had treated with indignity the robe of honour which was presented by the Fatimite ambassador. Yet the ungrateful Hashemite had changed with the change of fortune; he applauded the victory of Zendecan, and named the Seljukian sultan his temporal vicegerent over the Moslem world. As Togrul executed and enlarged this important trust, he was called to the deliverance of the caliph Cayem, and obeyed the holy summons, which gave a new kingdom to his arms. In the palace of Bagdad the commander of the faithful still slumbered, a venerable phantom. His servant or master, the prince of the Bowides, could no longer protect him from the insolence of meaner tyrants; and the Euphrates and the Tigris were oppressed by the revolt of the Turkish and Arabian emirs. The presence of a conqueror was implored as a blessing; and the transient mischiefs of fire and sword were excused as the sharp but salutary remedies which alone could restore the health of the republic. At the head of an irresistible force the sultan of Persia marched from Hamadan; the proud were crushed, the prostrate were spared; the prince of the Bowides disappeared; the heads of the most obstinate rebels were laid at the feet of Togrul; and he inflicted a lesson of obedience on the people of Mosul and Bagdad. After the chastisement of the guilty, and the restoration of peace, the royal shepherd accepted the reward of his labours; and a solemn comedy represented the triumph of religious prejudice over barbarian power. The Turkish sultan embarked on the Tigris, landed at the gate of Racca, and made his public entry on horseback. At the palace gate he respectfully dismounted, and walked on foot preceded by his emirs without arms. The caliph was seated behind his black veil; the black garment of the Abbassides was cast over his shoulders, and he held in his hand the staff of the Apostle of God. The conqueror of the East kissed the ground, stood some time in a modest posture, and was led toward the throne by the vizier and an interpreter. After Togrul had seated himself on another throne, his commission was publicly read, *which declared him the temporal lieutenant of the vicar of the*

---

* "As the Julian year equalled 365 days 6 hours, the Apocalyptic period would, on the year-day principle, be in amount as follows:—

A year = 365¼ days = 365 years + ¼ of a year.
A month = 30 days = 30 years.
A day = = 1 year.
                                    ─────────
                                    396 years.
¼ of a prophetic day or year (left out above) = 91¼ days.
An hour = $\frac{1}{24}$ of a prophetic day or year = 15$\frac{5}{6}$ days.
Total = years 396 + 106 days."
                                    Elliott, i. p. 498.

## CHAPTER IX.

*prophet*. He was successively invested with seven robes of honour, and presented with seven slaves, the natives of the seven climates of the Arabian empire. His mystic veil was perfumed with musk; two crowns were placed on his head; two scimetars were girded to his side, as the symbols of a double reign over the East and West. Their alliance was cemented by the marriage of Togrul's sister with the successor of the prophet," iv. 93, 94. This event, so described, was of sufficient importance, as constituting a *union* of the Turkish power with the Moslem faith, as making it practicable to move in their conquests toward the West, and as connected in its ultimate results with the downfall of the Eastern empire, to make it an *epoch* in the history of nations. In fact, it was *the* point which one would have particularly looked at, after describing the movements of the Saracens (ch. ix. 1-11), as the next event that was to change the condition of the world.

Happily we have also the means of fixing the exact date of this event, so as to make it accord with singular accuracy with the period supposed to be referred to. The *general* time specified by Mr. Gibbon is A.D. 1055. This, according to the two methods referred to of determining the period embraced in the "hour, and day, and month, and year," would reach, if the period were 391 years, to A.D. 1446; if the other method were referred to, making it 396 years and 106 days to A.D. 1451, with 106 days added, within less than two years of the actual taking of Constantinople. But there is a more accurate calculation as to the time than the *general* one thus made. In vol. iv. 93 Mr. Gibbon makes this remark:— "Twenty-five years after the death of Basil his successors were suddenly assaulted by an unknown race of barbarians, who united the Scythian valour with the fanaticism of new proselytes, and the art and riches of a powerful monarchy." He then proceeds (p. 94, seq.) with an account of the invasions of the Turks. In vol. iii. 307 we have an account of the death of Basil. "In the sixty-eighth year of his age his martial spirit urged him to embark in person for a holy war against the Saracens of Sicily; he was prevented by death, and Basil, surnamed the slayer of the Bulgarians, was dismissed from the world, with the blessings of the clergy and the curses of the people." This occurred A.D. 1025. "Twenty-five years" after this would make A.D. 1050. To this add the period here referred to, and we have respectively, as above, the years A. D. 1446, or A. D. 1451, and 106 days. Both periods are near the time of the taking of Constantinople and the downfall of the Eastern empire (A. D. 1453), and the latter strikingly so; and, considering the general nature of the statement of Mr. Gibbon, and the great indefiniteness of the dates in chronology, may be considered as remarkable.—But we have the means of a still more accurate calculation. It is by determining the exact period of the investiture of Togrul with the authority of caliph, or as the "temporal lieutenant of the vicar of the prophet." The time of this investiture, or coronation, is mentioned by Abulfeda as occurring on the 25th of Dzoulcad, in the year of the Hegira 449; and the date of Elmakin's narrative, who has given an account of this, perfectly agrees with this. Of this transaction Elmakin makes the following remark:— "There was now none left in Irak or Chorasmia who could stand before him." The *importance* of this investiture will be seen from the charge which the caliph is reported by Abulfeda to have given to Togrul on this occasion:— "The caliph commits to your care all that part of the world which God has committed to his care and dominion; and intrusts to thee, under the name of vicegerent, the guardianship of the pious, faithful, and God-serving citizens."\* The exact *time* of this investiture is stated by Abulfeda, as above, to be the 25th of Dzoulcad, A.H. 449. Now, reckoning this as the time, and we have the following result:—The 25th of Dzoulcad, A.H. 449, would answer to February 2, A.D. 1058. From this to May 29, 1453, the time when Constantinople was taken, would be 395 years and 116 days. The *prophetic* period, as above, is 396 years and 106 days—making a difference only of 1 year and 10 days—a result that cannot but be considered as remarkable, considering the difficulty of fixing ancient dates. Or if, with Mr. Elliott (i. 495-499), we suppose that the time is to be reckoned from the period when the Turkman

---

\* Mandat Chalifa tuæ curæ omne id terrarum quod Deus ejus curæ et imperio commisit; tibique civium piorum, fidelium, Deum colentium, tutclam sublocatorio nomine demandat.

power went forth from Bagdad on a career of conquest, the reckoning should be from the year of the Hegira 448, the year before the *formal* investiture, then this would make a difference of only 24 days. The date of that event was the 10th of Dzoulcad, A.H. 448. That was the day in which Togrul with his Turkmans, now the representative and head of the power of Islamism, quitted Bagdad to enter on a long career of war and conquest. "The part allotted to Togrul himself in the fearful drama soon to open against the Greeks was to extend and establish the Turkman dominion over the frontier countries of Irak and Mesopotamia, that so the requisite strength might be attained for the attack ordained of God's counsels against the Greek empire. The first step to this was the siege and capture of Moussul; his next of Singara. Nisibis, too, was visited by him; that frontier fortress that had in other days been so long a bulwark to the Greeks. Everywhere victory attended his banner—a presage of what was to follow." Reckoning from that time, the coincidence between the period that elapsed from that, and the conquest of Constantinople, would be 396 years and 130 days—a period that corresponds, with only a difference of 24 days, with that specified in the prophecy according to the explanation already given. It could not be expected that a coincidence more accurate than this could be made out on the supposition that the prophecy was designed to refer to these events; and if it *did* refer to them, the coincidence could have occurred only as a prediction by Him who sees with perfect accuracy all the future.

(13) *The effect.* This is stated, in ver. 20, 21, to be that those who survived these plagues did *not* repent of their wickedness, but that the abominations which existed before still remained. In endeavouring to determine the meaning of this, it will be proper, first, to ascertain the exact sense of the words used, and then to inquire whether a state of things existed subsequent to the invasions of the Turks which corresponded with the description here.

(*a*) The explanation of the language used in ver. 20, 21. ¶ *The rest of the men.* That portion of the world on which these plagues did not come. One-third of the race, it is said, would fall under these calamities, and the writer now proceeds to state what would be the effect on the remainder. The language used —"*the rest of the men*"—is not such as to designate with certainty any particular portion of the world, but it is implied that the things mentioned were of very general prevalence. ¶ *Which were not killed by these plagues.* The two-thirds of the race which were spared. The language here is such as would be used on the supposition that the crimes here referred to abounded in all those regions which came within the range of the vision of the apostle. ¶ *Yet repented not of the works of their hands.* To wit, of those things which are immediately specified. ¶ *That they should not worship devils.* Implying that they practised this before. The word used here—δαιμόνιον—means properly *a god, deity;* spoken of the heathen gods, Ac. xvii. 18; then a genius, or tutelary demon, *e.g.* that of Socrates; and, in the New Testament, a demon in the sense of an evil spirit. See the word fully explained in the Notes on 1 Co. x. 20. The meaning of the passage here, as in 1 Co. x. 20, "they sacrifice to devils," is not that they literally worshipped *devils* in the usual sense of that term, though it is true that such worship does exist in the world, as among the Yezidis (see Layard, *Nineveh and its Remains*, vol. i. pp. 225-254, and Rosenmüller, *Morgenland*, iii. 212-216); but that they worshipped beings *which were inferior to the Supreme God;* created spirits of a rank superior to men, or the spirits of men that had been enrolled among the gods. This last was a common form of worship among the heathen, for a large portion of the gods whom they adored were heroes and benefactors who had been enrolled among the gods—as Hercules, Bacchus, &c. All that is necessarily implied in this word is, that there prevailed in the time referred to the worship of spirits inferior to God, or the worship of the spirits of departed men. This idea would be more naturally suggested to the mind of a Greek by the use of the word than the worship of evil spirits as such—if indeed it would have conveyed that idea at all; and this word would be properly employed in the representation if there was *any* homage rendered to departed human spirits which came in the place of the worship of the true God. Comp. a dissertation on the meaning of the word used here, in

## CHAPTER IX.

Elliott on the *Apocalypse*, Appendix I. vol. ii. ¶ *And idols of gold, and silver*, &c. Idols were formerly, as they are now in heathen lands, made of all these materials. The most costly would, of course, denote a higher degree of veneration for the god, or greater wealth in the worshipper, and all would be employed as symbols or representatives of the gods whom they adored. The *meaning* of this passage is, that there would prevail, at that time, what would be properly called *idolatry*, and that this would be represented by the worship paid to these images or idols. It is not necessary to the proper understanding of this, to suppose that the images or idols worshipped were acknowledged *heathen idols*, or were erected in honour of *heathen gods*, as such. All that is implied is, that there would be such images — εἴδωλα — and that a degree of homage would be paid to them which would be in fact idolatry. The word here used — εἴδωλον, εἴδωλα — properly means an image, spectre, shade; then an idol-image, or that which was a representative of a heathen god; and then the idol-god itself — a heathen deity. So far as the *word* is concerned, it may be applied to any kind of image-worship. ¶ *Which neither can see, nor hear, nor walk*. The common representation of idol-worship in the Scriptures, to denote its folly and stupidity. See Ps. cxv.; comp. Is. xliv. 9-19. ¶ *Neither repented they of their murders*. This implies that, at the time referred to, murders would abound; or that the times would be characterized by that which deserved to be *called* murder. ¶ *Nor of their sorceries*. The word rendered *sorceries* — φαρμακεία — whence our word *pharmacy*, means properly *the preparing and giving of medicine*, Eng. *pharmacy* (Rob. *Lex.*). Then, as the art of medicine was supposed to have magical power, or as the persons who practised medicine, in order to give themselves and their art greater importance, practised various arts of incantation, the word came to be connected with the idea of magic, sorcery, or enchantment. See Schleusner, *Lex*. In the New Testament the word is *never* used in a good sense, as denoting the preparation of medicine, but always in this secondary sense, as denoting sorcery, magic, &c. Thus in Ga. v. 20, "the works of the flesh — idolatry, *witchcraft*," &c. Re. ix. 21, "Of their *sorceries*." Re. xviii. 23, "For by thy *sorceries* were all nations deceived." Re. xxi. 8, "Whoremongers, and *sorcerers*." The word does not elsewhere occur in the New Testament; and the *meaning* of the word would be fulfilled in anything that purposed to accomplish an object by sorcery, by magical arts, by trick, by cunning, by sleight of hand, or by *deceiving the senses in any way*. Thus it would be applicable to all jugglery and to all pretended miracles. ¶ *Nor of their fornication*. Implying that this would be a prevalent sin in the times referred to, and that the dreadful plagues which are here predicted would make no essential change in reference to its prevalence. ¶ *And of their thefts*. Implying that *this*, too, would be a common form of iniquity. The word used here — κλέμμα — is the common word to denote *theft*. The true idea in the word is that of privately, unlawfully, and feloniously taking the goods or movables of another person. In a larger and in the popular sense, however, this word might embrace all acts of taking the property of another by dishonest arts, or on false pretence, or without an equivalent.

(*b*) The next point then is, the inquiry whether there was any such state of things as is specified here existing in the time of the rise of the Turkish power, and in the time of the calamities which that formidable power brought upon the world. There are two things implied in the statement here: (1) that these things had an existence before the invasion and destruction of the Eastern empire by the Turkish power; and (2) that they continued to exist after that, or were not removed by these fearful calamities. The supposition all along in this interpretation is, that the eye of the prophet was on the Roman world, and that the design was to mark the various events which would characterize its future history. We look, then, in the application of this, to the state of things existing in connection with the Roman power, or that portion of the world which was then pervaded by the Roman religion. This will make it necessary to institute an inquiry whether the things here specified prevailed in that part of the world before the invasions of the Turks, and the conquest of Constantinople, and whether the judgments inflicted by that formidable Turkish invasion made any essential change in this respect.

(1) The statement that they wor-

shipped devils; that is, as explained, demons, or the deified souls of men. Homage rendered to the spirits of departed men, and substituted in the place of the worship of the true God, would meet all that is properly implied here. We may refer, then, to the worship of *saints* in the Romish communion as a complete fulfilment of what is here implied in the language used by John. The fact cannot be disputed that the invocation of saints took the place, in the Roman Catholic communion, of the worship of sages and heroes in heathen Rome, and that the canonization of saints took the place of the ancient deification of heroes and public benefactors. The same kind of homage was rendered to them; their aid was invoked in a similar manner, and on similar occasions; the effect on the popular mind was substantially the same; and the one interfered as really as the other with the worship of the true God. The decrees of the seventh general council, known as the second council of Nice, A.D. 787, authorized and established the worshipping (προσ-κυνέω — the same word used here — προσκυνήσωσι τὰ δαιμόνια) of the saints and their images. This occurred *after* the exciting scenes, the debates, and the disorders produced by the Iconoclasts, or image-breakers, and after the most careful deliberation on the subject. In that celebrated council it was decreed, according to Mr. Gibbon (iii. 341), "unanimously," "that the worship of images is agreeable to Scripture and reason, to the fathers and councils of the church; but they hesitate whether that worship be relative or direct; whether the Godhead and the figure of Christ be entitled to the same mode of adoration." This worship of the "saints," or prayer to the saints, asking for their intercession, it is well known, has from that time everywhere prevailed in the Papal communion. Indeed, a large part of the actual *prayers* offered in their services is addressed to the Virgin Mary. Mr. Maitland, "the able and learned advocate of the Dark Ages," says, "The superstition of the age supposed the glorified saint to know what was going on in the world; and to feel a deep interest, and to possess a considerable power, in the church militant on earth. I believe that they who thought so are altogether mistaken; and I lament, abhor, and am amazed at the superstition, *blasphemies*, and *ido*-*latries*, which have grown out of that opinion" (Elliott, ii. p. 10). As to the question whether this *continued* after the judgments brought upon the world by the hordes "loosed on the Euphrates," or whether they repented and reformed on account of the judgments, we have only to look into the Roman Catholic religion everywhere. Not only did the old practice of "dæmonolatry," or the worship of departed saints, continue, but *new* "saints" have been added to the number, and the list of those who are to receive this homage has been continually increasing. Thus in the year 1460, Catharine of Sienna was canonized by Pope Pius II.; in 1482, Bonaventura, the blasphemer,* by Sixtus IV.; in 1494, Anselm by Alexander VI. Alexander's bull, in language more heathen than Christian, avows it to be the pope's *duty* thus to choose out, and to hold up the illustrious dead, as their merits claim, for *adoration* and *worship*.†

(2) The statement that *idolatry* was practised, and continued to be practised, after this invasion:—"Repented not that they should not worship idols of gold, silver, and brass." On this point, perhaps it would be sufficient to refer to what has been already noticed in regard to the homage paid to the souls of the departed; but it may be farther and more clearly illustrated by a reference to the worship of *images* in the Romish communion. Anyone familiar with church history will recollect the long conflicts which prevailed respecting the worship of images; the establishment of images in the churches; the destruction of images by the "Iconoclasts;" and the debates on the subject by the council at Hiera; and the final decision in the second council of Nice, in which the propriety of image-worship was affirmed and established. See, on this subject, Bowers' *History of the Popes*, ii. 98, seq., 144, seq.; Gibbon, vol. iii. pp. 322–341. The importance of the question respecting *image-wor*-

* In the Hereford Discussion, between the Rev. J. Venn and Rev. James Waterworth, it was admitted by the latter, an able and learned Romish priest, that Bonaventura's Psalter to the Virgin Mary, turning the addresses to God into addresses to the Virgin, was *blasphemy* (Elliott, ii. 25).

† Romanus Pontifex viros claros, et qui sanctimoniâ floruerunt, et eorum exigentibus clarissimis meritis aliorum sanctorum numero aggregari merentur — inter sanctos prædictos debet collocare, et ut sanctos ab omnibus Christi fidelibus coli, venerari, et ADORARI mandare.

## CHAPTER IX.

ship may be seen from the remarks of Mr. Gibbon, iii. 322. He speaks of it as "a question of popular superstition which produced the revolt of Italy, the *temporal power of the popes*, and the restoration of the Roman empire in the West." A few extracts from Mr. Gibbon—who may be regarded as an impartial witness on this subject—will show what was the popular belief, and will confirm what is said in the passage before us in reference to the prevalence of *idolatry*. "The first introduction of a symbolic worship was in the veneration of the cross, and of relics. The saints and martyrs, when intercession was implored, were seated on the right hand of God; but the gracious, and often supernatural favours, which, in the popular belief, were showered round their tombs, conveyed an unquestionable sanction of the devout pilgrims who visited, and touched, and kissed these lifeless remains, the memorials of their merits and sufferings. But a memorial, more interesting than the skull or the sandals of a departed worthy, is a faithful copy of his person and features delineated by the arts of painting or sculpture. In every age such copies, so congenial to human feelings, have been cherished by the zeal of private friendship or public esteem; the images of the Roman emperors were adored with civil and almost religious honours; a reverence, less ostentatious, but more sincere, was applied to the statues of sages and patriots; and these profane virtues, these splendid sins, disappeared in the presence of the holy men who had died for their celestial and everlasting country. At first the experiment was made with caution and scruple, and the venerable pictures were discreetly allowed to instruct the ignorant, to awaken the cold, and to gratify the prejudices of the heathen proselytes. By a slow, though inevitable progression, the honours of the original were transferred to the copy; the devout Christian prayed before the image of a saint, and the Pagan rites of genuflexion, luminaries, and incense again stole into the Catholic church. The scruples of reason or piety were silenced by the strong evidence of visions and miracles; and the pictures which speak, and move, and bleed, must be endowed with a divine energy, and may be considered as the proper objects of religious adoration. The most audacious pencil might tremble in the rash attempt of defining, by forms and colours, the infinite Spirit, the eternal Father, who pervades and sustains the universe. But the superstitious mind was more easily reconciled to paint and worship the angels, and above all, the Son of God, under the human shape, which on earth they have condescended to assume. The Second Person of the Trinity had been clothed with a real and mortal body, but that body had ascended into heaven; and had not some similitude been presented to the eyes of his disciples, the spiritual worship of Christ might have been obliterated by the visible relics and representations of the saints. A similar indulgence was requisite, and propitious, for the Virgin Mary; the place of her burial was unknown; and the assumption of her soul and body into heaven was adopted by the credulity of the Greeks and Latins. *The use, and even the worship of images, was firmly established before the end of the sixth century;* they were fondly cherished by the warm imagination of the Greeks and Asiatics; *the Pantheon and the Vatican were adorned with the emblems of a new superstition;* but this semblance of idolatry was more coldly entertained by the rude barbarians and the Arian clergy of the West," vol. iii. p. 323. Again:—"Before the end of the sixth century these images, *made without hands* (in Greek it is a single word—ἀχειροποίητος), were propagated in the camps and cities of the Eastern empire; *they were the objects of worship*, and the instruments of miracles; and in the hour of danger or tumult their venerable presence could revive the hope, rekindle the courage, or repress the fury of the Roman legions," vol. iii. pp. 324, 325. So again (vol. iii. p. 340, seq.):—"While the popes established in Italy their freedom and dominion, the images, the first cause of their revolt, were restored in the Eastern empire. Under the reign of Constantine the Fifth, the union of civil and ecclesiastical power had overthrown the tree, without extirpating the root, of superstition. The *idols*, for such they were now held, were secretly cherished by the order and the sex most prone to devotion; and the fond alliance of the monks and females obtained a final victory over the reason and the authority of man." Under Irene a council was convened—the second council of Nice, or the seventh general council—in which, according to Mr. Gibbon (iii. 341), it was "unanimously pronounced that the worship of images is agreeable to Scripture and reason, to the fathers and councils of the church." The *arguments* which were urged in favour of the worship of images, in the council above referred to, may be seen in Bowers' *Lives of the Popes*, vol. ii. pp. 152-158, Dr. Cox's edition. The answer of the bishops in the council to the question of the empress Irene, whether they agreed to the decision which had been adopted in the council, was in these words:—"We all agree to it; we have all freely signed it; this is the faith of the apostles, of the fathers, and of the Catholic church; we all salute, honour, worship, and adore the holy and venerable images; be they accursed who do not honour, worship, and adore the adorable images" (Bowers' *Lives of the Popes*, ii. 159). As a matter of fact, therefore, no one can doubt that these images were *worshipped* with the honour that was due to God alone—or that the sin of *idolatry* prevailed; and no one can doubt that that has been continued, and is still, in the Papal communion.

(3) The next point specified is *murders* (ver. 21):—"Neither repented they of their murders." It can hardly be necessary to dwell on this to show that this was strictly applicable to the Roman power, and extensively prevailed, both before and after the Turkish invasion, and that that invasion had no tendency to produce repentance. Indeed, in nothing has the Papacy been more remarkably characterized than in the number of murders perpetrated on the innocent in persecution. In reference to the fulfilment of this we may refer to the following things:—(*a*) Persecution. This has been particularly the characteristic of the Roman communion, it need not be said, in all ages. The persecutions of the Waldenses, if there were nothing else, show that the spirit here referred to prevailed in the Roman communion, or that the times preceding the Turkish conquest were characterized by what is here specified. In the third Lateran council, A.D. 1179, an anathema was declared against certain dissentients and heretics, and then against the Waldenses themselves in Papal bulls of the years 1183, 1207, 1208. Again, in a decree of the fourth Lateran council, A.D. 1215, a *crusade*, as it was called, was proclaimed against them, and "plenary absolution promised to such as should perish in the holy war, from the day of their birth to the day of their death." "And never," says Sismondi, "had the cross been taken up with more unanimous consent." It is supposed that in this crusade against the Waldenses a million of men perished. (*b*) That this continued to be the characteristic of the Papacy *after* the judgments brought upon the Roman world by the Turkish invasion, or that those judgments had no tendency to produce repentance and reformation, is well known, and is manifest from the following things:—(1) The continuance of the spirit of persecution. (2) The establishment of the Inquisition. One hundred and fifty thousand persons perished by the Inquisition in thirty years; and from the beginning of the order of the Jesuits in 1540 to 1580, it is supposed that nine hundred thousand persons were destroyed by persecution. (3) The same spirit was manifested in the attempts to suppress the true religion in England, in Bohemia, and in the Low Countries. Fifty thousand persons were hanged, burned, beheaded, or buried alive, for the crime of heresy, in the Low Countries, chiefly under the Duke of Alva, from the edict of Charles V. against the Protestants to the peace of Chateau Cambresis in 1559. Comp. Notes on Da. vii. 24-28. To these are to be added all that fell in France on the revocation of the edict of Nantz; all that perished by persecution in England in the days of Mary; and all that have fallen in the bloody wars that have been waged in the propagation of the Papal religion. The number is, of course, unknown to mortals, though efforts have been made by historians to form some estimate of the amount. It is supposed that fifty millions of persons have perished in these persecutions of the Waldenses, Albigenses, Bohemian Brethren, Wycliffites, and Protestants; that some fifteen millions of Indians perished in Cuba, Mexico, and South America, in the wars of the Spaniards, professedly to propagate the Catholic faith; that three millions and a half of Moors and Jews perished, by Catholic persecution and arms, in Spain; and that thus, probably no less than sixty-eight millions and five hundred thousand human beings have been put to death by this one persecuting power. See Dr. Berg's *Lectures on Romanism*, pp. 6, 7. Assuredly, if this be true, it would be proper to characterize the times here

referred to, both before and after the Turkish invasion, as a time when *murders* would prevail.

(4) The fourth point specified is *sorceries*. It can hardly be necessary to go into detail to prove that *this* also abounded; and that delusive appeals to the senses; false and pretended miracles; arts adapted to deceive through the imagination; the supposed virtue and efficacy of relics; and frauds calculated to impose on mankind, have characterized those portions of the world where the Roman religion has prevailed, and been one of the principal means of its advancement. No Protestant surely would deny this, no intelligent Catholic can doubt it himself. All that is necessary to be said in regard to this is, that in this, as in other respects, the Turkish invasion, and the judgments that came upon the world, made no change. The very recent imposture of the "holy coat of Treves" is a full proof that the *disposition* to practise such arts still exists, and that the *power* to impose on a large portion of the world in that denomination has not died away.

(5) The fifth thing specified is *fornication*. This has abounded everywhere in the world; but the use of the term in this connection implies that there would be something *peculiar* here, and perhaps that it would be associated with the other things referred to. It is as unnecessary as it would be improper to go into any detail on this point. Anyone who is acquainted with the history of the Middle Ages—the period here supposed to be referred to—must be aware of the wide-spread licentiousness which then prevailed, especially among the clergy. Historians and poets, ballads, and acts of councils, alike testify to this fact.* It is to be remarked also, as illustrating the subject, that the dissoluteness of the Middle Ages was closely, and almost necessarily, connected with the worship of the images and the saints above referred to. The character of many of those who were worshipped as saints, like the character of many of the gods of the Pagan Romans, was just such as to be an incentive to every species of licentiousness and impurity. On this point Mr. Hallam makes the following remarks:—"That the exclusive worship of saints, under the guidance of an artful though illiterate priesthood, degraded the understanding, and begat a stupid credulity and fanaticism, is sufficiently evident. But it was also so managed as to loosen the bonds of religion, and pervert the standard of morality" (*Middle Ages*, vol. ii. pp. 249, 250; edit. Phil. 1824). He then, in a note, refers to the legends of the saints as abundantly confirming his statements. See particularly the stories in the *Golden Legend*. So, in speaking of the monastic orders, Mr. Hallam (*Middle Ages*, vol. ii. 253) says: "In vain new rules of discipline were devised, or the old corrected by reforms. Many of their worst vices grew so naturally out of their mode of life that a stricter discipline would have no tendency to extirpate them. Their extreme licentiousness was sometimes hardly concealed by the cowl of sanctity." In illustration of this we may introduce here a remark of Mr. Gibbon, made in immediate connection with his statement about the decrees respecting the worship of images. "I shall only notice," says he, "the judgment of the bishops on the comparative merit of image-worship and morality. A monk had concluded a truce with the demon of fornication, on condition of interrupting his daily prayers to a picture that hung in his cell. His scruples prompted him to consult the abbot. 'Rather than abstain from adoring Christ and his mother in their holy images, it would be better for you,' replied the casuist, 'to enter every brothel, and visit every prostitute in the city,'" iii. 341. So again, Mr. Gibbon, speaking of the pope, John XII., says: "His open simony might be the consequence of distress; and his blasphemous invocation of Jupiter and Venus, if it be true, could not possibly be serious. But we read with some surprise that the worthy grandson of Marozia lived in public adultery with the matrons of Rome; that the Lateran palace was turned into a place for prostitution, and that his rapes of virgins and of widows had deterred the female pilgrims from visiting the tomb of St. Peter, lest, in the devout act, they should be violated by his successor," iii. 353. Again, the system of *indulgences* led directly to licentiousness. In the pontificate of John XXII., about A.D. 1320, there was invented the celebrated Tax of Indulgences, of which more than forty editions are extant. According to this, *incest* was to cost, if

---

* "If you wish to see the horrors of these ages" (the Middle Ages), says Chateaubriand, *Dict. Hist.* tom. iii. 420, "read the *Councils*."

not detected, *five groschen;* if known and flagrant, *six.* A certain price was affixed in a similar way to adultery, infanticide, &c. See Merle D'Aubigné's *Reformation*, vol. i. p. 41. And farther, the very *pilgrimages* to the shrines of the saints, which were enjoined as a penance for sin, and which were regarded as a ground of merit, were occasions of the grossest licentiousness. So Hallam, *Middle Ages*, says: "This licensed vagrancy was naturally productive of dissoluteness, especially among the women. Our English ladies, in their zeal to obtain the spiritual treasuries of Rome, are said to have relaxed the necessary caution about one that was in their own custody," vol. ii. 255. The celibacy of the clergy also tended to licentiousness, and is known to have been everywhere productive of the very sin which is here mentioned. The state of the nunneries in the middle ages is well known. In the fifteenth century Gerson, the French orator so celebrated at the council of Constance, called them Prostibula meretricum. Clemangis, a French theologian, also contemporary, and a man of great eminence, thus speaks of them: Quid aliud sunt hoc tempore puellarum monasteria, nisi quædam non dico Dei sanctuaria, sed veneris execranda prostibula; ut idem sit hodie puellam velare, quod et publicè ad scortandum exponere (Hallam, *Middle Ages*, ii. 253). To this we may add the fact that it was a habit, not unfrequent, to license the clergy to live in concubinage (see the proof in Elliott, i. 447, note), and that the practice of auricular confession necessarily made "the tainting of the female mind an integral part of Roman priestcraft, and gave consecration to the communings of impurity." It hardly needs any proof that these practices continued *after* the invasions of the Turkish hordes, or that those invasions made no changes in the condition of the world in this respect. In proof of this we need refer only to Pope Innocent VIII., elected in 1484 to the Papacy;* to Alexander VI., his successor, who at the close of the fifteenth century stood before the world a monster, notorious to all, of impurity and vice; and to the general well-known character of the Romish clergy. "Most of the ecclesiastics," says the historian Infessura, "had their mistresses; and all the convents of the capital were houses of ill fame."

(6) The sixth thing specified (ver. 21) is *thefts;* that is, as explained, the taking of the property of others by dishonest arts, on false pretences, or without any proper equivalent. In the inquiry as to the applicability of this to the times supposed to be here referred to, we may notice the following things, as instances in which money was extorted from the people:— (*a*) The value fraudulently assigned to *relics.* Mosheim, in his historical sketch of the twelfth century, observes: "The abbots and monks carried about the country the carcasses and relics of saints, in solemn procession, and permitted the multitude to behold, touch, and embrace the sacred remains, *at fixed prices.*" (*b*) The exaltation of the miracle-working merit of particular saints, and the consecration of *new* saints, and dedication of *new* images, when the popularity of the former died away. Thus Mr. Hallam says: "Every cathedral or monastery had its tutelar saint, and every saint his legend; fabricated in order to enrich the churches under his protection; by exaggerating his virtues and his miracles, and consequently his power of serving those who paid liberally for his patronage." (*c*) The invention and sale of *indulgences*—well known to have been a vast source of revenue to the church. Wycliffe declared that indulgences were mere forgeries whereby the priesthood "*rob men of their money;* a subtle merchandise of Antichrist's clerks, whereby they magnify their own fictitious power, and instead of causing men to dread sin, encourage men to wallow therein as hogs." (*d*) The prescription of *pilgrimages* as penances was another prolific source of gain to the church that deserves to be classed under the name of *thefts.* Those who made such pilgrimage were expected and required to make an offering at the shrine of the saint; and as multitudes went on such pilgrimages, especially on the jubilee at Rome, the income from this source was enormous. An instance of what was offered at the shrine of Thomas à Becket will illustrate this. Through his reputation Canterbury became the Rome of England. A jubilee was celebrated every fiftieth year to his honour, with plenary indulgence to all such as visited his tomb; of whom one hundred thousand were registered at one time.

---

\* His character is told in the well-known epigram—
   Octo *nocens* pueros genuit, totidemque puellas:
   Hunc merito potuit dicere Roma *patrem.*

Two large volumes were filled with accounts of the miracles wrought at his tomb. The following list of the value of offerings made in two successive years to *his* shrine, the Virgin Mary's, and Christ's, in the cathedral at Canterbury, will illustrate at the same time the gain from these sources, and the *relative* respect shown to Becket, Mary, and the Saviour:—

| First Year. | £ | s. | d. |
|---|---|---|---|
| Christ's Altar................... | 3 | 2 | 6 |
| Virgin Mary's.................... | 63 | 5 | 6 |
| Becket's.......................... | 832 | 12 | 9 |
| Next Year. | | | |
| Christ's Altar................... | 0 | 0 | 0 |
| Virgin Mary's.................... | 4 | 1 | 8 |
| Becket's.......................... | 954 | 6 | 3 |

Of the jubilee of A.D. 1300 Muratori relates the result as follows:—"Papa innumerabilem pecuniam ab iisdem recepit; quia die et nocte duo clerici stabant ad altare Sancti Pauli, tenentes in eorum manibus rastellos, rastellantes pecuniam infinitam." "The pope received from them a countless amount of money; for two clerks stood at the altar of St. Paul night and day, holding in their hands little rakes, collecting an infinite amount of money" (Hallam). (*e*) Another source of gain of this kind was the numerous testamentary bequests with which the church was enriched—obtained by the arts and influence of the clergy. In Wycliffe's time there were in England 53,215 fœda militum, of which the religious had 28,000 —more than one-half. Blackstone says that, but for the intervention of the legislature, and the statute of mortmain, the church would have appropriated in this manner the whole of the land of England, vol. iv. p. 107. (*f*) The money left by the dying to pay for *masses*, and that paid by survivors for masses to release the souls of their friends from purgatory—all of which deserve to be classed under the word *thefts* as already explained—was another source of vast wealth to the church; and the practice was systematized on a large scale, and, with the other things mentioned, deserves to be noticed as a characteristic of the times. It is scarcely necessary to add, that the judgments which were brought upon the world by the Turkish invasions made no essential change, and wrought no repentance or reformation, and hence that the *language* here is strictly applicable to these things: "Neither *repented they* of their murders, nor of their sorceries, nor of their fornication, nor of their thefts."

## CHAPTER X.

### ANALYSIS OF THE CHAPTER.

This chapter contains the record of a sublime vision of an angel which, at this juncture, John saw descending from heaven, disclosing new scenes in what was yet to occur. The vision is interposed between the sounding of the sixth, or second woe-trumpet, and the sounding of the seventh, or third woe-trumpet, under which is to be the final consummation, ch. xi. 15, seq. It occupies an important *interval* between the events which were to occur under the sixth trumpet and the last scene—the final overthrow of the formidable power which had opposed the reign of God on the earth, and the reign of righteousness, when the kingdoms of the world shall become the kingdom of God, ch. xi. 15. It is, in many respects, an unhappy circumstance that this chapter has been separated from the following. They constitute one continued vision, at least to ch. xi. 15, where the sounding of the seventh and last trumpet occurs.

The tenth chapter contains the following things:—(1) An angel descends from heaven, and the attention of the seer is for a time turned from the contemplation of what was passing in heaven to this new vision that appeared on the earth. This angel is clothed with a cloud; he is encircled by a rainbow; his face is as the sun, and his feet like pillars of fire—all indicating his exalted rank, and all such accompaniments as became a heavenly messenger. (2) The angel appears with a small volume in his hand, ver. 2. This book is not closed and sealed, like the one in ch. v., but was "open"—so that it could be read. Such a book would indicate some new message or revelation from heaven; and the book would be, properly, a symbol of something that was to be accomplished *by* such an open volume. (3) The angel sets his feet upon the sea and the land, ver. 2:—indicating by this, apparently, that what he was to communicate appertained alike to the ocean and the land—to all the world. (4) The angel makes a proclamation—the nature of which is not here stated—with a loud voice, like the roaring of a lion, as if the nations were called to hear, ver. 3. (5) This cry or roar is responded to by heavy thunders, ver. 3. What those thunders uttered is not stated, but it was evidently so distinct that *John* heard it, for he says (ver. 4) that he was about to make a record of what was said. (6) John, about to make this record, is forbidden to do so by a voice from heaven, ver. 4. For some reason, not here stated, he was commanded not to disclose what was said, but so to seal it up that it should not be known. The *reason* for this silence is nowhere intimated in the chapter. (7) The angel lifts his hand to heaven in a most solemn manner, and swears by the Great Creator of all things that the time should not be yet — in our common version, "that there should be time no longer," ver. 5-7. It would seem that just at this period there would be an expectation that the reign of God was to begin upon the earth; but the angel, in the most solemn manner, declares that this was not *yet* to be, but that it would occur when the seventh angel should begin to sound. Then the great "mystery" would be complete, as it had been declared to the prophets. (8) John is then commanded, by the same voice which he heard from heaven, to go to the angel and take the little book from him which he held in his hand, and eat it—with the assurance that it would be found to be sweet to the taste, but would be bitter afterwards, ver. 8-10. (9) The chapter concludes with a declaration that he must yet prophesy before many people and nations (ver. 11), and then follows (ch. xi.) the commission to measure the temple; the command to separate the pure from the profane; the account of the prophesying, the death, and the resurrection to life of the two witnesses—all preliminary to the sounding of the seventh trumpet, and the introduction of the universal reign of righteousness.

The question to what does the chapter refer, is one which it is proper to notice before we proceed to the exposition. It is unnecessary to say, that on this question very various opinions have been entertained, and that very different expositions have been given of the chapter. Without going into an examination of these different opinions—which would be a task alike unprofitable and endless—it will be better to state what seems to be the fair interpretation and application of the symbol, in its connection with what precedes. A few remarks here, preliminary to the exposition and application of the chapter, may help us in determining the place which the vision is designed to occupy. (*a*) In the previous Apocalyptic revelations, if the interpretation proposed is correct, the *history* had been brought down, in the regular course of events, to the capture of Constantinople by the Turks, and the complete overthrow of the Roman empire by that event, A.D. 1453, ch. ix. 13-19. This was an important era in the history of the world; and if the exposition which has been proposed is correct, then the sketches of history pertaining to the Roman empire in the book of Revelation have been made with surprising accuracy. (*b*) A statement had been made (ch. ix. 20, 21) to the effect that the same state of things continued subsequent to the plagues brought on by those invasions, which had existed before, or that the effect had not been to produce any general repentance and reformation. God had scourged the nations; he had cut off multitudes of men; he had overthrown the mighty empire that had so long ruled over the world; but the same sins of superstition, idolatry, sorcery, murder, fornication, and theft prevailed *afterwards* that had prevailed before. Instead of working a change in the minds of men, the world seemed to be confirmed in these abominations more and more. In the exposition of that passage (ch. ix. 20, 21) it was shown that those things prevailed in the Roman church—which then embraced the whole Christian world—*before* the invasion of the Eastern empire by the Turks, and that they continued to prevail *afterwards:* that, in fact, the moral character of the world was not affected by those "plagues." (*c*) The next event, in the order of *time*, was the Reformation, and the circumstances in the case are such as to lead us to suppose that this chapter refers to that. For (1) the order of *time* demands this. This was the next important event in the history of the church and the world after the conquest of Constantinople producing the entire downfall of the Roman empire; and if, as is supposed in the previous exposition, it was the design of the Spirit of inspiration to touch on the great and material events in the history of the church and the world, then it would be natural to suppose that the Reformation would come next into view, for no previous event had more deeply or permanently affected the condition of mankind. (2) The state of the world, as described in ch.

# CHAPTER X.

AND I saw another mighty angel come down from heaven, clothed with a cloud; and a *a*rain-

*a* Eze.1.28.

bow *was* upon his head, and *b*his face *was* as it were the sun, and his feet as pillars of fire:

*b* ch.1.15,16; Mat.17.2.

ix. 20, 21, was such as to *demand* a reformation, or something that should be more effectual in purifying the church than the calamities described in the previous verse had been. The representation is, that God had brought great judgments upon the world, but that they had been ineffectual in reforming mankind. The same kind of superstition, idolatry, and corruption remained *after* those judgments which had existed before, and they were of such a nature as to make it every way desirable that a new influence should be brought to bear upon the world to purify it from these abominations. Some such work as the Reformation is, therefore, what we should naturally look for as the next in order; or, at least, such a work is one that well fits in with the description of the previous state of things. (*d*) It will be found, I apprehend, in the exposition of the chapter, that the symbols are such as accord well with the great leading events of the Protestant Reformation; or, in other words, that they are such that, on the supposition that it was intended to refer to the Reformation, these are the symbols which would have been appropriately employed. Of course it is not necessary to suppose that John understood distinctly *all* that was meant by these symbols, nor is it necessary to suppose that those who lived before the Reformation would be able to comprehend them perfectly, and to apply them with accuracy. All that is *necessary* to be supposed in the interpretation is, (1) that the symbol was designed to be of such a character as to give some *general* idea of what was to occur; and (2) that we should be able, now that the event has occurred, to show that it is fairly applicable to the event; that is, that on the supposition that this was designed to be referred to, the symbols are such as would properly be employed. This, however, will be seen more clearly after the exposition shall have been gone through.

With this general view of what we should naturally anticipate in this chapter, from the course of exposition in the preceding chapters, we are prepared for a more particular exposition and application of the symbols in this new vision. It will be the most convenient course, keeping in mind the general views presented here, to explain the symbols, and to consider their application as we go along.

1. *And I saw.* I had a vision of. The meaning is, that he saw this subsequently to the vision in the previous chapter. The attention is now arrested by a new vision—as if some new dispensation or economy was about to occur in the world. ¶ *Another mighty angel.* He had before seen the seven angels who were to blow the seven trumpets (ch. viii. 2), he had seen six of them successively blow the trumpet, he now sees *another* angel, different from them, and apparently having no connection with them, coming from heaven to accomplish some important purpose before the seventh angel should give the final blast. The angel is here characterized as a "*mighty*" angel—ἰσχυρόν—one of strength and power; implying that the work to be accomplished by his mission demanded the interposition of one of the higher orders of the heavenly inhabitants. The coming of an angel at all was indicative of some divine interposition in human affairs; the fact that he was one of exalted rank, or endowed with vast power, indicated the nature of the work to be done—that it was a work to the execution of which great obstacles existed, and where great power would be needed. ¶ *Clothed with a cloud.* Encompassed with a cloud, or enveloped in a cloud. This was a symbol of majesty and glory, and is often represented as accompanying the divine presence, Ex. xvi. 9, 10; xxiv. 16; xxxiv. 5; Nu. xi. 25; 1 Ki. viii. 10; Ps. xcvii. 2. The Saviour also ascended in a cloud, Ac. i. 9; and he will again descend in clouds to judge the world, Mat. xxiv. 30; xxvi. 64; Mar. xiii. 26; Re. i. 7. Nothing can be argued here as to the *purpose* for which the angel appeared, from his being encompassed with a cloud; nor can anything be argued from it in respect to the question *who* this angel was. The fair interpretation is, that this was one of the angels now represented as sent forth on an errand of mercy to man, and coming with appro-

priate majesty as the messenger of God. ¶ *And a rainbow was upon his head.* In ch. iv. 3 the throne in heaven is represented as encircled by a rainbow. See Notes on that verse. The rainbow is properly an emblem of peace. *Here* the symbol would mean that the angel came not for wrath, but for purposes of peace; that he looked with a benign aspect on men, and that the effect of his coming would be like that of sunshine after a storm. ¶ *And his face* was *as it were the sun.* Bright like the sun (Notes, ch. i. 16); that is, he looked upon men with (*a*) an *intelligent* aspect—as the sun is the source of light; and (*b*) with *benignity*—not covered with clouds, or darkened by wrath. The *brightness* is probably the main idea, but the appearance of the angel would, as here represented, naturally suggest the ideas just referred to. As an *emblem* or *symbol* we should regard his appearing as that which was to be followed by knowledge and by prosperity. ¶ *And his feet as pillars of fire.* See Notes on ch. i. 15. In this symbol, then, we have the following things:—(*a*) An angel—as the messenger of God, indicating that some new communication was to be brought to mankind, or that there would be some interposition in human affairs which might be well represented by the coming of an angel; (*b*) the fact that he was "mighty"—indicating that the work to be done required power beyond human strength; (*c*) the fact that he came in a cloud—on an embassage so grand and magnificent as to make this symbol of majesty proper; (*d*) the fact that he was encircled by a rainbow—that the visitation was to be one of peace to mankind; and (*e*) the fact that his coming was like the sun—or would diffuse light and peace.

Now, in regard to the *application* of this, without adverting to any other theory, no one can fail to see that, on the supposition that it was designed to refer to the Reformation, this would be the most striking and appropriate symbol that could have been chosen. For (*a*) as we have seen already, this is the *place* which the vision naturally occupies in the series of historical representations. (*b*) It was at a period of the world, and the world was in such a state, that an intervention of this kind would be properly represented by the coming of an angel from heaven. God had visited the nations with terrible judgments, but the effect had not been to produce reformation, for the same forms of wickedness continued to prevail which had existed before. Notes, ch. ix. 20, 21. In this state of things any new interposition of God for reforming the world would be properly represented by the coming of an angel from heaven as a messenger of light and peace. (*c*) The great and leading events of the Reformation were well represented by the *power* of this angel. It was not, indeed, physical power; but the work to be done in the Reformation was a *great* work, and was such as would be well symbolized by the intervention of a mighty angel from heaven. The task of reforming the church, and of correcting the abuses which had prevailed, was wholly beyond any ability which *man* possessed, and was well represented, therefore, by the descent of this messenger from the skies. (*d*) The same thing may be said of the *rainbow* that was upon his head. Nothing would better symbolize the general aspect of the Reformation, as fitted to produce peace, tranquillity, and joy upon the earth. And (*e*) the same thing was indicated by the splendour—the light and glory—that attended the angel. The symbol would denote that the new order of things would be attended with light; with knowledge; with that which would be benign in its influence on human affairs. And it need not be said, to anyone acquainted with the history of those times, that the Reformation was preceded and accompanied with a great increase of light; that at just about that period of the world the study of the Greek language began to be common in Europe; that the sciences had made remarkable progress; that schools and colleges had begun to flourish; and that, to a degree which had not existed for ages before, the public mind had become awakened to the importance of truth and knowledge. For a full illustration of this, from the close of the eleventh century and onward, see Hallam's *Middle Ages*, vol. ii. pp. 265-292, ch. ix. part ii. To go into any satisfactory detail on this point would be wholly beyond the proper limits of these Notes, and the reader must be referred to the histories of those times, and especially to Hallam, who has recorded all that is necessary to be known on the subject. Suffice it to say, that on the supposition that it was the intention to symbolize those times, no more appropriate emblem could have

## CHAPTER X.

**2 And he had in his hand a little book open: and he set his right foot upon the sea, and *his* left *foot* on the earth,**

been found than that of an angel whose face shone like the sun, and who was covered with light and splendour. These remarks will show, that if it be supposed it was intended to symbolize the Reformation, no more appropriate emblem could have been selected than that of such an angel coming down from heaven. If, after the events have occurred, we should desire to represent the same things by a striking and expressive symbol, we could find none that would better represent those times.

2. *And he had in his hand a little book open.* This is the first thing that indicated the purpose of his appearing, or that would give any distinct indication of the design of his coming from heaven. The general aspect of the angel, indeed, as represented in the former verse, was that of benignity, and his purpose, as there indicated, was light and peace. But still there was nothing which would denote the *particular* design for which he came, or which would designate the particular means which he would employ. Here we have, however, an *emblem* which will furnish an indication of what was to occur as the result of his appearing. To be able to apply this, it will be necessary, as in all similar cases, to explain the natural significancy of the emblem. (1) *The little book.* The word used here—βιβλαρίδιον—occurs nowhere else in the New Testament except in ver. 8, 9, 10 of this chapter. The word βιβλίον—*book*—occurs frequently:—Mat. xix. 7; Mar. x. 4—applied to a bill of divorcement; Lu. iv. 17, 20; Jn. xx. 30; xxi. 25; Ga. iii. 10; 2 Ti. iv. 13; He. ix. 19; x. 7. In the Apocalypse this word is of common occurrence: ch. i. 11; v. 1, 2, 3, 4, 5, 7, 8, 9; vi. 14, rendered *scroll;* xvii. 8; xx. 12; xxi. 27; xxii. 7, 9, 10, 18, 19. The word was evidently chosen here to denote something that was peculiar in the size or form of the book, or to distinguish it from that which would be designated by the ordinary word employed to denote a book. The word properly denotes a small roll or volume; a little scroll (Rob. *Lex., Pollux. Onomast.* 7. 210). It is evident that something was intended by the diminutive *size* of the book, or that it was designed to make a distinction between this and that which is indicated by the use of the word *book* in the other parts of the Apocalypse. It was, at least, indicated by this that it was something different from what was seen in the hand of him that sat on the throne in ch. v. 1. That was clearly a large volume; this was so small that it could be taken in the hand, and could be represented as eaten, ver. 9, 10. But of what is a book an emblem? To this question there can be little difficulty in furnishing an answer. A book seen in a dream, according to Artemidorus, signifies the life, or the acts of him that sees it (Wemyss). According to the Indian interpreters, a book is the symbol of power and dignity. The Jewish kings, when they were crowned, had the book of the law of God put into their hands (2 Ki. xi. 12; 2 Ch. xxiii. 11); denoting that they were to observe the law, and that their administration was to be one of intelligence and uprightness. The gift of a Bible now to a monarch when he is crowned, or to the officer of a corporation or society, denotes the same thing. A book, as such, thus borne in the hand of an angel coming down to the world, would be an indication that something of importance was to be communicated to men, or that something was to be accomplished by the agency *of a book.* It was not, as in ch. vi. 2, *a bow*—emblem of conquest; or ver. 4, *a sword*—emblem of battle; or ver. 5, *a pair of scales*—emblem of the exactness with which things were to be determined; but it was *a book*— a speechless, silent thing, yet mighty; not designed to carry desolation through the earth, but to diffuse light and truth. The natural interpretation, then, would be, that something was to be accomplished by the agency of a book, or that a book was to be the prominent characteristic of the times—as the bow, the sword, and the balances had been of the previous periods. As to the *size* of the book, perhaps all that can be inferred is, that this was to be brought about, not by extended tomes, but by a comparatively small volume—so that it could be taken in the hand; so that it could, without impropriety, be represented as *eaten* by an individual. (2) *The fact that it was open:* "a little book *open*"— ἀνεῳγμένον. The word here used means, properly, to open or unclose in respect to that which was

before fastened or sealed, as that which is covered by a door, Mat. ii. 11; tombs, which were closed by large stones, Mat. xxvii. 60, 66; a gate, Ac. v. 23; xii. 10; the abyss, Re. ix. 2—"since in the east pits or wells are closed with large stones, comp. Ge. xxix. 2" (Rob. *Lex.*). The meaning of this word, as applied to a book, would be, that it was now opened so that its contents could be read. The word would not *necessarily* imply that it had been sealed or closed, though that would be the most natural impression from the use of the word. Comp. for the use of the word rendered *open*, Re. iii. 8, 20; iv. 1; v. 2, 3, 4, 5, 9; vi. 1, 3, 5, 7, 9, 12; viii. 1; ix. 2; x. 8; xi. 19; xx. 12. This would find a fulfilment if some such facts as the following should occur:—(*a*) if there had been any custom or arrangement by which *knowledge* was kept from men, or access was forbidden to books or to some one book in particular; and (*b*) if something should occur by which that which had before been kept hidden or concealed, or that to which access had been denied, should be made accessible. In other words, this is the proper symbol of a diffusion of knowledge, or of *the influence of* A BOOK *on mankind*. (3) The fact that it was in the *hand* of the angel. All that seems to be implied in this is, that it was now *offered*, or was ready to be put in possession of John— or of the church—or of mankind. It was open, and was held out, as it were, for perusal.

In regard to the *application* of this, it is plain that, if it be admitted that it was the design of the author of the vision to refer to the Reformation, no more appropriate emblem could have been chosen. If *we* were now to endeavour to devise an emblem of the Reformation that would be striking and expressive, we could not well select one which would better represent the great work than that which is here presented. This will appear plain from a few considerations:—(1) The great agent in the Reformation, the moving cause of it, its suggestor and supporter, was a *book*— the *Bible*. Wycliffe had translated the New Testament into the English language, and though this was suppressed, yet it had done much to prepare the people for the Reformation; and all that Luther did can be traced to the discovery of the Bible, and to the use which was made of it. Luther had grown up into manhood; had passed from the schools to the university of Erfurt, and there having, during the usual four years' course of study, displayed intellectual powers and an extent of learning that excited the admiration of the university, and that seemed to open to his attainment both the honour and emolument of the world, he appeared to have been prepared to play an important part on the great drama of human affairs. Suddenly, however, to the astonishment and dismay of his friends, he betook himself to the solitude and gloom of an Augustinian monastery. There he found a *Bible*—a copy of the Vulgate—hid in the shelves of the university library. Till then he had supposed that there existed no other Gospels or Epistles than what were given in the Breviary, or quoted by the preachers.\* To the study of that book he now gave himself with untiring diligence and steady prayer; and the effect was to show to *him* the way of salvation by faith, and ultimately to produce the Reformation. No one acquainted with the history of the Reformation can doubt that it is to be traced to the influence of *the Bible;* that the moving cause, the spring of all that occurred in the Reformation, was the impulse given to the mind of Luther and his fellow-labourers by the study of that one book. It is this well-known fact that gives so much truth to the celebrated declaration of Chillingworth, that "the Bible is the religion of Protestants." If a symbol of this had been designed before it occurred, or if one should be sought for now that would designate the actual nature and influence of the Reformation, nothing *better* could be selected than that of an angel descending from heaven, with benignant aspect, with a rainbow around his head, and with light beaming all around him, holding forth to mankind *a book*. (2) This book had before been hidden, or closed; that is, it could not till then be regarded as an *open* volume. (*a*) It was in fact known by few even of the clergy, and it was not in the hands of the mass of the people at all. There is every reason to believe that the great body of the Romish clergy, in the time that preceded the Reformation, were even more ignorant of the Bible than Luther himself was. Many of them were unable to read; few had access to the Bible; and those who had, drew their doctrines

\* For the proof of this, see Elliott, ii. 92.

rather from the fathers of the church than from the Word of God. Hallam (*Middle Ages*, ii. 241) says: "Of this prevailing ignorance [in the tenth century and onward] it is easy to produce abundant testimony. In almost every council the ignorance of the clergy forms a subject for reproach. It is asserted by one held in 992, that scarcely a single person could be found in Rome itself who knew the first elements of letters. Not one priest of a thousand in Spain, about the age of Charlemagne, could address a letter of common salutation to another. In England, Alfred declares that he could not recollect a single priest south of the Thames (the best part of England), at the time of his accession, who understood the ordinary prayers, or who could translate the Latin into the mother tongue." There were few books of any kind in circulation, and even if there had been an ability to read, the *cost* of books was so great as to exclude the great mass of the people from all access to the sacred Scriptures. "Many of the clergy," says Dr. Robertson (*Hist. of Charles V.* p. 14, Harper's ed.), "did not understand the Breviary which they were obliged daily to recite; some of them could scarcely read it." "Persons of the highest rank, and in the most eminent stations, could neither read nor write." One of the questions appointed by the canons to be put to persons who were candidates for orders was this, "Whether they could read the Gospels and Epistles, and explain the sense of them at least literally?" For the causes of this ignorance see Robertson's *Hist. of Charles V.* p. 515. One of those causes was the *cost* of books. "Private persons seldom possessed any books whatever. Even monasteries of considerable note had only one *Missal*. The price of books became so high that persons of a moderate fortune could not afford to purchase them. The Countess of Anjou paid for a copy of the *Homilies of Haimon*, bishop of Alberstadt, two hundred sheep, five quarters of wheat, and the same quantity of rye and millet," &c. Such was the cost of books that few persons could afford to own a copy of the sacred Scriptures; and the consequence was, there were almost none in the hands of the people. The few copies that were in existence were mostly in the libraries of monasteries and universities, or in the hands of some of the higher clergy. (*b*) But there was another reason that was still more efficacious, perhaps, in keeping the people at large from the knowledge of the Scriptures. It was found in the prevailing views in the Roman Catholic communion respecting the private use and interpretation of the sacred volume. Whatever theory may now be advocated in the Roman Catholic communion on this point, as a matter of fact, the influence of that denomination has been to withhold the Bible from a free circulation among the common people. No one can deny that, in the times just preceding the Reformation, the whole influence of the Papal denomination was opposed to a free circulation of the Bible, and that one of the great and characteristic features of the Reformation was the fact, that the doctrine was promulgated that the Bible was to be freely distributed, and that the people everywhere were to have access to it, and were to form their own opinions of the doctrines which it reveals. (3) The Bible became, at the Reformation, in fact an "open" book. It was made accessible. It became *the* popular book of the world—the book that did more than all other things to change the aspect of affairs, and to give character to subsequent times. This occurred because (*a*) the art of printing was discovered just before the Reformation, as if, in the providence of God, it was *designed* then to give this precious volume to the world; and the Bible was, in fact, the first book printed, and has been since printed more frequently than any other book whatever, and will continue to be to the end of the world. It would be difficult to imagine now a more striking symbol of the art of printing, or to suggest a better device for it, than to represent an angel giving an open volume to mankind. (*b*) The leading doctrine of the Reformers was, that the Bible is the source of all authority in matters of religion, and, consequently, is to be accessible to all the people. And (*c*) the Bible was the authority appealed to by the Reformers. It became the subject of profound study; was diffused abroad; and gave form to all the doctrines that sprang out of the times of the Reformation. These remarks, which might be greatly expanded, will show with what propriety, on the supposition that the chapter here refers to the Reformation, the symbol of *a book* was selected. Obviously no other symbol would have been so appropriate; nothing else would have given so just a view of the lead-

3 And cried with a loud voice, as *when* a lion roareth: and when he had cried, seven ᶜthunders uttered their voices.

*c* ch. 8.5; 14.2.

ing characteristics of that period of the world.

¶ *And he set his right foot upon the sea, and* his *left* foot *upon the earth.* This is the *third* characteristic in the symbol. As a mere description this is eminently sublime. I was once (at Cape May, 1849) impressively reminded of this passage. My window was in such a position that it commanded a fine view at the same time of the ocean and the land. A storm arose such as I had never witnessed—the clouds from the different points of the compass seeming to come together over the place, and producing incessant lightning and thunder. As the storm cleared away the most magnificent rainbow that I ever saw appeared, arching the heavens, one foot of it far off on the sea, and the other on the land—an emblem of peace to both—and most strikingly suggesting to me the angel in the Apocalypse. The natural meaning of such a symbol as that represented here would be, that something was to occur which would pertain to the whole world, as the earth is made up of land and water. It is hardly necessary to say, that on the supposition that this refers to the Reformation, there is no difficulty in finding an ample fulfilment of the symbol. That great work was designed manifestly by Providence to affect all the world — the sea and the land — the dwellers in the islands and in the continents—those who "go down to the sea in ships, and do business in the great waters," and those who have a permanent dwelling on shore. It may be admitted, indeed, that, in itself, this one thing—the angel standing on the sea and the land, if it occurred alone, could not suggest the Reformation; and if there were nothing else, such an application might seem fanciful and unnatural; but, taken in connection with the other things in the symbol, and assuming that the whole vision was designed to symbolize the Reformation, it will not be regarded as unnatural that there *should* be some symbol which would intimate that the blessings of a reformed religion—a pure gospel—would be ultimately spread over land and ocean—over the continents and islands of the globe; in all the fixed habitations of men, and in their floating habitations on the deep. The symbol of a rainbow bending over the sea and land, would have expressed this; the same thing would be expressed by an angel whose head was encircled by a rainbow, and whose face beamed with light, with one foot on the ocean and the other on the land.

3. *And cried with a loud voice, as when a lion roareth.* The lion is the monarch of the woods, and his roar is an image of terror. The point of the comparison here seems to be the *loudness* with which the angel cried, and the *power* of what he said to awe the world —as the roar of the lion keeps the dwellers of the forest in awe. *What* he said is not stated; nor did John attempt to record it. Professor Stuart supposes that it was "a loud note of woe, some interjection uttered which would serve to call attention, and at the same time be indicative of the judgments which were to follow." But it is not necessary to suppose that this particular thing was intended. *Any* loud utterance—any solemn command —any prediction of judgment—any declaration of truth that would arrest the attention of mankind, would be in accordance with all that is said here. As there is no *application* of what is said, and no *explanation* made by John, it is impossible to determine with any certainty what is referred to. But, supposing that the whole refers to the Reformation, would not the loud and commanding voice of the angel properly represent the proclamation of the gospel as it began to be preached in such a manner as to command the attention of the world, and the reproof of the prevailing sins in such a manner as to keep the world in awe? The voice that sounded forth at the Reformation among the nations of Europe, breaking the slumbers of the Christian world, awaking the church to the evil of the existing corruptions and abominations, and summoning princes to the defence of the truth, might well be symbolized by the voice of an angel that was heard afar. In regard to the effect of the "theses" of Luther, in which he attacked the main doctrines of the Papacy, a contemporary writer says, "In the space of a fortnight they spread over Germany, and within a month they had run through all Christendom, *as if an-*

gels themselves had been the bearers of them to all men." To John it might not be known beforehand—as it probably would not be—what this symbolized; but could we now find a more appropriate symbol to denote the Reformation than the appearance of such an angel; or better describe the *impression* made by the first announcement of the great doctrines of the Reformation, than by the loud voice of such an angel? ¶ *And when he had cried, seven thunders uttered their voices.* Professor Stuart renders this, "*the* seven thunders uttered their voices," and insists that the article should be retained, which it has not been in our common version. So Elliott, Bishop Middleton, and others. Bishop Middleton says, "Why the article is inserted here I am unable to discover. It is somewhat remarkable that a few manuscripts and editions omit it in both places [ver. 3, 4]. Were the seven thunders anything well known and pre-eminent? If not, the omission must be right in the former instance, but wrong in the latter; if they were pre-eminent, then is it wrong in both. Bengel omits the article in ver. 3, but has it in ver. 4." He regards the insertion of the article as the true reading in both places, and supposes that there may have been a reference to some Jewish opinion, but says that he had not been able to find a vestige of it in Lightfoot, Schoettgen, or Meuschen. Storr supposes that we are not to seek here for any Jewish notion, and that nothing is to be inferred from the article (Middleton, on the *Greek Article*, p. 358). The best editions of the New Testament retain the article in both places, and indeed there is no authority for omitting it. The use of the article here naturally implies either that these seven thunders were something which had been before referred to, either expressly or impliedly; or that there was something about them which was so well known that it would be at once understood what was referred to; or that there was something in the connection which would determine the meaning. Comp. Notes on ch. viii. 2. It is plain, however, that there had been no mention of "seven thunders" before, nor had anything been referred to which would at once suggest them. The reason for the insertion of the article here must, therefore, be found in some pre-eminence which these seven thunders had; in some well-known facts about them; in something which would at once suggest them when they were mentioned— as when we mention *the* sun, *the* moon, *the* stars, though they might not have been distinctly referred to before. The number "seven" is used here either (*a*) as a general or perfect number, as it is frequently in this book, where we have it so often repeated—seven spirits; seven angels; seven seals; seven trumpets; or (*b*) with some specific reference to the matter in hand—the case actually in view of the writer. It cannot be doubted that it *might* be used in the former sense here, and that no law of language would be violated if it were so understood; as denoting *many* thunders; but still it is equally true that it *may* be used in a specific sense as denoting something that would be well understood by applying the number *seven* to it. Now let it be *supposed*, in regard to the application of this symbol, that the reference is to Rome, the seven-hilled city, and to the thunders of excommunication, anathema, and wrath that were uttered from that city against the Reformers; and would there not be *all* that is fairly implied in this language, and is not this such a symbol as *would be* appropriately used on such a supposition? The following circumstances may be referred to as worthy of notice on this point:—(*a*) the place which this occupies in the series of symbols—being just *after* the angel had uttered his voice as symbolical of the proclamation of the great truths of the gospel in the Reformation, if the interpretation above given is correct. The *next* event, in the order of nature and of fact, was the voice of excommunication uttered at Rome. (*b*) The word *thunder* would appropriately denote the bulls of excommunication uttered at Rome, for the name most frequently given to the decrees of the Papacy, when condemnatory, was that of Papal *thunders*. So Le Bas, in his *Life of Wycliffe*, p. 198, says: "The *thunders* which shook the world when they issued *from the seven hills* sent forth an uncertain sound, comparatively faint and powerless, when launched from a region of less devoted sanctity." (*c*) The number *seven* would, on such a supposition, be used here with equal propriety. Rome was built on 'seven hills; was known as the "seven-hilled" city, and the thunders from that city would seem to echo and re-echo from those hills. Comp. ch. xvii. 9. (*d*) This supposi-

4 And when the seven thunders had uttered their voices, I was about to write: and I heard a voice from heaven saying unto me, <sup>d</sup>Seal up those things which the seven

d Da.8.26; 12.4,9.

tion, also, will accord with the use of the article here, *as if* those thunders were something well known — "*the seven thunders;*" that is, the thunders which the nations were accustomed to hear. (*e*) This will also accord with the passage before us, inasmuch as the thunders would seem to have been of the nature of a response to what the angel said, or to have been sent forth *because* he had uttered his loud cry. In like manner, the anathemas were hurled from Rome because the nations had been aroused by the loud cry for reformation, as if an angel had uttered that cry. For these reasons there is a propriety in applying this language to the thunders which issued from Rome condemning the doctrines of the Reformation, and in defence of the ancient faith, and excommunicating those who embraced the doctrines of the Reformers. If we were *now* to attempt to devise a symbol which would be appropriate to express what actually occurred in the Reformation, we could not think of one which would be better fitted to that purpose than to speak of seven thunders bellowing forth from the seven-hilled city.

4. *And when the seven thunders had uttered their voices.* After he had listened to those thunders; or when they had passed by. ¶ *I was about to write.* That is, he was about to record what was uttered, supposing that that was the design for which he had been made to hear them. From this it would seem that it was not mere thunder—*brutum fulmen*—but that the utterance had a distinct and intelligible enunciation, or that *words* were employed that could be recorded. It may be observed, by the way, as Professor Stuart has remarked, that this proves that John wrote down what he saw and heard as soon as practicable, and in the place where he was; and that the supposition of many modern critics, that the Apocalyptic visions were written at Ephesus a considerable time after the visions took place, has no good foundation. ¶ *And I heard a voice from heaven saying unto me.* Evidently the voice of God: at all events it came with the clear force of command. ¶ *Seal up those things.* On the word *seal*, see Notes on ch. v. 1. The meaning here is, that he was not to record those things, but what he heard he was to keep to himself *as if* it was placed under a seal which was not to be broken. ¶ *And write them not.* Make no record of them. No reason is mentioned *why* this was not to be done, and none can now be given that can be proved to be the true reason. Vitringa, who regards the seven thunders as referring to the Crusades, supposes the reason to have been that a more full statement would have diverted the mind from the course of the prophetic narrative, and from more important events which pertained to the church, and that nothing occurred in the Crusades which was worthy to be recorded at length: Nec dignæ erant quæ prolixius exponerentur — "for," he adds, "these expeditions were undertaken with a foolish purpose, and resulted in real detriment to the church," pp. 431, 432. Professor Stuart (vol. ii. pp. 204–206) supposes that these "thunders" refer to the destruction of the city and temple of God, and that they were a sublime introduction to the last catastrophe, and that the meaning is not that he should keep "*entire* silence," but only that he should state the circumstances in a general manner, without going into detail. Mede supposes that John was commanded to keep silence because it was designed that the meaning should not then be known, but should be disclosed in future times; Forerius, because it was the design that the wise should be able to understand them, but that they were not to be disclosed to the wicked and profane. Without attempting to examine these and other solutions which have been proposed, the question which, from the course of the exposition, is properly before us is, whether, on the supposition that the voice of the seven thunders referred to the Papal anathemas, a rational and satisfactory solution of the reasons of this silence can be given. Without pretending to *know* the reasons which existed, the following may be referred to as not improbable, and as those which would meet the case:—(1) In these Papal anathemas there was nothing that was *worthy* of record; there was nothing that was important as history; there was nothing that com-

municated truth; there was nothing that really indicated *progress* in human affairs. In themselves there was nothing more that deserved *record* than the acts and doings of wicked men at any time; nothing that fell in with the main design of this book. (2) Such a record would have retarded the progress of the main statements of what was to occur, and would have turned off the attention from these to less important matters. (3) All that was necessary in the case was simply to state that such thunders were *heard:* that is, on the supposition that this refers to the Reformation, that that great change in human affairs would not be permitted to occur without opposition and noise— *as if* the thunders of wrath should follow those who were engaged in it. (4) John evidently *mistook* this for a real revelation, or for something that was to be recorded as connected with the divine will in reference to the progress of human affairs. He was naturally about to record this as he did what was uttered by the other voices which he heard; and if he had made the record, it would have been with this mistaken view. There was nothing in the voices, or in what was uttered, that would *manifestly* mark it as distinct from what had been uttered as coming from God, and he was about to record it under this impression. If this *was* a mistake, and if the record would do anything, as it clearly would, to perpetuate the error, it is easy to see a sufficient reason why the record should not be made. (5) It is remarkable that there was an entire correspondence with this in what occurred in the Reformation; in the fact that Luther and his fellow-labourers were, at first, and for a long time—such was the force of education, and of the habits of reverence for the Papal authority in which they had been reared— disposed to receive the announcements of the Papacy as the oracles of God, and to show to them the deference which was due to divine communications. The language of Luther himself, if the general view here taken is correct, will be the best commentary on the expressions here used. "When I began the affairs of the Indulgences," says he, "I was a monk, and a most mad Papist. So intoxicated was I, and drenched in Papal dogmas, that I would have been most ready to murder, or assist others in murdering, any person who should have uttered a syllable against the duty of obedience to the pope." And again: "Certainly at that time I adored him in earnest." He adds, "How distressed my heart was in that year 1517—how submissive to the hierarchy, not feignedly but really—those little knew who at this day insult the majesty of the pope with so much pride and arrogance. I was ignorant of many things which now, by the grace of God, I understand. I disputed; I was open to conviction; not finding satisfaction in the works of theologians, I wished to consult the living members of the church itself. There were some godly souls that entirely approved my propositions. But I did not consider their authority of weight with me in spiritual concerns. The popes, bishops, cardinals, monks, priests, were the objects of my confidence. After being enabled to answer every objection that could be brought against me from sacred Scripture, one difficulty alone remained, that *the Church ought to be obeyed.* If I had then braved the pope as I now do, I should have expected every hour that the earth would have opened to swallow me up alive, like Korah and Abiram." It was in this frame of mind that, in the summer of 1518, a few months after the affair with Tetzel, he wrote that memorable letter to the pope, the tenor of which can be judged of by the following sentences: and what could more admirably illustrate the passage before us, on the interpretation suggested, than this language? "Most blessed Father! Prostrate at the feet of thy blessedness I offer myself to thee, with all that I am, and that I have. Kill me, or make me live; call or recall; approve or reprove, as shall please thee. I will acknowledge *thy voice as the voice of Christ* presiding and speaking in thee." See the authorities for these quotations in Elliott, vol. ii. pp. 116, 117. (6) The command *not* to record what the seven thunders uttered was of the nature of a *caution* not to regard what was said in this manner; that is, not to be deceived by these utterances as if they were the voice of God. Thus understood, if this is the proper explanation and application of the passage, it should be regarded as an injunction *not* to regard the decrees and decisions of the Papacy as containing any intimation of the divine will, or as of authority in the church. That this is to be so regarded is the opinion of all Protestants; and if this is so, it is not a forced supposition

REVELATION. [A.D. 96.

thunders uttered, and write them not.

5 And the angel which I saw stand upon the sea and upon the earth ᵉlifted up his hand to heaven,

6 And sware by ᶠhim that liveth for ever and ever, who created heaven, and the things that therein are, and the earth, and the things that therein are, and the sea, and the things which are therein, ᵍthat there should be time no longer:

*e* Ex.6.8; De.32.40.   *f* ch.14.7; Ne.9.6.   *g* Da.12.6,7.

that this might have been intimated by such a symbol as that before us.

5. *And the angel which I saw stand,* &c. Ver. 2. That is, John saw him standing in this posture when he made the oath which he proceeds to record. ¶ *Lifted up his hand to heaven.* The usual attitude in taking an oath, as if one called heaven to witness. See Ge. xiv. 22; De. xxxii. 40; Eze. xx. 5, 6. Comp. Notes on Da. xii. 7.

6. *And sware by him that liveth for ever and ever.* By the ever-living God: a form of an oath in extensive use now. The essential idea in such an oath is an appeal to God; a solemn reference to Him as a witness; an utterance in the presence of Him who is acquainted with the truth or falsehood of what is said, and who will punish him who appeals to him falsely. It is usual, in such an oath, in order to give to it greater solemnity, to refer to some *attribute* of God, or something in the divine character on which the mind would rest at the time, as tending to make it more impressive. Thus, in the passage before us, the reference is to God as "ever-living;" that is, he is now a witness, and he ever will be; has now the power to detect and punish, and he ever will have the same power. ¶ *Who created heaven and the things that therein are,* &c. Who is the Maker of all things in heaven, on the earth, and in the sea; that is, throughout the universe. The design of referring to these things here is that which is just specified—to give increased solemnity to the oath by a particular reference to some one of the attributes of God. With this view nothing could be more appropriate than to refer to him as the Creator of the universe—denoting his infinite power, his right to rule and control all things. ¶ *That there should be time no longer.* This is a very important expression, as it is the substance of what the angel affirmed in so solemn a manner; and as the interpretation of the whole passage depends on it. It seems now to be generally agreed among critics that our translation does not give the true sense, inasmuch (*a*) as that was not the close of human affairs, and (*b*) as he proceeds to state what *would* occur *after* that. Accordingly, different versions of the passage have been proposed. Professor Stuart renders it, "that delay shall be no longer." Mr. Elliott, "that the time shall not yet be; but in the days of the voice of the seventh angel, whensoever he may be about to sound, then the mystery of God shall be finished." Mr. Lord, "that the time shall not be yet, but in the days of the voice of the seventh angel," &c. Andrew Fuller (*Works*, vol. vi. p. 113), "there should be no delay." So Dr. Gill. Mr. Daubuz, "the time shall not be yet." Vitringa (p. 432), *tempus non fore amplius*, "time shall be no more." He explains it (p. 433) as meaning, "not that this is to be taken *absolutely*, as if at the sounding of the seventh trumpet all things were then to terminate, and the glorious epiphany—ἐπιφανεια (or manifestation of Jesus Christ)—was then to occur, who would put an end to all the afflictions of his church; but in a limited sense—*restricte*—as meaning that there would be no *delay* between the sounding of the seventh trumpet and the fulfilment of the prophecies." The sense of this passage is to be determined by the meaning of the words and the connection. (*a*) The word *time*—χρόνος—is the common Greek word to denote *time*, and may be applied to time in general, or to any specified time or period. See Robinson, *Lex. sub voce*, (*a, b*). In the word itself there is nothing to determine its particular signification here. It might refer either to time in general, or to the time under consideration, and which was the subject of the prophecy. Which of these is the true idea is to be ascertained by the other circumstances referred to. It should be added, however, that the *word* does not of itself denote *delay*, and is never used to denote that directly. It can only denote that because *delay* occupies or consumes *time*, but this sense of the noun is not found in the New Testament. It is

found, however, in the verb χρονίζω, to linger, to delay, to be long in coming, Mat. xxv. 5; Lu. i. 21. (*b*) The absence of the article—"*time*," not "*the time*"—would naturally give it a general signification, unless there was something in the connection to limit it to some well-known period under consideration. See Notes on ch. viii. 2; x. 3. In this latter view, if the time referred to would be sufficiently definite *without* the article, the article need not be inserted. This is such a case, and comes under the rule for the omission of the article as laid down by Bishop Middleton, part i. ch. iii. The principle is, that when the copula, or verb connecting the subject and predicate, is the verb substantive, then the article is omitted. "To affirm the existence," says he, "of that of which the existence is already assumed, would be superfluous; to deny it, would be contradictory and absurd." As applicable to the case before us, the meaning of this rule would be, that the nature of the time here referred to is implied in the use of the substantive verb (ἔσται), and that consequently it is not necessary to specify it. All that needs to be said on this point is, that, on the supposition that John referred to a specified time, instead of time in general, it would not be necessary, under this rule, to insert the article. The reference would be understood without it, and the insertion would be unnecessary. This is substantially the reasoning of Mr. Elliott (vol. ii. p. 123), and it is submitted for what it is worth. My own knowledge of the usages of the Greek article is too limited to justify me in pronouncing an opinion on the subject, but the authorities are such as to authorize the assertion that, on the supposition that a particular well-known period were here referred to, the insertion of the article would not be necessary. (*c*) The particle rendered "longer"—ἔτι— "time shall be no *longer*"—means properly, according to Robinson (*Lex.*), *yet, still;* implying (1) *duration*—as spoken of the present time; of the present in allusion to the past, and, with a negative, *no more, no longer;* (2) implying accession, addition, *yet, more, further, besides.* According to Buttmann, *Gram.* § 149, vol. i. p. 430, it means, when alone, "yet still, yet farther; and with a negative, no more, no farther." The particle occurs often in the New Testament, as may be seen in the *Concordance.* It is more frequently rendered "*yet*" than by any other word (comp. Mat. xii. 46; xvii. 5; xix. 20; xxvi. 47; xxvii. 63; Mar. v. 35; viii. 17; xii. 6; xiv. 43—and so in the other Gospels, the Acts, and the Epistles); in all, fifty times. In the book of Revelation it is only once rendered "*yet*," ch. vi. 11, but is rendered "*more*" in ch. iii. 12; vii. 16; ix. 12; xii. 8; xviii. 21, 22 (three times), 23 (twice); xx. 3; xxi. 1, 4 (twice); "*longer*" in ch. x. 6; "*still*" in ch. xxii. 11 (four times). The usage, therefore, will justify the rendering of the word by "*yet*," and in connection with the negative, "not yet"—meaning that the thing referred to would not occur immediately, but would be hereafter. In regard to the general meaning, then, of this passage in its connection, we may remark, (*a*) That it cannot mean, literally, that there would be *time* no longer, or that the world would then come to an end absolutely, for the speaker proceeds to disclose events that would occur after that, extending far into the future (ch. x. 11), and the detail that follows (ch. xi.) before the sounding of the seventh trumpet is such as to occupy a considerable period, and the seventh trumpet is also yet to sound. No fair construction of the language, therefore, would require us to understand this as meaning that the affairs of the world were then to terminate. (*b*) The connection, then, apart from the question of grammatical usage, will require some such construction as that above suggested—"that the time," to wit, some certain, known, or designated time, "would not be *yet*," but would be in some future period; that is, as specified, ver. 7, "in the days of the voice of the seventh angel, when he shall begin to sound." *Then* "the mystery of God would be finished," and the affairs of the world would be put on their permanent footing. (*c*) This would imply that, at the time when the angel appeared, or in the time to which he refers, there would be some expectation or general belief that the "mystery was *then* to be finished, and that the affairs of the world were to come to an end. The proper interpretation would lead us to suppose that there would be so general an expectation of this, as to make the solemn affirmation of the angel proper to correct a prevailing opinion, and to show that the right interpretation was not put on what seemed to be the tendency of things. (d) As a matter of fact, we find that this expectation did actually exist at the time of the Reformation; that such an interpretation was put on the prophecies, and on the events that occurred; and that the impression that the Messiah was about to come, and the reign of saints about to commence, was so strong as to justify some interference, like the solemn oath of the angel, to correct the misapprehension. It is true that this impression had existed in former times, and even in the early ages of the church; but, as a matter of fact, it was true, and eminently true, in the time of the Reformation, and there was, on many accounts, a strong tendency to that form of belief. The Reformers, in interpreting the prophecies, learned to connect the downfall of the Papacy with the coming of Christ, and with his universal reign upon the earth; and as they saw the evidences of the approach of the former, they naturally anticipated the latter as about to occur. Comp. Da. ii. 34; xii. 11; 2 Th. ii. 3, 8. The anticipation that the Lord Jesus was about to come; that the affairs of the world, in the present form, were to be wound up; that the reign of the saints would soon commence; and that the permanent kingdom of righteousness would be established, became almost the current belief of the Reformers, and was frequently expressed in their writings. Thus Luther, in the year 1520, in his answer to the pope's bull of excommunication, expresses his anticipations: "Our Lord Jesus Christ yet liveth and reigneth; who, I firmly trust, will shortly come, and slay with the spirit of his mouth, and destroy with the brightness of his coming, that Man of Sin" (Merle D'Aubig., vol. ii. p. 166). After being summoned before the Diet at Worms, and after condemnation had been pronounced on him by the emperor, he fell back for comfort on the same joyous expectation. "For this once," he said, "the Jews, as on the crucifixion-day, may sing their pæan; but Easter will come for us, and then we shall sing Hallelujah" (D'Aubig., vol. ii. p. 275). The next year, writing to Staupitz, he made a solemn appeal against his abandoning the Reformation, by reference to the sure and advancing fulfilment of Daniel's prophecy. "My father," said he, "the abominations of the pope, with his whole kingdom, must be destroyed; and the Lord does this without hand, by the *Word* alone. The subject exceeds all human comprehension. I cherish the best hopes" (Milner, p. 692). In 1523 he thus, in a similar strain, expresses his hopes: "The kingdom of Antichrist, according to the prophet Daniel, must be broken *without hands;* that is, the Scriptures will be understood by and by; and every one will preach against Papal tyranny, from the Word of God, until the Man of Sin is deserted of all, and dies of himself" (Milner, p. 796). The same sentiments respecting the approach of the end of the world were entertained by Melancthon. In commenting on the passage in Daniel relating to the "little horn," he thus refers to an argument which has been prevalent: "The words of the prophet Elias should be marked by every one, and inscribed upon our walls, and on the entrances of our houses. Six thousand years shall the world stand, and after that be destroyed; two thousand years without the law; two thousand years under the law of Moses; two thousand years under the Messiah; and if any of these years are not fulfilled, they will be shortened (a shortening intimated by Christ also, on account of our sins)." The following manuscript addition to this argument has been found in Melancthon's hand, in Luther's own copy of the German Bible:—"Written A.D. 1557, and from the creation of the world, 5519; from which number we may see that this aged world is not far from its end." So also the British Reformers believed. Thus Bishop Latimer: "Let us cry to God day and night — Most merciful Father, let thy kingdom come! St. Paul saith, The Lord will not come till the swerving from the faith cometh (2 Th. ii. 3); which thing is already done and past. Antichrist is already known throughout all the world. Wherefore the day is not far off." Then, reverting to the consideration of the age of the world, as Melancthon had done, he says, "The world was ordained to endure, as all learned ones affirm, 6000 years. Now of that number there be past 5552 years, so that there is no more left but 448 years. Furthermore, those days shall be shortened for the elect's sake. Therefore, all those excellent and learned men, whom without doubt God hath sent into the world in these last days to give the world warning, do gather out of sacred Scrip-

7 But in the days of the voice of the *h*seventh angel, when he shall begin to sound, the *i*mystery

*h* ch.11.15.   *i* Ro.11.25; Ep.3.5-9.

of God should be finished, as he hath declared to his servants the prophets.

ture that the last day cannot be far off." So again, in a sermon on the nearness of the second advent, he says, "So that peradventure it may come in my days, old as I am, or in my children's days." Indeed, it is well known that this was a prevalent opinion among the Reformers; and this fact will show with what propriety, if the passage before us was *designed* to refer to the Reformation, this solemn declaration of the angel was made, that the "time would *not be yet* "—that those anticipations which would spring up from the nature of the case, and from the interpretations which would be put on what *seemed* to be the obvious sense of the prophecies, were unfounded, and that a considerable time must yet intervene before the events would be consummated. (*e*) The proper sense of this passage, then, according to the above interpretation would be—"And the angel lifted up his hand to heaven, and sware by him that liveth for ever and ever, That the time should not yet be; but, in the days of the voice of the seventh angel, when he shall begin to sound, the mystery of God shall be finished." Appearances, indeed, would then indicate that the affairs of the world were to be wound up, and that the prophecies respecting the end of the world were about to be fulfilled: but the angel solemnly swears "by Him who lives for ever and ever"—and whose reign therefore extends through all the changes on the earth—"by Him who is the Creator of all things," and whose purpose alone can determine when the end shall be, that the time would not be *yet.* Those cherished expectations would not yet be realized, but there was a series of important events to intervene before the end would come. Then—at the time when the seventh angel should sound—would be the consummation of all things.

7. *But in the days of the voice of the seventh angel.* The days in the period of time embraced by the sounding of the seventh trumpet. That is, the affairs of this world would not be consummated in that period embraced in the sounding of the sixth trumpet, but in that embraced in the sounding of the seventh and last of the trumpets.

Comp. ch. xi. 15-19. ¶ *When he shall begin to sound.* That is, the events referred to will *commence* at the period when the angel shall *begin* to sound. It will not be merely *during* or *in* that period, but the sounding of the trumpet, and the beginning of those events, will be contemporaneous. In other words, then would commence the reign of righteousness—the kingdom of the Messiah—the dominion of the saints on the earth. ¶ *The mystery of God should be finished.* On the meaning of the word *mystery*, see Notes on Ep. i. 9. It means here, as elsewhere in the New Testament, the purpose or truth of God which had been concealed, and which had not before been communicated to man. Here the particular reference is to the divine purpose which had been long concealed respecting the destiny of the world, or respecting the setting up of his kingdom, but which had been progressively unfolded by the prophets. That purpose would be "finished," or consummated, in the time when the seventh angel should begin to sound. Then all the "mystery" would be revealed; the plan would be unfolded; the divine purpose, so long concealed, would be manifested, and the kingdom of the Messiah and of the saints would be set up on the earth. Under that period, the affairs of the world would be ultimately wound up, and the whole work of redemption completed. ¶ *As he hath declared to his servants the prophets.* As he has from time to time disclosed his purposes to mankind through the prophets. The reference here is, doubtless, to the prophets of the Old Testament, though *the language* would include all who at any time had uttered any predictions respecting the final condition of the world. These prophecies had been scattered along through many ages; but the angel says that at that time all that had been said respecting the setting up of the kingdom of God, the reign of the saints, and the dominion of the Redeemer on the earth, would be accomplished. See Notes on ch. xi. 15. From the passage thus explained, if the interpretation is correct, it will follow that the sounding of the seventh trumpet (ch. xi. 15-18) is properly the conclusion of

8 And the *k* voice which I heard from heaven spake unto me again, and said, Go *and* take the little book which is open in the hand of the angel which standeth upon the sea and upon the earth.

*k* ver.4.

9 And I went unto the angel, and said unto him, Give me the little book. And he said unto me, *l* Take *it*, and eat it up; and it shall make thy belly bitter, but it shall be in thy mouth sweet as honey.

*l* Eze.3.1-3,14.

this series of visions, and denotes a "*catastrophe*" in the action, and that what follows is the commencement of a new series of visions. This is clear, because (*a*) the whole seven seals, comprising the seven trumpets of the seventh seal, must embrace *one* view of all coming events—since this embraced all that there was in the volume seen in the hand of him that sat on the throne; (*b*) this is properly implied in the word here rendered "should be finished"— τελέσθη—the fair meaning of which is, that the "mystery" here referred to— the hitherto unrevealed purpose or plan of God—would, under that trumpet, be consummated or complete (see the conclusive reasoning of Prof. Stuart on the meaning of the word, vol. ii. p. 210, foot-note); and (*c*) it will be found in the course of the exposition that, at ch. xi. 19, there commences a new series of visions, embracing a view of the world in its *religious* aspect, or *ecclesiastical* characteristics, reaching down to the same consummation, and stating at the close of that (ch. xx.) more fully what is here (ch. xi. 15-18) designated in a more summary way—the final triumph of religion, and the establishment of the kingdom of the saints. The present series of visions (ch. v.-xi. 18) relates rather to the outward or secular changes which would occur on the earth, which were to affect the welfare of the church, to the final consummation; the next series (ch. xi. 19; xii.-xx.) relates to the church internally, the rise of Antichrist, and the effect of the rise of that formidable power on the internal history of the church, to the time of the overthrow of that power, and the triumphant establishment of the kingdom of God. See the Analysis of the work, Intro. § 5. In other words, this series of visions, terminating at ch. xi. 18, refers, as the leading thing, to what would occur in relation to the Roman empire considered as a secular power, in which the church would be interested; that which follows (ch. xi. 19; xii.-xx.) to the Roman power considered as a great apostasy, and setting up a mighty and most oppressive domination over the true church, manifested in deep corruption and bloody persecutions, running on in its disastrous influence on the world, until that power should be destroyed, Babylon fall, and the reign of the saints be introduced.

8. *And the voice which I heard from heaven.* Ver. 4. This is not the voice of the angel, but a direct divine command. ¶ *Said, Go* and *take the little book that is open*, &c. That is, take it out of his hand, and do with it as you shall be commanded. There is a very strong resemblance between this passage and the account contained in Eze. ii. 9, 10; iii. 1-3. Ezekiel was directed to go to the house of Israel and deliver a divine message, whether they would hear or forbear; and in order that he might understand what message to deliver, there was shown to him a roll of a book, written within and without. That roll he was commanded to eat, and he found it to be "in his mouth as honey for sweetness." John has added to this the circumstance that, though "sweet in the mouth," it made "the belly bitter." The additional command (ver. 11), that he must yet "prophecy before many people," leads us to suppose that he had the narrative in Ezekiel in his eye; for, as the result of *his* eating the roll, he was commanded to go and prophesy to the people of Israel. The passage here (ver. 8) introduces a new symbol, that of "eating the book," and evidently refers to something that was to occur *before* the "mystery should be finished;" that is, before the seventh trumpet should sound. ¶ *Which is open in the hand*, &c. On the symbolical meaning of the word "open," as applied to the book, see Notes on ver. 2.

9. *And I went unto the angel.* This is symbolic action, and is not to be understood literally. As it is not necessary to suppose that an angel *literally* descended, and stood upon the sea and the land, so it is not necessary to suppose that there was a literal act of going to him, and taking the book from his hand and eating it. ¶ *Give me the little book.* In accordance with the com-

mand in ver. 8. We may suppose, in regard to this, (*a*) that the symbol was designed to represent that the book was to be used in the purpose here referred to, or was to be an important agent or instrumentality in accomplishing the purpose. The book is held forth in the hand of the angel as a striking emblem. There is a command to go and take it from his hand for some purpose not yet disclosed. All this seems to imply that the *book*—or that which is represented by it—would be an important instrument in accomplishing the purpose here referred to. (*b*) The application *for* the book might intimate that, on the part of him who made it, there would be some strong *desire* to possess it. He goes, indeed, in obedience to the command; but, at the same time, there would naturally be a *desire* to be in possession of the volume, or to know the contents (comp. ch. v. 4), and his approach to the angel for the book would be most naturally interpreted as expressive of such a wish. ¶ *And he said unto me, Take* it. As if he had expected this application; or had come down to furnish him with this little volume, and had anticipated that the request would be made. There was no reluctance in giving it up; there was no attempt to withhold it; there was no prohibition of its use. The angel had no commission, and no desire to retain it for himself, and no hesitation in placing it in the hands of the seer on the first application. Would not the readiness with which God gives his Bible into the hands of men, in contradistinction from all human efforts to restrain its use, and to prevent its free circulation, be well symbolized by this act? ¶ *And eat it up.* There is a similar command in Eze. iii. 1. Of course, this is to be understood figuratively, for no one would interpret literally a command to eat a manuscript or volume. We have in common use a somewhat similar phrase, when we speak of *devouring a book*, which may illustrate this, and which is not liable to be misunderstood. In Je. xv. 16, we have similar language: "Thy words were found, and I did eat them; and thy word was unto me the joy and rejoicing of my heart." Thus in Latin, the words *propinare, imbibere, devorare, deglutire*, &c., are used to denote the greediness with which knowledge is acquired. Comp. in the Apocrypha, 2 Esdras xiv. 38-40. The meaning here, then, is plain. He was to possess himself of the contents of the book; to receive it into his mind; to apply it, as we do food, for spiritual nourishment—truth having, in this respect, the same relation to the mind which food has to the body. If the little book was a symbol of the Bible, it would refer to the fact that the truths of that book became the nourisher and supporter of the public mind. ¶ *And it shall make thy belly bitter.* This is a circumstance which does not occur in the corresponding place in Eze. iii. 1-3. The expression here must refer to something that would occur *after* the symbolical action of "eating" the little book, or to some consequence of eating it—for the act of eating it is represented as pleasant: "in thy mouth sweet as honey." The meaning here is, that the effect which followed from eating the book was painful or disagreeable—as food would be that was pleasant to the taste, but that produced bitter pain when eaten. The fulfilment of this would be found in one of two things. (*a*) It might mean that the message to be delivered in consequence of devouring the book, or the message which it contained, would be of a painful or distressing character; that with whatever pleasure the book might be received and devoured, it would be found to contain a communication that would be indicative of woe or sorrow. This was the case with the little book that Ezekiel was commanded to eat up. Thus, in speaking of this book, it is said, "And it was written within and without: and there was written therein lamentations, and mourning, and woe," Eze. ii. 10. Comp. ch. iii. 4-9, where the contents of the book, and the effect of proclaiming the message which it contained, are more fully stated. So here the meaning may be, that, however gladly John may have taken the book, and with whatever pleasure he may have devoured its contents, yet that it would be found to be charged with the threatening of wrath, and with denunciations of a judgment to come, the delivery of which would be well represented by the "bitterness" which is said to have followed from "eating" the volume. Or (*b*) it may mean that the consequence of devouring the book, that is, of embracing its doctrines, would be persecutions and trouble—well represented by the "bitterness" that followed the "eating" of the volume. Either of these ideas would be a fulfilment of the

**10** And I took the little book out of the angel's hand, and ate it up; and it was in my mouth sweet as honey: and as soon as I had eaten it, my belly was bitter.

**11** And he said unto me, Thou must prophesy again before many peoples, and nations, and tongues, and kings.

proper meaning of the symbol; for, on the supposition that either of these occurred in fact, it would properly be symbolized by the eating of a volume that was sweet to the taste, but that made the belly bitter. ¶ *But it shall be in thy mouth sweet as honey.* So in Eze. iii. 3. The proper fulfilment of this it is not difficult to understand. It would well represent the pleasure derived from divine truth—the sweetness of the Word of God—the relish with which it is embraced by those that love it. On the supposition that the "little book" here refers to the Bible, and to the use which would be made of it in the times referred to, it would properly denote the relish which would exist for the sacred volume, and the happiness which would be found in its perusal; for this very image is frequently employed to denote this. Thus in Ps. xix. 10: "More to be desired are they than gold, yea, than much fine gold; sweeter also than honey and the honeycomb." Ps. cxix. 103: "How sweet are thy words unto my taste! yea, sweeter than honey to my mouth." We are then to look for the fulfilment of this in some prevailing delight or satisfaction, in the times referred to, in the Word of the Lord, or in the truths of revelation.

10. *And as soon as I had eaten it, my belly was bitter.* The effect immediately followed: that is, as soon as he was made acquainted with the contents of the book, either, as above explained, requiring him to deliver some message of woe and wrath which it would be painful to deliver, or that the consequence of receiving it was to bring on bitter persecutions and trials.

11. *And he said unto me.* The angel then said. ¶ *Thou must prophesy.* The word "*prophesy*" here is evidently used in the large sense of making known divine truth in general; not in the comparatively narrow and limited sense in which it is commonly used, as referring merely to the foretelling of future events. See the word explained in the Notes on Ro. xii. 6; 1 Co. xiv. 1. The meaning is, that, as a consequence of becoming possessed of the little volume and its contents, he would be called to proclaim divine truth, or to make the message of God known to mankind. The direct address is to John himself; but it is evidently not to be understood of him personally. *He* is represented as seeing the angel; as hearkening to his voice; as listening to the solemn oath which he took; as receiving and eating the volume; and then as prophesying to many people; but the reference is undoubtedly to the far-distant future. If the allusion is to the times of the Reformation, the meaning is, that the end of the world was not, as would be expected, about to occur, but that there was to be an interval long enough to permit the gospel to be proclaimed before "nations, and tongues, and kings;" that in consequence of coming into possession of the "little book," the Word of God, the truth was yet to be proclaimed far and wide on the earth. ¶ *Again*—πάλιν. This had been done before. That is, supposing this to refer to the time of the Reformation, it could be said, (*a*) that this had been done *before*—that the gospel had been in former times proclaimed in its purity before "many peoples, and nations, and tongues, and kings;" and (*b*) that it would be done "again;" that is, though the Word of God had been hidden, and a mass of corrupt traditions had taken its place, yet the time would come when those pure truths would be made known again to all lands. This will explain the word "*again*" in this place—not meaning that John would do this personally, but that this would be in fact the result of the restoration of the Bible to the church. ¶ *Before many peoples.* This word denotes people considered as *masses*, or as grouped together in masses, without reference to the manner in which it is done. It is used when we look on a *mass* of men, without taking into account the question whether they are of the same nation, or language, or rank. See Notes on ch. vii. 9. The plural is used here—"*peoples*"—perhaps to denote that those to whom the truth would be made known would be *very* numerous. They would not only be numerous in regard to the *individuals* to whom it would be communicated, but numerous considered as

communities or nations. ¶ *And nations.* The word *nations* here denotes people considered as separated by national boundaries, constitutions, laws, customs. See Notes on ch. vii. 9. ¶ *And tongues.* People considered as divided by languages—a division not always or necessarily the same as that denoted by the word "people," or "nations" as used in this passage. ¶ *And kings.* Rulers of the people. The meaning is, that the gospel would not only be borne before the *masses* of mankind, but in a special manner before kings and rulers. The effect of thus possessing the "little volume," or of the "open book" of revealed truth, would ultimately be that the message of life would be carried with power before princes and rulers, and would influence them as well as the common people.

In inquiring now for the proper application of this symbol as thus explained, we naturally turn to the Reformation, and ask whether there was anything in that of which this would be the proper emblem. The following things, then, are found in fact as occurring at that time, of which the symbol before us may be regarded as the proper representation:—

(1) The reception of the Bible as from the hand of an angel—or its recovery from obscurity and forgetfulness, *as if* it were now restored to the church by a heavenly interposition. The influence of the Bible on the Reformation; the fact that it was now recovered from its obscurity, and that it was made the grand instrument in the Reformation, has already been illustrated. See Notes on ver. 2. The symbolical action of taking it from the hand of an angel was not an improper representation of its reception again by the church, and of its restoration to its true place *in* the church. It became, as it is proper that it should always be, the grand means of the defence of the faith, and of the propagation of truth in the world.

(2) The statement that the little book when eaten was "in the mouth sweet as honey," is a striking and proper representation of the relish felt for the sacred Scriptures by those who love the truth (comp. Notes on ver. 9), and is especially appropriate to describe the interest which was felt in the volume of revealed truth in the time of the Reformation. For the Bible was to the Reformers emphatically a new book. It had been driven from common use to make way for the legends of the saints and the traditions of the church. It had, therefore, when translated into the vernacular tongue, and when circulated and read, the freshness of novelty — the interest which a volume of revealed truth would have if just given from heaven. Accordingly, it is well known with what avidity and relish the sacred volume was studied by Luther and his fellow-labourers in the Reformation; how they devoured its doctrines; how they looked to it for comfort in their times of trial; how sweet and sustaining were its promises in the troubles that came upon them, and in the labours which they were called to perform.

(3) The representation that, after it was eaten, it was "bitter," would not improperly describe the *effect*, in some respects, of thus receiving the Bible, and making it the groundwork of faith. It brought the Reformers at once into conflict with all the power of the Papacy and the priesthood; exposed them to persecution; aroused against them a host of enemies among the princes and rulers of the earth; and was the cause for which many of them were put to death. Such effects followed substantially when Wycliffe translated the Bible; when John Huss and Jerome of Prague published the pure doctrines of the New Testament; and when Luther gave to the people the Word of God in their own language. To a great extent this is always so— that, however sweet and precious the truths of the Bible may be to the preacher himself, one of the *effects* of his attempting to preach those truths may be such opposition on the part of men, such cold indifference, or such fierce persecution, that it would be well illustrated by what is said here, "it shall make thy belly bitter."

(4) The representation that, as a consequence of receiving that book, he would prophesy again before many people, is a fit representation of the effect of the reception of the Bible again by the church, and of allowing it its proper place there. For, (*a*) it led to *preaching*, or, in the language of this passage, "prophesying"—a thing comparatively little known before for many ages. The grand business in the Papal communion was not, and is not, *preaching*, but the performance of rites and ceremonies. Genuflexions, crossings, burning of incense, processions, music, constitute the characteristic

features of all Papal churches; the grand thing that distinguishes the Protestant churches all over the world, just in proportion as they *are* Protestant, is *preaching*. The Protestant religion—the pure form of religion as it is revealed in the New Testament—has few ceremonies: its rites are simple: it depends for success on the promulgation and defence of the *truth*, with the attending influence of the Holy Ghost; and for this view of the nature and degree of religion the world is indebted to the fact that the Bible was again restored to its true place in the church. (*b*) The Bible is the basis of all genuine *preaching*. Preaching will not be kept up in its purity, except in the places where the Bible is freely circulated, and where it is studied; and where it *is* studied, there will be, in the proper sense of the term, *preachers*. Just in proportion as the Bible is studied in the world, we may expect that preaching will be better understood, and that the number of preachers will be increased. (*c*) The study of the Bible is the foundation of all the efforts to spread the knowledge of the truth to "peoples, and nations, and tongues, and kings," in our own times. All these efforts have been originated by the restoration of the Bible to its proper place in the church, and to its more profound and accurate study in this age; for these efforts are but carrying out the injunction of the Saviour as recorded in this book—to "go into all the world, and preach the gospel to every creature." (*d*) The same thing will be true to the end of the world; or, in the language of the portion of the book of Revelation before us, till "the kingdoms of this world become the kingdoms of our Lord, and of his Christ; and he shall reign for ever and ever," ch. xi. 15. The fact of the restoration of the Bible to its proper place in the church will, therefore, ultimately be the means of the conversion of the whole world to God; and this fact, so momentous in its nature and its consequences, was worthy to be symbolized by the appearance of the "angel descending from heaven clothed with a cloud;" was properly represented by the manner in which he appeared—"his face radiant as the sun, and his feet as pillars of fire;" was worthy to be expressed by the position which he assumed, as "standing on the sea and the earth"—as if all the world were interested in the purpose of his mission, and was worthy of the loud proclamation which he made—as if a new order of things were to commence. Beautiful and sublime, then, as this chapter is, and always has been esteemed as a composition, it becomes still more beautiful and sublime if it be regarded as a symbol of the Reformation—an event the most glorious, and the most important in its issues, of any that has occurred since the Saviour appeared on the earth.

## CHAPTER XI.

ANALYSIS OF THE CHAPTER.

This chapter, which is very improperly separated from the preceding, and improperly *ended*—for it should have been closed at ver. 18—consists (excluding the last verse, which properly belongs to the succeeding chapter) essentially of three parts:—

I. The measuring of the temple, ver. 1, 2. A reed, or measuring-stick, is given to John, and he is directed to arise and measure the temple. This direction embraces two parts: (*a*) he was to measure, that is, to take an exact estimate of the temple, of the altar, and of the true worshippers; (*b*) he was carefully to separate this, in his estimate, from the outward court, which was to be left out and to be given to the Gentiles, to be trodden under foot forty-two months; that is, three years and a half, or twelve hundred and sixty days—a period celebrated in the book of Daniel as well as in this book.

II. The two witnesses, ver. 3-13. This is, in some respects, the most difficult portion of the book of Revelation, and its meaning can be stated only after a careful examination of the signification of the words and phrases used. The general statement in regard to these witnesses is, that they should have power, and should prophesy for twelve hundred and sixty days; that if anyone should attempt to injure them, they had power, by fire that proceeded out of their mouths, to devour and kill their enemies; that they had power to shut heaven so that it should not rain, and power to turn the waters of the earth into blood, and power to smite the earth with plagues as often as they chose; that when they had completed their testimony, the beast that ascends out of the bottomless pit would make war with them, and overcome them, and kill them; that their dead bodies

# CHAPTER XI.

AND there was given me a <sup>a</sup>reed like unto a rod: and the angel

<small>a ch.21.15; Zec.2.1.</small>

would lie unburied in that great city where the Lord was crucified three days and a half; that they that dwelt upon the earth would exult in their death, and send gifts to one another in token of their joy; that after the three days and a half the spirit of life from God would enter into them again, and they would stand up on their feet; that they would then be taken up into heaven, in the sight of their enemies; and that, at the time of their ascension, there would be a great earthquake, and a tenth part of the city would fall, and many (seven thousand) would be killed, and that the remainder would be affrighted, and would give glory to the God of heaven.

III. The sounding of the seventh trumpet, ver. 14–18. This is the grand consummation of the whole; the end of this series of visions; the end of the world. A rapid glance only is given of it here, for under another series of visions a more detailed account of the state of the world is given under the final triumph of truth. Here, as a proper close of the first series of visions, the result is merely glanced at or adverted to—that then the period would have arrived when the kingdoms of the world were to become the kingdoms of the Lord, and of his Christ, and when he should commence that reign which was to continue for ever. Then universal peace and happiness would reign, and the long-promised and expected kingdom of God on the earth would be established. The "nations" had been "angry," but the time had now come when a judgment was to be pronounced on the dead, and when the due reward was to be given to the servants of God—the prophets, and the saints, and those who feared his name, small and great—in the establishment of a permanent kingdom, and the complete triumph of the true religion in the world.

I regard this chapter, therefore, to ver. 18, as extending down to the consummation of all things, and as disclosing the last of the visions seen in the scroll or volume "sealed with the seven seals," ch. v. 1. For a reason above suggested, and which will appear more fully hereafter, the detail is here much less minute than in the earlier portions of the historic visions, but still it em-

stood, saying, Rise, and <sup>b</sup>measure the temple of God, and the altar, and them that worship therein.

<small>b Eze.xl.-xlviii.</small>

braces the whole period, and states in few words what will be the condition of things in the end. This was all that was necessary; this was, in fact, the leading design of the whole book. The end towards which all tended—that which John needed most to know and which the church needed most to know, was that religion *would* ultimately triumph, and that the period *would* arrive when it could be announced that the kingdoms of this world had become the kingdoms of God and of his Christ. That is here announced; and that is properly the close of one of the divisions of the whole book.

1. *And there was given me.* He does not say by whom, but the connection would seem to imply that it was by the angel. All this is of course to be regarded as symbolical. The representation undoubtedly pertains to a future age, but the language is such as would be properly addressed to one who had been a Jew, and the imagery employed is such as he would be more likely to understand than any other. The language and the imagery are, therefore, taken from the temple, but there is no reason to suppose that it had any *literal* reference to the temple, or even that John would so understand it. Nor does the language here used prove that the temple was standing at the time when the book was written; for, as it is symbolical, it is what would be employed whether the temple were standing or not, and would be as likely to be used in the one case as in the other. It is such language as John, educated as a Jew, and familiar with the temple worship, would be likely to employ if he designed to make a representation pertaining to the church. ¶ *A reed*—καλαμος. This word properly denotes a plant with a jointed hollow stalk, growing in wet grounds. Then it refers to the stalk as cut for use—as a measuring-stick, as in this place; or a mock sceptre, Mat. xxvii. 29, 30; or a pen for writing, 3 Jn. 13. Here it means merely a stick that could be used for measuring. ¶ *Like unto a rod.* This word—ῥάβδος—means properly a rod, wand, staff, used either for scourging, 1 Co. iv. 21; or for leaning upon in walking, Mat. x. 10; or for a sceptre, He. i. 8. Here the meaning

is, that the reed that was put into his hands was like such a rod or staff in respect to size, and was therefore convenient for handling. The word *rod* also is used to denote a measuring-pole, Ps. lxxiv. 2; Je. x. 16; li. 19. ¶ *And the angel stood, saying.* The phrase, "the angel stood," is wanting in many MSS. and editions of the New Testament, and is rejected by Professor Stuart as spurious. It is also rejected in the critical editions of Griesbach and Hahn, and marked as doubtful by Tittmann. The best critical authority is against it, and it appears to have been introduced from Zec. iii. 5. The connection does not demand it, and we may, therefore, regard the meaning to be, that the one who gave him the reed, whoever he was, at the same time addressed him, and commanded him to take a measure of the temple and the altar. ¶ *Rise, and measure the temple of God.* That is, ascertain its true dimensions with the reed in your hand. Of course, this could not be understood of the *literal* temple—whether standing or not—for the exact measure of that was sufficiently well known. The word, then, must be used of something which the temple would denote or represent, and this would properly be the church, considered as the abode of God on the earth. Under the old dispensation, the temple at Jerusalem was that abode; under the new, that peculiar residence was transferred to the church, and God is represented as dwelling in it. See Notes on 1 Co. iii. 16. Thus the word is undoubtedly used here, and the simple meaning is, that he who is thus addressed is directed to take an accurate estimate of the true church of God; *as* accurate as if he were to apply a measuring-reed to ascertain the dimensions of the temple at Jerusalem. In doing that, if the direction had been literally to measure the temple at Jerusalem, he would ascertain its length, and breadth, and height; he would measure its rooms, its doorways, its porticoes; he would take such a measurement of it that, in a description or drawing, it could be distinguished from other edifices, or that one could be constructed like it, or that a just idea could be obtained of it if it should be destroyed. If the direction be understood figuratively, as applicable to the Christian church, the work to be done would be to obtain an exact estimate or measurement of what the true church was—as distinguished from all other bodies of men, and as constituted and appointed by the direction of God; such a measurement that its characteristics could be made known; that a church could be organized according to this, and that the accurate description could be transmitted to future times. John has not, indeed, preserved the measurement; for the main idea here is not that he was to preserve such a model, but that, in the circumstances, and at the time referred to, the proper business would be to engage in such a measurement of the church that its true dimensions or character might be known. There would be, therefore, a fulfilment of this, if at the time here referred to there should be *occasion*, from any cause, to inquire what constituted the true church; if it was necessary to separate and distinguish it from all other bodies; and if there should be any such prevailing uncertainty as to make an accurate investigation necessary. ¶ *And the altar.* On the form, situation, and uses of the altar, see Notes on Mat. v. 23, 24; xxi. 12. The altar here referred to was, undoubtedly, the altar situated in front of the temple, where the daily sacrifice was offered. To measure that literally, would be to take its dimensions of length, breadth, and height; but it is plain that that cannot be intended here, for there was no such altar where John was, and, if the reference were to the altar at Jerusalem, its dimensions were sufficiently known. This language, then, like the former, must be understood metaphorically, and then it must mean—as the altar was the place of *sacrifice*—to take an estimate of the church considered with reference to its notions of sacrifice, or of the prevailing views respecting the sacrifice to be made for sin, and the method of reconciliation with God. It is by sacrifice that a method is provided for reconciliation with God; by sacrifice that sin is pardoned; by sacrifice that man is justified; and the direction here is equivalent, therefore, to a command to make an investigation on these subjects, and all that is implied would be fulfilled if a state of things should exist where it would be necessary to institute an examination into the prevailing views in the church on the subject of the atonement, and the true method of justification before God. ¶ *And them that worship therein.* In the temple, or, as the temple is the representation here of the church, of those who are in the church

2 But the ᶜcourt which is without the temple ¹leave out, and measure it not; for ᵈit is given unto the Gentiles: and the holy city shall they ᵉtread under foot forty and two months.

c Eze.40.17-20.   ¹ cast out.   d Lu.21.24.   e Da.7.25.

as professed worshippers of God. There is some apparent incongruity in directing him to "*measure*" those who were engaged in worship; but the obvious meaning is, that he was to take a correct estimate of their character; of what they professed; of the reality of their piety; of their lives, and of the general state of the church considered as professedly worshipping God. This would receive its fulfilment if a state of things should arise in the church which would make it necessary to go into a close and searching examination on all these points, in order to ascertain what was the true church, and what was necessary to constitute true membership in it. There were, therefore, three things, as indicated by this verse, which John was directed to do, so far as the use of the measuring-rod was concerned: (*a*) to take a just estimate of what constitutes the true church, as distinguished from all other associations of men; (*b*) to institute a careful examination into the opinions in the church on the subject of sacrifice or atonement—involving the whole question about the method of justification before God; and (*c*) to take a correct estimate of what constitutes true membership in the church; or to investigate with care the prevailing opinions about the qualifications for membership.

2. *But the court which is without the temple.* Which is outside of the temple proper, and, therefore, which does not strictly appertain to it. There is undoubtedly reference here to the "court of the Gentiles," as it was called among the Jews—the outer court of the temple to which the Gentiles had access, and within which they were not permitted to go. For a description of this, see Notes on Mat. xxi. 12. To an observer this would *seem* to be a part of the temple, and the persons there assembled a portion of the true worshippers of God; but it was necessarily neither the one nor the other. In forming an estimate of those who, according to the Hebrew notions, were true worshippers of God, only those would be regarded as such who had the privilege of access to the inner court, and to the altar. In making such an estimate, therefore, those who had no nearer access than that court, would be omitted; that is, they would not be reckoned as necessarily any part of those who were regarded as the people of God. ¶ *Leave out and measure it not.* Marg., *cast out.* So the Greek. The meaning is, that he was not to reckon it as appertaining to the true temple of worshippers. There is, indeed, a degree of force in the words rendered "*leave out*," or, in the margin, "*cast out*"—ἐκβαλλε ἔξω—which implies more than a mere *passing by*, or *omission.* The word (ἐκβάλλω) usually has the idea of *force* or *impulse* (Mat. viii. 12; xv. 17; xxv. 30; Mar. xvi. 9; Ac. xxvii. 38, *et al.*); and the word here would denote some decisive or positive act by which it would be indicated that this was *not* any part of the true temple, but was to be regarded as appertaining to something else. He was not merely *not* to mention it, or *not* to include it in the measurement, but he was to do this by some act which would indicate that it was the result of design in the case, and not by accidentally passing it by. ¶ *For it is given unto the Gentiles.* It properly appertains to them as their own. Though near the temple, and included in the general range of building, yet it does not pertain to those who worship there, but to those who are regarded as heathen and strangers. It is not said that it was *then* given to the Gentiles; nor is it said that it was given to them to be overrun and trodden down by them, but that it *appertained to them*, and was to be regarded as belonging to them. They occupied it, not as the people of God, but as those who were *without* the true church, and who did not appertain to its real communion. This would find a fulfilment if there should arise a state of things in the church in which it would be necessary to draw a line between those who properly constituted the church and those who did not; if there should be such a condition of things that any considerable portion of those who professedly appertained to the church ought to be *divided off* as not belonging to it, or would have such characteristic marks that it could be seen that they were strangers and aliens. The interpretation would demand that they should sustain *some* relation to the

church, or that they would *seem* to belong to it—as the court did to the temple; but still that this was in appearance only, and that in estimating the true church it was necessary to leave them out altogether. Of course this would not imply that there might not be some sincere worshippers among them as individuals—as there would be found usually, in the court of the Gentiles in the literal temple, some who were proselytes and devout worshippers, but what is here said relates to them as a mass or body—that they did not belong to the true church, but to the Gentiles. ¶ *And the holy city.* The *whole* holy city—not merely the outer court of the Gentiles, which it is said was given to them, nor the temple as such, but the *entire* holy city. There is no doubt that the words "the holy city" *literally* refer to Jerusalem—a city so called because it was the peculiar place of the worship of God. See Notes on Mat. iv. 5; comp. Ne. xi. 1, 18; Is. lii. 1; Da. ix. 24; Mat. xxvii. 53. But it is not necessary to suppose that this is its meaning here. The "holy city," Jerusalem, was regarded as sacred to God—as his dwelling-place on earth, and as the abode of his people, and nothing was more natural than to use the term as representing the church. Comp. Notes on Ga. iv. 26; He. xii. 22. In this sense it is undoubtedly used here as the whole representation is emblematical. John, if he were about to speak of anything that was to occur to the church, would, as a native Jew, be likely to employ such language as this to denote it. ¶ *Shall they tread under foot.* That is, the Gentiles above referred to; or those who, in the measurement of the city, were set off as Gentiles, and regarded as not belonging to the people of God. This is not spoken of the Gentiles in general, but only of that portion of the multitudes that seemed to constitute the worshippers of God, who, in measuring the temple, were set off or separated as not properly belonging to the true church. The phrase "should tread under foot" is derived from warriors and conquerors, who tread down their enemies, or trample on the fields of grain. It is rendered in this passage by Dr. Robinson (*Lex.*), "to profane and lay waste." As applied literally to a city, this would be the true idea; as applied to the church, it would mean that they would have it under their control or in subjection for the specified time, and that the practical effect of that would be to corrupt and prostrate it. ¶ *Forty and two months.* Literally this would be three years and a half; but if the time here is prophetic time—a day for a year—then the period would be twelve hundred and sixty years—reckoning the year at 360 days. For a full illustration of this usage, and for the reasons for supposing that this is prophetic time, see Notes on Da. vii. 25. See also Editor's Preface, p. xxv. In addition to what is there said, it may be remarked, in reference to this passage, that it is impossible to show, with any degree of probability, that the city of Jerusalem was "trampled under foot" by the Romans for the exact space of three years and a half. Professor Stuart, who adopts the opinion that it refers to the conquest of Jerusalem by the Romans, says, indeed, "It is certain that the invasion of the Romans lasted just about the length of the period named, until Jerusalem was taken. And although the city itself was not besieged so long, yet the metropolis in this case, as in innumerable others in both Testaments, appears to stand for the country of Judæa." But it is to be remembered that the affirmation here is, that "*the holy city*" was thus to be trodden under foot; and even taking the former supposition, in what sense is it true that the "whole country" was "trodden under foot" by the Romans only three years and a half? Even the wars of the Romans were not of that exact duration; and, besides, the fact was that Judæa was held in subjection, and trodden down by the Romans for centuries, and never, in fact, regained its independence. If this is to be literally applied to Jerusalem, it has been "trodden down by the Gentiles," with brief intervals, since the conquest by the Romans, to the present time. There has been no precise period of three years and a half, in respect to which the language here used would be applicable to the literal city of Jerusalem.

In regard, then, to the proper *application* of the language which has thus been explained (ver. 1, 2), it may be remarked, in general, that, for the reasons just stated, it is not to be taken *literally*. John could not have been directed literally to measure the temple at Jerusalem, and the altar, and the worshippers; nor could he have been requested literally to leave out, or "cast out" the court that was without; nor could it be meant that the holy city literally was to be trodden under foot for three years and a half. The language clearly is symbolical, and the reference must have been to something pertaining to the church. And, if the preceding exposition of the tenth chapter is correct, then it may be presumed that this would refer to something that was to occur at about the period there referred to. Regarding it, then, as applicable to the time of the Reformation, and as being a continuation of the vision in ch. x., we shall find, in the events of that period, what would be properly symbolized by the language here used. This will appear by reviewing the particulars which have been explained in these verses:—

(1) The command to "measure the temple of God," ver. 1. This, we have seen, was a direction to take an estimate of what constituted the true church; the very work which it was necessary to do in the Reformation, for this was the first point which was to be settled, whether the Papacy was the true church or was the Antichrist. This involved, of course, the whole inquiry as to what constitutes the church, alike in reference to its organization, its ministry, its sacraments, and its membership. It was long before the Reformers made up their minds that the Papacy was *not* the true church; for the veneration which they had been taught to cherish for that lingered long in their bosoms. And even when they were constrained to admit that that corrupt communion was the predicted form of the great apostasy—*Antichrist*—and had acquired boldness enough to break away from it for ever, it was long before they settled down in a uniform belief as to what *was* essential to the true church. Indeed, the differences of opinion which prevailed, the warm discussions which ensued, and the diversities of sect which sprang up in the Protestant world, showed with what intense interest the mind was fixed on this question, and how important it was to take an exact *measurement* of the real church of God.

(2) The direction to "measure the altar." This, as we have seen, would relate to the prevailing opinions on the subject of sacrifice and atonement; on the true method of a sinner's acceptance with God; and, consequently, on the whole subject of justification. As a matter of fact, it need not be said that this was one of the first questions which came before the Reformers, and was one which it was indispensable to settle, in order to a just notion of the church and of the way of salvation. The Papacy had exalted the Lord's supper into a real sacrifice; had made it a grand and essential point that the bread and wine were changed into the real body and blood of the Lord, and that a real offering of that sacrifice was made every time that ordinance was celebrated; had changed the office of the ministers of the New Testament from *preachers* to that of *priests;* had become familiar with the terms *altar*, and *sacrifice*, and *priesthood*, as founded on the notion that a real sacrifice was made in the "mass;" and had fundamentally changed the whole doctrine respecting the justification of a sinner before God. The altar in the Romish communion had almost displaced the pulpit; and the doctrine of justification by the merits of the great sacrifice made by the death of our Lord, had been superseded by the doctrine of justification by good works, and by the merits of the saints. It became necessary, therefore, to restore the true doctrine respecting sacrifice for sin, and the way of justification before God; and this would be appropriately represented by a direction to "measure *the altar*."

(3) The direction to take an estimate of those "who worshipped in the temple." This, as we have seen, would properly mean that there was to be a true estimate taken of what constituted membership in the church, or of the qualifications of those who should be regarded as true worshippers of God. This, also, was one of the first works necessary to be done in the Reformation. Before that, for ages, the doctrine of baptismal regeneration had been the established doctrine of the church; that all that was necessary to membership was baptism and confirmation, was the common opinion; the necessity of regeneration by the influences of the Holy Spirit, as a condition of church membership, was little understood, if not almost wholly unknown; and the grand requisition *in* membership was not holy living, but the observance of the rites and ceremonies of the church. One of the first things necessary in the Reformation was to restore to its true place the doctrine laid down by the Saviour, that a change

of heart—that regeneration by the Holy Ghost—was necessary to membership in the church, and that the true church was composed of those who had been thus renewed in the spirit of their mind. This great work would be appropriately symbolized by a direction to take an estimate of those who "worshipped in the temple of God;" that is, to settle the question who should be regarded as true worshippers of God, and what should be required of those who professed to be such worshippers. No more important point was settled in the Reformation than this.

(4) The direction to leave out, or to "cast out" the court without the temple. This, as we have seen, would properly mean that a separation was to be made between that which was the true church and that which was not, though it might seem to belong to it. The one was to be measured or estimated; the other was to be left out, as not appertaining to that, or as belonging to the Gentiles, or to heathenism. The idea would be, that though it professedly appertained to the true church, and to the worship of God, yet that it deserved to be characterized as heathenism. Now this will apply with great propriety, according to all Protestant notions, to the manner in which the Papacy was regarded by the Reformers, and should be regarded at all times. It claimed to be the true church, and to the eye of an observer would *seem* to belong to it, as much as the outer court seemed to pertain to the temple. But it had the essential characteristics of *heathenism*, and was, therefore, properly to be left out, or cast out, as not pertaining to the true church. Can anyone doubt the truth of this representation as applicable to the Papacy? Almost everything that was peculiar in the ancient heathen systems of religion had been introduced into the Roman communion; and a stranger at Rome would see more that would lead him to feel that he was in a heathen land, than he would that he was in a land where the pure doctrines of Christianity prevailed, and where the worship was celebrated which the Redeemer had designed to set up on the earth. This was true not only in the pomp and splendour of worship, and in the processions and imposing ceremonials; but in the worship of images, in the homage rendered to the dead, in the number of festival days, in the fact that the statues reared in heathen Rome to the honour of the gods had been reconsecrated in the service of Christian devotion to the apostles, saints, and martyrs; and in the robes of the Christian priesthood, derived from those in use in the ancient heathen worship. The direction was, that, in estimating the true church, this was to be "left out," or "cast out;" and, if this interpretation is correct, the meaning is, that the Roman Catholic communion, as an organized body, is to be regarded as no part of the true church—a conclusion which is inevitable, if the passages of Scripture which are commonly supposed by Protestants to apply to it are correctly applied. To determine this, and to separate the true church from it, was no small part of the work of the Reformation.

(5) The statement that the holy city was to be trodden under foot, ver. 2. This, as we have seen, must mean that the true church would thus be trodden down by those who are described as "Gentiles." So far as pure religion was concerned; so far as appertained to the real condition of the church, and the pure worship of God, it would be *as if* the whole holy city where God was worshipped were given into the hands of the Gentiles, and they should tread it down, and desecrate all that was sacred for the time here referred to. Everything in Rome at the time of the Reformation would sustain this description. "It is incredible," says Luther, on his visit to Rome, "what sins and atrocities are committed in Rome; they must be seen and heard to be believed. So that it is usual to say: 'If there be a hell, Rome is built above it; it is an abyss from which all sins proceed.'" So again he says: "It is commonly observed that he who goes to Rome for the first time, goes to seek a knave there; the second time he finds him; and the third time he brings him away with him under his cloak. But now, people are become so clever, that they make the three journeys in one." So Machiavelli, one of the most profound geniuses in Italy, and himself a Roman Catholic, said, "The greatest symptom of the approaching ruin of Christianity is, that the nearer we approach the capital of Christendom, the less do we find of the Christian spirit of the people. The scandalous example and crimes of the court of Rome have caused Italy to lose every principle of piety and every religious sentiment.

A.D. 96.]  CHAPTER XI.  273

3 And I will ²give *power* unto my ᶠtwo ᵍwitnesses, and they shall prophesy a thousand two hundred *and* threescore days, ʰclothed in sackcloth.

² or, *give unto my two witnesses that they may prophesy.*
ᶠ Mat.18.16.   ᵍ ch.20.4.
ʰ Is.22.12.

We Italians are principally indebted to the church and to the priests for having become impious and profane." See D'Aubigné's *History of the Reformation*, p. 54, ed. Phila. 1843. In full illustration of the sentiment that the church seemed to be trodden down and polluted by heathenism, or by abominations and practices that came out of heathenism, we may refer to the general history of the Romish communion from the rise of the Papacy to the Reformation. For a sufficient illustration to justify the application of the passage before us which I am now making, the reader may be referred to the Notes on ch. ix. 20, 21. Nothing would better describe the condition of Rome previous to and at the time of the Reformation—and the remark may be applied to subsequent periods also—than to say that it was a city which once seemed to be a Christian city, and was not improperly regarded as the centre of the Christian world and the seat of the church, and that it had been, as it were, overrun and trodden down by heathen rites and customs and ceremonies, so that, to a stranger looking on it, it would seem to be in the possession of the "Gentiles" or the heathens.

(6) The *time* during which this was to continue—"forty-two months;" that is, according to the explanation above given, twelve hundred and sixty years. This would embrace the whole period of the ascendency and prevalence of the Papacy, or the whole time of the continuance of that corrupt domination in which Christendom was to be trodden down and corrupted by it. The prophet of Patmos saw it in vision thus extending its dreary and corrupting reign, and during that time the proper influence of Christianity was trampled down, and the domination of practical heathenism was set up where the church should have reigned in its purity. Thus regarded, this would properly express the time of the ascendency of the Papal power, and the end of the "forty-two months," or twelve hundred and sixty years, would denote the time when the influence of that power would cease. If, therefore, the time of the *rise* of the Papacy can be determined, it will not be difficult to determine the time when it will come to an end. But for a full consideration of these points the reader is referred to the extended discussion on Da. vii. 25. See also Editor's Preface, p. xxv. As the point is there fully examined it is unnecessary to go into an investigation of it here.

The general remark, therefore, in regard to this passage (ver. 1, 2) is, that it refers to what would be necessary to be done at the Reformation in order to determine what is the true church and what are the doctrines on which it is based; and to the fact that the Romish communion, to which the church had been given over for a definite time, was to be set aside as not being the true church of Christ.

3. *And I will give* power *unto my two witnesses.* In respect to this important passage (ver. 3-13) I propose to pursue the same method which I have pursued all along in this exposition: first, to examine the meaning of the words and phrases in the symbol, with a purpose to ascertain the fair signification of the symbols; and, secondly, to inquire into the application—that is, to inquire whether any events have occurred which, in respect to their character and to the time of their occurrence, can be shown to be a *fair* fulfilment of the language. ¶ *And I will give* power. The word " power " is not in the original. The Greek is simply, "I will give"—that is, I will grant to my two witnesses the right or the power of prophesying during the time specified —correctly expressed in the margin, "give unto my two witnesses that they may prophesy." The meaning is not that he would *send* two witnesses to prophesy, but rather that these were *in fact* such " witnesses," and that he would during that time permit them to exercise their prophetic gifts, or give them the privilege and the strength to enunciate the truth which they were commissioned to communicate as his " witnesses" to mankind. Some word, then, like *power, privilege, opportunity*, or *boldness*, it is necessary to supply in order to complete the sense. ¶ *Unto my two witnesses.* The word "*two*" evidently denotes that the number would be small; and yet it is not necessary to confine it literally to two persons, or to two societies or communities. Perhaps the meaning is, that

**4** These are the *i*two olive-trees, and the two *k*candlesticks

*i* Je.11.16; Zec.4.3,11,14.   *k* ch.1.20.

as, under the law, two witnesses were required, and were enough, to establish any fact (Notes on Jn. viii. 17), such a number would during those times be preserved from apostasy as would be sufficient to keep up the evidence of truth; to testify against the prevailing abominations, errors, and corruptions; to show what was the real church, and to bear a faithful witness against the wickedness of the world. The law of Moses required that there should be *two* witnesses on a trial, and this, under that law, was deemed a *competent* number. See Num. xxxv. 30; De. xvii. 6; xix. 15; Mat. xviii. 16; Jn. v. 30-33. The essential meaning of this passage then is, that there would be *a competent number* of witnesses in the case; that is, as many as would be regarded as *sufficient* to establish the points concerning which they would testify, with perhaps the additional idea that the number would be *small*. There is no reason for limiting it strictly to two persons, or for supposing that they would appear in pairs, two and two; nor is it necessary to suppose that it refers particularly to two people or nations. The word rendered *witnesses*—μάρτυσί—is that from which we have derived the word *martyr*. It means properly one who bears testimony, either in a judicial sense (Mat. xviii. 16; xxvi. 65), or one who can in any way testify to the truth of what he has seen and known, Lu. xxiv. 48; Ro. i. 9; Phi. i. 8; 1 Th. ii. 10; 1 Ti. vi. 12. Then it came to be employed in the sense in which the word *martyr* is now—to denote one who, amidst great sufferings or by his death, bears witness to the truth; that is, one who is so confident of the truth, and so upright, that he will rather lay down his life than deny the truth of what he has seen and known, Acts xxii. 20; Rev. ii. 13. In a similar sense it comes to denote one who is so thoroughly convinced on a subject that it is not susceptible of being seen and heard, or who is so attached to one that he is willing to lay down his life as the evidence of his conviction and attachment. The word, as used here, refers to those who, during this period of "forty and two months," would thus be *witnesses* for Christ in the world; that is, who would bear their *testimony* to the truth of his religion, to the doctrines which he had revealed, and to what was required of man—who would standing before the God of the earth.

do this amidst surrounding error and corruption, and when exposed to persecutions and trials on account of their belief. It is not uncommon in the Scriptures to represent the righteous as *witnesses* for God. See Notes on Is. xliii. 10, 12; xliv. 8. ¶ *And they shall prophesy.* The word *prophesy* does not necessarily mean that they would predict future events; but the sense is, that they would give utterance to the truth as God had revealed it. See Notes on ch. x. 11. The sense here is, that they would in some public manner hold up or maintain the truth before the world. ¶ *A thousand two hundred* and *threescore days.* The same period as the forty and two months (ver. 2), though expressed in a different form. Reckoning a day for a year, this period would be twelve hundred and sixty years, or the same as the "time and times and the dividing of time" in Da. vii. 25. See Notes on that place; also Editor's Preface. The meaning of this would be, therefore, that during that long period, in which it is said that "the holy city would be trodden under foot," there would be those who might be properly called "witnesses" for God, and who would be engaged in holding up his truth before the world; that is, there would be no part of that period in which there would not be found *some* to whom this appellation could with propriety be given. Though the "holy city"—the church—would *seem* to be wholly trodden down, yet there would be a few at least who would assert the great doctrines of true godliness. ¶ *Clothed in sackcloth.* Sackcloth—σάκκους—was properly a coarse black cloth commonly made of hair, used for sacks, for straining, and for mourning garments. See Notes on ch. vi. 12; Is. iii. 24; and Mat. xi. 21. Here it is an emblem of mourning; and the idea is, that they would prophesy in the midst of grief. This would indicate that the time would be one of calamity, or that, in doing this, there would be occasion for their appearing in the emblems of grief, rather than in robes expressive of joy. The most natural interpretation of this is, that there would be but few who could be regarded as true witnesses for God in the world, and that they would be exposed to persecution.

4. *These are the two olive-trees.* These

5 And if any man will hurt them, *fire proceedeth out of their mouth, and devoureth their enemies: and if any man will hurt them, ᵐhe must in this manner be killed.

*l* Ps.18.8.     *m* Nu.16 35; IIo.6.5.

are represented by the two olive-trees, or these are what are symbolized by the two olive-trees. There can be little doubt that there is an allusion here to Zec. iv. 3, 11, 14, though the imagery is in some respects changed. The prophet (Zec. iv. 2, 3) saw in vision "a candlestick all of gold, with a bowl upon the top of it, and his seven lamps thereon, and seven pipes to the seven lamps, which were upon the top thereof; and two olive-trees by it, one upon the right side of the bowl, and the other upon the left side thereof." These two "olive branches" were subsequently declared (ver. 14) to be "the two anointed ones, that stand by the Lord of the whole earth." The olive-trees, or olive-branches (ver. 12), appear in the vision of the prophet to have been connected with the ever-burning lamp by golden pipes; and as the olive-tree produced the oil used by the ancients in their lamps, these trees are represented as furnishing a constant supply of oil through the golden pipes to the candlestick, and thus they become emblematic of the supply of grace to the church. John uses this emblem, not in the sense exactly in which it was employed by the prophet, but to denote that these two "witnesses," which might be compared with the two olive-trees, would be the means of supplying grace to the church. As the olive-tree furnished oil for the lamps, the two trees here would seem properly to denote ministers of religion; and as there can be no doubt that the candlesticks, or lamp-bearers, denote churches, the sense would appear to be that it was through the pastors of the churches that the oil of grace which maintained the brightness of those mystic candlesticks, or the churches, was conveyed. The image is a beautiful one, and expresses a truth of great importance to the world; for God has designed that the lamp of piety shall be kept burning in the churches by truth supplied through ministers and pastors. ¶ *And the two candlesticks.* The prophet Zechariah saw but *one* such candlestick or lamp-bearer; John here saw two--as there are two "witnesses" referred to. In the vision described in ch. i. 12, he saw seven—representing the seven churches of Asia.

For an explanation of the meaning of the symbol, see Notes on that verse. ¶ *Standing before the God of the earth.* So Zec. iv. 14, "These be the two anointed ones, that stand by the Lord of the whole earth." The meaning is, that they stood, as it were, in the very presence of God—as, in the tabernacle and temple, the golden candlestick stood "before" the ark on which was the symbol of the divine presence, though separated from it by a veil. Comp. Notes on ch. ix. 13. This representation, that the ministers of religion "stand before the Lord," is one that is not uncommon in the Bible. Thus it is said of the priests and Levites: "The Lord separated the tribe of Levi, to *stand before the Lord*, to minister unto him, and to bless his name," De. x. 8; comp. xviii. 7. The same thing is said of the prophets, as in the cases of Elijah and Elisha: "As the Lord liveth, *before whom I stand*," 1 Ki. xvii. 1; also, xviii. 15; 2 Ki. iii. 14; v. 16; comp. Je. xv. 19. The representation is, that they ministered, as it were, constantly in his presence, and under his eye.

5. *And if any man will hurt them.* This implies that there would be those who would be disposed to injure or wrong them; that is, that they would be liable to persecution. The word "*will*" is here more than the mere sign of the future; it denotes *intention, purpose, design* — θέλει — "if any man *wills* or *purposes* to injure them." See a similar use of the word in 1 Ti. vi. 9. The word *hurt* here means to do *injury* or *injustice*—ἀδικῆσαι—and may refer to wrong in any form—whether in respect to their character, opinions, persons, or property. The general sense is, that there would be those who would be disposed to do them harm, and we should naturally look for the fulfilment of this in some form of persecution. ¶ *Fire proceedeth out of their mouth.* It is, of course, not necessary that this should be taken literally. The meaning is, that they would have the power of destroying their enemies *as if* fire should proceed out of their mouth; that is, their words would be like burning coals or flames. There may possibly be an allusion here to 2 Ki. i. 10-14, where

6 These[n] have power to shut heaven, that it rain not in the days of their prophecy: and have [o] power over waters to turn them to blood, and to smite the earth with all plagues, as often as they will.

[n] 1 Ki.17.1.   [o] Ex.7.19.

it is said that Elijah commanded the fire to descend from heaven to consume those who were sent to take him (comp. Lu. ix. 54); but in that case Elijah commanded the fire to come "from heaven;" here it proceedeth "out of the mouth." The allusion here, therefore, is to the denunciations which they would utter, or the doctrines which they would preach, and which would have the same effect on their enemies as if they breathed forth fire and flame. So Je. v. 14, "Because ye speak this word, Behold, I will make my words in thy mouth fire and this people wood, and it shall devour them." ¶ *And devoureth their enemies.* The word *devour* is often used with reference to fire, which seems to *eat up* or *consume* what is in its way, or to *feed on* that which it destroys. This is the sense of the word here— κατισθίει — "to eat down, to swallow down, to devour." Comp. ch. xx. 9; Sept. Is. xxix. 6; Joel ii. 5; Le. x. 2. As there is no reason to believe that there would be literal *fire*, so it is not necessary to suppose that their enemies would be literally devoured or consumed. The meaning is fulfilled if their words should in any way produce an effect on their enemies *similar* to what is produced by fire: that is, if it should destroy their influence; if it should overcome and subdue them; if it should annihilate their domination in the world. ¶ *And if any man will hurt them.* This is repeated in order to make the declaration more intensive, and also to add another thought about the effect of persecuting and injuring them. ¶ *He must in this manner be killed.* That is, in the manner specified —by fire. It does not mean that he would be killed in the same manner in which the "witnesses" were killed, but in the method specified before—by the fire that should proceed out of their mouth. The meaning is, undoubtedly, that they would have power to bring down on them divine vengeance or punishment, so that there would be a just retaliation for the wrongs done them.

6. *These have power to shut heaven.* That is, so far as rain is concerned— for this is immediately specified. There is probably a reference here to an ancient opinion that the rain was kept in the clouds of heaven as in reservoirs or bottles, and that when they were opened it rained; when they were closed it ceased to rain. So Job, "He bindeth up the waters in his thick clouds, and the cloud is not rent under them," xxvi. 8. "Which the clouds do drop and distil upon man abundantly," Job xxxvi. 28. "Who can number the clouds in wisdom? or who can stay the bottles of heaven?" Job xxxviii. 37; comp. Ge. i. 7; vii. 12; viii. 2; 2 Ki. vii. 2. To *shut* or *close up the heavens*, therefore, is to restrain the rain from descending, or to produce a drought. Comp. Notes on Ja. v. 17. ¶ *That it rain not in the days of their prophecy.* In the time when they prophesy. Probably the allusion here is to what is said of Elijah, 1 Ki. xvii. 1. This would properly refer to some miraculous power; but still it *may* be used to denote merely that they would be clothed with the power of causing blessings to be withheld from men, *as if* rain were withheld; that is, that in consequence of the calamities that would be brought upon them, and the persecutions which they would endure, God would bring judgments upon men as if *they* were clothed with this power. The language, therefore, it seems to me, does not necessarily imply that they would have the power of working miracles. ¶ *And have power over waters to turn them to blood.* The allusion here is doubtless to what occurred in Egypt, Ex. vii. 17. Comp. Notes on Re. viii. 8. This, too, would literally denote the power of working a miracle; but still it is not absolutely necessary to suppose that this is intended. Anything that would be *represented* by turning waters into blood, would correspond with all that is necessarily implied in the language. If any great calamity should occur in consequence of what was done to them that would be properly represented by turning the waters into blood so that they could not be used, and that was so connected with the treatment which they received as to appear to be a judgment of heaven on that account, or that would appear to have come upon the world in consequence of their imprecations, it would be all that is necessarily implied in this language. ¶ *And to*

A.D. 96.]  CHAPTER XI.  277

7 And when they shall have finished their testimony *p* the beast that ascendeth out of the bottom-

*p* ch.17.8.

less pit shall *q* make war against them, and shall overcome them, and kill them.

*q* Da.7.21; Zec.14.2,&c.

*smite the earth with all plagues.* All kinds of plague or calamity; disease, pestilence, famine, flood, &c. The word *plague*—πληγἡ—which means, properly, *stroke, stripe, blow,* would include any or all of these. The meaning here is, that great calamities would follow the manner in which they were treated, *as if* the power were lodged in their hands. ¶ *As often as they will.* So that it would seem that they could exercise this power as they pleased.

7. *And when they shall have finished their testimony.* Professor Stuart renders this, "And whenever they shall have finished their testimony." The reference is undoubtedly to a period when they should have faithfully borne the testimony which they were appointed to bear. The word here rendered "shall have finished"—τελέσωσι, from τελέω—means properly to end, to finish, to complete, to accomplish. It is used, in this respect, in two senses—either in regard to *time* or in regard to the *end* or *object in view,* in the sense of *perfecting it,* or *accomplishing it.* In the former sense it is employed in such passages as the following:—"Till the thousand years should be *fulfilled,*" Re. xx. 3. "Ye shall not have gone over the cities of Israel [Gr., ye shall not have *finished* the cities of Israel] till the Son of man be come," Mat. x. 23; that is, ye shall not have finished passing through them. "When Jesus had made an end [Gr., *finished*] of commanding his twelve disciples," Mat. xi. 1. "I have *finished* my course," 2 Ti. iv. 7. In these passages it clearly refers to *time.* In the other sense it is used in such places as the following:—"And shall not the uncircumcision which is by nature, if it *fulfil* the law," Ro. ii. 27; that is, if it accomplish or come up to the demands of the law. "If ye *fulfil* the royal law according to the scriptures," Ja. ii. 8. The word, then, may here refer not to *time,* meaning that these events would occur at the *end* of the "thousand two hundred and threescore days," but to the fact that what is here stated would occur when they had completed their testimony in the sense of having testified all that they were *appointed* to testify; that is, when they had borne full witness for God, and fully uttered his truth. Thus understood, the meaning here may be that the event here referred to would take place, not at the *end* of the 1260 years, but at that period *during* the 1260 years when it could be said with propriety that they had accomplished their testimony in the world, or that they had borne full and ample witness on the points intrusted to them. ¶ *The beast.* This is the first time in the book of Revelation in which what is here called "the beast" is mentioned, and which has so important an agency in the events which it is said would occur. It is repeatedly mentioned in the course of the book, and always with similar characteristics, and as referring to the same object. Here it is mentioned as "ascending out of the bottomless pit;" in ch. xiii. 1, as "rising up out of the sea;" in ch. xiii. 11, as "coming up out of the earth." It is also mentioned with characteristics appropriate to such an origin, in ch. xiii. 2-4 (twice), 11, 12 (twice), 14 (twice), 15 (twice), 17, 18; xiv. 9, 11; xv. 2; xvi. 2, 10, 13; xvii. 3, 7, 8 (twice), 11, 12, 13, 16, 17; xix. 19, 20 (twice); xx. 4, 40. The word here used—θηρίον—means properly *a beast, a wild beast,* Mar. i. 13; Ac. x. 12; xi. 6; xxviii. 4, 5; He. xii. 20; Ja. iii. 7; Re. vi. 8. It is once used tropically of brutal or savage men, Tit. i. 12. Elsewhere, in the passages above referred to in the Apocalypse, it is used symbolically. As employed in the book of Revelation, the characteristics of the "beast" are strongly marked. (*a*) It has its *origin* from beneath—in the bottomless pit; the sea; the earth, ch. xi. 7; xiii. 1, 11. (*b*) It has great *power,* ch. xiii. 4, 12; xvii. 12, 13. (*c*) It claims and receives worship, ch. xiii. 3, 12, 14, 15; xiv. 9, 11. (*d*) It has a certain "seat" or throne from whence its power proceeds, ch. xvi. 10. (*e*) It is of scarlet colour, ch. xvii. 3. (*f*) It receives power conferred upon it by the kings of the earth, ch. xvii. 13. (*g*) It has a mark by which it is known, ch. xiii. 17; xix. 20. (*h*) It has a certain "*number;*" that is, there are certain mystical letters or figures which so express its name that it may be known, ch. xiii. 17, 18. These things serve to characterize the "beast" as distinguished from all other things, and they are so numerous and definite,

278 REVELATION. [A.D. 96.

8 And their ʳdead bodies *shall lie* in the street of the great city, which spiritually is called ˢSodom and ᵗEgypt, where also our Lord was crucified.

r He.13.12.   s Is.1.10.   t Ex.20.2.

that it would seem to have been intended to make it easy to understand what was meant when the power referred to should appear. In regard to the *origin* of the imagery here, there can be no reasonable doubt that it is to be traced to Daniel, and that the writer here means to describe the same "beast" which Daniel refers to in ch. vii. 7. The evidence of this must be clear to anyone who will compare the description in Daniel (ch. vii.) with the minute details in the book of Revelation. No one, I think, can doubt that John means to carry forward the description in Daniel, and to apply it to new manifestations of the same great and terrific power—the power of the fourth monarchy—on the earth. For full evidence that the representation in Daniel refers to the Roman power prolonged and perpetuated in the Papal dominion, I must refer the reader to the Notes on Da. vii. 25. It may be assumed here that the opinion there defended is correct, and consequently it may be assumed that the "beast" of this book refers to the Papal power. ¶ *That ascendeth out of the bottomless pit.* See Notes on ch. ix. 1. This would properly mean that its origin is the nether world; or that it will have characteristics which will show that it was from beneath. The meaning clearly is, that what was symbolized by the beast would have such characteristics as to show that it was not of divine origin, but had its source in the world of darkness, sin, and death. This, of course, could not represent the true church, or any civil government that is founded on principles which God approves. But if it represent a community pretending to be a church, it is an apostate church; if a civil community, it is a community the characteristics of which are that it is controlled by the spirit that rules over the world beneath. For reasons which we shall see in abundance in applying the descriptions which occur of the "beast," I regard this as referring to that great apostate power which occupies so much of the prophetic descriptions—the Papacy. ¶ *Shall make war against them.* Will endeavour to exterminate them by force. This clearly is not intended to be a general statement that they would be *persecuted*, but to refer to the particular manner in which the opposition would be conducted. It would be in the form of "*war;*" that is, there would be an effort to destroy them by arms. ¶ *And shall overcome them.* Shall gain the victory over them; conquer them—νικήσει αὐτούς. That is, there will be some signal victory in which those represented by the two witnesses will be subdued. ¶ *And kill them.* That is, an effect would be produced *as if* they were put to death. They would be overcome; would be silenced; would be apparently dead. Any event that would cause them to cease to bear testimony, *as if* they were dead, would be properly represented by this. It would not be necessary to suppose that there would be literally *death* in the case, but that there would be some event which would be well represented *by* death—such as an entire suspension of their prophesying in consequence of force.

8. *And their dead bodies* shall lie *in the street.* Professor Stuart, "Shall be in the street." The words "shall lie" are supplied by the translators, but not improperly. The literal rendering would be, "and their corpses upon the street of the great city;" and the meaning is, that there would be a state of things in regard to them which would be well represented by supposing them to lie unburied. To leave a body unburied is to treat it with contempt, and among the ancients nothing was regarded as more dishonourable than such treatment. See the *Ajax* of Sophocles. Among the Jews also it was regarded as a special indignity to leave the dead unburied, and hence they are always represented as deeply solicitous to secure the interment of their dead. See Ge. xxiii. 4. Comp. 2 Sa. xxi. 9–13; Ec. vi. 3; Is. xiv. 18–20; xxii. 16; liii. 9. The meaning here is, that, for the time specified, those who are here referred to would be treated with indignity and contempt. In the fulfilment of this, we are not, of course, to look for any *literal* accomplishment of what is here said, but for some treatment of the "witnesses" which would be well represented by this; that is, which would show that they were treated, after they were silenced, like unburied corpses putrefying in the sun. ¶ *Of*

*the great city.* Where these transactions would occur. As a great city would be the agent in putting them to death, so the result would be *as if* they were publicly exposed in its streets. The word "great" here supposes that the city referred to would be distinguished for its size—a circumstance of some importance in determining the place referred to. ¶ *Which spiritually is called*—πνευματικῶς. This word occurs only in one other place in the New Testament, 1 Co. ii. 14, "because they are *spiritually* discerned"—where it means, "in accordance with the Holy Spirit," or "through the aid of the Holy Spirit." Here it seems to be used in the sense of *metaphorically*, or *allegorically*, in contradistinction from the literal and real name. There may possibly be an intimation here that the city is so called by the Holy Spirit to designate its real character, but still the essential meaning is, that that was not its literal name. For some reason the real name is not given to it; but such descriptions are applied as are designed to leave no doubt as to what is intended. ¶ *Sodom.* Sodom was distinguished for its wickedness, and especially for that vice to which its abominations have given name. For the character of Sodom, see Ge. xviii., xix. Comp. 2 Pe. ii. 6. In inquiring what "city" is here referred to, it would be necessary to find in it such abominations as characterized Sodom, or so much wickedness that it would be proper to call it Sodom. If it shall be found that this was designed to refer to Papal Rome, no one can doubt that the abominations which prevailed there would justify such an appellation. Comp. Notes on ch. ix. 20, 21. ¶ *And Egypt.* That is, it would have such a character that the *name* Egypt might be properly given to it. Egypt is known in the Scriptures as the land of oppression — the land where the Israelites, the people of God, were held in cruel bondage. Comp. Ex. i.-xv. See also Eze. xxiii. 8. The particular idea, then, which seems to be conveyed here is, that the "city" referred to would be characterized by acts of oppression and wrong towards the people of God. So far as the *language* is concerned, it might apply either to Jerusalem or to Rome—for both were eminently characterized by such acts of oppression toward the true children of God as to make it proper to compare their cruelties with those which were inflicted on the Israelites by the Egyptians. Of whichever of these places the course of the exposition may require us to understand this, it will be seen at once that the language is such as is strictly applicable to either; though, as the reference is rather to Christians than to the ancient people of God, it must be admitted that it would be most natural to refer it to Rome. More acts authorizing persecution, and designed to crush the true people of God, have gone forth from Rome than from any other city on the face of the earth; and taking the history of the church together, there is no place that would be so properly designated by the term here employed. ¶ *Where also our Lord was crucified.* If this refers to Jerusalem, it is to be taken literally; if to another city, it is to be understood as meaning that he was *practically* crucified there: that is, that the treatment of his friends—his church—was such that it might be said that he was "crucified afresh" there; for what is done to his church may be said to be done to him. Either of these interpretations would be justified by the use of the language. Thus in He. vi. 6, it is said of apostates from the true faith (comp. Notes on the passage), that "they crucify to themselves the Son of God *afresh.*" If the passage before us is to be taken figuratively, the meaning is, that acts would be performed which might properly be represented as crucifying the Son of God; that, as he lives in his church, the acts of perverting his doctrines, and persecuting his people, would be, in fact, an act of crucifying the Lord again. Thus understood, the language is strictly applicable to Rome; that is, if it is admitted that John *meant* to characterize that city, he has employed such language as a Jewish Christian would naturally use. While, therefore, it must be admitted that the language is such as could be *literally* applied only to Jerusalem, it is still true that it is such language as might be figuratively applied to any other city strongly resembling that, and that in this sense it would characterize Rome above all other cities of the world. The common reading of the text here is "*our* Lord"—ἡμῶν; the text now regarded as correct, however (Griesbach, Tittmann, Hahn), is "*their* Lord"—αὐτῶν. This makes no essential difference in the sense, except that it directs the attention more particularly to the fact that they were treated like their own Master.

# REVELATION. [A.D. 96.

9 And they of the people, and kindreds, and tongues, and nations, shall <sup>u</sup>see their dead bodies three days and an half, and shall not suffer their dead bodies to be put in graves.

*u* Ps. 79. 3.

10 And they that dwell upon the earth shall rejoice over them, and make merry, and shall send gifts one to another; because these two prophets tormented them that dwelt on the earth.

---

9. *And they of the people.* Some of the people; a part of the people—ἐκ τῶν λαῶν. The language is such as would be employed to describe a scene where a considerable portion of a company of people should be referred to, without intending to include all. The essential idea is, that there would be an assemblage of different classes of people to whom their carcasses would be exposed, and that they would come and look upon them. We should expect to find the fulfilment of this in some place where, from any cause, a variety of people should be assembled—as in some capital, or some commercial city, to which they would be naturally attracted. ¶ *Shall see their dead bodies.* That is, a state of things will occur *as if* these witnesses were put to death, and their carcasses were publicly exposed. ¶ *Three days and an half.* This might be either literally three days and a half, or, more in accordance with the usual style of this book, these would be prophetic days; that is, three years and a half. Comp. Notes on ch. ix. 5, 15. ¶ *And shall not suffer their dead bodies to be put in graves.* That is, there would be a course of conduct in regard to these witnesses such as would be shown to the dead if they were not suffered to be decently interred. The language used here—"*shall not suffer*"—seems to imply that there would be those who might be disposed to show them the respect evinced by interring the dead, but that this would not be permitted. This would find a fulfilment if, in a time of persecution, those who had borne faithful testimony were silenced and treated with dishonour, and if there should be those who were disposed to show them respect, but who would be prevented by positive acts on the part of their persecutors. This has often been the case in persecution, and there could be no difficulty in finding numerous instances in the history of the church to which this language would be applicable.

10. *And they that dwell upon the earth shall rejoice over them.* Those dwelling in the land would rejoice over their fall and ruin. This cannot, of course, mean *all* who inhabit the globe; but, according to the usage in Scripture, those who dwell in the country where this would occur. Comp. Notes on Lu. ii. 1. We now affix to the word "earth" an idea which was not necessarily implied in the Hebrew word אֶרֶץ *ĕrĕtz* (comp. Ex. iii. 8; xiii. 5; De. xix. 2, 10; xxviii. 12; Ne. ix. 22; Ps. xxxvii. 9, 11, 22, 29; lxvi. 4; Pr. ii. 21; x. 30; Joel i. 2); or the Greek word γῆ—*gē*, comp. Mat. ii. 6, 20, 21; xiv. 15; Ac. vii. 7, 11, 36, 40; xiii. 17. Our word *land*, as now commonly understood, would better express the idea intended to be conveyed here; and thus understood, the meaning is, that the dwellers in the country where these things would happen would thus rejoice. The meaning is, that while alive they would, by their faithful testimony against existing errors, excite so much hatred against themselves, and would be so great an annoyance to the governing powers, that there would be general exultation when the voice of their testimony should be silenced. This, too, has been so common in the world that there would be no difficulty in applying the *language* here used, or in finding events which it would appropriately describe. ¶ *And make merry.* Be glad. See Notes on Lu. xii. 19; xv. 23. The Greek word does not necessarily denote the light-hearted mirth expressed by our word *merriment*, but rather joy or happiness in general. The meaning is, that they would be filled with joy at such an event. ¶ *And shall send gifts one to another.* As expressive of their joy. To send presents is a natural expression of our own happiness, and our desire for the happiness of others—as is indicated now by "Christmas" and "New Year's gifts." Comp. also Ne. viii. 10-12: "Then he said unto them, Go your way, eat the fat, and drink the sweet, and send portions unto them for whom nothing is prepared: for this day is holy unto our Lord: neither be ye sorry; for the joy of the Lord is your

11 And after three days and an half the ᵛSpirit of life from God entered into them, and they stood upon their feet; and great fear fell upon them which saw them.

12 And they heard a great voice

*v* Eze.37.5-14.

from heaven saying unto them, Come up hither. And they ʷascended up to heaven in a cloud; and ˣtheir enemies beheld them.

13 And the same hour was there a great earthquake, and the tenth

*w* 1 Th.4.17.   *x* Mal.3.18.

---

strength," &c. See also Es. ix. 19-22. ¶ *Because these two prophets tormented them that dwell on the earth.* They "tormented" them, or were a source of annoyance to them, by bearing testimony to the truth; by opposing the prevailing errors; and by rebuking the vices of the age: perhaps by demanding reformation, and by denouncing the judgment of heaven on the guilty. There is no intimation that they tormented them in any other way than by the truths which they held forth. See the word explained in the Notes on 2 Pe. ii 8.

11. *And after three days and an half.* See Notes on ver. 9. ¶ *The Spirit of life from God.* The living, or life-giving Spirit that proceeds from God entered into them. Comp. Notes on Job xxxiii. 4. There is evidently allusion here to Ge. ii. 7, where God is spoken of as the Author of life. The meaning is, that they would seem to come to life again, or that effects would follow *as if* the dead were restored to life. If, when they had been compelled to cease from prophesying, they should, after the interval here denoted by three days and a half, again prophesy, or their testimony should be again borne to the truth as it had been before, this would evidently be all that would be implied in the language here employed. ¶ *Entered into them.* Seemed to animate them again. ¶ *And they stood upon their feet.* As if they had come to life again. ¶ *And great fear fell upon them which saw them.* This would be true if those who were dead should be literally restored to life; and this would be the effect if those who had given great annoyance by their doctrines, and who had been silenced, and who *seemed* to be dead, should again, as if animated anew by a divine power, begin to prophesy, or to proclaim their doctrines to the world. The statement in the symbol is, that those who had put them to death had been greatly troubled by these "witnesses;" that they had sought to silence them, and in order to this had put them to death; that they then greatly rejoiced, as if they would no more be annoyed by them. The fact that they seemed to come to life again would, therefore, fill them with consternation, for they would anticipate a renewal of their troubles, and they would see in this fact evidence of the divine favour towards those whom they persecuted, and reason to apprehend divine vengeance on themselves.

12. *And they heard a great voice from heaven.* Some manuscripts read, "I heard"—ήκουσα—but the more approved reading is that of the common text. John says that a voice was addressed to *them* calling them to ascend to heaven. ¶ *Come up hither.* To heaven. ¶ *And they ascended up to heaven in a cloud.* So the Saviour ascended, Ac. i. 9; and so probably Elijah, 2 Ki. ii. 11. ¶ *And their enemies beheld them.* That is, it was done openly, so that their enemies, who had put them to death, saw that they were approved of God, *as if* they had been publicly taken up to heaven. It is not necessary to suppose that this would literally occur. All this is, manifestly, mere symbol. The meaning is, that they would triumph *as if* they should ascend to heaven, and be received into the presence of God. The sense of the whole is, that these witnesses, after bearing a faithful testimony against prevailing errors and sins, would be persecuted and silenced; that for a considerable period their voice of faithful testimony would be hushed as if they were dead; that during that period they would be treated with contempt and scorn, as if their unburied bodies should be exposed to the public gaze; that there would be general exultation and joy that they were thus silenced; that they would again revive, as if the dead were restored to life, and bear a faithful testimony to the truth again; and that they would have the divine attestation in their favour, *as if* they were raised up visibly and publicly to heaven.

13. *And the same hour.* In immediate connection with their triumph. ¶ *Was there a great earthquake.* An earth-

partʸ of the city fell, and in the earthquake were slain ³ of men seven thousand: and the remnant

y ch.16.19.   3 names of men.

were affrighted, and ᶻ gave glory to the God of heaven.

14 The ᵃ second woe is past; *and,* behold, the third woe cometh quickly.

z ch.14.7; Is.26.15,16.   a ch.8.13.

quake is a symbol of commotion, agitation, change; of great political revolutions, &c. See Notes on ch. vi. 12. The meaning here is, that the triumph of the witnesses, represented by their ascending to heaven, would be followed by such revolutions as would be properly symbolized by an earthquake. ¶ *And the tenth part of the city fell.* That is, the tenth part of that which is represented by the "city"—the persecuting power. A city would be the seat and centre of the power, and the acts of persecution would seem to proceed from it; but the destruction, we may suppose, would extend to all that was represented by the persecuting power. The word "tenth" is probably used in a general sense to denote that a considerable portion of the persecuting power would be thus involved in ruin; that is, that in respect to that power there would be such a revolution, such a convulsion or commotion, such a loss, that it would be proper to represent it by an earthquake. ¶ *And in the earthquake.* In the convulsions consequent on what would occur to the witnesses. ¶ *Were slain of men seven thousand.* Marg., as in the Greek, "names of men"—the name being used to denote the men themselves. The number here mentioned—seven thousand—seems to have been suggested because it would bear some proportion to the tenth part of the city which fell. It is not necessary to suppose, in seeking for the fulfilment of this, that just seven thousand would be killed; but the idea clearly is, that there would be such a diminution of numbers as would be well represented by a calamity that would overwhelm a tenth part of the city, such as the apostle had in his eye, and a proportional number of the inhabitants. The number that would be slain, therefore, in the convulsions and changes consequent on the treatment of the witnesses, might be numerically much larger than seven thousand, and might be as great as if a tenth part of all that were represented by the "city" should be swept away. ¶ *And the remnant were affrighted.* Fear and alarm came on them in consequence of these calamities. The "remnant" here refers to those who still remained in the "city"—that is, to those who belonged to the community or people designed to be represented here by the city. ¶ *And gave glory to the God of heaven.* Comp. Lu. v. 26: "And they were all amazed, and th y glorified God, and were filled with fear, saying, We have seen strange things to-day." All that seems to be meant by this is, that they stood in awe at what God was doing, and acknowledged his power in the changes that occurred. It does not mean, necessarily, that they would repent and become truly his friends, but that there would be a prevailing impression that these changes were produced by his power, and that his hand was in these things. This would be fulfilled if there should be a general willingness among mankind to acknowledge God, or to recognize his hand in the events referred to; if there should be a disposition extensively prevailing to regard the "witnesses" as on the side of God, and to favour their cause as one of truth and righteousness; and if these convulsions should so far change public sentiment as to produce an impression that theirs was the cause of God.

14. *The second woe is past.* That is, the second of the three that were announced as yet to come, ch. viii. 13; comp. ch. ix. 12. ¶ And, *behold, the third woe cometh quickly.* The last of the series. The meaning is, that that which was signified by the third "woe" would be the next, and final event, in order. On the meaning of the word "*quickly,*" see Notes on ch. i. 1; comp. ii. 5, 16; iii. 11; xxii. 7, 12, 20.

In reference now to the important question about the application of this portion of the book of Revelation, it need hardly be said that the greatest variety of opinion has prevailed among expositors. It would be equally unprofitable, humiliating, and discouraging to attempt to enumerate all the opinions which have been held; and I must refer the reader who has any desire to become acquainted with them to Poole's *Synopsis, in loco,* and to the copious statement of Professor Stuart, *Com.*

vol. ii. pp. 219-227. Professor Stuart himself supposes that the meaning is, that "a competent number of divinely-commissioned and faithful Christian witnesses, endowed with miraculous powers, should bear testimony against the corrupt Jews, during the last days of their commonwealth, respecting their sins; that they should proclaim the truths of the gospel; and that the Jews, by destroying them, would bring upon themselves an aggravated and an awful doom," ii. 226. Instead of attempting to examine in detail the opinions which have been held, I shall rather state what seems to me to be the fair application of the language used, in accordance with the principles pursued thus far in the exposition. The inquiry is, whether there have been any events to which this language is applicable, or in reference to which, if it be admitted that it was the design of the Spirit of inspiration to describe them, it may be supposed that such language would be employed as we find here.

In this inquiry it may be assumed that the preceding exposition is correct, and the application now to be made must accord with that—that is, it must be found that events occurred in such times and circumstances as would be consistent with the supposition that that exposition is correct. It is to be assumed, therefore, that ch. ix. 20, 21, refers to the state of the ecclesiastical world after the conquest of Constantinople by the Turks, and previous to the Reformation; that ch. x. refers to the Reformation itself; that ch. xi. 1, 2, refers to the necessity, at the time of the Reformation, of ascertaining what was the true church, of reviving the Scripture doctrine respecting the atonement and justification, and of drawing correct lines as to membership in the church. All this has reference, according to this interpretation, to the state of the church while the Papacy would have the ascendency, or during the twelve hundred and sixty years in which it would trample down the church *as if* the holy city were in the hands of the Gentiles. Assuming this to be the correct exposition, then what is here said (ver. 3–13) must relate to that period, for it is with reference to that same time—the period of "a thousand two hundred and threescore days," or twelve hundred and sixty years—that it is said (ver. 3) the witnesses would "prophesy," "clothed in sackcloth." If this be so, then what is here stated (ver. 3–13) must be supposed to occur during the ascendency of the Papacy, and must mean, in general, that during that long period of apostasy, darkness, corruption, and sin, there would be faithful witnesses for the truth, who, though they were few in number, would be sufficient to keep up the knowledge of the truth on the earth, and to bear testimony against the prevailing errors and abominations. The *object* of this portion of the book, therefore, is to describe the character of the faithful witnesses for the truth during this long period of darkness; to state their influence; to record their trials; and to show what would be the ultimate result in regard to them, when their "testimony" should become triumphant. This general view will be seen to accord with the exposition of the previous portion of the book, and will be sustained, I trust, by the more particular inquiry into the application of the passage to which I now proceed. The essential points in the passage (ver. 3-13) respecting the "witnesses" are six: (1) who are meant by the witnesses; (2) the war made on them; (3) their death; (4) their resurrection; (5) their reception into heaven; and (6) the consequences of their triumph in the calamity that came upon the city.

I. Who are meant by the witnesses, ver. 3-6. There are several specifications in regard to this point which it is necessary to notice. (*a*) The fact that, during this long period of error, corruption, and sin, there were those who were faithful witnesses for the truth—men who opposed the prevailing errors; who maintained the great doctrines of the Christian faith; and who were ready to lay down their lives in defence of the truth. For a full confirmation of this it would be necessary to trace the history of the church down from the rise of the Papal power through the long lapse of the subsequent ages; but such an examination would be far too extensive for the purpose contemplated in these Notes, and, indeed, would require a volume by itself. Happily, this has already been done ; and all that is necessary now is to refer to the works where the fact here affirmed has been abundantly established. In many of the histories of the church—Mosheim, Neander, Milner, Milman, Gieseler—most ample proof may be found, that amidst the general darkness and corruption there were those who faithfully adhered to the truth as it is in Jesus, and who, amidst many sufferings, bore their testimony against prevailing errors. The investigation has been made, also, with special reference to an illustration of this passage, by Mr. Elliott, *Horæ Apoca.* vol. ii. pp. 193-406; and although it must be admitted that some of the details are of doubtful applicability, yet the *main* fact is abundantly established, that during that long period there were "witnesses" for the pure truths of the gospel, and a faithful testimony borne against the abominations and errors of the Papacy. These "witnesses" are divided by Mr. Elliott into (1) the earlier Western witnesses—embracing such men, and their followers, as Serenus, bishop of Marseilles; the Anglo-Saxon church in England;* Agobard, archbishop of Lyons from A.D. 810 to 841, on the one side of the Alps, and Claude of Turin on the other; Gotteschalcus, A.D. 884; Berenger, Arnold of Brescia, Peter de Bruys, and his disciple Henry, and then the Waldenses. (2) The Eastern, or Paulikian line of witnesses, a sect deriving their origin, about A.D. 653, from an Armenian by the name of Constantine, who received from a deacon, by whom he was hospitably entertained, a present of two volumes, very rare, one containing the Gospels, and the other the Epistles of Paul, and who applied himself to the formation of a new sect or church, distinct from the Manicheans, and from the Greek Church. In token of the nature of their profession, they adopted the name by which they were ever after distinguished, Paulikiani, *Paulicians,* or "disciples of the disciple of Paul." This sect continued to bear "testimony" in the East from the time of its rise till the eleventh or twelfth centuries, when it commenced a migration to the West, where it bore the same honourable character for its attachment to the truth. See Elliott, ii. 233-246, 275-315. (3) Witnesses during the eleventh and twelfth centuries, up to the time of Peter Waldo. Among these are to be noticed those who were arraigned for heresy before the councils of Orleans, Arras, Thoulouse, Oxford, and

* "'An old Welsh Chronicle preserved at Cambridge says, 'After that by means of Austin the Saxons became Christians, in such sort as Austin had taught them, the Britons would not either eat or drink with or salute them; because they corrupted with *superstition, images,* and *idolatry,* the true religion of Christ.'" Cited in Hearn's *Man of Sin,* p. 21.—Elliott.

Lombers, in the years 1022, 1025, 1119, 1160, 1165, respectively, and who were condemned by those councils for their departure from the doctrines held by the Papacy. For a full illustration of the doctrines held by those who were thus condemned, and of the fact that they were "witnesses" for the truth, see Elliott, ii. 247-275. (4) The Waldenses and Albigenses. The nature of the testimony borne by these persecuted people is so well known that it is not necessary to dwell on the subject; and a full statement of their testimony would require the entire transcription of their history. No Protestant will doubt that they were "witnesses" for the truth, or that from the time of their rise, through all the periods of their persecution, they bore full and honourable testimony to the truth as it is in Jesus. The general ground of this claim to be regarded as Apocalyptic witnesses, will be seen from the following summary statements of their doctrines. Those statements are found in a work called *The Noble Lesson,* written within some twenty years of 1170. The treatise begins in this manner: "O brethren, hear a Noble Lesson. We ought always to watch and pray," &c. In this treatise the following doctrines are drawn out, says Mr. Elliott, "with much simplicity and beauty: the origin of sin in the fall of Adam; its transmission to all men, and the offered redemption from it through the death of Jesus Christ; the union and co-operation of the three persons of the blessed Trinity in man's salvation; the obligation and spirituality of the moral law under the gospel; the duties of prayer, watchfulness, self-denial, unworldliness, humility, love, as 'the way of Jesus Christ;' their enforcement by the prospect of death and judgment, and the world's near ending; by the narrowness, too, of the way of life, and the fewness of those who find it; as also by the hope of coming glory at the judgment and revelation of Jesus Christ. Besides which we find in it a protest against the Romish system generally, as one of soul-destroying idolatry; against masses for the dead, and therein against the whole doctrine of purgatory; against the system of the confessional, and asserted power of the priesthood to absolve from sin; this last point being insisted on as the most deadly point of heresy, and its origin referred to the mercenariness of the priesthood, and their love of money;—the iniquity further noticed of the Romish persecutions of good men and teachers that wished to teach the way of Jesus Christ; and the suspicion half-hinted, and apparently half-formed, that, though a personal Antichrist might be expected, yet Popery itself might be one form of Antichrist." In another work, the *Treatise of Antichrist*, there is a strong and decided identification of the Antichristian system and the Papacy. This was written probably in the last quarter of the fourteenth century. "From this," says Mr. Elliott (ii. 355), "the following will appear to have been the Waldensian views: that the Papal or Romish system was that of Antichrist; which, from infancy in apostolic times, had grown gradually by the increase of its constituent parts to the stature of a full-grown man; that its prominent characteristics were—to defraud God of the worship due to Him, rendering it to creatures, whether departed saints, relics, images, or Antichrist;—to defraud Christ, by attributing justification and forgiveness to Antichrist's authority and words, to saints' intercession, to the merits of men's own performances, and to the fire of purgatory; —to defraud the Holy Spirit, by attributing regeneration and sanctification to the *opus operatum* of the two sacraments; that the origin of this Antichristian religion was the covetousness of the priesthood; its tendency, to lead men away from Christ; its essence, a ceremonial; its foundation, the false notion of grace and forgiveness." This work is so important as a "testimony" against Antichrist, and for the truth, and is so clear as showing that the Papacy was regarded as Antichrist, that I will copy, from the work itself, the portion containing these sentiments —sentiments which may be regarded as expressing the uniform testimony of the Waldenses on the subject:—

"Antichrist is the falsehood of eternal damnation, covered with the appearance of the truth and righteousness of Christ and his spouse. The iniquity of such a system is with all his ministers, great and small: and inasmuch as they follow the law of an evil and blinded heart, such a congregation, taken together, is called Antichrist, or Babylon, or the Fourth Beast, or the Harlot, or the Man of Sin, who is the son of perdition.

"His first work is, that the service of *latria*, properly due to God alone, he perverts unto Antichrist himself and to his doings; to the poor creature, rational or irrational, sensible or insensible; as, for instance, to male or female saints departed this life, and to their images, or carcasses, or relics. His doings are the sacraments, especially that of the Eucharist, which he worships equally with God and Christ, prohibiting the adoration of God alone.

"His second work is, that he robs and deprives Christ of the merits of Christ, with the whole sufficiency of grace, and justification, and regeneration, and remission of sins, and sanctification, and confirmation, and spiritual nourishment; and imputes and attributes them to his own authority, or to a form of words, or to his own performances, or to the saints and their intercession, or to the fire of purgatory. Thus he divides the people from Christ, and leads them away to the things already mentioned; that so they may seek not the things of Christ, nor through Christ, but only the work of their own hands; not through a living faith in God, and Jesus Christ, and the Holy Spirit; but through the will and the work of Antichrist, agreeably to the preaching that man's salvation depends on his own deeds.

"His third work is, that he attributes the regeneration of the Holy Spirit to a dead outward faith; baptizing children in that faith, and teaching that by the mere outward consecration of baptism regeneration may be procured.

"His fourth work is, that he rests the whole religion of the people upon his Mass; for leading them to hear it, he deprives them of spiritual and sacramental manducation.

"His fifth work is, that he does everything to be seen, and to glut his insatiable avarice.

"His sixth work is, that he allows manifest sins without ecclesiastical censure.

"His seventh work is, that he defends his unity, not by the Holy Spirit, but by the secular power.

"His eighth work is, that he hates, and persecutes, and searches after, and robs and destroys the members of Christ.

"These things, and many others, are the cloak and vestment of Antichrist; by which he covers his lying wickedness, lest he should be rejected as a heathen

But there is no other cause of idolatry than a false opinion of grace, and truth, and authority, and invocation, and intercession; which this Antichrist has taken away from God, and which he has ascribed to ceremonies, and authorities, and a man's own works, and to saints, and to purgatory" (Elliott, ii. 354, 355).

It is impossible not to be struck with the application of this to the Papacy, and no one can doubt that the Papacy was intended to be referred to. And, if this be so, this was a bold and decided "testimony" against the abominations of that system, and they who bore this testimony deserved to be regarded as "witnesses" for Christ and his truth.

If to the "testimony" thus briefly referred to, we add that of such men as Wycliffe, John Huss, and Jerome of Prague, and then that of the Reformers, Luther, Calvin, Zuingle, Melancthon, and their fellow-labourers, we can see with what propriety it was predicted that even during the prevalence of the great apostasy there would be a competent number of "witnesses" to keep up the knowledge of the truth in the world. And supposing that this is what was designed to be represented, it is easy to perceive that the symbol which is employed is admirably appropriate. The design of what is here said is merely to show that during the whole of the period of the Papal apostasy—whenever it may be supposed to have begun, and whenever it shall cease, it is and will be true that the Saviour has had true "witnesses" on the earth — that there have been those who have "testified" against these abominations, and who, often at great personal peril and sacrifice, have borne a faithful testimony for the truth.

(*b*) The number of the witnesses. In ver. 3, this is said to be "two," and this has been shown to mean that there would be a *competent* number, yet probably with the implied idea that the number would not be large. The only question then is, whether, in looking through this long period, it would be found that, according to the established laws of testimony under the divine code, there was a *competent* number to bear witness to the truth. And of this no one can doubt, for, in respect to each and every part of the period of the great apostasy, it is possible now to show that there was a sufficient number of the true friends of the Redeemer to testify against all the great and cardinal errors of the Papacy. This simple and obvious interpretation of the language, it may be added, also, makes wholly unnecessary and inappropriate all the efforts which have been made by expositors to find precisely *two* such witnesses, or *two* churches or people with whom the line of the faithful testimony was preserved: all such interpretations as that the Old and New Testaments are referred to, as Melchior, Affelman, and Croly suppose; or that preachers are referred to who are instructed by the Law and the Gospel, as Pannonius and Thomas Aquinas, supposed; or that Christ and John the Baptist are referred to, as Ubertinus supposed; or that Pope Sylvester and Mena, who wrote against the Eutychians, are meant, as Lyranus and Ederus supposed; or that Francis and Dominic, the respective heads of two orders of monks, are intended, as Cornelius à Lapide supposed; or that the great *wisdom* and *sanctity* of the primitive preachers are meant, as Alcassar maintained; or that John Huss and Luther, or John Huss and Jerome of Prague, or the Waldenses and Albigenses, or the Jewish and Gentile Christians in Ælia, are intended, as others have supposed. According to the obvious and fair meaning of the language, all this is mere fancy, and can illustrate nothing but the fertility of invention of those who have written on the Apocalypse. All that is necessarily implied is, that the number of true and uncorrupted followers of the Saviour has been at all times sufficiently large to bear *a competent testimony* to the world, or to keep up the remembrance of the truth upon the earth—and the reality of this no one acquainted with the history of the church will doubt.

(*c*) The condition of the "witnesses" as "clothed in sackcloth," ver. 3. This has been shown to mean that they would be in a state of sadness and grief; and they would be exposed to trouble and persecution. It is unnecessary to prove that all this was abundantly fulfilled. The long history of those times was a history of persecutions; and if it be admitted that the passage before us was designed to refer to those above mentioned as "witnesses," no more correct description could be given of them than to say that they were "clothed in sackcloth."

(d) The power of the witnesses, ver. 5, 6. Of this there are several specifications. (1) They had power over those who should injure or hurt them, ver. 5. This is represented by "fire proceeding out of their mouth, and devouring their enemies." This has been shown to refer to the doctrines which they would proclaim, and the denunciations which they would utter, and which would resemble consuming fire. This would be accomplished or fulfilled if their solemn testimony—their proclamations of truth—and their denunciations of the wrath of God should have the effect ultimately to bring down the divine vengeance on their persecutors. And no one can doubt that this has had an ample fulfilment. That is, the effect of the testimony borne; of the solemn appeals made; of the denunciations of the judgment of heaven, has been to show that that great persecuting power that oppressed them is arrayed against God, and must be finally overthrown. In order to see the complete fulfilment of this, it would be necessary to trace all the effect of the testimony of the witnesses for the truth from age to age on that power, and to see how far it has been among the causes of the ultimate and final overthrow of the Papacy. Of course, it may be said that in an important sense it is *all* to be traced to that, since if they had forborne to bear that testimony, and to protest against those corruptions and abominations, that colossal power would have stood unshaken. But the solemn appeals made from age to age by the friends of truth, amidst much persecution, have contributed to weaken that power, and to prepare the world for its ultimate fall—as if fire from heaven fell upon it. The causes of the decline of the Papal power were, therefore, laid far back in the solemn truths urged by those persecuted "witnesses;" and the calamities which have ravaged Europe for these three hundred years, and the changes now occurring which make it so certain that this mighty power hastens to its fall, may all be the regular results of the "testimony" for the truths of a pure gospel borne long ago by the men that dwelt amidst the Alps, and their fellow-sufferers in persecution. (2) They "have power to shut heaven, that it rain not in the days of their prophecy," ver. 6. This has been shown to mean that they would have power to cause blessings to be withheld from men *as if* the rain were withheld. The reference here is probably to the spiritual heavens, and to that of which rain is the natural emblem—the influences of truth, and the influences of the Divine Spirit on the world. So Moses says, in De. xxxii. 2, "My doctrine shall drop as the rain, and my speech shall distil as the dew, as the small rain upon the tender herb, and as the showers upon the grass." So the psalmist (Ps. lxxii. 6), "He shall come down like rain upon the mown grass: as showers that water the earth." So Isaiah (lv. 10, 11), "For as the rain cometh down, and the snow from heaven, so shall my word be," &c. Comp. Mi. v. 7. The meaning here, then, must be, that spiritual influences would seem to be under their control; or that they would be imparted at their bidding, and withheld at their will. This found an ample fulfilment in the history of the church in those dark periods, in the fact that it was in connection with these "witnesses," and in answer to their prayers, that the influences of the Holy Spirit were imparted to the world, and that the true religion was kept up on the earth. "It is an historical fact," says the author of *The Seventh Vial* (p. 130), "that during the ages of their ministry, there was neither dew nor rain of a spiritual kind upon the earth, but at the word of the witnesses. There was no knowledge of salvation but by their preaching—no descent of the Spirit but in answer to their prayers; and, as the witnesses were shut out from Christendom generally, a universal famine ensued." (3) They had power over the waters to turn them to blood, and to smite the earth with all plagues, ver. 6. That is, as explained above, calamities would come upon the earth *as if* the waters were turned into blood, and this would be so connected with them, and with the treatment which they would receive, that these calamities would *seem* to have been called down from heaven in answer to their prayers, and in order to avenge their wrongs. And can anyone be ignorant that wars, commotions, troubles, disasters have followed the attempts to destroy those who have borne a faithful testimony for Christ in the dark period of the world here referred to? The calamities that have befallen the Papal communion from time to time may have been, and seem to have been, to a great degree, the consequence of its persecuting spirit, and of its attempts to quench the light of truth. When the oppressed and persecuted nations of Europe had borne it long, and when attempts had long been made to extinguish every spark of true liberty, the spirit of freedom and revenge was roused. The yoke was broken; and in the wars that ensued rivers of blood flowed upon the earth, as if these "witnesses" or martyrs had, by their own power and prayers, brought these calamities upon their oppressors. A philosophic historian carefully studying human nature, and the essential spirit of Christianity, might find in these facts a sufficient explanation of all the calamities that have come upon that once colossal power—the Papacy—and a full demonstration that, under the operation of these causes, that power must ultimately fall—*as if* in revenge called down from heaven by the martyrs for the wrongs done to them who had borne a faithful testimony to the truth.

II. The war against the witnesses, ver. 7. There are several circumstances stated in regard to this which demand explanation in order to a full understanding of the prophecy. Those circumstances relate to the time when this would occur; to the government by which this war would be waged; and to the victory.

(*a*) The time when the war referred to would be waged. The whole narrative (comp. ver. 3, 5) supposes that opposition would be made to them at all times, and that their condition would be such that they could properly be represented as always clothed in sackcloth; but it is evident that a particular period is here referred to, when there would be *such* a war waged with them that they would be for a time overcome, and would seem to be dead. This time is referred to by the phrase "when they shall have finished their testimony" (ver. 7); and it is to the period when this could be properly said of them that we are to look for the fulfilment of what is here predicted. This must mean, when they should have borne *full* or *ample* testimony; that is, when they had borne their testimony on all the great points on which they were appointed to bear witness. See Notes on ver. 7. This, then, must not be understood as referring to the time of the *completion* of the twelve hundred and sixty years, but to any time *during* that period when it could be said that they had borne a full and ample testimony for the truths of the gospel, and against the abominations and errors that prevailed. In this general expression there is not, indeed, anything that would accurately designate the time, but no one can doubt that this *had been done at the time of the Reformation*. In the preceding remarks it has been shown that there was a succession of faithful witnesses for the truth in the darkest periods of the church, and that to all the great points pertaining to the system of religion revealed in the gospel, as well as against the errors that prevailed, they had borne an unambiguous testimony. There is no impropriety, therefore, in fixing this period at about the time of the Reformation, for all that is necessarily implied in the language is fulfilled on such a supposition. Faithful testimony had been borne during the long period of the Papal corruptions, until it could be said that their peculiar work had been accomplished. The earlier witnesses for the truth—the Paulicians, the Waldenses, the Vaudois, and other bodies of true Christians—had borne an open testimony, from the beginning, against the various corruptions of Rome—her errors in doctrine, her idolatries in worship, and her immoralities, until in the end of the twelfth century—the same century in which, according to Mr. Gibbon, the meridian of Papal greatness was attained—they proclaimed her, as we have seen, to be the Antichrist of Scripture, the Harlot of the Apocalypse. Thus did they fulfil their testimony; and then was the war waged against them, with all the power of apostate Rome, to silence and to destroy them. This war was commenced in the edicts of councils, which stigmatized the pure doctrines of the Bible, and branded those who held them as heretics. The next step was to pronounce the most dreadful anathemas on those who were regarded as heretics, which were executed in the same remorseless and exterminating manner in which they were conceived. The confessors of the truth were denied both their natural and their civil rights. They were forbidden all participation in dignities and offices; their goods were confiscated; their houses were to be razed and never more to be rebuilt; and their lands were given to those who were able to seize them. They were shut out from the solace of human converse; no one might give them shelter while living, or Christian burial when dead. At length a crusade was proclaimed against them. Preachers were sent abroad through Europe to sound the trumpet of vengeance, and to assemble the nations. The pope wrote to all Christian princes, exhorting them to earn their pardon and win heaven rather by bearing the cross against heretics than by marching against the Saracens. The war, in particular, which was waged against the Waldenses, is well known, and the horror of its details is among the darkest pages of history. The peaceful and fertile valleys of the Vaudois were invaded, and speedily devastated with fire and sword; their towns and villages were burnt; while not one individual, in many cases, escaped to carry the tidings to the next valley. To all the cruelties of these wars, and to all the open persecutions which were waged, are to be added the horrors of the Inquisition, as an illustration of the fact that "wars" would be made against the true witnesses for Christ. Calculations, more or less accurate, have been made of the numbers that Popery has slain; and the lowest of those calculations would confirm what is said here, on the supposition that the reference is to the Papal power. From the year 1540 to the year 1570, comprehending a space of only thirty years, no fewer than nine hundred thousand Protestants were put to death by the Papists, in different countries of Europe. During the short pontificate of Paul the Fourth, which lasted only four years (A.D. 1555–1559), the Inquisition alone, on the testimony of Vergerius, destroyed a hundred and fifty thousand! When he died, the indignant populace of Rome crowded to the prison of the Inquisition, broke open the doors, and released seventeen hundred prisoners, and then set fire to the building (Bowers' *History of the Popes*, iii. 319, edit. 1845). Those who perished in Germany during the wars of Charles the Fifth, and in Flanders, under the infamous Duke of Alva, are reckoned by hundreds of thousands. In France several millions were destroyed in the innumerable massacres that took place in that kingdom. It has been computed that since the rise of the Papacy, not fewer than fifty millions of persons have been put to death on account of religion! Of this vast number the greater part have been cut off during the last six hundred years; for the Papacy persecuted very little during the first half of its existence, and it was in this way that it was not until the witnesses had "completed" their testimony, or had borne full and ample testimony, that it made war against them. Comp. *The Seventh Vial*, pp. 149–157. For a full illustration of the facts here referred to, see Notes on Da. vii. 21. There can be no reasonable doubt that Daniel and John refer to the same thing.

(*b*) By whom this was to be done. In ver. 7, it is said that it would be by "the beast that ascendeth out of the bottomless pit." This is undoubtedly the same as the fourth beast of Daniel (Da. vii.), and for a full illustration I must refer to the Notes on that chapter. It is necessary only to add here, if the above representation is correct, that it is easy to see the propriety of this application of the symbol to the Papacy. Nothing would better represent that cruel persecuting power "making war with the witnesses," than a fierce and cruel monster that seemed to ascend from the bottomless pit.

(*c*) The victory of the persecutors, and the death of the witnesses: "and shall overcome them, and kill them," ver. 7. That is, they would gain a temporary victory over them, and the witnesses would seem for a time to be dead. The subsequent statement shows, however, that they would revive again, and would again resume their prophesying. Comp. Notes on ch. ix. 20. The victory over them would appear to be complete, and the great object of the persecuting power would seem to have been gained. A few facts on this subject will show the propriety of the statement that "when they had finished," or *had fully borne their testimony*, a victory was obtained over them, and that they were so silenced that it might be said they were *killed*. The first will be in the words of Milner, in his account of the opening of the sixteenth century (*History of the Church*, p. 660, ed. Edin. 1835): "The sixteenth century opened with a prospect of all others the most gloomy, in the eyes of every true Christian. Corruption both in doctrine and in practice had exceeded all bounds; and the general face of Europe, though the name of Christ was everywhere professed, presented nothing that was properly evangelical. The Waldenses were too feeble to molest the popedom; and the Hussites, divided among themselves, and worn out by a long series of contentions, were reduced to silence. Among both were found persons of undoubted godliness, but they appeared incapable of making effectual impressions on the kingdom of Antichrist. The Roman pontiffs were still the uncontrolled patrons of impiety; neither the scandalous crimes of Alexander VI., nor the military ferocity of Julius II., seemed to have lessened the dominion of the court of Rome, or to have opened the eyes of men so as to induce them to make a sober investigation of the nature of true religion." The language of Mr. Cunninghame may here be adopted as describing the state of things at the beginning of the sixteenth century: "At the commencement of the sixteenth century, Europe reposed in the deep sleep of spiritual death, under the iron yoke of the Papacy. That haughty power, like the Assyrian of the prophet, said in the plenitude of his insolence, 'My hand hath found as a nest the riches of the people; and as one gathereth eggs, I have gathered all the earth; and there was none that moved the wing, *or opened the mouth*, or peeped.'" And in a similar manner, the writer of the article on the Reformation, in the *Encyclopædia Britannica*—in a statement made, of course, with no reference to the fulfilment of this passage—thus speaks of that period: "Everything was quiet; *every heretic was exterminated*, and the whole Christian world supinely acquiesced in the enormous absurdities inculcated by the Romish church." These quotations will show the propriety of the language used here by John, on the supposition that it was intended to refer to this period. No symbol would be more striking, or more appropriate to that state of things, than to represent the witnesses for the truth as overcome and slain, so that, for a time at least, they would cease to bear their testimony against the prevailing errors and corruptions. It will be remembered, also, that this occurred at a time when it might be said that they had "fulfilled" their testimony, or when, in a most solemn manner, they had protested against the existing idolatries and abominations.

III. The witnesses dead, ver. 8-10. The preceding verse contains the statement that they would be overcome and killed; these verses describe their treatment when they would be dead; that is, when they would be silenced. There are several circumstances referred to here which demand notice.

(*a*) The *place* where it is said that this would occur—that "great city which spiritually is called Sodom and Egypt, where also our Lord was crucified," ver. 8. In the explanation of this verse, it has been shown that the language used here is such as would be properly employed, on the supposition that the intention was to refer to Rome, or the Romish communion. A few testimonies may serve to confirm the interpretation proposed in the Notes on ver. 8, and to show farther the propriety of applying the appellation "Sodom" and "Egypt" to Rome. Thus among the Reformers, "Grosteste perceived that the whole scheme of the Papal government was enmity with God, and exclaimed that nothing but the sword could deliver the church from the *Egyptian* bondage" (D'Aubigné). Wycliffe compared the Romish priestcraft to "the accursed sorceries with which the sages of Pharaoh presumed to emulate the works of Jehovah" (Le Bas' *Wycliffe*, pp. 68, 147). Luther, in a letter to Melancthon, says, "Italy is plunged, as in ancient times in Egypt, in darkness that may be felt." And of Zuingle in Switzerland, they who longed for the light of salvation said of him, " He will be our Moses, to deliver us out of the darkness of Egypt." Any number of passages could be found in the writings of the Reformers, and even some in the writings of Romanists themselves, in which the abominations that prevailed in Rome are compared with those in Sodom. Comp. Elliott, ii. pp. 386, 387, notes. Assuming this to be the correct interpretation, the meaning is, that a state of things would exist after the silencing of the witnesses which would be well represented by supposing that their dead bodies would lie unburied; that is, that there would be dishonour and indignity heaped upon them, such as is shown to the dead when they are suffered to lie unburied. No one needs to be informed that this accurately represents the state of things throughout the Roman world. To the "witnesses" thus persecuted, downtrodden, and *silenced*, there was the same kind of indignity shown which there is when the dead are left unburied.

(*b*) The exposure of their bodies, ver. 8. That is, as we have seen, they would be treated with indignity, *as if* they were not worthy of Christian burial. Now this not only expresses what was in fact the general feeling among the Papists in respect to those whom they regarded as heretics, but it had a literal fulfilment in numerous cases where the rites of Christian burial were denied them. One of the punishments most constantly decreed and constantly enforced in reference to those who were called "heretics," was their exclusion from burial as persons excommunicated and without the pale of the church. Thus, in the third council of Lateran (A.D. 1179), Christian burial was denied to heretics; the same in the Lateran council A.D. 1215, and the Papal decree of Gregory IX., A.D. 1227; the same again in that of Pope Martin, A.D. 1422; and the same thing was determined in the council of Constance, A.D. 1422, which ordered that the body of Wycliffe should be exhumed, and that the ashes of John Huss, instead of being buried, should be collected and thrown into the lake of Constance. It may be added that Savonarola's ashes were in a similar manner cast into the Arno, A.D. 1498; and that in the first bull intrusted to the cardinal Cajetan against Luther, this was one of the declared penalties, that both Luther and his partisans should be deprived of ecclesiastical burial. See Waddington, p. 717; D'Aubigné, i. 355; Foxe, v. 677.

(*c*) The mutual congratulations of those who had put them to death; their exultation over them; and the expression of their joy by the interchange of presents: "And they that dwell upon the earth shall rejoice over them," &c., ver. 10. The language here used is expressive of general joy and rejoicing, and there can be no doubt that such joy and rejoicing occurred at Rome whenever a new victory was obtained over those who were regarded as heretics. Parcus remarks on the passage in Luke xv. 32, "It was meet that we should make merry," &c., that "when heretics are burnt, Papists play at frolicsome games, celebrate feasts and banquets, sing *Te Deum laudamus*, and wish one another joy." And so too Bullinger, *in loco*. But there was special rejoicing, which accorded entirely with the prediction here, at the close of the sessions of the Lateran council A.D. 1517, in the splendour of the dinners and fêtes given by the cardinals. The scene on the closing of the council is thus described by Dean Waddington: "The pillars of the Papal strength seemed visible and palpable; and Rome surveyed them with exultation from her golden palaces. The assembled princes and prelates separated from the council with *complacency*, *confidence*, and *mutual congratulations* on the peace, unity, and purity of the church." Still, while this was true of that particular council, it should be added that the language here used is general, and may be regarded as descriptive of the usual joy which would be felt, and which was felt at Rome, in view of the efforts made to suppress heresy in the church.

(*d*) The *time* during which the witnesses would remain "dead." This, it is said (ver. 9), would be for "three days and an half," during which time they would "not suffer their dead bodies to be put in graves;" that is, there would be a course of conduct, and a state of things, *as if* the dead were left unburied. This *time*, as we have seen (Notes on ver. 9), means probably three years and a half; and in the application of this we are to look for some striking event relating to the "witnesses," when they should have "finished their testimony," or when they had fully borne their testimony, that would fully correspond with this. Now it happens that there *was* a point of time, just previous to the Reformation, when it was supposed that a complete victory was gained for ever over those who were regarded as "heretics," but who were in fact the true witnesses for Christ. That point of time was during the session of the council of Lateran, which was assembled A.D. 1513, and which continued its sessions to May 16, 1517. In the ninth session of this council a remarkable proclamation was made, indicating that all opposition to the Papal power had now ceased. The scene is thus described by Mr. Elliott (ii. 396, 397): "The orator of the session ascended the pulpit; and, amidst the applause of the assembled council, uttered that memorable exclamation of triumph —an exclamation which, notwithstanding the long multiplied anti-heretical decrees of popes and councils, notwithstanding the yet more multiplied anti-heretical crusades and inquisitorial fires, was never, I believe, pronounced before, and certainly never since—'Jam nemo reclamat, nullus obsistit'—'There is an end of resistance to the Papal rule and religion; opposers there exist no more:'

and again, 'The whole body of Christendom is now seen to be subjected to its *Head, i.e.* to *Thee.*'" This occurred May 5, 1514. It is, probably, from this "time" that the three days and a half, or the three years and a half, during which the "dead bodies of the witnesses remained unburied," and were exposed to public gaze and derision, are to be reckoned.

But it was with remarkable accuracy that a period of three years and a half occurred from the time when this proclamation was made, and when it was supposed that these "witnesses" were "dead," to the time when the voice of living witnesses for the truth was heard again, as if those witnesses that had been silenced had come to life again; and "not in the compass of the whole ecclesiastical history of Christendom, except in the case of the death and resurrection of Christ himself, is there any such example of the sudden, mighty, and triumphant resuscitation of his church from a state of deep depression, as was, just after the separation of the Lateran council, exhibited in the protesting voice of Luther, and the glorious Reformation." All accounts agree in placing the beginning of the Reformation in A.D. 1517. See Bowers' *History of the Popes*, iii. 295; Murdock's *Mosheim*, iii. 11, note. The *effect* of this, as compared with the supposed suppression of heresy, or the death of the witnesses, and as an illustration of the passage before us, will be seen from the following language of a writer in the *Encyclopædia Britannica:*—"Everything was quiet; *every heretic exterminated;* and the whole Christian world supinely acquiescing in the enormous absurdities inculcated in the Romish church, when, in 1517, the empire of superstition received its first attack from Luther." Or, in the language of Mr. Cunninghame, "At the commencement of the sixteenth century, Europe reposed in the deep sleep of spiritual death, under the iron yoke of the Papacy. There was none that moved the wing, or opened the mouth, or peeped: when suddenly in one of the universities of Germany the voice of an obscure monk was heard, the sound of which rapidly filled Saxony, Germany, and Europe itself, shaking the very foundations of the Papal power, and arousing men from the lethargy of ages."

The remarkable coincidence in regard to *time*—supposing that three years and a half are intended—will be seen from the following statement. The day of the ninth session of the Lateran council, when the proclamation above referred to was made, was, as we have seen, May 5, 1514; the day of Luther's posting up his theses at Wittemberg (the well-known epoch of the beginning of the Reformation), was October 31, 1517. "Now, from May 5, 1514, to May 5, 1517, are three years; and from May 5, 1517, to October 31 of the same year, 1517, the reckoning in days is as follows:—

| May 5-31......27 | August 31......31 |
| June 30......30 | September 30......30 |
| July 31......31 | October 31......31 |

in all 180, or half of 360 days, that is, half a year; so that the whole interval is precisely, to a day, three and a half years" (Elliott, ii. 402, 403). But, without insisting on this very minute accuracy, anyone can see, and all must be prepared to admit, that, on the supposition that it was intended by the Spirit of God to refer to these events, this is the language which would be used; or, in other words, nothing would better represent this state of things than the declaration that the witnesses would be "slain," and would be suffered to "remain unburied" during this period of time, and that at the end of this period, a public testimony would be borne again for the truth, and against the abominations of the Papacy, as if "the Spirit of life from God should again enter into them, and they should stand upon their feet," ver. 11.

IV. The resurrection of the witnesses, ver. 11. Little need be added on this point, after what has been said on the previous portions of the chapter. We have seen (Notes on ver. 11) that this must mean that a state of things would occur which would be well represented by their being restored to life again; and if the previous illustrations are correct, there will be little difficulty in admitting that this had its fulfilment in the commencement of the Reformation. As to the *time* when they would revive, we have seen above how remarkably this accords with the commencement of the Reformation in 1517; and as to the correspondence of this with what is here symbolized, nothing would better represent this than to describe the witnesses as coming to life again. It was *as if* "the Spirit of life from God entered into" those who had been slain, and "they stood upon their feet" again, and again bore their solemn testimony to the truth as it is in Jesus. For (a) it was the same kind of testimony— testimony *to* the same truths, and *against* the same evils—which had been borne by the long array of the confessors and martyrs that had been put to death. The truths proclaimed by the Reformers on the great doctrines of grace were the same which had been professed by the Waldenses, by Wycliffe, by John Huss, and others; and the abominations of image-worship, of the invocations of the saints, of the arrogant claims of the pope, of the doctrine of human merit in justification, of the corruptions of the monastic systems, of the celibacy of the clergy, of the doctrine of purgatory, against which they testified, were the same. (b) That testimony was borne by men of the same spirit and character. In what would now be called *personal religious experience* there was the closest resemblance between the Waldenses and the other "witnesses" before the Reformation, and the Reformers themselves— between the piety of Huss, Jerome of Prague, Wycliffe, and Peter Waldo; and Luther, Melancthon, Zuingle, Calvin, Bucer, Latimer, Ridley, and Knox. They were men who belonged to the same spiritual communion, and who had been moulded and fashioned in their spiritual character by the same power from on high. (c) The testimony was borne with the same fearlessness, and in the midst of the same kind of persecution and opposition. All that occurred was *as if* the same "witnesses" had been restored to life and again lifted up their voice in the cause for which they had been persecuted and slain. The *propriety* of this language, as applied to these events, may be further seen from expressions used by the "witnesses" themselves, or by the persecuted friends of the truth. "And I," said John Huss, speaking of the gospel-preachers who should appear after he had suffered at the stake, "and I, *awaking as it were from the dead*, and *rising from the grave*, shall rejoice with exceeding great joy." Again, in 1523, after the Reformation had broken out, we find Pope Hadrian saying, in a missive addressed to the Diet at Nuremberg, "The heretics Huss and Jerome are now *alive again* in the person of Martin Luther" (*The Seventh Vial*, p. 190).

V. The ascension of the witnesses, ver. 12: "And they ascended to heaven in a cloud." We have seen (Notes on this verse) that this means that events would take place *as if* they should ascend in triumph to heaven, or which should be properly symbolized *by* such an ascent to heaven. All that is here represented would be fulfilled by a triumph of the truth under the testimony of the witnesses, or by its becoming gloriously established in view of the nations of the earth, *as if* the witnesses ascended publicly and were received to the presence of God in heaven. All this was fulfilled in the various influences that served to establish and confirm the Reformation, and to introduce the great principles of religious freedom, giving to that work ultimate triumph, and showing that it had the favour of God. This would embrace the whole series of events after the Reformation was begun, by which its triumph was secure, or by which that state of things was gradually introduced which now exists, in which the true religion is free from persecution, in which it is advancing into so many parts of the world where the Papacy once had the control, and in which, with so little molestation, and with such an onward march toward ultimate victory, it is extending its conquests over the earth. The triumphant ascent of the witnesses to heaven, and the public proof of the divine favour thus shown to them, would be an appropriate symbol of this.

VI. The consequences of the resurrection, ascension, and triumph of the witnesses, ver. 13. These are said to be, that there would be "in the same hour a great earthquake; that a tenth part of the city would fall; that seven thousand would be slain, and that the remainder would be affrighted and would give glory to the God of heaven."

(a) The earthquake. This, as we have seen (Notes on ver. 13), denotes that there would be a shock or a convulsion in the world, so that the powers of the earth would be shaken, as cities, trees, and hills are in the shocks of an earthquake. There can be little difficulty in applying this to the *shock* produced throughout Europe by the boldness of Luther and his fellow-labourers in the Reformation. No events have ever taken place in history that would be better compared with the shock of an earthquake than those which occurred when the long-established governments of Europe, and especially the domination of the Papacy, so long consolidated and confirmed, were shaken by the Reformation. In the suddenness of the attack made on the existing state of things, in the commotions which were produced, in the overthrow of so many governments, there was a striking resemblance to the convulsions caused by an earthquake. So Dr. Lingard speaks of the Reformation: "That religious revolution which astonished and *convulsed* the nations of Europe." Nothing would better represent the convulsions caused in Germany, Switzerland, Prussia, Saxony, Sweden, Denmark, and England by the Reformation than an earthquake.

(*b*) The fate of a part of the city: "And the tenth part of the city fell." That is, as we have seen (Notes on ver. 13), of that which is represented by the city, to wit, the Roman power. The fall of a "tenth part" would denote the fall of a considerable portion of that power; *as if*, in an earthquake, a tenth part of a city should be demolished. This would well represent what occurred in the Reformation, when so considerable a portion of the colossal Papal power suddenly fell away, and the immediate effect on the portions of Europe where the Reformation prevailed, as compared with the whole of that power, might well be represented by the fall of the *tenth* part of a city. It is true that a much larger proportion *ultimately* fell off from Rome, so that now the number of Romanists and Protestants is not far from being equal; but in the first convulsion—in what passed before the eye in vision as represented by the earthquake—that proportion would not be improperly represented by the tenth part of a city. The idea is, that the sudden destruction of a tenth part of a great city by an earthquake would well represent the convulsion at the breaking out of the Reformation, by which a considerable portion of the Papal power would fall.

(*c*) Those who were slain, ver. 13: "And in the earthquake were slain of men seven thousand." That is, as we have seen (Notes on ver. 13), a calamity would occur to this vast Papal power, *as if* this number should be killed in the earthquake, or which would be well represented by that. In other words, a portion of those who were represented by the city would be slain, which, compared with the whole number, would bear about the same proportion which seven thousand would to the usual dwellers in such a city. As the numbers in the city are not mentioned, it is impossible to form any exact estimate of the numbers that would be slain on this supposition. But if we suppose that the city contained a hundred thousand, then the proportion would be something like a fourteenth part; but if it were half a million, then it would be about a seventieth part; if it were a million, then it would be about a hundred and forty-fifth part; and, as we may suppose that John, in these visions, had his eye on Rome as it was in the age in which he lived, we may, if we can ascertain what the size of Rome was at that period, take that estimate as the basis of the interpretation. Mr. Gibbon (ii. 251, 252) has endeavoured to form an estimate of the probable number of the inhabitants of ancient Rome; and, after enumerating all the circumstances which throw any light on the subject, says: "If we adopt the same average which, under similar circumstances, has been found applicable to Paris, and indifferently allow about twenty-five persons for each house, of every degree, we may fairly estimate the inhabitants of Rome at twelve hundred thousand." Allowing this to be the number of the inhabitants of the city, then the number here specified that was slain—seven thousand—would be about the one hundred and seventieth part, or one in one hundred and seventy. This would, according to the purport of the vision here, represent the number that would perish in the convulsion denoted by the earthquake—a number which, though it would be large in the aggregate, is not probably too large in fact as referring to the number of persons that perished in Papal Europe in the wars that were consequent on the Reformation.

(*d*) The only other circumstance in this representation is, that "the remnant were affrighted and gave glory to the God of heaven," ver. 13. That is, as we have seen (Notes on ver. 13), fear and consternation came upon them, and they stood in awe at what was occurring, and acknowledged the power of God in the changes that took place. How well this was fulfilled in what occurred in the Reformation, it is hardly necessary to state. The events which then took place had every mark of being under the divine hand, and were such as to fill the minds of men with awe and to teach them to recognize the hand of God. The power which tore asunder that immense ecclesiastical establishment, that

## CHAPTER XI.

15 And the *b*seventh angel sounded; and there were great voices in heaven, saying, *c*The kingdoms of this world are become *the kingdoms* of our Lord, and of his Christ; and *d*he shall reign for ever and ever.

*b* ch.10.7.  *c* ch.12.10.  *d* Da.2.44; 7.14,18,27.

had so long held the whole of Europe in servitude; which dissolved the charm which had so long held kings, and princes, and people spell-bound; which rent away for ever so large a portion of the Papal dominions; which led kings to separate themselves from the control to which they had been so long subjected, and which emancipated the human mind, and diffused abroad the great principles of civil and religious liberty, was well adapted to fill the mind with awe, and to lead men to recognize the hand and the agency of God; and if it be admitted that the Holy Spirit in this passage *meant* to refer to these events, it cannot be doubted that the language here used is such as is well adapted to describe the effects produced on the minds of men at large.

15. *And the seventh angel sounded.* See Notes on ch. viii. 2, 6, 7. This is the last of the trumpets, implying, of course, that under this the series of visions was to end, and that this was to introduce the state of things under which the affairs of the world were to be wound up. The place which this occupies in the order of time, is when the events pertaining to the colossal Roman power—the fourth kingdom of Daniel (Da. ii.-vii.)—should have been completed, and when the reign of the saints (Da. vii. 9-14, 27, 28) should have been introduced. This, both in Daniel and in John, is to occur when the mighty power of the Papacy shall have been overthrown at the termination of the twelve hundred and sixty years of its duration. See Notes on Da. vii. 25. In both Daniel and John the termination of that persecuting power is the commencement of the reign of the saints; the downfall of the Papacy, the introduction of the kingdom of God, and its establishment on the earth. ¶ *And there were great voices in heaven.* As of exultation and praise. The grand consummation had come, the period so long anticipated and desired when God should reign on the earth had arrived, and this lays the foundation for joy and thanksgiving in heaven. ¶ *The kingdoms of this world.* The modern editions of the New Testament (see Tittmann and Hahn) read this in the singular number—"The kingdom of this world has become," &c. According to this reading, the meaning would be, either that the sole *reign* over this world had become that of the Lord Jesus; or, more probably, that the dominion over the earth had been regarded as one in the sense that Satan had reigned over it, but had now become the kingdom of God; that is, that "the kingdoms of this world are many considered in themselves; but in reference to the sway of Satan, there is only *one* kingdom ruled over by the 'god of this world'" (Professor Stuart). The sense is not materially different whichever reading is adopted; though the authority is in favour of the latter (Wetstein). According to the common reading, the sense is, that all the kingdoms of the earth, being many in themselves, had been now brought under the one sceptre of Christ; according to the other, the whole world was regarded as in fact one kingdom—that of Satan—and the sceptre had now passed from his hands into those of the Saviour. ¶ *The kingdoms of our Lord.* Or, the *kingdom* of our Lord, according to the reading adopted in the previous part of the verse. The word *Lord* here evidently has reference to God as such—represented as the original source of authority, and as giving the kingdom to his Son. See Notes on Da. vii. 13, 14; comp. Ps. ii. 8. The word *Lord*—Κυριος—implies the notion of possessor, owner, sovereign, supreme ruler—and is thus properly given to God. See Mat. i. 22; v. 33; Mar. v. 19; Lu. i. 6, 28; Ac. vii. 33; He. viii. 2, 10; Ja. iv. 15, *al. sæpe*. ¶ *And of his Christ.* Of his anointed; of him who is set apart as the Messiah, and consecrated to this high office. See Notes on Mat. i. 1. He is called "*his* Christ," because he is set apart by him, or appointed by him to perform the work appropriate to that office on earth. Such language as that which occurs here is often employed, in which God *and* Christ are spoken of as, in some respects, distinct—as sustaining different offices, and performing different works. The essential meaning here is, that the kingdom of this world had now become the kingdom of God *under*

16 And the *e*four and twenty elders, which sat before God on their seats, fell upon their faces, and worshipped God.

17 Saying, We give thee thanks,

*e* ch.4.4.

O Lord God Almighty, *f* which art, and wast, and art to come; because thou hast taken to thee thy great power, and *g* hast reigned.

*f* ch.16.5.     *g* ch.19.6.

---

Christ; that is, that that kingdom is administered by the Son of God. ¶ *And he shall reign for ever and ever.* A kingdom is commenced which shall never terminate. It is not said that this would be on the earth; but the essential idea is, that the sceptre of the world had now, after so long a time, come into his hands never more to pass away. The fuller characteristics of this reign are stated in a subsequent part of this book (ch. xx.-xxii.). What is here stated is in accordance with all the predictions in the Bible. A time is to come when, in the proper sense of the term, God is to *reign* on the earth; when his kingdom is to be universal; when his laws shall be everywhere recognized as binding; when all idolatry shall come to an end; and when the understandings and the hearts of men everywhere shall bow to his authority. Comp. Ps. ii. 8; Is. ix. 7; xi. 9; xlv. 22; lx.; Da. ii. 35, 44, 45; vii. 13, 14, 27, 28; Zec. xiv. 9; Mal. i. 11; Lu. i. 33. On this whole subject, see the very ample illustrations and proofs in the Notes on Da. ii. 44, 45; vii. 13, 14, 27, 28; comp. Notes on chap. xx.-xxii.

16. *And the four and twenty elders which sat*, &c. See Notes on ch. iv. 4. ¶ *Fell upon their faces, and worshipped God.* Prostrated themselves before him—the usual form of profound adoration. See Notes on ch. v. 8-14.

17. *Saying, We give thee thanks.* We, as the representatives of the church, and as identified in our feelings with it (see Notes on ch. iv. 4), acknowledge thy goodness in thus delivering the church from all its troubles, and having conducted it through the times of fiery persecution, thus establishing it upon the earth. The language here used is an expression of their deep interest in the church, and of the fact that they felt themselves identified with it. They, as representatives of the church, would of course rejoice in its prosperity and final triumph. ¶ *O Lord God Almighty.* Referring to God as all-powerful, because it was by his omnipotent arm alone that this great work had been accomplished. Nothing else could have defended the church in its many trials; nothing else could have established it upon the earth. ¶ *Which art, and wast, and art to come.* The Eternal One, always the same. See Notes on ch. i. 8. The reference here is to the fact that God, who had thus established his church on the earth, is unchanging. In all the revolutions which occur on the earth, he always remains the same. What he was in past times he is now; what he is now he always will be. The particular idea suggested here seems to be, that he had now shown this by having caused his church to triumph; that is, he had shown that he was the same God who had early *promised* that it should ultimately triumph; he had carried forward his glorious purposes without modifying or abandoning them amidst all the changes that had occurred in the world; and he had thus given the assurance that he would now remain the same, and that all his purposes in regard to his church would be accomplished. The fact that God remains always unchangeably the same is the sole reason why his church is safe, or why any individual member of it is kept and saved. Comp. Mal. iii. 6. ¶ *Because thou hast taken to thee thy great power.* To wit, by setting up thy kingdom over all the earth. Before that it *seemed* as if he had relaxed that power, or had given the power to others. Satan had reigned on the earth. Disorder, anarchy, sin, rebellion, had prevailed. It seemed as if God had let the reins of government fall from his hand. Now he came forth as if to resume the dominion over the world, and to take the sceptre into his own hand, and to exert his great power in keeping the nations in subjection. The setting up of his kingdom all over the world, and causing his laws everywhere to be obeyed, will be among the highest demonstrations of divine power. Nothing can accomplish this but the power of God; when that power is exerted nothing can prevent its accomplishment. ¶ *And hast reigned.* Professor Stuart, "and shown thyself as king"—that is, "hast become king, or acted as a king." The idea is, that he had now vindicated

## CHAPTER XI.

18 And the nations *ʰ* were angry, and thy wrath is come, and *ⁱ* the time of the dead, that they should be judged, and that thou *ᵏ* shouldest

*h* ver. 9.    *i* He. 9. 27.    *k* ch. 22. 12.

give reward unto thy servants the prophets, and to the saints, and them that fear thy name, *ˡ* small and great; and shouldest destroy them which ⁴ destroy the earth.

*l* ch. 19. 5.    ⁴ or, *corrupt.*

---

his regal power (Rob. *Lex.*)—that is, he had now set up his kingdom on the earth, and had truly begun to reign. One of the characteristics of the millennium—and indeed the main characteristic—will be that God will be everywhere obeyed; for when that occurs all will be consummated that properly enters into the idea of the millennial kingdom.

18. *And the nations were angry.* Were enraged against thee. This they had shown by their opposition to his laws; by persecuting his people; by slaying his witnesses; by all the attempts which they had made to destroy his authority on the earth. The reference here seems to be to the whole series of events preceding the final establishment of his kingdom on the earth; to all the efforts which had been made to throw off his government and to crush his church. At this period of glorious triumph it was natural to look back to those dark times when the "nations raged" (comp. Ps. ii. 1-3), and when the very existence of the church was in jeopardy. ¶ *And thy wrath is come.* That is, the time when thou wilt punish them for all that they have done in opposition to thee, and when the wicked shall be cut off. There will be, in the setting up of the kingdom of God, some manifestation of his wrath against the powers that opposed it; or something that will show his purpose to destroy his enemies, and to judge the wicked. The representations in this book lead us to suppose that the final establishment of the kingdom of God on the earth will be introduced or accompanied by commotions and wars which will end in the overthrow of the great powers that have opposed his reign, and by such awful calamities in those portions of the world as shall show that God has arisen in his strength to cut off his enemies, and to appear as the vindicator of his people. Comp. Notes on ch. xvi. 12-16; xix. 11-26. ¶ *And the time of the dead, that they should be judged.* According to the view which the course of the exposition thus far pursued leads us to entertain of this book, there is reference here, in few words, to the same thing which is more fully stated in ch. xx., and the meaning of the sacred writer will, therefore, come up for a more distinct and full examination when we consider that chapter. See Notes on ch. xx. 4-6, 12-15. The purpose of the writer does not require that a *detailed* statement of the order of the events referred to should be made here, for it would be better made when, after another line of illustration and of symbol (ch. xi. 19, xii.-xix.), he should have reached the same catastrophe, and when, in view of both, the mind would be prepared for the fuller description with which the book closes, ch. xx.-xxii. All that occurs here, therefore, is a very *general* statement of the final consummation of all things. ¶ *And that thou shouldest give reward unto thy servants.* The righteous. Comp. Mat. xxv. 34-40; Re. xxi., xxii. That is, in the final winding-up of human affairs, God will bestow the long-promised reward on those who have been his true friends. The wicked that annoyed and persecuted them will annoy and persecute them no more; and the righteous will be publicly acknowledged as the friends of God. For the *manner* in which this will be done, see the details in ch. xx.-xxii. ¶ *The prophets.* All who, in every age, have faithfully proclaimed the truth. On the meaning of the word, see Notes on ch. x. 11. ¶ *And to the saints.* To all who are holy—under whatever dispensation, and in whatever land, and at whatever time, they may have lived. Then will be the time when, in a public manner, they will be recognized as belonging to the kingdom of God, and as being his true friends. ¶ *And them that fear thy name.* Another way of designating his people, since religion consists in a profound veneration for God, Mal. iii. 16; Job i. 1; Ps. xv. 4; xxii. 23; cxv. 11; Pr. i. 7; iii. 13; ix. 10; Is. xi. 2; Ac. x. 22, 35. ¶ *Small and great.* Young and old; low and high; poor and rich. The language is designed to comprehend *all*, of every class, who have a claim to be numbered among the friends of God, and it furnishes a plain intimation that men of all classes will be found at last

among his true people. One of the glories of the true religion is, that, in bestowing its favours, it disregards all the artificial distinctions of society, and addresses man as man, welcoming all who are human beings to the blessings of life and salvation. This will be illustriously shown in the last period of the world's history, when the distinctions of wealth, and rank, and blood shall lose the importance which has been attributed to them, and when the honour of being a child of God shall have its true place. Comp. Ga. iii. 28. ¶ *And shouldest destroy them which destroy the earth.* That is, all who have, in their conquests, spread desolation over the earth, and who have persecuted the righteous, and all who have done injustice and wrong to any class of men. Comp. Notes on ch. xx. 13-15.

Here ends, as I suppose, the first series of visions referred to in the volume sealed with the seven seals, ch. v. 1. At this point, where the division of the chapter should have been made, and which is properly marked in our common Bibles by the sign of the paragraph (¶), there commences a new series of visions, intended also, but in a different line, to extend down to the consummation of all things. The former series traces the history down mainly through the series of *civil* changes in the world, or the *outward* affairs which affect the destiny of the church; the latter—the portion still before us — embraces the same period with a more direct reference to the rise of Antichrist, and the influence of *that* power in affecting the destiny of the church. When that is completed (ch. xi. 19, xii. - xix.), the way is prepared (ch. xx.-xxii.) for the more full statement of the final triumph of the gospel, and the universal prevalence of religion, with which the book so appropriately closes. That portion of the book, therefore, refers to the same period as the one which has just been considered under the sounding of the seventh trumpet, and the description of the final state of things would have immediately succeeded if it had not been necessary, by another series of visions, to trace more particularly the history of Antichrist on the destiny of the church, and the way in which that great and fearful power would be finally overcome. See the Analysis of the Book, part V. The way is then prepared for the description of the state of things which will exist when all the enemies of the church shall be subdued; when Christianity shall triumph; and when the predicted reign of God shall be set up on the earth, ch. xx.-xxii.

## CHAPTER XII.

ANALYSIS OF CH. XI. 19, XII.

This portion of the book commences, according to the view presented in the closing remarks on the last chapter, a new series of visions, designed more particularly to represent the internal condition of the church; the rise of Antichrist, and the effect of the rise of that formidable power on the internal history of the church to the time of the overthrow of that power, and the triumphant establishment of the kingdom of God. See the Analysis of the Book, part V. The portion before us embraces the following particulars:—

(1) A new vision of the temple of God as opened in heaven, disclosing the ark of the testimony, and attended with lightnings, and voices, and thunderings, and an earthquake, and great hail, ch. xi. 19. The view of the "*temple,*" and the "*ark,*" would naturally suggest a reference to the church, and would be an appropriate representation on the supposition that this vision related to the church. The attending circumstances of the lightnings, &c., were well fitted to impress the mind with awe, and to leave the conviction that great and momentous events were about to be disclosed. I regard this verse, therefore, which should have been separated from the eleventh chapter and attached to the twelfth, as the introduction to a new series of visions, similar to what we have in the introduction of the previous series, ch. iv. 1. The vision was of the temple—the symbol of the church —and it was "opened" so that John could see into its inmost part—even within the veil where the ark was—and could have a view of what most intimately pertained to it.

(2) A representation of the church, under the image of a woman about to give birth to a child, ch. xii. 1, 2. A woman is seen, clothed, as it were, with the sun—emblem of majesty, truth, intelligence, and glory; she has the moon under her feet, as if she walked the heavens; she has on her head a glittering diadem of stars; she is about to become a mother. This seems to have been designed to represent the church as about to be increased, and as in that

condition watched by a dragon—a mighty foe—ready to destroy its offspring, and thus compelled to flee into the wilderness for safety. Thus understood, the point of time referred to would be when the church was in a prosperous condition, and when it would be encountered by Antichrist, represented here by the dragon, and compelled to flee into the wilderness; that is, the church for a time would be driven into obscurity, and be almost unknown. It is no uncommon thing, in the Scriptures, to compare the church with a beautiful woman. See Notes on Isa. i. 8. The following remarks of Professor Stuart (vol. ii. 252), though he *applies* the subject in a manner very different from what I shall, seem to me accurately to express the general design of the symbol:—"The *daughter of Zion* is a common personification of the church in the Old Testament; and in the writings of Paul, the same image is exhibited by the phrase, *Jerusalem, which is the mother of us all; i.e.* of all Christians, Ga. iv. 26. The main point before us is the illustration of that church, ancient or later, under the image of a *woman*. If the Canticles are to have a spiritual sense given to them, it is plain enough, of course, how familiar such an idea was to the Jews. Whether the woman thus exhibited as a symbol be represented as *bride* or *mother* depends, of course, on the nature of the case, and the relations and exigencies of any particular passage."

(3) The dragon that stood ready to devour the child, ver. 3, 4. This represents some formidable enemy of the church, that was ready to persecute and destroy it. The real enemy here referred to is, undoubtedly, Satan, the great enemy of God and the church, but here it is Satan in the form of some fearful opponent of the church that would arise at a period when the church was prosperous, and when it was about to be enlarged. We are to look, therefore, for some fearful *manifestation* of this formidable power, having the characteristics here referred to, or some opposition to the church such as we may suppose Satan would originate, and by which the existence of the church might seem to be endangered.

(4) The fact that the child which the woman brought forth was caught up to heaven—symbolical of its real safety, and of its having the favour of God—a pledge that the ultimate prosperity of the church was certain, and that it was safe from real danger, ver. 5.

(5) The fleeing of the woman into the wilderness, for the space of a thousand two hundred and threescore days, or 1260 years, ver. 6. This act denotes the persecuted and obscure condition of the church during that time, and the period which would elapse before it would be delivered from this persecution, and restored to the place in the earth which it was designed to have.

(6) The war in heaven; a struggle between the mighty powers of heaven and the dragon, ver. 7-9. Michael and his angels contend against the dragon, in behalf of the church, and finally prevail. The dragon is overcome, and is cast out, and all his angels with him; in other words, the great enemy of God and his church is overcome and subdued. This is evidently designed to be symbolical, and the meaning is, that a state of things would exist in regard to the church, which would be well represented by supposing that such a scene should occur in heaven; that is, *as if* a war should exist there between the great enemy of God and the angels of light, and *as if*, being there vanquished, Satan should be cast down to the earth, and should there exert his malignant power in a warfare against the church. The general idea is, that his warfare would be *primarily* against heaven, as if he fought with the angels in the very presence of God, but that the form in which he would *seem* to prevail would be against the church, *as if*, being unsuccessful in his direct warfare against the angels of God, he was permitted, for a time, to enjoy the appearance of triumph in contending with the church.

(7) The shout of victory in view of the conquest over the dragon, ver. 10-12. A loud voice is heard in heaven, saying, that now the kingdom of God is come, and that the reign of God would be set up, for the dragon is cast down and overcome. The grand instrumentality in overcoming this foe was "the blood of the Lamb, and the word of their testimony;" that is, the great doctrines of truth pertaining to the work of the Redeemer would be employed for this purpose, and it is proclaimed that the heavens and all that dwell therein had occasion to rejoice at the certainty that a victory would be ultimately obtained over this great enemy of God. Still, however, his influence was not wholly at an end,

19 And the <sup>m</sup> temple of God was opened in heaven, and there was seen in his temple the ark of his

*m* ch.15.5,8.

for he would yet rage for a brief period on the earth.

(8) The persecution of the woman, ver. 13–15. She is constrained to fly, as on wings given her for that purpose, into the wilderness, where she is nourished for the time that the dragon is to exert his power—a "time, times, and half a time"—or for 1260 years. The dragon in rage pours out a flood of water, that he may cause her to be swept away by the flood: referring to the persecutions that would exist while the church was in the wilderness, and the efforts that would be made to destroy it entirely.

(9) The earth helps the woman, ver. 16. That is, a state of things would exist *as if*, in such a case, the earth should open and swallow up the flood. The meaning is, that the church would not be swept away, but that there would be an interposition in its behalf, *as if* the earth should, in the case supposed, open its bosom, and swallow up the swelling waters.

(10) The dragon, still enraged, makes war with all that pertains to the woman, ver. 17. Here we are told literally who are referred to by the "seed" of the woman. They are those who "keep the commandments of God, and have the testimony of Jesus Christ" (ver. 17); that is, the true church.

The chapter, therefore, may be regarded as a general vision of the persecutions that would rage against the church. It seemed to be about to increase and to spread over the world. Satan, always opposed to it, strives to prevent its extension. The conflict is represented *as if* in heaven, where war is waged between the celestial beings and Satan, and where, being overcome, Satan is cast down to the earth, and permitted to wage the war there. The church is persecuted; becomes obscure and almost unknown, but still is mysteriously sustained; and when most in danger of being wholly swallowed up, is kept *as if* a miracle were wrought in its defence. The *detail*—the particular form in which the war would be waged—is drawn out in the following chapters.

Ch. xi. 19. *And the temple of God was opened in heaven.* The temple of God testament: and there were <sup>n</sup> lightnings, and voices, and thunderings, and an <sup>o</sup> earthquake, and great hail.

*n* ch.8.5.    *o* ch.16.18,21.

at Jerusalem was a pattern of the heavenly one, or of heaven, He. viii. 1–5. In that temple God was supposed to reside by the visible symbol of his presence—the Shekinah—in the holy of holies. See Notes on He. ix. 7. Thus God dwells in heaven, as in a holy temple, of which that on earth was the emblem. When it is said that that was "opened in heaven," the meaning is, that John was permitted, as it were, to look *into* heaven, the abode of God, and to see him in his glory. ¶ *And there was seen in his temple the ark of his testament.* See Notes on He. ix. 4. That is, the very interior of heaven was laid open, and John was permitted to witness what was transacted in its obscurest recesses, and what were its most hidden mysteries. It will be remembered, as an illustration of the correctness of this view of the meaning of the verse, and of its proper place in the divisions of the book—assigning it as the opening verse of a new series of visions—that in the *first* series of visions we have a statement remarkably similar to this, ch. iv. 1: "After this I looked, and, behold, *a door was opened in heaven;*" that is, there was, as it were, an *opening* made into heaven, so that John was permitted *to look in* and see what was occurring there. The same idea is expressed substantially here, by saying that the very interior of the sacred temple where God resides was "opened in heaven," so that John was permitted to look in and see what was transacted in his very presence. This, too, may go to confirm the idea suggested in the Analysis of the Book, part V., that this portion of the Apocalypse refers rather to the *internal* affairs of the church, or the church itself—for of this the *temple* was the proper emblem. Then appropriately follows the series of visions describing, as in the former case, what was to occur in future times: this series referring to the internal affairs of the church, as the former did mainly to what would outwardly affect its form and condition. ¶ *And there were lightnings,* &c. Symbolic of the awful presence of God, and of his majesty and glory, as in the commencement of the first series of visions. See Notes on ch.

## CHAPTER XII.

AND there appeared a great ¹wonder in heaven; a *a* woman clothed with the *b*sun, and the moon under her feet, and upon her head a crown of twelve stars:

¹ or, *sign*.   *a* Is.54.6.   *b* Ps.84.11; Mal.4.2.

iv. 5. The *similarity* of the symbols of the divine majesty in the two cases may also serve to confirm the supposition that this is the beginning of a new series of visions. ¶ *And an earthquake.* Also a symbol of the divine majesty, and perhaps of the great convulsions that were to occur under this series of visions. Comp. Notes on ch. vi. 12. Thus, in the sublime description of God in Ps. xviii. 7, "Then the earth shook and trembled, the foundations also of the hills moved and were shaken, because he was wroth." So in Ex. xix. 18, "And Mount Sinai was altogether on a smoke — and the whole mount quaked greatly." Comp. Am. viii. 8, 9; Joel ii. 10. ¶ *And great hail.* Also an emblem of the presence and majesty of God, perhaps with the accompanying idea that he would overwhelm and punish his enemies. So in Ps. xviii. 13, "The Lord also thundered in the heavens, and the Highest gave his voice: hailstones and coals of fire." So also Job xxxviii. 22, 23:—

"Hast thou entered into the treasures of snow?
Or hast thou seen the treasures of the hail?
Which I have reserved against *the time of trouble*,
Against the day of *battle and war?*"

So in Ps. cv. 32:

"He gave them hail for rain,
And flaming fire in their land."

Comp. Ps. lxxviii. 48; Is. xxx. 30; Eze. xxxviii. 22.

Ch. xii. 1. *And there appeared a great wonder in heaven.* In that heavenly world thus disclosed, in the very presence of God, he saw the impressive and remarkable symbol which he proceeds to describe. The word *wonder*—σημεῖον—properly means something extraordinary, or miraculous, and is commonly rendered *sign*. See Mat. xii. 38, 39; xvi. 1, 3, 4; xxiv. 3, 24, 30; xxvi. 48; Mar. viii. 11, 12; xiii. 4, 22; xvi. 17, 20; — in all which, and in numerous other places in the New Testament, it is rendered *sign*, and mostly in the sense of *miracle*. When used in the sense of a miracle, it refers to the fact that the miracle is a *sign* or *token* by which the divine power or purpose is made known. Sometimes the word is used to denote *a sign of future things* — a portent or presage of coming events; that is, some remarkable appearances which foreshadow the future. Thus in Mat. xvi. 3: "*signs of the times;*" that is, the miraculous events which foreshadow the coming of the Messiah in his kingdom. So also in Mat. xxiv. 3, 30; Mar. xiii. 4; Lu. xxi. 7, 11. This seems to be the meaning here, that the woman who appeared in this remarkable manner was a portent or token of what was to occur. ¶ *A woman clothed with the sun.* Bright, splendid, glorious, *as if* the sunbeams were her raiment. Comp. ch. i. 16; x. 1; see also Ca. vi. 10—a passage which, very possibly, was in the mind of the writer when he penned this description: "Who is she that looketh forth as the morning, fair as the moon, clear as the sun, and terrible as an army with banners?" ¶ *And the moon under her feet.* The moon *seemed* to be under her feet. She seemed as if she stood on the moon, its pale light contrasted with the burning splendour of the sun, heightening the beauty of the whole picture. The woman, beyond all question, represents the church. See Notes on ver. 2. Is the splendour of the sunlight designed to denote the brightness of the gospel? Is the moon designed to represent the comparatively feeble light of the Jewish dispensation? Is the fact that she stood upon the moon, or that it was under her feet, designed to denote the superiority of the gospel to the Jewish dispensation? Such a supposition gives much beauty to the symbol, and is not foreign to the nature of symbolic language. ¶ *And upon her head a crown of twelve stars.* A diadem in which there were placed twelve stars. That is, there were twelve sparkling gems in the crown which she wore. This would, of course, greatly increase the beauty of the vision; and there can be no doubt that the number *twelve* here is significant. If the woman here is designed to symbolize the church, then the number twelve has, in all probability, some allusion either to the twelve tribes of Israel—as being a number which one who was born and educated as a Jew would be likely to use (comp. Ja. i. 1), or to the twelve apostles—an allusion which, it may be supposed, an apostle would be more

2 And she being with child cried, travailing in birth, and pained to be delivered.

likely to make. Comp. Mat. xix. 28; Re. xxi. 14.

2. *And she being with child cried, travailing in birth,* &c. That is, there would be something which would be properly represented by a woman in such circumstances.

The question now is, what is referred to by this woman? And here it need hardly be said that there has been, as in regard to almost every other part of the book of Revelation, a great variety of interpretations. It would be endless to undertake to examine them, and would not be profitable if it could be done; and it is better, therefore, and more in accordance with the design of these Notes, to state briefly what seems to me to be the true interpretation. (1) The woman is evidently designed to symbolize the church; and in this there is a pretty general agreement among interpreters. The image, which is a beautiful one, was very familiar to the Jewish prophets. See Notes on Is. i. 8; xlvii. 1; comp. Eze. xvi. (2) But still the question arises, *to what time* this representation refers: whether to the church before the birth of the Saviour, or after? According to the former of these opinions, it is supposed to refer to the church as giving birth to the Saviour, and the "man child" that is born (ver. 5) is supposed to refer to Christ, who "sprang from the church" —κατὰ σάρκα—according to the flesh (Professor Stuart, vol. ii. p. 252). The church, according to this view, is not simply regarded as Jewish, but, in a more general and theocratic sense, as *the people of God*. "From the Christian church, considered as Christian, he could not spring; for this took its rise only after the time of his public ministry. But from the bosom of the *people of God* the Saviour came. This church, *Judaical* indeed (at the time of his birth) in respect to rites and forms, but to become *Christian* after he had exercised his ministry in the midst of it, might well be represented here by the woman which is described in ch. xii." (Professor Stuart). But to this view there are some, as it seems to me, unanswerable objections. For, (a) there seems to be a harshness and incongruity in representing the Saviour as *the Son of the church*, or representing the church as giving birth to him. Such imagery is not found elsewhere in the Bible, and is not in accordance with the language which *is* employed, where Christ is rather represented as the *Husband* of the church than the *Son:* "Prepared as a bride adorned for her husband," Re. xxi. 2. "I will show thee the bride, the Lamb's wife," Re. xxi. 9; comp. Is. liv. 5; lxi. 10; lxii. 5. (*b*) If this interpretation be adopted, then this must refer to the *Jewish* church, and thus the woman will personify the Jewish community before the birth of Christ. But this seems contrary to the whole design of the Apocalypse, which has reference to the *Christian* church, and not to the ancient dispensation. (*c*) If this interpretation be adopted, then the statement about the dwelling in the wilderness for a period of 1260 days or years (ver. 14) must be assigned to the Jewish community—a supposition every way improbable and untenable. In what sense could this be true? When did anything happen to the Jewish people that could, with any show of probability, be regarded as the fulfilment of this? (*d*) It may be added, that the statement about the "man child" (ver. 5) is one that can with difficulty be reconciled to this supposition. In what sense was this true, that the "man *child*" was "caught up unto God, and to his throne?" The Saviour, indeed, ascended to heaven, but it was not, as here represented, that he might be *protected* from the danger of being destroyed; and when he *did* ascend, it was not as a helpless and unprotected babe, but as a man in the full maturity of his powers. The other opinion is, that the woman here refers to the Christian church, and that the object is to represent that church as about to be enlarged—represented by the condition of the woman, ver. 2. A beautiful woman appears, clothed with light—emblematic of the brightness and purity of the church; with the moon under her feet—the ancient and comparatively obscure dispensation now made subordinate and humble; with a glittering diadem of twelve stars on her head—the stars representing the usual well-known division of the people of God into twelve parts —as the stars in the American flag denote the original states of the Union; and in a condition (ver. 2) which showed that the church was to be increased. The time there referred to is at the

3 And there appeared another wonder[2] in heaven; and behold a [c]great red dragon, having seven heads and ten horns, and seven crowns upon his heads.

[2] or, *sign*.

[c] ver.9.

early period of the history of the church, when, as it were, it first appears on the theatre of things, and going forth in its beauty and majesty over the earth. John sees this church, as it was about to spread in the world, exposed to a mighty and formidable enemy—a hateful dragon—stationing itself to prevent its increase, and to accomplish its destruction. From that impending danger it is protected in a manner that would be well represented by the saving of the child of the woman, and bearing it up to heaven, to a place of safety—an act implying that, notwithstanding all dangers, the progress and enlargement of the church was ultimately certain. In the meantime, the woman herself flees into the wilderness—an act representing the obscure, and humble, and persecuted state of the church—till the great controversy is determined which is to have the ascendency—God or the Dragon. In favour of this interpretation, the following considerations may be suggested:—(*a*) It is the natural and obvious interpretation. (*b*) If it be admitted that John *meant* to describe what occurred in the world at the time when the true church seemed to be about to extend itself over the earth, and when that prosperity was checked by the rise of the Papal power, the symbol employed would be strikingly expressive and appropriate. (*c*) It accords with the language elsewhere used in the Scriptures when referring to the *increase* of the church. "Before she travailed, she brought forth; before her pain came, she was delivered of a man child. Who hath heard such a thing? As soon as Zion travailed, she brought forth her children," Is. lxvi. 7, 8. "Sing, O barren, thou that didst not bear; for more are the children of the desolate than the children of the married wife, saith the Lord," Is. liv. 1. "The children which thou shalt have, after thou shalt have lost the other, shall say again in thy ears, The place is too strait for me; give place to me that I may dwell," Is. xlix. 20. The comparison of the church to a woman as the mother of children, is one that is very common in the Scriptures. (*d*) The future destiny of the child and of the woman agrees with this supposition. The child is caught up to heaven, ver. 5—emble-

matic of the fact that God will protect the church, and not suffer its increase to be cut off and destroyed; and the woman is driven for 1260 years into the wilderness and nourished there, ver. 14—emblematic of the long period of obscurity and persecution in the true church, and yet of the fact that it would be protected and nourished. The *design* of the whole, therefore, I apprehend, is to represent the peril of the church at the time when it was about to be greatly enlarged, or in a season of prosperity, from the rise of a formidable enemy that would stand ready to destroy it. I regard this, therefore, as referring to the time of the rise of the Papacy, when, *but* for that formidable, corrupting, and destructive power, it might have been hoped that the church would have spread all over the world. In regard to the *rise* of that power, see all that I have to say, or can say, in the Notes on Da. vii. 24–28.

3. *And there appeared another wonder in heaven.* Represented as in heaven. See Notes on ver. 1. That is, he saw this as occurring *at the time* when the church was thus about to increase. ¶ *And behold a great red dragon.* The word rendered *dragon*—δράκων—occurs, in the New Testament, only in the book of Revelation, where it is uniformly rendered as here—*dragon:* ch. xii. 3, 4, 7, 9, 13, 16, 17; xiii. 2, 4, 11; xvi. 13; xx. 2. In all these places there is reference to the same thing. The word properly means a large serpent; and the allusion in the word commonly is to some serpent, perhaps such as the anaconda, that resides in a desert or wilderness. See a full account of the ideas that prevailed in ancient times respecting the dragon, in Bochart, *Hieroz.* lib. iii. cap. xiv., vol. ii. pp. 428–440. There was much that was fabulous respecting this monster, and many notions were attached to the dragon which did not exist in reality, and which were ascribed to it by the imagination at a time when natural history was little understood. The characteristics ascribed to the dragon, according to Bochart, are, that it was distinguished (*a*) for its vast size; (*b*) that it had something like a beard or dew-lap; (*c*) that it had three rows of teeth; (*d*) that *its* colour was black,

red, yellow, or ashy; (*e*) that it had a wide mouth; (*f*) that in its breathing it not only drew in the air, but also birds that were flying over it; and (*g*) that its hiss was terrible. Occasionally, also, feet and wings were attributed to the dragon, and sometimes a lofty crest. The dragon, according to Bochart, was supposed to inhabit waste places and solitudes (comp. Notes on Is. xiii. 22), and it became, therefore, an object of great terror. It is probable that the original of this was a huge serpent, and that all the other circumstances were added by the imagination. The prevailing ideas in regard to it, however, should be borne in mind, in order to see the force and propriety of the use of the word by John. Two special characteristics are stated by John in the general description of the dragon: one is, its *red colour;* the other, that it was *great.* In regard to the former, as above mentioned, the dragon was supposed to be black, red, yellow, or ashy. See the authorities referred to in Bochart, *ut sup.*, pp. 435, 436. There was doubtless a reason why the one seen by John should be represented as *red.* As to the other characteristic—*great*—the idea is that it was a huge monster, and this would properly refer to some mighty, terrible power which would be properly symbolized by such a monster. ¶ *Having seven heads.* It was not unusual to attribute many heads to monsters, especially to fabulous monsters, and these greatly increased the terror of the animal. "Thus Cerberus usually has three heads assigned to him; but Hesiod (*Theog.* 312) assigns him fifty, and Horace (Ode II. 13, 34) one hundred. So the Hydra of the Lake Lerna, killed by Hercules, had fifty heads (Virg. *Æn.* vi. 576); and in Kiddushim, fol. 29, 2, Rabbi Achse is said to have seen a demon like a dragon with seven heads" (Professor Stuart, *in loco*). The seven heads would somehow denote *power*, or seats of power. Such a number of heads increase the terribleness, and, as it were, the *vitality* of the monster. What is here represented would be *as* terrible and formidable as such a monster; or such a monster would appropriately represent what was designed to be symbolized here. The number seven *may* be used here "as a perfect number," or merely to heighten the terror of the image; but it is more natural to suppose that there would be something in what is here represented which would lay the foundation for the use of this number. There would be something either in the *origin* of the power; or in the union of various powers now combined in the one represented by the dragon; or in the *seat* of the power, which this would properly symbolize. Comp. Notes on Da. vii. 6. ¶ *And ten horns.* Emblems of power, denoting that, in some respects, there were *ten* powers combined in this one. See Notes on Da. vii. 7, 8, 20, 24. There can be little doubt that John had those passages of Daniel in his eye, and perhaps as little that the reference is to the same thing. The meaning is, that, in some respects, there would be a tenfold origin or division of the power represented by the dragon. ¶ *And seven crowns upon his heads.* Gr., *diadems*. See Notes on ch. ix. 7. There is a reference here to some *kingly* power, and doubtless John had some kingdom or sovereignty in his eye that would be properly symbolized in this manner. The method in which these heads and horns were arranged on the dragon is not stated, and is not material. All that is necessary in the explanation is, that there was *something* in the power referred to that would be properly represented by the seven heads, and *something* by the ten horns.

In the application of this, it will be necessary to inquire what was properly symbolized by these representations, and to refer again to these particulars with this view.

(*a*) *The dragon.* This is explained in ver. 9 of this chapter: "And the great dragon was cast out, that old serpent, called the Devil, and Satan, which deceiveth the whole world." So again, ch. xx. 2, "And he laid hold on the dragon, that old serpent, which is the Devil." Comp. Bochart, *Hieroz.* ii. pp. 439, 440. There can be no doubt, therefore, that the reference here is to Satan, considered as the enemy of God, and the enemy of the peace of man, and especially as giving origin and form to some mighty power that would threaten the existence of the church.

(*b*) *Great.* This will well describe the power of Satan as originating the organizations that were engaged for so long a time in persecuting the church, and endeavouring to destroy it. It was a work of vast power, controlling kings and nations for ages, and could have been accomplished only by one to whom the appellation here used could be given.

(c) *Red.* This, too, is an appellation properly applied here to the dragon, or Satan, considered as the enemy of the church, and as originating this persecuting power, either (1) because it well represents the bloody persecutions that would ensue, or (2) because this would be the favourite *colour* by which this power would be manifest. Comp. ch. xvii. 3, 4; xviii. 12, 16.

(d) *The seven heads.* There was, doubtless, as above remarked, something significant in these heads, as referring to the power designed to be represented. On the supposition that this refers to Rome, or to the power of Satan as *manifested* by Roman persecution, there can be no difficulty in the application; and, indeed, it is such an image as the writer would naturally use on the supposition that it had such a designed reference. Rome was built, as is well known, on seven hills (comp. Notes on ch. x. 3), and was called the seven-hilled city (*Septicollis*), from having been originally built on seven hills, though subsequently three hills were added, making the whole number ten. See Eschenburg, *Manual of Classical Literature*, p. 1, § 53. Thus Ovid:—

"Sed quæ de septem totum circumspicit orbem
Montibus, imperii Romæ Deûmque locus."

Horace:—

"Dis quibus septem placuere colles."

Propertius:—

"Septem urbs alta jugis, toti quæ præsidet orbi."

Tertullian:—"I appeal to the citizens of Rome, the populace that dwell on the seven hills" (Apol. 35). And again, Jerome to Marcella, when urging her to quit Rome for Bethlehem: "Read what is said in the Apocalypse of the seven hills," &c. The situation of the city, if that was destined to be represented by the dragon, would naturally suggest the idea of the seven-headed monster. Comp. Notes on ch. xiii. The explanation which is here given of the meaning of the "seven heads" is, in fact, one that is given in the book of Revelation itself, and there can be no danger of error in this part of the interpretation. See ch. xvii. 9: "The seven heads are seven mountains, on which the woman sitteth." Comp. ver. 18.

(e) *The ten horns.* These were emblems of power, denoting that in reference to that power there were, in some respects, *ten* sources. The same thing is referred to here which is in Da. vii. 7, 8, 20, 24. See the Notes on Da. vii. 24, where this subject is fully considered. The creature that John saw was indeed a *monster*, and we are not to expect entire congruity in the details. It is sufficient that the main idea is preserved, and that would be, if the reference was to Rome considered as the place where the energy of Satan, as opposed to God and the church, was centered.

(f) *The seven crowns.* This would merely denote that kingly or royal authority was claimed.

The *general* interpretation which refers this vision to Rome may receive confirmation from the fact that the *dragon* was at one time the Roman standard, as is represented by the annexed engraving from Montfauçon. Ammianus Marcellinus (xvi. 10) thus describes

Roman Standard.

this standard: "The dragon was covered with purple cloth, and fastened to the end of a pike gilt and adorned with precious stones. It opened its wide throat, and the wind blew through it; and it hissed as if in a rage, with its tail floating in several folds through the air." He elsewhere often gives it the epithet of *purpureus*—purple-red: *purpureum signum draconis*, &c. With

4 And his *d*tail drew the third part of the stars of heaven, and did cast them to the earth: and

*d* Is.9.15.

the dragon stood before the woman which was ready to be delivered, for to devour her child as soon as it was born.

---

this the description of Claudian well agrees also:—

"Hi volucres tollent aquilas; hi picta draconum
Colla levant: multumque tumet per nubila serpens,
Iratus stimulante noto, vivitque receptis
Flatibus, et vario mentitur sibila flatu."

The dragon was first used as an ensign near the close of the second century of the Christian era, and it was not until the third century that its use had become common; and the reference here, according to this fact, would be to that period of the Roman power when this had become a common standard, and when the applicability of this image would be readily understood. It is simply *Rome* that is referred to —Rome, the great agent of accomplishing the purposes of Satan towards the church. The *eagle* was the common Roman ensign in the time of the republic, and in the earlier periods of the empire; but in later periods the dragon became also a standard as common and as well known as the eagle. "In the third century it had become almost as notorious among Roman ensigns as the *eagle* itself; and is in the fourth century noted by Prudentius, Vegetius, Chrysostom, Ammianus, &c.; in the fifth, by Claudian and others" (Elliott).

4. *And his tail drew the third part of the stars of heaven.* The word rendered *drew* — σύρω — means to draw, drag, haul. Professor Stuart renders it "drew along;" and explains it as meaning that "the danger is represented as being in the upper region of the air, so that his tail may be supposed to interfere with and sweep down the stars, which, as viewed by the ancients, were all set in the visible expanse or welkin." So Daniel (viii. 10), speaking of the little horn, says that "it waxed great, even to the host of heaven, and it cast down some of the host and of the stars to the ground." See Notes on that passage. The main idea here undoubtedly is that of *power*, and the object of John is to show that the power of the dragon was *as if* it extended to the stars, and *as if* it dragged down a third part of them to the earth, or swept them away with its tail, leaving two-thirds unaffected. A power that would sweep them *all* away would be universal; a power that would sweep away one-third only would represent a dominion of that extent only. The dragon is represented as floating in the air—a monster extended along the sky—and one-third of the whole expanse was subject to his control. Suppose, then, that the dragon here was designed to represent the Roman Pagan power; suppose that it referred to that power about to engage in the work of persecution, and at a time when the church was about to be greatly enlarged, and to fill the world; suppose that it referred to a time when but one-third part of the Roman world was subject to Pagan influence, and the remaining two-thirds were, for some cause, safe from this influence,—all the conditions here referred to would be fulfilled. Now it so happens that at a time when the "dragon" had become a common standard in the Roman armies, and had in some measure superseded the eagle, a state of things *did* exist which well corresponds with this representation. There were times under the emperors when, in a considerable part of the empire, after the establishment of Christianity, the church enjoyed protection, and the Christian religion was tolerated, while in other parts Paganism still prevailed, and waged a bitter warfare with the church. "Twice, at least, before the Roman empire became divided permanently into the two parts, the Eastern and the Western, there was a *tripartite* division of the empire. The first occurred A.D. 311, when it was divided between Constantine, Licinius, and Maximin; the other A.D. 337, on the death of Constantine, when it was divided between his three sons, Constantine, Constans, and Constantius." "In two-thirds of the empire, embracing its whole European and African territory, Christians enjoyed toleration; in the other, or Asiatic portion, they were still, after a brief and uncertain respite, exposed to persecution, in all its bitterness and cruelty as before" (Elliott). I do not deem it absolutely essential, however, in order to a *fair* exposition of this passage, that we should

A.D. 96.]  CHAPTER XII.  307

5 And *she brought forth a man child, ᶠ who was to rule all nations
*e* Is.7.14.   *f* Ps.2.9.

with a rod of iron: and her child was caught up unto God, and *to* his throne.

be able to refer to minute historical facts with names and dates. A sufficient fulfilment is found if there was a period when the church, bright, glorious, and prosperous, was apparently about to become greatly enlarged, but when the monstrous Pagan power still held its sway over a considerable part of the world, exposing the church to persecution. Even after the establishment of the church in the empire, and the favour shown to it by the Roman government, it was long before the Pagan power ceased to rage, and before the church could be regarded as safe. ¶ *And the dragon stood before the woman which was ready to be delivered, for to devour her child.* To prevent the increase and spread of the church in the world.

5. *And she brought forth a man child.* Representing, according to the view above taken, the church in its increase and prosperity—*as if* a child were born that was to rule over all nations. See Notes on ver. 2. ¶ *Who was to rule all nations.* That is, according to this view, the church thus represented was destined to reign in all the earth, or all the earth was to become subject to its laws. Comp. Notes on Da. vii. 13, 14. ¶ *With a rod of iron.* The language here used is derived from Ps. ii. 9: "Thou shalt break them with a rod of iron." The form of the expression here used, "who was to rule"—ὃς μέλλει ποιμαίνειν—is derived from the Septuagint translation of the Psalm—ποιμανεῖς —"thou shalt *rule* them;" to wit, as a shepherd does his flock. The reference is to such control as a shepherd employs in relation to his flock—protecting, guarding, and defending them, with the idea that the flock is under his care; and, on the supposition that this refers to the church, it means that it would yet have the ascendency or the dominion over the earth. The meaning in the phrase, "with a rod of iron," is, that the dominion would be strong or irresistible—as an iron sceptre is one that cannot be broken or resisted. The thoughts here expressed, therefore, are, (*a*) that the church would become universal—or that the principles of truth and righteousness would prevail everywhere on the earth; (*b*) that the ascendency of religion over the understandings and consciences of men would be irresistible—as firm as a government administered under a sceptre of iron; yet (*c*) that it would be rather of a character of protection than of force or violence, like the sway which a shepherd wields over his flock. I understand the "man child" here, therefore, to refer to the church in its increase under the Messiah, and the idea to be, that that church was, at the time referred to, about to be enlarged, and that, though its increase was opposed, yet it was destined ultimately to assert a mild sway over all the world. The *time* here referred to would seem to be some period in the early history of the church when religion was likely to be rapidly propagated, and when it was opposed and retarded by violent persecution—perhaps the last of the persecutions under the Pagan Roman empire. ¶ *And her child was caught up unto God.* This is evidently a symbolical representation. Some event was to occur, or some divine interposition was to take place, *as if* the child thus born were caught up from the earth to save it from death, and was rendered secure by being in the presence of God, and near his throne. It cannot be supposed that anything like this would *literally* occur. Any divine interposition to protect the church in its increase, or to save it from being destroyed by the dragon — the fierce Pagan power—would be properly represented by this. Why may we not suppose the reference to be to the time of Constantine, when the church came under his protection; when it was effectually and finally saved from Pagan persecution; when it was rendered safe from the enemy that waited to destroy it? On the supposition that this refers to an increasing but endangered church, in whose defence a civil power was raised up, exalting Christianity to the throne, and protecting it from danger, this would be well represented by the child caught up to heaven. This view may derive confirmation from some well-known facts in history. The old Pagan power was concentrated in Maximin, who was emperor from the Nile to the Bosphorus, and who raged against the gospel and the church "with Satanic enmity." "Infuriate at the now imminent prospect of the Christian body

6 And the woman fled into the wilderness, where she hath a place prepared of God, that they should feed her there *a* a thousand two hundred *and* threescore days.

*g* ch. 11.3.

attaining establishment in the empire, Maximin renewed the persecution against Christians within the limits of his own dominion; prohibiting their assemblies, and degrading, and even killing their bishops." Comp. Gibbon, i. 325, 326. The last struggle of Pagan Rome to destroy the church by persecution, before the triumph of Constantine, and the public establishment of the Christian religion, might be well represented by the attempt of the dragon to destroy the child; and the safety of the church, and its complete deliverance from Pagan persecution, by the symbol of a child caught up to heaven, and placed near the throne of God. The persecution under Maximin was the last struggle of Paganism to retain the supremacy, and to crush Christianity in the empire. "Before the decisive battle," says Milner, "Maximin vowed to Jupiter that, if victorious, he would abolish the Christian name. The contest between Jehovah and Jupiter was now at its height, and drawing to a crisis." The result was the defeat and death of Maximin, and the termination of the efforts of Paganism to destroy Christianity by force. Respecting this event, Mr. Gibbon remarks, "The defeat and death of Maximin soon delivered the church from the last and most implacable of her enemies," i. 326. Christianity was, after that, rendered safe from Pagan persecution. Mr. Gibbon says, "The gratitude of the church has exalted the virtues of the generous patron *who seated Christianity on the throne of the Roman world.*" If, however, it should be regarded as a forced and fanciful interpretation to suppose that the passage before us refers to this *specific* event, yet the *general* circumstances of the times would furnish a fulfilment of what is here said. (*a*) The church would be well represented by the beautiful woman. (*b*) The prospect of its increase and universal dominion would be well represented by the birth of the child. (*c*) The furious opposing Pagan power would be well represented by the dragon in its attempts to destroy the child. (*d*) The safety of the church would be well represented by the symbol of the child caught up to God, and placed near his throne.

6. *And the woman.* The woman representing the church. Notes, ver. 1. ¶ *Fled.* That is, she fled in the manner, and at the time, stated in ver. 14. John here evidently anticipates, by a summary statement, what he relates more in detail in ver. 14-17. He had referred (ver. 2-5) to what occurred to the child in its persecutions, and he here alludes, in general, to what befell the true church as compelled to flee into obscurity and safety. Having briefly referred to this, the writer (ver. 7-13) gives an account of the efforts of Satan consequent on the removal of the child to heaven. ¶ *Into the wilderness.* On the meaning of the word *wilderness* in the New Testament, see Notes on Mat. iii. 1. It means a desert place, a place where there are few or no inhabitants; a place, therefore, where one might be concealed and unknown—remote from the habitations and the observations of men. This would well represent the fact, that the true church became for a time obscure and unknown —*as if* it had fled away from the habitations of men, and had retired to the solitude and loneliness of a desert. Yet even there (ver. 14, 16) it would be mysteriously nourished, though seemingly driven out into wastes and solitudes, and having its abode among the rocks and sands of a desert. ¶ *Where she hath a place prepared of God.* A place where she might be safe, and might be kept alive. The meaning is, that during that time the true church, though obscure and almost unknown, would be the object of the divine protection and care—a beautiful representation of the church during the corruptions of the Papacy and the darkness of the middle ages. ¶ *That they should feed her.* That they should *nourish* or *sustain* her—τρέφωσιν—to wit, as specified in ver. 14, 16. Those who were to do this, represented by the word "*they,*" are not particularly mentioned, and the simple idea is that she *would be* nourished during that time. That is, stripped of the figure, the church during that time would find true friends, and would be kept alive. It is hardly necessary to say that this has, in fact, occurred in the darkest periods of the history of the church. ¶ *A thousand two hundred* and *threescore days.* That

## CHAPTER XII.

**7 And there was war in heaven: Michael and his angels fought against the dragon; and the dragon fought and his angels.**

is, regarding these as prophetic days, in which a day denotes a year, twelve hundred and sixty years. The same period evidently is referred to in ver. 14, in the words "for a time, and times, and half a time." And the same period is undoubtedly referred to in Da. vii. 25: "And they shall be given into his hand until a time, and times, and the dividing of time." For a full consideration of the meaning of this language, and its application to the Papacy, see Notes on Da. vii. 25. The full investigation there made of the meaning and application of the language renders its consideration here unnecessary. I regard it here, as I do there, as referring to the proper continuance of the Papal power, during which the true church would remain in comparative obscurity, as if driven into a desert. Comp. Notes on ch. xi. 2. The meaning here is, that during that period the true church would not become wholly extinct. It would have an existence upon the earth, but its final triumph would be reserved for the time when this great enemy should be finally overthrown. Comp. Notes on ver. 14-17.

7. *And there was war in heaven.* There was a state of things existing in regard to the woman and the child—the church in the condition in which it would then be—which would be well represented by a war in heaven; that is, by a conflict between the powers of good and evil, of light and darkness. Of course it is not necessary to understand this *literally*, any more than the other symbolical representations in the book. All that is meant is, that a vision passed before the mind of John *as if* there was a conflict, in regard to the church, between the angels in heaven and Satan. There is a vision of the persecuted church—of the woman fleeing into the desert—and the course of the narrative is here interrupted by going back (ver. 7-13) to describe the conflict which led to this result, and the fact that Satan, as it were cast out of heaven, and unable to achieve a victory there, was suffered to vent his malice against the church on earth. The seat of this warfare is said to be heaven. This language sometimes refers to heaven as it appears to us—the sky—the upper regions of the atmosphere, and some have supposed that that was the place of the contest. But the language in ch. xi. 19, xii. 1 (see Notes on those places), would rather lead us to refer it to heaven considered as lying beyond the sky. This accords, too, with other representations in the Bible, where Satan is described as appearing before God, and among the sons of God. See Notes on Job i. 6. Of course this is not to be understood as a *real* transaction, but as a symbolical representation of the contest between good and evil—*as if* there was a war waged in heaven between Satan and the leader of the heavenly hosts. ¶ *Michael.* There have been very various opinions as to who Michael is. Many Protestant interpreters have supposed that Christ is meant. The reasons usually alleged for this opinion, many of which are very fanciful, may be seen in Hengstenberg (*Die Offenbarung des heiliges Johannes*), i. 611-622. The reference to *Michael* here is probably derived from Da. x. 13; xii. 1. In those places he is represented as the guardian angel of the people of God; and it is in this sense, I apprehend, that the passage is to be understood here. There is no evidence in the name itself, or in the circumstances referred to, that Christ is intended; and if he had been, it is inconceivable why he was not referred to by his own name, or by some of the usual appellations which John gives him. Michael, the archangel, is here represented as the guardian of the church, and as contending against Satan for its protection. Comp. Notes on Da. x. 13. This representation accords with the usual statements in the Bible respecting the interposition of the angels in behalf of the church (see Notes on He. i. 14), and is one which cannot be proved to be unfounded. All the analogies which throw any light on the subject, as well as the uniform statements of the Bible, lead us to suppose that good beings of other worlds feel an interest in the welfare of the redeemed church below. ¶ *And his angels.* The angels under him. Michael is represented as the archangel, and all the statements in the Bible suppose that the heavenly hosts are distributed into different ranks and orders. See Notes on Jude 9; Ep. i. 21. If Satan is permitted to make war against the church, there is no improbability in supposing that, in those higher regions where

8 And prevailed not; neither was their place found any more in heaven.

9 And the great dragon was cast out, that old *h*serpent, called

*h* Ge.3.1,4.

the *i*Devil, and *k*Satan, which deceiveth the whole world; he was cast out into the earth, and his angels were cast out with him.

i Jn.8.44.     k Zec.3.1.

---

the war is carried on, and in those aspects of it which lie beyond the power and the knowledge of man, good angels should be employed to defeat his plans. ¶ *Fought.* See Notes on Jude 9. ¶ *Against the dragon.* Against Satan. Notes, ver. 3. ¶ *And the dragon fought and his angels.* That is, the master-spirit — Satan, and those under him. See Notes on Mat. iv. 1. Of the nature of this warfare nothing is definitely stated. Its whole sphere lies beyond mortal vision, and is carried on in a manner of which we can have little conception. What weapons Satan may use to destroy the church, and in what way his efforts may be counteracted by holy angels, are points on which we can have little knowledge. It is sufficient to know that the fact of such a struggle is not improbable, and that Satan is successfully resisted by the leader of the heavenly host.

8. *And prevailed not.* Satan and his angels failed in their purpose. ¶ *Neither was their place found any more in heaven.* They were cast out, and were seen there no more. The idea is, that they were defeated and driven away, though for a time they were suffered to carry on the warfare elsewhere.

9. *And the great dragon was cast out.* See Notes on ver. 3. That there may be an allusion in the *language* here to what actually occurred in some far-distant period of the past, when Satan was ejected from heaven, there can be no reason to doubt. Our Saviour seems to refer to such an event in the language which he uses when he says (Lu. x. 18), "I beheld Satan as lightning fall from heaven;" and Jude, perhaps (ver. 6), may refer to the same event. All that we know on the subject leads us to suppose that at some time there was a revolt among the angels, and that the rebellious part were cast out of heaven, for an allusion to this is not unfrequent in the Scriptures. Still the event *here* referred to is a symbolical representation of what could occur at a later period, when the church would be about to spread and be triumphant, and when Satan would wage a deadly war against it. That opposition would be *as if* he made war on Michael the archangel, and the heavenly hosts, and his failure would be as great *as if* he were vanquished and cast out of heaven. ¶ *That old serpent.* This doubtless refers to the serpent that deceived Eve (Ge. iii. 1-11; Re. xx. 2; comp. Notes on 2 Co. xi. 3); and this passage may be adduced as a proof that the real tempter of Eve was the devil, who assumed the form of a serpent. The word *old* here refers to the fact that his appearance on earth was at an early stage of the world's history, and that he had long been employed in the work which is here attributed to him — that of opposing the church. ¶ *Called the Devil.* To whom the name *Devil* is given. That is, this is the same being that is elsewhere and commonly known by that name. See Notes on Mat. iv. 1. ¶ *And Satan.* Another name given to the same being—a name, like the other, designed to refer to something in his character. See it explained in the Notes on Job i. 6. ¶ *Which deceiveth the whole world.* Whose character is that of a deceiver; whose agency extends over all the earth. See Notes on Jn. viii. 44, and 1 Jn. v. 19. ¶ *He was cast out into the earth.* That is, he was not suffered to pursue his designs in heaven, but was cast down to the earth, where he is permitted for a time to carry on his warfare against the church. According to the interpretation proposed above, this refers to the period when there were indications that God was about to set up his kingdom on the earth. The *language*, however, is such as would be used on the supposition that there had been, at some period, a rebellion in heaven, and that Satan and his followers had been cast out to return there no more. It is difficult to explain this language except on that supposition; and such a supposition is, in itself, no more improbable than the apostasy and rebellion of man. ¶ *And his angels were cast out with him.* They shared the lot of their leader. As applicable to the state of things to which this refers, the meaning is, that *all* were overthrown; that no enemy of the church would remain

10 And I heard a loud voice saying in heaven, *Now is come salvation, and strength, and the kingdom of our God, and the power of his Christ: for the accuser of our brethren is cast down, which accused them before our God day and night.

*l* ch.11.15.

unsubdued; that the victory would be final and complete. As applicable to the event from which the language is supposed to have been derived—the revolt in heaven—the meaning is, that the followers in the revolt shared the lot of the leader, and that all who rebelled were ejected from heaven. The first and the only revolt in heaven was quelled; and the result furnished to the universe an impressive proof that none who rebelled there would be forgiven — that apostasy so near the throne could not be pardoned.

10. *And I heard a loud voice saying in heaven.* The great enemy was expelled; the cause of God and truth was triumphant; and the conquering hosts united in celebrating the victory. This representation of a song, consequent on victory, is in accordance with the usual representations in the Bible. See the song of Moses at the Red Sea, Ex. xv.; the song of Deborah, Ju. v.; the song of David when the Lord had delivered him out of the hand of all his enemies, 2 Sa. xxii.; and Is. xii., xxv. On no occasion could such a song be more appropriate than on the complete routing and discomfiture of Satan and his rebellious hosts. Viewed in reference to the *time* here symbolized, this would relate to the certain triumph of the church and of truth on the earth; in reference to the *language*, there is an allusion to the joy and triumph of the heavenly hosts when Satan and his apostate legions were expelled. ¶ *Now is come salvation.* That is, complete deliverance from the power of Satan. ¶ *And strength.* That is, now is the mighty power of God manifested in casting down and subduing the great enemy of the church. ¶ *And the kingdom of our God.* The reign of our God. See Notes on Mat. iii. 2. That is now established among men, and God will henceforward rule. This refers to the certain ultimate triumph of his cause in the world. ¶ *And the power of his Christ.* His anointed; that is, the kingdom of Christ as the Messiah, or as anointed and set apart to rule over the world. See Notes on Mat. i. 1. ¶ *For the accuser of our brethren is cast down.* The phrase "*our brethren*" shows by whom this song is celebrated. It is sung in heaven; but it is by those who belonged to the redeemed church, and whose brethren were still suffering persecution and trial on the earth. It shows the tenderness of the tie which unites all the redeemed as brethren, whether on earth or in heaven; and it shows the interest which they "who have passed the flood" have in the trials, the sorrows, and the triumphs of those who are still upon the earth. We have here another appellation given to the great enemy--"accuser of the brethren." The word here used—*κατήγορος*, in later editions of the New Testament *κατήγωρ*—means properly *an accuser*, one who blames another, or charges another with crime. The word occurs in Jn. viii. 10; Ac. xxiii. 30, 35; xxiv. 8; xxv. 16, 18; Re. xii. 10, in all which places it is rendered *accuser* or *accusers*, though only in the latter place applied to Satan. The verb frequently occurs, Mat. xii. 10; xxvii. 12; Mar. iii. 2; xv. 3, *et al.* The description of Satan as an *accuser* accords with the opinion of the ancient Hebrews in regard to his character. Thus he is represented in Job i. 9-11; ii. 4, 5; Zec. iii. 1, 2; 1 Ch. xxi. 1. The phrase "of the brethren" refers to Christians, or to the people of God; and the meaning here is, that one of the characteristics of Satan—a characteristic so well known as to make it proper to designate him by it—is that he is an *accuser* of the righteous; that he is employed in bringing against them charges affecting their character and destroying their influence. The propriety of this appellation cannot be doubted. It is, as it has always been, one of the characteristics of Satan—one of the means by which he keeps up his influence in the world—to bring accusations against the people of God. Thus, under his suggestions, and by his agents, they are charged with hypocrisy; with insincerity; with being influenced by bad motives; with pursuing sinister designs under the cloak of religion; with secret vices and crimes. Thus it was that the martyrs were accused; thus it is that unfounded accusations are often brought against

11 And they ᵐovercame him by the blood of the Lamb, and by the word of their testimony; and ⁿthey loved not their lives unto the death.

m Ro.8.33,37.
n Lu.14.26.

ministers of the gospel, palsying their power and diminishing their influence, or that when a professed Christian falls the church is made to suffer by an effort to cast suspicion on all who bear the Christian name. Perhaps the most skilful thing that Satan does, and the thing by which he most contributes to diminish the influence of the church, is in thus causing "accusations" to be brought against the people of God. ¶ *Is cast down.* The period here referred to was, doubtless, the time when the church was about to be established and to flourish in the world, and when accusations would be brought against Christians by various classes of calumniators and informers. It is well known that in the early ages of Christianity crimes of the most horrid nature were charged on Christians, and that it was by these slanders that the effort was made to prevent the extension of the Christian church. ¶ *Which accused them before our God.* See Notes on Job i. 9, 10. The meaning is, that he accused them, as it were, in the very presence of God. ¶ *Day and night.* He never ceased bringing these accusations, and sought by the perseverance and constancy with which they were urged to convince the world that there was no sincerity in the church and no reality in religion.

11. *And they overcame him.* That is, he was foiled in his attempt thus to destroy the church. The reference here, undoubtedly, is primarily to the martyr age and to the martyr spirit; and the meaning is, that religion had not become extinct by these accusations, as Satan hoped it would be, but lived and triumphed. By their holy lives, by their faithful testimony, by their patient sufferings, they showed that all these accusations were false, and that the religion which they professed was from God, and thus in fact gained a victory over their accuser. Instead of being themselves subdued, Satan himself was vanquished, and the world was constrained to acknowledge that the persecuted religion had a heavenly origin. No design was ever more ineffectual than that of crushing the church by persecution, no victory was ever more signal than that which was gained when it could be said that "the blood of the martyrs is the seed of the church." ¶ *By the blood of the Lamb.* The Lord Jesus—the Lamb of God. Notes, ch. v. 6; comp. Notes on Jn. i. 29. The blood of Christ was that by which they were redeemed, and it was in virtue of the efficacy of the atonement that they were enabled to achieve the victory. Comp. Notes on Phi. iv. 13. Christ himself achieved a victory over Satan by his death (see Notes on Col. ii. 15; He. ii. 15), and it is in virtue of the victory which he thus achieved that we are now able to triumph over our great foe.

" I ask them whence their victory came.
They, with united breath,
Ascribe their conquest to the Lamb,
Their triumph to his death."

¶ *And by the word of their testimony.* The faithful testimony which they bore to the truth. That is, they adhered to the truth in their sufferings, they declared their belief in it, even in the pains of martyrdom; and it was by this that they overcame the great enemy—that is, by this that the belief in the gospel was established and maintained in the world. The reference here is to the effects of persecution and to the efforts of Satan to drive religion from the world by persecution. John says that the result as he saw it in vision was, that the persecuted church bore a faithful testimony to the truth, and that the great enemy was overcome. ¶ *And they loved not their lives unto the death.* They did not so love their lives that they were unwilling to die as martyrs. They did not shrink back when threatened with death, but remained firm in their attachment to their Saviour, and left their dying testimony to the truth and power of religion. It was by these means that Christianity was established in the world, and John, in the scene before us, saw it thus triumphant, and saw the angels and the redeemed in heaven celebrating the triumph. The result of the attempts to destroy the Christian religion by persecution demonstrated that it was to triumph. No more mighty power could be employed to crush it than was employed by the Roman emperors; and when it was seen that Christianity could survive those efforts to crush it it was cer-

## CHAPTER XII.

12 Therefore° rejoice, ye heavens, and ye that dwell in them. Woe\^p to the inhabiters of the earth, and of the sea! for the devil is come down unto you, having great wrath, because ᵍ he knoweth that he hath but a short time.

13 And when the dragon saw that he was cast unto the earth, he persecuted the woman which brought forth the man *child*.

14 And to the woman were given two ʳ wings of a great eagle, that she might fly into the wilderness, into her place, where she is nourished for a time, and times, and half a time, from the face of the serpent.

o Ps.96.11; Is.49.13.   p ch.8.13.   q ch.10.6.   r Is.40.31.

---

tain that it was destined to live for ever.

12. *Therefore rejoice, ye heavens.* It is not unusual in the Scriptures to call on the heavens and the earth to sympathize with the events that occur. Comp. Notes on Is. i. 2. Here the heavens are called on to rejoice because of the signal victory which it was seen would be achieved over the great enemy. Heaven itself was secure from any further rebellion or invasion, and the foundation was laid for a final victory over Satan everywhere. ¶ *And ye that dwell in them.* The angels and the redeemed. This is an instance of the sympathy of the heavenly inhabitants—the unfallen and holy beings before the throne—with the church on earth, and with all that may affect its welfare. Compare Notes on 1 Pe. i. 12. ¶ *Woe to the inhabiters of the earth.* This is not an imprecation, or a wish that woe *might* come upon them, but a prediction that it *would*. The meaning is this: Satan would ultimately be entirely overcome—a fact that was symbolized by his being cast out of heaven; but there would be still temporary war upon the earth, as if he were permitted to roam over the world for a time and to spread woe and sorrow there. ¶ *And of the sea.* Those who inhabit the islands of the sea and those who are engaged in commerce. The meaning is, that the world as such would have occasion to mourn—the dwellers both on the land and on the sea. ¶ *For the devil is come down unto you.* As if cast out of heaven. ¶ *Having great wrath.* Wrath shown by the symbolical war with Michael and his angels (ver. 7); wrath increased and inflamed because he has been discomfited; wrath the more concentrated because he knows that his time is limited. ¶ *Because he knoweth that he hath but a short time.* That is, he knows that the time is limited in which he will be permitted to wage war with the saints on the earth. There is allu-

sion elsewhere to the fact that the time of Satan is limited, and that he is apprised of that. Thus in Mat. viii. 29, "Art thou come hither to torment us *before the time?*" See Notes on that passage. Within that limited space, Satan knows that he must do all that he ever can do to destroy souls, and to spread woe through the earth, and hence it is not unnatural that he should be represented as excited to deeper wrath, and as rousing all his energy to destroy the church.

13. *And when the dragon saw that he was cast unto the earth.* That is, when Satan saw that he was doomed to discomfiture and overthrow, *as if* he had been cast out of heaven; when he saw that his efforts must be confined to the earth, and that only for a limited time, he "persecuted the woman," and was more violently enraged against the church on earth. ¶ *He persecuted the woman which brought forth the man child.* See Notes on ver. 5. The child is represented as safe; that is, the ultimate progress and extension of the church was certain. But Satan was permitted still to wage a warfare against the church—represented here by his wrath against the woman, and by her being constrained to flee into the wilderness. It is unnecessary to say that, after the *Pagan* persecutions ceased, and Christianity was firmly established in the empire; after Satan saw that all hope of destroying the church in that manner was at an end, his enmity was vented in another form—in the rise of the Papacy, and in the persecutions under that—an opposition to spiritual religion no less determined and deadly than that which had been waged by Paganism.

14. *And to the woman were given two wings of a great eagle.* The most powerful of birds, and among the most rapid in flight. See Notes on ch. iv. 7. The meaning here is, that the

woman is represented as prepared for a rapid flight; so prepared as to be able to outstrip her pursuer, and to reach a place of safety. Divested of the figure, the sense is, that the church, when exposed to this form of persecution, would be protected *as if* miraculously supplied with wings. ¶ *That she might fly into the wilderness.* There is here a more full description of what is briefly stated in ver. 6. A wilderness or desert is often represented as a place of safety from pursuers. Thus David (1 Sa. xxiii. 14, 15) is represented as fleeing into the wilderness from the persecutions of Saul. So Elijah (1 Ki. xix. 4) fled into the wilderness from the persecutions of Jezebel. The simple idea here is, that the church, in the opposition which would come upon it, would find a refuge. ¶ *Into her place.* A place appointed for her; that is, a place where she could be safe. ¶ *Where she is nourished.* The word here rendered *nourished* is the same — τρέφω — which occurs in ver. 6, and which is there rendered *feed*. It means to feed, nurse, or nourish, as the young of animals (Mat. vi. 26; xxv. 37; Lu. xii. 24; Ac. xii. 20); that is, to sustain by proper food. The meaning here is, that the church would be kept alive. It is not indeed mentioned by whom this would be done, but it is evidently implied that it would be by God. During this long period in which the church would be in obscurity, it would not be suffered to become extinct. Comp. 1 Ki. xvii. 3-6. ¶ *For a time, and times, and half a time.* A year, two years, and half a year; that is, forty-two months (see Notes on ch. xi. 2); or, reckoning the month at thirty days, twelve hundred and sixty days; and regarding these as prophetic days, in which a day stands for a year, twelve hundred and sixty years. For a full discussion of the meaning of this language, see Notes on Da. vii. 25; and Editor's Pref. For the evidence, also, that the time thus specified refers to the Papacy, and to the period of its continuance, see the Notes on that place. The full consideration given to the subject there renders it unnecessary to discuss it here. For it is manifest that there is an allusion here to the passage in Daniel; that the twelve hundred and sixty days refer to the same thing; and that the true explanation must be made in the same way. The main difficulty, as is remarked on the Notes on that passage, is in determining the time when the Papacy properly commenced. If that could be ascertained with certainty, there would be no difficulty in determining when it would come to an end. But though there is considerable uncertainty as to the exact time when it arose, and though different opinions have been entertained on that point, yet it is true that all the periods assigned for the rise of that power lead to the conclusion that the time of its downfall cannot be remote. The meaning in the passage before us is, that during all the time of the continuance of that formidable, persecuting power, the true church would not in fact become extinct. It would be obscure and comparatively unknown, but it would still live. The fulfilment of this is found in the fact, that during all the time here referred to, there has been a true church on the earth. Pure, spiritual religion — the religion of the New Testament — has never been wholly extinct. In the history of the Waldenses, and Albigenses, the Bohemian brethren, and kindred people; in deserts and places of obscurity; among individuals and among small and persecuted sects; here and there in the cases of individuals in monasteries,[*] the true religion has been kept up in the world, as in the days of Elijah God reserved seven thousand men who had not bowed the knee to Baal: and it is possible now for us, with a good degree of certainty, to show, even during the darkest ages, and when Rome seemed to have entirely the ascendency, where the true church was. To find out this, was the great design of the Ecclesiastical History of Milner; it has been done, also, with great learning and skill, by Neander. ¶ *From the face of the serpent.* The dragon—or Satan represented by the dragon. Notes, ver. 3. The reference here is

[*] An affecting instance of this kind—perhaps one of many cases that existed—is mentioned by D'Aubigné (book i. p. 79, Eng. trans.), which came to light on the pulling down, in the year 1776, of an old building that had formed a part of the Carthusian convent at Basle. A poor Carthusian brother, by the name of Martin, had written the following confession, which he had placed in a wooden box, and inclosed in a hole which he had made in the wall of his cell, where it was found:—"O most merciful God, I know that I can only be saved, and satisfy thy righteousness, by the merit, the innocent suffering, and death of thy well-beloved Son. Holy Jesus! my salvation is in thy hands. Thou canst not withdraw the hands of thy love from me; for they have created and redeemed me. Thou hast inscribed my name with a pen of iron in rich mercy, and so as nothing can efface it, on thy side, thy hands, and thy feet," &c.

15 And the serpent cast out of his mouth water as a *flood, after the woman, that he might cause her to be carried away of the flood.

16 And the earth helped the woman, and the earth opened her mouth, and swallowed up the flood

*s* Is. 59. 19.

which the dragon cast out of his mouth.

17 And *t* the dragon was wroth with the woman, and went to make war with the remnant of her seed, which keep the commandments of God, and have the testimony of Jesus Christ.

*t* Ge. 3. 15.

---

to the opposition which Satan makes to the true church under the persecutions and corruptions of the Papacy.

15. *And the serpent cast out of his mouth water as a flood.* This is peculiar and uncommon imagery, and it is not necessary to suppose that anything like this literally occurs in nature. Some serpents are indeed said to eject from their mouths poisonous bile when they are enraged, in order to annoy their pursuers; and some sea-monsters, it is known, spout forth large quantities of water; but the representation here does not seem to be taken from either of those cases. It is the mere product of the imagination, but the sense is clear. The woman is represented as having wings, and as being able thus to escape from the serpent. But, as an expression of his wrath, and as if with the hope of destroying her in her flight by a deluge of water, he is represented as pouring a flood from his mouth, that he might, if possible, sweep her away. The figure here would well represent the continued malice of the Papal body against the true church, in those dark ages when it was sunk in obscurity, and, as it were, driven out into the desert. That malice never slumbered, but was continually manifesting itself in some new form, as if it were the purpose of Papal Rome to sweep it entirely away. ¶ *That he might cause her to be carried away of the flood.* Might cause the church wholly to be destroyed. The truth taught is, that Satan leaves no effort untried to destroy the church.

16. *And the earth helped the woman.* The earth *seemed* to sympathize with the woman in her persecutions, and to interpose to save her. The meaning is, that a state of things would exist in regard to the church thus driven into obscurity, which would be well represented by what is here said to occur. It was cut off from human aid. It was still in danger; still persecuted. In this state it was nourished from some unseen source. It was enabled to avoid the direct attacks of the enemy, and when he attacked it in a new form, a new mode of intervention in its behalf was granted, *as if* the earth should open and swallow up a flood of water. We are not, therefore, to look for any *literal* fulfilment of this, as if the earth interposed in some marvellous way to aid the church. The sense is, that, *in* that state of obscurity and solitude, the divine interposition was manifested, in an unexpected manner, *as if*, when an impetuous stream was rolling along that threatened to sweep everything away, a chasm should suddenly open in the earth and absorb it. During the dark ages many such interventions occurred, saving the church from utter destruction. Overflowing waters are often in the Scriptures an emblem of mighty enemies. Ps. cxxiv. 2–5, "If it had not been the Lord who was on our side, when men rose up against us; then they had swallowed us up quick, when their wrath was kindled against us: then the waters had overwhelmed us, the stream had gone over our soul: then the proud waters had gone over our soul." Ps. xviii. 16, "He sent from above, he took me, he drew me out of many waters." Je. xlvii. 2, "Behold, waters rise up out of the north, and shall be an overflowing flood, and shall overflow the land," &c. Comp. Je. xlvi. 7, 8, and Notes on Is. viii. 7, 8. ¶ *And the earth opened her mouth.* A chasm was made sufficient to absorb the waters. That is, John saw that the church was safe from this attack, and that, in order to preserve it, there was an interposition as marked and wonderful as if the earth should suddenly open and swallow up a mighty flood.

17. *And the dragon was wroth with the woman.* This wrath had been vented by his persecuting her (ver. 13); by his pursuing her; and by his pouring out the flood of water to sweep her away (ver. 15); and the same wrath was now vented against her children. As he could not reach and destroy the wo-

man herself, he turned his indignation against all who were allied to her. Stripped of the imagery, the meaning is, that as he could not destroy the church as such, he vented his malice against all who were the friends of the church, and endeavoured to destroy them. "The church, as such, he could not destroy; therefore he turned his wrath against individual Christians, to bring as many of them as possible to death" (De Wette). ¶ *And went to make war with the remnant of her seed.* No mention is made before of his persecuting the children of the woman, except his opposition to the "man child" which she bore, ver. 1-4. The "woman" represents the church, and the phrase "the remnant of her seed" must refer to her scattered children, that is, to the scattered members of the church, wherever they could be found. The reference here is to persecutions against individuals, rather than a general persecution against the church itself, and all that is here said would find an ample fulfilment in the vexations and troubles of individuals in the Roman communion in the dark ages, when they evinced the spirit of pure evangelical piety; in the cruelties practised in the Inquisition on individual Christians under the plea that they were heretics; and in the persecutions of such men as Wycliffe, John Huss, and Jerome of Prague. This warfare against individual Christians was continued long in the Papal church, and tens of thousands of true friends of the Saviour suffered every form of cruelty and wrong as the result. ¶ *Which keep the commandments of God.* Who were true Christians. This phrase characterizes correctly those who, in the dark ages, were the friends of God, in the midst of abounding corruption. ¶ *And have the testimony of Jesus Christ.* That is, they bore a faithful testimony to his truth, or were real *martyrs.* See ch. ii. 13.

The scene, then, in this chapter is this: John saw a most beautiful woman, suitably adorned, representing the church as about to be enlarged, and to become triumphant in the earth. Then he saw a great red monster, representing Satan, about to destroy the church: the Pagan power, infuriated, and putting forth its utmost energy for its destruction. He then saw the child caught up into heaven, denoting that the church would be ultimately safe, and would reign over all the world. Another vision appears. It is that of a contest between Michael, the protecting angel of the people of God, and the great foe, in which victory declares in favour of the former, and Satan suffers a discomfiture, *as if* he were cast from heaven to earth. Still, however, he is permitted for a time to carry on a warfare against the church, though certain that he would be ultimately defeated. He puts forth his power, and manifests his hostility, in another form—that of the Papacy—and commences a new opposition against the spiritual church of Christ. The church is, however, safe from *that* attempt to destroy it, for the woman is represented as fleeing to the wilderness beyond the power of the enemy, and is there kept alive. Still filled with rage, though incapable of destroying the true church itself, he turns his wrath, under the form of Papal persecutions, against individual Christians, and endeavours to cut them off in detail.

This is the *general* representation in this chapter, and on the supposition that it was *designed* to represent the various forms of opposition which Satan would make to the church of Christ, under Paganism and the Papacy, it must be admitted, I think, that no more expressive or appropriate symbols could have been chosen. This fact should be allowed to have due influence in confirming the interpretation suggested above; and *if* it be admitted to be a correct interpretation, it is conclusive evidence of the inspiration of the book. Further *details* of this opposition of Satan to the church under the *Papal* form of persecution are made in the subsequent chapters.

## CHAPTER XIII.

### ANALYSIS OF THE CHAPTER.

This chapter is closely connected with ch. xii., which is properly introductory to this and to the subsequent portions of the book to ch. xx. See the Analysis of the Book. The vision in this chapter is of two distinct "beasts," each with peculiar characteristics, yet closely related, deriving their power from a common source; aiding each other in the accomplishment of the same object, and manifestly relating to the same *power* under different forms. To see the design of the chapter, it will be necessary to exhibit the peculiar characteristics of the two "beasts," and

# CHAPTER XIII.

the points in which they resemble each other, and sustain each other.

I. THE CHARACTERISTICS OF THE BEASTS.

A. *The characteristics of the first beast,* ver. 1-10.

(*a*) It comes up out of the sea (ver. 1) —out of the commotion, the agitation of nations—a new power that springs up from those disturbed elements.

(*b*) It has seven heads and ten horns, and upon its horns ten crowns or diadems, ver. 1.

(*c*) In its general form it resembles a leopard; its feet are like those of a bear; its mouth like that of a lion. Its connection with the great "dragon"—with Satan—is indicated by the statement that it derives its "power, and its seat, and its authority" from him (ver. 2)—a striking representation of the fact that the civil or secular Roman power which supported the church of Rome through all its corrupt and bloody progress was the putting forth of the power of Satan on the earth.

(*d*) One of the heads of this beast is "wounded to death"—that is, with a wound that is in itself mortal. This wound is, however, in some way as yet unexplained, so healed that the vitality yet remains, and all the world pays homage to the beast, ver. 3. A blow is aimed at this authority which seems to be fatal; and there is some healing or restorative process by which its power is recovered, and by which the universality of its dominion and influence is again restored.

(*e*) The effect of this is, that the world renders homage really to the "dragon," the source of this power, though *in the form* of adoration of the "beast," ver. 4. That is, while the outward homage is rendered to the "beast," the real worship is that of the "dragon," or Satan. This beast is regarded as (1) *incomparable*--"Who is like unto the 'beast?'" and (2) *invincible*—"Who is able to war with him?"

(*f*) In this form the beast is endowed with a mouth that "speaks great things and blasphemies," ver. 5—that is, the power here referred to is arrogant, and reviles the God of heaven.

(*g*) The time during which he is to continue is "forty and two months"—that is, twelve hundred and sixty days, or twelve hundred and sixty years. See Notes on ch. xi. 2.

(*h*) The characteristics of this beast, and of his dominion, are these:—(1) He opens his mouth in blasphemy against God, and his church, and all holy beings, ver. 6. (2) He makes war with the saints and overcomes them, ver. 7. (3) He asserts his power over all nations, ver. 7. (4) He is worshipped by all that dwell on the earth, whose names are not in the book of life, ver. 8.

(*i*) All are called on to hear—as if the announcement were important for the church, ver. 9.

(*j*) The result or issue of the power represented by this monster, ver. 10. It had led others into captivity, it would itself be made captive; it had been distinguished for slaying others, it would itself feel the power of the sword. Until this is accomplished the patience and faith of the saints must be sorely tried, ver. 10.

B. *The characteristics of the second beast,* ver. 11-18.

(*a*) It comes out of the earth (ver. 11) —having a different origin from the former; not springing from troubled elements, as of nations at strife, but from that which is firm and established —like the solid earth.

(*b*) It has two horns like a lamb, but it speaks as a dragon (ver. 11). It is apparently mild, gentle, lamb-like, and inoffensive; but it is, in fact, arrogant, haughty, and imperative.

(*c*) Its dominion is coextensive with that of the first beast, and the effect of its influence is to induce the world to do homage to the first beast, ver. 12.

(*d*) It has the power of performing great wonders, and particularly of deceiving the world by the "miracles" which it performs. This power is particularly manifested in restoring what might be regarded as an "image" of the beast which was wounded, though not put to death, and by giving life to that image, and causing those to be put to death who will not worship it, ver. 13-15.

(*e*) This beast causes a certain mark to be affixed to all, small and great, and attempts a jurisdiction over all persons, so that none may buy or sell, or engage in any business, who have not the mark affixed to them—that is, the power represented attempts to set up a control over the commerce of the world, ver. 16, 17.

(*f*) The way by which the power here referred to may be known is by some proper application of the number 666. This is stated in an enigmatical form, and yet with such clearness that it is supposed that it would be sufficient to indicate the power here referred to.

## II. POINTS IN WHICH THE TWO BEASTS RESEMBLE OR SUSTAIN EACH OTHER.

It is manifest, on the slightest inspection of the characteristics of the "beasts" referred to in this chapter, that they have a close relation to each other; that, in important respects, the one is designed to sustain the other, and that both are manifestations or embodiments of that one and the same power represented by the "dragon," ver. 4. He is the great original source of power to both, and both are engaged in accomplishing his purposes, and are combined to keep up his dominion over the earth. The points of resemblance which it is very important to notice are the following:—

(1) They have the same origin—that is, they both owe their power to the "dragon," and are designed to keep up his ascendency in human affairs, ch. xii. 3; xiii. 2, 4, 12.

(2) They have the same extent of power and dominion.

### FIRST BEAST.

The world wonders after the beast, ver. 3. They worship the dragon and the beast, ver. 4; and all that dwell upon the earth shall worship him, ver. 8.

### SECOND BEAST.

He exercises all the power of the first beast, ver. 12. He causes the earth and them which dwell therein to worship the first beast, ver. 12. He has power to give life unto the image of the beast, ver. 15. He sets up jurisdiction over the commerce of the world, ver. 16, 17.

(3) They do the same things.

### FIRST BEAST.

The dragon gives power to the beast, ver. 4. There is given unto him a mouth speaking great things and blasphemies, ver. 5. He opens his mouth in blasphemy against God, ver. 6. It is given him to make war with the saints, and to overcome them, ver. 7.

### SECOND BEAST.

He exercises all the power of the first beast, ver. 12. He does great wonders, ver. 13. He makes fire come down from heaven in the sight of men, ver. 13. He performs miracles, ver. 14. He causes that as many as would not worship the first beast should be killed, ver. 15. He claims dominion over all, ver. 16, 17.

(4) The one is the means of healing the wounded head of the other, and of restoring its authority.

### FIRST BEAST.

One of his heads is, as it were, wounded to death: a wound that would be mortal if it were not healed, ver. 3.

### SECOND BEAST.

Has power to heal the wound of the first beast, ver. 12; for it is manifest that the *healing* comes from some influence of the second beast.

(5) The one restores life to the other when dying.

### FIRST BEAST.

Is wounded, ver. 3, and his power manifestly becomes exhausted.

### SECOND BEAST.

Causes an "image" of the first beast—something that should resemble that, or be the same power revived, to be made, and to be worshipped, ver. 15.

(6) They have the same general characteristics.

### FIRST BEAST.

Has a mouth given him to speak great things and blasphemies, ver. 5; opens his mouth in blasphemy, ver. 6; blasphemes the name of God, and his tabernacle, and his people, ver. 6; makes war with the saints and overcomes them, ver. 7.

### SECOND BEAST.

Speaks like a dragon, ver. 11; deceives those that dwell upon the earth, ver. 14; is a persecuting power—causing those who would not worship the image of the first beast to be killed, ver. 15.

From this comparison of the two beasts, the following things are plain: —(1) That the same *general* power is referred to, or that they are both modifications of one general dominion on the earth; having the same origin, having the same locality, and aiming at the same result. (2) It is the same general domination *prolonged*—that is, the one is, in another form, but the *continuation* of the other. (3) The one becomes weak, or is in some way likely to lose its authority and power, and is *revived* by the other—that is, the other restores its waning authority, and sets up substantially the same dominion again over the earth, and causes the same great power to be acknowledged on the earth. (4) The one *runs into* the other; that is, one naturally produces, or is followed by the other. (5) One *sustains* the other. (6) They, therefore, have a very close relation to each other: having the same object; possessing the same general characteristics; and accomplishing substantially the same thing on the earth. What this was, will be better seen after the exposition of the chapter shall have been made. It may be sufficient here to remark, that, on the very face of this statement, it is impossible not to have

## CHAPTER XIII.

A ND I stood upon the sand of the sea, and saw a *a* beast rise

*a* Da.7.2,&c.

the Roman power suggested to the mind, as a mighty persecuting power, in the two forms of the civil and ecclesiastical authority, both having the same origin; aiming at the same object; the one sustaining the other; and both combined to keep up the dominion of the great enemy of God and man upon the earth. It is impossible, also, not to be struck with the resemblance, in many particulars, between this vision and that of Daniel (ch. vii.), and to be impressed with the conviction that they are intended to refer to the same kingdom in general, and to the same events. But this will be made more manifest in the exposition of the chapter.

1. *And I stood upon the sand of the sea.* The sand upon the shore of the sea. That is, he seemed to stand there, and then had a vision of a beast rising out of the waters. The *reason* of this representation may, perhaps, have been that among the ancients the sea was regarded as the appropriate place for the origin of huge and terrible monsters (Professor Stuart, *in loco*). This vision strongly resembles that in Da. vii. 2, seq., where the prophet saw four beasts coming up in succession from the sea. See Notes on that place. In Daniel, the four winds of heaven are described as striving upon the great sea (ver. 2), and the agitated ocean represents the nations in commotion, or in a state of disorder and anarchy, and the four beasts represent four successive kingdoms that would spring up. See Notes on Da. vii. 2. In the passage before us, John indeed describes no storm or tempest; but the sea itself, as compared with the land (see Notes on ver. 11), represents an agitated or unsettled state of things, and we should naturally look for that in the rise of the power here referred to. If the reference be to the civil or secular Roman power that has always appeared in connection with the Papacy, and that has always followed its designs, then it is true that it rose amidst the agitations of the world, and from a state of commotion that might well be represented by the restless ocean. The sea in either case naturally describes a nation or people, for this image is fre- up out of the sea, *b* having seven heads and ten horns, and upon his horns ten crowns, and upon his heads the ¹name of blasphemy.

*b* ch.12.3; 17.3,9,12.   1 or, *names.*

quently so employed in the Scriptures. Comp., as above, Da. vii. 2, and Ps. lxv. 7; Je. li. 42; Is. lx. 5; Re. x. 2. The natural idea, therefore, in this passage, would be that the power that was represented by the "beast" would spring up among the nations, when restless or unsettled, like the waves of the ocean. ¶ *And saw a beast.* Daniel saw four in succession (ch. vii. 3–7), all different, yet succeeding each other; John saw two in succession, yet strongly resembling each other, ver. 1, 11. On the general meaning of the word *beast* —θηρίον—see Notes on ch. xi. 7. The beast here is evidently a symbol of some power or kingdom that would arise in future times. See Notes on Da. vii. 3. ¶ *Having seven heads.* So also the dragon is represented in ch. xii. 3. See Notes on that passage. The representation there is of Satan, as the source of all the power lodged in the two beasts that John subsequently saw. In ch. xvii. 9, referring substantially to the same vision, it is said that "the seven heads are seven mountains;" and there can be no difficulty, therefore, in referring this to the seven hills on which the city of Rome was built (comp. Notes on ch. xii. 3), and consequently this must be regarded as designed, in some way, to be a representation of Rome. ¶ *And ten horns.* See this also explained in the Notes on ch. xii. 3; comp. also the more extended illustration in the Notes on Da. vii. 25, seq. The reference here is to Rome, or the one Roman power, contemplated as made up of ten subordinate kingdoms, and therefore subsequently to the invasion of the Northern hordes, and to the time when the Papacy was about to rise. Comp. Re. xvii. 12: "And the ten horns which thou sawest are ten kings [marg. *kingdoms*], which have received no kingdom as yet, but receive power as kings with the beast." For a full illustration of this, see the copious Notes at the close of the seventh chapter of Daniel. ¶ *And upon his horns ten crowns.* Greek, *ten diadems.* See Notes on ch. xii. 3. These indicated dominion or authority. In ch. xii. 3, the "dragon is represented as having *seven* diadems on his head;"

2 And the beast which I saw was <sup>c</sup>like unto a leopard, and his feet were as *the feet* of a bear,

*c* Da.7.4-7.

here, the beast is represented as having *ten*. The dragon there represents the Roman domination, *as such*, the *seven-hilled*, or *seven-headed* power, and, therefore, properly described as having *seven* diadems; the beast here represents the Roman power, as now broken up into the ten dominations which sprung up (see Notes on Daniel as above) from the one original Roman power, and that became henceforward the supporters of the Papacy, and, therefore, properly represented here as having *ten* diadems. ¶ *And upon his heads the name of blasphemy.* That is, the whole power was blasphemous in its claims and pretensions. The word *blasphemy* here seems to be used in the sense that titles and attributes were claimed by it which belonged only to God. On the meaning of the word *blasphemy*, see Notes on Mat. ix. 3; xxvi. 65. The meaning here is, that each one of these heads appeared to have a frontlet, with an inscription that was blasphemous, or that ascribed some attribute to this power that properly belonged to God; and that the whole power thus assumed was in derogation of the attributes and claims of God. In regard to the propriety of this description considered as applicable to the Papacy, see Notes on 2 Th. ii. 4.

2. *And the beast which I saw was like unto a leopard.* For a description of the leopard, see Notes on Da. vii. 6. It is distinguished for bloodthirstiness and cruelty, and thus becomes an emblem of a fierce, tyrannical power. In its general character it resembles a lion, and the lion and the leopard are often referred to together. In this description, it is observable that John has combined in *one* animal or monster, all those which Daniel brought *successively* on the scene of action as representing different empires. Thus in Daniel (vii. 2-7) the *lion* is introduced as the symbol of the Babylonian power; the bear, as the symbol of the Medo-Persian; the leopard, as the symbol of the Macedonian; and a nondescript animal, fierce, cruel, and mighty, with two horns, as the symbol of the Roman. See Notes on that passage. In John there is one animal representing the Roman power, as if it were made up of

and his mouth as the mouth of a lion: and <sup>d</sup>the dragon gave him his power, and <sup>e</sup>his seat, and great authority.

*d* ch.12.9.   *e* ch.16.10.

all these: a *leopard* with the feet of a *bear*, and the mouth of a *lion*, with two horns, and with the general description of a fierce monster. There was an obvious propriety in this, in speaking of the Roman power, for it was, in fact, made up of the empires represented by the other symbols in Daniel, and "combined in itself all the elements of the terrible and the oppressive, which had existed in the aggregate in the other great empires that preceded it." At the same time there was an obvious propriety in the symbol itself; for the bloodthirstiness and cruelty of the leopard would well represent the ferocity and cruelty of the Roman power, *especially* as John saw it here as the great antagonistic power of the true church, sustaining the Papal claim, and thirsting for blood. ¶ *And his feet were as* the feet *of a bear.* See Notes on Da. vii. 5. The idea here seems to be that of *strength*, as the strength of the bear resides much in its feet and claws. At the same time, there is the idea of a combination of fierce qualities —*as if* the bloodthirstiness, the cruelty, and the agility of the leopard were united with the strength of the bear. ¶ *And his mouth as the mouth of a lion.* See Notes on Da. vii. 4. The mouth of the lion is made to seize and hold its prey, and is indicative of the character of the animal as a beast of prey. John has thus brought together the qualities of activity, bloodthirstiness, strength, ferocity, all as symbolical of the power that was intended to be represented. It is hardly necessary to say that this description is one that would apply well, in all respects, to Rome; nor is it necessary to say, that if it be supposed that he *meant* to refer to Rome, this is such a description as he would have adopted. ¶ *And the dragon.* See Notes on ch. xii. 3. ¶ *Gave him his power.* Satan claimed, in the time of the Saviour, all power over the kingdoms of the world, and asserted that he could give them to whomsoever he pleased. See Notes on Mat. iv. 8, 9. How far the power of Satan in this respect may extend, it may not be possible to determine; but it cannot be doubted that the Roman power *seemed* to have such an

A.D. 96.]  CHAPTER XIII.  321

3 And I saw one of his heads, as it were ²wounded to death; and

² *slain.*

his deadly wound was healed: and all *ᶠthe world wondered after the beast.

*ᶠ* ch. 17. 8.

origin, and that in the main it was such as, on that supposition, it would be. In its arrogance and haughtiness—in its thirst for dominion—in its persecutions—it had such characteristics as we may suppose Satan would originate. If, therefore, as the whole connection leads us to suppose, this refers to the Roman secular power, considered as the support of the Papacy, there is the most evident propriety in the representation. ¶ *And the seat*—θρόνον. Hence our word *throne*. The word properly means a seat; then a high seat; then a *throne*, as that on which a king sits. Here it refers to this power as exercising dominion on the earth. ¶ *And great authority*. The authority *was* great. It extended over a large part of the earth, and, alike in its extent and character, it was such as we may suppose Satan would set up in the world.

3. *And I saw one of his heads, as it were wounded to death.* The phrase "wounded to death" means properly that it received a mortal wound, that is, the wound would have been mortal if it had not been healed. A blow was struck that would be naturally fatal, but there was something that prevented the fatal result. John does not say, however, by whom the wound was inflicted, nor does he describe farther the nature of the wound. He says that "*one* of the heads"—that is, one of the seven heads—was thus wounded. In ch. xvii. 9, he says that "the seven heads are seven mountains on which the woman sitteth." In ch. xvii. 10, he says, "there are seven kings." And this would lead us to suppose that there were "seven" administrations, or forms of dominion, or dynasties, that were presented to the eye of John; and that while the number "seven," as applied to the "heads," so far identified the power as to fix its location on the seven "hills" (ch. xvii. 9), in another respect also the number "seven" suggested forms of administration of dynasties, ch. xvii. 10. What is meant by saying that one of these heads was wounded to death has been among the most perplexing of all the inquiries pertaining to the book of Revelation. The use of the word *seven*, and the explanation in ch. xvii. 9, make it morally certain that *Rome*, in some form of its administra-

tion, is referred to. Of this there can be no doubt, and in this all are agreed. It is not, however, the *Papal* power as such that is here referred to; for (*a*) the Papal power is designated under the image of the second beast; (*b*) the descriptions pertaining to the first beast are all applicable to a secular power; and (*c*) there was no form of the Papal spiritual dominion which would properly correspond with what is said in ch. xvii. 10. The reference in this place is, therefore, to Rome considered as a civil or secular power, yet Rome regarded as giving support to the second beast—the Papal power. The *general* idea here is, that a state of things would exist in regard to that power, at the time referred to, *as if* one of the seven heads of the monster should receive a wound which would be fatal, if it were not healed in some way. That is, its power would be weakened; its dominion would be curtailed, and that portion of its power would have come to an end, if there had not been something which would, as it were, restore it, and save it from the wrath that was impending. The great point of difficulty relates to the *particular* application of this; to the facts in history that would correspond with the symbol. On this there have been almost as many opinions as there have been interpreters of the Apocalypse, and there is no impropriety in saying that none of the solutions are wholly free from objection. The *main* difficulty, so far as the interpretation proposed above is concerned, is, in the fact that "*one*" of the seven heads is referred to as wounded unto death; as if one-seventh part of the power was endangered. I confess I am not able wholly to solve this difficulty; but, after all, is it certain that the meaning is that just *one-seventh part* of the power was in peril; that the blow affected just such a portion that it might be described as the one-seventh part? Is not the number *seven* so used in the Scriptures as to denote a considerable portion—a portion quite material and important? And may not all that is intended here be, that John saw a wound inflicted on that mighty power which would have been fatal if it had not been marvellously healed? And was it not true

## 322 REVELATION. [A.D. 96.

4 And they worshipped the dragon which gave power unto the beast: and they worshipped the beast, saying, Who *is* like unto the beast? *g* who is able to make war with him?

*g* ch.17.14.

that the Roman civil and secular power was *so* waning and decaying, that it might properly be represented *as if* one of the seven heads of the monster had received a fatal wound, until its power was restored by the influence of the spiritual domination of the church of Rome? If this be the correct exposition, then what is implied here may be thus stated : (*a*) The general subject of the representation is the Roman power, as seen at first in its vigour and strength; (*b*) then that power is said to be greatly weakened, as if one of its heads were smitten with a deadly wound; (*c*) then the wound was healed—this power was restored—by being brought into alliance with the Papacy; that is, the whole Roman power over the world would have died away, if it had not been restored and perpetuated by means of this new and mighty influence, ver. 12. Under this new form, Rome had all the power which it had ever had, and was guilty of all the atrocities of which it had ever been guilty: *it was Rome still.* Every wound that was inflicted on that power by the incursion of barbarians, and by the dividing off of parts of the empire, was healed by the Papacy, and under this form its dominion became as wide and as formidable as under its ancient mode of administration. If a more *particular* application of this is sought for, I see no reason to doubt that it may be found in the quite common interpretation of the passage given by Protestants, that the reference is to the *forms* of administration under which this power appeared in the world. The number of distinct forms of government which the Roman power assumed from first to last was the following:—kings, consuls, dictators, decemvirs, military tribunes, emperors. These *seven* forms of administration were, at least, sufficiently prominent and marked to be represented by this symbol, or to attract the attention of one contemplating this formidable power—for it was under these forms that its conquests had been achieved, and its dominion set up over the earth. In the time of John, and the time contemplated in this vision, all these had passed away but the *imperial.* That, too, was soon to be smitten with a deadly wound by the invasion of the Northern hordes; and that would have wholly and for ever ceased if it had not been restored—the deadly wound being healed—by the influence of the Papal power, giving Rome its former ascendency. See Notes at the close of ver. 15. ¶ *And his deadly wound was healed.* That is, as explained above, the waning Roman secular power was restored by its connection with the spiritual power—the Papacy. This was (*a*) a simple matter of fact, that the waning secular power of Rome was thus restored by connecting itself with the spiritual or ecclesiastical power, thus prolonging what might properly be called the *Roman* domination far beyond what it would otherwise have been; and (*b*) this would be *properly* represented by just the symbol employed here—the fatal wound inflicted on the head, and the healing of that wound, or preventing what would naturally be the effects. On the fulfilment of this, see Notes on ver. 15, at the close. ¶ *And all the world wondered after the beast.* The word here used—θαυμαζω—means, properly, to be astonished ; to be amazed ; then to wonder at; then to admire and follow (Rob. *Lex.*). In ver. 4, it is said that the world "*worshipped*" the beast; and the general idea is, that the beast received such universal reverence, or inspired such universal awe, as to be properly called worship or adoration. There can be no doubt of the propriety of this, considered as applicable to that secular Roman power which sustained the Papacy. The homage was as wide as the limits of the Roman empire had ever been, and might be said to embrace "all the world."

4. *And they worshipped the dragon which gave power unto the beast.* Notes, chap. xii. 3; xiii. 2. That is, they *in fact* worshipped him. The word *worship* —προσκυνέω—is not always, however, used in a *religious* sense. It means, properly, *to kiss;* to kiss towards anyone ; that is, to kiss his own hand and to extend it towards a person, in token of respect and homage (Rob. *Lex.*). Comp. Job xxxi. 27. Then it means to show respect to one who is our superior ; to kings and princes ; to parents ; and pre-eminently to God. See Notes on Mat. ii. 2. The word may be used here to mean that homage or reverence,

# CHAPTER XIII.

5 And there was given unto him a*ʰ* mouth speaking great things

*h* Da.7.8,11,25; 11.36.

as to a higher power, was rendered to the "dragon;" not strictly that he was openly *worshipped* in a religious sense as God. Can anyone doubt that this was the case under Papal Rome; that the power which was set up under that entire domination, civil and ecclesiastical, was such as Satan approved, and such as he sought to have established on the earth? And can anyone doubt that the homage thus rendered, so contrary to the law of God, and so much in derogation of his claims, was in fact homage rendered to this presiding spirit of evil? ¶ *And they worshipped the beast.* That is, they did it, as is immediately specified, by saying that he was *incomparable* and *invincible;* in other words, that he was superior to all others, and that he was almighty. For the fulfilment of this, see Notes on 2 Th. ii. 4. ¶ *Who is like unto the beast?* That is, he is to be regarded as unequalled and as supreme. This was, in fact, ascribing honours to him which belonged only to God; and this was the manner in which that civil and secular power was regarded in the period here supposed to be referred to. It was the policy of rulers and princes in those times to augment in every way possible the respect in which they were held; to maintain that they were the vicegerents of heaven; to claim for themselves sacredness of character and of person; and to secure from the people a degree of reverence which was in fact idolatrous. Never was this more marked than in the times when the Papacy had the ascendency, for it was its policy to promote reverence for the power that sustained itself, and to secure for itself the idolatrous veneration of the people. ¶ *Who is able to make war with him?* That is, he is invincible. They thus attributed to him omnipotence — an attribute belonging only to God. This found a fulfilment in the honour shown to the civil authority which sustained the Papacy; for the policy was to impress the public mind with the belief that that power was invincible. In fact, it was so regarded. Nothing was able to resist that absolute despotism; and the authority of princes and rulers that were allied with the Papal rule was of the most absolute kind, and the subjugation of the world was complete.

and blasphemies: and power was given unto him to ³continue *ⁱ*forty *and* two months.

³ *make war.* *i* ch.11.2,3; 12.6.

There was no civil, as there was no religious liberty; and the whole arrangement was so ordered as to subdue the world to an absolute and uncontrollable power.

5. *And there was given unto him a mouth speaking great things.* John does not say *by whom* this was given; but we may suppose that it was by the "dragon," who is said (ver. 2) to have given him his power, and seat, and authority. The fulfilment of this is found in the claims set up by the princes and rulers here referred to — that mighty secular power that sustained the Papacy, and that was, in some sort, a part of the Papacy itself. These arrogant claims consisted in the assertion of a divine right; in the power assumed over the liberty, the property, and the consciences of the people; in the arbitrary commands that were issued; and in the right asserted of giving absolute law. The language here used is the same as that which is found in Daniel (vii. 8) when speaking of the "little horn:" "In this horn were eyes like the eyes of a man, and a mouth speaking great things." For an illustration of the meaning of this, see Notes on that passage. Comp. Notes on Da. vii. 25. ¶ *And blasphemies.* That is, the whole power represented by the "beast" will be blasphemous. See Notes on ver. 1. Comp. Notes on Da. vii. 25. ¶ *And power was given unto him to continue forty and two months.* Three years and a half, reckoned as months; or twelve hundred and sixty days, reckoning thirty days for a month; or twelve hundred and sixty years, regarding the days as prophetic days. For the evidence that this is to be so regarded, see Notes on Da. vii. 25. This is the same period that we meet with in chap. xi. 2, and in chap. xii. 6. See Notes on those places. This fact proves that the same power is referred to in these places and in Daniel; and this fact may be regarded as a confirmation of the views here taken, that the power here referred to is designed to have a connection in some form with the Papacy. The duration of the existence of this power is the same as that which is everywhere ascribed to the Papacy, in the passages which refer to it; and

324 REVELATION. [A.D. 96.

6 And he opened his mouth in blasphemy against God, to blaspheme his name, and *k*his tabernacle, and *l*them that dwell in heaven.

7 And it was given unto him *m*to make war with the saints, and to

*k* Col.2.9; He.9.11,24.    *l* He.12.22,23.
*m* ch.11.7; 12.17; Da.7.21.

overcome them: and *n*power was given him over all kindreds, and tongues, and nations.

8 And all that dwell upon the earth shall worship him, whose names are not written in *o*the book of life of the Lamb slain *p*from the foundation of the world.

*n* Lu.4.6.    *o* ch.21.27; Da.12.1.    *p* ch.17.8.

all the circumstances, as before remarked, show that the same *general* power is referred to by the two "beasts" which are described in this chapter. If so, the continuance or duration may be supposed to be the same; and this is indicated in the passage before us, where it is said that it would be twelve hundred and sixty years. In regard to the application of this to the Papal power, and the manner in which the calculation is to be made of the duration of that power, see the Notes on Da. vii. 25, and the remarks at the end of that chapter. The meaning in the passage before us I take to be, that the Papal power, considered as a civil or secular institution, will have, from the time when that properly commenced, a duration of twelve hundred and sixty years. In the Scriptures there is nothing more definite in regard to any future event than this.

6. *And he opened his mouth in blasphemy against God, to blaspheme his name.* By his own arrogant claims; by his assumed authority in matters of conscience; by setting aside the divine authority; and by impious declarations in derogation of the divine claims. See Notes on ver. 1. ¶ *And his tabernacle.* Literally, his "tent" —σκηνήν. This is the word which is commonly applied to the sacred tent or tabernacle among the Hebrews, in which the ark was kept, and which was the seat of the Jewish worship before the building of the temple. It is thus used to denote a place of worship, considered as the dwelling-place of God, and is in this sense applied to heaven, He. viii. 2; ix. 11; Re. xv. 5. It seems to be used here in a general sense to denote the place where God was worshipped; and the meaning is, that there would be a course of conduct in regard to the true church—the dwelling-place of God on the earth—which could properly be regarded as blasphemy. Let anyone remember the anathemas and excommunications uttered against the Waldenses and Albigenses, and those of kindred spirit that appeared in the long period of the Papal rule, and he will find no difficulty in perceiving a complete fulfilment of all that is here said. ¶ *And them that dwell in heaven.* The true worshippers; the members of the true church, represented as dwelling in this holy tabernacle. No one acquainted with the reproaches cast on the devoted and sincere followers of the Saviour during the dark periods of the Papal rule can fail to see that there was in that a complete fulfilment of all that is here predicted.

7. *And it was given unto him.* By the same power that taught him to blaspheme God and his church. Notes on ver. 2, 5. ¶ *To make war with the saints.* See this fully illustrated in the Notes on the parallel passage in Da. vii. 21, and at the end of that chapter, (*f*). ¶ *And to overcome them.* In those wars. This was abundantly fulfilled in the wars with the Waldenses, the Albigenses, and the other sincere followers of the Saviour in the time of the Papal persecutions. The language here used is the same as that which is found in Da. vii. 21: "The same horn made war with the saints, and prevailed against them." See Notes on that passage. ¶ *And power was given him.* See Notes on ver. 2. ¶ *Over all kindreds, and tongues, and nations.* For the meaning of these words see Notes on ch. vii. 9. The meaning here is, that this dominion was set up over the world. Comp. Da. vii. 25. The fact that so large a portion of the kingdoms of the earth was under the influence of the Papacy, and sustained it, and the claim which it set up to universal dominion, and to the right of deposing kings and giving away kingdoms, corresponds entirely with the language here used.

8. *And all that dwell upon the earth shall worship him.* That is, as immediately stated, all whose names are not in the book of life. On the word *worship,* see Notes on ver. 4. ¶ *Whose*

**9** If any man have an ear, let him hear.

**10** He*q* that leadeth into captivity shall go into captivity: *r*he that killeth with the sword must be killed with the sword. Here is the *s*patience and the faith of the saints.

*q* Is.33.1.    *r* Ge.9.6.    *s* He.6.12.

---

names are not written in the book of life of the Lamb. That is, of the Lord Jesus—the Lamb of God. See Notes on Phi. iv. 3. Comp. Notes on Jn. i. 29. The representation here is, that the Lord Jesus keeps a book or register, in which are recorded the names of all who shall obtain everlasting life. ¶ *Slain from the foundation of the world.* See Notes on ch. v. 6. Comp. Notes on ch. iii. 5. The meaning here is, not that he was actually put to death "from the foundation of the world," but that the intention to give him for a sacrifice was formed then, and that it was so *certain* that it might be spoken of as actually then occurring. See Ro. iv. 17. The purpose was so certain, it was so constantly represented by bloody sacrifices from the earliest ages, all typifying the future Saviour, that it might be said that he was "slain from the foundation of the world." Professor Stuart, however (*Com. in loco*), supposes that this phrase should be connected with the former member of the sentence, "whose names are not written, from the foundation of the world, in the life-book of the Lamb, which was slain." Either construction makes good sense; but it seems to me that that which is found in our common version is the most simple and natural.

9. *If any man have an ear, let him hear.* See Notes on ch. ii. 7. The idea here is, that what was here said respecting the "beast" was worthy of special attention, as it pertained to most important events in the history of the church.

10. *He that leadeth into captivity.* This is clearly intended to refer to the power or government which is denoted by the beast. The form of expression here in the Greek is peculiar—"If any one leadeth into captivity," &c.—Εἴ τις αἰχμαλωσίαν συνάγει. The statement is *general*, and is intended to make use of a general or prevalent truth with reference to this particular case. The general truth is, that men will, in the course of things, be dealt with according to their character and their treatment of others; that nations characterized by war and conquests will be subject to the evils of war and conquest—or that they may expect to share the same lot which they have brought on others. This general statement accords with what the Saviour says in Mat. xxvi. 52: "All they that take the sword shall perish with the sword." This has been abundantly illustrated in the world; and it is a very important admonition to nations not to indulge in the purposes of conquest and to individuals not to engage in strife and litigation. The particular idea here is, that it would be a characteristic of the power here referred to that it would "lead others into captivity." This would be fulfilled if it was the characteristic of this power to invade other countries and to make their inhabitants prisoners of war; if it made slaves of other people; if it set up an unjust dominion over other people; or if it was distinguished for persecuting and imprisoning the innocent, or for depriving the nations of liberty. It is unnecessary to say that this is strikingly descriptive of Rome, considered in any and every point of view, whether under the republic or the empire, whether secular or ecclesiastical, whether Pagan or Papal. In the following forms there has been a complete fulfilment under that mighty power of what is here said: (*a*) In the desire of conquest or of extending its dominion, and, of course, leading others captive as prisoners of war or subjecting them to slavery. (*b*) In its persecutions of true Christians, alike pursued under the Pagan and the Papal form of the administration. (*c*) Especially in the imprisonments practised under the Inquisition, where tens of thousands have been reduced to the worst kind of captivity. In every way this description is applicable to Rome, as seeking to lead the world *captive* or to subject it to its own absolute sway. ¶ *Shall go into captivity.* As a just recompense for subjecting others to bondage, and as an illustration of a general principle of the divine administration. This is yet, in a great measure, to be fulfilled; and, as I understand it, it discloses the manner in which the Papal secular power will come to an end. It will be by being subdued, so that it might *seem* to be made captive and led off by some victorious host. Rome now is practically held in subjection by foreign arms,

11 And I beheld *another beast coming up out of the earth; and he had two horns like a lamb, and he spake as a dragon.

*t* ch.11.7.

and has no true independence; perhaps this will be more and more so as its ultimate fall approaches. ¶ *He that killeth with the sword.* See Notes, as above, on Mat. xxvi. 52. There can be no doubt that this is applicable to Rome in all the forms of its administration considered as a Pagan power; or considered as a nominally Christian power, either with reference to its secular or its spiritual dominion. Compute the numbers of human beings that have been put to death by that Roman power, and no better language could have been chosen to characterize it than that which is here used —"killed with the sword." Comp. Notes on Da. vii. 24–28, II. (3), (*g*). ¶ *Must be killed with the sword.* This domination must be brought to an end by war and slaughter. Nothing is more probable than this in itself; nothing could be more in accordance with the principles of the divine dealings in the world. Such a power as that of Rome will not be likely to be overcome but by the force of arms; and the probability is that it will ultimately be overthrown in a bloody revolution, or by foreign conquest. Indeed, there are not a few intimations now that this result is hastening on. Italy is becoming impatient of the secular power swayed in connection with the Papacy, and sighs for freedom; and it is every way probable that that land would have been free, and that the secular power of the Papacy, if not every form of the Papacy itself, would have come to an end in the late convulsion (1848), if it had not been for the intervention of France and Austria. The period designated by prophecy for the final overthrow of that power had not arrived; but nothing can secure its continuance for any very considerable period longer. ¶ *Here is the patience and the faith of the saints.* That is, the trial of their patience and of their faith. Nowhere on earth have the patience and the faith of the saints been put to a severer test than under the Roman persecutions. The same idea occurs in ch. xiv. 12.

11. *And I beheld another beast.* Comp. Notes on ver. 1. This was so distinct from the first that its characteristics could be described, though, as shown in the Analysis of the Chapter, there was in many points a strong resemblance between them. The relations between the two will be more fully indicated in the Notes. ¶ *Coming up out of the earth.* Professor Stuart renders this, "ascending from the land." The former was represented as rising up out of the sea (ver. 1); indicating that the power was to rise from a perturbed or unsettled state of affairs—like the ocean. This, from that which was more settled and stable—as the land is more firm than the waters. It may not be necessary to carry out this image; but the *natural* idea, as applied to the two forms of the Roman power supposed to be here referred to, would be that the former—the secular power that sustained the Papacy—rose out of the agitated state of the nations in the invasions of the northern hordes, and the convulsions and revolutions of the falling empire of Rome; and that the latter, the spiritual power itself—represented by the beast coming up from the land—grew up under the more settled and stable order of things. It was comparatively calm in its origin, and had less the appearance of a frightful monster rising up from the agitated ocean. Comp. Notes on ver. 1. ¶ *And he had two horns like a lamb.* In some respects he resembled a lamb; that is, he seemed to be a mild, gentle, inoffensive animal. It is hardly necessary to say that this is a most striking representation of the actual manner in which the power of the Papacy has always been put forth—putting on the apparent gentleness of the lamb; or laying claim to great meekness and humility, even when deposing kings, and giving away crowns, and driving thousands to the stake, or throwing them into the dungeons of the Inquisition. ¶ *And he spake as a dragon.* See Notes on ch. xii. 3. The meaning here is, that he spoke in a harsh, haughty, proud, arrogant tone—as we should suppose a dragon would if he had the power of utterance. The general sense is, that while this "beast" had, in one respect—in its resemblance to a lamb—the appearance of great gentleness, meekness, and kindness, it had, in another respect, a haughty, imperious, and arrogant spirit. How appropriate this is, as a symbol, to represent the Papacy, considered as a spiritual power, it is unnecessary to say. It will be admitted, whatever may be thought

**12 And he exerciseth all the power of the first beast before him, and causeth the earth and them which dwell therein to worship the first beast, *u* whose deadly wound was healed.**

*u* ver.3.

---

of the design of this symbol, that if it was in fact *intended* to refer to the Papacy, a more appropriate one could not have been chosen.

12. *And he exerciseth all the power of the first beast before him.* The same amount of power; the same kind of power. This shows a remarkable *relationship* between these two beasts; and proves that it was intended to refer to the same power substantially, though manifested in a different form. In the fulfilment of this, we should naturally look for some government whose authority extended far, and which was absolute and arrogant in its character, for this is the power attributed to the first beast. See Notes on ver. 2, 3, 4, 7, 8. This description had a remarkable fulfilment in the Papacy, considered as a spiritual dominion. The relation to the secular power is the same as would be indicated by these two beasts; the dominion was as wide-spread; the authority was as absolute and arrogant. In fact, on these points they have been identical. The one has sustained the other; either one would long since have fallen if it had not been upheld by the other. The Papacy, considered as a spiritual domination, was in fact a new power starting up in the same place as the old Roman dominion, to give life to that as it was tending to decay, and to continue its ascendency over the world. These two things, the secular and the spiritual power, constituting *the Papacy* in the proper sense of the term, are in fact but the continuance or the prolongation of the old Roman dominion—the fourth kingdom of Daniel—united so as to constitute in reality but one kingdom, and yet so distinct in their origin, and in their manifestations, as to be capable of separate contemplation and description, and thus properly represented by the two "beasts" that were shown in vision to John. ¶ *And causeth the earth and them which dwell therein to worship the first beast.* That is, to respect, to reverence, to honour. The word *worship* here refers to *civil* respect, and not to *religious* adoration. See Notes on ver. 4. The meaning here, according to the interpretation proposed all along in this chapter, is, that the Papacy, considered in its religious influence, or as a spiritual power —represented by the second beast— secured for the civil or secular power —represented by the first beast—the homage of the world. It was the means of keeping up that dominion, and of giving it its ascendency among the nations of the earth. The *truth* of this, as an historical fact, is well known. The Roman civil power would have long ago lost all its influence and been unknown, if it had not been for the Papacy; and, in fact, all the influence which it has had since the irruption of the northern barbarians, and the changes which their invasion produced, can be traced to that new power which arose in the form of the Papacy—represented in Daniel (ch. vii. 8) by the "little horn." That new power gave life and energy to the declining influence of Rome, and brought the world again to respect and honour its authority. ¶ *Whose deadly wound was healed.* See Notes on ver. 3. That is, was healed by the influence of this new power represented by the second beast. A state of things occurred, on the rise of that new power, *as if* a wound in the head, otherwise fatal, was healed. The striking applicability of this to the decaying Roman power—smitten as with a deadly wound by the blows inflicted by the northern hordes, and by internal dissensions—will occur to every one. It was as if a healing process had been imparted by some life-giving power, and, as a consequence, the Roman dominion—the prolongation of Daniel's fourth kingdom—has continued to the present time. Other kingdoms passed away—the Assyrian, the Babylonian, the Medo-Persian, the Macedonian; Rome alone, of all the ancient empires, has prolonged its power over men. In all changes elsewhere, an influence has gone forth from the seven-hilled city as wide and as fearful as it was in the brightest days of the republic, the triumvirate, or the empire, and a large part of the world still listens reverently to the mandates which issue from the seat which so long gave law to mankind. The fact that it *is* so is to be traced solely to the influence of that power represented here by the second beast that appeared in vision to John—the Papacy.

13 And he doeth *great wonders, so that he maketh fire come down from heaven on the earth in the sight of men,

14 And deceiveth them that dwell on the earth by *the means of*

*v* Mat.24.24; 2 Th.2.9,10.

those miracles which he had power to do in the sight of the beast; saying to them that dwell on the earth, that they should make an image to the beast, which had the *w* wound by a sword, and did live.

*w* ver.3,12.

---

**13.** *And he doeth great wonders. Signs* —σημεῖα—the word commonly employed to denote *miracles* (comp. Notes on Ac. ii. 19); and the representation here is, that the power referred to by the second beast would found its claim on pretended miracles, and would accomplish an effect on the world *as if* it actually did work miracles. The applicability of this to Papal Rome no one can doubt. See Notes on 2 Th. ii. 9. Comp. ver. 14. ¶ *That he maketh fire come down from heaven on the earth in the sight of men.* That is, he pretends this; he accomplishes an effect *as if* he did it. It is not necessary to suppose that he actually did this, any more than it is to suppose that he actually performed the other pretended miracles referred to in other places. John describes him as he saw him in the vision; and he saw him laying claim to this power, and actually producing an effect *as if* by a miracle he actually made fire to descend from heaven upon the earth. This is to be understood as included in what the apostle Paul (2 Th. ii. 9) calls "signs and lying wonders," as among the things by which the "man of sin and the son of perdition" would be characterized, and by which he would be sustained. See Notes on that passage. Why this particular pretended miracle is specified here is not certain. It may be because this would be among the most striking and impressive of the pretended miracles wrought—as if lying beyond all human power—as Elijah made fire come down from heaven to consume the sacrifice (1 Ki. xviii. 37, 38), and as the apostles proposed to do on the Samaritans (Lu. ix. 54), *as if* fire were called down on them from heaven. The phrase "in the sight of men" implies that this would be done publicly, and is such language as would be used of pretended miracles designed for purposes of ostentation. Amidst the multitudes of pretended miracles of the Papacy, it would probably not be difficult to find instances in which the very thing here described was attempted, in which various devices of pyrotechnics were shown off as miracles. For an illustration of the wonders produced in the dark ages in reference to fire, having all the appearance of miracles, and regarded *as* miracles by the masses of men, the reader is referred to Dr. Brewster's *Letters on Natural Magic*, particularly Letter xii.

**14.** *And deceiveth them that dwell on the earth by* the means of *those miracles.* Nothing could possibly be more descriptive of the Papacy than this. It has been kept up by deception and delusion, and its pretended miracles have been, and are to this day, the means by which this is done. Anyone in the slightest degree acquainted with the pretended miracles practised at Rome, will see the propriety of this description as applied to the Papacy. The main fact here stated, that the Papacy would endeavour to sustain itself by pretended miracles, is confirmed by an incidental remark of Mr. Gibbon, when speaking of the pontificate of Gregory the Great; he says: "The credulity or the prudence of Gregory was always disposed to confirm the truths of religion by the evidence of ghosts, *miracles*, and resurrections" (*Decline and Fall*, iii. 210). Even within a month of the time that I am writing (October 5, 1850), intelligence has been received in this country of extraordinary privileges conferred on some city in Italy, because the eyes of a picture of the Virgin in that city have miraculously moved—greatly to the "confirmation of the faithful." Such things are constantly occurring; and it is by these that the supremacy of the Papacy has been and is sustained. The *Breviary* teems with examples of miracles wrought by the saints. For instance: St. Francis Xavier turned a sufficient quantity of salt water into fresh to save the lives of five hundred travellers who were dying of thirst, enough being left to allow a large exportation to different parts of the world, where it wrought astonishing cures. St. Raymond de Pennafort laid his cloak on the sea, and sailed from Majorca to Barcelona, a distance of a hundred and

15 And he had power to give life[4] unto the image of the beast, that the image of the beast should

[4] breath.

both speak, and cause that as many as would not [x]worship the image of the beast should be killed.

[x] ch.16.2.

sixty miles, in six hours. St. Juliana lay on her death-bed; her stomach rejected all solid food, and in consequence she was prevented from receiving the Eucharist. In compliance with her earnest solicitations, the consecrated wafer was laid on her breast; the priest prayed; the wafer vanished, and Juliana expired. Many pages might be filled with accounts of modern miracles of the most ridiculous description, yet believed by Roman Catholics — the undoubted means by which Papal Rome "deceives the world," and keeps up its ascendency in this age. See Forsyth's *Italy*, ii. pp. 154-157; *Rome in the Nineteenth Century*, i. p. 40, 86, ii. p. 356, iii. pp. 193-201; Lady Morgan's *Italy*, ii. p. 306, iii. p. 189; Graham's *Three Months' Residence*, &c., p. 241. ¶ *Saying to them that dwell on the earth.* That is, as far as its influence would extend. This implies that there would be *authority*, and that this authority would be exercised to secure this object. ¶ *That they should make an image to the beast.* That is, something that would *represent* the beast, and that might be an object of worship. The word rendered *image* —εἰκών— means properly, (*a*) an image, effigy, figure, as an *idol*, image, or figure; (*b*) a likeness, resemblance, similitude. Here the meaning would seem to be, that, in order to secure the acknowledgment of the beast, and the homage to be rendered to him, there was something like a statue made, or that John saw in vision such a representation— that is, that a state of things existed *as if* such a statue were made, and men were constrained to acknowledge this. All that is stated here would be fulfilled if the old Roman civil power should become to a large extent dead, or cease to exert its influence over men, and if then the Papal spiritual power should cause a form of domination to exist, *strongly resembling* the former in its general character and extent, and if it should secure this result — that the world would acknowledge its sway or render it homage as it did to the old Roman government. This would receive its fulfilment if it be supposed that the first "beast" represented the ancient Roman civil power as such; that this died away—as if the head had received a fatal wound; that it was again revived under the influence of the Papacy; and that, under that influence, a civil government, *strongly resembling* the old Roman dominion, was caused to exist, depending for its vital energy on the Papacy, and, in its turn, lending its aid to support the Papacy. All this *in fact* occurred in the decline of the Roman power after the time of Constantine, and its final apparent extinction, as if "wounded to death," in the exile of the last of the emperors, the son of Orestes, who assumed the names of Romulus and Augustus, names which were corrupted, the former by the Greeks into *Momyllus*, and the latter by the Latins "into the contemptible diminutive *Augustulus.*" See Gibbon ii. 381. Under him the empire ceased, until it was revived in the days of Charlemagne. In the empire which then sprung up, and which owed much of its influence to the sustaining aid of the Papacy, we discern the "image" of the former Roman power; the prolongation of the Roman ascendency over the world. On the exile of the feeble son of Orestes (A.D. 476), the government passed into the hands of Odoacer, "the first barbarian who reigned in Italy" (Gibbon); and then the authority was divided among the sovereignties which sprang up after the conquests of the barbarians, until the "empire" was again restored in the time and the person of Charlemagne. See Gibbon, iii. 344, seq. ¶ *Which had the wound by a sword, and did live.* Which had a wound that was naturally fatal, but whose fatal consequences were prevented by the intervention of another power. See Notes on ver. 3. That is, according to the explanation given above, the Roman imperial power was "wounded with a fatal wound" by the invasions of the northern hordes—the sword of the conquerors. Its power, however, was restored by the Papacy, giving life to that which *resembled* essentially the Roman civil jurisdiction—the "image" of the former beast; and that power, thus restored, asserted its dominion again, as the prolonged Roman dominion—the fourth kingdom of Daniel (see Notes on Dan. vii. 19, seq.)—over the world.

15. *And he had power to give life unto the image of the beast.* That is, that image of the beast would be naturally powerless, or would have no life in itself. The second beast, however, had power to impart life to it, so that it would be invested with authority, and would exercise that authority in the manner specified. If this refers, as is supposed, to the Roman civil power—the power of the empire restored—it would find a fulfilment in some act of the Papacy by which the empire that resembled in the extent of its jurisdiction, and in its general character, the former Roman empire, received some vivifying impulse, or was invested with new power. That is, it would have power conferred on it through the Papacy which it would not have in itself, and which would confirm its jurisdiction. How far events actually occurred corresponding with this, will be considered in the Notes at the close of this verse. ¶ *That the image of the beast should both speak.* Should give signs of life; should issue authoritative commands. The *speaking* here referred to pertains to that which is immediately specified, in issuing a command that they who "would not worship the image of the beast should be killed." ¶ *And cause that as many as would not worship the image of the beast.* Would not honour it, or acknowledge its authority. The "worship" here referred to is *civil*, not *religious* homage. See Notes on ver. 4. The meaning is, that what is here called the "image of the beast" had power given it, by its connection with the second "beast," to set up its jurisdiction over men, and to secure their allegiance on pain of death. The power by which this was done was derived from the second beast; the obedience and homage demanded was of the most entire and submissive character; the nature of the government was in a high degree arbitrary; and the penalty enforced for refusing this homage was death. The *facts* that we are to look for in the fulfilment of this are, (1) that the Roman imperial power was about to expire—as if wounded to death by the sword; (2) that this was revived in the form of what is here called the "image of the beast"—that is, in a form closely resembling the former power; (3) that this was done by the agency of the Papal power, represented by the second beast; (4) that the effect of this was to set up over men a wide-extended secular jurisdiction, of a most arbitrary and absolute kind, where the penalty of disobedience to its laws was death, and where the infliction of this was, in fact, to be traced to the influence of the second beast—that is, the Papal spiritual power. The question now is, whether *facts* occurred that corresponded with this emblematic representation. Now, as to the leading fact, the decline of the Roman imperial power—the fatal wound inflicted on that by the "sword"—there can be no doubt. In the time of "Augustulus," as above stated, it had become practically extinct—"wounded as it were to death," and *so* wounded that it would never have been revived again had it not been for some foreign influence. It is true also, that, when the Papacy arose, the necessity was felt of allying itself with some wide-extended civil or secular dominion, that might be under its own control, and that would maintain its spiritual authority. It is true, also, that the empire was revived—the very "image" or copy, so far as it could be, of the former Roman power, in the time of Charlemagne, and that the power which was wielded in what was called the "empire," was that which was, in a great measure, derived from the Papacy, and was designed to sustain the Papacy, and was actually employed for that purpose. These are the main facts, I suppose, which are here referred to, and a few extracts from Mr. Gibbon will show with what propriety and accuracy the symbols here employed were used, on the supposition that this was the designed reference. (*a*) The rise, or restoration of this imperial power in the time and the person of Charlemagne. Mr. Gibbon says (iii. 342), "It was after the Nicene synod, and under the reign of the pious Irene, that the popes consummated the separation of Rome and Italy [from the Eastern empire] *by the translation of the empire* to the less orthodox Charlemagne. They were compelled to choose between the rival nations; religion was not the sole motive of their choice; and while they dissembled the failings of their friends, they beheld with reluctance and suspicion the Catholic virtues of their foes. The difference of language and manners had perpetuated the enmity of the two capitals [Rome and Constantinople]; and they were alienated from each other by the hostile opposition of seventy

years. In that schism the Romans had tasted of freedom, and the popes of sovereignty; their submission would have exposed them to the revenge of a jealous tyrant, and the revolution of Italy had betrayed the impotence as well as the tyranny of the Byzantine court." Mr. Gibbon then proceeds to state reasons why *Charlemagne* was selected as the one who was to be placed at the head of the revived imperial power, and then adds (p. 343), "The title of patrician was below the merit and greatness of Charlemagne; and *it was only by reviving the Western empire* that they could pay their obligations, or secure their establishment. By this decisive measure they would finally eradicate the claims of the Greeks; from the debasement of a provincial town the majesty of Rome would be restored; the Latin Christians would be united, under a supreme head, in their ancient metropolis; *and the conquerors of the West would receive their crown from the successors of St. Peter. The Roman church would acquire a zealous and respectable advocate;* and under the shadow of the Carlovingian power, the bishop might exercise, with honour and safety, the government of the city." All this seems as if it were a *designed* commentary on such expressions as these: "And he exerciseth all the power of the first beast, and causeth the earth and them which dwell therein to worship the first beast, whose deadly wound was healed," "saying to them that dwell on the earth that they should make an image to the beast which had the wound by a sword, and did live; and he had power to give life unto the image of the beast," &c. (b) Its extent. It is said (ver. 12), "And he exerciseth all the power of the first beast, and causeth the earth and them which dwell therein to worship the first beast, whose deadly wound was healed." Comp. ver. 14, 15. That is, the *extent* of the jurisdiction of the revived power, or the restored empire, would be as great as it was before the wound was inflicted. Of the *extent* of the restored empire under Charlemagne, Mr. Gibbon has given a full account, iii. pp. 546-549. The passage is too long to be copied here in full, and a summary of it only can be given. He says, "The empire was not unworthy of its title; and some of the fairest kingdoms of Europe were the patrimony or conquest of a prince who reigned at the same time in France, Spain, Italy, Germany, and Hungary. I. The Roman province of Gaul had been transformed into the name and monarchy of FRANCE, &c. II. The Saracens had been expelled from France by the grandfather and father of Charlemagne, but they still possessed the greatest part of Spain, from the rock of Gibraltar to the Pyrenees. Amidst their civil divisions, an Arabian emir of Saragossa implored his protection in the diet of Paderborn. Charlemagne undertook the expedition, restored the emir, and, without distinction of faith, impartially crushed the resistance of the Christians, and rewarded the obedience and service of the Mohammedans. In his absence he instituted the *Spanish March*, which extended from the Pyrenees to the river Ebro: Barcelona was the residence of the French governor; he possessed the counties of *Rousillon* and *Catalonia;* and the infant kingdoms of *Navarre* and *Aragon* were subject to his jurisdiction. III. As king of the Lombards, and patrician of Rome, he reigned over the greatest part of ITALY, a tract of a thousand miles from the Alps to the borders of Calabria, &c. IV. Charlemagne was the first who united GERMANY under the same sceptre, &c. V. He retaliated on the Avars, or Huns of Pannonia, the same calamities which they had inflicted on the nations: the royal residence of the Chagan was left desolate and unknown; and the treasures, the rapine of two hundred and fifty years, enriched the victorious troops, or decorated the churches of Italy and Gaul." "If we retrace the outlines of the geographical picture," continues Mr. Gibbon, "it will be seen that the empire of the Franks extended, between east and west, from the Ebro to the Elbe or Vistula; between the north and south, from the duchy of Beneventum to the river Eyder, the perpetual boundary of Germany and Denmark. Two-thirds of the Western empire of Rome were subject to Charlemagne, and the deficiency was amply supplied by his command of the inaccessible or invincible nations of Germany." (c) The dependence of this civil or revived secular power on the Papacy. "His deadly wound was healed." "And caused the earth to worship the first beast." "Saying to them that dwell on the earth, that they should make an image to the beast." "He had power to give life unto the image of the beast." Thus Mr. Gibbon

**16 And he caused all, both small and great, rich and poor, free and bond, to ⁵receive a mark in their right hand, or in their foreheads:**

⁵ *give them.*

(iii. 343) says, "From the debasement of a provincial town, the majesty of Rome would be restored; the Latin Christians would be united, under a supreme head, in their ancient metropolis; *and the conquerors of the West would receive their crown from the successors of St. Peter.*" And again (iii. 344) he says, "On the festival of Christmas, the last year of the eighth century, Charlemagne appeared in the church of St. Peter; and, to gratify the vanity of Rome, he had exchanged the simple dress of his country for the habit of a patrician. After the celebration of the holy mysteries, Leo *suddenly placed a precious crown on his head*, and the dome resounded with the acclamations of the people, 'Long life and victory to Charles, the most pious Augustus, *crowned by God the great and pacific emperor of the Romans!*' The head and body of Charlemagne were consecrated by the royal unction; his coronation oath represents a promise to maintain the faith and privileges of the church; and the first-fruits are paid in rich offerings to the shrine of the apostle. In his familiar conversation the emperor protested his ignorance of the intentions of Leo, which he would have disappointed by his absence on that memorable day. But the preparations of the ceremony must have disclosed the secret; and the journey of Charlemagne reveals his knowledge and expectation; he had acknowledged that the imperial title was the object of his ambition, and a Roman senate had pronounced that it was the only adequate reward of his merit and services." So again (iii. 350), Mr. Gibbon, speaking of the conquests of Otho (A.D. 962), and of his victorious march over the Alps, and his subjugation of Italy, says, "From that memorable era, two maxims of public jurisprudence were introduced by force and ratified by time. I. That the prince who was elected in the German diet, acquired from that instant the subject kingdoms of Italy and Rome. II. But that he might not legally assume the titles of emperor and Augustus, *till he had received the crown from the hands of the Roman Pontiff.*" In connection with these quotations from Mr. Gibbon, we may add, from Sigonius, the oath which the emperor took on the occasion of his coronation: "I, the Emperor, do engage and promise, in the name of Christ, before God and the blessed apostle Peter, that I will be a protector and defender of this holy church of Rome, in all things wherein I can be useful to it, so far as divine assistance shall enable me, and so far as my knowledge and power can reach" (quoted by Professor Bush, *Hieroph.* Nov. 1842, p. 141). We learn, also, from the biographers of Charlemagne that a commemorative coin was struck at Rome under his reign, bearing this inscription: "Renovatio Imperii Romani"—"*Revival of the Roman Empire*" (*Ibid.*). These quotations, whose authority will not be questioned, and whose authors will not be suspected of having had any design to illustrate these passages in the Apocalypse, will serve to confirm what is said in the Notes of the decline and restoration of the Roman secular power; of its dependence on the Papacy to give it life and vigour; and of the fact that it was designed to sustain the Papacy, and to perpetuate the power of Rome. It needs only to be added, that down to the time of Charles the Fifth—the period of the Reformation—nothing was more remarkable in history than the readiness of this restored secular power to sustain the Papacy and to carry out its designs; or than the readiness of the Papacy to sustain an absolute civil despotism, and to make the world subject to it by suppressing all attempts in favour of civil liberty.

16. *And he caused all.* He claims jurisdiction, in the matters here referred to, over all classes of persons, and compels them to do his will. This is the second beast, and, according to the interpretation given above, it relates to the Papal power, and to its claim of universal jurisdiction. ¶ *Both small and great.* All these expressions are designed to denote *universality*—referring to various divisions into which the human family may be regarded as divided. One of those divisions is into "small and great;" that is, into young and old; those small in stature and those large in stature; those of humble, and those of elevated rank. ¶ *Rich and poor.* Another way of dividing the human race, and denoting here, as in the former case, *all*—for it is a com-

A.D. 96.]  CHAPTER XIII.  333

**17 And that no man might buy or sell, save he that had the mark,** or the name of the beast, or ʸthe number of his name.

*y* ch.15.2.

mon method, in speaking of mankind, to describe them as "the rich and poor." ¶ *Free and bond.* Another method still of dividing the human race, embracing *all*—for all the dwellers upon the earth are either free or bond. These various forms of expression, therefore, are designed merely to denote, in an emphatic manner, *universality*. The idea is, that, in the matter referred to, none were exempt, either on account of their exalted rank, or on account of their humble condition; either because they were so mighty as to be beyond control, or so mean and humble as to be beneath notice. And if this refers to the Papacy, every one will see the propriety of the description. The jurisdiction set up by that power has been as absolute over kings as over the feeble and the poor; over masters and their slaves; alike over those in the humblest and in the most elevated walks of life. ¶ *To receive a mark in their right hand, or in their foreheads.* The word here rendered *mark*—χάραγμα—occurs only in one place in the New Testament except in the book of Revelation (Ac. xvii. 29), where it is rendered *graven*. In all the other places where it is found (Re. xiii. 16, 17; xiv. 9, 11; xv. 2; xvi. 2; xix. 20; xx. 4), it is rendered *mark*, and is applied to the same thing—the "mark of the beast." The word properly means something graven or sculptured; hence, (*a*) a graving, sculpture, sculptured work, as images or idols; (*b*) a mark cut in or stamped—as the stamp on coin. Applied to men, it was used to denote some stamp or mark on the hand or elsewhere—as in the case of a servant on whose hand or arm the name of the master was impressed; or of a soldier on whom some mark was impressed denoting the company or phalanx to which he belonged. It was no uncommon thing to mark slaves or soldiers in this way; and the design was either to denote their ownership or rank, or to prevent their escaping so as not to be detected.\* Most of us have seen such marks made on the hands or arms of sailors, in which, by a voluntary *tattooing*, their names, or the names of their vessels, were written, or the figure of an anchor, or some other device, was indelibly made by punctures in the skin, and by inserting some kind of colouring matter. The thing which it is here said was engraven on the hand or the forehead was the "name" of the beast, or the "number" of his name, ver. 17. That is, the "name" or the "number" was so indelibly inscribed either on the hand or the forehead, as to show that he who bare it appertained to the "beast," and was subject to his authority—as a slave is to his master, or a soldier to his commander. Applied to the Papacy, the meaning is, that there would be some mark of distinction; some indelible sign; something which would designate, with entire certainty, those persons who belonged to it, and who were subject to it. It is hardly necessary to say that, in point of fact, this has eminently characterized the Papacy. All possible care has been taken to designate with accuracy those who belong to that communion, and, all over the world, it is easy to distinguish those who render allegiance to the Papal power. Comp. Notes on ch. vii. 3.

17. *And that no man might buy or sell.* That is, this mighty power would claim jurisdiction over the traffic of the world, and endeavour to make it tributary to its own purposes. Comp. ch. xviii. 11-13, 17-19. This is represented by saying that no one might "buy or sell" except by its permission; and it is clear that where this power exists of determining who may "buy and sell," there is absolute control over the wealth of the world. ¶ *Save he that had the mark.* To keep it all among its own friends; among those who showed allegiance to this power. ¶ *Or the name of the beast.* That is, the "mark" referred to was *either* the name of the beast, or the number of his name. The meaning is, that he had something branded on him that showed that he

---

\*Among the Romans, slaves were stigmatized with the master's name or mark on their foreheads. So Valerius Maximus speaks of the custom for slaves, "literarum notis inuri;" and Plautus calls the slave "literatus." Ambrose (*De Obit. Valentin.*) says, Charactere Domini inscribuntur servuli. Petronius mentions the forehead as the place of the mark: Servitia ecce in frontibus cernitis. In many cases, soldiers bore the emperor's name or mark imprinted on the hand. Actius says, Stigmata vocant quæ in facie, vel in aliâ parte corporis, inscribuntur; qualia sunt militum in manibus. So Ambrose says, Nomine imperatoris signantur milites. Comp. Notes on Gal. vi. 17.

18 Here is wisdom. Let him that hath understanding count the number of the beast: for it is the number of a man; and his number *is* six hundred threescore *and* six.

belonged to the beast—as a slave had the name of his master; in other words, there was something that certainly showed that he was subject to its authority. ¶ *Or the number of his name.* In regard to what is denoted by the *number* of the beast, see Notes on ver. 18. The idea here is, that that "number," whatever it was, was so marked on him as to show to whom he belonged. According to the interpretation here proposed, the meaning of this passage is, that the Papacy would claim jurisdiction over traffic and commerce; or would endeavour to bring it under its control, and make it subservient to its own ends. Traffic or commerce is one of the principal means by which property is acquired, and he who has the control of this has, to a great degree, the control of the wealth of a nation; and the question now is, whether any such jurisdiction has been set up, or whether any such control has in fact been exercised, so that the wealth of the world has been subject to Papal Rome? For a more full illustration of this I may refer to the Notes on ch. xviii. 11-13, 16, 17; but at present it may be sufficient to remark, that the manifest aim of the Papacy, in all its history, has been to control the world, and to get dominion over its wealth, in order that it might accomplish its own purposes. But, besides this, there have been numerous specified acts more particularly designed to control the business of "buying and selling." It has been common in Rome to prohibit, by express law, all traffic with heretics. Thus a canon of the Lateran council, under Pope Alexander III., commanded that no man should entertain or cherish them in his house or land, or *traffic* with them (Hard. vi., ii. 1684). The synod of Tours, under the same Pope Alexander, passed the law that no man should presume to receive or assist the heretics, no, not so much as to exercise commerce with them in *selling* or *buying*. And so, too, the Constance council, as expressed in Pope Martin's bull (Elliott, vol. iii. pp. 220, 221).

18. *Here is wisdom.* That is, in what is stated respecting the name and the number of the name of the beast. The idea is, either that there would be need of peculiar sagacity in determining what the "number" of the "beast" or of his "name" was, or that peculiar "wisdom" was shown by the fact that the number could be thus expressed. The language used in the verse would lead the reader to suppose that the attempt to make out the "number" was not absolutely *hopeless*, but that the number was so far enigmatical as to require much skill in determining its meaning. It may also be implied that, for some reason, there was true "wisdom" in designating the name by this number, either because a more direct and explicit statement might expose him who made it to persecution, and it showed practical wisdom thus to guard against this danger; or because there was "wisdom" or skill shown in the fact that a number could be found which would thus correspond with the name. On either of these suppositions, peculiar wisdom would be required in deciphering its meaning. ¶ *Let him that hath understanding.* Implying (*a*) that it was *practicable* to "count the number of the name;" and (*b*) that it would require uncommon skill to do it. It could not be successfully attempted by all; but still there were those who might do it. This is such language as would be used respecting some difficult matter, but where there was hope that, by diligent application of the mind, and by the exercise of a sound understanding, there would be a prospect of success. ¶ *Count the number of the beast.* In ver. 16 it is "the number of his name." The word here rendered "count"—ψηφισάτω—means, properly, to count or reckon with pebbles, or counters; then to reckon, to estimate. The word here means *compute;* that is, ascertain the exact import of the number, so as to identify the beast. The "number" is that which is immediately specified, "six hundred threescore and six"—666. The phrase "the number of the beast" means, that somehow this number was so connected with the beast, or would so represent its name or character, that the "beast" would be identified by its proper application. The mention in ver. 17 of "the *name* of the beast," and "the *number* of his name," shows that this "number" was somehow connected with his proper designation, so that by

this he would be identified. The plain meaning is, that the number 666 would be so connected with his *name*, or with that which would properly designate him, that it could be determined who was meant by finding that number *in* his name or in his proper designation. This is the exercise of the skill or wisdom to which the writer here refers: substantially that which is required in the solution of a riddle or a conundrum. If it should be said here that this is undignified and unworthy of an inspired book, it may be replied, (*a*) that there might be some important reason why the name or designation should not be more plainly made; (*b*) that it was important, nevertheless, that it should be so made that it would be possible to ascertain who was referred to; (*c*) that this should be done only in some way which would involve the principle of the enigma—"where a known thing was concealed under obscure language" (Webster's *Dict.*); (*d*) that the use of symbols, emblems, hieroglyphics, and riddles was common in the early periods of the world; and (*e*) that it was no uncommon thing in ancient times, as it is in modern, to test the capacity and skill of men by their ability to unfold the meaning of proverbs, riddles, and dark sayings. Comp. the riddle of Samson, Ju. xiv. 12, seq. See also Ps. xlix. 4; lxxviii. 2; Eze. xvii. 2-8; Pr. i. 2-6; Da. viii. 23. It would be a *sufficient* vindication of the method adopted here if it was certain or probable that a direct and explicit statement of what was meant would have been attended with immediate danger, and if the object could be secured by an enigmatical form. ¶ *For it is the number of a man.* Various interpretations of this have been proposed. Clericus renders it, "The number is small, or not such as cannot be estimated by a man." Rosenmüller, "The number indicates *a man*, or a certain race of men." Professor Stuart, "The number is to be computed *more humano*, not *more angelico;*" "it is a man's number." De Wette, "It is such a number as is commonly reckoned or designated by men." Other interpretations may be seen in Poole's *Synopsis*. That which is proposed by Rosenmüller, however, meets all the circumstances of the case. The idea is, evidently, that the number indicates or refers to a certain man, or order of men. It does not pertain to a brute, or to angelic beings. Thus it would be understood by one merely interpreting the language, and thus the connection demands. ¶ *And his number is six hundred threescore and six.* The number of his name, ver. 17. This cannot be supposed to mean that his name would be composed of six hundred and sixty-six letters; and it must, therefore, mean that somehow the number 666 would be expressed by his name in some well-understood method of computation. The *number* here—six hundred and sixty-six—is, in Walton's *Polyglott*, written out in full: 'Εξακόσιοι ἑξάκοντα ἕξ. In Wetstein, Griesbach, Hahn, Tittmann, and the common Greek text, it is expressed by the characters χξς' =666. There can be no doubt that this is the correct number, though, in the time of Irenæus, there was in some copies another reading—χις'=616. This reading was adopted by the expositor Tychonius; but against this Irenæus inveighs (Liv. v. c. 30). There can be no doubt that the number 666 is the correct reading, though it would seem that this was sometimes expressed in letters, and sometimes written in full. Wetstein supposes that *both* methods were used by John; that in the first copy of his book he used the letters, and in a subsequent copy wrote it in full. This inquiry is not of material consequence.

It need not be said that much has been written on this mysterious "number," and that very different theories have been adopted in regard to its application. For the views which have been entertained on the subject, the reader may consult, with advantage, the article in Calmet's *Dict.*, under the word "Antichrist." It was natural for Calmet, being a Roman Catholic, to endeavour to show that the interpretations have been so various, that there could be no certainty in the application, and especially in the common application to the Papacy. In endeavouring to ascertain the meaning of the passage, the following *general* remarks may be made, as containing the result of the investigation thus far:—(*a*) There was some *mystery* in the matter—some designed concealment—some reason why a more explicit statement was not adopted. The reason of this is not stated; but it may not be improper to suppose that it arose from something in the circumstances of the writer, and that the adoption of this enigmatical expression was designed to avoid some peril to which he or others might be exposed if there were a more explicit statement. (*b*) It is implied, nevertheless, that it *could be* understood; that is, that the meaning was not so obscure that, by proper study, the designed reference could not be ascertained without material danger of error. (*c*) It required *skill* to do this; either natural sagacity, or particular skill in interpreting hieroglyphics and symbols, or uncommon spiritual discernment. (*d*) Some man, or order of men, is referred to that could properly be designated in this manner. (*e*) The method of designating persons obscurely by a reference to the numerical signification of the letters in their names was not very uncommon, and was one that was not unlikely, in the circumstances of the case, to have been resorted to by John. "Thus, among the Pagans, the Egyptian mystics spoke of Mercury, or Thouth, under the name 1218, because the Greek letters composing the word Thouth, when estimated by their numerical value, together made up that number. By others, Jupiter was invoked under the mystical number 717; because the letters of 'Η ΑΡΧΗ—*Beginning*, or *First Origin*, which was a characteristic of the supreme deity worshipped as Jupiter, made up that number. And Apollo under the number 608, as being that of νυς or υης, words expressing certain solar attributes. Again, the pseudo-Christian, or semi-Pagan Gnostics, from St. John's time and downwards, affixed to their gems and amulets, of which multitudes remain to the present day, the mystic word αβρασαξ [*abrasax*] or αβραξας [*abraxas*], under the idea of some magic virtue attaching to its number 365, as being that of the days of the annual solar circle," &c. See other instances referred to in Elliott, iii. 205. These facts show that John would not be unlikely to adopt some such method of expressing a sentiment which it was designed should be obscure in form, but possible to be understood. It should be added here, that this was more common among the Jews than among any other people. (*f*) It seems clear that some *Greek* word is here referred to, and that the mystic number is to be found in some word of that language. The *reasons* for this opinion are these: (1) John was writing in Greek, and it is most natural to suppose that this would be the reference; (2) he expected that his book would be read by those who understood the Greek language, and it would have been unnatural to have increased the perplexity in understanding what he referred to by introducing a word of a foreign language; (3) the first and last letters of the Greek alphabet, and not those of the Hebrew, are expressly selected by the Saviour to denote his eternity—"I am Alpha and Omega," ch. i. 8, 11; and (4) the numerals by which the enigma is expressed—χξς'—are Greek. It has indeed been supposed by many that the solution is to be found in the Hebrew language, but these reasons seem to me to show conclusively that we are to look for the solution in some *Greek* word.

The question now is, whether there is any word which corresponds with these conditions, and which would naturally be referred to by John in this manner. The exposition thus far has led us to suppose that the Papacy in some form is referred to; and the inquiry now is, whether there is any word which is so certain and determinate as to make it probable that John meant to designate that. The word Λατεινος—*Lateinos*, *the Latin* [Man]—actually has all the conditions supposed in the interpretation of this passage. From this word the number specified—666—is made out as follows:—

| Λ | Α | Τ | Ε | Ι | Ν | Ο | Σ |
|---|---|---|---|---|---|---|---|
| 30 | 1 | 300 | 5 | 10 | 50 | 70 | 200 = 666 |

In support of the opinion that this is the word intended to be referred to, the following suggestions may be made: (*a*) It is a Greek word. (*b*) It expresses the exact number, and corresponds in this respect with the language used by John. (*c*) It was early suggested as the probable meaning, and by those who lived near the time of John; who were intimately acquainted with the Greek language; and who may be supposed to have been familiar with this mode of writing. Thus it was suggested by Irenæus, who says, "It seems to me very probable; for this is a name of the last of Daniel's four kingdoms; they being *Latins* that now reign." It is true that he also mentions two other words as those which *may* be meant—ευανθας, a word which had been suggested by others, but concerning which he makes no remarks, and which, of course, must have been destitute of any probability in his view; and Τειταν, which he thinks has the clearest claims for admission—though he speaks of the word *Lateinos* as having a claim of probability. (*b*) This word would properly denote the Roman power, or the then *Latin* power, and would refer to that dominion as a Latin dominion—as it properly was; and if it be supposed that it was intended to refer to that, and, at the same time, that there should be some degree of obscurity about it, this would be more likely to be selected than the word *Roman*, which was better known; and (*e*) there was a *special* propriety in this, on the supposition that it was intended to refer to the *Papal* Latin power. The most *appropriate* appellation, if it was designed to refer to Rome as a *civil* power, would undoubtedly have been the word *Roman;* but if it was intended to refer to the *ecclesiastical* power, or to the Papacy, this is the *very* word to express the idea. In earlier times the more common appellation was *Roman*. This continued until the separation of the Eastern and Western empires, when the Eastern was called *Greek*, and the Western the *Latin;* or when the Eastern empire assumed the name of *Roman*, and affixed to the Western kingdoms one and all that were connected with Rome the appellation of *Latin*. This appellation, originally applied to the *language* only, was adopted by the Western kingdoms, and came to be that by which they were best designated. It was the Latin world, the Latin kingdom, the Latin church, the Latin patriarch, the Latin clergy, the Latin councils. To use Dr. More's words, "They *Latinize* everything: mass, prayers, hymns, litanies, canons, decretals, bulls, are conceived in Latin. The Papal councils speak in Latin, women themselves pray in Latin. The Scriptures are read in no other language under the Papacy than Latin. In short, all things are Latin." With what propriety, then, might John, under the influence of inspiration, speak, in this enigmatical manner, of the new power that was symbolized by the beast as *Latin*.

The only objection to this solution that has been suggested is, that the orthography of the Greek word is Λατινος —*Latinos*, and not Λατεινος—*Lateinos*, giving the number 661, and not 666; and Bellarmine asserts that this is the uniform method of spelling in Greek authors. All that is necessary in reply to this is to copy the following remark from Professor Stuart, vol. ii. p. 456:

"As to the form of the Greek word Λατεινος [*Lateinos*], viz., that ει is employed for the Latin long ī, it is a sufficient vindication of it to cite Σαβεινος, Φαυστεινος, Παυλεινος, Αντωνεινος, Ατειλιος, Μετειλιος, Παπειριος, Ουειβιος, &c. Or we may refer to the custom of the more ancient Latin, as in Plautus, of writing *i* by *ei*; *e.g.*, solitei, Diveis, captivei, preimus, Lateina, &c." See this point examined further, in Elliott, iii. 210–213.

As a matter of historical interest, it may be observed that the solution of the difficulty has been sought in numerous other words, and the friends of the Papacy and the enemies of the Bible have endeavoured to show that such terms are so numerous that there can be no certainty in the application. Thus Calmet (*Dict.* art. "Antichrist"), after enumerating many of these terms, says: "The number 666 is found in names the most sacred, the most opposite to Antichrist. The wisest and best way is to be silent."

We have seen that, besides the name *Lateinos*, two other words had been referred to in the time of Irenæus. Some of the words in which the mysterious number has been since supposed to be found are the following:—

נרון קסר Neron Cæsar = 50 + 200 + 6 + 50, and 100 + 60 + 200 = .......... 666
Diocles Augustus (Dioclesian) = .... DCLXVI.
C. F. Julianus Cæsar Atheus (the Apostate) = ..................... DCLXVI.
Luther— לוהתר = 200 + 400 + 30 + 6 + 30 = ...................................... 666
Lampetis, λαμπετις = 30 + 1 + 40 + 80 + 5 + 300 + 10 + 200 = ............... 666
η Λατινη βασιλεια = 8 + 30 + 1 + 300 + 10 + 50 + 8 + 2 + 1 + 200 + 10 + 30 + 5 + 10 + 1 = ...................... 666
Ιταλικα εκκλησια = 10 + 300 + 1 + 30 + 10 + 20 + 1 + 5 + 20 + 20 + 30 + 8 + 200 + 10 + 1 = ...................... 666
Αποστατης (the Apostate) = 1 + 80 + 70 + 6 + 1 + 300 + 8 + 200 = ......... 666
רומיית (Roman, sc. *Sedes*) = 200 + 6 + 40 + 10 + 10 + 400 = ............ 666
רמינוש (Romanus, sc. *Man*) = 200 + 40 + 70 + 50 + 6 + 300 = ............ 666

It will be admitted that many of these, and others that might be named, are fanciful, and perhaps had their origin in a determination, on the one hand, to find *Rome* referred to somehow, or in a determination, on the other hand, equally strong, *not* to find this; but still it is remarkable how many of the most obvious solutions refer to Rome and the Papacy. But the mind need not be distracted, nor need doubt be thrown over the subject, by the *number* of the solutions proposed. They show the restless character of the human mind, and the ingenuity of men; but this should not be allowed to bring into doubt a solution that is simple and natural, and that meets all the circumstances of the case. Such a solution, I believe, is found in the word Λατεινος— *Lateinos*, as illustrated above; and as that, if correct, settles the case, it is unnecessary to pursue the matter further. Those who are disposed to do so, however, may find ample illustration in Calmet, *Dict.* art. "Antichrist;" Elliott, *Horæ Apoca.* iii. 207-221; Prof. Stuart, *Com.* vol. ii. Excursus iv.; *Bibliotheca Sacra*, i. 84-86; Robert Fleming on the *Rise and Fall of the Papacy*, 28, seq.; De Wette, *Exegetisches Handbuch, N. T.*, iii. 140-142; Vitringa, *Com.* 625-637, Excursus iv.; *Nov. Tes. Edi. Koppianæ*, vol. x. *b*, pp. 235-265; and the Commentaries generally.

## CHAPTER XIV.

### ANALYSIS OF THE CHAPTER.

In the previous chapters (xii., xiii.) there is a description of the woes and sorrows which, for a long period, would come upon the church, and which would threaten to destroy it. It was proper that this gloomy picture should be relieved, and accordingly this chapter, having much of the aspect of an episode, is thrown in to comfort the hearts of those who should see those troublous times. There were bright scenes beyond, and it was important to direct the eye to them, that the hearts of the sad might be consoled. This chapter, therefore, contains a succession of symbolical representations designed to show the ultimate result of all these things— " to hold out the symbols of ultimate and certain victory" (Professor Stuart). Those symbols are the following:—

(1) The vision of the hundred and forty-four thousand on Mount Zion, as emblematical of the final triumph of the redeemed, ver. 1-5. They have the Father's name in their foreheads (ver. 1); they sing a song of victory (ver. 2, 3); they are found without fault before God—representatives, in this respect, of all that will be saved, ver. 4, 5.

(2) The vision of the final triumph of the gospel, ver. 6, 7. An angel is seen flying in the midst of heaven, having the everlasting gospel to preach to all that dwell upon the earth, and announcing that the end is near — a representation designed to show that the gospel *will* be thus preached among all nations; and when that is done, the time will draw on when the affairs of the world will be wound up.

(3) The fall of Babylon, the mighty Antichristian power, ver. 8. An angel is seen going forth announcing the glad tidings that this mighty power is overthrown, and that, therefore, its oppressions are come to an end. This, to the church in trouble and persecution, is one of the most comforting of all the assurances that God makes in regard to the future.

(4) The certain and final destruction of all the upholders of that Antichristian power, ver. 9-12. Another angel is seen making proclamation that all the supporters and abettors of this formidable power would drink of the wine of the wrath of God; that they would be tormented with fire and brimstone; and that the smoke of their torment would ascend up for ever and ever.

(5) The blessedness of all those who die in the Lord; who, amidst the persecutions and trials that were to come upon the church, would be found faithful unto death, ver. 13. They would rest from their labours; the works of mercy which they had done on the earth would follow them to the future world, securing rich and eternal blessings there.

(6) The final overthrow of all the enemies of the church, ver. 14-20. This is the grand completion; to this all things are tending; this will be certainly accomplished in due time. This is represented under various emblems: (*a*) The Son of man appears seated on a cloud, having on his head a golden crown, and in his hand a sharp sickle — emblem of gathering in the great harvest of the earth, and of his own glorious reign in heaven, ver. 14. (*b*) An angel is seen coming out of the temple, announcing that the time had come, and calling on the great Reaper to thrust in his sickle, for the harvest of the world was ripe, ver. 15. (*c*) He that has the sickle thrusts in his sickle to reap the great harvest, ver. 16. (*d*) Another angel is seen representing the final judgment of God on the wicked, ver. 17-20. He also has a sharp sickle; he is commanded by an angel that has power over fire to thrust in his sickle

## CHAPTER XIV.

AND I looked, and, lo, a *a* Lamb stood on the mount Zion, and with him *b* an hundred forty and four thousand, *c* having his Father's name written in their foreheads.

2 And I heard a voice from heaven, as *d* the voice of many waters, and as the voice of a great thunder: and I heard the voice of *e* harpers harping with their harps:

3 And they sung as it were *f* a new song before the throne, and before the four beasts, and the elders: and no man could learn

*a* ch.5.12.   *b* ch.7.4.   *c* ch.3.12.   *d* ch.19.6.   *e* ch.5.8,9.   *f* ch.15.3.

into the earth; he goes forth and gathers the clusters of the vine of the earth, and casts them into the great wine-press of the wrath of God.

This whole chapter, therefore, is designed to relieve the gloom of the former representations. The *action* of the grand moving panorama is stayed that the mind may not be overwhelmed with gloomy thoughts, but that it may be cheered with the assurance of the final triumph of truth and righteousness. The chapter, viewed in this light, is introduced with great artistic skill, as well as great beauty of poetic illustration; and, in its place, it is adapted to set forth this great truth, that, to the righteous, and to the church at large, in the darkest times, and with the most threatening prospect of calamity and sorrow, there is the certainty of final victory, and that this should be allowed to cheer and sustain the soul.

1. *And I looked.* My attention was drawn to a new vision. The eye was turned away from the beast and his image to the heavenly world — the Mount Zion above. ¶ *And, lo, a Lamb.* See Notes on ch. v. 6. ¶ *Stood on the mount Zion.* That is, in heaven. See Notes on He. xii. 22. Zion, literally the southern hill in the city of Jerusalem, was a name also given to the whole city; and, as that was the seat of the divine worship on earth, it became an emblem of heaven — the dwelling-place of God. The scene of the vision here is laid in heaven, for it is a vision of the ultimate triumph of the redeemed, designed to sustain the church in view of the trials that had already come upon it, and of those which were yet to come. ¶ *And with him an hundred forty* and *four thousand.* These are evidently the same persons that were seen in the vision recorded in ch. vii. 3-8, and the representation is made for the same purpose—to sustain the church in trial, with the certainty of its future glory. See Notes on ch. vii. 4. ¶ *Having his Father's name written in their foreheads.* Showing that they were his. See Notes on ch. vii. 3; xiii. 16. In ch. vii. 3, it is merely said that they were "sealed in their foreheads;" the passage here shows *how* they were sealed. They had the name of God so stamped or marked on their foreheads as to show that they belonged to him. Comp. Notes on ch. vii. 3-8.

2. *And I heard a voice from heaven.* Showing that the scene is laid in heaven, but that John in the vision was on the earth. ¶ *As the voice of many waters.* As the *sound* of the ocean, or of a mighty cataract. That is, it was so loud that it could be heard from heaven to earth. No comparison could express this more sublimely than to say that it was like the roar of the ocean. ¶ *As the voice of a great thunder.* As the loud sound of thunder. ¶ *And I heard the voice of harpers.* In heaven: the song of redemption accompanied with strains of sweet instrumental music. For a description of the *harp,* see Notes on Is. v. 12. ¶ *Harping with their harps.* Playing on their harps. This image gives new beauty to the description. Though the sound was loud and swelling, so loud that it could be heard on the earth, yet it was not mere shouting, or merely a tumultuous cry. "It was like the sweetness of symphonious harps." The music of heaven, though elevated and joyous, is sweet and harmonious; and perhaps one of the best representations of heaven on earth, is the effect produced on the soul by strains of sweet and solemn music.

3. *And they sung as it were a new song.* See Notes on ch. v. 9. It was proper to call this "*new,*" because it was on a new occasion, or pertained to a new object. The song here was in celebration of the complete redemption of the church, and was the song to be sung in view of its final triumph over all its foes. Comp. Notes on ch. vii. 9, 10. ¶ *Before the throne.* The throne of God in heaven. See Notes

340              REVELATION.              [A.D. 96.

that song but *g*the hundred *and* forty *and* four thousand, which were redeemed from the earth.

4 These are they which were not defiled with women; for they are

*g* ver.1.

*h* virgins. These are they *i* which follow the Lamb whithersoever he goeth. These were ¹redeemed from among men, *being* *k*the first-fruits unto God and to the Lamb.

*h* Ca.1.3; 6.8; 2 Co.11.2.  *i* Jn.10.27.
¹ *bought*, 1 Co.6.20.  *k* Ja.1.18.

on ch. iv. 2. ¶ *And before the four beasts.* See Notes on ch. iv. 6-8. ¶ *And the elders.* See Notes on ch. iv. 4. ¶ *And no man could learn that song,* &c. None could understand it but the redeemed. That is, none who had not been redeemed could enter fully into the feelings and sympathies of those who were. A great truth is taught here. To appreciate fully the songs of Zion; to understand the language of praise; to enter into the spirit of the truths which pertain to redemption; one must himself have been redeemed by the blood of Christ. He must have known what it is to be a sinner under the condemnation of a holy law; he must have known what it is to be in danger of eternal death; he must have experienced the joys of pardon, or he can never understand, in its true import, the language used by the redeemed. And this is only saying what we are familiar with in other things. He who is saved from peril; he who is rescued from long captivity; he who is pardoned at the foot of the scaffold; he who is recovered from dangerous illness; he who presses to his bosom a beloved child just rescued from a watery grave, will have an appreciation of the language of joy and triumph which he can never understand who has not been placed in such circumstances: but of all the joy ever experienced in the universe, so far as we can see, that must be the most sublime and transporting, which will be experienced when the redeemed shall stand on Mount Zion above, and shall realize that they are *saved.*

4. *These are they.* In this verse, and in the following verse, the writer states the leading characteristics of those who are saved. The *general* idea is, that they are chaste; that they are the followers of the Lamb; that they are redeemed from among men; and that they are without guile. ¶ *Which were not defiled with women.* Who were chaste. The word *defiled* here determines the meaning of the passage, as denoting that they were not guilty of illicit intercourse with women. It is unnecessary to show that this is a virtue everywhere required in the Bible, and everywhere stated as among the characteristics of the redeemed. On no point are there more frequent exhortations in the Scriptures than on this; on no point is there more solicitude manifested that the professed friends of the Saviour should be without blame. Comp. Notes on Ac. xv. 20; Ro. i. 24-32; 1 Co. vi. 18; He. xiii. 4. See also 1 Co. v. 1; vi. 13; Ga. v. 19; Ep. v. 3; Col. iii. 5; 1 Th. iv. 3. This passage cannot be adduced in favour of celibacy, whether among the clergy or laity, or in favour of monastic principles in any form; for the thing that is specified is, that they were not "*defiled* with women," and a lawful connection of the sexes, such as marriage, is *not* defilement. See Notes on He. xiii. 4. The word here rendered *defiled*—ἐμολύνθησαν, from μολύνω—is a word that cannot be applied to the marriage relation. It means properly *to soil, to stain, to defile.* 1 Co. viii. 7: "Their conscience being weak, is *defiled.*" Re. iii. 4: "Which have not *defiled* their garments." The word does not elsewhere occur in the New Testament, except in the passage before us, and it will be seen at once that it cannot be applied to that which is lawful and proper, and consequently that it cannot be construed as an expression against marriage and in favour of celibacy. It is a word that is properly expressive of illicit intercourse—of impurity and unchastity of life—and the statement is, that they who are saved are not impure and unchaste. ¶ *For they are virgins*—παρθένοι. This is the masculine form, but this form is found in the later Greek and in the Christian fathers. See Suidas and Suicer, *Thes.* The meaning of the word, when found in the feminine form, is well understood. It denotes a virgin, a maiden, and thence it is used to denote that which is chaste and pure: virgin modesty; virgin gold; virgin soil; virgin blush; virgin shame. The word in the masculine form must have a similar meaning as applied to men, and may denote

5 And in their mouth *l* was found no guile: for they are *m* without fault before the throne of God.

*l* Ps.32.2.
*m* Ep.5.27; Jude 24.

(*a*) those who are unmarried; (*b*) those who are chaste and pure in general. The word is applied by Suidas to Abel and Melchizedek. "The sense," says De Wette, *in loco*, "cannot be that all those 144,000 had lived an unmarried life; for how could the apostle Peter, and others who were married, have been excluded? But the reference must be to those who held themselves from all impurity—*unkeuschheit und hurerei*—which, in the view of the apostles, was closely connected with idolatry." Comp. Bleek, *Beitr.* i. 185. Professor Stuart supposes that the main reference here is to those who had kept themselves from idolatry, and who were thus pure. It seems to me, however, that the most obvious meaning is the correct one, that it refers to the redeemed as chaste, and thus brings into view one of the prominent things in which Christians are distinguished from the devotees of nearly every other form of religion, and, indeed, exclusively from the world at large. This passage, also, cannot be adduced in favour of the monastic system, because, (*a*) whatever may be said anywhere of the purity of virgins, there is no *such* commendation of it as to imply that the married life is impure; (*b*) it cannot be supposed that God meant in any way to reflect on the married life as in itself impure or dishonourable; (*c*) the language does not demand such an interpretation; and (*d*) the *facts* in regard to the monastic life have shown that it has had very little pretensions to a claim of virgin purity. ¶ *These are they which follow the Lamb.* This is another characteristic of those who are redeemed—that they are followers of the Lamb of God. That is, they are his disciples; they imitate his example; they obey his instructions; they yield to his laws; they receive him as their counsellor and their guide. See Notes on Jn. x. 3, 27. ¶ *Whithersoever he goeth.* As sheep follow the shepherd. Comp. Ps. xxiii. 1, 2. It is one characteristic of true Christians that they follow the Saviour *wherever* he leads them. Be it into trouble, into danger, into difficult duty; be it in Christian or heathen lands; be it in pleasant paths, or in roads rough and difficult, they commit themselves wholly to his guidance, and submit themselves wholly to his will. ¶ *These were redeemed from among men.* This is another characteristic of those who are seen on Mount Zion. They are there *because* they are redeemed, and they have the character of the redeemed. They are not there in virtue of rank or blood (Jn. i. 13); not on the ground of their own works (Tit. iii. 5); but because they are redeemed unto God by the blood of his Son. See Notes on ch. v. 9, 10. None will be there of whom it cannot be said that they are "redeemed;" none will be absent who have been truly redeemed from sin. ¶ *Being the first-fruits unto God.* On the meaning of the word *first-fruits*, see Notes on 1 Co. xv. 20. The meaning here would seem to be, that the hundred and forty-four thousand were not to be regarded as the *whole* of the number that was saved, but that they were *representatives* of the redeemed. They had the same characteristics which all the redeemed must have; they were a pledge that all the redeemed would be there. Professor Stuart supposes that the sense is, that they were, as it were, "an offering peculiarly acceptable to God." The former explanation, however, meets all the circumstances of the case, and is more in accordance with the usual meaning of the word. ¶ *And to the Lamb.* They stood there as redeemed by him, thus honouring him as their Redeemer, and showing forth his glory.

5. *And in their mouth was found no guile.* No deceit, fraud, hypocrisy. They were sincerely and truly what they professed to be—the children of God. This is the last characteristic which is given of them as redeemed, and it is not necessary to say that this is always represented as one of the characteristics of the true children of God. See Notes on Jn. i. 47. ¶ *For they are without fault before the throne of God.* The word here rendered *without fault*—ἀμωμοι—means, properly, *spotless, without blemish*, 1 Pe. i. 19. See Notes on Col. i. 22. This cannot be construed as meaning that they were by nature pure and holy, but only that they were pure as they stood before the throne of God in heaven—"having washed their robes, and made them pure in the blood of the Lamb." See Notes on ch. vii. 14. It will be certainly true that all who stand there will

6 And I saw another angel fly in the midst of heaven, having *ⁿ*the everlasting gospel to preach unto them that dwell on the earth, and to *ᵒ*every nation, and kindred, and tongue, and people,

*n* 2 Sa.23.5; Is.40.8.
*o* Ep.3.9.

be, in fact, pure, for nothing impure or unholy shall enter there, ch. xxi. 27.

The *design* of this portion of the chapter was evidently to comfort those to whom the book was addressed, and, in the same way, to comfort all the children of God in times of persecution and trial. Those living in the time of John were suffering persecution, and, in the previous chapters, he had described more fearful trials yet to come on the church. In these trials, therefore, present and prospective, there was a propriety in fixing the thoughts on the final triumph of the redeemed—that glorious state in heaven where all persecution shall cease, and where all the ransomed of the Lord shall stand before his throne. What could be better fitted than this view to sustain the souls of the persecuted and the sorrowful? And how often since in the history of the church—in the dark times of religious declension and of persecution—has there been occasion to seek consolation in this bright view of heaven? How often in the life of each believer, when sorrows come upon him like a flood, and earthly consolation is gone, is there occasion to look to that blessed world where all the redeemed shall stand before God; where all tears shall be wiped away from every face; and where there shall be the assurance that the last pang has been endured, and that the soul is to be happy for ever?

6. *And I saw another angel.* This must, of course, mean a different one from some one mentioned before; but no such angel is referred to in the previous chapters, unless we go back to ch. xii. 7. It is not necessary, however, to suppose that John refers to a particular angel immediately preceding this. In the course of these visions he had seen many angels; and now, accustomed to these visions, he says that he saw "another" one employed in a remarkable embassy, whose message was fitted to cheer the hearts of the desponding, and to support the souls of the persecuted and the sad—for his appearing was the pledge that the gospel would be ultimately preached to all that dwell upon the earth. The *design* of this vision is, therefore, substantially the same as the former—to cheer the heart, and to sustain the courage and the faith of the church, in the persecutions and trials which were yet to come, by the assurance that the gospel would be ultimately triumphant. ¶ *Fly in the midst of heaven.* In the air; so as to appear to be moving along the face of the sky. The scene cannot be *in* heaven, as the gospel is not to be preached there; but the word must denote heaven as it appears to us—the sky. Professor Stuart renders it correctly "mid-air." He is represented as *flying*, to denote the *rapidity* with which the gospel would spread through the world in that future period referred to. Comp. Notes on Is. vi. 2. ¶ *Having the everlasting gospel.* The gospel is here called everlasting or eternal, (*a*) because its great truths have always existed, or it is conformed to eternal truth; (*b*) because it will for ever remain unchanged—not being liable to fluctuation like the opinions held by men; (*c*) because its effects will be everlasting—in the redemption of the soul and the joys of heaven. In all the glorious eternity before the redeemed, they will be but developing the effects of that gospel on their own hearts, and enjoying the results of it in the presence of God. ¶ *To preach unto them that dwell on the earth.* To all men—as is immediately specified. Comp. Mat. xxviii. 19; Mar. xvi. 15. ¶ *And to every nation, and kindred,* &c. To all classes and conditions of men; to all men, without any distinction or exception. See Notes on ch. vii. 9. The truth here taught is, that the gospel is to be preached to all men as on an equality, without any reference to their rank, their character, or their complexion; and it is implied also, that at the time referred to this *will* be done. *When* that time will be the writer does not intimate farther, than that it would be *after* the beast and his adherents had attempted to stay its progress; and for the fulfilment of this, therefore, we are to look to a period subsequent to the rise and fall of that great Antichristian power symbolized by the beast and his image. This is in entire accordance with the prediction in Daniel. See Notes on Da. vii. 19-22.

7. *Saying with a loud voice.* As if

## CHAPTER XIV.

7 Saying with a loud voice, Fear God, and give glory to him; for the *p* hour of his judgment is come: and worship him that made heaven, and earth, and the sea, and the fountains of waters.

*p* ch. 15.4.

8 And there followed another angel, saying, *q* Babylon is fallen, is fallen, that great city, because she made all nations drink of the wine of the wrath of her fornication.

*q* ch.18.2,3; Is.21.9; Je.51.7,8.

all the nations were summoned to hear. ¶ *Fear God.* That is, reverence, honour, obey God. Render homage not to the beast, to his image, or to *any* idol, but to the only true God. This is the *substance* of the gospel—its end and design—to turn men from all forms of idol worship and superstition, to the worship of the only true God. ¶ *And give glory to him.* To give glory to him is to acknowledge him as the only true God; to set up his pure worship in the heart; and to praise him as the great Ruler of heaven and earth. ¶ *For the hour of his judgment is come.* His judgment on the beast and on those who worship him. The imagery here is substantially the same as in Da. vii. 9, 10, 14, 26, 27; and there can be no doubt that there is reference to the same subject. See Notes on those verses. The main idea is, that when God shall be about to cause his gospel to spread through the world, there will be, as it were, a solemn judgment on that Antichristian power which had so long resisted his truth and persecuted his saints, and that on the fall of that power his own kingdom will be set up on the earth; that is, in the language of Daniel, "the kingdom, and the dominion, and the greatness of the kingdom under the whole heaven, shall be given to the people of the saints of the Most High." ¶ *And worship him that made heaven, and earth,* &c. The true God, the Creator of all things. As already remarked, this is the ultimate design of the gospel, and, when this is accomplished, the great end for which it was revealed will be reached.

The design of this portion of the chapter (ver. 6, 7), also, was to comfort those to whom the book was addressed, and in the same way to comfort the church in all the persecution and opposition which the truth would encounter. The ground of consolation then was, that a time was predicted when the "everlasting gospel" would be made to fly speedily through the earth, and when it would be announced that a final judgment had come upon the Antichristian power which had prevented its being before diffused over the face of the world. The same ground of encouragement and consolation exists now, and the more so as we see the day approaching; and in all times of despondency we should allow our hearts to be cheered as we see that great Antichristian power waning, and as we see evidence that the way is thus preparing for the rapid and universal diffusion of the pure gospel of Christ.

8. *And there followed another angel.* That is, in the vision. It is not necessary to suppose that this would, in the fulfilment, succeed the other *in time.* The chapter is made up of a number of representations, all designed to illustrate the same general thing, and to produce the same general effect on the mind— that the gospel would be finally triumphant, and that, therefore, the hearts of the troubled and the afflicted should be comforted. The representation in this verse, bearing on this point, is, that Babylon, the great enemy, would fall to rise no more. ¶ *Babylon.* This is the first time that the word *Babylon* occurs in this book, though it is repeatedly mentioned afterwards, ch. xvi. 19; xvii. 5; xviii. 2, 10, 21. In reference to the literal Babylon, the word is used, in the New Testament, in Mat. i. 11-13; Ac. vii. 43; 1 Pe. v. 13. See Intro. to 1 Peter, § 2. Babylon was a well-known city on the Euphrates (for a full description of which see Notes on Isaiah, analysis of ch. xiii., xiv.), and was, in the days of its pride and glory, the head of the heathen world. In reference to the meaning of the word in this place, it may be remarked, (1) That the general characteristics of Babylon were, that it was proud, haughty, insolent, oppressive. It was chiefly known and remembered by the Hebrew people as a power that had invaded the Holy Land; that had reduced its capital and temple to ruins; that had destroyed the independence of their country, subjecting it to the condition of a province, and that had carried away the inhabitants into a long and painful captivity. It became,

therefore, the emblem of all that was haughty and oppressive, and especially of all that persecuted the church of God. (2) The word must be used here to denote some power that resembled the ancient and literal Babylon in these characteristics. The literal Babylon was no more; but the name might be properly used to denote a similar power. We are to seek, therefore, in the application of this, for some power that had the same general characteristics which the literal Babylon had. (3) In inquiring, then, what is referred to here by the word Babylon, we may remark, (*a*) that it could not be the *literal* Babylon on the Euphrates, for the whole representation here is of something *future*, and the literal Babylon had long since disappeared, never, according to the prophecies, to be rebuilt. See Notes on Is. xiii. 20–22. (*b*) All the circumstances require us to understand this of Rome, at some period of its history: for Rome, like Babylon, was the seat of empire, and the head of the heathen world; Rome was characterized by many of the same attributes as Babylon, being arrogant, proud, oppressive; Rome, like Babylon, was distinguished for its conquests, and for the fact that it made all other nations subject to its control; Rome had been, like Babylon, a desolating power, having destroyed the capital of the Holy Land, and burnt its beautiful temple, and reduced the country to a province. Rome, like Babylon of old, was the most formidable power with which the church had to contend. Yet (*c*) it is not, I suppose, Rome considered as *Pagan* that is here meant, but Rome considered as the prolongation of the ancient power in the *Papal* form. Alike in this book and in Daniel, Rome, Pagan and Papal, is regarded as *one* power, standing in direct opposition to the gospel of Christ, resisting its progress in the world, and preventing its final prevalence. See Notes on Da. vii. When that falls, the last enemy of the church will be destroyed, and the final triumph of the true religion will be speedy and complete. See Da. vii. 26, 27. (*d*) So it was understood among the early Christians. Mr. Gibbon, speaking of the expectations of the early Christians about the end of the world, and the glory of the literal reign of the Messiah, says, "Whilst the happiness and glory of a temporal reign were promised to the disciples of Christ, the most dreadful calamities were denounced against an unbelieving world. The edification of the New Jerusalem was to advance by equal steps with the destruction of the mystic Babylon; and as long as the emperors who reigned before Constantine persisted in the profession of idolatry, the epithet of Babylon was applied to the city and to the empire of Rome," vol. i. p. 263. ¶ *Is fallen.* That is, an event appeared in vision *as if* a mighty city fell to rise no more. ¶ *Is fallen.* This is repeated to give emphasis to the declaration, and to express the joyousness of that event. ¶ *That great city.* Babylon in its glory was the largest city of the world. Rome, in its turn, also became the largest; and the expression used here denotes that the power here referred to would be properly represented by cities of their magnitude. ¶ *Because she made all nations drink of the wine.* This language is probably taken from Je. li. 7: "Babylon hath been a golden cup in the Lord's hand, that made all the earth drunken: the nations have drunk of the wine, therefore the nations are mad." Babylon here, in accordance with the usual custom of the sacred writers when speaking of cities (see Notes on Is. i. 8), is represented as a female—here a female of abandoned character, holding in her hand a cup of wine to attract her lovers; that is, she allures and intoxicates them. This is a beautiful image to denote the *influence* of a great and corrupt city, and especially a city corrupt in its religion and devoted to idolatry and superstition, and may well be applied either to Babylon or Rome, literal or mystical. ¶ *Of the wrath.* There seems an incongruity in the use of this word here, and Professor Stuart proposes to render it "the inflammatory wine of her fornication;" that is, inebriating wine — wine that excited the passions and that led to uncleanness. He supposes that the word here used—θυμός—means *heat, inflammation,* corresponding to the Hebrew חֵמָה. There are no instances, however, in the New Testament in which the word is used in this sense. The common and proper meaning is *mind, soul,* then mind agitated with passion or under the influence of desire—a violent commotion of mind, as wrath, anger, indignation (Rob. *Lex.*). The *ground* of the representation here seems to be that Jehovah is often described as giving to the nations in his wrath an intoxicating cup so that they should reel and stagger to their destruction. Comp. Je. xxv. 15; li. 7. The mean-

## CHAPTER XIV.

9 And the third angel followed them, saying with a loud voice, If *r* any man worship the beast and his image, and receive *his* mark in his forehead, or in his hand,

10 The same shall *s* drink of the wine of the wrath of God, which is poured out without mixture into the cup of his indignation; and he shall be tormented *t* with fire and brimstone in the presence of the holy angels, and in the presence of the Lamb:

*r* ch.13.14-16.   *s* Ps.75.8.   *t* ch.19.20.

---

ing here is, that the nations had drunk of that cup which *brought on the wrath of God* on account of her "fornication." Babylon is represented as a harlot, with a cup of wine in her hand, and the *effect* of drinking that cup was to expose them to the wrath of God, hence called "the wine of the wrath of her fornication"— the alluring cup that was followed by wrath on account of her fornication. ¶ *Of her fornication.* Due to her fornication. The word "fornication" here is used to denote *spiritual* uncleanness; that is, heathen and superstitious rites and observances. The term is often used in the Scriptures as applicable to idolatry and superstition. The general meaning here is, that Rome—Papal Rome—would employ all forms of voluptuous allurements to bring the nations to the worship of the beast and his image, and that the "wrath" of God would be poured out on account of these abominations. The *design* of this verse also is to impart consolation by the assurance that this great enemy—this mighty, formidable, persecuting power—would be entirely overthrown. This is everywhere held up as the brightest hope of the church, for with this will fall its last great enemy, and the grand obstruction to the final triumph of the gospel on earth will be removed.

9. *And the third angel followed them.* This was a new vision designed to represent the removal of all the obstructions to the final prevalence of the gospel. We are not necessarily to suppose that this event would succeed those mentioned before in the order of time, though this would be the natural construction. The *design* of this is to show that the worshippers of the beast and his image would be certainly and finally destroyed. ¶ *Saying with a loud voice.* Making a loud proclamation. Ver. 7. ¶ *If any man worship the beast and his image.* See Notes on ch. xiii. 4, 8, 12, 15. This declaration is universal, affirming of *all* who thus render idolatrous reverence to the power represented by the beast and his image that they should drink of the wine of the wrath of God. The general meaning is, that they were guilty of idolatry of a gross form; and wherever this existed they who were guilty of it would come under the denunciations in the Scriptures against idolaters. And why should not such denunciations fall on idolaters under the Papacy as well as on others? Is it not true that there is as *real* idolatry there as in the heathen world? Is not the idolatry as gross and debasing? Is it not attended with as real corruption in the heart and the life? Is it not encompassed with as many things to inflame the passions, corrupt the morals, and alienate the soul from God? And is it not all the worse for being a perversion of Christianity, and practised under the forms of the religion of the Saviour? On what principle should idolatry be denounced and condemned anywhere if it is not in Papal Rome? Comp. Notes on 2 Th. ii. 4. ¶ *And receive* his *mark in his forehead or in his hand.* See Notes on ch. xiii. 16. The word "*receive*" here implies that there was, on their part, some degree of voluntariness: it was not a mark impressed *by force*, but a mark *received*. This is true in respect to all idolatry; and this lays the ground for condemnation. Whatever art is used to induce men to worship the beast and his image, it is still true that the worshippers are *voluntary*, and that, being voluntary, it is right that they should be treated as such. It is on this ground only that any idolaters, or any sinners of any kind, can be, in the proper sense of that term, *punished*.

10. *The same shall drink of the wine of the wrath of God.* See Notes on ver. 8. The "wine of the wrath of God" is the cup in the hand of the Lord, which, when drunk, makes them reel and fall. The image would seem to have been taken from the act of holding out a cup of poison to a condemned man that he might drink and die. See the sentiment here expressed illustrated in the Notes on Is. li. 17. ¶ *Which is poured*

11 And the ᵘsmoke of their torment ascendeth up for ever and ever: and they ᵛhave no rest day nor night, who worship the beast and his image, and whosoever receiveth the mark of his name.

*u* Is.34.10.    *v* Is.57.20,21.

*out without mixture.* Without being diluted with water—that is, in its full strength. In other words, there would be no mitigation of the punishment. ¶ *Into the cup of his indignation.* The cup held in his hand, and given them to drink. This is expressive of his indignation, as it causes them to reel and fall. The sentiment here is substantially the same, though in another form, as that which is expressed in 2 Th. ii. 12. See Notes on that verse. ¶ *And he shall be tormented.* Shall be punished in a manner that would be well represented by being burned with fire and brimstone. On the meaning of this word see Notes on ch. ix. 5; xi. 10. Comp. also ch. xviii. 7, 10, 15; xx. 10; Mat. viii. 29; Mar. v. 7; Lu. viii. 28. The word commonly denotes severe torture. ¶ *With fire and brimstone.* As if with burning sulphur. See Notes on Lu. xvii. 28–30. Comp. Ps. xi. 6; Job xviii. 15; Is. xxx. 33; Eze. xxxviii. 22. The imagery is taken from the destruction of Sodom and Gomorrah, Ge. xix. 24. The common representation of the punishment of the wicked is, that it will be in the manner here represented, Mat. v. 22; xiii. 42; xviii. 9; xxv. 41; Mar. ix. 44–48; 2 Pe. iii. 7; Jude 7; Re. xx. 14. Comp. Notes on Mat. v. 22; Mar. ix. 44. ¶ *In the presence of the holy angels.* This may mean either (*a*) that the angels will be present at their condemnation (Mat. xxv. 31), or (*b*) that the *punishment* will be actually witnessed by the angels, as it is most probable it will be. Comp. Is. lxvi. 24; Lu. xvi. 23–26. ¶ *And in the presence of the Lamb.* The Lamb of God—the final Judge. This also may mean either that the condemnation will occur in his presence, or that the punishment will be under his eye. Both of these things will be true in regard to him; and it will be no small aggravation of the punishment of the wicked, that it will occur in the very presence of their slighted and rejected Saviour.

11. *And the smoke of their torment.* The smoke proceeding from their place of torment. This *language* is probably derived from the account of the destruction of Sodom and Gomorrah, Ge. xix. 28: "And he [Abraham] looked toward Sodom and Gomorrah, and toward all the land of the plain, and beheld, and lo, the smoke of the country went up as the smoke of a furnace." The destruction of these cities is regarded as an emblem of the destruction of the wicked, and the smoke that ascended from them as a representation of that which ascends from the place where the wicked suffer for ever. See Notes on Jude 7. ¶ *Ascendeth up.* Continually rises from that world of woe. ¶ *For ever and ever.* See Notes on Jude 7. This does not indeed affirm that their individual sufferings would be eternal, since it is only a declaration that "the smoke of their torment ascends," but it is such language as would be used on the supposition that they would suffer for ever, and as can be explained only on that supposition. It implies that their torments continued, and were the cause of that ascending smoke; that is, that they were tormented *while* it ascended; and, as this is declared to be "for ever and ever," it implies that the sufferings of the wicked will be eternal: and this is such language as *would* not, and *could* not have been used in a revelation from God, unless the punishment of the wicked is eternal. Comp. Notes on Mat. xxv. 46. ¶ *And they have no rest day nor night.* "Day and night" include all time; and hence the phrase is used to denote perpetuity — *always.* The meaning here is, that they *never* have any rest — any interval of pain. This is stated as a circumstance strongly expressive of the severity of their torment. Here, rest comes to the sufferer. The prisoner in his cell lies down on his bed, though hard, and sleeps; the overworked slave has also intervals of sleep; the eyes of the mourner are locked in repose, and for moments, if not hours, he forgets his sorrows; no pain that we endure on earth can be so certain and prolonged that nature will not, sooner or later, find the luxury of sleep, or will find rest in the grave. But it will be one of the bitterest ingredients in the cup of woe, in the world of despair, that this luxury will be denied for ever, and that they who enter that gloomy prison sleep no more, never know the respite of a moment, never even lose the consciousness of their heavy doom. Oh how different from the condition of sufferers here! And oh how sad and strange

A.D. 96.]   CHAPTER XIV.   347

12 Here is the patience of the saints: here *are* they that keep the commandments of God, and the faith of Jesus.

13 And I heard a voice from heaven, saying unto me, Write,

Blessed *are* the dead which *w*die in the Lord ²from henceforth: Yea, saith the Spirit, that they may rest from their labours; and their works do follow them.

*w* 1 Th.4.14,16.
² or, *from henceforth saith the Spirit, Yea.*

---

that any of our race will persevere in sin, and go down to those unmitigated and unending sorrows! ¶ *Who worship the beast and his image.* See Notes on ch. xiii. 4, 15. ¶ *And whosoever receiveth the mark of his name.* See Notes on ch. xiii. 17. The meaning here is, that such worshippers will receive the punishment which other idolaters and sinners do. No exception will be made in favour of an idolater, though he worships idols under the forms of an abused Christianity; none will be made in favour of a sinner because he practised iniquity under the garb of religion.

12. *Here is the patience of the saints.* See Notes on ch. xiii. 10. ¶ *Here are they that keep the commandments of God.* That is, in exercising such patience. Those who exercise that "patience" in these long-continued persecutions and trials, will show that they belong to those who keep the commandments of God, and are his true children. Or perhaps the meaning may be, "Here is a disclosure respecting the final destiny of these persecutors, which is adapted to comfort and sustain the saints in the trials which they will endure; an encouragement to constancy in obeying the commands of God, and in evincing the meek faith of the gospel." ¶ *And the faith of Jesus.* To encourage persevering faith in the Saviour. In these times of trial it will be shown who are the friends of the Saviour; and in the prospect of the certain overthrow of all the enemies of God and his cause, there is a ground of encouragement for continued attachment to him.

The *design* of this portion of the chapter (ver. 9-12) is to encourage Christians in their trials by the assurance, that this formidable Antichristian power would be overthrown, and that all the enemies of God would receive their just doom in the world of despair. Fearful as that doctrine is, and terrible as is the idea of the everlasting suffering of any of the creatures of God, yet the final overthrow of the wicked is necessary to the triumph of truth and holiness, and there is consolation in the belief that religion will ultimately triumph. The desire for its triumph necessarily supposes that the wicked will be overthrown and punished; and indeed it is the aim of all governments, and of all administrations of law, that the wicked shall be overthrown, and that truth and justice shall prevail. What would be more consolatory in a human government than the idea that all the wicked would be arrested and punished as they deserve? For what else is government instituted? For what else do magistrates and police-officers discharge the functions of their office?

13. *And I heard a voice from heaven.* A voice that seemed to speak from heaven. ¶ *Saying unto me, Write.* Make a record of this truth. We may suppose that John was engaged in making a record of what he *saw* in vision; he was now instructed to make a record of what he *heard.* This passage may be referred to as a proof that he wrote this book while in Patmos, or as the heavenly disclosures were made to him, and not afterwards from memory. ¶ *Blessed* are *the dead.* That is, the condition of those who die in the manner which is immediately specified, is to be regarded as a blessed or happy one. It is much to be able to say of the dead that they are "blessed." There is much in death that is sad; we so much dread it by nature; it cuts us off from so much that is dear to us; it blasts so many hopes; and the grave is so cold and cheerless a resting-place, that we owe much to a system of religion which will enable us to say and to feel, that it is a blessed thing to die. Assuredly we should be grateful for any system of religion which will enable us thus to speak of those who are dead; which will enable us, with corresponding feeling, to look forward to our own departure from this world. ¶ *Which die in the Lord.* Not all the dead; for God never pronounces the condition of the wicked who die, blessed or happy. Religion guards this point, and confines the declaration to those who furnish evidence that they are prepared for

heaven. The phrase "to die in the Lord" implies the following things:—(1) That they who thus die are the friends of the Lord Jesus. The language "to be in the Lord" is often used to denote true attachment to him, or close union with him. Comp. Jn. xv. 4-7; Ro. xvi. 13, 22; 1 Co. iv. 17; vii. 39; Phi. i. 14; Col. iv. 7. The assurance, then, is limited to those who are sincere Christians; for this the language properly implies, and we are authorized to apply it only as there is evidence of true religion. (2) To "die in the Lord" would seem also to imply that there should be, at the time, the evidence of his favour and friendship. This would apply (*a*) to those who die as martyrs, giving their lives as a testimony to the truth of religion, and as an evidence of their love for it; and (*b*) to those who have the comforting evidence of his presence and favour on the bed of death. ¶ *From henceforth*—ἀπάρτι. This word has given no little perplexity to expositors, and it has been variously rendered. Some have connected it with the word *blessed*—"Blessed henceforth are the dead who die in the Lord;" that is, they will be ever-onward blessed: some with the word *die*, referring to the time when the apostle was writing —"Blessed are they who, *after this time*, die in the Lord;" designing to comfort those who were exposed to death, and who would die as martyrs: some as referring to the times contemplated in these visions—"Blessed will they be who shall die in those future times." Witsius understands this as meaning that, from the time of their death, they would be blessed, as if it had been said, *immediately* after their dissolution they would be blessed. Doddridge renders it, "Henceforth blessed are the dead." The language is evidently not to be construed as implying that they who *had* died in the faith before were not happy, but that in the times of trial and persecution that were to come, they were to be regarded as peculiarly blessed who should escape from these sorrows by a Christian death. Scenes of woe were indeed to occur, in which many believers would die. But their condition was not to be regarded as one of misfortune, but of blessedness and joy, for (*a*) they would die in an honourable cause; (*b*) they would emerge from a world of sorrow; and (*c*) they would rise to eternal life and peace. The *design*, therefore, of the verse is to impart consolation and support to those who would be exposed to a martyr's death, and to those who, in times of persecution, would see their friends exposed to such a death. It may be added that the declaration here made is true still, and ever will be. It is a blessed thing to die in the Lord. ¶ *Yea, saith the Spirit.* The Holy Spirit; "the Spirit by whose inspiration and command I record this" (Doddridge). ¶ *That they may rest from their labours.* The word here rendered *labour*—κόπος—means properly *wailing, grief*, from κόπτω, *to beat*, and hence a beating of the breast as in grief. Then the word denotes toil, labour, effort, Jn. iv. 38; 1 Co. iii. 8; xv. 58; 2 Co. vi. 5; x. 15; xi. 23, 27. It is here used in the sense of wearisome toil in doing good, in promoting religion, in saving souls, in defending the truth. From such toils the redeemed in heaven will be released; for although there will be employment there, it will be without the sense of fatigue or weariness. And in view of such eternal rest from toil, we may well endure the labours and toils incident to the short period of the present life, for, however arduous or difficult, it will soon be ended. ¶ *And their works do follow them.* That is, the *rewards* or the *consequences* of their works will follow them to the eternal world, the word *works* here being used for the *rewards* or *results* of their works. In regard to this, considered as an encouragement to labour, and as a support in the trials of life, it may be remarked, (*a*) that *all* that the righteous do and suffer here will be appropriately recompensed there. (*b*) This is *all* that *can* follow a man to eternity. He can take with him none of his gold, his lands, his raiment; none of the honours of this life; none of the means of sensual gratification. All that will go with him will be his character, and the results of his conduct here, and, in this respect, eternity will be but a prolongation of the present life. (*c*) It is one of the highest honours of our nature that we can make the present affect the future for good; that by our conduct on the earth we can lay the foundation for happiness millions of ages hence. In no other respect does man appear so dignified as in this; nowhere do we so clearly see the grandeur of the soul as in the fact, that what we do to-day may determine our happiness in that future period, when all the affairs of this world shall have been wound up, and when ages

[A.D. 96.] CHAPTER XIV. 349

14 And I looked, and behold a white cloud, and upon the cloud one sat ˣlike unto the Son of man, having on his head a golden crown, and in his hand a sharp sickle.
15 And another angel came out

x Eze.1.26; Da.7.13.

of the temple, crying with a loud voice to him that sat on the cloud, ʸThrust in thy sickle, and reap: for the time is come for thee to reap; for the ᶻharvest of the earth is ³ripe.

y Joel 3.13.   z Je.51.33; Mat.13.39.   3 or, *dried*.

---

which cannot now be numbered shall have rolled by. It is then a glorious thing to live, and will be a glorious thing to die. Comp. Notes on 1 Co. xv. 58.

14. *And I looked.* See Notes on ver. 1. His attention is arrested by a new vision. The Son of man himself comes forth to close the scene, and to wind up the affairs of the world. This, too, is of the nature of an episode, and the *design* is the same as the previous visions—to support the mind in the prospect of the trials that the church was to experience, by the assurance that it would be finally triumphant, and that every enemy would be destroyed. ¶ *And behold a white cloud.* Bright, splendid, dazzling—appropriate to be the seat of the Son of God. Comp. Notes on Mat. xvii. 5; Re. i. 7. See also Mat. xxiv. 30; xxvi. 64; Lu. xx. 27; Ac. i. 9; 1 Th. iv. 17; Re. x. 1. ¶ *And upon the cloud one sat like unto the Son of man.* Comp. Notes on ch. i. 13; Da. vii. 13. It is probable that there is here a designed reference to the passage in Daniel. The meaning is, that one appeared on the cloud in a human form, whom John at once recognized as he to whom the appellation of "the Son of man" peculiarly belonged—the Lord Jesus. The meaning of that term had not been fixed in the time of Daniel (vii. 13); subsequently it was appropriated by the Saviour, and was the favourite term by which he chose to speak of himself, Mat. viii. 20; ix. 6; x. 23; xi. 19; xii. 8, 32, 40, *et al.* ¶ *Having on his head a golden crown.* Appropriate to him as king. It was mainly in virtue of his kingly power and office that the work was to be done which John is now about to describe. ¶ *And in his hand a sharp sickle.* The word *sickle* here—δρέπανον—means a crooked knife or scythe for gathering the harvest, or vintage, by cutting off the clusters of grapes. See ver. 17. The image of a *harvest* is often employed in the New Testament to describe moral subjects, Mat. ix. 37, 38; xiii. 30, 39; Mar. iv. 29; Lu. x. 2;

Jn. iv. 35. Here the reference is to the consummation of all things, when the great harvest of the world will be reaped, and when all the enemies of the church will be cut off—for that is the grand idea which is kept before the mind in this chapter. In various forms, and by various images, that idea had already been presented to the mind, but here it is introduced in a grand closing image, as if the grain of the harvest-field were gathered in,—illustrating the reception of the righteous into the kingdom,—and the fruit of the vineyard were thrown into the wine-press, representing the manner in which the wicked would be crushed, ver. 19, 20.

15. *And another angel.* The fourth in order, ver. 6, 8, 9. ¶ *Came out of the temple.* See Notes on ch. xi. 19. Came, as it were, from the immediate presence of God; for the temple was regarded as his peculiar dwelling-place. ¶ *Crying with a loud voice to him that sat on the cloud.* To the Messiah, ver. 14. That is, the command was borne directly from God by the angel to the Messiah, to go forth and reap the great harvest of the world. It is not a command *of the angel*, but a command from God the Father to the Son. This is in accordance with all the representations in the New Testament, that the Son, as Messiah or Redeemer, is subordinate to the Father, and performs the work which has been given him to do. See Jn. iii. 16, 17; v. 19; x. 18; xii. 49; xiv. 31. Comp. Notes on Re. i. 1. ¶ *Thrust in thy sickle, and reap.* Into the great harvest of the world. ¶ *For the time is come for thee to reap.* That is, "the harvest which *thou* art to reap is ripe; the seed which *thou* hast sown has grown up; the earth which *thou* hast cultivated has produced this golden grain, and it is fit that *thou* shouldst now gather it in." This language is appropriately addressed to the Son of God, for all the fruits of righteousness on the earth may be regarded as the result of *his* culture. ¶ *For the harvest of the earth is ripe.* The "harvest" in

350 REVELATION. [A.D. 96.

16 And he that sat on the cloud thrust in his sickle on the earth; and the earth was reaped.

17 And another angel came out of the temple which is in heaven, he also having a sharp sickle.

18 And another angel came out from the altar, which had power over fire; and cried with a loud cry to him that had the sharp sickle,

saying, *a* Thrust in thy sharp sickle, and gather the clusters of the vine of the earth; for her grapes are fully ripe.

19 And the angel thrust in his sickle into the earth, and gathered the vine of the earth, and cast *it* into the great *b* wine-press of the wrath of God.

*a* ver.15.   *b* ch.19.15.

reference to the righteous—the fruit of the good seed sown by the Saviour and his apostles and ministers. The *time* alluded to here is the end of the world, when the affairs of earth shall be about to be wound up. The design is to state that the Redeemer will then gather in a great and glorious harvest, and by this assurance to sustain the hearts of his people in times of trial and persecution.

16. *And he that sat on the cloud.* The Saviour, ver. 14. ¶ *Thrust in his sickle on the earth.* To cut down the harvest —that is, to gather his people to himself. ¶ *And the earth was reaped.* So far as the righteous were concerned. The end had come; the church was redeemed; the work contemplated was accomplished; and the results of the work of the Saviour were like a glorious harvest.

17. *And another angel.* The fifth in order. This angel came for a different purpose—with reference to the cutting off of the enemies of God, represented by the gathering of a vintage. Comp. Mat. xiii. 41; xxiv. 31. ¶ *Came out of the temple which is in heaven.* Sent or commissioned by God. See Notes on ver. 15. ¶ *He also having a sharp sickle.* On the word *sickle*, see Notes on ver. 14.

18. *And another angel.* The sixth in order. He came, like the angel in ver. 15, with a command to him who had the sickle to go forth and execute his commission. ¶ *Came out from the altar.* This stood in the front of the temple (see Notes on Mat. xxi. 12; comp. Notes on Mat. v. 23, 24), and was the place where burnt-sacrifices were made. As the work now to be done was a work of destruction, this was an appropriate place in the representation. ¶ *Which had power over fire.* As if he kept the fire on the altar. Fire is the usual emblem of *destruction;* and as the work now to be done was such, it was proper

to represent this angel as engaged in it. ¶ *And cried with a loud cry,* &c. See ver. 15. That is, he came forth, as with a command from God, to call on him who was appointed to do the work of destruction, now to engage in performing it. The time had fully come. ¶ *Thrust in thy sharp sickle.* Ver. 15. ¶ *And gather the clusters of the vine of the earth.* That portion of the earth which might be represented by a vineyard in which the grapes were to be gathered and crushed. The image here employed occurs elsewhere to denote the destruction of the wicked. See the very beautiful description in Is. lxiii. 1-6, respecting the destruction of Edom, and the Notes on that passage. ¶ *For her grapes are fully ripe.* That is, the time has come for the ingathering; or, to apply the image, for the winding up of human affairs by the destruction of the wicked. The *time* here, as in the previous representation, is the end of the world; and the design is, to comfort the church in its trials and persecutions, by the assurance that all its enemies will be cut off.

19. *And the angel thrust in his sickle into the earth.* That is, into that part of the earth which might be represented by a vineyard; or the earth considered as having been the abode of wicked men. ¶ *And cast it into the great wine-press of the wrath of God.* See Is. lxiii. 1-6. That is, the wine-press where the grapes are crushed, and where the juice, resembling blood, flows out, may be used as a symbol to denote the destruction of the wicked in the last day; and as the *numbers* will be immensely great, it is called the "*great* wine-press of divine wrath." The symbol appears to be used here alike with reference to the *colour* of the wine resembling blood, and the *pressure* necessary to force it out; and thus employed it is one of the most striking emblems conceivable to denote the final destruction of the wicked.

A.D. 96.] CHAPTER XV. 351

20 And the wine-press was <sup>c</sup>trodden <sup>d</sup>without the city, and <sup>e</sup>blood came out of the wine-press, <sup>f</sup>even unto the horse-bridles, by the space of a thousand *and* six hundred furlongs.

c Is.63.3.   d He.13.11,12.   e Is.34.7.   f ch.19.14.

20. *And the wine-press was trodden without the city.* The representation was made *as if* it were outside of the city—that is, the city of Jerusalem, for that is represented as the abode of the holy. The word *trodden* refers to the manner in which wine was usually prepared, by being trodden by the feet of men. See Notes on Is. lxiii. 2. The wine-press was usually in the vineyard—not in the city — and this is the representation here. As appearing to the eye of John, it was not within the walls of any city, but standing without. ¶ *And blood came out of the wine-press.* The representation is, that there would be a great destruction which would be well represented by the juice flowing from a wine-press. ¶ *Even unto the horse-bridles.* Deep, as blood would be in a field of slaughter where it would come up to the very bridles of the horses. The idea is, that there would be a *great* slaughter. ¶ *By the space of a thousand and six hundred furlongs.* That is, two hundred miles; covering a space of two hundred miles square—a lake of blood. This is designed to represent a *great* slaughter; but why the space here employed to describe it was chosen is unknown. Some have supposed it was in allusion to the length of Palestine. Professor Stuart supposes that it refers to the *breadth of Italy*, and that the allusion is to the attack made on the city of the beast. But it is impossible to determine *why* this space was chosen, and it is unnecessary. The idea is, that there would be a slaughter so great, as it were, as to produce a lake or sea of blood; that the enemies of the church would be completely and finally overthrown, and that the church, therefore, delivered from all its enemies, would be triumphant.

The *design* of this, as of the previous representations in this chapter, is to show that *all* the enemies of God will be destroyed, and that, therefore, the hearts of the friends of religion should be cheered and consoled in the trials and persecutions which were to come upon it. What could be better fitted to sustain the church in the time of trial, than the assurance that every foe will be ultimately cut off? What is better fitted to sustain the heart of the individual believer, than the assurance that all *his* foes will be quelled, and that he will ere long be safe in heaven?

## CHAPTER XV.
ANALYSIS OF THE CHAPTER.

This chapter has a close connection in design with the previous chapter. In that, pledges and assurances had been given that all the enemies of religion would be cut off, and that the church would be ultimately triumphant, and particularly that that formidable Antichristian power represented by the "beast" would be destroyed. This chapter commences the statement in regard to the manner in which these pledges would be accomplished, and the statement is pursued through the subsequent chapters, giving in detail what is here promised in a general manner. The vision in this chapter may be thus described:—

I. The writer sees a new sign or wonder in heaven. Seven angels appear, having the seven last plagues that fill up or complete the wrath of God; representing the wrath that is to come upon the beast, or the complete overthrow of this formidable Antichristian power, ver. 1.

II. Those who in former times had "gotten the victory over the beast," now appear standing on a sea of glass, rejoicing and rendering thanks for the assurance that this great enemy of the church was now to be destroyed, and that now all nations were to come and worship before God, ver. 2-4.

III. The writer sees the interior of the temple opened in heaven, and the seven angels, having the seven plagues, issuing forth to execute their commission. They come clothed in pure and white linen, and girded with golden girdles. One of the four beasts before the throne forthwith gives them the seven golden vials full of the wrath of God, to empty them upon the earth—that is, to bring upon the beast the predicted destruction. The temple is immediately filled with smoke, so that no one might enter; that is, no one could now approach to make intercession, and the destruction of this great enemy's power is now certain, ver. 5-8.

This chapter, therefore, is merely introductory to what follows, and its

## CHAPTER XV.

AND I saw another sign in heaven, great and marvellous, seven angels having the seven last plagues; for in them is filled up the *a* wrath of God.

2 And I saw as it were a *b* sea of glass *c* mingled with fire: and them

*a* ch.14.10.   *b* ch.4.6.   *c* Is.4.4,5.

---

interpretation is attended with no particular difficulty. It is a beautiful scenic representation preparatory to the infliction of predicted judgments, and designed to introduce the account of those judgments with suitable circumstances of solemnity.

1. *And I saw another sign in heaven.* Another wonder or extraordinary symbol. The word *sign* here—σημεῖον—is the same which in ch. xii. 1, 3; xiii. 13, is rendered *wonder* and *wonders,* and in ch. xiii. 14; xvi. 14; xix. 20, *miracles.* The word is not elsewhere found in the book of Revelation, though it is of frequent occurrence in other parts of the New Testament. See it explained in the Notes on ch. xii. 1. Here it is used to denote something wonderful or marvellous. This is represented as appearing in heaven, for the judgments that were to fall upon the world were to come thence. Comp. ch. xl. 19; xiv. 1, 6, 13, 14, 17. ¶ *Great and marvellous.* Great and wonderful, or fitted to excite admiration—θαυμαστόν. The subsequent statements fully justify this, and show that the vision was one of portentous character, and that was fitted to hold the mind in astonishment. ¶ *Seven angels.* Comp. Notes on ch. i. 4. ¶ *Having the seven last plagues.* The article here, "*the* seven last plagues," would seem to imply that the plagues referred to had been before specified, or that it would be at once understood what is referred to. These plagues, however, have not been mentioned before, and the reason why the article is used here seems to be this: the destruction of this great Antichristian power *had been* distinctly mentioned, ch. xiv. That might be spoken of as a thing now well known, and the mention of it would demand the article; and as that was well known, and would demand the article, so any allusion to it, or description of it, might be spoken of in the same manner, as a thing that was definite and fixed, and hence the mention of the plagues by which it was to be accomplished would be referred to in the same manner. The word *plagues* — πληγάς, from πληγή — means properly a wound caused by a stripe or blow, and is frequently rendered *stripe* and *stripes,* Lu. xii. 48; Ac. xvi. 23, 33; 2 Co. vi. 5; xi. 23. It does not elsewhere occur in the New Testament, except in the book of Revelation. In this book it is rendered *wound* in ch. xiii. 3, 12, 14; and *plagues* in ch. ix. 20; xi. 6; xv. 1, 6, 8; xvi. 9, 21; xviii. 4, 8; xxi. 9; xxii. 18. It does not occur elsewhere. The secondary meaning of the word, and the meaning in the passage before us, is *a stripe* or *blow inflicted by God;* calamity or punishment. The word "last" means those under which the order of things here referred to would terminate; the winding up of the affairs respecting the beast and his image—not necessarily the closing of the affairs of the world. Important events were to occur subsequent to the destruction of this Antichristian power (xix.-xxii.), but *these* were the plagues which would come finally upon the beast and his image, and which would terminate the existence of this formidable enemy. ¶ *For in them is filled up the wrath of God.* That is, in regard to the beast and his image. All the expressions of the divine indignation towards that oppressive and persecuting power will be completed or exhausted by the pouring out of the contents of these vials. Comp. Notes on ch. x. 7, where the word rendered *filled up*—ἐτελέσθη—is rendered *finished.*

2. *And I saw as it were a sea of glass.* In ch. iv. 6, a similar vision is recorded—"And before the throne there was a sea of glass, like unto crystal." See the Notes on that passage. The sea of *glass* here means a sea clear, pellucid, like glass: an expanse that seemed to be made of glass. There it was entirely clear; here it is mingled with fire. ¶ *Mingled with fire.* That is, a portion of the sea was red like fire. It was not all clear and pellucid, as in ch. iv. 6, but it was as it were a tesselated expanse, composed in part of what seemed to be glass, and in part of a material of a red or fiery colour. In the former case (ch. iv. 6), the emblem was designed

that had gotten the victory *d*over the beast, and over his image, and over his mark, *and* over the number of his name, stand on the sea of glass, having the *e* harps of God.

3 And they sing the *f* song of Moses the servant of God, and the *g* song of the Lamb, saying, Great and marvellous *are* thy works, Lord God Almighty; *h* just and true *are* thy ways, thou King of ¹saints.

*d* ch.13.15-17.   *e* ch.14.2.
*f* Ex.15.1-19; De.32.1-43.
*g* ch.14.3.   *h* Ho.14.9.
¹ or, *nations*, or *ages*, ch.17.14.

---

to represent the pure worship of heaven without reference to any other symbolic design, and hence the sea is wholly clear and pellucid; here, in connection with the purpose of furnishing an appropriate symbol of the divine majesty, there is united the idea of punishment on the foes of God, represented by the fiery or red colour. If it is proper, from conjecture, to suggest the meaning of this as an emblem, it would be that the foundation—the main element—of all the divine dealings is justice or holiness—represented by the portion of the sea that seemed to be glass; and that there was, in this case, intermingled with that, the image of wrath or anger—represented by the portion that was fiery or red. The very sight of the pavement, therefore, on which they stood when worshipping God, would keep before their minds impressive views of his character and dealings. ¶ *And them that had gotten the victory over the beast.* Ch. xiii. 11. That is, they who had gained a victory in times of persecution and temptation; or they whom the "beast" had not been able, by arts or arms, to subdue. The persons referred to here, I suppose, are those who in the long dominion of the Papal power, and amidst all its arts and corruptions—its threats and persecutions—had remained steadfast in the truth, and who might thus be said to have gained *a victory*—for such victories of piety, virtue, and truth, amidst the corrupting influences of sin and error, and the intimidations of power, are the most important that are gained in this world. ¶ *And over his image.* See Notes on ch. xiii. 14, 15. The meaning is, that they had not been led to apostatize by the dread of the power represented here by the "image of the beast." In all the attempts of that power to subdue them —to intimidate them—to induce them to give up their attachment to the truth as it is in Jesus—they had remained steadfast in the faith, and had triumphed. ¶ *And over his mark.* See Notes on ch. xiii. 16. Over all the attempts of the beast to fix his mark upon them, or to designate them as his own. ¶ *And over the number of his name.* See Notes on ch. xiii. 17, 18. Over all the attempts to fix upon them that mysterious number which expressed his name. The general sense is, that in times of general error and corruption; when the true friends of Christ were exposed to persecution; when every effort was made to induce them to become the followers of the "beast," and to yield to the corrupt system represented by the "beast," they remained unmoved, and adhered firmly to the truth. The number of such in the aggregate was not small; and with great beauty and propriety they are here represented as rejoicing and giving thanks to God on the overthrow of that corrupt and formidable power. ¶ *Stand on the sea of glass.* That is, before God. They are now seen in heaven, redeemed and triumphant. ¶ *Having the harps of God.* Harps that pertained to the worship of God; harps to be employed in his praise. See Notes on ch. xiv. 2.

3. *And they sing the song of Moses the servant of God.* A song of thanksgiving and praise, such as Moses taught the Hebrew people to sing after their deliverance from Egyptian bondage. See Ex. xv. The meaning here is, not that they would sing that identical song, but that, as Moses taught the people to celebrate their deliverance with an appropriate hymn of praise, the redeemed would celebrate their delivery and redemption in a similar manner. There is an obvious propriety here in referring to the "song of Moses," because the circumstances are very similar; the occasion of the redemption from that formidable Antichristian power here referred to, had a strong resemblance to the rescue from Egyptian bondage. ¶ *And the song of the Lamb.* The hymn which is sung in honour of the Lamb, as their great deliverer.

4 Who*i* shall not fear thee, O Lord, and glorify thy name? for *thou* *k*only *art* holy: for *l*all nations shall come and worship before thee; for thy judgments are made manifest:

5 And after that I looked, and behold, the *m*temple of the taber-

*i* Je.10.7.   *k* 1 Sa.2.2.   *l* Is.45.23.

*m* ch.11.19.

Comp. Notes on ch. v. 9, 10, 12, 13. ¶ *Saying, Great and marvellous are thy works.* See Notes on ver. 1. The meaning is, that great *power* was evinced in redeeming them; and that the interposition of the divine goodness in doing it was *marvellous*, or was such as to excite wonder and admiration. ¶ *Lord God Almighty.* This would seem to mean the same thing as the expression so common in the Old Testament, "Jehovah, God of hosts." The union of these appellations give solemnity and impressiveness to the ascription of praise, for it brings into view the fact, that he whose praise is celebrated is *Lord* — the JEHOVAH — the uncreated and eternal One; that he is *God* — the creator, upholder, and sovereign of all things; and that he is *Almighty* — having all power in all worlds. All these names and attributes are suggested when we think of redemption; for all the perfections of a glorious God are suggested in the redemption of the soul from death. It is the *Lord*—the Ruler of all worlds; it is *God*—the Maker of the race, and the Father of the race, who performs the work of redemption; and it is a work which could be accomplished only by one who is *Almighty*. ¶ *Just and true.* The attributes of *justice* and *truth* are brought prominently into view also in the redemption of man. The fact that God is just, and that in all this work he has been careful to maintain his justice (Ro. iii. 26); and the fact that he is true to himself, true to the creation, true to the fulfilment of all his promises, are prominent in this work, and it is proper that these attributes should be celebrated in the songs of praise in heaven. ¶ *Are thy ways.* Thy ways or *dealings* with us, and with the enemies of the church. That is, all the acts or "ways" of God in the redemption of his people had been characterized by justice and truth. ¶ *Thou King of saints.* King of those who are holy; of all who are redeemed and sanctified. The more approved reading here, however, is *King of nations* — ὁ βασιλεὺς τῶν ἐθνῶν — instead of *King of saints*—τῶν ἁγίων. So it is read in the critical editions of Griesbach, Tittmann, and Hahn. The sense is not materially affected by the difference in the reading.

4. *Who shall not fear thee, O Lord.* Reverence and adore thee; for the word *fear*, in the Scriptures, is commonly used in this sense when applied to God. The sense here is, that the judgments about to be inflicted on the beast and his image should and would teach men to reverence and adore God. There is, perhaps, included here also the idea of awe, inasmuch as this would be the effect of punishment. ¶ *And glorify thy name.* Honour thee—the *name* being put for the person who bare it. The sense is, that, as a consequence of these judgments, men would be brought to honour God, and to acknowledge him as the Ruler of the earth. ¶ *For* thou *only* art *holy.* That is, in these judgments he would show himself to be a holy God; a God hating sin, and loving righteousness and truth. When it is said that he "*only*" is holy, the expression is used, of course, in a comparative sense. He is *so* pure that it may be said that, in comparison with him, no one else is holy. Comp. Notes on Job iv. 18; xv. 15. ¶ *For all nations shall come and worship before thee.* That is, as the result of these punishments inflicted on this dread Antichristian power, they shall come and worship thee. Everywhere in the New Testament the destruction of that power is connected with the promise of the speedy conversion of the world. ¶ *For thy judgments are made manifest.* To wit, on the beast. That formidable power is overthrown, and the grand hindrance to the universal spread of the true religion is now taken away. Comp. Notes on Is. xxvi. 9.

5. *And after that I looked.* After I had seen in vision the redeemed thus referred to, celebrating the praises of God, I saw the preparation made for the execution of these purposes of judgment. ¶ *And behold, the temple of the tabernacle of the testimony.* Not the *whole* temple, but only that part to which this name was given. The word *tabernacle* —σκηνή—means properly a booth, hut, tent, and was the name commonly given

nacle of the testimony in heaven was opened:

6 And the seven angels came out of the temple, having the seven plagues, clothed in pure and white linen, and having their breasts girded with golden girdles.

7 And one of the four beasts

to the *tent* or *tabernacle* that was erected in the wilderness for the service of God. See Notes on Ac. vii. 44. The same word came naturally to be applied to the temple that was reared for the same purpose in Jerusalem. It is called the "tabernacle of testimony," because it was a *testimony* or *witness* of the presence of God among the people—that is, it served to keep up the remembrance of him. See Notes as above on Ac. vii. 44, where the same Greek phrase is used as here—rendered there "tabernacle *of witness.*" The word *temple* here —ναός—does not refer to the *whole* of the building called the "temple," but to the holy of holies. See Notes on He. ix. 3. This was regarded as the peculiar dwelling-place of God; and it was this sacred place, usually closed from all access, that now seemed to be opened, implying that the command to execute these purposes came directly from God himself. ¶ *In heaven.* That is, that part of heaven which corresponds to the most holy place in the temple was opened; to wit, that which is the peculiar residence of God himself. ¶ *Was opened.* Was thrown open to the view of John, so that he was permitted to look, as it were, upon the very dwelling-place of God. From his holy presence now came forth the angels to execute his purposes of judgment on that Antichristian power which had so long corrupted religion and oppressed the world.

6. *And the seven angels.* See Notes on ver. 1. ¶ *Came out of the temple.* Were seen to come from the temple; that is, from the immediate presence of God. ¶ *Having the seven plagues.* See Notes on ver. 1. Each one intrusted with a single "plague" to be executed upon the earth. The meaning here is, that they were designated or appointed to execute those plagues in judgments. The *symbols* of their office—the golden vials—were given to them afterwards, ver. 7. ¶ *Clothed in pure and white linen.* The emblem of holiness—the common representation in regard to the heavenly inhabitants. See Notes on ch. iii. 4; vii. 13. Comp. Mat. xvii. 2; Lu. ix. 29; Mar. xvi. 5. ¶ *And having their breasts girded with golden girdles.* See Notes on ch. i. 13. The meaning is, that they were attired in a manner befitting their rank and condition.

7. *And one of the four beasts.* See Notes on ch. iv. 6, 7. *Which* one of the four is not mentioned. From the explanation given of the design of the representation of the "four beasts," or *living creatures,* in the Notes on ch. iv. 6, 7, it would seem that the meaning here is, that the great principles of that divine government would be illustrated in the events which are now to occur. In events that were so closely connected with the honour of God and the triumph of his cause on the earth, there was a propriety in the representation that these living creatures, symbolizing the great principles of divine administration, would be particularly interested. ¶ *Gave unto the seven angels seven golden vials.* The word here used—φιάλη— means properly, "a bowl or goblet, having more breadth than depth" (Rob. *Lex.*). Our word vial, though derived from this, means rather a thin long bottle of glass, used particularly by apothecaries and druggists. The word would be better rendered by *bowl* or *goblet,* and probably the representation here was of such bowls as were used in the temple service. See Notes on ch. v. 8. They are called in ch. xvi. 1, "vials of the wrath of God;" and here they are said to be "full of the wrath of God." The allusion seems to be to a drinking cup or goblet filled with poison, and given to persons to drink— an allusion drawn from one of the methods of punishment in ancient times. See Notes on ch. xiv. 10. These vials or goblets thus became emblems of divine wrath, to be inflicted on the beast and his image. ¶ *Full of the wrath of God.* Filled with that which represented his wrath; that is, they seemed to be filled with a poisonous mixture, which being poured upon the earth, the sea, the rivers, the sun, the seat of the beast, the river Euphrates, and into the air, was followed by severe divine judgments on this great Antichristian power. See ch. xvi. 2-4, 8, 10, 12, 17. ¶ *Who liveth for ever and ever.* The eternal God.

gave unto the seven angels seven golden vials, full of the wrath of God, who liveth for ever and ever.

8 And the temple was *filled with

n Is.6.4.

The particular object in referring to this attribute here appears to be, that though there may seem to be delay in the execution of his purposes, yet they will be certainly accomplished, as he is the ever-living and unchangeable God. He is not under a necessity of abandoning his purposes, like men, if they are not soon accomplished.

8. *And the temple was filled with smoke.* The usual symbol of the divine presence in the temple. See Notes on Is. iv. 5; vi. 4. ¶ *From the glory of God.* From the manifestation of the divine majesty. That is, the smoke was the proper accompaniment of the Divine Being when appearing in majesty. So on Mount Sinai he is represented as appearing in this manner: "And mount Sinai was altogether on a smoke, because the Lord descended on it in fire: and the smoke thereof ascended as the smoke of a furnace, and the whole mount quaked greatly," Ex. xix. 18. The purpose *here* seems to have been, partly to represent the smoke as the proper symbol of the divine presence, and partly to represent it as so filling the temple that no one could enter it until the seven plagues were fulfilled. ¶ *And from his power.* Produced by his power; and the symbol of his power. ¶ *And no man was able to enter into the temple, till the seven plagues of the seven angels were fulfilled.* Till those vials had been poured out, and all that was indicated by them was accomplished. The meaning here seems to be, that no one would be permitted to enter to make intercession—to turn away his wrath—to divert him from his purpose. That is, the purpose of punishment had been formed, and would certainly be executed. The agents or instrumentalities in this fearful work had been now sent forth, and they would by no means be recalled. The mercy-seat, in this respect, was inaccessible; the time of judgment on the great foe had come, and the destruction of the grand enemy of the church was certain. The point, therefore, at which this vision leaves us is, that where all the preparations are made for the infliction of the threatened punishment smoke from the *o* glory of God, and from his power; and no man was able to enter into the temple, till the seven plagues of the seven angels were fulfilled.

o Ps.29.9.

on the grand Antichristian power which had so long stood up against the truth; where the agents had prepared to go forth; and where no intercession will ever avail to turn away the infliction of the divine wrath. The detail follows in the next chapter.

## CHAPTER XVI.

### ANALYSIS OF THE CHAPTER.

The previous chapter had described the preparation for the last plagues that were to come upon that mighty Antichristian power to which this series of prophetic visions refers. All is now ready; and this chapter contains the description of those seven last "plagues" under which this power would reel and fall. These "plagues" are described *as if* they were a succession of physical calamities that would come upon this Antichristian power, and bring it to an end; though perhaps it is not necessary to look for a *literal* infliction of such calamities. The course of the exposition thus far will lead us to regard this chapter as a description of the *successive blows by which the Papacy will fall.* A part of this is still undoubtedly future, though perhaps not far distant; and, in reference to this, and to some portions of the remainder of the book, there may be more difficulty in satisfying the mind than in the portions which pertain to past events.

The chapter comprises statements on the following points:—

A command is issued from the temple to the seven angels, to go and execute the commission with which they were intrusted, ver. 1.

The first angel pours out his vial upon the earth—followed by a plague upon those who had worshipped the beast and his image, ver. 2.

The second angel pours out his vial upon the sea—followed by the death of all that were in the sea, ver. 3.

The third angel pours out his vial upon the rivers and fountains of waters, and they become blood. This is followed by an ascription of praise from the angel of the waters, because God had given to those who had shed the blood

# CHAPTER XVI.

AND I heard a great voice out of the temple saying to the seven[a] angels, Go your ways, and pour out the vials of the wrath of God upon the earth.

a ch.15.1,7.

of the saints blood to drink, with a response from the altar that this was just, ver. 4-7.

The fourth angel pours out his vial upon the sun, and an intenser heat is given to it to scorch men. The consequence is, that they blaspheme the name of God, but repent not of their sins, ver. 8, 9.

The fifth angel pours out his vial upon the very seat of the beast, and his kingdom is full of darkness. Men still blaspheme the name of God and repent not of their sins, ver. 10, 11.

The sixth angel pours out his vial upon the great river Euphrates. The consequence is, that the waters of the river are dried up, so that the way of the kings of the East might be prepared. The writer sees also, in this connection, three unclean spirits like frogs come out of the mouth of the dragon, and out of the mouth of the beast, and out of the mouth of the false prophet, that go forth into all the earth to gather all nations to the great day of the battle of God Almighty, ver. 12-16.

The seventh angel pours out his vial into the air, and a voice is heard answering that "it is done:" the time of the consummation has come—the formidable Antichristian power is to come to an end. The great city is divided into three parts; the cities of the nations fall; great Babylon thus comes up in remembrance before God to receive the punishment which is her due. This terrific scene is accompanied with voices, and thunderings, and lightnings, and an earthquake, and with great hail—a tempest of wrath beating upon that formidable power that had so long stood up against God, ver. 17-21. The *detail* of the actual destruction of this power is carried forward in the subsequent chapters.

1. *And I heard a great voice out of the temple.* A loud voice out of the temple as seen in heaven (Notes on ch. xi. 19), and that came, therefore, from the very presence of God. ¶ *Saying to the seven angels.* That had the seven vials of wrath. Notes on ch. xv. 1, 7.

2 And the first went, and poured out his vial [b] upon the earth; and there fell a noisome and grievous [c] sore upon the men which had the [d] mark of the beast, and upon them which worshipped his image.

b ch.8.7.    c Ex.9.8-11.    d ch.13.15-17.

¶ *Go your ways.* Your respective ways, to the fulfilment of the task assigned to each. ¶ *And pour out the vials of the wrath of God.* Empty those vials; cause to come upon the earth the plagues indicated by their contents. The *order* in which this was to be done is not intimated. It seems to be supposed that that would be understood by each. ¶ *Upon the earth.* The particular part of the *earth* is not here specified, but it should not be inferred that it was to be upon the earth in general, or that there were any calamities, in consequence of this pouring out of the vials of wrath, to spread over the whole world. The subsequent statements show what parts of the earth were particularly to be affected.

2. *And the first went.* Went forth from heaven, where the seat of the vision was laid. ¶ *And poured out his vial upon the earth.* That is, upon the *land,* in contradistinction from the sea, the rivers, the air, the seat of the beast, the sun, as represented in the other vials. In ver. 1, the word *earth* is used in the general sense to denote this world as distinguished from heaven; in this verse it is used in the specific sense, to denote *land* as distinguished from other things. Comp. Mar. iv. 1; vi. 47; Jn. vi. 21; Ac. xxvii. 29, 43, 44. In many respects there is a strong resemblance between the pouring out of those seven vials, and the sounding of the seven trumpets, in ch. viii., ix., though they refer to different events. In the sounding of the first trumpet (ch. viii. 7), it was the *earth* that was particularly affected in contradistinction from the sea, the fountains, and the sun: "The first angel sounded, and there followed hail and fire mingled with blood, and they were cast *upon the earth.*" Comp. ch. viii. 8, 10, 12. In regard to the symbolical meaning of the term *earth,* considered with reference to divine judgments, see Notes on ch. viii. 7. ¶ *And there fell a noisome and grievous sore.* The judgment here is specifically different from that inflicted under the first trumpet, ch.

viii. 7. There it is said to have been that "the third part of trees was burnt up, and all green grass was burnt up." Here it is that there fell upon *men* a "noisome and grievous sore." The two, therefore, are designed to refer to different events, and to different forms of punishment. The word rendered *sore* properly denotes a *wound* (Hom. *Il.* xi. 812), and then, in later writers, an *ulcer* or *sore*. It is used in the New Testament only in the following places: Lu. xvi. 21, "The dogs came and licked his *sores;*" and in Re. xvi. 2, 11, where it is rendered *sore*, and *sores*. It is used in the Septuagint, in reference to the *boils* that were brought upon the Egyptians, in Ex. ix. 9-12, and probably De. xxviii. 27; in reference to the leprosy, Le. xiii. 18-20, 23; in reference to the boil, ulcer, or elephantiasis brought upon Job, ch. ii. 7; and in reference to any sore or ulcer, in De. xxviii. 35. In all these places it is the translation of the word שְׁחִין *shehhin*—rendered in our English version *boil*, Ex. ix. 9-11; Le. xiii. 18-20, 23; 2 Ki. xx. 7; Job ii. 7; Is. xxxviii. 21; and *botch*, De. xxviii. 27, 35. The proper meaning, therefore, is that of a sore, ulcer, or boil of a severe and painful character; and the most obvious reference in the passage, to one who was accustomed to the language of Scripture, would be to some fearful plague like that which was sent upon the Egyptians. In the case of Hezekiah (2 Ki. xx. 7; Is. xxxviii. 21), it was probably used to denote a *plague-boil*, or the black leprosy. See Notes on Is. xxxviii. 21. The word "noisome"—κακόν, *evil*, *bad*—is used here to characterize the plague referred to as being peculiarly painful and dangerous. The word *grievous*—πονηρόν—*bad*, *malignant*, *hurtful*—is further used to increase the intensity of the expression, and to characterize the plague as particularly severe. There is no reason to suppose that it is meant that this would be *literally* inflicted, any more than it is in the next plague, where it is said that the "rivers and fountains became *blood*." What is obviously meant is, that there would be some calamity which would be well represented or symbolized by such a fearful plague. ¶ *Upon the men*. Though the plague was poured upon "*the earth*," yet its effects were seen upon "*men*." Some grievous calamity would befall them, *as if* they were suddenly visited with the plague. ¶ *Which had the mark of the beast*. Notes on ch. xiii. 16, 17. This determines the portion of the earth that was to be afflicted. It was not the whole world; it was only that part of it where the "beast" was honoured. According to the interpretation proposed in ch. xiii., this refers to those who are under the dominion of the Papacy. ¶ *And upon them which worshipped his image*. See Notes on ch. xiii. 14, 15. According to the interpretation in ch. xiii., those are meant who sustained the civil or secular power to which the Papacy gave life and strength, and from which it, in turn, received countenance and protection.

In regard to the application or fulfilment of this symbol, it is unnecessary to say that there have been very different opinions in the world, and that very different opinions still prevail. The great mass of Protestant commentators suppose that it refers to the Papacy; and of those who entertain this opinion, the greater portion suppose that the calamity referred to by the pouring out of this vial is already past, though it is supposed by many that the things foreshadowed by a part of these "vials" are yet to be accomplished. As to the true meaning of the symbol before us, I would make the following remarks:—

(1) It refers to the Papal power. This application is demanded by the results which were reached in the examination of ch. xiii. See the remarks on the "beast" in the Notes on ch. xiii. 1, 2, 11, and on "the image of the beast" in the Notes on ch. xiii. 14, 15. This one mighty power existed in two forms closely united, and mutually sustaining each other—the civil or secular, and the ecclesiastical or spiritual. It is this combined and consolidated power—the Papacy as such—that is referred to here, for this has been the grand Antichristian power in the world.

(2) It refers to some grievous and fearful calamity which would come upon that power, and which would be *like* a plague-spot on the human body—something which would be of the nature of a divine judgment, resembling that which came upon the Egyptians for their treatment of the people of God.

(3) The course of this exposition leads us to suppose, that this would be the beginning in the series of judgments,

which would terminate in the complete overthrow of that formidable power. It is the *first* of the vials of wrath, and the whole description evidently contemplates a *series* of disasters, which would be properly represented by these successive vials. In the application of this, therefore, we should naturally look for the first of a series of such judgments, and should expect to find some facts in history which would be properly represented by the vial "poured upon the earth."

(4) In accordance with this representation, we should expect to find such a series of calamities gradually weakening, and finally terminating the Papal power in the world, as would be properly represented by the number *seven*.

(5) In regard now to the *application* of this series of symbolical representations, it may be remarked, that most recent expositors—as Elliott, Cunninghame, Keith, Faber, Lord, and others—refer them to the events of the French revolution, as important events in the overthrow of the Papal power; and this, I confess, although the application is attended with some considerable difficulties, has more plausibility than any other explanation proposed. In support of this application, the following considerations may be suggested:—

(*a*) France, in the time of Charlemagne, was the kingdom to which the Papacy owed its civil organization and its strength—a kingdom to which could be traced all the civil or secular power of the Papacy, and which was, in fact, a restoration or reconstruction of the old Roman power—the fourth kingdom of Daniel. See Notes on Da. vii. 24-28; and comp. Notes on Re. xiii. 3, 12-14. The restoration of the old Roman dominion under Charlemagne, and the aid which he rendered to the Papacy in its establishment as to a temporal power, would make it probable that this kingdom *would be* referred to in the series of judgments that were to accomplish the overthrow of the Papal dominion.

(*b*) In an important sense France has always been the head of the Papal power. The king of France has been usually styled, by the popes themselves, "the eldest son of the church." In reference to the whole Papal dominion in former times, one of the principal reliances has been on France, and, to a very large extent, the state of Europe has been determined by the condition of France. "A revolution in France," said Napoleon, "is sooner or later followed by a revolution in Europe" (Alison). Its central position; its power; its direct relation to all the purposes and aims of the Papacy, would seem to make it probable that, in the account of the final destruction of that power, this kingdom would not be overlooked.

(*c*) The scenes which occurred in the times of the French revolution were such as would be properly symbolized by the pouring out of the first, the second, the third, and the fourth vials. In the passage before us—the pouring out of the first vial—the symbol employed is that of "a noisome and grievous sore"—boil, ulcer, plague-spot—"on the men which had the mark of the beast, and on them which worshipped his image.' This representation was undoubtedly derived from the account of the sixth plague on Egypt (Ex. ix. 9-11); and the sense here is, not that this would be literally inflicted on the power here referred to, but that a calamity would come upon it which would be *well represented* by that, or of which that would be an appropriate emblem. This interpretation is further confirmed by ch. xi. 8, where Rome is referred to under the name of *Egypt*, and where it is clear that we are to look for a course of divine dealing, in regard to the one, resembling that which occurred to the other. See Notes on that passage. Now, this "noisome and grievous sore" would well represent the moral corruption, the pollution, the infidelity, the atheism, the general dissolution of society, that preceded and accompanied the French revolution; for that was a universal *breaking out* of loathsome internal disease — of corruption at the centre — and in its general features might be represented as a universal plague-spot on society, extending over the countries where the beast and his image were principally worshipped. The symbol would properly denote that "tremendous outbreak of social and moral evil, of democratic fury, atheism, and vice, which was specially seen to characterize the French revolution: that of which the ultimate source was in the long and deep-seated corruption and irreligion of the nation; the outward vent, expression, and organ of its Jacobin clubs, and seditious and atheistic publications; the result, the dissolution of all society, all morals, and all

3 And the second angel poured out his vial $^e$ upon the sea; and it became as the $^f$ blood of a dead man: and every living soul died in the sea.

$e$ ch.8.8.
$f$ Ex.7.17-20.

religion; with acts of atrocity and horror accompanying, scarce paralleled in the history of men; and suffering and anguish of correspondent intensity throbbing throughout the social mass and corroding it; that which, from France as a centre, spread like a plague throughout its affiliated societies to the other countries of Papal Christendom, and was, wherever its poison was imbibed, as much the punishment as the symptoms of the corruption within." Of this sad chapter in the history of man, it is unnecessary to give any description here. For scenes of horror, pollution, and blood, its parallel has *never* been found in the history of our race, and, as an event in *history*, it was worthy of a notice in the symbols which portrayed the future. The full details of these amazing scenes must be sought in the histories which describe them, and to such works as Alison's *History of Europe*, and Burke's *Letters on a Regicide Peace*, the reader must be referred. A few expressions copied from those letters of Mr. Burke, penned with no design of illustrating this passage in the Apocalypse, and no expectation that they would be ever so applied, will show with what propriety the spirit of inspiration suggested the phrase, "a noisome and grievous sore" or plaguespot, on the supposition that the design was to refer to these scenes. In speaking of the revolutionary spirit in France, Mr. Burke calls it "the fever of aggravated Jacobinism," "the epidemic of atheistical fanaticism," "an evil lying deep in the corruptions of human nature," "the malignant French distemper," "a plague, with its fanatical spirit of proselytism, that needed the strictest quarantine to guard against it," whereof, though the mischief might be "skimmed over" for a time, yet the result, into whatever country it entered, was "the corruption of all morals," "the decomposition of all society," &c. But it is unnecessary to describe those scenes farther. The "world has them by heart," and they can never be obliterated from the memory of man. In the whole history of the race there has never been an outbreak of evil that showed so deep pollution and corruption within.

(d) The result of this was to affect the Papacy—a blow, in fact, aimed at that power. Of course, all the infidelity and atheism of the French nation, before it struck so strongly Papal, went just so far in weakening the power of the Papacy; and in the ultimate result it will perhaps yet be found that the horrid outbreaks in the French revolution were the first in the series of providential events that will result in the entire overthrow of that Antichristian power. At all events, it will be admitted, I think, that, on the supposition that it was *intended* that this should be descriptive of the scenes that occurred in Europe at the close of the last century, no more expressive symbol could have been chosen than has been employed in the pouring out of this first vial of wrath.

3. *And the second angel poured out his vial upon the sea.* So the second trumpet (ch. viii. 8), "And the second angel sounded, and as it were a great mountain burning with fire was cast into the sea; and the third part of the sea became blood." For the meaning of this as a symbol, see Notes on that verse. ¶ *And it became as the blood of a dead man.* "Either very bloody, like a mangled corse, or else coloured, as it were, with the dark and almost black blood of a dead man" (Professor Stuart, *in loco*). The latter would seem to be, most probably, the meaning; implying that the ocean would become discoloured, and indicating that this was the effect of blood shed in great quantities on its waters. In ch. viii. 8 it is, "the sea became blood;" here the allusion to the blood of a dead man would more naturally suggest the idea of naval conflicts, and of the blood of the slain poured in great quantities into the deep. ¶ *And every living soul died in the sea.* In ch. viii. 9 it is said that "the third part of the creatures that were in the sea died, and the third part of the ships were destroyed." Here the destruction is more general; the calamity is more severe and awful. It is as if *every living thing*—πᾶσα ψυχὴ ζῶσα—had died. No emphasis should be put on the word *soul* here, for the word means merely a creature, a living thing, an animal, Ac. ii. 43; iii. 23; Ro. xiii. 1; 1 Co. xv. 45. See Rob. *Lex. sub voce*, c.

A.D. 96.] CHAPTER XVI. 361

4 And the third angel poured out his vial *g* upon the rivers and fountains of waters; and they became blood.

*g* ch.8.10.

The sense here is, that there would be some dreadful calamity, *as if* the sea were to be changed into dark blood, and as if every living thing in it were to die.

In inquiring into the proper application of this, it is natural to look for something pertaining to the sea, or the ocean (see Notes on ch. viii. 8, 9), and we should expect to find the fulfilment in some calamity that would fall on the marine force, or the commerce of the power that is here referred to; that is, according to the interpretation all along adopted, of the Papal power; and the proper application, according to this interpretation, would be the complete destruction or annihilation of the naval force that contributed to sustain the Papacy. This we should look for in respect to the naval power of France, Spain, and Portugal, for these are the only Papal nations that have had a navy. We should expect, in the fulfilment of this, to find a series of naval disasters, reddening the sea with blood, which would tend to weaken the power of the Papacy, and which might be regarded as *one* in the series of events that would ultimately result in its entire overthrow. Accordingly, in pursuance of the plan adopted in explaining the pouring out of the first vial, it is to be observed that immediately succeeding, and connected with, the events thus referred to, there was a series of naval disasters that swept away the fleets of France, and that completely demolished the most formidable naval power that had ever been prepared by any nation under the Papal dominion. This series of disasters is thus noticed by Mr. Elliott (iii. 329, 330):—"Meanwhile, the great *naval* war between France and England was in progress; which, from its commencement in February, 1793, lasted for above twenty years, with no intermission but that of the short and delusive peace of Amiens; in which war the maritime power of Great Britain was strengthened by the Almighty Providence that protected her to destroy everywhere the French ships, commerce, and smaller colonies; including those of the fast and long-continued allies of the French, Holland and Spain. In the year 1793, the greater part of the French fleet at Toulon was destroyed by Lord Hood; in June, 1794, followed Lord Howe's great victory over the French off Ushant; then the taking of Corsica, and nearly all the smaller Spanish and French West India Islands; then, in 1795, Lord Bridport's naval victory, and the capture of the Cape of Good Hope; as also soon after of a French and Dutch fleet, sent to retake it; then, in 1797, the victory over the Spanish fleet off Cape St. Vincent; and that of Camperdown over the Dutch; then, in succession, Lord Nelson's three mighty victories—of the Nile in 1798, of Copenhagen in 1801, and in 1805 of Trafalgar. Altogether in this naval war, from its beginning in 1793, to its end in 1815, it appears that there were destroyed near 200 ships of the line, between 300 and 400 frigates, and an almost incalculable number of smaller vessels of war and ships of commerce. The whole history of the world does not present such a period of naval war, destruction, and bloodshed." This brief summary may show, if this was referred to, the propriety of the expression, "The sea became as the blood of a dead man;" and may show also that, on the supposition that it was intended that these events should be referred to, an appropriate symbol has been employed. No language could more strikingly set forth these bloody scenes.

4. *And the third angel poured out his vial upon the rivers and fountains of waters.* This coincides also with the account of the sounding of the third trumpet (ch. viii. 10, 11):—"And the third angel sounded, and there fell a great star from heaven, burning as a lamp, and it fell upon the third part of the rivers, and upon the fountains of waters." As to the meaning of the phrase, "rivers and fountains of waters," see Notes on that passage. We found, it was supposed, in the application of that passage, that the invasion of the Roman empire by Attila, king of the Huns, was referred to, affecting mainly those parts of the empire where the rivers and streams had their origin. The *analogy* would lead us, in the fulfilment of the passage before us, to look for some similar desolations on those portions of Europe. See Notes at the close of ver. 7. ¶ *And they became blood.* This would properly mean that they became *as* blood; or became red

5 And I heard the angel of the waters say, *h* Thou art righteous, O Lord, which art, and wast, and shalt be, because thou hast judged thus.
6 For they have shed the blood of saints and prophets, and *i* thou

*h* ver.7.   *i* De.32.42,43; Is.49.26.

hast given them blood to drink; for they are worthy.
7 And I heard another out of the altar say, Even so, *k* Lord God Almighty, true and righteous *are* thy judgments.

*k* ch.15.3; 19.2.

*with* blood; and it would be fulfilled if bloody battles were fought near them, so that they seemed to run blood.
5. *And I heard the angel of the waters say.* The angel who presides over the element of water; in allusion to the common opinion among the Hebrews that the angels presided over elements, and that each element was committed to the jurisdiction of a particular angel. Comp. Notes on ch. vii. 1. ¶ *Thou art righteous, O Lord.* In view of the judgments that reddened these streams and fountains with the blood of men, the angel ascribes righteousness to God. These judgments seemed terrible—the numbers slain were so vast—the bloody stream indicated so great slaughter, and such severity of the divine judgment; yet the angel sees in all this only the act of a righteous God bringing just retribution on the guilty. ¶ *Which art, and wast, and shalt be.* That is, who art *eternal*—existing now; who hast existed in all past time; and who will exist ever onward. See Notes on ch. i. 8. The *reason* why this attribute of God is here referred to, seems to be that the mind of the angel adverts to it in the *changes* and *desolations* that were occurring around him. In such overturnings among men—such revolutions of kingdoms—such desolations of war—the mind naturally turns to one who is unchanging; to one whose throne is from everlasting to everlasting. ¶ *Because thou hast judged thus.* Hast suffered these wars to occur that have changed rivers and fountains to blood.
6. *For they have shed the blood of saints.* The nations here referred to. They have been engaged in scenes of bloody persecution, and this is a just recompense. ¶ *And prophets.* Teachers of religion; ministers of truth. It is not necessary to understand the word *prophets* here in its technical sense, as denoting those who are raised up by God and sent forth as inspired men, but it may be understood in its more common signification in the New Testament as denoting teachers of religion in general. See Notes on Ro. xii. 6; 1 Co.

xiv. 1. ¶ *And thou hast given them blood to drink.* To wit, by turning the streams and fountains into blood, ver. 4. Blood had been poured out in such abundance that it seemed to mingle with the very water that they drank. This was a recompense for their having, in those very regions, poured out so much blood in persecuting the saints and prophets—the pious private members of the church, and the public teachers of religion. ¶ *For they are worthy.* That is, they deserve this; or this is a just recompense for their sins. It is not intended that those who would thus suffer had been individually guilty of this, or that this was properly a punishment on *them;* but it is meant that in those countries there had been bloody persecutions, and that this was a fit recompense for what had there occurred.
7. *And I heard another.* Evidently another *angel*, though this is not specified. ¶ *Out of the altar.* Either the angel *of* the altar—that is, who presided over the altar (Professor Stuart), or an angel whose voice seemed to come from the altar. The sense is essentially the same. The writer seemed to hear a voice coming from the altar responding to what had just been said in regard to the judgment of God, or to his righteousness in bringing the judgment upon men, ver. 5. This was evidently the voice of some one who was interested in what was occurring, or to whom these things particularly appertained; that is, one who was particularly connected with the *martyrs* referred to, whose blood was now, as it were, to be avenged. We are naturally reminded by this of the martyr-scene in ch. vi. 9–11, in the opening of the fifth seal, though it cannot be supposed that the same *events* are referred to. There "the souls of those that had been slain for the word of God" are represented as being " under the altar," and as crying to God to "avenge their blood on them who dwelt on the earth." Here a voice is heard with reference to martyrs, as of one interested *in* them,

ascribing praise to God for *having brought a righteous judgment on those who had shed the blood of the saints.* They are both, for similar reasons, connected with the "altar," and the voice is heard proceeding from the same source. In regard to the meaning of the word *altar* here, and the reason why the martyrs are represented in connection with it, see Notes on ch. vi. 9.

¶ *True and righteous are thy judgments.* Responding to what is said in ver. 5. That is, God is "true" or faithful to his promises made to his people, and "righteous" in the judgments which he has now inflicted. These judgments had come upon those who had shed the blood of the martyrs, and they were just.

In regard to the application of this there are several things to be said. The following points are clear:—(*a*) That this judgment would *succeed* the first-mentioned, and apparently at a period not remote. (*b*) It would occur in a region where there had been much persecution. (*c*) It would be in a country of streams, and rivers, and fountains. (*d*) It would be a just retribution for the bloody persecutions which had occurred there. The question now is, where we shall find the fulfilment of this, assuming that the explanation of the pouring out of the first vial is correct. And here, I think, there can be no mistake in applying it to the events bearing on the Papacy, and the Papal powers, which followed the French revolution. The next material event, after that revolution, was the invasion of Italy, where Napoleon began his career of victories, and where he first acquired his fame. At this stage of my examination of this passage, I looked into Alison's *History of Europe* to see what events, in fact, followed the scenes of confusion, crime, blood, atheism, and pollution in the French revolution, and I found that the next chapters in these eventful scenes, were such as would be well represented by the vial poured upon the rivers and fountains, and by their being turned into blood. The detail would be too long for my limits, and I can state merely a summary of a few of the chapters in that history. Ch. xix. contains the "History of the French Republic from the fall of Robespierre to the establishment of the Directory"—comprising properly the closing scenes of "the Reign of Terror." Ch. xx. contains an account of the campaign in Italy in 1796, embracing, as stated in the summing up of contents in this chapter, the "Battles of Montenotte, Millesimo, Dego; the passage of the bridge of Lodi, and fall of Milan; the siege of Mantua, and the battle of Castiglione; the battles of Caldero and Arcola; and the battles of Rivoli and Mantua." This is followed (ch. xxiii.) with an account of the campaign of 1797, which closed with the fall of Venice; and this is followed (ch. xxvi.) with an account of the invasion of Switzerland, &c. It is unnecessary to dwell on the details of the wars which followed the French revolution on the Rhine, the Po, and the Alpine streams of Piedmont and Lombardy. The slightest acquaintance with that history will show the propriety of the following remarks:—(*a*) These wars occurred in regions under the influence of the Papacy, for these were all Papal states and territories. (*b*) These scenes followed closely on the French revolution, and grew out of it as a natural consequence, and would be properly represented as a second "vial" poured out immediately after the first. (*c*) The country is such as here supposed—"of rivers and fountains"—for, being mostly a mountainous region, it abounds with springs, and fountains, and streams. Indeed, on the supposition that this is the land referred to, a more appropriate description could not have been given of it than is found in this passage. One has only to look upon a map of Northern Italy to see that there is no other portion of the world which would more naturally be *suggested* when speaking of a country abounding in "rivers and fountains of water." The admirable map of this region prefixed to the volume, for which I am indebted to the work of Dr. Alexander Keith, on the *Signs of the Times*, will clearly illustrate this passage, and the corresponding passage in ch. viii. 10, 11. Let anyone look at the Po and its tributaries on the map, and then read with attention the twentieth chapter of Alison's *History of Europe* (vol. i. pp. 391-424), and he will be struck with the appropriateness of the description, on the supposition that this portion of the book of Revelation was designed to refer to these scenes; for he cannot but see that the battles there described were fought in a country in every way corresponding with the statement here. (*d*) This country corresponds with the description here given in another respect. In

8 And the fourth angel poured out his vial *upon the sun: and power was given unto him to scorch men ᵐwith fire.

*l* ch.8.12.   *m* ch.9.17.

ver. 5, 6 there is a tribute of praise rendered to God, in view of these judgments, because he was righteous in bringing them upon a land where the blood of saints and prophets had been shed—a land of martyrs. Now this is applicable to the circumstances supposed, not only in the sense that Italy in general had been the land where the blood of martyrs had been shed—the land of Roman persecution, alike under Paganism and the Papacy—but true in a more definite sense, from the fact that this was the very region where the persecutions against the Waldenses and the Albigenses had been carried on—*the valleys of Piedmont*. In the times of Papal persecution these valleys had been made to flow with the blood of the saints; and it *seemed*, at least, to be a righteous retribution that these desolations of war, these conflagrations, and these scenes of carnage, should occur in that very land, and that the very fountains and streams which had before been turned into blood, by the slaughter of the friends of the Saviour, should now be reddened with the blood of men slain in battle. This is, perhaps, what John saw in vision: a land where persecution had raged, and the blood of the holy had flowed freely, and then the same land brought under the awful judgments of God, and the fountains and streams reddened with the blood of the slain. There was a propriety, therefore, that a voice should be heard ascribing righteousness to God for avenging the blood of the saints (ver. 5, 6), and that another voice should be heard from the "altar" of the martyrs (ver. 7) responding and saying, "Even so, Lord God Almighty, true and righteous are thy judgments."
(*e*) It may be added, to show the propriety of this, that this was *one* of the series of events which will be found in the end to have contributed to the overthrow of the Papal power; for a blow was struck, in the French invasion of Italy, from which Rome has never recovered, and sentiments were diffused as the result in favour of liberty which it has been difficult ever since to suppress, and which are destined yet to burst out in favour of freedom, and to

9 And men were ¹scorched with great heat, and ⁿblasphemed the name of God, which hath power over these plagues: and ᵒthey repented not, to give him glory.

¹ or, *burned*.   *n* ver.11,21.   *o* ch.9.20; Da.5.22,23.

be one of the means of the final destruction of the power. Comp. Alison's *History of Europe*, vol. i. p. 403.
8. *And the fourth angel poured out his vial upon the sun.* Toward the sun, or so as to reach the sun. The effect was *as if* it had been poured *upon* the sun, giving it an intense heat, and thus inflicting a severe judgment upon men. This corresponds also with the fourth trumpet (ch. viii. 12), where it is said, that the "third part of the sun was smitten, and the third part of the moon, and the third part of the stars." For the general meaning of this symbol see Notes on that place. The idea is, that a scene of calamity and woe would occur *as if* the sun should be made to pour forth such intense heat that men would be "scorched." It cannot be supposed that the sun would be *literally* made hotter, or that the exact nature of these calamities would be that men would be consumed by its rays. ¶ *And power was given unto him.* To the sun. The meaning is, that a calamity would follow *as if* such an increased power should be given to its rays. ¶ *To scorch men with fire.* Literally, "And it was given him to scorch men with fire"—that is, with heat so great that it *seemed* to be fire. The Greek word—καυματίσαι—meaning *to burn, to scorch*—is used in the New Testament only in Mat. xiii. 6; Mar. iv. 6; Re. xvi. 8, 9, in all which places it is rendered *scorch* and *scorched*. Compare, however, the use of the word καῦμα, in Re. vii. 16; xvi. 9; καῦσις, in He. vi. 8; καυσόω, in 1 Pe. iii. 10, 12; and καύσων, in Mat. xx. 12; Lu. xii. 55; Ja. i. 11. The notion of intense or consuming heat is implied in all the forms of the word; and the reference here is to some calamity that would be well represented by such an increased heat of the sun.
9. *And men were scorched with great heat.* That is, as above expressed, calamity came upon them which would be well represented by such heat. It is said that this calamity would come upon *men*, and we are to suppose that it would be such that human life would be particularly affected; and as that heat of the

sun must be exceedingly intense which would cut down *men*, we are to suppose that the judgment here referred to would be intensely severe. ¶ *And blasphemed the name of God.* The effect would be to cause them to blaspheme God or to reproach him as the author of these calamities; and in the fulfilment of this we are to look for a state of things when there would be augmented wickedness and irreligion, and when men would become worse and worse, notwithstanding the woes that had come upon them. ¶ *Which hath power over these plagues.* Who had brought these plagues upon them, and who had power to remove them. ¶ *And they repented not.* The effect was not to produce repentance, though it was manifest that these judgments had come upon them on account of their sins. Comp. Notes on ch. ix. 21. ¶ *To give him glory.* To turn from sin; to honour him by lives of obedience. Comp. Notes on Jn. ix. 24.

In regard to the *application* of this the following things may be remarked: —(*a*) That the calamity here referred to was one of the series of events which would precede the overthrow of the "beast," and contribute to that, for to this all these judgments tend. (*b*) In the order in which it stands it is to follow, and apparently to follow *soon*, the third judgment—the pouring of the vial upon the fountains and streams. (*c*) It would be a calamity such *as if* the sun, the source of light and comfort to mankind, were smitten, and became a source of torment. (*d*) This would be attended by a great destruction of *men*, and we should naturally look in such an application for calamities in which multitudes of *men* would be, as it were, consumed. (*e*) This would *not* be followed, as it might be hoped it would, by repentance, but would be attended with reproaches of God, with profaneness, with a great increase of wickedness.

Now, on the supposition that the explanation of the previous passages is correct, there can be no great difficulty in supposing that this refers to the wars of Europe following the French revolution, the wars that preceded the direct attack on the Papacy and the overthrow of the Papal government, for these events had all the characteristics here referred to. (*a*) They were one of a series in weakening the Papal power in Europe—heavy blows that will yet be seen to have been among the means preliminary to its final overthrow. (*b*) They followed in their order the invasion of Northern Italy, for one of the purposes of that invasion was to attack the *Austrian* power there, and ultimately through the Tyrol to attack Austria itself. Napoleon, after his victories in Northern Italy, above referred to (comp. ch. xx. of Alison's *History of Europe*), thus writes to the French Directory: "Coni, Ceva, and Alexandria are in the hands of our army; if you do not ratify the convention I will keep these fortresses and march upon Turin. Meanwhile I shall march to-morrow against Beaulieu, and drive him across the Po; I shall follow close at his heels, overrun all Lombardy, and in a month be in the Tyrol, join the army of the Rhine, and carry our united forces into Bavaria. *That design is worthy of you, of the army, and of the destinies of France*" (Alison, i. 401). (*c*) The campaign in Germany in 1796 followed immediately this campaign in Italy. Thus, in ch. xx. of Alison's *History*, we have an account of the campaign in Italy; in ch. xxi. we have the account of the campaign in Germany; and the other wars in Europe that continued so long, and that were so fierce and bloody, followed in quick succession—all tending, in their ultimate results, to weaken the Papal power and to secure its final overthrow. (*d*) It is hardly necessary to say here that these wars had all the characteristics here supposed. It was *as if* the sun were smitten in the heavens and power were given to scorch men with fire. Europe seemed to be on fire with musketry and artillery, and presented almost the appearance of the broad blaze of a battle-field. The number that perished was immense. These wars were attended with the usual consequences—blasphemy, profaneness, and reproaches of God in every form. And yet there was another effect wholly in accordance with the statement here, that none of these judgments brought men to "repentance, that they might give God the glory." Perhaps these remarks, which might be extended to great length, will show that, on the supposition that it was *intended* to refer to those scenes by the outpouring of this vial, the symbol was well chosen and appropriate.

10. *And the fifth angel poured out his*

beast; and his kingdom was full of ᵠdarkness; and they gnawed their tongues for pain,

*q* ch.9.2.

*vial upon the seat of the beast.* The previous judgments had been preparatory to this. They all had a bearing on this, and were all preliminary to it; but the "seat"—the home, the centre of the power of the beast—had not yet been reached. Here, however, there was a direct blow aimed at that power, still not such yet as to secure its *final* overthrow, for that is reserved for the pouring out of the last vial, ver. 17–21. All that is represented here is a heavy judgment which was merely *preliminary* to to that final overthrow, but which affected *the very seat of the beast.* The phrase "the seat of the beast"—τὸν θρόνον τοῦ θηρίου—means the *seat* or *throne* which the representative of that power occupied, the central point of the Antichristian dominion. Comp. Notes on ch. xiii. 2. See also ch. ii. 13. I understand this as referring to the very seat of the Papal power—Rome—the Vatican. ¶ *And his kingdom was full of darkness.* Confusion—disorder—distress, for darkness is often the emblem of calamity, Is. lix. 9, 10; Je. xiii. 16; Eze. xxx. 18; xxxii. 7, 8; xxxiv. 12; Joel ii. 2. ¶ *And they gnawed their tongues for pain.* This is a "most significant expression of the writhings of anguish." The word here rendered *gnawed* does not occur elsewhere in the New Testament, nor is the expression elsewhere used in the Bible; but its meaning is plain—it indicates deep anguish.

11. *And blasphemed the God of heaven.* The same effect which it was said would be produced by the pouring out of the fourth vial, ver. 9. ¶ *Because of their pains and their sores.* Of the calamities that had come upon them. ¶ *And repented not of their deeds.* See Notes on ver. 9. Comp. ch. ix. 21.

In regard to the fulfilment and application of this, the following general remarks may be made here:—(*a*) It would succeed, at no great interval probably, what is referred to under the previous "vials," and would be one in the series tending to the same result. (*b*) It would fall directly on the seat of the authority of the "beast" —on the central power of the Papacy, according to the interpretation of the

11 And blasphemed the God of heaven because of ʳtheir pains and their sores, and repented not of their deeds.

*r* ver.2.

other symbols; and we should look, therefore, for some calamity that would come upon Rome itself, and still more specifically upon the pope himself, and those immediately around him. (*c*) This would be attended with deep distress and darkness in the Papal dominions. (*d*) There would be an increase of what is here called "blasphemy;" that is, of impiety and reproaches of the Divine Being. (*e*) There would be no repentance produced. There would be no reformation. The system would be as corrupt as it was before, and men would be as much under its influence. And (*f*) we should not expect that this would be the *final* overthrow of the system. *That* is reserved for the outpouring of the seventh and last vial in the series (ver. 17–21), and under that the system would be overthrown, and would come to an end. This is distinctly stated in the account of that "vial;" and therefore we are not to expect to find, in the application of the fifth "vial," that the calamity brought upon "the seat of the beast" would be such that it would not recover for a time, and maintain, apparently, in some good degree, its former power and influence.

With this view of what we are to expect, and in connection with the explanations of the previous symbols, it seems to me that there can be no hesitation in applying this to the direct attacks on the Papal power and on the pope himself, as one of the consequences of the French revolution, and to the calamities that were thus brought upon the Papal States. In order to show the appropriateness of this application, I will state a few facts which will show that, on the supposition that it was the *intention* in this symbol to refer to the Papal power at that time, the symbol has been well chosen, and has been fulfilled. And, in doing this, I will merely copy from Alison's *History of Europe* (vol. i. pp. 542–546) a few statements, which, like many that have been quoted from Mr. Gibbon in the former part of these Notes, would seem almost to have been penned in view of this prophecy, and with a view to record its fulfilment. The statement is as follows:—

"The Ecclesiastical States were the

next object of attack. It had long been an avowed object of ambition with the Republican government to revolutionize the Roman people, and plant the tricolour flag in the city of Brutus," and fortune at length presented them with a favourable opportunity to accomplish the design.

"The situation of the pope had become, since the French conquests in Italy, in the highest degree precarious. Cut off by the Cisalpine Republic from any support from Austria; left by the treaty of Campo Formio entirely at the mercy of the French republic; threatened by the heavings of the democratic spirit within his own dominions; and exposed to all the contagion arising from the complete establishment and close vicinity of republican governments in the north of Italy, he was almost destitute of the means of resisting so many seen and unseen enemies. The pontifical treasury was exhausted by the immense payments stipulated by the treaty of Tolentino; while the activity and zeal of the revolutionary clubs in all the principal towns of the Ecclesiastical States was daily increasing with the prospect of success. To enable the government to meet the enormous demands of the French army, the principal Roman families, like the pope, had sold their gold, their silver, their jewels, their horses, their carriages—in a word, all their valuable effects; but the exactions of the republican agents were still unabated. In despair they had recourse to the fatal expedient of issuing a paper circulation; but that, in a country destitute of credit, soon fell to an inconsiderable value, and augmented rather than relieved the public distress. Joseph Bonaparte, brother to Napoleon, had been appointed ambassador at the court of Rome; but as his character was deemed too honourable for political intrigue, Generals Duphot and Sherlock were sent along with him, the former of whom had been so successful in effecting the overthrow of the Genoese aristocracy. The French embassy, under their direction, soon became the centre of the revolutionary action; and those numerous ardent characters with which the Italian cities abound, flocked there as to a common focus, from whence the next great explosion of democratic power was to be expected. In this extremity, Pius VI., who was above eighty years of age, and sinking into the grave, called to his counsels the Austrian general Provera, already distinguished in the Italian campaigns; but the Directory soon compelled the humiliated pontiff to dismiss that intrepid counsellor. As his recovery then seemed hopeless, the instructions of government to their ambassador were to delay the proclamation of a republic till his death, when the vacant chair of St. Peter might be overturned with little difficulty; but such was the activity of the revolutionary agents, that the train was ready to take fire before that event took place, and the ears of the Romans were assailed by incessant abuse of the ecclesiastical government, and vehement declamations in favour of republican freedom.

"The resolution to overturn the Papal government, like all the other ambitious projects of the Directory, received a very great impulse from the re-ascendent of Jacobin influence at Paris, by the results of the revolution of 18th Fructidor. One of the first measures of the new government was to despatch an order to Joseph Bonaparte at Rome, to promote, by all the means in his power, the approaching revolution in the Papal States; and, above all things, to take care that at the pope's death no successor should be elected to the chair of St. Peter. Napoleon's language to the Roman pontiff became daily more menacing. Immediately before setting out for Rastadt, he ordered his brother Joseph to intimate to the pope that three thousand additional troops had been forwarded to Ancona; that if Provera was not dismissed within twenty-four hours, war would be declared; that if any of the revolutionists who had been arrested were executed, reprisals would forthwith be exercised on the cardinals; and that, if the Cisalpine Republic was not recognized, it would be the signal for immediate hostilities. At the same time ten thousand troops of the Cisalpine Republic advanced to St. Leon, in the Papal duchy of Urbino, and made themselves masters of that fortress; while at Ancona, which was still garrisoned by French troops, notwithstanding its stipulated restoration by the treaty of Tolentino to the Holy See, the democratic party openly proclaimed the 'Anconite Republic.' Similar revolutionary movements took place at Corneto, Civita Vecchia, Pesaro, and Senigaglia; while at Rome itself, Joseph

Bonaparte, by compelling the Papal government to liberate all persons confined for political offences, suddenly vomited forth upon the capital several hundreds of the most heated republicans in Italy. After this great addition, measures were no longer kept with the government. Seditious meetings were constantly held in every part of the city; immense collections of tricolour cockades were made to distinguish the insurgents, and deputations of the citizens openly waited on the French ambassador to invite him to support the insurrection, to which he replied, in ambiguous terms—'The fate of nations, as of individuals, being buried in the womb of futurity, it is not given to me to penetrate its mysteries.'

"In this temper of men's minds, a spark was sufficient to occasion an explosion. On the 27th of December, 1797, an immense crowd assembled, with seditious cries, and moved to the palace of the French ambassador, where they exclaimed, 'Vive la République Romaine!' and loudly invoked the aid of the French to enable them to plant the tricolour flag on the Capitol. The insurgents displayed the tricolour cockade, and evinced the most menacing disposition; the danger was extreme; from similar beginnings the overthrow of the governments of Venice and Genoa had rapidly followed. The Papal ministers sent a regiment of dragoons to prevent any sortie of the revolutionists from the palace of the French ambassador; and they repeatedly warned the insurgents that their orders were to allow no one to leave its precincts. Duphot, however, indignant at being restrained by the pontifical troops, drew his sword, rushed down the staircase, and put himself at the head of one hundred and fifty armed Roman democrats, who were now contending with the dragoons in the courtyard of the palace. He was immediately killed by a discharge ordered by the sergeant commanding the patrol of the Papal troops; and the ambassador himself, who had followed to appease the tumult, narrowly escaped the same fate. A violent scuffle ensued; several persons were killed and wounded on both sides; and, after remaining several hours in the greatest alarm, Joseph Bonaparte, with his suite, retired to Florence.

"This catastrophe, however, obviously occasioned by the revolutionary schemes which were in agitation at the residence of the French ambassador, having taken place within the precincts of his palace, was, unhappily, a violation of the law of nations, and gave the Directory too fair a ground to demand satisfaction. But they instantly resolved to make it the pretext for the immediate occupation of Rome and overthrow of the Papal government. The march of troops out of Italy was countermanded, and Berthier, the commander-in-chief, received orders to advance rapidly into the Ecclesiastical States. Meanwhile, the democratic spirit burst forth more violently than ever at Ancona and the neighbouring towns, and the Papal authority was soon lost in all the provinces on the eastern slope of the Apennines. To these accumulated disasters the pontiff could only oppose the fasts and prayers of an aged conclave—weapons of spiritual warfare little calculated to arrest the conquerors of Arcola and Lodi.

"Berthier, without an instant's delay, carried into execution the orders of the Directory. Six thousand Poles were stationed at Rimini to cover the Cisalpine Republic; a reserve was established at Tolentino, while the commander-in-chief, at the head of eighteen thousand veteran troops, entered Ancona. Having completed the work of revolution in that turbulent district, and secured the fortress, he crossed the Apennines; and, advancing by Foligno and Narni, appeared on the 10th of February before the Eternal City. The pope, in the utmost consternation, shut himself up in the Vatican, and spent night and day at the foot of the altar in imploring the divine protection.

"Rome, almost defenceless, would have offered no obstacle to the entrance of the French troops; but it was part of the policy of the Directory to make it appear that their aid was invoked by the spontaneous efforts of the inhabitants. Contenting himself, therefore, with occupying the castle of St. Angelo, from which the feeble guards of the pope were soon expelled, Berthier kept his troops for five days encamped without the walls. At length, the revolutionists having completed their preparations, a noisy crowd assembled in the Campo Vaccino, the ancient Forum; the old foundations of the Capitol were made again to resound with the cries, if not the spirit, of freedom, and the venerable ensigns, S. P. Q. R., after the lapse of fourteen hundred years, again floated in the winds. The multitude tumultuously demanded the overthrow of the Papal authority; the French troops were invited to enter; the conquerors of Italy, with a haughty air, passed the gates of Aurelian, defiled through the Piazza del Popolo, gazed on the indestructible monuments of Roman grandeur, and, amid the shouts of the inhabitants, the tricolour flag was displayed from the summit of the Capitol.

"But while part of the Roman populace were surrendering themselves to a pardonable intoxication upon the fancied recovery of their liberties, the agents of the Directory were preparing for them the sad realities of slavery. The pope, who had been guarded by five hundred soldiers ever since the entry of the republicans, was directed to retire into Tuscany; his Swiss guard relieved by a French one; and he himself ordered to dispossess himself of all his temporal authority. He replied, with the firmness of a martyr, 'I am prepared for every species of disgrace. As supreme pontiff, I am resolved to die in the exercise of all my powers. You may employ force—you have the power to do so; but know that, though you may be masters of my body, you are not so of my soul. Free in the region where it is placed, it fears neither the events nor the sufferings of this life. I stand on the threshold of another world; there I shall be sheltered alike from the violence and impiety of this.' Force was soon employed to dispossess him of his authority; he was dragged from the altar by his palace, his repositories all ransacked and plundered, the rings even torn from his fingers, the whole effects in the Vatican and Quirinal inventoried and seized, and the aged pontiff conducted, with only a few domestics, amid the brutal jests and sacrilegious songs of the French dragoons, into Tuscany, where the generous hospitality of the grand-duke strove to soften the hardships of his exile. But, though a captive in the hands of his enemies, the venerable old man still retained the supreme authority in the church. From his retreat in the convent of the Chartreuse, he yet guided the counsels of the faithful; multitudes fell on their knees wherever he passed, and sought that benediction from a captive which they would, perhaps, have disregarded from a ruling pontiff.

"The subsequent treatment of this venerable man was as disgraceful to the republican government as it was honourable to his piety and constancy as the head of the church. Fearful that from his virtues and sufferings he might have too much influence on the continent of Italy, he was removed by their orders to Leghorn, in March, 1799, with the design of transferring him to Cagliari in Sardinia; and the English cruisers in the Mediterranean redoubled their vigilance in the generous hope of rescuing the father of an opposite church from the persecution of his enemies. Apprehensive of losing their prisoner, the French altered his destination; and forcing him to traverse, often during the night, the Apennines and the Alps in a rigorous season, he at length reached Valence, where, after an illness of ten days, he expired, in the eighty-second year of his age, and the twenty-fourth of his pontificate. The cruelty of the Directory increased as he approached their dominions, all his old attendants were compelled to leave him, and the father of the faithful was allowed to expire, attended only by his confessor. Yet even in this disconsolate state he derived the highest satisfaction from the devotion and reverence of the people in the provinces of France through which he passed. Multitudes from Gap, Vizelle, and Grenoble flocked to the road to receive his benediction; and he frequently repeated, with tears in his eyes, the words of Scripture: 'Verily, I say unto you, I have not seen such faith, no, not in Israel.'

"But long before the pope had sunk under the persecution of his oppressors, Rome had experienced the bitter fruits of republican fraternization. Immediately after the entry of the French troops, commenced the regular and systematic pillage of the city. Not only the churches and the convents, but the palaces of the cardinals and of the nobility, were laid waste. The agents of the Directory, insatiable in the pursuit of plunder, and merciless in the means of exacting it, ransacked every quarter within its walls, seized the most valuable works of art, and stripped the Eternal City of those treasures which had survived the Gothic fire and the rapacious hands of the Spanish soldiers. The bloodshed was much less, but the spoil collected incomparably greater,

**12** And the sixth angel poured out his vial upon ⁸the great river Euphrates; and the water thereof was ᵗdried up, that the way of the kings of the east might be prepared.

s ch.9.14.   t Is.42.15; Je.50.38; 51.36.

than at the disastrous sack which followed the death of the Constable Bourbon. Almost all the great works of art which have since that time been collected throughout Europe, were then scattered abroad. The spoliation exceeded all that the Goths or Vandals had effected. Not only the palaces of the Vatican, and the Monte Cavallo, and the chief nobility of Rome, but those of Castel Gandolfo, on the margin of the Alban Lake, of Terracina, the Villa Albani, and others in the environs of Rome, were plundered of every article of value which they possessed. The whole sacerdotal habits of the pope and cardinals were burned, in order to collect from the flames the gold with which they were adorned. The Vatican was stripped to its naked walls; the immortal frescoes of Raphael and Michael Angelo, which could not be removed, remained in solitary beauty amid the general desolation. A contribution of four millions in money, two millions in provisions, and three thousand horses, was imposed on a city already exhausted by the enormous exactions it had previously undergone. Under the direction of the infamous commissary Haller, the domestic library, museum, furniture, jewels, and even the private clothes of the pope were sold. Nor did the palaces of the Roman nobility escape devastation. The noble galleries of the Cardinal Braschi, and the Cardinal York, the last relic of the Stuart line, underwent the same fate. Others, as those of the Chigi, Borghese, and Doria palaces, were rescued from destruction only by enormous ransoms. Everything of value that the treaty of Tolentino had left in Rome became the prey of republican cupidity, and the very name of freedom soon became odious, from the sordid and infamous crimes which were committed in its name.

"Nor were the exactions of the French confined to the plunder of palaces and churches. Eight cardinals were arrested and sent to Civita Castellana, while enormous contributions were levied on the Papal territory, and brought home the bitterness of conquest to every poor man's door. At the same time the ample territorial possessions of the church and the monasteries were confiscated, and declared national property—a measure which, by drying up at once the whole resources of the affluent classes, precipitated into the extreme of misery the numerous poor who were maintained by their expenditure, or fed by their bounty. All the respectable citizens and clergy were in fetters; and a base and despicable faction alone, among whom, to their disgrace be it told, were found fourteen cardinals, followed in the train of the oppressors; and, at a public festival, returned thanks to God for the miseries they had brought upon their country."*

**12.** *And the sixth angel poured out his vial upon the great river Euphrates.* On the situation of that river, and the symbolical meaning of this language, see Notes on ch. ix. 14–21. The reference there was supposed to be to the Turkish power, and the analogy of interpretation would seem to require that it should be so understood here. There is every reason, therefore, to suppose that this passage has reference to something in the future history of the Turkish dominions, and to some bearing of the events which are to occur in that history on the ultimate downfall of the Antichristian power referred to by the "beast." ¶ *And the water thereof was*

---

* In this connection, I may insert here the remarkable calculation of Robert Fleming, in his work, entitled, *Apocalyptical Key*, or *The Pouring Out of the Vials*, first published in 1701. It is in the following words:—"The fifth vial (ver. 10, 11), which is to be poured out *on the seat of the beast, or the dominions which more immediately belong to, and depend on, the Roman see; that, I say, this judgment will probably begin about the year 1794, and expire about A.D. 1848*; or that the duration of it upon this supposition will be the space of fifty-four years. For I do suppose that, seeing the pope received the title of Supreme Bishop no sooner than A.D. 606, he cannot be supposed to have any vial poured upon his seat immediately (so as to ruin his authority so signally as this judgment must be supposed to do) *until the year* 1848, *which is the date of the twelve hundred and sixty years in prophetical account, when they are reckoned from* A.D. 606. But yet we are not to imagine that this will totally destroy the Papacy (though it will exceedingly weaken it), for we find that still in being and alive when the next vial is poured out" [pp. 124, 125, Cobbin's edition]. It is a circumstance remarkably in accordance with this calculation, that in the year 1848 the pope was actually driven away to Gaeta, and that at the present time (1851) he is restored, though evidently with diminished power.

13 And I saw three unclean spirits like frogs *come* out of the mouth of *u*the dragon, and out of

*u* ch.12.3,9.

the mouth of *v*the beast, and out of the mouth of *w*the false prophet.

*v* ch.13.2.   *w* ch.19.20.

*dried up, that the way of the kings of the east might be prepared.* That is, as the effect of pouring out the vial. There is an allusion here, undoubtedly, to the dividing of the waters of the Red Sea, so that the children of Israel might pass. See Ex. xiv. 21, 22. Comp. Notes on Is. xi. 15. In this description the Euphrates is represented as *a barrier* to prevent the passage of "the kings of the East," on their way to the West for some purpose not yet specified; that is, applying the symbol of the Euphrates as being the seat of the Turkish power, the meaning is, that *that power* is such a hindrance, and that, in some way that hindrance is to be removed *as if* the waters of an unbridged and unfordable river were dried up so as to afford a safe and easy passage through. Still there are several inquiries as to the application of this, which is not easy, and, as it refers to what is still future, it may be impossible to answer. The *language* requires us to put upon it the following interpretation : -- (*a*) The persons here referred to as "kings of the East," were ready to make a movement towards the West, over the Euphrates, and would do this if this obstruction were not in their way. *Who* these "kings of the East" are is not said, and perhaps cannot be conjectured. The natural interpretation is, that they are the kings that reign in the East, or that preside over the countries of the eastern hemisphere. *Why* there was a proposed movement to the West is not said. It might have been for conquest, or it might have been that they were to bring their tribute to the spiritual Jerusalem, in accordance with what is so often said in the prophets, that under the gospel kings and princes would consecrate themselves and their wealth to God. See Ps. lxxii. 10, 11: "The kings of Tarshish and of the isles shall bring presents: the kings of Sheba and Seba shall offer gifts. Yea, all kings shall fall down before him." So also Is. lx. 4-6, 9, 11: "Thy sons shall come from far.—The forces of the Gentiles shall come unto thee.—All they from Sheba shall come: they shall bring gold and incense.—The isles shall wait for me, and the ships of Tarshish first, to bring thy sons from far, their silver and their gold with them.—Thy gates shall be open continually; they shall not be shut day nor night; that men may bring unto thee the forces of the Gentiles, and that their kings may be brought." All that is *fairly* implied in the language used here is, that the kings of the East would be converted to the true religion, or that they were, at the time referred to, in a state of readiness to be converted, if there were no hindrance or obstruction. (*b*) There was some hindrance or obstruction to their conversion; that is, as explained, from the Turkish power : in other words, they would be converted to the true faith if it were not for the influence of that power. (*c*) The destruction of that power, represented by the drying up of the Euphrates, would remove that obstruction, and the way would thus be "prepared" for their conversion to the true religion. We should most naturally, therefore, look, in the fulfilment of this, for some such decay of the Turkish power as would be followed by the conversion of the rulers of the East to the gospel.

13. *And I saw three unclean spirits.* They assumed a visible form which would well represent their odiousness—that of frogs—but still they are spoken of as " spirits." They were evil powers, or evil influences (ver. 14, "spirits of devils"), and the language here is undoubtedly designed to represent some such power or influence which would, at that period, proceed from the dragon, the beast, and the false prophet. ¶ *Like frogs*—βατραχοι. This word does not occur in the New Testament except in the passage before us. It is properly translated *frogs*. The *frog* is here employed clearly as a *symbol*, and it is designed that certain qualities of the "spirits" here referred to should be designated by the symbol. For a full illustration of the meaning of the symbol, the reader may consult Bochart, *Hieroz.* P. II. lib. v. cap. iv. According to Bochart, the frog is characterized, as a symbol, (1) for its rough, harsh, coarse voice; (2) on this account, as a symbol of complaining or reproaching ; (3) as a symbol of empty loquacity; (4) as a symbol of heretics and philosophers, as understood by Augustine ; (5) because the frog has its origin in

mud, and lives in mud, as a symbol of those who are born in sin, and live in pollution; (6) because the frog endures all changes of the season—cold and heat, summer, winter, rain, frost—as a symbol of *monks* who practise self-denial; (7) because the frog, though abstemious of food, yet lives in water and drinks often, as a symbol of drunkards; (8) as a symbol of impudence; (9) because the frog swells his size, and distends his cheeks, as a symbol of pride. See the authorities for these uses of the word in Bochart. How many or few of these ideas enter into the symbol here, it is not easy to decide. We may suppose, however, that the spirits referred to would be characterized by pride, arrogance, impudence, assumption of authority; perhaps impurity and vileness, for all these ideas enter into the meaning of the symbol. They are not here, probably, symbols of *persons*, but of *influences* or *opinions* which would be spread abroad, and which would characterize the age referred to. The reference is to what the "dragon," the "beast," and the "false prophet" would *do* at that time in opposing the truth, and in preparing the world for the great and final conflict. ¶ *Out of the mouth of the dragon.* One of which seemed to issue from the mouth of the dragon. On the symbolic meaning of the word "dragon," see Notes on ch. xii. 3. It, in general, represents Satan, the great enemy of the church; perhaps here Satan under the form of heathenism or paganism, as in ch. xii. 3, 4. The idea then is, that, at the time referred to, there would be some manifestation of the power of Satan in the heathen nations, which would be bold, arrogant, proud, loquacious, hostile to truth, and which would be well represented by the hoarse murmur of the frog. ¶ *And out of the mouth of the beast.* The Papacy, as above explained, ch. xiii. That is, there would be some putting forth of arrogant pretensions; some loud denunciation or complaining; some manifestation of pride and self-consequence, which would be well represented by the croaking of the frog. We have seen above (Notes on ver. 5, 6), that although the fifth vial was poured upon "the seat of the beast," the effect was not to crush and overthrow that power entirely. The Papacy would still survive, and would be finally destroyed under the outpouring of the seventh vial, ver. 17-21. In the passage before us we have a representation of it as still living; as having apparently recovered its strength; and as being as hostile as ever to the truth, and able to enter into a combination, secret or avowed, with the "dragon" and the "false prophet," to oppose the reign of truth upon the earth. ¶ *And out of the mouth of the false prophet.* The word rendered *false prophet*—ψευδοπροφήτου—does not before occur in the book of Revelation, though the use of the article would seem to imply that some well-known power or influence was referred to by this. Comp. Notes on ch. x. 3. The word occurs in other places in the New Testament, Mat. vii. 15; xxiv. 11, 24; Mar. xiii. 22; Lu. vi. 26; Ac. xiii. 6; 2 Pe. ii. 1; 1 Jn. iv. 1; and twice elsewhere in the book of Revelation, with the same reference as here, ch. xix. 20; xx. 10. In both these latter places it is connected with the "beast:" "And the beast was taken, and with him the false prophet;" "And the devil that deceived them was cast into the lake of fire and brimstone, where the beast and the false prophet are." It would seem, then, to refer to some power that was similar to that of the beast, and that was to share the same fate in the overthrow of the enemies of the gospel. As to the application of this, there is no opinion so probable as that it alludes to the Mahometan power—not strictly the *Turkish* power, for that was to be "dried up," or to diminish; but to the Mahometan power as such, that was still to continue for a while in its vigour, and that was yet to exert a formidable influence against the gospel, and probably in some combination, in fact, if not in form, with Paganism and the Papacy. The *reasons* for this opinion are: (*a*) that this was referred to, in the former part of the book, as one of the formidable powers that would arise, and that would materially affect the destiny of the world—and it may be presumed that it would be again referred to in the account of the final consummation, see ch. ix. 1-11; (*b*) the name "*false prophet*" would, better than any other, describe that power, and would naturally suggest it in future times—for to no one that has ever appeared in our world could the name be so properly applied as to Mahomet; and (*c*) what is said will be found to agree with the facts in regard to that power, as, in connection with the Papacy and with Paganism, constituting the sum of the

14 For they are the *x*spirits of devils, *y*working miracles, which go forth unto the kings of the earth and of *z*the whole world, to gather them to the *a*battle of that great day of God Almighty.

*x* 1 Ti.4.1.   *y* 2 Th.2.9
*z* 1 Jn.5.19.   *a* ch.19.19.

15 Behold, *b*I come as a thief. Blessed *is* he that watcheth, and keepeth his garments, lest he walk *c*naked, and they see his shame.

16 And he gathered them together into a place called in the Hebrew tongue Armageddon.

*b* 2 Pe.3.10.   *c* ch.3.4,18.

obstruction to the spread of the gospel around the world.

14. *For they are the spirits of devils.* On the meaning of the word used here, see Notes on ch. ix. 20. It is used here, as it is in ch. ix. 20, in a bad sense, as denoting *evil* spirits. Comp. Notes on Mat. iv. 1, 2, 24. ¶ *Working miracles.* Working what *seemed* to be miracles; that is, such wonders as to deceive the world with the belief that they were miracles. See Notes on ch. xiii. 13, 14, where the same power is ascribed to the "beast." ¶ *Which go forth unto the kings of the earth.* Which particularly affect and influence kings and rulers. No class of men have been more under the influence of Pagan superstition, Mahometan delusion, or the Papacy, than kings and princes. We are taught by this passage that this will continue to be so in the circumstances referred to. ¶ *And of the whole world.* That is, so far that it might be represented as affecting the whole world—to wit, the heathen, the Mahometan, and the Papal portions of the earth. These still embrace so large a portion of the globe, that it might be said, that what would affect those powers now would influence the whole world. ¶ *To gather them.* Not literally to assemble them all in one place, but so to unite and combine them that it might be represented as an assembling of the hosts for battle. ¶ *To the battle of that great day of God Almighty.* Not the day of judgment, but the day which would determine the ascendency of true religion in the world—the final conflict with those powers which had so long opposed the gospel. It is not necessary to suppose that there would be a literal "*battle*," in which God would be seen to contend with his foes; but there would be that which might be properly *represented* as a battle. That is, there would be a combined struggle against the truth, and in that God would appear by his providence and Spirit on the side of the church, and would give it the victory. It accords with all that has occurred in the past, to suppose that there will be such a combined struggle before the church shall finally triumph in the world.

15. *Behold, I come as a thief.* That is, suddenly and unexpectedly. See Notes on Mat. xxiv. 43; 1 Th. v. 2. This is designed evidently to admonish men to watch, or to be in readiness for his coming, since, whenever it would occur, it would be at a time when men were not expecting him. ¶ *Blessed* is *he that watcheth.* Comp. Mat. xxiv. 42-44. The meaning here is, that he who watches for these events, who marks the indications of their approach, and who is conscious of a preparation for them, is in a better and happier state of mind than he on whom they come suddenly and unexpectedly. ¶ *And keepeth his garments.* The allusion here seems to be to one who, regardless of danger, or of the approach of an enemy, should lay aside his garments and lie down to sleep. Then the thief might come and take away his garments, leaving him naked. The essential idea, therefore, here, is the duty of vigilance. We are to be awake to duty and to danger; we are not to be found sleeping at our post; we are to be ready for death—ready for the coming of the Son of man. ¶ *Lest he walk naked.* His raiment being carried away while he is asleep. ¶ *And they see his shame.* Comp. Notes on ch. iii. 18. The meaning here is, that, as Christians are clothed with the garments of righteousness, they should not lay them aside, so that their spiritual nakedness should be seen. They are to be always clothed with the robes of salvation; always ready for any event, however soon or suddenly it may come upon them.

16. *And he gathered them together.* Who gathered them? Professor Stuart renders it, "*they* gathered them together," supposing that it refers to the "spirits" —πνεύματα—in ver. 13, and that this is the construction of the neuter plural with a singular verb. So De Wette understands it. Hengstenberg supposes

that it means that *God* gathered them together; others suppose that it was the sixth angel; others that it was Satan; others that it was the beast; and others that it was Christ. See Poole's *Synopsis, in loco*. The authority of De Wette and Professor Stuart is sufficient to show that the construction which they adopt is authorized by the Greek, as indeed no one can doubt, and perhaps this accords better with the context than any other construction proposed. Thus, in ver. 14, the spirits are represented as going forth into the whole world for *the purpose* of gathering the nations together to the great battle, and it is natural to suppose that the reference is to them here as having accomplished what they went forth to do. But who are to be gathered together? Evidently those who, in ver. 14, are described by the word "*them*"—the "kings of the earth, and the whole world;" that is, there will be a state of things which would be well described by a universal gathering of forces in a central battle-field. It is by no means necessary to suppose that what is here represented will *literally* occur. There will be a mustering of spiritual forces; there will be a combination and a unity of opposition against the truth; there will be a rallying of the declining powers of Heathenism, Mahometanism, and Romanism, *as if* the forces of the earth, marshalled by kings and rulers, were assembled in some great battle-field, where the destiny of the world was to be decided. ¶ *Into a place called in the Hebrew tongue Armageddon*. The word *Armageddon*—'Ἀρμαγεδδών—occurs nowhere else in the New Testament, and is not found in the Septuagint. It seems to be formed from the Hebrew הר מגדו *Har Megiddo—Mountain of Megiddo*. Comp. 2 Ch. xxxv. 22, where it is said that Josiah "came to fight *in the valley of Megiddo*." Megiddo was a town belonging to Manasseh, although within the limits of Issachar, Jos. xvii. 11. It had been originally one of the royal cities of the Canaanites (Jos. xii. 21), and was one of those of which the Israelites were unable for a long time to take possession. It was rebuilt and fortified by Solomon (1 Ki. ix. 15), and thither Ahaziah king of Judah fled when wounded by Jehu, and died there, 2 Ki. ix. 27. It was here that Deborah and Barak destroyed Sisera and his host (Ju. v. 19); and it was in a battle near this that Josiah was slain by Pharaoh-Necho, 2 Ki. xxiii. 29, 30; 2 Ch. xxxv. 20-25. From the great mourning held for his loss, it became proverbial to speak of any grievous mourning as being "like the mourning of Hadadrimmon in the valley of Megiddon," Zec. xii. 11. It has not been found easy to identify the place, but recent searches have made it probable that the vale or plain of Megiddo comprehended, if it was not wholly composed of, the prolongation of the plain of Esdraelon, towards Mount Carmel; that the city of Megiddo was situated there; and that the waters of Megiddo, mentioned in Ju. v. 19, are identical with the stream Kishon in that part of its course. See *Biblical Repository*, vol. i. pp. 602, 603. It is supposed that the modern town called *Lejjûn* occupies the site of the ancient Megiddo (Robinson's *Biblical Researches*, vol. iii. pp. 177-180). Megiddo was distinguished for being the place of the decisive conflict between Deborah and Sisera, and of the battle in which Josiah was slain by the Egyptian invaders; and hence it became emblematic of *any* decisive battle-field—just as Marathon, Leuctra, Arbela, or Waterloo is. The word "mountain," in the term Armageddon —"Mountain of Megiddo"—seems to have been used because Megiddo was in a mountainous region, though the battles were fought in a *valley* adjacent. The meaning here is, that there would be, as it were, a decisive battle which would determine the question of the prevalence of true religion on the earth. What we are to expect as the fulfilment of this would seem to be, that there will be some mustering of strength— some rallying of forces—some opposition made to the kingdom of God in the gospel, by the powers here referred to, which would be decisive in its character, and which would be well represented by the battles between the people of God and their foes in the conflicts in the valley of Megiddo.

As this constitutes, according to the course of the exposition by which we have been conducted, an important division in the book of Revelation, it may be proper to pause here and make a few remarks. The previous parts of the book, according to the interpretation proposed, relate to the past, and thus far we have found such a correspondence between the predictions and facts which have occurred as to lead us to suppose that these predictions have

## CHAPTER XVI.

been fulfilled. At this point, I suppose, we enter on that part which remains yet to be fulfilled, and the investigation must carry us into the dark and unknown future. The remaining portion comprises a very general sketch of things down to the end of time, as the previous portion has touched on the great events pertaining to the church and its progress for a period of more than one thousand eight hundred years. A few general remarks, therefore, seem not inappropriate at this point.

(*a*) In the previous interpretations, we have had the facts of history by which to test the accuracy of the interpretation. The plan pursued has been, first, to investigate the meaning of the words and symbols, entirely independent of any supposed application, and then to inquire whether there have been any facts that may be regarded as corresponding with the meaning of the words and symbols as explained. Of this method of testing the accuracy of the exposition, we must now take our leave. Our sole reliance must be in the exposition itself, and our work must be limited to that.

(*b*) It is always difficult to interpret a prophecy. The language of prophecy is often apparently enigmatical; the symbols are sometimes obscure; and prophecies relating to the same subject are often in detached fragments, uttered by different persons at different times; and it is necessary to collect and arrange them, in order to have a full view of the one subject. Thus the prophecies respecting the Messiah were many of them obscure, and indeed apparently contradictory, before he came; they were uttered at distant intervals, and by different prophets; at one time one trait of his character was dwelt upon, and at another another; and it was difficult to combine these so as to have an accurate view of what he would be, until he came. The result has shown what the meaning of the prophecies was; and at the same time has demonstrated that there was entire consistency in the various predictions, and that to one who could have comprehended all, it would have been *possible* to combine them so as to have had a *correct* view of the Messiah, and of his work, even before he came. The same remark is still more applicable to the predictions in the book of Revelation, or to the similar predictions in the book of Daniel, and to many portions of Isaiah.

It is easy to see how *difficult* it would have been, or rather how *impossible* by any human powers, to have applied these prophecies in detail before the events occurred; and yet, now that they have occurred, it may be seen that the symbols were the happiest that could have been chosen, and the only ones that could with propriety have been selected to describe the remarkable events which were to take place in future times.

(*c*) The same thing we may presume to be the case in regard to events which are to occur. We may expect to find (1) language and symbols that are, in themselves, capable of clear interpretation as to their proper meaning; (2) the events of the future so sketched out by that language, and by those symbols, that we may obtain a *general* view that will be accurate; and yet (3) an entire impossibility of filling up beforehand the minute details.

In regard, then, to the application of the particular portion now before us, ver. 12-16, the following remarks may be made:—

(1) The Turkish power, especially since its conquest of Constantinople under Mahomet II. in 1453, and its establishment in Europe, has been *a* grand hindrance to the spread of the gospel. It has occupied a central position; it has possessed some of the richest parts of the world; it has, in general, excluded all efforts to spread the pure gospel within its limits; and its whole influence has been opposed to the spread of pure Christianity. Comp. Notes on ch. ix. 14-21. "By its laws it was death to a Mussulman to apostatize from his faith, and become a Christian; and examples, not a few, have occurred in recent times to illustrate it." It was not until quite recently, and that under the influence of missionaries in Constantinople, that evangelical Christianity has been tolerated in the Turkish dominions.

(2) The prophecy before us implies that there would be a *decline* of that formidable power—represented by the "drying up of the great river Euphrates." See Notes on ver. 12. And no one can be insensible to the fact that events are occurring which would be properly represented by such a symbol; or that there is, in fact, now such a decline of that Turkish power, and that the beginning of that decline closely followed, in regard to *time*, if not in regard to the *cause*, the events which it is sup-

posed were designated by the previous vials—those connected with the successive blows on the Papacy and the seat of the beast. In reference, then, to the decline of that power, we may refer to the following things:—(*a*) The first great cause was *internal revolt and insurrection*. In 1820 Ali Pasha asserted his independence, and by his revolt precipitated the Greek insurrection which had been a long time secretly preparing—an insurrection so disastrous to the Turkish power. (*b*) The Greek insurrection followed. This soon spread to the Ægean isles, and to the districts of Northern Greece, Epirus, and Thessaly; while at the same time the standard of revolt was raised in Wallachia and Moldavia. The progress and issue of that insurrection are well known. A Turcoman army of 30,000 that entered the Morea to reconquer it was destroyed in 1823 in detail, and the freedom of the peninsula was nearly completed by the insurgents. By sea the Greeks emulated their ancestors of Salamis and Mycale; and, attended with almost uniform success, encountered and vanquished the superior Turkish and Egyptian fleets. Meanwhile the sympathies of Western Christendom were awakened in behalf of their brother Christians struggling for independence; and just when the tide of success began to turn, and the Morea was again nearly subjected by Ibrahim Pasha, the united fleets of England, France, and Russia (in contravention of all their usual principles of policy) interposed in their favour; attacked and destroyed the Turco-Egyptian fleets in the battle of Navarino (September, 1827), and thus secured the independence of Greece. Nothing had ever occurred that tended so much to weaken the power of the Turkish empire. (*c*) The rebellion of the great Egyptian pasha, Mehemet Ali, soon followed. The French invasion of Egypt had prepared him for it, by having taught him the superiority of European discipline, and thus this event was one of the proper results of those described under the first four vials. Mehemet Ali, through Ibrahim, attacked and conquered Syria; defeated the sultan's armies sent against him in the great battles of Hems, of Nezib, and of Iconium; and, but for the intervention of the European powers of England, Russia, Prussia, and Austria, by which he was driven out of Syria, and forced back to his proper pashalic, Egypt, he would probably have advanced to Constantinople and subdued it. (*d*) There has been for centuries a gradual weakening of the Turkish power. It has done nothing to extend its empire by arms. It has been resting in inglorious ease, and, in the meantime, its wealth and its strength have been gradually decreasing. It has lost Moldavia, Wallachia, Greece, Algiers, and, practically, Egypt; and is doing nothing to recruit its wasted and exhausted strength. Russia only waits for a favourable opportunity to strike the last blow on that enfeebled power, and to put an end to it for ever. (*e*) The general condition of the Turkish empire is thus described by the Rev. Mr. Walsh, chaplain to the British ambassador to Constantinople:—"The circumstances most striking to a traveller passing through Turkey is its *depopulation*. Ruins where villages had been built, and fallows where land had been cultivated, are frequently seen with no living thing near them. This effect is not so visible in larger towns, though the cause is known to operate there in a still greater degree. Within the last twenty years, Constantinople has lost more than half its population. Two conflagrations happened while I was in Constantinople, and destroyed fifteen thousand houses. The Russian and Greek wars were a constant drain on the janizaries of the capital; the silent operation of the plague is continually active, though not always alarming; it will be no exaggeration to say that, within the period mentioned, from three to four hundred thousand persons have been swept away in one city in Europe by causes which were not operating in any other—*conflagration, pestilence, and civil commotion*. The Turks, though naturally of a robust and vigorous constitution, addict themselves to such habits as are very unfavourable to population—the births do little more than exceed the ordinary deaths, and cannot supply the waste of casualties. The surrounding country is, therefore, continually drained to supply this waste in the capital, which, nevertheless, exhibits districts *nearly depopulated*. We see every day life going out in the fairest portion of Europe; *and the human race threatened with extinction* in a soil and climate capable of supporting the most abundant population" (Walsh's *Narrative*, pp. 22-26, as quoted in Bush *on the Millennium*, 243, 244). The probability now is, that this gradual decay

17 And the seventh angel poured out his vial into the air; and there came a great voice out of the temple of heaven, from the throne, saying, *d* It is done.

*d* ch.21.6.

18 And there were voices, and thunders, and lightnings; and there was a *e* great earthquake, *f* such as was not since men were upon the earth, so mighty an earthquake, *and* so great.

*e* ch.11.13.   *f* Da.12.1.

will be continued; that the Turkish power will more and more diminish; that one portion after another will set up for independence; and that, by a gradual process of decline, this power will become practically extinct, and what is here symbolized by the "drying up of the great river Euphrates" will have been accomplished.

(3) This obstacle removed, we may look for a general turning of the princes, and rulers, and people of the Eastern world to Christianity, represented (ver. 12) by its being said that "the way of the kings of the East might be prepared." See Notes on that verse. It is clear that nothing would be more *likely* to contribute to this, or to prepare the way for it, than the removal of that Turcoman dominion which for more than four hundred years has been an effectual barrier to the diffusion of the gospel in the lands where it has prevailed. How rapidly, we may suppose, the gospel would spread in the East, if all the obstacles thrown in its way by the Turkish power were at once removed!

(4) In accordance with the interpretation suggested on ver. 13, 14, we may look for something that would be well represented by a combined effort on the part of Heathenism, Mahometanism, and Romanism, to stay the progress and prevent the spread of evangelical religion. That is, according to the fair interpretation of the passage, we should look for some simultaneous movement *as if* their influence was to be about to cease, and as if it were necessary to arouse all their energies for a last and desperate struggle. It may be added that, in itself, nothing would be more *probable* than this; but when it will occur, and what form the aroused enemy will assume, it would be vain to conjecture.

(5) And in accordance with the interpretation suggested on ver. 15, we are to suppose that something will occur which would be well represented by the decisive conflicts in the valley of Megiddo; that is, something that will determine the ascendency of true religion in the world, *as if* these great powers of Heathenism, Mahometanism, and Romanism should stake all their interests on the issue of a single battle. It is not necessary to suppose that this will *literally* occur, and there are no certain intimations as to the time when what is represented will happen; but all that is meant may be, that events will take place which would be well represented by such a conflict. Still, nothing in the prophecy prevents the supposition that these combined powers *may be* overthrown in some fierce conflict with Christian powers.

17. *And the seventh angel poured out his vial into the air.* This introduces the final catastrophe in regard to the "beast"—his complete and utter overthrow, accompanied with tremendous judgments. Why the vial was poured into *the air* is not stated. The most probable supposition as to the idea intended to be represented is, that, as storms and tempests seem to be engendered in the air, so this destruction would come from some supernatural cause, as if the whole atmosphere should be filled with wind and storm; and a furious and desolating whirlwind should be aroused by some invisible power. ¶ *And there came a great voice out of the temple of heaven.* The voice of God. See Notes on ch. xi. 19. ¶ *From the throne.* See Notes on ch. iv. 2. This shows that it was the voice of God, and not the voice of an angel. ¶ *Saying, It is done.* The series of judgments is about to be completed; the dominion of the beast is about to come to an end for ever. The meaning here is, that that destruction was so certain, that it might be spoken of as now actually accomplished.

18. *And there were voices, and thunders, and lightnings.* Accompanying the voice that was heard from the throne. See Notes on ch. iv. 5; xi. 19. ¶ *And there was a great earthquake,* &c. See Notes on ch. vi. 12; xi. 19. The meaning is, that a judgment followed *as if* the world were shaken by an earthquake, or which would be properly represented by that. ¶ *So mighty an*

19 And the *great city was divided into three parts, and the cities of the nations fell: and great Babylon came in remembrance before God, to give unto her the *cup of the wine of the fierceness of his wrath.

20 And *every island fled away, and the mountains were not found.

*g* ch.14.8.    *h* Is.51.17,23; Je.25.15,16.    *i* ch.6.14.

*earthquake*, and *so great*. All this is intensive, and is designed to represent the severity of the judgment that would follow.

19. *And the great city was divided into three parts.* The city of Babylon; or the mighty power that was represented by Babylon. See Notes on ch. xiv. 8. The division here mentioned into three parts was manifestly with reference to its destruction—either that one part was smitten and the others remained for a time, or that one form of destruction came on one part, and another on the others. In ch. xi. 13 it is said, speaking of "the great city spiritually called Sodom and Egypt"—representing Rome, that "the tenth part of the city fell, and in the earthquake were slain of men seven thousand" (see Notes on that place); here it is said that the whole city, in the calamities that came upon it, was divided into three portions, though it is evidently implied that, in these calamities, the *whole* city was sooner or later destroyed. Professor Stuart (*in loco*) supposes that the number *three* is used here, as it is throughout the book, "in a symbolical way," and that the meaning is, that "the city was severed and broken in pieces, so that the whole was reduced to a ruinous state." He supposes that it refers to Pagan Rome, or to the Pagan Roman persecuting power. Others refer it to Jerusalem, and suppose that the allusion is to the divisions of the city, in the time of the siege, into Jewish, Samaritan, and Christian parties; others suppose that it refers to a division of the Roman empire under Honorius, Attalus, and Constantine; others to the fact, that when Jerusalem was besieged by Titus, it was divided into three factions; and others, that the number three is used to denote *perfection*, or the total ruin of the city. All that, it seems to me, can be said now on the point is, (*a*) that it refers to Papal Rome, or the Papal power; (*b*) that it relates to something yet future, and that it may not be possible to determine with precise accuracy what will occur; (*c*) that it probably means that, in the time of the final ruin of that power, there will be a threefold judgment—either a different judgment in regard to some threefold manifestation of that power, or a succession of judgments, *as if* one part were smitten at a time. The certain and entire ruin of the power is predicted by this, but still it is not improbable that it will be by such divisions, or such successions of judgments, that it is proper to represent the city as divided into three portions. ¶ *And the cities of the nations fell.* In alliance with it, or under the control of the central power. As the capital fell, the dependent cities fell also. Considered as relating to Papal Rome, the meaning here is, that what may be properly called "the cities *of the nations*" that were allied with it would share the same fate. The cities of numerous "nations" are now, and have been for ages, under the control of the Papal power, or the spiritual Babylon; and the calamity that will smite the central power *as such*—that is, *as* a spiritual power—will reach and affect them all. Let the central power at Rome be destroyed; the Papacy cease; the superstition with which Rome is regarded come to an end; the power of the priesthood in Italy be destroyed, and however widely the Roman dominion is spread now, it cannot be kept up. If it falls *in* Rome, there is not influence enough *out of* Rome to continue it in being—and in all its extended ramifications it will die as the body dies when the head is severed; as the power of provinces ceases when ruin comes upon the capital. This the prophecy leads us to suppose will be the final destiny of the Papal power. ¶ *And great Babylon.* See Notes on ch. xiv. 8. ¶ *Came in remembrance before God.* That is, for purposes of punishment. It had been, as it were, overlooked. It had been permitted to carry on its purposes, and to practise its abominations, unchecked, as if God did not see it. Now the time had come when all that it had done was to be remembered, and when the long-suspended judgment was to fall upon it. ¶ *To give unto her the cup of the wine,* &c. To punish; to destroy her. See Notes on ch. xiv. 10.

A.D. 96.]  CHAPTER XVII.  379

21 And there fell upon men a great *k*hail out of heaven, *every stone* about the weight of a talent:

*k* ch.11.19.

and men blasphemed God because of the plague of the hail; for the plague thereof was exceeding great.

20. *And every island fled away.* Expressive of great and terrible judgments, *as if* the very earth were convulsed, and everything were moved out of its place. See Notes on ch. vi. 14. ¶ *And the mountains were not found.* The same image occurs in ch. vi. 14. See Notes on that place.

21. *And there fell upon men a great hail out of heaven.* Perhaps this is an allusion to one of the plagues of Egypt, Ex. ix. 22-26. Comp. Notes on ch. xi. 19. For a graphic description (by Com. Porter) of the effects of a hailstorm, see Notes on Is. xxx. 30. Comp. Notes on Job xxxviii. 22. ¶ *Every stone about the weight of a talent.* The Attic talent was equal to about 55 lbs. or 56 lbs. Troy weight; the Jewish talent to about 113 lbs. Troy. Whichever weight is adopted, it is easy to conceive what must be the horror of such a storm, and what destruction it must cause. We are not, of course, to suppose necessarily, that this would literally occur; it is a frightful image to denote the terrible and certain destruction that would come upon Babylon—that is, upon the Papal power. ¶ *And men blasphemed God.* See Notes on ver. 9. ¶ *Because of the plague of the hail.* Using the word *plague* in allusion to the plagues of Egypt. ¶ *For the plague thereof was exceeding great.* The calamity was great and terrible. The design of the whole is to show that the destruction would be complete and awful.

This finishes the summary statement of the final destruction of this formidable Antichristian power. The details and the consequences of that overthrow are more fully stated in the subsequent chapters. The *fulfilment* of what is here stated will be found, according to the method of interpretation proposed, in the ultimate overthrow of the Papacy. The process described in this chapter is that of successive calamities that would weaken it and prepare it for its fall; then a rallying of its dying strength; and then some tremendous judgment that is compared with a storm of hail, accompanied with lightning, and thunder, and an earthquake, that would completely overthrow all that was connected with it. We are not, indeed, to suppose that this will *literally* occur; but the fair interpretation of prophecy leads us to suppose that that formidable power will, at no very distant period, be overthrown in a manner that would be well represented by such a fearful storm.

CHAPTER XVII.

ANALYSIS OF THE CHAPTER.

This chapter properly commences a more detailed description of the judgment inflicted on the formidable Antichristian power referred to in the last chapter, though under a new image. It contains an account of the sequel of the pouring out of the last vial, and the description, in various forms, continues to the close of ch. xix. The whole of this description (ch. xvii.-xix.) constitutes the last great catastrophe represented under the seventh vial (ch. xvi. 17-21), at the close of which the great enemy of God and the church will be destroyed, and the church will be triumphant, ch. xix. 17-21. The image in this chapter is that of a harlot, or abandoned woman, on whom severe judgment is brought for her sins. The action is here *delayed*, and this chapter has much the appearance of *an explanatory episode*, designed to give a more clear and definite idea of the character of that formidable Antichristian power on which the judgment was to descend. The chapter, without any formal division, embraces the following points:—

(1) Introduction, ver. 1-3. One of the seven angels intrusted with the seven vials comes to John, saying that he would describe to him the judgment that was to come upon the great harlot with whom the kings of the earth had committed fornication, and who had made the dwellers upon the earth drunk by the wine of her fornication—that is, of that Antichristian power so often referred to in this book, which by its influence had deluded the nations, and brought their rulers under its control.

(2) A particular description of this Antichristian power—represented as an abandoned and attractive female, in the usual attire of an harlot, ver. 3-6. She is seated on a scarlet-coloured beast, covered over with blasphemous names—a beast with seven heads and

## CHAPTER XVII.

AND there came one of the seven angels which had the seven vials, and talked with me, saying

---

ten horns. She is arrayed in the usual gorgeous and alluring attire of an harlot, clothed in purple, decked with gold, and precious stones, and pearls, with a golden cup in her hand full of abomination and filthiness. She has on her forehead a name expressive of her character. She is represented as drunken with the blood of the saints, and is such as to attract attention and excite wonder.

(3) An explanation of what is meant by this scarlet-clothed woman, and of the design of the representation, ver. 7-18. This comprises several parts: (a) A promise of the angel that he would explain this, ver. 7. (b) An enigmatical or symbolical representation of the design of the vision, ver. 8-14. This description consists of an account of the beast on which the woman sat, ver. 8; of the seven heads of the beast, as representing seven mountains, ver. 9; of the succession of kings or dynasties represented, ver. 9-11; of the ten horns as representing ten kings or kingdoms giving their power and strength to the beast, ver. 12, 13; and of the conflict or warfare of all these confederated or consolidated powers with the Lamb, and their discomfiture by him, ver. 14. (c) A more literal statement of what is meant by this, ver. 15-18. The waters on which the harlot sat represent a multitude of people subject to her control, ver. 15. The ten horns, or the ten kingdoms, on the beast, would ultimately hate the harlot, and destroy her, *as if* they should eat her flesh, and consume her with fire, ver. 16. This would be done *because* God would put it into their hearts to fulfil his purposes, alike in giving their kingdom to the beast, and then turning against it to destroy it, ver. 17. The woman referred to is at last declared to be the great city which reigned over the kings of the earth, ver. 18. For particularity and definiteness, this is one of the most remarkable chapters in the book, and there can be no doubt that it was the design in it to give such an *explanation* of what was referred to in these visions, that there could be no mistake in applying the description. "All that remains between this and

unto me, Come hither; I will show unto thee the judgment of the *a*great whore that *b*sitteth upon many waters:

*a* ch.19.2; Na.3.4.   *b* Je.51.13.

the twentieth chapter," says Andrew Fuller, "would in modern publications be called *notes of illustration*. No new subject is introduced, but mere enlargement on what has already been announced" (*Works*, vi. 205).

1. *And there came one of the seven angels which had the seven vials*. See Notes on ch. xv. 1, 7. Reference is again made to these angels in the same manner in ch. xxi. 9, where one of them says that he would show to John "the bride, the Lamb's wife." No particular one is specified. The general idea seems to be, that to those seven angels was intrusted the execution of the last things, or the winding up of affairs introductory to the reign of God, and that the communications respecting those last events were properly made through them. It is clearly quite immaterial by which of these it is done. The expression "which had the seven vials," would seem to imply that though they had emptied the vials in the manner stated in the previous chapter, they still retained them in their hands. ¶ *And talked with me*. Spake to me. The word *talk* would imply a more protracted conversation than occurred here. ¶ *Come hither*. Gr., δεῦρο—"Here, hither." This is a word merely calling the attention, as we should say now, "*Here*." It does not imply that John was to leave the place where he was. ¶ *I will show thee*. Partly by symbols, and partly by express statements; for this is the way in which, in fact, he showed him. ¶ *The judgment*. The condemnation and calamity that will come upon her. ¶ *Of the great whore*. It is not uncommon in the Scriptures to represent a city under the image of a woman—a pure and holy city under the image of a virgin or chaste female; a corrupt, idolatrous, and wicked city under the image of an abandoned or lewd woman. See Notes on Is. i. 21: "How is the faithful city become an harlot!" Comp. Notes on Is. i. 8. In ver. 18 of this chapter it is expressly said that "this woman is that great city which reigneth over the kings of the earth"—that is, as I suppose, Papal Rome; and the design here is to represent it as resembling an abandoned female—fit representative of an apos-

2 With<sup>c</sup> whom the kings of the earth have committed fornication, and the inhabitants of the earth have been made drunk with the wine of her fornication.

c ch. 18. 3.

---

tate, corrupt, unfaithful church. Comp. Notes on ch. ix. 21. ¶ *That sitteth upon many waters.* An image drawn either from Babylon, situated on the Euphrates, and encompassed by the many artificial rivers which had been made to irrigate the country, or Rome, situated on the Tiber. In ver. 15 these waters are said to represent the peoples, multitudes, nations, and tongues over which the government symbolized by the woman ruled. See Notes on that verse. Waters are often used to symbolize nations.

2. *With whom the kings of the earth have committed fornication.* Spiritual adultery. The meaning is, that Papal Rome, unfaithful to God, and idolatrous and corrupt, had seduced the rulers of the earth, and led them into the same kind of unfaithfulness, idolatry, and corruption. Comp. Jer. iii. 8, 9; v. 7; xiii. 27; xxiii. 14; Eze. xvi. 32; xxiii. 37; Ho. ii. 2; iv. 2. How true this is in history need not be stated. All the princes and kings of Europe in the dark ages, and for many centuries were, and not a few of them are now, entirely under the influence of Papal Rome. ¶ *And the inhabitants of the earth have been made drunk with the wine of her fornication.* The alluring cup which, as an harlot, she had extended to them. See this image explained in the Notes on ch. xiv. 8. There it is said that Babylon—referring to the same thing—had "made them drink of the wine *of the wrath* of her fornication;" that is, of the cup that led to wrath or punishment. Here it is said that the harlot had made them "*drunk* with the wine of her fornication;" that is, they had been, as it were, intoxicated by the alluring cup held out to them. What could better describe the influence of Rome on the people of the world, in making them, under these delusions, incapable of sober judgment, and in completely fascinating and controlling all their powers?

3. *So he carried me away in the spirit.* In vision. He *seemed* to himself to be thus carried away; or the scene which he is about to describe was made to

3 So he carried me away in the spirit into the wilderness; and I saw a woman sit upon a <sup>d</sup>scarlet-coloured beast, full of names of blasphemy, <sup>e</sup>having seven heads and ten horns.

d ch. 12. 3.     e ch. 13. 1.

pass before him *as if* he were present. ¶ *Into the wilderness.* Into a desert. Comp. Notes on ch. xii. 6. Why this scene is laid in a wilderness or desert is not mentioned. Professor Stuart supposes that it is because it is "appropriate to symbolize the future condition of the beast." So De Wette and Rosenmüller. The imagery is changed somewhat from the first appearance of the harlot in ver. 1. There she is represented as "sitting upon many waters." Now she is represented as "riding on a beast," and of course the imagery is adapted to that. Possibly there may have been no intentional significancy in this; but on the supposition, as the interpretation has led us to believe all along, that this refers to Papal Rome, may not the propriety of this be seen in the condition of Rome and the adjacent country, at the rise of the Papal power? That had its rise (see Notes on Da. vii. 25, seq.) after the decline of the Roman civil power, and properly in the time of Clovis, Pepin, or Charlemagne. Perhaps its first *visible* appearance, as a power that was to influence the destiny of the world, was in the time of Gregory the Great, A.D. 590-605. On the supposition that the passage before us refers to the period when the Papal power became thus marked and defined, the state of Rome at this time, as described by Mr. Gibbon, would show with what propriety the term *wilderness* or *desert* might be then applied to it. The following extract from this author, in describing the state of Rome at the accession of Gregory the Great, has almost the appearance of being a designed *commentary* on this passage, or is, at anyrate, such as a partial interpreter of this book would *desire* and *expect* to find. Speaking of that period, he says (*Decline and Fall*, iii. 207-211): —"Rome had reached, about the close of the sixth century, the lowest period of her depression. By the removal of the seat of empire, and the successive loss of the provinces, the sources of public and private opulence were exhausted; the lofty tree under whose shade the nations of the earth had reposed was deprived of its leaves and branches, and the sapless trunk was left to wither on the ground. The ministers of command and the messengers of victory no longer met on the Appian or Flaminian Way; and the hostile approach of the Lombards was often felt and continually feared. The inhabitants of a potent and peaceful capital, who visit without an anxious thought the garden of the adjacent country, will faintly picture in their fancy the distress of the Romans; they shut or opened their gates with a trembling hand, beheld from the walls the flames of their houses, and heard the lamentations of their brethren who were coupled together like dogs, and dragged away into distant slavery beyond the sea and the mountains. Such incessant alarms must annihilate the pleasures, and interrupt the labours of a rural life; *and the Campagna of Rome was speedily reduced to the state of a dreary* WILDERNESS, *in which the land is barren, the waters are impure, and the air is infectious.* Curiosity and ambition no longer attracted the nations to the capital of the world; but if chance or necessity directed the steps of a wandering stranger, he contemplated with horror *the vacancy and solitude of the city; and might be tempted to ask, Where is the Senate, and where are the people?* In a season of excessive rains, the Tiber swelled above its banks, and rushed with irresistible violence into the valleys of the seven hills. A pestilential disease arose from the stagnation of the deluge, and so rapid was the contagion that fourscore persons expired in an hour in the midst of a solemn procession which implored the mercy of Heaven. A society in which marriage is encouraged, and industry prevails, soon repairs the accidental losses of pestilence and war; but as the far greater part of the Romans was condemned to hopeless indigence and celibacy, *the depopulation was constant and visible, and the gloomy enthusiasts might expect the approaching failure of the human race.* Yet the number of citizens still exceeded the measure of subsistence; their precarious food was supplied from the harvests of Sicily or Egypt; and the frequent repetition of famine betrays the inattention of the emperor to a distant province. *The edifices of Rome were exposed to the same ruin and decay; the mouldering fabrics were easily overthrown by inundations, tempests, and earthquakes; and the monks who had occupied the most advantageous stations exulted in their base triumph over the ruins of antiquity.*

"Like Thebes, or Babylon, or Carthage, the name of Rome might have been erased from the earth, if the city had not been animated by a vital principle which again restored her to honour and dominion. The power as well as the virtue of the apostles resided with living energy in the breast of their successors; and the chair of St. Peter, under the reign of Maurice, was occupied by the first and greatest of the name of Gregory. The sword of the enemy was suspended over Rome; it was averted by the mild eloquence and seasonable gifts of the pontiff, who commanded the respect of heretics and barbarians." Comp. Rev. xiii. 3, 12-15. On the supposition, now, that the inspired author of the Apocalypse had Rome, in that state when the civil power declined and the Papacy arose, in his eye, what more expressive imagery could he have used to denote it than he has employed? On the supposition—if such a supposition could be made—that Mr. Gibbon *meant* to furnish a commentary on this passage, what more appropriate language could *he* have used? Does not this language look as if the author of the Apocalypse and the author of the *Decline and Fall* meant to play into each other's hands?

And, in further confirmation of this, I may refer to the testimony of two Roman Catholic writers, giving the same view of Rome, and showing that, in their apprehension also, it was only by the reviving influence of the Papacy that Rome was saved from becoming a total waste. They are both of the middle ages. The first is Augustine Steuchus, who thus writes:—"The empire having been overthrown, unless God had raised up the *pontificate*, Rome, resuscitated and restored by none, would have become uninhabitable, and been a most foul habitation thenceforward of cattle. But in the pontificate it revived as with a *second birth;* its empire in magnitude not indeed equal to the old empire, but its form not very dissimilar: because all nations, from East and from West, venerate the pope, not otherwise than they before obeyed the emperor." The other is Flavio Blondas:—"The princes of the world now adore and worship as

A.D. 96.]  CHAPTER XVII.  383

4 And the woman was arrayed in purple and scarlet colour, and decked[1] with gold and precious

[1] gilded.

stones and pearls,[f] having a golden cup in her hand full of abominations of filthiness of her fornication:

[f] Je.51.7.

*perpetual dictator* the successor not of Cæsar but of the fisherman Peter; that is, the *supreme pontiff*, the substitute of the aforesaid emperor." See the original in Elliott, iii. 113.

¶ *And I saw a woman.* Evidently the same which is referred to in ver. 1. ¶ *Sit upon a scarlet-coloured beast.* That is, either the beast was itself naturally of this colour, or it was covered with trappings of this colour. The word *scarlet* properly denotes a bright red colour—brighter than crimson, which is a red colour tinged with blue. See Notes on Is. i. 18. The word here used — κόκκινον — occurs in the New Testament only in the following places:— Mat. xxvii. 28; He. ix. 19; Re. xvii. 3, 4; xviii. 12, 16 — in all which places it is rendered *scarlet*. See Notes on Mat. xxvii. 28 and He. ix. 19. The colour was obtained from a small insect which was found adhering to the shoots of a species of oak in Spain and Western Asia. This was the usual colour in the robes of princes, military cloaks, &c. It is applicable in the description of Papal Rome, because this is a favourite colour there. Thus it is used in ch. xii. 3, where the same power is represented under the image of a "red dragon." See Notes on that passage. It is remarkable that nothing would better represent the favourite colour at Rome than this, or the actual appearance of the pope, the cardinals, and the priests in their robes, on some great festival occasion. Those who are familiar with the descriptions given of Papal Rome by travellers, and those who have passed much time in Rome, will see at once the propriety of this description, on the supposition that it was intended to refer to the Papacy. I caused this inquiry to be made of an intelligent gentleman who had passed much time in Rome—without his knowing my design — what would strike a stranger on visiting Rome, or what would be likely particularly to arrest his attention as remarkable there; and he unhesitatingly replied, "The scarlet colour." This is the colour of the dress of the cardinals—their hats, and cloaks, and stockings being always of this colour. It is the colour of the carriages of the cardinals, the entire body of the carriage being scarlet, and the trappings of the horses the same. On occasion of public festivals and processions, scarlet is suspended from the windows of the houses along which processions pass. The inner colour of the cloak of the pope is scarlet; his carriage is scarlet; the carpet on which he treads is scarlet. A large part of the dress of the body-guard of the pope is scarlet; and no one can take up a picture of Rome without seeing that this colour is predominant. I looked through a volume of engravings representing the principal officers and public persons of Rome. There were few in which the scarlet colour was not found as constituting some part of their apparel; in not a few the scarlet colour prevailed almost entirely. And in illustration of the same thought, I introduce here an extract from a foreign newspaper, copied into an American newspaper of Feb. 22, 1851, as an illustration of the fact that the scarlet colour is characteristic of Rome, and of the readiness with which it is referred to in that respect:— "*Curious Costumes.* — The three new cardinals, the archbishops of Thoulouse, Rheims, and Besançon, were presented to the president of the French Republic by the Pope's nuncio. They wore red caps, red stockings, black Roman coats lined and bound with red, and small cloaks." I conclude, therefore, that if it be admitted that it was *intended* to represent Papal Rome in the vision, the precise description would have been adopted which is found here. ¶ *Full of names of blasphemy.* All covered over with blasphemous titles and names. What could more accurately describe Papal Rome than this? Comp. for some of these names and titles the Notes on 2 Th. ii. 4; 1 Ti. iv. 1-4; and Notes on Re. xiii. 1, 5. ¶ *Having seven heads and ten horns.* See Notes on ch. xiii. 1.

4. *And the woman was arrayed in purple and scarlet colour.* On the nature of the *scarlet colour*, see Notes on ver. 3. The *purple* colour — πορφύρα — was obtained from a species of shell-fish found on the coasts of the Mediterranean, which yielded a reddish-purple dye, much prized by the ancients. Robes dyed in that colour were com-

5 And upon her forehead *was* a name written, *g*MYSTERY, BABYLON THE GREAT, THE MOTHER OF ²HARLOTS AND ABOMINATIONS OF THE EARTH.

*g* 2 Th. 2. 7.   ² or, *fornications.*

monly worn by persons of rank and wealth, Mar. xv. 17, 20; Lu. xvi. 19. The purple colour contains more blue than the crimson, though the limits are not very accurately defined, and the words are sometimes interchanged. Thus the mock robe put on the Saviour is called in Mar. xv. 17, 20, πορφύραν — *purple*, and in Mat. xxvii. 28, κοκκίνην — *crimson.* On the applicability of this to the Papacy, see Notes on ver. 3. ¶ *And decked with gold.* After the manner of an harlot, with rich jewelry. ¶ *And precious stones.* Sparkling diamonds, &c. ¶ *And pearls.* Also a much-valued female ornament. Comp. Notes on Mat. vii. 6; xiii. 46. ¶ *Having a golden cup in her hand.* As if to entice lovers. See Notes on ch. xiv. 8. ¶ *Full of abominations.* Of abominable things; of things fitted to excite abhorrence and disgust; things unlawful and forbidden. The word, in the Scriptures, is commonly used to denote the impurities and abominations of idolatry. See Notes on Da. ix. 27. The meaning here is, that it seemed to be a cup filled with wine, but it was in fact a cup full of all abominable drugs, leading to all kinds of corruption. How much in accordance this is with the fascinations of the Papacy, it is not necessary now to say, after the ample illustrations of the same thing already furnished in these Notes. ¶ *And filthiness of her fornication.* The image here is that of Papal Rome, represented as an abandoned woman in gorgeous attire, alluring by her arts the nations of the earth, and seducing them into all kinds of pollution and abomination. It is a most remarkable fact that the Papacy, as if *designing* to furnish a fulfilment of this prophecy, has chosen to represent itself almost precisely in this manner—as a female extending an alluring cup to passers by—as will be seen by the engraving on this page. Far as the design of striking this medal may have been from confirming this portion of the book of Revelation, yet no one can fail to see that if this *had* been the design, no more happy illustration could have been adopted. Apostate churches, and guilty nations, often furnish the very proofs necessary to confirm the truth of the Scriptures.

5. *And upon her forehead.* In a circlet around her forehead. That is, it was made prominent and public, *as if* written on the forehead in blazing capitals. In ch. xiii. 1 it is said that "the name of blasphemy" was written on the "heads" of the beast. The meaning in

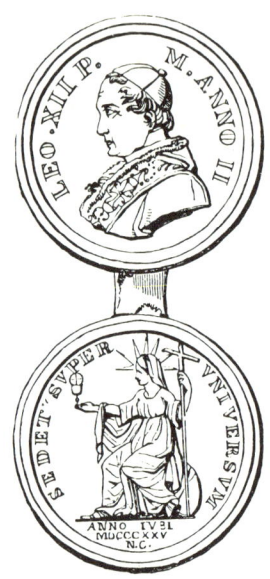

Medal of Pope Leo XII.

both places is substantially the same, that it was prominent and unmistakable. See Notes on that verse. Comp. Note on ch. xiv. 1. ¶ *Was a name written.* A title, or something that would properly indicate her character. ¶ *Mystery.* It is proper to remark that there is nothing in the original as written by John, so far as now known, that corresponded with what is implied in placing this inscription in capital letters; and the same remark may be made of the "title" or inscription that was placed over the head of the Saviour on the cross, Mat. xxvii. 37; Mar. xv. 26; Lu. xxiii. 38; Jn. xix. 19. Our translators have adopted this form, apparently for the sole purpose of denoting that it *was* an inscription or title. On the meaning of the word *mystery*, see Notes on 1 Co. ii. 7. Comp. Notes on

A.D. 96.]  CHAPTER XVII.  385

6 And I saw the woman *h*drunken with the blood of the saints, and with the blood of the martyrs of Jesus: and when I saw her I wondered with great admiration.

7 And the angel said unto me, Wherefore didst thou marvel? I

*h* ch.16.6.

will tell thee the mystery of *i*the woman, and of *k*the beast that carrieth her, which hath the seven heads and ten horns.

8 The beast that thou sawest was, and is not; and shall *l*ascend out of the bottomless pit, and *m*go

*i* ver.1.   *k* ver.3.   *l* ch.11.7.   *m* ver.11.

1 Ti. iii. 16. Here it seems to be used to denote that there was something hidden, obscure, or enigmatical, under the title adopted; that is, the word *Babylon*, and the word *mother*, were symbolical. Our translators have printed and pointed the word *mystery* as if it were part of the inscription. It would probably be better to regard it as referring to the inscription, thus: "a name was written—a *mysterious* name, to wit, Babylon," &c. Or, "a name was written mysteriously." According to this, it would mean, not that there was any wonderful "mystery" about the thing itself, whatever might be true on that point, but that the *name* was enigmatical or symbolical; or that there was something *hidden* or *concealed* under the name. It was not to be literally understood. ¶ *Babylon the great.* Papal Rome, the nominal head of the Christian world, as Babylon had been of the heathen world. See Notes on ch. xiv. 8. ¶ *The mother of harlots.* (*a*) Of that spiritual apostasy from God which, in the language of the prophets, might be called adultery. See Notes on ch. xiv. 8. (*b*) The promoter of lewdness by her institutions. See Notes on ch. ix. 21. In both these senses, there never was a more expressive or appropriate title than the one here employed. ¶ *And abominations of the earth.* Abominable things that prevail on the earth, ver. 4. Comp. Notes on ch. ix. 20, 21.

6. *And I saw the woman drunken with the blood of the saints.* A reeling, intoxicated harlot, for that is the image which is kept up all along. In regard to the phrase "drunken with blood," comp. Je. xlvi. 10. "The phraseology is derived from the barbarous custom (still extant among many Pagan nations) of drinking the blood of the enemies slain in the way of revenge. The effect of drinking blood is said to be to exasperate, and to intoxicate with passion and a desire of revenge" (Prof. Stuart, *in loco*). The meaning here is, that the persecuting power referred to had shed the blood of the saints; and that, in its

fury, it had, as it were, drunk the blood of the slain, and had become, by drinking that blood, intoxicated and infuriated. No one need say how applicable this has been to the Papacy. Compare, however, the Notes on Da. vii. 21, 25; Re. xii. 13, 14; xiii. 15. ¶ *And with the blood of the martyrs of Jesus. Especially* with their blood. The meaning is, that the warfare, in which so much blood was shed, was directed against the *saints as such*, and that, in fact, it terminated particularly on those who, amidst cruel sufferings, were faithful *witnesses* for the Lord Jesus, and deserved to be called, by way of eminence, *martyrs*. Comp. Notes on ch. ii. 13; vi. 9; xi. 5, 7. How applicable this is to the Papacy, let the blood shed in the valleys of Piedmont; the blood shed in the Low Countries by the Duke of Alva; the blood shed on St. Bartholomew's day; and the blood shed in the Inquisition, testify. ¶ *And when I saw her, I wondered with great admiration.* I was astonished at her appearance, at her apparel, and at the things which were so significantly symbolized by her.

7. *And the angel said unto me, Wherefore didst thou marvel?* He was doubtless struck with the appearance of John as he stood fixed in astonishment. The question asked him, *why* he wondered, was designed to show him that the cause of his surprise would be removed or lessened, for that he would proceed so to explain this that he might have a correct view of its design. ¶ *I will tell thee the mystery of the woman.* On the word *mystery*, see Notes on ver. 5. The sense is, "I will explain what is meant by the symbol—the hidden meaning that is couched under it." That is, he would so far explain it that a just view might be obtained of its signification. The explanation follows, ver. 8-18. ¶ *And of the beast that carrieth her,* &c. Ver. 3.

8. *The beast that thou sawest was, and is not.* In the close of the verse it is added, "and yet is"—"the beast that was, and is not, and yet is." There are

**386** REVELATION. [A.D 96.

into perdition, and they that dwell on the earth shall *n* wonder, whose names were not written in the book of life from the foundation of the world, when they behold the beast that was, and is not, and yet is.

*n* ch.13.3,8.

9 And here *is* the mind which hath wisdom. The *o* seven heads are seven mountains, on which the woman sitteth.

10 And there are seven kings: five are fallen, and one is, *and* the

*o* ch.13.1.

---

three things affirmed here: first, that there is a sense in which it might be said of the power here referred to, that it "was," or that, *before* this, it had an existence; second, that there was a sense in which it might be said that it is "not," that is, that it had become practically extinct; and third, that there is a sense in which that power would be so *revived* that it might be said that it "still is." The "beast" here referred to is the same that is mentioned in ver. 3 of this chapter, and in ch. xiii. 1, 3, 11-16. That is, there was one great formidable power, having essentially the same origin, though manifested under somewhat different modifications, to one and all of which might, in their different manifestations, be given the same name, "*the beast.*" ¶ *And shall ascend out of the bottomless pit*—ἐκ τῆς ἀβύσσου. On the meaning of the word here used, see Notes on ch. ix. 1. The meaning here is, that this power would *seem* to come up from the nether world. It would appear at one time to be extinct, but would revive again *as if* coming from the world over which Satan presides, and would, in its revived character, be such as might be expected from such an origin. ¶ *And go into perdition.* That is, its end will be destruction. It will not be permanent, but will be overthrown and destroyed. The word *perdition* here is properly rendered by Prof. Stuart *destruction*, but nothing is indicated by the word of the *nature* of the destruction that would come upon it. ¶ *And they that dwell on the earth.* The inhabitants of the earth generally; that is, the matter referred to will be so remarkable as to attract general attention. ¶ *Shall wonder.* It will be so contrary to the regular course of events, so difficult of explanation, so remarkable in itself, as to excite attention and surprise. ¶ *Whose names were not written in the book of life from the foundation of the world.* See this explained in the Notes on ch. xiii. 8. The idea seems to be, that those whose names *are* written in the book of life, or who are truly the friends of God, would not be drawn off in admiration of the beast, or in rendering homage to it. ¶ *When they behold the beast that was, and is not, and yet is.* That is, the power that once was mighty; that had declined to such a state that it became, as it were, extinct; and that was revived again with so much of its original strength, that it might be said that it still exists. The fact of its being revived in this manner, as well as the nature of the power itself, seemed fitted to excite this admiration.

9. *And here is the mind which hath wisdom.* Here is that which requires wisdom to interpret it; or, here is a case in which the mind that shows itself able to explain it will evince true sagacity. So in ch. xiii. 18. See Notes on that place. Prof. Stuart renders this, "Here is a meaning which compriseth wisdom." It is undoubtedly implied that the symbol *might* be understood— whether in the time of John, or afterwards, he does not say; but it was a matter which could not be determined by ordinary minds, or without an earnest application of the understanding. ¶ *The seven heads are seven mountains.* Referring, undoubtedly, to Rome—the seven-hilled city — *Septicollis Roma.* See Notes on ch. xii. 3, (*d*). ¶ *On which the woman sitteth.* The city represented as a woman, in accordance with a common usage in the Scriptures. See Notes on Is. i. 8.

10. *And there are seven kings.* That is, seven in all, as they are enumerated in this verse and the next. An *eighth* is mentioned in ver. 11, but it is, at the same time, said that this one so pertains to the seven, or is so properly in one sense of the number seven, though, in another sense, to be regarded as an eighth, that it may be properly reckoned as the seventh. The word *kings*— βασιλεῖς—may be understood, so far as the meaning of the word is concerned, (*a*) literally, as denoting a king, or one who exercises royal authority; (*b*) in a more general sense, as denoting one of distinguished honour—a viceroy, prince, leader, chief, Mat. ii. 1, 3, 9; Lu. i. 5; Ac. xii. 1; (*c*) in a still larger sense,

other is not yet come; and when he cometh, he must continue a short space.

as denoting a dynasty, a form of government, a mode of administration, as that which, in fact, *rules*. See Notes on Da. vii. 24, where the word *king* undoubtedly denotes a dynasty, or form of rule. The notion of *ruling*, or of authority, is undoubtedly in the word, for the verb βασιλεύω means *to rule*, but the word may be applied to anything in which sovereignty resides. Thus it is applied to a king's son, to a military commander, to the gods, to a Greek archon, &c. See Passow. It would be contrary to the whole spirit of this passage, and to what is demanded by the proper meaning of the word, to insist that the word should denote literally *kings*, and that it could not be applied to emperors, or to dictators, or to dynasties. ¶ *Five are fallen.* Have passed away as if fallen; that is, they have disappeared. The language would be applicable to rulers who have died, or who had been dethroned; or to dynasties or forms of government that had ceased to be. In the fulfilment of this, it would be necessary to find *five* such successive kings or rulers who had died, and who appertained to one sovereignty or nation; or five such dynasties or forms of administrations that had successively existed, but which had ceased. ¶ *And one is.* That is, there is one—a sixth—that now reigns. The proper interpretation of this would be, that this existed in the time of the writer; that is, according to the view taken of the time of the writing of the Apocalypse (see Intro., § 2), at the close of the first century. ¶ *And the other is not yet come.* The sixth one is to be succeeded by another in the same line, or occupying the same dominion. ¶ *And when he cometh.* When that form of dominion is set up. No intimation is yet given as to the *time* when this would occur. ¶ *He must continue a short space*—ὀλίγον. A short time; his dominion will be of short duration. It is observable that this characteristic is stated as applicable *only* to this one of the seven; and the fair meaning would seem to be, that the time would be short *as compared* with the six that preceded, and as compared with the one that followed—the *eighth*—into which it was to be merged, ver. 11.

11. *And the beast that was, and is*

11 And the beast that was, and is not, even he is the eighth, and is of the seven, and goeth into perdition.

*not.* That is, the one power that was formerly mighty; that died away so that it might be said to be extinct; and yet (ver. 8) that "still is," or has a prolonged existence. It is evident that, by the "beast" here, there is some one power, dominion, empire, or rule, whose essential identity is preserved through all these changes, and to which it is proper to give the same name. It finds its termination, or *its last form*, in what is here called the "eighth;" a power which, it is observed, sustains such a peculiar relation to the seven, that it may be said to be "of the seven," or to be a mere prolongation of the same sovereignty. ¶ *Even he is the eighth.* The eighth in the succession. This form of sovereignty, though a mere prolongation of the former government, so much so as to be, in fact, but keeping up the same empire in the world, appears in such a novelty of form, that, in one sense, it deserves to be called the *eighth* in order, and yet is so essentially a mere concentration and continuance of the one power, that, in the general reckoning (ver. 10), it might be regarded as pertaining to the former. There was a sense in which it was proper to speak of it as the eighth power; and yet, viewed in its relation to the whole, it so essentially combined and concentrated all that there was *in* the seven, that, in a general view, it scarcely merited a separate mention. We should look for the fulfilment of this in some such concentration and embodiment of all that it was, in the previous forms of sovereignty referred to, that it perhaps would deserve mention as an *eighth* power, but that it was, nevertheless, such a mere prolongation of the previous forms of the one power, that it might be said to be "*of* the seven;" so that, *in this view*, it would not claim a separate consideration. This seems to be the fair meaning, though there is much that is enigmatical in the form of the expression. ¶ *And goeth into perdition.* See Notes on ver. 8.

In inquiring now into the application of this very difficult passage, it may be proper to suggest some of the principal opinions which have been held, and then to endeavour to ascertain the true meaning.

I. The principal opinions which have been held may be reduced to the following:—

(1) That the seven kings here refer to the succession of Roman emperors, yet with some variation as to the manner of reckoning. Prof. Stuart begins with Julius Cæsar, and reckons them in this manner:—the "five that are fallen" are Julius Cæsar, Augustus, Tiberius, Caligula, Claudius. Nero, who, as he supposes, was the reigning prince at the time when the book was written, he regards as the sixth; Galba, who succeeded him, as the seventh. Others, who adopt this literal method of explaining it, suppose that the time begins with Augustus, and then Galba would be the sixth, and Otho, who reigned but three months, would be the seventh. The expression, "the beast that was, and is not, who is the eighth," Prof. Stuart regards as referring to a general impression among the heathen and among Christians, in the time of the persecution under Nero, that he would again appear after it was reported that he was dead, or that he would rise from the dead and carry on his persecution again. See Prof. Stuart, *Com.* vol. ii., Excur. iii. The *beast*, according to this view, denotes the Roman emperors, specifically Nero, and the reference in ver. 8 is to "the well-known hariolation respecting Nero, that he would be assassinated, and would disappear for a while, and then make his appearance again to the confusion of all his enemies." "What the angel," says he, "says, seems to be equivalent to this—'The *beast* means the Roman emperors, specifically Nero, of whom the report spread throughout the empire that he will revive, after being apparently slain, and will come, as it were, from the abyss or Hades, but he will perish, and that speedily,'" vol. ii. p. 323.

(2) That the word "kings" is not to be taken literally, but that it refers to forms of government, dynasties, or modes of administration. The general opinion among those who hold this view is, that the first six refer to the forms of the Roman government—(1) kings; (2) consuls; (3) dictators; (4) decemvirs; (5) military tribunes; (6) the imperial form, beginning with Augustus. This has been the common Protestant interpretation, and in reference to these *six* forms of government there has been a general agreement. But, while the mass of Protestant interpreters have supposed that the "six" heads refer to these forms of administration, there has been much diversity of opinion as to the seventh; and here, on this plan of interpretation, the main, if not the sole difficulty lies. Among the opinions held are the following:—

(*a*) That of Mr. Mede. He makes the seventh head what he calls the "Demi-Cæsar," or the "Western emperor who reigned after the division of the empire into East and West, and which continued, after the last division, under Honorius and Arcadius, about sixty years—a short space" (*Works*, book iii. ch. 8; book v. ch. 12).

(*b*) That of Bishop Newton, who regards the sixth or imperial "head" as continuing uninterruptedly through the line of Christian as well as Pagan emperors, until Augustulus and the Heruli; and the seventh to be the *Dukedom* of Rome, established soon after under the exarchate of Ravenna (*Prophecies*, pp. 575, 576).

(*c*) That of Dr. More and Mr. Cunninghame, who suppose the Christian emperors, from Constantine to Augustulus, to constitute the seventh head, and that this had its termination by the sword of the Heruli.

(*d*) That of Mr. Elliott, who supposes the seventh head or power to refer to a new form of administration introduced by Diocletian, changing the administration from the *original imperial character* to that of *an absolute Asiatic sovereignty*. For the important changes introduced by Diocletian that justify this remark, see the *Decline and Fall*, vol. i. pp. 212-217.

Numerous other solutions may be found in Poole's *Synopsis*, but these embrace the principal, and the most plausible that have been proposed.

II. I proceed, then, to state what seems to me to be the true explanation. This must be found in some *facts* that will accord with the explanation given of the meaning of the passage.

(1) There can be no doubt that this refers to Rome, either Pagan, Christian, or Papal. All the circumstances combine in this; all respectable interpreters agree in this. This would be naturally understood by the symbols used by John, and by the explanations furnished by the angel. See ver. 18: "And the woman which thou sawest is that great city, which reigneth over the kings of the earth." Every circumstance combines here in leading to the conclu-

## CHAPTER XVII.

sion that Rome is intended. There was no other power or empire on the earth to which this could be properly applied; there was everything in the circumstances of the writer to lead us to suppose that this was referred to; there is an utter impossibility now in applying the description to anything else.

(2) It was to be a *revived* power; not a power in its original form and strength. This is manifest, because it is said (ver. 8) that the power represented by the beast "was, and is not, and yet is"—that is, it was once a mighty power; it then declined so that it could be said that "it is *not;*" and yet there was so much remaining vitality in it, or so much revived power, that it could be said that it "still is"—καίπερ ἐστίν. Now, this is strictly applicable to Rome when the Papal power arose. The old Roman might had departed; the glory and strength evinced in the days of the consuls, the dictators, and the emperors, had disappeared, and yet there was a lingering vitality, and a reviving of power under the Papacy, which made it proper to say that it still continued, or that that mighty power was prolonged. The civil power connected with the Papacy was a revived Roman power—the Roman power prolonged under another form—for it is susceptible of clear demonstration that, if it had not been for the rise of the Papal power, the sovereignty of Rome, as such, would have been wholly extinct. For the proof of this, see the passages quoted in the Notes on ver. 3. Comp. Notes on ch. xiii. 3, 12, 15.

(3) It was to be a power emanating from the "abyss," or that would seem to ascend from the dark world beneath. See ver. 8. This was true in regard to the Papacy, either (*a*) as apparently ascending from the lowest state and the most depressed condition, *as if* it came up from below (see Notes on ver. 3, comp. ch. xiii. 11); or (*b*) as, in fact, having its origin in the world of darkness, and being under the control of the prince of that world, which, according to all the representations of that formidable Antichristian power in the Scriptures, is true, and which the whole history of the Papacy, and of its influence on religion, confirms.

(4) One of the powers referred to *sustained* the other. "The seven heads are seven mountains on which the woman *sitteth,*" ver. 9. That is, the power represented by the harlot was *sustained* or *supported* by the power represented by the seven heads or the seven mountains. Literally applied, this would mean that the Papacy, as an ecclesiastical institution, was sustained by the civil power, with which it was so closely connected. For the illustration and support of this, see Notes on ch. xiii. 2, 3, 12, 15. In the Notes on those passages it is shown that the support was *mutual;* that while the Papacy, in fact, *revived* the almost extinct Roman civil power, and gave it new vitality, the price of that was, that *it* should be, in its turn, sustained by that revived Roman civil power. All history shows that that has been the fact; that in all its aggressions, assumptions, and persecutions, it has, *in fact*, and *professedly*, leaned on the arm of the civil power.

(5) A more important inquiry, and a more serious difficulty, remains in respect to the statements respecting the "seven kings," ver. 10, 11. The statements on this point are, that the whole number properly was seven; that of this number five had fallen or passed away; that one was in existence at the time when the author wrote; that another one was yet to appear who would continue for a little time; and that the general power represented by all these would be embodied in the "beast that was, and is not," and that might, in some respects, be regarded as an "eighth." These points may be taken up in their order.

(*a*) The first inquiry relates to the five that were fallen and the one that was then in existence—the first six. These may be taken together, for they are manifestly of the same class, and have the same characteristics, at least so far as to be distinguished from the "seventh" and the "eighth." The meaning of the word "*kings*" here has been already explained, ver. 10. It denotes ruling power, or forms of power; and, so far as the signification of the *word* is concerned, it might be applicable to royalty, or to any other form of administration. It is not necessary, then, to find an exact succession of *princes* or *kings* that would correspond with this—five of whom were dead, and one of whom was then on the throne, and all soon to be succeeded by one more, who would soon die.

The true explanation of this seems to be that which refers this to the forms of the Roman government or administration. These six "heads," or forms of administration, were, in their order, *Kings, Consuls, Dictators, Decemvirs, Military Tribunes,* and *Emperors.* Of these, five had passed away in the time when John wrote the Apocalypse; the sixth, the imperial, was then in power, and had been from the time of Augustus Cæsar. The only questions that can be raised are, whether these forms of administration were so *distinct* and *prominent,* and whether in the times previous to John they so embraced the whole Roman power, as to justify this interpretation—that is, whether these forms of administration were so marked in this respect that it may be supposed that John would use the language here employed in describing them. As showing the probability that he would use this language, I refer to the following arguments, viz.: (1) The authority of Livy, lib. vi. cap. 1. Speaking of the previous parts of his history, and of what he had done in writing it, he says: "Quæ ab condita urbe Roma ad captam eandem urbem, Romani sub *regibus* primum, *consulibus* deinde ac *dictatoribus, decemviris* ac *tribunis consularibus* gessere, foris bella, domi seditiones, quinque libris exposui." That is, "In five books I have related what was done at Rome, pertaining both to foreign wars and domestic strifes, from the foundation of the city to the time when it was taken, as it was governed by *kings,* by *consuls,* by *dictators,* by the *decemvirs,* and by *consular tribunes.*" Here he mentions *five* forms of administration under which Rome had been governed in the earlier periods of its history. The imperial power had a later origin, and did not exist until near the time of Livy himself. (2) The same distribution of power, or forms of government, among the Romans, is made by Tacitus, *Annal.* lib. i. cap. 1: "Urbem Romam à principio *reges* habuere. Libertatem et *consulatum* L. Brutus instituit. *Dictaturæ* ad tempus sumebantur. Neque *decemviralis potestas* ultrà biennium, neque *tribunorum militum consulare jus* diu valuit. Non Cinnæ, non Syllæ longa dominatio: et Pompeii Crassique potentia cito in Cæsarem, Lepidi atque Antonii arma in Augustum cessere; qui cuncta, discordiis civilibus fessa, nomine *principis* sub *imperium* accepit." That is, "In the beginning, Rome was governed by *kings.* Then L. Brutus gave to her liberty and the *consulship.* A temporary power was conferred on the *dictators.* The authority of the *decemvirs* did not continue beyond the space of two years: neither was the consular power of the *military tribunes* of long duration. The rule of Cinna and Sylla was brief; and the power of Pompey and Crassus passed into the hands of Cæsar; and the arms of Lepidus and Antony were surrendered to Augustus, who united all things, broken by civil discord, under the name of *prince* in the *imperial* government." Here Tacitus distinctly mentions the *six forms of administration* that had prevailed in Rome, the last of which was the imperial. It is true, also, that he mentions the brief rule of certain *men* —as Cinna, Sylla, Antony, and Lepidus; but these are not forms of *administration,* and their temporary authority did not indicate any change in the *government*—for some of these men were *dictators,* and none of them, except Brutus and Augustus, established any permanent form of administration. (3) The same thing is apparent in the usual statements of history, and the books that describe the forms of government at Rome. In so common a book as Adam's *Roman Antiquities,* a description may be found of the forms of Roman administration that corresponds almost precisely with this. The forms of *supreme* power in Rome, as enumerated there, are what are called *ordinary* and *extraordinary* magistrates. Under the former are enumerated kings, consuls, prætors, censors, quæstors, and tribunes of the people. But of these, in fact, the *supreme* power was vested in two; for there were, under this, but *two* forms of administration—that of kings and consuls; the offices of prætor, censor, quæstor, and tribune of the people being merely subordinate to that of the consuls, and no more a new form of administration than the offices of secretary of the state, of war, of the navy, of the interior, are now. Under the latter—that of *extraordinary* magistrates—are enumerated *dictators, decemvirs, military tribunes,* and the *interrex.* But the *interrex* did not constitute a *form* of administration, or a change of government, any more than, when the President or Vice-president of the United States should die, the performance of the duties of the office of president by the speaker of the senate would indicate a change, or than the regency of the Prince of Wales in the time of George III. constituted a new form of government. So that, in fact, we have enumerated, as constituting *the supreme power* at Rome, kings, consuls, dictators, decemvirs, and military tribunes—five in number. The imperial power was the sixth. (4) In confirmation of the same thing, I may refer to the authority of Bellarmine, a distinguished Roman Catholic writer. In his work *De Pontiff.*, cap. 2, he thus enumerates the changes which the Roman government had experienced, or the forms of administration that had existed there: 1. Kings; 2. Consuls; 3. Decemvirs; 4. Dictators; 5. Military Tribunes with consular power; 6. Emperors. See Poole's *Synop., in loco*. And (5) it may be added, that this would be *understood* by the contemporaries of John in this sense. These forms of government were so marked that, in connection with the mention of the "seven mountains," designating the city, there could be no doubt as to what was intended. Reference would at once be made to the *imperial* power as then existing, and the mind would readily and easily turn back to the five main forms of the supreme administration which had existed before.

(*b*) The next inquiry is, what is denoted by *the seventh*. If the word "kings" here refers, as is supposed (Notes on ver. 10), to a form of government or administration; if the "five" refer to the forms previous to the imperial, and the "sixth" to the imperial; and if John wrote *during* the imperial government, then it follows that this must refer to some form of administration that was to succeed the imperial. If the Papacy was "the eighth," and of the "seventh," then it is clear that this must refer to some form of civil administration lying *between* the decline of the *imperial* and the rise of the *Papal* power: that "short space"—for it *was* a short space that intervened. Now, there can be no difficulty, I think, in referring this to that form of administration over Rome—that "dukedom" under the exarchate of Ravenna, which succeeded the decline of the imperial power, and which preceded the rise of the Papal power;—between the year 566 or 568, when Rome was reduced to a dukedom, under the exarchate of Ravenna, and the time when the city revolted from this authority and became subject to that of the pope, about the year 727. This period continued, according to Mr. Gibbon, about two hundred years. He says, "During a period of two hundred years, Italy was unequally divided between the kingdom of the Lombards and the exarchate of Ravenna. The offices and professions, which the jealousy of Constantine had separated, were united by the indulgence of Justinian; and eighteen successive exarchs were invested, *in the decline of the empire, with the full remains of civil, of military, and even of ecclesiastical power*. Their immediate jurisdiction, *which was afterwards consecrated as the patrimony of St. Peter*, extended over the modern Romagna, the marshes or valleys of Ferrara and Commachio, five maritime cities from Rimini to Ancona, and a second inland Pentapolis, between the Adriatic coast and the hills of the Apennine. The duchy of Rome appears to have included the Tuscan, Sabine, and Latian conquests, *of the first four hundred years of the city;* and the limits may be distinctly traced along the coast, from Civita Vecchia to Terracina, and with the course of the Tiber from Ameria and Narni to the port of Ostia" (*Dec. and Fall*, iii. 202). How accurate is this if it be regarded as a statement of a *new* power or form of administration that succeeded the imperial—a power that was, in fact, a prolongation of the old Roman authority, and that was designed to constitute and embody it all! Could Mr. Gibbon have furnished a *better* commentary on the passage if he had adopted the interpretation of this portion of the Apocalypse above proposed, and if he had *designed* to describe this as the seventh power in the successive forms of the Roman administration? It is worthy of remark, also, that this account in Mr. Gibbon's history immediately *precedes* the account of the rise of the Papacy; the record respecting the exarchate, and that concerning Gregory the Great, described by Mr. Gibbon as "the Saviour of Rome," occurring in the same chapter, vol. iii. 202-211.

(*c*) This was to "continue for a short space"—for a little time. If this refers to the power to which in the remarks above it is supposed to refer, it is easy to see the propriety of this statement. Compared with the previous form of administration — the imperial—it was of short duration; absolutely considered, it was brief.

12 And the *p*ten horns which thou sawest are ten kings, which

*p* Da.7.20; Zec.1.18-21.

Mr. Gibbon (iii. 202) has marked it as extending through "a period of two hundred years;" and if this is compared with the form of administration which preceded it, extending to more than five hundred years, and more especially with that which followed—the Papal form—which has extended now some twelve hundred years, it will be seen with what propriety this is spoken of as continuing for a "short space."

(*d*) "The beast that was, and is not, even he is the eighth, and is of the seven," ver. 11. If the explanations above given are correct, there can be no difficulty in the application of this to the Papal power; for (1) all this power was concentrated in the Papacy, all that revived or prolonged Roman power had now passed into the Papacy, constituting that mighty dominion which was to be set up for so many centuries over what had been the Roman world. See the statements of Mr. Gibbon (iii. 207-211), as quoted in the Notes on ver. 3. Compare also, particularly, the remarks of Augustine Steuchus, a Roman Catholic writer, as quoted in the Notes on that verse: "The empire having been overthrown, unless God had raised up the *pontificate*, Rome, resuscitated and restored by none, would have become uninhabitable, and been thenceforward a most foul habitation of cattle. But in the pontificate it revived as with a *second birth;* its empire in magnitude not indeed equal to the old empire, but its form not very dissimilar: because all nations, from East and from West, venerate the pope, not otherwise than they before obeyed the emperor." (2) This was an *eighth* power or form of administration—for it was different, in many respects, from that of the kings, the consuls, the dictators, the decemvirs, the military tribunes, the emperors, and the dukedom—though it comprised substantially the power of all. Indeed, it could not have been spoken of as identical with either of the previous forms of administration, though it concentrated the power which had been wielded by them all. (3) It was "*of* the seven;" that is, it pertained to them; it was a prolongation of the same power. It had the same central seat—Rome; it extended over the same territory, and have received no kingdom as yet; but receive power as kings one hour with the beast.

it embraced sooner or latter the same nations. There is not one of those forms of administration which did not find a prolongation in the Papacy; for it aspired after, and succeeded in obtaining, all the authority of kings, dictators, consuls, emperors. It was in fact still the *Roman* sceptre swayed over the world; and with the strictest propriety it could be said that it was "*of* the seven," as having sprung out of the seven, and as perpetuating the sway of this mighty domination. For full illustration of this, see the Notes on Da. vii. and Re. xiii. (4) It would "go into perdition;" that is, it would be under this form that this mighty domination that had for so many ages ruled over the earth would die away, or this would be the *last* in the series. The *Roman* dominion, as such, would not be extended to a ninth, or tenth, or eleventh form, but would finally expire under the eighth. Every indication shows that this is to be so, and that with the decline of the Papal power the *whole Roman domination*, that has swayed a sceptre for two thousand five hundred years, will have come for ever to an end. If this is so, then we have found an ample and exact application of this passage even in its most minute specifications.

12. *And the ten horns which thou sawest.* On the scarlet-coloured beast, ver. 3. ¶ *Are ten kings.* Represent or denote ten kings; that is, kingdoms or powers. See Notes on Da. vii. 24. ¶ *Which have received no kingdom as yet.* That is, they were not in existence when John wrote. It is implied, that during the period under review they *would* arise, and would become connected, in an important sense, with the power here represented by the "beast." For a full illustration respecting the ten "kings," or kingdoms here referred to, see Notes on Da. vii., at the close of the chapter, II. (2). ¶ *But receive power.* It is not said from what *source* this power is received, but it is simply implied that it would in fact be conferred on them. ¶ *As kings.* That is, the power would be that which is usually exercised by kings. ¶ *One hour.* It cannot be supposed that this is to be taken *literally.* The meaning clearly is, that this would be brief and tempo-

13 These have one mind, and shall give their power and strength unto the beast.

14 These shall $^q$ make war with the Lamb, and the Lamb $^r$ shall

<sub>q ch.19.19.    r Je.50.44.</sub>

overcome them: for he is $^s$ Lord of lords, and King of kings: and $^t$ they that are with him are $^u$ called, and $^v$ chosen, and $^w$ faithful.

<sub>s ch.19.16; De.10.17; 1 Ti.6.15.    t Mi.5.8,9.
u Ro.8.30,37.    v Jn.15.16.    w ch.2.10.</sub>

rary; that is, it was a form of administration which would be succeeded by one more fixed and permanent. Any one can see that, in fact, this is strictly applicable to the governments, as referred to in the Notes on Daniel, which sprang up after the incursion of the northern barbarians, and which were finally succeeded by the permanent forms of government in Europe. Most of them were very brief in their duration, and they were soon remodelled in the forms of permanent administration. Thus, to take the arrangement proposed by Sir Isaac Newton, (1) the kingdom of the Vandals and Alans in Spain and Africa; (2) the kingdom of the Suevians in Spain; (3) the kingdom of the Visigoths; (4) the kingdom of the Alans in Gallia; (5) the kingdom of the Burgundians; (6) the kingdom of the Franks; (7) the kingdom of the Britons; (8) the kingdom of the Huns; (9) the kingdom of the Lombards; (10) the kingdom of Ravenna—how *temporary* were most of these; how soon they passed into the more permanent forms of administration which succeeded them in Europe! ¶ *With the beast.* With that rising Papal power. They would exercise their authority in connection with that, and under its influence.

13. *These have one mind.* That is, they are united in the promotion of the same object. Though in some respects wholly independent of each other, yet they may be regarded as, in fact, so far united that they tend to promote the same ultimate end. As a fact in history, all these kingdoms, though of different origin, and though not unfrequently engaged in war with each other, became Roman Catholics, and were united in the support of the Papacy. It was with propriety, therefore, that they should be regarded as so closely connected with that power that they could be represented as "ten horns" on the seven-headed monster. ¶ *And shall give their power and strength unto the beast.* Shall lend their influence to the support of the Papacy, and become the upholders of that power. The meaning, according to the interpretation above proposed, is, that they would all become Papal kingdoms, and supporters of the Papal power. It is unnecessary to pause to show how true this has been in history. At first, most of the people out of whom these kingdoms sprang were Pagans; then many of them embraced Christianity under the prevailing form of Arianism, and this fact was for a time a bar to their perfect adhesion to the Roman see; but they were all ultimately brought wholly under its influence, and became its supporters. In A.D. 496, Clovis, the king of the Franks, on occasion of his victory over the Allemanni, embraced the Catholic faith, and so received the title, transmitted downward through nearly thirteen hundred years to the French kings as his successors, of "*the eldest son of the church;*" in the course of the sixth century, the kings of Burgundy, Bavaria, Spain, Portugal, England, embraced the same religion, and became the defenders of the Papacy. It is well known that each one of the powers above enumerated as constituting these ten kingdoms, became subject to the Papacy, and continued so during their separate existence, or when merged into some other power, until the Reformation in the sixteenth century. *All* "their power and strength was given unto the beast;" all was made subservient to the purposes of Papal Rome.

14. *These shall make war with the Lamb.* The Lamb of God — the Lord Jesus (Notes, ch. v. 6); that is, they would combine with the Papacy in opposing evangelical religion. It is not meant that they would *openly* and *avowedly* proclaim *war* against the Son of God, but that they would *practically* do this in sustaining a persecuting power. It is unnecessary to show how true this has been in history; how entirely they sustained the Papacy in all its measures of persecution. ¶ *And the Lamb shall overcome them.* Shall ultimately gain the victory over them. The meaning is, that they would not be able to extinguish the true religion. In spite of all opposition and persecution, that would still live in the world, until it would be said that a complete triumph

15 And he saith unto me, *ˣ*The waters which thou sawest, where the whore sitteth, are *ʸ*peoples, and multitudes, and nations, and tongues.

*x* ver.1; Is.8.7.     *y* ch.13.7.

was gained. ¶ *For he is Lord of lords, and King of kings.* He has supreme power over all the earth, and all kings and princes are subject to his control. Comp. ch. xix. 16. ¶ *And they that are with him.* The reference is to the persecuted saints who have adhered to him as his faithful followers in all these protracted conflicts. ¶ *Are called.* That is, called by him to be his followers; as if he had selected them out of the world to maintain his cause. See Notes on Ro. i. 7. ¶ *And chosen.* See Notes on Jn. xv. 16, and 1 Pe. i. 2. In their steadfast adherence to the truth, they had shown that they were truly *chosen* by the Saviour, and could be relied on in the warfare against the powers of evil. ¶ *And faithful.* They had shown themselves faithful to him in times of persecution, and in the hour of darkness.

15. *And he saith unto me.* The angel, ver. 7. This commences the more *literal* statement of what is meant by these symbols. See the Analysis of the chapter. ¶ *The waters which thou sawest.* See Notes on ver. 1. ¶ *Are peoples, and multitudes, and nations, and tongues.* For an explanation of these terms, see Notes on ch. vii. 9. The meaning here is, (*a*) that these waters *represent* a multitude of people. This is a common and an obvious symbol—for outspread seas or raging floods would naturally represent such a multitude. See Is. viii. 7, 8; xvii. 12, 13; Je. xlvii. 2. Comp. *Iliad*, v. 394. The sense here is, that vast numbers of people would be subject to the power here represented by the woman. (*b*) They would be composed of different nations, and would be of different languages. It is unnecessary to show that this, in both respects, is applicable to the Papacy. Nations have been, and are subject to its control, and nations speaking a large part of the languages of the world. Perhaps under no one government—not even the Babylonian, the Macedonian, or the ancient Roman —was there so great a diversity of people, speaking so many different languages, and having so different an origin.

16 And the ten horns which thou sawest upon the beast, *ᶻ*these shall hate the whore, and shall *ᵃ*make her desolate and naked, and shall eat her flesh, and *ᵇ*burn her with fire.

*z* Je.50.41,42.    *a* Eze.16.37-44.    *b* ch.18.8,18.

16. *And the ten horns which thou sawest upon the beast.* Ver. 3. The ten powers or kingdoms represented by those horns. See Notes on ver. 12. ¶ *These shall hate the whore.* There *seems* to be some incongruity between this statement and that which was previously made. In the former (ver. 12-14), these ten governments are represented as in alliance with the beast; as "giving all their power and strength" unto it; and as uniting with it in making war with the Lamb. What is here said must, therefore, refer to some subsequent period, indicating some great change in their feelings and policy. We have seen the evidence of the fulfilment of the former statements. This statement will be accomplished if these same powers, represented by the ten horns, that were formerly in alliance with the Papacy, shall become its enemy, and contribute to its final overthrow. That is, it will be accomplished if the nations of Europe, embraced within the limits of those ten kingdoms, shall become hostile to the Papacy, and shall combine for its overthrow. Is anything more probable than this? France (see Notes on ch. xvi.) has already struck more than one heavy blow on that power; England has been detached from it; many of the states of Italy are weary of it, and are ready to rise up against it; and nothing is more probable than that Spain, Portugal, France, Lombardy, and the Papal States themselves, will yet throw off the yoke for ever, and put an end to a power that has so long ruled over men. It was with the utmost difficulty, in 1848, that the Papal power was sustained, and this was done only by foreign swords; the Papacy could not probably be protected in another such outbreak. And this passage leads us to anticipate that the period will come—and that probably not far in the future—when those powers that have for so many ages sustained the Papacy will become its determined foes, and will rise in their might and bring it for ever to an end. ¶ *And shall make her desolate and naked.* Strip her of all her power and all her attractive-

A.D. 96.]   CHAPTER XVIII.   395

17 For <sup>c</sup>God hath put in their hearts to fulfil his will, and to agree, and give their kingdom unto the beast, <sup>d</sup>until the words of God shall be fulfilled.

<small>c Ac.4.27,28.   d ch.10.7.</small>

18 And the woman which thou sawest is <sup>e</sup>that great city, which reigneth over the kings of the earth.

<small>e ch.16.19.</small>

ness. That is, applied to Papal Rome, all that is so gorgeous and alluring—her wealth, and pomp, and splendour—shall be taken away, and she will be seen as she is, without anything to dazzle the eye or to blind the mind. ¶ *And shall eat her flesh.* Shall completely destroy her—*as if* her flesh were consumed. Perhaps the image is taken from the practice of cannibals eating the flesh of their enemies slain in battle. If so, nothing could give a more impressive idea of the utter destruction of this formidable power, or of the feelings of those by whom its end would be brought about. ¶ *And burn her with fire.* Another image of total destruction. Perhaps the meaning may be, that after her *flesh* was eaten, such parts of her as remained would be thrown into the fire and consumed. If this be the meaning, the image is a very impressive one to denote absolute and total destruction. Comp. Notes on ch. xviii. 8.

17. *For God hath put in their hearts to fulfil his will.* That is, in regard to the destruction of this mighty power. They would be employed as his agents in bringing about his designs. Kings and princes are under the control of God, and, whatever may be their own designs, they are in fact employed to accomplish *his* purposes, and are instruments in *his* hands. See Notes on Is. x. 7. Comp. Ps. lxxvi. 10. ¶ *And to agree.* See ver. 13. That is, they act harmoniously in their support of this power, and so they will in its final destruction. ¶ *And give their kingdom unto the beast.* Notes, ver. 13. ¶ *Until the words of God shall be fulfilled.* Not for ever; not as a permanent arrangement. God has fixed a limit to the existence of this power. When his purposes are accomplished, these kingdoms will withdraw their support, and this mighty power will fall to rise no more.

18. *And the woman which thou sawest.* Ver. 3. ¶ *Is that great city.* Represents that great city. ¶ *Which reigneth over the kings of the earth.* Rome would of course be understood by this language in the time of John, and all the circumstances, as we have seen, combined to show that Rome, in some form of its dominion, is intended. Even the *name* could hardly have designated it more clearly, and all expositors agree in supposing that Rome, either as Pagan or as Christian, is referred to. The chapter shows that its power is limited; and that, although for purposes which he saw to be wise, God allows it to have a wide influence over the nations of the earth, yet, in his own appointed time, the very powers that have sustained it will become its foes, and combine for its overthrow. Europe needs but little farther provocation, and the fires of liberty, which have been so long pent up, will break forth, and that storm of indignation which has expelled the Jesuits from all the courts of Europe; which has abolished the Inquisition; which has more than once led hostile armies to the very gates of Papal Rome, will again be aroused in a manner which cannot be allayed, and that mighty power, which has controlled so large a part of the nations of Europe for more than a thousand years of the world's history, will come to an end.

## CHAPTER XVIII.
### ANALYSIS OF THE CHAPTER.

This chapter may be regarded as a still further *explanatory episode* (comp. Anal. to ch. xvii.), designed to show the *effect* of pouring out the seventh vial (ch. xvi. 17-21) on the formidable Antichristian power so often referred to. The description in this chapter is that of a rich merchant-city reduced to desolation, and is but carrying out the general idea under a different form. The chapter comprises the following points:—

(1) Another angel is seen descending from heaven, having great power, and making proclamation that Babylon the great is fallen, and is become utterly desolate, ver. 1-3.

(2) A warning voice is heard from heaven, calling on the people of God to come out of her, and to be partakers neither of her sins nor her plagues. Her torment and sorrow would be proportionate to her pride and luxury; and her plagues would come upon her sud-

## CHAPTER XVIII.

AND after these things I saw another angel come down from heaven, having great power; and the[a] earth was lightened with his glory.

2 And he cried mightily with a

a Eze.43.2.

strong voice, saying, [b]Babylon the great is fallen, is fallen, and is [c]become the habitation of devils, and the hold of every foul spirit, and a cage of every unclean and hateful bird.

b ch.14.8; Is.13.19; 21.9; Je.51.8.
c ch.17.2; Is.34.11,14; Je.50.39; 51.37.

denly; death, and mourning, and famine, and consumption by fire, ver. 4-8.

(3) Lamentation over her fall—by those especially who had been connected with her; who had been corrupted by her; who had been profited by her, ver. 9-19. (a) By kings, ver. 9, 10. They had lived deliciously with her, and they would lament her. (b) By merchants, ver. 11-17. They had trafficked with her, but now that traffic was to cease, and no man would buy of her. Their business, so far as she was concerned, was at an end. All that she had accumulated was now to be destroyed; all her gathered riches were to be consumed; all the traffic in those things by which she had been enriched was to be ended; and the city that was more than all others enriched by these things, as if clothed in fine linen, and purple, and scarlet, and decked with gold, and precious stones, and pearls, was to be destroyed for ever. (c) By ship-masters and seamen, ver. 17-19. They had been made rich by this traffic, but now all was ended; the smoke of her burning is seen to ascend, and they stand afar off and weep.

(4) Rejoicing over her fall, ver. 20. Heaven is called upon to rejoice, and the holy apostles and prophets, for their blood is avenged, and persecution ceases in the earth.

(5) The final destruction of the city, ver. 21-24. A mighty angel takes up a stone and casts it into the sea as an emblem of the destruction that is to come upon it. The voice of harpers, and musicians, and pipers would be heard no more in it; and no craftsmen would be there, and the sound of the millstone would be heard no more, and the light of a candle would shine no more there, and the voice of the bridegroom and bride would be heard no more.

1. *And after these things.* After the vision referred to in the previous chapter. ¶ *I saw another angel come down from heaven.* Different from the one that had last appeared, and therefore coming to make a new communication to him. It is not unusual in this book that different communications should be intrusted to different angels. Comp. ch. xiv. 6, 8, 9, 15, 17, 18. ¶ *Having great power.* That is, he was one of the higher rank or order of angels. ¶ *And the earth was lightened with his glory.* The usual representation respecting the heavenly beings. Comp. Ex. xxiv. 16; Mat. xvii. 2; Lu. ii. 9; Ac. ix. 3. This would, of course, add greatly to the magnificence of the scene.

2. *And he cried mightily.* Literally, "he cried with a strong great voice." See ch. x. 3. ¶ *Babylon the great is fallen, is fallen.* See Notes on ch. xiv. 8. The proclamation here is substantially the same as in that place, and no doubt the same thing is referred to. ¶ *And is become the habitation of devils.* Of demons—in allusion to the common opinion that the demons inhabited abandoned cities, old ruins, and deserts. See Notes on Mat. xii. 43-45. The language here is taken from the description of Babylon in Is. xiii. 20-22; and for a full illustration of the meaning, see Notes on that passage. ¶ *And the hold of every foul spirit*—φυλακή. A watch-post, station, haunt of such spirits. That is, they, as it were, *kept guard* there; were stationed there; haunted the place. ¶ *And a cage of every unclean and hateful bird.* That is, they would resort there, and abide there as in a cage. The word translated "cage" is the same which is rendered "hold"—φυλακή. In Is. xiii. 21, it is said, "and owls shall dwell there;" and in Is. xiv. 23, it is said that it would be a "possession for the bittern." The idea is that of utter desolation; and the meaning here is, that spiritual Babylon—Papal Rome (ch. xiv. 8)—will be reduced to a state of utter desolation resembling that of the real Babylon. It is not necessary to suppose this of the *city* of Rome itself—for that is not the object of the representation. It is the *Papacy*, re-

3 For ᵈall nations have drunk of the wine of the wrath of her fornication, and the kings of the earth have committed fornication with her, and the ᵉmerchants of the earth are waxed rich through the ¹abundance of her delicacies.

4 And I heard another voice from heaven, saying, ᶠCome out of her,

d Is. 47.15.   e ver. 11, 15.
¹ or, *power*.
f Is. 48.20; 52.11; Je. 50.8; 51.6, 45; 2 Co. 6.17.

presented under the image of the city, and having its seat there. *That* is to be destroyed as utterly as was Babylon of old; that will become as odious, and loathsome, and detestable as the literal Babylon, the abode of monsters is.

3. *For all nations have drunk of the wine of the wrath of her fornication.* See Notes on ch. xiv. 8. This is given as a *reason* why this utter ruin had come upon her. She had beguiled and corrupted the nations of the earth, leading them into estrangement from God, and into pollution and sin. See Notes on ch. ix. 20, 21. ¶ *And the kings of the earth have committed fornication with her.* Spiritual adultery; that is, she has been the means of seducing them from God and leading them into sinful practices. ¶ *And the merchants of the earth are waxed rich through the abundance of her delicacies.* The word rendered "*abundance*" here, means commonly *power*. It might here denote *influence*, though it may also mean *number*, *quantity*, *wealth*. Comp. ch. iii. 8, where the same word is used. The word rendered *delicacies*—στρῆνους—occurs nowhere else in the New Testament. It properly means *rudeness, insolence, pride;* and hence *revel, riot, luxury.* It may be rendered here properly luxury, or proud voluptuousness; and the reference is to such luxuries as are found commonly in a great, a gay, and a splendid city. These, of course, give rise to much traffic, and furnish employment to many merchants and sailors, who thus procure a livelihood, or become wealthy as the result of such traffic. Babylon—or Papal Rome—is here represented under the image of such a luxurious city; and of course, when she falls, they who have thus been dependent on her, and who have been enriched by her, have occasion for mourning and lamentation. It is not necessary to expect to find a *literal* fulfilment of this, for it is emblematic and symbolical. The image of a great, rich, splendid, proud and luxurious city having been employed to denote that Antichristian power, all that is said in this chapter follows, of course, on its fall. The general idea is, that she was doomed to utter desolation, and that all who were connected with her, far and near, would be involved in her ruin.

4. *And I heard another voice from heaven.* He does not say whether this was the voice of an angel, but the idea seems rather to be that it is the voice of God. ¶ *Come out of her, my people.* The reasons for this, as immediately stated, are two: (*a*) that they might not participate in her sins; and (*b*) that they might not be involved in the ruin that would come upon her. The language seems to be derived from such passages in the Old Testament as the following:—"Go ye forth of Babylon, flee ye from the Chaldeans, with a voice of singing," Is. xlviii. 20. "Flee out of the midst of Babylon, and deliver every man his soul; be not cut off in her iniquity," Je. li. 6. "My people, go ye out of the midst of her, and deliver ye every man his soul from the fierce anger of the Lord," Je. li. 45. Comp. Je. l. 8. ¶ *That ye be not partakers of her sins.* For the meaning of this expression, see Notes on 1 Ti. v. 22. It is implied here that by remaining in Babylon they would lend their sanction to its sins by their presence, and would, in all probability, become contaminated by the influence around them. This is an universal truth in regard to iniquity, and hence it is the duty of those who would be pure to come out from the world, and to separate themselves from all the associations of evil. ¶ *And that ye receive not of her plagues.* Of the punishment that was to come upon her—as they must certainly do if they remained in her. The judgment of God that was to come upon the guilty city would make no discrimination among those who were found there; and if they would escape these woes they must make their escape from her. As applicable to Papal Rome, in view of her impending ruin, this means, (*a*) that there might be found in her some who were the true people of God; (*b*) that it was their duty to separate wholly from her—a command that will not only justify the Reformation, but which would have made a longer continuance in commun-

my people, that ye be not partakers of her sins, and that ye receive not of her plagues.

5 For her sins have *g*reached unto heaven, and God hath *h*remembered her iniquities.

6 Reward *i* her even as she rewarded you, and double unto her

*g* Je.51.9.    *h* ch.16.19.
*i* Ps.137.8; Je.50.15,29.

double according to her works: in the cup which she hath filled, fill to her double.

7 How much she hath glorified herself, and lived deliciously, so much torment and sorrow give her; for she saith in her heart, *k* I sit a queen, and am no widow, and shall see no sorrow.

*k* Is.47.7-11; Zep.2.15.

ion with the Papacy, when her wickedness was fully seen, an act of guilt before God; (*c*) that they who remain in such a communion cannot but be regarded as partaking of her sin; and (*d*) that if they remain, they must expect to be involved in the calamities that will come upon her. There never was any duty plainer than that of withdrawing from Papal Rome; there never has been any act attended with more happy consequences than that by which the Protestant world separated itself for ever from the sins and the plagues of the Papacy.

5. *For her sins have reached unto heaven.* So in Je. li. 9, speaking of Babylon, it is said, "For her judgment reacheth unto heaven, and is lifted up even to the skies." The meaning is not that the sins of this mystical Babylon were like a mass or pile so high as to reach to heaven, but that it had become so prominent as to attract the attention of God. Comp. Ge. iv. 10, "The voice of thy brother's blood crieth unto me from the ground." See also Ge. xviii. 20. ¶ *And God hath remembered her iniquities.* He had *seemed* to forget them, or not to notice them, but now he acted as if they had come to his recollection. See Notes on ch. xvi. 19.

6. *Reward her even as she rewarded you.* It is not said to whom this command is addressed, but it would seem to be to those who had been persecuted and wronged. Applied to mystical Babylon—Papal Rome—it would seem to be a call on the nations that had been so long under her sway, and among whom, from time to time, so much blood had been shed by her, to arise now in their might, and to inflict deserved vengeance. See Notes on ch. xvii. 16, 17. ¶ *And double unto her double according to her works.* That is, bring upon her double the amount of calamity which she has brought upon others; take ample vengeance upon her. Comp. for similar language, Is. xl. 2,

"She hath received of the Lord's hand *double* for all her sins." "For your shame ye shall have double," Is. lxi. 7. ¶ *In the cup which she hath filled.* To bring wrath on others. Notes, ch. xiv. 8. ¶ *Fill to her double.* Let her drink abundantly of the wine of the wrath of God—double that which she has dealt out to others. That is, either let the *quantity* administered to her be doubled, or let the ingredients in the cup be doubled in intensity.

7. *How much she hath glorified herself.* Been proud, boastful, arrogant. This was true of ancient Babylon, that she was proud and haughty; and it has been no less true of mystical Babylon—Papal Rome. ¶ *And lived deliciously.* By as much as she has lived in luxury and dissoluteness, so let her suffer now. The word used here and rendered *lived deliciously* — ἐστρηνίασε — is derived from the noun — στρῆνος — which is used in ver. 3, and rendered *delicacies.* See Notes on that verse. It means properly, "to live strenuously, rudely," as in English, "to live *hard;*" and then to revel, to live in luxury, riot, dissoluteness. No one can doubt the propriety of this as descriptive of ancient Babylon, and as little can its propriety be doubted as applied to Papal Rome. ¶ *So much torment and sorrow give her.* Let her punishment correspond with her sins. This is expressing substantially the same idea which occurs in the previous verse. ¶ *For she saith in her heart.* This is the estimate which she forms of herself. ¶ *I sit a queen.* Indicative of pride, and of an asserted claim to rule. ¶ *And am no widow.* Am not in the condition of a widow—a state of depression, sorrow, and mourning. All this indicates security and self-confidence, a description in every way applicable to Papal Rome. ¶ *And shall see no sorrow.* This is indicative of a state where there was nothing feared, notwithstanding all the indications which existed of approaching calamity. In

8 Therefore shall her plagues come in one day, death, and mourning, and famine; and she shall be utterly *l*burned with fire: for *m*strong *is* the Lord God who judgeth her.

*l* ch.17.16.   *m* Ps.62.11; Je.50.34.

this state we may expect to find Papal Rome, even when its last judgments are about to come upon it; in this state it has usually been; in this state it is now, notwithstanding all the indications that are abroad in the world that its power is waning, and that the period of its fall approaches.

8. *Therefore.* In consequence of her pride, arrogance, and luxury, and of the calamities that she has brought upon others. ¶ *Shall her plagues come in one day.* They shall come in a time when she is living in ease and security; and they shall come at the same time— so that all these terrible judgments shall seem to be poured upon her at once. ¶ *Death.* This expression, and those which follow, are designed to denote the same thing under different images. The general meaning is, that there would be utter and final destruction. It would be *as if* death should come and cut off the inhabitants. ¶ *And mourning.* As there would be where many were cut off by death. ¶ *And famine.* As if famine raged within the walls of a besieged city, or spread over a land. ¶ *And she shall be utterly burned with fire.* As completely destroyed *as if* she were entirely burned up. The certain and complete destruction of that formidable Antichristian power is predicted under a great variety of emphatic images. See ch. xiv. 10, 11; xvi. 17-21; xvii. 9, 16. *Perhaps* in this so frequent reference to a final destruction of that formidable Antichristian power by *fire*, there may be more intended than merely a figurative representation of its final ruin. There is some degree of probability, at least, that Rome itself will be literally destroyed in this manner, and that it is in this way that God intends to put an end to the Papal power, by destroying that which has been so long the seat and the centre of this authority. The extended prevalence of this belief, and the grounds for it, may be seen from the following remarks:—(1) It was an early opinion among the Jewish rabbies that Rome would be thus destroyed. Vitringa, on the Apocalypse, cites some opinions of this kind; the Jewish expectation being founded, as he says, on the passage in Is. xxxiv. 9, as Edom was supposed to mean Rome. "This chapter," says Kimchi, "points out the future destruction of Rome, here called Bozra, for Bozra was a great city of the Edomites." This is, indeed, *worthless* as a proof or an interpretation of Scripture, for it is a wholly unfounded interpretation; it is of value only as showing that somehow the Jews entertained this opinion. (2) The same expectation was entertained among the early Christians. Thus Mr. Gibbon (vol. i. p. 263, ch. xv.), referring to the expectations of the glorious reign of the Messiah on the earth (comp. Notes on ch. xiv. 8), says, speaking of Rome as the mystic Babylon, and of its anticipated destruction: "A regular series was prepared [in the minds of Christians] of all the moral and physical evils which can afflict a flourishing nation; intestine discord, and the invasion of the fiercest barbarians from the unknown regions of the north; pestilence and famine, comets and eclipses, earthquakes and inundations. All these were only so many preparatory and alarming signs of the great catastrophe of Rome, when the country of the Scipios and Cæsars should be consumed by a flame from heaven, and the city of the seven hills, with her palaces, her temples, and her triumphal arches, should be buried in a vast lake of fire and brimstone." So even Gregory the Great, one of the most illustrious of the Roman pontiffs, himself says, acknowledging his belief in the truth of the tradition: Roma à Gentilibus non exterminabitur; sed tempestatibus, coruscis turbinibus, ac terræ motu, in se marcescet (*Dial.* ii. 15). (3) Whatever may be thought of these opinions and expectations, there is *some* foundation for the opinion in the nature of the case. (*a*) The region is adapted to this. "It is not Ætna, the Lipari volcanic islands, Vesuvius, that alone offer visible indications of the physical adaptedness of Italy for such a catastrophe. The great Apennine mountain-chain is mainly volcanic in its character, and the country of Rome more especially is as strikingly so almost as that of Sodom itself." Thus the mineralogist Ferber, in his *Tour in Italy*, says: "The road from Rome to Ostia is all volcanic ashes till within two miles of Ostia." "From Rome to Tivoli I went on fields and hills of vol-

400 REVELATION. [A.D. 96.

9 And the <sup>n</sup>kings of the earth, who have committed fornication and lived deliciously with her, shall bewail her, and lament for her, when they shall see the smoke of her burning,

*n* Eze.26.16,17.

---

canic ashes or *tufa*." "A volcanic hill in an amphitheatrical form includes a part of the plain over Albano, and a flat country of volcanic ashes and hills to Rome. The ground about Rome is generally of that nature," pp. 189, 191, 200, 234. (*b*) Mr. Gibbon, with his usual accuracy, *as if* commenting on the Apocalypse, has referred to the physical adaptedness of the soil of Rome for such an overthrow. Speaking of the anticipation of the end of the world among the early Christians, he says: "In the opinion of a general conflagration, the faith of the Christian very happily coincided with the tradition of the East, the philosophy of the Stoics, and the analogy of nature; *and even the country, which, from religious motives, had been chosen for the origin and principal scene of the conflagration, was the best adapted for that purpose by natural and physical causes;* by its deep caverns, beds of sulphur, and numerous volcanoes, of which those of Ætna, of Vesuvius, and of Lipari, exhibit a very imperfect representation," vol. i. p. 263, ch. xv. As to the *general* state of Italy, in reference to volcanoes, the reader may consult, with advantage, Lyell's *Geology*, book ii. ch. ix.-xii. See also Murray's *Encyclopædia of Geography*, book ii. ch. ii. Of the country around Rome it is said in that work, among other things: "The country around Rome, and also the hills on which it is built, is composed of tertiary marls, clays, and sandstones, and intermixed with a preponderating quantity of granular and lithoidal volcanic tufas. The many lakes around Rome are formed by craters of ancient volcanoes." "On the road to Rome is the Lake of Vico, formerly the Lacus Cimini, which has all the appearance of a crater."

The following extract from a recent traveller will still further confirm this representation:—"I behold everywhere —in Rome, near Rome, and through the whole region from Rome to Naples —most astounding proof, not merely of the possibility, but the probability, that the whole region of central Italy will one day be destroyed by such a catastrophe [by earthquakes or volcanoes]. The soil of Rome is *tufa*, with a volcanic subterranean action going on. At Naples the boiling sulphur is to be seen bubbling near the surface of the earth. When I drew a stick along the ground, the sulphurous smoke followed the indentation; and it would never surprise me to hear of the utter destruction of the southern peninsula of Italy. The entire country and district is volcanic. It is saturated with beds of sulphur and the substrata of destruction. It seems as certainly prepared for the flames, as the wood and coal on the hearth are prepared for the taper which shall kindle the fire to consume them. The divine hand alone seems to me to hold the element of fire in check by a miracle as great as that which protected the cities of the plain, till the righteous Lot had made his escape to the mountains" (Townsend's *Tour in Italy* in 1850). ¶ *For strong is the Lord God who judgeth her.* That is, God has ample power to bring all these calamities upon her.

9. *And the kings of the earth.* This verse commences the description of the *lamentation* over the fall of the mystical Babylon (see the Analysis of the chapter). ¶ *Who have committed fornication.* That is, who have been seduced by her from the true God, and have been led into practical idolatry. Notes on ch. xiv. 8. The *kings* of the earth seem to be represented as among the chief mourners, because they had derived important aid from the power which was now to be reduced to ruin. As a matter of fact, the kings of Europe have owed much of their influence and power to the support which has been derived from the Papacy, and when *that* power shall fall, there will fall much that has contributed to sustain oppressive and arbitrary governments, and that has prevented the extension of popular liberty. In fact, Europe might have been long since free, if it had not been for the support which despotic governments have derived from the Papacy. ¶ *And lived deliciously with her.* In the same kind of luxury and dissoluteness of manners. See ver. 3, 7. The courts of Europe, under the Papacy, have had the same general character for dissoluteness and licentiousness as Rome itself. The same views of religion produce the same effects everywhere. ¶ *Shall bewail her, and lament for her.* Because their ally is destroyed, and

10 Standing afar off for the fear of her torment, saying, Alas, alas, that great city Babylon, that mighty city! for °in one hour is thy judgment come.

11 And the ᵖmerchants of the earth shall weep and mourn over her; for no man buyeth her merchandise any more;

<sub>o ver.17,19.      p Eze.27.27-36.</sub>

12 The merchandise of ᑫgold, and silver, and precious stones, and of pearls, and fine linen, and purple, and silk, and scarlet, and all ²thyine wood, and all manner vessels of ivory, and all manner vessels of most precious wood, and of brass, and iron, and marble,

<sub>q ch.17.4.      2 or, sweet.</sub>

the source of their power is taken away. The fall of the Papacy will be the signal for a general overturning of the thrones of Europe. ¶ *When they shall see the smoke of her burning.* When they shall see her on fire, and her smoke ascending towards heaven. Notes on ch. xiv. 11.

10. *Standing afar off for the fear of her torment.* Not daring to approach, to attempt to rescue and save her. They who had so long contributed to the support of the Papal power, and who had, in turn, been upheld by that, would not now even attempt to rescue her, but would stand by and see her destroyed, unable to render relief. ¶ *Alas, alas, that great city Babylon.* The language of lamentation that so great and so mighty a city should fall. ¶ *For in one hour is thy judgment come.* See Notes on ver. 8. The general sentiment here is, that, in the final ruin of Papal Rome, the kings and governments that had sustained her, and had been sustained by her, would see the source of their power taken away, but that they would not, or could not attempt her rescue. There have been not a few indications already that this will ultimately occur, and that the Papal power will be left to fall, without any attempt, on the part of those governments which have been so long in alliance with it, to sustain or restore it.

11. *And the merchants of the earth.* Who have been accustomed to traffic with her, and who have been enriched by the traffic. The image is that of a rich and splendid city. Of course, such a city depends much on its merchandise; and when it declines and falls, many who had been accustomed to deal with it, as merchants or traffickers, are affected by it, and have occasion to lament its fall. ¶ *Shall weep and mourn over her; for no man buyeth their merchandise any more.* The merchandise which they were accustomed to take to the city, and by the sale of which they lived. The enumeration of the articles of merchandise which follows, seems to have been inserted for the purpose of filling out the representation of what is usually found in such a city, and to show the desolation which would occur when this traffic was suspended.

12. *The merchandise of gold, and silver.* Of course, these constitute an important article of commerce in a great city. ¶ *And precious stones.* Diamonds, emeralds, rubies, &c. These have always been important articles of traffic in the world, and, of course, most of the traffic in them would find its way to great commercial cities. ¶ *And pearls.* See Notes on Mat. vii. 6; xiii. 46. These, too, have been always, and were, particularly in early times, valuable articles of commerce. Mr. Gibbon mentions them as among the articles that contributed to the luxury of Rome in the age of the Antonines: "precious stones, among which the pearl claimed the first rank after the diamond," vol. i. p. 34. ¶ *And fine linen.* This was also a valuable article of commerce. It was obtained chiefly from Egypt. See Notes on Is. xix. 9. Linen, among the ancients, was an article of luxury, for it was worn chiefly by the rich, Ex. xxviii. 42; Le. vi. 10; Lu. xvi. 19. The original word here is βύσσος, *byssus*, and it is found in the New Testament only in this place, and in Lu. xvi. 19. It was a "species of fine cotton, highly prized by the ancients." Various kinds are mentioned—as that of Egypt, the cloth which is still found wrapped around mummies; that of Syria, and that of India, which grew on a tree similar to the poplar; and that of Achaia, which grew in the vicinity of Elis. See Rob. *Lex.* ¶ *And purple.* See Notes on Lu. xvi. 19. Cloth of this colour was a valuable article of commerce, as it was worn by rich men and princes. ¶ *And silk.* Silk was a very valuable article of commerce, as it was costly, and could be worn only by the

13 And cinnamon, and odours, and ointments, and frankincense, and wine, and oil, and fine flour, and wheat, and beasts, and sheep, and horses, and chariots, and ³slaves, and ʳsouls of men.

³ or, *bodies*.     ʳ Eze. 27. 13.

rich. It is mentioned by Mr. Gibbon as such an article in Rome in the age of the Antonines:—"Silk, a pound of which was esteemed not inferior in value to a pound of gold," vol. i. p. 34. On the cultivation and manufacture of silk by the ancients, see the work entitled, *The History of Silk, Cotton, Linen, and Wool*, &c., published by Harper Brothers, New York, 1845, pp. 1–21. ¶ *And scarlet.* See Notes on ch. xvii. 3. ¶ *And all thyine wood.* The word here used — θύϊνον — occurs nowhere else in the New Testament. It denotes an evergreen African tree, from which statues and costly vessels were made. It is not agreed, however, whether it was a species of cedar, savin, or lignum-vitæ, which latter constitutes the modern genus *Thuja*, or *Thyia*. See Rees' *Cyclo.*, art. "Thuja." ¶ *And all manner vessels of ivory.* Everything that is made of ivory. Ivory, or the tusk of the elephant, has always been among the precious articles of commerce. ¶ *And all manner vessels of most precious wood.* Furniture of costly wood—cedar, the citron tree, lignum-vitæ, &c. ¶ *And of brass, and iron, and marble.* Brass or copper would, of course, be a valuable article of commerce. The same would be the case with iron; and so marble, for building, for statuary, &c., would likewise be.

13. *And cinnamon.* Cinnamon is the aromatic bark of the *Laurus Cinnamomum*, which grows in Arabia, India, and especially in the island of Ceylon. It was formerly, as it is now, a valuable article in the Oriental trade. ¶ *And odours.* Aromatics employed in religious worship, and for making perfumes. Mr. Gibbon (vol. i. p. 34) mentions, among the articles of commerce and luxury, in the age of the Antonines, "a variety of aromatics that were consumed in religious worship and the pomp of funerals." It is unnecessary to say that the use of such odours has been always common at Rome. ¶ *And ointments.* Unguents—as spikenard, &c. These were in common use among the ancients. See Notes on Mat. xiv. 7; Mar. xiv. 3. ¶ *And frankincense.* See Notes on Mat. ii. 11. It is unnecessary to say that *incense* has been always much used in public worship in Rome, and that it has been, therefore, a valuable article of commerce there. ¶ *And wine.* An article of commerce and luxury in all ages. ¶ *And oil.* That is, olive oil. This, in ancient times, and in Oriental countries particularly, was an important article of commerce. ¶ *And fine flour.* The word here means the best and finest kind of flour. ¶ *And beasts, and sheep, and horses.* Also important articles of merchandise. ¶ *And chariots.* The word here used — ῥεδῶν — means, properly a carriage with four wheels, or a carriage drawn by mules (Prof. Stuart). It was properly a travelling carriage. The word is of Gallic origin (Quinctil. i. 9; Cic. *Mil.* 10; *Att.* v. 17; vi. 1. See Adam's *Rom. Ant.* p. 525). It was an article of luxury. ¶ *And slaves.* The Greek here is σωμάτων—"*of bodies.*" Prof. Stuart renders it *grooms*, and supposes that it refers to a particular kind of slaves who were employed in taking care of horses and carriages. The word properly denotes *body—an animal body—*whether of the human body, living or dead, or the body of a beast; and then the external man—the person, the individual. In later usage, it comes to denote a slave (see Rob. *Lex.*), and in this sense it is used here. The traffic in slaves was common in ancient times, as it is now. We know that this traffic was carried on to a large extent in ancient Rome, the city which John probably had in his eye in this description. See Gibbon, *Dec. and Fall*, vol. i. pp. 25, 26. Athenæus, as quoted by Mr. Gibbon (p. 26), says that "he knew very many Romans who possessed, not for use, but for ostentation, ten, and even twenty thousand slaves." It should be said here, however, that although this refers evidently to traffic in slaves, it is not necessary to suppose that it would be literally characteristic of Papal Rome. All this is symbolical, designed to exhibit the Papacy under the image of a great city, with what was customary in such a city, or with what most naturally presented itself to the imagination of John as found in such a city; and it is no more necessary to suppose that the Papacy would be engaged in the traffic of slaves, than in the traffic of cinnamon, or fine flour, or sheep and horses.

14 And the fruits that thy soul lusted after are departed from thee, and all things which were dainty and goodly are departed from thee, and thou shalt find them no more at all.

15 The merchants of these things, which were made rich by her, shall stand afar off for the fear of her torment, weeping and wailing,

16 And saying, Alas, alas, that great city, that was $^s$clothed in fine linen, and purple, and scarlet, and decked with gold, and precious stones, and pearls!

17 For in one hour so great riches is come to nought. And $^t$every ship-master, and all the company in ships, and sailors, and as many as trade by sea, stood afar off,

$s$ Lu.16.19,&c.   $t$ Is.23.14.

¶ *And souls of men.* The word used, and rendered *souls* — ψυχὰς — though commonly denoting the soul (properly the breath, or vital principle), is also employed to denote the living thing—the animal—in which the soul or vital principle resides; and hence may denote a person or a man. Under this form it is used to denote a *servant* or *slave*. See Rob. *Lex.* Professor Robinson supposes that the word here means *female slaves*, in distinction from those designated by the previous word. Professor Stuart (*in loco*) supposes that the previous word denotes a particular kind of slaves—those who had the care of horses—and that the word here is used in a generic sense, denoting slaves in general. This kind of traffic in the "persons" or *souls* of men is mentioned as characterizing ancient Tyre, in Eze. xxvii. 13: "Javan, Tubal, and Meshech, they were thy merchants; they traded in the persons of men." It is not quite clear why, in the passage before us, this traffic is mentioned in two forms, as that of the *bodies* and the *souls* of men; but it would seem most probable that the writer meant to designate *all* that would properly come under this traffic, whether male or female slaves were bought and sold; whether they were for servitude, or for the gladiatorial sports (see Wetstein, *in loco*); whatever might be the *kind* of servitude that they might be employed in, and whatever might be their condition in life. The use of the *two* words would include all that is implied in the traffic, for, in most important senses, it extends to the body and the soul. In slavery both are purchased; both are supposed, so far as he can avail himself of them, to become the property of the master.

14. *And the fruits that thy soul lusted after.* Literally, "the fruits of the desire of thy soul." The word rendered fruits — ὀπώρα — properly means, *late summer; dog-days*, the time when Sirius, or the Dog-star, is predominant. In the East this is the season when the fruits ripen, and hence the word comes to denote *fruit*. The reference is to any kind of fruit that would be brought for traffic into a great city, and that would be regarded as an article of luxury. ¶ *Are departed from thee.* That is, they are no more brought for sale into the city. ¶ *And all things which were dainty and goodly.* These words "characterize all kinds of furniture and clothing which were gilt, or plated, or embroidered, and therefore were bright or splendid" (Professor Stuart). ¶ *And thou shalt find them no more at all.* The address here is decidedly to the city itself. The meaning is, that they would no more be found there.

15. *The merchants of these things.* Who trafficked in these things, and who supplied the city with them, ver. 11. ¶ *Which were made rich by her.* By traffic with her. ¶ *Shall stand afar off.* Ver. 10. ¶ *For fear of her torment.* Struck with terror by her torment, so that they did not dare to approach her, ver. 10.

16. *And saying, Alas, alas,* &c. Notes on ver. 10. ¶ *That was clothed in fine linen.* In the previous description (ver. 12, 13), these are mentioned as articles of traffic; here the city, under the image of a female, is represented as clothed in the most rich and gay of these articles. ¶ *And purple, and scarlet.* See Notes on ch. xvii. 3, 4. Comp. ver. 12 of this chapter. ¶ *And decked with gold, and precious stones, and pearls.* Notes on ch. xvii. 4.

17. *For in one hour.* In a very brief period—so short, that it seemed to them to be but one hour. In the prediction (ver. 8), it is said that it would be "in one day" (see Notes on that place); here it is said that, to the lookers-on, it *seemed* to be but an hour. There is no inconsistency, therefore, between the

18 And cried when they saw the smoke of her burning, saying, What [u] *city is* like unto this great city!

19 And they [v] cast dust on their heads, and cried, weeping and wailing, saying, Alas, alas, that great

u Je.51.37.   v Jos.7.6; Job 2.12; Eze.27.30.

city, wherein were made rich all that had ships in the sea by reason of her costliness! for in one hour is she made desolate.

20 Rejoice [w] over her, *thou* heaven, and *ye* holy apostles and prophets; for God hath [x] avenged you on her.

w Je.51.48.   x ch.19.2; De.32.43; Lu.18.7,8.

two statements. ¶ *So great riches is come to nought.* All the accumulated wealth of so great and rich a city. This should have been united with ver. 16, as it is a part of the lamentation of the merchants, and as the lamentation of the mariners commences in the other part of the verse. It is so divided in the Greek Testaments. ¶ *And every ship-master.* This introduces the lamentation of the mariners, who would, of course, be deeply interested in the destruction of a city with which they had been accustomed to trade, and by carrying merchandise to which they had been enriched. The word *ship-master* —κυβερνήτης—means, properly, a *governor;* then a governor of a ship—the *steersman* or *pilot,* Ac. xxvii. 11. ¶ *And all the company in ships.* Professor Stuart renders this *coasters.* There is here, however, an important difference in the reading of the text. The commonly received text is, πᾶς ἐπὶ τῶν πλοίων ὁ ὅμιλος—"the whole company in ships," as in our common version; the reading which is now commonly adopted, and which is found in Griesbach, Hahn, and Tittmann, is ὁ ἐπὶ τόπον πλέων—"he who sails to a place;" that is, he who sails from one place to another along the coast, or who does not venture out far to sea; and thus the phrase would denote a secondary class of sea-captains or officers—those less venturesome, or experienced, or bold than others. There can be little doubt that this is the correct reading (comp. Wetstein, *in loco*); and hence the class of seamen here referred to is *coasters.* Such seamen would naturally be employed where there was a great and luxurious maritime city, and would have a deep interest in its fall. ¶ *And sailors.* Common seamen. ¶ *And as many as trade by sea.* In any kind of craft, whether employed in a near or a remote trade. ¶ *Stood afar off.* Notes on ver. 10.

18. *And cried,* &c. That is, as they had a deep interest in it, they would, on their own account, as well as hers, lift up the voice of lamentation. ¶ *What* city is *like unto this great city?* In her destruction. What calamity has ever come upon a city like this?

19. *And they cast dust on their heads.* A common sign of lamentation and mourning among the Orientals. See Notes on Job ii. 12. ¶ *By reason of her costliness.* The word rendered *costliness*—τιμιότητος—means, properly, *preciousness, costliness;* their magnificence, costly merchandise. The luxury of a great city enriches many individuals, however much it may impoverish itself. ¶ *For in one hour is she made desolate.* So it seemed to them. Notes on ver. 17.

20. *Rejoice over her.* Over her ruin. There is a strong contrast between this language and that which precedes. Kings, merchants, and seamen, who had been countenanced and sustained by her in the indulgence of corrupt passions, or who had been enriched by traffic with her, would have occasion to mourn. But not so they who had been persecuted by her. Not so the church of the redeemed. Not so heaven itself. The great oppressor of the church, and the corrupter of the world, was now destroyed; the grand hindrance to the spread of the gospel was now removed, and all the holy in heaven and on earth would have occasion to rejoice. This is not the language of vengeance, but it is the language of exultation and rejoicing in view of the fact, that the cause of truth might now spread, without hindrance, through the earth. ¶ *Thou heaven.* The inhabitants of heaven. Comp. Notes on Is. i. 2. The meaning here is, that the dwellers in heaven—the holy angels and the redeemed—had occasion to rejoice over the downfall of the great enemy of the church. ¶ *And ye holy apostles.* Professor Stuart renders this, "Ye saints, and apostles, and prophets." In the common Greek text, it is, as in our version, "holy apostles and prophets." In the text of Griesbach, Hahn, and Tittmann, the word καὶ (*and*) is interposed between the word "*holy*" and "*apostle.*" This

21 And a mighty angel took up a stone like a great millstone, and cast *it* into the sea, saying, *y* Thus with violence shall that great city Babylon be thrown down, and shall be found no more at all.

22 And the voice of harpers, and musicians, and of pipers, and trumpeters, shall be heard no more at all in thee; and no craftsman, of whatsoever craft *he be*, shall be found any more in thee; and *z* the sound of a millstone shall be heard no more at all in thee;

*y* Je.51.64.     *z* Je.25.10.

is, doubtless, the true reading. The meaning, then, is that the *saints* in heaven are called on to rejoice over the fall of the mystical Babylon. ¶ *Apostles.* The twelve who were chosen by the Saviour to be his *witnesses* on earth. See Notes on 1 Co. ix. 1. The word is commonly limited to the twelve, but, in a larger sense, it is applied to other distinguished teachers and preachers of the gospel. See Notes on Ac. xiv. 14. There is no impropriety, however, in supposing that the apostles are referred to here *as* such, since they would have occasion to rejoice that the great obstacle to the reign of the Redeemer was now taken away, and that that cause in which they had suffered and died was now to be triumphant. ¶ *And prophets.* Prophets of the Old Testament and distinguished teachers of the New. See Notes on Ro. xii. 6. All these would have occasion to rejoice in the prospect of the final triumph of the true religion. ¶ *For God hath avenged you on her.* Has taken vengeance on her for her treatment of you. That is, as she had persecuted the church *as such*, they all might be regarded as interested in it and affected by it. All the redeemed, therefore, in earth and in heaven, are interested in whatever tends to retard or to promote the cause of truth. All have occasion to mourn when the enemies of the truth triumph; to rejoice when they fall.

21. *And a mighty angel.* Notes on ver. 1. This seems, however, to have been a different angel from the one mentioned in ver. 1, though, like that, he is described as having great power. ¶ *Took up a stone like a great millstone.* On the structure of mills among the ancients see Notes on Mat. xxiv. 41. ¶ *And cast* it *into the sea.* As an emblem of the utter ruin of the city; an indication that the city would be as completely destroyed as that stone was covered by the waters. ¶ *Saying, Thus with violence.* With force, as the stone was thrown into the sea. The idea is, that it would not be by a gentle and natural decline, but by the application of foreign power. This accords with all the representations in this book, that violence will be employed to overthrow the Papal power. See ch. xvii. 16, 17. The origin of this image is probably Je. li. 63, 64: "And it shall be, when thou hast made an end of reading this book, that thou shalt bind a stone to it, and cast it into the midst of Euphrates; and thou shalt say, Thus shall Babylon sink, and shall not rise from the evil that I will bring on her."

22. *And the voice of harpers.* Those who play on the harp. This was usually accompanied with singing. The idea, in this verse and the following, is substantially the same as in the previous parts of the chapter, that the mystical Babylon—Papal Rome—would be brought to utter desolation. This thought is here exhibited under another form—that all which constituted festivity, joy, and amusement, and all that indicated thrift and prosperity, would disappear. Of course, in a great and gay city, there would be all kinds of music; and when it is said that this would be heard there no more it is a most striking image of utter desolation. ¶ *And musicians.* Musicians in general; but perhaps here *singers*, as distinguished from those who played on instruments. ¶ *And of pipers.* Those who played on pipes or flutes. See Notes on 1 Co. xiv. 7; Mat. xi. 17. ¶ *And trumpeters.* Trumpets were common instruments of music, employed on festival occasions, in war, and in worship. Only the principal instruments of music are mentioned here, as representatives of the rest. The general idea is, that the sound of music, as an indication of festivity and joy, would cease. ¶ *Shall be heard no more at all in thee.* It would become utterly and permanently desolate. ¶ *And no craftsman, of whatsoever craft.* That is, artificers of all kinds would cease to ply their trades there. The word here used—τεχνίτης—would include all artisans or mechanics, all who were engaged in any kind of trade or craft. The meaning here is, that all these would disappear, an image,

406 REVELATION. [A.D. 96.

23 And the light of a candle shall shine no more at all in thee; and the *a*voice of the bridegroom and of the bride shall be heard no more at all in thee: for thy *b*merchants were the great men of the earth;

*a* Je.7.34; 16.9; 33.11.   *b* Is.23.8.

for by thy *c*sorceries were all nations deceived.

24 And in her was found the blood of prophets, and of saints, and of *d*all that were slain upon the earth.

*c* 2 Ki.9.22; Na.3.4.   *d* Je.51.49.

of course, of utter decay. ¶ *And the sound of a millstone shall be heard no more.* Taylor (*Frag. to Cal. Dict.* vol. iv. p. 346) supposes that this may refer not so much to the rattle of the mill as to the voice of singing, which usually accompanied grinding. The sound of a mill is cheerful, and indicates prosperity; its ceasing is an image of decline.

23. *And the light of a candle shall shine no more at all in thee.* Another image of desolation, as if every light were put out, and there were total darkness. ¶ *And the voice of the bridegroom and of the bride shall be heard no more at all in thee.* The merry and cheerful voice of the marriage procession in the streets (Notes on Mat. xxv. 1-7), or the cheerful, glad voice of the newly-married couple in their own dwelling (Notes on Jn. iii. 29). ¶ *For thy merchants were the great men of the earth.* Those who dealt with thee were the rich, and among them were even nobles and princes; and now that they trade with thee no more there is occasion for lamentation and sorrow. The contrast is great between the time when distinguished foreigners crowded thy marts, and now, when none of any kind come to traffic with thee. The origin of this representation is probably the description of Tyre in Eze. xxvii. ¶ *For by thy sorceries were all nations deceived.* This is stated as a reason for the ruin that had come upon her. It is a common representation of Papal Rome that she has *deceived* or *deluded* the nations of the earth (see Notes on ch. xiii. 14), and no representation ever made accords more with facts as they have occurred. The word *sorceries* here refers to the various arts the tricks, impostures, and false pretences by which this has been done. See Notes on ch. ix. 21.

24. *And in her.* When she came to be destroyed, and her real character was seen. ¶ *Was found the blood of prophets.* Of the public teachers of the true religion. On the word *prophets* see Notes on ver. 20. ¶ *And of saints.* Of the holy. See Notes on ver. 20. ¶ *And of all that were slain upon the earth.* So numerous have been the slain, so constant and bloody have been the persecutions there, that it may be said that all the blood ever shed has been poured out there. Comp. Notes on Mat. xxiii. 35. No one can doubt the propriety of this representation with respect to Pagan and Papal Rome.

In regard to the general meaning and application of this chapter the following remarks may be made:—

(1) It refers to Papal Rome, and is designed to describe the final overthrow of that formidable Antichristian power. The whole course of the interpretation of the previous chapters demands such an application, and the chapter itself naturally suggests it.

(2) If it be asked why so much of this imagery is derived from the condition of a *maritime* power, or pertains to *commerce*, since both Babylon and Rome were at some distance from the sea, and neither could with propriety be regarded as seaport towns, it may be replied, (*a*) that the main idea in the mind of John was that of a rich and magnificent city; (*b*) that all the things enumerated were doubtless found, in fact, in both Babylon and Rome; (*c*) that though not properly seaport towns, they were situated on rivers that opened into seas, and were therefore not unfavourably situated for commerce; and (*d*) that, in fact, they traded with all parts of the earth. The leading idea is that of a great and luxurious city, and this is filled up and decorated with images of what is commonly found in large commercial towns. We are not, therefore, to look for a *literal* application of this, and it is not necessary to attempt to find *all* these things, in fact, in the city referred to. Much of the description may be for the mere sake of *keeping*, or ornament.

(3) If this refers to Rome, as is supposed, then, in accordance with the previous representations, it shows that the destruction of the Papal power is to be complete and final. The image which John had in his eye as illustrating that was undoubtedly ancient Baby-

Ion as prophetically described in Is. xiii., xiv., and the destruction of the power here referred to is to be as complete as was the destruction described there. It would not be absolutely necessary in the fulfilment of this to suppose that Rome itself is to become a heap of ruins like Babylon, whatever may be true on that point, but that the Papal power, as such, is to be so utterly destroyed that the ruins of desolate Babylon would properly represent it.

(4) If this interpretation is correct, then the Reformation was in entire accordance with what God would have his people do, and was demanded by solemn duty to him. Thus, in ver. 4 of this chapter, his people are expressly commanded to "come out of her, that they might not be partakers of her sins, nor of her plagues." If it had been the design of the Reformers to perform a work that should be in all respects a fulfilling of the command of God, they could have done nothing that would have more literally met the divine requirement. Indeed, the church has never performed a duty more manifestly in accordance with the divine will, and more indispensable for its own purity, prosperity, and safety, than the act of separating entirely and for ever from Papal Rome.

(5) The Reformation was a great movement in human affairs. It was the index of great progress already reached, and the pledge of still greater. The affairs of the world were at that period placed on a new footing, and from the period of the Reformation, and just in proportion as the principles of the Reformation are acted on, the destiny of mankind is *onward*.

(6) The fall of Papal Rome, as described in this chapter, will remove one of the last obstructions to the final triumph of the gospel. In the Notes on ch. xvi. 10–16, we saw that *one* great hindrance to the spread of the true religion would be taken away by the decline and fall of the Turkish power. A still more formidable hindrance will be taken away by the decline and fall of the Papal power; for that power holds more millions of the race under its subjection, and with a more consummate art, and a more powerful spell. The Papal influence has been felt, and still is felt, in a considerable part of the world. It has churches, and schools, and colleges, in almost all lands. It exercises a vast influence over governments. It has powerful societies organized for the purpose of propagating its opinions; and it so panders to some of the most powerful passions of our nature, and so converts to its own purposes all the resources of superstition, as still to retain a mighty, though a waning hold on the human mind. When this power shall finally cease, anyone can see that perhaps *the* most mighty obstruction which has ever been on the earth for a thousand years to the spread of the gospel will have been removed, and the way will be prepared for the introduction of the long-hoped-for millennium.

## CHAPTER XIX.
### ANALYSIS OF THE CHAPTER.

This chapter, as well as the last, is an episode, delaying the final catastrophe, and describing more fully the effect of the destruction of the mystical Babylon. The chapter consists of the following parts:—

I. A hymn of the heavenly hosts in view of the destruction of the mystical Babylon, ver. 1–7. (*a*) A voice is heard in heaven shouting Hallelujah, in view of the fact that God had judged the great harlot that had corrupted the earth, ver. 1, 2. (*b*) The sound is echoed and repeated as the smoke of her torment ascends, ver. 3. (*c*) The four and twenty elders, and the four living creatures, as interested in all that pertains to the church, unite in that shout of Hallelujah, ver. 4. (*d*) A voice is heard from the throne commanding them to praise God, ver. 5; and (*e*) the mighty shout of Hallelujah is echoed and repeated from unnumbered hosts, ver. 6, 7.

II. The marriage of the Lamb, ver. 8, 9. The Lamb of God is united to his bride—the church—never more to be separated; and after all the persecutions, conflicts, and embarrassments which had existed, this long-desired union is consummated, and the glorious triumph of the church is described under the image of a joyous wedding ceremony.

III. John is so overcome with this representation, that in his transports of feeling he prostrates himself before the angel who shows him all this, ready to *worship* one who discloses such bright and glorious scenes, ver. 10. He is gently rebuked for allowing himself to be so overcome that he would render divine homage to any creature, and is told that he who communicates this to

## CHAPTER XIX.

AND after these things I heard a *a*great voice of much people in heaven, saying, *b*Alleluia; *c*Salvation, and glory, and honour, and power, unto the Lord our God:

2 For *d*true and righteous *are* his judgments: for he hath judged

<small>a ch.11.15.    b ver.3,4,6.<br>c ch.7.10,12.    d ch.16.7.</small>

the great whore, which did corrupt the earth with her fornication, and hath *e*avenged the blood of his servants at her hand.

3 And again they said, Alleluia. And her *f*smoke rose up for ever and ever.

4 And the four and twenty elders

<small>e ch.18.20.    f ch.18.9,18; Is. 34.10.</small>

him is but a fellow-servant, and that God only is to be worshipped.

IV. The final conquest over the beast and the false prophet, and the subjugation of all the foes of the church, ver. 11-21. (*a*) A description of the conqueror—the Son of God, ver. 11-16. He appears on a white horse—emblem of victory. He has on his head many crowns; wears a vesture dipped in blood; is followed by the armies of heaven on white horses; from his mouth goes a sharp sword; and his name is prominently written on his vesture and his thigh—all emblematic of certain victory. (*b*) An angel is seen standing in the sun, calling on all the fowls of heaven to come to the great feast prepared for them in the destruction of the enemies of God—*as if* there were a great slaughter sufficient to supply all the fowls that feed on flesh, ver. 17, 18. (*c*) The final war, ver. 19, 21. The beast, and the kings of the earth, and their armies are gathered together for battle; the beast and the false prophet are taken, and are cast into the lake that burns with fire and brimstone; and all that remain of the enemies of God are slain, and the fowls are satisfied with their flesh. The last obstacle that prevented the dawn of the millennial morning is taken away, and the church is triumphant.

1. *And after these things.* The things particularly that were exhibited in the previous chapter. See Notes on ch. xviii. 1. ¶ *I heard a voice of much people in heaven.* The voice of the worshippers before the throne. ¶ *Saying, Alleluia.* The Greek method of writing *Hallelujah.* This word—ἀλληλούϊα—occurs in the New Testament only in this chapter, ver. 1, 3, 4, 6. The Hebrew phrase—הַלְלוּ יָהּ *Hallelujah*—occurs often in the Old Testament. It means, properly, *Praise Jehovah,* or *Praise the Lord.* The occasion on which it is introduced here is very appropriate. It is uttered by the inhabitants of heaven, in the immediate presence of God himself, and in view of the final overthrow of the enemies of the church, and the triumph of the gospel. In such circumstances it was fit that heaven should render praise, and that a song of thanksgiving should be uttered in which all holy beings could unite. ¶ *Salvation.* That is, the salvation is to be ascribed to God. See Notes on ch. vii. 10. ¶ *And glory, and honour.* Notes on ch. v. 12. ¶ *And power.* Notes on ch. v. 13. ¶ *Unto the Lord our God.* That is, all that there is of honour, glory, power, in the redemption of the world belongs to God, and should be ascribed to him. This is expressive of the true feelings of piety always; this will constitute the song of heaven.

2. *For true and righteous are his judgments.* That is, the calamities that come upon the power here referred to are deserved. ¶ *For he hath judged the great whore.* The power represented by the harlot. See Notes on ch. xvii. 1. ¶ *Which did corrupt the earth with her fornication.* See Notes on ch. xiv. 8; xvii. 2, 4, 5; xviii. 3. Comp. Notes on ch. ix. 21. ¶ *And hath avenged the blood of his servants.* See Notes on ch. xviii. 20, 24. ¶ *At her hand.* Shed by her hand.

3. *And again they said, Alleluia.* Notes on ver. 1. The event was so glorious and so important; the final destruction of the great enemy of the church was of so much moment in its bearing on the welfare of the world, as to call forth repeated expressions of praise. ¶ *And her smoke rose up for ever and ever.* See Notes on ch. xiv. 11. This is an image of final ruin; the image being derived probably from the description in Genesis of the smoke that ascended from the cities of the plain, Ge. xix. 28. On the joy expressed here in her destruction, comp. Notes on ch. xviii. 20.

4. *And the four and twenty elders and the four beasts.* See Notes on ch. iv. 4, 6, 7. As representatives of the church,

and the four beasts fell down and worshipped God that sat on the throne, saying, Amen; Alleluia.

5 And a voice came out of the throne, saying, *g* Praise our God, all ye his servants, and ye that fear him, both small and great.

*g* Ps.135.1.

and as interested in its welfare, they are now introduced as rejoicing in its final triumph, and in the destruction of its last foe. ¶ *Fell down.* Prostrated themselves—the usual posture of worship. ¶ *And worshipped God that sat on the throne.* Ch. iv. 2, 3, 10. That is, they now adored him for what he had done in delivering the church from all its persecutions, and causing it to triumph in the world. ¶ *Saying, Amen.* See Notes on Mat. vi. 13. The word here is expressive of approbation of what God had done; or of their solemn assent to all that had occurred in the destruction of the great enemy of the church. ¶ *Alleluia.* Notes on ver. 1. The repetition of this word so many times shows the intenseness of the joy of heaven in view of the final triumph of the church.

5. *And a voice came out of the throne.* A voice seemed to come from the very midst of the throne. It is not said by whom this voice was uttered. It cannot be supposed, however, that it was uttered by God himself, for the command which it gave was this: "Praise *our* God," &c. For the same reason it seems hardly probable that it was the voice of the Messiah, unless it be supposed that he here identifies himself with the redeemed church, and speaks of God as *his* God and *hers*. It would seem rather that it was a responsive voice that came from those nearest the throne, calling on all to unite in praising God in view of what was done. The meaning then will be, that all heaven was interested in the triumph of the church, and that one portion of the dwellers there called on the others to unite in offering thanksgiving. ¶ *Praise our God.* The God that we worship. ¶ *All ye his servants.* All in heaven and earth; all have occasion for thankfulness. ¶ *And ye that fear him.* That reverence and obey him. The fear of the Lord is a common expression in the Scriptures to denote true piety. ¶ *Both small and great.* All of every class and condition—poor and rich—young and old; those of humble and those of exalted rank. Comp. Ps. cxlviii. 7–13.

6 And I heard as it were the voice of a great multitude, and as the voice of many waters, and as the voice of many thunderings, saying, Alleluia; *h* for the Lord God omnipotent reigneth.

*h* Ps.97.1,12.

6. *And I heard as it were the voice of a great multitude.* In ver. 1 he says that he "heard a great voice of much people;" here he says he "heard *as it were* a voice of a great multitude." That is, in the former case he heard a shout that he at once recognized as the voice of a great multitude of persons; here he says that he heard a sound not distinctly recognized at first as such, but which *resembled* such a shout of a multitude. In the former case it was *distinct;* here it was confused—bearing a resemblance to the sound of roaring waters, or to muttering thunder, but less distinct than the former. This phrase would imply (*a*) *a louder* sound; and (*b*) that the sound was more remote, and therefore less clear and distinct. ¶ *And as the voice of many waters.* The comparison of the voices of a host of people with the roar of mighty waters is not uncommon in the Scriptures. See Notes on Is. xvii. 12, 13. So in Homer:—

"The monarch spoke, and straight a murmur rose,
Loud as the surges when the tempest blows;
That dash'd on broken rocks tumultuous roar,
And foam and thunder on the stony shore."

¶ *And as the voice of mighty thunderings.* The loud, deep, heavy voice of thunder. The distant shouts of a multitude may properly be represented by the sound of heavy thunder. ¶ *Saying, Alleluia.* Notes on ver. 1. This is the *fourth* time in which this is uttered as expressive of the joy of the heavenly hosts in view of the overthrow of the enemies of the church. The occasion will be worthy of this emphatic expression of joy. ¶ *For the Lord God omnipotent reigneth.* Jehovah—God Almighty—the true God. The meaning is, that as the last enemy of the church is destroyed, he now truly reigns. This is the result of his *power,* and therefore it is proper that he should be praised as the *omnipotent* or *Almighty God*—for he has shown that he can overcome all his enemies, and bring the world to his feet.

7 Let us be glad and rejoice, and give honour to him: for the *marriage of the Lamb is come, and his *wife hath made herself ready.

8 And to her was granted that she should be *arrayed in fine linen, clean and ¹white: for the fine linen is the *righteousness of saints.

9 And he saith unto me, Write, *Blessed are they which are called unto the *marriage-supper of the

*i* Mat.25.10.   *k* Is.52.1.   *l* ch.3.4; Is.61.10.   ¹ or, *bright*.   *m* Ps.132.9.   *n* Lu.14.15.   *o* ch.3.20.

7. *Let us be glad and rejoice.* Let all in heaven rejoice—for all have an interest in the triumph of truth; all should be glad that the government of God is set up over an apostate world. ¶ *And give honour to him.* Because the work is glorious; and because it is by his power alone that it has been accomplished. Notes on ch. v. 12. ¶ *For the marriage of the Lamb is come.* Of the Lamb of God—the Redeemer of the world. Notes on ch. v. 6. The relation of God, and especially of the Messiah, to the church, is often in the Scriptures represented under the image of marriage. See Notes on Is. liv. 4–6; lxii. 4, 5; 2 Co. xi. 2; Ep. v. 23-33. Comp. Je. iii. 14; xxxi. 32; Ho. ii. 19, 20. The idea is also said to be common in Arabic and Persian poetry. It is to be remembered, also, that Papal Rome has just been represented as a gay and meretricious woman; and there is a propriety, therefore, in representing the true church as a pure bride, the Lamb's wife, and the final triumph of that church as a joyous marriage. The meaning is, that the church was now to triumph and rejoice as if in permanent union with her glorious head and Lord. ¶ *And his wife hath made herself ready.* By putting on her beautiful apparel and ornaments. All the preparations had been made for a permanent and uninterrupted union with its Redeemer, and the church was henceforward to be recognized as his beautiful bride, and was no more to appear as a decorated harlot —as it had during the Papal supremacy. Between the church under the Papacy, and the church in its true form, there is all the difference which there is between an abandoned woman gaily decked with gold and jewels, and a pure virgin chastely and modestly adorned, about to be led to be united in bonds of love to a virtuous husband.

8. *And to her was granted.* It is not said here *by whom* this was granted, but it is perhaps implied that this was conferred by the Saviour himself on his bride. ¶ *That she should be arrayed in fine linen, clean and white.* See Notes on ch. iii. 4, 5, 18; vii. 13. *White* has, perhaps, in all countries been the usual colour of the bridal dress—as an emblem of innocence. ¶ *For the fine linen is the righteousness of saints.* Represents the righteousness of the saints; or is an emblem of it. It should be remarked, however, that it is implied here, as it is everywhere in the Scriptures, that this is not their *own* righteousness, for it is said that this was "*given*" to the bride—to the saints. It is the gracious bestowment of their Lord; and the reference here must be to that righteousness which they obtain by faith—the righteousness which results from justification through the merits of the Redeemer. Of this Paul speaks, when he says (Phi. iii. 9), "And be found in him, not having mine own righteousness, which is of the law, but that which is through the faith of Christ, the righteousness which is of God by faith." Comp. Notes on Ro. iii. 25, 26.

9. *And he saith unto me.* The angel who made these representations to him. See ver. 10. ¶ *Write, Blessed are they.* See Notes on ch. xiv. 13. ¶ *Which are called unto the marriage-supper of the Lamb.* The idea of a festival, or a marriage-supper, was a familiar one to the Jews to represent the happiness of heaven, and is frequently found in the New Testament. Comp. Notes on Lu. xiv. 15, 16; xvi. 22; xxii. 16; Mat. xxii. 2. The image in the passage before us is that of many *guests* invited to a great festival. ¶ *And he saith unto me, These are the true sayings of God.* Confirming all by a solemn declaration. The importance of what is here said; the desirableness of having it fixed in the mind, amidst the trials of life and the scenes of persecution through which the church was to pass, makes this solemn declaration proper. The idea is, that in all times of persecution—in every dark hour of despondency—the church, as such, and every individual member of the church, should receive it as a solemn truth never to be doubted, that the religion of Christ would finally

Lamb. And he saith unto me, These*p* are the true sayings of God.

10 And*q* I fell at his feet to worship him. And he said unto

*p* ch.22.6.   *q* ch.22.8,9.

me, See *thou do it* not: I am thy fellow-servant, and of thy brethren that have the testimony of Jesus; worship God: for the *r* testimony of Jesus is the spirit of prophecy.

*r* Ac.10.43; 1 Pe.1.10,11.

prevail, and that all persecution and sorrow here would be followed by joy and triumph in heaven.

10. *And I fell at his feet to worship him.* At the feet of the angel. Notes on ver. 9. This is a common posture of adoration in the East. See Rosenmüller's *Morgenland, in loco.* Notes on 1 Co. xiv. 25. John was entirely overcome with the majesty of the heavenly messenger, and with the amazing truths that he had disclosed to him, and in the overflowing of his feelings he fell upon the earth in the posture of adoration. Or it may be that he mistook the rank of him who addressed him, and supposed that he was the Messiah whom he had been accustomed to worship, and who had first (ch. i.) appeared to him. If so, his error was soon corrected. He was told by the angel himself who made these communications that he had no claims to such homage, and that the praise which he offered *him* should be rendered to God alone. It should be observed that there is not the slightest intimation that this *was* the Messiah himself, and consequently this does not contain any evidence that it would be improper to worship him. The only fair conclusion from the passage is, that it is wrong to offer religious homage to an angel. ¶ *And he said unto me, See* thou do it *not.* That is, in rendering the homage which you propose to me, you would in fact render it to a creature. This may be regarded as an admonition to be *careful* in our worship; not to allow our feelings to overcome us; and not to render that homage to a creature which is due to God alone. Of course, this would prohibit the worship of the Virgin Mary, and of any of the saints, and all that homage rendered to a created being which is due to God only. Nothing is more carefully guarded in the Bible than the purity and simplicity of worship; nothing is more sternly rebuked than idolatry; nothing is more contrary to the divine law than rendering in any way that homage to a creature which belongs of right to the Creator. It was necessary to guard even John, the beloved disciple, on that subject; how much more needful, therefore, is it to guard the church at large from the dangers to which it is liable. ¶ *I am thy fellow-servant.* Evidently this was an angel, and yet he here speaks of himself as a "fellow-servant" of John. That is, he was engaged in the service of the same God; he was endeavouring to advance the same cause, and to honour the same Redeemer. The sentiment is, that in promoting religion in the world, we are associated with angels. It is no condescension in them to be engaged in the service of the Redeemer, though it seems to be condescension for them to be associated with us in anything; it constitutes no ground of merit in us to be engaged in the service of the Redeemer (comp. Lu. xvii. 10), though we may regard it as an honour to be associated with the angels, and it may raise us in conscious dignity to feel that we are united with them. ¶ *And of thy brethren.* Of other Christians; for all are engaged in the same work. ¶ *That have the testimony of Jesus.* Who are witnesses for the Saviour. It is possible that there may be here a particular reference to those who were engaged in preaching the gospel, though the language will apply to all who give their testimony to the value of the gospel by consistent lives. ¶ *Worship God.* He is the only proper object of worship; he alone is to be adored. ¶ *For the testimony of Jesus.* The meaning here seems to be, that this angel, and John, and their fellow-servants, were all engaged in the same work—that of bearing their testimony to Jesus. Thus, in this respect, they were on a level, and one of them should not worship another, but all should unite in the common worship of God. No one in this work, though an angel, could have such a pre-eminence that it would be proper to render the homage to him which was due to God alone. There *could be* but one being whom it was proper to worship, and they who were engaged in simply bearing *testimony* to the work of the Saviour should not worship one another. ¶ *Is the spirit of prophecy.*

11 And I saw heaven opened, and behold, a *white horse; and he that sat upon him *was* ᵗcalled Faithful and True, and ᵘin righteousness he doth judge and make war.

*s* ch.6.2.   *t* ch.3.14.   *u* Ps.45.3,4; Is.11.4.

12 His ᵛ eyes *were* as a flame of fire, and on his head *were* ʷmany crowns; and he had a ˣname written, that no man knew but he himself.

13 And he *was* clothed with a

*v* ch.1.14; 2.18.
*w* ch.6.2; Ca.3.11; Is.62.3; Zec.9.16; He.2.9.
*x* ch.3.12.

The design of prophecy is to bear testimony to Jesus. The language does not mean, of course, that this is the *only* design of prophecy, but that this is its great and ultimate end. The word *prophecy* here seems to be used in the large sense in which it is often employed in the New Testament—meaning to make known the divine will (see Notes on Ro. xii. 6), and the *primary* reference here would seem to be to the preachers and teachers of the New Testament. The sense is, that their grand business is to bear testimony to the Saviour. They are all—whether angels, apostles, or ordinary teachers—appointed for this, and therefore should regard themselves as "fellow-servants." The *design* of the angel in this seems to have been, to state to John what was his own specific business in the communications which *he* made, and then to state a universal truth applicable to *all* ministers of the gospel, that they were engaged in the same work, and that no one of them should claim adoration from others. Thus understood, this passage has no direct reference to the prophecies of the Old Testament, and teaches nothing in regard to their design, though it is *in fact* undoubtedly true that their grand and leading object was to bear testimony to the future Messiah. But this passage will not justify the attempt so often made to "find Christ" everywhere in the prophecies of the Old Testament, or justify the many forced and unnatural interpretations by which the prophecies are often applied to him.

11. *And I saw heaven opened.* He saw a new vision, *as if* an opening were made through the sky, and he was permitted to look *into* heaven. See Notes on ch. iv. 1. ¶ *And behold, a white horse.* On the white horse as a symbol, see Notes on ch. vi. 2. He is here the symbol of the final victory that is to be obtained over the beast and the false prophet (ver. 20), and of the final triumph of the church. ¶ *And he that sat upon him was called Faithful and True.* He is not designated here by his usual and real name, but by his attributes. There can be no doubt that the Messiah is intended, as he goes forth to the subjugation of the world to himself. The attributes here referred to—*faithful* and *true*—are peculiarly appropriate, for they are not only strongly marked attributes of his character, but they would be particularly manifested in the events that are described. He would thus show that he was *faithful*—or worthy of the confidence of his church in delivering it from all its enemies; and *true* to all the promises that he has made to it. ¶ *And in righteousness he doth judge.* All his acts of judgment in determining the destiny of men are righteous. See Notes on Is. xi. 3-5. ¶ *And make war.* That is, the war which he wages is not a war of ambition; it is not for the mere purpose of conquest; it is to save the righteous, and to punish the wicked.

12. *His eyes* were *as a flame of fire.* See Notes on ch. i. 14. ¶ *And on his head* were *many crowns.* Many diadems, indicative of his universal reign. It is not said *how* these were worn or arranged on his head—perhaps the various diadems worn by kings were in some way *wreathed* into one. ¶ *And he had a name written.* That is, probably on the frontlet of this compound diadem. Comp. Notes on ch. xiii. 1; xiv. 1. ¶ *That no man knew but he himself.* See Notes on ch. ii. 17. This cannot here mean that no one could *read* the name, but the idea is, that no one but himself could fully understand its import. It involved a depth of meaning, and a degree of sacredness, and a relation to the Father, which he alone could apprehend in its true import. This is true of the name here designated—"the Word of God"—the *Logos*—Λόγος; and it is true of *all* the names which he bears. See Mat. xi. 27. Comp. a quotation from Dr. Buchanan* in the *Asiatic Researches*, vol. i. vi. p. 264, as quoted by Rosenmüller, *Morgenland, in loco.*

13. *And he was clothed with a vesture*

A.D. 96.] CHAPTER XIX. 413

vesture dipped in blood: and his name is called *y* The Word of God.

14 And the armies *which were* in heaven followed him upon white horses, *z* clothed in fine linen, white and clean.

15 And *a* out of his mouth goeth

*y* Jn.1.1.   *z* Mat.28.3.   *a* ch.1.16.

a sharp sword, that with it he should smite the nations: and he shall rule them with a *b* rod of iron: and *c* he treadeth the wine-press of the fierceness and wrath of Almighty God.

16 And he hath on *his* vesture

*b* Ps.2.9.   *c* Is.63.3.

*dipped in blood.* Red, *as if* dipped in blood — emblem of slaughter. The original of this image is probably Is. lxiii. 2, 3. See Notes on that passage. ¶ *And his name is called The Word of God.* The name which in ver. 12, it is said that no one knew but he himself. This name is 'Ο λόγος τοῦ Θεοῦ, or "the Logos of God." That is, this is his peculiar name; a name which belongs only to him, and which distinguishes him from all other beings. The name *Logos*, as applicable to the Son of God, and expressive of his nature, is found in the New Testament only in the writings of John, and is used by him to denote the higher or divine nature of the Saviour. In regard to its meaning, and the reason why it is applied to him, see Notes on Jn. i. 1. The reader also may consult, with great advantage, an article by Professor Stuart in the *Bibliotheca Sacra*, vol. vii. pp. 16-31. The following *may be* some of the reasons why it is said (ver. 12) that no one understands this but he himself:— (1) No one but he can understand its *full import*, as it implies so high a knowledge of the nature of the Deity; (2) no one but he can understand the *relation* which it supposes in regard to God, or the relation of the Son to the Father; (3) no one but he can understand what is implied in it, regarded as the method in which God reveals himself to his creatures on earth; (4) no one but he can understand what is implied in it in respect to the manner in which God makes himself known to other worlds. It may be added, as a further illustration of this, that none of the attempts made to explain it have left the matter so that there are no questions unsolved which one would be glad to ask.

14. *And the armies* which were *in heaven followed him*. The heavenly hosts; particularly, it would seem, the redeemed, as there would be some incongruity in representing the angels as riding in this manner. Doubtless the original of this picture is Is. lxiii. 3: "I have trodden the wine-press *alone*, and of the people there was none with me." These hosts of the redeemed on white horses accompany him to be witnesses of his victory, and to participate in the joy of the triumph, not to engage in the work of blood. ¶ *Upon white horses.* Emblems of triumph or victory. See Notes on ch. vi. 2. ¶ *Clothed in fine linen, white and clean.* The usual raiment of those who are in heaven, as everywhere represented in this book. See ch. iii. 4, 5; iv. 4; vii. 9, 13; xv. 6.

15. *And out of his mouth goeth a sharp sword.* See Notes on ch. i. 16. In that place the sword seems to be an emblem of his *words* or *doctrines*, as penetrating the hearts of men; here it is the emblem of a work of destruction wrought on his foes. ¶ *That with it he should smite the nations.* The nations that were opposed to him; to wit, those especially who were represented by the beast and the false prophet, ver. 18-20. ¶ *And he shall rule them with a rod of iron.* See Notes on ch. ii. 27; xii. 5. ¶ *And he treadeth the wine-press of the fierceness and wrath of Almighty God.* This language is probably derived from Is. lxiii. 1-4. See it explained in the Notes on that place, and on ch. xiv. 19, 20. It means here that his enemies would be certainly crushed before him — as grapes are crushed under the feet of him that treads in the wine-vat.

16. *And he hath on his vesture.* That is, this name was conspicuously written on his garment — probably his military robe. ¶ *And on his thigh.* The robe or military cloak may be conceived of as open and flowing, so as to expose the limbs of the rider; and the idea is, that the name was conspicuously written not only on the flowing robe, but on the other parts of his dress, so that it *must* be conspicuous whether his military cloak were wrapped closely around him, or whether it was open to the breeze. Grotius supposes

and on his thigh a name written, KING[d] OF KINGS, AND LORD OF LORDS.

17 And I saw an angel standing in the sun; and he cried with a loud voice, saying to all the fowls that fly in the midst of heaven,

d ch.17.14.

[e]Come and gather yourselves together unto the supper of the great God;

18 That ye may eat the flesh of kings, and the flesh of captains, and the flesh of mighty men, and the flesh of horses, and of them

e Eze.39.17-20.

that this name was on the edge or hilt of the sword which depended from his thigh. ¶ *A name written.* Or a title descriptive of his character. ¶ *King of kings, and Lord of lords.* As in ch. xvii. 5, so here, there is nothing in the original to denote that this should be distinguished, as it is, by capital letters. As a conspicuous title, however, it is not improper. It means that he is, in fact, the sovereign over the kings of the earth, and that all nobles and princes are under his control —a rank that properly belongs to the Son of God. Comp. Notes on Ep. i. 20-22. See also ver. 12 of this chapter. The custom here alluded to of inscribing the name or rank of distinguished individuals on their garments, so that they might be readily recognized, was not uncommon in ancient times. For full proof of this, see Rosenmüller, *Morgenland*, vol. iii. pp. 232-236. The authorities quoted there are, Thevenot's *Travels*, vol. i. p. 149; Gruter, p. 989; Dempster's *Etruria Regalis*, t. ii. tab. 93; Montfauçon, *Antiq. Expliq.* t. iii. tab. 39. Thus Herodotus (vol. ii. p. 196), speaking of the figures of Sesostris in Ionia, says that, "Across his breast, from shoulder to shoulder, there is this inscription in the sacred characters of Egypt, 'I conquered this country by the force of my arms.'" Comp. Cic. *Verr.* iv. 23; Le Moyne *ad* Jer. xxiii. 6; Münter, *Diss. ad Apoc.* xvii. 5, as referred to by Professor Stuart, *in loco*.

17. *And I saw an angel standing in the sun.* A different angel evidently from the one which had before appeared to him. The *number* of angels that appeared to John, as referred to in this book, was very great, and each one came on a new errand, or with a new message. Everyone must be struck with the image here. The description is as simple as it can be; and yet as sublime. The fewest words possible are used; and yet the image is distinct and clear. A heavenly being stands in the blaze of the brightest of the orbs that God permits us here to see—yet not consumed, and himself so bright that he can be distinctly seen amidst the dazzling splendours of that luminary. It is difficult to conceive of an image more sublime than this. *Why* he has his place in the sun is not stated, for there does not *appear* to be anything more intended by this than to give grandeur and impressiveness to the scene. ¶ *And he cried with a loud voice.* So that all the fowls of heaven could hear. ¶ *Saying to all the fowls that fly in the midst of heaven.* That is, to all the birds of prey—all that feed on flesh—such as hover over a battle-field. Comp. Notes on Is. xviii. 6; lvi. 9. See also Je. vii. 33; xii. 9; Eze. xxxix. 4-20. ¶ *Come and gather yourselves together.* All this imagery is taken from the idea that there would be a great slaughter, and that the bodies of the dead would be left unburied to the birds of prey. ¶ *Unto the supper of the great God.* As if the great God were about to give you a feast — to wit, the carcasses of those slain. It is called "*his* supper" because he gives it; and the image is merely that there would be a great slaughter of his foes, as is specified in the following verse.

18. *That ye may eat the flesh of kings.* Of the kings under the control of the beast and the false prophet, ch. xvi. 14; xvii. 12-14. ¶ *And the flesh of captains.* Of those subordinate to kings in command. The Greek word is χιλιάρχων— *chiliarchs*—denoting captains of a thousand, or, as we should say, commanders of a regiment. The word *colonel* would better convey the idea with us; as he is the commander of a regiment, and a regiment is usually composed of about a thousand men. ¶ *And the flesh of mighty men.* The word here means *strong*, and the reference is to the robust soldiery — rank and file in the army. ¶ *And the flesh of horses, and of them that sit on them.* Cavalry — for most armies are composed in part of horsemen. ¶ *And the flesh of all* men, both *free* and *bond.* Freemen and

that sit on them, and the flesh of all *men, both* free and bond, both small and great.

19 And I saw the beast, and the kings of the earth, and their armies, gathered*ᶠ* together to make war

*f* ch. 16. 14, 16.

against him that sat on the horse, and against his army.

20 And the *ᵍ*beast was taken, and with him the false prophet that wrought miracles before him, with which he deceived them that had

*g* ch. 16. 13, 14.

---

slaves. It is not uncommon that freemen and slaves are mingled in the same army. This was the case in the American Revolution, and is common in the East. ¶ *Both small and great.* Young and old; of small size and of great size; of those of humble, and those of exalted rank. The later armies of Napoleon were composed in great part of conscripts, many of whom were only about eighteen years of age, and to this circumstance many of his later defeats are to be traced. In the army that was raised after the invasion of Russia no less than one hundred and fifty thousand of the conscripts were between eighteen and nineteen years of age (Alison's *History of Europe*, vol. iv. p. 27). Indeed, it is common in most armies that a considerable portion of the enlistments are from those in early life; and besides this, it is usual to employ mere boys on various services about a camp.

19. *And I saw the beast.* Notes on ch. xiii. 1, 11. Comp. ch. xvii. 13. ¶ *And the kings of the earth, and their armies, gathered together.* There is allusion here to the same assembling of hostile forces which is described in ch. xvi. 13, 14, for the great decisive battle that is to determine the destiny of the world—the question whether the Messiah or Antichrist shall reign. There can be no doubt that the writer in these passages designed to refer to the same events—the still future scenes that are to occur when the Roman, the Pagan, and the Mahometan powers shall be aroused to make common cause against the true religion, and shall stake all on the issue of the great conflict. See the Notes on ch. xvi. 13, 14. ¶ *Against him that sat on the horse.* The Messiah—the Son of God. Notes on ver. 11. ¶ *And against his army.* The hosts that are associated with him — his redeemed people. Notes on ver. 14.

20. *And the beast was taken.* That is, was taken alive, to be thrown into the lake of fire. The hosts were slain (ver. 21), but the leaders were made prisoners of war. The *general* idea is, that these armies were overcome, and that the Messiah was victorious; but there is a propriety in the representation here that the leaders — the authors of the war—should be taken captive, and reserved for severer punishment than death on the battle-field would be—for they had stirred up their hosts, and summoned these armies to make rebellion against the Messiah. The *beast* here, as all along, refers to the Papal power; and the idea is that of its complete and utter overthrow, *as if* the leader of an army were taken captive and tormented in burning flames, and all his followers were cut down on the field of battle. ¶ *And with him the false prophet.* As they had been *practically* associated together, there was a propriety that they should share the same fate. In regard to the false prophet, and the nature of this alliance, see Notes on ch. xvi. 13. ¶ *That wrought miracles before him.* That is, the false prophet had been united with the beast in deceiving the nations of the earth. See Notes on ch. xvi. 14. ¶ *With which he deceived them that had received the mark of the beast.* Notes on ch. xiii. 16-18. By these arts they had been deceived—that is, they had been led into the alliance, and had been sustained in their opposition to the truth. The whole representation is that of an alliance to prevent the spread of the true religion, *as if* the Papacy and Mahometanism were combined, and the one was sustained by the pretended miracles of the other. There would be a practical array against the reign of the Son of God, *as if* these great powers should act in concert, and *as if* the peculiar claims which each set up in behalf of its own divine origin became a claim which went to support the whole combined organization. ¶ *These both were cast alive into a lake of fire.* The beast and the false prophet. That is, the overthrow will be as signal, and the destruction as complete, *as if* the leaders of the combined hosts should be taken alive, and thrown into a pit or lake that burns with an intense heat. There is no necessity for supposing that this

received the mark of the beast, and them that worshipped his image. These both were *h* cast alive into a lake of fire burning with brimstone.

*h* ch.20.10; Da.7.11.

21 And the remnant were *i* slain with the sword of him that sat upon the horse, which *sword* proceeded out of his mouth; and *k* all the fowls were filled with their flesh.

*i* ver.15; ch.1.16.   *k* ver.17,18.

is to be *literally* inflicted—for the whole scene is symbolical—meaning that the destruction of these powers would be as complete *as if* they were thrown into such a burning lake. Comp. Notes on ch. xiv. 10, 11. ¶ *Burning with brimstone.* Sulphur—the usual expression to denote intense heat, and especially as referring to the punishment of the wicked. See Notes on ch. xiv. 10.

21. *And the remnant.* The remainder of the assembled hosts—the army at large, in contradistinction from the leaders. ¶ *Were slain with the sword.* Cut down with the sword; not rescued for protracted torment. A proper distinction is thus made between the deceived multitudes and the leaders who had deceived them. ¶ *Of him that sat upon the horse.* The Messiah, ver. 11. ¶ *Which* sword *proceeded out of his mouth.* Notes on ver. 15. That is, they were cut down by a *word*. They fell before him as he spake, as if they were slain by the sword. Perhaps this indicates that the effect that is to be produced when these great powers shall be destroyed is a *moral* effect; that is, that they will be subdued by the word of the Son of God. ¶ *And all the fowls were filled with their flesh.* Notes on ver. 17. An effect was produced *as if* the fowls of heaven should feed upon the carcasses of the slain.

The general idea here is, that these great Antichristian powers which had so long resisted the gospel, and prevented its being spread over the earth; which had shed so much blood in persecution, and had so long corrupted and deceived mankind, would be subdued. The true religion would be as triumphant as if the Son of God should go forth as a warrior in his own might, and secure their leaders for punishment, and give up their hosts to the birds of prey. This destruction of these great enemies—which the whole course of the interpretation leads us to suppose is still future—prepares the way for the millennial reign of the Son of God—as stated in the following chapter. The "beast" and the "false prophet" are disposed of, and there remains only the subjugation of the great dragon—the source of all this evil—to prepare the way for the long-anticipated triumph of the gospel. The subjugation of the great original source of all those evil influences is stated in ch. xx. 1-3; and then follows the account of the thousand years' rest of the saints, the resurrection of the dead, and the final judgment.

## CHAPTER XX.

### ANALYSIS OF THE CHAPTER.

This chapter, like chapters xvi. 12-21, xvii., xviii., xix., pertains to the future, and discloses things which are yet to occur. It is not to be wondered at, therefore, for the reason stated in the Notes on ch. xvi. 16, that much obscurity should hang over it, nor that it is difficult to explain it so as to remove all obscurity. The statement in this chapter, however, is distinct and clear in its *general* characteristics, and time will make all its *particular* statements free from ambiguity.

In the previous chapter, an account is given of the final destruction of *two* of the most formidable enemies of the church, and consequently the removal of two of the hindrances to the universal spread of the gospel—the beast and the false prophet—the Papal and the Mahometan powers. But one obstacle remains to be removed—the power of Satan as concentrated and manifested in the form of *Pagan* power. These three powers it was said (ch. xvi. 13, 14) would concentrate their forces as the time of the final triumph of Christianity drew on; and with these the last great battle was to be fought. Two of these have been subdued; the conquest over the other remains, and Satan is to be arrested and bound for a thousand years. He is then to be released for a time, and afterwards finally destroyed, and at that period the end will come.

The chapter comprises the following parts:—

I. The binding of Satan, ver. 1-3. An angel comes down from heaven with the key of the bottomless pit, and a great chain in his hand, and seizes upon the dragon, and casts him into the pit, that for a thousand years he should deceive the nations no more. The great enemy of God and his cause is thus made a prisoner, and is restrained from making war in any form against the church. The way is thus prepared for the peace and triumph which follow.

II. The millennium, ver. 4-6. John sees thrones, and persons sitting on them; he sees the souls of those who were beheaded for the witness of Jesus, and for the word of God—those who had not worshipped the beast nor his image—living and reigning with Christ during the thousand years: the spirits of the martyrs revived, and becoming again the reigning spirit on earth. This he calls the first resurrection; and on all such he says the second death has no power. Temporal death they might experience—for such the martyrs had experienced—but over them the second death has no dominion, for they live and reign with the Saviour. This is properly the millennium—the long period when the principles of true religion will have the ascendency on the earth, *as if* the martyrs and confessors—the most devoted and eminent Christians of other times—should appear again upon the earth, and as if their spirit should become the reigning and pervading spirit of all who professed the Christian name.

III. The release of Satan, ver. 7, 8. After the thousand years of peace and triumph shall have expired, Satan will be released from his prison, and will be permitted to go out and deceive the nations which are in the four quarters of the earth, and gather them together to battle; that is, a state of things will exist *as if* Satan were then released. There will be again an outbreak of sin on the earth, and a conflict with the principles of religion, as if an innumerable multitude of opposers should be marshalled for the conflict by the great author of all evil.

IV. The final subjugation of Satan, and destruction of his power on the earth, ver. 9, 10. After the temporary and partial outbreak of evil (ver. 7, 8), Satan and his hosts will be entirely destroyed. The destruction will be *as if* fire should come down from heaven to devour the assembled hosts (ver. 9), and as if Satan, the great leader of evil, should be cast into the same lake where the beast and false prophet are to be tormented for ever. Then the church will be delivered from *all* its enemies, and religion henceforward will be triumphant. How *long* the interval will be between *this* state and that next disclosed (ver. 11-15)—the final judgment—is not stated. The eye of the seer glances from one to the other, but there is nothing to forbid the supposition, that, according to the laws of prophetic vision, there may be a long interval in which righteousness shall reign upon the earth. Comp. Intro. to Isaiah, § 7, III. (3)-(5).

V. The final judgment, ver. 11-15. This closes the *earthly* scene. Henceforward (ch. xxi., xxii.) the scene is transferred to heaven—the abode of the redeemed. The last judgment is the winding up of the earthly affairs. The enemies of the church are all long since destroyed; the world has experienced, perhaps for a long series of ages, the full influence of the gospel; countless millions have been, we may suppose, brought under its power; and then at last, in the winding up of human affairs, comes the judgment of the great day, when the dead, small and great, shall stand before God; when the sea shall give up its dead; when death and hell shall give up the dead that are in them; when the records of human actions shall be opened, and all shall be judged according to their works; and when all who are not found written in the book of life shall be cast into the lake of fire. This is the earthly consummation; henceforward the saints shall reign in glory—the New Jerusalem above, ch. xxi., xxii.

In order to prepare the way for a proper understanding of this chapter, the following additional remarks may be here made:—

(*a*) The design of this book did not demand a minute *detail* of the events which would occur in the consummation of human affairs. The main purpose was to trace the history of the chuch to the scene of the final triumph when all its enemies would be overthrown, and when religion would be permanently established upon the earth. Hence, though in the previous chapters we have a detailed account of the persecutions that would be endured; of the enemies that would rise up against the church, and of their complete ultimate overthrow—leaving religion triumphant on the earth—yet we have no minute statement of what will occur in the millennium. A rapid view is taken of the closing scenes of the earth's history, and the general results only are stated. It would not be strange, therefore, if there should be much in this that would seem to be enigmatical and obscure, especially as it is now all in the future.

(*b*) There may be long intervening periods between the events thus thrown together into the final grouping. We are not to suppose necessarily that these events will succeed each other immediately, or that they will be of short duration. Between these events thus hastily sketched, there may be long intervals that are not described, and whose general character is scarcely even glanced at. This results from the very nature of the prophetic vision, as described in the Intro. to Isaiah, § 7, III. (3)-(5). This may be illustrated by the view which we have in looking at a landscape. When one is placed in a favourable situation, he can mark distinctly the *order* of the objects in it —the succession—the *grouping*. He can tell what objects appear to him to lie *near* to each other, and are apparently in juxtaposition. But there are objects which, in such a vision, the eye cannot take in, and which would not be exhibited by any description which might be given of the view taken. Hills in the distant view may seem to lie near each other; one may seem to rise just back of another, and to the eye they may seem to constitute parts of the same mountain, and yet *between* them there may be deep and fertile vales, smiling villages, running streams, beautiful gardens and waterfalls, which the eye cannot take in, and the *extent* of which it may be wholly impossible to conjecture; and a description of the whole scene, as it *appears* to the observer, would convey no idea of the actual extent of the intervals. So it is in the prophecies. Between the events which are to occur hereafter, as seen in vision, there may be long intervals, but the length of these intervals the prophet may have left us no means of determining. See these thoughts more fully illustrated in the Introduction to Isaiah, as above referred to.

What is here stated may have occurred in the vision which John had of the future, as described in this chapter. Time is marked in the prophetic description until the fall of the great enemy of the church; beyond that it does not seem to have been regarded as necessary to determine the actual duration of the events referred to. Comp. Professor Stuart, *Com.* ii. 353, 354.

(*c*) These views are sustained by the most cursory glance of the chapter before us. There is none of the *detail* which we have found in the previous portions of the book—for such detail was not necessary to the accomplishment of the design of the book. The grand purpose was to show *that Christianity would finally triumph*, and hence the detailed description is carried on until that occurs, and beyond that we have only the most *general* statements. Thus, in this chapter, the *great* events that are to occur are merely hinted at. The events of a thousand years; the invasion by Gog and Magog; the ultimate confinement and punishment of Satan; the general judgment,—are all crowded into the space of *twelve* verses. This shows that the distant future is only *glanced at* by the writer; and we should not wonder, therefore, if it should be found to be obscure, nor should we regard it as strange that much is left to be made clear by the events themselves when they shall occur.

(*d*) The *end* is triumphant and glorious. We are assured that every enemy of the church will be slain, and that there will be a long period of happiness, prosperity, and peace. "The eye of hope," says Professor Stuart, beautifully, "is directed forward, and sees the thousand years of uninterrupted prosperity; then the sudden destruction of a new and fatal enemy; and all the rest is left to joyful anticipation. When all clouds are swept from the face of the sky, why should not the sun shine forth in all his glory? I cannot, therefore, doubt that the setting sun of the church on earth is to be as a heaven of unclouded splendour. Peaceful and triumphant will be her latest age. The number of the redeemed will be augmented beyond all computation; and the promise made from the beginning, that 'the seed of the woman should bruise the serpent's head,' will be fulfilled in all its extent, and with a divine plenitude of meaning. The understanding and pious reader closes the book with admiration, with wonder, with delight, with lofty anticipations of the future, and with undaunted resolution to follow on in the steps of those who, through faith and patience, have inherited the promises, and entered into everlasting rest," vol. ii. pp. 354, 355.

## CHAPTER XX.

AND I saw an angel come down from heaven, having the ᵃkey

a ch.1.18; 9.1.

of the bottomless pit and a great chain in his hand.

2 And he laid hold on the ᵇdra-

b ch.12.9.

1. *And I saw an angel come down from heaven.* Comp. Notes on ch. x. 1. He does not say whether *this* angel had appeared to him before, but the impression is rather that it was a different one. The whole character of the composition of the book leads us to suppose that different angels were employed to make these communications to John, and that, in fact, in the progress of things disclosed in the book, he had intercourse with a considerable number of the heavenly inhabitants. The scene that is recorded here occurred *after* the destruction of the beast and the false prophet (ch. xix. 18-21), and therefore, according to the principles expressed in the explanation of the previous chapters, what is intended to be described here will take place *after* the final destruction of the Papal and Mahometan powers. ¶ *Having the key of the bottomless pit.* See Notes on ch. i. 18; ix. 1. The fact that he has the key of that underworld is designed to denote here, that he can fasten it on Satan so that it shall become his prison. ¶ *And a great chain in his hand.* With which to bind the dragon, ver. 2. It is called *great* because of the strength of him that was to be bound. The chain only appears to have been in his hand. Perhaps the key was suspended to his side.

2. *And he laid hold on.* Seized him by violence—ἐκράτησε. The word denotes the employment of strength or force; and it implies that he had power superior to that of the dragon. Comp. Mat. xiv. 3; xviii. 28; xxi. 46; xxii. 6; xxvi. 4. We can at once see the propriety of the use of this word in this connection. The great enemy to be bound has himself mighty power, and can be overcome only by a superior. This may teach us that it is only a power from heaven that can destroy the empire of Satan in the world; and *perhaps* it may teach us that the interposition of angels will be employed in bringing in the glorious state of the millennium. Why should it not be? ¶ *The dragon.* See Notes on ch. xii. 2. Comp. ch. xii. 4, 7, 13, 16, 17; xiii. 2, 4, 11; xvi. 13. There can be no doubt as to the meaning of the word here; for it is expressly said to mean the devil, and Satan. It would seem, however, that it refers to some manifestation of the power of Satan that would exist *after* the beast and false prophet—that is, the Papacy and Mahometanism—should be destroyed, and probably the *main* reference is to the still existing power of Paganism. Comp. Notes on ch. xvi. 13, 14. It *may* include, however, all the forms of wickedness which Satan shall have kept up on the earth, and all the modes of evil by which he will endeavour to perpetuate his reign. ¶ *That old serpent.* This is undoubtedly an allusion to the serpent that deceived our first parents (Ge. iii. 1, seq.), and therefore a proof that it was Satan that, under the form of a serpent, deceived them. Comp. Notes on ch. xii. 3. ¶ *Which is the Devil.* On the meaning of this word, see Notes on Mat. iv. 1. ¶ *And Satan.* On the meaning of this word, see Notes on Job i. 6. In regard to the *repetition* of the names of that great enemy of God and the church here, Mr. Taylor, in the *Fragments to Calmet's Dictionary*, No. 152, says that this "almost resembles a modern Old Bailey indictment, in which special care is taken to identify the culprit, by a sufficient number of *aliases*. An angel from heaven, having the key of the prison of the abyss, and a great chain to secure the prisoner, 'apprehended the dragon, *alias* the old serpent, *alias* the devil, *alias* the Satan, *alias* the seducer of the world,' who was sentenced to a thousand years' imprisonment." The *object* here, however, seems to be not so much to *identify* the culprit by these *aliases*, as to show that under whatever forms, and by whatever names he had appeared, it was always the same being, and that now the author of the whole evil would be arrested. Thus the one great enemy sometimes has appeared in a form that would be best represented by a fierce and fiery dragon; at another, in a form that would be best represented by a cunning and subtle serpent; now in a form to which the word devil, or accuser, would be most appropriate; and now in a form in which the word Satan—an adversary—would be most expressive of what he does. In these various forms, and under these various names, he has ruled the

gon, that old serpent, which is the Devil, and Satan, and <sup>c</sup>bound him a thousand years,

3 And cast him into the bottomless pit, and shut him up, and <sup>d</sup>set a seal upon him that he should deceive the nations no more, till the thousand years should be fulfilled: and after that he must be loosed a little season.

c 2 Pe.2.4; Jude 6.  d Da.6.17.

fallen world; and when this one great enemy shall be seized and imprisoned, all these forms of evil will, of course, come to an end. ¶ *A thousand years.* This is the period usually designated as the MILLENNIUM—for the word millennium means *a thousand years.* It is on this passage that the whole doctrine of the millennium *as such* has been founded. It is true that there are elsewhere in the Scriptures abundant promises that the gospel will ultimately spread over the world; but the notion of a *millennium as such* is found in this passage alone. It is, however, enough to establish the doctrine, if its meaning be correctly ascertained; for it is a just rule in interpreting the Bible, that the clearly-ascertained sense of a single passage of Scripture is sufficient to establish the truth of a doctrine. The fact, however, that this passage stands alone in this respect, makes it the more important to endeavour accurately to determine its meaning. There are but three ways in which the phrase "a thousand years" can be understood here: either (*a*) literally; or (*b*) in the prophetic use of the term, where a day would stand for a year, thus making a period of three hundred and sixty thousand years; or (*c*) figuratively, supposing that it refers to a long but indefinite period of time. It may be impossible to determine *which* of these periods is intended, though the first has been generally supposed to be the true one, and hence the common notion of the millennium. There is nothing, however, in the use of the language here, as there would be nothing contrary to the common use of symbols in this book in regard to time, in the supposition that this was designed to describe the longest period here suggested, or that it is meant that the world shall enjoy a reign of peace and righteousness during the long period of three hundred and sixty thousand years. Indeed, there are some things in the arrangements of nature which look as if it were contemplated that the earth would continue under a reign of righteousness through a vastly long period in the future.

3. *And cast him into the bottomless pit.* See Notes on ch. ix. 1. A state of peace and prosperity would exist *as if* Satan, the great disturber, were confined in the nether world as a prisoner. ¶ *And shut him up.* Closed the massive doors of the dark prison-house upon him. Comp. Notes on Job x. 21, 22. ¶ *And set a seal upon him.* Or, rather, "upon *it*"—ἐπάνω αὐτοῦ. The seal was placed upon the *door* or *gate* of the prison, not because this would fasten the gate or door of itself, and make it secure, for this was secured by the key, but because it prevented intrusion, or any secret opening of it without its being known. See Notes on Da. vi. 17, and Mat. xxvii. 66. The idea here is, that every precaution was taken for absolute security. ¶ *That he should deceive the nations no more.* That is, during the thousand years. Comp. Notes on ch. xii. 9. ¶ *Till the thousand years should be fulfilled.* That is, during that period there will be a state of things upon the earth *as if* Satan should be withdrawn from the world, and confined in the great prison where he is ultimately to dwell for ever. ¶ *And after that he must be loosed a little season.* See ver. 7, 8. That is, a state of things will then exist, for a brief period, *as if* he were again released from his prison-house, and suffered to go abroad upon the earth. The phrase "a little season"—μικρὸν χρόνον, *little time*—denotes properly that this would be brief as compared with the thousand years. No intimation is given as to the exact time, and it is impossible to conjecture how long it will be. All the circumstances stated, however, here and in ver. 7-10, would lead us to suppose that what is referred to will be like the sudden outbreak of a rebellion in a time of general peace, but which will soon be quelled.

§ *a.—Condition of the world in the period referred to in ver. 1-3.*

It may be proper, in order to a correct understanding of this chapter, to present a brief summary under the different parts (see the Analysis of the chapter) of what, according to the interpretation proposed, may be expected to be the condition of things in the time referred to.

On the portion now before us (ver. 1-3), according to the interpretation proposed, the following suggestions may be made:—

(1) This will be subsequent to the downfall of the Papacy and the termination of the Mahometan power in the world. Of course, then, this lies in the future—how far in the future it is impossible to determine. The interpretation of the various portions of this book, and the book of Daniel, have, however, led to the conclusion that the termination of those powers cannot now be remote. If so, we are on the eve of important events in the world's history. The affairs of the world look as if things were tending to a fulfilment of the prophecies so understood.

(2) It will be a condition of the world *as if* Satan were bound; that is, where his influences will be suspended, and the principles of virtue and religion will prevail. According to the interpretation of the previous chapters, it will be a state in which all that has existed, and that now exists, in the Papacy to corrupt mankind, to maintain error, and to prevent the prevalence of free and liberal principles, will cease; in which all that there now is in the Mahometan system to fetter and enslave mankind—now controlling more than one hundred and twenty millions of the race—shall have come to an end; and in which, in a great measure, all that occurs under the direct influence of Satan in causing or perpetuating slavery, war, intemperance, lust, avarice, disorder, scepticism, atheism, will be checked and stayed. It is proper to say, however, that this passage does not require us to suppose that there will be a *total cessation* of Satanic influence in the earth during that period. Satan will, indeed, be bound and restrained as to his former influence and power. But there will be no change in the character of man as he comes into the world. There will still be corrupt passions in the human heart. Though greatly restrained, and though there will be a general prevalence of righteousness on the earth, yet we are to remember that the race is fallen, and that even then, if restraint should be taken away, man would act out his fallen nature. This fact, if remembered, will make it appear less strange that, after this period of prevalent righteousness, Satan should be represented as loosed again, and as able once more for a time to deceive the nations.

(3) It will be a period of long duration. On the supposition that it is to be literally a period of one thousand years, this is in itself long, and will give, especially under the circumstances, opportunity for a vast progress in human affairs. To form some idea of the length of the period, we need only place ourselves in imagination *back* for a thousand years—say in the middle of the ninth century—and look at the condition of the world then, and think of the vast changes in human affairs that have occurred during that period. It is to be remembered, also, that if the millennial period were soon to commence, it would find the world in a far different state in reference to future progress from what it was in the ninth century, and that it would *start off*, so to speak, with all the advantages in the arts and sciences which have been accumulated in all the past periods of the world. Even if there were no special divine interposition, it might be presumed that the race, in such circumstances, would make great and surprising advances in the long period of a thousand years. And here a very striking remark of Mr. Hugh Miller may be introduced as illustrating the subject. "It has been remarked by some student of the Apocalypse," says he, "that the course of predicted events at first moves slowly, as one after one, six of seven seals are opened; that, on the opening of the seventh seal, the progress is so considerably quickened that the seventh period proves as fertile in events—represented by the sounding of the seven trumpets—as the foregoing six taken together; and that on the seventh trumpet, so great is the further acceleration, that there is an amount of incident condensed in this seventh part of the seventh period equal, as in the former case, to that of all the previous six parts in one. There are three cycles, it has been said, in the scheme—cycle within cycle—the second comprised within a seventh portion of the first, and the third within a seventh portion of the second. Be this as it may, we may, at least, see something that exceedingly resembles it in that actual economy of change and revolution manifested in English history for the last two centuries. *It would seem as if events, in their downward course,*

had come under the influence of that *law of gravitation through which falling bodies increase in speed, as they descend, according to the squares of the distance"* (*First Impressions of England and its People*, pp. vii. viii.). If to this we add the supposition, which we have seen (Notes on ver. 2) to be by no means improbable, that it is intended, in the description of the millennium in this chapter, that the world will continue under a reign of peace and righteousness for the long period of three hundred and sixty thousand years, it is impossible to anticipate what progress will be made during that period, or to enumerate the numbers that will be saved. On this subject, see some very interesting remarks in the *Old Red Sandstone*, by Hugh Miller, pp. 248-250, 258, 259. Comp. Professor Hitchcock's *Religion and Geology*, pp. 370-409.

(4) What, then, will be the state of things during that long period of a thousand years?

(*a*) There will be a great increase in the population of the globe. Let wars cease, and intemperance cease, and slavery cease, and the numberless passions that now shorten life be stayed, and it is easy to see that there must be a vast augmentation in the number of the human species.

(*b*) There will be a general diffusion of intelligence upon the earth. Every circumstance would be favourable to it, and the world would be in a condition to make rapid advances in knowledge, Da. xii. 4.

(*c*) That period will be characterized by the universal diffusion of revealed truth, Is. xi. 9; xxv. 7.

(*d*) It will be marked by unlimited subjection to the sceptre of Christ, Ps. ii. 7; xxii. 27-29; Is. ii. 2, 3; lxvi. 23; Zec. ix. 10; xiv. 9; Mat. xiii. 31, 32; Re. xi. 15.

(*e*) There will be great progress in all that tends to promote the welfare of man. We are not to suppose that the resources of nature are exhausted. Nature gives no signs of exhaustion or decay. In the future there is no reason to doubt that there will yet be discoveries and inventions more surprising and wonderful than the art of printing, or the use of steam, or the magnetic telegraph. There are profounder secrets of nature that may be delivered up than any of these, and 'the world is tending to their development.

(*f*) It will be a period of the universal reign of peace. The attention of mankind will be turned to the things which tend to promote the welfare of the race, and advance the best interests of society. The single fact that wars shall cease will make an inconceivable difference in the aspect of the world; for if universal peace shall prevail through the long period of the millennium, and the wealth, the talent, and the science now employed in human butchery shall be devoted to the interests of agriculture, the mechanical arts, learning, and religion, it is impossible now to estimate the progress which the race will make, and the changes which will be produced on the earth. For Scripture *proofs* that it will be a time of universal peace, see Is. ii. 4; xi. 6-9; Mi. iv. 3.

(*g*) There will be a *general* prevalence of evangelical religion. This is apparent in the entire description in this passage, for the two most formidable opposing powers that religion has ever known—the beast and the false prophet—will be destroyed, and Satan will be bound. In this long period, therefore, we are to suppose that the gospel will exert its fair influence on governments, on families, on individuals; in the intercourse of neighbours, and in the intercourse of nations. God will be worshipped in spirit and in truth, and not in the mere *forms* of devotion; and temperance, truth, liberty, social order, honesty, and love, will prevail over the world.

(*h*) It will be a time when the Hebrew people—the Jews—will be brought to the knowledge of the truth, and will embrace the Messiah whom their fathers crucified, Zec. xii. 10; xiii. 1; Ro. xi. 26-29.

(*i*) Yet we are not necessarily to suppose that *all* the world will be absolutely and entirely brought under the power of the gospel. There will be still on the earth the remains of wickedness in the corrupted human heart, and there will be so much *tendency* to sin in the human soul, that Satan, when released for a time (ver. 7, 8), will be able once more to deceive mankind, and to array a formidable force, represented by Gog and Magog, against the cause of truth and righteousness. We are not to suppose that the nature of mankind, as fallen, will be essentially changed, or that there may not be sin enough in the human heart to make it capable of the same opposition to the

# CHAPTER XX.

**4** And I saw *ethrones, and they sat upon them, and ƒjudgment was given unto them: and *g I saw* the souls of them that were beheaded

*e* Da.7.9,22,27; Lu.22.30.  ƒ 1 Co.6.2,3.  *g* ch.6.9.

gospel of God which has thus far been evinced in all ages. From causes which are not fully stated (ver. 8, 9), Satan will be enabled once more to rouse up their enmity, and to make one more desperate effort to destroy the kingdom of the Redeemer by rallying his forces for a conflict. See these views illustrated in the work entitled *Christ's Second Coming*, by Rev. David Brown, of St. James' Free Church, Glasgow, pp. 398-442; New York, 1851.

4. *And I saw thrones*—θρόνους. See ch. i. 4; iii. 21; iv. 3, 4. John here simply says, that he saw in vision *thrones*, with persons sitting on them, but without intimating who they were that sat on them. It is not the throne of God that is now revealed, for the word is in the plural number, though the writer does not hint how *many* thrones there were. It *is* intimated, however, that these thrones were placed with some reference to pronouncing a judgment, or determining the destiny of some portion of mankind, for it is immediately added, "and judgment was given unto them." There is considerable resemblance, in many respects, between this and the statement in Daniel (vii. 9): "I beheld till the thrones were cast down, and the Ancient of days did sit;" or, as it should be rendered, "I beheld"—that is, I continued to look—"until the thrones were *placed* or *set*," to wit, for the purposes of judgment. See Notes on that passage. So John here sees, as the termination of human affairs approaches, thrones placed with reference to a determination of the destiny of some portion of the race, *as if* they were now to have a trial, and to receive a sentence of acquittal or condemnation. The *persons* on whom this judgment is to pass are specified, in the course of the verse, as those who were "beheaded for the witness of Jesus, who had the word of God, who had not worshipped the beast," &c. The *time* when this was to occur manifestly was at the beginning of the thousand years. ¶ *And they sat upon them.* Who sat on them is not mentioned. The natural construction is, that *judges* sat on them, or that persons sat on them to whom judgment was intrusted. The language is such as would be used on the supposition either that he had mentioned the subject before, so that he would be readily understood, or that, from some other cause, it was so well understood that there was no necessity for mentioning who they were. John seems to have assumed that it would be understood who were meant. And yet to us it is not entirely clear; for John has not before this given us any such intimation that we can determine with certainty what is intended. The probable construction is, that those are referred to to whom it appropriately belonged to occupy such seats of judgment, and who they are is to be determined from other parts of the Scriptures. In Mat. xix. 28, the Saviour says to his apostles, "When the Son of man shall sit on the throne of his glory, ye also shall sit upon twelve thrones, judging the twelve tribes of Israel." In 1 Co. vi. 2, Paul asks the question, "Do ye not know that the saints shall judge the world?" The meaning as thus explained is, that Christians will, in some way, be employed in judging the world; that is, that they will be exalted to the right hand of the Judge, and be elevated to a station of honour, *as if* they were associated with the Son of God in the judgment. Something of that kind is, doubtless, referred to here; and John probably means to say that he saw the thrones placed on which those will sit who will be employed in judging the world. If the apostles are specially referred to, it was natural that John, eminent for modesty, should not particularly mention them, as he was one of them, and as the true allusion would be readily understood. ¶ *And judgment was given unto them.* The power of pronouncing sentence in the case referred to was conferred on them, and they proceeded to exercise that power. This was not in relation to the whole race of mankind, but to the martyrs, and to those who, amidst many temptations and trials, had kept themselves pure. The sentence which is to be passed would seem to be that in consequence of which they are to be permitted to "live and reign with Christ a thousand years." The *form* of this expressed approval is that of a resurrection and judgment; whether this be the *literal* mode is another inquiry, and will properly be considered when the exposition

for the witness of Jesus, and for the word of God, and which had not worshipped the beast, neither his image, neither had received *his*

of the passage shall have been given. ¶ *And* I saw *the souls of them*. This is a very important expression in regard to the meaning of the whole passage. John says he saw *the souls*—not *the bodies*. If the obvious meaning of this be the correct meaning; if he saw the *souls* of the martyrs, not the *bodies*, this would seem to exclude the notion of a *literal* resurrection, and consequently overturn many of the theories of a literal resurrection, and of a literal reign of the saints with Christ during the thousand years of the millennium. The doctrine of the last resurrection, as everywhere stated in the Scripture, is, that the *body* will be raised up, and not merely that the *soul will live* (see 1 Co. xv., and the Notes on that chapter); and consequently John must mean to refer in this place to something different from that resurrection, or to *any* proper resurrection of the dead as the expression is commonly understood. The doctrine which has been held, and is held, by those who maintain that there will be a *literal resurrection* of the saints to reign with Christ during a thousand years, can receive no support from this passage, for there is no ambiguity respecting the word *souls*—ψυχάς—as used here. By no possible construction can it mean the *bodies* of the saints. If John had intended to state that the saints, as such, would be raised as they will be at the last day, it is clear that he would not have used this language, but would have employed the common language of the New Testament to denote it. The language here does not express the doctrine of the resurrection of the body; and if no other language but this had been used in the New Testament, the doctrine of the resurrection, as now taught and received, could not be established. These considerations make it clear to my mind that John did not mean to teach that there would be a *literal* resurrection of the saints, that they might live and reign with Christ personally during the period of a thousand years. There was undoubtedly something that might be *compared* with the resurrection, and that might, in some proper sense, be *called* a resurrection (ver. 5, 6), but there is not the slightest intimation that it would be a resurrection of the *body*, or that it would be identical with the *final* resurrection.

John undoubtedly intends to describe some honour conferred on the *spirits* or *souls* of the saints and martyrs during this long period, *as if* they were raised from the dead, or which might be represented by a resurrection from the dead. What that honour is to be, is expressed by their "*living* and *reigning* with Christ." The meaning of this will be explained in the exposition of these words; but the word used here is fatal to the notion of a literal resurrection and a personal reign with Christ on the earth. ¶ *That were beheaded*. The word here used—πελεκίζω—occurs nowhere else in the New Testament. It properly means, *to axe*, that is, to hew or cut with an axe—from πέλεκυς, axe. Hence it means to behead with an axe. This was a common mode of execution among the Romans, and doubtless many of the Christian martyrs suffered in this manner; but "it cannot be supposed to have been the intention of the writer to confine the rewards of martyrs to those who suffered in this particular way; for this specific and ignominious method of punishment is designated merely as the symbol of any and every kind of martyrdom" (Professor Stuart). ¶ *For the witness of Jesus*. As witnesses of Jesus; or bearing in this way their testimony to the truth of his religion. See Notes on ch. i. 9; comp. ch. vi. 9. ¶ *And for the Word of God*. See Notes on ch. i. 9. ¶ *Which had not worshipped the beast*. Who had remained faithful to the principles of the true religion, and had resisted all the attempts made to seduce them from the faith, even the temptations and allurements in the times of the Papacy. See this language explained in the Notes on ch. xiii. 4. ¶ *Neither his image*. Notes on ch. xiii. 14, 15. ¶ *Neither had received* his *mark upon their foreheads, or in their hands*. See Notes on ch. xiii. 16. ¶ *And they lived*—ἔζησαν, from ζάω, *to live*. Very much, in the whole passage, depends on this word. The meanings given to the word by Professor Robinson (*Lex*.) are the following:—(*a*) to live, to have life, spoken of physical life and existence; (*b*) to live, that is, to sustain life, to live *on* or *by* anything; (*c*) to live in any way, to pass one's life in any manner; (*d*) to live and prosper; to be blessed. It *may* be applied to those who were before dead (Mat. ix. 18; Mar.

mark upon their foreheads, or in their hands; and they lived and

xvi. 11; Lu. xxiv. 23; Jn. v. 25; Ac. i. 3; ix. 41), but it does not necessarily imply this, nor does the mere use of the word *suggest* it. It is the proper notion of living, or having life *now*, whatever was the former state — whether nonexistence, death, sickness, or health. The mind, in the use of this word, is fixed on the *present as a state of living*. It is not necessarily in contrast with a former state *as dead*, but it is on the fact that they are now *alive*. As, however, there is reference, in the passage before us, to the fact that a portion of those mentioned had been "beheaded for the witness of Jesus," it is to be admitted that the word here refers, in some sense, to that fact. They were put to death in the body, but their "*souls*" were now seen to be alive. They had not ceased *to be*, but they lived and reigned with Christ *as if* they had been raised up from the dead. And when this is said of the "*souls*" of those who were beheaded, and who were seen to reign with Christ, it cannot mean (*a*) that their *souls* came to life again, for there is no intimation that they had for a moment ceased to exist; nor (*b*) that they then became *immortal*, for that was always true of them; nor (*c*) that there was any literal *resurrection of the body*, as Professor Stuart (ii. 360, 475, 476) supposes, and as is supposed by those who hold to a literal reign of Christ on the earth, for there is no intimation of the resurrection of the *body*. The meaning, then, so far as the language is concerned, must be, that there would exist, at the time of the thousand years, a state of things *as if* the martyrs were raised up from the dead—an honouring of the martyrs *as if* they should live and reign with Christ. Their names would be vindicated; their principles would be revived; they would be exalted in public estimation above other men; they would be raised from the low rank in which they were held by the world in times of persecution to a state which might well be represented by their sitting with Christ on the throne of government, and by their being made visible attendants on his glorious kingdom. This would not occur in respect to the rest of the dead—even the pious dead (ver. 5)—for *their* honours and rewards would be reserved for the great day when *all* the dead should be judged ac-

*h* reigned with Christ a thousand years.

*h* ch. 5.10.

cording to their deeds. In this view of the meaning of this passage there is nothing that forbids us to suppose that the martyrs will be *conscious* of the honour thus done to their names, their memory, and their principles on earth, or that this consciousness will increase their joy even in heaven. This sense of the passage is thus expressed, substantially, by Archbishop Whately (*Essays on the Future State*): "It may signify not the literal raising of dead men, but the raising up of an increased Christian zeal and holiness; the revival in the Christian church, or in some considerable portion of it, of the *spirit* and *energy* of the noble martyrs of old (even as John the Baptist came in the spirit and power of Elias), so that Christian principles shall be displayed in action throughout the world in an infinitely greater degree than ever before." This view of the signification of the word *lived* is sustained by its use elsewhere in the Scriptures and by its common use among men. Thus in this very book, ch. xi. 11: "And after three days and a half, the Spirit of *life* from God entered into them, and they stood upon their feet." So in Ezekiel, in speaking of the restoration of the Jews: "Thus saith the Lord God, O my people, *I will open your graves, and cause you to come up out of your graves*, and bring you into the land of Israel. And ye shall know that I am the Lord, when I have opened your graves, and brought you up out of your graves, and shall put my Spirit in you, and ye shall *live*," ch. xxvii. 12-14. So in Ho. vi. 2: "After two days he will *revive* us [cause us to live again]; in the third day he will raise us up, and we shall *live* in his sight." So in the parable of the prodigal son: "This thy brother was *dead*, and *is alive again*," Lu. xv. 32. So in Is. xxvi. 19: "Thy dead men shall *live*, together with my dead body shall they arise." The following extract, from D'Aubigné's *History of the Reformation*, will show how natural it is to use the *very* language employed here when the idea is intended to be conveyed of reviving former principles *as if* the men who held them should be raised to life again. It is the language of the martyr John Huss, who, in speaking of himself in view of a remarkable dream that he had, said, "I am no dreamer, but I maintain this for

# REVELATION. [A.D. 96.

**5** But the rest of the dead lived not again till the thousand years were finished. This *is* the first resurrection.

**6** Blessed and holy *is* he that hath part in the first resurrection: on such the *ⁱsecond death hath no

*i* ch.2.11; 21.8.

certain, that the image of Christ will never be effaced. They [his enemies] have wished to destroy it, but it shall be painted afresh in all hearts by much better preachers than myself. The nation that loves Christ will rejoice at this. *And I, awaking from among the dead, and rising, so to speak, from my grave, shall leap with great joy.*" So a Brief addressed by Pope Adrian to the Diet at Nuremberg contains these words: "The heretics Huss and Jerome *are now alive again* in the person of Martin Luther." For a further illustration of the passage see the remarks which follow (§ *b*) on the state of things which may be expected to exist in the time referred to in ver. 4-6. ¶ *And reigned with Christ.* Were exalted in their principles, and in their personal happiness in heaven, *as if* they occupied the throne with him, and personally shared his honours and his triumphs. Who can tell, also, whether they may not be employed in special services of mercy, in administering the affairs of his government during that bright and happy period? ¶ *A thousand years.* During the period when Satan will be bound, and when the true religion will have the ascendency in the earth. Notes on ver. 2.

5. *But the rest of the dead.* In contradistinction from the beheaded martyrs, and from those who had kept themselves pure in the times of great temptation. The phrase "rest of the dead" here would most naturally refer to the *same general class* which was before mentioned—the pious dead. The meaning is, that the martyrs would be honoured as if they were raised up and the others not—that is, that special respect would be shown to their principles, their memory, and their character. In other words, *special* honour would be shown *to a spirit of eminent piety* during that period above the *common* and *ordinary* piety which has been manifested in the church. The "rest of the dead"—the pious dead—would indeed be raised up and rewarded, but they would occupy comparatively humble places, *as if* they did not partake in the exalted triumphs when the world should be subdued to the Saviour. Their places in honour, in rank, and in reward would be *beneath* that of those who in fiery times had maintained unshaken fidelity to the cause of truth. ¶ *Lived not.* On the word *lived* see Notes on ver. 4. That is, they lived not during that period in the peculiar sense in which it is said (ver. 4) that the eminent saints and martyrs lived. They did not come into remembrance; their principles were not what then characterized the church; they did not see, as the martyrs did, *their* principles and mode of life in the ascendency, and consequently they had not the augmented happiness and honour which the more eminent saints and martyrs had. ¶ *Until the thousand years were finished.* Then all who were truly the children of God, though some might be less eminent than others had been, would come into remembrance, and would have their proper place in the rewards of heaven. The *language* here is not necessarily to be interpreted as meaning that they *would* be raised up then, or would live then, whatever may be true on that point. It is merely an emphatic mode of affirming that *up to that period they would not live* in the sense in which it is affirmed that the others would. But it is not affirmed that they would even then "live" immediately. A long interval *might* elapse before that would occur in the general resurrection of the dead. See the Analysis of the chapter. ¶ *This* is *the first resurrection.* The resurrection of the saints and martyrs, as specified in ver. 4. It is called the *first* resurrection in contradistinction from the second and last—the general resurrection—when all the dead will be *literally* raised up from their graves and assembled for the judgment, ver. 12. It is not necessary to suppose that what is called here the "first resurrection" will resemble the real and literal resurrection in every respect. All that is meant is, that there will be such a resemblance as to make it proper to call it *a* resurrection—a coming to life again. This will be, as explained in the Notes on ver. 4, in the honour done to the martyrs, in the restoration of their principles as the great actuating principles of the church, and perhaps in the increased happiness conferred on them in heaven, and in their being employed in promoting the cause of truth in the world.

6. *Blessed.* That is, his condition is to be regarded as a happy or a

power, but they shall be *k*priests of God and of Christ, and shall reign with him a thousand years.

*k* ch.1.6; Is.61.6.

favoured one. This is designed apparently to support and encourage those who, in the time of John, suffered persecution, or who might suffer persecution afterwards. ¶ *And holy.* That is, no one will be thus honoured who has not an established character for holiness. Holy principles will then reign, and none will be exalted to that honour who have not a character for eminent sanctity. ¶ *That hath part in the first resurrection.* That participated in it; that is, who is associated with those who are thus raised up. ¶ *On such the second death hath no power.* The "second death" is properly the death which the wicked will experience in the world of woe. See ver. 14. The meaning here is, that all who are here referred to as having part in the first resurrection will be secure against that. It will be one of the blessed privileges of heaven that there will be absolute security against DEATH in any and every form; and when we think of what death *is* here, and still more when we think of "the bitter pains of the second death," we may well call that state "blessed" in which there will be eternal exemption from either. ¶ *But they shall be priests of God and of Christ, and shall reign with him.* Notes ch. i. 6; v. 10.

§ *b.—Condition of the world in the period referred to in ver. 4-6.*

I. It is well known that this passage is the principal one which is relied on by those who advocate the doctrine of the literal reign of Christ on the earth for a thousand years, or who hold what are called the doctrines of the "second advent." The points which are maintained by those who advocate these views are substantially, (*a*) that at that period Christ will descend from heaven to reign personally upon the earth; (*b*) that he will have a central place of power and authority, probably Jerusalem; (*c*) that the righteous dead will then be raised, in such bodies as are to be immortal; (*d*) that they will be his attendants, and will participate with him in the government of the world; (*e*) that this will continue during the period of a thousand years; (*f*) that the world will be subdued and converted during this period, not by moral means, but by "a new dispensation"—by the power of the Son of God; and (*g*) that at the close of this period all the remaining dead will be raised, the judgment will take place, and the affairs of the earth will be consummated.

The opinion here adverted to was held substantially by Papias, Justin Martyr, Irenæus, Tertullian, and others among the Christian Fathers, and, it need not be said, is held by many modern expositors of the Bible, and by large numbers of Christian ministers of high standing, and other Christians. See the *Literalist, passim.* The opinion of the Christian Fathers, with which the modern "literalists," as they are called, substantially coincide, is thus stated by Mr. Elliott: "This resurrection is to be literally that of departed saints and martyrs, then at length resuscitated in the body from death and the grave; its *time* to synchronize with, or follow instantly after, the destruction of the beast Antichrist, on Christ's personal second advent; the *binding* of Satan to be an absolute restriction of the power of hell from tempting, deceiving, or injuring mankind, throughout a literal period of a thousand years, thence calculated; the *government of the earth* during its continuance to be administered by Christ and the risen saints— the latter being now ἰσάγγελοι—in nature like angels; and under it, all false religion having been put down, the Jews and saved remnant of the Gentiles been converted to Christ, the earth renovated by the fire of Antichrist's destruction, and Jerusalem made the universal capital, there will be a realization on earth of the blessedness depicted in the Old Testament prophecies, as well as perhaps of that too which is associated with the New Jerusalem in the visions of the Apocalypse—until at length this millennium having ended, and Satan gone forth to deceive the nations, the final consummation will follow; the new-raised enemies of the saints, Gog and Magog, be destroyed by fire from heaven: and then the general resurrection and judgment take place, the devil and his servants be cast into the lake of fire, and the millennial reign of the saints extend itself into one of eternal duration" (Elliott on the Apocalypse, iv. 177, 178).

Mr. Elliott's own opinion, representing, it is supposed, that of the great body of the "*literalists,*" is thus expressed: "It would seem, therefore, that in this state of things and of feeling in professing Christendom [a feeling of carnal security], all suddenly, and unexpectedly, and conspicuous over the world as the lightning that shineth from the east even unto the west, the second advent and appearing of Christ will take place; that at the accompanying voice of the archangel and trump of God, the departed saints of either dispensation will rise from their graves to meet him—alike patriarchs, and prophets, and apostles, and martyrs, and confessors—all at once and in the twinkling of an eye; and then instantly the saints living at the time will be also caught up to meet him in the air; these latter being separated out of the ungodly nations, as when a shepherd divides his sheep from the goats, and all, both dead and living saints, changed at the moment from corruption to incorruption, from dishonour to glory, though with very different degrees of glory; and so in a new angelic nature, to take part in the judging and ruling in this world. Meanwhile, with a tremendous earthquake accompanying, of violence unknown since the revolutions of primeval chaos, an earthquake under which the Roman world at least is to rock to and fro like a drunken man, the solid crust of this earth shall be broken, and fountains burst forth from its inner deep, not as once of water, but of liquid fire; and that the flames shall consume the Antichrist and his confederate kings, while the sword also does its work of slaughter; the risen saints being perhaps the attendants of the Lord's glory in this destruction of Antichrist, and assessors in his judgment on a guilty world. And then immediately the renovation of this our earth is to take place, its soil being purified by the very action of the fire, and the Spirit poured out from on high, to renew, in a yet better sense, the moral face of nature; the Shekinah, or personal glory of Christ amidst his saints, being manifested chiefly in the Holy Land and at Jerusalem, but the whole earth partaking of the blessedness; and thus the regeneration of all things, and the world's redemption from the curse, having their accomplishment, according to the promise, at the manifestation of the sons of God," iv. 224-231.*

* I have slightly abridged this passage, but have retained the sense.

To this account of the prevailing opinion of the "literalists" in interpreting the passage before us, there should be added that of Professor Stuart, who, in general, is as far as possible from sympathizing with this class of writers. He says, in his explanation of the expression "*they lived,*" in ver. 4, "There would seem to remain, therefore, only one meaning which can be consistently given to ἔζησαν [*they lived*]; viz., that they (the martyrs who renounced the beast) are now *restored to life,* viz., such life as implies the vivification of the body. Not to a union of the soul with a gross material body indeed, but with such an one as the saints in general will have at the final resurrection—a spiritual body, 1 Co. xv. 44. In no other way can this resurrection be ranked as *correlate* with the second resurrection named in the sequel,' vol. ii. p. 360. So again, Excursus vi. (vol. ii. p. 476), he says, " I do not see how we can, on the ground of exegesis, fairly avoid the conclusion that John has taught in the passage before us, that *there will be a resurrection of the martyr-saints, at the commencement of the period after Satan shall have been shut up in the dungeon of the great abyss.*" This opinion he defends at length, pp. 476-490. Professor Stuart, indeed, maintains that the martyrs thus raised up will be taken to heaven and reign with Christ *there,* and opposes the whole doctrine of the literal reign on the earth, vol. ii. p. 480. The risen saints and martyrs are to be "*enthroned* with Christ; that is, they are to be where he dwells, and where he will continue to dwell, until he shall make his descent at the final judgment day."

II. In regard to these views, as expressive of the meaning of the passage under consideration, I would make the following remarks:—

(1) There is strong *presumptive* evidence against this interpretation, and especially against the main point in the doctrine, that there will be a *literal resurrection* of the bodies of the saints at the beginning of that millennial period, to live and reign with Christ on earth, from the following circumstances:—(*a*) It is admitted, on all hands, that this doctrine, if contained in the Scriptures at all, is found in this one passage only. It is not pretended that there is, in any other place, a direct affirmation that this will literally occur, nor would the advocates for that opinion undertake

to show that it is fairly implied in any other part of the Bible. But it is strange, not to say improbable, that the doctrine of the literal resurrection of the righteous, a thousand years before the wicked, should be announced in one passage only. If it were so announced in plain and unambiguous language, I admit that the believer in the divine origin of the Scriptures would be bound to receive it; but this is so contrary to the usual method of the Scriptures on all great and important doctrines, that this circumstance should lead us at least to doubt whether the passage is correctly interpreted. The resurrection of the dead is a subject on which the Saviour often dwelt in his instructions; it is a subject which the apostles discussed very frequently and at great length in their preaching, and in their writings; it is presented by them in a great variety of forms, for the consolation of Christians in time of trouble, and with reference to the condition of the world at the winding up of human affairs; and it is strange that, in respect to so important a doctrine as this, if it be true, there is not elsewhere, in the New Testament, a hint, an intimation, an allusion, that would lead us to suppose that the righteous are to be raised in this manner. (*b*) If this is a true doctrine, it would be reasonable to expect that a clear and unambiguous statement of it would be made. Certainly, if there is but *one* statement on the subject, that might be expected to be a perfectly clear one, it would be a statement about which there could be no diversity of opinion, concerning which those who embraced it might be expected to hold the same views. But it cannot be pretended that this is so in regard to this passage. It occurs in the book which, of all the books in the Bible, is most distinguished for figures and symbols; it cannot be maintained that it is *directly* and *clearly* affirmed; and it is *not* so taught that there is any uniformity of view among those who profess to hold it. In nothing has there been greater diversity among men than in the opinions of those who profess to hold the "*literal*" views respecting the personal reign of Christ on the earth. But this fact assuredly affords *presumptive* evidence that the doctrine of the literal resurrection of the saints a thousand years before the rest of the dead, is not intended to be taught. (*c*) It is presumptive proof against this, that nothing is said of the employment of those who are raised up; of the reason why they are raised; of the new circumstances of their being; and of their condition when the thousand years shall have ended. In so important a matter as this, we can hardly suppose that the whole subject would be left to a single hint in a symbolical representation, depending on the doubtful meaning of a single word, and with nothing to enable us to determine, with absolute certainty, that this *must* be the meaning. (*d*) If it be meant that this is a description of the resurrection of the *righteous* as such—embracing *all* the righteous—then it is wholly unlike all the other descriptions of the resurrection of the righteous that we have in the Bible. Here the account is confined to "those that were beheaded for the witness of Jesus," and to "those who had not worshipped the beast." If the righteous, as such, are here referred to, why are these particular classes specified? Why are not the usual general terms employed? Why is the account of the resurrection confined to these? Elsewhere in the Scriptures, the account of the resurrection is given in the most *general* terms (comp. Mat. xxv. 41; Jn. iv. 54; v. 28, 29; Ro. ii. 7; 1 Co. xv. 23; Phi. iii. 20, 21; 2 Th. i. 10; He. ix. 28; 1 Jn. ii. 28, 29; iii. 2); and if this had been the designed reference here, it is inconceivable why the statement should be limited to the martyrs, and to those who have evinced great fidelity in the midst of temptations and allurements to apostasy. These circumstances furnish strong *presumptive* proofs, at least, against the doctrine that there is to be a literal resurrection of *all* the saints at the beginning of the millennial period. Comp. *Christ's Second Coming*, by Rev. David Brown, p. 219, seq.

(2) In reference to many of the views necessarily implied in the doctrine of the "second advent," and avowed by those who hold that doctrine, it cannot be pretended that they receive any countenance or support from this passage. In the language of Professor Stuart (*Com.* vol. ii. p. 479), there is "not a word of Christ's descent to the earth at the beginning of the millennium. Nothing of the literal assembling of the Jews in Palestine; nothing of the Messiah's temporal reign on *earth;* nothing of the overflowing abun-

dance of worldly peace and plenty." Indeed, in all this passage, there is not the remotest hint of the grandeur and magnificence of the reign of Christ as a literal king upon the earth; nothing of his having a splendid capital at Jerusalem, or anywhere else; nothing of a new dispensation of a miraculous kind; nothing of the renovation of the earth to fit it for the abode of the risen saints. All this is the mere work of fancy, and no man can pretend that it is to be found in this passage.

(3) Nor is there anything here of a literal resurrection of the *bodies* of the dead, as Professor Stuart himself supposes. It is not a little remarkable that a scholar so accurate as Professor Stuart is, and one, too, who has so little sympathy with the doctrines connected with a literal reign of Christ on the earth, should have lent the sanction of his name to perhaps the most objectionable of all the dogmas connected with that view—the opinion that the *bodies* of the saints will be raised up at the beginning of the millennial period. Of this there is not one word, one intimation, one hint, in the passage before us. John says expressly, *and as if to guard the point from all possible danger of this construction*, that he " saw the SOULS of them that were beheaded for the witness of Jesus;" he saw them "*living*" and "reigning" with Christ—raised to the exalted honour during that period, as if they had been raised from the dead; but he nowhere mentions or intimates that they were raised up from their graves; that they were clothed with bodies; that they had their residence now literally on the earth; or that they were, in any way, otherwise than disembodied spirits. There is not even one word of their having "*a spiritual body.*"

(4) There are *positive* arguments, which are perfectly decisive, against the interpretation which supposes that the bodies of the saints will be raised up at the beginning of the millennial period, to reign with Christ on the earth for a thousand years. Among these are the following:—

(*a*) If the "first resurrection" means rising from the grave in immortal and glorified bodies, we do not need the assurance (ver. 6), that "on such the second death hath no power;" that is, that they would not perish for ever. That would be a matter of course, and there was no necessity for such a statement. But if it be supposed that the main idea is that the *principles* of the martyrs and of the most eminent saints would be revived and would live, *as if* the dead were raised up, and would be manifested by those who were in *mortal* bodies—men living on the earth—then there would be a propriety in saying that all such were exempt from the danger of the *second* death. *Once*, indeed, they would die; but the *second* death could not reach them. Comp. Re. ii. 10, 11.

(*b*) In the whole passage there are but two classes of men referred to. There are those " who have part in the first resurrection;" that is, according to the supposition, *all* the saints; and there are those over whom " the second death" *has* power. Into which of these classes are we to put the myriads of men having flesh and blood who are to people the world during the millennium? They have no part in "the first resurrection," if it be a bodily one. Are they then given over to the power of the "second death?" But if the "first resurrection" be regarded as figurative and spiritual, then the statement that those who are actuated by the spirit of the martyrs and of the eminent saints, shall not experience the "second death," is seen to have meaning and pertinency.

(*c*) The mention of the *time* during which they are to reign, if it be literally understood, is contrary to the whole statement of the Bible in other places. They are to "live and reign with Christ" *a thousand years*. What, then? Are they to live no longer? Are they to reign no longer with him? This supposition is entirely contrary to the current statement in the Scriptures, which is, that they are to live and reign with him *for ever:* 1 Th. iv. 17, "*And so shall we ever be with the Lord.*" According to the views of the "literalists," the declaration that they "should live and reign with Christ," considered as the characteristic features of the millennial state, is to terminate with the thousand years—for this is the promise, according to that view, that they should thus live and reign. But it need not be said that this is wholly contrary to the current doctrine of the Bible, that they are to live and reign with him for ever.

(*d*) A further objection to this view is, that the wicked part of the world—"the rest of the dead who lived not again *until* the thousand years were finished"—must of course be expected to "live again" in the same bodily sense *when* those thousand years were finished. But, so far from this, there is no mention of their living then. When the thousand years are finished, Satan is loosed for a season; then the nations are roused to opposition against God; then there is a conflict, and the hostile forces are overthrown; and then comes the final judgment. During all this time we read of no resurrection at all. The period after this is to be filled up with something besides the resurrection of the rest of the dead." There is no intimation, as the *literal* construction, as it is claimed, would demand, that immediately after the "thousand years are finished" the "rest of the dead"— the wicked dead—would be raised up; nor is there any intimation of such a resurrection until *all* the dead are raised up for the final trial, ver. 12. But every consideration demands, if the interpretation of the "literalists" be correct, that the "rest of the dead" —the unconverted dead—should be raised up immediately after the close of the millennial period, and be raised up as a distinct and separate class.

(*e*) There is no intimation in the passage itself that the *righteous* will be raised up *as such* in this period, and the proper interpretation of the passage is contrary to that supposition. There are but two classes mentioned as having part in the first resurrection. They are those who were "beheaded for the witness of Jesus," and those who "had not worshipped the beast"—that is, the martyrs, and those who had been eminent for their fidelity to the Saviour in times of great temptation and trial. There is no mention of the resurrection of the righteous *as such*—of the resurrection of the great body of the redeemed; and if it could be shown that this refers to a *literal* resurrection, it would be impossible to apply it, according to any just rules of interpretation, to any more than the two classes that are specified. By what rules of interpretation is it made to to teach that *all* the righteous will be raised up on that occasion, and will live on the earth during that long period? In this view of the matter, the passage *does not* express the doctrine that the whole church of God will be raised bodily from the grave. And supposing it had been the design of the Spirit of God to teach this, is it credible, when there are so many clear expressions in regard to the resurrection of the dead, that so important a doctrine should have been reserved for one single passage so obscure, and where the great mass of the readers of the Bible in all ages have failed to perceive it? That is not the way in which, in the Scriptures, great and momentous doctrines are communicated to mankind.

(*f*) The fair statement in ver. 11-15 is, that *all* the dead will then be raised up and be judged. This is implied in the general expressions there used—"the dead, small and great;" the "book of life was opened"—as if *not* opened before; "the dead"—*all* the dead—"were judged out of those things which were written in the books;" "the sea gave up the dead which were in it, and death and hell (hades) delivered up the dead which were in them." This is entirely inconsistent with the supposition that a large part of the race—to wit, all the righteous—had been before raised up; had passed the solemn judgment; had been clothed with their immortal bodies, and had been admitted to a joint reign with the Saviour on his throne. In the last judgment what place are *they* to occupy? In what sense are *they* to be raised up and judged? *Would* such a representation have been made as is found in ver. 11-15, if it had been designed to teach that a large part of the race had been already raised up, and had received the approval of their judge?

(*g*) This representation is wholly inconsistent, not only with ver. 11-15, but with the uniform language of the Scriptures, *that all the righteous and the wicked will be judged together, and both at the coming of Christ*. On no point are the statements of the Bible more uniform and explicit than on this, and it would seem that the declarations had been of design so made that there should be no possibility of mistake. I refer for full proof on this point to the following passages of the New Testament:—Mat. x. 32, 33, compared with Mat. vii. 21-23; xiii. 30, 38-43; xvi. 24-27; xxv. 10, 31-46; Mar. viii. 38; Jn. v. 28, 29; Ac. xvii. 31; Ro. ii. 5-16; xiv. 10, 12; 1 Co. iii. 12-15; iv. 5; 2 Co. v. 9-11; 2 Th. i. 6-10; 1 Ti. v. 24, 25; 2 Pe. iii. 7, 10, 12; 1 Jn. ii. 28; iv. 17; Re. iii. 5; xx. 11-15; xxii. 12-15. It is utterly *impossible* to explain these passages on any other supposition than that they are intended to teach that

7 And when the thousand years are expired, Satan shall be loosed out of his prison,

the righteous and the wicked will be judged together, and both at the coming of Christ. And if this is so, it is of course impossible to explain them consistently with the view that all the righteous will have been already raised up at the beginning of the millennium in their immortal and glorified bodies, and that they have been solemnly approved by the Saviour, and admitted to a participation in his glory. Nothing could be more irreconcilable than these two views; and it seems to me, therefore, that the objections to the literal resurrection of the saints at the beginning of the millennial period are insuperable.

III. The following points, then, according to the interpretation proposed, are implied in this statement respecting the "first resurrection," and these will clearly comprise *all* that is stated on the subject.

(1) There will be a reviving, and a prevalence of the spirit which actuated the saints in the best days, and a restoration of their principles as the grand principles which will control and govern the church, *as if* the most eminent saints were raised again from the dead, and lived and acted upon the earth.

(2) Their memory will then be sacredly cherished, and they will be honoured on the earth with the honour which is due to their names, and which they should have received when in the land of the living. They will be no longer cast out and reproached; no longer held up to obloquy and scorn; no longer despised and forgotten; but there will be a reviving of sacred regard for their principles, *as if* they lived on the earth, and had the honour which was due to them.

(3) There will be a state of things upon the earth as if they thus lived and were thus honoured. Religion will no longer be trampled under foot, but will triumph. In all parts of the earth it will have the ascendency, as if the most eminent saints of past ages lived and reigned with the Son of God in his kingdom. A spiritual kingdom will be set up with the Son of God at the head of it, which will be a kingdom of eminent holiness, as if the saints of the best days of the church should come back to the earth and dwell upon it. The ruling influence in the world will be the religion of the Son of God, and the principles which have governed the most holy of his people.

(4) It may be implied that the saints and martyrs of other times will be employed by the Saviour in embassies of mercy; in visitations of grace to our world to carry forward the great work of salvation on earth. Nothing forbids the idea that the saints in heaven may be thus employed, and in this long period of a thousand years, it may be that they will be occupied in such messages and agencies of mercy to our world as they have never been before—*as if* they were raised from the dead, and were employed by the Redeemer to carry forward his purposes of mercy to mankind.

(5) In connection with these things, and in consequence of these things, they may be, during that period, exalted to higher happiness and honour in heaven. The restoration of their principles to the earth; the Christian remembrance of their virtues; the prevalence of those truths to establish which they laid down their lives, would in itself exalt them, and would increase their joy in heaven. All this would be well represented, in vision, by a resurrection of the dead; and admitting that this was all that was intended, the representation of John here would be in the highest degree appropriate. What could better symbolize it—and we must remember that this is a symbol—than to say that at the commencement of this period there was, as it were, a solemn preparation for a judgment, and that the departed dead seemed to stand there, and that a sentence was pronounced in their favour, and that they became associated with the Son of God in the honours of his kingdom, and that their principles were now to reign and triumph in the earth, and that the kingdom which they laboured to establish would be set up for a thousand years, and that, in high purposes of mercy and benevolence during that period, they would be employed in maintaining and extending the principles of religion in the world? Admitting that the Holy Spirit intended to represent these things, and these only, no more appropriate symbolical language could have been used; none that would more accord with the general style of the book of Revelation.

7. *And when the thousand years are*

8 And shall go out to deceive the nations which are in the four quarters of the earth, *'*Gog and Magog, to *ᵐ*gather them together to battle: the number of whom *is* as the sand of the sea.

*l* Eze.38.2; 39.1.     *m* ch.16.14.

---

*expired*. See ver. 2. ¶ *Satan shall be loosed out of his prison*. See ver. 3. That is, a state of things will then occur as if Satan should be for a time let loose again, and should be permitted to go as formerly over the world. No intimation is given *why* or *how* he would be thus released from his prison. We are not, however, to infer that it would be a mere arbitrary act on the part of God. All that is necessary to be supposed is, that there would be, in certain parts of the world, a temporary outbreak of wickedness, *as if* Satan were for a time released from his chains.

8. *And shall go out to deceive the nations*. See Notes on ch. xii. 9. The meaning here is, that he would again, for a time, act in his true character, and in some way delude the nations once more. In what way this would be done is not stated. It would be, however, clearly an appeal to the wicked passions of mankind, exciting a hope that they might yet overthrow the kingdom of God on the earth. ¶ *Which are in the four quarters of the earth*. Literally, *corners* of the earth, as if the earth were one extended square plain. The earth is usually spoken of as divided into four parts or quarters—the eastern, the western, the northern, and the southern. It is implied here that the deception or apostasy referred to would not be confined to one spot or portion of the world, but would extend afar. The idea seems to be, that during that period, though there would be a *general* prevalence of the gospel, and a *general* diffusion of its blessings, yet that the earth would not be entirely under its influence, and especially that the native character of the human heart would not be changed. Man, under powerful temptations, would be liable to be deluded by the great master spirit that has so often corrupted the race. Once more he would be permitted to make the trial, and then his power would for ever come to an end. ¶ *Gog and Magog*. The name *Gog* occurs as the name of a prince in Eze. xxxviii. 2, 3, 16, 18; xxxix. 1, 11. "He is an invader of the land of Israel, the chief prince of Meshech and Tubal," Eze. xxxviii. 2. *Magog* is also mentioned in Eze. xxxviii. 2, "the land of Magog;" and in Eze. xxxix. 6, "I will send a fire on Magog." As the terms are used in the Old Testament, the representation would seem to be that *Gog* was the king of a people called *Magog*. The signification of the names is unknown, and consequently nothing can be determined about the meaning of this passage from that source. Nor is there much known about the *people* who are referred to by Ezekiel. His representation would seem to be, that a great and powerful people, dwelling in the extreme recesses of the north (ch. xxxviii. 15; xxxix. 2), would invade the Holy Land after the return from the exile, ch. xxxviii. 8-12. It is commonly supposed that they were *Scythians*, residing between the Caspian and Euxine Seas, or in the region of Mount Caucasus. Thus Josephus (*Ant*. i. 6, 3) has dropped the Hebrew word *Magog*, and rendered it by Σκύθαι—*Scythians*; and so does Jerome. Suidas renders it Πέρσαι—Persians; but this does not materially vary the view, since the word *Scythians*, among the ancient writers, is a collective word, to denote all the north-eastern, unknown, barbarous tribes. Among the Hebrews, the name *Magog* also would seem to denote all the unknown barbarous tribes about the Caucasian mountains. The fact that the names Gog and Magog are, in Ezekiel, associated with Meshech and Tubal, seems to determine the locality of these people, for those two countries lie between the Euxine and Caspian Seas, or at the south-east extremity of the Euxine Sea (Rosenmüller, *Bib. Geog*. vol. i. p. 240). The people of that region were, it seems, a terror to Middle Asia, in the same manner as the Scythians were to the Greeks and Romans. Intercourse with such distant and savage nations was scarcely possible in ancient times; and hence, from their numbers and strength, they were regarded with great terror, just as the Scythians were regarded by the ancient Greeks and Romans, and as the Tartars were in the middle ages. In this manner they became an appropriate symbol of rude and savage people; of enemies fierce and warlike; of foes to be dreaded; and as such they were referred to by both Ezekiel and John. It has been made

a question whether Ezekiel and John do not refer to the same period, but it is not necessary to consider that question here. All that is needful to be understood is, that John means to say that at the time referred to there would be formidable enemies of the church who might be compared with the dreaded dwellers in the land of Magog; or, that after this long period of millennial tranquillity and peace, there would be a state of things which might be properly compared with the invasion of the Holy Land by the dreaded barbarians of Magog or Scythia. It is not necessary to suppose that any particular *country* is referred to, or that there would be any one portion of the earth which the gospel would not reach, and which would be still barbarous, heathen, and savage; all that is necessary to be supposed is, that though religion would generally prevail, human nature would remain essentially corrupt and unchanged; and that, therefore, from causes which are not stated, there might yet be a fearful apostasy, and a somewhat general prevalence of iniquity. This would be nothing more than *has* occurred after the most favoured times in the church, and nothing more than human nature would exhibit at any time, if all restraints were withdrawn, and men were suffered to act out their native feelings. *Why* this will be permitted ; what causes will bring it about; what subordinate agencies will be employed, is not said, and conjecture would be vain. The reader who wishes more information in regard to Gog and Magog may consult Professor Stuart on this book, vol. ii. pp. 364-368, and the authorities there referred to. Comp. especially Rosenmüller on Eze. xxxviii. 2. See also Sale's *Koran*, Pre. Dis. § 4, and the *Koran* itself, Sura xviii. 94; and xxi. 95. ¶ *To gather them together to battle.* *As if* to assemble them for war; that is, a state of things would exist in regard to the kingdom of God and the prevalence of the true religion *as if* distant and barbarous nations should be aroused to make war on the church of God. The meaning is, that there would be an awakened hostility against the kingdom of Christ in the earth. See Notes on ch. xvi. 14. ¶ *The number of whom* is *as the sand of the sea.* A common comparison in the Scriptures to denote a great multitude, Ge. xxii. 17; xxxii. 12; xli. 49; 1 Sa. xiii. 5; 1 Ki. iv. 20, *et al.*

§ *c.—Condition of things in the period referred to in ver.* 7, 8.

(1) This will occur *at the close of the* millennial period — the period of the thousand years. It is not said, indeed, that it would be *immediately* after that; but the statement is explicit that it will be *after* that, or "when the thousand years are expired." There may be an interval before it shall be accomplished of an indefinite time; the alienation and corruption may be gradual; a considerable period may elapse before the apostasy shall assume an organized form, or, in the language of John, before the hosts shall "be gathered to battle," but it is to be the *next* marked and prominent event in the history of the world, and is to precede the final consummation of all things.

(2) This will be a *brief period.* Compared with the long period of prosperity that preceded it, and *perhaps* compared with the long period that shall follow it before the final judgment, it will be short. Thus, in ver. 3, it is said that Satan "must be loosed *a little season.*" See Notes on that verse. There is no way of determining the time with exactness; but we are assured that it will not be long.

(3) What will be the exact state of things then can be only a matter of conjecture. We may say, however, that it will *not* be (*a*) necessarily *war.* The language is figurative and symbolical, and it is not necessary to suppose that an actual and bloody warfare will be literally waged against the church. Nor (*b*) will there be a literal invasion of the land of Palestine as the residence of the saints and the capital of the Redeemer's visible empire, for there is not a hint of this—not a word to justify such an interpretation. Nor (*c*) is it necessary to suppose that there will be literally such nations as will be then called "*Gog* and *Magog*," for this language is figurative, and designed to characterize the foes of the church—as being in some respects formidable and terrible as were those ancient nations.

We may thus suppose that at that time, from causes which are unexplained, there will be (*a*) a revived opposition to the truths of religion; (*b*) the prevalence, to a greater or less extent, of infidelity; (*c*) a great spiritual declension; (*d*) a combination of interests opposed to the gospel; (*e*) possibly some new form of error and delusion that shall extensively prevail. Satan may set up some new form of religion, or he may breathe into those that may already exist a spirit of worldliness and vanity—some new manifestation of the religion of forms—that shall for a limited period produce a general decline and apostasy. As there is, however, no distinct specification of what will characterize the world at that time, it is impossible to determine what is referred to any more than in this general manner.

(4) A few remarks may, however, be made on the *probability* of what is here affirmed, for it seems contrary to what we should suppose would be the characteristics of the closing period of the world. The following remarks, then, may show that this anticipated state of things is not improbable :—(*a*) We are to remember that human nature will then be essentially the same as now. There is no intimation that man, as born into the world, will be then different from what he is now, or that any of the natural corrupt tendencies of the human heart will be changed. Men will be *liable* to the same outbreaks of passion, to be influenced by the same forms of temptation, to fall into the same degeneracy and corruption, to feel the same unhappy influences of success and prosperity as now, for all this appertains to a fallen nature, except as it is checked and controlled by grace. We often mistake much in regard to the millennial state by supposing that all the evils of the apostasy will be arrested and that the *nature* of man will be as wholly changed as it will be in the heavenly world. (*b*) The whole history of the church has shown that there is a liability to *declension* even in the best state and in the condition of the highest spiritual prosperity. To see this we have only to remember the example of the Hebrews, and how readily they apostatized after the most striking manifestation of the divine mercies; the early Christian church, and how soon it declined; the seven churches of Asia Minor, and how soon their spirituality departed; the various revivals of religion that have occurred from time to time, and how soon they have been succeeded by coldness, worldliness, and error; the fact that great religious denominations, which have begun their career with zeal and love, have so soon degenerated in spirit, and fallen into the same formality and worldliness which they have evinced who have gone before them; and the case of the individual Christian, who from the most exalted state of love and joy so soon often declines into a state of conformity to the world. These are sad views of human nature, even under the influence of true religion; but the past history of man has given but too much occasion for such reflections, and too much reason to apprehend that the same things may occur, for a time, even under the best forms in which religion may manifest itself in a fallen world. Man's nature will be better in heaven, and religion there, in its purest and best form, will be permanent; here we are not to be surprised at *any* outbreak of sin or any form of declension in religion. What has often occurred in the world on a small scale we may suppose may then occur on a larger scale. "Just as on a small scale, in some little community like that of Northampton, as described by President Edwards, after the remarkable sense of God's presence over the whole town had begun to wax feeble, the still unconverted persons of it, though subdued and seemingly won over to Christ, would by little and little recover themselves, and at length venture forth in their true character; so it will be, in all probability, on a vast scale, at the close of the latter day. The unconverted portion of the world—long constrained by the religious influences everywhere surrounding them to fall in with the spirit of the day, catching apparently its holy impulses, but never coming savingly under its power—this portion of mankind, which we have reason to fear will not be small, will now be freed from these irksome restraints, no longer obliged to breathe an atmosphere uncongenial to their nature" (Brown on the *Second Coming of Christ*, p. 442). "No oppression is so grievous to an unsanctified heart as that which arises from the purity of Christianity. A desire to shake off this yoke is the true cause of the opposition which Christianity has met with in the world in every period, and will, it is most likely, be the chief motive to influence the followers of Gog in his time" (Frazer's *Key*, p. 455). (*c*) The representations of the New Testament elsewhere confirm this view in regard to the latter state of the world—the state when the Lord Jesus shall come to judgment. "When the Son of man cometh, shall he find faith on the earth?" Lu. xviii. 8. "There shall come in the last days scoffers, walking after their own lusts, and saying, Where is the promise of

9 And *ⁿ*they went up on the breadth of the earth, and compassed the camp of the saints about, and the beloved city: and fire came down from God out of heaven, and devoured them.

*n* Is.8.8; Eze.38.9,16.

his coming?" 2 Pe. iii. 3, 4. "The day of the Lord so cometh as a thief in the night. For when they shall say, Peace and safety, then sudden destruction cometh upon them, as travail upon a woman with child, and they shall not escape," 1 Th. v. 2, 3. See especially Lu. xvii. 26–30: "As it was in the days of Noe, so shall it be also in the days of the Son of man. They did eat, they drank, they were given in marriage, until the day that Noe entered into the ark, and the flood came and destroyed them all. Likewise also as it was in the days of Lot; they did eat, they drank, they bought, they sold, they planted, they builded; but the same day that Lot went out of Sodom it rained fire and brimstone from heaven, and destroyed them all. *Even thus shall it be in the day when the Son of man is revealed.*"

9. *And they went up on the breadth of the earth.* They spread over the earth in extended columns. The image is that of an invading army that seems, in its march, to spread all over a land. The reference here is to the hosts assembled from the regions of Gog and Magog; that is, to the formidable enemies of the gospel that would be roused up at the close of the period properly called the *millennial* period— the period of the thousand years. It is not necessary to suppose that there would be *literally* armies of enemies of God summoned from lands that would be called lands of "Gog and Magog;" but all that is necessarily implied is, that there will be a state of hostility to the church of Christ which would be well illustrated by such a comparison with an invading host of barbarians. The expression "the breadth of the land" occurs in Hab. i. 6, in a description of the invasion of the Chaldeans, and means there *the whole extent of it;* that is, they would spread over the whole country. ¶ *And compassed the camp of the saints about.* Besieged the camp of the saints considered as engaged in war, or as attacked by an enemy. The "camp of the saints" here seems to be supposed to be *without* the walls of the city; that is, the army was drawn out for defence. The fact that the foes were able to "compass this camp about," and to encircle the city at the same time, shows the greatness of the numbers of the invaders. ¶ *And the beloved city.* Jerusalem—a city represented as beloved by God and by his people. The whole imagery here is derived from a supposed invasion of the land of Palestine—imagery than which nothing could be more natural to John in describing the hostility that would be aroused against the church in the latter day. But no just principle of interpretation requires us to understand this *literally.* Comp. He. xii. 22. Indeed, it would be absolutely *impossible* to give this chapter throughout a *literal* interpretation. What would be the *literal* interpretation of the very first verses? "I saw an angel come down from heaven, having the *key* of the bottomless pit, and *a great chain* in his hand; and he laid hold on the *dragon* and *bound* him." Can anyone believe that there is to be a literal *key,* and a *chain,* and an act of seizing a *serpent,* and *binding* him? As little is it demanded that the passage before us should be taken *literally;* for if it is maintained that this should be, we may insist that the same principle of interpretation should be applied to every part of the chapter, and every part of the book. ¶ *And fire came down from God out of heaven, and devoured them.* Consumed them—fire being represented as *devouring* or *eating.* See Notes on ch. xvii. 16. The meaning is, that they would be destroyed *as if* fire should come down from heaven, as on Sodom and Gomorrah. But it is not necessary to understand *this* literally, any more than it is the portions of the chapter just referred to. What is obviously meant is, that their destruction would be sudden, certain, and entire, and that thus the last enemy of God and the church would be swept away. Nothing can be determined from this about the *means* by which this destruction will be effected; and that must be left for time to disclose. It is sufficient to know that the destruction of these last foes of God and the church will be certain and entire. This *language,* as denoting the final destruction of the enemies of God, is often employed in the Scriptures. See Ps. xi. 6; Is. xxix. 6; Eze. xxxviii. 22; xxxix. 6.

A.D. 96.]  CHAPTER XX.  437

10 And the devil that deceived them was cast into the *lake of fire and brimstone, where the beast

*o* ch.19.20.

and the false prophet *are*, and shall be tormented day and night for ever and ever.

---

10. *And the devil that deceived them.* See Notes on ver. 3, 8. ¶ *Was cast into the lake of fire and brimstone.* In ch. xix. 20, it is said of the beast and the false prophet that they were "cast alive into a lake of fire, burning with brimstone." Satan, on the other hand, instead of being doomed at once to that final ruin, was confined for a season in a dark abyss, ch. xx. 1–3. As the final punishment, however, he is appropriately represented as consigned to the same doom as the beast and the false prophet, that those great enemies of God, that had been associated and combined in deceiving the nations, might share the same appropriate punishment in the end. Comp. ch. xvi. 13, 14. ¶ *Where the beast and the false prophet are.* Notes on ch. xix. 20. ¶ *And shall be tormented day and night for ever.* Comp. Notes on ch. xiv. 11. All the great enemies of the church are destroyed, and henceforward there is to be no array of hostile forces; no combination of malignant powers against the kingdom of God. The gospel triumphs; the way is prepared for the final consummation.

§ *d.—Condition of things in the period referred to in ver. 9, 10.*

(1) There will be, after the release of Satan, and of course at the close of the millennial period properly so called, a state of things which may be well represented by the invasion of a country by hostile, formidable forces. This, as shown in the exposition, need not be supposed to be literal; but it is implied that there will be decided hostility against the true religion. It may be an organization and consolidation, so to speak, of infidel principles, or a decided worldly spirit, or some prevalent form of error, or some new form of depravity that shall be developed by the circumstances of that age. What it will be it is impossible now to determine; but, as shown above (§ *c*, (4) ), it is by no means improbable that this will occur even at the close of the millennium.

(2) There will be a decided defeat of these forces thus combined, *as if* fire should come down from heaven to destroy an invading army. The *mode* in which this will be done is not indeed stated, for there is no necessity of understanding the statement in ver. 9 *literally*, any more than the other parts of the chapter. The fair inference, however, is that it will be by a manifest divine agency; that it will be sudden, and that the destruction will be entire. We have no reason, therefore, to suppose that the outbreak will be of long continuance, or that it will *very* materially disturb the settled order of human affairs on the earth—any more than a formidable invasion of a country does, when the invading army is suddenly cut off by some terrible judgment from heaven.

(3) *This* overthrow of the enemies of God and of the church will be *final*. Satan will be "cast into the lake of fire and brimstone, to be tormented day and night for ever." The beast and the false prophet are already there (ch. xix. 20); that is, they will have ceased long since, even before the beginning of the millennial period (ch. xix. 20, compared with ch. xx. 1–3), to have opposed the progress of truth in the world, and their power will have been brought to an end. Satan now, the last enemy, will be doomed to the same hopeless woe; and *all* the enemies that have ever opposed the church—in all forms of Paganism, Mahometanism, Popery, and delusion—will be destroyed for ever. The world then will have peace; the church will have rest; the great triumph will have been achieved.

(4) For reasons stated in the Analysis of the Chapter, V. (*c*), it is possible that there will be a long period of continued prosperity and peace between the events stated in ver. 9, 10, and the final judgment, as described in ver. 11–15. If so, however, the purpose of the book did not require that that should be described at length, and it must be admitted that the most *obvious* interpretation of the New Testament would not be favourable to such a supposition. Comp. Lu. xvii. 26–30; xviii. 8; 1 Th. v. 2, 3; 2 Pe. iii. 3, 4. The great glory of the world will be the millennial period; when religion shall have the ascendency and the race shall have reached its highest point of progress on earth, and the blessings of liberty, intelligence, peace, and piety, shall have during that period been spread over the globe. In

11 And I saw a great white throne, and him that sat on it, from whose face the *p*earth and the heaven fled away; and there was found no place for them.

*p* 2 Pe.3.10,12.

12 And I saw the dead, small and great, stand before God; and the *q*books were opened: and *r*another book was opened, which is *the book* of life: and the dead were

*q* Da.7.10.   *r* ch.21.27; Da.12.1.

that long duration, who can estimate the numbers that shall be redeemed and saved? That period passed, the great purpose contemplated by the creation of the earth—the glory of God in the redemption of a fallen race, and in setting up a kingdom of righteousness in a world of apostasy—will have been accomplished, and there will be no reason why the final judgment should not then occur. "The work of redemption will now be finished. The end for which the means of grace have been instituted shall be obtained. All the effect which was intended to be accomplished by them shall now be accomplished. All the great wheels of Providence have gone round—all things are ripe for Christ's coming to judgment" (President Edwards' *History of Redemption*).

11. *And I saw a great white throne.* This verse commences the description of the final judgment, which embraces the remainder of the chapter. The first thing seen in the vision is the burning throne of the Judge. The things that are specified in regard to it are, that it was *great*, and that it was *white*. The former expression means that it was high or elevated. Comp. Is. vi. 1. The latter expression—*white*—means that it was *splendid* or *shining*. Comp. 1 Ki. x. 18–20. The throne here is the same which is referred to in Mat. xxv. 31, and called there "the throne *of his glory*." ¶ *And him that sat on it.* The reference here undoubtedly is to the Lord Jesus Christ, the final Judge of mankind (comp. Mat. xxv. 31), and the scene described is that which will occur at his second advent. ¶ *From whose face.* Or, from whose presence; though the word *may* be used here to denote more strictly his *face*—as illuminated, and shining like the sun. See ch. i. 16, "And his countenance was as the sun shineth in his strength." ¶ *The earth and the heaven fled away.* That is, as the stars, at the rising of the sun, seem to flee to more remote regions, and vanish from human view, so when the Son of God shall descend in his glory to judge the world, the earth and all other worlds shall seem to vanish. Every one must admire the sublimity of this image; no one can contemplate it without being awed by the majesty and glory of the final Judge of mankind. Similar expressions, where the natural creation shrinks back with awe at the presence of God, frequently occur in the Bible. Comp. Ps. xviii. 7–15; lxxvii. 16–19; cxiv. 3–5; Hab. iii. 6, 10, 11. ¶ *And there was found no place for them.* They seemed to flee *entirely* away, as if there was *no* place where they could find a safe retreat, or which would receive and shelter them in their flight. The image expresses, in the most emphatic manner, the idea that they entirely disappeared, and *no* language could more sublimely represent the majesty of the Judge.

12. *And I saw the dead, small and great.* All the dead—for this language would express that—the whole race being composed of the "small and great." Thus, in other language, the same idea might be expressed by saying, the young and old; the rich and poor; the bond and free; the sick and well; the happy and the unhappy; the righteous and the wicked; for all the human family might, in these respects, be considered as thus divided. The fair meaning in this place therefore is, that *all* the dead would be there, and of course this would preclude the idea of a *previous* resurrection of any part of the dead, as of the saints, at the beginning of the millennium. There is no intimation here that it is the *wicked* dead that are referred to in this description of the final judgment. It is the judgment of *all* the dead. ¶ *Stand before God.* That is, they appear thus to be judged. The word "God" here must naturally refer to the final Judge on the throne, and there can be no doubt (see Mat. xxv. 31) that this is the Lord Jesus. Comp. 2 Co. v. 10. None can judge the secrets of the heart; none can pronounce on the moral character of all mankind, of all countries and ages, and determine their everlasting allotment, but he who is Divine.

A.D. 96.]  CHAPTER XX.  439

judged out of those things which were written in the books, *according to their works.

13 And the sea gave up the dead which were in it; and death and

¹hell delivered up the dead which were in them: and they were judged every man according to their works.

14 And ᵗdeath and hell were

*s* Je.32.19; Mat.16.27.   1 *the grave.*   *t* Ho.13.14; 1 Co.15.26,54.

¶ *And the books were opened.* That is, the books containing the record of human deeds. The representation is, that all that men have done is recorded, and that it will be exhibited on the final trial, and will constitute the basis of the last judgment. The imagery seems to be derived from the accusations made against such as are arraigned before human courts of justice. ¶ *And another book was opened, which is the book of life.* The book containing the record of the names of all who shall enter into life, or into heaven. See Notes on ch. iii. 5. The meaning here is, that John saw not only the general books opened containing the records of the deeds of men, but that he had a distinct view of the list or roll of those who were the followers of the Lamb. It would seem that in regard to the multitudes of the impenitent and the wicked, the judgment will proceed *on their deeds* in general; in regard to the righteous, it will turn on the fact that their names had been enrolled in the book of life. That will be sufficient to determine the nature of the sentence that is to be passed on them. He will be safe whose name is found in the book of life; no one will be safe who is to have his eternal destiny determined by his own deeds. This passage proves *particularly* that the righteous dead are referred to here as being present at the final judgment; and is thus an additional argument against the supposition of a resurrection of the righteous, and a judgment on them, at the beginning of the millennium. ¶ *And the dead were judged out of those things which were written in the books.* The records which had been made of their deeds. The final judgment will proceed on the record that has been made. It will not be arbitrary, and will not be determined by rank, condition, or profession, but it will be according to the record. ¶ *According to their works.* See Notes on 2 Co. v. 10. The fact that the name of anyone was found in the book of life would seem, as above remarked, to determine the *certainty* of salvation; but the amount of reward would be in proportion to the service rendered to the Redeemer, and the attainments made in piety.

13. *And the sea gave up the dead which were in it.* All that had been buried in the depths of ocean. This number in the aggregate will be great. If we include all who were swept off by the flood, and all who have perished by shipwreck, and all who have been killed in naval battles and buried in the sea, and all who have been swept away by inundations of the ocean, and all who have peacefully died at sea, as sailors, or in the pursuits of commerce or benevolence, the number in the aggregate will be immense—a number so vast that it was proper to notice them particularly in the account of the general resurrection and the last judgment. ¶ *And death and hell delivered up the dead which were in them.* That is, *all* the dead came, from all regions where they were scattered—on the land and in the ocean—in this world and in the invisible world. "Death and hell" are here personified, and are represented as having dominion over the dead, and as now *delivering* up, or *surrendering* those who were held under them. On the meaning of the words here used, see Notes on ch. i. 18; vi. 8. Comp. Notes on Mat. x. 23; Job x. 21, 22; Is. xiv. 9. This whole representation is entirely inconsistent with the supposition that a large part of the dead had been already raised up at the beginning of the millennial period, and had been permitted, in their glorified bodies, to reign with Christ. ¶ *And they were judged,* &c. All these were judged—the righteous and the wicked; those buried at sea, and those buried on the land; the small and the great; the dead, in whatever world they may have been.

14. *And death and hell were cast into the lake of fire.* Death and Hades (*hell*) are here personified, as they are in the previous verse. The declaration is equivalent to the statement in 1 Co. xv. 26: "The last enemy that shall be destroyed is *death.*" See Notes on that passage. The idea is, that death, considered as the separation of soul and body, with

cast into the lake of fire. This is the second death.

15 And whosoever was not found written in the book of life was ᵘcast into the lake of fire.

u Mat. 25. 41.

all the attendant woes, will exist no more. The righteous will live for ever, and the wicked will linger on in a state never to be terminated by death. The reign of Death and Hades, as such, would come to an end, and a new order of things would commence where *this* would be unknown. There might be that which would be properly called death, but it would not be death in this form; the soul would live for ever, but it would not be in that condition represented by the word ᾅδης — *hades*. There would be *death* still, but a "second death differs from the first, in the fact that it is not a separation of the soul and body, but a state of *continual agony* like that which the first death inflicts — like that in intensity, but not in kind" (Professor Stuart). ¶ *This is the second death.* That is, this whole process here described—the condemnation, and the final death and ruin of those whose names are "not found written in the book of life"—properly constitutes the second death. This proves that when it is said that "death and hell were cast into the lake of fire," it cannot be meant that all punishment will cease for ever, and that all will be saved, for the writer goes on to describe what he calls "the second death" as still existing. See ver. 15. John describes this as the second death, not because it in all respects resembles the first death, but because it has so many points of resemblance that it may be properly called *death*. Death, in any form, is the penalty of law; it is attended with pain; it cuts off from hope, from friends, from enjoyment; it subjects him who dies to a much-dreaded condition, and in all these respects it was proper to call the final condition of the wicked *death*—though it would still be true that the soul would live. There is no evidence that John meant to affirm that the second death would imply an extinction of *existence*. Death never does that; the word does not naturally and properly convey that idea.

15. *And whosoever.* All persons, of all ranks, ages, and conditions. No word could be more comprehensive than this. The single condition here stated, as being that which would save *any* from being cast into the lake of fire, is, that they are "found written in the book of life." All besides these, princes, kings, nobles, philosophers, statesmen, conquerors; rich men and poor men; the bond and the free; the young and the aged; the gay, the vain, the proud, and the sober; the modest and the humble, will be doomed to the lake of fire. Unlike in all other things, they will be alike in the only thing on which their eternal destiny will depend—that they have not *so* lived that their names have become recorded in the book of life. As they will also be destitute of true religion, there will be a propriety that they shall share the same doom in the future world. ¶ *Written in the book of life.* See Notes on ch. iii. 5. ¶ *Was cast into the lake of fire.* See Notes on Mat. xxv. 41. That is, they will be doomed to a punishment which will be well represented by their lingering in a sea of fire for ever. This is the termination of the judgment—the winding up of the affairs of men. The vision of John here rests for a moment on the doom of the wicked, and then turns to a more full contemplation of the happy lot of the righteous, as detailed in the two closing chapters of the book.

§ *e.—Condition of things referred to in ver. 11-15.*

(1) There will be a general resurrection of the dead—of the righteous and the wicked. This is implied by the statement that the "dead, small and great," were seen to stand before God; that "the sea gave up the dead which were in it;" that "Death and Hades gave up their dead." All were there whose names were or were not written in the book of life.

(2) There will be a solemn and impartial judgment. How long a time this will occupy is not said, and is not necessary to be known—for time is of no consequence where there is an eternity of devotion—but it *is* said that they will be all judged "according to their works"—that is, strictly according to their character. They will receive no arbitrary doom; they will have no sentence which will not be just. See Mat. xxv. 31-46.

(3) This will be the *final* judgment. After this, the affairs of the race will be put on a different footing. This will be the end of the present arrangements;

the end of the present dispensations; the end of human probation. The great question to be determined in regard to our world will have been settled; what the plan of redemption was intended to accomplish on the earth will have been accomplished; the agency of the Divine Spirit in converting sinners will have come to an end; and the means of grace, as such, will be employed no more. There is not here or elsewhere an intimation that beyond this period any of these things will exist, or that the work of redemption, as such, will extend into the world beyond the judgment. As there is no intimation that the condition of the righteous will be changed, so there is none that the condition of the wicked will be; as there is no hint that the righteous will ever be exposed to temptation, or to the danger of falling into sin, so there is none that the offers of salvation will ever again be made to the wicked. On the contrary, the whole representation is, that all beyond this will be fixed and unchangeable for ever. See Notes on ch. xxii. 11.

(4) The wicked will be destroyed, in what may be properly called the *second* death. As remarked in the Notes, this does not mean that this death will in all respects resemble the first death, but there will be so many points of resemblance that it will be proper to call it *death*. It does not mean that they will be *annihilated*, for *death* never implies that. The meaning is, that this will be a cutting off from what is properly called *life*, from hope, from happiness, and from peace, and a subjection to pain and agony, which it will be proper to call *death*—death in the most fearful form; death that will continue for ever. No statements in the Bible are more clear than those which are made on this point; no affirmation of the eternal punishment of the wicked *could be* more explicit than those which occur in the sacred Scriptures. See Notes on Mat. xxv. 46, and 2 Th. i. 9.

(5) This will be the end of the woes and calamities produced in the kingdom of God by sin. The reign of Satan and of Death, so far as the Redeemer's kingdom is concerned, will be at an end, and henceforward the church will be safe from all the arts and efforts of its foes. Religion will be triumphant, and the affairs of the universe be reduced to permanent order.

(6) The preparation is thus made for the final triumph of the righteous—the state to which all things tend. The writer of this book has conducted the prospective history through all the times of persecution which awaited the church, and stated the principal forms of error which would prevail, and foretold the conflicts through which the church would pass, and described its eventful history to the millennial period, and to the final triumph of truth and righteousness; and now nothing remains to complete the plan of the work but to give a rapid sketch of the final condition of the redeemed. This is done in the two following chapters, and with this the work is ended.

## CHAPTER XXI.

ANALYSIS OF CHAP. XXI., XXII. 1-5.

The whole of ch. xxi., and the first five verses of ch. xxii., relate to scenes beyond the judgment, and are descriptive of the happy and triumphant state of the redeemed church, when all its conflicts shall have ceased, and all its enemies shall have been destroyed. That happy state is depicted under the image of a beautiful city, of which Jerusalem was the emblem, and it was disclosed to John by a vision of that city—the New Jerusalem—descending from heaven. Jerusalem was regarded as the peculiar dwelling-place of God, and to the Hebrews it became thus the natural emblem or symbol of the heavenly world. The conception having occurred of describing the future condition of the righteous under the image of a beautiful city, all that follows is in *keeping* with that, and is merely a carrying out of the image. It is a city with beautiful walls and gates; a city that has no temple—for it is all a temple; a city that needs no light—for God is its light; a city into which nothing impure ever enters; a city filled with trees, and streams, and fountains, and fruits—the *Paradise Regained*.

The description of that blessed state comprises the following parts:—

I. A vision of a new heaven and a new earth, as the final abode of the blessed, ver. 1. The first heaven and the first earth passed away at the judgment (ch. xx. 11-15), to be succeeded by a new heaven and earth fitted to be the abode of the blessed.

II. A vision of the holy city—the New Jerusalem—descending from heaven, as the abode of the redeemed, prepared as a bride adorned for her husband—representing the fact that God would truly abide with men, ver. 2–4. Now all the effects of the apostasy will cease; all tears will be wiped away, and in that blessed state there will be no more death, or sorrow, or pain. This contains the *general* statement of what will be the condition of the redeemed in the future world. God will be there; and all sorrow will cease.

III. A command to make a record of these things, ver. 5.

IV. A general description of those who should dwell in that future world of blessedness, ver. 6–8. It is for all who are athirst; for all who desire it, and long for it; for all who "overcome" their spiritual enemies, who maintain a steady conflict with sin, and gain a victory over it. But all who are fearful and unbelieving—all the abominable, and murderers, and sorcerers, and idolaters, and liars—shall have their part in the lake that burns with fire and brimstone. That is, that world will be pure and holy.

V. A minute description of the city, representing the happy abode of the redeemed, ver. 9–26. This description embraces many particulars:—

(1) Its general appearance, ver. 11, 18, 21. It is bright and splendid—like a precious jasper-stone, clear as crystal, and composed of pure gold.

(2) Its walls, ver. 12, 18. The walls are represented as "great and high," and as composed of "jasper."

(3) Its gates, ver. 12, 13, 21. The gates are twelve in number, three on each side; and are each composed of a single pearl.

(4) Its foundations, ver. 14, 18–20. There are twelve foundations, corresponding to the number of the apostles of the Lamb. They are all composed of precious stones—jasper, sapphire, chalcedony, emerald, sardonyx, sardius, chrysolite, beryl, topaz, chrysoprasus, jacinth, and amethyst.

(5) Its size, ver. 15–17. It is square—the length being as great as the breadth, and its height the same. The extent of each dimension is twelve thousand furlongs—a length on each side and in height of three hundred and seventy-five miles. It would seem, however, that though the *city* was of that height, the *wall* was only an hundred and forty-four cubits, or about two hundred and sixteen feet high. The idea seems to be that the city—the dwellings within it—towered high above the wall that was thrown around it for protection. This is not uncommon in cities that are surrounded by walls.

(6) Its light, ver. 23, 24; ch. xxii. 5. It has no need of the sun, or of the moon, or of a lamp (ch. xxii. 5) to lighten it; and yet there is no night there (ch. xxii. 5), for the glory of God gives light to it.

(7) It is a city without a temple, ver. 22. There is no one place in it that is peculiarly sacred, or where the worship of God will be exclusively celebrated. It will be all a temple, and the worship of God will be celebrated in all parts of it.

(8) It is always open, ver. 25. There will be no need of closing it as walled cities on earth are closed to keep enemies out, and it will not be shut to prevent those who dwell there from going out and coming in when they please. The inhabitants will not be prisoners, nor will they be in danger, or be alarmed by the prospect of an attack from an enemy.

(9) Its inhabitants will all be pure and holy, ver. 27. There will in no wise enter there anything that defiles, or that works abomination, or that is false. They only shall dwell there whose names are written in the Lamb's book of life.

(10) Its inclosures and environs, ch. xxii. 1, 2. A stream of water, pure as crystal, proceeds from the throne of God and the Lamb. That stream flows through the city, and on its banks is the tree of life constantly bearing fruit—fruit to be partaken of freely. It is Paradise regained—a holy and beautiful abode, of which the garden of Eden was only an imperfect emblem, where there is no prohibition, as there was there, of anything that grows, and where there is no danger of falling into sin.

(11) It is a place free, consequently, from the curse that was pronounced on man when he forfeited the blessings of the first Eden, and when he was driven out from the happy abodes where God had placed him.

(12) It is a place where the righteous shall reign for ever, ch. xxii. 5. Death shall never enter there, and the presence and glory of God shall fill all with peace and joy.

Such is an outline of the figurative and glowing description of the future blessedness of the redeemed; the eternal abode of those who shall be saved.

## CHAPTER XXI.

AND I saw a *a*new heaven and a new earth: for the first heaven and the first earth were

*a* Is.65.17-19; 66.22; 2 Pe.3.13.

passed away; and there was no more sea.

2 And I John saw the *b*holy city, new Jerusalem, coming down from

*b* Is.52.1; He.11.10; 12.22.

It is poetic and emblematical; but it is elevating, and constitutes a beautiful and appropriate close, not only of this single book, but of the whole sacred volume — for to this the saints are everywhere directed to look forward; this is the glorious termination of all the struggles and conflicts of the church; this is the result of the work of redemption in repairing the evils of the fall, and in bringing man to more than the bliss which he lost in Eden. The mind rests with delight on this glorious prospect; the Bible closes, as a revelation from heaven should, in a manner that calms down every anxious feeling; that fills the soul with peace, and that leads the child of God to look forward with bright anticipations, and to say, as John did, "Come, Lord Jesus," ch. xxii. 20.

1. *And I saw a new heaven and a new earth.* Such a heaven and earth that they might properly be called *new;* such transformations, and such changes in their appearance, that they seemed to be just created. He does not say that they *were* created now, or anew; that the old heavens and earth were annihilated; — but all that he says is, that there were such changes that they *seemed* to be new. If the earth is to be renovated by fire, such a renovation will give an appearance to the globe as if it were created anew, and might be attended with such an apparent change in the heavens that they might be said to be *new.* The description here (ver. 1) relates to scenes *after* the general resurrection and the judgment—for those events are detailed in the close of the previous chapter. In regard to the meaning of the language here, see Notes on 2 Pe. iii. 13. Compare, also, *The Religion of Geology and its Connected Sciences*, by Edward Hitchcock, D.D., LL.D., pp. 370-408. ¶ *For the first heaven and the first earth were passed away.* They had passed away by being changed, and a renovated universe had taken their place. See Notes on 2 Pe. iii. 10. ¶ *And there was no more sea.* This change struck John more forcibly, it would appear, than anything else.

Now, the seas and oceans occupy about three-fourths of the surface of the globe, and, of course, to that extent prevent the world from being occupied by men— except by the comparatively small number that are mariners. There, the idea of John seems to be, the whole world will be inhabitable, and no part will be given up to the wastes of oceans. In the present state of things, these vast oceans are necessary to render the world a fit abode for human beings, as well as to give life and happiness to the numberless tribes of animals that find their homes in the waters. In the future state, it would seem, the present arrangement will be unnecessary; and if man dwells upon the earth at all, or if he visits it as a temporary abode (see Notes on 2 Pe. iii. 13), these vast wastes of water will be needless. It should be remembered that the earth, in its changes, according to the teachings of geology, has undergone many revolutions quite as remarkable as it would be if all the lakes, and seas, and oceans of the earth should disappear. Still, it is not certain that it was intended that this language should be understood literally as applied to the material globe. The object is to describe the future blessedness of the righteous; and the idea is, that that will be a world where there will be no such wastes as those produced by oceans.

2. *And I John saw the holy city, new Jerusalem, coming down from God out of heaven.* See the Analysis of the chapter. On the phrase "new Jerusalem," see Notes on Ga. iv. 26, and He. xii. 22. Here it refers to the residence of the redeemed, the heavenly world, of which Jerusalem was the type and symbol. It is here represented as "coming down from God out of heaven." This, of course, does not mean that this great city was *literally* to descend upon the *earth,* and to occupy any one part of the renovated world; but it is a symbolical or figurative representation, designed to show that the abode of the righteous will be splendid and glorious. The idea of a city literally descending from heaven, and being set upon the earth with such proportions—three hun-

God, out of heaven, prepared as *c* a bride *d* adorned for her husband.

3 And I heard a great voice out of heaven, saying, Behold, the *e* tabernacle of God *is* with men, and he will dwell with them, and they shall be *f* his people, and God himself shall be with them, *and be* their God.

4 And God shall *g* wipe away all tears from their eyes; and there shall be *h* no more death,

*c* Is.54.5.   *d* Ps.45.9-14.   *e* 2 Co.6.16.   *f* Zec.8.8.   *g* ch.7.17; Is.25.8.   *h* 1 Co.15.26,54.

dred and seventy miles high (ver. 16), made of gold, and with single pearls for gates, and single gems for the foundations—is absurd. No man can suppose that this is literally true, and hence this must be regarded as a figurative or emblematic description. It is a representation of the heavenly state under the image of a beautiful city, of which Jerusalem was, in many respects, a natural and striking emblem. ¶ *Prepared as a bride adorned for her husband.* See Notes on Is. xlix. 18; lxi. 10. The purpose here is, to represent it as exceedingly beautiful. The comparison of the church with a bride, or a wife, is common in the Scriptures. See Notes on ch. xix. 7, 8, and on Is. i. 21. It is also common in the Scriptures to compare a city with a beautiful woman, and these images here seem to be combined. It is a beautiful city that seems to descend, and this city is itself compared with a richly-attired bride prepared for her husband.

3. *And I heard a great voice out of heaven.* As if uttered by God himself, or the voice of angels. ¶ *Behold the tabernacle of God is with men.* The *tabernacle*, as that word is commonly used in the Scriptures, referring to the sacred *tent* erected in the wilderness, was regarded as the peculiar dwelling-place of God among his people—as the temple was afterwards, which was also called a *tabernacle*. See Notes on He. ix. 2. The meaning here is, that God would now dwell with the redeemed, *as if* in a tabernacle, or in a house specially prepared for his residence among them. It is not said that this would be *on the earth*, although that *may* be; for it is possible that the earth, as well as other worlds, may yet become the abode of the redeemed. See Notes on 2 Pe. iii. 13. ¶ *And he will dwell with them.* As in a tent, or tabernacle—σκηνώσει. This is a common idea in the Scriptures. ¶ *And they shall be his people.* He will acknowledge them in this public way as his own, and will dwell with them as such. ¶ *And God himself shall be with them.* Shall be permanently with them; shall never leave them. ¶ *And be their God.* Shall manifest himself as such, in such a manner that there shall be no doubt.

4. *And God shall wipe away all tears from their eyes.* This will be one of the characteristics of that blessed state, that not a tear shall ever be shed there. How different will that be from the condition here—for who is there here who has not learned to weep? See Notes on ch. vii. 17. Comp. Notes on Is. xxv. 8. ¶ *And there shall be no more death.* In all that future world of glory, not one shall ever die; not a grave shall ever be dug! What a view do we begin to get of heaven, when we are told there shall be no *death* there! How different from earth, where death is so common; where it spares no one; where our best friends die; where the wise, the good, the useful, the lovely die; where fathers, mothers, wives, husbands, sons, daughters, all die; where we habitually feel that we must die. Assuredly we have here a view of heaven most glorious and animating to those who dwell in a world like this, and to whom nothing is more common than death. In all their endless and glorious career, the redeemed will never see death again; they will never themselves die. They will never follow a friend to the tomb, nor fear that an absent friend is dead. The slow funeral procession will never be witnessed there; nor will the soil ever open its bosom to furnish a grave. See Notes on 1 Co. xv. 55. ¶ *Neither sorrow.* The word *sorrow* here—πένθος—denotes sorrow or *grief* of any kind; sorrow for the loss of property or friends; sorrow for disappointment, persecution, or care; sorrow over our sins, or sorrow that we love God so little, and serve him so unfaithfully; sorrow that we are sick, or that we must die. How innumerable are the sources of sorrow here; how constant is it on the earth! Since the fall of man there has not been a day, an hour, a moment, in which this has not been a sorrowful world; there has not been a nation, a tribe—a city or a village—nay, not a family, where there has

A.D. 96.]  CHAPTER XXI.  445

neither *sorrow, nor crying, neither shall there be any more pain: for the former things are passed away.

5 And he that sat upon the throne said, Behold, I make all things new. And he said unto me,

*i* Is.35.10.

Write: for these words are true and faithful.

6 And he said unto me, *k* It is done. I *l* am Alpha and Omega, the beginning and the end. I *m* will

*k* ch.16.17.  *l* ch.1.8; 22.1
*m* ch.22.17; Is.55.1; Jn.4.10,14; 7.37.

not been grief. There has been no individual who has been always perfectly happy. No one rises in the morning with any certainty that he may not end the day in grief; no one lies down at night with any assurance that it may not be a night of sorrow. How different would this world be if it were announced that henceforward there would be no sorrow! How different, therefore, will heaven be when we shall have the assurance that henceforward grief shall be at an end! ¶ *Nor crying—κραυγὴ.* This word properly denotes a cry, an outcry, as in giving a public notice; a cry in a tumult—a clamour, Ac. xxiii. 9; and then a cry of sorrow, or wailing. This is evidently its meaning here, and it refers to all the outbursts of grief arising from affliction, from oppression, from violence. The sense is, that as none of these *causes* of wailing will be known in the future state, all such wailing will cease. This, too, will make the future state vastly different from our condition here; for what a change would it produce on the earth if the cry of grief were never to be heard again! ¶ *Neither shall there be any more pain.* There will be no sickness, and no calamity; and there will be no mental sorrow arising from remorse, from disappointment, or from the evil conduct of friends. And what a change would *this* produce—for how full of *pain* is the world now! How many lie on beds of languishing; how many are suffering under incurable diseases; how many are undergoing severe surgical operations; how many are pained by the loss of property or friends, or subjected to acuter anguish by the misconduct of those who are loved! How different would this world be, if all *pain* were to cease for ever; how different, therefore, must the blessed state of the future be from the present! ¶ *For the former things are passed away.* The world as it was before the judgment.

5. *And he that sat upon the throne said.* Probably the Messiah, the dispenser of the rewards of heaven. See Notes on ch. xx. 11. ¶ *Behold, I make all things new.* A new heaven and new earth (ver. 1), and an order of things to correspond with that new creation. The former state of things when sin and death reigned will be changed, and the change consequent on this must extend to everything. ¶ *And he said unto me, Write.* Make a *record* of these things, for they are founded in truth, and they are adapted to bless a suffering world. Comp. Notes on ch. xiv. 13. See also ch. i. 19. ¶ *For these words are true and faithful.* They are founded in truth, and they are worthy to be believed. See Notes on ch. xix. 9. Comp. also Notes on Da. xii. 4.

6. *And he said unto me.* That is, he that sat on the throne—the Messiah. ¶ *It is done.* It is finished, complete; or, still more expressively, *it is—γέγονε.* An expression remarkably similar to this occurs in John xix. 30, when the Saviour on the cross said, "It is finished." The meaning in the passage before us evidently is, "The great work is accomplished; the arrangement of human affairs is complete. The redeemed are gathered in; the wicked are cut off; truth is triumphant, and all is now complete—prepared for the eternal state of things." ¶ *I am Alpha and Omega, the beginning and the end.* This language makes it morally certain that the speaker here is the Lord Jesus, for it is the very language which he uses of himself in ch. i. 11. See its meaning explained in the Notes on ch. i. 8. If it *is* applied to him here, it proves that he is divine, for in the following verse (7) the speaker says that he would be a *God* to him who should "overcome." The meaning of the language as here used, regarded as spoken by the Redeemer at the consummation of all things, and as his people are about entering into the abodes of blessedness, is, "I am now *indeed* the Alpha and the Omega—the first and the last. The attributes implied in this language which I claimed for myself are now verified in me, and it is seen that these properly belong to me. The scheme for setting up a kingdom in the lost world began in me, and it ends in me—the glorious

give unto him that is athirst of the fountain of the water of life freely.

7 He that overcometh shall inherit ¹all things; and I will be his God, and he shall be my son.

8 But the ⁿfearful, and ᵒunbelieving, and the ᵖabominable, and murderers,ᑫ and ʳwhoremongers,

<small>1 or, these.    n Lu.12.4-9.    o 1 Jn.5.4,10.
p 1 Co.6.9,10.    q 1 Jn.3.15.    r He.13.4.</small>

and ˢsorcerers, and ᵗidolaters, and all ᵘliars, shall have their part in the lake which burneth with fire and brimstone: which is the second death.

9 And there came unto me one of the ᵛseven angels which had the seven vials full of the seven last plagues, and talked with me, say-

<small>s Mal.3.5.    t 1 Co.10.20,21
u ch.22.15; Pr.19.5,9.    v ch.15.1,6,7.</small>

and triumphant king." ¶ *I will give unto him that is athirst.* See Notes on Mat. v. 6; Jn. iv. 14; vii. 37. ¶ *Of the fountain of the water of life.* An image often used in the Scriptures to represent salvation. It is compared with a fountain that flows in abundance, where all may freely slake their thirst. ¶ *Freely.* Without money and without price (Notes on Is. lv. 1; Jn. vii. 37); the common representation in the Scriptures. The meaning here is, not that he would do this *in the future*, but that he had shown that this was his character, as he had claimed, in the same way as he had shown that he was the Alpha and the Omega. The freeness and the fulness of salvation will be one of the most striking things made manifest when the immense hosts of the redeemed shall be welcomed to their eternal abodes.

7. *He that overcometh.* See Notes on ch. ii. 7. ¶ *Shall inherit all things.* Be an heir of God in all things. See Notes on Ro. viii. 17. Comp. Re. ii. 7, 11, 17, 26; iii. 5, 12, 21. ¶ *And I will be his God.* That is, *for ever.* He would be to them all that is properly implied in the name of *God;* he would bestow upon them all the blessings which it was appropriate for God to bestow. See Notes on 2 Co. vi. 18; He. viii. 10. ¶ *And he shall be my son.* He shall sustain to me the relation of a son, and shall be treated as such. He would ever onward sustain this relation, and be honoured as a child of God.

8. *But the fearful.* Having stated, in general terms, who they were who would be admitted into that blessed world, he now states explicitly who would *not.* The *fearful* denote those who had not firmness boldly to maintain their professed principles, or who were afraid to avow themselves as the friends of God in a wicked world. They stand in contrast with those who "*overcome*," ver. 7. ¶ *And unbelieving.* Those who have

not true faith; avowed infidels; infidels at heart; and all who have not the sincere faith of the gospel. See Notes on Mar. xvi. 16. ¶ *And the abominable.* The verb from which this word is derived means to excite disgust; to feel disgust at; to abominate or abhor; and hence the participle—"the abominable" —refers to all who are detestable, to wit, on account of their sins; all whose conduct is offensive to God. Thus it would include those who live in open sin; who practise detestable vices; whose conduct is fitted to excite disgust and abhorrence. These must all, of course, be excluded from a pure and holy world; and this description, alas! would embrace a lamentably large portion of the world as it has hitherto been. See Notes on Ro. i. 26, seq. ¶ *And murderers.* See Notes on Ro. i. 29; Ga. v. 21. ¶ *And whoremongers.* See Notes on Ga. v. 19. ¶ *And sorcerers.* See the word here used — φαρμακεῦσι — explained in the Notes on Ga. v. 19, under the word *witchcraft.* ¶ *And idolaters.* 1 Co. vi. 9; Ga. v. 19. ¶ *And all liars.* All who are false in their statements, their promises, their contracts. The word would embrace all who are false towards God (Ac. v. 1-3), and false towards men. See Ro. i. 31. ¶ *Shall have their part in the lake which burneth,* &c. Notes on ch. xx. 14. That is, they will be excluded from heaven, and punished for ever. See Notes on 1 Co. vi. 9, 10; Ga. v. 19-21.

9. *And there came unto me one of the seven angels,* &c. See Notes on ch. xvi. 6, 7. Why one of these angels was employed to make this communication is not stated. It may be that as they had been engaged in bringing destruction on the enemies of the church, and securing its final triumph, there was a propriety that that triumph should be announced by one of their number. ¶ *And talked with me.* That is, in regard to what he was about to show me.

ing, Come hither, I will show thee the *w* bride, the Lamb's wife.

10 And he carried me away in the spirit to a great and high mountain, and showed me *x* that great city, the holy Jerusalem, descending out of heaven from God,

11 Having the *y* glory of God: and her light *was* like unto a stone most precious, even like a jasper stone, clear as crystal;

*w* ch.19.7.   *x* Eze.xl.-xlviii.   *y* Is.60.1,2.

12 And had a wall great and high, *and* had *z* twelve gates, and at the gates twelve angels, and names written thereon, which are *the names* of the twelve tribes of the children of Israel:

13 On the east three gates; on the north three gates; on the south three gates; and on the west three gates.

*z* Eze.48.31-34.

¶ *I will show thee the bride, the Lamb's wife.* I will show you what represents the redeemed church now to be received into permanent union with its Lord—as a bride about to be united to her husband. See Notes on ver. 2. Comp. ch. xix. 7, 8.

10. *And he carried me away in the spirit.* Gave him a *vision* of the city; seemed to place him where he could have a clear view of it as it came down from heaven. See Notes on ch. i. 10. ¶ *To a great and high mountain.* The elevation, and the unobstructed range of view, gave him an opportunity to behold it in its glory. ¶ *And showed me that great city,* &c. As it descended from heaven. Notes on ver. 2.

11. *Having the glory of God.* A glory or splendour such as became the dwelling place of God. The nature of that splendour is described in the following verses. ¶ *And her light.* In ver. 23 it is said that "the glory of God did lighten it." That is, it was made light by the visible symbol of the Deity—the *Shekinah.* See Notes on Lu. ii. 9; Ac. ix. 3. The word here rendered *light* —φωστήρ—occurs nowhere else in the New Testament except in Phi. ii. 15. It means, properly, a light, a lightgiver, and, in profane writers, means commonly *a window.* It is used here to denote the brightness or shining of the divine glory, as supplying the place of the sun, or of a window. ¶ *Like unto a stone most precious.* A stone of the richest or most costly nature. ¶ *Even like a jasper stone.* On the *jasper,* see Notes on ch. iv. 3. It is used there for the same purpose as here, to illustrate the majesty and glory of God. ¶ *Clear as crystal.* Pellucid or resplendent like crystal. There are various kinds of jasper — as red, yellow, and brown, brownish yellow, &c. The stone is essentially a quartz, and the word *crys-* *tal* here is used to show that the form of it referred to by John was clear and bright.

12. *And had a wall great and high.* Ancient cities were always surrounded with walls for protection, and John represents this as inclosed in the usual manner. The word *great* means that it was thick and strong. Its height also is particularly noticed, for it was unusual. See ver. 16. ¶ *And had twelve gates.* Three on each side. The number of the gates correspond to the number of the tribes of the children of Israel, and to the number of the apostles. The idea seems to be that there would be ample opportunity of access and egress. ¶ *And at the gates twelve angels.* Stationed there as guards to the New Jerusalem. Their business seems to have been to watch the gates that nothing improper should enter; that the great enemy should not make an insidious approach to this city as he did to the earthly paradise. ¶ *And names written thereon.* On the gates. ¶ *Which are* the names *of the twelve tribes of the children of Israel.* So in the city which Ezekiel saw in vision, which John seems also to have had in his eye. See Eze. xlviii. 31. The inscription in Ezekiel denoted that that was the residence of the people of God; and the same idea is denoted here. The New Jerusalem is the eternal residence of the children of God, and this is indicated at every gate. None can enter who do not belong to that people; all who are within are understood to be of their number.

13. *On the east three gates,* &c. The city was square (ver. 16), and the same number of gates is assigned to each quarter. There does not appear to be any special significancy in this fact, unless it be to denote that there is access to this city from all quarters of the world, and that they who dwell there will have come from each of the

448                    REVELATION.                    [A.D. 96.

14 And the wall of the city had twelve foundations, and *a* in them the names of the twelve apostles of the Lamb.

15 And he that talked with me had a golden *b* reed to measure the

*a* Ep.2.20.    *b* ch.11.1; Eze.40.3; Zec.2.1.

city, and the gates thereof, and the wall thereof.

16 And the city lieth four-square, and the length is as large as the breadth: and he measured the city with the reed, twelve thousand furlongs. The length, and the breadth, and the height of it are equal.

---

great divisions of the earth—that is, from every land.

14. *And the wall of the city had twelve foundations.* It is not said whether these foundations were twelve rows of stones placed one above another under the city, and extending round it, or whether they were twelve stones placed at intervals. The former would seem to be the most probable, as the latter would indicate comparative feebleness and liability to fall. Compare Notes on ver. 19. ¶ *And in them.* In the foundation of stones. That is, the names of the apostles were cut or carved in them so as to be conspicuous. ¶ *The names of the twelve apostles of the Lamb.* Of the Lamb of God; the Messiah. For an illustration of this passage, see Notes on Ep. ii. 20.

15. *And he that talked with me.* The angel, ver. 9. ¶ *Had a golden reed to measure the city.* See Notes on ch. xi. 1. The reed, or measuring rod, here, is of gold, because all about the city is of the most rich and costly materials. The rod is thus suited to the personage who uses it, and to the occasion. Compare a similar description in Eze. xl. 3–5; xliii. 16. The object of this measuring is to show that the city has proper architectural proportions. ¶ *And the gates thereof*, &c. To measure every part of the city, and to ascertain its exact dimensions.

16. *And the city lieth four-square.* It was an exact square. That is, there was nothing irregular about it; there were no crooked walls; there was no jutting out, and no indentation in the walls, as if the city had been built at different times without a plan, and had been accommodated to circumstances. Most cities have been determined in their outline by the character of the ground—by hills, streams, or ravines; or have grown up by accretions, where one part has been joined to another, so that there is no regularity, and so that the original plan, if there was any, has been lost sight of. The New Jerusalem, on the contrary, had been built according to a plan of the utmost regularity, which had not been modified by the circumstances, or varied as the city grew. The idea here may be, that the church, as it will appear in its state of glory, will be in accordance with an eternal plan, and that the great original design will have been fully carried out. ¶ *And the length is as large as the breadth. The height also of the city was the same* —so that it was an exact square. ¶ *And he measured the city with the reed, twelve thousand furlongs.* As eight furlongs make a mile, the extent of the walls, therefore, must have been three hundred and seventy-five miles. Of course, this must preclude all idea of there being such a city literally in Palestine. This is clearly a figurative or symbolical representation; and the idea is, that the city was on the most magnificent scale, and with the largest proportions, and the description here is adopted merely to indicate this vastness, without any idea that it would be understood *literally*. ¶ *The length, and the breadth, and the height of it are equal.* According to this representation, the height of the *city*, not of the *walls* (comp. ver. 17), would be three hundred and seventy-five miles. Of course, this *cannot* be understood literally, and the very idea of a literal fulfilment of this shows the absurdity of that method of interpretation. The idea intended to be conveyed by this immense height would seem to be that it would contain countless numbers of inhabitants. It is true that such a structure has not existed, and that a city of such a height may seem to be out of all proportion; but we are to remember (*a*) that this is a *symbol;* and (*b*) that, considered as one mass or pile of buildings, it may not seem to be out of proportion. It is no uncommon thing that a house should be as high as it is long or broad. The idea of *vastness* and of *capacity* is the main idea designed to be represented. The image before the mind is, that the numbers of the redeemed will be immense.

## CHAPTER XXI.

17 And he measured the wall thereof, an hundred and forty and four cubits, according to the measure of a man, that is, of the angel.

18 And the building of the wall of it was *of* jasper; and the city *was* pure gold, like unto clear glass.

17. *And he measured the wall thereof.* In respect to its *height*. Of course, its *length* corresponded with the extent of the city. ¶ *An hundred* and *forty* and *four cubits.* This would be, reckoning the cubit at eighteen inches, two hundred and sixteen feet. This is less than the height of the walls of Babylon, which Herodotus says were three hundred and fifty feet high. See Introduction to ch. xiii. of Isaiah. As the walls of a city are designed to protect it from external foes, the height mentioned here gives all proper ideas of security; and we are to conceive of the city itself as towering immensely *above* the walls. Its glory, therefore, would not be obscured by the wall that was thrown around it for defence. ¶ *According to the measure of a man.* The measure usually employed by men. This seems to be added in order to prevent any mistake as to the size of the city. It is an *angel* who makes the measurement, and without his explanation it might perhaps be supposed that he used some measure not in common use among men, so that, after all, it would be impossible to form any definite idea of the size of the city. ¶ *That is, of the angel.* That is, "which is the measure employed by the angel." It was, indeed, an angel who measured the city, but the measure which he employed was that in common use among men.

18. *And the building of the wall of it.* The material of which the wall was composed. This means the wall *above* the foundation, for that was composed of twelve rows of precious stones, ver. 14, 19, 20. The height of the foundation is not stated, but the entire wall above was composed of jasper. ¶ *Was* of *jasper.* See Notes on ch. iv. 3. Of course, this cannot be taken *literally;* and an attempt to explain all this literally would show that that method of interpreting the Apocalypse is impracticable. ¶ *And the city was pure gold.* The material of which the edifices were composed. ¶ *Like unto clear glass.* The word rendered *glass* in this place — ὕαλος — occurs in the New Testament only here and in ver. 21 of this chapter. It means, properly, "anything transparent like water;" as, for example, any transparent stone or gem, or as rock-salt, crystal, glass (Rob. *Lex.*). Here the meaning is, that the golden city would be so bright and burnished that it would seem to be glass reflecting the sunbeams. Would the appearance of a city, as the sun is setting, when the reflection of its beams from thousands of panes of glass gives it the appearance of burnished gold, represent the idea here? If we were to suppose a city made entirely of glass, and the setting sunbeams falling on it, it might convey the idea represented here. It is certain that, as nothing could be more magnificent, so nothing could more beautifully combine the two ideas referred to here—that of *gold* and *glass.* Perhaps the reflection of the sunbeams from the "Crystal Palace," erected for the late "industrial exhibition" in London, would convey a better idea of what is intended to be represented here than anything which our world has furnished. The following description from one who was an eye-witness, drawn up by him at the time, and without any reference to this passage, and furnished at my request, will supply a better illustration of the passage before us than any description which I could give:—"Seen as the morning vapours rolled around its base — its far-stretching roofs rising one above another, and its great transept, majestically arched, soaring out of the envelope of clouds—its pillars, window-bars, and pinnacles, looked literally like a castle in the air; like some palace, such as one reads of in idle tales of Arabian enchantment, having about it all the ethereal softness of a dream. Looked at from a distance at noon, when the sunbeams came pouring upon the terraced and vaulted roof, it resembles a regal palace of silver, built for some Eastern prince; *when the sun at eventide sheds on its sides his parting rays, the edifice is transformed into a temple of gold and rubies;* and in the calm hours of night, when the moon walketh in her brightness, the immense surface of glass which the building presents looks like a sea, or like throwing back, in flickering smile, the radiant glances of the queen of heaven."

19 And the *c*foundations of the wall of the city were garnished with all manner of precious stones. The first foundation was jasper; the second, sapphire; the third, a chalcedony; the fourth, an emerald;

*c* Is. 54.11.

20 The fifth, sardonyx; the sixth, sardius; the seventh, chrysolite; the eighth, beryl; the ninth, a topaz; the tenth, a chrysoprasus; the eleventh, a jacinth; the twelfth, an amethyst.

19. *And the foundations of the wall of the city.* Notes on ver. 14. ¶ *Were garnished.* Were adorned, or decorated. That is, the foundations were *composed* of precious stones, giving them this highly ornamented and brilliant appearance. ¶ *The first foundation.* The first *row*, *layer*, or *course.* Notes on ver. 14. ¶ *Was jasper.* See Notes on ch. iv. 3. ¶ *The second, sapphire.* This stone is not elsewhere mentioned in the New Testament. It is a precious stone, next in hardness to the diamond, usually of an azure or sky-blue colour, but of various shades. ¶ *The third, a chalcedony.* This word occurs nowhere else in the New Testament. The stone referred to is an uncrystallized translucent variety of quartz, having a whitish colour, and of a lustre nearly like wax. It is found covering the sides of cavities, and is a deposit from filtrated silicious waters. When it is arranged in *stripes*, it constitutes *agate;* and if the stripes are horizontal, it is the *onyx.* The modern *carnelian* is a variety of this. The carnelian is of a deep flesh red, or reddish-white colour. The *name* chalcedony is from *Chalcedon*, a town in Asia Minor, opposite to Byzantium, or Constantinople, where this stone was probably first known (Webster's *Dict.*). ¶ *The fourth, an emerald.* See Notes on Re. iv. 3. The emerald is green.

20. *The fifth, sardonyx.* This word does not occur elsewhere in the New Testament. The *name* is derived from *Sardis*, a city in Asia Minor (Notes on ch. iii. 1), and ὄνυξ, *a nail*—so named, according to Pliny, from the resemblance of its colour to the flesh and the nail. It is a silicious stone or gem, nearly allied to the onyx. The colour is a reddish yellow, nearly orange (Webster, *Dict.*). ¶ *The sixth, sardius.* This word does not elsewhere occur in the New Testament. It is also derived from *Sardis*, and the name was probably given to the gem because it was found there. It is a stone of a blood-red or flesh colour, and is commonly known as a *carnelian.*

It is the same as the *sardine* stone mentioned in Re. iv. 3. See Notes on that place. ¶ *The seventh, chrysolite.* This word does not elsewhere occur in the New Testament. It is derived from χρυσὸς, *gold*, and λίθος, *stone*, and means *golden stone*, and was applied by the ancients to all gems of a golden or yellow colour, probably designating particularly the topaz of the moderns (Rob. *Lex.*). But in Webster's *Dict.* it is said that its prevalent colour is green. It is sometimes transparent. This is the *modern* chrysolite. The ancients undoubtedly understood by the name a *yellow* gem. ¶ *The eighth, beryl.* This word occurs nowhere else in the New Testament. The beryl is a mineral of great hardness, and is of a green or bluish-green colour. It is identical with the emerald, except in the colour, the emerald having a purer and richer green colour, proceeding from a trace of oxide of chrome. Prisms of beryl are sometimes found nearly two feet in diameter in the state of New Hampshire (Webster). ¶ *The ninth, a topaz.* This word does not elsewhere occur in the New Testament. The topaz is a well-known mineral, said to be so called from *Topazos*, a small island in the Arabian Gulf. It is generally of a yellowish colour, and pellucid, but it is also found of greenish, bluish, or brownish shades. ¶ *The tenth, a chrysoprasus.* This word does not elsewhere occur in the New Testament. It is derived from χρυσὸς, *gold*, and πράσον, *a leek*, and denotes a precious stone of greenish golden colour, like a leek; that is, "apple-green passing into a grass-green" (Rob. *Lex.*). "It is a variety of quartz. It is commonly apple-green, and often extremely beautiful. It is translucent, or sometimes semi-transparent; its hardness little inferor to flint" (Webster, *Dict.*). ¶ *The eleventh, a jacinth.* The word does not elsewhere occur in the New Testament. It is the same word as *hyacinth*—ὑάκινθος—and denotes properly the well-known flower of that name, usually of a deep purple or reddish blue. Here it denotes a gem of this colour. It is a

A.D. 96.]  CHAPTER XXI.  451

21 And the twelve gates *were* twelve pearls; every several gate was of one pearl: and the street of the city *was* pure gold, as it were transparent glass.

22 And I saw no temple therein: for the Lord God Almighty and the Lamb are the temple of it.

23 And the city *d*had no need of the sun, neither of the moon, to shine in it; for the glory of God

*d* ch.22.5; Is.60.19,20.

did lighten it, and *e* the Lamb *is* the light thereof.

24 And the *f* nations of them which are saved shall walk in the light of it: and the *g* kings of the earth do bring their glory and honour into it.

25 And the gates of it shall not be shut at all by day; for *h* there shall be no night there.

*e* Jn.1.4.  *f* Is.60.3-11; 66.10-12.
*g* Ps.72.11.  *h* Zec.14.7.

red variety of *zircon*. See Webster's *Dict.* under the word *hyacinth*. ¶ *The twelfth, an amethyst*. This word, also, is found only in this place in the New Testament. It denotes a gem of a deep purple or violet colour. The *word* is derived from α, priv., and μεθύω, to be intoxicated, because this gem was supposed to be an antidote against drunkenness. It is a species of quartz, and is used in jewelry.

21. *And the twelve gates*. Ver. 12. ¶ *Were twelve pearls*. See Notes on ch. xvii. 4; Mat. xiii. 46. ¶ *Every several gate was of one pearl*. Each gate. Of course, this is not to be understood literally. The idea is that of ornament and beauty, and nothing could give a more striking view of the magnificence of the future abode of the saints. ¶ *And the street of the city was pure gold*. Was paved with gold; that is, all the vacant space that was not occupied with buildings was of pure gold. See Notes on ver. 18.

22. *And I saw no temple therein*. No structure reared expressly for the worship of God; no particular place where he was adored. It was *all* temple—nothing but a temple. It was not like Jerusalem, where there was but one house reared expressly for divine worship, and to which the inhabitants repaired to praise God; it was all one great temple reared in honour of his name, and where worship ascended from every part of it. With this explanation, this passage harmonizes with what is said in ch. ii. 12; vii. 15. ¶ *For the Lord God Almighty and the Lamb are the temple of it*. They are present in all parts of it in their glory; they fill it with light; and the splendour of their presence may be said *to be* the temple. The idea here is, that it would be a holy world—*all* holy. No particular portion would be set apart for purposes of public worship, but in all places God would be adored, and every portion of it devoted to the purposes of religion.

23. *And the city had no need of the sun, neither of the moon, to shine in it*. This imagery seems to be derived from Is. lx. 19, 20. See Notes on those verses. No language could give a more striking or beautiful representation of the heavenly state than that which is here employed. ¶ *For the glory of God did lighten it*. By the visible splendour of his glory. See Notes on ver. 11. That supplied the place of the sun and the moon. ¶ *And the Lamb is the light thereof*. The Son of God; the Messiah. See Notes on ch. v. 6; Is. lx. 19.

24. *And the nations of them which are saved*. All the nations that are saved; or all the saved considered *as* nations. This imagery is doubtless derived from that in Isaiah, particularly ch. lx. 3-9. See Notes on that passage. ¶ *Shall walk in the light of it*. Shall enjoy its splendour, and be continually in its light. ¶ *And the kings of the earth do bring their glory and honour into it*. All that they consider as constituting their glory, treasures, crowns, sceptres, robes. The idea is, that all these will be devoted to God in the future days of the church in its glory, and will be, as it were, brought and laid down at the feet of the Saviour in heaven. The language is derived, doubtless, from the description in Is. lx. 3-14. Comp. Is. xlix. 23.

25. *And the gates of it shall not be shut at all by day*. It shall be constantly open, allowing free ingress and egress to all who reside there. The language is derived from Is. lx. 11. See Notes on that place. Applied to the future state of the blessed, it would seem to mean, that while this will be their per-

26 And they shall bring the glory and honour of the nations into it.

27 And *there shall in no wise enter into it any thing that defileth, neither *whatsoever* worketh abomination, or *maketh* a lie: but they which are written in the *Lamb's book of life.

*i* Is.35.8; 52.1; 60.21; Joel 3.17; Mat.13.41; 1 Co.6.9,10; Ga.5.19-21; Ep.5.5; He.12.14.   *k* ch.13.8.

manent abode, yet that the dwellers there will not be *prisoners*. The universe will be open to them. They will be permitted to go forth and visit every world, and survey the works of God in all parts of his dominions. ¶ *For there shall be no night there.* It shall be all day; all unclouded splendour. When, therefore, it is said that the gates should not be "shut *by day*," it means that they would *never* be shut. When it is said that there would be no *night* there, it is, undoubtedly, to be taken as meaning that there would be no *literal* darkness, and nothing of which night is the emblem: no calamity, no sorrow, no bereavement, no darkened windows on account of the loss of friends and kindred. Comp. Notes on ver. 4.

26. *And they shall bring,* &c. See Notes on ver. 24. That blessed world shall be made up of all that was truly valuable and pure on the earth.

27. *And there shall in no wise.* On no account; by no means. This strong language denotes the absolute exclusion of all that is specified in the verse. ¶ *Anything that defileth.* Literally, anything "*common.*" See Notes on Ac. x. 14. It means here that nothing will be found in that blessed abode which is unholy or sinful. It will be a pure world, 2 Pe. iii. 13. ¶ *Neither whatsoever worketh abomination, or maketh a lie.* See Notes on ver. 8. ¶ *But they which are written in the Lamb's book of life.* Whose names are there recorded. See Notes on ch. iii. 5. Comp. Notes on ver. 8.

## CHAPTER XXII.

For the analysis of the first five verses of this chapter, see the Analysis of ch. xxi. The chapter comprises the remainder of the description of the "New Jerusalem"—the blessed abode of the saints (ver. 1-5), and then (ver. 6-21) the conclusion or epilogue of the whole book. It is difficult to conceive what induced the author of the division of the

## CHAPTER XXII.

AND he showed me a pure river of water of life, clear as crystal, proceeding out of the throne of God and of the Lamb.

2 In*a* the midst of *b* the street of it, and on either side of the river, *was there* *c* the tree of life, which

*a* Eze.47.1,12.   *b* ch.21.21.   *c* ch.2.7.

New Testament into chapters, to separate the first five verses of this chapter from the preceding chapter. A new chapter should have commenced at ver. 6 of ch. xxii.; for the remainder properly comprises the conclusion of the whole book. Comp. Intro. to Notes on the Gospels, vol. i. pp. vii. viii.

1. *And he showed me a pure river of water of life.* In the New Jerusalem; the happy abode of the redeemed. The phrase "water of life," means *living* or *running* water, like a spring or fountain, as contrasted with a stagnant pool. See Notes on John iv. 14. The allusion here is doubtless to the first Eden, where a river watered the garden (Gen. ii. 10, seq.), and as this is a description of Eden recovered, or Paradise regained, it was natural to introduce a river of water also, yet in such a way as to accord with the general description of that future abode of the redeemed. It does not spring up, therefore, from the ground, but flows from the throne of God and the Lamb. Perhaps, also, the writer had in his eye the description in Eze. xlvii. 1-12, where a stream issues from under the temple, and is parted in different directions. ¶ *Clear as crystal.* See Notes on ch. iv. 6. ¶ *Proceeding out of the throne of God and of the Lamb.* Flowing from the foot of the throne. Comp. ch. iv. 6. This idea is strictly in accordance with Oriental imagery. In the East, fountains and running streams constituted an essential part of the image of enjoyment and prosperity (see Notes on Is. xxxv. 6), and such fountains were common in the courts of Oriental houses. Here, the river is an emblem of peace, happiness, plenty; and the essential thought in its flowing from the throne is, that all the happiness of heaven proceeds from God.

2. *In the midst of the street of it.* Professor Stuart renders this, "between the street thereof and the river;" and says that "the writer conceives of the river as running through the whole city;

# CHAPTER XXII. 453

bare twelve *manner of* fruits, *and* yielded her fruit every month: and then of streets parallel to it on either side; and then, on the banks of the river, between the water and the street, the whole stream is lined on either side with two rows of the tree of life." The more common interpretation, however, is doubtless admissible, and would give a more beautiful image; that in the street, or streets of the city, as well as on the banks of the river, the tree of life was planted. It abounded everywhere. The city had not only a river passing through it, but it was pervaded by streets, and all those streets were lined and shaded with this tree. The idea in the mind of the writer is that of *Eden* or *Paradise;* but it is not the Eden of the book of Genesis, or the Oriental or Persian Paradise: it is a picture where all is combined, that in the view of the writer would constitute beauty, or contribute to happiness. ¶ *And on either side of the river.* As well as in all the streets. The writer undoubtedly conceives of a single river running through the city—probably as meandering along—and that river lined on both sides with the tree of life. This gives great beauty to the imagery. ¶ Was there *the tree of life.* Not a single tree, but it abounded everywhere—on the banks of the river, and in all the streets. It was the *common* tree in this blessed Paradise—of which all might partake, and which was everywhere the emblem of immortality. In this respect, this new Paradise stands in strong contrast with that in which Adam was placed at his creation, where there seems to have been a single tree that was designated as the tree of life, Ge. iii. 22, 23. In the future state of the blessed, that tree will abound, and all may freely partake of it; the emblem, the pledge of immortal life, will be constantly before the eyes, whatever part of the future abode may be traversed, and the inhabitants of that blessed world may constantly partake of it. ¶ *Which bare twelve* manner of *fruits.* "Producing twelve fruit-harvests; not (as our version) twelve manner of fruits" (Professor Stuart). The idea is not that there are twelve kinds of fruit on the same tree, for that is not implied in the language used by John. The literal rendering is, "producing twelve *fruits*"—ποιοῦν καρποὺς δώδεκα. The word "*manner*" has been introduced by the translators without authority. The idea is, that the tree bore every month in the year, so that there were twelve fruit-harvests. It was not like a tree that bears but once a year, or in one season only, but it *constantly* bore fruit—it bore every month. The idea is that of *abundance,* not *variety.* The supply never fails; the tree is never barren. As there is but a single class of trees referred to, it might have been supposed, perhaps, that, according to the common method in which fruit is produced, there would be sometimes plenty and sometimes want; but the writer says that, though there *is* but one kind, yet the supply is ample. The tree is everywhere; it is constantly producing fruit. ¶ And *yielded her fruit every month.* The word "*and*" is also supplied by the translators, and introduces an idea which is not in the original, as if there was not only a *succession* of harvests, which *is* in the text, but that each one differed from the former, which is *not* in the text. The proper translation is, "producing twelve fruits, yielding or rendering its fruit in each month." Thus there is, indeed, a succession of fruit-crops, but it is the same kind of fruit. We are not to infer, however, that there will not be *variety* in the occupations and the joys of the heavenly state, for there can be no doubt that there will be ample diversity in the employments, and in the sources of happiness, in heaven; but the single thought expressed here is, that the means of life *will be abundant:* the trees of life will be everywhere, and they will be constantly yielding fruit. ¶ *And the leaves of the tree.* Not only the *fruit* will contribute to give life, but even the *leaves* will be salutary. Everything about it will contribute to sustain life. ¶ Were *for the healing.* That is, they contribute to impart life and health to those who had been diseased. We are not to suppose that there will be sickness, and a healing process in heaven, for that idea is expressly excluded in ch. xxi. 4; but the meaning is, that the life and health of that blessed world will have been imparted by partaking of that tree; and the writer says that, in fact, it was owing to it that they who dwell there had been healed of their spiritual maladies, and had been made to live for ever. ¶ *Of the nations.* Of all the nations assembled there, ch. xxi.

3 And <sup>d</sup>there shall be no more curse: but the <sup>e</sup>throne of God and of the Lamb shall be in it; and his <sup>f</sup>servants shall serve him:

<small>d Zec.14.11.  e Eze.48.35.  f ch.7.15.</small>

4 And <sup>g</sup> they shall see his face; and <sup>h</sup>his name *shall be* in their foreheads.

5 And <sup>i</sup> there shall be no night

<small>g Mat.5.8; Jn.12.26; 17.24; 1 Co.13.12; 1 Jn.3.2.
h ch.3.12.   i ch.21.23,25.</small>

24. There is a close resemblance between the language here used by John and that used by Ezekiel (xlvii. 12), and it is not improbable that both these writers refer to the same thing. Comp. also in the Apocrypha, 2 Esdras ii. 12; viii. 52–54.

3. *And there shall be no more curse.* This is doubtless designed to be in strong contrast with our present abode; and it is affirmed that what now properly comes under the name of a *curse*, or whatever is part of the curse pronounced on man by the fall, will be there unknown. The earth will be no more cursed, and will produce no more thorns and thistles; man will be no more compelled to earn his bread by the sweat of his brow; woman will be no more doomed to bear the sufferings which she does now; and the abodes of the blessed will be no more cursed by sickness, sorrow, tears, and death. ¶ *But the throne of God and of the Lamb shall be in it.* God will reign there for ever; the principles of purity and love which the Lamb of God came to establish, will pervade that blessed abode to all eternity. ¶ *And his servants shall serve him.* All his servants that are there; that is, all the inhabitants of that blessed world. For the meaning of this passage, see Notes on ch. vii. 15.

4. *And they shall see his face.* See Notes on Mat. xviii. 10. They would be constantly in his presence, and be permitted continually to behold his glory. ¶ *And his name* shall be *in their foreheads.* They shall be designated as his. See Notes on ch. iii. 12; vii.3; xiii.16.

5. *And there shall be no night there.* Notes on ch. xxi. 25. ¶ *And they need no candle.* No lamp; no artificial light, as in a world where there is night and darkness. ¶ *Neither light of the sun; for the Lord God*, &c. Notes on ch. xxi. 23. ¶ *And they shall reign for ever and ever.* That is, with God; they shall be as kings. See Notes on ch. v. 10; xx. 6. Comp. Notes on Ro. viii. 16; 2 Ti. ii. 11, 12.

REMARKS ON CHAP. XXI., XXII. 1-5.

This portion of the Apocalypse contains the most full and complete continuous description of the state of the righteous, in the world of blessedness, that is to be found in the Bible. It seems to be proper, therefore, to pause on it for a moment, and to state in a summary manner what will be the principal features of that blessedness. All can see that, as a description, it occupies an appropriate place, not only in regard to this book, but to the volume of revealed truth. In reference to this particular book, it is the appropriate close of the account of the conflicts, the trials, and the persecutions of the church; in reference to the whole volume of revealed truth, it is appropriate because it occurs in the last of the inspired books that was written. It was proper that a volume of revealed truth given to mankind, and designed to describe a great work of redeeming mercy, *should* close with a description of the state of the righteous after death.

The principal features in the description are the following:—

(1) There will be a new heaven and a new earth: a new order of things, and a world adapted to the condition of the righteous. There will be such changes produced in the earth, and such abodes fitted up for the redeemed, that it will be proper to say that they are *new*, ch. xxi. 1.

(2) The *locality* of that abode is not determined. No particular *place* is revealed as constituting heaven; nor is it intimated that there would be such a *place*. For anything that appears, the universe at large will be heaven— the earth and all worlds; and we are left free to suppose that the redeemed will yet occupy any position of the universe, and be permitted to behold the peculiar glories of the divine character that are manifested in each of the worlds that he has made. Comp. Notes on 1 Pe. i. 12. That there may be some one place in the universe that will be their permanent home, and that will be more properly called *heaven*, where the glory of their God and Saviour will be peculiarly manifested, is not improbable; but still there is nothing to prevent the hope and the belief that in the infinite duration that awaits them they will be permitted to

there: and they need no candle, neither light of the sun; for *k*the *l*they shall reign for ever and ever.

*k* Ps.36.9.     *l* Ro.5.17.

visit all the worlds that God has made, and to learn in each, and from each, all that he has peculiarly manifested of his own character and glory there.

(3) That future state will be entirely and for ever free from all the consequences of the apostasy as now seen on the earth. There will be neither tears, nor sorrow, nor death, nor crying, nor pain, nor curse, ch. xxi. 4; xxii. 3. It will, therefore, be a perfectly happy abode.

(4) It will be pure and holy. Nothing will ever enter there that shall contaminate and defile, ch. xxi. 8, 27. On this account, also, it will be a happy world, for (*a*) all real happiness has its foundation in holiness; and (*b*) the source of all the misery that the universe has experienced is sin. Let that be removed, and the earth would be happy; let it be extinguished from any world, and its happiness will be secure.

(5) It will be a world of perfect light, ch. xxi. 22-25; xxii. 5. There will be (*a*) literally no night there; (*b*) spiritually and morally there will be no darkness—no error, no sin. Light will be cast on a thousand subjects now obscure; and on numerous points pertaining to the divine government and dealings which now perplex the mind there will be poured the splendour of perfect day. All the darkness that exists here will be dissipated there; all that is now obscure will be made light. And in view of this fact, we may well submit for a little time to the mysteries which hang over the divine dealings here. The Christian is destined to live for ever and ever. He is capable of an eternal progression in knowledge. He is soon to be ushered into the splendours of that eternal abode where there is no need of the light of the sun or the moon, and where there is no night. In a little time—a few weeks or days—by removal to that higher state of being, he will have made a degree of progress in true knowledge compared with which all that can be learned here is a nameless trifle. In that future abode he will be permitted to know all that is to be known in those worlds that shine upon his path by day or by night; all that is to be known in the character of their Maker, and the principles of his government; all that is to be known of the glorious plan of redemption; all that is to be known of the reasons why sin and woe were permitted to enter this beautiful world. There, too, he will be permitted to enjoy all that there is to be enjoyed in a world without a cloud and without a tear; all that is beatific in the friendship of God the Father, of the Ascended Redeemer, of the Sacred Spirit; all that is blessed in the goodly fellowship of the angels, of the apostles, of the prophets; all that is rapturous in reunion with those that were loved on the earth. Well, then, may he bear with the darkness and endure the trials of this state a little longer.

(6) It will be a world of surpassing splendour. This is manifest by the description of it in ch. xx., as a gorgeous city, with ample dimensions, with most brilliant colours, set with gems, and composed of pure gold. The writer, in the description of that abode, has accumulated all that is gorgeous and magnificent, and doubtless felt that even *this* was a very imperfect representation of that glorious world.

(7) That future world will be an abode of the highest conceivable happiness. This is manifest, not only from the fact stated that there will be no pain or sorrow here, but from the positive description in ch. xxii. 1, 2. It was, undoubtedly, the design of the writer, under the image of a *Paradise*, to describe the future abode of the redeemed as one of the highest happiness—where there would be an ample and a constant supply of every want, and where the highest ideas of enjoyment would be realized. And,

(8) All this will be eternal. The universe, so vast and so wonderful, seems to have been made to be fitted to the eternal contemplation of created minds, and *in* this universe there is an adaptation for the employment of mind for ever and ever.

If it be asked now why John, in the account which he has given of the heavenly state, adopted this figurative and emblematic mode of representation, and why it did not please God to reveal *any more* respecting the nature of the employments and enjoyments of the heavenly world, it may be replied, (*a*) That this method is eminently in accordance with the general character of the book, as a book of symbols and emblems. (b) He has stated *enough* to give us a general and a most attractive view of that blessed state. (c) It is not certain that we would have appreciated it, or could have comprehended it, if a more minute and literal description had been given. That state may be so unlike this that it is doubtful whether we could have comprehended *any* literal description that could have been given. How little of the future and the unseen can ever be known by a mere description; how faint and imperfect a view can we ever obtain of anything by the mere use of words, and especially of objects which have no resemblance to anything which we have seen! Who ever obtained any adequate idea of Niagara by a mere description? To what Greek or Roman mind, however cultivated, could there have been conveyed the idea of a printing-press, of a locomotive engine, of the magnetic telegraph, by mere description? Who can convey to one born blind an idea of the prismatic colours; or to the deaf an idea of sounds? If we may imagine the world of insect tribes to be endowed with the power of language and thought, how could the gay and gilded butterfly that to-day plays in the sunbeam impart to its companions of yesterday—low and grovelling worms—any adequate idea of that new condition of being into which it had emerged? And how do we know that *we* could comprehend *any* description of that world where the righteous dwell, or of employments and enjoyments so unlike our own?

I cannot more appropriately close this brief notice of the revelations of the heavenly state than by introducing an ancient poem, which seems to be founded on this portion of the Apocalypse, and which is the original of one of the most touching and beautiful hymns now used in Protestant places of worship — the well-known hymn which begins, "Jerusalem! my happy home!" This hymn is deservedly a great favourite, and is an eminently beautiful composition. It is, however, of Roman Catholic origin. It is found in a small volume of miscellaneous poetry, sold at Mr. Bright's sale of manuscripts in 1844, which has been placed in the British Museum, and now forms the additional MS. 15,225. It is referred, by the lettering on the book, to the age of Elizabeth, but it is supposed to belong to the subsequent reign. The volume seems to have been formed by or for some Roman Catholic, and contains many devotional songs or hymns, interspersed with others of a more general character. See Littell's *Living Age*, vol. xxviii. pp. 333–336. The hymn is as follows:—

A SONG MADE BY F. B. P.
*To the tune of "Diana."*

Jerusalem! my happy home!
  When shall I come to thee?
When shall my sorrows have an end—
  Thy joys when shall I see?

O happy harbour of the saints—
  O sweet and pleasant soil!
In thee no sorrow may be found,
  No grief, no care, no toil.

In thee no sickness may be seen,
  No hurt, no ache, no sore;
There is no death, no ugly deil,*
  There's life for evermore.

No dampish mist is seen in thee,
  No cold nor darksome night;
There every soul shines as the sun,
  There God himself gives light.

There lust and lucre cannot dwell,
  There envy bears no sway;
There is no hunger, heat, nor cold,
  But pleasure every way.

Jerusalem! Jerusalem!
  God grant I once may see
Thy endless joys, and of the same
  Partaker aye to be.

Thy walls are made of precious stones,
  Thy bulwarks diamonds square;
Thy gates are of right orient pearl,
  Exceeding rich and rare.

Thy turrets and thy pinnacles
  With carbuncles to shine;
Thy very streets are paved with gold,
  Surpassing clear and fine.

Thy houses are of ivory,
  Thy windows crystal clear;
Thy tiles are made of beaten gold—
  O God, that I were there!

Within thy gates no thing doth come
  That is not passing clean;
No spider's web, no dirt, no dust,
  No filth may there be seen.

Ah, my sweet home, Jerusalem!
  Would God I were in thee;
Would God my woes were at an end,
  Thy joys that I might see!

Thy saints are crown'd with glory great,
  They see God face to face;
They triumph still, they still rejoice—
  Most happy is their case.

We that are here in banishment
  Continually do moan;
We sigh and sob, we weep and wail,
  Perpetually we groan.

* Devil, in MS., but it must have been pronounced *Scoticè*, "deil."

6 And he said unto me, These sayings *are* faithful and true: and the Lord God of the holy prophets ᵐsent his angel to show unto his

*m* ch.1.1.

> Our sweet is mixed with bitter gall,
> Our pleasure is but pain;
> Our joys scarce last the looking on,
> Our sorrows still remain.
>
> But there they live in such delight,
> Such pleasure, and such play,
> As that to them a thousand years
> Doth seem as yesterday.
>
> Thy vineyards and thy orchards are
> Most beautiful and fair;
> Full furnished with trees and fruits,
> Most wonderful and rare.
>
> Thy gardens and thy gallant walks
> Continually are green;
> There grow such sweet and pleasant flowers
> As nowhere else are seen.
>
> There's nectar and ambrosia made,
> There's musk and civet sweet;
> There many a fair and dainty drug
> Are trodden under feet.
>
> There cinnamon, there sugar grows,
> There nard and balm abound;
> What tongue can tell, or heart conceive,
> The joys that there are found?
>
> Quite through the streets, with silver sound,
> The flood of life doth flow;
> Upon whose banks, on every side,
> The wood of life doth grow.
>
> There trees for evermore bear fruit,
> And evermore do spring;
> There evermore the angels sit,
> And evermore do sing.
>
> There David stands with harp in hand,
> As master of the quire;
> Ten thousand times that man were blest
> That might this music* hear.
>
> Our Lady sings *Magnificat*,
> With tune surpassing sweet;
> And all the virgins bear their parts,
> Sitting above her feet.
>
> *Te Deum* doth Saint Ambrose sing,
> Saint Austin doth the like;
> Old Simeon and Zachary
> Have not their song to seek.
>
> There Magdalene hath left her moan,
> And cheerfully doth sing
> With blessed saints, whose harmony
> In every street doth ring.
>
> Jerusalem, my happy home!
> Would God I were in thee;
> Would God my woes were at an end,
> Thy joys that I might see!

ANALYSIS OF CHAPTER XXII. 6-20.

This portion of the book of Revelation is properly the epilogue, or conclusion. The main purposes of the vision are accomplished; the enemies of the church are quelled; the church is triumphant; the affairs of the world are wound up; the redeemed are received to their blissful, eternal abode; the wicked are cut off; the earth is purified, and the affairs

* Musing, in MS.

of the universe are fixed on their permanent foundation. A few miscellaneous matters, therefore, close the book.

(1) A solemn affirmation on the part of him who had made these revelations, that they are true, and that they will be speedily accomplished, and that he will be blessed or happy who shall keep the sayings of the book, ver. 6, 7.

(2) The effect of all these things on John himself, leading him, as in a former case (ch. xix. 10), to a disposition to worship him who had been the medium in making to him such extraordinary communications, ver. 8, 9.

(3) A command not to seal up what had been revealed, since the time was near. These things would soon have their fulfilment, and it was proper that the prophecies should be unsealed, or open, both that the events might be compared with the predictions, and that a persecuted church might be able to see what would be the *result* of all these things, and to find consolation in the assurance of the final triumph of the Son of God, ver. 10.

(4) The fixed and unchangeable state of the righteous and the wicked, ver. 11-13.

(5) The blessedness of those who keep the commandments of God, and who enter into the New Jerusalem, ver. 14, 15.

(6) Jesus, the root and the offspring of David, and the bright and morning star, proclaims himself to be the Author of all these revelations by the instrumentality of an angel, ver. 16.

(7) The universal invitation of the gospel—the language of Jesus himself —giving utterance to his strong desire for the salvation of men, ver. 17.

(8) A solemn command not to change anything that had been revealed in this book, either by adding to it or taking from it, ver. 18, 19.

(9) The assurance that he who had made these revelations would come quickly, and the joyous assent of John to this, and prayer that his advent might soon occur, ver. 20.

(10) The benediction, ver. 21.

6. *And he said unto me.* The angel-interpreter, who had showed John the vision of the New Jerusalem, ch. xxi. 9, 10. As these visions are now at an

458   REVELATION.   [A.D. 96.

servants the things which must shortly be done.

7 Behold, [n]I come quickly: blessed *is* he that keepeth the sayings of the prophecy of this book.

8 And I John saw these things, and heard *them.* And when I had heard and seen, I fell down to worship before the feet of the angel which showed me these things.

[n] ver.10,12,20.

9 Then saith he unto me, See *thou do it* not: for I am thy fellow-servant, and of thy brethren the prophets, and of them which keep the sayings of this book: worship God.

10 And he saith unto me, [o]Seal not the sayings of the prophecy of this book: for the time is at hand.

[o] Da.8.26.

end, the angel comes to John directly, and assures him that all these things are true—that there has been no deception of the senses in these visions, but that they were really divine disclosures of what would soon and certainly occur. ¶ *These sayings are faithful and true.* These communications — all that has been disclosed to you by symbols, or in direct language. See Notes on ch. xxi. 5. ¶ *And the Lord God of the holy prophets.* The same God who inspired the ancient prophets. ¶ *Sent his angel.* See Notes on ch. i. 1. ¶ *To show unto his servants.* To all his servants—that is, to all his people, by the instrumentality of John. The revelation was made to him, and he was to record it for the good of the whole church. ¶ *The things which must shortly be done.* The beginning of which must soon occur—though the series of events extended into distant ages, and even into eternity. See Notes on ch. i. 1-3.

7. *Behold, I come quickly.* See Notes on ch. i. 3. The words here used are undoubtedly the words of the Redeemer, although they are apparently repeated by the angel. The meaning is, that they were used by the angel as the words of the Redeemer. See ver. 12. 20. ¶ *Blessed is he that keepeth the sayings of the prophecy of this book.* That receives them as a divine communication; that makes use of them to comfort himself in the days of darkness, persecution, and trial; and that is obedient to the precepts here enjoined. See Notes on ch. i. 3.

8. *And I John saw these things, and heard* them. That is, I *saw* the parts that were disclosed by pictures, visions, and symbols; I *heard* the parts that were communicated by direct revelation. ¶ *And when I had heard and seen, I fell down to worship before the feet of the angel,* &c. As he had done on a former occasion. See Notes on ch. xix. 10. John appears to have been entirely overcome by the extraordinary nature of the revelations made to him, and not improbably entertained some suspicion that it was the Redeemer himself who had manifested himself to him in this remarkable manner.

9. *Then saith he unto me, See* thou do it *not.* See Notes on ch. xix. 10. ¶ *For I am thy fellow-servant.* Notes on ch. xix. 10. ¶ *And of thy brethren the prophets.* In ch. xix. 10, it is "of thy brethren that have the testimony of Jesus." Here the angel says that, in the capacity in which he appeared to John, he belonged to the general rank of the prophets, and was no more entitled to worship than any of the prophets had been. Like them, he had merely been employed to disclose important truths in regard to the future; but as the prophets, even the most eminent of them, were not regarded as entitled to worship on account of the communications which they had made, no more was he. ¶ *And of them which keep the sayings of this book.* "I am a mere creature of God. I, like men, am under law, and am bound to observe the law of God." The "sayings of this book" which he says he kept, must be understood to mean those great principles of religion which it enjoined, and which are of equal obligation on men and angels. ¶ *Worship God.* Worship God only. Notes on ch. xix. 10.

10. *And he saith unto me.* The angel. ¶ *Seal not the sayings of the prophecy of this book.* That is, seal not the book itself, for it may be regarded altogether as a prophetic book. On the sealing of a book, see Notes on ch. v. 1. Isaiah (viii. 16; xxx. 8) and Daniel (viii. 26; xii. 4, 9) were commanded to seal up their prophecies. Their prophecies related to far-distant times, and the idea in their being commanded to seal them was, that they should make the record

A.D. 96.]  CHAPTER XXII.  459

11 He*p* that is unjust, let him be unjust still: and he which is filthy, let him be filthy still: and

*p* Pr.1.24-33; Ec.11.3; Mat.25.10; 2 Ti.3.13.

*q*he that is righteous, let him be righteous still: and he that is holy, let him be holy still.

*q* Pr.4.18; Mat.5.6.

sure and unchangeable; that they should finish it, and lay it up for future ages; so that, in far-distant times, the events might be compared with the prophecy, and it might be seen that there was an exact correspondence between the prophecy and the fulfilment. Their prophecies would not be immediately demanded for the use of persecuted saints, but would pertain to future ages. On the other hand, the events which John had predicted, though in their ultimate development they were to extend to the end of the world, and even into eternity, were about to *begin* to be fulfilled, and were to be of immediate use in consoling a persecuted church. John, therefore, was directed *not* to seal up his predictions; not to lay them away, to be opened, as it were, in distant ages; but to leave them *open*, so that a persecuted church might have access to them, and might, in times of persecution and trial, have the assurance that the principles of their religion would finally triumph. See Notes on ch. x. 2. ¶ *For the time is at hand.* That is, they are soon to *commence.* It is not implied that they would be soon *completed.* The idea is, that as the scenes of persecution were soon to open upon the church, it was important that the church should have access to these prophecies of the final triumph of religion, to sustain it in its trials. Comp. Notes on ch. i. 1, 3.

11. *He that is unjust, let him be unjust still.* This must refer to the scenes beyond the judgment, and must be intended to affirm an important truth in regard to the condition of men in the future state. It cannot refer to the condition of men on this side the grave, for there is no fixed and unchangeable condition in this world. At the close of this book, and at the close of the whole volume of revealed truth, it was proper to declare, in the most solemn manner, that when these events were consummated, everything would be fixed and unchanging; that all who were then found to be righteous would remain so for ever; and that none who were impenitent, impure, and wicked, would ever change their character or condition. That this is the meaning here seems to me to be plain; and this sentiment accords with all that is said in the Bible of the final condition of the righteous and the wicked. See Mat. xxv. 46; Ro. ii. 6-9; 1 Th. i. 7-10; Da. xii. 2; Ec. xi. 3. Every assurance is held out in the Bible that the righteous will be secure in holiness and happiness, and that there will be no danger—no possibility—that they will fall into sin, and sink to woe; and by the same kind of arguments by which it is proved that their condition will be unchanging, is it demonstrated that the condition of the wicked will be unchanging also. The argument for the eternal punishment of the wicked is as strong as that for the eternal happiness of the righteous; and if the one is open to doubt, there is no security for the permanence of the other. The word *unjust* here is a general term for an unrighteous or wicked man. The meaning is, that he to whom that character properly belongs, or of whom it is properly descriptive, will remain so for ever. The design of this seems to be, to let the ungodly and the wicked know that there is no change beyond the grave, and by this solemn consideration to warn them *now* to flee from the wrath to come. And assuredly no more solemn consideration can ever be presented to the human mind than this. ¶ *And he which is filthy, let him be filthy still.* The word *filthy* here is, of course, used with reference to *moral* defilement or pollution. It refers to the sensual, the corrupt, the profane; and the meaning is, that their condition will be fixed, and that they will remain in this state of pollution for ever. There is nothing more awful than the idea that a polluted soul will be always polluted; that a heart corrupt will be always corrupt; that the defiled will be put for ever beyond the possibility of being cleansed from sin. ¶ *And he that is righteous, let him be righteous still.* The just, the upright man — in contradistinction from the *unjust* mentioned in the first part of the verse. ¶ *And he that is holy, let him be holy still.* He that is pure, in contradistinction from the *filthy* mentioned in the former part of the verse. The righteous and the holy will be confirmed in their character and condition, as well as the wicked. The affirmation

460 REVELATION. [A.D. 96.

12 And behold, ʳI come quickly; and my reward *is* with me, ˢto give every man according as his work shall be.

13 Iᵗ am Alpha and Omega, the beginning and the end, the first and the last.

14 Blessed ᵘ *are* they that do his commandments, that they may have

*r* Zep.1.14.  *s* ch.20.12.  *t* Is.44.6.  *u* Lu.12.37,38.

right to the tree of life, and may enter in through the gates into the city.

15 For ᵛwithout *are* ʷdogs, and sorcerers, and whoremongers, and murderers, and idolaters, and whosoever loveth and maketh a lie.

16 I Jesus have sent mine angel to testify unto you these things in

*v* ch.21.8,27.  *w* Phi.3.2.

that their condition will be fixed is as strong as that that of the wicked will be—and no stronger; the entire representation is, that all beyond the judgment will be unchanging for ever. Could any more solemn thought be brought before the mind of man?

12. *And behold, I come quickly.* See Notes on ch. i. 1, 3. These are undoubtedly the words of the Redeemer; and the meaning is, that the period when the unchanging sentence would be passed on each individual—on the unjust, the filthy, the righteous, and the holy—would not be remote. The *design* of this seems to be to impress on the mind the solemnity of the truth that the condition hereafter will soon be fixed, and to lead men to prepare for it. In reference to each individual, the period is near when it is to be determined whether he will be holy or sinful to all eternity. What thought could there be more adapted to impress on the mind the importance of giving immediate attention to the concerns of the soul? ¶ *And my reward is with me.* I bring it with me to give to every man: either life or death; heaven or hell; the crown or the curse. He will be prepared immediately to execute the sentence. Compare Mat. xxv. 31-46. ¶ *To give every man according as his work shall be.* See Notes on Mat. xvi. 27; Ro. ii. 6; 2 Co. v. 10.

13. *I am Alpha and Omega*, &c. See Notes on ch. i. 8, 11. The idea here is, that he will thus show that he is the first and the last—the beginning and the end. He originated the whole plan of salvation, and he will determine its close; he formed the world, and he will wind up its affairs. In the beginning, the continuance, and the end, he will be recognized as the same being presiding over and controlling all.

14. *Blessed* are *they that do his commandments.* See Notes on ch. i. 3; xxii. 7. ¶ *That they may have right.* That they may be entitled to approach the tree of life; that this privilege may be granted to them. It is not a *right* in the sense that they have *merited* it, but in the sense that the privilege is conferred on them as one of the rewards of God, and that, in virtue of the divine arrangements, they will be entitled to this honour. So the word here used —ἐξουσία—means in Jn. i. 12, rendered *power*. The *reason* why this right or privilege is conferred is not implied in the use of the word. In this case it is by *grace*, and all the *right* which they have to the tree of life is founded on the fact that God has been pleased graciously to confer it on them. ¶ *To the tree of life.* See Notes on ver. 2. They would not be forbidden to approach that tree as Adam was, but would be permitted always to partake of it, and would live for ever. ¶ *And may enter in through the gates into the city.* The New Jerusalem, ch. xxi. 2. They would have free access there; they would be permitted to abide there for ever.

15. *For without* are *dogs.* The wicked, the depraved, the vile: for of such characters the dogs, an unclean animal among the Jews, was regarded as a symbol, De. xxiii. 18. On the meaning of the expression, see Notes on Phi. iii. 2. The word "without" means that they would not be admitted into the heavenly city, the New Jerusalem, ch. xxi. 8, 27. ¶ *And sorcerers,* &c. All these characters are specified in ch. xxi. 8, as excluded from heaven. See Notes on that verse. The only change is, that those who "love and make a lie" are added to the list; that is, who delight in lies, or that which is false.

16. *I Jesus.* Here the Saviour appears expressly as the speaker—ratifying and confirming all that had been communicated by the instrumentality of the angel. ¶ *Have sent mine angel.* Notes on ch. i. 1. ¶ *To testify unto you.* That is, to be a witness for me in communi-

## CHAPTER XXII.

the churches. I am *the root and the offspring of David, *and* the bright and morning star.

*x* ch.5.5.

cating these things to you. ¶ *In the churches.* Directly and immediately to the seven churches in Asia Minor (ch. ii. iii.); remotely and ultimately to all churches to the end of time. Comp. Notes on ch. i. 11. ¶ *I am the root.* Not the root in the sense that David sprang from him, as a tree does from a root, but in the sense that he was the "*root-shoot*" of David, or that he himself sprang from him, as a sprout starts up from a decayed and fallen tree—as of the oak, the willow, the chestnut, &c. See this explained in the Notes on Is. xi. 1. The meaning then is, not that he was the *ancestor* of David, or that David sprang from him, but that he was the offspring of David, according to the promise in the Scripture, that the Messiah should be descended from him. No argument, then, can be derived from this passage in proof of the pre-existence, or the divinity of Christ. ¶ *And the offspring.* The descendant; the progeny of David; "the seed of David according to the flesh." See Notes on Ro. i. 3. It is not unusual to employ two words in close connection to express the same idea with some slight shade of difference. ¶ *And the bright and morning star.* See Notes on ch. ii. 28. It is not uncommon to compare a prince, a leader, a teacher, with that bright and beautiful star which at some seasons of the year precedes the rising of the sun, and leads on the day. Comp. Notes on Is. xiv. 12. The reference here is to that star as the harbinger of day; and the meaning of the Saviour is, that he sustains a relation to a dark world similar to this beautiful star. At one time he is indeed compared with the sun itself in giving light to the world; here he is compared with that morning star rather with reference to its *beauty* than its *light.* May it not also have been one object in this comparison to lead us, when we look on that star, to think of the Saviour? It is perhaps the most beautiful object in nature; it succeeds the darkness of the night; it brings on the day—and as it mingles with the first rays of the morning, it seems to be so joyous, cheerful, exulting, bright, that nothing can be better adapted to remind us of Him who came to lead on eternal day. Its

17 And the Spirit and *y*the bride say, *z*Come. And let him that heareth say, Come. And *a*let him

*y* ch.21.2,9.   *z* Is.2.5.   *a* ch.21.6.

*place*—the first thing that arrests the eye in the morning—might serve to remind us that the Saviour should be the first object that should draw the eye and the heart on the return of each day. In each trial—each scene of sorrow—let us think of the bright star of the morning as it rises on the darkness of the night—emblem of the Saviour rising on our sorrow and our gloom.

17. *And the Spirit and the bride say, Come.* That is, come to the Saviour; come and partake of the blessings of the gospel; come and be saved. The construction demands this interpretation, as the latter part of the verse shows. The design of this whole verse is, evidently, to show the freeness of the offers of the gospel; to condense in a summary manner all the invitations of mercy to mankind; and to leave on the mind at the close of the book a deep impression of the ample provision which has been made for the salvation of a fallen race. Nothing, it is clear, could be more appropriate at the close of this book, and at the close of the whole volume of revealed truth, than to announce, in the most clear and attracting form, that salvation is free to all, and that whosoever will may be saved. ¶ *The Spirit.* The Holy Spirit. He entreats all to come. This he does (*a*) in all the recorded invitations in the Bible—for it is by the inspiration of that Spirit that these invitations are recorded; (*b*) by all his influences on the understandings, the consciences, and the hearts of men; (*c*) by all the proclamations of mercy made by the preaching of the gospel, and by the appeal which friend makes to friend, and neighbour to neighbour, and stranger to stranger—for all these are methods in which the Spirit invites men to come to the Saviour. ¶ *And the bride.* The church. See Notes, ch. xxi. 2, 9. That is, the church invites all to come and be saved. This it does (*a*) by its ministers, whose main business it is to extend this invitation to mankind; (*b*) by its ordinances—constantly setting forth the freeness of the gospel; (*c*) by the lives of its consistent members — showing the excellency and the desirableness of true religion; (*d*) by all its efforts to do good in the world; (*e*) by the example of

that is athirst come: and whosoever will, let him take the water of life freely.

18 For I testify unto every man that heareth the words of the prophecy of this book, *b* If any man shall add unto these things, God shall add unto him the plagues that are written in this book:

*b* Pr. 30. 6.

---

those who are brought into the church—showing that all, whatever may have been their former character, may be saved; and (*f*) by the direct appeals of its individual members. Thus a Christian parent invites his children; a brother invites a sister, and a sister invites a brother; a neighbour invites his neighbour, and a stranger a stranger; the master invites his servant, and the servant his master. The church on earth and the church in heaven unite in the invitation, saying, Come. The living father, pastor, friend, invites—and the voice of the departed father, pastor, friend, now in heaven, is heard re-echoing the invitation. The once-loved mother that has gone to the skies still invites her children to come; and the sweet-smiling babe that has been taken up to the Saviour stretches out its arms from heaven, and says to its mother — *Come.* ¶ *Say, Come.* That is, come to the Saviour; come into the church; come to heaven. ¶ *And let him that heareth say, Come.* Whoever hears the gospel, let him go and invite others to come. Nothing could more strikingly set forth the freeness of the invitation of the gospel than this. The authority to make the invitation is not limited to the ministers of religion; it is not even confined to those who accept it themselves. All persons, even though *they* should not accept of it, are authorized to tell others that they may be saved. One impenitent sinner may go and tell another impenitent sinner that if he will he may find mercy and enter heaven. How *could* the offer of salvation be made more freely to mankind? ¶ *And let him that is athirst come.* Whoever desires salvation, as the weary pilgrim desires a cooling fountain to allay his thirst, let him come as freely to the gospel as that thirsty man would stoop down at the fountain and drink. See Notes on Is. lv. 1. Comp. Notes on Mat. v. 6; Jn. vii. 37; Re. xxi. 6. ¶ *And whosoever will, let him take the water of life freely.* Ch. xxi. 6. Every one that is disposed to come, that has any sincere wish to be saved, is assured that he may live. No matter how unworthy he is; no matter what his past life has been; no matter how old or how young, how rich or how poor; no matter whether sick or well, a freeman or a slave; no matter whether educated or ignorant; no matter whether clothed in purple or in rags—riding in state or laid at the gate of a rich man full of sores, the invitation is freely made to all to come and be saved. With what more appropriate truth *could* a revelation from heaven be closed?

18. *For I testify.* The writer does not specify who is meant by the word "*I*" in this place. The most natural construction is to refer it to the writer himself, and not to the angel, or the Saviour. The meaning is, "I bear this solemn witness, or make this solemn affirmation, in conclusion." The object is to guard his book against being corrupted by any interpolation or change. It would seem not improbable, from this, that as early as the time of John, books were liable to be corrupted by additions or omissions, or that at least there was felt to be great danger that mistakes might be made by the carelessness of transcribers. Against this danger, John would guard this book in the most solemn manner. Perhaps he felt, too, that as this book would be necessarily regarded as obscure from the fact that symbols were so much used, there was great danger that changes would be made by well-meaning persons with a view to make it appear more plain. ¶ *Unto every man that heareth the words of the prophecy of this book.* The word "heareth" seems here to be used in a very general sense. Perhaps in most cases persons would be made acquainted with the contents of the book by hearing it read in the churches; but still the spirit of the declaration must include all methods of becoming acquainted with it. ¶ *If any man shall add unto these things.* With a view to furnish a more full and complete revelation; or with a profession that new truth had been communicated by inspiration. The reference here is to the book of Revelation only—for at that time the books that now constitute what we call *the Bible* were not collected into a single volume. This

**19** And if any man shall take away from the words of the book of this prophecy, ᶜGod shall take away his part ¹out of the book of life, and out of the holy city, and *from* the things which are written in this book.

**20** He which testifieth these

<small>c ch.3.5.    ¹ or, *from the tree.*</small>

passage, therefore, should not be adduced as referring to the whole of the sacred Scriptures. Still, the *principle* is one that is thus applicable; for it is obvious that no one has a right to change any part of a revelation which God makes to man; to presume to add to it, or to take from it, or in any way to modify it. Comp. Notes, 2 Ti. iii. 16. ¶ *God shall add unto him the plagues that are written in this book.* These "plagues" refer to the numerous methods described in this book as those in which God would bring severe judgment upon the persecutors of the church and the corrupters of religion. The meaning is, that such a person would be regarded as an enemy of his religion, and would share the fearful doom of all such enemies.

19. *And if any man shall take away from the words of the book of this prophecy.* If he shall reject the book altogether; if he shall, in transcribing it, designedly strike any part of it out. It is conceivable that, from the remarkable nature of the communications made in this book, and the fact that they seemed to be unintelligible, John supposed there might be those who would be inclined to omit some portions as improbable, or that he apprehended that when the portions which describe Antichrist were fulfilled in distant ages, those to whom those portions applied would be disposed to strike them from the sacred volume, or to corrupt them. He thought proper to guard against this by this solemn declaration of the consequence which would follow such an act. The whole book was to be received —with all its fearful truths—as a revelation from God; and however obscure it might seem, in due time it would be made plain; however faithfully it might depict a fearful apostasy, it was important, both to show the truth of divine inspiration and to save the church, that these disclosures should be in their native purity in the possession of the people of God. ¶ *God shall take away his part out of the book of life.* Perhaps there is here an intimation that this would be most likely to be done by those who professed to be Christians, and who supposed that their names were in the book of life. In fact, most of the corruptions of the sacred Scriptures have been attempted by those who have professed some form of Christianity. Infidels have but little interest in attempting such changes, and but little influence to make them received by the church. It is most convenient for them, as it is most agreeable to their feelings, to reject the Bible altogether. When it said here that "God would take away his part out of the book of life," the meaning is not that his name *had been written* in that book, but that he would take away the part which he *might* have had, or which he *professed* to have in that book. Such corruption of the divine oracles would show that they had no true religion, and would be excluded from heaven. On the phrase "book of life," see Notes on ch. iii. 5. ¶ *And out of the holy city.* Described in ch. xxi. He would not be permitted to enter that city; he would have no part among the redeemed. ¶ *And* from *the things which are written in this book.* The promises that are made; the glories that are described.

20. *He which testifieth these things.* The Lord Jesus; for he it was that had, through the instrumentality of the angel, borne this solemn witness to the truth of these things, and this book was to be regarded as *his* revelation to mankind. See Notes on ch. i. 1; xxii. 16. He here speaks of himself, and vouches for the truth and reality of these things by saying that he "*testifies*" of them, or bears witness to them. Comp. Jn. xviii. 37. The fact that Jesus himself vouches for the truth of what is here revealed, shows the propriety of what John had said in the previous verses about adding to it, or taking from it. ¶ *Saith, Surely I come quickly.* That is, the development of these events will soon *begin* — though their consummation may extend into far distant ages, or into eternity. See Notes on ch. i. 1, 3; xxii. 7, 10. ¶ *Amen.* A word of solemn affirmation or assent. See Notes on Mat. vi. 13. Here it is to be regarded as the expression of John, signifying his solemn and cheerful assent to what the Saviour had said, that he

things saith, <sup>d</sup>Surely I come quickly; Amen. Even<sup>e</sup> so, come, Lord Jesus.

<small>d ver.7,12.   e He.9.28; Is.25.9.</small>

21 The<sup>f</sup> grace of our Lord Jesus Christ *be* with you all. Amen.

<small>f 2 Th.3.18.</small>

---

would come quickly. It is the utterance of a strong desire that it might be so. He longed for his appearing. ¶ *Even so.* These, too, are the words of John, and are a response to what the Saviour had just said. In the original, it is a response in the same *language* which the Saviour had used, and the beauty of the passage is marred by the translation "*Even so.*" The original is, "He which testifieth to these things saith, *Yea*—ναι—I come quickly. Amen. *Yea*—ναι—come, Lord Jesus." It is the utterance of desire in the precise language which the Saviour had used—heart responding to heart. ¶ *Come, Lord Jesus.* That is, as here intended, "Come in the manner and for the objects referred to in this book." The *language*, however, is expressive of the feeling of piety in a more extended sense, and may be used to denote a desire that the Lord Jesus would come in any and every manner; that he would come to impart to us the tokens of his presence; that he would come to bless his truth and to revive his work in the churches; that he would come to convert sinners, and to build up his people in holiness; that he would come to sustain us in affliction, and to defend us in temptation; that he would come to put a period to idolatry, superstition, and error, and to extend the knowledge of his truth in the world; that he would come to set up his kingdom on the earth, and to rule in the hearts of men; that he would come to receive us to his presence, and to gather his redeemed people into his everlasting kingdom. It was appropriate to the aged John, suffering exile in a lonely island, to pray that the Lord Jesus would speedily come to take him to himself; and there could have been no more suitable close of this marvellous book than the utterance of such a desire. And it is appropriate for us as we finish its contemplation, disclosing so much of the glories of the heavenly world, and the blessedness of the redeemed in their final state, when we think of the earth, with its sorrows, trials, and cares, to respond to the prayer, and to say, "Come, Lord Jesus, come quickly." For that glorious coming of the Son of God, when he shall gather his redeemed people to himself, may all who read these Notes be finally prepared. Amen.

21. *The grace of our Lord Jesus Christ be with you all. Amen.* The usual benediction of the sacred writers. See Notes on Ro. xvi. 20.